Old World,
New World

Also by Kathleen Burk

War and the State: The Transformation of British Government, 1914–1919 *(editor)*

Britain, America and the Sinews of War 1914–1918

The First Privatisation: The Politicians, the City and the Denationalisation of Steel

Morgan Grenfell 1838–1988: The Biography of a Merchant Bank

'Goodbye, Great Britain': The 1976 IMF Crisis
(with Alec Cairncross)

Deutsche Bank in London 1873–1998 *(with Manfred Pohl)*

The United States and the European Alliance Since 1945
(editor with Melvyn Stokes)

Troublemaker: The Life and History of A.J.P. Taylor

The Short Oxford History of the British Isles: The British Isles Since 1945 *(editor)*

Old World, New World

Great Britain and America from the Beginning

KATHLEEN BURK

Atlantic Monthly Press
New York

First published in Great Britain in 2007 by Little Brown
an imprint of Little, Brown Book Group, London

Published simultaneously in Canada
Printed in the United States of America

FIRST AMERICAN EDITION OCTOBER 2008

ISBN-10: 0-87113-971-5
ISBN-13: 978-0-87113-971-9

Atlantic Monthly Press
an imprint of Grove/Atlantic, Inc.
841 Broadway
New York, NY 10003
Distributed by Publishers Group West
www.groveatlantic.com

08 09 10 11 12   10 9 8 7 6 5 4 3 2 1

Quattuor amicis criticis ac fidelibus

Jane Card

David d'Avray

David French

Jeremy Wormell

I have not the least hesitation in saying that I aspire to write in such a way that it wd. be impossible to an outsider to say whether I am, at a given moment, an American writing about England or an Englishman writing about America (dealing as I do with both countries,) & so far from being ashamed of such an ambiguity I should be exceedingly proud of it, for it would be highly civilized.

Henry James

Contents

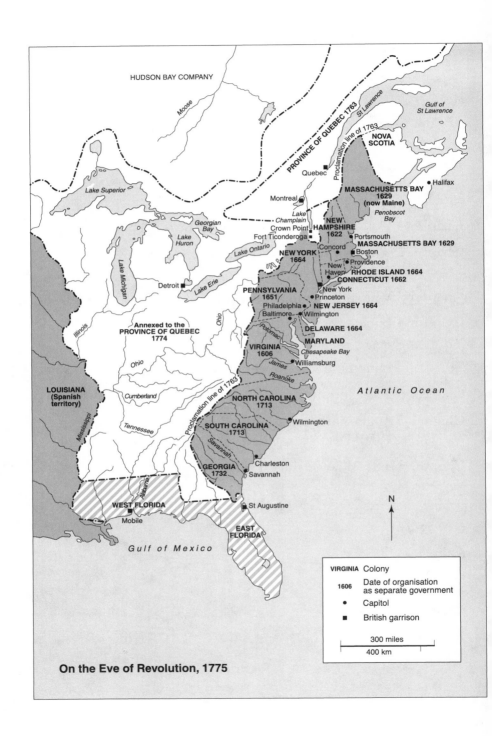

HUDSON BAY COMPANY

Moose

PROVINCE OF QUEBEC 1763

St Lawrence

Gulf of St Lawrence

Proclamation line of 1763

NOVA SCOTIA

Quebec

• Halifax

Lake Superior

Montreal •

MASSACHUSETTS BAY 1629 (now Maine)

Penobscot Bay

Georgian Bay

Lake Champlain
Crown Point ■
Fort Ticonderoga ■

NEW HAMPSHIRE 1622

Portsmouth •

MASSACHUSETTS BAY 1629

Lake Huron

Lake Ontario

Concord •
Boston ■

NEW YORK 1664

New • • Providence
Haven **RHODE ISLAND 1664**
CONNECTICUT 1662

Detroit ■
Lake Erie

Lake Michigan

PENNSYLVANIA 1651

New York •
Princeton •

Annexed to the PROVINCE OF QUEBEC 1774

Ohio

Philadelphia • **NEW JERSEY 1664**
Baltimore • • Wilmington

DELAWARE 1664

Illinois

Potomac

MARYLAND

Ohio

VIRGINIA 1606

Chesapeake Bay

James

LOUISIANA (Spanish territory)

Cumberland

Williamsburg •

Roanoke

Atlantic Ocean

Tennessee

Proclamation line of 1763

NORTH CAROLINA 1713

Mississippi

SOUTH CAROLINA 1713

Wilmington •

Savannah

GEORGIA 1732

Charleston •

Savannah •

Alabama

WEST FLORIDA

■ St Augustine

Mobile ■

N ↑

EAST FLORIDA

Gulf of Mexico

VIRGINIA Colony

1606 Date of organisation as separate government

• Capitol

■ British garrison

300 miles
400 km

On the Eve of Revolution, 1775

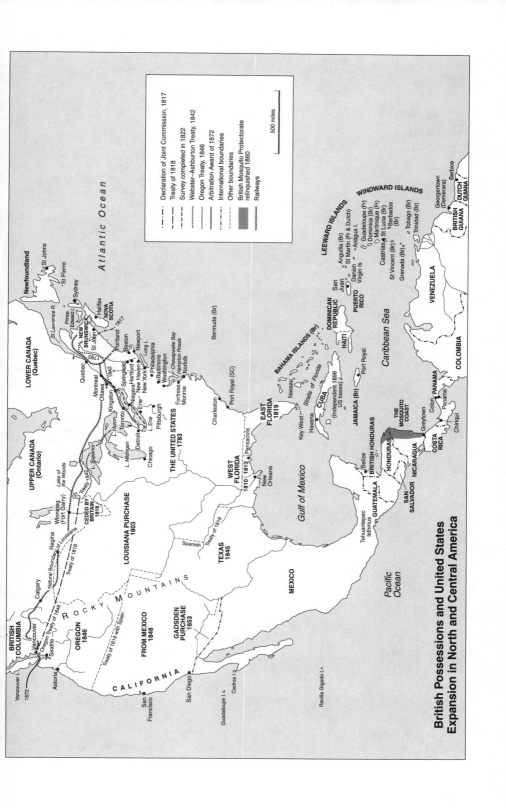

British Possessions and United States
Expansion in North and Central America

Legend:
- Declaration of Joint Commission, 1817
- Treaty of 1818
- Survey completed in 1822
- Webster–Ashburton Treaty, 1842
- Oregon Treaty, 1846
- Arbitration Award of 1872
- International boundaries
- Other boundaries
- British Mosquito Protectorate relinquished 1860
- Railways

500 miles

Atlantic Ocean

Newfoundland
St Johns
St Pierre

LOWER CANADA (Quebec)

Prince Edward I.
Sydney
Halifax
NEW BRUNSWICK
NOVA SCOTIA
St John
Portland 1817
Boston
Newport
Long I.
New Haven
New York
Philadelphia
Baltimore
Washington
Norfolk
Chesapeake Bay
Hampton Roads
Fortress Monroe

St Lawrence R.
Quebec
Montreal
Ottawa
Kingston
Toronto
Niagara
Hartford
Springfield
1842

UPPER CANADA (Ontario)

L. Superior
L. Huron
L. Michigan
L. Erie
Erie
Detroit
Chicago
Pittsburgh

THE UNITED STATES 1783

Bermuda (Br)

Charleston
Port Royal (SC)

EAST FLORIDA 1819

WEST FLORIDA 1810 1813
Pensacola
New Orleans

Key West
Havana

CUBA (Independent 1898 US bases)

BAHAMA ISLANDS (Br)
Nassau
Straits of Florida
Port Royal

DOMINICAN REPUBLIC
HAITI
PUERTO RICO
San Juan
Danish Virgin Is
Virgin Is

LEEWARD ISLANDS
Anguilla (Br)
St Martin (Fr & Dutch)
Antigua I.
Guadeloupe (Fr)
Dominica (Br)

WINDWARD ISLANDS
Martinique (Fr)
St Lucia (Br)
Castries
St Vincent (Br)
Barbados (Br)
Grenada (Br)
Tobago (Br)
Trinidad (Br)

Caribbean Sea

Georgetown
Berbice
BRITISH GUIANA
DUTCH GUIANA
(Demerara)

VENEZUELA

COLOMBIA

PANAMA
Colon, PANAMA
Panama
Chiriqui

COSTA RICA

THE MOSQUITO COAST
Greytown

NICARAGUA
HONDURAS
BRITISH HONDURAS
Belize
JAMAICA (Br)

SAN SALVADOR

GUATEMALA

Gulf of Mexico

Tehuantepec Isthmus

MEXICO

TEXAS 1845

Treaty of 1819

Spanish

LOUISIANA PURCHASE 1803

Lake of the Woods
Treaty 1842

Winnipeg (Fort Garry)

CEDED BY BRITAIN 1818

Regina
Natural Boundary
Treaty of 1818

Calgary

BRITISH COLUMBIA
Vancouver I.
1872
Vancouver
Seattle
Astoria

Oregon Treaty of 1846

Treaty of 1819 with Spain

R O C K Y   M O U N T A I N S

OREGON 1846

FROM MEXICO 1848

GADSDEN PURCHASE 1853

CALIFORNIA

San Francisco
San Diego

Guadaloupe I.
Cedros I.

Revilla Gigedo I.

Pacific Ocean

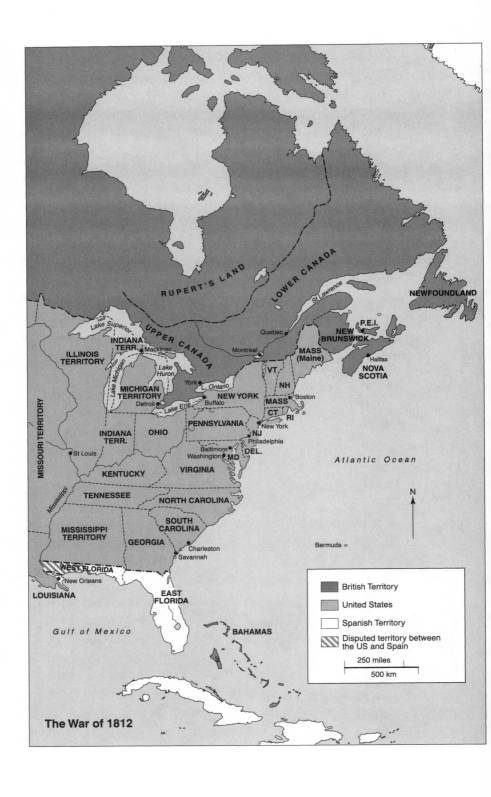

The War of 1812

British Territory
United States
Spanish Territory
Disputed territory between the US and Spain

250 miles
500 km

RUPERT'S LAND

LOWER CANADA

UPPER CANADA

NEWFOUNDLAND

St Lawrence

Quebec

Montreal

York

P.E.I.

NEW BRUNSWICK

MASS (Maine)

Halifax

NOVA SCOTIA

ILLINOIS TERRITORY

INDIANA TERR.

Mackinac

Lake Superior

Lake Michigan

Lake Huron

MICHIGAN TERRITORY

Detroit

Lake Erie

Ontario

Buffalo

VT

NH

NEW YORK

MASS

CT

RI

Boston

New York

MISSOURI TERRITORY

INDIANA TERR.

OHIO

PENNSYLVANIA

NJ

Philadelphia

DEL.

MD

St Louis

Mississippi

Baltimore

Washington

KENTUCKY

VIRGINIA

Atlantic Ocean

TENNESSEE

NORTH CAROLINA

MISSISSIPPI TERRITORY

SOUTH CAROLINA

GEORGIA

Charleston

Savannah

Bermuda

WEST FLORIDA

New Orleans

LOUISIANA

EAST FLORIDA

Gulf of Mexico

BAHAMAS

N

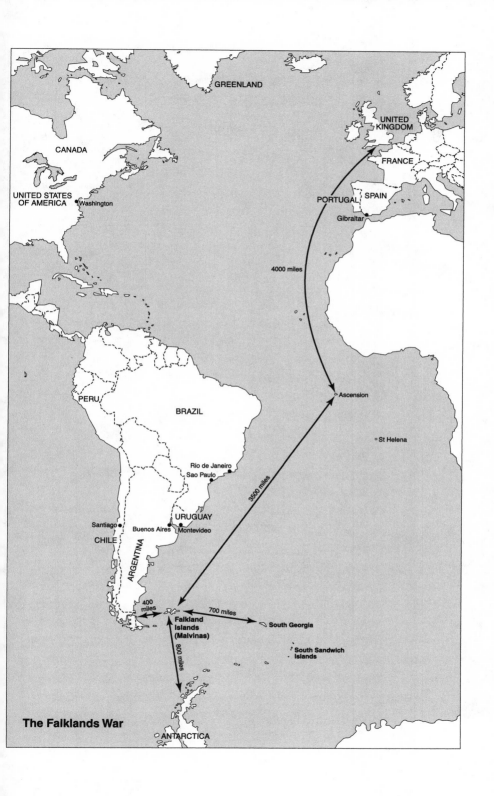

The Falklands War

Preface and Acknowledgements

There are a number of reasons for writing a book covering Anglo-American relations over a period of five centuries. It has never been done, not even by Churchill, and there is the attraction of doing something for the first time. I should add that Churchill had a much rosier view of the relationship than I do, so the reader who wishes for a concentration on the sunlit uplands should stop right here. I also wanted to answer the question, why is the Anglo-American relationship different from those of any two other countries? One may approve or disapprove, but the fact is undeniable. I have tried to explain why this is the case. It is a formidable challenge to attempt a many-layered history of one country: this book seeks to be a many-layered history of the relationship between two. It also makes a rather good story. And, finally, there is my very strong conviction that the academy and the general reader have drifted too far apart, and that those who take the public penny have a responsibility to convey the results of their research to the public. The public can then decide whether to read this book, but at least the opportunity is there.

I want to pay tribute to my agents and editors. Bill Hamilton and I have worked together for some years. After a somewhat offhand comment on my part about this topic, he encouraged me to widen, lengthen and deepen my ideas about what I could do. Going over my proposal with him was rather like having a DPhil supervision, and I have repeatedly benefited from both his encouragement and his critical eye. Emma Parry, who takes care of my interests in America, combines ideas and strength of purpose. Both she and Bill have acted and occasionally fought on my behalf, to my great benefit. My editor at Little, Brown, Stephen Guise, has been wonderfully supportive, especially when my academic load and bouts of ill health meant that I was somewhat wayward in meeting deadlines. The

Atlantic Ocean has prevented the same sort of easy contact with my editor at Grove/Atlantic, Jofie Ferrari-Adler, but he has none the less made certain that distance has not precluded their taking close account of my wishes and preferences. I recommend them all unreservedly.

I have spent the past seven years researching and writing this book, but it was built on the foundation of my earlier research on the subject, and on fifteen years of teaching Anglo-American relations to both undergraduates and postgraduates. It is an academic mantra to pay homage to one's students, but in this case it is justified. UCL pulses with intellectual energy, and this attracts students who can be spectacularly good. I have benefited from teaching some of the best, and the need to combine lucidity with acuity has kept me on the alert. I also have colleagues with whom anyone would be proud to be associated, and their expectation that this book would be completed, and would be halfway decent, was not unimportant.

Some of my students and former students were very helpful. I did virtually all of my own research, but scarce time was saved by not myself having to track down certain files in the UK National Archive for photocopying or to check references in the British Library. I am pretty obsessive about accuracy, and all quotations and references from secondary sources had to be verified. Tim Crockford, Matthew Edwards and particularly Clare Walsh were of inestimable help in carrying out these tasks.

And then you tap your friends on the shoulder and hand them a stack of paper. They all rallied. Richard Rathbone read the Prologue, and was deeply encouraging about my wanderings through time and space. Stephen Conway sacrificed part of his summer and read the chapter on the colonisation of America. I gave a short and early version of Chapter 4 as the Commonwealth Fund Lecture, and the pointed remarks of members of the audience were absorbed and appreciated. Six of the chapters made early appearances as public lectures whilst I was the Gresham Professor of Rhetoric in the City of London, and questions from the audience showed me where I had been unclear. My colleague Adam Smith read all of the chapters on the nineteenth century, and made comments of critical power. Thomas Otte read the sections dealing with nineteenth-century diplomacy, and gave me the benefit of his impressive and wide-ranging command of the subject and its sources. My former student Giora Goodman, now an academic in Israel, read several of the chapters, in one case whilst in some physical danger. He knows a great deal about the subject, and I suspect that he took some pleasure in marking up my manuscript as I used to mark up his. My colleague Bernhard Rieger and my former student and now academic James Vaughan attempted to remedy my lamentable ignorance about popular culture, with mixed results. Michael Jewess, a scientist and the other half of my personal Anglo-American relationship, drew the map showing the discovery of North America; he was also of very great help whilst I was writing the Prologue, as some of the footnotes betray. He read several of the chapters, and was instrumental in my dumping some sections in the bin. My daughter Miranda Jewess came to my rescue at the end by reading a second set of proofs.

Four friends and colleagues deserve special thanks, because they read not only this book chapter by chapter, but also my previous one. Jane Card, Head of History at Didcot Girls' School in South Oxfordshire, played her usual encouraging role as my Intelligent General Reader and finder of illustrations. My colleagues David d'Avray and David French read the chapters with critical care: the former concentrated on the flow of the prose, stopping occasionally to make percipient comments, particularly on the sections dealing with religion; the latter was more interested in the political, diplomatic and military discussions, and he seldom held himself back when he thought that my explanations were less than adequate. Jeremy Wormell is a special case, because he has read every monograph I've written since the late 1980s. His speciality is financial and economic history, and since a significant part of this book deals with political economy, his comments were of great importance. I grew used to receiving chapters back from him covered in red ink. I am profoundly grateful to all four of them, and it is to them that this book is dedicated.

As is usual for writers of non-fiction, I have accumulated numerous debts of gratitude to staff members in the archives which I visited whilst conducting the research for this book. Naturally, I visited many more archives, as I read many more books and articles, than are listed in the Bibliography; I have restricted myself to those which produced material which I have cited. In the UK I want to acknowledge the UK National Archive in Kew, London; the Bank of England; the British Library; the Anthony Wedgwood Benn Archive in London; the National Maritime Museum, Greenwich; the London School of Economics; Churchill College, Cambridge; the Guildhall Library, London; the House of Lords Record Office; and the Courtauld Institute, London. Special mention must be made of the University of London's Institute of Historical Research, a block from my office, with its hundreds of feet of printed sources and small, quiet rooms in which to work for an hour or a day. In the US I wish to acknowledge the US National Archives in Washington, D.C. and Maryland; the Gerald D. Ford Presidential Library in Ann Arbor, Michigan; the Franklin D. Roosevelt Presidential Library in Hyde Park, New York; the Harry S Truman Presidential Library in Independence, Missouri; Princeton University Library; the Library of Congress; Yale University Library; and the University of Kentucky Library. I am grateful to them all. The usual disclaimers apply.

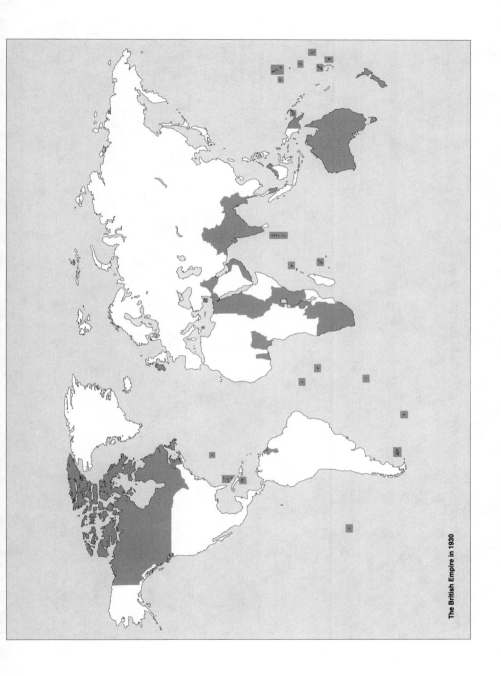

The British Empire in 1930

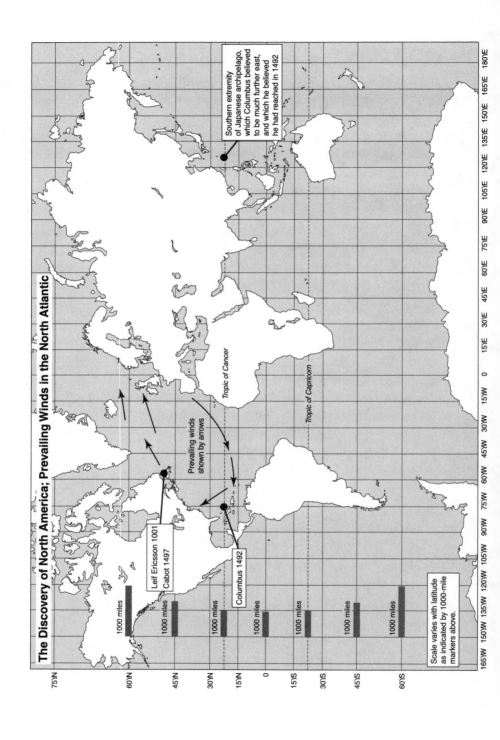

The Discovery of North America; Prevailing Winds in the North Atlantic

Southern extremity of Japanese archipelago, which Columbus believed to be much further east, and which he believed he had reached in 1492

Leif Ericsson 1001
Cabot 1497

Columbus 1492

Prevailing winds shown by arrows

Tropic of Cancer

Tropic of Capricorn

1000 miles

Scale varies with latitude as indicated by 1000-mile markers above.

PROLOGUE

Looking Westwards

In the yere of our Lord 1497 John Cabot a Venetian, and his sonne
Sebastian (with an English fleet set out from Bristoll) discovered that
land which no man before that time had attempted, on the 24 of June,
about five of the clocke early in the morning.

Richard Hakluyt, *The Principal Navigations, Voyages,*
Traffiques & Discoveries of the English Nation (1600)[1]

Licence my roving hands, and let them goe
Behind, before, above, between, below.
Oh my America, my new founde lande,
My kingdome, safeliest when with one man man'd,
My myne of precious stones, my Empiree
How blest am I in this discovering thee.

John Donne, 'To His Mistris
Going to Bed' (1596)[2]

The map[3] opposite is familiar to the modern reader, but is the result
of an enormous effort of intellect and exploration beginning in the
late fifteenth century. It shows how it was that Norsemen came upon
North America in the late tenth century AD; at northerly latitudes,
they could hop between land masses from Europe to America by
means of relatively short sea-crossings. The map also shows the prevailing winds which led eventually to the standard practice for
sailing ships of crossing to North America by routes nearer to the
Equator and then returning to Europe by more northerly routes.
Although the southerly routes are considerably longer in distance,
the currents and winds ensured that they were faster and more reliable until the advent of steamships.

At the beginning of the so-called 'Age of Discovery' in the early
fifteenth century, most mariners were skilled in 'pilotage', that is,
travelling within sight ('ken') of land and using landmarks to find

their way. 'Navigation', the art of finding one's way on the open sea, was only developed during the Age of Discovery. Navigation was a key aspect of the new scientific and technological age, since mariners needed to use the products of mathematicians and scientists (in particular cartographers and astronomers): better maps, and instruments to ascertain just where on the map they were. Columbus in 1492 depended on the Pole Star, his compass and dead reckoning,[4] but those sailing to Virginia a century later had the advantage of the new methods. What they had in common was travelling to the west for wealth or a new life.

I

Men from the western European tradition looked to the west. The east was known and often dangerous: trade came from the east, but also conquerors. The west was unknown, and ripe for speculation, myth and hopes. True, sunset is a universal metaphor for the end of life, the inescapable fate of all, but for some this could lead to bliss. For Homer, although the mouth of Hades was in the west, so were the Elysian Fields, the place of the blessed. The Hesperides of Greek myth, the three maidens who guarded the tree with the golden apples (some of which were stolen by Heracles), resided in the 'gardens of the west'.[5] The Ocean Sea was west beyond the Pillars of Heracles (the Strait of Gibraltar), the sea route out of the otherwise land-locked Mediterranean. This was the domain of the god Oceanus and his wife Tethys, parents of three thousand sons, the gods of all of the rivers of the world, and of three thousand daughters, the sea- and river-nymphs. For ancient geographers, Oceanus was a swift and unbounded stream that encircled the world. What was there? For two millennia the assumption was islands, rich and alluring – plentiful food, long life, no need to work – or dangerous and terrifying. One man put a name and a structure to such an island. That man was Plato, and the island was Atlantis.[6]

In the *Timaeus*, Plato relates that Socrates' guest Critias had heard of this island from the Athenian lawgiver Solon, who had been told of it by a very old Egyptian priest in Saïs, who knew of the written record about Atlantis which was kept in a very old temple, and who retailed the happenings of nine thousand years before: 'There was an island opposite the strait which you call . . . the Pillars of Heracles, an island larger than Libya and Asia combined; from it travellers could in those days reach the other islands, and from them the whole opposite continent which surrounds what can truly be called the ocean.' But 'there were earthquakes and floods of extraordinary violence . . . and the island of Atlantis was . . . swallowed up by the sea and vanished'.[7] The story of Atlantis has shown an inexplicable durability,[8] but what is of more importance in this context is the old Egyptian's description of an ocean and an opposite continent. This was possibly the inspiration of Seneca the Younger (1 BC–AD 65) for the meditation of the Chorus in his play, *Medea*:

> There will come an age,
> a distant Chinese year when
> Ocean will lose its
> power to limit knowledge,
> and the gigantic earth will open to us.
> Tethys, sea goddess,
> will disclose whole new worlds;
> no more will Iceland
> be our far horizon.[9]

But equally possible is that Seneca had read Strabo's compendious gazetteer, *Geographia*, or the writings of the historian Polybius about Pytheas of Massilia, who in 330 BC had reached Britain, the Shetlands and then Iceland, which he called Ultima Thule.[10] Iceland, in any case, brings a shock of the real to the speculation. There is evidence of an early sighting of North America by the Norseman Bjarni Herjolfsson about AD 985, followed by a planned exploration by Leif Ericsson, who landed at Newfoundland in 1001, followed by the first attempted colonisation of the continent by Thorfinn Karlsefni. Because of the trading links with Iceland and Norway, as well as the large Viking population around York, some in Britain would probably have heard about Ericsson's discovery, which was recorded in the *Vinland Sagas* (although evidence appears to

demonstrate that the Vinland Map is a fake).[11] However, there is no
record of anyone following up these rumours. Probably because
intellectual exchange between Scandinavia and the Mediterranean
was at best limited, the stories apparently had no influence in the
development of the Age of Discovery,[12] although it is possible that
such tales were told in sailors' and fishermen's haunts. Therefore, by
the time the Iberians and then the English set sail over the western
sea, there was little knowledge as to what, if anything, lay to the west
before the Indies. Yet, driven by the desire to evade tolls – imposed
in the Mediterranean by the Venetians and the Genoese with their
formidable navies – and by the wish to bypass the long and dangerous overland journey to India and Cathay, these explorers, and the
rulers who encouraged and sponsored them, looked for an alternative sea route. By 1420, the Portuguese had landed and settled in
Madeira. The Indies still awaited discovery.

There were, of course, always myths and speculation about
elsewhere, probably encouraged by the fact that, during the fifteenth
century, islands in the Atlantic kept being discovered: besides
Madeira, the Portuguese also happened upon the Azores and the
Cape Verde Islands. Furthermore, by the early fifteenth century
there were a number of books about the world outside Europe, and
particularly about Asia, which were available for the interested (and
the learned). There were academic treatises, some incorporating
material from Arabic sources gained, for example, by Iberian Jewish
cartographers of the fourteenth century, living as they did on the borders of the Muslim and Christian worlds. However, much more
numerous were the books of travels, in particular about Asia, the
Divisament dou monde of Marco Polo being the best known as well as
one of the most informative. But probably even more widely read,
with much of it falling into the category of fictional travellers' tales,
was *The Voyages and Travels of Sir John Mandeville, Knight*.

Mandeville set off in 1322 from St Albans in England on pilgrimage to Jerusalem. He apparently returned thirty-four years later,
claiming to have visited not only the Holy Land, but China, India,
Java and Sumatra. His written account of his putative adventures
became the fourteenth-century equivalent of a bestseller: at least
three hundred handwritten copies exist, and it was translated into

every European language, major and minor. Mandeville's manuscript was important because he stimulated the imagination of
numerous men as to what lay in the unknown parts of the world.

In his *Travels*, plausible descriptions of Cyprus, Egypt, Jerusalem
and Syria are followed by wildly fictitious tales of distant and
unknown lands. Part of its attraction lay in the descriptions of the
strange men, women and monsters which he claimed to have met. In
a group of fifty-four islands, for example,

> there are ugly folk without heads, who have eyes in each shoulder;
> their mouths are round, like a horseshoe, in the middle of their chest.
> In yet another part there are headless men whose eyes and mouths
> are on their backs ... In another isle there are ugly fellows whose
> upper lip is so big that when they sleep in the sun they cover all their
> faces with it. In another isle there are people whose ears are so big
> that they hang down to their knees ... There is another isle where
> the people are hermaphrodite, having the parts of each sex, and
> each has a breast on one side. When they use the male member, they
> beget children; and when they use the female, they bear children.[13]

But the main attractions for the early explorers were more likely to
have been his descriptions of China and India, allegedly abounding
in gold and silver, and his insistence that the wealth of the east could
be reached by sailing west. He was aware that the earth was spher-
ical, and even knew its size approximately, asserting that 'a man
could go all round the world, above or below, and return to his own
country, provided he had his health, good company, and a ship ...
And all along the way he would find men, lands, islands, cities and
towns, such as there are in those countries.'[14] Christopher Columbus
(1451–1506) was profoundly influenced by Mandeville; Sir Walter
Ralegh, initially sceptical, concluded on the basis of his own travels
that much of his story was true; and Sir Martin Frobisher took a
copy with him on his journey to find a north-west passage.[15]

Cartography was crucial to oceanic travel. Before the rediscovery
of the writings of ancient geographers, the dominant conceptual
map of the Christian west was the *mappa-mundi*, the round
mediaeval map of the world with Jerusalem at the centre and the

continents spaced symetrically around. With the recovery in particular of the *Geography* of Ptolemy (written around AD 150), however, men's views of the world outside Europe were modified almost beyond recognition.[16] Claudius Ptolemaeus had been a Hellenised Egyptian who, in response to a demand for a complete description of the Roman Empire, had set out to summarise in his writings the entire geographical and cosmographical knowledge of his day, based on many earlier works of Greek geographers, mathematicians and astromomers. He produced the first bound collection of maps suitable for both learning and administration. His book, the main part of which was an exhaustive gazetteer of places arranged by region, with a latitude and longitude assigned to each place, was translated into Latin by 1406. The second part of the *Geography* comprised a single world map and some regional maps. Ptolemy was the best that was available and as such profoundly influential.

A map published in Ulm in 1482 and based on Ptolemy's description shows, incorrectly, the mainland of China going off the edge at longitude 157 degrees east (calculated relative to the Greenwich meridian, the modern basis of longitude). D'Ailly's *Imago Mundi* of 1410, a copy of which Columbus possessed, argued that Ptolemy had underestimated the eastern extension of Asia. Columbus also possessed a 1484 edition of the works of Marco Polo, describing his thirteenth-century travels. According to Marco Polo, the island of Cipangu (Japan) lay fifteen hundred miles to the east of the Chinese coast. Taking encouragement from such sources, each grossly exaggerating the eastern extent of Asia, and disregarding contrary counsel from the geographers of the Court of Castile, Columbus sailed west from the Spanish port of Palos in 1492. After thirty-three days at sea he arrived at the outer cays of the Bahamas (longitude 75 degrees west), believing these to be part of the Japanese archipelago, whose actual longitude at the latitude of Columbus' crossing is 125 degrees east. Thus, by a cartographical error amounting to 160 degrees of longitude – over 40 per cent of the entire globe, occupied by North America and the Pacific Ocean – Columbus 'discovered' the New World.[17]

By the late fifteenth century there was growing dissatisfaction with maps based on Ptolemy, and by the first quarter of the sixteenth century they were seen to be wrong. There was also increasing knowledge about the lands which could be reached by sailing west. The map of the known world printed by Henricus Martellus in 1489 – the world of Columbus before he sailed – does not show the New World. The oldest manuscript showing the continent is Juan de la Cosa's map of 1500. La Cosa had been Columbus's pilot, and his map correctly showed that there was a solid land barrier to expansion in the west, even if Columbus thought that it was Asia and therefore not New. The first printed world map to show the New World was that published by Matteo Giovanni Contarini in 1506. Here discoveries made in North America are shown as the eastern coast of a greatly extended Asian mainland, and there is a wide ocean gap between North and South America. It is the map printed in 1507 by the German cartographer Martin Waldseemüller (c. 1470–1518), the second printed map of America, which so names it, after the Italian navigator Amerigo Vespucci (1454–1512).[18]

The practical experience of explorers such as Columbus, Vasco da Gama (who sailed around the tip of Africa in 1497 and reached India in 1498) and Ferdinand Magellan (who circumnavigated the globe in 1519–22), the tales of travellers such as Marco Polo and Mandeville, and the theoretical and practical capabilities of one of the most famous of all mapmakers, Gerald Mercator, all came together in 1569 to produce a world map which resembled the modern map in most significant qualitative respects. Mercator, working in the Low Countries, had published his first map (of the Holy Land) in 1537, and was making globes in 1541.[19] His world map of 1569 was particularly important for the means by which he 'projected' the curved surface of the terrestrial globe onto a flat sheet of paper. Mercator's 'cylindrical conformal projection' (as used in the map at the beginning of this Prologue) meant that if the longitude and latitude of a starting-point and destination were known and marked on the map, the mariner could determine the direction in which he needed to travel (his 'bearing') simply by drawing a straight line between them. The use of the correct bearing was crucial for navigation across the ocean, where many days were spent sailing out of sight of land.[20]

Mercator's projection provided, in principle, a sound basis for navigation and for recording locations discovered by exploration. But the calculations on which the projection was based needed some refinement and the principles had to be explained in textbooks before they could be practically applied. Work on this by Simon Stevin, a mathematician of Bruges, and Edward Wright, a Cambridge mathematician, was published in 1599. Richard Hakluyt (*c.* 1552–1616), whose role in promoting English colonisation of North America is described below, published a world map constructed by Wright in Mercator's projection in the same year.[21]

II

Much transpired in Mexico and South America during the sixteenth century, with the Spanish and Portuguese *conquistadores* taking possession. Hernán Cortés conquered the Aztecs in 1519 and Francisco Pizarro the Incas in 1531–3. They and others devoted themselves to acquiring a wealth of gold and silver, carving out and ruling colonies, and enslaving and converting the natives. Their hold was so strong that there was no question of their being supplanted by the adventurers of any other nations. Instead, outsiders, particularly French, Dutch and English privateers, had to content themselves with attacking Spanish and Portuguese treasure ships and stealing their booty.

North America was another matter. Englishmen, primarily men of Bristol and the West Country, now appear on the stage. Bristol had strong links with Lisbon, Seville and Madeira, as well as with Ireland and Iceland, and during the later fifteenth century its citizens were active in exploring North America. The summer of 1480 saw the first recorded voyage of discovery from the city: under the command of one Thloyde, a ship of eighty tons sailed for the legendary island of Brasylle, which was believed to lie to the west of Ireland. This was followed by a second journey the following year, and then perhaps others. It is likely that the English were searching for new fishing grounds, given the ferocious German competition for those around Iceland; the great increase in the European population required ever-larger quantities of fish.[22]

It was late in the following decade when men from Bristol landed on North America. In 1494 or 1495 John Cabot, a Venetian, came to Bristol with his three sons. On 5 March 1496, King Henry VII granted the family a patent authorising them to occupy such lands as they might discover in 'the eastern, western and northern sea', and to establish trade with them. However, that year's voyage was unsuccessful. In May 1497 Cabot and his son Sebastian tried again, sailing from Bristol in the *Mathew*, a ship of fifty tons, with a crew of twenty. They first sailed to the west of Ireland, and then set course due west on a latitude of possibly 55 degrees north; thirty-five days later, they made landfall. It is unknown precisely where he landed, but he spent a month exploring the coast, and it has been estimated that he ranged between 54 and 42 degrees north, or – very roughly – from around Hamilton Islet in Newfoundland down to just north of Plymouth Rock. His return to Bristol was greeted with acclaim in both that city and London, and a handsome pension of twenty pounds a year from the King. Economically, the great discovery was that the area was swarming with fish. Unfortunately, a voyage of five ships the following year was a disaster, and Cabot was lost at sea. Nevertheless, his achievement was recognised abroad, and La Cosa's map of 1500 shows a long coastline dotted with English flags.[23]

In 1517 Sir Thomas More's brother-in-law, John Rastell, a lawyer, publisher and writer, led a voyage of two ships to explore the North American coast. Unfortunately, it failed even to reach Ireland: he was abandoned by his crew off the Irish coast when he refused to turn pirate.[24] Rastell's prescience deserved better. He and More, the future Chancellor of England, shared a profound interest in the discoveries of the New World. More had utilised the reports for his *Utopia* of 1515, which he located in the Atlantic. The peg on which he hung his satirical and philosophical tale was an experienced traveller, Raphael Hythloday, who had just returned from a voyage with Americus Vesputius to the 'unknown peoples and lands' of the New World.[25] Rastell looked for more practical results. He recognised that it was a continent, not just an island, and that it possessed valuable forests and coastal waters. Furthermore, he stated that he wanted it to be taken and occupied by the English, and that his whole purpose had been to initiate this.[26] Yet, it was to be over a half-century before the English again made a serious effort to explore, and then to colonise, North America.

Why the delay? First, it was not profitable. The interest of men from Bristol faded, and any ventures during the next fifty years were typically the initiatives of kings, courtiers, or Italian bankers with spare funds to invest. King Henry VIII supported several such ventures, but the interest of most merchants in the City of London was tepid at best; profits were more certain from the trade with Muscovy or with western Europe. There was little intellectual interest in England in the new geography – Rastell was unusual. Furthermore, during the latter part of Henry VIII's reign, and in those of Edward VI and Mary, attention was diverted by religious turmoil and European politics, so it was only midway through the reign of Elizabeth I (1558–1603) that interest in ventures across the North Atlantic rekindled.

Everyone could see the economic benefits, particularly the gold and silver, which flowed to Spain and Portugal from their South and Central American and Mexican colonies. From 1504, French privateers attacked Spanish shipping on their final leg home, whilst from the 1530s, French corsairs extended their activities into the Caribbean. These raids mirrored the Franco-Spanish conflict in Europe itself. It did not take long for the English to join in. The lead was again taken by men of the West Country, both gentry and merchants, who supported, and were often related to, the sea-dogs who captained the ships – Sir Francis Drake, Sir John, Richard and William Hawkins, and Sir Richard Grenville. They were driven by the desire for wealth, sometimes by a militant Protestantism, and always by a hatred of Spain. As Kenneth R. Andrews has described it:

> From the first this was an aggressive drive by armed traders bent on breaking into the Portuguese and Spanish Atlantic trades, an unofficial war of trade and reprisals in the course of which emerged ambitions to colonize . . . [The] anti-Catholic edge of English Protestantism was turned against Spain and militant puritanism fused with aggressive nationalism in that fanatical, psalm-singing, image-breaking 'cause' espoused by Francis Drake and not a few of his piratical companions. It was in this form, as an ingredient of national feeling, that religion made its chief contribution to the movement of overseas expansion in the period.[27]

The early English attempts at the colonisation of North America were largely driven by private enterprise, by men who were eager for moveable wealth and for great landed estates. Their expectations of easily acquired fortunes, to be gained from the labour of a docile native population, from gold lying around on the ground and from land so rich that crops grew without the need for cultivation, were part of a common European currency which stretched back centuries. Ben Jonson satirised this belief in his 1605 play, *Eastward Ho!*, when he had Captain Seagull insist that 'I tell thee, gold is more plentiful there than copper is with us . . . Why, man, all their dripping pans and their chamber pots are pure gold; . . . and for rubies and diamonds, they go forth on holidays and gather 'em by the seashore, to hang on their children's coats.'[28] Yet, there were also those who hoped to find a new Arcadia, a land of long life and happiness. All peoples have had a concept of a past Golden Age, but in addition many believed that there might still be lands and peoples existing in this state of wondrous nature. Europe was corrupt; the New World was innocent. Europeans could be barbaric; the New World would, or at least might, be inhabited by noble savages who could be converted to civility and the Christian religion. Fundamentally, the New World would allow freedom, and the chance for new beginnings.[29]

III

It was Sir Humfrey Gilbert (*c.* 1539–1583) who was the first Englishman to plan and lead a serious attempt to colonise North America. Gilbert was one of a number of ambitious and rapacious Elizabethans who burned to acquire land and treasure for themselves and for England. The southern parts of the New World were entirely locked up by Spain (which annexed Portugal in 1580), and therefore the English turned their attention to the north. Some wished to continue the attempts to find a north-west passage to Asia, whilst others looked to the coast of America itself, where they confidently expected to find precious metals and other valuable goods, and land to colonise. To embark on such a venture, Gilbert needed the permission of Queen Elizabeth, and, ideally, a patent giving sole rights under the Crown to whatever he discovered. In 1566 he petitioned the Queen for permission to organise a voyage to find a north-west passage, but she refused. In 1574 he presented his 'Discourse to prove a Passage by the North West to Cathaia', but again she refused. In both cases, his request infringed the monopoly of the Muscovy Company to northerly navigation, and the Company objected. Instead, the royal licence to seek a north-west passage was given to another sea-dog, Martin Frobisher (c. 1535–94), who had the support of influential people. Frobisher made three voyages between 1576 and 1578, and although much geographical information was obtained, he was frustrated by the Arctic ice.[30]

Suddenly, the Queen changed her mind about Gilbert. It has been suggested that politically engaged Protestants associated with Sir Francis Walsingham (c. 1532–90), Secretary of State and head of intelligence, with the aid of propagandists employed by them, 'sought to alert the nation and the state to the advantages that their Spanish adversaries had gained over them through transoceanic exploits'.[31] For whatever reason, on 11 June 1578 she granted Gilbert a royal patent for six years 'for the inhabiting and planting of our people in America'. He was to 'discover, finde, searche out, and view such remote, heathen and barbarous lands . . . as to him . . . shall seem good', as well as inhabit 'such remote lands, countreys and territories'.[32] The expedition set off three months later, but initially it was beaten back by the weather. Having set off again, it was attacked by the Spanish off the Cape Verde Islands. The remainder of the fleet crawled back to Plymouth, utterly demoralised. Gilbert had sunk much of his personal fortune into the venture, and he was forced into semi-retirement.

The Queen, however, was persuaded to let him have another go, in spite of his reputation, as the Queen herself put it, as 'a man noted of not good happ at sea'. In June 1583 Gilbert sailed with five vessels (although one had to return after just two days), reaching Newfoundland seven weeks later. In August he found some thirty-six fishing vessels of various nationalities at St John's harbour, who all gave way to him when he produced the Queen's patent. He then formally claimed possession of four hundred miles of the coast. A colony now existed, at least in theory, and Gilbert was free to renew his patent. He and his men spent a fortnight prospecting, in particular for metals, but during this period sickness overwhelmed many of his crew. Many died, others remained too ill to work, still others deserted, and some refused to continue on the voyage. One ship, the *Swallow*, returned to England with the sick; another, the *Delight*, was wrecked upon shoals.

Demoralised and in great distress, the crew of the remaining two vessels refused to do anything other than return to England, and Gilbert had to agree. With the wreck of one of his ships he had lost his books and maps, in particular that sketching out the new colony, as well as his samples of ore, but he refused to admit defeat. He remained on his eight-ton frigate, the *Squirrel*, refusing to leave it for the forty-ton *Golden Hind*, a safer vessel. He met his death in a 'mood of defiant bravado' on 9 September 1583, as described by the captain of the *Golden Hind*:

> very foule weather, and terrible seas, breaking short and high, Pyramid wise, . . . the Generall sitting abaft with a booke in his hand, cried out unto us in the Hind (so oft as we did approch within hearing), We are as neere to heaven by sea as by land. Reiterating the same speech, well beseeming a souldier, resolute in Jesus Christ, as I can testifie he was. The same Monday night, about twelve of the clocke . . . suddenly her lights were out, whereof as it were in a moment, we lost sight, and withall our watch cryed, the Generall was cast away, which was too true.'[33]

Gilbert's patent was taken up by Sir Walter Ralegh (1552–1618), his half-brother. This may have been partly a result of the Queen's well-known affection for Ralegh, who was one of her favourite courtiers. Ralegh was about thirty-two, and a younger son who could expect little in the way of an inheritance from his father. But he was ambitious, and had made his way from Devon to London and the Court. He was, a contemporary wrote, 'an outward man, a good presence, in a handsome and well compacted person, a strong natural wit, and a better judgement, with bold and plausible tongue, where he could set out his parts to the best advantage. He was an indefatigable reader . . . and none of the least observers both of men and of the times.' Another wrote that he was 'a tall, handsome and bold man, but . . . damnably proud'.[34] Ralegh had long believed in the possibility of an English settlement in North America, and he interested seafaring men such as Drake and Grenville.

Much more important in terms of public relations, however, were the writings of Richard Hakluyt, and his editions of the writings of others about the explorations by Englishmen. His 'Discourse of Western Planting', written primarily for the Queen and Walsingham, was issued in 1584, on the eve of Ralegh's first effort to establish a colony in Virginia, and provided a summary of the arguments and justifications for colonisation in America which were then circulating in England. The first benefit, Hakluyt claimed, would be the conversion of 'these simple people', with this 'most godly and Christian work' being best carried out, of course, by the Protestant English. It is likely that Hakluyt genuinely believed this, since militant Protestantism and anti-Catholicism were becoming entwined with a hatred and fear of Spain. Yet, he devoted much more time to explaining how colonising America would enhance the wealth and power of England, not so much through gold and jewels as through the enhancement of production and trade. It lay in latitudes similar to those stretching from Scandinavia to the Mediterranean. 'The soils, as reported by Huguenot colonists for southeastern North America, had such "fertilitie and riches" as to suggest that North America, or Virginia, as the English called this vast region, might supply England with virtually every commodity it then obtained from the Levant, Muscovy, and other parts of Europe.' Hakluyt envisaged the development of many profitable plantations (colonies) and a vast and lucrative trade.[35]

Hakluyt was part of a circle which included John Dee (1527–1608), a pioneer of the mathematics of navigation (and astrologer to Queen Mary, in which subject he had instructed the young Princess Elizabeth), and an early proponent of English expansion. Dee invented the phrase 'Brytish Impire' and sketched out the English claim to an empire of the North Atlantic, which he set down in 1578 in a statement for his erstwhile pupil of 'Her Majesty's Title Royal' to the lands in question, depicted in his 1580 map of Atlantis (the continent of North America). Hakluyt, Dee and others argued that if England would but grab the opportunities provided by North

America, there would be substantial benefits. First of all, England's trading fortunes, currently restricted by Spain and other nations, would be revitalised. Furthermore, the country's naval and military resources would increase significantly. The colonies could also be used as bases from which to launch attacks against Spanish, French and Portuguese shipping. This would lessen the funds available to these countries, especially Spain, and so limit their threat to the Protestant countries of Europe and their interests. At the domestic level, a substantial emigration to American plantations would be a solution to overpopulation and underemployment. England was 'swarming with lustie youthes that be turned to no profitable use'; setting up colonies would improve their economic circumstances and therefore their happiness. Finally, Hakluyt argued, America could provide a religious as well as an economic refuge, not for the English but for those 'from all partes of the worlde' who were 'forced to flee for the truthe of gods worde'.[36]

It can be argued that at least some of this was cant. 'In pleading with the powers of heaven to favour one's design it was certainly the best argument known. Likewise it appealed to the Protestant conscience, which Hakluyt and the Virginia Company's hired preachers duly prodded by reminding Englishmen how much the Catholic church had done to bring a falsified Christianity to the heathen, and how little the Protestants had done to spread the true word.' Although such exhortations, when uttered by well-meaning believers, should not be condemned as hypocritical – it seems that Dee at least was sincere in wanting to convert the infidels – they had little effect: 'The missionary ideal was not a major stimulus to English colonial endeavour and the nation's record in this field remained poor.'[37]

Their views of the peoples of the New World seem to have been of a matter-of-fact nature. In Spain and France, the previous century had seen learned treatises about the inhabitants of the Americas, whether they were Noble Savages or just savage, and 'on the whole, the image of the innocent Indian was most easily maintained by those Europeans who had never actually seen one. Europeans who had experienced any contact with him were as likely as not to swing sharply to the other extreme . . . The theme of the bestiality of the Indian, alternating with the theme of his primeval innocence, runs through the early literature of discovery and settlement.'[38] One historian argues that the English did not then have a racial ideology or a set of ethnic stereotypes which they could apply to the Native Americans whom they were to meet (although one should not forget the racial ideas inherent in Shakespeare's *The Tempest*), possibly because the occasions for meeting Africans or Asians on their own ground had been relatively few.

> They began, it is true, with the simple and vague idea of Christianizing and civilizing them, but by and large they did not care enough about savages to make much effort to save their souls . . . Contempt alternates with respect for their mental, physical and moral qualities. There is admiration as well as revulsion for their culture. The idea that colonists regarded the Indians as irremediably savage is not borne out by the documentary evidence which survives . . . There is no agreed picture of the Indian, but a confusion of images, behind which lay, thinly if at all concealed, one constant drive: to acquire and exploit that land, with or without its people.[39]

This was certainly the intention of Ralegh. But he also wanted this colony to act as a base from which to launch assaults on the Spanish treasure fleet as it made its annual journey back to Spain. The key was the direction of the winds. In the southern latitudes, the Trade Winds blow from east to west all year round; in the northern, the Westerlies blow from west to east. In other words, ships taking advantage of the winds and currents sailed clockwise, rather than straight across the Atlantic. Ralegh and his colleagues therefore wanted a naval base on the coast of North America, far enough from the Spanish colony in Florida to be hidden from it, but near enough to attack the treasure fleet as it sailed up the coast to catch the Westerlies.

On 25 March 1584, Ralegh received his Letters Patent from the Queen, which stated that the whole unoccupied coast of America was his to plant with colonies that he might hold for ever.[40] His first move was to send out two ships, captained by Philip Amadas and Arthur Barlowe, to conduct a reconnaissance. They sailed from Plymouth on 27 April, beat their way south against contrary winds to the Canaries, picked up the Trade Winds on 10 May, and reached the Caribbean a month later. They then had to negotiate the passage from the Caribbean into the Florida Channel – 'a tricky piece of navigation for mariners not yet familiar with the currents there'.[41] They first sighted land on 4 July. As they later wrote to Ralegh, 'the second of July, we found shole [shallow] water, wher we smelt so sweet, and so strong a smel, as if we had bene in the midst of some delicate garden abounding with all kinde of odoriferous flowers, by which we were assured, that the land could not be farre distant'. They skirted the Carolina Banks, and eventually found an inlet lying between Roanoke and Hatarask islands to the south. On 13 July they landed on Hatarask, and claimed it for the Queen. They made contact with the natives of Roanoke Island (later they brought 'two of the Savages being lustie men' back to England with them) and found what seemed a land of abundance: the crops grew almost without labour, the water was alive with fish and the air was thick with fowl; and the natives were either friendly or easily cowed by the Europeans' superior weaponry.[42] Amadas and Barlowe's report, suitably edited and published, provided welcome publicity to attract support for the next stage of the project: the founding of a colony.

In spite of Hakluyt's 'Discourse' and Ralegh's energetic lobbying for funds, the Queen's support was restricted largely to that of her approval, but without which he could not have gone. This also gave him some advantages with regard to supplies. She did send one of her own ships, the 160-ton *Tiger*, but otherwise the funds came from Ralegh himself and a number of subscribers, including Walsingham, Lord Charles Howard, the Lord High Admiral, and Sir Richard Grenville (1542–91). In early April 1585, a flotilla of five large and two smaller ships, carrying about six hundred men in all, left Plymouth. Besides the *Tiger*, they included Ralegh's own ship, the 140-ton *Roebuck*. The command was held by Grenville, who captained the *Tiger*; the soldiers, who were to form the main body of the colony, were under Ralph Lane, an experienced soldier released from his command in Ireland. There were two others of note on the voyage: the artist John White, who may have been on the previous voyage and the scientist Thomas Hariot, a graduate of Oxford and an intimate member of Dee's circle. Hariot, a pioneer of astronomy, mathematics and navigation, had joined Ralegh's household in about 1580 to instruct him and his sea-captains in mathematics, presumably for use in navigation. White and Hariot together would produce a vivid picture of Virginia in words, drawings and maps, describing the fish, animals, birds, plants, people and their habitats, and surveying and mapping the region.[43]

The main intention of the expedition was to set up a permanent military base. After gathering at Puerto Rico, the ships made their way through the Bahamas and reached the Carolina Banks at the end of June. But then disaster struck: trying to negotiate an inlet, the *Tiger* ran aground. Although they managed to ground her with her back unbroken, a substantial proportion of the provisions for the colony had been ruined by the saltwater, jeopardising the expedition and making it dangerously dependent on the generosity of the local population. However, friendly relations were established with the Roanoke tribe, who agreed to allow the English to build a fort and some cottages on the north end of the island. It was decided that Lane would remain with just over a hundred men, a much smaller colony than had been planned, but now they would have to live off the country. In late August Grenville departed for England in the *Tiger*, taking optimistic letters from Lane to Walsingham, and capturing a rich Spanish prize on the way.

The area around Roanoke was unsuitable for a naval base, but the Indians indicated that waters north might be useful, so Lane sent a reconnaissance party to find a satisfactory harbour. They discovered Chesapeake Bay, and explored the surrounding countryside, which seemed fertile with a temperate climate. Lane wanted to relocate the colony there as soon as the expected relief arrived from England.

By this time the Indians were turning hostile. The English had arrived too late to sow seed, and therefore had to look to the natives for food. They expected supplies to arrive from England before Easter and so lacked any strong incentive to produce their own. In any case, being soldiers and gentlemen, it was beneath them to grow their own food, although they did hunt. But as the Indians' own food supplies dwindled, they refused to meet the colonists' demands. In March Lane discovered that the Indians were planning to move against them, surprised them in council, and took hostages; the Indians then left, taking all of their corn. By April, things had quietened down, and the Indians allowed the colony enough land and seed corn for a year's crop. But this would not be ready until July, and meanwhile famine threatened. In May Lane realised that the Indians were planning a general assault, so on 1 June the colonists attacked first, slaughtered many, and effectively crushed the opposition.

A week later they sighted a great fleet. The fear was that it was Spanish, but to their relief it was Sir Francis Drake (*c.* 1543–96), who had come from sacking some of the most important Spanish towns in the Caribbean. He found the colonists in a poor state, and in the end took them all back to England, excepting three who were upcountry and therefore abandoned. Ironically, Ralegh had in fact organised a relief expedition, which arrived at Roanoke before the end of June, only to find it deserted. It returned to England, but meanwhile Grenville as well had set out with substantial reinforcements aboard a squadron of West Country privateers. On their way they took prizes, which delayed their arrival at Roanoke until after the colonists' departure. Grenville, 'finding the places which they [the colonists] inhabited desolate, yet unwilling to loose the possession of the countrey which Englishmen had so long held: after good deliberation, hee determined to leave some men behinde to reteine possession of the Countrey: whereupon he landed fifteene men in the Isle of Roanoak, furnished plentifully with all maner of provision for two yeeres, and so departed for England.'[44] These fifteen, of course, had no chance at all against the hostile Indian population. A war party of thirty Indians arrived. They beckoned to 'two of the chiefest of our Englishmen' with 'friendly signs' and while 'one of the savages traitorously embraced one, the other with his sword of wood . . . stroke him upon the head and slew him'. The remaining twenty-eight Indians sprang from cover and a running fight developed between the Indians and the colonists, who used 'such weapons as came first to hand'. The Englishmen, 'some of them hurt, retired fighting to the water side, where their boat lay, with which they fled'. The survivors were last seen regrouping on an off-shore island. This did not save them.[45]

The colony was probably doomed from the beginning. In the first place, Ralegh did not have, and could not raise, enough resources for such a plantation so far from home and amidst a hostile population. Secondly, the earlier reconnaissance had been cursory, whilst the report on the land and its population had been doctored so that it was unremittingly positive. It had failed, for example, to mention that Roanoke was swampy and disease-ridden. Most important of all, the wrong kind of settlers had been sent: soldiers of fortune, not colonists, who lacked practical skills and motivation – they wanted to seize wealth, not create it themselves. Lane was to complain that he was in charge of wild men amongst savages.[46]

By this time, Ralegh's enthusiasm was waning, since he now had estates in Ireland to build up and his attempt in America had ended so ignominiously. However, Hakluyt, John White and others encouraged him to make another attempt, this time to settle in the Chesapeake Bay area, which had better harbour facilities and friendlier Indians. By the beginning of 1587, he had decided to do so. This time, though, it would be (at White's urging) a mixed civilian colony, an agricultural rather than a military one. For the first time, the colonists themselves, many of them artisans and farmers, as well as some educated middle-class couples, would have a stake in the colony: each was to receive five hundred acres of land. Furthermore, they were to bring their families, make a living in the country, and create the City of Ralegh in Virginia. John White was to be the Governor; he was accompanied by his pregnant daughter and her husband.

On 8 May 1587, eighty-five men, seventeen women and eleven children set sail in three vessels. From the beginning the venture was wracked with dissension and ill luck. According to White's journal, there were continual quarrels between himself and the master of the flagship, the *Lion*: the master saw the Caribbean as an area for privateering, whilst White viewed it as a source of supplies; as a result, they got neither plunder nor supplies. There was also bad feeling between the emigrants and the sailors. Upon reaching Hatarask on 22 July, White wanted to take one of the small ships and go up the Roanoke River in search of the fifteen men left there by Grenville; he then wanted the ships to take them to Chesapeake Bay to establish the colony, as Ralegh had instructed. Unfortunately, because the ship had been late in departing from England, 'the

Summer was farre spent, wherefore hee [the captain] would land all the planters in no other place'. Because the men left by Grenville had disappeared, no crops had been sown, nor were there habitable cottages. In the circumstances, it was decided that White should return to England and bring back supplies. He was very reluctant to leave, fearing that he would be blamed for having abandoned the colony. But his fellow planters insisted, and on 27 August he departed, leaving behind 117 colonists, including his daughter and his new granddaughter Virginia.[47] He was never to see them again.

White reached England in November 1587, and Ralegh ordered a ship to take out supplies as soon as possible, to be followed in the summer of 1588 by a fleet under Grenville. Neither was to depart, because of the conflict with Spain. Hostility had been growing between the two countries since the 1560s, and by 1585 they were in open conflict. In May of that year, Philip II of Spain ordered the arrest of English ships, men and goods in Spanish harbours, at which English privateers began a campaign of reprisal against Spanish shipping. In August, England became formally allied with the Protestant Dutch in their rebellion against Spanish occupation of the Netherlands and sent an army to engage the Spaniards. This convinced Philip that he needed to eliminate England from the struggle, so in 1586 he began the preparations for the Invincible Armada. If Spain could gain control of the waters between the Strait of Gibraltar and the North Sea, supplies for the Spanish troops in Flanders could be carried directly by water rather than by the circuitous 'Spanish Road'. But the alliance of the English, the Dutch and the Huguenots (French Protestants) had controlled this route since the late 1560s. The 'logic of the situation demanded that if Philip could neither keep Elizabeth out of the war nor persuade her to withdraw, he must try to knock her out of it by a frontal assault'. Hence the Armada of 1588, the 'Enterprise of England'.[48]

Elizabeth had never been an imperialist – her focus had always been on European politics and the threats from France and Spain. White's return to England coincided with increasing apprehension of the danger from Spain, with the result that Ralegh was forbidden to send out the supplies; the government had already ordered a general stay of shipping in English ports. Nevertheless, Grenville continued to prepare for the expedition to Virginia and he was ready by the end of March, but at that point it was cancelled and the ships sent to Plymouth to reinforce Drake's fleet, which he was to lead against the Armada. White finally received permission to send out two small boats with fifteen planters and supplies, but once out of port the sailors began chasing ships for plunder. Ultimately, both ships returned to England, having abandoned the voyage.

It was not until 1590 that a full expedition was allowed to go to Virginia. Its primary purpose was privateering in the West Indies, but it took along White. The ships departed from Plymouth on 20 March and anchored off Hatarask on 15 August. Three days later they found the Roanoke fort; it was deserted, and no houses remained. What stood there now was a high palisade of trees, on one of which the single word 'CROATOAN' was carved in capital letters; on another tree was 'CRO'. According to a code arranged before White's departure, the colonists had signalled their departure for Croatoan Island. The code also stipulated that if they were in danger or distress they were to include a Maltese cross. There was no cross, and White was therefore 'greatly joyed that I had safely found a certaine token of their safe being at Croatoan', where the 'Savages of the Iland' were friendly. The captain agreed to take them to Croatoan, but foul weather prevented it. With White's agreement, the captain decided to take the ship back to the West Indies for the winter, but, beset by heavy storms, the course was changed for the Azores and thence for England, reaching Plymouth in October 1590.[49] The Lost Colony was now effectively abandoned.

For almost a century the English had made sporadic attempts to explore North America, but the lack of sustained interest or effort ensured failure. Roanoke was the most obvious failure, one which occasioned speculation for years: had the colonists survived? For decades there were reports of blond, blue-eyed Indians. Had they been slaughtered? Had they attempted to escape by boat and drowned? No archeological remains have ever been found. It would take the success of the next attempt to colonise Virginia, the Jamestown settlement, to relegate Roanoke to history.

CHAPTER 1

Conquest and Colonisation: 1607–1763

And in regions far
Such heroes bring ye forth
As those from whom we came,
And plant our name
Under that star
Not known unto our north
. . .
Thy voyages attend,
Industrious HACKLUTT,
Whose readings shall inflame
Men to seek fame,
And much commend
To after-times thy wit.

Michael Drayton, 'Ode to the
Virginian Voyage'

Not such as *Europe* breeds in her decay;
Such as she bred when fresh and young,
When heav'nly Flame did animate her Clay,
By future Poets shall be sung.

Westward the Course of Empire takes its Way;
The four first Acts already past,
A fifth shall close the Drama with the Day;
Time's noblest Offspring is the last.

George Berkeley, 'On the Prospect of Planting
Arts and Learning in America' (1752)

The English had tried, and failed, to establish viable colonies. The funds had been too meagre; the knowledge of geography had been too scant; and the colonists themselves had failed to adapt to their new environment. From 1607, however, new attempts were made, and this time they were more successful. The first colony, that of Virginia, was organised by a joint stock company, and thus had access to much more capital than previous attempts. Its primary motive was to make money. Another successful colony, the Massachusetts Bay Colony, was established in 1630 by Puritans, who yearned for the freedom to practise their own form of Protestantism. A third was Pennsylvania, which was a proprietary colony established in 1682 by a single proprietor, William Penn, both to make money and to carry out a 'holy experiment' for complete religious freedom. And a fourth was New York, acquired in 1674 by conquest from the Dutch. Other colonies were variations on these themes, or the result of internal settlement beyond initial colonial boundaries.

The land, of course, was not empty, and one theme during the entire colonial period was repeated conflict with the Native Americans, as colonists steadily pushed their farmsteads further west. Yet the Indians were sometimes allies, because another major theme of the period was conflict with the French to the north and west, and, to a lesser extent, with the Spanish to the south. As an increasingly important part of the British Empire, which was locked in combat with the French Empire around the world, the colonies were sucked into a series of wars.

Another thread was the political development of the colonies. Colonists from England (and, after the Union of 1707 with Scotland, Great Britain) believed that they brought with them their rights as 'free-born Englishmen', and early on established legislative assemblies. The question was, what relation did these colonies have with Great Britain? Were they subject entirely to the wishes of the Crown (or of the 'Crown-in-Parliament') or were they fundamentally self-governing? This question became one of increasing urgency.

The American colonies were also part of the wider social, intellectual and religious world. Colonists received London periodicals, English and French books, including novels and political philosophy. They also followed London fashions, and social and political gossip. London was the social and intellectual capital of the empire, of which the American elite felt themselves a part.

It is a mistake, when looking at the colonial period, to see the colonies as a unity, for the colonists themselves certainly did not. Each colony was an individual enterprise, and, although they are sometimes spoken of in groups – New England, the 'Middle Colonies', the Chesapeake colonies, the Carolinas – their modes of colonisation, religions and political structures made them very different from each other. These differences continued into the period of the Revolution and independence.

I

Let England knowe our willingnesse,
For that our worke is good.
Wee hope to plant a nation,
Where none before hath stood . . .

'Newes from Virginia . . .'[1]

Some Englishmen had never entirely given up the desire to colonise North America, but with the war against Spain, and the failure of earlier attempts, from 1586 to 1603 there had been little governmental support. Furthermore, public opinion did not support further ventures. Nevertheless, 'the sea war of the 1580s and 1590s helped to forge the tools of Empire, developing the ships, men, and capital needed for seaborne expansion'.[2] The conflict with Spain had been predominantly a sea war, although not one between navies: rather, for the English it had been a privateering war – even a privatised war. The Crown licensed the privateers, and in return gained a percentage of their takings; it has been estimated that from 1585 onwards, between one hundred and two hundred vessels, ranging from small barques of less than fifty tons to three-hundred-ton men-of-war, put out to sea in search of Spanish ships to capture. These privateers were encouragingly successful, the annual value of their prizes amounting to at least £200,000, and the lure of such profit attracted interest and participation from a wide spectrum of society.[3] One result was a shipbuilding boom, which laid the basis of an ocean-going merchant marine, manned and led by seamen whose knowledge of the east coast of America was unrivalled. This was vital for subsequent colonisation. In addition, the war had tended to concentrate much of the profit in the hands of a group of London merchants who, even before the war was over, were consolidating themselves into a powerful group favouring overseas trade and colonial settlement. After 1604, part of their capital was redeployed to promote colonial enterprise in America.

The year 1604 is important, because it signalled the end of formal hostilities with Spain. Upon the death of Queen Elizabeth in 1603, James VI of Scotland acceded to the throne of England as James I, inheriting the peace negotiations with Spain. By the Treaty of Tordesillas (1494), the Spanish monarchy had gained the right to explore and hold the lands of Latin America roughly west of modern Brazil. The relevance of this both before and after 1604 was that the Spanish hold on South America was such that the English had no real chance of breaking it. However, the Anglo-Spanish Treaty of London (1604), by not resolving the issue of who had the right to commercial and colonial enterprise in North America as a whole, left it open to the English to claim that whichever parts were not already occupied by a Christian nation were available for others to settle. More important, however, was that the end of the Anglo-Spanish War made it much safer to venture onto the ocean.

Yet for a time, those who were eager to resume such ventures were confounded. James refused to abandon the English claims to parts of North America, in spite of Spain's strong disapproval; Sir Walter Ralegh's charter rights had reverted to James in 1603, and he was determined to defend them in principle. The Spanish, however, made it clear to James that they disliked the English encroachment on territory which they considered to be within their sphere, Virginia (where they actually had no presence) and the Caribbean. James was torn. On the one hand, he refused to concede his rights; on the other, he disliked and disapproved of privateering, and many of those who most supported colonial enterprise in North America were amongst the most famous and successful of that trade. He was particularly hostile to Ralegh, most voluble in his support of the Virginia enterprise, whom he was to have executed in 1618 at the behest of the Spanish Ambassador. He disapproved of adventuring in the Caribbean, a particularly rich area for the plundering of Spanish ships and islands; and he very much wished to conclude a Spanish marriage for his son.[4] The result of all of this uncertainty was a temporary suspension of endeavour until men were more certain which way the wind would blow.

At the same time, interest in North America was stimulated by French efforts to carve out a sphere of influence there. The surge in the European population by the 1580s had increased the demand for fish, which abounded in the waters off the upper North American coast, and in the last years of the sixteenth century colonisation there became a serious French objective. The English first made a bid for influence in the Gulf of St Lawrence (in what is now Canada) in the 1590s, but in 1597 they were easily beaten off by Basque and Breton fishermen, ferocious in defence of their claims to control the fishing in the area. However, news came in 1603 that the French were sending out expeditions under Samuel de Champlain to explore the area of the St Lawrence, and this was seen by the English as a serious challenge.

There were many reasons for a renewed focus on colonies. For one thing, there was a belated realisation that there were alternative paths to wealth to seizing it, and alternative commodities to gold and silver. Spices, of course, had for centuries provided riches to those who sold or traded them, but now coffee, sugar, tobacco, cotton, furs and other goods might have equal value. The shipping industry itself benefited greatly, as did those who financed trade. Another stimulus was the continuing rise in the population, which increased by 40 per cent between 1580 and 1640,[5] and the accompanying rise in unemployment; disorder was feared. Unemployment in England was not confined to the unskilled, but included tenant farmers, who had lost their land through enclosure, and skilled workers in the woollen industry, which had been in decline for some decades. A particularly important spur was religious dissent, which would assume even greater importance after James's son, Charles I, came to the throne in 1625.

Much of the support for colonial enterprises came from the West Country, as had the earlier privateers. It was centred on Plymouth in Devon, which was noticeable for the dangerous scale of unemployment amongst soldiers and sailors arising from the end of the war against Spain. Furthermore, it was home to another generation of Gilberts, sons of the Elizabethan pioneer Sir Humfrey, who were 'fired by their father's old ambition'.[6] They were joined by some of the leading West Country merchants and politicians, with the latter uniting local interests with those of the City of London, whose wealth enabled an organisation to be set up on terms which the King would approve.

Towards the end of 1605, a group of merchants and their friends petitioned the Crown for a charter incorporating two joint-stock companies, whose purpose would be to establish colonies in North America. Earlier attempts, such as those of Ralegh, had foundered partly on a lack of finance, since support normally came from one or, at most, a few men. Indeed, a significant difference between the colonising efforts of the English and those of Spain, France, the Netherlands and Portugal, and a significant factor in its weakness, was the fact that the state played little part in the enterprise. Queen Elizabeth licensed such attempts but gave very little economic support. The rise of the joint-stock company transformed colonial potential: shares in an enterprise could be sold, thereby attracting investment from many individuals who would not otherwise have dared to lock up their capital.[7]

The King agreed to the issuing of a charter which authorised the two companies. One was created by seven men from the City of London and was called the Virginia Company of London, or London Company. The other was organised by men from the ports of Bristol, Exeter and Plymouth and was called the Plymouth Company. The charter authorised the companies to establish two colonies in that part of America 'commonly called Virginia',[8] which was defined as lying between latitudes 34 and 45 degrees north, outside the areas dominated by France and Spain. The Plymouth Company was allocated 'North Virginia' (between 38 and 45 degrees north), which would later be called New England, and the London Company 'South Virginia' (between 34 and 41 degrees north). This, of course, meant there was overlap, but this was not seen as a problem because neither company was particularly interested in this area. However, just in case, settlements were forbidden within a hundred miles of each other.

In May 1607, the Plymouth Company sent two ships with about 120 men to establish a settlement on the Sagadahoc River (modern Kennebec) on the coast of Maine. Disputes soon broke out: as reported back to London, 'the Childish factions, ignorent timerous, and ambitiouse persons . . . hath bread an unstable resolution, and a general confusion, in all theyr affayres'.[9] The Indians, at the outset friendly to the colonists, soon responded by withholding their aid and trade, with the result that the venture could not send back the furs and other goods which had been expected. Supplies of food ran low. The Plymouth expedition failed because of these disappointing returns from the fur trade, the fact that the land was not particularly suitable for agriculture, and the ferocity of the winter of 1607–8. When a relief ship arrived in the spring of 1608, the survivors refused to stay. The colonisation of New England had to await the second attempt in 1620 for sustained settlement.[10]

Meanwhile, the London Company also organised an expedition, led by Captain Christopher Newport, 'a Marriner well practised for the Westerne parts of America',[11] to establish a colony in South Virginia. Three ships, the *Susan Constant*, the *Discovery* and the *Godspeed*,[12] set sail from Blackwall Dock on 19 December 1606 with 104 settlers: thirty-five 'gentlemen', an Anglican minister, a doctor, forty soldiers, and a variety of artisans and labourers. For six weeks adverse winds kept them just twenty miles off the coast of England; they then sailed via the Canaries, and arrived off Chesapeake Bay in late April 1607. Newport had been instructed to find a site that was secure from Spanish attack, but had access to the sea; there he was to build a fort and town, and explore the surrounding countryside. In order to meet all of the criteria, he sailed fifty miles up the James River, where he found a narrow-necked peninsula of land which was joined to the shore by a thin natural causeway, making it more defensible than would be a settlement on the shore. The settlement would also be near a deep-water channel, allowing ships to anchor near by. However, it was unhealthy, low-lying and marshy.

From the first, the settlement was wracked with dissension. It originated shortly after the ships set sail, with bickering between Edward Maria Wingfield and John Smith, both experienced soldiers. 'Never a reticent man, Smith had offended the highborn and well-connected Wingfield, who took the captain's ready opinions as a sign of disrespect for his betters.'[13] Once the settlers arrived, a sealed letter from the London Company revealed who was to serve on the resident council, and Smith was one of those named. However,

Wingfield was chosen President, and succeeded in keeping Smith off the council.[14] This was unfortunate, since Wingfield lacked leadership qualities and thus authority. Strong government was required, not least because the gentlemen colonists disliked hard work and discipline. Quarrels, intrigue and the death of supporters led to Wingfield's deposition and replacement by the inept, indolent John Ratcliffe, captain of the *Discovery*; John Smith finally assumed his place on the council in the summer of 1607. Continuing petty malice and factious feuding amongst the leaders, one of whom was executed for treason, were disastrous. Worse, when more settlers arrived in January and April 1608, 56 out of the total of 190 were gentlemen. Furthermore, too many of the remainder were specialised craftsmen: the London Company expected that iron, soap-ash, olive oil, silk and other commodities would be produced almost immediately for their profit. 'Those listed as "labourers" in the first group of planters numbered only twelve, and Smith complained that "the labour of 30 of the best only preserved in Christianitie by their industrie the idle livers of neare 200 of the rest".'[15]

Because many would not work, and others wasted their time trying to grow olive trees or produce glass, even elementary self-sufficiency was impossible. The colony depended on shipments of food from home, on what they could forage during certain seasons – 'the winter approaching, the rivers became so covered with swans, geese, duckes, and cranes, that we daily feasted with good bread, Virginia pease, pumpions, and putchamins, fish, fowle, and diverse sorts of wild beasts as far as we could eate them'[16] – and on corn, which they received from the natives in exchange for cloth, tools and even weapons. The importance of the natives to the settlement became starkly clear in the hot, muggy summer and then winter of 1607–8, as related by George Percy, one of the leaders: 'Our men were destroyed with cruell diseases as Swellings, Fluxes, Burning Fevers, and by warres, and some departed suddenly, but for the most part they died of meere famine.'[17] From mid-July to September, about half of the colonists died; of the original 104, only 38 survived the winter.

Relations between the settlers and the natives were fragile, with friction and conflict common. The settlers wanted food, and if they could not acquire it legally, they tried to seize it. The great chief was Powhatan, who held sway over the tribes of the greater part of tidewater Virginia, a considerable empire with a complex societal structure. The English expected to overawe the natives, but they themselves were awed by Powhatan's power.[18] Conversely, Powhatan had little reason to fear or admire the English, who seemingly could hardly take care of themselves and were dying like flies. He did, however, appreciate their weapons, and thought that they might be useful allies against other tribes, whom he reckoned more dangerous than the white men. The approaches of the English varied. Newport, for example, tried to induct the Indians into accepting English sovereignty and law; this was the policy of the London promoters, who sent back to Virginia with Newport a crown and regalia so that he could crown Powhatan a king under James. Smith, however, thought that this was stupid, 'for we had his favour much better, onlie for a poore peece of Copper, till this stately kinde of soliciting made him so much overvalue himselfe, that he respected us as much as nothing at all'.[19] Soon the company reversed itself, and decided that Powhatan's power should be destroyed and the tribes brought under the control of the English as tributaries. This was easier to decide than to implement.

One episode between John Smith and Powhatan has entered American mythology. When Ratcliffe became President, he appointed Smith as Master of Supply. The latter 'set some to mow, others to binde thatch, some to build houses, others to thatch them, himselfe alwayes bearing the greatest taske for his owne share, so that in short time, he provided most of them lodgings, neglecting any for himselfe'.[20] After whipping the colony into some shape, he set out on two successive voyages to 'search the Country for trade' (i.e., to find some supplies). In December 1607, he was captured by the natives after a ferocious fight, and then kept prisoner for six or seven weeks, which at least ensured that he was better fed than his companions back at Jamestown.

> At last they brought him to Meronocomo, where was Powhatan
> their Emperor . . . At his entrance . . . all the people gave a great
> shout . . . [H]aving feasted him after best barbarous manner they

could, a long consultation was held, but the conclusion was, two great stones were brought before Powhatan: then as many as could layd hands on him, dragged him to them, and thereon laid his head, and being ready with their clubs, to beate out his braines, Pocahontas the Kings dearest daughter, when no intreaty could prevaile, got his head in her armes, and laid her owne upon his to save him from death: whereat the Emperor was contented he should live.[21]

Smith took over the leadership of the colony in September 1608, whereupon he again put the men to building houses, digging a well and stockpiling corn. To deal with the problem of lazy and complaining colonists, he instituted two rules: those who did not work would not eat; and they would live under military discipline. He taught them how to use weapons and made them drill daily. Healthy, well-drilled colonists were more likely to survive both the climate and the natives, but not all of them buckled down to work willingly. In July 1609, a single ship straggled into anchorage. It brought news of another supply vessel, which was welcome, but also of a pending reorganisation of the colony's government. This emboldened dissidents to try to overthrow Smith. This was unsuccessful, but an accidental gunpowder explosion badly injured him, and he returned to England in October 1609 for medical treatment. An unforeseen but unfortunate consequence was that 'the Savages no sooner understood Smith was gone, but they all revolted, and did spoile and murther all they incountered'.[22]

Meanwhile, back in London, investors in the London Company, who had expected to recover their investment after two years, had decided to reorganise the colony and the company in fundamental ways. This required a new charter, which James granted early in 1609. The sale of new shares met with an enthusiastic response, and the company chose a new Governor, Lord De la Warr, who had both political and military experience. A pair of soldiers, Sir Thomas Gates and Sir Thomas Dale, were hired as his assistants. (In due course, each became Governor.) Five hundred men, women and children were recruited as colonists, and nine vessels sailed from Plymouth for Virginia on 2 June 1609. Because De la Warr was unable to leave England at that time, Gates was named leader. He, Newport and the admiral, Sir George Somers, quarrelled over precedent, and as a result they all sailed on the flagship, the *Sea Venture*, instead of travelling separately. Adverse winds prevented the convoy from sailing beyond sight of England for weeks, and after seven weeks at sea a gale overwhelmed the fleet near the Azores, sinking one of the ships. Seven of the others carried on to Virginia, but the *Sea Venture* was forced by gales in a different direction. A hurricane blew up off the West Indies, driving the *Sea Venture* onto a reef off Bermuda, the uninhabited 'Island of Devils', the impact of which destroyed the ship's hull. However, all of the passengers survived and struggled to dry land, where they wintered. Using the native red cedar, they built two new ships, the *Deliverance* and the *Patience*, and in the spring they filled them with provisions and sailed north-west to Virginia. William Strachey, the Secretary to the Colony who had also travelled on the *Sea Venture*, wrote a powerful description of the wrecking of the ship; this inspired Shakespeare's *The Tempest*, first performed at court in 1611.[23]

Meanwhile, the other ships, carrying four hundred colonists but none of the expedition's leaders, had dropped anchor at Jamestown in August 1609. This was disastrous. There was no time to raise food to feed another four hundred people, as the growing season was nearly at an end. Furthermore, the newcomers had been so weakened by the crossing – dozens had died of the plague – that they lacked the strength to ward off disease or prepare for the coming winter. As piercingly cold weather set in, so did famine. Those who could ate roots, nuts, acorns, horsehide – and much worse besides. As one survivor recalled,

> so great was our famine, that a Savage we slew, and buried, the poorer sort tooke him up againe and eat him, and so did divers one another boyled and stewed with roots and herbs: And one amongst the rest did kill his wife, powdered [salted] her, and had eaten part of her before it was knowne, for which hee was executed, as hee well deserved; now whether shee was better roasted, boyled or carbonado'd, I know not, but of such a dish as powdered wife I never heard of. This was that time, which still to this day we called the starving time.[24]

When the *Deliverance* and the *Patience* arrived at Jamestown on 23 May 1610, they found a starving remnant of the settlement numbering only sixty. Gates decided that the colony was beyond repair, and he decided to abandon it. He loaded up the survivors, and the ships were making their way down the James River when word reached them that Lord De la Warr was in the bay. His arrival with ample supplies and new settlers on 10 June 1610, the 'Day of Providence', saved Jamestown.[25]

There was still a fundamental problem: how to make the colony an economic success. The hero of this part of the story was John Rolfe, one of the passengers on the *Sea Venture*. Some of Ralegh's colonists had introduced tobacco to the court, and it had become fashionable to smoke it. Rolfe himself was addicted. The Indians also smoked the local plant, but it was very bitter; the only really acceptable variety was one grown in the Spanish Indies. However, it was not clear which strains would adapt to Virginia, nor how tobacco might be cured for transport to England. After two years' experimentation, Rolfe produced his first four barrels, which Gates took with him to England in 1614. At last, there was something which, in the words of fellow-colonist Ralph Hamor, 'everyman may plant, and with the least part of his labour, tend and cure and returns him both cloaths and other necessaries'. And everyman did, planting everywhere possible, even in 'the market-place, and the streets, and all the other spare places' about Jamestown. By 1618, more than fifty thousand pounds of tobacco leaf had been shipped back to England, and the survival, and success, of the colony was assured.[26] It was also the beginning of Virginia's career as a colony, and then state, with a one-crop, slave-supported economy.

Relations with Powhatan's confederacy were a continuing problem. Hostility was never far below the surface. The English felt contempt for the Indians, who were neither white nor Christian, and insulted them by not marrying their women; the Indians increasingly realised that the English meant to remain, and feared the loss of both land and culture. An accomplishment of Gates and Dale was the calming of relations between the two nations, not least by taking Pocahontas hostage during a raid in 1613. During her period of confinement, she converted to Christianity and met John Rolfe, although it is not clear which came first. Rolfe was then a widower: his pregnant wife had accompanied him on the *Sea Venture*, but had died on Bermuda. In 1614, Rolfe petitioned Governor Dale to be allowed to marry Pocahontas; it is clear that he anticipated possible objections to the union, and feared that he was giving way to carnal lust, since there were very few women in Jamestown:

> Let therefore this [constitute] my well advised protestation ... if my chiefest intent and purpose be not to strive with all my power of body and mind, in the undertaking of so mighty a matter, no way led (so far forth as man's weakness may permit) with the unbridled desire of carnal affection: but for the good of this plantation, for the honour of our country, for the glory of God, for my own salvation, and for the converting to the true knowledge of God and Jesus Christ, an unbelieving creature, namely Pokahuntas, to whom my hearty and best thoughts are, and have a long time been so intangled ...[27]

They were allowed to marry, and had a son, Thomas.

Another explanation for the marriage is more political and economic. Rolfe himself acknowledged that he needed to placate the Indians in order to save his nascent tobacco enterprise, and, apparently, the marriage did improve relations, since the intermittent tribal attacks ceased, at least for a time. In 1616 the family travelled to London, where Pocahontas, known as Lady Rebecca Rolfe, was taken up by the fashionable set, and had her portrait painted. This journey was also intended to serve a political purpose. Governor Dale accompanied them, taking along a party of Algonquins, supposedly Christian converts, to demonstrate the success of the Company's 'civilising' mission and encourage more of the better sort to emigrate. ('In 1616, the English in Virginia still numbered only 350, among whom Dale discerned "a generall desire in the best sort to returne for England".') Pocahontas, as an Indian princess, was highly esteemed and, in recognition of her relationship to the 'Emperor' Powhatan, she was given a generous living allowance by James I whilst staying in England.[28] However, on 21 March 1617, on beginning their journey back to Virginia, she died of smallpox at the age of just twenty-two. She was buried at Gravesend, Kent.

Within a year, the relationship between the colonists and the Indians had begun to unravel. One reason was that Powhatan died in 1618, and he was succeeded as leader of the Confederacy by, successively, two of his brothers, the second of whom, Opechancanough, detested the English. He bided his time. Another was the increase in the number of colonists, which put more pressure on tribal lands. To encourage the growth of the colony, in 1618 the Company partially suspended Dale's strict laws, instituted a general assembly at Jamestown with advisory and legislative powers, and, from 1618 to 1621, sent out another four thousand emigrants, including batches of paupers, convicts and ragged children. Disease did for most of them, so that by March 1621 the population was only 843, but these survivors took more and more land, moving out from Jamestown to live next to the Indians and consuming resources and living space.[29]

All the Indians knew of Opechancanough's passion to destroy the English, but he knew that surprise was his only chance, and pretended friendship, 'even vowing that the heavens should fall before *he* would break the peace'. Meanwhile, he surreptitiously amassed his warriors, for a sudden, massive and simultaneous attack on the entire line of English settlements. He struck on 22 March 1622. According to a contemporary account,

> And by this meanes that fatall Friday morning, there fell under the bloudy and barbarous hands of that perfidious and inhumane people, contrary to all lawes of God and men, of Nature and Nations, three hundred forty seven men, women, and children, mostly by their own weapons; and not being content with taking away life alone, they fell after againe upon the dead, making as well as they could, a fresh murder, defacing, dragging, and mangling the dead carkasses into many pieces, and carrying some parts away in derision, with base and brutish triumph.[30]

This was one-third of the colony's population. Jamestown itself escaped only because the inhabitants learned about the attack in time and because Opechancanough failed to press the attack, which allowed the English time to pull themselves together and fight back, destroying all of the Indian settlements near Jamestown and the lower peninsula. The result was a nasty and brutish war. As the Secretary to the Virginia Company noted, 'Our hands which before were tied with gentleness and faire usage, are now set at liberty by the treacherous violence of the Savages . . . [We] may now by right of War, and law of nations, invade the country and destroy them who sought to destroy us.' What this meant was that over the following decade, expeditions were sent out three times a year to kill the Indians, seize their crops and prevent their return. Peace was achieved in the early 1630s, when the two sides decided to maintain a strict separation by a line across the Jamestown Peninsula, with limited contacts for trade. This uneasy truce lasted until the second war between the colonists and the Indians from 1644 to 1646, when Openchancanough again made a surprise attack, killing five hundred settlers. But the settlers were too strong for the Indians to regain their lands. Openchancanough was captured and killed in Jamestown. The Indians were now banned from the Jamestown Peninsula, and had to acknowledge the King of England as their sovereign; nor could they prevent their remaining lands on the north side of the York River from being colonised.[31]

Nevertheless, conflict with the Indians and the accompanying loss of property (1622 saw the destruction of several major plantations and an iron works), when combined with famine and further loss of life in 1623, killed off the London Company, whose shareholders lost all desire to continue. In November 1623, the Company was taken to court by the Attorney-General, and the following year it lost its charter. James I died on 27 March 1625, to be succeeded by his son, Charles I. Within six weeks, Charles proclaimed Virginia a royal colony. In this guise, the Crown commissioned successive governors to rule with the advice of an appointed council, who were answerable to the King. The colonists seem to have preferred this to Company control, since it allowed them to make their own way so long as the Stuart regime was preoccupied with domestic crises.[32] The governors soon realised that, lacking both soldiers and bureaucracy, they had to govern with the consent of the colonists. The

Assembly of Burgesses, established in 1618, was a useful body for the necessary dialogue. However, Charles I did not grant it formal recognition until 1639, when he authorised the Governor to summon the burgesses 'as formerly once a year or oftener, if urgent occasion shall require', conceding the fundamental, and crucial, point that the assembly 'together with the governor and council shall have power to make acts and laws for the government of that plantation, correspondent as near as may be to the laws of England'.[33]

The years from the accession of Charles I to the restoration of his son Charles II in 1660 saw the colony grow steadily in wealth but slowly in population. By 1640, the production of tobacco had reached one million pounds in weight, and the population eight thousand, but the need for labour was constant if the economy were to expand. This came from two sources: indentured servants and slaves. Indentured servants might best be described as temporary slaves. Overwhelmingly, they were young white males – during one period there were six men for every woman who travelled to the Chesapeake Bay region – who, in exchange for having their passage paid, agreed to work for nothing for four years. Put to work in disease-ridden, unfamiliar territory, they died like flies. Even if they did not, there were so few women – those who emigrated were almost as likely to die – that marriage, or even cohabitation, was difficult to arrange. Few women, in fact, went of their own free will; indeed, some were 'trepanned', that is, ensnared or lured.[34] Thus, the native-born population grew slowly. Of those who were born there, half died before the age of twenty; those who survived could expect only another twenty years of life. Indeed, during the seventeenth century, 75 per cent of children lost at least one parent by the age of eighteen.[35] This cycle of emigration, death and more emigration could be broken only when the population developed more resistance to the local diseases and there were more women. It took until the turn of the eighteenth century for native-born whites to outnumber white emigrants. There was a gradual shift to African slave labour (by 1680, it constituted 8 per cent of the population in Virginia and Maryland), which took off around 1700 when its availability vastly increased with the breaking of the monopoly of the Royal Africa Company. Suddenly the slave trade was thrown open to all.[36] For nearly two more centuries, Virginia would be dominated by the economic and social effects of slavery.

The guiding ethos of the social elite in Virginia for over a century was the 'Cavalier ethic', which celebrated hierarchy, male (especially patriarchal) dominance, freedom for those who ruled, and the virtues of the gentleman – truth, fidelity, courtesy to both his equals and his inferiors, and responsibility. More practically, a gentleman also abstained from any sort of work, although of necessity this was more honour'd in the breach than the observance. The ideal of the Virginian would for generations be the English gentleman. Transplanting this ethos was the conscious project of Sir William Berkeley, Governor of the Virginia colony from 1642, when he was appointed by Charles I, until 1676. The period up to 1660 was one of civil war and loss for Royalists: not only were the forces of Charles I defeated by those who supported Parliament, but the King himself lost his head in 1649. During the 1650s, the dominant Puritan oligarchy in England used force to impose their beliefs, and many of the King's supporters fled to the Continent, but Berkeley convinced a good number to emigrate to Virginia. He then promoted many to high office and granted them large estates, thereby creating an enduring oligarchy of his own.

The context in England, beyond war and loss, was the dominance of primogeniture, which determined that the bulk of an estate passed to the eldest son. This left most younger sons with a taste for the way of life of gentry or aristocrat but without the means to support it. Berkeley recruited these younger sons. In 1663 he published a pamphlet addressed to the younger sons of England's great families, in which he wrote that 'A small sum of money will enable a younger brother to erect a flourishing family in a new world; and add more strength, wealth and honour to his native country, than thousands did before, that dyed [sic] forgotten and unrewarded in an unjust war [the English Civil War] . . . men of as good families as any subjects in England have resided there'. Berkeley's campaign was successful: nearly all of Virginia's ruling families were founded by younger sons of eminent English families during his period as Governor.[37]

The period from 1647 to 1660 saw the bulk of this Cavalier

migration, during which names famous in American history make their first appearance, with the first Madison (James Madison was the fourth President) receiving a grant of land in 1653 and the first Washington in 1657. They, along with the meaner sort, came overwhelmingly from the south and west of England, bounded by the western border of the Weald of Kent in the east, by Devon in the west, and by Warwickshire in the north – the area roughly coterminous with the Wessex of the novelist Thomas Hardy and the kingdoms of Wessex and Mercia of the England of the seventh, eighth and ninth centuries. The Royalists were bound together by politics, religion – they were fervent members of the Church of England – and region; furthermore, once in Virginia, they married each other. As a result, they soon constituted an unusually integrated elite, which went on to exhibit remarkable staying power. In the mid-seventeenth century, they essentially captured control of the Royal Council, which functioned as the governor's cabinet, as the upper house of the legislature and as the colony's supreme court of law. As early as 1660, every seat on the Council was filled by members of five interrelated families, whilst as late as 1775, every member of the Council was descended from a member of that 1660 Council. Membership of the Council had practical economic effects, because it controlled the distribution of land, the greater share of which went to twenty-five families who filled two-thirds of the seats from 1680 to 1775. With this economic power went political power over the poorer sort: as one emigrant related, 'John Randolph [a prominent member of the elite], in speaking of the disposition of the Virginians, very freely cautioned us against disobliging or offending any person of note in the Colony . . .; for says he, either by blood or marriage, we are almost all related, and so connected in our interests, that whoever of a stranger presumes to offend any one of us will infallibly find an enemy of the whole. Nor, right or wrong, do we forsake him, till by one means or other his ruin is accomplished.'[38] The dominance of this elite would be shaken in the mid-seventeenth century by a religious revival amongst the meaner sort, but the Revolutionary period would demonstrate that their essential position remained unchanged.

II

My Brethren all attend,
And list to my relation:
This is the day, mark what I say, Tends to your
renovation;
Stay not among the Wicked,
Lest that with them you perish,
But let us to New-England go,
And the Pagan People cherish; . . .
When we, that are elected, Arrive in that fair Country,
Even by our faith, as the Brethren saith,
We will not fear our entry . . .

'Zealous Puritans 1639'[39]

Although Virginia was the first of the American colonies, many Americans appear to believe that the Pilgrim Fathers were the first settlers of the future United States. They were, in fact, the second, and their motives and backgrounds were somewhat different from most of those who went out to Virginia. Importantly, they were dissenters in both politics and religion, in contrast to the Virginian colonists, who were supporters of both the King and the established Church. Yet, religious as the first New England colonists were, they had no intention of sailing into unnecessary poverty, and nor did the group who embarked for America a decade after them – the Puritans.

The failure in 1608 of the colony at Sagadahoc on the coast of Maine did not discourage interest in north-eastern America, since its fish-filled waters continued to attract West Country men, particularly members of the Plymouth Company, and certain islands became centres of the fur as well as the fish trade. The men of the Jamestown colony found it a welcome source of supply, and in 1611 the Earl of Southampton sent a ship to prospect the whole of the New England shore, during which time it drove off a French intruder. Two years later, a ship from Virginia sailed up to attack French settlements in Acadia (later Nova Scotia), thereby preserving

New England as an English sphere of influence. This all made the area less of a forbidding unknown.

The Pilgrim Fathers were not Puritans,[40] who wished to reform the Anglican Church, but Separatists, who believed that the Church was so corrupt that nothing would do but to leave it. This particular group had left Scrooby in Lincolnshire some time in 1605–6 and spent the subsequent eleven or twelve years in Leyden (Leiden), in the Netherlands.[41] However, in 1617, their leader William Bradford later wrote, they began to think of moving to America, since the coming to an end of the Dutch–Spanish truce threatened renewed war (and 1618–48 did indeed see the Thirty Years War, during which the Catholic powers tried to stamp out Protestantism). The congregation was made up largely of unskilled and illiterate people, who found themselves ground down and 'could not endure yt great labor and hard fare'. Of equal importance, they were fearful that their children would be corrupted, 'the which as it did not a litle wound ye tender harts of many a loving father & mother', since 'many of their children, by these occasions, and ye great licentiousness of youth in yt countrie, and ye manifold temptations of the place, were drawne away by evill examples into extravagante & dangerous courses'. According to Bradford, 'The place they had thoughts on was some of those vast & unpeopled countries of America, which are frutfull & fitt for habitation, being devoyd of all civill inhabitants, wher ther are only salvage & brutish men, which range up and downe, litle otherwise than ye wild beasts of the same.' Almost in the same breath he spoke of 'propagating & advancing ye gospell of ye kingdom of Christ in those remote parts of ye world'[42] – a remarkable indication 'of the divided attitude of the godly towards those whose land they proposed to appropriate'.[43]

The Separatists decided to apply for a licence to settle in America, and they looked to the Plymouth Company. After the failure of Sagadahoc, the company tended to limit itself to licensing voyages of exploration, but one of the few remaining shareholders, the West Countryman Sir Fernando Gorges, looked favourably on the suggestion, made by John Smith and others, that a permanent settlement be established in the area to dry and cure cod for export to England. However, Gorges decided that a new and more tightly drawn charter was needed, or else any settlement would be wracked with dissension as had Sagadahoc (and Jamestown in its early years). Therefore, he proposed to limit the new organisation to forty eminent persons, who would be co-opted rather than elected to positions of authority. It was to be called the Council of New England. He was also aware of the non-profitability of the earlier ventures, so the new company would only patent an area and lay down its judicial and administrative structures. The costs and risks of colonisation would be left to others.

It was to this new organisation that the Separatists made their application, influenced by the offer of financial help from some London merchants if they applied to the Council, rather than to the Virginia Company. In any case, the Jamestown colony was Anglican. However, the delay of the Council of New England in obtaining their own patent from the Crown meant that the Separatists received their licence from the Virginia Company, although it is probable that they always intended to sail north to New England. Whilst their primary reason for emigrating was religious, they were not unworldly, and drove a hard bargain with the merchants – their corporate unity enabled them to secure far better terms than those which had been available to colonists bound for Jamestown. Each colonist had a share in the enterprise equal to the share held by a merchant; they also had standing equal to that of the merchants in England, and were not required to accept their advice. In July 1620 a voluntary stock company was set up between the merchants and the Separatists; the agreement was that the colonists would farm, build houses, and fish for seven years, after which the profits would be shared between the two parties.

The 101 colonists who on 16 September 1620 departed on the *Mayflower*, a ship of 180 tons, included the Separatists from Leyden but also non-Separatists from London and Southampton, among their number fourteen servants and artisans hired for wages, as well as relatives of the Leyden group. There were eighteen wives and thirty-one children on board. The two-month journey was long and hard, and during this period they considered how the colony was to be governed. This was particularly important because of the presence of the non-Separatists, who, it was decided, must not be allowed to influence the nature of the settlement. Therefore, on 21 November 1620, forty-one of the men drew up the agreement known to history as the 'Mayflower Compact', a declaration of intent rather than a form of government:

> We whose names are underwritten . . . having undertaken for the glory of God and advancement of the Christian faith, and the honour of our King and country, a voyage to plant the first colony in the northern parts of Virginia, do, by these presents, covenant and combine ourselves into a civil body politic for our better ordering and preservation and furtherance of the ends aforesaid; and by virtue hereof do enact, constitute, and frame such just and equal laws, ordinances, acts, constitutions, and officers, from time to time, as shall be thought most meet and convenient for the general good of the colony, to which we promise all due submission and obedience.[44]

It is generally thought in the United States that this introduced democracy into the new land; on the contrary, the intention was to preserve authority in the hands of the self-chosen few. It was to be an oligarchy, not a democracy.

The Separatists, known to history as the Pilgrim Fathers (Pilgrim Mothers are seldom mentioned),[45] arrived at New Plymouth in mid-December. On Christmas Day they began to erect simple frames covered by rough planks. After constructing a common storehouse, each family built its own shelter. They had brought enough supplies to last through the winter, in addition to which they took a store of local corn belonging to the Indians. Nevertheless, and in spite of a relatively mild winter, 'in 2. or 3. moneths time halfe of their company dyed, espetialy in Jan: & February, being ye depth of winter, and wanting houses & other comforts; being infected with ye scurvie & other diseases, which this long vioage & their inacomodate condition had brought upon them'. [46] In the contemporary parlance, they did not survive 'seasoning'.

In the spring, the survivors sowed their first crop of Indian corn (corn on the cob), and in March 1621 an Indian named Samoset walked into the settlement. He spoke a little English, but having left he returned shortly with another Indian named Squanto. Squanto had been kidnapped in 1615 to be a slave but had somehow made his way to England, where he had met Sir Fernando Gorges, who had sent him back to Cape Cod. Upon his return he had discovered, undoubtedly to his great sorrow, that his tribe, the Patuxet, had been wiped out by bubonic plague. This had been brought to the area by European visitors, and had reduced the Massachusetts tribes to a fraction of their former numbers. Squanto nevertheless welcomed the settlers. He showed them how to plant squashes between the rows of corn and how to fertilise the land with fish, as well as 'wher to take fish, and to procure other comodities, and was also their pilott to bring them to unknowne places for their profitt, and never left them till he dyed'.[47] He also opened negotiations on behalf of the settlers with the chief of the local Wampanaog nation, Massasoit, who made a treaty with them later that month. The result of this treaty was that the Pilgrims were able to harvest their first crops in safety. In recognition of this divine providence, they shot some wild turkeys, invited some of the Indians to join them, and in October 1621 celebrated Thanksgiving.[48]

Through their hard work and the help of Squanto and the other Indians, the colony survived, although it grew only slowly, having 124 inhabitants in 1624 and barely 300 by 1630. During this period it evolved from a collective community dependent on the help of the Indians to a family-based farming society, which also engaged in some trade in fish and furs. Meanwhile, the London merchants lost both their money and their patience with the Pilgrims, and in November 1626 they pulled out. Plymouth therefore became a self-governing colony under the nominal rule of the Council of New England. The colony never really throve: as a Separatist settlement, it was adrift from mainstream Puritanism, and thus could not recruit from a wider population; it also lacked the financial resources to expand; and nor did it have a decent harbour or a substantial commodity to trade. There was little ambition amongst the colonists beyond survival and the desire to worship in their own fashion.[49] It never received a royal charter from the Crown establishing an independent legal status, and it was eventually annexed by Massachusetts in 1691.

The Separatists may have been a tiny vanguard, but the Puritans who crossed the Atlantic from 1629 to 1640 constituted a migration. There were more of them, they were better off, they had greater political and social support and they were highly educated. They did not wish to leave the world; rather, they left England to establish a New England with religion reformed and purified. They detested the reforms being made to the Anglican Church by Charles I's Archbishop of Canterbury, William Laud, but they were also encouraged to leave because of political changes and economic depression. In 1640, when Charles was forced to recall Parliament, the great migration stopped, and even reversed, as colonists returned to England to join other Dissenters working against the King. But by this time, the Massachusetts Bay Colony was firmly established.

Upon his accession to the throne in 1625, Charles I displayed tendencies both in politics and religion that increasingly disturbed those subjects who considered themselves to be amongst 'the godly', and whom others referred to as 'Puritans'. These were people who believed that the Church of England should be purged of the traditions and ceremonies inherited from Rome – in short, purified. However, this is to ignore the theology which accompanied their hatred of institutional accretions, and which can be described as Calvinist, after the sixteenth-century French theologian John Calvin. Firstly, there was the overwhelming idea of depravity – that, because of Adam's original sin, man was totally corrupt; accompanying this was the belief that evil was present in the world, and the universe was the stage for a cosmic struggle between good and evil. Secondly, there was the belief that there was a covenant between God and man, based on God's agreement with Abraham in the book of Genesis: Abraham received unconditional salvation, but took on many obligations. This is worth emphasising, because the idea of the covenant dominated relationships between God and man, ministers and congregations, magistrates and members of the community, and men and their families. All of these were envisioned in terms of a covenant or contract that rested on consent and mutual responsibilities.[50] Thirdly, there was a conviction that only a few humans were admitted to this covenant: one of Calvinism's doctrines was that of limited atonement – that Christ died only for the elect, not for all of humanity. Fourthly, there was the idea of grace, more difficult to describe but seen as God's gift to the elect, a sense of spiritual freedom which Puritans called 'soul liberty'. And fifthly, there was the assurance, for the elect, of divine love, that men were so unworthy that salvation came only because of God's infinite love and mercy; good deeds were a symptom, not a cause, of salvation. A saving aspect of this for common human relations was that Puritans were bound to love each other in this godly way: people were asked to 'lovingly give, as well as lovingly take, admonitions', a vital principle.[51] This could twist believers into knots. As Edmund S. Morgan has described it, 'Puritanism demanded more of the individual than it did of the church. Once it took possession of a man, it was seldom shaken off and would shape – some people would say warp – his whole life.'[52]

Puritans and Puritanism had been influential in the Anglican Church and English politics since the reign of Edward VI, the only son of the instigator of the English Reformation, Henry VIII; it had, however, received a sharp setback during the reign of the Catholic Queen Mary, who tried to wrench England back to the 'True Faith'. However, with the accession to the throne of Elizabeth I, the Church preached a moderate Calvinist theology, which most Puritans very reluctantly accepted, although they continued to work for further purification of Anglicanism. With the accession of James I, this became more difficult: he made no secret of his intense dislike of Puritans and his desire to drive them out of England, but he talked more than he acted. Indeed, his Archbishop of Canterbury, George Abbot, leaned towards Puritanism himself. Nevertheless, Puritans were apprehensive, fearing that God would not hold back for ever from visiting His wrath upon the sinful country of England, which had a government that tolerated so many evils.

Their fears for England were heightened enormously by Charles I, for whom his father had failed to find a Spanish wife. His wife, Queen Henrietta Maria, instead was French and, ominously, a Catholic. During the reign of James, many Anglican leaders had embraced the Arminian 'heresy', which taught that men by their own willpower could achieve faith and thus win salvation, and that good works were themselves necessary to merit salvation. This was a doctrine which could hardly be further from that of the Puritans, who carried out good works because they were already saved. Furthermore, collective worship based on the *Book of Common Prayer* and an emphasis on ritual, rather than plain preaching, formed church services. Charles made plain his own acceptance of Arminianism, and in 1628 appointed an Arminian, William Laud, as the Bishop of London. This was bad enough, but Charles also threatened the current political balance of the country. When the first Parliament he called refused to grant him the funds he requested and began to speak of policies, he dissolved it. When he summoned a new one, he had Bishop Laud preach to the members on the duty of obedience and warned them himself 'that Parliaments are altogether in my power for their calling, sitting, and dissolution; therefore, as I find the fruits of them good or evil, they are to continue, or not to be'. When they again spoke of policies, he dissolved Parliament and began to raise a forced loan, demanding it from taxpayers as though Parliament had levied it as a tax. Archbishop Abbot daringly opposed the loan, and found himself deprived of his authority in church courts, which was transferred to a commission headed by Laud. (In 1633 Charles would make Laud Archbishop of Canterbury.) The Puritans, through preaching and pamphlets, encouraged Parliament to stand fast, not least because they saw it as a bulwark against Arminianism. The House of Commons responded by demanding an end to unparliamentary taxation and the suppression of Arminianism in the Church, even passing a resolution that anyone who tried to bring in Arminianism or popery would be deemed an enemy of the King and kingdom. This meant that Charles's greatest enemy was deemed to be Charles, so a week later, on 10 March 1629, he formally dissolved Parliament and made it plain that he would not summon another.[53]

In 1628 the Council of New England had granted a charter for settlement on their land to a group of Puritan merchants organised as the New England Company. This authorised the company to settle and govern the area from three miles south of the Charles River to three miles north of the Merrimac River. However, there was some doubt as to the validity of the charter, and the shareholders of the company wanted their title to be more secure. On 4 March 1629, just a week before the dissolution of Parliament, they managed to obtain a royal charter confirming the grant and changing the name of the New England Company to the Governor and Company of the Massachusetts Bay in New England. There was, however, an omission from the charter which would prove of overwhelming importance in determining the nature of the new colony: the usual condition in a charter that the company had to maintain its headquarters in England was missed out. If the headquarters was in London, anyone, not just Puritans, could buy shares in the company, and the King and bishops could keep an eye on its activities. But with the headquarters in America, the Puritans could control their own colony. Reassured, a number of Puritans planned their emigration; as the Governor of the Massachusetts Bay Company, and therefore the Governor of the colony, they elected John Winthrop, a Suffolk lawyer and landowner.

There were a number of reasons why families of some substance elected to leave their native land. One of the most important, of course, was mounting religious pressure. Puritans were frequently deprived of their pulpits, and recalcitrant churchwardens in local parishes were admonished for the inaccurate placement of altars and communion tables. Increasingly strict laws were being promulgated, and enforced, by the Church.[54] There was also growing apprehension about the war in Europe, where the Protestant forces were being repeatedly defeated in battle. If the Continent became entirely controlled by Catholics, what would happen to England? Along with religious apprehension came political fears. Charles I had dissolved Parliament – what would now save the Puritan cause? Was England to go the way of the European monarchies, few of whom were constrained by any countervailing domestic political power? Curiously, though, this list of threats was at least as likely to keep men in England as to persuade them to flee: some feared that they would be abandoning England to the wrath of God, and that they should stay and fight the good fight. This certainly worried John Winthrop himself.

Winthrop was one of the 60 per cent of emigrants to Massachusetts who came from nine counties in the east of England, made up of East Anglia, eastern Lincolnshire, eastern Cambridgeshire, and the northeastern part of Kent; three of the largest contingents were from

Suffolk, Essex and Norfolk. This is important because this area was the centre of the textile trade, which was in deep depression due to wars with Spain (1625–30) and France (1627–9) and general commercial decline. Half of the adult population of Essex was employed in the cloth trade. Bernard Bailyn points out, however, that the East Anglian population had been accustomed for generations to moving about geographically for employment and stability. Thus, the Puritan migration was nothing unusual. Three times the number of those who left for Massachusetts left for other colonies in America and the West Indies or Ireland, so 'Amid this continuous circulation of people throughout the greater British world, the relocation of religious groups like the Puritans, seeking relief and self-determination, was by no means "unique in the annals of migration".'[55] Beyond economic problems, however, there was concern about the temptations available to lure many, and especially the young, away from God. As Winthrop wrote, 'The fountaine of Learning & Religion are so corrupted as . . . most children (even the best wittes & of fairest hopes) are perverted, corrupted, & utterly overthrown by the multitude of evil examples.' One of those most concerned about this was Winthrop himself, whose younger brother Henry was one of those so lured.[56]

The result was that on 7 April 1630, a group of men, women and children set sail in the *Arbella*, bound for America. She was the first of seventeen ships which sailed for Massachusetts that year. Over the eleven years of the so-called Great Migration, nearly 200 ships carried about 21,200 emigrants to Massachusetts.[57] During this first journey, Winthrop thought about the nature of the covenant which the Puritans had with God, and the type of society they hoped to establish in Massachusetts. This was to be a holy commonwealth, a Christian community, where the wealthy were to show charity and refrain from exploiting their poorer brethren, and the poor were to work diligently. He set it down in an essay, 'A Modell of Christian Charity', the ending of which remains part of the currency of American politics:

Thus stands the case between God and us. We are entered into covenant with Him for this work . . . But if we neglect to observe these articles, . . . the Lord will surely break out in wrath against us . . . Now the only way to avoid this shipwreck and to provide for our posterity is to follow the counsel of Micah: to do justly, to love mercy, to walk humbly with God. For this end we must be knit together in this work as one man . . . So we shall keep the unity of the spirit in the bond of peace . . . We shall find that the God of Israel is among us, and ten of us shall be able to resist a thousand of our enemies. The Lord will make our name a praise and glory, so that men shall say of succeeding plantations: 'The Lord make it like that of New England.' For we must consider that we shall be like a City upon a Hill; the eyes of all people are on us.[58]

Early in June 1630, men on the *Arbella* sighted the shore of Maine, and sailed south until they reached the vicinity of the Charles River, where they noticed a thin neck of land protruding into the bay, central and defensible. Here they landed, and called it Boston, after the town in Lincolnshire which had been home to some of the emigrants. The settlers were weak with exhaustion and scurvy, and fevers swept through the camp. As one of them recalled, 'The first beginning of this work seemed very dolorous . . . almost in every family, lamentation, mourning and woe was heard.' When the ship returned to England nearly a hundred settlers returned with it.[59] But the remaining colonists pulled themselves together and began to set up homes. Some remained where they had landed, but lack of space and water to support everyone encouraged others to create settlements around the bay. These were organised in congregations: a group of people would pool their resources and apply to the Council for a grant of land, would make a covenant to create a godly community, and would then build a church and clear enough land to support themselves. By the end of 1630, eleven towns had been established with a total of over a thousand inhabitants. They had little trouble with the Indians, since the tribes had been devastated by disease before their arrival. And the colonists had another advantage over their fellow-colonists in Virginia: the climate. True, it was harsh and cold in the winter, but this meant that there were far fewer insect-borne diseases than pervaded the hot and disease-ridden settlements further south, and little typhoid, because the water of Massachusetts Bay was so cold.[60]

The political organisation of the community had to be established. According to the charter, the members of the Company, known as 'freemen', were to meet four times a year in a 'Great and General Court' to make laws for both the Company and the colony. Once a year at one of these Courts, they were to elect a governor, a deputy-governor, and eighteen 'assistants' for the coming year, who would manage affairs between meetings of the Court. In short, Winthrop and the dozen or so members who emigrated with him had the power to impose whatever type of government they chose over the other settlers. The only restriction imposed by the charter was that they could pass no laws repugnant to the laws of England. Certainly, they did not open the door to the influence of others because of incipient feelings about equality of station and therefore of influence; in the same essay in which he had proclaimed New England a city upon a hill, he also reminded the other passengers that 'God Almightie in his most holy and wide providence hath soe disposed of the Condicion of mankinde, as in all times some must be rich some poore, some highe and eminent in power and dignitie; others meane and in subjeccion.' God intended government to be in the hands of men such as the members of the Company, not in those of the generality of people, since the latter was not sanctioned by Scripture; furthermore, they were not fit to rule, and would be dangerous to the well-being of the community.[61]

It was, then, a somewhat remarkable decision to widen the franchise as they did. It is probable that the reasons were that the colonists were predominantly farmers, artisans, craftsmen, merchants and traders, the 'sturdy middle class of England', rather than labourers,[62] and that full-hearted mutual support was vital for the survival of the community. Winthrop believed that extending to church members a voice in selecting the men who were to exercise authority over them increased the practical strength of the government, since they would submit more readily if they had a voice in choosing it.[63] Winthrop summoned the General Court on 19 October 1630, but this time attendance was not limited to the Governor and the members of the Company; rather, it included the settlers. What was proposed, and what the General Court assented to, was that the assistants were to be elected by all of the freemen, and then these assistants were to choose the governor and deputy-governor. A 'freeman' was no longer a term for a member of the Company but for a citizen of the colony, with the right to vote and hold office. By electing a council, it was transformed into a legislative assembly. But the question remained: who were the freemen? This was decided at the next meeting of the General Court, when 116 people, most of the adult males of the colony (excepting the servants), were admitted as freemen, without needing to purchase their membership, as had the original members of the Company.[64]

No one was automatically a full citizen, with voting rights; he (never a she) had to be a full member of the Church, that is, one of the elect, or a saint. This was not easy. The supplicant had to make it clear, before the assembly of those already qualified as 'visible saints', or church members, that he or she (women *could* be church members, although not voters) had entered into a full covenant of grace with God, and this required a public confession of faith, including an exhaustive account of sins overcome.[65] But even church members could stray into wrongdoing, and here it was the duty of the magistracy to use its coercive power as a 'guardian of the [colony's] divine Commission'. The magistrates must punish those who preached heresies and uttered blasphemies if they threatened social order.[66] What kept the Bay Colony from being a full-blown theocracy was that there was a formal separation between the Church and the state, although it must be said that the magistrates and the church elders were often one and the same. The people themselves constituted the police, who reported, or denounced, wrongdoers, since an unpunished sin might bring down the wrath of God on them all. 'Families became little cells of righteousness where the father and mother disciplined not only their children but also their servants and any boarders they might take in. In order that no one should escape this wholesome control, it was forbidden for anyone to live alone: unmarried men and maids were required to place themselves in some family if their own had been left behind . . . [C]hurch members guarded each other's morals by censuring or excommunicating those who strayed from the straight path.' Such methods of enforcement were normally successful, particularly for less serious transgressions, but in the last analysis enforcement fell to the state, which was responsible for suppressing heresy, as well as drunkenness, theft and murder.[67]

In the beginning, Winthrop as Governor and his colleagues as assistants promulgated and enforced the laws and levied taxes in the Bay Colony, but over the decade, pressures from the community forced them to open up the process of government, including the extension of representation. They had to recognise that by the charter – which Winthrop kept to himself for several years until the General Court demanded to see it – it was the duty of the Court, not the Governor and his assistants, to levy taxes. By 1640, the colony was a bit less of a semi-theocracy and more of a semi-democracy.

The colony had a continuing struggle to keep its identity as a holy commonwealth, with the inhabitants devoted to living a life of righteousness in a manner agreed to by all. Internally, there was a recurring problem with those Puritans who took an even purer view of religion than the generality. Some are famous, such as Roger Williams, who argued the case for establishing a separation of Church and state. A trained minister, he came to Massachusetts in 1631, and argued passionately that outward conformity – dear to the hearts of most Puritans – did not mean salvation. This belief led him into Separatism, and he stayed for two years in Plymouth with the Pilgrim Separatists (where William Bradford, still Governor of Plymouth plantation, described him as 'godly and zealous . . . but very unsettled in judgement'). He then moved to Salem, where a number of the settlers shared his leanings. Between 1633 and 1635, he began to call for the separation of the Church he had founded from other New England congregations, on the grounds that they had not disavowed the Church of England; in 1635 the General Court expelled the representatives from Salem. Williams then denied that the General Court had any authority over spiritual matters, arguing for the complete separation of Church and state. At this point the Massachusetts General Court lost patience with him, and in October 1635 he was banished from the colony.[68] With a few faithful adherents, he moved south and founded Providence plantation near Narragansett Bay in 1636. However, both Massachusetts and Plymouth claimed parts of this territory, and maintained a hostile attitude. Williams accordingly sailed to England in 1643 and secured a patent in March 1644, which granted the petitioners a charter 'with full Power and Authority to rule themselves', qualified only by the customary warning that all laws should 'be conformable to the Laws of England'. This was the future state of Rhode Island. Williams remained a Christian but accepted no creed, and Rhode Island never had an established Church.[69] This is an example of a recurring phenomenon in New England: disagreement within the congregation leading to the departure of dissidents to found a new settlement.

There were also external challenges to the Bay Colony. First of all, the members of the Company had to fight off attempts by members of the Council of New England in London to assert authority over the colony. Although the colony had its charter from the Council, the Council realised that it had virtually no control over the plan of government or anything else in the colony. It therefore petitioned the King to rescind the Charter. In 1637 Charles I did so, and proclaimed the Massachusetts Bay Colony a royal colony; this meant that he would govern Massachusetts as he did Virginia, through a governor and council. However, by that time, his attention was dominated by the increasing domestic conflict, and attempts to enforce the change were unsuccessful.

A second challenge, curiously, came from Parliament, which in 1629 had been a strong supporter of Puritanism. In 1640 Charles was forced to summon Parliament, and this was the signal to committed Puritans that there was now 'an opportunity to serve the faith in the home country, not in a wilderness periphery'; it has been estimated that between 8 and 17 per cent of the population returned to England.[70] However, rather than being a Puritan Parliament, it was now dominated by Presbyterians, with whom the Puritans had a number of doctrinal differences, not least over the fact that Presbyterians, unlike the Puritans (who were also called Congregationalists), believed in a ministerial hierarchy. It was a Presbyterian, Dr Robert Child, who mounted the next challenge. Having first visited Massachusetts in 1641, he returned in 1645, following Parliament's victory over the King in the Civil War. In 1646 he and several others wrote *A Remonstrance and Humble Petition*, in which he charged that his rights as an Englishman were being infringed, that Massachusetts laws did not conform to those of England, and that the Church lacked proper regulation, since it excluded most inhabitants from the sacrament and their children from baptism (only the children of members were allowed baptism). The conclusion was that a Presbyterian system alone would remedy these faults. Naturally, the Puritan leadership refused to admit any wrongdoing, and Child was charged with writing 'divers false and scandalous passages . . . against the Churches of Christ and the civil government here established'. The Court determined to impose a stiff fine, but when Child and his co-authors intimated that they would appeal to Parliament, they were imprisoned whilst the Court sent its own messenger to London. Fortunately for the Bay Colony, the Independents (as the congregational Puritans were known in England) took control from the Presbyterians, and in 1648 the Colony seemed to be safe in its relationship with the London government.[71] Indeed, this remained the case until the Restoration of Charles II in 1660, which would open a new phase in the recurring conflict between England and the Massachusetts Bay Colony.

III

Religious dissent also played a part in the establishment of two examples of a different type of colony, known as a 'proprietary' colony, which was one set up by a proprietor rather than by a joint-stock company. Two examples were Maryland and Pennsylvania, both of whose proprietors shared a desire to enrich themselves whilst providing a place of refuge for their co-religionists, Catholic and Quaker respectively. The proprietor of Maryland eventually, and the proprietor of Pennsylvania from the outset, allowed freedom of religion – anathema to both Massachusetts and Virginia. Each proprietor received his charter in part because of friendship with the current King. But the two colonies diverged sharply from each other in terms of their social and economic systems, and of their political cultures.

George Calvert, the first Lord Baltimore and a Catholic convert, was an investor in the Virginia Company. The Company, however, would not allow Catholics to become full citizens – part of a general discrimination against them at the time. Guy Fawkes and a group of fellow radical Catholics had reportedly planned to kill James I on 5 November 1605 by blowing up Parliament with the King inside; this so-called Gunpowder Plot had led to a considerable tightening of laws against the Catholics.[72] Furthermore, England was at war with Spain, the leader of Catholic Europe, from 1625 to 1630. The result was apprehension about and fear of Catholicism. But Baltimore was a peer and close to Charles I and his Catholic wife. He was awarded a grant to colonise land in the Chesapeake region that had yet to be claimed, named it Maryland after the Queen, and on 20 June 1632 received a charter. (Or, rather, his son George, the second Lord Baltimore, received the charter, his father having died.) As sole proprietor, Baltimore received extensive powers over land rights, natural resources, and trade, customs and other revenues in the colony. Furthermore, he had powers which can only be called feudal: he could incorporate towns, hold courts of justice and, should he so desire, allow for a variety of religious faiths to worship as they pleased, by licensing churches. He also had 'full, and absolute Power . . . to ordain, Make, and Enact Laws', subject to 'the Advice, Assent, and Approbation of the Free Men of the same Province . . . or of their Delegates or Deputies'. No one really knows why Baltimore included this last clause, which limited his powers. It has been suggested by Richard Middleton that perhaps it was because he would have to compete with Virginia for settlers, and Virginia had a representative body. However, in an emergency, the Lord Proprietor could unilaterally issue ordinances or proclaim martial law. The only restriction, as usual, was that all laws should be 'agreeable to the Laws, Statues, Customs and Rights' of England.[73] In exchange, the duties the Lord Proprietor owed to the Crown were limited in scope: the Crown would receive 20 per cent of any precious metals, and two arrows, a year.

Baltimore's prime concern had been to increase his landed estates and their earnings, always, in an aristocratic society, the road to wealth and power. To those investors who purchased one thousand or more acres he granted manorial rights, which meant that they could hold courts, dispense justice and collect dues. Sixty manors, ranging from one thousand to six thousand acres, were eventually created, with most of the first lords of the manor being Catholic gentry, who emigrated with their servants. He also, for convoluted political and economic reasons, called a representative assembly to meet on 25 January 1638, which passed a number of Acts. One was an oath of allegiance to the King, in order to reassure the Crown that Maryland was not going to be a haven for potential regicides such as Guy Fawkes; the fear of some of the Protestant representatives was that all non-Anglican faiths might be suppressed if they did not openly support the King. The second Act established the form of the future legislature, modelled on Parliament, with a governor and council, the lords of the manor as an upper house, and one or two freemen elected from every hundred (a local government jurisdiction, later replaced by the parish) making up a lower house. The third Act stipulated that an assembly was to be summoned at least every three years, with 'the like power, privileges, authority, and jurisdiction . . . as in the House of Commons'. Baltimore's response was that the assembly had had no legal right to initiate this legislation, and he nullified all of the Acts. The following year, however, he allowed the Governor of the colony, his brother Leonard Calvert, to be more flexible, and most of the laws were accepted.[74]

The security of Baltimore's proprietorship of the colony waxed and waned between 1642 and 1656. The outbreak of the English Civil War in 1642 occasioned great suspicion of the Catholic Baltimore, and some of his Protestant enemies took the opportunity to take over the colony in the name of securing Protestantism (Calvert had returned to England to consult his brother). Upon his return, however, Calvert enlisted the aid of the Governor of Virginia, Sir William Berkeley, and in 1644 he recaptured the colony. Baltimore's influence at court meant that for a time he could stave off further attacks, but in 1649, the year Charles I was executed, he decided it was politic to appoint a Protestant governor. He also introduced a Bill for religious toleration in the Maryland assembly, partly in answer to Protestant pressure in the colony itself – four hundred zealous Puritans had been expelled from Virginia by Berkeley and had crossed the border to settle in Maryland – and partly to save his proprietorship, since a radical Puritan bloc controlled the so-called 'Rump Parliament' in London. However, these moves did not save his position. In 1650 Parliament sent a commission to seize several of the colonies, including Maryland, and Baltimore was ousted.

In late 1653 Oliver Cromwell, one of the leaders of the Parliamentary forces during the Civil War, took up the reins of government as Lord Protector. He eventually decided that it was dangerous to have an unstable colony with a radical Puritan element in charge, and in 1657 Baltimore was reinstated. 'An Act Concerning Religion' was then passed. This was a remarkable document, unique in its scope and purpose: 'And whereas the enforcing of conscience in matters of religion has frequently [proved] of dangerous consequence in those commonwealths where it has been practiced[,] . . . no person or persons . . . professing to believe in Jesus Christ, shall, from henceforth, be any way troubled . . . in respect of his or her religion, nor in the free exercise thereof, nor any way compelled to the belief or exercise of any other religion against his or her consent'.[75]

After the Restoration of the monarchy in 1660 and the accession of Charles II, Baltimore consolidated his hold on the colony. It was not to last. He sent first his brother and then his son out as Governor, and his friends controlled the Council, but more and more Protestants were being elected to the Assembly, which eventually precipitated a clash between it and the proprietary faction. The accession of James II, the brother of Charles II, to the throne in 1685 exacerbated tensions. James II was a Catholic; he also strove to recover the powers of the monarchy and centralise the making and administration of policy. As many of his subjects correctly perceived, he was trying to impose the Continental model of absolutism on England and Scotland. Protestants both at home and in the colonies were increasingly alarmed. Many of the Maryland Protestants grew convinced that there were plans afoot to attack their religion, and in 1688 they formed an 'association in arms for the defence of the Protestant Religion'. There was deep suspicion between the colonial government and the Protestant Association, but matters were soon settled with the Glorious Revolution of 1688.

In the spring of 1688 James II's second wife, Mary Beatrice of Modena, gave birth to a son, thereby raising the probability of a Catholic succession and the continuance of James's centralising policies. The assumption had always been that James's daughter Mary Stuart, a Protestant, would succeed him, but she had now been removed from the immediate succession. This galvanised much of the political nation, who looked around for an alternative. Fortunately, one was immediately to hand: Mary and her husband, William of Orange, Stadholder and captain-general of Protestant Holland. Accordingly, in June 1688, seven prominent Englishmen wrote to William, asking him to come to the rescue of the people of England. He was only too happy to oblige: Holland was threatened by the Catholic Louis XIV, and William wanted to co-opt English resources and power for the struggle against France. He put together a fleet four times the size of any Spanish armada, and, in the autumn of 1688, led a successful Dutch invasion of England, landing in the West Country at Torbay. Marching towards London, he was everywhere greeted with acclaim. By the middle of November, James had given up and fled to France, throwing the Great Seal of England into the River Thames as he departed.

Parliament offered the Crown to Mary, but she had already told William, and insisted to Parliament, that he should not be considered merely her consort, but should reign with her as King, with full executive authority during his lifetime. In April 1689 they were crowned as William III and Mary II, thereby securing the Protestant succession and eventual parliamentary supremacy. [76] Once reports of the succession made their way to Maryland, the Protestant Association took matters into their own hands, and on 16 July 1689 they took over the State House and then laid siege to Lord Baltimore's country house, forcing the Deputy Governor to flee. With this, the proprietary government collapsed, and Maryland became a royal colony, with the governor appointed by the Crown.

Meanwhile, it had developed both economically and socially. The new colony had learned from the mistakes of Virginia, and the colonists in the first years concentrated on clearing the land for corn, planting apple trees for cider,[77] and raising pigs and cattle. Once the basic economy for survival was established, the settlers planted tobacco, a cash crop with a ready market. This required labour and, as did Virginia, Maryland developed on the backs of indentured servants. They were both Chesapeake colonies, and shared the same disease-ridden climate and high mortality rates. Before 1640, the population was about 400; by 1660 the white population had risen to 8,400, but this was through immigration, not natural increase; only at the turn of the century did native-born inhabitants provide a larger increase in the population than did immigrants. As in Virginia, when the arrival of indentured servants began to decline – and in the later seventeenth century the numbers emigrating fell by 3 per cent each year – planters began to buy slaves. By 1700, out of a population of 29,600, over 3,000 were slaves.[78] As in Virginia, a nascent aristocracy began to build and furnish in a manner which reflected its social ambitions; indeed, in many ways, the two Chesapeake colonies grew alike. Virginia and Maryland both developed into stable societies, but with one-crop, slave-holding economies.

IV

Come Friends, let's away,
Since our Yea and Nay
In England is now slighted,
To the Indies wee'll goe,
And our Lights to them show,
That they be no longer
benighted.

'The Quakers Farewell
to England . . .'[79]

A second proprietary colony, Pennsylvania, had a very different trajectory. It was a Quaker colony, one of several, although it was the largest and richest. William Penn, the founder of Pennsylvania, was a complex man. He was born in 1644 into a military family, nearly became a professional soldier, and always celebrated the virtues of the warrior, even when a pacifist. As one historian has described him,

William Penn was a bundle of paradoxes – an admiral's son who
became a pacifist, an undergraduate at Oxford's Christ Church
who became a pious Quaker, a member of Lincoln's Inn [where
lawyers were trained] who became an advocate of arbitration, a
Fellow of the Royal Society [for scientists] who despised pedantry,
a man of property who devoted himself to the welfare of the poor,
a polished courtier who preferred the plain style, a friend of kings
who became a radical Whig, and an English gentleman who
became one of Christianity's great spiritual leaders.[80]

He also, it must be said, grew in self-regard, and by the later years of
his life could not understand why the colonists were not more grateful and willing to follow his advice.

Penn had been involved in grants for East and West Jersey, the
latter of which became a Quaker colony, whilst East Jersey was the
first to be dominated by Scottish proprietors, but he found that there
were too many others involved. Furthermore, his room for manoeuvre was limited, since he lacked the power to establish freedom of
worship for the Quakers. He decided to seek another personal and
more substantial grant. Through his involvement in colonial activities, he knew that the lands behind the Delaware River remained
unclaimed; he was also urged by George Fox, the founder of the
Quakers, who had visited the area in 1672, to plant his colony
there.[81] It had fertile soil, large deposits of iron ore, coal, copper and
other useful minerals, forests of oak, walnut and chestnut, lots of
creeks and rivers running into the Delaware itself, a temperate climate, and friendly natives. Penn decided to seek a formal charter
from the King.

He was fortunate that his father, Sir William Penn, who had been
an admiral in the Royal Navy during the First and Second Anglo-
Dutch Wars (the two countries went to war three times between
1652 and 1674) and a member of the Restoration Privy Council, had
introduced him to both Charles II and his brother the Duke of York
(later King James II): this personal connection was to be of immense
value. There were probably four main reasons why Penn was successful in gaining a charter. First of all, the King had borrowed
heavily from Penn's father, and the grant was made in lieu of

repaying the debt of £16,000; secondly, establishing a colony which would be a refuge for the Quakers would solve their plight, one with which the King had sympathy; thirdly, the land which Penn wanted was the only unsettled territory between existing English colonies, and was therefore open to French encroachment; and fourthly, Penn, although a Whig and Dissenter, had not been part of the attempt in 1680–1 to exclude the Duke of York from the succession to the throne on the grounds of his religion.[82] (It also did not hurt that his wife, Gulielma Springett, a high-born lady celebrated for her blond beauty and her Quaker piety, had many connections in English society.[83]) Penn received his charter in 1681 and held the land in 'free and common socage' for payment of a small annual quitrent.[84] He was free to grant land on whatever terms he chose, could make all laws, and could raise taxes subject to 'the advice, assent, and approbation of the Freemen of the said Country'. There were, however, checks on his power: all laws had to be sent to the Privy Council within five years, and those inconsistent with the laws of England would be disallowed; unlike Massachusetts Bay, he also had to maintain an agent in London to answer for any infractions of his patent; and all commerce had to be carried out according to English law. In exchange, the King promised not to levy taxes except with the 'consent of the Proprietary, or chief, governor, or assembly, or by act of Parliament in England'. For Penn, this was an opportunity to increase his personal wealth by dealing in land and developing the fur trade; it also, more immediately, allowed him to raise money from quitrents to pay off his own large debts, thereby keeping him out of prison.[85]

But what was equally, if not more, important to him was that he could now implement his Quaker beliefs by setting up a 'holy experiment': believing, as he did, that all people had within them a 'spark of the divine', he envisioned a colony wherein a common Christian faith transcended sectarian differences. But this would depend on the correctness of two further assumptions: first, that only pious people would come as settlers; and second, that they would put what Penn thought to be the public interest above their own private interests. Neither of these assumptions proved to be correct. Quakerism celebrated the individual conscience, and Quakers

maintained their own convictions about theology, church organisation and religious practices. These would have public repercussions –
what does a pacifist do about defence? – because elected representatives did not cease to be Quakers of various sorts when sitting in a
legislature. In the end, therefore, Penn's 'holy experiment' would
fail,[86] but the legacy it left behind was not at all contemptible.

It is difficult to imagine now, but the Quakers were originally considered radical and religiously subversive. In common with other
Protestant sects, they were devoted readers of the Bible, but unlike
the Puritans, they tended to concentrate on the New Testament:
their God was not angry and ferocious, judgemental and damning
but a God of love and light. A central tenet of the Quakers was 'the
doctrine of the inner light, which held that an emanation of divine
goodness and virtue passed from Jesus into every human soul. They
believed that this "light within" brought the means of salvation
within reach of everyone who awakened to its existence. They
believed that Christ died not merely for a chosen few, but for all
humanity.' Most Quakers believed that they could achieve their
own salvation by their own efforts. Therefore, they did not have a
liturgy, nor a hierarchy of clergy (they relied on licensed members to
do any preaching), nor did they build churches as such, nor have
ordinations or church taxes of any type. What they had were meetings. Indeed, the Society of Friends was organised as a structure of
meetings – men's meetings, women's meetings,[87] meetings for study,
for business, meetings meeting monthly, quarterly, and yearly.
Within these meetings, no one led a service; rather, all sat quietly,
focusing on their inner light, and occasionally standing up and speaking to the other Friends. They had leadership figures, specifically
the elders and what were called overseers, whose duties were to
teach and support; authority, however, resided in the Society itself,
manifested by a 'rigorous system of collective discipline'. This discipline extended from business and law to matters of marriage and
dress.[88]

It is not difficult to see how the Quakers could enrage both
Anglicans and Puritans. Religion, after all, was a foundation of society and state alike, and the Quakers denied all hierarchy and
deference. They refused to take their hats off to their superiors, to

give 'hat honour', which often drove those superiors to beat them. Instead of bowing and scraping, Quakers offered to shake hands. They refused to use social titles, but called everyone 'Friend', regardless of age or rank. Worse, there was a great deal more equality between the sexes. Women were even allowed to preach. As George Fox wrote, 'I met with a sort of people that held women have no souls, adding in a light manner, no more than a goose. I reproved them, and told them that was not right, for Mary said, "My soul doth magnify the Lord"', whilst Penn himself wrote that '*Sexes make no Difference; since in Souls there is none*'.[89] The Quaker missionary Mary Dyer, 'a comely woman and a grave matron', who repeatedly refused to stop preaching to the townsfolk, was hanged by the Puritans on a high hill in Boston in 1660.[90] The horror of a preaching woman was memorably expressed by Samuel Johnson to his friend James Boswell: 'Boswell: Next day, Sunday, July 3, I told him I had been that morning at a meeting of the people called Quakers, where I had heard a woman preach. Johnson: Sir, a woman's preaching is like a dog's walking on his hind legs. It is not done well; but you are surprised to find it done at all.'[91]

The first Quakers in the 'Friends' Migration' took ship in 1675, landing in West Jersey at what they were to call Salem. Two years later, on a spring day in 1677, 230 Quakers, mainly from Yorkshire, departed in the *Kent* for the Delaware River, and also landed in West Jersey. It was not until 1682 that William Penn and seventy or so colonists (over a hundred had set off, but thirty died of smallpox *en route*), travelling in the *Welcome*, landed in Delaware Bay to found the colony of Pennsylvania (Charles II had himself added the 'Penn' to the proposed name 'Sylvania'). Another twenty-two ships with over two thousand colonists arrived during the year, and a total of ninety shiploads of settlers had landed by the end of 1685. Altogether, 23,000 settlers came to the Delaware Valley between 1675 and 1715.[92] They came from all over England, but they were concentrated in specific areas, just as the Puritan immigrants had been in the 1630s. They came from the north Midlands, particularly from the counties of Cheshire, Lancashire, Nottinghamshire, Yorkshire and Derbyshire; as well, they tended to come from the Pennine moors and uplands, from the Peak District of Derbyshire northwards to the

Fells of Yorkshire and Cumberland. This had been the area con-quered and held by the Vikings in the tenth century, a not unimportant ancestry. As Hugh Barbour has described it, 'In the central region of the North, the Pennine moorland, where Quakerism was strongest, the villages were mainly Norse in origin and name, and Norse had been spoken there in the Middle Ages. From the Norsemen came the custom of moots or assemblies in the open at a standing-stone or hilltop grave, which may have influenced the Quakers' love for such meeting places.'[93] Their enemies were contemptuous of their supposed place in society – 'The Quaker is an upstart branch of the Anabaptists, lately sprung up but thickest in the North parts, the body of this Heresie is composed and made up out of the dregs of the common people'[94] – but in fact the Quakers were largely of the lower middling sort, shepherds and farmers, whose evangelical Protestantism set them apart from the Royalist local gentry; overall, very few of the English elite adopted Quakerism. There was certainly no love lost between the two groups, with the Norse past again of significance in the north, in that the Norse custom involved individual ownership of homes and fields, whilst the Norman custom of feudal manors, imposed during the twelfth century, was never accepted and always resented. There were also groups of Quakers from Wales, and from London, but they, too, tended to be lower middling – shopkeepers, traders and artisans. A 'solid core of the poorer sort' was largely limited to Somerset and Essex, and possibly Cheshire. Quakerism was, above all, overwhelmingly rural.[95] Interestingly, they tended to settle in separate parts of the new colony, with, for example, London Quakers in Philadelphia and Philadelphia County.[96] Philadelphia grew to about two thousand inhabitants within the first two decades, stretching thinly along the banks of the Delaware River. Much of that growth was attributable to the commercial success of Quaker merchants, who aggressively made their place in the Atlantic commercial world, trading with fellow-Quakers in London, Bristol and the West Indies.[97]

Pennsylvania was the greatest proprietary grant ever made, stretching, as it did, from Delaware Bay to the Great Lakes. Penn had drawn up a system of government: power was to be vested in him as Governor, together with the freemen of the province, meeting as an elected provincial council or general assembly. A freeman was defined as any male who owned fifty acres of at least partially cultivated land, or who paid the local taxes. Penn also set out his ideal settlement plan for townships, which was a quiet and open countryside, dotted with small clusters of independent farms. (It is notable that this pattern of settlement had long existed in the north of England.) By 1685, there were more than fifty townships in Pennsylvania. He also wanted there to be common lands and pastures attached to the townships, but these were not supported by the settlers and so failed to develop.[98]

From the beginning, politics developed in a style very different from that which Penn had anticipated. From 1682 to 1755, Quakers generally controlled the politics of Pennsylvania, from which one might assume that public life was reasonably calm. However, Quaker individuals were devoted to their political principles and habitually involved themselves in public activity; the result, more often than not, was furious public debate over public questions. They were all against evil in government, but they had considerable trouble in agreeing on what was evil and what to do about it. One consequence was the emergence of political parties at a very early date: by 1701, there were two stable parties, both consisting largely of Quakers. The issues tended to centre on the relative powers of the Proprietor (and his heirs) and the Assembly, the relative importance of property rights and personal liberties, and the control of the judiciary.

There was another notable political aspect, which would today be called the politics of ethnicity. Once Penn had obtained his charter, he sent a pamphlet around England and Wales, and parts of Holland and Germany, where the Society of Friends was well established. A number of non-Quaker English and Welsh groups, as well as English and Welsh Quakers, responded, but unfortunately, tensions between the English and Welsh had arisen by 1680, and this carried over to the colony. In the early eighteenth century Penn sent his agents around Germany to recruit settlers; among those most eager to emigrate were members of various German Protestant sects, in particular the Pietists. In addition, from 1717, large numbers of Scottish

Borderers and Scotch-Irish from Ulster began to arrive. Their rude demeanour and sometimes brutal actions soon alienated the Quakers (see below). Settlement was uncontrolled by the centre, and colonists fanned out from their ports of debarkation, following rivers or the contours of the countryside to establish farms and homes. The colony, therefore, was a political checkerboard. The Quakers, however, had suffered as outsiders in their own homeland, and as a result, the prevailing political culture 'encouraged the rapid development of political pluralism'.[99]

One continuing source of tension, especially during the eighteenth century, was religion. Pennsylvania shared with Rhode Island and Maryland a policy of religious toleration, which, Penn had assumed, would conduce to religious peace. However, he had reckoned without the Anglicans, who emigrated to Pennsylvania in increasing numbers. Coming from a country where they had formed the established Church, they found it very difficult to cope with minority status. The eighteenth century therefore saw repeated attempts by them to increase their power and influence, which bore fruit as members of the old Quaker elite became Anglicans, even including members of the Penn family. The Anglicans were also not slow in appealing to London for support. London, though, was largely powerless to interfere with any effect, although there were still imbroglios between the colonial government and the London bureaucracy. In particular, a great deal of acrimony was caused by the Quaker elevation of a personal belief in pacifism to an unshakeable principle of government. The late seventeenth and eighteenth centuries saw a series of wars between England (or Great Britain after 1707) and France, the Netherlands and Spain. Fighting was not confined to the European Continent or the seas, but usually also broke out in the colonies, where the rival empires struggled for supremacy. For the North American colonies, there was the added threat of attacks by the Indians, either alone or in alliance with France. However, the Quaker lawmakers refused to take military measures against the hostile natives, much to the rage of those frontier settlements which took the brunt of the attacks; as a consequence, the colonial government was accused of refusing to protect its citizens. London respected the Quakers' pacifism and did not try to force them to field an army, but they wanted Pennsylvania at least to raise the funds to support, for example, the New York militia. The Assembly refused. Penn himself was sometimes caught between London and the Assembly. Whilst he shared his co-religionists' pacifism, he had little objection to others fighting – he had once been a soldier himself, after all. His attempts at mediation were unsuccessful. Only in 1748 did the Assembly agree to support a voluntary militia, thereby conceding to non-Quakers at least the means to defend themselves.[100]

By then, Pennsylvania was a thriving colony, rich from agriculture and trade. It had a culture of minimal and relatively uncorrupt government and religious toleration. It was true that political controversy could be ferocious and party conflict intense. It was also true that the eastern part of the colony, the borderland, could be rough and violent. But on the whole, it was a desirable destination for emigrants – certainly more so than, for example, the Carolinas.

V

> North Carolina . . . is very hot in Summer, and not very cold in Winter . . . and has been very indifferently managed. It is a very fruitful Country . . . South Carolina . . . is very hot and has but very little winter. Its produce is the same with that of North Carolina; but its principal Produce is Rice, with which it supplies almost all Europe.[101]

The Carolinas were border country. Carved out of the original Virginia grant – as would be Georgia – English colonisation threatened the Spanish territory of Florida. Because much of the colonial expansion in North America took place during a period of repeated imperial conflict, it is probable that defence as well as expansion was in the mind of the King when he acceded to the request of eight men that he grant them a proprietorial colony to the south of Virginia. In the event, there was relatively little actual fighting with the Spanish; it was in conflict with the Indians, whose land the grant was intended to appropriate, that most blood was shed.

The settlement of the Carolinas had begun in an unplanned manner, as English settlers around 1650 began to show an interest in the land south of Chesapeake Bay. By 1655, they had crossed over the border from southern Virginia to the area around Albemarle Sound. However, the threat of Spanish retaliation, along with the presence of numerous Indian tribes, retarded further movement. New Englanders also showed interest, and a 'committee for Cape Faire at Boston', supported by both merchants and those concerned about the diminishing amount of open land in the Bay Colony, sent the *Adventure* under Captain William Hilton to explore around the Cape Fear River, where they arrived on 4 October 1662. They brought back very favourable reports of the area, and this encouraged a colonising attempt from Boston in the spring of 1663. However, the settlers soon returned, discouraged.[102]

Meanwhile, more organised colonisation of the Carolinas was being planned. The leader in promoting colonisation in this area was Sir John Colleton, a Royalist who had fought for Charles I and then fled to Barbados to become a planter. This was an island which was experiencing difficulties. During the 1640s, planters had switched from tobacco to sugar, a very lucrative export, one result of which was 'fabulous wealth for some and abject poverty for others, who were described by contemporaries as "poor men that are just permitted to live . . . derided by the Negroes, and branded with the Epithite of white slaves"'. There was a rapid increase in the number of African slaves, as well as of whites lured by the promise of wealth, and Barbados was soon among the most densely populated areas in the English-speaking world. This meant a severe shortage of land for both poor and wealthy, the latter finding it nearly impossible to expand their holdings or to provide for younger sons. Thus, there was a growing discontented mass of younger sons and poor planters, who would probably be glad to take up opportunities elsewhere. As it happened, a group of Barbadians had also commissioned Captain Hilton to explore the area, and he investigated Port Royal Sound, praising its anchorage and good soil.[103]

After the Restoration in 1660, Colleton returned to London to claim his reward for faithful service. He joined with Sir William Berkeley, the erstwhile Governor of Virginia, who had spent the Cromwell years in Paris and then became Governor again at the Restoration, and his brother John, Lord Berkeley of Stratton. Their resources were limited, but they won the support of the Duke of

York and Sir George Carteret. Colleton was also connected with the Duke of Albemarle, whose march from Scotland had made possible the Restoration, and he soon joined them, along with the Earl of Clarendon (Charles II's chief minister and father-in-law of the Duke of York), the Earl of Craven (a friend of the Duke), and an ambitious and liberal young politician who had once owned a plantation in Barbados, Anthony Ashley Cooper, the future Earl of Shaftesbury. The King was financially indebted to some of these men and politically indebted to all of them, and therefore he agreed to a grant – not the last time that he would discharge a debt by giving away part of North America. He seems to have hoped that the grant would produce tractable colonies, unlike, for example, the Massachusetts Bay Colony. In the event, he issued a charter on 24 March 1663 for 'ALL that Territory or Tract of ground' from the Virginia border southward to Spanish Florida and westward 'as far as the South Seas': that is, all the lands from Luck Island on the 36th parallel to the St Matthias River on the border of the Spanish territory of Florida. Two years later he was to issue another charter, extending the boundaries of the colony to take in everything between latitudes 29 degrees and 36 degrees 30 minutes north, which included the Spanish settlement of St Augustine in the south as well as some existing English settlements on Albemarle Sound. This was done in part to put pressure on Spain. In response, the Spanish authorities signed the Treaty of Madrid, which recognised England's claim to the territory which was effectively occupied north of what is now Charleston.[104]

The eight men were to be 'absolute Proprietors of the Country', holding the land in free and common socage for a nominal rent. They could make all laws and raise taxes, subject to 'the advice, assent and approbation of the freemen of the said province'. They could lease or sell land, establish courts of justice, bestow titles of nobility (as long as they were different from those in England), make war in defence of the territory, declare martial law in an emergency, and provide religious toleration if they thought it was appropriate and reasonable.

First of all, however, they had to find some colonists. Colleton, at least, was familiar with the problems of new settlers being mown down by disease, and none of them wanted to bear the expense of bringing them from England. Thus they decided to try to lure those already in the American colonies. Possibilities were men who found New England too cold, or who lacked land in Barbados: the new colony was warm and had rich alluvial soil along its many rivers. As noted above, some New Englanders tried it but decided not to stay. A number came from Barbados, but they disliked the demand for rent, even though they were to receive fifty acres each – and besides, they had come to one of the less fertile parts of the Carolinas, the Cape Fear region; after two years, they went elsewhere, some to Virginia and others back to Barbados.

Such failure was depressing for the Proprietors, but they had to try again or lose their grant, since the Privy Council had recently announced that such grants would lapse if there was no successful settlement within a reasonable period. Another incentive was the treaty with Spain which had finally ended the country's claims to North America, thereby (it was hoped) rendering the area safe from Spanish attack. The result was the decision to recruit settlers from England. To encourage this, the Proprietors issued the Concessions and Agreements of 1665, which, they anticipated, would lure colonists with the promise of 150 acres (rather than the earlier 50) for each family member and the grant of an assembly, which would have the exclusive right to levy taxes on the inhabitants. In exchange, the Proprietors retained the power to veto legislation and to charge a quitrent of a halfpenny per acre per year.[105]

But the colony still lacked a system of government. The intention was to provide one with the 'Fundamental Constitutions of Carolina', devised by the Earl of Shaftesbury and his secretary, the philosopher John Locke. These were unusual, complicated and never implemented. The stated purpose of the Constitutions was the 'better settlement of the government', which was to be carried out by instituting an oligarchy and 'avoid erecting a numerous democracy'.[106] One principle was liberty of conscience. Although the Anglican Church was to be established to the extent that it was to be supported by taxes, and the hope was that Jews and heathens would convert after 'having an opportunity of acquainting them-selves with [Anglicanism's] truth and reasonableness', they would in any case be tolerated. This reflected the personal beliefs of Shaftesbury and Locke, but, more importantly, the King had insisted that the settlers be allowed liberty of conscience, as long as they periodically affirmed their loyalty to the throne. Furthermore, the Indians would also be shown 'forbearance' (whatever that meant), as their 'idolatory, ignorance, or mistake gives us no right to expel or use them ill'. As it happened, the plan was a dead letter, because settlers rejected virtually all of it and refused to move to the region until it was replaced by a more 'democratic' system of government. In fact, the government of the colony from the outset resembled those of the other colonies, which was that a governor appointed by the Proprietors consulted a council and what came to be called the Commons House of Assembly, meeting in Charles Town (later Charleston). Yet, it was an original and interesting attempt to plan the structure of both society and government in the New World.[107]

The first settlers, financed by a contribution of five hundred pounds from each of the Proprietors (Shaftesbury had talked the others into it), left England in August 1669; they stopped off in Barbados, where they recruited additional settlers, and arrived at the mouth of the Ashley River in April 1670. Here they established Charles Town; two years later the colony had 271 men and 69 women. The Governor, Sir John Yeamans, summoned the first Assembly in July 1671 and instituted a survey of lands, vital if it was to be accurately allocated.[108] This, though, turned out to be unnecessary, because most of the settlers preferred trading in furs with the Indians to farming. In 1682 another attempt to create a farming economy was made, with more surveys and the promise of a free fifty acres (a 'headright') to indentured servants at the end of their period of service. However, there was a quitrent of a penny an acre, not a crippling charge, but resented nevertheless, not least because the landlords declined sharing in the hardship and remained across the Atlantic. It is true to say that turbulent and factional, even violent, politics characterised both of the Carolinas during these early years.

A continuing problem was that the Proprietors had high hopes for the colony while the settlers tended to have low ones. The former insisted that members of the Council swear to 'doe equal right to the rich and to the poore', and not offer 'Councill for favor or affection, in any difference or quarrell depending before you', but to behave themselves 'as to equity and justice appertaines'. The settlers, on the other hand, were naturally driven by self-interest, enslaving the Indians and refusing to accept the rights of the Proprietors. Yet, the Proprietors' upright intentions ring strangely today – a warning not to read current preoccupations back into history. For one thing, they had no doubt as to the justification for their appropriation of the Indians' lands. In *The Second Treatise of Government* (1690), Locke would write that 'in the beginning all the World was *America*', by which he meant that America was still in a state of nature. 'God gave the world to men in common; but since he gave it them for their benefit and the greatest conveniences of life they were capable to draw from it, it cannot be supposed he meant it should always remain common and uncultivated. He gave it to the use of the industrious and rational.' And, he asked, 'whether in the wild woods and uncultivated waste of America, left to nature, without any improvement, tillage, or husbandry, a thousand acres yield the needy and wretched inhabitants as many conveniences of life as ten acres of equally fertile land do in Devonshire, where they are well cultivated'? The answer was obvious: God intended that the English should take the land and make it productive. Locke failed to justify the use of slaves, but in order to attract Barbadians and other slaveholders to the colony, the Proprietors made slavery legal from the outset. (Governor Yeamans was one of the first to import a substantial number of slaves.)[109]

In common with other colonies, most of the energy in the early years was spent on finding a place to settle and getting established, whether as a farmer or a trader. There was a certain amount of wandering around, as settlers searched for somewhere better. The two provinces developed in a very different manner. Albemarle in the north was controlled by Berkeley, again Governor of Virginia, since most of the settlers were coming from that colony. There were attempts to sell land to settlers in a controlled manner, but some of them simply bought titles from the local inhabitants without regard to the rights of the Proprietors. There were renewed attempts to survey Albemarle, but the resources to enforce the rules were not provided, since the Proprietors had decided that there was little, and perhaps no, profit to be made there. The land was neither terribly fertile nor conducive to a cash crop such as tobacco or rice; the inhabitants were mostly self-sufficient white families who exported lumber and pitch, which was used for shipbuilding. There was really no chance that, as the Proprietors had planned, a structured society, with landlords great and small, would take root in the north. Consequently, they lost interest in Albemarle, and instead concentrated their attention on Clarendon in the south.

When the Barbadians went to Clarendon, they took with them their mode of farming: large landholdings devoted to cash crops and worked primarily by slaves. They brought along their existing black slaves, then bought more or enslaved the Indians. Indeed, in alliance with the Creek and Yamasee tribes, they set up a profitable trade in surplus Indian slaves destined for the West Indies. This caused anger among the victimised tribes, and destabilised the region. In September 1711, the Tuscarora Indians in Albemarle Province, who had grown increasingly angry at the abuses of the traders and the encroachment of whites on their lands, rose up and massacred the coastal settlement of New Bern. Aid came from Virginia, from Clarendon Province and from their Indian allies, who destroyed the Tuscarora. In due course, however, the Yamasee themselves and the settlers came into conflict: once-plentiful game had been over-hunted and was now scarce; the white population had, by the turn of the century, reached ten thousand; the fraudulent practices of the traders kept many of the Indians in perpetual debt; and, because of the deteriorating relations, traders began bypassing the Yamasee altogether, dealing instead with the Cherokee and other Indian nations to the west. War broke out in 1715 between the settlers and the Yamasee and their allies, the Creeks. It was extremely serious, not just a series of small skirmishes. Indeed, the Yamasee brought war to the gates of Charleston, killing over four hundred settlers. The colonists appealed to the Proprietors for aid, but received no response. Desperation drove them into arming their own slaves. The tide turned when the Cherokee decided to support the settlers: the Yamasee were hunted down and killed, sold into slavery, or driven into Florida.[110]

The failure of the Proprietors to defend the colonists against the

Indians led eventually to a change in the constitutional status of the colony. Already in the 1690s, a separate assembly had begun meeting in Albemarle, since Charleston was so far away. It was very active, largely because most of the settlers had come from Virginia, where they had a thriving House of Burgesses (the Virginian term for their assembly). By this time, references were made to North and South Carolina, rather than to their provincial names of Albemarle and Clarendon; this popular separation was legalised in 1712, when the Proprietors appointed a separate governor for North Carolina, thereby re-establishing two separate colonies. When rumours of an impending Spanish attack reached Charleston in 1719, and there was, of course, no expectation of aid from the Proprietors, the Assembly proclaimed itself a 'convention of the people' and chose a new governor to replace the one appointed by the Proprietors. They then requested that King George I take over the local government. In response, George appointed a provisional governor for South Carolina. In North Carolina the Proprietors' appointee remained in place during negotiations between them and the King. In 1729 the Crown bought out seven of the eight Proprietors, with only Sir George Carteret continuing to hold title to the northern half of North Carolina until the American Revolution. The Carolinas had therefore become royal colonies.[111]

The land cleared was devoted to ever-larger estates growing the new cash crop, rice, which made Clarendon Province, unlike Albemarle, profitable. It is ironic that the new crop, which drove the need for more and more slaves, was probably brought to South Carolina by the Africans themselves. As a result, a slave-based society developed in the Carolinas much earlier than in Virginia and Maryland. By 1708, one-half of the non-Indian population was black, whilst by 1720 the figure was two-thirds. In some rice-growing areas, the ratio was eight slaves to one white. By the mid-eighteenth century, successive waves of white migration to the backcountry restored the racial balance of the colony as a whole, but the coastal lowcountry continued to resemble Barbados. This kept alive apprehension of a slave revolt.

South Carolina during its first fifty years was a desperately unhealthy place for anyone to live, with the low-lying coastal areas a death-trap. As their gift to their new home, slaves brought virulent forms of yellow fever and malaria to which they, but not the whites, had partial immunity. 'The resulting devastation prompted many sayings during the eighteenth century to the effect that "they who want to die quickly, go to Carolina", which was "in the spring a paradise, in the summer a hell, and in the autumn a hospital".' One result was that in some regions of the lowcountry until well into the eighteenth century, only 14 per cent of children reached adulthood. Population increase therefore depended on immigration.[112]

Beginning in about 1717, the Carolinas received successive waves of immigrants, predominantly from counties bordering the Irish Sea – Ulster, the lowlands of Scotland, and the northern counties of England. A quarter of a million came to the colonies between 1717 and 1776, driven partly by political and partly by economic changes. From 1040 to 1745, Scottish and English kings fought over the border territories, where there lived powerful warlike families and clans who fought both on the battlefield and in private raids for plunder. In this world of danger and treachery, blood relationships were extremely important. The social order was organised to provide fighting men, and the King's law ran only intermittently, justice being doled out by the nobles, gentry and clan chiefs. With the uniting of the Scottish and English crowns under James VI of Scotland and I of England in 1603, the endemic border violence began to be suppressed. But the 'pacification' was as violent as the culture it destroyed, with entire families outlawed or exterminated, and others forcibly resettled in Ulster, where they became known as the Scotch-Irish, carrying their violent border culture with them. Many of these were later banished from Ulster to the colonies.

Emigration was also driven by crop failures and famine, especially those of 1727, 1740 and 1770, each of which was followed by a surge of emigration. Between 1718 and 1775, the number of emigrants from Ireland, Scotland and the north of England averaged more than 5,000 a year, with at least 150,000 coming from Ulster alone. The violence of northern Britain had prevented ordinary economic growth, and many were in search of material benefits, such as lower rents, longer leases, higher wages and lower taxes, not to mention food.

The social composition of the emigrants was mixed. There was a small but significant minority of gentry from the ruling order in England, Scotland and Ulster, whose families were destined to become eminent in American affairs. Although they constituted only 1 to 2 per cent of the numbers, they included, for example, the families of the future presidents Andrew Jackson and James K. Polk, of Patrick Henry of the Revolution and of John C. Calhoun of states' rights and the Civil War. A second and somewhat larger group were independent yeomen (small farmers who owned land), who had achieved a measure of independence from the great landlords who dominated the Border region. Most emigrants, however, came from the ranks below them, farmers and farm labourers who were landless and worked as tenants and undertenants. A large minority were semi-skilled craftsmen and small traders, with only a small minority unskilled labourers. Remarkably few came as indentured servants, not least because Irish servants were disliked in the colonies, where they were felt to be 'violent, ungovernable and very apt to assault their masters'. The poorest did not come, since the cost of the journey was prohibitive. What all the emigrants shared was a fierce and stubborn pride, which 'was a source of irritation to their English neighbours, who could not understand what they had to feel proud about'.[113]

The principal port of entry for these emigrants was Philadelphia, where their usual mode of behaviour upset even the Quakers: they were audacious and disorderly, and particularly belligerent towards other ethnic groups. The combination of poverty and pride set them 'squarely apart from other English-speaking people in the American colonies. Border emigrants demanded to be treated with respect even when dressed in rags. Their humble origins did not create the spirit of subordination which others expected of the "lower ranks". This fierce and stubborn pride would be a cultural fact of high importance in the American region which they came to dominate.'[114] The Quakers quickly encouraged them to move westward from Philadelphia into the rolling hills of the interior, and they drifted south and west along the Appalachian Mountains of Maryland, Virginia and especially the Carolinas. They became the dominant English-speaking culture in a broad belt of territory that extended from the highlands of Appalachia through the old Southwest. This may well have been because their culture was appropriate for survival. It was a violent and dangerous land with hostile natives, and the extended family was central. Institutionally, this was the 'derbfine', which encompassed all kin within the span of four generations and had been recognised in northern Britain and Ireland as the unit which defined the descent of property and power. Nevertheless, the abundance of water meant that small family farms could flourish without aid, further encouraging a stubborn independence. Furthermore, not only family loyalties but family enemies could survive the crossing, and much of the most brutal and ferocious fighting during the Revolution would be centred in these old feuds, now given new political clothes.[115] Within the context of the Carolinas themselves, the contrast between the plantation-dominated lowlands with their huge slave population and the backcountry dominated by fiercely independent farmers prone to violence was a political fact of prime importance, not least because the lowlands were Anglican and the backcountry Dissenters.

VI

New York, Delaware and New Jersey became English colonies by conquest. Their origin lay in the quest for a Northwest Passage to the East. In 1609, the Englishman Henry Hudson, sailing in the *Half Moon* on behalf of the Dutch East India Company, located Delaware Bay, discovered the Hudson River, and sailed up it to the site of modern Albany.[116] This was then settled by the Dutch West India Company as New Netherland. The area claimed by the Company was conquered by the English in 1664 and called New York, reconquered by the Dutch in 1673 and renamed New Netherland, and finally reacquired by the English and renamed New York as part of the treaty ending the Third Anglo-Dutch War of 1672–4. For some decades thereafter there was domestic political conflict within the colony between the Dutch and the English, between different religions, and between classes. As for Delaware, Dutch claims extended to the Delaware River, and although Swedes settled in that area, the Dutch never recognised Sweden's claim to the region, and took it over in 1655. New Jersey was amputated from New York and granted to friends of the Duke of York in 1674.

After Hudson's discovery, the Dutch East India Company established a trading post at present-day Albany in 1613. The Company was interested primarily in the fur trade, rather than in settlements, and this was just another outpost in its global trading empire. Having proved unprofitable, it was abandoned after two years. When in 1620 it appeared that Spain and the Netherlands might again go to war, Dutch interest in the area revived, because a base might be required for operations against Spanish interests in the New World. A new corporation, the Dutch West India Company, was formed to exploit commercial opportunities, and in 1624 a group of settlers was despatched to the area, travelling up to the site of the old trading post, now called Fort Orange, soon to be the principal place for Dutch commerce. Another detachment went to the Delaware Valley, establishing Fort Nassau near the site of the future Philadelphia. The following year, as more settlers arrived, a post was set up on Manhattan Island, called New Amsterdam, where a fort, church and director-general's residence were built. This was to be the centre of the settlement. The position was legalised by the purchase by Willem Verhulst and Peter Minuit of Manhattan from the Manhattan Indians for sixty guilders in 1626 (in American storybooks the price was twenty-four or twenty-eight dollars).[117] The fact that the Indians did not see the sale as irrevocable, while the settlers did, would cause much trouble and strife in the future.

The colony did not flourish as might have been expected, given the fertility of the soil and the Company's gifts to settlers of land, livestock, tools and grain. There were only about three hundred inhabitants by 1630. One reason was that the Netherlands itself was prospering, whilst if anyone wished to try his fortune elsewhere, there were better prospects in Ceylon, the East Indies or Brazil.[118] Another was that the Company had granted much of the best of the accessible arable land in the Hudson Valley as vast 'patroonships' (manors) to its most important, or at least most aggressive, promoters. Another was the autocratic nature of its government. For most of its history, New Netherland was ruled by the director-general and a few officials who implemented Company policy, dispensed justice and levied the Company's dues; there were no elected representatives. Indeed, it appears that in the early years, there was little pressure for this, possibly because the Netherlands itself did not elect representatives in the English mode.

During the 1640s the nature of the settlement began to change, as its policy of religious toleration attracted Jews, French Huguenots, Catholics, Africans and various Protestants; the largest element in the population was probably Finnish. It also changed in a manner which had political repercussions, as a number of New Englanders began settling on Long Island. By the 1650s, both Dutch and English villages began to demand local government. In due course this was granted, but the officials were appointed by the director-general, not elected by the inhabitants. After pressure, there were two attempts to establish an elected representative body, but both times the director-general saw them as transgressing the boundary protecting the Company's rights when they presumed to propose policies and taxes, and he dismissed them. At the point when the settlement became a British colony, its political development had therefore been somewhat retarded.[119]

Delaware's history as a colony began at roughly the same time as New York's, and the Dutch never accepted that the region had a legal existence separate from New Netherland. Rather, when Peter Minuit, who had helped to buy Manhattan Island, was recalled by the Company in 1631, he travelled on to Sweden, where King Augustus Adophus chartered a general company to trade with Africa, Asia and America. However, it achieved little until 1636, when a new charter was secured specifically for the Delaware region. In 1637, Minuit led the earliest colonising expedition to the area, founding Fort Christiana, the first settlement of New Sweden, at modern Wilmington in 1638. (He died at sea whilst returning to Sweden.) New Sweden never throve, having only about four hundred colonists when it was taken over by the Dutch, because it was starved of both attention – the King was focused on the Thirty Years War – and investment, and in 1655 Swedish control ended with the Dutch capture of Fort Casimir.[120]

Dutch control of both New York and Delaware effectively came to an end in 1664. New Netherland was sandwiched between two fast-growing areas of English settlement – New England and the Chesapeake colonies – and London saw it as a real problem: coastal trading was calling there in order to evade English navigation laws. The resulting conflict was part of the Second Anglo-Dutch War, fought from 1664 to 1667. An equally important reason for moving against the Dutch colony was the ambition of the Duke of York; he wanted to enlarge his estates, and the New World was an obvious place to effect this. His brother Charles II agreed, and on 12 March 1664 a charter was issued granting to James the area between the Connecticut and Delaware rivers with full powers. He was given all of the lands in free and common socage, with the right to make laws and appoint officials as he wished, provided that the laws were 'as conveniently may be, agreeable to the laws, statutes and government of this our realm of England'. Agreeably to the Duke, there was no mention of an assembly in the charter.[121]

Richard Nicholls subsequently led a fleet from England to capture the territory for James. The Governor wanted to resist, but the Dutch colonists persuaded him to yield. Nicholls then renamed it New York, New Amsterdam was renamed New York City, and Fort Orange up the Hudson River became Albany (now the capital of New York). However, the colony was not safely the Duke's until it was confirmed by the Treaty of Westminster in 1674. As Proprietor, the Duke had the power of an absolute monarch. 'William Penn thought his government of New York was a model of what he planned for England "if the Crown should ever devolve upon his head".' To shore up that power, he continued the patroonships and furthered the system by granting large manors to his favourites. A most generous grant went to Sir George Carteret and Lord Berkeley, two of the Proprietors of the Carolinas: James severed New Jersey from New Netherland and presented it to them. (They retained the colony as given until 1676, when they divided it and Berkeley sold the western half to a group of London-based Quakers; in 1682 Carteret sold his eastern half to another group of Quakers.[122]) In 1702 the Crown reunited East and West Jersey into the royal colony of New Jersey.

New York differed from other English colonies. First of all, there were no elections to an assembly or town meetings; even Nicholls admitted that 'our new laws are not contrived so democratically as the rest'. More unusually, there was a strong military presence in the colony, with New York City becoming the base for the first regular garrison of soldiers in British America; furthermore, James appointed an army officer, Major Sir Edmund Andros, as Governor. Andros's government was arbitrary, provoking calls from some quarters for a representative assembly. James refused, because to concede such a body would be 'of dangerous consequence, nothing being more known than the aptness of such bodies to assume to themselves many privileges which prove destructive to, or very oft disturb, the peace of the government wherein they are allowed'. He was, of course, correct. Yet, Andros found it difficult to raise taxes without the consent of a representative assembly. This was the chink in James's armour. He had spent two thousand pounds of his own money to acquire the colony, and he wanted to make it up and then turn a profit; but perhaps more important, he saw the colonies as cash cows to provide funds to support his plans for the centralisation of government and power in England (and, after his succession in 1685, in his own hands). Over the succeeding several years, there was intermittent non-violent conflict between James and Governor Andros and various citizens of New York, as well as with citizens in the successor colonies of Delaware and New Jersey. Taxes were demanded, customs and trading laws were imposed or eliminated, and long-standing customary privileges were suppressed. Discontent boiled over in 1680, with many merchants refusing to pay a number of levies; furthermore, they took the collector to court. The grand jury demanded that James place the province 'upon equal ground with our fellow Brethren and subjects of the realm of England', meaning the granting of an assembly.[123]

James gave in, perhaps deciding that the colonists were best placed to extract the desired money, or, more likely, that he would be unable to extract *any* without this concession. Deciding to make a fresh start, he replaced Andros as Governor with Thomas Dongan, and then agreed to the calling of an assembly, even giving its deputies full 'liberty to consult and debate among themselves all matters' for the drafting of 'laws for the good government of the said colony'. However, the revenues were to be levied in the Duke's name, not that of New York, and he privately told Dongan to raise sufficient revenue to render unnecessary any further meetings of the Assembly. (There would be no further Assemblies for five years.[124]) The first Assembly met in October 1683. Although a majority were from Dutch towns, the English settlers from Long Island rapidly took the lead, since they were considerably more familiar with such institutions than were the Dutch. The deputies began by designing a system of government. Under the Proprietor (the Duke of York), supreme legislative authority was to lie with the Governor, Council and 'the people in general assembly', who were to meet at least every three years, 'according to the usage, custom and practice of the realm of England'. All freeholders or freemen were to have the vote. Deputies were to have all the privileges of a parliament: freedom from arrest, free speech and the right to adjourn; furthermore, together with the Governor and Council, they, not the Proprietor, were to impose all taxes. They then drew up what was essentially a bill of rights, based almost entirely on English precedents. There was to be trial by jury, the observance of due process of law, and punishment was to fit the crime. ('The Duke's Laws' of 2 April 1664 had mandated execution for at least eleven offences, including adultery, denying the true God, and the smiting of a mother or father by their child over the age of sixteen, if the parents wished it. Homosexuality and copulating with beasts were also punishable by death.) In accordance with an Act of 1679, no soldiers were to be quartered on the settlers against their will, and martial law was to apply only to the military. Lands could not be seized arbitrarily, and women with property could sell it. Middleton points out that this was a remarkable document: other fundamental sets of rules in other American colonies (e.g., the Mayflower Compact) had been designed to protect the interests of the dominant group; in the case of New York, because there was no dominant group, 'the assembly had to devise a bill establishing the rights of all its settlers'.[125]

This was accepted by the Governor and the Duke; Dongan had secured a substantial revenue as the price for the convening of the Assembly. The colony now had a widely accepted form of government, but the composition of the Assembly had reflected the ethnic lines which would have repercussions: of the 15,000 colonists, 1,500 almost exclusively Dutch were in Albany; 6,000 were on Long Island, divided between five Dutch and two English settlements; and New York City had 3,000 inhabitants, consisting of Dutch, English and many other nationalities, but assimilation even there was limited. Other problems remained as well: taxes were high, large land grants went to favoured individuals, and New York City monopolised the trade of the colony. Tensions resulting from these issues would explode with the flight of James II and the Glorious Revolution of 1688 – or 1689 in the colonies.[126]

VII

There were five other colonies, the first four of which were settled by farmers from existing colonies; the fifth had a philanthropic origin. Connecticut was colonised partly by settlers from England and New Netherland, but most importantly by congregations from Massachusetts who had become increasingly dissatisfied with the arbitrary actions of the General Court and the restrictive nature of church membership. This local migration was led by Thomas Hooker, who established a settlement at Hartford in 1637. A frame of government was decided upon in 1638, and the following three towns, including Hartford, came together and agreed to govern themselves under the Fundamental Orders of Connecticut. New Haven was founded as a separate settlement in 1638. In 1662 Connecticut won legal standing from Charles II as a charter colony, and then annexed New Haven, thereby achieving the territory it has today.

In the spring of 1623 David Thomson founded the first European settlement in New Hampshire at modern Rye on the Piscataqua River estuary. This territory was included in the claim of the Plymouth Company under William Bradford, but in 1629 these claims were acquired by John Mason. He wished to establish a proprietary colony, but was frustrated by the aggression of the Massachusetts Bay Colony, which annexed the New Hampshire towns in 1640. However, on 18 September 1680, it was separated from Massachusetts and made a royal colony.

As for Maine, the Plymouth Company settlement of 1607 on the Sagadahoc River was abandoned the following year, and the next settlement was only established in 1622, when the Council of New England authorised grants to those who would settle there. Over the next several years, fishing and trading posts sprang up, including one established by the Plymouth Pilgrims. Sir Fernando Gorges assumed the Plymouth Company's claims to the area and obtained a royal charter as Proprietor of the 'Province of Maine'. However, he was unable to prevent its annexation by Massachusetts on 31 May 1652, which claimed that it was part of its original grant; in 1677 Gorges's heirs sold his claims to Maine to Massachusetts. It gained a separate identity only when it became the twenty-third state in 1820.

Vermont did not receive its first Anglo-American settlement until 1724, when one was founded at Fort Drummer, near modern Brattleboro. In 1749, New Hampshire began issuing land grants west of the Connecticut River, an area which formed part of New York's legal jurisdiction. In 1767, after the Privy Council in London ordered New Hampshire to stop, almost half of the modern state had been granted to speculators, by which point hundreds of settlers, mostly from Connecticut, had founded nearly a hundred towns. In 1764, New York had begun issuing its own land grants to speculators, who were expected to evict the New Hampshire claimants in court. Ethan Allen's Green Mountain Boys, soon to be a formidable force during the Revolution, countered this with threats and violence. In 1777, during the Revolution, a convention at Windsor declared Vermont an independent state and wrote a constitution which was the first to abolish slavery and allow universal manhood suffrage. However, the Continental Congress, the governing institution of the newly declared United States, would agree to Vermont's inclusion only with New York's agreement, and this was withheld until 1789. It became the fourteenth state in 1791.

Finally, there was Georgia. On 20 June 1732, King George II issued a charter to twenty-one trustees, who were responsible for overseeing the colony for twenty-one years. A group of philanthropists, they hoped to send as colonists those who had been imprisoned for debt and Protestant refugees from Europe, believing that this would give them a chance for a better life. The following year, James Oglethorpe founded Savannah. He planned to treat the Indians as civilised men, agreeing treaties which would be observed, but in this he was confounded by the settlers themselves, as had happened in Pennsylvania despite the intentions of Penn. The trustees also hoped to create a silk industry, presumably with the aid of French Huguenot refugees. Nevertheless, the colony failed to develop satisfactorily, for economic reasons and because of the constant threat from both Indians and Spanish Florida to the south. It was only after 1750, when slavery was legalised and Georgia became a centre of rice production, that it began to grow rapidly. By 1775, its population was 33,000, of whom 15,000 were slaves.

As can be seen from the accounts above, all of the colonial endeavours were different. Partly it was the differing ways in which they were colonised; partly it was geography and the crops which were grown; and, connected with this, partly it was the differing farming and economic systems which developed. New England was the home of the 'middling sort', farmers and artisans with no aristocratic pretensions, family farms rather than plantations, a reasonably healthy climate, and dissenting religions. The 'middle colonies' – especially Pennsylvania, but also Delaware, New Jersey and New York – had rich agricultural land and grew corn, livestock, and children. The Chesapeake colonies, Maryland and Virginia, so called because they shared the coastline of Chesapeake Bay, were aristocratic, Anglican (or Catholic in Maryland) and slave-owning, with large plantations dominating the good land and poor white farmers forced to frontier areas to fight it out with the Indians. The Carolinas could be awful – slave-owning and disease-ridden in the low-lying coastal area and poor and violent in the backcountry. New England, and to a lesser extent the middle colonies and the backcountry of the Carolinas, tended to have immigrants in family groups; the Chesapeake and the more southern colonies had largely young, male indentured servants, those who bought their passage by essentially enslaving themselves for four years. Population grew slowly in the south, because there were relatively few women and disease was rife. But overall, the English poured in: during the Great Migration of 1630–60, at least 214,000 emigrants, nearly 4 per cent of the population of England, crossed the Atlantic. Nearly all of them had in common an urgent and even reckless desire to own land, to push back the frontiers if necessary, to take over the wilderness and make it productive. If this meant war with Native Americans, and it often did, they would take their chances.

VIII

From the vantage point of the colonies, the central concerns of each were its own economic and political interests. London was aware of the diversity of the American colonies – particularly of the trouble-maker, the Massachusetts Bay Colony – but the tendency, for policy-making purposes, was to view them as a group. They were increasingly considered a very important component of the empire, which could be exploited in order to increase the wealth and power of the mother country; indeed, as has been the case with every empire, the economic benefits of the colonies were intended to accrue primarily to the imperial centre. In support of this axiom, London made repeated attempts to impose economic and political restrictions on the colonies. In America, the colonists struggled for a decade or so against some of the more onerous impositions, but gradually they came to terms with them.

From the 1630s on, the colonial governments passed measures to support their own trade. This habit increased during the period of the English Civil War, with the breakdown of the metropolitan government and the onset of a severe depression in the colonies themselves. Most importantly in this context, they increasingly traded with the Dutch at New Amsterdam, not least because their charges were roughly a third less than those of British shippers. In short, the Dutch were creaming off much of the colonial carrying trade, to the detriment of England, and London decided that this had to be stopped.

There were other considerations arising from this beyond the immediate loss of revenue by the Exchequer to the Dutch. During most of the seventeenth and eighteenth centuries, what was termed 'mercantilism' tended to determine English and then British political economy. This assumed that the volume of international commerce in both commodities and services would continue to grow slowly, if at all, and that national success depended on the sustained use of force, backed up by the skilful deployment of diplomacy, in order to make and retain economic gains at the expense of major rivals. In other words, there was only a small international economic pie, and more for the Dutch (or the French or the Spaniards) meant less for the English. The government had the duty to increase national wealth and power, and therefore to shape the economy in a manner that would enable it to pay for the ships and trained sailors who would drive other nations out of overseas markets. In the mid-seventeenth century the Dutch dominated the international trading system. Once the Thirty Years War was ended by the Treaty of Utrecht in 1648, Anglo-Dutch unity, forged in the conflict with the Catholic powers, dissolved, and they became bitter commercial rivals.

Why did the American colonies matter in all this? First of all, their purchase of imports stimulated British domestic manufactures and increased their exports; secondly, since most British imports from the colonies were raw materials, the requirement that they be processed in England before domestic use or re-export provided additional employment; and thirdly, their imports, particularly tobacco and sugar, some dyestuffs, and timber and other naval stores, meant that England did not have to pay Portugal, Spain and Scandinavia for such goods with gold and silver, but instead could pay its own subjects, thereby keeping the money in its own system. America's importance in all three areas would increase sharply up to the Revolution.[127]

It is not surprising, then, that the Rump Parliament decided in 1650 that it would have to intervene to recover and secure its interests in America. The Netherlands controlled much of England's European trade; the fear was that she was engrossing much of the colonial trade as well. The legislative reaction consisted of four Navigation Acts over the following quarter of a century, whilst the military reaction comprised three Anglo-Dutch wars. Historians differ as to whether these wars were caused by the cries of London and Bristol merchants, to which Parliament responded, or were fought simply to increase national and thus international power.[128]

Either way, for the American colonies, it was the consequences, not the causes, which mattered.

The Commonwealth Parliament in 1651 passed the first Navigation Act, which stated that all commodities imported into England from the colonies had to be carried in English ships. The definition of an English ship was one that was built within the empire, that was owned and captained by English subjects, and that was sailed by a crew that was at least three-quarters English. In this, there was no discrimination between English and colonial subjects. The Dutch saw this Act as specifically aimed at destroying their interests. However, England was in dire economic straits as a result of the Civil War, harvest failure, plague and the disruption of foreign trade, and increasing national income was absolutely necessary. The Dutch demanded the Act's repeal, but Parliament refused. There followed from 1652 to 1654 a purely naval, and inconclusive, war.[129]

In 1660 the Restoration Parliament passed the second Navigation Act. In addition to incorporating the provisions of the first, it stipulated that certain colonial items, the so-called 'enumerated commodities', could be exported only to England or other English colonies. The Second Anglo-Dutch War of 1665–7, it must be said, was the result of English aggression, rather than due to Dutch reaction to the new Act: pressure was applied by the English in the expectation that the Dutch would make concessions rather than engage in another war. For the purposes of the colonies, the most important result was the conquest of New Netherland by Richard Nicholls and its transformation into New York; as a consequence, colonists now had to submit to the Navigation Laws.

The third Navigation Act was passed in 1673, after a period of deep depression culminated in the 'Stop of the Exchequer' in 1672, when Charles II suspended payment on outstanding government obligations. The intention of this Act was to increase government revenue by the better enforcement of the 1660 Act. The Third (and final) Anglo-Dutch War of 1672–4 was not, therefore, a result of newly imposed restrictions: rather, J.R. Jones calls it a 'deliberate and contrived war' against the Netherlands, which was agreed to in the secret Treaty of Dover of June 1670 between Charles II and King Louis XIV of France. The main publicly stated aim of the

English Crown was sovereignty over the seas, whilst the French wanted to control the Netherlands itself. A more important English motive was the desire of the King, his brother the Duke of York and certain ministers to increase the power of the Crown by moving to a French alliance at the expense of the Netherlands. As it happened, the war became highly unpopular, and ended with few gains for either side. Although the Dutch had recaptured New York in 1673 and renamed it New Netherland, they agreed to return it to England, as well as agreeing that, as a courtesy, they would salute the English flag at sea.[130]

For the Americans, the reacquisition of New York was one notice-able result of the war. Another was the fact that the Royal Navy could now attend to the enforcement of the Navigation Acts. To the surprise of many colonists they benefited, because there was now a closed trading system, within which only subjects of the British Empire had the right to trade. This meant that the men of Boston had the same opportunites as those of Bristol, and the colonists moved to exploit the system. In certain cases – the smuggling of non-English Caribbean sugar, molasses and rum into North America after 1733, and the trade with the enemy during the War of the Austrian Succession of 1740–8 and the Seven Years' War of 1756–63 – the possible gains made the risks worth while. But 'by the end of the War of the Spanish Succession in 1713, colonial trade conformed in almost every particular to the navigation system'.[131]

IX

The imposition by the London government of these new commer-cial policies was just one aspect of the drive from the Restoration of Charles II in 1660, and especially after about 1675, to centralise in London the making and implementation of policy, and particularly to bind the colonies closer to the metropolis – to reduce the colonies to what the government called an 'absolute obedience to the King's authority'.[132] It had become increasingly clear to the government how valuable they were, but it was also apparent how unruly and ungovernable – in London terms – they could be. Differing ideas as to their rights and obligations brought the colonies into repeated conflict with London. Each colony had a charter – between the King and the joint-stock company, or the King and the Proprietor or the King and the corporation. In each it was made clear that the colony was not 'Part of the Realm of England', but 'Separate and Distinct Dominions'. Therefore, each was an individual corporate entity with distinct circumstances and thus distinct institutions, laws, customs and, eventually, identity.[133] But it was agreed that the colonists were Englishmen, as demonstrated by the charters of both Virginia and the Massachusetts Bay Colony: those emigrating were to 'enjoy all Liberties and immunities of free and natural Subjects . . . as if born within the Realm of England'. This was of fundamental importance, because the colonists in later days would argue that the King-in-Parliament refused to accept that they possessed the liberties of free-born Englishmen. These charters also usually provided for an elected assembly and a governor appointed by the Crown. (Connecticut and Rhode Island were exceptions, in that they elected their governors.) There was a property qualification for voting, but the widespread ownership of land ensured that the political class was much broader than that in England and then Britain.

Emphatically, the colonies were not independent from the British Empire, and until the third quarter of the eighteenth century, they did not wish to be. They shared 'the British Constitution', referring to the structure of government, the way it conducted itself, and the powers that it held, which derived from traditional practice and revered documents, such as the Magna Carta of 1215 and the 1689 Bill of Rights. Colonists were proud of being part of a liberal empire, one whose power and glory derived from those very liberties which the Americans claimed as part of their birthright.[134] Yet, from the very beginning, there was conflict over the nature of the relationship between the London government and the American colonies. What was the political relationship between the imperial centre and its subordinate colonies? There were, broadly, two answers to this crucial question. First, the view from London: it was evident that the colonies were subject to the will of the Crown, or, in the eighteenth century, the Crown-in-Parliament, that they were 'inferiour dominion[s]' which had to remain subordinate to the 'Dominion

Superiour';[135] it then followed that the legislative powers the colonial legislatures exercised, the laws they promulgated, depended on the consent of the King, by the King's grace, as the phrase went.[136] Secondly, the view from the colonies: yes, they were subjects of the King, but from the first they had had the rights and liberties of freeborn Englishmen, possessing not only laws, but customs made sacred by usage, and these could not be erased simply by the will of the King. These included both their individual and their local corporate liberties.

The Crown-in-Parliament never conceded that it did not possess almost absolute power. However, the pressure put on the colonies to conform waxed and waned, although at a low level it was constant. They were a long way away and the attention of London was often distracted by war elsewhere. The attention paid to the governance of the colonies was therefore episodic, but there were periods when pressure to conform was intense. The crux was the status and power of the colonies' legislative assemblies. What was their power in relation to the royal governors and the Crown? Once a Bill was passed by an assembly, it had to be approved by that colony's governor before it became law, which was the same as the legislative relationship between Parliament and the King. This became a problem if the governor approved laws which the London government did not. But why should this happen, when the governor had been appointed by the Crown? Circumstances often determined outcomes: they depended on the power wielded by the governor, and this depended on his support amongst the colonial legislators. It became increasingly difficult for a governor to buy support with patronage, such as office or land, because the London government increasingly kept its use in its own hands. Julian Hoppit has described the 'rage of party', the conflict between political parties, which was particularly ferocious during the reign of Queen Anne (1702–13) but continued in one form or another for the remainder of the eighteenth century. Preoccupation with the rewards of office had noticeable effects on the governing of the Empire. Sir Robert Walpole (Prime Minister 1721–42) and the fourth Duke of Newcastle (Prime Minister 1754–6, 1757–62) both used patronage to sustain a majority in the House of Commons, and not the least of the rewards were concessions on import duties and trade legislation, a number of which affected the colonies.[138]

Although parties polarised around Tories and Whigs, they lacked a formal basis. Tories 'had largely come into being in the late 1670s to defend the royal prerogative, hereditary succession, and ideas of passive obedience ... The Whig party had cut its teeth between 1679 and 1681 in the failed attempts to exclude James from the succession ... [T]hough they were as profoundly anti-Catholic as the Tories, they were markedly more tolerant to Protestant Dissent ... Many were deeply suspicious of the royal prerogative and stressed the need for a shift of authority from the executive to the legislature to produce a better balanced political system.'[138] They operated at all levels of English society; at Westminster, most Members of Parliament, whether in the House of Commons or peers in the House of Lords, followed a consistent party line. But within each party were factions, the leaders of which competed for influence, both for power for themselves and for offices with which to reward their followers. They did not necessarily confine themselves to emoluments available in England itself; rather, over the following decades, those available in the colonies were increasingly appropriated, and this limited the extent to which royal governors could utilise patronage to influence colonial legislatures.[139]

A further reason for a governor's approval of laws which he suspected might not be to the taste of London was that the legislatures annually voted on his salary, a situation which London tried and largely failed to change (its only success was in Virginia). As a consequence, most governors allied themselves with the strongest elements in the local political elite, and their interests frequently conflicted with those of the Crown. The latter tried to insist that no colonial legislative Act was lawful until the monarch, not just the governor, had approved it, but there were also ferociously competing interests in London, and approval or disapproval could take so long that laws were passed in the colonies which were stated to be temporarily lawful, until the Crown's verdict arrived. This often exacerbated local difficulties, and was a conflict which increased markedly after 1763. It was only resolved by the outcome of the Revolution.

X

A primary reason why these conflicts never became critical before 1763 was the position of the colonies on the borderlands of the British Empire when it was expanding and consolidating, constituting as they did the frontier against French and Spanish territory in North America, and that of their Indian allies. Between 1689 and 1763, the British fought four wars with France and its allies, against French predominance in Europe, for mastery of the colonies, and for control of the shipping lanes across the Atlantic and Indian oceans. As a consequence, constitutional conflicts became of less urgent interest to London, not least because they wanted the colonies to provide money and troops.

The wars came in two cycles. Between 1689 and 1697, there was the War of the League of Augsburg, called King William's War in America, and from 1702 to 1713 the War of the Spanish Succession, called Queen Anne's War in the colonies. There were then roughly twenty-five years of peace. The second cycle began with war with Spain from 1739 to 1744, the War of Jenkins' Ear; this war then broadened to include conflict with France from 1744 to 1748, the War of the Austrian Succession, known in America as King George's War and later as the Old French War. Eight years later came the Seven Years' War, from 1756 to 1763, in America called the French and Indian War or simply the French War. The first three of these wars focused on Europe, with the colonial conflicts as by-products, whilst the fourth treated Europe as a by-product of the war for colonies.

France threatened the American colonies on two fronts: from French Canada in the north and from French-controlled territory in the west, running from Canada down the Mississippi River to Louisiana. The French controlled their territory with the general acquiescence of the Indians. One reason for this was that there were far fewer French than British settlers – in the mid-eighteenth century, there were 1.5 million British colonists to only 70,000 French. The predominant French interest in the west for some decades had been fur-trading with the Indians, which they protected with a series of forts and trading settlements south of the Great Lakes and along the Mississippi; they were, therefore, not threatening to push the Indians off their land. Furthermore, the French, as a matter of policy, treated the Indians with some respect and humanity, not normally the British approach.[140] Nevertheless, on occasions the British were able to entice Indian allies, particularly the Iroquois, who hated and distrusted the French, whose soldiers had been party to a massacre of the tribe in 1609.[141] The British maintained relatively few troops on the mainland. Until the French and Indian War, defence against other imperial powers was more important for the rich and vulnerable West Indian sugar islands, and the few soldiers on the mainland were there for protection against Indians, not to attack the French. For all of the wars, the British depended on the Royal Navy to destroy coastal defences and to transport troops as and when they were needed. Thus, military success on the frontier could very well depend on which side received news of the outbreak of war first.

During the first cycle of wars, from 1689 to 1713, conflict in America was essentially a sideshow, with war in Europe the main event. During the War of the League of Augsburg, Britain had to protect herself and her Dutch allies against invasion by a powerful France led by Louis XIV. Any resources sent out to America went to defend the West Indies; the mainland colonies were largely left to fend for themselves. New England, Massachusetts Bay and the Canadian colonies attempted to mount an attack on French-held Quebec, but the result was ignominious. Although Great Britain and her allies were successful in forestalling the French in Europe, the English colonists were repeatedly defeated by New France, as French Canada was called, and her Indian allies. Their cause was not helped by their own bitter infighting and lack of unity.[142]

The end of the war did not mean the end of irregular conflict in America, since shifting and dangerous frontiers remained. In 1697, for instance, Indians from Maine made a raid into Massachusetts:

A war party of Abenakis fell on several farmhouses near Haverhill . . . In one lived the Dustin family. Mrs. Hannah Dustin had just been delivered of her eighth child the week before and was being nursed by one Mary Neff. Mr. Dustin had taken the seven children to the field with him. When the savages struck, he sent the children running to a fortified house while he started to rescue his wife. The savages turned on him, and he found he could only retreat and keep firing to give his children the time they needed. Mrs. Dustin, her baby, and the nurse were carried off and the house set afire.

Because the baby cried, a warrior seized it by the feet and bashed its head against a tree. The benumbed mother and frightened nurse were driven deeper into the forest where they soon came to a rendezvous of more Indians and captive neighbors. Some of the prisoners were now killed – there were twenty-seven victims altogether of the raid – and others were divided among the captors. Mrs. Dustin, Mary Neff, and a neighbor lad were assigned to a party of two warriors, three squaws, and seven children. They continued northward, hunting along the way. Night and morning the Catholic Indians prayed with their rosaries. The captives carried heavy loads and were frequently abused. The women were told that when they reached the home village they would be stripped and made to run the gauntlet. After six weeks *en route* Mrs. Dustin decided that a break for freedom must be made. She whispered her plan to the nurse and the boy. On the night of April 29, after all the Indians were sleeping around a dying fire, the three prisoners got up noiselessly and each procured a hatchet. In concert they moved around the circle of twelve Indians and killed all but one old squaw and a boy, who ran off screaming into the woods. Then they waited by their victims until dawn, when the frugal Hannah Dustin proceeded to scalp each one. With their grisly trophies they started back home and made it safely to Haverhill. Massachusetts promptly paid them £50 bounty for the ten scalps, and Mr. Dustin was reunited with his truly formidable wife.[143]

The War of the Spanish Succession was caused by the French attempt to unite the Catholic kingdoms of France and Spain, and again the first priority for England was to defend herself and the Netherlands. This time, England won a series of land battles in Europe as well as naval battles, including the Battle of Blenheim in 1704. This marked the emergence of England as a first-rank power. Unfortunately, the English war effort again faltered in the colonies.

It is argued that England did not take much notice of the gradual French encirclement of her colonies, and the mainland colonies involved in the fighting, which was confined to New England, Florida and the Carolinas, were largely left on their own. London promised aid, and then laid aside the plans without telling the colonists. Unsurprisingly, this did not increase colonial trust in the mother country. Great Britain also abandoned her European allies and signed the Peace of Utrecht in 1713. As a result, what are now Newfoundland, Nova Scotia and Hudson Bay became British, leaving the territory of Quebec and the settlements down the Mississippi River still in French hands.[144]

The outcome of this war marked a change of direction for Great Britain: she was now giving a new priority to overseas expansion, retaining territory rather than trading it for European concessions (although in the next war, some North American territory would be traded for holdings in India), and committing her empire to the control of maritime commerce rather than European territory. This dramatic shift elevated the American colonies to new importance. As noted above, they were important economically to Great Britain, but they were also important strategically, given that the eye of London was fixed ambitiously upon the remainder of the French Empire in the Caribbean and North America. The War of the Austrian Succession – was Maria Theresa, or some male Habsburg, to succeed to the Austrian throne? – did not precisely develop out of an Anglo-Spanish war, the War of Jenkins' Ear,[145] but it was natural in the circumstances of this war that France and Spain should become allies against Great Britain.

A major victory in the colonies was the capture of the vital Fort Louisbourg, situated on Cape Breton Island, which controlled the entrance to the St Lawrence River. This was a siege undertaken and directed by American militias, without the help of British officers:

> planned by a lawyer, executed by a merchant commanding undisciplined farmers, fishermen and mechanics, it was successful because of initial luck (which the Yankees quickly forgot), followed up by enthusiastic action . . . Louisbourg, therefore,

emerged from the war as a symbol of American prowess, as if a new military power had appeared in the New World . . . Consequently, the rashest measure Great Britain could take was to hand Louisbourg back to the French as if it were a bauble or a remote barren island [it was exchanged for Madras in the Treaty of Aix-la-Chapelle of 1748] . . . American pride was insulted, and New England turned bitter. Americans would not respond so enthusiastically in the next war with France. As they clearly foresaw, in another war Louisbourg would have to be taken again, and the lobster-backs could jolly well do the job themselves. When the necessity did arise, it required nine thousand British regulars and forty ships of war.[146]

John Adams, the second President of the United States, remembered as an old man that his father and others in Braintree, Massachusetts had cursed the British for the surrender of Louisbourg to the French. Because London had abandoned it, the colonists of New France were free once again to arm their Indian allies to 'take to the warpath' on the New England frontier. This made it clear just where the colony fitted into London's priorities.[147]

The Seven Years' War, or the French and Indian War (1756–63), was a conflict of a different type. After the end of the previous war, the French had resumed their advances into the rich Ohio Valley; at roughly the same time, the British had begun to realise that controlling this territory was more important than, for example, possessing fishing rights off the coast of Newfoundland. The French wanted to join Canada and Louisiana both by the Mississippi River and by a belt of forts and missions across the Ohio Valley. The British were keen on expanding inland, beyond the Appalachian Mountains. It was therefore vital that the French were not allowed to build a barrier down the western side of the colonies. There was fighting in North America between the two sides even whilst the countries were formally at peace, with four battles fought in the year before England declared war on France in May 1756. Even with war in Europe, the British decided to make the war in North America the priority, seeking to expand the empire deep into the continent by investing men and money as never before to conquer New France.

British success also threatened the Indians, because they had long depended on playing off the two empires against each other, partly to maintain their own independence and partly to co-opt one side as an ally against other tribes. Without the French counterweight, the British could thrust deep into the interior, transforming the lands of the Indians into farms and settlements. Many Indians sided with the French for that very reason, but the Iroquois, amongst the strongest of the tribes, fought with the British.[148]

The Seven Years' War was a war primarily against France, in which Great Britain, Prussia and Hanover (total population: twelve million people) faced Russia, Poland, Sweden, Saxony, France and Austria (ninety million). But the fact was that it was truly a world war, with battles in Europe, America, the West Indies, Africa, India and even the Philippines, and this required that British supremacy at sea be fully exploited. The war was notable for other reasons, too. First of all, previous colonial wars had been sideshows of European conflicts which had begun first; in this one, hostilities began in America and spread slowly to the mother countries. And secondly, William Pitt the Elder, who as Secretary of State managed the war, was convinced that France could be humbled by taking possession of her colonies, rather than trying – for the fourth time – to defeat her large army in Europe. 'Consequently, the focus of the war was now outside the continent, with a kind of holding operation in Europe by the Prussian and British armies and especially by the British navy.'[149]

In July 1758, Fort Louisbourg was retaken, whilst September 1759 saw the Anglo-American capture of Quebec in possibly the most famous battle of the war, that between General James Wolfe and the Marquis de Montcalm on the Plains of Abraham, during which both commanders were killed. An American innovation which had proved its worth – the organisation of rangers, a company of woodsmen to scout, bring in prisoners for information, and generally act as the eyes and ears of the army – was soon adopted by the British army. The British also, for the first time, decided to raise an enormous new regiment of American soldiers, to be paid by London, rather then depending on the separate colonies to do so. In this way, the Americans would serve in the regular army, but would fight together. The regiment was called the Royal Americans, and was numbered the 62nd and then the 60th. Its descendants still form part of the British army.[150] In the end, the French and their Indian allies lost, and all of New France became part of the British Empire. The British had simply overwhelmed New France through sheer numbers of soldiers and sailors, warships and cannon. That ability to project military power across the Atlantic Ocean reflected British superiority in shipping, finance and organisation. But it was something of a pyrrhic victory for Great Britain: the post-war attempts to centralise imperial relations, and to tax the colonies far more heavily in order to pay off the huge national debt arising from the wars and to finance colonial defence, constituted the catalyst for the American Revolution.[151]

XI

Anglo-American relations during the colonial period were not limited to domestic and imperial conflict. On the contrary, there were increasing links between the centre and the periphery, not only economic, but also social and cultural, intellectual and religious. These links in their turn depended on a great improvement in communications: by 1730, instead of needing to wait days or weeks for the next ship to sail in order to send news, sailings were sufficiently frequent, and the American postal service had increased sufficiently in range and frequency, to allow friends, relatives and political and intellectual contacts something approaching regular, if still slow, correspondence. As an important consequence, Ned Landsman has argued, Americans came to view themselves as more truly British than they had done before about 1680, when their identification was almost entirely with their particular colony, seeing themselves as men of Massachusetts or as Virginians. An identity as provincial Britons (and Protestants), rather than colonists, began to develop. These were full members of a rich and successful British Empire.

Americans were conscious of living in a relatively rude, unpolished society, one situated on the edge of, and threatened by, barbarism. The Indians and Africans were savage, not 'civil'. By civility, the colonists tended to mean societies organised according to the rule of law, although many colonial settlements frequently failed to exhibit such devotion. Nevertheless, colonists considered this a primary mark of their difference from the Indians.[152] Colonists were also, of course, civilised in their mode of living, but here they realised that there was room for improvement. The members of the colonial elites, in particular, were aware of the relative lack of polish of their societies, and even of themselves, and looked to London to provide it. As Paul Langford has pointed out, 'The English gentleman's claim to fame . . . was that he uniquely combined good nature with civilized manners.'[153]

One reason why they were self-conscious in this matter was that the concept of politeness, of a 'polite' society, was increasingly important in Great Britain itself.[154] The term 'polite' had a more substantive meaning than today's use of it to mean manners or etiquette: it meant not using violence and the sword to deal with opposition, nor even sharp command or aggressive argument, but persuasion; it meant a lack of bigotry in religion or politics; it meant depending on reason and reflection, not tradition or ancient authorities, when coming to a decision. It was a means of uplifting society, of separating it from barbarity, of 'polishing' rude manners. The characteristic polite literary form was the essay, and the most important publication conveying this form of persuasion was the periodical *The Spectator*, published only from 1711 to 1714, but the essays from which were still being published in book form on both sides of the Atlantic over a century later. 'It was renowned for its graceful, "polite" style, which was affable in tone . . . and spread a moderate but uplifting influence both in manners and in taste. It was meant to persuade, rather than to argue or command, as much on the basis of style and sentiment as on the specifics of the case; . . . Its characteristic form was the essay, shorter and less definitive than the treatise, but more substantial than mere assertion – the perfect form to achieve its goal of persuasion.'[155]

One American set out to learn to write from the *The Spectator*. In his *Autobiography*, Benjamin Franklin tells how he decided to improve his manner of writing after his father had pointed out its lack of elegance of expression and inadequate organisation of arguments. Franklin recalled that 'About this time, I met with an odd

Volume of the Spectator . . . I thought the Writing excellent, & wish'd if possible to imitate it. With that View, I took some of the Papers, & making short Hints of the Sentiment in each Sentence, laid them by a few Days, and then without looking at the Book, try'd to compleat the Papers again, by expressing each hinted Sentence at length & as fully as it had been express'd before, in any suitable Words that should come to hand.' He was particularly interested in the method of marshalling, and then expressing, arguments: Mr Spectator often stated his arguments with a pleasing uncertainty, rather than hurling them at his opponent, as Franklin admitted he had been wont to do, taking his cue from religious disputations.[156]

Colonial Americans were able to acquire and read the *The Spectator* because they were part of a transatlantic literary world, the term for which in the eighteenth century was the 'republic of letters'. Periodicals and books crossed the ocean, with the first half of the eighteenth century seeing the development of a thriving transatlantic book trade, complementing the increasing printing capabilities in America itself – Franklin himself made his living for some years as a printer in Philadelphia. Although many of the books from Great Britain were religious, there were also increasing numbers of histories, poetry and novels.

The century saw the development of the novel in Great Britain, and Americans did not long remain ignorant of it. This was linked with an increase in the reading public and particularly with an increasingly literate sector of urban women. The dominant subjects were probably men's career and especially women's (and men's) marriage choices in an increasingly commercial society. Because of the subject matter, which was often seduction and romance, the novel was condemned by leaders of society and of the Church – certainly Jane Austen mentioned the disdain often shown to novels.[157] One reaction was to supplant the authors of these dangerous books by writing, as the prosperous London printer and Dissenter Samuel Richardson did, novels which were morally instructive. His *Pamela, or Virtue Rewarded* (1740) is considered by many to be the first proper English novel – it was certainly the first to be published in the American colonies, including an edition by Franklin in 1742. It was so popular that teacups emblazoned with her image were produced. Pamela is a fifteen-year-old girl, pious and virtuous, the daughter of a former schoolmaster now down on his luck. She is maidservant to an old woman who dies, and she is then kept on by the lady's son. He conceives a passion for her, and much of the book is taken up with his attempts to seduce her, by word or deed, and her repeated success in fending him off. He then accepts her virtue, and marries her – her virtue is rewarded. The book's wild success attracted disparagement: Henry Fielding, author of the popular novel *Tom Jones*, remarked that its popularity owed less to its moral pronouncements than to its ability to titillate – and considering the scene describing an attempted rape, he may well have been correct. It certainly retains its sheer readability.

Pamela as a manual showing the individual how to live a moral and virtuous life did have a place in American female society. Esther Edwards Burr, the daughter of Jonathan Edwards, an influential theologian and preacher, devoted a steady correspondence with a friend in 1754 to discussing the novel and drawing moral reflections from it. They were typical of the urban, educated women who read novels. Curiously, there seems to have been a geographical divide in America over types of novel: the north preferred the moralism of *Pamela*, whilst the southern colonies liked the wittier *Tom Jones*[158] – choices perhaps determined, even if unconsciously, by the religious origins of New England versus those of the South.

Besides histories and novels, there were two other categories of books sent from Europe to the colonies, and these linked Americans to the European political and scientific Enlightenment. Politically, as Bernard Bailyn has pointed out,

It is not simply that the great *virtuosi* of the American Enlightenment – Franklin, [John] Adams, [Thomas] Jefferson – [read] the classic Enlightenment texts . . . They did so; but they were not alone. The ideas and writings of the leading secular thinkers of the European Enlightenment – reformers and social critics like Voltaire, Rousseau, and Beccaria as well as conservative analysts like Montesquieu – were quoted everywhere in the colonies, by everyone who claimed a broad awareness. In pamphlet after pamphlet the American writers cited Locke on natural rights and on social and governmental contract, Montesquieu and later Delolme on the character of British liberty and on the institutional requirements for its attainment, Voltaire on the evils of clerical oppression.[159]

As for science, this was also the period of scientific 'virtuosi', men of education and leisure who took a strong, if sometimes shallow, interest in developments in science. Americans were part of this community, although their relative isolation kept most of them from contributing much to demonstrations and discussions. But not all of them: Franklin, a printer, inventor, later Founding Father and general Renaissance man, was at the centre of the scientific revolution. He it was who flew a kite connected to a key in the middle of a thunderstorm to find out whether lightning was indeed electricity – he was lucky not to have electrocuted himself – and went on to invent the lightning rod, which directs lightning harmlessly into the earth. The respect for him in London was so great that he was elected a Fellow of the Royal Society in 1756, a position of great intellectual eminence then as today.

Indeed, the creation of scientific societies was one of the characteristic features of this period in both Great Britain and America. The establishment of such societies in America was one means by which local educated, and would-be better-educated, men, and some women, tried to improve the level of their culture in order to catch up with that of Great Britain. The areas in which they could match, and sometimes even better, European efforts were natural history, especially botany – there were thousands of previously unknown plants in the colonies – and the study of humanity, as it was termed then (what is now called anthropology or ethnology). Here, of course, the Indians were natural subjects. As citizens of the New World, in this area of study at least Americans had much to teach the Old, and there was widespread transatlantic correspondence between members of the respective societies.

But probably the most public demonstration of strong Anglo-American links was the impact of evangelical religious revival in both countries, called the 'Great Awakening' in America.[160] This revival had already begun when the British Anglican preacher

George Whitfield arrived in October 1739 and began a spectacular, year-long preaching tour of the colonies from New England to Georgia, taking the Gospel to the people – seeking out the consumer, as it were, rather than waiting for him to come to the shop. He was not alone in his itinerancy, and this brought a new force into religion. Before, each parish tended to control what went on inside its boundaries, with preachers licensed to preach in the parish church. But itinerant preachers on both sides of the Atlantic outflanked these regulations in at least two ways: they preached in open places such as parks or public squares, or in taverns, as an alternative to the church; and they engaged in aggressive advertising before their arrival, including a measure of hype detailing previous sermons and their success. Indeed, Franklin decided that the itinerants had a competitive edge over the settled ministry because they could hone their delivery by endlessly repeating the same sermons.[161]

The emphasis for most of these preachers, as well as that of the most fervent revivalists, tended to be on emotion rather than reason, and on personal, even public, conversion. It also tended towards the anti-intellectual, and particularly appealed to women and the powerless. One of the most famous sermons in American history was preached in the summer of 1741 by the New England preacher Jonathan Edwards. This was 'Sinners in the Hand of an Angry God', in which Edwards compared the sinner to a 'loathsome insect' suspended by only a thread over a 'bottomless pit, full of the fire of wrath', into which sinners, if the hand of God were withdrawn, would simply fall by the weight of their own sins into exquisite and eternal torture. Not surprisingly, his congregations reacted with moans and shrieks of terror, lifting up their hands and falling down in despair and repentance. This was not to everyone's taste, and the Great Awakening divided the American religious community and caused schisms that rent congregations and denominations asunder from north to south.

The close links forged between British and American evangelical communities, exemplified by correspondence and meetings between groups on both sides of the Atlantic, fostered otherwise unlikely contacts between groups of like-minded souls. These connections would never entirely disappear, even with the Revolution, and would re-emerge in the nineteenth century with transatlantic reform movements, including the most famous, that devoted to the abolition of slavery.

These links also conveyed very strongly the extent to which the American colonists were part of a larger entity, the British Empire: they might be American British, but they were still British. They saw themselves as having the same political rights, developing the same civil society, and following, as best they could, the same intellectual pursuits as other Britons. They might be separate, but they were equal. The rapid development of a nascent American identity came in reaction to later British attempts to force American obedience to damaging laws and regulations that they had had no part in drafting and for which they were not allowed to vote. The result of British benign neglect was that the American colonies were in the habit of governing themselves, and did not take kindly to the metropolitan government's attempts to reverse the process.[162]

But in 1763, that was in the future. A look backwards over the previous 160 years shows the amazing changes wrought on the eastern edge of the North American continent by the English, the Welsh, the Irish and the Scots. From a wilderness covered by trees, there was a large and rapidly expanding swath which was now British territory. Furthermore, at least along the coast, there were towns and cities where the material benefits of civilisation were widely spread, and social as well as political equality far outstripped that found in Great Britain itself. There were also costs: tens of thousands of colonists had died from disease and warfare. But the greatest sufferers were the Native Americans, who had lost land and lives, driven further and further west by the seemingly unstoppable hordes of settlers eager for land. By 1763, settlers were already spilling over and through the Appalachian Mountains into the rich Ohio Valley, and not the least of the causes of the American Revolution would be the attempts of the British government to stem that tide.

CHAPTER 2

The War for American Independence: 1763–1783

[Y]ou may depend on My firm and stedfast Resolution to withstand every Attempt to weaken or impair the supreme Authority of the Legislature over all the Dominions on My Crown, the Maintenance of which I consider as essential to the Dignity, the Safety, and the Welfare of the *British* Empire.

George III, 30 November 1774[1]

Let the colonies always keep the idea of their civil rights associated with your government; they will cling and grapple to you; and no force under heaven will be of power to tear them from their allegiance. But let it be once understood that your government may be one thing, and their privilege another . . . that these two things may exist without any mutual relation; the cement is gone; the cohesion is loosened; and every thing hastens to decay and dissolution.

Edmund Burke, 22 March 1775[2]

By the rude bridge that arched the flood,
Their flag to April's breeze unfurled;
Here once the embattled farmers stood,
and fired the shot heard round the world.

Ralph Waldo Emerson,
'The Concord Hymn' (1837)[3]

What is meant by the Revolution? The War? That was no part of the Revolution. It was only an Effect and Consequence of it. The Revolution was in the minds of the People, and this was effected, from 1760 to 1775, in the course of fifteen Years before a drop of blood was drawn at Lexington.

John Adams to Thomas Jefferson, 24 August 1815[4]

The Revolution is the American Foundation Myth, a tale of unity and valour, of right versus wrong, of the simple, God-fearing

American fighting for his home and his liberty against the arrogant, freedom-destroying Briton. But things were infinitely more complicated.[5] First of all, this was a civil war, not only between the British and the American colonists, but within America itself, between the Loyalists and the rebels, or Patriots, as they were often styled within America. As with all civil wars, it was nasty, ferocious and bloody. And secondly, whilst for the colonies this was a local conflict, for Great Britain it soon became a global war, in which Britain was ranged alone against France, Spain and the Netherlands. Within less than three years, the war in America had, for Great Britain, become almost a sideshow, as she defended the rest of her empire.

Fundamentally, the war was fought over a constitutional issue: who was to control the American colonies, Parliament or the colonies' own legislative assemblies? Who was to govern, and who was to choose the governors? British attempts after 1763 to impose a control which, although intended since 1607, had not before been successfully enforced in a sustained manner caused the Americans to declare independence. No single date or event marks the beginning of separation. The Stamp Act of 1765, which produced the slogan (now it would be called a soundbite) 'no taxation without representation', was crucial in mobilising the colonists against British taxation policies; the Boston Tea Party of December 1773 was the event after which the British government decided that strong measures had to be taken to bring the Americans to heel; and the shooting of Americans by British soldiers on Lexington Common on 19 April 1775 was the beginning of the war. But it is probable that even had there not been a war, separation was well-nigh inevitable. The island could not for long have controlled the continent. Or, as a French officer said in 1782, after the fighting was over, 'No opinion was clearer than that though the *people* of America might be conquered by well disciplined European troops, the *country* of America was unconquerable.'[6]

The colonists were seldom united. The middle colonies, comprising New York, Pennsylvania, New Jersey and Delaware, hesitated the longest before joining the others in preparing for war and agreeing to the Declaration of Independence in July 1776, and although Loyalists (to the Crown) lived in every part of the country, they were especially clustered in New York and the southern colonies. Furthermore, most localities saw civil war, as one side or the other coerced, terrified and then attacked the local minority. But even the rebels were never truly united, and their cause had virtually ceased to attract active support by the time of the Battle of Yorktown in 1781.

The British were rather more united, but, nevertheless, there was a great deal of political conflict over the war, sometimes for its own sake and sometimes reflecting political rivalries between His Majesty's Government under the leadership of Lord North, First Minister (Prime Minister) from 1767 to 1781, and the opposing factions. It is important also to remember the dozens of Members of Parliament who were independent, because they held the balance of political power. The defeat at Yorktown in 1781 broke the government: North resigned, and the Opposition formed the government and negotiated the terms of independence and peace.

The Americans owed their victory at Yorktown largely to the French fleet, which prevented the Royal Navy from coming to the aid of the British army under Lord Cornwallis. Indeed, it is incontrovertible that without the aid of France, the American Revolution would not have succeeded. This was not only because of the economic and military aid it provided: the Franco-American Treaty of 1778, followed by the decisions of Spain and the Netherlands to support the Americans in 1779, turned what had been essentially a colonial police action for Great Britain into an imperial war, and one in which the home islands were threatened. Yorktown did not end the state of war between Great Britain and the American colonies – this only came with the Treaty of Paris in 1783 – but Great Britain turned her attention to fighting France in the West Indies and elsewhere. Meanwhile, the Americans were left to pick up the pieces and attempt to turn a group of colonies into a country and a group of colonists into a nation: the 'American people', as such, did not yet exist.

I

The nature and extent of Great Britain's control of her colonies had been an issue since the beginning of colonisation. In 1650 Parliament had passed an Act to 'reduce . . . all . . . parts and places belonging to the Commonwealth of England'. Its intent was to bring those colonies which had issued proclamations of loyalty to Charles II under the legal control of Parliament; in essence it wished to cancel their charters. The Act declared that as the colonies had been 'planted at the Cost, and setled by the People, and by Authority of this Nation', they were subject to the laws of the English nation in Parliament. As Robert Bliss has pointed out, 'the far-reaching implications of this doctrine were made clear later on the same day when, by mere parliamentary order, the letters patent of the colonies which supported the King were required to be brought to the House "to be disposed of as the Parliament shall think fit"'.[7] The implications of this order were obvious to all of the colonies, in that it struck at the foundation of their authority to govern by subjecting them to an imperial legislature, and they united in defence of the powers they had obtained by charter or precedence and custom. As the Massachusetts General Court pointed out, planters, not 'those who stay[ed] at home', had paid and suffered for the colonies. Once given and paid for, the rights of government could not be taken away by 'a Parliament in which we have no representatives'.[8] This was a defence which would recur again, and with more force, in the period after 1763.

The North American colonies were different from Great Britain's other imperial possessions, in that they were settler colonies peopled by the British or other Europeans, rather than conquered colonies with the British maintaining military and economic control. The new additions to the empire in India, Africa and Asia, resulting from the Peace of Paris in 1763, increased both defence and administrative costs whilst 'encouraging more authoritarian experiments'.[9] According to Stephen Conway, this included treating the American colonies primarily as part of the dependent empire, rather than as fellow-Englishmen over the ocean. The American colonists, on the other hand, believed that they had taken with them their rights and liberties as free-born Englishmen, as set out in their charters; but over the decades, their perceptions and those of the English (and then British) government as to the limitations on these rights increasingly diverged. A clear theme during this period of British history is the supplantation of the powers of the Crown by the powers of Parliament: a parliamentary monarchy replaced a divine-right monarchy.[10] Notable in the Anglo-American context is the attempt of the Crown to retain and extend the more direct and even arbitrary powers which it claimed it had over colonies and which it no longer claimed to exercise in Great Britain itself. London never formally altered its position that the colonial assemblies were granted as privileges by the Crown, rather than being an inherent right of the colonists as Englishmen.[11]

The Americans by 1763 were in a political maze. They saw the power of Great Britain personified by the Crown-appointed governors, and they needed to try to influence these and lesser appointments. At the same time, they had to lobby Members of Parliament in order to influence legislative enactments. Because special-interests groups, such as the City of London and West Indian sugar planters, were so powerful, they also had to make contact with them. And all this had to be done from four thousand miles away in a shifting political kaleidoscope. Each colony as well as some local governments maintained agents in London – Benjamin Franklin was the agent for Philadelphia for most of the Seven Years' War – but the security and economic interests of the American colonies were priorities for no one in Great Britain. Indeed, according to Michael Kammen, by the late 1760s and early 1770s, colonial agents had lost much of their ability to influence British policy as the constitutional disputes between the two sides increased in importance.[12] The inability of the Americans to convince British politicians and the Crown to pay more attention to their interests bred a continuing, and increasing, frustration which eroded the fundamental loyalty of the colonists to Great Britain.

The story begins in 1763, at the end of the Seven Years' War. Great Britain emerged from her fourth war in seventy-five years against France and her allies almost unimaginably victorious. From France she took her North American possessions, including Quebec and all of her land east of the Mississippi River, with the sole exception of New Orleans, whilst from Spain she took East and West Florida. The result was that Great Britain had established her claim to the whole of the continent east of the Mississippi to the Atlantic Ocean, from the Gulf of Mexico in the south to Hudson Bay in the north. In addition, she took from France most of her possessions in India,[13] the West Indian sugar islands – among the richest of her acquisitions – Senegal in Africa and Minorca. But she also gained Spanish and French enmity, along with that of the other European Powers. Great Britain was perceived as over-mighty, a threat to the Balance of Power, and, as a result, she was isolated. Isolation can be threatening, and within three years of the beginning of the War for American Independence, Great Britain would be profoundly threatened: France and Spain signed an alliance, with the object of invading and defeating Britain.

Meanwhile, the British moved to reorganise their empire in North America. The urgent need to do so was underlined by Pontiac's War, when eight of the western Indian nations under the leadership of the Ottawa chief went on the warpath in May 1763 against the British. One of the agreements the British had made with their Indian allies was to evacuate all of the military posts west of the Allegheny Mountains; once the war was over, however, the British made it clear that they had no further use for their allies and would renege on this agreement, even going so far as to build new outposts south of the Great Lakes. The Indians had other grievances: the supply of gifts had ceased – the British had no concept of the importance of gift culture to the Indians – at a time when war had disrupted their hunting and planting cycles; the British made no effort to control the traders, whose goods tended to be shoddy and overpriced; furthermore, the traders often used rum as a negotiating tool to cheat the Indians out of their furs; the British demanded the return of all prisoners, including those who had been adopted into the tribes and did not want to return; and they seemed unable to control the flood of settlers flowing into the western lands. The Indians were not defeated until November 1764, but the government had by then decided that the former French territories would be reserved for the Indians.[14] Therefore, by the Royal Proclamation of 4 October 1763,[15] a 'Proclamation Line' was drawn which, beginning at the Gulf of the St Lawrence River, connected a series of mountains, from the Green Mountains in what later became Vermont, to the Adirondacks in New York, down to the Alleghenies in Virginia and Pennsylvania, to the Blue Ridge Mountains in the Carolinas, and to the Great Smokey Mountains in Georgia, with the Line continuing to the border with Florida. By this Proclamation, the lands west of this line and extending to the Mississippi River were 'Reserved for the Indians', and colonial settlement was forbidden; instead, would-be settlers were encouraged to move north to Quebec and Nova Scotia or south to the Floridas. Great Britain had created three new colonies from these territories, and desired Anglo-Saxon Protestants to migrate there, thereby making them easier to control than if they were dominated by resentful French or Spanish residents.

The colonists objected violently to the British government's attempt to prevent their spilling west over the mountains and set-tling in the new territories sweeping down to the Mississippi. Indeed, it was impossible to prevent their doing so, and the attempt was abandoned by London in 1772. Yet, it could be asked why the British were prepared to support the interests of the Indians against those of the colonists in the first place. As noted above, an important consideration was the desire to funnel settlers north and south. But Conway has pointed out possibly the primary reason: disquiet amongst most British politicians at what was seen as 'the growing insubordination of the Americans, together with an associated con-cern about the increasing difficulty of imposing control and direction from London'.[16] It was not an independent country the British feared – an idea inconceivable not only to the British, but to most colonists before the mid-1770s – but effective disintegration, with the individual colonies becoming ungovernable, the rise of internal disorder, and even conflict between the colonies. The apprehen-sion was that as the North American empire fell apart, the French would step in and pick off the colonies one by one.[17] Control was therefore essential, and coastal colonies, it was believed, could, if necessary, be controlled by the Royal Navy. However, the lack of navigable rivers from the coast – and over the mountains – meant that the rapid disposition of troops was impossible, and ensured that Great Britain would soon lose control over any colonies which devel-oped further west.[18]

Yet it was not only the new territories which held the attention of the government. The war had brought into relief irritation and even anger at the behaviour of the colonists. During the war, the

Americans had traded with the enemy – the Royal Navy had discovered that some of them had helped to resupply French West Indian islands – whilst some of the assemblies had failed to vote the funds required to support even local troops, many of whom had in any case performed poorly. Partly because the colonial troops were so inadequately trained and led, the British government decided that a large regular army needed to be stationed in the colonies for defence against the French and Spanish, and for control of the Indian territories and the new colonies. Indeed, Pontiac's War had emphasised this need: except for New York, no colony had given significant help, leaving it to the British regulars to do all of the fighting. Furthermore, there was a strong feeling in London that the war was the fault of the colonies, in that they had let the traders cheat the Indians and had not tried to prevent settlers from squatting on Indian territory.[19]

Leaving an army of ten thousand men to garrison the new territories and police the frontier was a new departure for Great Britain, which had heretofore managed to patrol her empire with a relatively small force.[20] It had horrendous financial implications: the average annual cost of the army in North America would be £385,000,[21] or a tenth of the Crown's disposable income. How was it to be paid? The government had a real problem. The Seven Years' War had caused the National Debt to balloon from £74.6 million in 1756 to £132.6 million in 1763:[22] the annual interest on the debt alone was £5 million – and the Crown's annual income was only £8 million. Traditionally, responsibility for raising and paying for the army had been the duty of the King, who then had control over it, but from the accession of William and Mary in 1689 at the invitation of Parliament, this had ceased to be acceptable. Now Parliament insisted that *it* controlled the army, but this meant that Parliament had to finance it, which meant levying even higher taxes. The burden on the British taxpayer was already seen as unacceptably high, and most British politicians thought it entirely fair that the North American colonies should contribute to the cost of their own defence.

This was certainly the conviction of the young King and his administration. Born in England in 1738, George III had ascended the throne in 1760. If one takes as correct the character portrayed in American demonology, he was a man determined to exercise almost autocratic power. However, one could equally see him as a man imbued with proper constitutional ideas: 'his tutor Lord Bute taught the young Prince to revere the constitution as established by the [Glorious] Revolution Settlement'. This was the system of checks and balances between monarch and legislature. Indeed, as Peter Thomas has pointed out, 'by 1760 the Prince had begun to think for himself, and perceived two royal threats to the balance of the constitution, the unfettered power of the Crown to create peers, and the existence of an army under royal control. That in an essay on the British constitution, written only a few months before his accession, George III privately showed this concern about the potential danger to liberty from the monarchy is an ironic contrast to much contemporary and historical portrayal of his behaviour as King.'[23]

However, he also believed that it was his right and duty to select his ministers, and these did not include many of the Whig grandees who had pretty well controlled politics and patronage since the Glorious Revolution. As a result, he had driven into opposition the ablest men in politics: 'the aristocratic Rockingham group, who numbered one in seven of the House of Commons and commanded in [Edmund] Burke, [Richard] Sheridan and [Charles James] Fox a peerless team of orators; and Lord Chatham's [William Pitt the Elder] odd and brilliant political heir Lord Shelburne, with about ten votes in the House'. He had also unleashed what was perhaps the most faction-ridden and thus turbulent period in British politics since the time of Queen Anne. In addition to the Opposition of about eighty Members and the Court Party of about two hundred, made up of all of those who held office, pensions and sinecures, there were the independent Members, who then numbered about three hundred and therefore held the balance of power in the Commons. These independents tended to support the administration in power, but they could also be convinced by a good speech – hence the importance of Burke, Sheridan and Fox – and were thus not wholly dependable in a political conflict. And it was the House of Commons which mattered: in spite of the fact that all of the leaders of the factions sat in the House of Lords, the latter was more of a propaganda chamber, one which acted as a sounding board. A defeat in the Lords was an irritant; a defeat in the Commons could be serious. The King would continue to insist on appointing his ministers until forced to give way to the political opposition and name their leaders as ministers after the British defeat at Yorktown in 1781. Nevertheless, and despite his determination to play an active role in politics, he did not impose his views on his ministers; once he had made his representations, he supported their policies.[24]

Across the Atlantic, politics could be equally fractious. Most of the thirteen colonies had the following organisational pattern: a governor appointed by the Crown, a council appointed by the governor, and an elected legislative assembly. There were variations; in Massachusetts, for example, the most radical of the colonies, there were town meetings with rights of governance and elected juries,[25] whilst in Virginia, power was much more in the hands of large property-holders. One very important difference between Great Britain and the colonies was the franchise, although the fundamental basis in both was the ownership of land. In Great Britain very few could vote – during the eighteenth century about one in six adult males – and in some parliamentary constituencies there were no voters at all. Two of the most notorious were Old Sarum, which was essentially a field of sheep with the landlord naming the MP, and Dunwich, which some time before had slid into the North Sea. Conversely, in America about two out of every three adult males, excepting slaves and Indians, could vote.[26] These differing structures of politics would be fundamental to the growing conflict between the imperial centre and its colonies.

II

In April 1763, George Grenville, Chatham's brother-in-law, became Prime Minister. Grenville's personal following in the House of Commons numbered about forty, but he could also call on the Court Party and most of the independents. He had firm convictions as to the role of Parliament as an imperial legislature, including its right to tax the colonies if necessary, and these were shared by the overwhelming majority of the Commons. Therefore, he had the support of the House for the two Bills passed to finance the British army in North America, the Sugar Act of 1764 and the Stamp Act of 1765.

The Sugar Act was important because it was the first attempt to tax the colonies for revenue rather than only to regulate trade. Ostensibly, it provided for a reduction of the duty on foreign molasses (used to make rum), set at sixpence a gallon by the Molasses Act of 1733. This duty was so high that it encouraged smuggling; as a result, instead of an annual revenue of £200,000, based on a trade of about eight million gallons, the government received only £700. Therefore, the Treasury Board proposed that it should be lowered to threepence, which, it was estimated, would raise £78,000. It was also the firm intention of the administration that this time it would be enforced – an unfamiliar prospect for many in the colonies. Furthermore, because those accused of violating the Act were to be tried in vice-admiralty courts, which had traditionally been used only in cases involving maritime law, it appeared to threaten the right to trial by jury. The proposal was introduced to the Commons on 9 March 1764 as part of the Budget, with Grenville justifying it by reminding the MPs of Britain's vast expenditure in the colonies during the Seven Years' War. He pointed out that it was designed to regulate trade, in that there would be no duty on molasses from the British West Indies; but it was also a measure to raise revenue, since he was 'convinced this country had the right to impose an inland tax'. There was very little criticism. It seemed only fair that the colonists help pay for their own defence, and besides, the right of Parliament to mandate such taxation was generally assumed.[27]

The Stamp Act of 1765 was of a different order entirely. The duty on molasses was a familiar form of revenue-raising, levied as it was on an import (the colonists had never denied that Great Britain had the right to regulate trade). But the Stamp Tax was an internal tax, and this was entirely new and shocking. It was a tax on anything deemed to require a stamp: newspapers, many legal documents, ships' clearance documents, calendars, dice, land grants, liquor licences, press advertisements, pamphlets and playing cards. Virtually everyone would be taxed in some form or other. There had been Stamp Taxes in Great Britain itself since the time of William III, so Grenville thought that the colonists would accept the American version, although under protest. The Bill was drafted to meet all reasonable objections: the tax burden would be small, the revenue would not be remitted to Great Britain but retained in the colonies to support the army,[28] and it would be administered by Americans, not by British officials. (Benjamin Franklin, in London as the agent for Philadelphia, secured some of these posts for friends in America.) Grenville met some of the American agents, but they had no alternative proposal, except for the Crown to revert to requisitioning funds, and Grenville found this inadequate. Nevertheless, 'it was common doctrine that legislation affecting the colonies should be delayed, as of course the Stamp Act was, for a session, until American opinion was heard'.[29]

The news of the passage of the Act in March 1765, with its promise of new taxes, reached the colonies in April, at a time when they were already suffering from a post-war economic depression. The first reaction was more of resignation than of revolt, but soon there was an electrifying protest which galvanised the colonies. On 29 May, at a session of the Virginia House of Burgesses (a mere one-third full), the twenty-nine-year-old lawyer Patrick Henry, himself a member for only nine days, proposed seven resolutions, of which five were carried. These declared *inter alia* that the rights of Englishmen guaranteed in Virginia's royal charters stipulated that Virginians could be taxed only by legislators whom they had elected; hence, as the fifth resolution concluded, any such attempt to contravene these had 'a manifest tendency to destroy British as well as American freedom'. The following day, this resolution was expunged, the majority of the Burgesses fearing that it was too inflammatory, but it was too late: newspapers throughout the colonies printed it. Furthermore, they printed a further two, which Henry had proposed but which had not been passed: that the colonists were not obliged to obey the law, and that anyone who attempted to obey the Act would be deemed 'an enemy to this His Majesty's Colony'. 'No taxation without representation' now became the rallying cry throughout the colonies – the Virginia Resolves had changed the mood of America.[30]

There followed a domino effect, demonstrated by the decisions of
the state assemblies as they met in the autumn. In September
Rhode Island voted as Virginia had done, followed by Pennsylvania
and Maryland. By the end of 1765, Connecticut, Massachusetts,
South Carolina, New Jersey and New York had all done the same.
The crucial decision was that of eight of the colonies which
responded to the call of Massachusetts to send delegates to a meeting in October, known as the Stamp Act Congress, to frame a
petition to the King.[31] The outcome was the thirteen Resolves. After
a clause declaring their allegiance to the Crown and subordination to
Parliament, they asserted that 'his Majesty's liege subjects in these
colonies are entitled to all the inherent rights and liberties of his natural born subjects within the kingdom of Great Britain'. Furthermore,
that 'it is inseparably essential to the freedom of a people, and the
undoubted right of Englishmen, that no taxes should be imposed on
them, but with their own consent, given personally, or by their representatives'. However, 'the people of these colonies are not, and
from their local circumstances, cannot be represented in the House
of Commons of Great Britain', and, therefore, 'the only representatives of the people of these colonies, are persons chosen therein, by
themselves; and that no taxes ever have been, or can be constitutionally imposed on them, but by their respective legislature'.[32] In
other words, no taxation without representation.

This question of representation was complex, reflecting the dia-
metrically opposed theories of the British and the Americans. The
latter argued that because they had no direct representatives in the
House of Commons,[33] they were not represented and thus could not
constitutionally be taxed; and in any case, their charters stated that
taxes would be raised only by a vote in their own legislative assemblies.[34] The response in Great Britain had two parts. First, the
growth in the constitutional doctrine of the supremacy of Parliament
implied that it had the power to make any law appertaining to anything anywhere in the empire, and this certainly included taxation.
And second, and this was the British response in these early days of
the conflict, the Americans were indeed represented in Parliament,
by means of 'virtual representation'. Most British males could not
vote, and urban centres such as Manchester and Birmingham sent no

representatives. Why should the Americans be treated any differently? Ministers had a ready response for anyone who claimed that their lack of a vote meant they were being treated unfairly: 'none are actually, all are virtually represented', the argument being that there were many MPs who would speak for them, as well as for their own constituents.[35]

This, though, was unacceptable to many Americans, even to those not directly involved in politics, and a number of people in Boston had resorted to direct action even before their legislature debated the issue. The events on 14 August 1765 were initiated by the 'Loyal Nine', 'a social club of respectable merchants and tradesmen that later became the town's organized Sons of Liberty'.[36] (This sobriquet was the invention of Colonel Isaac Barré MP, who had referred to the colonists as 'Sons of Liberty' during the parliamentary debate over the Stamp Act.[37]) They decided to target Andrew Oliver, who was both the stamp distributor ('stamp man') for Massachusetts and the Secretary of the colony. Having arranged for working-class groups from both the northern and southern areas of Boston to unite (they were ordinarily enemies), the Loyal Nine made effigies of Oliver and others. 'When daylight came on that Wednesday, it revealed an effigy of Oliver along with one of the devil peeping out of a boot. The effigies dangled from the Liberty Tree, a large old elm located in South End near the Boston Common . . . which became a staging area for anti-British activities. The effigy of Oliver carried the verse "A goodlier sight who e'er did see? A Stamp-Man hanging on a tree!"' Thousands saw them, whilst Northsiders guarded them throughout the day to prevent their being torn down. That evening, a crowd of perhaps three thousand people paraded the effigies through the streets, ending up at the stamp distribution office, which they destroyed. They then marched to Fort Hill, where they beheaded the Oliver effigy and burned it and all of the others. The Loyal Nine then left, but the crowd went to Oliver's home, attempted to burn his coach, smashed his windows, destroyed garden furniture and drank some of his wine. Oliver resigned the stamp distributorship the next day.[38]

Clearly, the crowd was now out of the control of the Loyal Nine, and on 26 August they sought out another target: Thomas

Hutchinson, the Boston-born Lieutenant-Governor. 'Catching the chief justice and his family at the dinner table, the crowd smashed in the doors with axes, sent the family packing, and then systematically reduced the furniture to splinters, stripped the walls bare, chopped through inner partitions until the house was a hollow shell, destroyed the formal gardens in the rear of the mansion, drank the wine cellar dry, stole £900 sterling in coin, and carried off every moveable object of value except some of Hutchinson's books and papers, which were left to scatter in the wind.'[39] 'Crowds did not normally steal personal property. The theft of personal property and the lower-class character of the crowd suggests Hutchinson was targeted in part because he was a rich aristocrat.'[40] For some contemporaries, this implied the threat of an American class war on top of the colonial–British conflict.[41]

As news of the riots in Boston spread to other colonies, so did violence and threats of violence. From Rhode Island to South Carolina, local groups organised themselves to resist the Act. 'In many places fire and artillery companies, artisan associations, and other fraternal bodies formed the basis for these emerging local organizations, which commonly called themselves Sons of Liberty. Led mostly by the middle ranks – shopkeepers, printers, master mechanics, small merchants – these Sons of Liberty burned effigies of royal officials, forced stamp agents to resign, compelled businessmen and judges to carry on without stamps, . . . generally enforced nonimportation of British goods, and managed antistamp activities throughout the colonies.'[42] By 1 November 1765, there was no stamp man left to enforce the Stamp Act in any of the thirteen colonies (although in Georgia a non-American stamp man arrived on 4 January 1766 and acted for some weeks, until he was persuaded to desist).

Meanwhile, in London there was a change of government and a change of mind, if not necessarily a change of political philosophy. News of American resistance to the Stamp Act gradually reached Great Britain over the summer and autumn of 1765. It was clearly going to be impossible to enforce the Act in the face of such vigorous hostility, but its abandonment would have been impossible for Grenville, who was and remained a confirmed supporter of the Stamp Act. However, his government fell, and the new administration was led by the Marquess of Rockingham, the main opposition leader against the various governments of George III until his death in July 1782, four months after becoming Prime Minister against the wishes of the King. He had no real commitment to the Stamp Act, but repealing it would be difficult, because MPs would consider that the government was bowing before the mob.

Even more important was the question of the supremacy of Parliament. In the debates, Grenville had emphasised that it was not just a revenue which was at stake: rather, it was the question of whether Parliament was the supreme legislature of the British Empire, whose powers of taxation were unquestionable. As Gordon Wood has pointed out, 'What made this British argument so powerful was its basis in the widely accepted doctrine of sovereignty – the belief that in every state there could be only one final, indivisible, and uncontestable supreme authority. This was the most important concept of eighteenth-century English political theory.'[43] Rockingham did not disagree with Grenville on this point, although he seems to have believed that whilst supremacy should be declared, it should not be unnecessarily emphasised.[44] Most of the political nation was adamant that repeal of the Stamp Act must be accompanied by a strong assertion of Parliamentary supremacy, or should not take place at all. But without repeal, the colonies would continue in an uproar. A powerful argument for repeal was made during the House of Commons debate on the Stamp Act on 14 January 1766. The speaker was William Pitt the Elder, returning to the Commons after a two-year absence because of gout. After Grenville called for its enforcement, Pitt responded: 'That House has no right to lay an internal tax upon America, that country not being represented', and, although 'I assert the authority of this kingdom over the colonies, to be sovereign and supreme, in every circumstance of government and legislation whatsoever, . . . Taxation is no part of the governing or legislative power.' Referring to the theory of 'virtual representation of *America* in this House', he called it 'the most contemptible idea that ever entered the head of man' and declared, 'I rejoice that America has resisted', ending with the demand that 'the Stamp Act be repealed absolutely, totally and immediately'. But he also called for the sovereign authority of Great Britain over the colonies to 'be asserted in as strong terms as can be devised, and be made to extend to every point of legislation whatsoever. That we may bind their trade, confine their manufactures, and exercise every power whatsoever, except that of taking their money out of their pockets without their consent!'[45]

On 27 January, the petition of the Stamp Act Congress was presented to the Commons.[46] The Rockingham ministry was split over the proper reaction: the Congress was considered an illegal body, and it had denied Parliament's right to tax the colonies, but they believed that the Act was not now enforceable. To ease the way for repeal, on 3 February 1766 the ministry introduced a resolution declaring that Parliament 'had, hath, and of right ought to have, full power and authority to make laws and statutes, of sufficient force and validity, to bind the colonies and people of America, subject to the crown of Great Britain in all cases whatsoever'. Pitt, however, was not convinced. Demanding that the words 'in all cases whatsoever' be omitted from the declaration in order to make it clear that taxation was not included, he ended with a warning: 'Bind them with the golden cord of equity and [moderation] [sic]. Cords of iron will not hold them. If you have this resolution like an eagle hanging over them I believe they will never go to rest.'[47] His warning fell on stone, and the Declaratory Act was passed on 18 March 1766, the same day as the Stamp Act was repealed.[48]

III

In America the colonists would now regard any British policy proposals with suspicion. From their point of view, this wariness was eminently justified by the next proposals for raising revenue, the Townshend duties. The Prime Minister was now Pitt the Elder, who had accepted a peerage from George III as the Earl of Chatham; the Rockingham faction, along with two others, once again became the Opposition. The Chatham administration reasserted Parliamentary sovereignty over the colonies, whilst framing the proposals to accord with what they believed was the American distinction between external and internal taxes: external, such as customs duties, were acceptable; internal, such as the Stamp Tax, were not. Benjamin Franklin had emphasised this during questioning in the House of Commons on 13 February 1766:

> Q. You say the colonies have always submitted to external taxes, and object to the right of parliament only in laying internal taxes; now can you shew that there is any kind of difference between the two taxes to the colony on which they may be laid?
>
> A. I think the difference is very great. An external tax is a duty laid on commodities imported; that duty is added to the first cost, and other charges on the commodity, and when it is offered to sale, makes a part of the price. If the people do not like it at that price, they refuse it; they are not obliged to pay it. But an internal tax is forced from the people without their consent, if not laid by their own representatives. The stamp act says, we shall have no commerce, make no exchange of property with each other, neither purchase nor grant, nor recover debts; we shall neither marry nor make our wills, unless we pay such and such sums, and thus it is intended to extort our money from us, or ruin us by the consequences of refusing to pay it.[49]

The new Chancellor of the Exchequer, Charles Townshend, told the House of Commons on 18 February 1767 that he intended to follow the colonial distinction, even though it was 'not founded on reason'.[50] He did so, but as he developed his programme, its intended beneficiary changed. The revenue to be raised from the Sugar and Stamp Acts had been intended to support the army in America; now the goal was to free the colonial governments from financial dependence on the colonial assemblies by using the proceeds of the tax to pay the salaries of governors, judges and other officials.[51]

The Townshend Revenue Act, with its moderate taxes on glass, painters' colours, red and white lead, tea, and various kinds of coloured papers for furniture (Townshend had told Parliament on 26 January that his duties 'would not be heavy in any manner upon the people in the colonies'[52]), was published on 1 June 1767 and signed by the King on 2 July. The dutiable articles formed a curious group, but they were apparently chosen because the size of imports was quite small and would not disturb patterns of trade; England monopolised trade in them and the colonists had no other source; and, given that Franklin had pointed out during his questioning in the House that the colonists might begin to make their own manufactures if Britain imposed import duties,[53] Townshend chose items which were difficult to produce and probably impossible to do so in the colonies. The amount to be raised by these duties was not large (between thirty and forty thousand pounds each year[54]), although sufficient to pay the salaries of the royal officers in America, but 'new tax measures are often small and increase only after the taxpayer has grown accustomed to paying them'.[55] More alarming to the colonists was that the British were determined to enforce them: another part of the Bill established an American Board of Customs, which was supported a few months later by the setting-up of another three vice-admiralty courts in Boston, Philadelphia and Charles Town, to join that already in Halifax, where those found evading the duties would be tried. Furthermore, Royal Navy cruisers were now to be used for customs enforcement, a provocative act in itself. Townshend realised that his plan might exacerbate relations between Great Britain and her colonies, but, he told the House of Commons on 13 May 1767, the quarrel 'must soon come to an issue. The superiority of the mother country can at no time be better exerted than now.'[56] American matters were now so wide-ranging and taking up so much time that in January 1768 the office of Secretary of State for America was established to co-ordinate colonial policy.

The reaction in America to news of the Townshend duties was at first somewhat muted, but it then grew stronger. Crucially, opinion against the duties was mobilised by the publication of twelve *Letters from a Farmer in Pennsylvania*, written by John Dickinson, a prominent Philadelphia lawyer and landlord. Beginning with the *Pennsylvania Chronicle and Universal Advertiser* of 2 December 1767, they were reproduced in nineteen of the twenty-three English-language colonial newspapers and in seven pamphlets, as well as in two editions in Europe. Dickinson's arguments were relatively familiar. He warned against letting the executive override the liberties of assemblies, the dangers of a standing army, and the threat of allowing the Act to set a precedent. The Townshend duties were not intended to regulate trade, but were taxes to raise revenue, and taxes disguised as trade duties were a dangerous innovation. Even more fundamental, he argued, Great Britain could not constitutionally levy a tax of any sort on the colonists because the latter had no representatives in Parliament. His main suggestions to the colonists were to petition the King and to boycott British goods until their grievances were rectified.[57]

The Massachusetts Assembly followed his advice, and between 30 December 1767 and mid-January 1768, it drew up 'remonstrances', among which was the 'Circular Letter'. Sent on 11 February 1768 to all of the colonial assemblies, the Letter conceded that Parliament was 'the supreme legislative power over the whole empire', but echoed Dickinson by arguing that the Townshend Act was a breach of the colonists' rights as British subjects, because they were not represented in Parliament. It also stated that no people could enjoy full freedom if the monarch could both appoint and pay the salaries of colonial officials, and that Parliament had no right to tax the colonies for the sole purpose of raising revenue. The letter was largely the work of Samuel Adams, the Clerk of the Lower House, who was one of the most brilliant politicians of his day, a man of 'puritanical zeal, organizational skill, and deep hatred of crown authority'.[58] He was a – possibly *the* – power in the Boston Caucus, which largely ran the politics of the city.[59] He also clearly realised the power that accrues to the person who drafts letters, agreements or manifestos. News of the Circular Letter brought a swift riposte from the British government: on 21 April the colonial governors were ordered not to permit any reply from their assemblies, leading all of them to prorogue or dissolve them. (The Virginia House of Burgesses drafted its own circular letter and was promptly dismissed.)

Meanwhile, colonists in the major seaports were organising non-importation agreements to boycott British goods, led by the town meeting in Boston in March 1768. Others soon followed, although not all were equally keen – Philadelphia, for example, was notably unenthusiastic. Unlike the boycotts organised against the Stamp

Act, this time the merchant community was divided. Those involved in the transatlantic trade were against it – not surprisingly, since it was their livelihood which was at risk – whilst those involved in the coastal trade or in trade with the West Indies tended to be strong supporters. One of the latter was John Hancock, who, as President of the Continental Congress, would be the sole signatory of the published Declaration of Independence.[60] One of the richest men in Boston, not least from his smuggling activities (not looked upon in the colonies as particularly reprehensible), he worked closely with Sam Adams. An American historian writing in the early twentieth century referred to him thus: 'Owing to the lightness of his character, his excessive vanity, and love of popularity, unballasted by either moral depth or intellectual ability, his motives for joining the patriot party are difficult to appraise correctly or even, perhaps, fairly, but there was no question of patriotism in much of his smuggling. That was for profit.'[61]

Beyond the merchant community, there was widespread support for non-importation. Artisans thought it would give them more work, because American-made goods would have to be substituted for British ones; many women prevented tea being drunk or produced linen and woollen cloth; and many supported it because they believed that Americans were becoming too materialistic, and by importing luxuries they were helping Great Britain to enslave America. Many ordinary people therefore seized the chance of taking exciting, and often effective, action.[62]

Hancock was soon the centre of a contretemps in Boston which would trigger an ominous response from Great Britain. The new American Board of (Customs) Commissioners had just arrived in the town, where Hancock was leading the resistance to the local collectors. A popular nineteenth-century American historian described what happened next:

The commissioners of customs and the master of a sloop-of-war which, at their request, had come to Boston from Halifax, now assumed the utmost insolence of manner and speech toward the people. New England men were impressed into the British naval service, and in June, the sloop *Liberty*, belonging to John Hancock, whom the crown officials cordially hated because of his opposition to them, was seized under peculiar circumstances. She had come into the harbor with a cargo of Madeira wine. Just at sunset, the 'tide-waiter' in the employ of the commissioners went on board, and took his seat in the cabin, as usual, to drink punch[63] with the master until the sailors should land the cargo of dutiable goods. Hancock had resolved to resist the obnoxious revenue laws; and at about nine o'clock in the evening, his captain and others in his employ entered the cabin, confined the tidewaiter, and proceeded to land the wine without entering it at the custom-house or observing any other formula. So great were the exertions of the master of the *Liberty* that night, that he died from their effects before morning.

The sloop was now seized by the officers of the customs for a violation of the revenue laws. A crowd of citizens quickly gathered at the wharf, and as the proceedings went on, a part of them, of the lower order, became a mob under the lead of Malcom, a bold smuggler. The collector (Harrison) and the controller (Hallowell)[64] were there to enforce the law. The former thought the sloop might remain at Hancock's wharf with the broad arrow upon her (a mark designating her legal position); but the latter had determined to have her moored under the guns of the war-vessel (*Romney*, of sixty guns), and had sent for her boats to come ashore. An exciting scene now occurred, which Mr Bancroft[65] has described as follows: 'You had better let the vessel be at the wharf,' said Malcom. 'I shall not,' said Hallowell, and gave directions to cut the fasts. 'Stop, at least, till the owner comes,' said the people who crowded round. 'No, damn you,' cried Hallowell, 'cast her off.' 'I'll split out the brains of any man that offers to receive a fast or stop the vessel,' said the master of the *Romney*; and he shouted to the marines to fire. 'What rascal is that who dares to tell the marines to fire?' cried a Bostoneer; and turning to Harrison, the collector, a well-meaning man, who disapproved the violent manner of the seizure, he added: 'The owner is sent for; you had better let her lie at the wharf till he comes down.' 'No, she shall go,' insisted the controller [Hallowell]; 'show me the man who dares oppose it.' 'Kill the damned scoundrel,' cried the master. 'We will throw the people from the *Romney* overboard,' said Malcom, stung with anger. 'By God she shall go,' repeated the master, and he more than once called to the marines, 'Why don't you fire?' and bade them fire. So they cut her moorings, and with ropes in the barges the sloop was towed away to the *Romney*.

This act excited the hot indignation of the people. A mob, led by Malcom, followed the custom-house officers, pelted them with stones and other missiles, and broke the windows of their offices. The mob seized a pleasure-boat belonging to the collector, and after dragging it through the town, burned it on the Common. Then they quietly dispersed. The commissioners were unhurt, but greatly alarmed. They applied to the governor for protection, but he, as much frightened as they, told them he was powerless. They finally fled to the *Romney* and thence to Castle William, nearly three miles southeast of the city, where a company of British artillery were stationed.[66]

The British response was swift. Believing that Boston was essentially out of control, on 27 July the ministry sent four regiments to sustain the civil government, two from Nova Scotia and two from Ireland. 'The first units began landing on 1 October 1768, covered by the menacing guns of several warships. By the end of the year the garrison consisted of the 14th, 29th, 64th, and 65th regiments plus part of the 59th. These were sufficient to prevent all but petty harrassment by the sullen inhabitants, who viewed the soldiers as the arm of ministerial oppression.' This was the first time that the British government had sent a large number of troops to enforce their authority in the colonies – four thousand for a population of fifteen thousand. After the situation had stabilised, General Thomas Gage, Commander-in-Chief of the British troops in America, whose headquarters were in New York, eventually withdrew most of the troops, 'leaving only about 600 men to shiver through the winter of 1769–70 under the taunt of "lobsterback" and even less flattering epithets hurled by Boston's gamins'.[67]

There was violence in New York that winter as well. Elsewhere in the colonies there was tension wherever and whenever redcoats and colonists came together. Tempers were short, and neither side gave quarter, each willing to believe the worst about the other. By this time, many colonists had lost all trust in the British government, with the result that its every pronouncement and every move were met with suspicion and hostility: 'as the Americans moved in definable stages away from their loyalty of 1765, so they abandoned step by step the tactic of resistance that opposed only discrete aspects of London's rule for revolution and a rejection of all British authority'.[68] At the same time, however, many other colonists were opposed to the actions of the radicals; these included people of the 'middling sort' as well as many of the wealthy. In community after community, this led to local-based conflict in addition to that with Great Britain. Indeed, traditional estimates have been that the colonists eventually fell into the following positions: one-third pro-independence, one-third loyal to the British connection and one-third concerned primarily with daily life and work and wanting only to keep their heads down. The third group was increasingly squeezed between the other two.

In London, most politicians, and other members of the political nation, truly did not understand why the Americans reacted as they did. They took it as given that London should control the Empire in all things; furthermore, it seemed only right that the Americans should help to pay for their own defence. And as long as Birmingham had no vote, it did not seem particularly anomalous that nor did Boston. (In response to this, a number of Americans did not see this as a commanding argument: if this was indeed the case, Birmingham ought to have its own representatives.) The British could only ascribe the defiance and uproar to troublemakers – and the greatest centre of trouble was Boston. London gradually came to the conclusion that if they could suppress Boston, all of the colonies would quieten down and again act as subjects should.

The so-called Boston Massacre has traditionally been seen as one outcome of this policy. It is famous largely because of an engraving by the silversmith Paul Revere, one of the Boston Sons of Liberty, entitled *Fruits of Arbitrary Power, or the Bloody Massacre Perpetuated in King Street*. Revere was economical with the truth, but as one American historian points out, the engraving 'helped to create an image of British tyranny and American innocence that still shapes our memory of the event'.[69] It showed a group of respectable citizens on the left being shot down by a rank of British soldiers on the right, with an officer clearly giving the order to fire.

The truth is more complicated. There had been an increasing number of small but hostile conflicts between soldiers and colonists, with taunts and occasional blows being exchanged. On 5 March 1770, things rapidly became more serious. There were a number of fights that evening, which 'intensified when several soldiers attacked and beat two boys, one 11 years old and the other 14. A crowd gathered and in a frenzy attempted to charge into the main barracks after the soldiers. Several officers held off the mob with their swords. Frustrated and hearing the noise of another group not far away, the mob departed. Shortly thereafter several of its members broke into the meeting house and began to ring its bell, the signal for fire, bringing hundreds of people into the streets.'[70] Standing in King Street with their backs pressed against the customs house, Captain Thomas Preston and a small contingent of soldiers faced a milling, taunting crowd.

'Fire, damn you! Fire!' someone shouted. Those in the rear pressed the front of the mob towards the pointed bayonets. A stick flew out of the darkness, striking the gun barrel of Private Hugh Montgomery. He stepped back, or slipped on the icy street, and fired his weapon. Knocked to the ground, he screamed to the other soldiers, 'Fire! Fire!' Panicked by now, the troopers followed Montgomery's example and shot point-blank into the mass of bodies. The solid mass flew apart as the mob shoved and pushed and trampled to escape the line of fire. One soldier was apparently seen to take careful aim at the back of a fleeing youngster, but his shot missed. Within seconds King Street was deserted except for the soldiers, the wounded, and the dead. There were eleven casualties: three were killed outright, including Crispus Atticus, a runaway slave and the first African-American to die in the revolutionary conflict, two lay mortally wounded, and six others were less seriously wounded. The meeting house bells continued to chime and were soon supported by the staccato drum beat of the call to arms.[71]

Immediately there was tumult, as the streets filled with ferociously angry and armed colonists, whilst express letters were sent to neighbouring towns asking for armed aid against the British army.

Meanwhile, men raced to the Governor, Thomas Hutchinson, who responded

> instantly to the plea 'For God's sake . . . go to King Street' or 'the town would be all in blood.' He had plunged into the great press and confusion of the mob in King Street, 'some brandishing their bludgeons and some their cutlasses'; had been thrown up against the soldiers' bayonets; in the tumult had shouted at Captain Preston, 'How came you to fire without orders from a civil magistrate!'; and had been forced up by the crowd into the Council chamber. From the balcony he had somehow managed to control the mob, promising them a full and impartial inquiry ('The law shall have its course! I will live and die by the law!'),[72] and had convinced them to disperse.

The following morning, Boston selectmen (elected local board members) told Hutchinson that if he did not order the removal of the troops from the town, there would be 'blood and carnage'; the public temper grew more violent, and by midday the selectmen had told Hutchinson that if the troops did not leave, 'the people of Boston would drive them out, with the help of the men from the surrounding towns if need be'. Hutchinson refused for some time, convinced that if the troops were forced to retreat to Castle William, this would be the turning point in the ability of Great Britain to maintain its authority in the American colonies. But he 'finally, and wearily, "under duress", conceded. Five days later the last of the royal troops, ignominiously patrolled by the town's militia, left Boston.'[73]

Ironically also on 5 March 1770 a motion was brought before Parliament to repeal all of the Townshend duties – except, fatally, that on tea. This was retained for two reasons: it brought in three-quarters of the revenue produced by the duties; and its retention was a symbol of parliamentary supremacy. One historian has claimed that the American boycott of British imports had little influence on the decision, because although British exports to America had fallen by 38 per cent in 1769 as compared to 1768, the American market represented only 16 per cent of Britain's total export trade, with the bulk of it going to Europe. On the other hand, the absolute numbers are significant: only £21,000 in new duties were collected, whilst sales of British goods to the colonies fell by more than £700,000. After the debate, the motion passed, and the Bill was signed into law on 12 April. Its effect in America was to split the colonies. First, New York decided to end the boycott, except for tea; other ports feared that all of the carrying trade would go to New York, so that Philadelphia soon adopted the New York agreement, followed by Boston (widely suspected of cheating by the other colonies). By the end of 1770, the policy appeared to have been a success.[74]

The British administration responsible for this apparent triumph was headed by Lord North.[75] He had succeeded Townshend as Chancellor of the Exchequer in 1767 at the age of thirty-five, becoming the First Lord of the Treasury – in effect, Prime Minister – at the end of January 1770. He held both posts until 1782. He had opposed repeal of the Stamp Act in 1766, and would be responsible for steering through the House of Commons the disciplinary legislation against the colonies until the outbreak of war. Under North, 'nearly all those politicians who had supported firm colonial measures were gathered together, while the Opposition groups under Rockingham and Chatham contained those who had displayed a more conciliatory disposition'.[76] North was an excellent parliamentary manager but a hopeless head of administration, incapable of ensuring the co-ordination of departments or of providing firm leadership. George III would spend a significant amount of time bucking him up.

IV

The following two years were superficially calm, with no significant conflicts. But that interlude ended on 9 June 1772, with the wreck of the *Gaspée*. This was a Royal Navy cutter, engaged in what men of Rhode Island considered to be heavy-handed enforcement of the Navigation Acts. It ran aground in Narragansett Bay, upon which

Rhode Islanders boarded it, wounded the captain and burned the ship. North's administration immediately established a royal commission to inquire into the sinking, empowered to send those charged back to Great Britain for trial. Unfortunately for the government, nothing came of this, because no one would talk to the commission. But it caused great damage because of the threat to send those accused back to London for trial: an ancient right of Englishmen was to be tried at the scene of their alleged crimes, and this seemed to be seriously threatened. In Virginia, several of the younger members of the political elite, including Thomas Jefferson and Patrick Henry, feared a conspiracy by the government to strip them of their rights. They decided to set up intercolonial committees of correspondence on the Boston model – the Boston Committee of Correspondence had been established at the suggestion of Sam Adams in September 1771 – to monitor British activities throughout the colonies; the Virginia House of Burgesses called for this in March 1773, and twelve colonies agreed, with only pacifist Pennsylvania declining. These provincial committees of correspondence met regularly, whether the elected assemblies were sitting or not, forming an alternative structure for mobilising public opinion in the face of increasing efforts by the governors to prevent such activity by dissolving the assemblies.[77] They were thus in place when the final act began.

A major outcome of the boycott on British tea in the colonies since 1767[78] had been an increasing strain on the East India Company,[79] and by 1773 it was on the verge of bankruptcy. The company had large stocks of tea in its warehouses, which were not getting any fresher, and the government decided to help the Company to sell it. The idea was that the price of tea in the colonies should be lowered, and sales would therefore increase. One way of doing this could have been to repeal the threepence tax on tea in the colonies, but this was unacceptable to the government, since the tax symbolised Parliament's right to tax them. However, since all tea imported had to land in Great Britain to be taxed before being exported to America and elsewhere, it was arranged that this tax would be rebated. Therefore, the cost of the tea to the Americans was reduced by the amount of the tax. In another provision of the

Tea Act the Company was granted permission to choose those to whom it would consign the tea, thereby giving these agents a monopoly and cutting out the rest. With this Act, the North administration managed to outrage three different groups: 'professional patriots' charged that lowering the price of tea whilst maintaining the colonial tax constituted another attempt to 'trick' them into accepting taxation; colonial merchants were apprehensive that the precedent of allowing the Company to choose its own factors could presage similar arrangements in the future;[80] and smugglers were irritated by the prospect of lower prices on tea, since it was likely that people would prefer these lower prices on legal British tea to higher prices on smuggled Dutch tea. Together, these groups constituted a formidable opposition.

In the summer of 1773, the company sent shipments of tea to the four major ports in the colonies: Charles Town, Philadelphia, New York and Boston. In New York and Philadelphia the colonists refused to allow the tea to be unloaded, and the ships left the harbours; in Charles Town the tea was eventually unloaded and stored without paying the tax. In Boston the result was violence. On 28 November the *Dartmouth* arrived with 114 chests of tea. Governor Hutchinson believed that the people of Boston had become a mob and that the government's authority must be restored. He decided to utilise the shipment of tea to do this. 'Once the ships had entered the harbor, British law forbade their leaving until all taxes had been paid. Fortuitously, . . . the guns of Castle William controlled egress from the harbor and permitted Hutchinson to stop the ships from leaving Boston.' The point was that, by law, the tea could not be returned to England, and if a ship and its cargo waited in port for three weeks without paying the tax, the authorities were authorised to unload it. Hutchinson intended to do just that, presumably by using military force.[81]

During these three weeks, thousands of citizens in Boston and the surrounding towns met repeatedly to discuss possible strategies. Meanwhile, a number of people kept continuous watch over the *Dartmouth* and the other two ships which joined it at Griffin's Wharf. The Boston town meeting was extended to include 'the whole body of the people'. On 16 December 1773, the day before customs officials were legally entitled to seize the tea and land it themselves, 'an estimated five thousand people travelled through a cold, steady rain to gather at the Old South Meeting House'. The meeting decided to send Captain Francis Rotch, commander of the three vessels, to make a final appeal to Hutchinson to allow the ship to return to England, carrying its cargo of tea. When Rotch returned at 5.45 p.m., the Old South was lit by candles.[82] 'Samuel Adams, serving as moderator . . ., listened to Rotch explain Hutchinson's final refusal to permit the ships to leave. Then, according to tradition, he banged his gavel three times and declared that since "this meeting" could do no more to protect the rights of America it stood adjourned.'[83]

That night, as thousands stood on the quayside to watch, a group of men disguised as 'Mohawk Indians' boarded the ship. According to one of them, Joshua Wyeth, a journeyman blacksmith, 'It was proposed that young men, not much known in town and not liable to be easily recognised should lead in the business . . . [M]ost of the persons selected for the occasion were apprentices and journeymen, as was the case with myself.'[84] Another participant, the poor shoe-maker George Hewes, described the action:

I fell in with many who were dressed, equipped and painted as I was . . . When we arrived at the wharf, there were three of our number who assumed authority to direct our operations, to which we readily submitted. They divided us into three parties, for the purpose of boarding the three ships . . . The commander of the division to which I belonged . . . ordered me to go to the captain and demand of him the keys to the hatches and a dozen candles. I made the demand accordingly, and the captain promptly replied, and delivered the articles; but requested me at the same time to do no damage to the ship or rigging. We then were ordered by our commander to open the hatches, and take out all the chests of tea and throw them overboard, and we immediately proceeded to execute his orders; first cutting and splitting the chests with our tomahawks, so as thoroughly to expose them to the effects of the water. In about three hours from the time we went on board, we had thus broken and thrown overboard every tea chest to be found in the ship; while those in the other ships were disposing of the tea in the same way, at the same time. We were surrounded by British armed ships, but no attempt was made to resist us. We then quietly retired to our several places of residence, without having any conversation with each other, or taking any measures to discover who were our associates.[85]

According to Ray Raphael, 'Unlike the mob of the Stamp Act riots . . . this was a contained and disciplined cadre. No extraneous looting or destruction of property was permitted. A padlock accidently broken was supposedly replaced, while the few men who tried to grab some tea for themselves were severely reprimanded and ridiculed.'[86]

The British government decided that the time had come to restore its authority in the colonies, even though none of the others had reacted with such violence; indeed, many colonists had decidedly mixed feelings about the action in Boston. One such was Benjamin Franklin, who wrote that he was shocked by 'the act of violent injustice on our part', given that the East India Company was not an enemy of the colonists, and that it was wrong 'to destroy private property'.[87] Another who expressed reservations was a Virginia planter, George Washington. The news of the Tea Party reached London on 19 January 1774, the Philadelphia tea ship arrived on 25 January, and by the 29th the administration knew of the failure to sell the tea at the other three ports, and that New York intended resistance. There was universal condemnation, with even the sympathisers of the colonists unwilling to support the flouting of the laws of property; Rockingham and Chatham were as appalled as the supporters of the government. Consequently, the North administration anticipated few objections when it decided to use the occasion to restore its full authority in the colonies, because if they did not, this authority would continue to bleed away.[88]

The first thought of the government was to take direct administrative action, by closing Boston Harbour, moving the Massachusetts seat of government from the town, and punishing the individuals responsible. However, government lawyers said that there was not enough evidence to convict anyone. The administration accepted this, but then took a fateful decision: rather than rely on the administrative authority of the Crown, they decided to adopt the suggestion of Lord Dartmouth, the Secretary of State for America, to take legislative powers to close Boston Harbour until the town paid financial compensation to the East India Company, to change the system of justice, and to alter the Massachusetts Charter of 1691. This raised the stakes tremendously, because any resistance by the Americans now would be seen as a direct challenge not to the authority of the Crown or ministers but to the authority of Parliament.

Between 31 March and 22 June 1774, Parliament passed four separate Acts, known as the Coercive Acts (and in America as the Intolerable Acts). The first was the Boston Port Act, introduced on 14 March 1774: this forbade ships to enter or leave the port until compensation for the lost tea was paid to the East India Company (in which many MPs held stock), and until the King deemed that shipping was safe in the area. There was no division (vote) on it, and the bill passed on 31 March. Second was the Massachusetts Government Act, introduced in the House of Commons on 28 March, whose intent was to curtail the more 'democratic' elements of New England government. This abrogated the Massachusetts Charter, and restructured colonial and local government: first, whilst before the Council had been selected by the Governor from a list drawn up by the Assembly, the members were now to be appointed solely by the King (the Mandamus Council), as in the other colonies; furthermore, the Act gave the Governor greater control over local government, by allowing town meetings to be held but once a year and forbidding them to consider anything but purely local matters. He would also now name magistrates – they had previously been elected – and the local selection of juries was abolished. The third Act was the Administration of Justice Act, introduced on 15 April by Lord North as a temporary measure, the remit of which was to protect British officials who were trying to enforce sometimes unpopular laws. In capital cases, government officials or their subordinates were to be protected from blatantly prejudiced juries by authorising a change of venue to another colony or to London. And finally, the fourth Act was the Quartering Act, introduced by Lord Barrington, the Secretary at War, which aimed to place the authority for billeting soldiers in the hands of the governors, and which stipulated that when colonies offered quarters for soldiers which were unacceptable, the governors could place them in 'uninhabited houses, outhouses, barns or other buildings' – but not private homes. General Thomas Gage, the Commander-in-Chief of the British army in North America, who was then home on leave, was named Governor of Massachusetts to replace the now discredited Hutchinson and instructed to move the capital of the colony from Boston to Salem.[89]

A fifth Act was passed at roughly the same time, but this one had nothing to do with the thirteen colonies. Nevertheless, in their suspicious and fevered condition, colonists saw it as part of the package. This was the Quebec Act, ironically an enlightened approach to the newly conquered Catholic French-speaking colony, constructed with the intention of reconciling the French inhabitants to the change of identity and government. It allowed the Catholic Church to retain a semi-established position; retained French civil law, which, however, did not guarantee trial by jury; and set up a government without an elected assembly (having an assembly seemed inexpedient, given that the French colonists both lacked such experience and currently outnumbered the English colonists). To many colonists, this seemed a warning of British intentions towards their own colonies. But what was immediately enraging was that the government added to Quebec the Old Northwest Territory, where Virginia, Massachusetts and Connecticut all had charter rights, and a number of the colonists had land claims. The government's hope was that the new colony would control the fur trade and thus keep down costs.[90]

The North administration paid a heavy price for the passage of the Coercive Acts: the destruction of the Parliamentary consensus on America. Whilst the Boston Port Act was seen as an appropriate response to the wanton destruction of private property, the others met with a barrage of criticism from the Opposition. For example, the Massachusetts Government Act was seen for what it was: a violation of charter rights. Yet, even had North wished to be more conciliatory, he would probably have been prevented from being so by the adamant refusal of his backbench supporters to countenance any softening of his stance. Furthermore, even the Opposition admitted that public opinion was behind him.[91]

General Gage and the text of the Boston Port Act arrived together in early May. Acting quickly, the Boston Committee of Correspondence arranged for a joint meeting with the committees of eight neighbouring towns on 12 May. Just before that meeting opened, the Speaker of the Rhode Island Assembly electrified the Bostonians by informing them that every colonial assembly (except Nova Scotia's) had indicated that it would join in united action for 'preserving the Liberties and promoting the Union of the American Colonies'. Why not Nova Scotia or, for that matter, Newfoundland and Quebec? For Nova Scotia, it was the fact that Halifax was the main North American base for the Royal Navy. The economic and social interests of the colony were intertwined with those of the Navy, while military force would have easily prevented any movement southwards by the colonists. The Royal Navy would also have prevented any attempt by colonists from Newfoundland to join. The fact that both territories were far away from the southern mainland colonies must not be forgotten. As for Quebec, Protestant New Englanders would have been horrified if Catholics from Quebec had joined them. In any case, there is little evidence of any desire of the colonists from north of the St Lawrence River to join those in the south.

The meeting chose Sam Adams as its chairman, and approved sending to all of the other colonies and the port cities a letter claiming that the Port Act was intended to intimidate Boston, and that if the town failed to resist – and, by implication, if the other colonies failed to help her – they would all be threatened with the loss of their freedom and liberties. In the letter, the joint committees called on the other colonies to 'come into a joint Resolution, to stop all Importations from Great Britain & Exportations to Great Britain & every part of the West Indies' until Parliament repealed the Boston Port Act.[92]

The situation changed dramatically a few weeks later. On 1 June 1774, the Boston Port Act, which effectively closed the port, took effect, and Bostonians walked the streets in mourning clothes as church bells tolled. In Philadelphia the church bells 'rang out a muffled tolling', and the flags of the ships in the harbour flew at half-mast.

When in Williamsburg, the capital of Virginia, the House of Burgesses proposed a day of fasting and prayer for 1 June, the Governor suspended it; as head of the Church of England in Virginia, he himself was the only person with the authority formally to decree such a day. Nevertheless, most of Virginia anyhow observed a day of fasting. The following day, Boston learned of the next two Coercive Acts, the Massachusetts Government and the Administration of Justice Acts. The Boston Committee of Correspondence drew up a Solemn League and Covenant (a name which alluded to the alliance against Charles I during the English Civil War), which was a programme of fierce economic warfare against Great Britain: there should be no imports from Britain, and no one should use anything manufactured there. Everyone should sign this pledge, and if they refused, or contravened it, they should be boycotted and ostracised for ever. Sam Adams, who was instrumental in drawing up the Covenant, distrusted merchants, who would not lightly resign their livelihoods, and thus intended to mobilise the people – the 'yeomanry', as he called them – to enforce it.[93]

These two new Acts increased support for a meeting of representatives from the colonies, and Adams manoeuvred to ensure that it took place. On 9 June the Massachusetts House of Representatives appointed him to head a committee to report on the state of the colony and the Port Act. Not all members of the committee were as radical as Adams, and he and like-minded members met secretly at night, devising plans to call for an intercolonial congress and agreeing on a slate of delegates.

> [A]fter getting the gallery cleared and the House door shut and locked, Adams unveiled the results of the nighttime meetings. His committee proposed that all colonies send delegates to a congress that would convene in Philadelphia on September 1, 1774. The congressmen would 'deliberate and determine upon wise and proper Measures to be recommended by them to all the Colonies, for the Recovery and Establishment of their just Rights and Liberties civil and religious, and the Restoration of Union and Harmony between Great-Britain and the Colonies, most ardently desired by all good Men'.

The members of the House agreed that the proposal would be sent to all of the other colonies.[94] All except Georgia, which laboured under imminent war with the Creek Indians, agreed: the anger in the other colonies was so great that, even when their governors had dissolved their assemblies in order to prevent the election of delegates,[95] informal assemblies were called for the election of representatives to attend the Congress, ensuring an unusually broad basis of support for the delegates.

On 5 September 1774, the fifty-five delegates to the First Continental Congress began their deliberations in Carpenter Hall in Philadelphia. Opposition to the 1774 legislation was taken as a given, so the debates focused on the best course of action. The Congress was split. The more conservative (middle) colonies of New York, Pennsylvania and New Jersey, who were led by the leader of the Pennsylvania delegation, Joseph Galloway,[96] wanted to send a remonstrance to the King, but the New England and southern colonies successfully insisted on a boycott of British goods. Their conflict was fundamental: Galloway and the conservatives wanted to renegotiate the imperial relationship, whilst the radicals (the 'ardent Whigs'), led by the cousins John and Sam Adams of Massachusetts and by Patrick Henry and Richard Henry Lee of Virginia,[97] wanted Parliament to resign entirely its claim to sovereignty over the colonies. Independence was not yet an issue for the overwhelming majority of delegates, but the radicals narrowly won. On 16 September, Paul Revere arrived in Philadelphia with a copy of the fiery Suffolk County (Massachusetts) Resolves,[98] which wanted outright resistance to the Coercive Acts. These Acts were 'the attempts of a wicked administration to enslave America', and the Resolves called for taxpayers in Massachusetts to withhold their taxes, the militia to be readied for action, and colonial officials to obey their elected county conventions, rather than royal officials. Fundamentally, they advanced the argument that citizens need not obey unjust laws. On 18 September they were endorsed by the Congress.[99]

This was an expression of solidarity with the colonists of Massachusetts, but it was not the line which most of the delegates necessarily wished their own colonies to follow. There were three main questions to be answered. First of all, what were their (that is, colonial) rights? They proposed to draw up a clear statement of those rights, but were unable to agree on such a list. Whilst they all rejected Parliament's right to tax the colonies, to interfere with trial by jury, and to adopt the Coercive Acts, they split over whether Parliament had the right to regulate trade. This part of the report was fudged. Secondly, which Acts of Parliament violated those rights? None before 1763, they decided, the year when relations began to break down. Those Acts passed thereafter were listed in a Statement of Rights and Grievances, which was published on 14 October. Six days later, the Congress decided to concentrate on the 1774 legislation, together with the revenue measures. And thirdly, what measures should the colonists take to force Parliament to repeal the offending Acts? Although some of the more radical delegates, in particular Sam Adams and Richard Henry Lee, had argued that the Congress should call on the colonists to prepare for war, the majority decided against such a momentous course. Instead, it was again decided simply to boycott British goods. It had worked before – why should it not this time? On 27 September, the Congress unanimously called upon Americans to cancel orders sent to, and to cease importing goods from, Great Britain on 1 December 1774. A few days later, it decreed that 'non-exportation' of all goods to Great Britain and the British West Indies would begin on 10 September 1775 if American grievances had not been redressed. There was a very practical reason for the different dates: the tobacco colonies insisted on the opportunity to sell the following year's crop, and fairness dictated that this window of opportunity remain open for others.

But how were these decisions to be enforced, given the divisions between the moderates and the radicals? The answer was the Continental Association, whose proposed duties and powers were described in the document issued by the Continental Congress on 20 October 1774. The cause of the anxiety of 'We, his Majesty's most loyal subjects . . . [was] the present unhappy situation of our affairs . . . occasioned by a ruinous system of colony administration, adopted by the British ministry about the year 1763, evidently calculated for enslaving these colonies, and with them, the British Empire.' The decision of the Congress, therefore, was that 'a committee be chosen in every county, city, and town by those who are qualified to vote for representatives in the legislature, whose business it shall be attentively to observe the conduct of all persons touching this Association'; if a person 'violated' the Association, his name would be published and he would be ostracised.[100]

This call encouraged the breakdown of the established systems of local government. Committees of Inspection were swiftly appointed by town and county meetings in New England and the southern colonies, with the exception of Georgia. In the middle colonies the response was more mixed. Whilst the embargo was effective in the major port cities of New York and Philadelphia, the evidence for the more inland areas is fragmented, and even the New York Assembly refused to ratify the Association. But the significance of the Committees of Inspection was profound in the 'development of revolutionary government in the colonies' because thousands of colonists 'were brought into the movement through their activities' as members of them. Their activities differed: in the port cities, much time was spent in inspecting ships and associated activities, whilst in other towns individual colonists were challenged on their activities or loyalties. 'Newspapers reported a number of incidents in which individuals were forced to recant before local committees for having cast aspersions on various members or on the committee itself. As the crisis deepened, the Committees of Inspection gradually evolved into Committees of Safety and took upon themselves responsibility for such governmental policies as collecting taxes for the revolutionary governments and recruiting soldiers.' It was significant that the Committees believed that they derived their authority from the Continental Congress, not from the provincial assemblies or congresses.[101]

There was often violence. Groups of men, numbering from a few dozen to several thousand, claiming to speak for 'the body of the people', ranged 'through villages and city streets searching out enemies of the people. Suspected enemies, under threat of being tarred and feathered, were often forced to take back unfriendly words or designs against the public, to sign confessions of guilt and repentance, and to swear new oaths of friendship to the people.'[102] Tarring and feathering combined pain and humiliation:

The following is the Recipe for an effectual Operation. 'First, strip a Person naked, then heat the Tar until it is thin, & pour it upon the naked Flesh, or rub it over with a Tar Brush . . . After which, sprinkle decently upon the Tar, whilst it is yet warm, as many Feathers as will stick to it. Then hold a lighted Candle to the Feathers, & try to set it all on Fire; if it will burn so much the better. But as the Experiment is often made in cold Weather; it will not then succeed – take also an Halter & put it round the Person's Neck, & then cart him the Rounds.'[103]

A letter from a Loyalist lady described an actual event:

[H]e was stript Stark naked, one of the severest cold nights this Winter, his body covered all over with Tar, then with feathers, his arm dislocated in tearing off his cloaths, he was drag'd in a Cart with thousands attending, some beating him w'th clubs & Knocking him out of the Cart, then in again. They gave him several severe whipings, at different parts of the Town. This Spectacle of horror & sportive cruelty was exhibited for about five hours . . . They bro't him to the Gallows & put a rope about his neck say'g they woud hang him he said he wished they woud, but that they could not for God was above the Devil. The Doctors say it is imposible this poor creature can live. They say his flesh comes off his back in Stakes.[104]

One recipient of attention from his local association was a Church of England priest in Maryland, who had been a friend and dinner guest of George Washington before their friendship broke. In his memoirs, the Rev. Jonathan Bouchier described the growing pressure put on him to conform: 'The first open and avowed violence I met with was on account of my expressly declining, when applied to by some noisy patriots heretofore of no great note, to preach a sermon to recommend the suffering people of Boston to the charity of my parish . . . [T]he true motive was by those means to raise a sum sufficient to purchase arms and ammunition.' The threats increased: 'I received sundry messages and letters threatening me with the most fatal consequences if I did not . . . preach what should be agreeable to the friends of America . . . And for more than six months I preached . . . with a pair of loaded pistols lying on the cushion.' In due course, one Sunday two hundred armed men arrived in his church. He tried to go up to his pulpit with his sermon in one hand and a loaded pistol in the other, but he was prevented by a friend who knew that he would be killed.

> Seeing myself thus circumstanced, it occurred to me that things seemed now indeed to be growing alarming, and . . . there was but one way to save my life. This was by seizing Sprigg [the ring-leader], as I immediately did, by the collar, and with my cocked pistol in the other hand, assuring him that if any violence was offered to me I would immediately blow his brains out, as I most certainly would have done. I then told him that if he pleased he might conduct me to my horse, and I would leave them. This he did, and we marched together upwards of a hundred yards, I with one hand fastened in his collar and a pistol in the other, guarded by his whole company, whom he had the meanness to order to play on their drums the Rogues' March all the way we went, which they did.

The attacks 'became so frequent and so furious, and the time, more-over, was coming on fast when if I did not associate, and take the oaths against legal government, I should certainly be proscribed, and, what seemed still worse, not have it in my power to get out of their clutches; for on the 10th of September all further intercourse with Great Britain was to be stopped; so I now began to have serious thoughts of making my retreat to England'. And so on 10 September 1775, the day non-exportation was to begin, Bouchier and his family slipped away.[105]

Earlier that year, the reaction of the British government – as soon as the Christmas holidays were over – was firm rather than concilia-tory. There were two decided convictions: that the resistance was the work of the rabble led by a few radicals, and that a show of firmness and even force would bring them to heel. The particular concern was Massachusetts Bay, seen as in open rebellion against the imperial government. The belief was that if this could be suppressed, the other colonies would submit quietly and accept their rightful place in the British Empire, which included acceptance of the rights and duties of Parliament. General Gage, however, was finding Massachusetts almost impossible to govern. For example, Parliament had ruled that town meetings should be held only once a year, but Boston got around that by adjourning from week to week. Before leaving Great Britain, Gage had believed that the colonists could be brought to submit by determination and the show of force, but late in 1774 he had written to the Cabinet suggesting that the Coercive Acts be suspended until they could be enforced. One reason was that he had finally realised that resistance was not driven only by a few upstart leaders, but was supported by the great and the good of the colony as well. The response in London was derision, and even the suggestion by some that Gage was afraid to enforce the Acts. The fact that his position was supported by other British officials in America, who also wrote to London that the colonists were determined to resist the Coercive Acts, was discounted. The government continued to believe in the efficacy of force.[106]

V

Early in 1775 Lord Dartmouth, Secretary of State for the Colonies as well as Lord North's stepbrother, sent a letter to Gage instructing him to make a show of force in the countryside around Boston, perhaps by confiscating military stores; in addition, a further three thousand soldiers were sent out to join the four thousand already there. Whether a show of force would trigger a civil war, as Gage feared, was immaterial; the Cabinet believed that if war were inevitable, it would be better to begin it immediately, rather than allow the colonists the time to prepare. However, it appears never to have occurred to the Cabinet that the colonists would, or could, resist. In fact, Massachusetts (along with several other colonies) was already preparing itself, acquiring and storing guns and ammunition, and patrolling the roads leading out of Boston in order to warn the countryside when the British finally marched.[107]

Gage had in March sent out three soldiers on a secret scouting trip from Boston to Roxbury and thence through several villages to Concord. 'The three were well armed and so strikingly disguised in "brown cloathes and reddish handkerchiefs" that they were readily recognised as spying British soldiers.'[108] Nevertheless, they managed to gather useful information about the nature of the landscape and, more important, were told by a Loyalist of the military stores being collected at Concord.[109] Gage decided to send a force to confiscate or destroy the arsenal at Concord, where the illegal Provincial Congress had just met, and, if possible, to capture the rebel leaders Sam Adams and John Hancock, who had attended it.[110] So, on the night of 18 April 1775, the British soldiers quietly left their barracks and marched towards Concord. A number of horsemen were awaiting a signal as to the route of the march. Amongst them was Paul Revere, the most famous because of a poem by Henry Wadsworth Longfellow that generations of American schoolchildren would subsequently recite:

> Listen, my children and you shall hear,
> Of the midnight ride of Paul Revere,
> On the eighteenth of April, in Seventy-five,
> Hardly a man is now alive
> Who remembers that famous day and year.
>
> He said to his friend, 'If the British march
> By land or sea from the town to-night,
> Hang a lantern aloft in the belfry-arch
> Of the North Church tower as a signal light,
> One, if by land, and two, if by sea;[111]
> And I on the opposite shore will be,
> Ready to ride and spread the alarm
> Through every Middlesex village and farm,
> For the country-folk to be up and arm.' . . .[112]

In essence alone the poem is not untrue, but the actual events were more complicated, and, indeed, more interesting, than those portrayed by Longfellow, 'who was utterly without scruple in his manipulation of historical fact'.[113] First of all, with soldiers billeted around the town, the colonists soon knew that something was up.

Revere joined some thirty other men, who had the Green Dragon tavern as their unofficial headquarters, gathering intelligence; they soon knew the destination of the soldiers, but not the route they were to take. They might march across Boston Neck through Roxbury, or travel by boat across to East Cambridge and join the Concord Road there. Dr Joseph Warren, chairman of the Boston Committee of Safety, sent William Dawes, a tanner, across the Neck on horseback to Lexington.[114] Meanwhile, when it became clear that the soldiers were loading into boats, Revere gave the go-ahead for the prearranged signal of two lanterns in the steeple of Old North Church to warn the colonists watching from across the water.[115] Revere himself and a few others crossed the Charles River in a boat with muffled oars.[116] At Charlestown, he was provided with a horse, and set off towards Lexington.

By the time the eight to nine hundred British regulars had gathered on an empty beach near Back Bay at 10 p.m.,[117] the expedition was already doomed to fail. The previous day the Committee of Safety had ordered the dispersal of the stores from Concord to outlying farms and the surrounding towns, and as the soldiers readied to march, men, women and children worked through the night, loading the arms and ammunition onto ox carts to carry them away to new hiding places, putting them into barrels, hauling them into attics and covering them with feathers, or burying them in the fields and woods. A yoke of oxen was hitched to a plough and furrows were turned up in a field, into which were laid the barrels of light cannon and muskets.[118] Furthermore, word of their coming had been spread by others who had seen British soldiers marching towards Concord in advance of the main body of troops. By the time the latter reached the Concord Road, alarm bells and cannon were rousing the countryside.

Revere, meanwhile, was making his midnight ride towards Lexington, where he stopped to warn Hancock and Adams to flee. When a member of the Lexington militia refused him permission to pass, saying that the family in the house where the two were staying did not want any noise, Revere cried out, 'Noise! You'll have noise enough before long. The Regulars are coming out!'[119] William Dawes met Revere there, and the two set off for Concord. They were soon joined by a Concord man, Dr Samuel Prescott, who had spent the evening in Lexington with his sweetheart. This was fortunate: a few miles further on, their progress was halted by British sentries, who confiscated Revere's horse, forcing him to walk back to Lexington in his silver spurs and heavy riding boots. Contrary to Longfellow's account, Revere's ride was therefore completed by Prescott, who jumped his horse over a stone wall and escaped through back roads and over fields.

There were two types of American fighters who fought at Lexington and Concord, militia and Minutemen. Companies of militia had existed for some time, but since they consisted of all able-bodied men between the ages of sixteen and thirty, and since their numbers were dispersed on farms around the countryside, they could not readily be summoned. Accordingly, beginning in September 1774, certain Massachusetts militia began reorganising themselves, forming about a third of their members into companies that could be assembled 'at a minute's notice'. These were the Minutemen. On 26 September the townsmen of Concord voted 'that there be one or more Companys Raised in this Town by Enlistment and that they Chuse their officers out of the Body So Inlisted and that Said Company or Companies Stand at a minutes warning in Case of an alarm'.[120] The same occurred in the neighbouring towns and villages.

The first blood of the Revolution was shed at Lexington, not Concord. At 12.30 a.m. on 19 April, William Dawes arrived at Lexington and gave the alarm, at which the bell began to ring. In response, 130 members of the Lexington militia, under the command of Captain John Parker, assembled on Lexington Green. However, no British soldiers were in the neighbourhood, so they were dismissed, although with orders to reassemble at the beating of the drum. At 4.30 a.m., it was reported that the British were within a half-mile of Lexington and the drum was beaten to recall the militia. Major John Pitcairn, in command of the British Marines, saw the militia lined up and formed his own men into line of battle. 'Captain Parker then gave his famous order to his company: "Stand your ground! Don't fire unless fired upon! But if they mean to have a war, let it begin here!" Whereupon Pitcairn rode to the front of his ranks and shouted to the men in Parker's lines, "Lay down your arms, you damned rebels and disperse!"'[121] Realising at last how badly he was outnumbered and how futile his situation was, Parker ordered his men to file away. But then a shot was fired – no one knows by whom – and the British in response fired a volley. Another followed, and then the British soldiers charged with fixed bayonets. Eight men were killed – one dying on his doorstep at the feet of his wife – and another ten wounded. 'The main body of the British soon came upon the Green. A cheer rose up in token of the victory and "the musick struck up" as the troops started down the road for Concord.'[122]

By this time, men with their guns were streaking to Concord from all over the countryside, and word of the fatalities at Lexington soon spread. The British reached Concord about 7 a.m., at the same time as large numbers of militia and Minutemen assembled at various points around the town. For the next couple of hours, the British soldiers searched for the military stores. About 9 a.m., the Americans on the top of a nearby hill saw smoke rising from the town – the British had set fire to the courthouse – and feared the worst. They decided to march to its defence, and were joined by a number of groups from other towns and villages. The Americans met the British at the North Bridge, and after several bursts of fire from each side, the Americans stepped onto the bridge. At this point, with artillery shells falling amongst them, the British retreated. The confrontation at the North Bridge, celebrated in Emerson's 'The Concord Hymn', was all over in two or three minutes.

The main body of the British troops reassembled in the middle of Concord, rested for a couple of hours, and then began the return to Boston. It was a nightmare. As word of the fighting spread across the countryside, militiamen converged in their thousands on the Concord to Boston road. As the soldiers marched in ranks down the road, the Americans hid behind boulders and in wooded groves and picked them off, or ambushed them from behind stone fences, shooting and then running to the next vantage point.[123] Some were caught by the British flankers (light infantry who fanned out from the main troops), but the skirmishing took place under conditions overwhelmingly favourable to the Americans. The troops reached Lexington at about 2 p.m., and were met by a volley of shots from the Lexington Minutemen. During their march, often under fire, the British regulars repeatedly fell into disarray, and their officers had great difficulty keeping them together and under control. They were also exhausted, most having been on the march for over twenty-four hours by the time the last of them reached Boston at midnight. The cost of the day was 273 British and 95 Americans dead; the result was a countryside in open revolt.

On 10 May, the Second Continental Congress convened in Philadelphia. It had a momentous decision to take – was there to be war or peace? Apparently, there was to be both: they would prepare for war by establishing a Continental Army, but they would continue to send petitions to Parliament and hope for peace and a return to a united British Empire. The context was a divided American social and political elite. There were the radicals, who had little hope of reconciliation and, to a greater or lesser extent, hoped for, or at least were prepared for, independence. They included John and Samuel Adams, Benjamin Franklin, Thomas Jefferson and George Washington. There were the conservatives, who, although determined to protect American rights and liberties, hoped that the petitions and general moderation would change the British Cabinet's mind without the need for military measures. They included John Dickinson, who had written *Letters from a Philadelphia Farmer*, and John Jay of New York, who would become the first Chief Justice of the Supreme Court. And in between were the moderates, who wanted the colonies to resume their place in the empire, and hoped, but did not really believe, that this could be accomplished peacefully; therefore, they supported military measures as the only way to convince the British to grant colonial demands. This group included John Hancock. However, over the following year all three groups, with the significant exception of some of the conservatives, would decide that the only remedy was independence.[124]

But in May 1775, the most urgent matter for the Congress was whether or not to establish an army. After Lexington and Concord, thousands of American militiamen had swarmed to Boston, which they surrounded, and many were anxious to attack the British. Some organisation would be useful. In any case, the delegates of the First Congress had promised Massachusetts that if they refrained from aggressive action against the British but were still attacked by the redcoats, the other colonies would come to their aid. The British had attacked: now it was time for the Congress to act on its promise.

Meanwhile, a group of irregulars under Ethan Allen and Captain
Benedict Arnold of the Connecticut Militia, the latter the most
famous of American traitors, had obtained a commission from the
Massachusetts Committee of Safety to attack and capture the
British arsenal at Fort Ticonderoga on Lake Champlain; the idea
was to pre-empt an attack on the colonies from British Canada. The
attack was successful. This, of course, was unwarranted aggression
by the colonies against the mother country, and it worried many of
the delegates. In the end, they decided that the colonists involved
should make an inventory of all arms and supplies taken from the
fort, so that, once the dispute was over, they could be returned to
Great Britain. (Washington, in November 1775, ordered the fort's
heavy artillery to be transported to Boston.)[125]

But should there be a Continental Army? And if so, who was to
command it? With these questions in mind, two of the most important delegates were John Adams of Massachusetts and George
Washington of Virginia. Each was ready for war, but each underplayed his views.[126] As John Feiling points out, 'Adams' first task was
to create a national army. Washington's first objective was to be
chosen commander of that army. To publicly avow anything more
radical than resistance to British policies would have jeopardised
the immediate goal of each man.'[127] Washington, not very subtle,
wore his Virginia Regiment uniform to these sessions. It took thirty-
five days for the Continental Congress to create a Continental Army,
since it was necessary for the moderates and especially the conservatives to conclude that London was so hostile that the colonies had
to be prepared to counter force with force. Immediately after the
decision was taken, Adams nominated Washington as Commander-
in-Chief. The New England delegates were desperate that it be a
truly national army, and appointing Washington as its commander
would cement the southern states to the north. But there were other
reasons for his appointment. He had been a soldier for five years,
during the French and Indian War (although, it must be said, with no
great success). Nevertheless, he at least knew which end of a gun
was which. He was wealthy, relatively young (forty-three), and in
good health. He was tall and imposing, and exuded an air of
authority which made men want to follow his leadership. He was

both charismatic and dignified. He firmly believed in civilian control of and jurisdiction over the army. And he was a convinced republican – one who would not, Adams believed, be tempted to become a tyrant or a king.[128] He was appointed on 15 June, departed later that month, and reached Boston on 2 July.

Congress, however, continued with its other responses to the emergency. One was to draft a statement setting out why the colonists felt the need to take up arms against the mother country. This became the 'Declaration of the Causes and Necessity of Taking Up Arms', largely drafted by another delegate from Virginia, Thomas Jefferson. It was strongly anti-monarchical and anti-British, accusing Great Britain of a design to 'erect a despotism of unlimited extent' over the colonists, and it entirely put off some of the delegates, who hoped for reconciliation. Jefferson was therefore forced to moderate some of the language. At the same time, Dickinson and his supporters argued for what came to be called the Olive Branch Petition, an appeal to the King. The delegates adopted them both at the same time.[129] Given that the official creation of an army was the action of a sovereign power, it is curious, to say the least, that Congress kept insisting that it was not bidding for independence.

Meanwhile, twenty thousand New Englanders were camped around Boston and besieging the city, under the collective command of the Massachusetts Committee of Safety;[130] this cut the British army off from the countryside, and within days provisions were running short. Gage was reluctant to move against the besiegers, conscious of his relative lack of troops, but the arrival of substantial reinforcements (seven battalions of infantry and a cavalry regiment) from Britain six weeks after Lexington and Concord, along with two major-generals, a third general and an admiral, probably emboldened him to attempt to break out of the city and gain access to the countryside; for one thing, he feared that he would be replaced if something was not done. He was correct: the two major-generals, Sir William Howe and Sir Henry Clinton, succeeded him as commander in October 1775 and March 1778 respectively. As described by Hugh Bicheno, 'In order of seniority they were William Howe, younger brother of Admiral Lord Howe, who together with his brother implemented a doomed policy of limited warfare to encourage reconciliation; Henry Clinton who took over from him and drifted from stalemate to defeat; and John Burgoyne who was to sacrifice an army to his vanity.'[131]

But the change in command was in the future. For the time being, Gage was still in charge, but his attempted breakout was badly, even stupidly, organised, and a monument to the contempt with which the British army regarded the fighting ability of the colonists. From their fortifications on the tops of Brede's Hill and Bunker Hill, the Americans could look down over the town and harbour, and over the British soldiers, who would have to fight marching uphill and in the open. The American positions were not softened up by gunfire from the ships in the harbour. Furthermore, the British had no reserves prepared, and no arrangements were made to take care of the wounded. Nevertheless, the British soldiers fought gallantly on Brede's Hill, and their bayonet charges finally forced the Americans to retreat and then run away. Although there were many excellent shots amongst the Americans, and they were famously ordered by their captain not to fire 'until you can see the whites of their eyes', smoke soon covered the field and their marksmanship fell before the organised advance of the British. The Americans lost 140 killed and 271 injured at what was called the Battle of Bunker Hill. This was seen by them as a humiliating defeat, leading to a surge of desertions and the court martial and dismissal of a colonel and five captains. (Bicheno, however, has argued that this was a 'moral victory of the highest order for the men who held Brede's Hill, despite shameful lack of support from their fellows at Bunker Hill and on the mainland'.[132]) It was a victory for the British, but it was gained at great cost: of the 2,300 soldiers involved, 226 were killed and 828 wounded, with an unusually high proportion dying of infected wounds.[133] In other words, the British had lost 40 per cent of their attacking force. Amongst the dead was Major Pitcairn, who had led his men at Lexington, and who was shot down as he led his Marines on the final assault on the hill.[134]

The battle changed Gage's perceptions of the Americans' ability to fight and of what the British had to do to defeat them. As he wrote to the Secretary at War, Lord Barrington, on 26 June, nine days after the battle: 'These people show a spirit and courage against us they never showed against the French, and everybody has judged them from their formal appearance and behaviour when joined with the King's forces in the last war; which has led many into great mistakes. They are now spirited up by a rage and enthusiasm as great as ever people were possessed of, and you must proceed in earnest or give the business up.'[135] Gage finally asked permission in late August to leave Boston and relocate the army in New York, but by the time permission was received in early October, he had been replaced as Commander-in-Chief by Howe.

On 25 July 1775, London learned of Bunker Hill. The Cabinet accepted that an escalation of the conflict was inevitable, and Lord North wrote to the King the following day that 'the war is now grown to such a height, that it must be treated as a foreign war',[136] not merely as a coercive action by the mother country against her colonies. North then tried to conciliate the Americans, authorising the Howe brothers to offer the colonists the right to tax themselves, if only they would accept the sovereignty of Parliament. This was too little too late. The King was more determined. Already, on 18 November 1774, he had written to North that 'the New England governments are in a state of rebellion, blows must decide whether they are to be subject to this country or independent'.[137] Now the Privy Council on his behalf issued on 23 August 1775 the Royal Proclamation of Rebellion, declaring that 'not only all our officers, civil and military, are obliged to exert their utmost endeavours to suppress such rebellion and to bring the traitors to justice; but that all our subjects of this realm and the dominions thereunto belonging are bound by law to be aiding and assisting in the suppression of such rebellion'.[138] Consequently, when the Olive Branch Petition was presented on 1 September to the Secretary of State for America, Lord Dartmouth, he effectively ignored it, and no answer was given by the King.

VI

Nevertheless, Lord North still hoped for peace and the reintegration of the colonies into the empire. His vehicle was to be a Peace Commission. However, it was so convoluted an idea that it was entirely misunderstood by the colonists. The idea was that the Peace Commission should be able to conduct genuine negotiations. To do this, North believed, there had to be something which the colonists would not like, and which the Commission could then lift. This was the American Prohibitory Act: it repealed the Boston Port Act and the two Acts of 1775 that banned American trade, but prohibited all colonial trade, which meant that colonial ships were now fair game for the Royal Navy. To underline the peril of the Americans, they were declared to be beyond the King's protection. (According to Conway, 'John Adams . . . astutely observed that the British had in effect proclaimed American independence.'[139]) The Peace Commission was authorised to lift this ban on individual colonies if they acccepted North's Conciliatory Proposition: when any colony offered to pay for its civil government and its share of defence costs, Parliament would not tax that colony for revenue. The sting, of course, was that Parliament could decide on the sum. The Opposition offered little debate when it was introduced by North on 20 November,[140] and the King signed it into law on 22 December 1775.

The ministry then turned to preparations for war. Early in 1776, subsidy treaties were concluded with two German states, arranging for five thousand Brunswickers and twelve thousand Hessians to travel to North America. As for strategy, General Howe and the new Secretary at War, Lord George Germain, agreed that New York should be the British Army's headquarters, not least because it would divide the colonies in two. Meanwhile, on the Peace Commission, Richard Howe, one of Britain's finest admirals, was appointed a commissioner as well as being named the naval commander for America. Germain appointed the admiral's brother, William Howe, as the second commissioner. It was a ridiculous arrangement: the two men empowered to secure peace were at the same time the two men empowered to wage war on land and sea. One task would have to give way. As it happened, the Peace Commission, as represented by Richard Howe, only arrived in the colonies on 12 July 1776, eight days after the Declaration of Independence had been published, thus rendering the whole exercise nugatory. His brother told him that peace negotiations would now have to await the defeat of the Americans.[141]

It was ironic that since the previous autumn, opinion in favour of independence – a minority conviction in any case – had been cooling, and more colonists were shifting back in favour of reconciliation. In the closing months of 1775, the legislatures of Delaware, New Jersey, New York, Pennsylvania and South Carolina had all instructed their delegates to the Continental Congress not to vote for independence, and the Maryland legislature did the same in January 1776.[142] There were several reasons for this. For one thing, fear: could the colonies stand up militarily to Great Britain? Furthermore, one should not underestimate the pride much of the population felt in being British, a patriotism heightened by the French and Indian War and the victory over France. On the whole, people were conservative: the decision to change one's traditional loyalty to Great Britain would not have been an easy one for most of them to take. Fundamentally, 'Americans took particular pride in being governed under Britain's unwritten constitution, which they considered the most perfect form of government ever invented "by the wit of man".'[143] For many, it was not obvious that they would be better off outside the Empire. Allied to this, many saw the Crown's American policy as part of a drive to accumulate such power that the balance of this exemplary constitution would be destroyed. 'To resist such an effort was conservative since it sought to preserve Britain's historic system of governance.'[144] This was not a drive for independence.

The question of independence, however, burst upon the consciousness of the general public in January 1776, with the publication of a pamphlet by the Englishman Thomas Paine entitled *Common Sense; Addressed to the Inhabitants of America*. Paine had been a corsetmaker and then excise officer in England. It had therefore been his job to collect duties, such as those on tea. He had also written a pamphlet on behalf of his fellow-excisemen calling for higher wages. Although that pamphlet had little impact, it whetted his appetite for politics and journalism. He was now bankrupt, separated from his wife, and jobless, so he decided to go to America. Through connections made during his unsuccessful attempt at lobbying in London, he was introduced to Benjamin Franklin, who gave him some letters of introduction to take with him to Pennsylvania, and in late 1774, aged thirty-seven, he arrived in Philadelphia, where he became a newspaperman. During the following year, he wrote a number of articles on the unacceptability of British actions; it did not take him long to make contact with the radicals, and he was encouraged to write his pamphlet. He began drafting it in November 1775.

In a coincidence of which most writers can only dream, *Common Sense* was published on the same day that Philadelphians first read the text of the King's speech of 26 October 1775 to Parliament, in which he had accused the colonists of aiming for independence and pledged to put 'a speedy End to these disorders by the most decisive Exertions'.[145] The *Pennsylvania Evening Post*, in its issue of 9 January 1776, published both the text of the speech and the first advertisement for Paine's pamphlet.[146] Available for sale the following day, it sold some 120,000 copies during the following three months. It went through twenty-five editions in 1776 alone, and one estimate is that it sold half a million copies that year.[147]

Probably the most original element of Paine's pamphlet was its charging the King – the 'Royal Brute of Britain' – rather than his ministers and Parliament with the attempts to extirpate freedom in the colonies.[148] The arguments by Americans against the actions of Great Britain had been arguments against Parliament, particularly against its claim to be sovereign over all parts of the British Empire. The direct representation of Americans in Parliament – or, rather, the lack of such representation – had been the gravamen of colonial opposition to its decision. Now, here was Paine writing that Parliament was, if not exactly irrelevant, of considerably less importance than the King, who could control it by bribing Members with pensions and places. Therefore, Americans should recognise the fact that the monarchy, supported by an unelected, hereditary aristocracy, was the true enemy.[149]

Paine did not stop there. People remember that he called for independence from Great Britain – 'Every thing that is right or natural pleads for separation. The blood of the slain, the weeping voice of nature cries, "TIS TIME TO PART"';[150] but he went further, and sketched out a new form of government. It was probably the case that many who trembled on the edge of decision were more than a little apprehensive as to what might replace the form of government they knew. Paine gave them an alternative: a republic. This would be founded purely on popular choice, with no hereditary elements. There would be a president, more equal representation for voters, who would elect assemblies annually, and a constitution, called a Continental Charter, or Charter of the United Colonies, 'answering to what is called the Magna Charta [sic] of England'.[151] This was worth fighting for, and Paine insisted that they could defeat Great Britain: the Americans had men, matériel, solidarity, and the expectation of foreign aid.

Indeed, the fear of what independence might give rise to greatly influenced many to hold back. According to Pauline Maier, Paine's plan for a republic stimulated even more opposition than did his call for independence. She quotes John Adams, one of the most important of the radicals, as lamenting that by its 'crude, ignorant Notion of a Government by one assembly', Common Sense would 'do more Mischief in dividing Friends of Liberty, than all the Tory Writings together'. Paine was 'a keen Writer, but very ignorant of the Science of Government'.[152] All around them, there was tumult and a world threatening to slide into disorder, with mobs letting debtors out of prison, violent disputes over land, fear of restive slaves who heard about freedom, a series of temporary assemblies and local governments, and the apprehension that in some places the military power was threatening the supremacy of the civil power. Delaying action, in the hope that Great Britain would be more conciliatory, became increasingly dangerous. Therefore, on 10 May 1776, the Continental Congress recommended to 'the respective Assemblies and Conventions of the United Colonies, where no Government sufficient to the exigencies of their affairs has been hitherto established, to adopt such Government as shall, in the opinion of the Representatives of the People, best conduce to the happiness and safety of their constituents in particular and America in general'.[153] In short, any authority which the Crown still possessed was to be eliminated.

The resolution required a preface, and on 15 May the Congress issued it. As Paine had done, the Congress pinned responsibility for the grievances of the colonies firmly on the King. The charges against him were few in number but powerful in effect: he had consented to the Prohibitory Act, which formally excluded Americans from his protection; he had refused to answer their petitions for redress, such as the Olive Branch Petition; and he was bringing against them 'the whole force of the Kingdom, aided by foreign Mercenaries'. The last was a new charge. Rumours had abounded earlier in the year that the King was looking to hire foreign troops – something which had been done before, of course, but against *foreign* enemies – but it was not until early May that Americans learned from a Cork newspaper that Great Britain was sending some forty thousand additional soldiers, including 'Hessians, Hanoverians, [and] Mechlenburghers'. According to Maier, 'Five days later, Congress received – through a mysterious emissary who came from London with documents sewn in his clothes – copies of the treaties George III had concluded with the Duke of Brunswick, the Landgrave of Hesse Cassel, and the Count of Hanau, each of which specified the terms on which German-speaking soldiers would be supplied for the King's service in America. Within a week the treaties were published in Pennsylvania newpapers. The effect was electrifying.'[154]

Events now accelerated. An American invasion of Canada, intended to extend the rebellion and 'free' the French Canadians, which had begun in the autumn of the previous year, had by May 1776 turned into an unmitigated disaster.[155] Furthermore, it now seemed that the home territory was increasingly at risk. The British army, which had withdrawn from Boston on 17 March, had regrouped in Halifax and was expected to land somewhere on the Atlantic seaboard at any time. The Americans needed foreign help, but would, for example, France give aid if the Americans were still deemed to be British subjects? Many, of course, questioned whether it was wise to turn to the traditional enemy, Catholic France, for assistance. But they, and others who delayed for other reasons, were undermined by the news that in early May, the City of London had presented a petition asking the King to set out the terms of a just peace before attacking the colonies, and that the King had rejected it: he would be 'ready and happy to alleviate those miseries, by acts of mercy and clemency, whenever that authority is established, and the now existing rebellion is at an end. To obtain these salutary purposes, I will inevitably pursue the most proper and effectual means.'[156] The war drums were already sounding.

On 7 June, Richard Henry Lee, a delegate to the Continental Congress from Virginia, moved three resolutions on the instructions of the Virginia Convention, which were seconded by John Adams:

> That these United Colonies are, and of right ought to be, free and independent States, that they are absolved from all allegiance to the British Crown, and that all political connection between them and the State of Great Britain is, and ought to be, totally dissolved.
>
> That it is expedient forthwith to take the most effectual measures for forming foreign Alliances.
>
> That a plan of confederation be prepared and transmitted to the respective Colonies for their consideration and approbation.[157]

Then ensued some days of debate. It was soon clear that the middle colonies were not yet ready finally to break the connection with Great Britain. The delegates decided to postpone a decision on this declaration of independence for three weeks, so that minds could be changed. Meanwhile, in order that time should not be lost if the resolutions were accepted, the Congress on 11 June appointed a committee of five to prepare a declaration of independence. They were John Adams, Benjamin Franklin, Thomas Jefferson, Robert R. Livingston and Roger Sherman;[158] Jefferson was given the task of writing the first draft, which was presented to Congress seventeen days later. By this time, only Maryland and New York still awaited permission from their assemblies to vote for independence; that night, the Maryland delegation learned that they could go ahead. In the end, the New York delegation had to abstain.

During this period, frightening news was received about the movements of the British. Washington learned that on 9 June a fleet of 132 ships had sailed from Halifax under General Howe; it was expected that he would attack New York City, and the surrounding states were asked to send their militias to help in its defence. On 29 June Washington reported the arrival of fifty ships on the New Jersey shore near the entrance to New York Harbour; within days, there were twice the number. By 1 July, Congress had learned that another fifty-three British ships were outside Charles Town, South Carolina;

they had also learned of the fate of the American invasion of Canada. In other words, it had become appallingly clear that this was a decision for war, the outcome of which would render them either traitors hanged by Great Britain or the founders of a new nation. Debate on the resolutions began on 1 July, and on the following day the Congress voted to declare independence from Great Britain. They then devoted the following two days to editing Thomas Jefferson, to his great rage: the draft was cut and pared by a quarter, and he had to sit there and listen to it happening. 'The more alterations Congress made on his draft, the more miserable Jefferson became.'[159] But the outcome was a compelling piece of prose:

> . . . We hold these truths to be self-evident, that all men are created equal, that they are endowed by their Creator with certain inalienable Rights, that among these are Life, Liberty and the pursuit of Happiness. That to secure these rights, Governments are instituted among Men, deriving their just powers from the consent of the governed. That whenever any Form of Government becomes destructive to these ends, it is the Right of the People to alter or to abolish it, and to institute new Government, laying its foundation on such principles and organizing its powers in such form, as to them shall seem most likely to effect their Safety and Happiness.

The document was signed by John Hancock as the President of the Continental Congress. It was, in effect, a declaration of treason. As Hancock declared, 'There must be no pulling different ways[.] We must all hang together' and Franklin famously replied, 'Yes, we must, indeed, all hang together, or most assuredly we shall all hang separately.'[160] Only on 18 January 1777, after the Americans had won two victories in New Jersey, did the rest affix their signatures and the Congress send signed copies to all of the states. The Declaration was read out in Philadelphia on 8 July with appropriate ceremonial, but there is no record of the Liberty Bell – or any other bell – being rung. Washington also chose to inform and, he hoped, inspire the soldiers of the Continental Army in New York City by having it read out to them: on 9 July, 'with the British "constantly in view, upon and at Staten-Island," as one participant recalled, the brigades were "formed in hollow squares on their respective parades," where they heard the Declaration read, as the General [Washington] had specified, "with an audible voice".'[161] The Americans had proclaimed their independence; now they would have to fight for it.

VII

The year 1777 was crucial for both sides. The British needed to cut the colonies in two, so that the southern ones would be unable to aid New England, particularly Massachusetts, seen as the fomenter of the rebellion. Their strategy, therefore, was for a northern army of ten thousand to drive the Americans from Canada, and then to proceed down into New York via Lake Champlain to meet up with the main army under General Howe in the lower Hudson Valley. This was a decision based on maps rather than on local knowledge. As Bicheno points out, placing the British strategy in geographic context:

Before the advent of railways, significant military forces seldom strayed far from coasts and rivers. Nor did they need to, for human habitation and wealth was always concentrated in littoral areas. The 'roads' of America were primitive tracks, as they were everywhere else in the world at this time with the sole exception of the remarkable English turnpike system. The novelty was not that land communications were appalling but that they ran through woods of an extent and density not seen in Europe since the time of the Roman Empire. Far more significant to a maritime power like Britain were the four great hydrographic systems, the St. Lawrence, the Hudson, the Delaware and the Chesapeake Bay catchment area. Of these, the first two were linked by an almost continuous ribbon of water reaching from Canada to New York along the Richelieu River, Lake Champlain and Lake George, which exerted a fatal fascination over strategists on both sides. Fatal, because the 'almost' in that description was a nearly impenetrable watershed between the ends of lakes and the northern-most curl of the navigable Hudson. Both sides were to find defeat by crossing it.[162]

The British troops in Canada, under the command of General John Burgoyne, began to advance south in June 1777. The main army, under the command of General Howe, moved by sea to the rebel capital, Philadelphia. The plan was to lure the Continental Army to a decisive battle and thereby destroy the rebel forces, but Washington refused to be lured. Meanwhile, the army under Burgoyne faced great difficulties, not least the need to build forty bridges; it took twenty-four days to travel twenty-three miles. The troops became exhausted and supplies diminished alarmingly. Furthermore, it became clear that the British had underestimated the dangers posed by the New England militias. Burgoyne sent out a group of soldiers to capture an enemy magazine. As described by Piers Mackesy,

> The commander he chose was a brave German dragoon called Colonel Baum, who qualified for marching through a country of mixed friends and foes by speaking no English. His force was remarkable. He had fifty picked British marksmen and 100 German grenadiers and light infantry; 300 Tories, Canadians and Indians; to preserve secrecy, a German band; to speed the column, 170 dismounted German dragoons in search of horses, marching in their huge top boots and spurs and trailing their sabres. This was reinforced on the march by fifty Brunswick Jäger and ninety local Tories who brought Baum's force to 800 men.[163]

They were defeated by parts of the New Hampshire, Massachusetts and Vermont militias at Bennington, Vermont, and this discouraged many local Loyalists, whose support melted away. Indeed, one of the advantages of the Americans came in the form of these backwoods riflemen, mounted light infantry and militias, who fought a guerrilla war: they interrupted communications and supply lines, harassed flanks of the army and raided isolated outposts. The British continued to meet heavy resistance and Burgoyne called for reinforcements, but they failed to arrive. The result was the defeat of the fewer than six thousand British troops at Saratoga by an American force nearly twice its size, with capitulation on 17 October 1777. This changed the nature, and the outcome, of the war.[164]

What changed was the entry of France into the war. France had decided in early May 1776 to provide arms for the Americans.[165] This was not for love of Americans but through hatred of Great Britain. The French Foreign Minister, Charles Gravier, Comte de Vergennes, argued that the British economy and the Royal Navy were dependent on Great Britain's maintaining her monopoly of American trade; hence, France should aid the American rebellion. Vergennes wanted to distract Great Britain from paying too much attention to French activities in the eastern parts of Europe. Shipments of arms, ammunition (particularly gunpowder) and clothing came through the French Caribbean islands of Martinique, Guadeloupe and St Domingue (now Haiti), as well as the Dutch Caribbean island of St Eustatius. Because Lord North had not ordered a full-scale naval mobilisation, superior British sea power was unable to cut off this aid entirely. France also allowed rebel privateers and the tiny Continental Navy the clandestine use of her ports. However, she had held back from open material support until there was evidence that the rebels proved a serious threat to Great Britain. British defeats and difficulties in 1777, culminating in the defeat at Saratoga, emboldened France to sign treaties of commerce and alliance with the 'United States' on 6 February 1778. The Treaty of Amity and Commerce gave America most-favoured-nation status, whilst by the Treaty of Alliance, France rejected any claim to Canada (excepting the rich Newfoundland fisheries), promised not to make peace until Great Britain recognised American independence, and guaranteed in perpetuity American 'liberty, sovereignty and independence'. The two countries agreed that neither would make a separate peace with Great Britain, and that Spain would be asked to join the alliance. Copies were sent to Philadelphia, where the Congress ratified them on 4 May 1778. The British knew about the 'secret' treaties, but chose to ignore them. France, however, announced the Treaty of Amity and Commerce on 13 March, though not that of Alliance; Great Britain then withdrew her ambassador from the French court, and France withdrew hers from the Court of

St James's and recognised the American representatives in Paris, who included Benjamin Franklin, as diplomats. The British understood this for what it was: a declaration by France that she intended that Great Britain should lose the most important group of colonies in her empire. The two countries began to prepare for war.[166]

In Great Britain, news of the defeat at Saratoga came as a great shock. It caused a huge political crisis for the North administration, and his support became increasingly fragile. As one historian has emphasised, politics during the North ministry reached heights of bitterness not seen for nearly fifty years and, because the ministry was a coalition, the Cabinet reflected these competing interests and factions. North's skills were those of a man of peace and a manager of the House of Commons, not of a great war leader. He saw politics at home, not the American problem, as his major concern, and had refrained from increasing the strength of the army and navy so that taxes need not be raised. This had more than one impact on the military services. Increasing their size would have increased the scope for patronage, because they were dominated by the spoils system. For most MPs, a seat in the House of Commons was less an instrument to govern the country than an instrument for gaining promotions, prizes and places. Indeed, the twenty-three generals in the House of Commons in 1780 (including Howe, Burgoyne and Cornwallis) shared between them twenty-one colonelcies, nine governorships and around six staff appointments, and criticism by North of a military failure by a dependant of any of them would probably send the MP and his supporters into opposition. Social ties therefore clashed with the military hierarchy, in that the aristocratic structure of the army and navy affected discipline. The Royal Navy was less affected than the army, since efficiency and quality were vital to the very safety of the realm. But Saratoga was so catastrophic that ferocious feuding between ministers and the naval and military commanders broke out, and all of the Commanders-in-Chief in America in due course resigned, General Sir Guy Carleton (in Canada) and William Howe by the end of 1777, and Richard Howe during 1778.[167]

Of far greater importance was that the conflict had now ceased to be a police action by an imperial power against a colonial rebellion and had become a worldwide war, one in which all British imperial possessions were at risk. This had profound implications for naval strategy. Whilst Great Britain controlled the high seas, she could isolate conflicts in any part of the world by preventing aid from reaching her opponents. But when her command of the oceans was threatened, all strategic decisions were interrelated. If she gave priority to protecting the rich West Indian islands, she exposed the North American colonies to danger. If, as she must, she made protecting the home islands the priority, this made it more likely that the French would try to recover India. In short, sea power, which had had remarkably little effect during the first phase of the war, now became paramount, as the defence of the far-flung maritime empire and the safety of the home islands, rather than the crushing of the American rebellion, became the strategic priorities.

The danger to Great Britain of the challenge was considerable, because the outcome of the Seven Years' War had had unexpected results. As Mackesy puts it, although she had crushed her opponents, she had also lost her friends: her former ally Austria was now obsessed by the rise of Prussia, and looked to France; Prussia, another former ally, had been alienated by Great Britain's ignoring Prussian interests; the Netherlands could no longer be considered a Great Power; and Spain and France had both been defeated and yearned for revenge.[168] Britain not only had no friends, she was effectively surrounded by enemies, and became increasingly outgunned. To look ahead: in 1778 the French had fifty-two ships of the line (large warships) against the British sixty-six; in June 1779, Spain joined the alliance, and Great Britain now faced the combined force of the second and third largest navies in the world, her ninety ships facing the 121 ships of her opponents' combined fleets; and when in 1781 the Dutch joined the anti-British alliance, Great Britain's fleet of ninety-four ships was opposed by an allied fleet of 137.

Lord Sandwich, the First Lord of the Admiralty, saw as his main responsibility the defence of the British Isles, which were weakly garrisoned and vulnerable to invasion. As soon as the government learned of the signing of the Treaty of Alliance, the Admiralty ordered twenty of Lord Howe's ships to return to Great Britain and another thirteen to sail to the West Indies. This was the overall naval picture: in July 1778, with Great Britain newly at war with France, 47 per cent of

British ships of the line were in Europe, 8 per cent in the West Indies, 3 per cent in India and 41 per cent in North America. In July 1779, a month after Spain joined the war, 49 per cent were in Europe, 33 per cent in the West Indies, 9 per cent in India – and only 9 per cent in North America. There was a similar shift in the disposition of the British army. In February 1778, 26 per cent of its forces were stationed in Great Britain, 2 per cent in the West Indies, 7 per cent in the Mediterranean, none in India, and 65 per cent in North America. By September 1780, 55 per cent were in Great Britain, 8 per cent in the West Indies, 6 per cent in the Mediterranean, 1 per cent in India – and only 29 per cent in North America, a decline of 36 per cent.[169] It is not surprising that the British continued to rely on German mercenaries.

France wanted to seize the initiative, and on 11 April 1778 twelve ships of the line (including a fifty-gun ship) and four frigates, carrying four thousand soldiers, left the naval base at Toulon under the command of Admiral le Comte d'Estaing and headed directly towards New York.[170] The French hoped that the British would fear an invasion and keep their fleet in the Channel, rather than reinforcing New York, since their plan was to capture the city before the British realised what was happening and end the war at a stroke. Lord Sandwich duly fulfilled their hope. The French fleet arrived off Sandy Hook on 11 July, causing some alarm, since Admiral Howe's fleet was undermanned. Washington had concocted a plan for a Franco-American attack on New York, but d'Estaing's pilots discovered that the channel in New York was too shallow for the French vessels. The decision was then taken to attack Newport, but before it could take place, d'Estaing's fleet was badly damaged by a sudden and violent storm. It left for Boston for repairs, later sailing from there to the West Indies.

Events in 1777 had driven the British to two decisions. The first was to revise entirely their military strategy. Because the British were now facing a much greater threat – that of France probably allied to Spain – than any the Americans could provide, their response was to relegate the American problem very much to second place.[171] The British decided to change the centre of operations from the northern to the southern colonies and the West Indies, and the disposition of the armed forces was therefore drastically changed.

And secondly, there was an attempt to remove the Americans from the equation by coming to terms with them, but in a manner which would enable Great Britain to retain at least a nominal sovereignty over her erstwhile colonies.

On 8 March 1778, Secretary at War Germain instructed William Henry Clinton, successor to General Howe as Commander-in-Chief of the British army in America, to prepare for a predominantly naval war. This was to be conducted from New York and Nova Scotia, the latter a safer base than most further south because that colony was not in rebellion, and was the home of the Halifax naval base. He suggested that they abandon Philadelphia and change to a 'southern strategy': Georgia, South Carolina and North Carolina were seen as full of Loyalists who could be called upon to control the territory whilst the army cleaned out the rebels, and thereafter. Then, five days later, came the announcement of the Franco-American Treaty, and this strategy was quickly revised. Consideration was given to withdrawing completely from the thirteen colonies in the face of the imminent French danger, but this was rejected. Instead, it was decided to concentrate on attacking the rich French West Indian islands before France could come to their defence, with the American South a secondary theatre of operations. Clinton was ordered to send eight thousand of his troops south, with the remainder to be withdrawn to New York. This was done in November 1778.

Before any of this, however, the second tactic of the North administration had been implemented. North had promised the House of Commons before the Christmas 1777 recess that he would introduce new peace proposals, and duly in February 1778 another set of Conciliatory Propositions was passed 'by a silent and gloomy House'. By these Propositions, the Coercive Acts were repealed, the Renunciation Act renounced the right of Parliament to tax the colonies except for the regulation of trade, the colonists were to be allowed to maintain their own army, and, if they chose, the Continental Congress could remain in being as a subordinate branch of the imperial Parliament. A new Peace Commission under the leadership of the Earl of Carlisle was appointed with full powers to negotiate for any terms short of independence. Whilst North was convinced that the terms did not exist which would be acceptable both to

Great Britain and to the Congress, domestic opinion was beginning to change. The main threat was France, and even American independence might be a price worth paying to safeguard Britain. This opinion was now held even by the King, who by this time was primarily concerned with the situation in Canada, Nova Scotia and Florida, colonies still loyal to the Crown. The Commissioners sailed for America on 16 April. They offered Congress a union of Great Britain and America under a common sovereign 'on a basis of equal freedom and mutual safety'. Congress refused to treat with Carlisle, and reasserted American independence: negotiations for peace would take place when Great Britain recognised that independence and had withdrawn her military forces. Such a response could not have been unexpected, given that the Americans had secured the alliance with France, and French troops were actually on the coast.[172] The only alternatives for the British were to fight or to concede. The decision was to fight, in the hope that they might reclaim at least the southern colonies, which were particularly valuable and complementary to Britain's Caribbean possessions.[173]

As the new Franco-American alliance stimulated apprehension in the British, it brought hope to the Americans. Washington and the Continental Army by now had had very mixed results against the British. Bunker Hill – strictly speaking a defeat, but morally a victory – and Saratoga had been followed by a series of stand-offs and reverses, countered by small-scale but significant victories at Trenton and Princeton, New Jersey, in 1776 and 1777, respectively. The winter of 1777–8 at Valley Forge, difficult as it was,[174] had at least seen some serious training of the Americans by Baron Friedrich von Steuben, a former Prussian general, which gave the army a much greater degree of professionalism.[175] But 1776 to 1778 also saw continuing conflict between Washington and the Continental Congress, which failed to provide him with necessary supplies and pay for his soldiers; he was also enraged by the shameless profiteering indulged in by many of its members.[176] Although Washington knew that the French alliance was vital to American victory, he also saw it as a danger. Many Americans now expected France to win the war for them, and this alarmed Washington. Active support for the war slackened, and he was convinced that without high morale and determination on the part of the Americans themselves, the war would be lost.

On 18 June 1778, the three thousand Loyalists who had decided to leave Philadelphia with the British withdrawal sailed to New York, whilst the bulk of the British army travelled by land. The supply wagons alone stretched for twelve miles, and progress was slow. *En route*, the Continental Army under Washington shadowed the British and engaged in an inconclusive battle at Monmouth Court House on 27 June. A temperature of 100 degrees Fahrenheit prostrated both sides, and in due course the British disengaged and continued to New York, which they reached on 6 July.[177] Most of those who were not sent south in November stayed there for some two and a half years, watched by Washington from a short distance away. Both Clinton and Washington wanted to defeat the other in a climactic battle; the latter, in fact, grew obsessed by this, convinced that a great victory in New York, and probably only in New York, would end the war. He knew, however, that he would need French help, which the French were unwilling to provide: the French commander, the Comte de Rochambeau, who arrived in May 1780 with 6,500 troops, was opposed to close co-operation with the Americans, stating that his instructions were to remain close to the French navy. Meanwhile, the activities of both sides were limited to the occasional raiding expedition.[178]

The exception in 1779 was Washington's despatch of troops commanded by Major-General John Sullivan to fight the Iroquois Indians on the New York frontier. Indeed, where war raged unceasingly in the North was on the frontier. Fighting was centred on the Pennsylvania and New York frontiers: here there was both fighting between the colonists and the Indians and civil war between Loyalists and Patriots. Both American sides allied themselves with Indian tribes; both found the Indians impossible to control. This contributed to unspeakably bloody conflicts, reprisals and counter-reprisals. Loyalists took revenge for the tribulations which they had suffered at the hands of the Patriots during the previous several years, and both sides were far more brutal than the British. There was also intermingling: British-led Loyalist units in the later stages of the war included deserters from the Continental Army, and their increasing desperation led to even greater ruthlessness.[179]

The three thousand troops sent by Clinton to Georgia in

November 1778 were meant to reconquer the South. The expectation was that disaffected and war-weary Americans would support British attempts to restore royal authority. Successes in Georgia in the winter of 1778–9, including the breaking of a Franco-American siege of Savannah, seemed to support this, as did comparable successes in South Carolina. Yet there was a drawback for Loyalists: the British army would advance and the Loyalists would emerge; then the British would withdraw, leaving the Loyalists at the mercy of their rebel neighbours. The Loyalists in the southern tidewater areas rapidly learned discretion. But, as in the North, when they were themselves in the ascendant, they were equally unforgiving towards their local opponents.

This was particularly the case in the South Carolina backcountry, the location for what has been termed the 'Second Revolution'. On 26 December 1779, Clinton set sail from New York with 7,600 troops to take Charles Town, South Carolina, which capitulated on 12 May 1780. This success, plus other local victories against the Americans, convinced Clinton that the British hold on the tidewater could be extended to the backcountry. It was with confidence that he sailed back to New York with four thousand troops to parry a reported French threat, leaving General the Earl Cornwallis in command of operations in the South. Yet within a few weeks, 'the backcountry had burst into flame'. Why? First of all, 'the plundering, assaults and rapes committed by members of the army on South Carolinians almost certainly played a part; [Lieutenant-Colonel Banastre] Tarleton's British Legion gained a special notoriety in this respect. The newly-formed loyalist militia were perhaps even more guilty, using their position of power to settle old scores.' Secondly, the country had already been stripped of supplies by the American army at Charles Town, and the entry of the British only exacerbated shortages. Thirdly, ethnic rivalries which pre-dated the rebellion, between the Scotch-Irish and the Germans, heated up: when the Germans backed the British, the Scotch-Irish joined the revolutionaries. Fourthly, resistance could be easily sustained by revolutionary support from across the border: as one British officer noted, the revolutionary militia in North Carolina 'over awes great part of the Country and Keeps the Candle of Rebellion still Burning'. And finally, the perception that revolution was thriving in North Carolina encouraged its supporters. As a result, from June 1780, attacks against the British rapidly increased, whilst persistent rumours of the imminent arrival of Continental Army and French troops helped to keep the rebellion alive.[180]

This energetic fighting in the backcountry was in stark contrast to the draining away of support for the revolution elsewhere. During 1780, the American cause reached its nadir. The British naval blockade was increasingly damaging the economic life of the country. The Continental Congress was forced to declare bankruptcy, and its authority appeared to be slipping away. Whilst the French alliance seemed to have added little to American strength, it constituted, Washington thought, a threat to American independence itself. Early in 1780,

> Washington's spirits reached low ebb . . . America's cascading willpower and disintegrating economy had rendered it incapable of winning the war without still more French assistance. Two years after the alliance had been consumated, the United States had grown utterly dependent on France. America could no longer raise an effective army without French economic assistance. Once raised, the Continental army would do nothing unless it was assisted by the French navy. In fact, the American army was so debilitated that even with the support of a French fleet it might no longer be sufficient to score a great victory.

John Adams went further, believing that Vergennes wished America to be a French vassal.[181] On 30 July 1780, Washington acknowledged to Congress that there was 'a total stagnation of military business', which he attributed to the absence of the French navy. He also added, however, that he could do nothing in any case, because only 6,000 of the 16,500 men whom Congress had decided to raise that year were under arms.[182] This was, perhaps, not surprising. Many soldiers were neither fed nor paid. In January 1781 mutinies were to erupt in regiments from Pennsylvania and New Jersey, whilst the following month Massachusetts and New Jersey troops clashed in a serious riot at Princeton.

At least as dangerous to the American cause was the French reaction to the apparent collapse of the American army, which was to consider evacuating their forces.[183] They might even have withdrawn their aid entirely. During the latter part of 1780, the French Economics Minister feared collapse and urged Louis XVI to end the war. Furthermore, Vergennes, the French Foreign Minister, knew that if the Franco-American alliance were not soon victorious, economic disaster might well force France to leave the war and accept the best possible peace terms. Then, in the spring of 1781, a diplomatic threat to the Americans came from a different direction: just as word of the mutinies reached Europe, Russia and Austria proposed a conference of the European Great Powers to end the war through mediation and to resolve the status of the American 'colonies'. The conference never met, but this was not because of French resolve: rather, Russia lost interest in the proposal, the Americans (especially John Adams, the American representative in Paris) fought frantically against it, and the British rejected it, believing that America's mounting problems meant the war could be won.[184] A Spanish threat to Britain had also lessened temporarily, although it was to be crucial later in the year. To France's great relief, Spain had entered the war as an ally on 12 April 1779; by that time, the French believed that without the contribution of the fifty Spanish ships of the line, the war would be lost. Spain, however, insisted on two provisos in the Convention of Aranjuez: that the two countries invade Great Britain, which was organised but aborted in 1779; and that France not make peace until Spain had captured Gibraltar from the British. The alliance was also vital to the Americans, because it is probable that she would have been unable to defeat Great Britain without the contribution of Spain. However, in January 1780 the Royal Navy defeated the Spanish in the waters around Gibraltar.[185]

Fortunately for the rebel cause, Great Britain had her own problems. When, on 2 May 1780, the 6,500 men under the command of the Comte de Rochambeau sailed from France for Newport, Rhode Island, the British failed to stop them; they also failed to intercept French and Spanish reinforcements for the West Indies. A wholly unexpected development centred in Northern Europe also vastly increased the pressure on Britain. Since the beginning of the conflict in America, Britain had used her naval superiority to limit the ability of the neutral countries to ship supplies to America and later to France. Not surprisingly, these countries, particularly the Dutch, had objected. On 28 February 1780, Empress Catherine II of Russia announced the formation of a League of Armed Neutrality to protect the rights of neutral shippers. According to Jonathan Dull, her 'action stunned the British, who considered themselves particular friends of Russia and who had hoped for Catherine's support'.[186] Russia was joined by Denmark, Sweden, Prussia, Portugal, Austria and Naples. Furthermore, relations between the British and the Dutch deteriorated, and the latter opened negotiations with Russia to join the League. 'Panic-stricken at the possibility of Russia's providing military support to the Dutch, the British [on 20] December 1780 declared war on the Netherlands so as to preclude a Russo-Dutch treaty.' The immediate result was to add the fifteen Dutch ships of the line to her enemies' naval strength and open the North Sea as another possible theatre of operations for the already over-stretched Royal Navy. However, the paucity of Dutch ships meant that the conflict with the British was a huge disaster for the Netherlands, and the Dutch threat receded.[187]

In the face of the war with France, Spain and now the Netherlands, and the threat from the League, domestic support in Great Britain for continuing the war in America lessened considerably, not least because it was proving unexpectedly difficult to defeat the rebels. Furthermore, there were political upheavals at home. On 6 April 1780 there was a bruising debate in the House of Commons on a resolution to limit the King's powers: the Commons adopted, by a majority of eighteen, a resolution by John Dunning MP 'that the influence of the crown has increased, is increasing, and ought to be diminished'.[188] At the very least, this result threatened the North administration and, by implication, the continuance of the war against America. This was followed in London by the anti-Catholic Gordon Riots of June 1780, the worst in the city's history, which saw the mob raging through the streets for ten days: the City of London was abandoned to arson and pillage, the prisons were burst open, the Bank of England assaulted, and the homes of many prominent Catholics burned. The King finally authorised the use of armed force, and between three hundred and seven hundred people were killed. As troops were called to the capital, those remaining in the South-East were warned to watch the enemy coast in case the French should seize the opportunity to raid the coastline.[189]

By 1781, then, both sides were war-weary. On the American side, support for the revolution was dying away, and there was increasing talk of coming to terms with Great Britain.[190] On the British side, the American rebellion had long before been relegated to second place in comparison with the imperial war against France, Spain and, to a lesser extent, the Netherlands. However, the British still had some hope that the southern strategy would succeed. With the apparent success of operations in Georgia and South Carolina – before guerrilla warfare spread over the backcountry – London believed that it would take only a short time to bring North Carolina and Virginia back into the empire. However, Clinton and Cornwallis had different approaches to this theatre. The former believed that the latter should not launch a northward thrust until South Carolina was completely pacified. The impetuous and dashing Cornwallis, however, wasted little time before launching an invasion of North Carolina. As a result, in Georgia and South Carolina, the Americans rolled up and eliminated British outposts, so that the British lost control of the interior, keeping only Savannah and Charles Town until they were evacuated in 1782.

Just outside North Carolina, frontiersmen destroyed Cornwallis's Loyalist left wing on 7 October 1780 at Kings Mountain. Another American army of about two thousand men, both regulars and militia, commanded by General Nathanael Greene, later entered South Carolina. Opinion is divided about Greene. Don Higginbotham calls him 'Washington's ablest lieutenant and former quartermaster-general . . . a flexible, resourceful general'. Bicheno reckons he was the 'deeply corrupt quartermaster-general of the Continental Army between 1778 and 1780, the period of its greatest privation. In the South he lost every battle he fought despite invariably enjoying significant numerical advantage and subordinates who included some of the most talented American cavalry and guerrilla commanders of the war.'[191] In this instance, Greene divided his army. Whilst his division remained to watch Cornwallis, he sent about seven hundred Continentals and militia under General Daniel Morgan to collect provisions and probe British defences in the backcountry; Morgan advanced south-westwards into the state, rallying the rebels and checking the Loyalists.[192] Morgan was a ranger, a frontier rifleman standing six feet two inches tall, who wore homemade fringed buckskins and moccasins. He was a master of terrain and tactics.[193] Cornwallis decided to destroy part of Greene's army, and he sent Banastre Tarleton's Tory Legion of 1,100 troops after Morgan. Tarleton made one of his 'trademark overnight marches' and on 17 January 1781 at Cowpens caught up with Morgan, who had chosen his ground and tactics carefully. Tarleton launched an immediate dawn attack. The Americans made mistakes, but they recovered to secure a significant victory. Morgan made skilful use of his militia; he also pretended to withdraw, luring the British infantry out of rank, and then counter-attacked. Tarleton made no egregious errors: 'he simply ran into a better combination of soldiers and officers than any previous experience in America could have prepared him for'. Morgan was an inspirational leader, but he also made certain that his officers and men knew exactly what they were expected to do – rarer, perhaps, than it ought to have been. The battle was disastrous for the British, since Tarleton lost eight hundred British regulars and Loyalist light troops, whilst Morgan lost only seventy-two.[194]

As Higginbotham describes it, 'now began a merry chase, with Cornwallis setting out after the retreating Morgan, and with Greene endeavoring to reunite with Morgan before Cornwallis overtook his subordinate'. The Americans linked up, and then challenged Cornwallis at Guilford Courthouse on 15 March 1781. The British 'won', but they lost twice as many men as did the Americans. After the battles of Kings Mountain, Cowpens and Guilford Courthouse, Cornwallis's army was no longer an effective fighting force. They slowly made their way to Wilmington on the coast, and thence to Virginia. After two months of indecisive wanderings, they retired to Yorktown. Cornwallis had been instructed to fortify a base for the use of the Royal Navy as a winter anchorage, and early in August they began to erect fortifications.[195]

On 15 August 1781, Rochambeau received a despatch from

Admiral de Grasse in the West Indies, stating that he was sailing to Chesapeake Bay, where he would be by the end of the month, with twenty ships of the line, 3,000 soldiers, and 1,200,000 livres borrowed from the Spanish. Two days later, Washington and Rochambeau wrote to him that they would hasten southwards to co-operate in trapping Cornwallis on the peninsula, and on 19 August four thousand French and two thousand American troops began to do just that. A few days later, Admiral de Barras sailed from Newport with siege guns to meet de Grasse. Admiral Thomas Graves, since July the British naval commander in America, on 31 August set sail with nineteen ships of the line for the Chesapeake, in order to prevent the juncture of the two French fleets. De Grasse had already arrived and disembarked his troops. On 5 September Graves and de Grasse fought a two-hour battle; neither lost a ship, but there was considerable damage and Graves sailed back to New York for a refit. Meanwhile, de Grasse transported the regiments of Washington and Rochambeau from Chesapeake Bay to the James River; a small American force under the Marquis de Lafayette positioned itself up the peninsula to block any attempt of the British to escape. Clinton sent word to Cornwallis on 2 September warning him of the approaching enemy. He finally decided that circumstances were so desperate that he would himself lead five thousand troops to relieve Yorktown. However, it took so long to repair the ships that he did not set sail until 19 October; by then, Yorktown had already fallen.

The allied army of about sixteen thousand troops had taken up positions on the night of 28 September, preparing to lay siege. Cornwallis abandoned his outer defences in order to concentrate his forces. Food was scarce and disease rife: according to one of the soldiers, 'we get terrible provisions now . . . putrid meat and wormy biscuits that have spoiled on the ships. Many of the men have been taken sick with . . . the bloody flux and diarrhoea. Foul fever is spreading . . . we have had little rest night or day.'[196] The allies began bombarding the British on 6 October, and by the 10th, when the French brought the harbour under direct fire and sank several British ships, any hope of help from the sea had evaporated. A line of French ships prevented any possibility of rescue by a British fleet. (According to Dull, because a Franco-Spanish fleet massed off the English coast in 1781 and a Dutch fleet appeared in the North Sea, British forces in America received virtually no naval reinforcements during the campaign which ended with Yorktown.) On 14 October the French and Americans stormed two British redoubts. 'Thanks to the exquisite tact of Rochambeau the Americans were permitted to play a significant role in the siege, including an assault made by light infantry under Alexander Hamilton, . . . but otherwise they were paid spectators at an event managed by the French.' An account written by a German officer pointed out that a quarter of the Continental Army soldiers were African-American, with the all-black 1st Rhode Island Regiment 'the most neatly dressed, the best under arms, and the most precise in its manoeuvres'. Cornwallis was now trapped by land and sea. On 16 October he made his only attempt at escaping. Under cover of darkness, he tried to get his men across the York River and make a run for it, but was foiled by a storm that broke after sunset. He now accepted that he had no hope of breaking the siege, and on the morning of 17 October, a drummer beat the call for a parley from the parapet. At 10 a.m. he sent a messenger under a white flag to Washington's headquarters, where he requested a meeting 'to settle terms of the surrender'. At 2 p.m. on 19 October, the British garrison marched out to the popular song 'The World Turned Upside Down'.[197]

A small footnote: no sooner were the capitulation proceedings ended than 'the French officers entertained their British and German peers lavishly and even lent Cornwallis 300,000 livres to pay his troops. Jean-François-Louis, Comte de Clermont-Crevecoeur[,] noted: ". . . when the Americans expressed their displeasure on this subject we replied that good upbringing and courtesy bind men together, and that since we had reason to believe the Americans did not like us, they should not be surprised at our preference."'[198] Prickly Franco-American relations have a long history.

Military operations against the British in America now virtually ceased, although some fighting continued in the South, and Greene put a blockade around Savannah. (Not until February and April 1783 did Parliament and Congress, respectively, proclaim an official

ceasefire.) Although the Americans controlled the hinterland around
the remaining British enclaves, Savannah, New York and Charles
Town, without French naval aid they could do no more, and this aid
was denied. The decisive defeat of the British army at Yorktown was
unexpected by both sides. It was fortuitous, and the victory was not
that of the Americans alone, but of the alliance. It need not have
effectively been the end of the fighting, but it was – the will to continue had disappeared. When word of Yorktown reached Lord North
on 25 November, he exclaimed, 'Oh God! It is all over!' His
Parliamentary support drained away. On 4 February 1782, the House
of Commons passed a resolution that all who sought to prosecute the
war against the Americans would be regarded as enemies of their
country; on the 27th at 2 a.m., the House approved by a majority of
nineteen General Henry Conway's motion condemning the 'offensive War in America' and calling for direct peace negotiations 'with
the revolted colonies'.[199] On 15 March the North administration's
majority on a vote of confidence was only nine votes, and five days
later he resigned.

VIII

North was succeeded by his old adversary, the aged Rockingham,
with Charles James Fox as Foreign Secretary and Lord Shelburne as
Secretary of State for Home and Colonial Affairs. The Rockingham
administration was committed to ending the war with America. But
Fox, who was very anti-French, wanted to grant American independence without delay, in order to allow Great Britain to deal more
effectively with her European enemies, whilst Shelburne, who
claimed that negotiations with the Americans came under his
purview, wanted to withhold recognition until a comprehensive
peace settlement with the former colonies had been secured.
Rockingham's Cabinet reflected the confusion in Parliament and
public opinion as to relations with America: there was a general
desire to end the war but also considerable reluctance to recognise
American independence. To look ahead, on 1 July, Fox and
Shelburne fought a climactic battle in Cabinet over the American

negotiations, and Shelburne won. On the following day Rockingham died of influenza, the King asked Shelburne to form the new ministry, and Fox resigned.[200]

From the dying days of the North ministry, Great Britain had intended that, if independence had to be granted, it would be on the basis of *uti possidetis*: each belligerent would keep the territory that it held at the end of the war, and Great Britain would therefore retain the relevant French, Spanish and Dutch territory. She was also determined to separate America from France, realising that the latter hoped to use America to threaten Canada. Shelburne proposed to France in mid-March 1782 that peace be concluded on the basis of *uti possidetis*, but Vergennes replied that a peace agreement could be negotiated only if Great Britain dealt on an equal basis with France's ally, America. It was this response that triggered North's resignation on 20 March, since he and the King had no more room for manoeuvre. For some months, Shelburne continued to hope that the two countries could remain united under the King, parts of the same empire, but each having its own sovereign parliament (although it is unclear just how this was supposed to work in practice). Support for complete independence amongst MPs and the public in Great Britain was patchy, not least because of concern for the fate and property of Loyalists. Shelburne proposed his plan to Franklin, and the British Commander-in-Chief in America, General Sir Guy Carleton, proposed it to Washington, but the response of both was that Great Britain had to negotiate with France and America together. Thus far, the allies appeared to be standing together, but it was all part of the preliminary probing and jockeying for position.[201]

Certainly, France wanted to control negotiations on behalf of both the Americans and herself. Central to the peace negotiations was the question of whether the recognition of American independence should be part of a future treaty with France or be separately negotiated and conceded – although fighting by British regulars had ceased on the American mainland, conflict with France had, if anything, increased. France wanted recognition to appear to be a gift from herself; she also wanted to limit its extent to the 1763 Proclamation Line within the Allegheny Mountains, so that Canada (Quebec) might be French in essence if not in ownership and the

Mississippi Valley Spanish, thereby staunching American expansion. For the British negotiators, on the other hand, the new western boundary of America would be the Mississippi River, and would therefore include what Great Britain had acquired from France in 1763, except for Canada, which would remain British.

Thomas Grenville met Vergennes on 9 May 1782, and told him that with Great Britain conceding independence to the Americans, France was expected to restore to Britain her conquests of British territory. Not surprisingly, the meeting between the two was cool. On 18 May the Cabinet gave Grenville full powers to negotiate a peace based on American independence and the 1763 Treaty of Paris, which had ended the Seven Years' War and would require the return of some British territory. On the same day news reached London that a fleet of the Royal Navy in the West Indies had on 12 April beaten the French in battle. The British had captured seven battleships, including Admiral de Grasse's 110-gun *Ville de Paris*. Of course, this disrupted plans for a Franco-Spanish assault on Jamaica. Vergennes had hoped to use this treaty to undo some French losses in Africa and Asia in 1763, but now he abandoned the idea. France became much more 'tractable', which made both Shelburne's and Franklin's negotiating roles easier.[202]

After becoming First Minister on 1 July, Shelburne himself kept control of the negotiations, although British representatives continued to carry out the day-to-day discussions in Paris: they were Richard Oswald, 'an elderly amateur diplomat', who was an old acquaintance of Franklin; Thomas Grenville, son of the former First Minister George Grenville, 'whose superb political connections were recompense for his lack of experience'; and, later, Benjamin Vaughan, Franklin's editor and a friend of Shelburne.[203] They were, frankly, not equal to the American peace commissioners. John Adams, who would become the second President of the USA, had been named the sole commissioner in 1779, so the appointment by the Congress of others in 1781 angered him greatly. However, the others named were men of very high calibre: Benjamin Franklin, minister to France, old, wise, and a networker of prodigious ability; John Jay, minister to Spain and the first Chief Justice of the US Supreme Court; Thomas Jefferson, main draftsman of the Declaration of Independence, who would be the third President of the USA; and Henry Laurens, named Minister to the Netherlands in 1779, but captured by the British *en route* and imprisoned in the Tower of London, until he was released in 1781 to take up his duties as commissioner. Jefferson refused to leave the US in time, and Laurens, weakened by his imprisonment, refused to serve. But the three remaining commissioners were experienced diplomats and skilled politicians; usefully, Adams and Jay were also distinguished lawyers, 'adept at disputation and repartee'.[204]

The objectives of both countries naturally changed over the period of negotiations, as the international situation developed and opportunities rose and receded. The American negotiators might have been gravely hampered by the Congress's stipulation in June 1781 (nearly five months *before* the British surrender at Yorktown, when French aid was still crucial) that the peace commissioners were to 'make the most candid and confidential communication upon all subjects to the ministers of our generous ally, the King of France; to undertake nothing in the negotiations for peace or truce without their knowledge and concurrence; and ultimately to govern yourselves by their advice and opinion'[205] in making agreements with Great Britain. Furthermore, by the 1778 Treaty of Alliance with France, neither side was to make a separate peace with Britain. The three commissioners, however, agreed at their first meeting together in the last week of October 1782 that they would not be bound by the Congressional requirement and would proceed without consulting the French;[206] nor, in due course, would they feel bound by their treaty obligation.

For the Americans, the foremost objective was not independence – this they already had. The war had not been fought to defeat Great Britain, which would have been impossible, but to hold out long enough for the British to recognise this independence, and thus its legitimacy, in a peace treaty. They considered this objective non-negotiable. Closely related was the withdrawal of all British military forces from American territory. Next in importance was control of the territory west of the states to the Mississippi River; they also wanted freedom of navigation of that river, so that the western farmers could send their goods to market. Adams was equally determined to achieve for Massachusetts the extent of her claims to territory to the north, and a share in the Newfoundland fisheries. They called for the cession of Canada and Nova Scotia, with Adams believing that 'we shall have perpetual wars with Britain while she has a foot of ground in America'.[207] (Vergennes indeed hoped that Great Britain would continue to hold some ground, having two months before written to Conrad-Alexandre Gérard, the French minister in America, that France wished Canada to remain in British hands to assure American dependence on French support.[208]) Finally, they wanted freedom to trade with the British West Indies.

Franklin, as did Shelburne, wanted Anglo-American reconciliation, but there was to be no compromise on American independence. He eventually managed to convince Shelburne that 'if Britain offered sufficiently generous peace terms America would help Britain reach agreement with France and Spain by threatening to make a separate peace', which would release tens of thousands of British troops for military operations against the West Indies. (Vergennes was also receiving news of an ominous crisis in the Crimea, which increased the pressure on him to come to a quick agreement.) A quick agreement might have been reached, but Franklin fell seriously ill with a kidney stone, and negotiations were taken over by Jay. He became convinced that France and Great Britain were preparing to come to an agreement at America's expense. His suspicions were increased when Joseph-Mathias Gérard de Rayneval, Vergennes's closest confidant, went to London in mid-August (on non-American business). At the same time, the British leaked to him a letter indicating that France was hostile to American claims of fishing rights off Newfoundland. Without consulting Franklin, Jay sent word to Shelburne that the United States was prepared to abandon the French alliance. This broke the impasse in the Anglo-American negotiations.[209]

The final push came during late October and November with the arrival of Adams, and of Henry Laurens for the final session. By this time, Franklin and Jay had given up the attempt to acquire Canada, but Great Britain had conceded the West to the Mississippi. However, Adams was dismayed to learn that New England had not fared so well: they had not only agreed to a United States–Canadian boundary line far lower than Massachusetts's historic claim, but had accepted less than advantageous terms for the fishing industry. He determined to fight for full rights to the fisheries: not only was this crucial for New England, it was important to the United States as a whole, since the fishing industry would be 'a Nursery of Seamen and a source of naval power', which was a traditional British claim as well. Adams also determined to fight for the right of navigation on the Mississippi River, because the farmers would need it to get their goods to market. Furthermore, if denied this access to markets, 'the western farmers would be ripe for the machinations of the European power that controlled the Mississippi'.[210]

On 30 October the final negotiations began. The British negotiating team was now led by Henry Strachey, an undersecretary of state. He was assisted by Alleyne Fitzherbert, an able twenty-nine-year-old career diplomat, but he spent most of his time negotiating with Spain and France. Vaughan was still there, as was Oswald, but the latter was by now in 'the clutches of dementia'. Adams took a leading part in the negotiations, and managed to claw back part of what the others had conceded with regard to the Massachusetts boundary. The United States forfeited southern Ontario and gave the Canadians access to the Great Lakes, but acquired the northern reaches of present Minnesota (where the Mesabi Iron Range is situated). They also agreed on navigation rights for both on the Mississippi. As for the fisheries issue, American fishermen received the 'liberty' to fish on the Newfoundland Banks and the 'right' to fish in the Gulf of St Lawrence, as well as the right to dry their catches on the uninhabited coasts of Nova Scotia, Labrador and the Magdalen Islands.[211] The final, and ferociously contentious, issue was the treatment of the Loyalists. Late in the war, virtually all of the states had confiscated and sold Loyalist property to raise funds, and the British wanted them compensated. Jay and Franklin – whose son had been a Loyalist – absolutely refused, and the best that the British could achieve was the promise that the Congress would recommend to the states that they compensate the Loyalists. This was predictably unsuccessful.[212]

On 30 November the American and British commissioners signed the Preliminary Articles. The British accepted American independence and promised to withdraw their troops; the Americans received generous boundaries – Vergennes wrote to Rayneval that 'the English buy peace rather than make it. Their concessions exceed all that I should have thought possible' – fishing rights, and a share in the British right to navigation on the Mississippi. The Americans were fortunate that Shelburne strongly desired close Anglo-American ties; indeed, it has been argued that he valued international commerce more highly than territorial empire, and thus wanted to establish an atmosphere in which trade would flourish. He also wished to push France, Spain and the Netherlands into making peace. However, his fall from office in early 1783, caused largely by the feeling that he had been too generous to the Americans, meant that any ambiguities in the treaty, such as the exact nature of American fishing rights, were interpreted in Britain's favour. Furthermore, America's failure to comply with the provisions of the treaty with regard to the payment of debts to British creditors and compensation to the Loyalists gave the British an excuse not to leave nine frontier posts situated within American territory.[213] This perhaps correctly reflected the fact that a 'willingness to engage in double-dealing was characteristic of all parties'.[214] After all, crucial to Anglo-American agreement had been American betrayal (by making a separate peace) of the Treaty of Alliance with France. But, subject to the acceptance of the Preliminary Articles by both Great Britain and the United States in 1783, the war was over.

There was now a United States of America recognised by the Great Powers and poised to grow rapidly in extent and power. It had been only twenty years since the end of the Seven Years' War, or the French and Indian War, but those two decades had seen disaffection, revolution and final separation. Shelburne's hope for reconciliation and economic, if not political, links would take many more decades to bear fruit. Before that could happen, the two countries had to settle outstanding problems connected to both war and peace, and even to begin to settle them required a second war, in 1812. Thereafter, although there were some sharp crises during the nineteenth century, as far as international relations were concerned, the two countries spent much of the following century ignoring each other.

CHAPTER 3

War and Rumours of War: 1783–1872

Oh, say, can you see, by the dawn's early light,
What so proudly we hail'd at the twilight's last gleaming?
Whose broad stripes and bright stars, thro' the perilous fight,
O'er the ramparts we watch'd, were so gallantly streaming?
And the rockets' red glare, the bombs bursting in air,
Gave proof to the night that our flag was still there.
O say, does that star-spangled banner yet wave
O'er the land of the free and the home of the brave?

. . .

O, thus be it ever when freemen shall stand,
Between their lov'd homes and the war's desolation;
Blest with vic'try and peace, may the heav'n-rescued land
Praise the Pow'r that hath made and preserv'd us as a nation!
Then conquer we must, when our cause is just,
And this be our motto: 'In God is our trust.'
And the star-spangled banner in triumph shall wave
O'er the land of the free and the home of the brave!

Francis Scott Key, 'The Defense of Fort McHenry',
20 September 1814[1]

[I]t is proper you should understand what I deem the essential
principles of our Government, and consequently those which ought to
shape its Administration . . . [P]eace, commerce, and honest friendship
with all nations, entangling alliances with none.

President Thomas Jefferson's first inaugural address, 4 March 1801[2]

Wherever the standard of freedom and independence has been or shall
be unfurled, there will her heart, her benedictions and her prayers be.
But she goes not abroad, in search of monsters to destroy. She is the well-
wisher to the freedom and independence of all. She is the champion and
vindicator only of her own . . . She well knows that by once enlisting
under other banners than her own, were they even the banners of
foreign independence, she would involve herself beyond the power of
extrication . . . The fundamental maxims of her policy would insensibly
change from *liberty* to *force* . . . She might become the dictatress of the
world. She would be no longer the ruler of her own spirit.

John Quincy Adams, 'An Address . . . Celebrating the Anniversary of
Independence, at the City of Washington on the Fourth of July 1821'

Nobody doubts any more that the United States is a power of the first class, a nation which it is very dangerous to offend and almost impossible to attack.

The Spectator, 1866

By the Treaty of Paris in 1783, the government of Great Britain recognised American independence and its withdrawal from the British Empire. This set the stage for nearly a century of unfriendly and sometimes threatening relations. It was difficult for both countries to accept the changed relationship, and mutual suspicion was rife. For the entire period Great Britain was the greatest naval power in the world, a position which enabled her to support the maintenance of the world's largest empire, which, indeed, continued to grow. But the American empire also grew. Until the final third of the nineteenth century, they clashed repeatedly on the water – on rivers, lakes and oceans – as well as on land, and a theme here, as in the last chapter, is the constraint frequently placed on strategic British power in the Western Hemisphere by threats elsewhere. This period was brought to a close by the 1871 Treaty of Washington and its implementation.

For Americans, it was a time of fundamental uncertainty. Would the United States continue to exist in an unfriendly world? The unshakeable assumption was that Great Britain disliked intensely the loss of her colonies, and would do whatever she could to undermine the new state. If this was the case, to whom could the United States turn? Not to France, certainly, with whom she continued to have a relationship tinged with suspicion. And once the country threatened to rip itself apart with Civil War, it was the actions of Great Britain that most enraged Americans both North and South, since this was the country most able to harm her. In short, the dislike and fear of Great Britain was widespread and constant.

For the first forty years after 1783, many Britons indeed found it difficult to accept that the United States was an independent, and equal, country, rather than a colony,[3] and should not be treated with a contemptuous disregard of the rights inherent in this sovereignty. Certainly, most European countries assumed that, more likely than not, its existence in its current form was transitory. As Bradford Perkins points out, as late as 1814 a normally friendly London newspaper, the *Morning Chronicle*, in its issue of 20 October referred 'quite naturally' to the United States as 'the Colonies'.[4] For its part, the United States found it difficult to accept that the rights and privileges which it had enjoyed as a member of the British Empire, particularly commercial rights, no longer obtained. Each tended to think the worst of the other, and the two countries stumbled into the War of 1812. Strictly speaking, neither won nor lost that war, but it has been argued that for the United States, it constituted the 'second war for independence',[5] the term used by, for example, Senator James Henry Hammond in a speech to the Senate on 4 March 1858.[6] This period was brought to an end by the proclamation by President James Monroe in 1823 of what came to be called the Monroe Doctrine, which stated that the Western Hemisphere would no longer be open to colonisation or recolonisation by the European powers and that it was thereafter the sphere of influence of the US. Monroe also declared the lack of any American interest in Continental European affairs. The United States turned her primary attention to North and Central America.

Thus began the period of Manifest Destiny, the American drive for dominion from sea to shining sea. The most important question now was: what were to be the boundaries of the United States? Many Americans assumed that in due course they would absorb the entire continent. With the exception of some dabbling in the 'Texas Question' – Was it part of Mexico, or the Texas Republic? Was it to remain a republic, or become an American state? – Great Britain had relatively little to do with the southern boundary. But she had everything to do with the boundary between the USA and the British colony Canada. There were conflicts between Maine and New Brunswick, New Hampshire and Quebec, in New York along the Niagara boundary, and just west of the Great Lakes around the Pigeon River Falls, but by far the most important and long-lasting conflict was over the Oregon Country, which was 500,000 square miles in size, roughly the combined areas of Great Britain, Ireland, France, Germany, Belgium and the Netherlands. It took a series of negotiations[7] to come to what seemed to be a final agreement, achieved in 1903, although not without ferocious (if largely empty) threats from the United States.

With the outbreak of the most important event in nineteenth-century American history, the Civil War of 1861 to 1865, Great Britain proclaimed her neutrality. The Union (or the North) reacted with fury, since this implied that the rebels had some international standing, and it confirmed the belief of many that Britain implicitly supported the South. This set the stage for another series of conflicts between the two. Early on in the war, the USA and Great Britain themselves came closer to going to war than at any time since 1815 – this time, ironically, over American interference with British neutral rights and in contravention of international law. There were other crises, several of them very serious indeed, and it took until 1871 for a settlement to be reached. The legacy in the USA was renewed dislike and bitterness, but until the end of the century, diplomatic relations between the two were relatively peaceful.

I

At the end of the Revolutionary War, the United States was made up of thirteen semi-sovereign states. They were loosely grouped together under the Articles of Confederation,[8] according to which they each retained all of their powers save those which they had voluntarily ceded to the central government, with Congress as the decision-making body. This was a remarkably weak system of government, with the central government lacking the powers to tax and to conduct a strong foreign policy. Consequently, Congress was unable to carry out its treaty obligations or to force the states to do so. At the same time, partly in response, Great Britain failed to fulfil some of her own obligations. It is likely that without the ratification of the new Constitution in 1789, many of the states of the Union would have gone their own way; it is certainly the case that their ability to stand up successfully to the British Empire would have approached nil. By means of the Constitution, the Federal government gained the right to set duties and tariffs, as well as the responsibility for formulating and implementing foreign policy, the latter the duty of the President.[9]

Both the United States itself and the individual states were encumbered with heavy debts and a depreciated currency, with a restless frontier threatened by several enemies, foreign and domestic, and with an acute dependence on international trade and shipping, which Great Britain had the power to curtail. Without commerce, the country could not function, because the revenue which enabled the government to do so came from import and export duties; and because most US commerce was still with Great Britain, Anglo-American relations in the decades after 1783 were critical. They were also suffused with distrust, and, often, contempt and hatred. Boswell recorded Samuel Johnson's tirade: '"I am willing to love all mankind, *except an American*" . . . calling them, "Rascals–robbers–pirates;" and exclaiming, he'd "burn and destroy them" . . . [he] roared out another tremendous volley, which one might fancy could be heard across the Atlantic.'[10]

The British were determined to protect and expand both the Royal Navy and the merchant marine, with the intention of securing British primacy at sea. The separation of the United States from the Empire had meant the loss of easy access to American timber and other naval stores, and to ships. Indeed, American ships, so long part of the imperial strength, would now be foreign competitors. Furthermore, they might continue the alliance with France, and, with or without France, the British West Indies lay uncomfortably close to the USA. Therefore, the primary goal of Great Britain was to strengthen her own shipping, ideally at the expense of the Americans' carrying trade. The Crown issued an Order-in-Council on 2 July 1783 which, amongst other things, provided for the rigid exclusion of all American ships from the West Indies: this meant that any American exports to or imports from the West Indies had to be carried in British ships. The American response was outrage: in July 1785 John Adams, then American Minister in London, wrote to Jefferson that 'The disigns [*sic*] of ruining, if they can our carrying trade, and annihilating all our Navigation, and Seamen is too apparent.'[11] The possibility that Great Britain had a legitimate interest in building up her own sea power apparently escaped the Americans. The British in any case thought that the Americans were naive if they assumed that they could continue to enjoy the commercial advantages of being part of the Empire which they had just violently rejected. There was 'commercial reciprocity', according to Prime Minister William Pitt and his colleagues in London, because the ports of the two home countries were open to each other's ships and goods. Access to the British Empire for American goods carried in American ships, however, was a privilege, not a right, and a privilege which Great Britain was in no mood to extend. The loss of this trade was galling, and it would take a half-century to regain it.[12]

With British primacy at sea secured, the British government moved to recover its pre-war position as European entrepôt for American trade. By an Order-in-Council issued on 26 December 1783, American goods were to be admitted as though they were colonial, there would be duty-free importation of indigo and naval stores (e.g., tar, turpentine, pitch, masts and bowsprits), American tobacco would have advantageous import rules, and many other American goods would be liable for lower duties than the same goods from other countries. Another factor which tied American merchants to Great Britain was the fact that British credit was irreplaceable: French and Dutch merchants demanded immediate cash, which the Americans lacked. However, massive exports soon glutted the American market, American merchants found it difficult to pay, and debts mounted alarmingly; there was then a sharp recession, and numerous American debtors defaulted. This caused the British to look again at the American market, and although once the recession ended Anglo-American trade again expanded, the Americans would find it difficult to shake a reputation for commercial irresponsibility.[13]

British contempt was encouraged by the treatment of Loyalists and by the refusal of thousands of Americans to repay their British creditors. By the treaty ending the war, Congress was obliged to try to convince the states to compensate the Loyalists, many of whom had been forced to abandon their property and flee their homes, either north to Great Britain's other North American colonies or to England. However, the Confederation was so weak that it was unable to force, or even to convince, the states to fulfil these treaty obligations. Great Britain eventually took on the burden of compensation herself, which by 1789 had cost the Exchequer £7.5 million. But much more of a problem for Britain, because it touched so many exporters and merchants, was the refusal of roughly thirty thousand Americans to pay the debts owed to these men. These debtors were supported by the state legislatures, many of whom refused to remove legal obstacles to the collection of pre-war debts, no matter what the Treaty of Paris stipulated. Indeed, many of the states reinforced their laws discriminating against British creditors. Maryland and Virginia were the worst – as a committee of British merchants complained bitterly, in these two states there was 'more Ability than Inclination' to pay the debts.[14] In their turn, the Americans demanded compensation for the slaves 'abducted' – or freed – by the British at the end of the war.[15] The entire mess only encouraged European scepticism about the permanence of the American experiment.

Another area of conflict was the Old Northwest. This was the territory from which the states of Ohio, Indiana, Illinois, Michigan and Wisconsin would be carved out, and where Great Britain continued to occupy seven forts which she had, by Article VII of the Treaty of Paris, agreed to vacate.[16] As described by the historian Samuel Flagg Bemis nearly a century ago,

> Garrisoned by a few hundred British soldiers and supported by a horde of savage allies, . . . these forts had enabled England to protect Canada during the American Revolution. They had helped her to harass the whole line of settlements south of the Ohio and in western New York and Pennsylvania. Held in British possession at the peace, they became important military positions in the rear of the American states. They protected the fur trade. They overawed the souls of the savage allies who more and more were coming to depend on purchasing with their furs their luxuries, even their very subsistence, from the traders sheltered under the guns of the forts.[17]

Why had Great Britain not withdrawn from the forts, as she had promised to do? In 1923 Bemis ascribed most blame to the fur trade, 'at that time the greatest and most profitable single industry in North America'. By the signing of the peace treaty, he pointed out, the trade amounted to £200,000 annually; it was estimated in 1790 that one-half of this annual yield was collected in the 'countries to the southward of the Great Lakes'. If the terms of the treaty were carried out and the new boundary recognised without some provision for the protection of the fur trade, it was feared by the British that the commercial prosperity of Britain's other North American colonies would be threatened, not to mention that of the traders and those who utilised the pelts in Britain itself. Fur traders of Quebec had been outraged at the abandonment of hunting areas and centres of supply and transportation, and interest groups made their views known to government ministers.[18]

However, by 1784, the fur trade had ceased to play quite such an important role in the development of British policy, although it was not entirely irrelevant. Of continuing concern were the interests of the Loyalists, but of considerably greater importance was the need to secure British lives and property against the Indians, particularly those who had been allies of the Americans during the war. There was also apprehension about American threats against Canada, a concern which would repeatedly recur over the following sixty years. The British knew that they could not occupy these forts indefinitely; in the meantime, however, the occupation could be used as leverage: as Abigail Adams, the wife of John Adams, rightfully said, it was 'a rod over our heads'.[19] By the autumn of 1784, the Americans had realised that Great Britain would remain in occupation until the US also complied with the treaty, particularly with regard to the repayment of debts.

John Adams was sent to London in May 1785 as the first American Minister to the Court of St James's – a curious choice, since it was well known that he hated England with a passion. To his fury, he found that many Britons assumed that, sooner or later, the USA would return to the Empire. As he wrote to Richard Henry Lee of Virginia on 26 August 1785,

There is a strong propensity in this people to believe that America is weary of her independence; that she wishes to come back; that the states are in confusion; Congress has lost its authority; the governments of the states have no influence; no laws, no order, poverty, distress, ruin, and wretchedness; that no navigation acts that we can make will be obeyed; no duties we lay on can be collected ... that smuggling will defeat all our prohibitions, imposts and revenues ... This they love to believe.

The attitude to America was, he decided, virtually as hostile as it had been during the war.[20]

The resentment which all of this engendered did nothing to soften Adams' naturally abrasive approach to diplomacy. Nevertheless, in the early stages of trying to sort out, in particular, the issue of the debts, he seemed to be making some progress. However, he made an important strategic error: instead of confining himself to the issue of the debts, he attempted to use the opportunity to force a comprehensive settlement of all of the conflicts between the two countries, including the goal of securing a commercial agreement which would eliminate the restrictions against American trade with the British Empire. On 17 June 1785, Adams met with the British Foreign Secretary, Lord Carmarthen. In a calm and sensible manner each set out the issues as he saw them; Carmarthen suggested that Adams put the issues in writing and, since the question of the forts seemed the most important to the Americans, he could begin with that. Then Adams indiscreetly told the Foreign Secretary that he was instructed by Congress 'to require' evacuation of the posts: had orders perhaps already gone out for British withdrawal? Adams' assumption that Great Britain would naturally do as the Americans wished put Carmarthen on his guard, and he asked Adams to put Congress's requirement in writing as well.

On 24 August, Adams met with Pitt, who was ready to settle the problem of the abducted slaves. But, 'as to the posts [forts], says he, that is a point connected with some others, that I think must be settled at the same time'. These were the debts, and it was now clear that the issues of the forts and the debts would not be disentangled.[21] Shortly thereafter, Pitt also decided that there would be no commercial negotiations until the problem of the debts was resolved, a decision which would be a particular blow to Adams, who was keen to secure a commercial treaty. The British government now concentrated on gathering information on the debts from the creditors, both as to the amounts involved and the details of their attempts to collect them through the American courts. It was not until 28 February 1786 that Adams received the government's answer to his memorandum setting out the American position.

Adams had grown more optimistic in the interim, and the uncompromising British answer was unexpected. Carmarthen's memorandum claimed that the King's fixed determination was always to act in conformity with principles of justice and good faith; the Americans, however, had flagrantly violated the treaty, whose stipulations were mutually and equally binding on the contracting parties. It was folly and injustice to think that Great Britain alone was obliged to adhere strictly to its terms whilst the US was 'free to deviate from its own engagements as often as convenience might render such deviation necessary though at the expense of its own National Credit and Importance'. When justice was done to British creditors and the US manifested a 'real determination to fulfil her part of the Treaty', then Great Britain would quickly prove her sincere desire to co-operate in putting the treaty of peace 'into real and compleat Effect'.[22]

Why such a cold response? Charles Ritcheson's argument is compelling:

> The explanation must lie . . . in Adams' maladroit use of the debt issue and, even more rankling, in his 'requirement.' Here was the envoy of a government unable to make its writ run in its own land, . . . paying no attention at all to serious British grievances, yet 'requiring' Britain to act at America's good pleasure, and demanding in the bargain a new commercial accord directly conflicting with British maritime interests. It was impudent and absurd, and, Pitt and his colleagues must have concluded, fully deserving Carmarthen's tough answer.[23]

Both the British government and important interest groups had decided that the Americans were asking for too much and offering too little in their usual arrogant and slippery manner. And besides, could the Americans be depended upon to carry out their agreements? It seemed unlikely.

In 1789, Great Britain's official position remained the same: it continued to occupy the seven forts on American territory because the US had failed to fulfil Article IV of the peace treaty, which stated that there would be no unlawful impediment to the recovery of pre-war debts owed to British creditors, and Article V, which stipulated that Congress should recommend to the states the restitution of estates confiscated from the Loyalists. But there were more commanding reasons than American non-compliance. As noted above, the need to protect the fur trade controlled by Montreal merchants retained some of its importance; there was also the desirability of maintaining contact with its former Indian allies in the Old North-west Territory, now caught between the US and Canada, with the associated idea of carving out an independent Indian state north-west of the Ohio River, which would nullify the cession of the territory to the US in 1783; and there was the need to protect Canada against 'pushful and procreative American pioneers'.[24] As for the Americans, they were increasingly angered by the British refusal to comply with Article VII of the treaty, which provided for the evacuation of American territory 'with all convenient speed'; furthermore, after the proclamation of peace, but before the treaty was signed, certain British subjects had 'abducted' slaves, the property of Americans, and refused to give them back.[25] Many of those 'abducted' had fought for the British, and might well have preferred abduction and the chance of freedom to returning to their former masters and certain slavery.

Relations between the two countries continued to deteriorate. There was an added dimension in the US when the new Constitution was ratified by the states and a much stronger central government was in place. To the dismay of George Washington and others, 'factions' played an increasing role in politics, and in due course became organised political parties. Washington's Secretary of the Treasury, Alexander Hamilton, was a leader of the pro-British faction; he was convinced of the United States' need to secure revenue from trade, primarily with Britain and the Empire, to allow the new Federal government to function – the lack of revenue had rendered the Confederation government virtually powerless. This faction supported a strong central government, and developed into the Federalist Party, with its main support in New York and the

North-east. On the opposite side, Thomas Jefferson, Washington's Secretary of State, had retained his loyalty to the French treaty of 1778 and to France itself. The faction he led became known as the Republicans. (The party split between 1828 and 1832, and orthodox party members were thereafter called the Democratic Party.) They were supporters of weak central government, fearing that a strong one might develop into a tyranny and oppress the states. Their stronghold lay in the southern and western states. Jefferson's political links with France encouraged Great Britain to act ruthlessly against American trade once Britain and France went to war in 1793.

By that year, British public opinion had shifted dramatically: differences between Great Britain and the US were recognised but were now much less important than before, and wartime bitterness had faded, along with the sharp feelings of betrayal caused by the American alliance with France, Britain's traditional enemy. There were even signs that links between the two countries were growing. Trade between the two countries was expanding rapidly, so that by 1790 Great Britain was receiving almost one-half of America's exports and supplied more than four-fifths of her imports. Furthermore, in the years after the Revolution, the USA had become the granary for the so-called 'North Atlantic triangle' – Great Britain, Canada, the West Indies and the US herself, which balanced America's economic dependence on Great Britain. A significant proportion of the American national debt was now funded by British capital, proof of a more sanguine attitude about American financial probity than had obtained during the Confederation period. There was also some Anglo-American co-operation in trading with the East. Finally – but less legally – a great subterranean network of smuggling (particularly of tobacco), collusion (with the West Indies, who co-operated in large-scale smuggling) and clandestine partnerships (false registers of American ships as British) developed, infuriating the British government but constituting a source of mutual profit to its British and American participants. According to one historian, the ultimate importance of this private Anglo-American co-operation lay in the development of a pattern of commercial intercourse which survived even the outbreak of the Anglo-French War in 1793.[26]

In 1792 the armies of Revolutionary France had overrun the

Austrian Netherlands (today's Belgium); the following year France annexed Belgium, and was poised to invade the Netherlands. On 1 February 1793 the French declared war on the Netherlands and Great Britain. The Royal Navy had over 600 vessels manned by 100,000 men. Its responsibilities were to blockade the Continent and to sweep any enemy fleet from the seas. What Great Britain wanted from the US, above all, was neutrality, but she feared American support for France. Indeed, France hoped to sign a new treaty with the US, and in February 1793 sent the thirty-year-old, handsome and patriotic Edmond Charles Genêt, 'Citizen Genêt', to America as its envoy. France wanted American ports closed to British shipping and a renewal of the American guarantee of her Caribbean possessions; she also wanted certain provisions of the 1778 Treaty of Amity and Commerce to be strictly observed, especially that allowing each to bring prizes from privateering into the ports of the other, whilst denying the same to those at war with France or the US. French privateers should be allowed to recruit and equip in American ports – and, indeed, anti-British privateers had already begun to sail out of Charleston harbour. France also wanted America's remaining debt to her, about $5.6 million, to be paid back early in order to secure arms, food and provisions for the French West Indies and France itself. And, finally, France wanted to use American territory as a base to reconquer Canada and conquer Louisiana and the Floridas, the latter territories belonging to Spain.[27]

However, in mid-March, news arrived in Washington of the decapitation of Louis XVI on 21 January, followed in early April by the news that France had declared war on Great Britain. The American government's response, after a great deal of memorandum-writing and heated discussion, was a proclamation of neutrality by President Washington on 22 April 1793.[28] The French were outraged, and Genêt spent a good deal of time over the following months trying to evade the restrictions. He appeared to have great public support, and decided to go over the head of the President and appeal to Congress and the people. This was too much, and on 1 August the Cabinet decided to ask for his recall. As it turned out, Genêt's supporters in France, the Girondists, had been overthrown by the Jacobins, who had called him an enemy of the Republic and recalled him to face trial and, doubtless, the guillotine. Washington offered him a refuge in the US and there he remained, marrying the daughter of the Governor of New York and living out his life as a gentleman farmer.

In late August the Americans learned of a British Order-in-Council of 8 June. As always, Great Britain claimed the right to control the shipping of contraband by neutrals in time of war. But what constituted contraband? The Americans agreed that neutrals should not furnish implements of war to belligerents and should not trade at blockaded ports; beyond that, they insisted, 'free ships made free goods'. However, by this Order, the British were focusing on the shipment of American grain and flour to France: any ships bound for enemy ports with grain, flour or meal would be intercepted and detained, and the shipowner would receive a fair price (as, however, determined by the British) and the freight charges, or could dispose of his cargo in a friendly port. The American response was predictable, but the Jeffersonian counter-attack was undercut by the news that even before the Order had been promulgated, the French Assembly had itself decreed the seizure of neutral vessels carrying provisions to enemy ports – in direct violation of the 1778 Franco-American Treaty.[29]

Over the following months Great Britain and the US moved towards war. The initial conflict was over neutral rights, but events in the Old Northwest also enflamed matters. The situation seemed to be reeling out of control when in mid-March 1794 news arrived of an extraordinary seizure of American vessels in West Indian waters by British cruisers. An Order-in-Council dated 6 November 1793, and issued in great secrecy, had instructed commanders of royal warships and privateers to seize 'all ships laden with goods the produce of any colony belonging to France or carrying provisions or other supplies for the use of any such colony'. The idea was to trap unsuspecting ships, and the Order was not published in London until 26 December. In February 1793, France had thrown open her sugar islands to American vessels, whilst in May of that year rumours began to circulate that the British West Indies might be open to American vessels. The combination of British and French needs had since drawn an extraordinary number of profit-seeking American merchantmen into West Indian waters, and when British men-of-war and privateers suddenly swooped, some 250 American vessels were seized and 150 condemned – roughly one-half of the entire American merchant marine. Furthermore, the manner of capture, adjudication and condemnation by the British authorities in the islands could be brutal.

The US reaction was outrage, whilst that of London merchants trading with the US was hardly less heated. A new Order of 8 January 1794 now allowed direct trade between the US and the French West Indian islands, except for contraband, but it also restated the so-called 'Rule of the War of 1756'. This unilateral British rule stated that if trade was not allowed in peacetime, it was not allowed by the British in wartime. In other words, since France had not allowed the US to participate in the trade between France and its sugar colonies before the war, Americans could not now do so. As far as Great Britain was concerned, she was fighting for her liberty, and the arguments of the Americans over neutral rights were irrelevant. On 26 March, a thirty-day embargo on all foreign trade was passed by Congress and proclaimed by the President, which was preferable to continued British confiscation of American ships.[30]

The second dangerous point of conflict was the Old Northwest, from which Great Britain had still not withdrawn her garrisons in the seven forts. In February 1794, prompted by the encroachment of Vermont citizens on British territory, and convinced that the restless expansion of the Americans made war highly probable, Lord Dorchester, the Governor-General of Canada, made a wholly unauthorised speech to a gathering of Indians: if war broke out between the British and the Americans, which he predicted would happen within a year, the Indians would have to draw a line with their tomahawks. (A version of the speech appeared in the American press on 26 March.) A week later, General John Simcoe, Lieutenant-Governor since 1791 of the new province of Upper Canada, was instructed by Dorchester to reoccupy Fort Miami at the foot of the Maumee River, twenty miles south of Lake Erie; it had been established during the war, but then abandoned in 1783 as unnecessary and expensive. The two were now 'nearly frantic with fear'[31] that the American Major-General Anthony Wayne, who was preparing a decisive push against the Indians north-west of the Ohio River, meant to seize Fort Detroit by force and thereby prevent British contact with their Indian allies. They also feared that Wayne would then turn the Indians against the British. Simcoe's reoccupation of the post would present a challenge to Wayne, but the former probably had a second goal, which was to co-ordinate activities with the Spanish colony of Louisiana in case of war with the US (Spain and Great Britain were then allies). On 20 August 1794 Wayne defeated the Indians at the Battle of Fallen Timbers, after which he advanced to within range of the British guns at the fort at Maumee and demanded that the British evacuate it. The Canadians believed that war was imminent, and so, apparently, did Wayne. But the restraints placed upon both Wayne and the Canadian commanders by their respective governments meant that peace was preserved, but it was a close-run thing.[32]

On 10 March 1794, a group of Federalist Senators from seafaring states met in the Philadelphia office of Senator Rufus King of New York (one of the Founding Fathers). They proposed that 'an Envoy extraordinary should be sent to England to require satisfaction for the loss of our Property, and to adjust those points which menaced a War between the two Countries'. Two days later, they presented their suggestion to President Washington. He delayed his decision for some weeks, during which time several events convinced him that this was the best course of action. First of all, on 28 March, news arrived from London that the 6 November 1793 Order had been superseded by the somewhat more liberal Order of 8 January 1794. Rufus King himself had learned, and informed Washington, that Pitt had responded to the voluminous complaints of London merchants about the wholesale condemnation of American cargoes by promising 'the most ample compensation'. (According to John Ehrman, British ministers, amazingly, had not anticipated the enraged American reaction to the November Order.) On 3 April, a message arrived from the American Minister in London, Thomas Pinckney, 'containing reassuring words' about the future treatment of American ships from Lord Grenville, the British Foreign Secretary. News also arrived about the French recapture of Toulon on 19 December: this would certainly divert any thoughts which the British might be entertaining about war with the US.[33] Finally, a letter from Alexander Hamilton suggested that the time was 'peculiarly favourable' for an envoy's mission, and the political parties apparently agreed that one should be sent. Some were still arguing for reprisals first and then negotiations, but, Hamilton said, it was obvious that Great Britain could not settle under such pressure 'without renouncing her pride and her dignity, without losing her consequence and weight in the scale of nations; and, consequently, it is morally certain that she will not do it'. It should also be obvious that 'she would be less disposed to receive the law from us than from any other nation – a people recently become a nation, not long since one of her dependencies, and as yet if a Hercules – a Hercules in the cradle'. The US should negotiate, whilst taking defensive measures, so as not to deliberately antagonise Great Britain: 'Tis our error to overrate ourselves and underrate Great Britain; we forget how little we can annoy, how much we may be annoyed . . . To precipitate a great conflict of any sort is utterly unsuited to our condition, to our strength, or to our resources.'[34] (The former British Minister to the US later wrote that Americans held such an 'overweening idea of American Prowess and American Talents that they do not scruple to talk of the United States as singly an overmatch for any nation in Europe'.[35])

On 15 April, as suggested by Hamilton in his letter, Washington offered the position of envoy to John Jay, the Chief Justice of the Supreme Court. Jay was not overjoyed, writing to his wife on 19 April that 'no appointment ever operated more unpleasantly upon me; but the public considerations which were urged, and the manner in which it was pressed, strongly impressed me with a conviction that to refuse it would be to desert my duty'.[36] Jay's instructions, dated 6 May, were drafted by the Secretary of State, Edmund Randolph, although they were substantially based on points made by Hamilton, King and one or two other Federalists. Not surprisingly, given that the Federalists' stronghold was the North-east, the centre of the shipping trade, the primary objects were, first, that Great Britain should recognise America's neutral rights and that '[c]ompensation for all the injuries sustained, and captures, will be strenuously pressed by you . . . A Second cause of your mission, but not inferior in dignity to the preceding . . . is to draw to a conclusion all points of difference between the United States and Great Britain, concerning the treaty of peace.' It was obvious to the Americans that Britain would insist upon negotiations over the debts owed, but Jay was instructed to say that they should not be the object of diplomatic discussions, but were 'certainly of a judicial nature; to be decided by our Courts'. Of course, the refusal of the British to withdraw from the forts was an issue: 'one of the consequences of holding the posts has been much bloodshed on our frontiers by the Indians, and much expense'. The third object, but one which Jay had full discretion to propose or not as he thought fit, was a commercial treaty. However, Randolph conceded that, given the great distance between the US and Great Britain and 'the present instability of public events' – that is, the war against France – Jay was to consider these as recommendations only, excepting two 'immutable' cases: he was not to derogate from the American treaties and engagements with France (it was naturally assumed that the British would encourage him to do so);[37] and he was not to conclude any treaty of commerce contrary to this prohibition.[38] On 12 May, Jay set sail for Great Britain, arriving in London on 14 June.

The fact that his mission was crucial to Anglo-American relations came as a surprise to the British ministry, who had not, until May 1794, realised that a peaceful relationship was at risk. However, shortly before Jay's arrival in London came the reports from the Canadian governors and a mass of private and official letters and reports. (Indeed, reports from the US were so confusing that 'only two days before landing the envoy was still expected to be Jefferson'.[39]) Realisation finally dawned that, because of the increasing and ruthless depradations on American shipping, Lord Dorchester's speech to Britain's Indian allies and Simcoe's march to the Maumee River, the two countries were on the verge of war. Yet, formal negotiations were delayed for two months: Jay needed to gather information on the West Indian seizures of American ships earlier in the year;[40] the Pitt ministry was going through a crisis which resulted in a reorganisation of the government; and the ministry was mesmerised with horror at the emerging catastrophe in Flanders, where the British army was about to be defeated by the

Seventeenth-century depiction of early English traders and Native Americans.

Captain John Smith, without whom Jamestown would not have survived.

Sir Walter Ralegh, a favourite of Queen Elizabeth, and founder of an unsuccessful colony in Virginia.

Powhatan, father of Pocahontas, Chief of the Powhatan Confederacy, with whom the colonists at Jamestown had to deal.

A nineteenth-century painting showing the Pilgrims embarking for America in 1620.

A nineteenth-century heliotrope showing the landing of the Pilgrims at Plymouth in December 1620.

hn Winthrop, leader of the Puritans during the Migration and early years of the Massachusetts Bay Colony.

Thomas Hutchinson, age thirty, later the British Governor of Massachusetts at the outbreak of the Revolution.

George Washington, Commander of the Continental Army and first President, after the battle at Princeton in 1777.

Benjamin Franklin, Founding Father and Renaissance man, who represented the United Colonies in Paris during the Revolution.

George III became king in 1760 at the age of twenty-one.

General Thomas Gage, Commander-in-Chief of the British Army in America at the beginning of the Revolution.

Lord North, George III's First (Prime) Minister during the War for American Independence.

William Pitt the Younger, who became Prime Minister in 1783 at the age of twenty-four.

Eighteenth-century depiction of the Boston Tea Party, 16 December 1773.

Boston residents tar and feather the tax collector John Malcolm in 1774.

Collection of the New-York Historical Society/Bridgeman Art Library

New Yorkers tear down a statue of George III on 9 July 1776.
The torso was melted down for bullets and the head stuck up
a pike in the Blue Bell Tavern in New York City.

Paul Revere, master goldsmith and Son of Liberty, and star of Longfellow's nationalistic poem, 'The Midnight Ride of Paul Revere'.

Paul Revere's engraving of the Boston Massacre on 5 March 1770. For propaganda purposes, he heavily falsified the event.

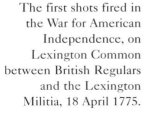

The first shots fired in the War for American Independence, on Lexington Common between British Regulars and the Lexington Militia, 18 April 1775.

French. Furthermore, in Paris the Terror was in full and sickening swing, with more than fifteen hundred men and women guillotined during June and July.[41] Radicalism of a paler sort also existed in Great Britain. Only a few yearned for an English Revolution on the French model, but a considerable number called for parliamentary reform, with the more fearless holding mass meetings. In response, the Pitt government arrested a dozen radicals and charged them with treason, Parliament suspended *habeas corpus*, and the militia was organised and armed. (The fear of a French invasion was the main reason for the last of these actions, but some also feared domestic rebellion.)

Jay arrived in the midst of all of this, and met the Foreign Secretary on 27 June. William Wyndham Grenville, Lord Grenville, the Foreign Secretary from 1791 to 1801, was thirty-four, the son of former Prime Minister George Grenville of the Stamp Act, and a cousin of Pitt. According to one historian, he was aristocratic, reserved, intensely English, cold in appearance and forbidding in personality, argumentative, dogmatic and obstinate, scornful of public opinion and awkward in dealing with colleagues and subordinates. Yet, the same historian considers him the major architect of an Anglo-American rapprochement.[42] An important reason for this may have been Jay's perception of him, which was that he was 'liberal, candid & temperate'.[43] Jay himself was stuffy and long-winded, but he was also honest, and secure enough not to feel the urge to take umbrage nor the need to score points. The two worked easily together, meeting frequently and alone, and their discussions tended towards the informal rather than the wary.

On 31 July, Jay presented Grenville with a Note on spoliations, arguing that 'a very considerable number of american vessels have been irregularly captured and *as improperly condemned*'.[44] Grenville responded the following day, evidence, perhaps, that the two had already discussed the subject informally – Jay had, in fact, written to Randolph on the 31st that he was led to believe that Grenville's response 'will in some Respect meet our wishes'.[45] Sent the very next day, it did exactly that. Although he took the opportunity to remind the Americans of the context of their complaints – 'All experience shews that a Naval War extending over the four Quarters of the Globe must unavoidably be productive of some inconveniences to the Commerce of Neutral Nations, and that no care can prevent some irregularities in the course of those proceedings' – nevertheless, the King wanted these 'irregularities' to be limited, and compensation would be considered. Grenville also assured Jay that 'if in any instance American Seamen have been impressed into the King's Service, it has been contrary to the King's desire; though cases may have occasionally arisen from the difficulty discriminating between British and American Seamen', and, pointedly, 'especially where there so often exists an interest and intention to deceive'. But it was the King's desire that justice be done and, if the facts were satisfactorily established, the person concerned should be released.[46] With regard to the Old Northwest, Dorchester was reprimanded both for his inflammatory speech to the Indians and for authorising Simcoe to send regular troops southward into American territory. The King himself, on meeting Jay, remarked, 'Well, sir, I imagine you begin to see that your mission will probably be successful.'[47]

Jay presented Grenville with a draft treaty on 6 August, which emphasised the evacuation of the forts by 1 June 1795, British compensation for injuries suffered by American shipping, American compensation to creditors injured by the lack of legal redress, and access by US ships of up to a hundred tons to the West Indies. There would also be no privateering in an Anglo-American war, and the border disputes involving Maine and the upper Mississippi were to be settled by mixed and impartial commissions. Grenville replied with his own draft treaties on 30 August, one dealing with commercial issues and the other with military and legal disputes. There was substantial agreement on issues of compensation; on evacuation of the forts, except that the date would be 1 June 1796 – how could the treaty be accepted and ratified, and distant traders and trading settlements notified, in less than a year? – and both British subjects and Indians should have free access and trading rights in the relevant territory; and that American vessels of up to seventy (rather than one hundred) tons would have access to the West Indies for up to two years after the end of the current war.[48]

Negotiations then continued over the following months, with a great deal of give-and-take, and the occasional alarm. For example, was the US about to join the League of Armed Neutrality against, essentially, British depredations against neutral rights? Britain was also apprehensive that the USA might support France in the war, and this undoubtedly played its part in encouraging a spirit of compromise in the Pitt ministry. In early September, James Monroe, recently appointed American Minister to France, 'arrived in Paris, was greeted with a kiss by the President of the National Convention, and then gave a stirring speech to the Convention on French–American friendship. Monroe presented, and the British newspapers published, a letter from Secretary of State Randolph which also seemed to support France in its war against Britain.'[49] However, Grenville could be pretty certain that the US would not join the League and take overt action against Great Britain: Hamilton had assured the British Minister that this would not happen, an assurance which was, strictly speaking, a betrayal of his colleagues in the government; but in any case, Grenville had Jay's cypher, and could read his post.[50]

At the end of September Jay presented Grenville with a revised draft treaty, which included a number of new provisions. Some were accepted, such as the proposal that the treaty would begin with professions of undying peace and friendship between the two countries – this was, essentially, Article 1 of the final treaty – and access for American shippers to East Indian ports. One of the proposals which was not accepted, that neither country would keep armed vessels on the Great Lakes, was too radical; it had to wait until 1818, when it formed one of the provisions of the Convention of 1818. Jay was also unsuccessful in trying to narrow significantly the definition of contraband. However, whilst the question of whether food would be considered contraband was left undecided (left 'to the law of nations'), Grenville accepted Jay's suggestion that if food were seized, there would always be compensation.[51] Nevertheless, in early October, Grenville wrote to Jay that there was so much new material in his latest draft that it would take some time before negotiations could move to a conclusion. In mid-October John Quincy Adams, son of John Adams and in due course the sixth President, who was travelling to take up his post as minister to the Netherlands, stopped in London for a fortnight. Jay took the opportunity to go over the draft treaty line by line with him and Pinckney. The response of Adams, widely known as being anti-British, was valuable to Jay: Adams wrote in his diary that the draft was not very satisfactory, but 'with some alterations', which the British would probably accept, it seemed to all three of the Americans that it was 'preferable to a war'.[52] Discussions continued until finally, on 19 November 1794, Grenville and Jay signed the formal treaty. Jay, enclosing it in a rapidly scribbled eleven-page gloss, sent it off to the US the same day.[53]

How far did Jay achieve the objects which Randolph had set out in his instructions of 6 May? By Article 2, Great Britain was to withdraw all troops and garrisons from American territory before 1 June 1796; by Article 3, British subjects, American citizens and Indians were all free to 'pass and repass' by land or inland navigation into their respective territories – for the British, freedom to navigate the Mississippi River was reaffirmed – but the Article did not include freedom for Americans to sail into the ports, bays or creeks and rivers of Great Britain's North American colonies, thereby closing off illegal fishing and invasion routes; by Articles 4 and 5, there would be joint surveys to sort out the boundary between Canada and the US – this would produce much conflict in the future; by Article 6, if British creditors were unable to obtain 'full and adequate' compensation from the American debtors, the US would pay the compensation, thereby eliminating this holdover from the Revolution; by the same token, in Article 7, the British government agreed to compensate American shipowners and merchants for their losses if these had arisen from irregular or illegal captures or condemnations; by Article 13, American vessels were free to trade with the East Indies, and American trade with India would thereby increase massively; Article 18 set out a comprehensive list of what constituted contraband, and when they could not agree – such as over provisions – they would be purchased instead of condemned as a prize; this article also stated that if a ship sailed to a port without knowing that it was being blockaded or besieged, the ship would be turned away but not detained (to forestall a repeat of the British swoop on American vessels in the West Indies); and finally, by Article 28, only the first ten Articles were to be permanent, thereby ensuring political uproar over renewal, as each element would again be subject to attack.[54]

In its final form the Treaty of Amity, Commerce and Navigation – or 'Mr Jay's Treaty', as it was known – finally laid to rest the problems of the debts and the forts, hangovers from the Treaty of 1783. However, impressment was not mentioned: particularly during a time of war, the Royal Navy, badly in need of manpower, was not going to forgo the possibility of hauling men it considered to be British subjects off of American merchant ships and onto its own. Jay realised this. He also knew that Great Britain was not going to concede that free ships made free goods nor accept other restraints on her maritime power when each such concession would damage her in the French wars. He also recognised that Great Britain was not going to offer compensation for slaves taken away during the Revolution. Bemis condemns Jay for accepting terms 'which might have been bettered by an abler negotiator' and considers that Grenville was a 'more able and a more experienced diplomat than John Jay'. Grenville was certainly more experienced, but he also represented a much more powerful country than was the US: Jay had the nous not to try to bluff when it would have been easy for his bluff to have been called. And it was noteworthy that Great Britain signed any treaty at all with the US in this period. Captain Alfred Thayer Mahan, an American naval theorist and historian in the final years of the nineteenth century, pointed out that this was an event of 'epochal significance', a recognition of the existence of American nationality of far greater importance than the technical recognition of independence forced from George III in 1783. Furthermore, '[h]er consenting now to modify her position was an implicit admission that in trade, as in political existence, the former mother country recognized at last the independence of her offspring'.[55] Finally, it prevented war between the US and Great Britain – at least for a time.

The response in the United States was not nearly so generous: both Jay and the treaty were excoriated. When Washington received the treaty in March 1795, he decided to keep its terms secret and thus presented it in secret to the Senate for its consent. In late June, on a party-line vote (twenty Federalists versus ten Republicans), the treaty was ratified (except for an article limiting exports to the West Indies, which was struck out). However, once the terms were made public by a leak to a Republican newspaper, there was uproar, which continued for some six weeks. 'Jay reacted to all this . . . with philosophic calm. He reportedly joked that he could, if he wanted, make his way from one end of the country to the other by the light of burning effigies of himself.'[56] Washington held off signing the treaty until mid-August. When the question of funding it finally came to a vote in the House of Representatives in late April 1796, the House approved the Bill. Passions had died down; the removal of the British from the forts and thus the elimination of their support for the Indians would make easier the move west for thousands; and in the seaports and elsewhere the current economic boom would collapse if trade with Great Britain were to be cut off. And, at least until 1805, an Anglo-American war never seriously threatened.

II

There are two major themes of the period from 1795 up to the outbreak of the War of 1812. First was the general increase in, or at least maintenance of, trade between the two countries, regardless of the legal constraints in force. Great Britain retained her primacy in the American market, whilst American merchants who were engaged in trade with the British were amongst the loudest advocates of friendly relations. The British were heavy investors in US bonds, accounting for more than one-half of the stock held abroad – it was even reported in 1795 that George III held a substantial number.[57] From 1795 to 1800, American exports to the United Kingdom rose by 300 per cent, and from 1802 to 1812, an annual average of 45 per cent of all American exports went to British possessions. And, just as Great Britain was the United States' most important customer, the reverse was also true: for example, from 1802 to 1804, Britain provided approximately one-half of all American imports.[58] Beyond its own value, the volume of this trade had an impact on foreign policy: as Henry Dundas, the Secretary for War, wrote to Grenville in October 1800, 'The Americans are egregiously in the wrong, but they are so much in debt to this country that we scarcely dare to quarrel with them.'[59]

Indeed, trade was at the core of American relations with Great Britain and, increasingly, with France, and the second major theme is the fact that the strength or weakness of relations between Britain and the United States tended to vary according to the state of Anglo-French relations. France assumed that she could bully the US into actions desirable to France, and the outcome was nearly war. The cause of this spectacular dive in relations was the Jay Treaty: James Monroe, the Minister to France (and later the fifth President), had insisted to the Directory in Paris that the US would never sign a treaty with Great Britain which compromised America's strongly felt grievances, and thus the signature and even more the ratification of the treaty stimulated French denunciations of President Washington and of the US as disloyal to republicanism. France suspended the Treaty of 1778 and then diplomatic relations. Early in 1798 it decreed that any British goods found on board a neutral vessel would subject the entire cargo and the ship itself to condemnation. Heavy French attacks on American commerce – about 830 ships fell victim to French warships and privateers, especially in the Caribbean – led Congress to declare the Treaty of 1778 null and void, and the two countries moved into what is termed the Quasi-War from 1798 to 1800. In May 1798, Congress established the Department of the Navy, which by January 1799 had outfitted fourteen men-of-war and two hundred privateers to implement armed neutrality against French aggression.

This drove the US, temporarily, into the arms of Great Britain. The former was allowed to purchase military stores in the latter, but far more important was the support of the Royal Navy. At the beginning of the Quasi-War, American commerce was almost completely dependent on it for protection. The Royal Navy's American Squadron was reinforced as French activities off the American coast increased. The British and the Americans arranged convoys for the ships of both countries. The US, realising that her tiny navy would be of limited use if spread thinly, let Great Britain roam the ocean whilst they concentrated in the Caribbean, where her frigates and smaller vessels were a match for French corsairs. In addition, Anglo-American co-operation in intelligence was close and effective.[60]

Although the Quasi-War came to an end in 1800, there was still conflict between the two, this time in North America. Jefferson became President in 1801, with James Madison, also an ardent Republican, his Secretary of State. They wanted to keep open the chance to transport goods down the Mississippi and into the Gulf, and the cession of Louisiana by Spain to France in 1802 was alarming: they feared that Napoleon would try to occupy New Orleans and close it to non-French traders and, threateningly, that a strong power was about to be established along the Mississippi River. Jefferson warned that this would throw the US into the arms of Great Britain: 'the day that France takes possession of New Orleans', he wrote to Robert Livingston, the American Minister to France, on 18 April 1802, 'we must marry ourselves to the British fleet and nation'.[61] Of course, Jefferson did not want an alliance with Great Britain, and he hoped that Napoleon would turn his attention elsewhere. However, in April 1802, he and the Cabinet agreed that, if France seemed determined on war with the US, or 'had formed projects which will constrain the United States to resort to hostilities', the Secretary of State would open negotiations with Britain for an alliance.[62]

Events, however, determined otherwise. Spain had ceded Louisiana to the French in 1800. Napoleon was short of funds, and his sale of Louisiana to the US in 1803 removed France as a rival in North America, leaving Great Britain as the major hostile power. Great Britain was still locked in battle with France, which was now no longer a republic but an empire led by Napoleon, and one which controlled a substantial part of the Continent. The need to fight him ruthlessly meant that, in 1805, Anglo-American relations deteriorated sharply. There were many reasons for this – continuing depredations against American commerce and new tensions in the Northwest were again important – but three events stand out: the *Essex* decision, the Battle of Trafalgar and the publication of a pamphlet, *War in Disguise*. The American ship *Essex* in 1799 had carried wine from Barcelona to Salem, Massachusetts. After complying with American customs law, she set sail for Havana with the same cargo. *En route*, she was captured by the British privateer *Favourite* and taken into New Providence, where the *Essex* and her cargo were condemned. The ship was deemed to be carrying the wine from Spain to her colony Cuba, and had stopped in Salem only as a subterfuge; she had thereby contravened Great Britain's 'Rule of 1756' by trading between a country and its colony when this would not have been allowed in peacetime. The decision was appealed, but confirmed in 1805. This ruling set a precedent, which was that the burden of proof now lay with the owner of the ship that was seized, rather than with the captor. Before the American merchant marine knew of the decision – it was not immediately made public – the British had begun to seize dozens of ships engaged in such indirect trade between Europe and enemy islands in the Caribbean. The attacks soon increased. On 21 October Admiral Horatio Nelson smashed the Franco-Spanish line of battle and destroyed the French fleet at Trafalgar, thereby considerably lessening the need for Great Britain to be considerate towards neutrals. On the same day a pamphlet entitled *War in Disguise; Or, the Frauds of the Neutral Flags*, written by a lawyer, James Stephen, was published in London. He argued that most of the so-called neutral trade, particularly the American, was fraudulently sheltering enemy property. Thus, 'the encroachments and frauds of the neutral flags . . . [are the] channels of revenue, which sustains the ambition of France, and prolongs the miseries of Europe'. In order to deprive Napoleon of war supplies and the neutrals of their dishonest profits, Stephens urged that there should be a ruthless execution of Great Britain's maritime code and a complete shutting down of the enemy's colonial trade carried out by neutrals. Widely read, *War in Disguise* 'crystallized British opinion, [and] consolidated it behind a policy that showed little respect for neutrals'.[63] This opinion remained, and supported the British government when, from 1812 to 1814, it fought a sideshow war against the Americans.

President Jefferson was in a quandary. First of all, he believed that almost any type of peace was preferable to war. Secondly, he shared with his Secretary of State, James Madison (his successor as President), the conviction that American trade was vital to Great Britain and could be used against her – had it not worked against the Stamp Act and the Navigation Acts? Like almost all Republicans, he detested standing armies and navies, fearing them as weapons of tyranny.[64] Finally, he supported the traditional links with revolutionary and republican France, although his faith had been shaken by the vicious and predatory policies of Napoleonic France, policies which were also directed against the US. This adherence by Jefferson and Madison to principles admirable in the abstract but unworkable in reality contributed to the absolute failure of American policy towards Great Britain and encouraged a relentless stumble into war with the greatest naval power in the world. They also nearly destroyed the unity of the American Republic.

During the period 1803–15, when she was at war with Napoleonic France, Great Britain was convinced that she was fighting for her life as an independent country. Indeed, she saw herself as the saviour of the world against the man who wanted to control it. In this context, the US could not be permitted to get in the way. Further, the British believed that the US herself would benefit by the defeat of Napoleon, as his contemptuous decrees against American trade manifestly showed (see below). On a lower level, Britain also welcomed one result of her policies against neutral trading, which was to ensure that her own merchant marine benefited. The argument was that Britain needed a strong economy to finance the fight with France and her allies. British merchants did not object. The certainty of rectitude held by both the British and the American leaderships made a settlement between the two increasingly difficult.

Between 1807 and 1812, the US was squeezed between the two belligerent Great Powers. Napoleon might have encouraged American trade with Europe, which would have helped France directly by giving her access to useful supplies, and might also have embroiled the US in war with Great Britain much earlier than actually happened. Yet, he chose rather to restrict it. On 21 November 1806, he issued the Berlin Decree, which declared a blockade of the British Isles – although he hardly had the naval forces to enforce it, given their destruction at Trafalgar – and prohibited all trade with the British or in British merchandise. Vessels coming from British ports were ordered seized and brought into ports controlled by France. This was followed on 23 November and 17 December 1807 by the Milan Decrees, which stipulated that ships which submitted to British regulations as to areas open to trade or allowed themselves to be searched at sea by the

Royal Navy would be considered to have lost their neutral status and were therefore subject to confiscation. Consequently, the French seizure of American ships began immediately.[65]

Yet, British seizures of American ships exceeded those of the French. From 1805 to 1808, according to James Monroe (by then Minister to Great Britain), the Royal Navy seized an American ship as a prize every two days. Particularly infuriating to the Americans were British actions within American territorial waters, with cruisers mounting an almost continuous blockade. Off New York City, the British frequently halted almost every ship leaving the harbour, and there was often a queue of a dozen or so ships awaiting British inspection. This led to numerous complaints against the Admiralty courts, which were supposed to apply the law impartially but did not. British ships, desperately short of sailors, also continued to impress those seamen whom they considered to be British subjects. Admittedly, thousands of British seamen did leave British ships and join the crews of American merchantmen; this is not surprising when one compares British wages (about seven dollars a month) with those paid by the Americans (between twenty-five and thirty-five dollars a month, and this for much less onerous work). In 1812 the Admiralty claimed that at least twenty thousand Britons, British even by American definition, were serving under the American flag; this meant that about one-half of the seamen on American ships trading abroad were British. The Americans did not disagree, but they argued that many of the seamen, having taken American citizenship, were no longer British. The British insisted that once a British subject, always a British subject, pointing out that American courts had themselves sometimes ruled that once an American, always an American.[66] The American Secretary of the Treasury, Albert Gallatin, estimated in February 1812 that the Americans recruited about 2,500 British sailors each year. However, as Perkins points out, 'These opposing definitions, a tendency on both sides to doctor figures for political purposes, and delayed and incomplete reports make it extremely difficult to establish the precise dimensions of flight from British service on the one hand and impressment on the other.'[67]

Whatever the exact numbers were, this continual bleeding away of seamen encouraged individual British commanders to strain, and sometimes to overstep, the limits of official British policy. The *Chesapeake* affair was one of the most notorious examples. In the spring of 1807, a number of deserters from the Royal Navy received protection from local authorities in Chesapeake Bay. One of them, a former London tailor called Jenkin Ratford, enlisted on the warship USS *Chesapeake* 'and railed at British officers on the quays and streets of Norfolk'. Vice-Admiral Sir George Cranfield Berkeley, MP, was the Commander-in-Chief on the American station, and a man who believed that the Americans would always back down if Great Britain did not.[68] He told his subordinates that if they met with the *Chesapeake* outside of American territorial waters, they were to show the captain Berkeley's order demanding the right to board the ship and search for Ratford. On 22 June 1807, Captain Salusbury P. Humphreys of Berkeley's flagship, the *Leopard*, sailed to Norfolk. When, a day later, the *Chesapeake* set sail for the Mediterranean, it was hailed by the *Leopard*. Because, by their own rules, the British were not to challenge neutral warships but only merchantmen, the *Chesapeake*'s commander, Commodore Barron, came to. The ship was boarded, fruitless arguments followed, and the British withdrew. Humphreys continued the argument through a hailing trumpet, and then fired a shot across the *Chesapeake*'s bow. This did not convince the Americans to obey the order. Humphreys believed that he had to follow his orders, and, therefore, for ten minutes the *Leopard* fired into the *Chesapeake*, killing three Americans and driving Barron to surrender. A second party boarded the ship, dragged Ratford and three others out of hiding, and took them to Halifax, where Ratford was soon hanged.

American sovereignty had therefore been comprehensively violated. All supplies to British ships were cut off, in response to which the British interfered even more with American shipping. Militia patrolled the coasts to prevent supplies reaching the ships, public meetings bayed for British blood, and those British in the country, official or private, had to take great care. Some Americans urged a declaration of war. However, within a month the uproar had died down. Jefferson apparently hoped to keep up the pressure short of war so that the British would settle the affair and end impressment, but this hope was pathetically futile.[69] By October 1807, Jefferson and his Cabinet knew that Great Britain would not end impressment, although the British government did disavow the attack on the *Chesapeake* and reaffirmed that it did not claim the right to search warships.[70]

What was soon to come was worse. On 11 and 25 November 1807, the British proclaimed two new Orders-in-Council.[71] These Orders have a strong claim to consideration as the most important 'cause' of the War of 1812. All ports from which British ships were excluded were declared to be under blockade. Neutrals were permitted to trade with enemy colonies, to sail from them to certain ports in the Empire, and to carry British produce to Europe (it was assumed that these concessions would be enough to keep the US satisfied), but foreign cargoes bound for Europe had first to be landed at a British port, where a duty would be levied on the reshipment of freight and a licence obtained to trade with Europe. Besides raising funds, this secured for Great Britain a near monopoly of trade with the Continent. Indeed, Mahan later wrote that the taxation by Great Britain of American goods bound for Europe was 'literally, and in no metaphorical sense, the reimposition of colonial regulation'.[72] Spencer Perceval, the Prime Minister, set out in a memorandum of 11 October the arguments which would form the core of the British defence of the Orders for the subsequent five years, until war with the US loomed: neutrals, 'if they complain justly, . . . will direct their complaint against those whose proceedings against us & our Trade, make it indispensable . . . to retaliate'. In any case, neutrals had abandoned their privileged status, since a state that failed to force Napoleon to observe its rights 'ceases to be a Neutral, by ceasing to observe that impartiality which is the very life and soul of neutrality'.[73] This was remarkably similar to Napoleon's justification for imposing the Milan Decrees the following month. The result of the British Orders plus the Milan Decrees was to bring international trade virtually to a standstill.

The *Chesapeake* affair and then the Orders drove Jefferson and his Cabinet to tighten their policy. An attempt had been made, clearly unsuccessfully, to change British attitudes by passing the ineffectual Non-Importation Act in March 1806. Now Jefferson, supported by Secretary of State Madison and the rest of the Cabinet, signed the

Embargo Act on 22 December 1807. Madison had two firm beliefs about the British Empire which encouraged his strong support of the embargo: one was an overestimation of the strength of the Empire within the United States, supported, he thought, by the 'anglomen', particularly in the North-east, whose adherence to British interests would be undercut by such an embargo; the other was his perception of the Empire as vulnerable to economic pressures, making it safe to challenge.[74] Both assumptions turned out to be wrong. The purpose of the embargo was to forbid the departure of all ships from US ports, be they American or foreign. To be successful, such a law would require the whole-hearted co-operation of Americans, because acute self-denial would be vital; this co-operation was also required in order to convince the British that the Americans would continue the embargo for as long as was necessary. Precisely because he doubted that Americans would be so self-denying, Secretary of the Treasury Gallatin only reluctantly supported the embargo. He 'never forgot the value a dollar had to Americans. He knew that the nation's love for the main chance piled massive obstacles in the path of both embargo enforcement and war preparation.' Jefferson 'reacted more emotionally and violently to evasions of the law. He blamed the embargo's travail on merchant sharpsters and Federalist politicians, "parracides" he called them, who were no better than "unprincipled adventurers" . . . Expecting more from the American people [than Gallatin did], he was more easily disappointed and outraged.'[75] Nevertheless, he refused to justify his policy publicly until August 1808; by then, events were beginning to spiral out of control.

In the interval between the passing of the Act and the establishment of a system to enforce it, American shipowners sent hundreds of ships to sea. During the summer, there were numerous attempts to smuggle goods across the Canadian border, to be exported via the St Lawrence River. However, it was only at the end of 1808,

> as it became apparent that not war but a long embargo was most likely, and as the [domestic] political climate became more and more hostile to the whole system, did there arise the last great surge of criminality which destroyed the Embargo . . . Areas contiguous to British possessions developed an unaccountable

demand for goods of all sorts, a high proportion of which slipped across the border by land or water. Nineteen thousand barrels of flour reached Passamaquoddy Bay, for example, in the first week of May. Many ships found themselves forced by often imaginary bad weather or constructed circumstances to run to foreign ports for safety, sometimes all the way across the Atlantic.[76]

Most damagingly, the embargo ripped apart domestic relations. 'The government marched troops to the frontiers, sent gunboats and frigates scurrying up and down the coast, passed law after law and issued directive after directive. And yet violations continued.' As a result, many Americans came to believe that the Republicans had adopted coercive and even tyrannical methods akin to those of the British which could not be justified, while at the same time, 'violations strengthened the conviction of America's enemies abroad that her republican form of government made any forceful policy impossible'. In January 1809, in spite of ferocious opposition from the Congressional representatives from the North-east, Congress passed a law which permitted seizures of ships which officials suspected were about to sail illegally, forbade the loading of ships without the permission of Federal officials, provided for the arrest of goods travelling towards the border with Canada by road, and authorised the increased use of force at sea and by the militia. This all showed how pervasive were the violations of the embargo, how authoritarian Jefferson was prepared to be to enforce it, and how weak the American government actually was.[77]

In short, the embargo was a thunderous failure. Napoleon did not care about it, since the Royal Navy had already stopped most trade with Europe and he was indifferent to the fate of the French colonies. Great Britain suffered much less economically than did the US herself: the embargo promised to end the problem of American trade with France, and it enabled Britain to capture a near monopoly of trade with the neutrals. Unemployed sailors began to return from American to British ships. Indeed, the British government viewed the embargo with contempt, since Jefferson appeared a coward and the US showed that it could bluster rather more than it could implement a policy; it also demonstrated that such a policy hurt the US more than its intended victims. In a contest of British will against American, the Americans gave way. But most of all, the whole exercise destroyed American unity. The North-east was in virtual revolt, and the unenforceable law only encouraged contempt for the government and for Federal law-making.

The next three and a half years saw a bumpy slide into war. First of all, Congress passed the Non-Intercourse Act, which came into effect on 15 March 1809, eleven days after Madison had succeeded Jefferson as President. This was 'a mere sham of a law'.[78] Its purpose was to close all trade, export and import, with Great Britain and France whilst permitting it with all other countries, but its main result was to spawn a massive evasion of the law: who could tell where a ship would go after leaving port? (In the first months of the Act, seventy-nine ships sailed from New York in order, it was claimed, to find markets in the Azores.[79]) Naturally, it was Great Britain which benefited, since the Royal Navy could intercept ships bound for France whilst France was unable to retaliate in kind. Indeed, it did not take long for British and American merchants to resume their evasion of these sorts of restrictions, and a lively business grew up in neutral ports, as British ships carrying British manufactures exchanged cargoes with American ships carrying American raw materials. By spring 1810, the Non-Intercourse Act was admitted by most to have been a fiasco, and on 1 May, in an attempt to resolve the diplomatic impasse, Congress passed the Macon's No. 2 Act. This repealed all restrictions on trade, but stipulated that if either Great Britain or France removed their restrictions on American trade, the US would renew non-intercourse with the other.

Meanwhile, in retaliation for the Non-Intercourse Act, Napoleon in March 1810 had issued the Rambouillet Decree, which ordered all American ships which entered French ports to be seized, without exception. A few months later, however, he appeared to reverse his position, probably to encourage Anglo-American conflict. On 5 August 1810, the Duke of Cadore, the French Foreign Minister, gave to John Armstrong, the American Minister to France, a declaration by Napoleon that if the US again prohibited trade with Britain (or if Britain repealed the Orders-in-Council), the Berlin and Milan

Decrees would no longer be enforced after 1 November. However, Napoleon then quietly imposed other restrictions which effectively nullified this concession, as well as ordering the sale of all American vessels and their cargoes which had been seized in French ports since the previous spring. Nevertheless, '[w]ith the confidence that, we may presume, has characterised fish from time immemorial, President Madison believed it possible to feed on the bait without swallowing the visible hook'.[80] On 2 November, Madison announced that since France had revoked the Decrees, the US would resume trading with her. Then, in February 1811, British ships and goods were forbidden to enter American ports. Trusting Napoleon was a risk because he might easily swing back (as in fact he had already done), but Madison hoped to use this agreement to force Britain to repeal the Orders-in-Council. The British government, however, believed that the Americans had been tricked, and refused to do so. They also believed that Madison would soon accept that he had been duped and would modify American policy, but this also failed to happen. In September 1811 new Orders-in-Council were issued. These excluded American salted fish from the West Indian colonies, and imposed heavy duties on other imports from the US.

Meanwhile, rumours of a new Indian war sped along the Western frontier. News came that Indians who had crossed into Canada were receiving subsidies from the British, who were encouraging them to attack Americans. The former was true, but the latter was not. If there was another war between the US and Great Britain, the British assumed that the Indians would not remain neutral and, in that case, they wanted them on their side. Added to this was the news that Tecumseh, chief of the Shawnee tribe, who in 1805 had begun to create a new Indian league, had gone south to try to convince other tribes to join.[81] General William Henry Harrison, who in 1809 had 'convinced' the Indians to cede nearly three million acres in the Old Northwest, gathered a mixed force of regulars and volunteers, dashed north, and defeated the Indians at the Battle of Tippecanoe on 7 November 1811. News of this quickly spread, and, because conflict with the Indians tended to accompany conflict with the British, Americans believed that the British were supporting the Indian military alliance. As a result, many were determined to drive the British out of Canada and attach it to the US. Indeed, during the War of 1812, Tecumseh fought on the side of the British.

This western disaffection was partly responsible for the emergence of a more militantly anti-British attitude in Congress, signalled by a group of Republican representatives returned from the southern and western states and dubbed the War Hawks, who made up about one-third of the House of Representatives. They were intensely nationalistic and supported an expansionist Republic willing to defend its interests. If the US continued to be humiliated, the Republican Party, and, indeed, republican institutions, would be threatened. If diplomacy did not work, war had to come. (The House also contained a number of 'scarecrow men', those who hoped to frighten Great Britain by apparently preparing for war, although many were reluctant to go to war if the bluff failed.[82]) One of the War Hawks, Henry Clay from Kentucky, would become Speaker of the House of Representatives in 1811. However, important though they were in raising Anglo-American tensions even further, the western problems probably played a lesser role than the Orders-in-Council in nudging the US towards a declaration of war. On 5 November 1811, in his Annual Message to Congress, Madison recommended that military preparations should begin.

In Great Britain, for most of the period from 1809, American activities seemed of relatively little importance.[83] September 1809 saw the fall of the ministry after a crisis lasting over two months, resulting in an absence of effective government for more than three weeks. When the new Prime Minister, Spencer Perceval, finally presented his Cabinet, the public response was to wonder at the collective lack of talent and experience.[84] Thereafter, the government had to worry about the cost, and results, of the campaign against France in the Iberian Peninsula led by the future Duke of Wellington; about the colonial campaigns of 1809 to 1811, which were prompted either by enemy weakness or by strategic necessity (although as, one by one, French and Dutch colonies were picked off, they were transformed into sources of raw materials and markets, and Great Britain increasingly supplanted Spain and Portugal in Latin American trade);[85] about George III's illness and possible insanity in 1810 and the Regency crisis (whether Parliament should restrict the powers of the

Prince Regent to exercise the royal authority), which ended only in February 1811 with the passing of the Regency Bill;[86] about the need to try to assemble, and keep together, a coalition of allies with Russia at its heart; and, overarching all, about the need to fight Napoleon. During this whole period, successive ministries believed that the US was too cowardly, too disorganised and too greedy to fight, and that there was thus no need to make concessions. Furthermore, the desirability of making concessions was nil compared to the overwhelming necessity of maintaining every weapon against Napoleon which the country possessed.

What began to modify this approach was that from the end of 1810, Great Britain began to suffer from her worst economic depression since 1797. This was caused by a combination of a series of bad harvests, inflation caused by the printing of paper money to finance the war, the strains of rapid industrialisation, and the concomitant glut of goods in factories and warehouses arising from the reduction in trade with Europe and the US. Production in Lancashire dropped by 40 per cent and imports from the US declined sharply. More importantly, whilst in 1810 roughly 17 per cent of British exports went to the USA, in 1811 it was less than 5 per cent. From late 1810 until 1812, all trade declined by a quarter. In the spring of 1812 a series of riots swept through the Midlands.[87]

Around the same time, news of the so-called War Hawk Congress and of Madison's Annual Message to Congress began to arrive. This allowed the Opposition in Parliament and its supporters outside to emphasise the threat to Great Britain. But in the House of Commons, Samuel Whitbread declared: 'War with America . . . would be a great evil: and war once commenced, no man could tell what might follow . . . [I]t was not in the power of England to annihilate her, and it was therefore the interest of England to be her friend.'[88] The *Morning Chronicle* of 27 January pointed out that war with the United States would divert the Royal Navy and thereby give Napoleon the chance to rebuild the French fleet, whilst the need to send troops to Canada would weaken the British effort in Spain and elsewhere. However, just in case, the government ordered that three regiments be sent to Canada, but the War Office so little anticipated that they would be needed that it instructed the

Canadian commander to be prepared to return two of them for service elsewhere if and when the threat of war receded.[89]

The main effect of the news from America seems to have been to stimulate to protest those in Great Britain who had suffered from, and therefore opposed, the Orders-in-Council. Prime Minister Perceval, a model of inflexibility, gave no sign that he intended to compromise on the issue, but a parliamentary struggle was developing. This was led by the Scot Henry Brougham, MP,[90] a man of energy who succeeded in marshalling the anti-Orders troops. They included: manufacturers from the Midlands;[91] the 'Friends of Peace', opponents of the war outside Parliament (also called liberals); merchants with interests in American trade; a section of the press; and many, both in and out of Parliament, who thought that Great Britain did not need another war, since it would only divert men and supplies from the main fight against Napoleon. The manufacturers, merchants and liberals overwhelmed the government with facts and petitions, but it held firm,[92] fearing that conciliation would be interpreted as surrender to this bumptious young Republic and a betrayal of maritime rights vital to the safety of the realm.

On 10 April, as the price demanded by the Viscount Sidmouth for his support of the government, Perceval, both to silence his parliamentary enemies and to offer a concession to the US, agreed to end the system of licences for trading with the Continent. But then the government made a serious mistake: on 21 April it issued a statement intended to convince the British public and 'reasonable' Americans that the Perceval ministry's refusal to repeal the Orders-in-Council had been forced on it by the French. It insisted that France was tricking the US, and declared that the Orders would remain in force until France stated that it would repeal its own decrees. '[I]n America people assumed the ministry had decided to stand on the Orders in Council, and this declaration played a decisive part in the American decision for war.'[93]

It took the assassination of the Prime Minister on 11 May to begin to break the impasse. The new ministry under Lord Liverpool agreed that the Orders had to be repealed, but it was apprehensive about appearing to have been driven to this by the Opposition, and in particular by extra-parliamentary pressure, especially that of the middle and working classes. Nevertheless, it was domestic considerations, both political and economic, not the fear of war with the US, which drove ministers towards repeal of the Orders.

Several months earlier, on 20 March 1812, the British minister to the United States, Augustus John Foster, had received from Lord Wellesley, the Foreign Secretary, a despatch containing the unchanging British argument that since the French repeal in the Duke of Cadore's letter was fraudulent, Britain would continue the Orders-in-Council. On 1 April Madison, in a one-sentence message to Congress, recommended a general embargo, which was then passed in a secret session of the Senate. Once news of the embargo was made public, however, there was the predictable flight of hundreds of merchant ships from American ports, nullifying the point of the embargo and again shaming the US. Carl Benn believes, however, that the embargo was the opening move in the war, arguing that the Americans implemented it in order to get their merchant ships, which were at sea, into port and so prevent their falling into the hands of the British.[94]

The point of decision had now come. If the US wished to maintain her honour and regain the respect of other countries, she had to declare war, although, it must be said, war fever had hardly swept the country. Indeed, the war was to see significant internal dissent, with New England in particular practically in a state of revolt. Nevertheless, on 1 June 1812, President Madison recommended a declaration of war against Great Britain. 'British cruisers', he pointed out, 'have been in the continued practice of violating the American flag on the great highway of nations, and of seizing and carrying off persons sailing under it, not in the exercise of a belligerent right founded on the law of nations against an enemy, but of a municipal prerogative over British subjects. British jurisdiction is thus extended to neutral vessels in a situation where no laws can operate but the law of nations and the laws of the country to which the vessels belong'. And instead of being fairly judged in a proper court, 'these rights are subjected to the will of every petty commander'. (Between 1807 and 1812, Great Britain and France had together seized roughly nine hundred American ships.[95]) 'Whether the

United States shall continue passive under these progressive usurp-
ations and these accumulated wrongs, or, opposing force to force in
defense of their national rights, . . . is a solemn question which the
Constitution wisely confides to the legislative department of the
Government.'[96] According to the Constitution, war had to be
declared by Congress and then agreed to by the President; he could
not declare it on his own.

Because the War Hawks came from the South and West, it might
seem as though the vote was entirely sectional. Certainly, except for
three Congressmen from North Carolina, those from the states south
of Virginia voted as a bloc. However, these constituted fewer than
one-third of the votes for war in the House of Representatives. Most
of the rest came from Pennsylvania, Maryland and Virginia. On the
whole, the North-east was opposed. More important than geography
was party membership: 90 per cent of Congressmen who voted for
the war were Republicans. They had continuously threatened and
then retreated, and to do so again might well cost them the next
election or even permanently cripple the party. Worst of all, 'what
was catastrophic, in the view of most Republicans and many citizens,
was the challenge to the honor of the nation, to the effectiveness of
republican polity'. In the House the vote was seventy-nine to forty-
nine. In the Senate, where the sentiments were largely the same, the
vote was much closer: nineteen to thirteen. (When news of the votes
arrived in the North-east, in many of the seaports church bells tolled
a dirge, shops closed, and ships' flags flew at half-mast.) On 18 June
1812, the date the declaration of war passed Congress, Madison
called in Foster, the British minister, to inform him officially of the
decision. At noon on 25 June, Foster left Washington for a leisurely
journey to New York, from where he set sail on 12 July.[97]

In London, the Orders-in-Council had finally been repealed on 16
June (although not announced until the following week), two days
before the declaration of war. Five weeks later, news of the repeal
reached the US. The British government fully expected that this
would result in withdrawal of the declaration, but Madison noted
that Lord Castlereagh, the new Foreign Secretary, had reserved the
right to reimpose the Orders in May 1813 if French or American
conduct required it.[98] The President therefore concluded that the

repeal was a ruse to trick the US into stopping the war. The British were 'astonished' that the Americans had begun to fight, decided that it was probably a misunderstanding, and in August offered to negotiate. But when Jonathan Russell, the American Minister to Great Britain, insisted at a meeting with Castlereagh on 17 September that in addition to the repeal of the Orders, there had to be an end to impressment, the Foreign Secretary referred to 'the inherent difficulty of the matter' and declared that 'no administration could expect to remain in power that should consent to renounce the right of impressment or to suspend the practice, without the certainty of an arrangement . . . to secure its object'.[99] For the British, war against the US now commenced in earnest, although it is undeniable that, with war against Napoleon still being waged – June had also seen his invasion of Russia – the conflict with the Americans was a secondary consideration.

The Americans had already begun, but their preparation had been minimal. They were confident in their local superiority, given that the British garrison in Upper and Lower Canada numbered only seven thousand soldiers in 1812 and that the war with France would preclude sending the reinforcements necessary to enable the provinces to withstand an American attack. Furthermore, as noted above, Americans distrusted standing military forces, with many, including Madison, having great faith in the capabilities of a citizen militia against regular forces. So how did the two forces compare?

The US navy was largely composed of professional officers and experienced voluntary seamen, but it was underfunded. It only possessed thirteen operational vessels, but three of them were so-called 'super frigates' designed and built by Joshua Humphreys. Congress had decided that no ships of the line (huge vessels with massive firepower meant to fight in the line of battle) could be built, but the super frigate carried more men (up to 450 – needed for boarding enemy ships during combat and for sailing captured vessels), more guns (up to 54), more armour in the hulls, and more sail than ordinary frigates. They could outrun and outmanoeuvre ordinary frigates, too. 'They were fast enough to cut ships out of British convoys, fight them down, and slip away.'[100] Furthermore, most sea captains were under forty and eager to fight. The Royal Navy was the largest and most powerful in the world, but the numbers of vessels which were fighting fit were fewer than would have been ideal. The French were still a threat, and Great Britain's global responsibilities meant that crews were often ill-trained and partly impressed, under strength, and sailing in badly built vessels, often constructed from inferior timber.

The armies both had a mixture of line and light (mounted) infantry, artillery and cavalry; both drew on part-time civilian militiamen (the US called out 450,000 during the war). The US army seemed larger, with an authorised strength of 35,600, but at the outbreak of war only 13,000 had actually enlisted, and many were untrained recruits. However, there was clearly scope for a rapid increase. The British had stronger leadership and better training. Most of the American generals were nearly or over sixty, and had been appointed simply because they had gained experience in the Revolutionary War and were Republicans – not, perhaps, ideal, since the result more often than not was an ageing political appointee. One example was Major-General Henry Dearborn, a veteran of Saratoga, Valley Forge and Yorktown, Secretary of War in both of Jefferson's administrations, and now sixty-one.[101] As a local source for soldiers, the US had a population of 7.5 million, whilst the British North American population was only 500,000. Indeed, the province of Upper Canada, which was directly in the sights of the Americans, had a population of only seventy to eighty thousand, and although many were former Loyalists, many others were recent American immigrants. Crucially, the British supply lines extended to the West Indies or across the Atlantic.

What were the objectives for each? For the US, there were two territorial ambitions: to conquer Canada, and therefore most of the fighting took place along the upper St Lawrence River and through the Great Lakes region; and to eliminate, if possible, the ability of the Indians to block western expansion, with the assumption being that the fall of Canada would deprive them of supplies and support. As a result, American forces crossed into Canada in 1812, 1813 and 1814, and won a few victories; but in only one of eight attempts did they succeed in occupying British territory for more than a short period, and even that exception, in south-western Upper Canada, was returned to Britain in the peace treaty. To support the fight for Canada, the US navy and privateers were to attack British merchantmen and naval vessels.

For Great Britain, the war was defensive, in that her primary goal was to retain Canada, and in general to end the ability of the USA to threaten her American colonies. She embarked on both land and sea offensives, over the border from Canada and along the Atlantic and Gulf coasts. She wanted to avenge the sufferings of the Canadians and, if possible, to redraw the Canadian–American border in order to make it more defensible. It is also likely that she wanted to humble the Americans.

The Americans assumed that it would be easy to conquer Canada. Thomas Jefferson wrote in August 1812 that 'The acquisition of Canada this year, as far as the neighborhood of Quebec, will be a mere matter of marching, and will give us experience for the attack of Halifax the next, and the final expulsion of England from the American continent.'[102] On 12 July the Americans invaded Canada from Detroit, part of a planned three-pronged attack which also included crossing the Niagara frontier and advancing along the Champlain corridor to Montreal. (Montreal was particularly crucial, since it kept open the St Lawrence River, allowing troops and supplies to travel to Upper Canada.) However, the limitations of being led by political appointees and the armies' lacking a staff or a supply system meant that the Americans lost every campaign of significance: the British captured Detroit in August, the Niagara invasion force was defeated in October at the Battle of Queenston Heights, and the Champlain incursion never really got under way.[103]

They were, however, more successful the following year. For political reasons – the pro-war Governor of New York, Daniel Tompkins, was up for re-election and needed movement on the Canadian front – it was decided to attack York (now Toronto), the capital of Canada, which was vulnerable and thinly defended. On 27 April 1813, the Americans launched an amphibious assault against the village, driving out the British and seizing a large quantity of supplies.[104] But they failed to capture two ships – one had left shortly before the attack and the British burned the other – and upon their departure the British also blew up a gunpowder magazine, killing 250 Americans and depriving them of a large cache of ammunition.

The Americans occupied York for a week. A surrender agreement was negotiated, whereby the US commanders (including Dearborn) agreed to respect private property, allow the civil government to function, and permit doctors to attend to the British wounded. Despite the agreement, American soldiers, including some officers, broke into homes, robbed the Canadians, pillaged the church, and locked up the British and Canadian wounded without food, water or medical attention for two days. At one point, the priest, John Strachan, rescued a woman who was about to be shot by the Americans whilst they were looting her house. Strachan's own pregnant wife was assaulted, robbed and probably raped by a gang of American soldiers. When the Americans withdrew, they set fire to the parliament buildings and the Governor's home[105] – the Canadian equivalent of the Capitol and the White House.

During 1813 the American campaigns in the York–Niagara and Montreal regions came to nothing, but they had some military success in south-western Upper Canada, driving the British and the Indians led by Tecumseh from Ohio territory back into Canada. They also won, at the Battle of Put-in-Bay on Lake Erie, one of the decisive battles of the war. The British dominated the Great Lakes, with a squadron of freshwater ships on Lakes Ontario and Erie. The Americans needed to break this hold. The Admiralty sent reinforcements, including carpenters, to build more ships; the Americans did the same, with more need. The twenty-seven-year-old Oliver Hazard Perry was sent to Sackett's Harbor to take command of the American squadron and build some ships for it, arriving in March 1813. The problem was that at the mouth of the harbour the water's depth was only six feet, and it was therefore vital to build shallow-draft boats. This had to be done in the intense cold.

Captain Robert Barclay arrived in June to take command of the British squadron. Desperate for men, he commandeered foot soldiers from Fort Erie, and then tried to blockade Perry. On 31 July, by which time he had nine warships, Perry saw that the British had disappeared from the mouth of the harbour, and he decided to try to get his vessels over the bar. Some of the ships to have their rigging and guns removed to allow it, but it was an impressive exploit, and Perry went without sleep for the three days whilst overseeing it. The boats then took up their anchorage at Put-in-Bay on Gibraltar Island. By this time the British squadron was short of men and supplies, and the Americans prevented reinforcement. In the end the British had six ships with 440 men, of whom only sixty were trained sailors; against this were the Americans' nine ships with 530 men, a larger proportion of whom were trained sailors. In addition, the Americans' firepower was almost twice that of the British. At dawn on 10 September, American lookouts announced that the British fleet was in view, and Perry sailed out to engage them. It was close-fought and bloody. Four hours later, the ship's commander and his deputy in every British ship had been killed or wounded, and the 'murderous raking fire' of the Americans had tipped the balance. At 4 p.m., Perry wrote to the American Secretary of War to report the victory, and a shorter note to General William Henry Harrison: 'We have met the enemy and they are ours – two ships, two brigs, one schooner, and a sloop.'[106]

Perry then ferried Harrison and his army of 3,500 men, including 250 Indians from the Ohio country, across Lake Erie. They caught the British and their allies, including Tecumseh, at Moraviantown, where they defeated them on 5 October at the Battle of the Thames. Tecumseh was killed. However, within six weeks of this destruction of British power, the term of service of many of the western militiamen expired, which somewhat limited the possibilities of a further advance.[107] But with the death of Tecumseh the dream of an independent Indian homeland also died. These victories, which gave the Americans control of Lake Erie and part of Upper Canada, were their only campaign successes on the northern front during the war.

Further east, when the term of service of many American militiamen expired in December, the British decided to push forward. The Americans retreated across the border to consolidate their forces. *En route*, they pursued something of a scorched-earth policy, turning the people of Niagara out into the snow and burning their houses, then destroying part of Queenston by firing red-hot cannon balls to set it on fire. The tactical argument was that this prevented the use of both towns by the British. The new British commander in Upper

Canada, Lieutenant-General Gordon Drummond, determined to avenge the destruction. He crossed the Niagara River, defeated the American garrison at Fort Niagara, and drove the Americans out of the region completely. Over the next several days the British torched the settlements on the American side of the river. Drummond captured Buffalo, destroyed four ships of the Lake Erie squadron which were wintering there, and then retired to the Canadian side. There continued to be sporadic fighting on the northern frontier for the remainder of the war. Most importantly, the American victory on 11 September 1814 at the Battle of Plattsburg Bay on Lake Champlain stopped a British invasion force, which had intended to slice the Union in two.

By the end of 1813, the Americans had regained most of the lost territory in the West, had destroyed for ever the possibility of an Indian homeland in the Ohio territory, and had occupied part of south-western Upper Canada. But they had not, as anticipated, conquered all of Upper Canada – and they would never do so. On the ocean, although the American navy could not begin to match the Royal Navy in size, it had a number of unexpected (by the British) successes. For example, the USS *Constitution*, after making a dramatic escape from a British squadron in July, on 19 August 1812 defeated HMS *Guerrière* in a bloody encounter (it was primarily an artillery duel, with the ships running side by side); on 25 October the USS *United States* defeated and captured the British frigate HMS *Macedonian*; and on 29 December the *Constitution* defeated HMS *Java* off the coast of Brazil.[108] (The *Constitution* was nicknamed 'Old Ironsides' by its sailors as several of the *Guerrière*'s cannon balls bounced off her hull.) As a result of these and other clashes, the British sent out a secret order discouraging single combat.[109]

Nevertheless, the US navy itself was no match for the Royal Navy. With the onset of war, the latter had to pay much greater attention to protecting convoys from American frigates, which were soon to show their mettle, and privateers; furthermore, it had to blockade the American coastline in order to destroy American trade and prevent her naval operations. Early in 1812, there were seventy-seven major warships off the American coast and in the Caribbean, but by early 1813 this number had risen to 105. A very important part of the naval conflict was the use by both countries of their warships against merchant vessels.[110] The US navy seized 165 British vessels and some troop transports whilst the Royal Navy captured 1,400 merchantmen and privateers. Both countries licensed privateers, with mixed success. The Americans licensed 526, of which 207 took a prize and 148 were captured or destroyed; the British privateers, most of them from the maritime provinces of Canada, in turn took several hundred American ships, many of them coastal traders. In the Galapagos Islands during the summer of 1813, the British whaling industry was devastated by the USS *Essex*, which captured all of the ships known to be in the area. In the British Empire American privateers captured nearly 1,400 merchantmen, although almost 750 of them were subsequently recaptured by the British.[111]

The greatest impact on the ocean war was the Royal Navy's blockade of the Atlantic Coast, which began with twenty ships and ended with 135. From the beginning of the war until May 1814, New England was exempted: the British army required American grain, and the Americans were happy to ship it in vessels licensed by the British. Once Napoleon abdicated, however, and the supplies were no longer needed, New England was blockaded as well. There were two major impacts of the blockade: it paralysed the US navy, since it was extremely difficult for American warships to leave port, which meant that even the six super frigates built during the war had to sit it out; and it devastated America's international trade. In 1811 the value of American exports and imports totalled $192 million; in 1814 this had fallen to $31 million. In the same period customs revenues fell from $13 million to $6 million. By 1814, according to Benn, only one out of twelve ships even dared to leave port. By contrast, Great Britain's international trade grew from £91 million in 1811 to £152 million in 1814.[112]

Beginning in February 1813, the Royal Navy and the British army launched raids in the Chesapeake region, not least because it was the base of many of the privateers – the British referred to Baltimore as a nest of pirates. Resistance on the whole was patchy, and they destroyed military and industrial property and captured a large number of ships. If the Americans opened fire, the British often torched or plundered. If the Americans stayed at home, they were generally left alone and were paid for the supplies taken by the British. Upon Napoleon's abdication in May 1814, resources were released for the American war, and by the end of May the blockade extended the entire length of the Atlantic Coast.

On 20 May 1814, Lord Bathurst, the Secretary for War and the Colonies, instructed Major-General Robert Ross, a veteran of the Peninsular War against the French, '"to effect a diversion on the coasts of the United States of America in favor of the army employed in the defence of Upper and Lower Canada" . . . [The] force was not intended for "any extended operation at a distance from the coast"', nor was Ross to hold permanent possession of any captured district. Furthermore, '"If in any descent you shall be enabled to take such a position as to threaten the inhabitants with the destruction of their property, you are hereby authorized to levy upon them contributions in return for your forbearance"', but the government's munitions, harbours and shipping were to be taken away or destroyed. These orders were strictly carried out: the American historian Henry Adams was later to write that Ross's troops 'showed unusual respect for private property'.[113]

In August 1814 the British landed four thousand men near Washington. (A twenty-one-gun salute was fired as they sailed past Washington's tomb at Mount Vernon.) The American army had no system of scouts, no means of gathering and assessing information in a systematic fashion. Scouts had not even been placed on the Chesapeake to count the number of British ships, and 'even Monroe, the secretary of state, rode as close as he dared to the enemy, trying to assess troop strength'.[114] On 24 August, twenty-six hundred British soldiers met six thousand Americans, made up of regulars, sailors and militia, at Bladensburg. An American officer later remarked that 'we were outflanked and defeated in as short a time as such an operation could well be performed'.[115] The American Mahan wrote nearly a century later that in this battle 'was realized Jefferson's ideal of a citizen soldiery, unskilled, but strong in the love of home, flying to arms to oppose an invader; and they had every inspiring incentive to tenacity, for they, and they only, stood between the enemy and the centre and heart of national life. The position they occupied, though unfortified, had many natural advantages; while the enemy had to cross a river which, while in part fordable, was nevertheless an obstacle to rapid action, especially when confronted by the superior artillery the Americans had.'[116] Nevertheless, terrified by the British soldiers, whom they also outnumbered by two to one, the mostly untrained Americans simply bolted.

It was only four o'clock in the afternoon when the battle ended. The British rested for two hours, and then marched the six miles to Washington. Meanwhile, according to Adams,

> the President [had] left Bladensburg battlefield toward two o'clock. He had already ridden in the early morning from the White House to the navy-yard, and thence to Bladensburg – a distance of eight miles at the least. He had six miles to ride, on a very hot August day, over a road encumbered by fugitives. He was sixty-three years old, and had that day already been in the saddle since eight o'clock in the morning, probably without food. Soon after three o'clock he reached the White House, where all was confusion and flight.[117]

Madison was concerned that his wife Dolly should get away safely; she had already done so, taking a few belongings with her and in particular cutting Gilbert Stuart's full-length and now iconic portrait of George Washington out of its frame, rolling it up, and handing it to men who would safeguard it. Meanwhile, at the State Department, the Declaration of Independence and the official diary of the Constitutional Convention were also spirited away. Before six o'clock, Madison crossed the Potomac River in a boat from the White House grounds, climbed into a carriage, and travelled westward, but not before giving orders that the bridge should be broken up, leaving others attempting to flee Washington marooned on the opposite side of the river.[118]

G.R. Gleig, then an officer in the Light Brigade, later described the burning of Washington: 'As it was not the intention of the British government to attempt permanent conquests in this part of America; and as the General [Ross] was well aware that, with a handful of men, he could not pretend to establish himself, for any length of time, in an enemy's capital, he determined to lay it under contribution, and to return quietly to the shipping.' By the normal rules of war, those who conquered were entitled to any public property they could take; Ross was suggesting that if the citizens paid ransom, as it were, the town would not be destroyed.

> Such being the intention of General Ross, he did not march the troops immediately into the city, but halted them upon a plain in its immediate vicinity, whilst a flag of truce was sent in with terms. But . . . scarcely had the party bearing the flag entered the street, than they were fired upon from the windows of one of the houses, and the horse of the General himself, who accompanied them, killed . . . All thoughts of accommodation were instantly laid aside; the troops advanced forthwith into the town, and having first put to the sword all who were found in the house from which the shots were fired, and reduced it to ashes, they proceeded, without a moment's delay, to burn and destroy every thing in the most distant degree connected with government. In this general devastation were included the Senate-house, the President's palace, an extensive dock-yard and arsenal', and a number of military buildings, equipment and stores. 'But, unfortunately, it did not stop here; a noble library, several printing offices, and all the national archives were likewise committed to the flames, which, no doubt the property of government, might better have been spared.

Nevertheless, British troops 'spared as far as was possible, all private property, not a single house in the place being plundered or destroyed, except that from which the general's horse had been killed; and those which were accidently thrown down by the explosion of the [gunpowder] magazines'.[119] Meanwhile, other British soldiers and naval forces were moving upriver, and took Alexandra on 27–8 August, seizing twenty-one ships as prizes.[120]

'The British then moved against Baltimore, home of much of the privateering fleet and hence a city that deserved, in the minds of many officers, to be either destroyed or compelled to pay an enormous tribute in order to be spared'.[121] Unlike the citizens of

Washington, however, those of Baltimore had supported the building of fortifications since 1813, and when news of the capture of Washington arrived, they worked night and day to complete them. The city was surrounded by entrenchments, with semicircular batteries at a number of points, mounted with cannon and connected by a line of works. The population also built a formidable line of redoubts, which would give some cover to the militia who were expected to defend the city. The British would therefore need many more troops than had sufficed to take Washington, even if aided by the Royal Navy. Roughly thirteen thousand troops plus nine hundred officers were ready to defend the city, but 'the fortifications chiefly decided the result. No army on either side during the war succeeded in storming works in face, except by surprise; and to turn the works of Baltimore a larger army was required than Ross had at his command.' The British had only about five thousand troops.[122]

At 3 a.m. on 12 September, the Royal Navy began landing troops at the mouth of the Patapsco River, and then carried on to Baltimore. The troops marched towards the city, and in a skirmish with some American riflemen Ross was killed. A few minutes later the British came upon six or seven thousand American soldiers blocking the way, protected by small lakes to either side and well wooded. Both sides had artillery and brave troops who stayed their fire until they were a hundred yards apart. Then the Americans fired, the British answered, and kept moving towards the American line. However, the British were experienced with the bayonet, and at twenty yards the American left flank fled. Thereafter, it was a rout.

On the evening of 13 September the British reached a ridge of hills which concealed Baltimore from view, and on which were stationed twenty thousand American troops, formidably entrenched. It was decided to wait until dark, and then, 'assisted by the frigates and bombs . . . to try the fortune of a battle'.[123] The problem was that it would be suicide to storm the Americans. However, the left of the American army extended to Fort McHenry, built upon the edge of the river. If the ships could shell and silence the fort, the Americans' flank would be turned, the British could push a column into their midst, and the Americans would be caught between two fires. But this all depended on the aid of the British fleet. It had begun a twenty-five-hour bombardment of Fort McHenry with artillery and rockets; it was this bombardment which was watched by Francis Scott Key, and which inspired his poem, 'The Defense of Fort McHenry', soon to be sung as 'The Star-Spangled Banner'. Unfortunately for the British, they could not get close enough to do much damage: the river was so shallow that only the very lightest craft could make their way within six miles of the town, and men from Baltimore had sunk twenty-four merchant vessels to block the way. The ships could therefore barely get within a shell's longest range of the fort. In addition, a squadron of American gunboats threatened their rear. A British officer stole around the right of the American lines to reach the river and make contact with the fleet; conducted to Admiral Cochrane, he was told that no effectual support could be given to the land forces, and that it would be wise to withdraw. The following day the soldiers marched back to the ships.[124] Baltimore had been saved, thanks to the geography of the river and its citizens' well-managed preparations.

In the autumn of 1814 the Royal Navy moved to attack the Gulf Coast in the south, arriving at Mobile Point in September. They hoped to seize the lower part of the Mississippi River and use it as a bargaining chip in future peace negotiations; they may also have mooted carving out a separate state, independent of the US. An assault against New Orleans had to await the end of the hurricane season, but after assembling 7,500 troops in Bermuda and the West Indies, the British arrived there in December. The American Major-General Andrew Jackson sent a flotilla of gunboats to guard one of the approaches, but Royal Marines in small ships' rowboats attacked them on 14 December and captured all of the American ships. The British then landed near the city with help from Spanish and Portuguese fishermen. 'However, unusually cold weather, combined with the deep swamps and difficult terrain, made the advance on the city very difficult, created serious supply problems, and contributed to a large number of deaths through illness and exposure.' On 23 December Jackson led a combined naval and land attack against the British camp, but the latter held their own in the 'confused night action', and the Americans pulled back.[125]

Jackson fortified the approach to New Orleans at the Rodriguez

Canal. On 28 December the British, led by their commander, Major-General Sir Edward Pakenham (Wellington's brother-in-law), made a reconnaissance in force against Jackson's line; they nearly broke one of the American flanks, but were forced to withdraw. On 1 January 1815, the British bombarded the Americans in an attempt to take out their guns, but they had too little ammunition, and American artillery fire inflicted considerable damage on the British position in return. The British continued towards New Orleans, continuously harried by the Americans. Then, on 8 January, the British soldiers were flung into a frontal assault against the American line behind the Rodriguez Canal; the Americans were sheltered by ramparts, and protected by the Mississippi on one side and a swamp on the other. The British overwhelmed one of the American batteries at bayonet point; but the main assault collapsed, not least because Colonel Mullens of the 44th Regiment forgot the scaling ladders, and Pakenham was killed. The British withdrew, having suffered their worst defeat in the war.[126] They, like the Americans, did not yet know that terms of peace had been agreed on Christmas Eve. Indeed, they continued their assaults, and in the final battle of the war took Fort Bowyer on 11 February in preparation for a move against Mobile. The next day, however, word of the peace treaty finally arrived.

Desultory attempts at beginning peace negotiations had been going on for most of the war. As early as August 1812, the Russian Chancellor, Count Rumiantzov, proposed mediation, with Tsar Alexander promising support for freedom of the seas. (The fact that Alexander and John Quincy Adams, the son of John Adams and since 1809 the American Minister to Russia, were close friends was significant.) However, Great Britain rejected the proposal out of hand: the Cabinet did not expect defeat and thus had no desire for mediation; nor was the possibility of a US–Russian common front in favour of neutral rights welcome. In Washington, President Madison in January 1813 also at first received the mediation proposal coolly, but by the following month the news of Napoleon's defeat in Russia had arrived, and the President knew that Britain's position had thereby vastly improved. Acceptance of the offer was announced in Washington, and peace commissioners appointed: they were John Quincy Adams; Albert Gallatin, the Secretary of the Treasury; and

James A. Bayard, a former Senator from Delaware. As for London, it was the opinion of the Secretary of State that although 'it is not known that Great Britain has acceded to the proposition, . . . it is presumed that she will not decline it'.[127]

London, however, continued to decline. Direct negotiations were different from Russian-controlled mediation, however, and in July Castlereagh sent such an offer to St Petersburg. Rumiantzov, still wishing to mediate, concealed this offer from the Americans for months. Finally, in November 1813, Castlereagh wrote to Secretary of State Monroe offering negotiations, although neutral rights would not be discussed. Madison and Monroe did not allow this reservation to prevent acceptance of the suggestion: news of American defeats on the Niagara frontier and of Napoleon's at Leipzig had arrived just before Castlereagh's offer, and it was accepted in January 1814.[128]

This time there were to be five American peace commissioners, with Adams, Gallatin and Bayard joined by Jonathan Russell, the former chargé d'affaires in London and now the newly appointed American Minister to Sweden, and Henry Clay, the Speaker of the House of Representatives. Adams was highly intelligent, experienced in diplomacy, pugnacious and self-righteous. Gallatin was the peacemaker, particularly between Adams and Clay; he was also good at reconciling the innumerable drafts of notes and reports.[129] Clay 'was ever the beguiling and affable politician',[130] who combined a responsible attitude to the negotiations with a penchant for card-playing. Bayard's coolness and tact were as important in settling disputes amongst his colleagues as in conducting negotiations with his opposite numbers. Russell wielded less influence than the others. They grated on each other and quarrels were the result, but they did not let these show to the British negotiators. In any case, they were as one in defence of US interests, although they sometimes differed as to just what these interests were.

The commissioners received their instructions from Monroe. Great Britain had to be convinced to abandon some of her claims to belligerent rights on the seas – for example, no blockade would be legal if there was no adequate force to enforce it, and the rights of neutrals were to be respected. Impressment – 'this degrading practice' – must cease, 'our flag must protect the crew, or the United

States, cannot consider themselves an independent Nation'. In exchange for this, the President was willing to exclude all British seamen from American vessels and to surrender those who had deserted in American ports.[131] The Commissioners were 'to bring to view, the advantages to both Countries which is promised, by a transfer of the upper parts and even the whole of Canada to the United States'.[132] Fundamentally, however, their object was 'to secure to the United States . . . a safe and honorable peace',[133] with the emphasis on the honorable. The venue for negotiations moved from St Petersburg, which Great Britain did not want, to Castlereagh's suggestion of London, which the Americans did not want, to Göteborg in Sweden in response to the Americans' wish for a neutral venue, and finally to Ghent in Belgium for convenience. Adams and Russell arrived on 24 June 1814, and were soon joined by the other three.

The British delegation arrived six weeks later. The first member was Vice-Admiral Lord Gambier, a veteran of forty-five years in the Royal Navy, whose experience included service in the War of Independence; he would play a minor role in the negotiations. (He was also vice-president of the English Bible Society and prayed a lot.) Secondly, there was Dr William Adams, a blunt Admiralty lawyer. The third member was Henry Goulburn, MP, Under-Secretary for War and the Colonies. He brought his wife and small child with him, but Mrs Goulburn was plagued with an unshakeable cold and childcare problems.[134] Goulburn was the most active of the negotiators, but because he doubted whether the Americans really wanted peace, he often held to a more rigid line than his superiors strictly wanted. Henry Adams was later to write that 'he had as little idea of diplomacy as was to be expected from an Under-Secretary of State for the colonies'. He also sometimes engaged in public arguments with the Americans, and especially with John Quincy Adams, himself a short-tempered and highly argumentative man. The positions and talents of the British delegation were substantially below those of the Americans, which was unsurprising because the senior British diplomats would be fully occupied in Paris and Vienna, working out Europe's future after Napoleon's defeat. However, the major thrust was clear: 'all Englishmen wanted to cripple the United

States. Their demands varied in detail but might, the *Times* said, "be couched in a single word, submission"'.[135]

Castlereagh's instructions to the British commissioners, dated 28 July, 'reflected the demands of the press'. The starting point was *uti possidetis* – that each belligerent would keep the territory it held at the end of the war. Gallatin had already written to Washington on 13 June, warning that fifteen to twenty thousand men were on their way to America, and that the best that could be expected from the negotiations was the *status quo ante bellum* – the situation before the beginning of the war. The British expected that victory would enable them to annex to Canada substantial portions of the northern US territories. The Americans were also required to concede at the outset as a *sine qua non* (that is, without which there would be no negotiations) that the Indians of the Old Northwest should be included, and that territory should be assigned to them with boundaries guaranteed by both the US and Great Britain. There were other points, particularly that the Americans should no longer fish in British waters nor land and dry fish on British territory, but these were the three major conditions of a peace treaty.[136]

The first meeting of the two delegations took place at 1 p.m. on 8 August 1814. There were the usual civilities, but then Goulburn laid out the points the British wished to discuss; the Americans did the same the following day. The British then made more specific demands and the Americans recognised that their answers to these demands – that they could not accept them – would end the negotiations. On 20 August the British sent an official note containing the demands, which the Americans forwarded to Washington. They then worked until 11 p.m. on 24 August, drafting and redrafting their answer, which they assumed would end any chance of peace, at the same time as the British were burning Washington. On the 25th, they sent the reply to the British commissioners, and began arrangements to return to America.

Castlereagh, in Paris, received letters from Goulburn describing the negotiations. He was annoyed that Great Britain had been put into the position of appearing to be engaged on a war of conquest, and that negotiations were breaking on that point. Castlereagh wrote to Bathurst, the Secretary for War and the Colonies and in charge of the negotiations in his absence, setting out the choice: to continue the war for territorial arrangements, or to make peace, claiming the fisheries and leaving the territorial questions to be discussed later. Should they take a chance on future victories and then formulate their demands based on circumstances? Prime Minister Lord Liverpool shared Castlereagh's disapproval; if there was a rupture in the negotiations, it had to be the fault of the Americans. Popular approval of the war was fragile, and opposition could easily grow. The Americans should be humbled, but after sixteen years of war, people – and taxpayers especially – were weary. From 1812 to 1815, government expenditure totalled £550,000,000, and although it had been necessary to fight Napoleon, most saw this outlay as draining the country's real strength to purchase military victory. Was conquest in America worth it? Even if it were, could it be guaranteed?[137]

The Americans remained in Ghent, but over the following two months negotiations went on at a slow pace, as the British hoped for news of victories. The victories at Bladenburg and Washington were encouraging, but they were counteracted by Baltimore and by the defeat at Plattsburg. The financial burden assumed ever more importance, until by November 1814, according to the Chancellor of the Exchequer, Nicholas Vansittart, 'Economy & relief from taxation are not merely the War Cry of Opposition, but they are the real objects to which public attention is turned'. Between March and November 1813 alone Great Britain had paid out more than eleven million pounds in subsidies to various European allies. The Prime Minister agreed, chafing under the 'prodigious expense' of a war in which there was little chance of a sweeping victory: 'We must expect . . . to hear it said that the property-tax is continued for the purpose of securing a better frontier for Canada.' By the end of November, again according to the Chancellor, public opinion was 'very indifferent . . . to the final issue of the War, provided it be not dishonorable'.[138]

There was another set of pressures on Great Britain, and especially on Castlereagh, during this period. In October he was in a contest with Tsar Alexander over the future of Poland, and early in November the Tsar and Castlereagh's brother Lord Stewart each spoke of war to the other. At the peak of this tension, the Cabinet decided not to pursue territorial claims against the US. Then there were the claims on Saxony by both Austria and Prussia. In short, during the whole of the negotiations with the US, Great Britain was urgently trying to defuse crises which might drag her into another European war. The discussions at Ghent, and British claims on the USA, declined in importance.[139]

The negotiations were a series of hard-fought battles; indeed, for the Americans, they were amongst themselves as much as with the British. But step by step, each side gave way on one issue after another. By mid-October, incredibly, the issue of impressment had disappeared: the British were not going to give it up, but the Americans decided that, with the war over, it would not again be an issue, at least not before they would be strong enough to resist it successfully. After four statements by the British and four American rejoinders, the issue of a guaranteed territory for the Indians also vanished. The Americans were not going to concede this, whilst the British learned that, after the Battle of the Thames, a number of their tribal allies had become allies of the Americans, and thus no longer deserved British concern. The question of Canada was rather easily answered. The Americans in Ghent (if not in Washington) knew that Great Britain would never cede it, and thus they never demanded it. Indeed, Clay had claimed the year before that the invasion of Canada had been 'not the end but the means' of putting pressure on Britain for the 'redress of injuries'.[140] It was to be the Duke of Wellington who soon put an end to the British claims.

On 3 November 1814, the Cabinet for the first time met to consider the Ghent negotiations. The European situation was threatening: the Polish crisis had almost reached its peak (it was on the following day that Tsar Alexander and Lord Stewart would threaten each other). In Paris, there were threats on the life of Wellington, who was the British Ambassador, and partly to get him out of Paris and partly to rescue the American situation, the Cabinet offered him the chief command in America. He did not refuse, but did not anticipate much success: there were enough troops, but the lack of naval superiority on the Great Lakes was crucial; without it, the Americans could not be prevented from invading Canada and nor could the British press southwards. He also told the Cabinet bluntly his opinion of their claims to *uti possidetis*: 'I think you have no right from the state of the war to demand any concession of territory from America . . . [Y]ou have not been able to carry it into the enemy's territory . . . and have not even cleared your own territory of the enemy on the point of attack. You cannot then . . . claim a cession of territory excepting in exchange for other advantages which you have in your power.'[141] As Henry Adams pointed out, 'after such an opinion from the first military authority of England, the British Ministry had no choice but to abandon its claim for territory'.[142]

The final conflict – and one which nearly reduced Henry Clay and John Quincy Adams to blows – was over the rights to the British fisheries for the Americans and the right to navigate the Mississippi for the British, which had been coupled in the treaty of 1783. Adams absolutely refused to admit that the Americans did not have a 'natural right' to continue to fish in British waters and dry fish on British soil, as they had done when subjects of the Empire. This was of interest only to Massachusetts, but, significantly, it had been Adams' father John who had fought to get it in the earlier treaty. For his part, Clay violently opposed a renewal of the Mississippi privilege: he, with most westerners, believed that it was Canadian traders who had encouraged Indian attacks on settlers, and he swore he would sign no treaty which contained this article. The patience and skill of Gallatin over the following month saved the situation; in the end, neither issue was mentioned in the treaty.[143]

The Treaty of Peace and Amity was curiously hollow. Five of the articles pointed out the lack of agreed boundaries around islands, on land and on the Great Lakes, and set out arrangements for commissions to survey and decide on them. The US agreed to cease hostilities against the Indians and to restore to them what they had enjoyed in 1811, provided that the Indians ceased hostilities against Americans. Both Britain and the US agreed to work together to abolish the slave trade. And that, essentially, was it. Nothing on impressment or neutral rights, nothing on ceding lands, nothing on fisheries or navigation down the Mississippi. Nevertheless, it can be argued that the treaty was a remarkable achievement for the US, a country internally divided, militarily weak and nearly bankrupt, and that without Great Britain's European difficulties, the outcome of both the war and the negotiations would almost certainly have been different. In the event, neither won and neither lost. As with the War of Independence, the US survived, and Great Britain had to accept that it was no longer a quasi-colony. The Americans, however, did not see the outcome as a stalemate. Because the news of the peace treaty arrived in the US shortly after the news of the Battle of New Orleans, Americans believed that they had won the war against Great Britain, the most powerful country in the world.[144] They were thus a match for any country and essentially unconquerable, and pride and patriotism blossomed accordingly. A separation movement in Massachusetts collapsed, along with the remnants of the Federalist Party. As for economic relations, during 1815 the US shipped more goods to the British Empire than in any year since 1807. For Great Britain, there was relief from what Castlereagh called 'the millstone of an American war'.[145] Lord Liverpool's ministry could now concentrate on the European threat – the Battle of Waterloo was shortly to take place.

III

The following years were diplomatically somewhat difficult for Great Britain. The final Great Power allies against France – the British, Austrian and Russian Empires, as well as the Kingdom of Prussia – agreed to meet periodically in Congress (as in the 1815 Congress of Vienna, which settled the terms of the Treaty ending the Napoleonic Wars) for the foreseeable future in order to sort out European problems before they reached the state of war. The difficulty was that the Continental Great Powers had a different interpretation from Britain as to what constituted a problem. For example, what about liberal unrest within a country? Or colonies which revolted against one of the European countries, as Spain's Latin American colonies were doing? Autocratic powers all, they decided that they had a right and a duty to intervene. In response, Castlereagh on 5 May 1820 issued a State Paper in which he laid out the principles which were to set Great Britain apart from the other Great Powers: '[T]his Alliance . . . was an union for the Reconquest and liberation of a great proportion of the Continent of Europe from the Military Domination of France . . . It never was however intended as an Union for the Government of the World, or for the Superintendence of the Internal Affairs of other States . . . We shall be found in our place when actual danger menaces the System of Europe, but this Country cannot, and will not, act upon abstract and speculative Principles of Precaution.'[146]

In August 1822, Castlereagh, in the throes of mental illness, slit his own throat with his razor, and George Canning succeeded him as Foreign Secretary. This had a certain irony: Canning had been Foreign Secretary from 1807 to 1809, when his intrigues against Castlereagh had led to his retirement from the Cabinet and a duel with Castlereagh, by whom he was wounded. (Indeed, Castlereagh's widow vigorously opposed Canning's appointment.) Canning had very little time for the so-called Congress System of the other Great Powers, and particularly for the 'Holy Alliance' of Russia, Prussia and Austria, and he rather supported the attempts of Spain's Latin American colonies to maintain their independence (although he also hoped that some of them, such as Mexico, would become monarchies). This was less from a heartfelt devotion to freedom than from a desire for the consolidation of British commercial dominance in Latin America. A French agent in Colombia wrote in 1823 that 'The power of England is without a rival in America; no fleets but hers to be seen; her merchandises are bought almost exclusively; her commercial agents, her clerks and brokers, are everywhere to be met with.'[147] But it was not just Spain which threatened British interests there. Early in 1823, France, which again had a Bourbon king, invaded Spain in order to defeat the constitutional government and restore the Bourbon Ferdinand VII to the throne. France also wished to place Bourbon princes on the thrones of ex-Spanish colonies such as Mexico, Colombia, Peru and Chile; her influence in Spain would facilitate this. In short, France wanted to succeed to the power in Latin America which Spain had lost. Russia, too, had a project to expand in Spanish America, in this case down the Pacific Coast, and it was this which triggered the attention and then activity of John Quincy Adams, since 1817 the US Secretary of State. It was Canning, however, who began the 'Great Flirtation', intended to produce a joint Anglo-American front against the other Great Powers.

Early in November 1822, Canning told the Duke of Wellington, by then Master-General of the Ordnance and a member of the Cabinet, that he was increasingly convinced that 'the American questions are out of all proportion more important to us than the European, and that if we do not seize and turn them to our advantage in time, we shall rue the loss of an opportunity never, never to be recovered'.[148] The fundamental question was, should Great Britain recognise the independence of the former Spanish colonies? Doing so would anger the Great Powers as well as Spain, so would there be compensating advantages? British commerce in the Caribbean was suffering greatly from the attacks of pirates, and could not be effectively protected unless there was co-operation amongst the new authorities along the coasts. As well, recognition of the new states would gain their gratitude and cement the commercial advantages the British already enjoyed. On the other hand, there was formidable opposition to recognition in the Cabinet and from the King. Any immediate hope that Canning might have had about his policy of recognition was destroyed by the French invasion of Spain, yet the Cabinet was united against any extension of French influence to Latin America. This was conclusive, and in August 1823, Canning decided to try another tack to contain the French: a joint Anglo-American diplomatic offensive.

The Americans, too, had contemplated recognition for some years. They had been held back by the desire not to antagonise Spain unduly until they had acquired Florida, and until the would-be republics had achieved some stability. In 1819 Spain ceded Florida to the US, whilst by 1822 the fortunes of war seemed to be against Spain. Therefore, in March 1822, President Monroe asked Congress for funds to support diplomatic posts in five of the new states: Argentina, Chile, Gran Colombia, Mexico and Peru. The Americans, too, were concerned about Great Power intentions towards Latin America, but by 1823 there was a further challenge in the hemisphere, a Russian Ukase (edict) of 7 September 1821. Largely because it was irritated by the activities of American fishing vessels, Russia decided to claim the Pacific Coast from Behring's Straits south to the fifty-first parallel, including part of Vancouver Island, and the adjacent sea to one hundred miles from the shore; all foreign vessels were forbidden to trade within this limit. Both the US and British governments protested vigorously,[149] but the former had a further reason beyond fish. The Secretary of State, John Quincy Adams, was a fervent nationalist, having proclaimed in a Cabinet meeting in 1819 that the world must be 'familiarized with the idea of considering our proper dominion to be the continent of North America'.[150] He would devote the remainder of his official life to this.

By a formal letter dated 31 March 1823, Canning informed the British Ambassador to Paris, Sir Charles Stuart, that, although the question of formal recognition by Great Britain of the independence of the would-be new states was still undecided, 'events appear to have substantially decided the question of the separation of these colonies from the Mother Country'. The King also 'disclaimed all intention of appropriating to himself the smallest portion of the late Spanish possessions in America'. The letter was then published. It was very favourably received in the United States, the effect being, according to the British Minister, Sir Stratford Canning, 'of making the English almost popular'.[151] Possibly because of this change in temperature, Canning responded to a suggestion made by Richard Rush, the American Minister to London, on 16 August that 'England would not remain passive' under any attempt by France to bring the ex-colonies under her control by asking Rush what he thought the American government 'would say to going hand in hand with England in such a policy? He did not think that concert of action would become necessary . . . This belief was founded, he said, upon the large share of the maritime power of the world which Great Britain and the United States held, and the consequent influence which the knowledge of their common policy, on a question involving such important maritime interests, present and future, could not fail to produce every where.'[152] Canning followed up this opening four days later in a private letter to Rush, in which he suggested that the two countries make a joint declaration of this nature: 'I am persuaded, there has seldom, in the history of the world, occurred an opportunity, when so small an effort, of two friendly Governments, might produce so unequivocal a good and prevent such extensive calamities.'[153] Then, on the 25th, at a dinner in Liverpool, Canning made an important comment while proposing the health of the

American Minister to Sweden, alluding to the two countries as united in their true interests 'by a common language, a common spirit of commercial enterprise, and a common regard for well-regulated liberty'. Dissensions had been forgotten, 'the force of blood again prevails, and the daughter and mother stand together against the world'.[154]

When the two met again on 28 August, Rush offered, although without instructions, that the US would 'not remain inactive under an attack upon the independence of those States by the Holy Alliance' – provided that Great Britain would herself immediately recognise their independence. Canning was unprepared for this, and responded coldly on the 31st.[155] Yet he remained apprehensive about the French, and on 18 September, speaking with some passion, he again raised the issue with Rush. The latter had previously pointed out that he had no instructions from his government; furthermore, the US tradition was not to become involved in European affairs. However, as he wrote to Adams the next day, 'words so remarkable could not fail to make a distinct impression upon me'. He told Canning, 'Let Great Britain immediately and unequivocally *acknowledge the Independence of the new States*. This will put an end to all difficulty.' Then Rush would stand upon his general powers as Minister and associate the US with the proposed declaration warning France against interfering in Latin America.[156] A week later Canning declared that the 'government felt great embarrassment as regarded the immediate recognition of these new states . . . and asked whether I could not give my assent to his proposals on a promise by Great Britain of *future* acknowledgment. To this intimation I gave an immediate and unequivocal refusal.' The US required a *previous* and explicit recognition as the price of its co-operation.[157] There was to be no Anglo-American diplomatic barrier.

Faced with Rush's refusal, Canning dropped the proposal.[158] Instead, he approached the Prince de Polignac, the French Ambassador in London, for a discussion about French policy towards Latin America. With a wonderfully adroit manoeuvre, he finessed the French, and extracted from de Polignac a Minute of their meeting in which the Ambassador declared unequivocally that France had no 'intention or desire' to take over any Spanish American territory, nor did they seek any exclusive advantages. Canning had not needed to state that British naval power would prevent any such French attempt. The Polignac Memorandum, which for some time tied the hands of the French Government, was an important diplomatic victory for Canning, and was widely acknowledged as such by all of the other Great Powers.[159]

Meanwhile, Rush's despatches of 19, 23 and 28 August had reached Washington on 9 October. On 17 October, President Monroe sent to ex-President Jefferson copies of the two despatches from Rush which contained the letters from Canning proposing Anglo-American co-operation. Monroe's own impression was 'that we ought to meet the proposal of the British govt', but he wanted Jefferson's comments, as well as those of ex-President Madison.[160] Jefferson responded on 24 October, stating, 'Great Britain is the nation which can do us the most harm of any one, or all on earth; and with her on our side we need not fear the whole world. With her then, we should most sedulously cherish a cordial friendship; and nothing would tend more to knit our affections than to be fighting once more, side by side, in the same cause.' He concluded by advising the acceptance of the British proposal, noting, however, that it might also prevent the US's acquisition of, for example, Cuba, a colony which he had always considered 'the most interesting addition which could ever be made to our system of States'.[161] Given the history of the previous quarter century, in which Jefferson had played a leading role, it must be said that this is a mildly astonishing letter. Madison agreed with Jefferson, writing on 30 October that 'It is particularly fortunate that the policy of G. Britain, tho' guided by calculations different from ours, has presented a co-operation for an object the same with ours. With that co-operation we have nothing to fear from the rest of Europe, and with it the best assurance of success to our laudable views. There ought not, therefore, to be any backwardness, I think, in meeting her in the way she has proposed'.[162]

Early in November, Monroe returned to Washington, and for the following several weeks he discussed a number of interrelated problems with four members of his Cabinet; Secretary of State Adams and Secretary of War John C. Calhoun dominated the discussions. 'Because they had only Rush's despatches, a handful of reports from other American diplomats in Europe, and some newspaper clippings to inform them, they were in a sense feeling their way in a dimly lit room.'[163] Monroe called a Cabinet meeting for 7 November to discuss Rush's despatches and Canning's proposals. Adams, nationalist and anglophobe, naturally knew immediately what Canning was up to: 'The object of Canning appears to have been to obtain some public pledge from the Government of the United States, ostensibly against the forcible interference of the Holy Alliance between Spain and South America; but really or especially against the acquisition to the United States themselves of any part of the Spanish-American possessions.' This was not the case, but Adams' antipathy drove his policy. Monroe himself 'was averse to any course which should have the appearance of taking a position subordinate to that of Great Britain'. Adams then had a brilliant idea: 'I remarked that the communications recently received from the Russian Minister . . . afforded . . . a very suitable and convenient opportunity for us to take our stand against the Holy Alliance, and at the same time to decline the overture of Great Britain. It would be more candid, as well as more dignified, to avow our principles explicitly to Russia and France, than to come in as a cock boat in the wake of the British man-of-war. This idea was acquiesced in on all sides.'[164]

Monroe continued to worry, showing Adams the letters of Jefferson and Madison on 15 November; Calhoun, too, was urging that the US not ignore the chance to save Latin America from attack. But Adams was robust: the threat was probably not real; if it was, it would not permanently succeed; and if the rebels were as weak as Calhoun feared, the US should not become involved. However, the following day, Rush's despatches of 2 and 10 October arrived, and these changed the whole tenor of the discussion. The President believed that Canning was now less alarmed by the French threat than he had appeared to be, and that he believed the danger of intervention had passed. As far as Adams was concerned, 'My own opinion is confirmed that the alarm was affected; that the object was to obtain by a sudden movement a premature commitment of the American Government against any transfer of the island of Cuba to France, or the acquisition of it by ourselves; and, failing in that point, he has returned to the old standard of British belligerency.'[165] The

President decided not to accept Canning's proposal, and on 30 November a polite refusal was sent. (Rush could not convey it to Canning until 1 February 1824.)[166]

Monroe did, however, decide to state publicly American policy. The occasion was his annual Message to Congress on 2 December 1823. The ideas of the three significant paragraphs – the non-colonisation doctrine, and America's policies of non-intervention and isolation – came from Adams, as did much of the language used to express them.[167]

> In the wars of the European powers in matters relating to themselves we have never taken any part, nor does it comport with our policy to do so. It is only when our rights are invaded or seriously menaced that we resent injuries or make preparation for our defense. With the movements in this hemisphere we are of necessity more immediately concerned . . . We owe it, therefore, to candor and to the amicable relations existing between the United States and those powers to declare that we should consider any attempt on their part to extend their system to any portion of this hemisphere as dangerous to our peace and safety. With the existing colonies or dependencies of any European power we have not interfered and shall not interfere. But with the Governments who have declared their independence and maintained it, and whose independence we have, on great consideration and on just principles, acknowledged, we could not view any interposition for the purpose of oppressing them, or controlling in any other manner their destiny, by any European power in any other light than as the manifestation of an unfriendly disposition toward the United States.

He noted that '[o]ur policy with regard to Europe . . . is, not to interfere in the internal concerns of any of its powers'. But 'it is impossible that the allied powers should extend their political system to any portion of either continent without endangering our peace and happiness'[168] – a warning to Russia, but also to Great Britain.[169]

The Continental European Great Powers at first assumed that

the Message was the result of a secret understanding between the US and Great Britain, but once they understood that this was not the case, they did not take Monroe's pronouncements particularly seriously. Canning's response was more equivocal. On the one hand, the declaration essentially reinforced the Polignac Memorandum; in this sense, Canning believed that he had gained as much from the President's pronouncement as he would have done from a joint declaration. But he strongly disapproved of two claims. First of all, he disliked the American attempt to make Latin America the preserve of republics, just as the Holy Alliance was trying to make Europe a preserve of monarchies – he preferred diversity and balance. More importantly, he refused absolutely to accept the attempted American prohibition of further colonisation in the hemisphere. Indeed, what about the conflicting British and American claims in Oregon (see below)? The US could not have enforced this doctrine against the might of the Royal Navy. Indeed, she made no attempt to do so in 1833, for example, when Britain annexed the Falkland Islands off the coast of Argentina. In fact, on commercial grounds, American officials encouraged the British annexation.[170]

Canning was also determined to prevent an American propaganda victory over Great Britain. Adams had taken every opportunity to remind representatives of the South American republics of how desirous the US was that they retain their independence, and how earnestly she was pressing Great Britain to acknowledge it. What Canning did was to launch an impressive publicity campaign. Copies of the Polignac Memorandum of 9 October (apparently one of the first documents to be lithographed) were circulated to British diplomats in Europe with instructions to make discreet use of them. Canning underlined the importance of emphasising the date (9 October), which demonstrated that the British had been much quicker than the Americans to warn off the French from intervening in South America. Copies were also given to the new consuls setting sail for South America in early 1824. 'They were told to use them to show "how early and how anxiously Great Britain declared against any project of bringing back the late Spanish colonies under the dominion of the mother country by foreign aid".' On 30 March, Canning laid the Memorandum before Parliament and had it published in the press; by midsummer, it was appearing in South American newspapers, where it was greeted with acclaim: 'The Chilean authorities even went so far as to describe Canning as the "Redeemer of Chile".' That the US had recognised the new republics whilst Great Britain had not was now of little account: much more important was that the Royal Navy could offer better protection than could the US. Furthermore, Great Britain recognised three of the new republics at the end of the year.

Adams therefore lost this particular battle for hearts and minds.[171] And, after all of this effort, it is perhaps surprising the extent to which the entire world, including the US, ignored the Monroe Doctrine: only when the US decided to enforce it near the end of the century did it gain any significance.

IV

An important focus of Anglo-American diplomatic relations for the remainder of the period was the North American continent. Fundamentally, the US wanted to spread as far and wide as possible, whilst Great Britain wanted to contain this expansion as much as possible. The most important issue for Britain was the Canadian boundary; a secondary concern was whether Texas remained a republic or joined the US. With regard to the boundary, good fences make good neighbours. With regard to Texas – given Great Britain's desire to create a balance of power on the continent, to safeguard Canada by limiting the power of the US – she wanted it to remain independent. Sometimes the strands remained separate, but by the mid-1840s they were intertwined, and war appeared to threaten. But nothing happened. Nor did an Anglo-American war break out during the American Civil War, although it came very close to doing so. Thereafter, the Treaty of Washington in 1871 not only largely settled the remaining questions of the boundary but resolved the causes of Anglo-American conflict arising from the Civil War.

A focus of the fighting during the War of 1812 had been the Great Lakes, and at the end of that war both sides were madly building ships, especially on Lake Ontario. Peace (merely a truce, according to John Quincy Adams) saw continuing suspicion on both sides, and each kept watch on the other's naval and military activities. Many Britons and Canadians argued that since the US could more easily throw substantial military forces into any conflict, Britain had to maintain naval superiority. Shortly after the end of the war, Congress was swept by a gust of economy, and on 27 February 1815 it ordered the dismantling of most of the ships on the Lakes. However, mostly false rumours from London indicated that Great Britain intended to keep building. Consequently, in November 1815, John Quincy Adams, then Minister in London, was instructed 'to propose ... such an arrangement respecting the naval forces to be kept on the Lakes by both governments, as will demonstrate their pacific policy and secure their peace'.[172]

Lord Castlereagh, then Foreign Secretary, was more than receptive. He was 'the first British statesman to recognize that the friendship of the United States was a major asset to Britain, and to use in his relations with her a language that was neither superior nor intimidating'.[173] Castlereagh believed, as he himself wrote, that 'there are no two States whose friendly relations are of more practical value to each other, or whose hostility so inevitably and so immediately entails upon both the most serious mischiefs'.[174] He rejected the idea that Great Britain had to maintain naval superiority on the Lakes, not least because it would be ruinously expensive, and told Adams that he would look favourably upon any reasonable American proposal. President Madison, aware that this would weaken Britain's ability to defend Canada, was intensely suspicious of Castlereagh's motives, as was Secretary of State Monroe. At one point in May 1816, when negotiations in Washington seemed to flag, Madison threatened that unless Great Britain ceased her (non-existent) building programme, Congress would probably require that the US herself resume ship construction.[175]

Finally, in August 1816, agreement was reached: the naval forces on each side would be limited to one ship on Lake Champlain, one on Lake Ontario, and two more on the upper Lakes; construction would cease; and the ships would be used only to enforce revenue laws. These were American stipulations and Great Britain made the concessions, but Castlereagh knew that American superiority on the continent would only increase relative to that of Canada, and thus he believed that it was better to come to an agreement. London was very dilatory in accepting it, however – Castlereagh wrote to the British Minister in Washington, Sir Charles Bagot, that the summer holidays would delay approval – and this reactivated Monroe's simmering distrust. 'Not until the end of January, 1817, did Castlereagh, with embarrassed apologies, forward his government's official assent.' The Americans, however, were equally dilatory, and Senate approval of the Rush–Bagot Agreement only came in April 1818. The result was not exactly transforming: although there was virtual disarmament on the Great Lakes, both sides continued to fortify the land frontier.[176]

This was the next question: where, precisely, was the frontier between the US and British North America?[177] The treaty ending the War of 1812 had pointed out the lack of agreed boundaries, and set out arrangements for commissions to survey and decide on them. As it happened, the questions of the boundaries were taken together with negotiations for a commercial treaty, the decades-old problem of compensation for slaves taken during the Revolution, and control of a small settlement at the mouth of the Columbia River. A combination of rampant American nationalism and suspicion of Great Britain, the need for Castlereagh to give priority to European affairs when rationing his time, and the complicated group of topics made for a confused beginning.

On 3 January 1818, Richard Rush, the American Minister to London, handed to Castlereagh a set of proposals for negotiation, which the latter laid before the Cabinet. Castlereagh and Rush then met on 1 February and touched on all of the topics, but Castlereagh then had to concentrate on European matters – as Rush noted later, 'he had the whole European relations of Britain at that time in his hands, with those of the continent also to discuss' (the Congress at Aix-la-Chapelle was imminent) – and turned the negotiations over to others. In July President Monroe, wishing to strengthen the American team, instructed Albert Gallatin, now Minister to France, to join Rush in London. On 27 August negotiations began in earnest.[178]

Rush spoke truly when he wrote about the negotiations that 'the subjects were multifarious. All demanded attention; some, copious discussions. These, with the documents at large, the protocols, the projets and counter-projets, debated and modified by the scrutiny of each side, would present a mass of matter through which the diplomatist or politician might perhaps wade; but be little attractive to any one else.' Suffice it to say, then, that 'neither side yielded its convictions to the reasoning of the other. This being exhausted, there was no resource left with nations disposed to peace, but a compromise', and on 20 October 1818 Rush and Gallatin transmitted to Adams the text of the Convention which they had that day concluded with the British negotiators.[179]

The plenipotentiaries agreed to extend a commercial convention of 1815 regulating Anglo-American trade, to a temporary settlement of the fisheries question (as noted above, an obsession of both John Adams and his son John Quincy Adams), to compensation for the slaves, and to an arrangement over the Columbia River. The most important decision, however, was to draw the Canadian–American boundary from the Lake of the Woods to the 'Stony Mountains' (the Rockies) along the forty-ninth parallel. At the outset, Gallatin had made a suggestion of major importance: to delimit the claims of both the US and Great Britain to the Oregon Country by drawing the border along the forty-ninth parallel all the way to the Pacific. The British refused, and the result was an agreement on joint occupation for ten years. The American offer could be seen as amazing, in that it limited American claims, but there are two possible explanations: the first is that a number of Americans, including President Monroe, anticipated that the Oregon Country would constitute an independent republic, since it was so distant from the United States, and arguing over a border was therefore not worth the effort; the second is that the expectation was that American settlers would in due course flow into the area and therefore, as Rush put it, 'time is, for the United States, the best negotiator'.[180]

V

The period from the mid-1820s to the 1840s was one of serious Anglo-American animosity. In Great Britain, dislike of the US was a habit of many, but contempt also stemmed from the Conservative Party's fight against political reform, which encouraged a dim view of American 'mobocracy', particularly in view of the increased political influence of backwoodsmen from the states across the Appalachian Mountains, symbolised by the election of Andrew Jackson from Tennessee as President in 1828. The growth of tension between the northern and southern states encouraged ideas of a future break-up of the US. As the British Minister to Washington wrote in 1827, it was 'with reason that an opinion is generally entertained in Europe of the instability of the Union between these states so jealous of the distinct and separate sovereignty which they exercise within the limits of their own territories'.[181] This opinion would greatly influence the British response to the conflict over Texas. In the US, dislike and distrust of Great Britain was bred in the bones of most Americans. This was only aggravated by the dozens of critical books and articles written about the Republic by British travellers (see Chapter 4).

Real conflict erupted in the late 1830s, in both the South and the North. In the former, the focus was Texas. Since its independence in 1821, Mexico had encouraged Americans to move into its northern province, Texas. By 1830, they numbered thirty thousand, and the Mexican government, fearing loss of control, imposed restrictions. The Americans disliked these, and feared that the government would enforce in Texas the Mexican law of 1829 against slavery (about a quarter of the Americans owned slaves, and many others wished to do so). Resistance to the new regime culminated in a declaration of Texan independence in March 1836. That September a plebiscite was held over whether to join the US, and the vote in favour was overwhelming. In March 1837 the US recognised the Texas Republic, and in August it was proposed that Texas be annexed. As it happened, though, this was a bad moment because of growing sectional conflict in the US between 'slave states' and 'free states', and thus the suggestion to admit what would be another slave state came to nothing. But the continuing threat of a Mexican counter-attack encouraged the Texas Republic to turn to Great Britain for support; it is also likely that this was done in the hope that it might stimulate the Americans to look more favourably upon annexation. In 1837 a Texan agent arrived in Great Britain seeking recognition, but this was delayed until June 1842. For one thing, it was a 'ramshackle republic',[182] with ten different capitals in ten years; as Lord Palmerston, the Foreign Secretary, wrote to a colleague in October 1837, 'We cannot pretend to exert much influence on the destiny of Texas; ... we must see whether the Band of outlaws who occupy Texas will be able to constitute themselves into such a community as it would be decent for us to make a Treaty with.'[183] The British government hoped to increase its influence in both Texas and Mexico, but above all, they wanted a peaceful solution to the crisis. (They had competing concerns: the First Afghan War [1839–42], the second Egyptian Crisis [1839–41] and the First Opium War with China [1839–42].) Palmerston told the Mexican government in 1840 that its hope of recovering Texas was 'visionary'; but for that government, giving up the idea of recovering Texas was politically impossible. On 28 June 1842, the British government finally ratified a Treaty of Amity and Commerce with Texas. Partly through this, the British hoped that the development of the Texan cotton industry would undermine the American monopoly and that an independent Texas would help to balance American power, thereby lessening the threat to Canada. In fact, the treaty vastly increased the chances of Anglo-American conflict on the US's southern border.[184]

The British Consul-General and chargé d'affaires to the Republic of Texas, Captain Charles Elliot, was instructed to try to mediate between Texas and Mexico, but this proved impossible; indeed, on 18 April 1844, the Secretary of State, John C. Calhoun, wrote to Richard Pakenham, the British Minister to Washington, defending slavery as a positive good and announcing that Texas was being annexed as a counter-measure against plotting by British supporters of the abolition of slavery. This upset the northern states, and his treaty of annexation was defeated in the Senate. In the autumn the President of Mexico agreed to the urgings of Great Britain that Texan independence should be recognised, on the proviso that it must promise not to join another country; the Colorado River would be the frontier. Great Britain and France were to guarantee the border, and instructions to Elliot arrived on 20 March 1845.

However, a day or two before, he and the French chargé d'affaires had heard that Congress had passed a resolution in favour of annexation. Elliot and the French diplomat set out posthaste for the Texan capital to urge the government to accept the Mexican offer. This might have happened, but the French government then withdrew its offer of a guarantee, and by May 1845 the British Foreign Office regarded US annexation as inevitable. It was: on 4 July, Texas agreed to annexation and in December Congress ratified it.[185]

In the north of the continent, conflict was triggered by a Canadian drive for independence from Great Britain, something with which most Americans sympathised. In November 1837, rebellion broke out against the British regime, and recruitment quickly began on the American side of the border, where sympathy for the rebels was noisy and widespread. On 30 December, a Canadian government force crossed the Niagara River and burned the American ship the *Caroline*, which had been used to supply the rebels.[186] The British government was already bringing ten thousand militia into active service and planning to increase the regular soldiery from two thousand to ten thousand; when news of the *Caroline* incident arrived in February, London added a further two regiments.

By 1840, the number of regulars in Canada was nearly 11,500. Although this increased military strength was aimed primarily at ending the rebellion and calming the border, it also reflected a growing apprehension of war with the US. As Henry Fox, the British Minister to Washington, wrote on 15 March 1838 to Admiral Sir Charles Paget, the Commander-in-Chief of the North American Squadron, 'I do not wish to excite unnecessary alarm; but I would venture, confidentially, to recommend to Your Excellency, so to regulate the situation of your squadron, as to render it most available in the event of war breaking out . . . if we should unfortunately be forced into a war with the Americans, it would be of immense importance for us to be enabled to commence that war by an astounding blow upon their navigation and commerce.'[187] From the other direction, during 1838, several attacks on Canada were staged from the American side of the border. It was very difficult for President Martin Van Buren to take effective action: the rebels were popular, his constitutional powers were limited, and the available military forces were derisory. However, military efforts were made, and as the revolt petered out in the second half of the year, 'American opinion generally began to appreciate that most Canadians did not wish to join the Republic'.[188]

However, the whole northern frontier remained dangerous. In March 1839, news arrived in Washington of the 'brawling between rival lumberjacks [that] escalated into the "Aroostook War" over the almost unpopulated area of extreme northern Maine, where the boundary with New Brunswick was disputed'. Only at this point did the American government seriously consider the military implications of war with Great Britain, and recognise that they were seriously underprepared. Late in 1840, Alexander McLeod, a Canadian who boasted in New York that he had been one of the party who had boarded the *Caroline* in 1837 and killed one of her crew, was promptly arrested, charged with arson and murder, and threatened with execution. Great Britain protested that the arrest was a violation of international law, and Foreign Secretary Palmerston told Andrew Stevenson, the American Minister in London, 'not officially but as a Private Friend', that 'if McLeod is executed there must be war'. Fortunately, after eleven months the jury let everyone off the hook by acquitting him.[189] This opened the way for Great Britain and the US to clear up other disagreements.

The focus of negotiations was what President Andrew Jackson, in his Annual Message of 3 December 1833, had called 'the interesting question of our north-eastern boundary'. The cause was the lack of geographical knowledge of the area when the treaty ending the War of Independence was drafted, giving rise to several ambiguities. There had been an attempt to sort things out by commissions or arbitration after the War of 1812, but these had foundered, as had a further attempt in the early 1830s. The Aroostook Valley fell within the disputed area, and the eponymous 'war' encouraged the attempt to establish the border once and for all. In September 1841 Palmerston was succeeded as Foreign Secretary by the Earl of Aberdeen, mild-mannered, hard-working, and a fervent believer in Anglo-American amity. He appointed as British plenipotentiary Lord Ashburton, the former Alexander Baring, head of the rich and powerful merchant (investment) bank, the House of Baring, which had huge interests in the US. Ashburton also had an American wife, and a tremendous knowledge of business and American affairs; furthermore, he had negotiated the financing of the Louisiana Purchase in 1803, and was on friendly terms with the Secretary of State, Daniel Webster. He seemed ideal.[190] Although he believed that the Americans made 'troublesome neighbours' with whom 'nothing [was] more easy than to get into war ... any morning with a very good cause', he also believed that a good Anglo-American relationship was vital for both countries. Webster shared that belief.[191]

Unsurprisingly, the two men soon reached an agreement. The most difficult clause was that on the northern Maine boundary. The Maine legislators were adamant about what they considered to be their rights, and Webster was reluctant to go ahead without their consent. Because of the mutual trust between Ashburton and Webster, however, the two entered, 'while in the preliminary stages of the Maine discussions, into a virtual conspiracy with each other to disarm the intransigeants on that issue in each other's public and to make possible a compromise settlement.' The final agreement was a compromise which broadly favoured the British, and the other decisions were seen as equitable.[192]

Of much more moment, and the cause of much more conflict, was the Oregon Territory, by which was meant almost all of the western part of North America between California and Alaska. It will be recalled that in 1818 Gallatin and Rush had suggested that the US–Canadian border be continued to the Pacific Ocean on the forty-ninth parallel. The British had refused, since they would lose the southern tip of Vancouver Island and Puget Sound, and a joint occupation for ten years was agreed; it could be denounced by either side with a year's notice. Shortly after his inauguration on 4 March 1845, President James K. Polk instructed the Secretary of State, James Buchanan, to repeat to Richard Pakenham, the British Minister to Washington, the offer made by the previous administration to settle at the forty-ninth parallel. Holding to the letter of his instructions, rather than adopting the more pacific suggestions made to him by Foreign Secretary Aberdeen in private, Pakenham rejected the offer, refusing even to forward the offer to London.[193] Polk then withdrew it, gave the required notice, and in April 1846 denounced the

Joint Occupation. (Earlier, he had claimed the whole of the territory in his Inaugural Address.)[194]

Why the change? First of all, the idea that the US's 'Manifest Destiny' was dominion over the entire continent had an unbreakable grip on the public imagination, and the election of 1844 had been partly fought on the issue. The Democrats' election manifesto had included the claim that 'our title to the whole Territory of Oregon is clear and unquestionable': this was trumpeted by the Senator from Ohio, William 'Foghorn Bill' Allen, as 'Fifty-four forty or fight!'[195] Southern expansionists who wanted Texas and whatever else they could get supported Northern expansionists who wanted all of the Oregon Territory; they expected that the latter would reciprocate. Secondly, in the early 1840s, American settlers had begun to arrive in droves, and by 1844 there were several thousand of them in the Willamette Valley. Thirdly, the area which both nations claimed included valuable ports on Puget Sound and on the tip of Vancouver Island, and Polk was somewhat obsessive about the need for the US to gain ports on the Pacific Ocean (California, then Mexican territory, was annexed only in 1850). And finally, there was great expectation that the railways would soon reach the Pacific Northwest, linking its seaports with the rest of the US.

London wanted the border to run along the Columbia River, which would have placed it roughly between today's Washington and Oregon states; the US had offered a border between Washington and British Columbia. In November 1845 Polk heard from London that Aberdeen favoured a peaceful approach, and regretted Pakenham's rejection of the administration's proposal. This, of course, only encouraged the President's hard line. The following month, the British seemed pliable, and Polk continued his demand for most if not all of the Oregon Territory; he asked Congress to extend American laws to Oregon and recommended a military build-up (this was inconsistent, since his budget called for a reduction in military spending). In late January 1846, Aberdeen learned that on 3 January Buchanan had rejected a new offer of arbitration from Pakenham. Already disgusted with Polk's bombastic threats, Aberdeen called in the American Minister to London, Louis McLane, and 'complained of the terms and manner in which it had been declined'. He then warned him that he would withdraw his opposition to preparations 'founded upon the contingency of war with the United States'; these would be preparations 'not only for the defence of the Canadas, but for offensive operations', including 'the immediate equipment of thirty ships of the line, besides steamers and other vessels of war'.[196] Great Britain then did indeed begin active preparations in Canada.

Meanwhile, in Washington: on 29 January 1846, a few days after having received a rather mild warning from Aberdeen, Buchanan authorised McLane to tell the Foreign Secretary 'cautiously and informally' that whilst the President still claimed the whole Territory, he would nevertheless submit to the Senate a new offer on the lines of that made to Pakenham the previous summer.[197] On 26 February, after receiving word of Aberdeen's more stern warning, there was an urgent Cabinet meeting; the invitation to Great Britain to settle at the forty-ninth parallel was revived, accompanied by a private letter from Buchanan assuring Aberdeen that the Senate would accept the compromise. (Polk had written in his diary on 21 February that the news from London 'was not altogether of so pacific a character as the accounts given in the English newspapers had led me to believe'.[198]) The problem for the US was that she was woefully unprepared for war with Great Britain. There were only 480 men on the northern frontier; even worse was the navy, with only one ship of the line, six frigates, and another twenty vessels of various types. The real weakness was the shortage of steamships: the US had seven steamships, mounting some thirty-nine guns, whilst Great Britain had 146, mounting 698 guns. Polk's problem here was that his party had always been against the creation of an ocean-going navy, and thus it would be embarrassing to ask Congress for one now. (Only in December, in the face of war with Mexico, did Congress provide the funds for a few ships.[199])

In London, Aberdeen produced a new proposal, giving up the line of the forty-ninth parallel to the US and thereby losing Washington State, but reserving the whole of Vancouver Island and the free navigation of the Columbia River. Consequently, the US would receive the lion's share of the Oregon Territory, including the harbours of Puget Sound. This proposal arrived in Washington on 6

June 1846, and at the end of the month Aberdeen learned that Polk had passed it on to the Senate.[200] Democrats in the South were not interested in vast territories in the North, but they were concerned that British markets for their cotton remained available; as a result, intransigent Northern senators could not muster the required votes to reject it. In the event, more than the necessary two-thirds of the Senate approved the draft treaty immediately with no changes, and the Treaty in Regard to Limits Westward of the Rocky Mountains was signed on 15 June.[201] The British had lost the chance to establish a balance of power in North America as some protection for Canada. The United States could now concentrate on a war with Mexico, at the end of which she controlled all of the territory from Canada to Mexico and from the East to the West coast.

What followed was a drive for expansion and power by the US into Central America and the Caribbean, and a determined defence by Great Britain of her possessions and sea power.[202] The Clayton–Bulwer Treaty of 1850, by which it was agreed that neither country was to fortify or exercise exclusive control over any future canal linking the Atlantic and Pacific oceans, calmed the most dangerous rivalry. However, the dislike – even hatred – and distrust engendered by this competition ensured that an episode during the American Civil War nearly precipitated another Anglo-American war. But this episode and other conflicts were finally resolved in 1872, and whilst the two countries clashed thereafter, war between them was never again a truly serious option for either side.

VI

The victory of the Republican candidate, Abraham Lincoln, in the election of November 1860 was the signal for the secession of a number of southern states from the United States. In February 1861 they formed the Confederate States of America, and in June, a few miles outside Washington, D.C., the Confederates won the Battle of Bull Run, the first pitched battle of the War Between the States. As a result, most European states assumed that the South would win, with the result that there would be at least two countries where before there had existed one. This was seen as rather a good thing, since it would undermine the growing power of the US. Great Britain would not mind the grave weakening of a competitor, while the French welcomed the opportunities this promised for an expansion of their influence in Latin America.

Most British politicians and newspaper editors had welcomed Lincoln's election, seeing it as a barrier to the march of slavery. However, once it became clear that his priority was to save the Union, he was dismissed as just another supporter of empire. As the Foreign Secretary, Lord John Russell, said in October, slavery was not the issue between the North and the South: rather, they were 'contending, as so many States of the Old World have contended, the one for empire and the other power'.[203] There was also the economic issue: the South backed low tariffs, the North protectionism. There was, therefore, no reason of either British national interest or morality to support the North as a matter of course. Indeed, conservatives welcomed the dissolution of a republic – as one peer commented, 'I see in America the trial of Democracy and its failure' – whilst R.J.M. Blackett has argued that support for the Confederacy was more widespread than earlier historians had recognised.[204] Nevertheless, there were still many supporters of the North; it was just that most doubted that they would win.

What conditioned the North's reaction to Great Britain during the Civil War was the reception of Confederate emissaries by Russell in May 1861, and his announcement that Britain recognised the belligerency of the Confederacy, and would remain neutral in the conflict. This was the announcement that greeted the newly arrived American Minister to London, Charles Francis Adams – John Quincy Adams' son – when he stepped off the boat at Liverpool on 13 May. As his own son, his private secretary, later wrote, 'no one in England – literally no one – doubted that Jefferson Davis [President of the Confederacy] had made or would make a nation, and nearly all were glad of it, though not often saying so'. As the philosopher John Stuart Mill, a supporter of the North as a force against slavery, wrote a few years later, 'it may be imagined with what feelings I contemplated the rush of nearly the whole upper and middle classes of my own country, even those who passed for Liberals, into a furious pro-Southern partisanship: the working classes, and some of the literary and scientific men, being almost the sole exceptions to the general frenzy'.[205] Furthermore, Henry Adams later wrote, 'the Governments and society of Europe, for a year at least, regarded the Washington Government as dead'.[206] It would therefore be foolish to alienate the South. However, it would also be foolish to push this view on the North: Canada was a hostage, and the Secretary of State, William H. Seward, was a ferocious Anglophobe and bellicose (the bellicosity calmed down, but the Anglophobia did not). He was matched, possibly, by Foreign Secretary Russell, who believed that 'Americans were bullies – brash, boorish, crafty, pushy, cowardly, and entirely unamenable to logical argument or conciliatory persuasion.'[207] Only with the Union victory at the Battle of Gettysburg on 4 July 1863 did Great Britain generally accept that the North would win and the US survive.

This was the context in which three great Anglo-American crises were played out: the *Trent* affair; the British desire to mediate; and the *Alabama* depradations and subsequent claims for compensation. On 8 November 1861, Captain Charles Wilkes of the USS *San Jacinto* stopped the British mail packet, the *Trent*, off Cuba. It was carrying two Confederate agents, James Murray Mason and John Slidell, who had managed to slip through the Union blockade and were *en route* to Great Britain to represent the Confederacy. Against international law, and the advice of his subordinates, Wilkes seized the envoys and their secretaries and carried them off to Boston and prison. In Washington, the House of Representatives urged the President to give Wilkes a gold medal; in Great Britain, there was 'an explosion of feeling . . . the expectation, which prevailed for some weeks, of war with the United States, and the warlike preparations actually commenced on this side'.[208] Certainly Prime Minister Palmerston seriously considered sending the Royal Navy's Channel Squadron across the Atlantic, and the government did send another 10,500 regular soldiers to the Canadian frontier, with the possibility of more if required.[209] The assumption was that peace was most likely if the Americans realised that the British were prepared for war and, as Charles Francis Adams wrote to William Seward on 12 December, 'all the preparations for warfare are going on at the different Depôts and magazines with great energy'. True, the Prime Minister and his colleagues thought it would be madness for the North to provoke war at such a time, but this, they thought, 'was just the sort of insanity to be expected from Americans'. The British government was supported by public opinion: according to Adams, 'the feeling is running very high on this side, and little confidence is entertained of the possibility of preserving peaceful relations'; there was 'an almost universal demand for satisfaction for the insult and injury'. One historian reckons that 'the *Trent* crisis was the most dangerous single incident of the Civil War and perhaps in the whole course of Anglo-American relations since 1815'.[210]

The British government sent a protest of unusual bluntness, and demanded the release of the four men. Although Russell did not press Seward for an immediate reply, he instructed Lord Lyons, the British Minister at Washington, to make clear to Seward that if his response was not satisfactory, the result would be a break in relations.[211] But Seward and Lyons appear to have found a means to defuse the situation, with the latter making every effort to give the former the time he required to arrange matters satisfactorily. Seward convinced Lincoln that Wilkes' action should be repudiated, pointing out that international law would then be upheld and that the US would thereby be acting just as it wished Great Britain and other nations to act. Possibly he was influenced by Adams' descriptions of the 'absolute torrent of warlike preparations' in Great Britain. His reply to Lyons' demands reached London on 8 January 1862, by which time the four men had been released. Interestingly, the response in one respect was similar on both sides. With regard to the *Trent* case, Adams insisted that 'the apparent victory of Great Britain involves in reality the necessary surrender of one of her most odious assumptions of power over the ocean'; on the other hand, Britain more often than not respected the inadequate blockade proclaimed by the North on the grounds that this only strengthened the case for the Royal Navy to continue to use similar (but more effective) measures during time of war.[212]

The second crisis arose from the proposal for mediation made in a speech at a banquet in Newcastle on 7 October 1862 by William Gladstone, the Chancellor of the Exchequer, in which he claimed that 'Jefferson Davis and the leaders of the South have made an army; they are making, it appears, a navy; and they have made, what is more than either – they have made a nation.'[213] He called on the Union to 'drink the cup'. A few weeks earlier, Palmerston and Russell had agreed 'that the time is come for offering mediation to the United States Government, with a view to the recognition of the independence of the Confederates', but the success of the Union army at turning back the Confederate invasion of the North at the Battle of Antietam on 17 September had undermined the conviction that the South was bound to win, and the project was laid aside. Furthermore, Lincoln's Proclamation of Emancipation of the Slaves on 22 September also encouraged public support for the North. Gladstone, however, remained concerned. Yet the response to his speech was, to him, unexpected, suggesting a 'widespread disinclination to extend recognition to the South at this time', although Russell resumed his support for the idea. Hearing reports of this, Seward instructed Adams to warn the government that an offer of mediation would be considered a declaration of war. Palmerston and the Cabinet then decided that 'we must continue merely to be lookers-on till the war shall have taken a more decided turn'. In mid-November the plan was shelved for good.[214]

The third major crisis of the war was that relating to a Confederate ship, the *Alabama*. Under both domestic and international law, British firms could sell arms to the belligerents, and both North and South took advantage of this. Ships were more complicated, though: shipbuilding for belligerents was allowed only if the ships were not armed; consequently, they were built, and then outfitted with guns elsewhere. In the case of the Confederacy, most of the ships had careers as commerce-raiders (privateers). One such was the *Alabama*, currently being completed in Liverpool. Adams made a number of increasingly urgent representations to the British government, and whilst Russell and his colleagues were sympathetic to his complaints, they could not find a legal means of stopping the building of what was, on the surface, a perfectly legal ship. On 24 July 1862 Adams sent a letter to Russell containing detailed information about the ship and included counsel's opinion that, under English law, the ship should be detained. On Saturday 26 July, Russell was given the letter and he quickly referred the case to the Queen's Advocate, Sir John Harding, for an opinion. On that same Saturday, James Bulloch, the southern agent in charge of acquiring ships for the Confederate navy, 'received information from a private but most reliable source, that it would not be safe to leave the ship in Liverpool another forty-eight hours'.[215] Fortunately for Bulloch, Sir John had just gone insane, and his wife, not surprisingly, neglected to send the packet back to the Foreign Office until Monday the 28th. That evening, the Attorney-General and the Solicitor-General considered the papers, and advised that the ship should indeed be detained. But that same evening, she had already left the Birkenhead docks, with a brass band and well-dressed ladies on her deck, ostensibly for a few hours of steaming trials. However, once the ship reached Holyhead, the musicians and passengers were put ashore. She then raced out into the Atlantic, evaded the USS *Tuscarora*, which was waiting for her, and steamed to the Azores, where the guns and ammunition which would convert her into a Confederate cruiser had already been delivered by British merchant ships.

During her subsequent career, the *Alabama* 'captured and burned ten Union ships in the mid-Atlantic, sank the USS *Hatteras* in an engagement of only thirteen minutes in the dark in the Gulf of Mexico, turned down the coast of Brazil towards the Cape of Good Hope and then sailed around the world, capturing another eighty-two merchant ships in the process'. She was finally defeated and sunk off Cherbourg in June 1864. Most of her crew, including the captain, were picked up by spectators, including the owner of a British yacht.[216]

The end of the Civil War on 9 April 1865 left serious conflicts between the US and Great Britain, not least the issue of claims for compensation arising from the depredations of the *Alabama*. Over the period of her career, Adams had kept a detailed record of the losses and of the claims arising from them. By 1869, these had still not been settled, and President Ulysses S. Grant told the British Minister to Washington, Edward Thornton, that 'the *Alabama* claims were the only grave question which the United States had at issue with any nation'. Indeed, American public opinion, or at least the Northern section, remained incensed about the losses caused by the

ship and the encouragement it had given to the South, and they
fully supported the US government's determination that Great
Britain should make reparation for those losses: 'the ghost of the
departed *Alabama* was poisoning Anglo-American relations'.[217]
Senator Charles Sumner, Chairman of the Senate Committee on
Foreign Relations, made a speech on 13 April 1869 during which he
claimed that Britain owed $15 million to private Americans for their
losses, and $110 million for the losses to the nation, including the
rise in the rate of marine insurance and the decrease in the tonnage
of ships flying the American flag. Not surprisingly, Lord Clarendon,
the British Foreign Secretary, intimated to the American Minister in
London that the speech had had an 'unfortunate effect' on the government and people of Great Britain.[218]

The deadlock was broken in November 1870 by the suggestion of
Lord Tenterden, the Assistant Under-Secretary in the Foreign
Office, that a joint commission to decide how to deal with the claims
be set up.[219] It sat in Washington from March to May 1871, and, by
all accounts, the members worked very well together. Senator
Sumner had in January made another suggestion: in exchange for a
settlement of the claims, the British should completely withdraw
'from the whole hemisphere, including the islands, and the
American flag should fly in its stead'. A copy was given by the
Secretary of State, Hamilton Fish, to Sir John Rose, a Canadian who
was acting as a non-official diplomat, who communicated it to the
British Commissioners. In the course of the conference, 'Mr Fish
threw out a hint to Lord de Grey that the cession of Canada might
end the quarrel. The English envoy contented himself with the dry
remark that he did not find such a suggestion in his Instructions.'[220]
On 8 May 1871, the Treaty of Washington was signed. In it, the
British Government expressed its regret for the escape of the
Alabama. In order to deal with the claims, a tribunal of five arbitrators
was to be set up – one each to be appointed by the governments of
the US, Great Britain, Italy, Switzerland and Brazil – which would
meet in Geneva; rules as to the law were set out for their guidance,
and their decision would be final. The opportunity was also taken for
decisions to be made on other outstanding problems, primarily matters of fishing and the rights to navigation of certain rivers.

There was a postscript to this. Early in January 1872, the British government was shocked by the fact that the American case was in fact a claim not merely for direct damages inflicted by the *Alabama* and other such ships, but for all 'indirect, constructive and consequential loss'. In other words, the whole cost of the war since the Battle of Gettysburg, on the grounds that thereafter the South conducted the war only at sea, and that Great Britain did not prevent the Confederates from acquiring their ships from British shipyards. In Parliament, the Leader of the Opposition, Benjamin Disraeli, spoke of the indirect claims as 'preposterous and wild', whilst Gladstone, now Prime Minister, was in favour of breaking off the arbitration, rather than submitting. Then followed five months of discussion and exchange of diplomatic cables back and forth across the Atlantic. The Gordian knot was cut by Charles Francis Adams, now one of the arbitrators, who waived the indirect claims. The final award, which decided that Great Britain had not used 'due diligence in the performance of her neutral obligations', cost her $15.5 million in gold, but the Tribunal had also decided that indirect claims could not be admitted. This was just as well, because states facing such claims might prefer war to arbitration.[221]

There were to be other conflicts, such as over the right to kill seals in the Bering Sea, but the attention of each country now turned elsewhere. Great Britain had to protect India from Russia, and her interests in China and Africa from all of the Great Powers, but Tenterden's memorandum had emphasised the interrelationship between Anglo-American relations and imperial and European problems. A stimulus for his suggestion of a joint commission had been his fear that if there were an Anglo-Russian war, as then seemed possible, the US would probably support Russia. A year earlier, Lord Clarendon, the Foreign Secretary, had made the same point in a letter to Queen Victoria: 'It is the unfriendly state of our relations with America that to a great extent paralyses our action in Europe. There is not the smallest doubt that if we were engaged in a Continental quarrel we should immediately find ourselves at war with the United States.'[222] Thus, for Great Britain, her consciousness of power was tempered by an awareness of her vulnerability, to which the US made a significant contribution.

As for the United States, she continued her drive westwards to fill up her territories and resumed her predations in Central America, but British actions during the Civil War had embittered Americans in both the North and the South. The former did not forget that Great Britain had recognised the South as a belligerent, and appeared ready to recognise her as a country. The latter remembered that Great Britain had not supported them; had she done so, the South might well have won. As a result, Anglophobia continued to permeate American public affairs for the remainder of the century.

CHAPTER 4

Nineteenth-Century Travellers' Tales

It is an absorbing thing to watch the process of world-making:- both the formation of the natural and the conventional world. I witnessed both in America; and when I look back upon it now, it seems as if I had been in another planet.

Harriet Martineau, *Society in America* (1837)[1]

There is every thing to connect the past in mournful interest with the present and the future. English names are plentiful around you, and many objects within view have an English look about them. Yet, when the Englishman steps ashore, it is on a foreign, though a friendly land.

Alexander Mackay, *The Western World* (1849)[2]

Jonathan may bless his vanity. He is encased in it from top to toe; it is a panoply of truth, which renders him invulnerable equally to ridicule and argument.

Thomas Hamilton, *Men and Manners in America* (1833)[3]

I never stood in an English crowd without being conscious of hereditary sympathies. Nevertheless, it is undeniable that an American is continually thrown upon his national antagonism by some acrid quality in the moral atmosphere of England. These people think so loftily of themselves, and so contemptuously of everybody else, that it requires more generosity than I possess to keep always in perfectly good humor with them.

Nathaniel Hawthorne, *Our Old Home* (1863)[4]

One of the consequences of the War of American Independence was the tearing apart of the concept as well as the reality of a transatlantic British identity. Its loss invited alternative identities to fill the gap. The populations of the United States and Great Britain knew to their own satisfaction what constituted these identities, and, in any case, that is not the subject of this chapter. Rather, the focus is on the perceptions of the Americans by the British, and of the British by the

Americans. To narrow it down: what did the intrepid middle-class traveller think, the man or woman who actually made the journey across the ocean to see for him- or herself? It was, it must be said, primarily the British who were curious, and early in the life of the new Republic they began to tour America and write about what they had found. They wanted to know the nature of the new American democracy, and if it was a good thing. Some Americans made the reverse journey, although not nearly as many – they were busy building a country – and they, too, described their experiences. By the end of the nineteenth century, there had been hundreds of these travel books published.[5] Whilst always thought-provoking, they can also be by turns depressing and hilarious. Nowadays, the term normally used is 'national identity'; then, they spoke of 'national character'.

In both cases a faint trajectory can be traced. During the first three-quarters of the century most British visitors, to varying degrees, disliked what they saw: the vulgarity, the lack of distance, the slavery. After 1870, however, there was more acceptance and even admiration expressed about the US, and less contempt. The idea of an 'Anglo-Saxon race' captured many, since it was an idea which emphasised similarity rather than strangeness. The response of Americans visiting England was more equivocal. Many visited who felt their English heritage strongly, particularly those from New England, and went to experience the landscape and historical remains and to make literary pilgrimages to living poets and prose writers. Others went expecting to dislike what they saw, alert to those aspects of England which highlighted American superiority. They, too, found what they sought. But, naturally, this is far too simple, and Mark Twain was only one of many who loved England and the English, but hated some of its institutions.

Two points are important. First of all, others besides the middle classes visited the US: Irish revolutionaries, Chartist radicals, and many members of the working classes who came to scout the possibilities. Nevertheless, with a few notable exceptions, it was members of the middle and upper-middle classes who wrote most of the books. And secondly, the public context was repeated Anglo-American crises and heightened American nationalism, which only exacerbated the existing mutual antipathy.

I

In 1782 a book entitled *Letters from an American Farmer* was published in England. The author was J. Hector St John Crèvecoeur, a French emigrant who had farmed for a few years in New York State, before fleeing back to France at the outbreak of the American Revolution, unwilling to take sides. Once the war was over, interested Europeans were asking: what is an American? This was the first new nation: it had not evolved, it had been created. It was no longer part of the British Empire, so its citizens were not Britons. But what was an American? According to Crèvecoeur, 'he is an American, who, leaving behind him all his antient [*sic*] prejudices and manners, receives new ones from the new mode of life he has embraced, the new government he obeys and the new rank he holds'. In the new United States, 'individuals of all nations are melted into a new race of men, whose labours and posterity will one day cause great changes in the world'. In sum, 'the American is a new man, who acts upon new principles; he must therefore entertain new ideas and form new opinions'.[6]

And so, Europeans wanted to know, what were the principles, ideas and opinions of Americans? How did Americans think, look, act? In one sense, it could be argued, the United States was tacked on to the idea of the Grand Tour. During the eighteenth century, upper-class Britons, most of them young, toured Europe, travelling in particular to Paris, Venice, Rome, Florence and Naples, with the more intellectual or adventurous also visiting Berlin or travelling over the Swiss Alps. Some went for the landscape or the antiquities; others, especially the young men, wished to gain social polish; most were keen to ascertain the character of the Italians, the French or the Germans.[7] In the same manner, in the nineteenth century, travellers visited the United States to marvel at the landscape, to study the political and social systems, to see how people lived and what they were like. Paul Langford argues that the comparison is not valid because the Grand Tour was embarked on by the upper classes, and those who travelled to America were largely middle class. Thus, their tours were not Grand. In this sense, he is, of course, entirely correct, but in the larger context the comparison remains valid.[8]

The classic treatment of the subject of the United States, the one by which all others are measured, is *Democracy in America*, written by the Frenchman Alexis de Tocqueville, and published in two volumes in 1835 and 1840. De Tocqueville, an aristocratic young administrator who was disillusioned with the outcome of the Revolution in France, went with a friend to America in 1831 for ten months to study 'the future in the present'. To do so, he made a wide sweep from Newport, Rhode Island to Boston, down to New Orleans, over to Macon, Georgia, and up to Michigan, which was then on the very edge of western civilisation. Indeed, he spent a good proportion of his time in the frontier area, where individualism was certainly at its rawest. He wanted to see for himself the effects of this individualism, of freedom and equality, the better to understand their future in Europe. As he wrote, in Europe 'I saw the equality of conditions that, without having reached its extreme limits as it had in the United States, was approaching them more each day; and the same democracy reigning in American societies appeared to me to be advancing rapidly toward power in Europe.'[9] In short, 'it appears to me beyond doubt that sooner or later we shall arrive, like the Americans, at an almost complete equality of conditions'.[10] What were the implications of this?

The context for de Tocqueville was the fact that 'the social state of the Americans is eminently democratic. It has had this character since the birth of the colonies; it has it even more in our day.'[11] His viewpoint was that of the aristocrat viewing an egalitarian society, and he made observations which in one way or another would repeatedly pop up in other accounts. Because there was little concern for social distinctions, no one donned their clothes very well – the women dressed at 7 a.m. and remained in the same dress all day! The sequence of foods at dinner was barbaric. There was no feeling for language and American orators were pompous. Wealth, not birth, was everything, and thus what social distinctions there were could be overturned; indeed, 'the whole of society seems to have melted into a middle class',[12] and one recurring theme over the century was the boring, conformist, religious nature of the American middle class. Furthermore, everything changed extremely rapidly: new life? just up stakes and move further west or to the city. Tired of being a farmer? Try being a merchant. Begin as a ploughboy, end as a land speculator. There was little stability and few roots. There were family ties but, in the end, individualism was more important.

And yet, de Tocqueville believed, the young Republic was saved from the worst threat – to be driven by greed and selfish individualism – by its genuine concern for the liberty of others and for the well-being of the community. As he wrote, 'I must say that I often saw Americans make great and genuine sacrifices for the public, and I remarked a hundred times that, when needed, they almost never fail to lend faithful support to one another.'[13] In short, if individualism is not absolute, not entirely selfish, if it has room for the rights of others, for others' individualism, liberty may triumph. In the United States it had done so. This was helped by the fact that Americans were not ideological – 'In America, personalities are everything, principles are insignificant',[14] and thus the citizenry were not riven by ideological quarrels. (De Tocqueville was to die before the Civil War began in 1861.) Another lubricant of social relations was religion: within a month of his arrival in the US, de Tocqueville was musing that he had 'never . . . been so conscious of the influence of religion on the morals and the social and political state of a nation'.[15] In France during the Revolution, freedom and religion had been on opposite sides of the barricades; in the United States they 'united intimately with one another'.[16]

Crucially, private and public interests were easily reconciled because of the genius of Americans for forming associations. As de Tocqueville wrote, 'Americans of all ages, all conditions, all minds constantly unite . . . Americans use associations to give fêtes, to found seminaries, to build inns, to raise churches, to distribute books, to send missionaries to the antipodes; in this manner they create hospitals, prisons, schools.'[17] Living, as most did, in small and local communities, Americans constantly came into contact with one another in circumstances which forced them to help one another: you help me build my barn and I'll help you build yours; or, we need a school, so we'll all build one together.

De Tocqueville did identify two less desirable attributes of Americans, and his comments were echoed by visitor after visitor over the century. One was the tyranny of the majority. He posited that 'The moral empire of the majority is founded in part on the idea that there is more enlightenment and wisdom in many men united than in one alone... It is the theory of equality as applied to intellects.'[18] As a result, 'I do not know any country where, in general, less independence of mind and genuine freedom of discussion reign than in America... [A]s long as the majority is doubtful, one speaks; but when it has irrevocably pronounced, everyone becomes silent and friends and enemies alike then seem to hitch themselves together to its wagon.'[19] The other was the incessant demand by Americans for praise about America – its institutions, its people, its habits, its future, its actual being: 'Americans, in their relations with foreigners, appear impatient at the least censure and insatiable for praise. The slimmest eulogy is agreeable to them and the greatest is rarely enough to satisfy them; they pester you at every moment to get you to praise them; and if you resist their entreaties, they praise themselves.'[20] The denial of this praise in any sense was a cause for condemnation of the transgressor, amongst whom, again, were many of the British commentators on America. As it happened, Americans did like de Tocqueville, largely because they saw him as a 'first-class philosophical thinker'[21] and his book as transcending political and social disputes. They were willing to accept from him criticisms that they denounced in others: he seemed sympathetic, he had studied America thoroughly, and his conclusions, even when unfavourable, were presented in a dispassionate manner. De Tocqueville was a perspicacious commentator who was sometimes invoked by later, British, commentators.[22] Fundamentally, he decided that the Republic was an experiment which was working, and in the direction towards which European society would eventually develop.

This was not necessarily the view taken by some of the earliest, and most widely read, English travellers. Indeed, the very idea filled some of them with repulsion. Thomas Hamilton, who admitted that he 'may have been influenced by the prejudices natural to an Englishman', wrote in *Men and Manners in America* (1833) that 'when I found the institutions and the experiences of the United States quoted in the reformed Parliament, as affording safe precedent for British legislation, and learned that the drivellers who uttered such nonsense, instead of encountering merited derision, were listened to with patience and approbation, by men as ignorant as themselves, I certainly did feel that another work on America was yet wanted'.[23] In this context, it is useful to remember that the 1830s and 1840s in Great Britain were a period of passionate internal debate between Tories and Liberal Radicals on the desirability or otherwise of the spread of democracy within the realm.[24] American democracy was a central part of this debate, and writers on the US tended to take positions accordingly. An American commentator seventy-five years later felt that much British opinion during the first half of the century had been formed by reading the works of Hamilton, Basil Hall, Frances Trollope and Charles Dickens;[25] a glance at them suggests reasons for the adverse and even contemptuous nature of much of that opinion.

Hall, the son of a baronet, a captain in the Royal Navy and Fellow of the Royal Society, travelled with his wife, his daughter Eliza and a maid as far north as Quebec, as far south as New Orleans and Savannah, Georgia, and as far west as Missouri. His three-volume work, *Travels in North America in the Years 1827 and 1828*,[26] was published in 1830, half a decade before that of de Tocqueville. Hall's volumes were rather more descriptive than de Tocqueville's, and laden more with illustrative stories and anecdotes, but his work was based on close observation and many notes, and was referred to by many later travellers. His social standing and his 'anti-democratic haughteur'[27] appealed to many of his British readers, and his strictures frequently supported pre-existing prejudices. A major problem was that America was not like England,[28] and since this was the standard by which the Halls judged it, they found it wanting.

One dislike was the absence of social classes and, therefore, of class distinctions. These distinctions contributed to the general happiness, as (he said) he told an American:

> with us, all men are divided into ranks or classes, which, although they blend insensibly, and intermix with one another where they meet, are yet very obviously distinguished, while the acknowledged rights and privileges of each are scrupulously preserved. Every one finds out, also, in the long run, that his best chance of

success and of happiness, consists in conforming as nearly as possible to the established habits of that branch of society in which he
happens to be born, or which he may reach by dint of extraordinary industry or good fortune. I may even add, that without doing
so, no man is considered respectable. [Furthermore,] the lowest
and most numerous orders in England cheerfully and wisely
submit [in legislating for and governing the land] to those immediately above them, who are somewhat more fortunately
circumstanced, and who, from enjoying that casual, but not invid-
ious advantage, have leisure to acquire knowledge, or power, call
it what you will, by which those about them and below them are
willing to be influenced. These again, in the very same
manner, . . . are under the influence of a still higher class, whose
means are proportionately greater; and so on, through a hundred
gradations, many of them almost insensible, to the top of the scale.

By this means, the opinions of the lowest are not disregarded, but
'sifted'. In this case, Hall has considered the same problem as de
Tocqueville, but has not the same faith in the system to mediate the
desires of the populace, because, unfortunately, 'In America, every
public man may be said to live upon popularity',[29] thereby reducing
politics to the pursuit of the lowest common denominator.

The Americans suffered socially and culturally as well from 'the
total absence of a permanent money-spending class in the society, . . . to serve as models in this difficult art'. The general division
of property, as opposed to primogeniture, 'seldom gives to each sufficient means to enable him to live independently of business'. And
even if only one son inherits, how is he to live happily? 'Where,
when, and with whom? How is he to find companionship? How
expect sympathy from the great mass of all the people he mixes
amongst, whose habits and tastes lie in totally different directions?'[30]
Hall may well have lost some of his American readers at this point.

A second point of contention between Hall and the Americans
was the English language. Whilst visiting New Haven, Connecticut,
home of Yale College, Hall was introduced to Noah Webster, whom
he described as having spent forty years in compiling a dictionary of
the English language.[31] Webster believed fervently that the new

American nation needed a language and literature of its own, and he devoted his life to providing the language. From 1783 to 1785, he had published a three-volume *Grammatical Institute of the English Language,* Part I of which – commonly known as *Webster's Spelling Book* or the *Blue-Backed Speller* – was used in all schools, sold some sixty million copies over the following century, and helped to make American spelling uniform. In 1807 he published *A Philosophical and Practical Grammar of the English Language.* Webster believed that English grammars were objectionable in that they conformed too much to the grammars of Latin and Greek: the American language was 'rude and irregular' in comparison, and could not be reduced to the same orderly system.[32] His greatest work, however, was *An American Dictionary of the English Language.* Revised a number of times over the following two centuries, it remains the best known of American dictionaries. Webster was responsible for taking the 'u' out of 'labour' and 'neighbour'.

Hall treated Webster with much more respect than he had shown many others in his writing, and even allowed himself to admit of being mistaken. Take the question of new words, 'Americanisms' according to Hall. Webster contended that Americans not only had a right, they had an obligation to modify the language to suit new circumstances, geographical and political, although he agreed that where there was an equally expressive English word, it ought to be used in preference to the new word.

> 'Nevertheless,' said [Webster], 'it is quite impossible to stop the progress of language – it is like the course of the Mississippi . . . [which] possesses a momentum quite irresistible . . . [I]n process of time, your new words find their way across the Atlantic, and are incorporated in the spoken language here. In like manner,' he added, 'many of our words, heretofore not used in England, have gradually crept in there, and are now an acknowledged part of the language. The interchange, in short, is inevitable; and, whether desirable or not, cannot be stopped, or even essentially modified.'[33]

There were many other American opinions, habits and institutions which Hall disliked, but slavery, which might have caused great and unmixed repugnance, was for him a complex problem which argued against moral certainties. After viewing his first slave sale, he 'ran off as fast as I could down one of the avenues [in Washington, D.C.], hoping, by change of place, to get rid of the entanglement of many unpleasant thoughts which crowded upon me during the sale'.[34] Yet, he later refers to 'judicious and kind-hearted slave-owners – for many such there are in America'.[35] He spent some time in the South, and

> found my ideas on the intricate and formidable subject of slavery becoming rather less clear than I fancied they had formerly been . . . Men of sense and feeling use their slaves well in every State, not only because it is much more agreeable to be kind than to be cruel to them, but because the pecuniary advantages are always greater. Men who have no sense or command of temper, are sure to disregard the feelings of those over whom they have such unlimited authority. Consequently, wherever there is slavery, there must be more or less cruelty and injustice, if – as in America – the checks to the intemperate use of irresponsible power are merely nominal.[36]

It seemed clear to Hall that no man in a 'Slave State' could hope to change matters, because members of the legislature are 'taken exclusively from amongst the slave-holders; a class of men who are naturally in the highest degree jealous of any attempts to tamper with a subject, upon which their fortunes and even their very lives depend'.[37] Yet, nor could the Federal government interfere, since

> Congress has not, by the terms of the Constitution, the slightest shadow of right to meddle with the internal concerns of the States, and least of all with those which relate to Slavery. Any assumption of such pretensions on the part of Congress, would be so instant-aneously resisted – by actual force, if that were necessary – by the whole mass of the slave-holding States, that the idea could not exist one hour. If such intentions of interference with the slave system should ever, by any strange infatuation, be seriously con-templated, either by a powerful Executive, or by a majority of the

members of Congress from the non-slave-holding States, the inevitable consequence would be a division of the Union.[38]

Hall's clear-eyed realism drove him to conclude that 'it is useless, then, for foreigners to hold the language of reproach or of appeal to America'.[39]

The American reaction to Hall's volumes was recorded by another traveller, Mrs Frances Trollope. After referring to 'one of the most remarkable traits in the national character of the Americans; namely, their exquisite sensitiveness and soreness respecting every thing said or written concerning them', she adduced as evidence 'the effect produced on nearly every class of readers by the appearance of Captain Basil Hall's "Travels in North America"'. In fact it was a sort of moral earthquake, and the vibration it occasioned through the nerves of the Republic, from one corner of the Union to the other, was by no means over two years later.[40] Mrs Trollope, mother of the more famous Anthony, was the redoubtable wife of a somewhat inef-fectual husband, a querulous and failing lawyer. With the family teetering on the edge of bankruptcy, and her marriage by now a sham, in late 1827 she sailed with three of her children and a young French artist[41] to America. Certainly, the journey 'presented her with the perfect opportunity to live apart from her husband without the stigma of separation',[42] but she also grabbed the opportunity to travel with Fanny Wright, the radical, free-thinking and charismatic reformer,[43] who intended to establish a new settlement for ex-slaves in Nashoba, Tennessee. Trollope planned to stay there for a time. Her son Henry expected to work in Nashoba as a teacher, and his mother wanted to see him established. She also hoped to take the strain off the family finances by living cheaply in the backwoods settlement.[44]

Mrs Trollope and her entourage – her son, her two daughters age nine and eleven, two servants, and the artist – along with Fanny Wright and hers landed in New Orleans and sailed up the Mississippi River, a boring and uncomfortable journey. Nashoba turned out to be a disaster – the entire settlement consisted of three roofless log cabins[45] – and Mrs Trollope and her group continued north. They set up house and shop in the booming frontier town of

Cincinnati, Ohio. The shop was named the Bazaar, decorated in an unusually extravagant manner for Cincinnati, and filled with high-priced goods of variable desirability. But illness, scandal and predictable business failure combined to drive them out of Cincinnati, and they travelled back to the East, visiting Virginia, Baltimore, Washington, the Hudson Valley and Niagara Falls, before returning to England in the summer of 1831. Upon reaching home, she turned the saga into a book, *Domestic Manners of the Americans* (1832). At the outset, the impression given is that she was prepared to like America – why else plan to go there for such a long period of time? – but experience convinced her of the worth of what she had left behind.

In one respect, Mrs Trollope gave her game away in the intro-duction: In the third person she wrote:

> She leaves to abler pens the more ambitious task of commenting on the democratic form of the American government; while, by describing, faithfully, the daily aspect of ordinary life, she has endeavoured to show how greatly the advantage is on the side of those who are governed by the few, instead of the many. The chief object she has had in view is to encourage her countrymen to hold fast by a constitution that ensures all the blessings which flow from established habits and solid principles. If they forgo these, they will incur the fearful risk of breaking up their repose by introducing the jarring tumult and universal degradation which invariably follow the wild scheme of placing all the power of the State in the hands of the populace.[46]

She was a Tory, and as such she was arguing against the passage of the 1832 Reform Bill, which began the widening of the franchise in Britain. What she described in America was the result of such folly.

What she most hated was the lack of deference, the assumption of equality. She was mortified at having to share a coach; she disliked shopkeepers dressing and acting as though they were aristocrats at a ball; she found the rude indifference of American children repellent. As for the demeanour of a self-defined 'lady' in Virginia: 'To say she addressed us in a tone of equality, will give no adequate idea of her manner; I am persuaded that no misgiving on the subject ever entered her head.' Not surprisingly, she thoroughly detested the incessant, remorseless and nearly universal habit of chewing tobacco, referring to 'the loathsome spitting, from the contamination of which it was absolutely impossible to protect our dresses'.[47] On the frontier, it was apparently the custom for people to wander into their neighbour's house without invitation, and to stay for what seemed to be hours; having herself experienced this, Mrs Trollope did not like it.[48] Early on in her travels, she decided that the greatest difference between England and the US was the lack of refinement in the latter; by now, she begins to sound like one of Jane Austen's less attractive characters:

[T]he theory of equality may be very daintily discussed by English gentlemen in a London dining-room, where the servant, having placed a fresh bottle of cool wine on the table, respectfully shuts the door, and leaves them to their walnuts and their wisdom; but it will be found less palatable when it presents itself in the shape of a hard greasy paw, and is claimed in accents that breathe less of freedom than of onions and whisky. Strong, indeed, must be the love of equality in an English breast, if it can survive a tour through the Union.[49]

As did de Tocqueville, she commented on how religious the Americans were, having attended some alarming evangelical religious meetings:

[T]wo or three of the priests walked down from the tribune, and going, one to the right, and the other to the left, began whispering to the poor tremblers seated there. These whispers were inaudible to us, but the sobs and groans increased to a frightful excess. Young creatures, with features pale and distorted, fell on their knees on the pavement, and soon sunk forward on their faces; the most violent cries and shrieks followed, while from time to time a voice was heard in convulsive accents, exclaiming, 'O Lord!' 'O Lord Jesus!' 'Help me, Jesus!' and the like.[50]

But while de Tocqueville saw religion as helping to knit the population together, Mrs Trollope emphasised its unbridled and ignorant nature, lamenting, 'I believe I am sufficiently tolerant; but this does not prevent my seeing that the object of all religious observances is better obtained, when the government of the church is confided to the wisdom and experience of the most venerated among the people, than when it is placed in the hands of every tinker and tailor who chooses to claim a share in it'.[51]

And like religion, like politics. Where de Tocqueville saw the force of democratic politics moderated by community spirit, she saw only corruption, ignorance, lack of ability and of stability. As she wrote, with mounting hostility,

> The small patrician band is a race apart; they live with each other, and for each other; mix wondrously little with the high matters of state, which they seem to leave rather supinely to their tailors and tinkers . . . I speak not of these, but of the population generally, as seen in town and country, among the rich and the poor, in the slave states and the free states. I do not like them. I do not like their principles, I do not like their manners, I do not like their opinions. Both as a woman, and as a stranger, it might be unseemly for me to say that I do not like their government, and therefore I will not say so.[52]

Mrs Trollope's book sold thousands on both sides of the Atlantic. For many Britons, it confirmed their suspicions that by winning independence from the mother country, the Americans had gone astray. The Americans hated this implication, but also possibly hated the fact that in many cases she was telling the truth. After all, she had not just visited America: she had lived there. The Englishman E.T. Coke wrote from New York that 'the commotion it created amongst the good citizens is truly remarkable . . . At every table d'hôte, on board of every steam-boat, in every stage-coach, and in all societies, the first question was, "Have you read Mrs Trollope?"'[53]

Five years later another intrepid British woman, Harriet Martineau, published her own two volumes on the United States, entitled *Society in America*. Deaf (she travelled with two ear trumpets) and virtually devoid of the senses of smell and taste, but a widely famous writer of tales of political economy, in 1834, at the age of thirty-two, she set off across the Atlantic. Whilst Frances Trollope had been keen on the landscape and the horrible people, Miss Martineau was much more interested in the social and political systems. She wanted to compare this society with the ideals set out by the Founding Fathers in the Declaration of Independence: 'every true citizen of [the US] must be content to have his self-government tried by the test of these principles, to which, by his citizenship, he has become a subscriber'.[54] She made a familiar journey – beginning with New York, the Hudson Valley and Niagara, she went to Philadelphia, Baltimore, Washington and Virginia, across to New Orleans, up the Mississippi to Cincinatti (five years after Mrs Trollope had left it), back to Virginia by boat, up to New England, back to Ohio, then to New York and home on 1 August 1836, two years after setting out.[55]

She was a good, and tolerant, traveller (unlike Mrs Trollope) and found American 'society' of great interest. Whilst Mrs Trollope had thought American children rude and indifferent, Martineau felt 'the independence and fearlessness of children was a perpetual charm in my eyes'.[56] Everywhere, she found interesting people with whom to talk – or *at* whom to talk, since she was rather given to garrulity: 'Sydney Smith, the editor of the *Edinburgh Review*, dreamed he "was chained to a rock and being talked to death by Harriet Martineau and Macaulay".'[57] She was especially struck by the treatment of individuals: 'the English insolence of class to class, of individuals towards each other, is not even conceived of, except in the one highly disgraceful instance of the treatment of the people of colour. Nothing in American civilisation struck me so forcibly and so pleasurably as the invariable respect paid to man, as man. Nothing since my return to England has given me so much pain as the contrast here.'[58] As may be inferred from that quotation, she hated slavery, believing that it was degrading to master and slave alike, and beneficial to no one: 'A large proportion of the labour of the United States is held on principles wholly irreconcilable with the principles of the constitution: whatever may be true about its origin, it is now inefficient, wasteful, destructive, to a degree which soon must cause a change of plan.'[59]

Slavery elicited a mixture of responses from British visitors. Thomas Hamilton described in 1833 how 'there are slave auctions almost every day in the New Orleans Exchange. I was frequently present at these, and the man who wants an excuse for misanthropy, will nowhere discover better reason for hating and despising his species. The usual process differs in nothing from that of selling a horse.'[60] Charles Dickens, who visited the US in 1842, divided the upholders of slavery there into three great classes: the more moderate and rational 'owners of human cattle', who knew it was wrong and perceived its dangers to society; then there were those who 'cannot bear a superior, and cannot brook an equal . . . whose pride, in a land where voluntary servitude [i.e., being a servant] is shunned as a disgrace, must be ministered to by slaves'; and the largest group, 'all those owners, breeders, users, buyers and sellers of slaves, who will, until the bloody chapter has a bloody end, own, breed, use, buy, and sell them at all hazards; who doggedly deny the horrors of the system, in the teeth of such a mass of evidence as never was brought to bear on any other subject, . . . who, when they speak of Freedom, mean the Freedom to oppress their kind'.[61]

Others, however, approved of slavery, or at least did not disapprove. The novelist William Makepeace Thackeray, who travelled in the US in the spring of 1853, wrote letters home to his daughters and friends that were 'filled with jokes, ridicule, contempt and condescensions for the black people that he met in the South. "They are not my fellow men and brethren".'[62] Of course, very few white people could honestly claim a close kinship with slaves; for example, even 'most female abolitionists of the period spoke of the black woman not as an equal but as a "daughter"'.[63] Basil Hall, as described above, was pulled in several directions, as was Frances Trollope. On the one hand, she wrote that 'the effect produced upon English people by the sight of slavery in every direction is very new, and not very agreeable, and it is not the less painfully felt from hearing upon every breeze the mocking words "All men are born free and equal"'. On the other, she decided that 'to emancipate them entirely throughout the Union, cannot, I conceive, be thought of, consistently with the safety of the country'; but if slaves were treated more kindly, 'the negro population of the Union might cease to be a terror, and their situation no longer be a subject either of indignation or of pity'.[64] However, once resettled in England, and as opinions in both the US and Europe polarised, her antipathy towards slavery increased, and she produced in 1836 *The Life and Adventures of Jonathan Jefferson Whitlaw; or Scenes on the Mississippi*, the first anti-slavery novel, which was published fifteen years before Harriet Beecher Stowe's *Uncle Tom's Cabin*.[65]

Harriet Martineau never wavered. Before arriving in America, she had a reputation of sympathising with abolition based on one of her tales, 'Demerara', which dealt with the treatment of West Indian slaves with great compassion. Indeed, upon arriving in New York, the captain tried to dissuade her from landing, fearing that she might be lynched.[66] At her time of arrival, the rise of the abolitionist movement had created a violent, pro-slavery backlash, and she was to suffer because of it. Although many doors were opened to her, many others were closed. This was particularly the case after an episode in Boston. She had decided that, however strongly she felt about slavery, she would not denounce it publicly, since she felt that, as a visitor, she ought not to comment. But this reticence soon gave way, and at a meeting of the Boston Female Anti-Slavery Society on 18 November 1835, as a mob outside threw mud at the windows, she came out as an abolitionist: 'I consider Slavery as inconsistent with the law of God, and as incompatible with the course of his Providence . . . [It is an] utter abomination and I now declare that in your *principles* I fully agree.'[67] The result was death threats – this time she was threatened with lynching – and widespread social rejection. Of course, in certain parts of the country, such as New England, she spoke with many of the converted, and these remained friends even after her return to Britain. Nevertheless, she was shocked at the virulent pro-slavery public opinion which she found even in Boston.

But how did she ultimately answer her question, her comparison of the proclaimed ideals of the Founding Fathers and the sordid realities? She wanted to find the US the hope of the future, and learn that the evils she discovered, pre-eminently that of slavery, were temporary. She wrote, 'The striking effect upon a stranger of witnessing, for the first time, the absence of poverty, of gross ignorance, of all servility, of all insolence of manner, cannot be exaggerated in description. I had seen every man in the towns an independent citizen; every man in the country a land-owner. I had seen that the villages had their newspapers, the factory girls their libraries. I had witnessed the controversies between candidates for office on some difficult subjects, of which the people were to be the judges.'[68] One can only wonder whether Mrs Trollope and Miss Martineau had visited the same country. Of course, the latter had a few small criticisms. She found the general health of Americans poor, possibly because their rooms were too hot and their baths too few. And, like de Tocqueville, she emphasised their great terror of adverse opinion along with a continual demand for flattery. As for the condition of women: 'While woman's intellect is confined, her morals crushed, her health ruined, her weakness encouraged, and her strength punished, she is told that her lot is cast in the paradise of women: and there is no country in the world where there is so much boasting of the "chivalrous" treatment she enjoys.'[69]

In her introduction, Miss Martineau claimed that she had never intended to write a book – 'I had again and again put away the idea of saying one word in print on the condition of society in the United States.' Yet, 'men will never arrive at a knowledge of each other, if those who have the opportunity of foreign observation refuse to relate what they think they have learned; or even to lay before others the materials from which they themselves hesitate to construct a theory, or draw larger conclusions'.[70] So she published her book. The Americans hated and resented it;[71] the English admired it. She said that she did not mind, and she remained optimistic about American developments. But the Civil War dimmed her enthusiasm, and the aftermath, with its political and economic corruption and its crushing of the hopes of the newly freed slaves, nearly destroyed it. Her last recorded words on America were, 'I am, like many others, almost in despair for the great Republic.'[72]

Charles Dickens similarly set off for America expecting to like it, but felt that his 'young enthusiasm' was 'anything but prepared' for what he found there. As he later wrote, 'no stranger could have set foot upon those shores with a feeling of livelier interest in the country, and stronger faith in it'.[73] Only twenty-nine when he went, he had written five novels in five years and wanted new experiences; he also planned to write an account of his trip, but he was clever enough not to reveal this to his American friends. Although he hardly expected the New Jerusalem, as an ardent radical at home, concerned for the plight of the poor and other social evils – think of *Oliver Twist* – he certainly expected to find the situation better in the US. He also wanted to be lionised, as his American friends had promised he would be: 'Washington Irving writes me that if I went, it would be such a triumph from one end of the States to the other, as was never known in any other Nation.'[74] This happened at first, and Dickens returned the compliment; but then his perceptions, and his ideas, changed.

His opinion turned because of two issues: the lack of international copyright protection and the scurrility of the newspapers. The US had refused to make a reciprocal agreement with Britain by which authors could claim royalties in the other country. Thus, Americans read and loved Dickens, but refused to pay him. He complained publicly,[75] and many of the newspapers, who had been amongst those who had effectively stolen his work, retaliated with vigour: 'You must drop that, Charlie, or you will be dished; it smells of the shop-rank,' wrote one Boston newspaper.[76] Lies started to be printed about him. Furthermore, the adulation began to pall, particularly when his and his wife's privacy was invaded, with, for example, crowds peering through the windows whilst they were dressing. As a nineteenth-century commentator on his work wrote, 'another cause of his discontent with the United States was the infinite fatigue he underwent, owing to the rush of the people to see him and welcome him. It is cruel to make one man shake hands with a nation of men. The ovations were pleasant enough at first, but when the charm of novelty wore off they became an insufferable bore.'[77]

By the time they returned home, there was much about America that he intensely disliked, which became very obvious when he published *American Notes* in 1842, and then the novel based on those notes, *Martin Chuzzlewit*[78] – Americans could hardly decide which they disliked the more. According to Malcolm Bradbury, *American Notes* 'breached some implied rule of American hospitality, and no book more soured literary relations between the countries as well as between Dickens and his American readers'.[79] Tobacco-chewing and spitting, mentioned by virtually all British travellers, appeared: 'As Washington may be called the headquarters of tobacco-tinctured saliva, the time is come when I must confess, without any disguise, that the prevalence of those two odious practices of chewing and expectorating began about this time to be anything but agreeable, and soon became most offensive and sickening.' Let no stranger 'persuade himself (as I once did, to my shame), that previous tourists have exaggerated its extent. The thing itself is an exaggeration of nastiness which cannot be outdone.'[80] He also excoriated the picking of teeth in public, bolting food, the men's neglecting to change their linen, and the wearing of their hats indoors, all of which were also mentioned by Mrs Trollope. He particularly disliked those aspects of America which he attributed to money-grasping. Americans, Dickens wrote, admired a man who was 'smart', who got ahead whether or not he did it honestly: 'I recollect . . . remarking on the bad effects such gross deceits must have when they exploded, in generating a want of confidence abroad, and discouraging foreign investment; but I was given to understand that this was a very smart scheme by which a deal of money had been made, and that its smartest feature was that they forgot these things abroad, in a very short time, and speculated again as freely as ever.'[81] An American, in short, was an economic animal. (A later writer, the journalist W.E. Adams, wrote in *Our American Cousins* (1883) that things changed so quickly in America that 'many of the descriptions which Dickens gave to the public in his *American Notes* . . . are now totally inaccurate'.[82]) Dickens himself later modified his views to the extent that in a lecture tour to the US during the winter of 1867–8 he could pay tribute to the 'amazing changes'[83] he had observed. But glad confident morning never came again.

By the 1880s, there were hundreds of books about America written by British travellers and residents, and the stream continued. One, however, stands out because of its quality: James Bryce's *The American Commonwealth* (1888) is the only book of this type which can bear comparison with de Tocqueville's *Democracy in America* – indeed, Bryce himself made a direct comparison.[84] Bryce was a brilliant academic and sometime Professor of Jurisprudence at Oxford; a Liberal politician with a seat in Gladstone's Cabinet; and British Ambassador to the United States from 1907 to 1913. As a young man in 1870, he made the first of three trips to the US, with the object of studying American constitutional government. He travelled by railroad to Chicago and, after studying the city's co-educational system, became a convinced supporter of education for girls.[85] He travelled down the Mississippi, and then returned to New York, where he watched city government and politics in action; this convinced him that 'Hardly anyone seems to think any principle is at stake in this context; it is simply [a struggle] for place and power.'[86] Yet his impressions of America were on the whole favourable.

It was on his second visit in 1881, when he already held the chair in law at Oxford, that the idea of a major work on American democracy began to take shape. The third trip in 1883 was used to collect more material and to talk with other scholars, state and Federal officials, newspaper editors, lawyers and others. He then wrote the book, which ranged over every aspect of American society and quickly became a classic. Notably, Bryce did not allow his distaste for certain aspects, such as the monotony of American cities, 'which haunts one like a nightmare',[87] to interfere with his objective purpose: 'during the last fifty years no author has proposed to himself the aim of portraying the whole political system of the country in its practice as well as its theory . . . [including] the ideas, temper, habits of the sovereign people . . . To present such a general view of the United States both as a Government and as a Nation is the aim of the present book.'[88]

This is not to say that he refrained from comment on many American customs and mores. He was astounded at the American love, almost worship, of bigness for its own sake, and at a tendency 'to seek truth only in the voice of the majority, to mistake prosperity for greatness'.[89] He joined other writers in emphasising 'the extraordinary mobility of the population',[90] one result of which was that their loyalty was not to a locality, but to institutions. (Others referred to the cult of the Constitution.) His major criticism was directed at the political bosses who controlled city administrations: 'There is no denying that the government of cities is the one conspicuous failure of the United States . . . The faults of the State governments are insignificant compared with the extravagance, corruption, and mismanagement which mark the administrations of most of the great cities.'[91] But the implication of this comment was that the remainder of the political system worked, in its own peculiar manner. In this, Bryce agreed with de Tocqueville.

This is a minute sample of the hundreds of books written during the nineteenth century by the British on America and the Americans. In the first half of the century, the British were ignorant of the US, but curious. There was a democratic experiment being carried out on the other side of the Atlantic, and, particularly during the 1830s and 1840s, many toured through the States to investigate and to judge. As Bryce put it, it was 'a sense of the immense curiosity of Europe regarding the social and political life of America, and of the incomparable significance of American experience, that has led and will lead so many travellers to record their impressions of the Land of the Future'.[92]

For the British themselves, there was the added piquancy that the Americans had cut themselves off from Great Britain, had violently exiled themselves from the great Empire. Because of this separation, and the immediate need to deal with the wars with France, attention wandered from the United States. As a consequence, most visitors came unprepared for what they were to see. The reaction was primarily one of shock, at the fact that it was all so un-English. The British resonated with condescension, reinforced by an automatic assumption of superiority to the social values and cultural life of America. They recoiled from the assertive egalitarianism. William Austin, an American who resided in London from 1802 to 1803, clearly sympathised with this instinctive reaction, remarking in a letter that 'The English people are more civil than ours . . . [Americans] seem to carry the Declaration of Independence in their pockets, and regard the least degree of urbanity which may possibly be construed into obsequiousness, a breach of the constitution.'[93] The British were on the whole repulsed by the lack of refinement and social distinctions which met them in America, by the oft-stated assumptions of Americans that they could do as they liked because they were free, by the invasive nature of American curiosity, by the uniformity of American culture – as Matthew Arnold put it, 'what really dissatisfies in American civilization is the want of the *interesting*'.[94] And everyone was stunned by the truly horrible nature of the newspapers: 'The absence of truth and soberness in them, the poverty in serious interest, the personality and sensation-mongering, are beyond belief.'[95] These Americans were essentially foreigners to the visiting British.

Over the century, however, views became more favourable. Americans became more 'civilised' to British eyes – most men ceased to spit in public, for one thing. A wealthy social elite had emerged, and its members tended to visit Europe and absorb selected European customs and mores.[96] There was also increased British traffic to the US and, more specifically, to the West – for the younger sons of the gentry and aristocracy a favourite place to visit, and even to ranch. Then the fact of the Civil War, and its outcome, stimulated a great change in the nature of commentaries on the US: the Americans would and could fight for an idea, and the Union had survived.[97] On another plane, increased international tension, and the concomitant perceived threats to the British Empire, caused many Britons to see the US in a new light, as a country which shared British ideals. The Americans were increasingly powerful, and the two countries were, after all, related – 'these children of our own', according to Anthony Trollope; 'our American Cousins', according to W.E. Adams; 'the English people on the other side of the Atlantic', according to Matthew Arnold[98] – and war between them was becoming unthinkable. As the future Prime Minister A.J. Balfour stated in 1896, 'the idea of a war with the United States of America carries with it something of the unnatural horror of civil war'.[99] Perhaps, instead, they could be allies. Indeed, the turn of the century saw Great Britain settling outstanding problems with the United States – one historian has referred to the period from 1895 to 1914 as the 'great rapprochement'.[100] The concept of the 'special relationship' was gradually developing, at least on the British side.

II

There was much less traffic in the other direction, and it was of a different sort. The British went to the United States as to a foreign land, in a spirit of adventure. Many Americans ventured to Britain in a spirit of pilgrimage, particularly an historical and literary pilgrimage, in a conscious return home. Many of those who wrote about their travels were writers themselves, professional men, scholars, journalists or diplomats; in other words, they were members of the professional and intellectual classes. They also, more likely than not, came from the East Coast and especially from New England, whose professional and social elites considered their region to be akin to England itself. There were, of course, others – one example was the journal of a landscape gardener who walked over England looking at noblemen's parks[101] – but many of the more memorable books were written by professional writers.

One such was Washington Irving. He was physically delicate, and although he had trained as a lawyer, his family allowed him a life as a man of letters and diplomat. He had written a number of essays and a book before his voyage to Europe in 1815, which had been occasioned by the death of his fiancée; he remained there for seventeen years, accepting a post in the US Embassy in Madrid for financial reasons. Before travelling to Spain, however, he travelled around England, and in 1820 he published in London his best-known book, *The Sketch Book of Geoffrey Crayon, Gent.*, a series of essays and stories.[102] Its claim to enduring fame rests on two of the tales, those of Rip Van Winkle and 'The Legend of Sleepy Hollow'. In the nineteenth century, however, his most influential essay, which also appeared in *The Sketch Book*, was 'Stratford-on-Avon', written in the whimsical but slightly ponderous style of the narrator. The result was both comic and ironic. Crayon followed the well-established routines of visitors to Stratford: he looked for the names of the great amongst the mass of those scribbled on the whitewashed walls of Shakespeare's house; and he sat on Shakespeare's chair, but commented that 'whether this be done with the hope of imbibing any of the inspiration of the bard I am at loss to say'.[103]

Americans tended to call Shakespeare 'the Bard'. Indeed, the American tourist went to Stratford, as Irving wrote, 'on a poetical pilgrimage';[104] more than that, according to Christopher Mulvey, he went on a national mission to establish for himself and for the world that Shakespeare belonged to America, that he was America's national bard as much as he was England's. (The British began to pay real attention to Shakespeare combined with Stratford only when the Germans began to refer to him as *unser Shakespeare*.) Crayon's essay was particularly important because it was probably read by every American traveller to Stratford. This was because, upon publication, *The Sketch Book* was widely praised in England, which ensured that it was widely read in the US.[105]

It was not only Shakespeare who attracted the educated tourist, it was all of English literature. What is important here is that many of these Americans claimed English literature for their own. One who tried to argue against this was Ralph Waldo Emerson, the Transcendentalist philosopher and essayist, who made two long visits to England, in 1832 and 1847. During the first he sought out Wordsworth, Coleridge and Shelley, although the result was disappointing; he wrote of Wordsworth, for example, that 'He has written longer than he was inspired.' Emerson admitted that 'Every book we read, every biography, play, romance, in whatever form, is still English history and manners',[106] and asserted that America had to develop her own modes of thought, her own literary culture.[107] De Tocqueville had earlier written that there were no writers in America because freedom of opinion did not exist: 'the majority draws a formidable circle around thought. Inside those limits, the writer is free; but unhappiness awaits him if he dares to leave them.'[108]

In his *English Traits* (first published in 1856 and enjoying numerous reprints), Emerson ventured far beyond Britain's literary dominance in the English-speaking world. Instead, he attempted to analyse Great Britain and the British by approaching them from other vantage points:

The problem of the traveller landing at Liverpool is, Why England is England? What are the elements of power which the English hold over other nations? If there be one test of national genius universally accepted, it is success; and if there be one successful country in the universe for the last millennium, that country is England. A wise traveller will naturally choose to visit the best of actual nations; and an American has more reasons than another to draw him to Britain. In all that is done or begun by the Americans towards right thinking or practice, we are met by a civilization already settled and overpowering. The culture of the day, the thoughts and aims of men, are English thoughts and aims . . . The practical common-sense of modern society, the utilitarian direction which labor, laws, opinion, religion take, is the natural genius of the British mind.[109]

He then set out to look more closely at the elements which make up this English genius. One was the importance of private life as opposed to public life. The French noble lived at court, when there was one; the English aristocrat preferred to live on his estate. This dedication to the home extended down the social scale: the Englishman dearly loved his house, and spared no expense on it, gardening outside and decorating within – 'Tis a passion which survives all others, to deck and improve it.' The private man 'keeps his promises, never so trivial . . . To be king of their word', Emerson stated, 'is their pride.' Furthermore, 'An Englishman understates, avoids the superlative, checks himself in compliments'. He emphasised the role of English stolidity, combined with their brute force and power, in their security and stability, and claimed that 'The stability of England is the security of the modern world.' The 'English stand for liberty', and the genius of English society writ large was that private life had the place of honour. And so did work: even then, according to Emerson, the Englishman worked three times as many hours in a year as any other European. The result was the wealth of England, which, he argued, was a main fact of modern history. It was the foundation of British power.[110]

Emerson was not blind to the many faults of the English, but he remained an Anglophile. However, he was an American first, as he made clear:

I saw everywhere [in England] proofs of sense and spirit, and success of every sort: I like the people: they are as good as they are handsome; they have everything, and can do everything: but meantime, I surely know, that, as soon as I return to Massachusetts, I shall lapse at once into the feeling, which the geography of America inevitably inspires, that we play the game with immense advantage; that there and not here is the seat and center of the British race; and that no skill or activity can long compete with the prodigious natural advantages of that country, in the hands of the same race; and that England, an old and exhausted island, must one day be contented, like other parents, to be strong only in her children. But, this is a proposition which no Englishman of whatever condition can easily entertain.[111]

A more famous American author, whom even the British recognised, was Nathaniel Hawthorne, author of *The Scarlet Letter*, one of the few American novels which British critics deemed a masterpiece. From 1853 to 1857 Hawthorne was the American consul in Liverpool. This was an interesting vantage point, because most ships from America docked in Liverpool, so he had a constant stream of American visitors, more often than not seamen, and thus every opportunity to compare the two peoples. Hawthorne expressed the confusion that many American visitors must have felt when he wrote in his book of travels, *Our Old Home*, that 'after all these bloody wars and vindictive animosities, we still have an unspeakable yearning towards England'.[112] The title, which at first glance promises sentimental musings, in fact contains both beauty and beasts. He was profoundly drawn towards the great English writers, particularly Shakespeare, and to the architecture and landscape: 'visiting these famous localities, and a great many others, I hope that I do not compromise my American patriotism by acknowledging that I was often conscious of a fervent hereditary attachment to the native soil of our forefathers, and felt it to be our own Old Home'.[113] He made a pilgrimage to Westminster Abbey, the beauty of which continued to overwhelm and inspire him. His writing up of this experience in *Our Old Home* was the occasion for a disquisition on time, history, kingship, poetry and beauty. In particular, he tried to convey in his writings the beauty and grandeur, the special quality, of Gothic architecture, which did not exist at home.[114] Great Britain had the history, and its artefacts, which the United States lacked.

Yet, for Hawthorne, his delight in and admiration for the beauty and culture of England was matched by a growing impatience with British hostility towards the US and the Britons' abrasive manner towards Americans. He hated 'American' jokes. Stronger even than his resentment was his contempt for the aristocratic system, which he felt was deeply unjust: the accident of birth should not alone determine the course of a person's life, whether for good or ill. When he left England for Italy, he felt intensely and proudly American.[115]

This disdain for the aristocratic system was shared by a frequent visitor, Mark Twain. In *A Yankee at the Court of King Arthur*, set in an imaginary sixth century and published in 1889, he has an arresting set piece which makes his opinion clear:

And the people! They were the quaintest and simplest and trustingest race – why, they were nothing but rabbits. It was piti- ful for a person born in a wholesome free atmosphere to listen to their humble and hearty outpourings of loyalty toward their King and Church and nobility; as if they had any more occasion to love and honour King and Church and noble, than a slave has to love and honour the lash, or a dog has to love and honour the stranger that kicks him! Why, dear me, *any* kind of royalty, howsoever mod- ified, *any* kind of aristocracy, howsoever pruned, is rightly an insult; but if you are born and brought up under that sort of arrangement you probably never find it out for yourself, and don't believe it when somebody else tells you.[116]

But Twain differed from Hawthorne in an important way: he loved England and the English. British critics had admired his work long before the Americans. According to Benjamin Lease, 'He had been involved, since his first visit in 1872, in a love affair with England (marked by the occasional stormy misunderstandings that accompany such deep attachments); "I would like to stay here about fifteen or seventy-five years," he wrote to [a friend] during his first visit.' This regard was returned. In 1907, when he was given an honorary D.Litt. degree at Oxford University, Rudyard Kipling, who was receiving the same degree, noted that 'even those distinguished old dons stood up and yelled'.[117]

Another writer who loved England was Henry James, one of the most famous Americans in England in the late nineteenth and early twentieth centuries. James needed European culture more than American democracy. He came from a distinguished family – his grandfather had been one of the first millionaires in America[118] – and grew up equally in the United States and Europe. He always wrote, and at twenty-one he published his first short story. In his twenties he made his first independent trip to Europe, and this apparently was the seed of his fascination with the theme of the American in Europe. In 1875 he moved abroad permanently, first to Paris and then to England, where he lived for the rest of his life. His explanation for this was not that he was anti-American; rather, he felt that American culture was not yet developed enough to support, intellectually rather than financially, a writer. As he wrote in his short biography of Hawthorne, 'it takes such an accumulation of history and custom, such a complexity of manners and types, to form a fund of suggestion for a novelist . . . [O]ne might enumerate the items of high civilization, as it exists in other countries, which are absent from the texture of American life, until it should become a wonder to know what was left.'[119] He loved the US; he just could not live there. He remained an American citizen until the year before his death in 1916, when, as a sign of his support of Great Britain during the First World War, he became a British subject.

James and Irving are different from the other authors mentioned, in that their approach to, and feelings about, the American abroad were primarily expressed in fictional form. James's theme gradually developed into one focusing on the international confrontation of American and European civilisation; it also evolved from the idea of the American innocent abroad meeting evil to one of recognition that innocence can, quite unknowingly, trigger evil in others.[120] Alongside his novels, however, he compiled and published a volume called *English Hours* (1905),[121] thirty years' worth of travel essays, in which he conveyed the feeling that the essence of England could be found in her landscape, in a coincidence of time and place which produced an emotion which could only be termed transcendental. As he wrote in a letter to his father,

> The other afternoon I trudged over to Worcester – thro' a region so thick-sown with good old English 'effects' – with elm-scattered meadows and sheep-cropped commons and ivy-smothered dwellings of small gentility, and high-gabled, heavy-timbered, broken-plastered farm-houses and stiles leading to delicious meadow footpaths and lodge-gates leading to far-off manors – with all things suggestive of the opening chapters of half-remembered novels, devoured in my infancy – that I felt as if I were pressing all England to my soul.[122]

James shared with many other American visitors the feeling of the strong link in England between landscape and literature, one source of the lure of Stratford, and of Warwickshire in general. This landscape often brought a shock of recognition to these visitors: through family ties, or inclination during the Revolution, or from the tales and poetry of England which they had learned, many felt that they had come home. Harriet Beecher Stowe wrote in *Sunny Memories of Foreign Lands* that 'Say what you will, an American, particularly a New Englander, can never approach the old country without a kind of thrill and pulsation of kindred . . . Our very life-blood is English life-blood. It is Anglo-Saxon vigor that is spreading our country from Atlantic to Pacific.'[123] Can there be a better example of an hereditary identification with England? Indeed, there is a recurring motif in these writings – call it appropriation or co-optation or what you will. Shakespeare is as much American as English; English literature is also American literature; in Irving's tale of Rip Van Winkle, a pub sign showing George III mutates during his twenty years' sleep into a pub sign of George Washington – this is evolution, not revolution. Indeed, the great events in English history, such as Magna Carta and the Glorious Revolution, are also part of the American past. Emerson wrote that 'The American is only the continuation of the English genius into new conditions, more or less propitious.'[124] This may be simple pride or realistic acceptance, but it could also betray insecurity, even a feeling of impoverishment. American travellers coming to England were hit in the face with what they lacked. All they could do was celebrate what they had: land, people, vitality, and the certainty of a glorious future – much better than merely a glorious past.

Fundamentally, this was all about definition. British travellers to America tried to define an American. American travellers to Great Britain tried to define an Englishman (the term almost invariably used for all the inhabitants of the British Isles), but each individual traveller was really defining her- or himself. This is an American; this is not me; therefore a Briton and an American are different species, and this is how you can tell. In short, each defined her- or himself against the other. In all of these, and in many other books of travels published during the nineteenth century, the authors had in common the conviction that they had ascertained, and then revealed to others, the key to the essence of the American and America, of the Briton and Great Britain.

CHAPTER 5

Some Elements of Everyday Life in the Nineteenth and Twentieth Centuries

The natural resource of new countries is to borrow the capital of old countries.

The Economist, 18 May 1872[1]

In the four quarters of the globe, who reads an American book?

Sydney Smith, *Edinburgh Review*, January 1820[2]

Once upon a time, America was our hope and our enchantment... Now we yearn for America to be, not itself – a greedy, domineering, isolated, stomping, hypocritical land of political correctness at home and blatant savagery abroad – but the self we always believed it to be. And *that*, more than anything else, is why we are so angry. We have been let down. The America we yearned for has gone.

Michael Bywater, *Lost Worlds* (2004)[3]

The official Anglo-American relationship was grounded in war and diplomacy: they provided the context and set the boundaries within which Britons and Americans conducted many aspects of their daily lives. But outside of periods of crisis and war (and sometimes even within them), the habitual modes of intercourse continued. In endless ways, British and American individuals and groups communicated, met, co-operated or argued. As they shared a language as well as historical legacies, it would have been amazing if this had not been the case.

The economic relationship was crucial. For the whole of the nineteenth century the strength of the trading relationship was very important to both countries. Almost as vital for the US was British investment: the US was a developing country, and British funds were significant in the financing of the American infrastructure.

Much of this was so-called 'portfolio investment', the purchasing of stocks and bonds, as opposed to direct investment. However, an increasing amount of direct investment by the British took place in the final third of the century. Notably, they invested in tracts of land, a habit from colonial times. In this case it was often used for cattle ranching, which sometimes led to conflict between farmers (or 'nesters') and cattlemen.[4] For the British, then, the US remained a very important focus for investment and trade; for many Americans, the fear was that their country would remain an economic colony of Britain, as the thirteen colonies had been before the Revolution. But the economic relationship shifted in the twentieth century, with the US economy becoming the most powerful in the world.

The religious links between the two countries were of the utmost strength and importance during the first half of the nineteenth century. These links were consciously exploited, both to foster religion and to achieve social reforms; they were, for example, important in the drive to abolish slavery in the American South. However, the growing crisis between the states which ended in the Civil War tended to separate religious groups in the South and Great Britain from each other, just as it split denominations between the North and South of the US. Many of the institutional religious links as such never recovered their former potency, although informal organisations and private beliefs retained or regained their importance, both for the encouragement of religion itself and in the support of social reforms.

After the Civil War, slavery having been abolished, social reformers concentrated more on alleviating the consequences of industrialisation and unbridled capitalism, including the growth of slums. In this area most ideas originated in Great Britain, although the US took the lead in educational reform. Interestingly, after 1850, those working for women's rights on both sides looked across the Atlantic less frequently than might have been expected.

For the US reading public, the literary relationship in the nineteenth century was a mass rather than an elite phenomenon, given the relatively high level of literacy. Influence flowed primarily from Great Britain to America, where British novels and poetry were likely to be read in American-printed pirate editions. As pointed out in Chapter 4, this meant that no royalties were paid to the authors, to the incandescent rage of Charles Dickens and others. Dickens probably did not realise – and would not have cared – that American publishers themselves frequently acted in the same manner towards native authors. (And it is only fair to add that British publishers occasionally did the same to American writers.) This is not to say that the British did not read any American writers: Nathaniel Hawthorne and James Fenimore Cooper were both widely read, and the poetry of Henry Wadsworth Longfellow – he of 'The Midnight Ride of Paul Revere' – swept Britain (he was later referred to as 'the best known poet of the nineteenth century'[5]), as did, to a lesser extent, the anti-slavery poetry of John Greenleaf Whittier.[6] After the Civil War, however, as a united US now seemed a permanent entity, there was a – possibly related – rapid growth of an American literature which was self-consciously 'American'. For many years, it still had relatively little impact in Britain. Only in the twentieth century was the opposite the case.

A theme which emerges is that in spite of the growing power and wealth of the US, in spite of the fact that, by 1870, she was a united, continent-wide country, she was still, for most purposes during the nineteenth century, a social and intellectual colony of Great Britain. Furthermore, for most of the century, she remained something of an economic one. The American public realised this, and many of them repeatedly called for the driving out of British investors, British exporters, British landowners. These calls largely went unanswered.

During the twentieth century, in a reflection of the change in the balance of power between the US and Great Britain, the latter's social and cultural influence on the former ineluctably declined. Conversely, the impact of America on Great Britain became substantial. The influences were economic and commercial, social and intellectual. By the mid-twentieth century, American cultural influence was pervasive. The impact stimulated adverse comments about American 'cultural hegemony', but by the end of the twentieth century, these claims appeared to have been somewhat exaggerated.

I

The close economic relationship continued after 1815, but this is not particularly surprising given the established business and financial relationships. Indeed, as was noted in Chapter 3, many of these continued even when they were illegal, as during the Jeffersonian embargo. Dealing with those whom you knew was particularly important when distance made it difficult to assess the quality and solvency of unknown firms. There was the added consideration that, again as noted in Chapter 3, British merchants often provided credit whilst most Dutch and French would not. Furthermore, the established trade played to the strengths of each country. On the whole, the US exported raw materials and foodstuffs to Great Britain, which in turn exported manufactured goods to the US. This largely remained the case for most of the nineteenth century. Yet, from about 1870, the US bounded into its own industrial revolution, the products of which were increasingly exported, not least to Britain.

The data for American trade with Great Britain show that during the first half of the century it followed an upward trajectory. In 1821, 35 per cent of American exports went to Great Britain;[7] by 1850, it was nearly half. For most of the remainder of the century it continued at a little over half, before falling in the final decade to 38 per cent by 1900. The overwhelming categories of these exports were raw materials and foodstuffs, especially raw cotton, wheat and tobacco. The flow of cotton reflected the growth in British textile manufacturing, whilst the increased British imports of wheat and flour reflected population growth, the increasing consumption of bread made from wheat rather than rye, and the much cheaper cost of American wheat.[8] As for American imports, in 1821, 44 per cent came from Great Britain, at which level they remained until 1850. There was then a gentle decline, with an average from the 1860s to the 1890s of a third, then falling to just under a fifth by 1900.[9]

The record from a British perspective is different, in that the US was always a less important destination for her exports than Britain was for those of the US. However, there were periods when British exporters were encouraged to focus on the US for reasons besides making money. As Henry Brougham recommended in a speech to the House of Commons in 1816, British traders should dump their exports on the US, even if they had to take a loss, because this glut of goods would 'stifle in the cradle those rising manufactures in the United States which the war had forced into existence contrary to the natural course of things'.[10] The outraged American reaction to this may be imagined, but Brougham's rhetoric seems to have had little impact: in 1821, 44 per cent of US imports came from Britain, whilst exports to the US were only 17 per cent of Britain's total. By mid-century, the US market accounted for 25 per cent of all British exports, but then the proportion fell significantly: it stood at 17 per cent a decade later, 10 per cent in 1890, and only 8 per cent in 1900.[11] This decline reflected the growing industrialisation of the US, and the consequent reduced demand for manufactured products from Britain.

In the earlier part of the century the US was a developing country. With a largely agricultural economy, although there was commercial activity on the seaboard and growing industrialisation in the North and Middle Atlantic states, she needed to import both labour and capital. Immigrants were required to develop the millions of acres of available land, both for agriculture and for mining, and to provide the manpower for the gradually evolving industrial sector. British subjects from England, Scotland and Wales constituted a varying proportion of these immigrants: in 1820, for example, they made up 29 per cent of the total, falling to 5 per cent in 1830; for Ireland, the figures are 43 per cent and 12 per cent, respectively, showing an analogous decline.[12] By 1850, the percentage for emigrants from England, Scotland and Wales was 14 per cent of the total, which increased to 27 per cent in 1870 and fell to just 3 per cent in 1900; the Irish percentages were 45 per cent – clearly owing to the Potato Famine – 15 per cent and 8 per cent for the same years.[13] Sharing a language, often a (Protestant) religion, and many aspects of culture, British immigrants (but not the Irish Catholics) found it relatively easy to assimilate and 'blend in',[14] and certain principles that they shared with Americans – sanctity of the family, equality before the law, the importance of private property – reinforced their importance to American culture.

British immigrants were also significant because they brought with them new technologies in, for example, mining and textiles. According to Frank Thistlethwaite, British miners arrived at shallow American coal pits and showed the Americans how to burrow into deep seams. They also established the basis for the metalworking industries: as early as 1820, Cornish tin miners were working lead mines on the Upper Mississippi, and they and their successors opened up the copper and iron beds of Lake Superior. More importantly, 'the primitive, charcoal-burning iron trade was transformed into a vigorous, progressive industry not only by British techniques but by British technicians'. But the most important of all 'industrial immigrants' were those with expertise in textiles. People from Lancashire, the West Riding of Yorkshire and Scotland illegally slipped away from Great Britain, since those possessing knowledge of new and important technologies were discouraged from emigrating. They then sold this knowledge, which facilitated the establishment of an American textile industry, the first of Great Britain's new industries to be established in the US.[15]

Capital was also required to develop the country. Short-term funds were needed to finance a substantial proportion of American imports and, especially, exports, but they were needed even more to finance 'internal improvements', particularly the building of canals and railways. The demand for primary products such as cotton, tobacco and wheat from the South and West fuelled the need for improved transportation networks: the South needed western foodstuffs, whilst both regions needed to get their goods to foreign markets. Turnpike (toll) roads were built, including a Federally financed National Road from Baltimore to Columbus, Ohio, but the latter was essentially a failure: it was covered with gravel, which sank into the mud during the winter and then baked during the summer, and it was prone to landslides. This experience convinced many that there must be an alternative. They joined critics who believed that the Federal government should in any case stay out of internal improvements, especially those which benefitted only some of the states.[16]

The alternative was canals. The Americans had before them the example of the British, who since the 1770s had experienced something of a mania for building canals. The 3rd Duke of Bridgewater, owner of a number of coal mines at Worsley in Lancashire, wanted to transport his coal to the rapidly growing city of Manchester, six miles to the south-east. It was being shipped by road, but this was very slow and expensive. Completed in 1761, the Bridgewater Canal was an immediate success, reducing the price of coal in Manchester by one-half in one year, and repaying the cost of construction within just a few years. Its success triggered the investment of huge sums, and within a few years there were four thousand miles of canals in Great Britain, which facilitated rapid industrialisation.[17]

If not the Federal government, it would have to be the states which organised the construction and financing of canals, since no group of private individuals would take the huge financial risk. New York State took the lead.[18] In 1817 the State Legislature authorised the construction of the Erie Canal, to run from Buffalo on the eastern shore of Lake Erie to the Hudson River; ships could then continue to the port of New York. Certainly a major motivation was to link the Great Lakes with the Atlantic Ocean, but of equal importance was that the canal would help open up to settlers the Old Northwest, now the states of Ohio, Illinois and Indiana. No longer would people or produce have to go over the Appalachian Mountains. Before the canal, it cost between $90 and $125 to ship a ton of cargo by road from Buffalo to New York City; within a few years of its opening in 1825, the cost had dropped to $4 a ton. It was also an investment success: within twelve years, it had recouped its cost of construction. Unsurprisingly, this stimulated a canal boom.

The Erie Canal was financed to a great extent by British investors, but they seldom invested directly. For example, for an importer buying goods from Great Britain, it was safer to pay in bonds than in gold. An American importer might therefore purchase some of the bonds issued by New York State to pay for the construction of the Canal, then send them to London as payment for his goods. These bonds were a great success, because the interest on them was paid promptly each year at a rate of interest twice that obtaining in London, and they were redeemable early at a premium. The result was a tremendous burst of enthusiasm in London for American state securities.

This enthusiasm was not just for any investment, however. British investors were drawn to what were termed 'productive purposes', investments that paid for themselves by producing an income stream. A prime subject was canals, which had been immensely profitable in Great Britain; the bulk of the American state securities bought by British investors in the 1830s were for the construction of canals. The interest rates on the securities, at 5 to 6 per cent, were high, the US was evidently prosperous, and British trade would benefit from the production of American exports and the consequent increased ability of Americans to buy British imports. Leland Jenks argues that there were also 'imponderables' which led British investors to turn eagerly to American stocks: kinship, language and the common law. The result was the elevation of the US above all other regions as the focus for British investment. It is estimated that the total of British capital invested in American securities in the 1830s was roughly equivalent to the states' debts: by 1835, this invested capital amounted to $66 million; three years later the sum was $174 million.[19]

However, in July 1836, President Andrew Jackson signed the Specie Circular, which required that all public land sales be settled in gold, not paper money. His intention was to quash land speculation funded by an outpouring of promissory notes printed by so-called 'wildcat banks', state-chartered and lacking adequate reserves to support their notes. Jackson wanted to lower land prices for settlers, but his policy merely created a demand for specie (coinage rather than paper money). This soon led to pressure on banks on the Atlantic Coast to acquire gold bullion. At roughly the same time, the Bank of England raised interest rates to reduce the outflow of gold from its reserves, which had fallen from eleven million to seven million pounds in just four years.[20] There were no immediate repercussions, but conditions were now ripe for a crisis.

In 1837 there was an unusually large cotton crop, and cotton prices fell by 25 per cent during February and March. The result was calamity. The three main 'American houses' in England suspended payment to their creditors,[21] and hundreds of American banks, which had lent money on the security of crops, also suspended payment. Farmers, planters, traders and speculators throughout the US went bankrupt. Nine out of ten factories in the eastern states shut down, and 50 per cent of commercial employees were sacked. In Great Britain the crisis was limited to the American trade – that with Africa, the Continent and the colonies continued – and there was no commercial depression. But for the US, the Panic of 1837 was a disaster.[22]

A scheme to alleviate it was organised by Nicholas Biddle, former president of the defunct Second Bank of the United States, which was reborn as a Pennsylvanian institution (headed by Biddle). He established various unorthodox ways to raise finance so that producers and brokers could hold cotton back from sale until the price rose. This worked for some months, but in 1838 events conspired against the plan. The British wheat crop failed, which meant that most available British credit went into importing more grain. At the same time, the new textile industries of Prussia, Belgium and Saxony cut back on their demand for English yarn, which resulted in British manufacturers cutting back their orders for raw cotton from the US. Producers and brokers could not continue to hold stocks of cotton because the flow of credit funds from London had dried up. The attempts in the US to support the price of cotton failed, and this resulted in a deeper crisis. There were further bankruptcies, and, by the states, a widespread repudiation of debts. As a consequence, 'there were few regions in the world whose public treasuries and private enterprises had as little credit as those of the United States'.[23] For older Britons, this was all too reminiscent of the states' responses to pre-Revolutionary War debts.

In 1842, Illinois, Indiana, Louisiana, Michigan, Alabama, Maryland, Mississippi, Pennsylvania and the territory of Florida either defaulted on the interest due on their state bonds or repudiated them altogether. (Indeed, Mississippi continues to repudiate them.) As a result, the sale of American securities in London became almost impossible. Americans blamed London. As Sydney Smith, clergyman and editor of the influential *Edinburgh Review*, wrote:

> Angered at the folly with which they had incurred indebtedness, American Commonwealths sought to vent their rage upon the obliging creditors. And . . . there arose a debacle of American credit as complete as the confidence which it had formerly elicited

had been unquestioning . . . What caused American stocks to join those of Portugal and Mexico and Greece in the ghettoes of finance was the failure of nine sovereign commonwealths to pay the interest upon their debts.[24]

The British lobbied to have the Federal government assume the obligations of the defaulting states, and when they failed, the reaction was ferocious. Smith wrote in 1843 that he never met a citizen of Pennsylvania (some of whose securities Smith himself held) at a London dinner 'without feeling a disposition to seize and divide him – to allot his beaver [hat] to one sufferer and his coat to another – to appropriate his pocket handkerchief to the orphan and to comfort the widow with his silver watch, Broadway rings, and the London Guide which he always carried in his pockets . . . He has no more right to eat with honest men than a leper has to eat with clean.'[25] This bitterness extended to the Federal government. In the summer of 1842, when agents of the US Treasury came to Europe to raise a loan to cover the decline in customs receipts, they were essentially thrown out of bankers' offices: '"You may tell your government," said the Paris Rothschild to Duff Green, the American agent, "that you have seen the man who is at the head of the finances of Europe, and that he has told you that they cannot borrow a dollar, not a dollar."'[26]

Although the three most substantial London 'American houses' went down in the crisis, one American house survived and prospered. This was the firm headed by George Peabody, an American who had begun by dealing in dry goods and later moved into American securities, for which, during the 1840s, he seems to have been the major London specialist. He bought and sold them in the London market; he also took part in new issues in the US and sold them in London, usually on joint account with Baring Brothers, then the most important English house in American finance. After the repudiations by the states, American securities were, not surprisingly, seen as dangerously risky, and Peabody was active in trying to restore confidence in them. He genuinely had great faith in their ultimate value, so he was prepared to buy at low prices, confident that he would eventually reap a profit. Indeed, because there was now no regular market for American securities in England, Peabody, as a large and constant buyer, reaped many advantages. He made his office a centre of transactions, and he developed the reputation of being willing to buy or sell any American securities – which he sometimes did only to keep that reputation intact. In short, Peabody was, in modern parlance, a 'market-maker', someone whose willingness to buy and sell even when the market is volatile provides the investor with liquidity. He was arguably the man most responsible for keeping alive the market for American securities in London, and when the mood of the market changed in the late 1840s he was able to sell many which he himself owned, reaping his just rewards.[27] His activities put his firm on a solid foundation of reputation and solvency, and he established two branches: one became Morgan Grenfell in London and the other J.P. Morgan (and its 1930s offshoot, Morgan Stanley) in New York.

The mood of the London market had changed in 1848 for a number of reasons. Throughout the decade reviving commerce had gradually swelled the revenues of American public bodies, and dividend payments were resumed by all but three states. This encouraged the hope that the others might do so and, in general, that American state bonds were becoming a reasonable risk. Furthermore, renewed attention was being paid to the basic strengths of the US, such as its population and natural resources, its growing manufacturing base and its developing infrastructure. The fact that Federal securities were selling very well in the US encouraged confidence. In Continental Europe the spate of revolutions in 1848 caused 'nervous money' to buy American bonds. And finally, later in 1848, gold was discovered in California.[28] This was all just in time for the railway boom.

What initiated the boom of the 1850s was the passage in 1850 of the Illinois Central Land Grant Bill. This granted land to the railroad via the state to extend the line through Federal territories (those which were neither part of nor under the control of a state). It provided for a right-of-way along the route of the railway two hundred feet wide and alternate larger sections of land on either side. 'The pattern was like that of a checkerboard: for every mile of track laid, the government granted to the railroad company every other square mile of land on both sides of the track to a depth of six square miles (the reds), while retaining ownership of the bypassed square miles (the blacks) for itself.' The idea was that the railways could market their bonds because they owned land which could serve as collateral, whilst the government could sell its plots of land at a much higher price because of the value created by the existence of the railway.[29] Other railway companies then also received Federal and state land grants, and this, plus the relative ease of building railways on level ground, set imaginations flying. Railway mileage tripled from 1849 to 1856, with most of the increase taking place in the West or in East–West connecting lines.[30]

Jay Sexton points out that whilst American capital funded the majority of railways built during this period, foreign investment was crucial to the building of several 'significant' lines, including the Illinois Central. One important reason for raising funds in Great Britain was to facilitate the purchase of British steel, greatly superior to any other, and in high demand during the 1850s. Indeed, 'for a brief period following their initial public issuance abroad in 1852, American railroad bonds were the "prime glamour issue" in London', with British investment in American railways doubling between 1848 and 1852, from £12 million to £24 million ($60 million to $120 million).[31] But British investment was not the dominant element in the feverish speculation in railways during the mid-1850s; rather, it was the Americans themselves. However, this was curtailed by the Panic of 1857: the combination of railway speculation, a sharp decline in agricultural exports to Europe, the failure of a major insurance company, and the collapse of land speculation led to the withdrawal of British funds from American banks, casting grave doubts on the strength of the US economy. This was soon followed by the Civil War, and it was only when that was over that American railways again became the principal attraction for foreign investors.[32]

There was a recurring problem for foreign investors in American railways, however: the apparent endemic corruption which weakened and sometimes destroyed them. One notorious exponent of this was Jay Gould, the robber baron who eventually controlled both the Atlantic and Great Western Railroad and the Erie Railroad. After the Civil War, British investors probably held fifty million out of the

Erie's seventy-million-dollar capital stock, and one-third of the Atlantic and Great Western's funded debt. They were therefore sharply attuned to rumours of corruption in the management of both companies. For example, in their desire to wrest control of the Erie from Cornelius Vanderbilt, Gould and his two partners, amongst other questionable activities, issued fraudulent stock to themselves and their supporters in order to gain a majority stake in the company. Charles Francis Adams Jr.'s report on this corruption, published in 1871 as *Chapters of Erie*, was crucial in forming the investors' views of American railways in general. 'Dubbed a "swindler" by *The Economist*, Jay Gould did little to win over British investors when he infamously predicted that "there will be icicles in Hell when Erie common [stock] pays a dividend".'[33] Dorothy Adler reports the then-current claim that British investors lost between ten and twenty million pounds in the two railways, thereby underlining the 1869 advice of the *Bankers' Magazine* that 'the English public should refrain, as much as possible, from making investments in American railway shares'.[34]

Once memories of the Erie scandal began to fade, however, British investors again began to invest in American railways. The railways at that point were the country's second-largest employer (after agriculture), and involved huge amounts of risk. The failure of the Northern Pacific Railroad, established in order to build a second transcontinental railway, triggered the Panic of 1873 and the 'Long Depression', which lasted until 1877. It has been estimated that of the $390 million of American railway bonds and shares held abroad in December 1874 (not all by British investors), $148 million or 38 per cent were in default. Again, foreign investors held back, but by the 1880s a very active market for US railway securities abroad had resumed. There was a separate section of the London Stock Exchange for trades in them, and in 1913 their nominal value quoted on the Exchange came to $8.4 billion, or about 42 per cent of the entire nominal capitalisation of US railways. This did not entirely reflect British holdings, but it shows the importance they had in portfolio investment,[35] as well as the fundamental optimism of the British investor in America.

There was much less direct than indirect investment in the US in the nineteenth century, but one important example of the former was investment in land. Since the colonial period the British upper classes had bought land in America. However, in the late nineteenth century, in the Great Plains states and territories – west of the Mississippi and east of the Rocky Mountains, from Texas in the South to Montana in the North – 'alien [foreign] ownership' stimulated rage and fear, with Scots the most heavily involved.[36] A chief concern was that available supplies of free or low-cost land were dwindling; and, indeed, they had essentially dried up by about 1890, when the Bureau of the Census announced that, after four hundred years, the frontier line had closed – there was no more cheap public land available to purchase.[37] In this situation, it was easy to blame British owners: they were normally absent, and their holdings were large, even, in some cases, huge. The assumption was that these owners were hated aristocrats, and some certainly were – Lord Dunraven owned several thousand acres, and fellow cattle barons included the Duke of Sutherland and the Marquis of Tweeddale – but most of the land was actually owned by corporations (although aristocrats might of course be directors or shareholders): by the end of 1883, there were incorporated in Great Britain twenty-one major western cattle companies. If American farmers lost their farms, they might have to become tenants. Not only was this virtually unAmerican – an American farmer should own his land, not rent it – but millions of Irish immigrants had stories to tell of what being a tenant of a British landlord could mean. In 1880, 26 per cent of farms were held by tenants; by 1890, this had increased to 34 per cent.[38]

There was a further clash, in that the owners of these huge tracts of land were not arable farmers; rather, as noted above, they were cattle ranchers. Furthermore, they were – quite legally – grazing their livestock on public land, although some were fencing it off (as were many of the American landowners). This led to violence in the Great Plains and especially in Texas, where settlers began to cut the fences. These attacks, plus floods of petitions against foreign landlords, led Congress to pass on 25 February 1885 a law prohibiting enclosures on the public domain which would prevent a person from entering peaceably to visit or establish a settlement or residence on public land. The intention of the government to enforce this law was

made clear by the issuing on 7 August of a proclamation by President
Grover Cleveland ordering all unlawful fences to be torn down.[39]
One hundred thousand cattle belonging to the (Scottish) Prairie
Cattle Company ranged over at least one million acres of land, whilst
in the spring of 1884 it was estimated that the total Scottish investment in land and cattle came to twenty-five million dollars. The
House of Representatives' 'Report on Land Titles to Aliens in the
United States' revealed that the British controlled at least twenty-
five million acres, chiefly in the West.[40] It was, however, the
movement of settlers into western Nebraska, Kansas, Texas and
eastern Colorado which produced strong and general hostility to
British cattle ranches. Between 1883 and 1887, anger grew as new
settlers bumped up against the ranchers' fences. The Prairie Cattle
Company and the Arkansas Valley Land and Cattle Company were
each reported to have fenced a million acres in Colorado, as well as
long stretches of the Arkansas River. In truth, American cattlemen
far outnumbered the British in these conflicts, but it was the activities of the British which were publicised and thus stoked the wrath
of western farmers and their supporters.[41]

This intense dislike of the British gave a special twist to the fear
of the end of the frontier and therefore of supplies of cheap land.
'British' stood for the subjection of other peoples, for financial
power, and for aristocratic institutions. It was believed dangerous for
American soil to pass into the hands of foreigners 'whose birth and
education create and foster sentiments inimical to the country from
which they are attempting to derive wealth'. A western newspaper
put it more simply: 'England by stratagem and purchase [is] getting
back what she lost in war.'[42]

This was a period of intense agrarian discontent and even revolt,
and an article of faith was the need to forbid the foreign ownership
of land. In December 1883 an (unsuccessful) Bill was introduced in
the House of Representatives in Washington to prohibit the acquisition of Federal territorial land by absentee 'aliens' or by companies
in which more than 20 per cent of the stock was held by aliens. In
January 1885 there was an extended debate following the report of
the House of Representatives' Committee on Public Lands. The
objections were to the ownership and control of the lands, not to the

investment of foreign money; the committee proposed to guarantee that 'American soil should be owned exclusively by American citizens'. There was some fear that such a law would drive out British capital, but a Bill was finally agreed upon and signed by President Cleveland in March 1887. It forbade any absentee alien, or resident alien who had not declared the intention of becoming an American citizen, from gaining possession of real property in the territories, unless it was inherited or was payment for debts already contracted. Furthermore, at least four-fifths of the stock of any corporation acquiring land in the territories had to be held by Americans. Finally, no company, whether American or foreign, could own more than five thousand acres of land, unless they were building transport services, such as roads or railways. Domestic opinion was widely supportive, and a number of states hastened to pass similar legislation.[43]

However, states and territories which were home to considerable mining interests objected to this legislation; they needed capital for development, and London was a major source. Their fears were realised, and the flow of capital virtually dried up; at the same time, mining and other deals about to be finalised in Great Britain and Europe were cancelled. The flotation of mining companies on the London Stock Exchange was abruptly checked. The prosperity of the affected territories suffered severely. Yet, by the mid-1890s, foreign investments in mining had revived, and investment had resumed. What did not recover was the drive to put together large land companies for investment, but in any case, their era seemed to have passed.[44]

Trade and British investment in the US were probably the major elements in the Anglo-American economic relationship during the nineteenth century. Nevertheless, it is obvious that business dealings between individuals and firms spanned the spectrum. There were other agricultural products and commodities sold besides wheat and cotton. Many industrial products were sold, primarily by Britain to the US before the Civil War, but increasingly in the reverse direction as American industry expanded after 1870. The number of Americans investing in Britain also now grew. In short, the asymmetry began to lessen. Finally, it is worth remembering that economic issues could be difficult to disentangle from politics and diplomacy: as *The Economist* wrote in October 1860, 'According to general estimation . . . political circumstances are the most influential in determining the price of the funds.'[45] The settlement of the Oregon border, of future control of any isthmian canal by the Clayton–Bulwer Treaty in 1850, and of the *Alabama* claims in 1872 all encouraged British investors to assess the US as a better risk than before. On the other side, the Americans might hate the British, but they needed their investment.

II

Ritcheson has argued that 'aside from nationality itself, the Christian religion, and, more especially the Protestant variation of it, constituted the greatest common denominator of life in both Britain and America in the first half of the nineteenth century'.[46] In general terms this was probably true, but the varieties of Protestantism were remarkably varied, and denominations varied in the strength of their transatlantic links. The Church of England or Anglican Church and the Protestant Episcopal Church in the US were linked in the Anglican Communion, as were the British and American Quakers in the Society of Friends. The dissenting or nonconformist Churches, notably the Methodists, had strong but informal links with their brethren across the Atlantic. All of these links were shaken by the Civil War. Afterwards, however, a continuing interest in propagating the faith or in working for social reforms encouraged the re-establishment of closer ties during the remainder of the century.

Transatlantic links were particularly strong between evangelical nonconformist groups, and pre-eminent here were the Methodists. Methodism had originated in Great Britain, and until the death in 1791 of John Wesley, one of its founders, it was a subset of the Church of England. It then broke away, constituting a separate and evangelical Church, but with several branches of its own. For decades, British Methodists predominated in the relationship with American Methodists. Their influence was based on producing the overwhelming majority of evangelical publications, on ministerial visits, and on emigration, the latter two benefitting from the increased number, speed and regularity of sailings. The visiting ministers increased the number of 'circuit riders', the itinerant evangelical ministers who made regular preaching circuits through the less inhabited parts of the US; the immigrants swelled the ranks of those who taught Sunday school and distributed religious tracts. The British Methodists also brought polish and relative refinement to American revivalist habits, which helped to bring in more sophisticated, urban audiences. Nevertheless, they tended not to challenge the methods and mores of American revivalism, which had evolved from the indigenous social and cultural environment. Influence and aid did not flow in one direction only, however, since many British Methodists took inspiration from the American example.

The dynamic force behind most American Protestant denominations – of which there was a bewildering array – was evangelicalism, the drive to convert. In the United States it was an accelerating force from the time of the Great Awakening in the 1730s and 1740s, and independence only increased the momentum. Gordon S. Wood argues that 'the religious transformation that took place as a result of the Revolution could not have been more radical. Ordinary people asserted themselves during the Revolution in unprecedented numbers, and they brought their egalitarian religious enthusiasm with them.'[47] Indeed, by the 1820s, popular evangelical Christianity had become a force of such strength that it was dubbed the 'Second Great Awakening'. But the revival of the nineteenth century was different from the first in at least one important respect. The eighteenth-century Awakening had stressed the inherently sinful nature of man, and his utter incapacity to overcome his depravity without the direct action of God working through the Holy Spirit.[48] In the nineteenth century the emphasis was on sin as human action: humans repenting and turning away from sinful behaviour.[49] The Second Great Awakening was about convincing people that they could and should do so.

The primary method used was the revival. This term developed from the earlier idea of churches experiencing a religious revival, an unexpected awakening and outpouring of spiritual conviction and concern. The core of nineteenth-century evangelicalism was conversion, which was fundamentally an emotional experience. The convert did not merely believe: he or she experienced an overpowering catharsis. Of supreme importance in encouraging conversion was the revival or camp meeting, which emerged at the turn of the nineteenth century. Charles Grandison Finney, evangelical preacher and later president of Oberlin College, 'the most influential American revivalist of the nineteenth century', explained the importance of the revival: 'Almost all the religion in the world has been produced by revivals. God has found it necessary to take advantage of the excitability there is in mankind, to produce powerful excitements among them, before he can lead them to obey.'[50] Revivals were first held in rural western Virginia and North Carolina, and on the Kentucky and Ohio frontiers, and were organised by Presbyterians and Baptists as well as by Methodists. The most famous of these meetings took place at Cane Ridge, Kentucky, in 1801. Hundreds and sometimes thousands of people came to this camp in the wilderness, drawn from villages and farmsteads from miles around, remaining for four days to a week. While there, they listened to sermons each day, given by preachers who could combine conviction, energy and simplicity of speech, sang dozens of hymns, and went through the stages to conversion: public confessions of sin and avowals to put the devil behind oneself, personal witness to the workings of the spirit, sometimes screaming, yelling, rolling on the ground, and eventually the conviction of being saved and entering a new life.[51]

This was more or less the pattern of revivals for the following half-century in the US, although in many areas, such as New England, they were normally not quite so unbridled. The American writer James Fenimore Cooper described some meetings as 'impressive and beautiful. The Methodists have, at stated periods, what are called camp meetings. They assemble in thousands in some wood, and hold their religious festivals in a manner that is as striking by its peculiar simplicity, as it is touching by the interest and evident enjoyment they experience.'[52] Whether by camp meetings or urban meetings, fixed churches or itinerant preachers, the revival became a distinguishing characteristic of American evangelical churches.

Revivalism as a tool of conversion, and of the renewal and

maintenance of strong belief in God and Jesus Christ, was also present in Great Britain, but Richard Carwardine has pointed out that 'revivalism never held as religiously prominent or socially acceptable a place in Britain as in America', although it was a mark of all evangelical churches. (Wood states that by the early nineteenth century, 'enthusiastic groups of revivalist Baptists and Methodists had moved from the margins to the center of American society'.) The American-style revival meeting had a lesser place in British than in American evangelical culture. The British tended to distrust so much emotion, and many came increasingly to believe that it was better to use such meetings as an occasional method of supporting existing belief, rather than, as in the US, using repeated and protracted camp meetings as primarily conversion events. In due course doubts grew in Britain about the theology, practices and general emotional excitement of American revivalism, with a developing feeling that this excitement did not necessarily reflect true religion. There was an upsurge of revivalism in the late 1850s, first in the US and then in Britain, but thereafter it declined in importance in most churches,[53] although it continued in others, particularly in rural America.

Daniel Walker Howe argues that the segment of British society which identified with bourgeois evangelicalism, usually thought to be the 'most characteristically Victorian', actually tended to live at the periphery of polite society and political power: middle-class standards had to contend with the patterns of aristocratic culture. (However, as always, there were exceptions: one such was Gladstone, four times Prime Minister.) Conversely, in the US, such people dominated economic, social and political institutions, since aristocratic cultural patterns were weak, if they existed at all beyond southern plantation culture. As a consequence, 'Victorian' culture was felt more strongly in the US. On the other hand, evangelical groups there had to contend with an ethnic diversity that simply did not exist in Britain.[54] These differences did not, however, prevent the two religious cultures co-operating as members of a joint mission to convert and save the world, and during the Second Great Awakening there was much transatlantic travel. All of the Protestant denominations, bar the Anglicans and Unitarians, engaged in this, but Methodists were probably more powerfully driven than the others.

In Britain, the Church of England during the first half of the century experienced something approaching turmoil. By repute, according to Ralph Waldo Emerson (who was himself a Unitarian, a faith which denied the Trinity), the Church exhibited a notable lack of fervour, apparently acting as an occupational home for the younger sons of the gentry and the aristocracy, and possessing a fox-hunting clergy: 'The curates are ill paid, and the prelates are overpaid. This abuse draws into the church the children of the nobility, and other unfit persons, who have a taste for expense.'[55] During the first half of the century, Ritcheson states, both branches 'were in deep lethargy, identified in England with rankest conservatism in the Age of Reform; in America, tarred with the Tory brush, suffering from poor organization, and indulging in a cold and lifeless formalism little adapted to the evangelical spirit of the times'.[56]

In truth, fervour as such was not lacking in the Church of England: the issue for reformers was to confront this lethargy, and the irrelevance of the Church to great swaths of the lower classes, both working and non-working. To do so would require some change of direction. The question was, in which direction? One possibility was to become more High Church, a position identified with the Oxford Movement. The origins of the Oxford Movement itself lends some credence to Emerson's comment. Its begetters were a group of Anglican academics and clergymen resident in Oxford, fundamentally a conservative city – it had supported Charles I against the Parliamentarians during the Civil War – with a conservative university. These men were 'increasingly unhappy with the lack of seriousness with which the establishment regarded its religious duties'.[57] They wished to rekindle appreciation of and adherence to the pre-Reformation Catholic heritage and theological insights; they attacked doctrinal laxity, and political trends which appeared to be leading to the Church's disestablishment (as was being discussed and would in due course happen in Ireland).

The most prominent spokesman of the movement was John Henry Newman, Fellow of Oriel College, Oxford, and vicar of the University Church, St Mary's. According to Owen Chadwick,

Newman was in the beginning 'sensitive, shy and complicated, puritan in austerity, somewhat introverted, aloof by reason of nervousness and not from sense of superiority'. During the 1820s and early 1830s he moved steadily to the right in both doctrine and politics; it was the struggle for the Great Reform Bill of 1832 that confirmed him as a conservative high churchman.[58] Newman was the author of the majority of the ninety 'Tracts for the Times' – hence the Movement's other name, the Tractarians – the first of which was published in 1833. They argued in general that the truth of Anglican doctrine rested on the modern Church's position as the direct descendant of the Apostles' Church, a position which emphasised the influence of Catholic doctrine and denied the legitimacy of most of the other reform movements.

'The Oxford Movement added a conservative option to the lively atmosphere of Victorian religious debate. The Victorians who abhorred the atheism of the Unitarians and the agnosticism of the scientists, were put off by the enthusiasm of the Evangelicals, found the Broad Church [see below] too latitudinarian to have any meaning left to its doctrine, and yet could not stomach going over to Rome, found these High Church Anglicans a perfect conservative solution.'[59] Newman, however, was to undercut the popularity and even acceptability of this movement. Tract No. 90, published in 1841, argued that the fundamental basis of the Anglican Church, the Thirty-Nine Articles, did not necessarily conflict with Roman Catholic doctrine. But this appeared to many to open the Church to Catholic infiltration, and Newman's conversion to Catholicism in 1845 came as a thunderbolt to many. It appeared to demonstrate that being a Tractarian led one inevitably to Rome, and this, in conjunction with a theological (and marital) crisis occasioned by another Tractarian, H.G. Ward (who also converted to Catholicism), effectively destroyed the movement's influence and soon the Movement itself.[60]

An alternative course for the Anglican Church was to develop in the direction of a broad church that eschewed narrow expressions of doctrine as espoused by Anglo-Catholics (high churchmen) or evangelicals (low churchmen). This was argued for by a tiny and unorganised group of Anglican intellectuals who believed that, whilst the Bible was in some sense divinely inspired, it should not be taken as literal truth, a position supported by work (especially by German scholars) on Jesus as an historical figure and on biblical and related non-biblical texts. This was a position which divided them sharply from Tractarians, Anglo-Catholics and evangelicals. (An alternative term for the position, hurled by Newman as an insult, was 'liberalism'.) These men welcomed, or at least tolerated, a broad range of approaches to religious observance, and strove to be inclusive rather than exclusive.

Many of them also believed strongly that people should worship Christ by working for social justice, an idea which would produce the Social Gospel Movement (see below). Probably the most famous of these, although he died young (in 1842), was Dr Thomas Arnold, the headmaster of Rugby School (and father of Matthew Arnold). His influence is celebrated by a novel written by Thomas Hughes, *Tom Brown's School Days*; Hughes was a schoolboy at Rugby. He asks why three hundred boys should feel gripped by the headmaster's sermon? His answer was that 'we listened . . . to a man whom we felt to be, with all his heart and soul and strength, striving against whatever was mean and unmanly and unrighteous in our little world'.[61] This highlights a main principle of Arnold and other supporters of this liberal approach: that a man should work against injustice and for the amelioration of conditions which drag men down. This ethos would drive forward British and imperial social reforms in the second half of the century as it was adopted by the middle and upper classes, largely through its promulgation by the public schools and some university leaders, such as Benjamin Jowett, Master of Balliol College, Oxford, a nursery for administrators of the Empire.

The third possible new direction for the Anglican Church was to increase its commitment to evangelicalism. This was not really a sharply defined position, as was the case with liberalism: rather, evangelical beliefs already informed or at least touched many aspects of the Church. For example, both the Tractarians and the evangelicals emphasised inner religion, rather than outward rituals (although the term 'High Church' also came to designate those who did require 'bells and smells'). Gladstone was only one example of a high churchman who had strong evangelical convictions. Earlier Anglican evangelicals included the Clapham Sect, conservative and socially prominent, who were central in the campaign to abolish slavery. The high churchmen and the evangelicals could, when necessary, unite against the liberals. All of these groups had their supporters; what was increasingly unacceptable was to do nothing and let the Church drift.

All three branches of the Church of England had links with the American Protestant Episcopal Church, which had been formally reorganised in 1789 as the successor to the Anglican Church in the colonies. Their situations, however, were very different. The Anglican Church was the Established Church, supported and sometimes directed by the government; the Episcopal Church was not established, and it faced the hostility of the various political and cultural establishments, which overwhelmingly had their roots in dissent. This may have made it difficult for some to avow openly their sense of togetherness with the Anglican Church. In any case, the Episcopal Church did not depend wholly on the English Church for its inspiration; rather, it tended to look back to the early Church. This, of course, was not unlike the Oxford Movement's pre-Reformation focus, which probably made the exchange of ideas easier.

In the 1840s, it has been argued, the ideas of the Oxford Movement encouraged changes in the American Church, particularly in the conduct of worship and in the tightening of spiritual discipline. Larry Crockett, however, suggests that this has been vastly overstated, that the American Church pre-dated the British in some of its reforms, and that Newman himself wrote about this in the October 1839 issue of the *British Critic*, suggesting that the Anglican Church could learn from its American brethren, because they were implementing Catholic reforms free from the interference of the state.[62] The idea of a broad church was also influential in the American Episcopal Church, but in this case influence was not brought to bear on the procedures or prayers of the churches themselves. Rather, emphasis in the USA shifted to working in the world for the physical as well as the religious improvement of human beings, which transformed the Episcopal Church from a conservative organisation into a leading exponent of the Social Gospel.

Finally, there were the Quakers. From the seventeenth century until the mid-nineteenth, the transatlantic connection was very strong, with the two groups linked by trade as well as by families and religion, and constituting a single Society of Friends. Virtually every year after 1672 saw a 'gospel visit' by English Quakers to America, giving encouragement and support; occasionally American Quakers visited England, but the traffic from east to west was far greater and of more importance in terms of forms of religious thought, church organisation and governance, and methods of transacting business. Countless tracts, books and sermons in letters – the 'epistles' – from the British Yearly Meetings poured across the Atlantic. The pre-dominance of the London Society, given its size, experience and wealth, not surprisingly continued for most of the first half of the nineteenth century.[63]

The separate national approaches to religion sometimes precipi-tated a gradual but tangible lessening of institutional religious links during the first half of the century, the Quakers excepted, but of more direct importance was the clash over slavery (see below). The British simply could not understand why the American churches did not all condemn it, and the growing habit of southern churchmen of citing the Bible in support of the system sickened them. There was also considerable support for slavery in the North, as Harriet Martineau discovered in Boston (see Chapter 4).[64] Nevertheless, this did not prevent many northern churches from calling on their southern brethren to take a stand against slavery; the Quakers as well as the Methodist and Baptist churches effectively split over the issue (although not the Episcopal Church). American evangelical aboli-tionists called on their British co-religionists to help, but the result was the general condemnation of British interference and the cutting of many transatlantic religious ties. It took some years to repair the rents in the fabric, but the process was facilitated by the end of slav-ery and by the growing involvement of church members in social reform movements.

III

The relationship between British and American social reform move-ments was lopsided, in that the predominant influence was British.

The majority of ideas about types of reform and the methodology to accomplish their adoption most often originated in Great Britain. These ideas were carried across the Atlantic by visitors and in journals, reports and books, and they led to the growth and development of analogous reform groups in the US. In the earlier part of the century, evangelicals on both sides of the Atlantic came together in the anti-slavery movement. After the Civil War, although there was some concern for the freedmen, the focus of social reformers was the plight of the working man and his family, and in particular the squalor of the great cities where they lived. Here, the Social Gospel Movement was of prime importance in the US, with some of its proponents becoming part of the more secular Progressive movement. In Great Britain, whilst there were strong supporters of the tenets of the Social Gospel Movement, the Christian Socialist Movement was also important. However, of equal significance were secular intellectuals and publicists, in particular the Fabians. Both British and American reformers were part of what Kenneth O. Morgan called 'a world-wide quest to control urbanization and industrialization',[65] but the problems in the US and Great Britain were of primary importance to both.

The move to abolish the international slave trade and then slavery itself in the US was a prominent example of the link between religion and social reform in the first half of the century. Although the eighteenth-century campaign to abolish the slave trade had supporters in both countries, the British had led the way in developing techniques to mobilise middle-class opinion in support of legislation. During the period from the abolition of the slave trade within the British Empire in 1807 to the final abolition of slavery itself in the Empire in 1833, anti-slavery leaders perfected their methods. The first step was to establish the facts. Quaker bankers and merchants financed research into the conditions of West Indian slavery, at that time their focus, and then arranged for the distribution of pamphlets disseminating the results of this research to nonconformists, who were keen readers, and to the wider public. 'From 1823 onwards the British Anti-Slavery Society . . . conducted a paper war against the West Indian planters of modern dimensions.' During 1823 alone, nearly 250,000 anti-slavery pamphlets were distributed in Great

Britain; no one had any excuse for not knowing the facts of the matter.[66]

But knowing the facts and deploring them, and then making a conscience-soothing financial contribution to the cause, was not enough. By the end of the 1820s, more radical elements decided that this gradual, almost well-mannered, approach to the elimination of slavery had to be supplanted by repeated, and often loud, demands for its immediate abolition. This was justified by the invocation of a Higher Law, a moral approach that made the movement more of an evangelical crusade than akin to a modern political campaign. With money and prodding from the Quakers, a British Agency Committee was set up; this employed six paid agitators to speak to religious groups up and down the country. 'These, and especially one, George Thompson, an agitator of great rhetorical gifts and personal magnetism, were responsible for the formation of hundreds of new antislavery societies [which] organised meetings and speakers, compiled circulation lists, distributed tracts, drafted petitions to Parliament, boycotted slave produce, and raised funds by holding bazaars and fairs.'[67] They also organised a placard campaign to reach those who had only the rudiments of reading. As one historian has pointed out, 'A central committee controlling policy, publications and funds, with hundreds of local auxiliary societies to stimulate and discipline the converts, in Britain . . . was to become the framework of party organization.'[68] The result of this agitation, when joined with skilful parliamentary debate, was the passing in 1833 of the West Indian Emancipation Act, abolishing slavery in its last foothold in the British Empire.

The attention of the radicals then finally turned to the US. The importation of slaves had been outlawed in 1807, but when southerners formed the American Colonization Society in 1816 to send free, and freed, blacks to the new country of Liberia on the West Coast of Africa, British anti-slavery groups condemned the scheme[69] as a palliative as well as an evasion of the real problem. At this point, most activity in the US was focused on this scheme, since to many it appeared to encourage emancipation. There were, however, zealots in favour of immediate abolition, such as the charismatic William Lloyd Garrison, a convert from the Colonization Society. He had decided that many of the society's members did not, in fact, believe in emancipation; rather, they wanted to reduce the numbers of free blacks in the US to help preserve slavery.[70] On 1 January 1831, Garrison published the first issue of the *Liberator* and began his crusade; as he wrote, rather vehemently, 'I do not wish to think, or speak, or write, with moderation . . . I am in earnest – I will not equivocate – I will not excuse – I will not retreat a single inch – AND I WILL BE HEARD.'[71] The first Anti-Slavery Society in America was founded by Lewis and Arthur Tappan in New York; in 1832 Garrison helped found the New England Anti-Slavery Society; and the following year, inspired by the British Emancipation Act, they co-operated in founding the American Anti-Slavery Society in Philadelphia, which had nearly a hundred thousand members by the end of the decade, some of whom were black.[72]

The American Society was unashamedly based on the British model. The idea was to go beyond the middle and upper-middle classes and reach mass audiences, using the methods developed by the British: endless numbers of newspaper articles and pamphlets, petition drives and lectures. This mobilisation of the masses would be critical, because Garrison and his colleagues stood out in their ferocious conviction of the sinfulness of slavery and the absolute need to eliminate it at once. Even in the North, abolitionists were very much in the minority in the early 1830s, with most people either pro-slavery or supporters of only very gradual change. Abolitionists were attacked, their meetings were broken up, and presses which printed their anti-slavery pamphlets were wrecked. Even before the British Emancipation Act was passed, Garrison had travelled to London to ask for help and support for the American effort from British anti-slavery interest groups. (Whilst there, he walked in Westminster Abbey behind the bier of William Wilberforce the Emancipator, who had led the fight against the slave trade.) But there was perturbation amongst some of the British as to the propriety of their interfering in the American effort; even Joseph Sturge, a Quaker who had been instrumental in setting up the British Agency Committee, and who was distressed at the apparent lack of anti-slavery conviction amongst American Quakers, was doubtful.[73] Garrison managed to convince some of the British activists otherwise.

He decided that the American cause especially needed the help of George Thompson, the 'ace agitator',[74] and he invited him to come to the US. In 1834 Thompson arrived and proceeded to address meetings all around the North, his efforts leading to the founding of some 150 anti-slavery societies. However, he was often threatened by mobs: in Boston the following year he escaped death only by fleeing in a small rowing boat to a British vessel, which took him to New Brunswick, where he caught a ship for England. His visit had probably done more harm than good. It was condemned by President Jackson, and 'by his rhetorical gifts and tactless energy he succeeded, almost singlehandedly, in provoking the first great wave of Southern bitterness against Northern interference'. It also aroused hostility against foreign interference in both the North and the South, and it helped to give the anti-slavery movement a 'foreign and alien character'.[75] However, this nationwide adverse reaction did not prevent the American Anti-Slavery Society from copying this technique and setting up its own Agency Committee; indeed, rather than six, as in the British Society, they had seventy paid itinerant anti-slavery lecturers.

One such was Mauris Robinson, who wrote to his wife Emily on 25 January 1837:

Since I wrote you a week since I have been upon the go-go-go. Have spoken ten times, been mobbed thrice, once most rousingly ... The mob was in the vicinity of the house where I was, when I made my appearance they commenced their ribaldry and shouts, pushing each other upon me, etc. Then they made a rush ahead of me for the [meeting-]house. I finally got in, took my stand on the seat of the pulpit and made an effort to be heard. Succeeded in pronouncing one sentence so as to be heard and then confusion, curses, cries of drag him out, kill him, etc., accompanied with brandishing of clubs succeeded. Finally their Captain General got as near me as he could and with his club raised proposed terms to me. They were that in twenty minutes I should leave town never to return or lecture there again. I told them that I was an American citizen and could not so far forget my duty and my rights as such to render obedience to their direction. By this time I had opened the door of the room thinking that a retreat to the open air would give me a better field for action. One of the mobocrats in obedience to the cry, drag him out, aided me in my design, as he seized me by the left arm and pulled away with all his might to drag me from the pulpit. I finally got out of doors. About a half dozen of the men had hold of me in the public square for a half hour . . . Suffice it to say that the Lord delivered me out of their hands and that evening I lectured four miles distant and formed a society . . . The Lord is my protection.[76]

Robinson's work as a lecturer was at least partly the result of Thompson's lead, although it is difficult to imagine the latter being subjected to the same type of harassment in Great Britain.

Besides sending out a raft of lecturers, the American Anti-Slavery Society organised further activities based on the British model: they lobbied state and Federal governments, sent petitions, published and distributed tracts, and continued to found new local societies. The two national societies maintained close relations, reinforced by correspondence between Joseph Sturge in London and Lewis Tappan in New York,[77] through a frequent exchange of newspapers, pamphlets and intelligence, and with yearly visits across the ocean. The pinnacle was the General or World Anti-Slavery Convention, which consisted of between five and six hundred delegates, conceived by the Americans, organised by Sturge, and held in London in June 1840. The chief object of the meeting was to mobilise Anglo-American opinion against American slavery. There were fifty-three American delegates, in some sense representing the Society's 250,000 members, but six were women, and this caused a temporary crisis. The clergy of both countries were overwhelmingly against them. Sturge had thought that their appearance would be outrageous and had countermanded the invitations, but the half-dozen managed to slip in to the convention. They were ejected and in the end had to sit behind a curtain. Notably, however, when William Lloyd Garrison arrived a little later, he insisted on joining the women in protest. The controversy 'stirred profoundly the women who experienced it. The young Elizabeth Cady Stanton . . . shared her indignation with Lucretia Mott, and learned from the older woman ideas which were to shape her life . . . As the two went about London . . . they decided to call that woman's rights convention which ultimately took place eight years later at Seneca Falls, New York.'[78]

The Anti-Slavery Convention was a scene of moral outrage, as debates and resolutions resonated for a week through Exeter Hall, where each May missionary societies held their yearly meetings. The idea was to mobilise opinion, and in particular Christian opinion, against the Southern planters, to make war on their consciences and, if that did not work, to cut them off from decent people. As far as many of the British delegates were concerned, the Americans were not as eager to smite the unrighteous as they ought to have been. One stark example was that of the American Quakers. Although committed to anti-slavery, they shrank from radical abolition; reprehensibly, their meetings were segregated. In Great Britain the Quakers had taken the lead in the movement and they simply could not understand the timidity of their American co-religionists. As for the Methodists and Baptists, their internal conflicts over slavery would lead to schism between the northern and southern churches in 1842 and 1845, respectively, and their growing crises were only made more unsolvable by the resolutions of the convention. The Americans made it clear that they welcomed British help, but would have appreciated more understanding. As one of the delegates stated, 'To be an abolitionist in England and in America are very different things; and if I may be permitted to say so, but a few of your abolitionists have stood the fire on our side of the Atlantic.' In short, '[i]n American eyes, British antislavery was drawing room philanthropy'. For this reason, perhaps, Garrison and the other radicals seemed as lions in the eyes of many of the British delegates.[79]

The British abolitionists had for years possessed the added advantage, compared to the Americans, of going with the grain of their government's policies. The context in the US was the increasing tension between the slave and the free states and the slide to civil war; it is also well to remember that the Federal government did not have the constitutional authority to outlaw slavery, even had it wished to do so. Conversely, ever since the abolition of the trade in slaves in the British Empire in 1807, successive British governments had led the attempts to suppress it entirely. The US had showed some interest after the end of the War of 1812, and by Article 10 of the Treaty of Ghent, as noted above, both she and Great Britain had committed themselves to using 'their best endeavours' to accomplish the 'entire abolition' of the trade. Further, in 1820, Congress had also outlawed the slave trade, referring to it as piracy and thereby determining that anyone convicted of it would be executed; however, it must be said that no one suffered such a punishment until the Civil War.

The problem was, how to catch the slavers? For Great Britain, the answer was obvious: ships should be stopped and searched. During one of the conferences associated with the ending of the wars with France, at Aix-la-Chapelle in 1818, Castlereagh had gained the agreement of the European states to the mutual search of ships for slaves in peacetime. But what about the US? It was not the only country receiving slaves – Brazil welcomed many more – but it was the country most active in the trade. Many slavers found that their only immunity from search was to fly the American flag, a ruse which made most ships doing so of intense interest to ships of the British Africa Squadron.[80] But stopping suspected slavers and searching them for slaves was all too reminiscent of the British tradition of stopping American ships and searching them for contraband or sailors. It would have been politically impossible for any American government to agree to the Royal Navy's stopping a ship flying the American flag to ascertain if it was a slaver. Repeated discussions on the matter during the 1820s were unsuccessful.[81] According to John Quincy Adams in 1824, the real problem was the fear of many in the South that 'this concert between the United States and Great Britain for suppressing the slave-trade should turn to a concert for the abolition of slavery'.[82]

In 1833, having abolished slavery within the Empire, the British redoubled their efforts to suppress the trade. By 1840, several European and Latin American countries were co-operating with the Royal Navy in this endeavour, with the US the only seafaring nation of any size which refused to join them. The vessels of this group patrolled great parts of the West Coast of Africa and stationed blockades at the mouths of major rivers.[83] But the US saw this as a matter of principle. Adams himself was a staunch abolitionist, but when Stratford Canning, the British Minister to Washington, had asked him in 1822 if he 'could conceive of a greater or more atrocious evil than the slave trade', Adams had replied with defiance, 'Yes: admitting the right of search by foreign officers of our vessels upon the seas in time of peace; for that would be making slaves of ourselves.'[84]

The year 1840, then, saw deadlock between the British and American navies in the fight against the African slave trade. But the same year was also the high point in the united attempts of the British and American abolitionists to convince the state governments to outlaw domestic slavery, since they had the constitutional power to do so. The follow-up to the 1840 convention, held three years later, however, was essentially a damp squib. Both the British and the American economies were going into recession, which undercut the ability of businessmen in either country to finance interest groups. Furthermore, the agitators had held exaggerated ideas of the efficacy of moral exhortation to move governments: instead, although opinion was organised, nothing tangible had resulted. When the British groups attempted to work through their own government by supporting the Aberdeen administration's attempt to support Texan independence to prevent its becoming a slave state, the result was northern support for its annexation. Politics in the US became more embittered as they took on an increasingly sectional focus, and any comment by the British, public or private, was dismissed with contemptuous resentment by most of the population.

In the UK, the outcome of the movement's activities was to sensitise much of the population to the abhorrent nature of American slavery. Important to this was Harriet Beecher Stowe's *Uncle Tom's Cabin* (1852), which was, according to the journalist and reformer W.T. Stead, 'the first American work which had literally a world-wide audience' (it sold over a million copies in the UK in its first year[85]). Stead points out that 'Mrs Stowe was fortunate in her subject, fortunate in the moment when she published her book, and specially fortunate in the spirit with which she handled her story . . . [T]he book came as a revelation, not merely of the realities of slavery in the Southern States, but of the existence of a high and noble humanity under the skin of a coloured man . . . The white man had never before realised the essential humanity of the negro.'[86] As noted above, this extension of knowledge and transformation of perception was to be of some importance in the British reaction to the Civil War.

IV

In the broader field of social reforms, most Anglo-American collaboration had to await the end of the Civil War, when a new generation of concerned individuals saw new problems to be tackled. A stimulus for such collaboration was the recognition that they shared certain economic developments, in particular the increasing dominance of finance and industrial capitalism. As Daniel T. Rodgers has pointed out, the 'new Atlantic economy of the late nineteenth century was to encourage a new Atlantic-wide politics. From its first stirrings in the 1890s, the new social politics was to emerge as a powerful political force by the 1910s, with representatives in every capital in the North Atlantic world. Even the Americans, so distant from the chief centers of policy and intellectual innovation, were to be drawn in.' The vast range of reformers never found a common name; however, the term 'Progressive' was used in both countries as a unifying term for both reformers and their movement. It arose out of London municipal politics in the 1890s, where Progressives formed a subset of the Liberal Party, and crossed the Atlantic in the first decade of the twentieth century.[87]

In this new social politics, the focus of reformers in Great Britain turned from worrying about electoral and political structures to concentrating on changing many of the structures and activities of everyday life, with a particular concern being the rise of working-class resentments. In the US, the Constitution was never the issue, although corrupt municipal politics was, but there as well reformers concentrated on the awfulness of everyday life in the slums and the factories. The implementation and administration of policies assumed much greater importance: who, for example, should control the provision of water? The public or the private sector? Much of the information about what was happening in each country was gained by reading the new newspapers and journals of information and opinion, such as the British *Review of Reviews* and the American *New Republic*. On both sides of the Atlantic, Protestants were again of great importance in the reform movement, which Rodgers characterises as one of Progressive politics entangled with social Protestantism.[88]

In the US, now in the throes of its own industrial revolution, there was an increasing awareness of the cost to the individual of this accelerating growth of a pitiless process and the concomitant growth of overcrowded and unhealthy big cities. It was the danger to the morals and religious beliefs of the working man and his family, however, that first aroused the concern of leaders of various Protestant denominations, a concern out of which developed the theological movement called the Social Gospel. Traditionally, American Protestants believed that if the individual was saved, he or she would become a better person, and this would result in social improvements. The ideas of the Social Gospel Movement were the reverse: individuals were sinful largely because of their social and economic situations, and thus if the situations were changed, or the individuals taken out of such situations, they would leave behind their sinful lifestyles. Therefore, adherents of the Social Gospel tended to believe that social reform was more important than the conversion of individuals, since the latter would follow the former.

Social Gospel ideas, a result of the ideas of Arnold and other members of the Broad Church Movement, had a dominant influence in both the US and Great Britain, with the addition in the latter of Christian Socialists. This group was founded in April 1848,[89] a year of revolutions all over Europe, by, amongst others, the Anglican priest and reformer F.D. Maurice, who became the leader, and Thomas Hughes and Charles Kingsley, author of *The Water Babies*, advocates of what both contemporaries and posterity called 'muscular Christianity'.[90] A primary goal was to prevent revolution by alleviating the reasonable grievances of the working class, to be achieved by a programme of education and legislative reform. Allied to this was the hope of convincing property owners to practise Christian ethics in their dealings with the poor. Maurice rejected competitive and selfish individualism and suggested a co-operative, socialist approach as an alternative to the prevailing economic belief in *laissez-faire*. Journals were founded and some workingmen's associations established, but disagreements among the members in the mid-1850s resulted in the movement's remaining in a moribund state until the late 1870s. The following decade saw a revival, but the movement's influence now lay primarily in the activities of individuals embued with its principles.

The Fabian Society, which was to be of very great influence, was an association of Christian Socialists founded in 1884 by a small group of middle-class intellectuals, including Sidney Webb and the playwright George Bernard Shaw. They believed in gradual change, with reforms based on extensive research and careful consideration of causes and effects, in evolution rather than revolution. (The name came from Quintus Fabius Maximus Cunctator ('the delayer'), a third-century BC Roman general, who wore out the invading forces of Hannibal by avoiding direct engagements and leading him on marches and counter-marches.) Fabians researched the problems, wrote reports and pamphlets, and frequently travelled to the US, constituting something of a transatlantic network of their own. In 1898, for example, Sidney and Beatrice Webb travelled from New York to San Francisco, talking to a number of like-minded individuals; however, they refused to travel there again, being stunned by the 'infantile' character of American politics. Other Fabians were not so squeamish, and formed lasting connections; indeed, in general, American Progressives had their closest rapport with the Fabians.[91]

Americans learned much about the ideas being discussed and the activities taking place in Great Britain (as well as in other parts of Europe) through journals. As Paul A. Kramer has pointed out, 'Anglo-American dialogues . . . were . . . given life by a publishing revolution in the 1890s.' There were a number of Anglo-American 'literary-political magazines' published through 'transatlantic houses with joint centers in New York and London'. These included the *Atlantic Monthly*, the *North American Review*, the *Fortnightly Review* and *Nineteenth Century*, which 'burdened late-Victorian tabletops on both sides of the Atlantic'.[92] In most areas of late nineteenth- and early twentieth-century social reform, ideas flowed from Great Britain to the US far more than in the opposite direction; Americans were very aware of being at the periphery as far as information and ideas were concerned, and they wanted to learn. The US government's Bureau of Labor, 'founded as a sop to the labor vote in 1865', was one of the earliest investigators, and soon emerged as the 'key social investigative agency in Washington'. It published in its *Bulletin* detailed accounts of social policies – or the lack of them and the consequences of that lack – for a number of countries; examples for Great Britain were labour conciliation agencies and city-owned public utilities, such as water and gas. The result was information, official links, and men experienced in social policy: the Bureau's John Graham Brooks became the first president of the National Consumers' League, whilst his colleague, Walter Wehl, co-founded the *New Republic* magazine.[93]

Then there was the important Social Gospel link. One member of this movement was the Englishman W.T. Stead, a prominent figure on both sides of the Atlantic, who was a crusading journalist and founder of the *Review of Reviews*. The son of a Congregational minister, at the age of twenty-two he became the editor of the Darlington *Northern Echo*, declaring soon after that 'the Press is the greatest agency for influencing public opinion in the world' and 'the true and only lever by which thrones and governments could be shaken and the masses of the people raised'.[94] In 1883 he became the editor of a London newspaper, the *Pall Mall Gazette*, which he soon livened up by the use of American techniques: sensational headlines, short paragraphs, a readable style, and the frequent use of diagrams, maps and illustrations to break up the text. He campaigned for a number of reforms. One was the exposure of white slavery in London, in which he was joined by Josephine Butler, a feminist who worked to ameliorate the lives of prostitutes, and Bramwell Booth, son of the founders of the Salvation Army and its leader himself from 1912. In July 1885 Stead bought the thirteen-year-old Eliza Armstrong, daughter of a chimney-sweep. He paid five pounds to the girl's drunken mother, had her virginity certified by a midwife, had her delivered to a brothel in London, and, finally, transported her to France. He then published the story over several days as 'Maiden Tribute of Modern Babylon' in the *Pall Mall Gazette*. His intention was to demonstrate how easily young girls could be sold into prostitution, but he and five others were sent to trial for unlawfully kidnapping a minor and jailed for three months. The whole episode had been intended to force the House of Commons to pass the Criminal Law Amendment Act, raising the age of consent from thirteen to sixteen, and this was accomplished.[95] Nor did sinful and outrageous activities in the US escape his attention. In 1893 he travelled to Chicago to investigate corruption and immorality; the result was a ferocious assault on the city in his book *If Christ Came to Chicago*, published the following year.[96]

One of the most famous, and useful, results of the transatlantic links between social Protestants was the settlement house. The first was Toynbee Hall, established in 1884 in Whitechapel in the East End of London by the Christian Socialists Samuel and Henrietta Barnett; Samuel, the vicar of St Jude's, Whitechapel, was its first warden. The idea was to enable graduates, primarily from Oxford, to live and work amongst the poor in order to improve the latter's lives. It provided free legal advice, promoted affordable workers' housing, and worked to improve the educational and cultural lives of the poor, with the Workers' Educational Association, the establishment of the Whitechapel Art Gallery, and a varied series of lectures and classes. The goal was to make Christianity relevant to the workers by contributing to the solution of social problems. From its opening, it was a magnet for American visitors; Jane Addams, a visitor in 1887, 1888 and 1889, established in 1889 the most famous of the American settlement houses, Hull House Settlement in Chicago, which itself then became a magnet for British visitors. Addams, the house's principal, was, according to Beatrice Webb, 'a remarkable woman, an interesting combination of the organiser, the enthusiast and the subtle observer of human characteristics'.[97]

Although settlement house workers on both sides of the Atlantic were very conscious of belonging to the same movement, the American system developed in a different direction from the English one. The movement was rooted in a women's college network – a situation virtually unknown in England – and was 'much more quickly and deeply feminized than its English model. Sharing neither the Oxford cultural pretensions of Toynbee Hall (with its fine arts exhibits and reading rooms wreathed in pipe smoke) nor its residents' easy, Oxbridge-greased access to government policy making, the American settlement houses were more alert to issues of family, immigrants, and neighborhoods.'[98] In Hull House, Addams concentrated on the women of the neighbourhood, with classes in housewifery along with those for learning English; she also encouraged immigrants to retain their own cultures. However, in spite of Beatrice Webb's praise for Addams, she was distinctly underwhelmed by her visit to Chicago. As she wrote in her diary, the 'days of our stay at Hull House are so associated in my memory with sore throat and fever, with the dull heat of the slum, the unappetising food of the restaurant, the restless movements of the residents from room to room, the rides over impossible streets littered with unspeakable garbage, that they seem like one long bad dream lightened now and again by Miss Addams' charming grey eyes and gentle voice and graphic power of expression'.[99] It is unclear whether it was Chicago or specifically Hull House which she disliked so much, but a patrician note certainly comes through.

The American settlement houses worked very hard to retain their links with their British counterparts. They became involved in their own social investigations, and this following of the London model ensured that they remained more than sources of charity in their neighbourhoods. Their streams of British visitors kept them in touch with developments in social policy-making and reform, whilst also tightening personal transatlantic links. Touchingly, Jane Addams read Henrietta Barnett's letters aloud at dinner.

Another area where Britain led the US was in actually achieving many of their reform goals. Politics was nearly all. Municipal politics in Great Britain was considerably less corrupt than in the US. Furthermore, the British had earlier success in putting together the urban political coalitions necessary to legislate for social reform and then to maintain the control necessary to ensure that the reforms' administration was not perverted. American social reformers tried to import a number of ideas and policies from Britain, but they frequently lacked a local supporting political structure. For one thing, the US judiciary blocked many of the attempts at reform, on the ground that they were beyond the constitutional powers of government. For most of this period, US municipal government was a byword for corruption. This meant that there were often two choices when establishing, say, a new utility: the city could control it, thereby enabling the politicians to exploit the organisation for patronage, or it could be offered to the private sector, enabling bribes for successful bids. This situation was not universal, but it was very widespread. A successful clean-up movement could cost many jobs, a high price, it could be argued, for honesty in government, since the poor would lose and the well-off would win. The National Municipal League was established in 1894 to reform local politics and administration. It argued for a merit-based civil service, and in general advocated replacing the graft-ridden, patronage-driven, corrupt political machines with non-partisan, businesslike administrations subject to control by the voters rather than the bosses. Success was not impossible, but it could be slow to achieve.[100]

Successful electoral reforms were often state-based, particularly in those states which had the strength of the rural Populist as well as the urban Progressive movements behind them. In a number of states, most of them west of the Mississippi River, the electorates agreed to fundamental changes in governance – the initiative, recall and referendum, each of which depended on a successful petition campaign by voters: the initiative empowered them to force a Bill or constitutional amendment to be placed on the ballot at the next election; the recall allowed the electorate to propose a special election to vote on the dismissal of an elected official; and the referendum allowed the electorate to approve a measure rejected by their legislature or to repeal a measure already enacted. Of greater importance were the laws passed by the Federal government, including the Sherman Antitrust Act (1890) to break up the great monopolies and trusts, such as John D. Rockefeller's Standard Oil Company of New Jersey, and the Owen–Glass Act (1913), which established a central banking system, the Federal Reserve, for the first time since the 1830s. In its example of a successful central bank, and in the evidence it provided, the Bank of England was of significant help in the establishment of the Federal Reserve System. Few other Federal reforms, however, owed much to the British example; what is relevant in this context is that the very existence of reform movements on both sides of the Atlantic encouraged the feeling for many of being part of a larger movement with the wind in its sails.

There was a short period, from about 1906 to 1916, when there were Progressive governments in both countries: the Liberals in Great Britain, and the Republican administrations of Theodore Roosevelt (1901–8) and, to a lesser extent, of William Howard Taft (1909–12) and the Democratic administration of Woodrow Wilson (1912–16) in the US. Yet discussions between the governments tended to be over foreign policy and military issues, not social reform. This was the era in Great Britain which saw the establishing of targeted (rather than universal) state-supported old-age pensions, labour exchanges for the unemployed, and national health insurance. The way in the US was far harder for these types of reform: the individualistic ethos discouraged organised collective pressure; the sanctity of private property precluded the passage of laws which appeared to threaten such property; and the judiciary took a very narrow view of what the state could be allowed to do, striking down many reform Acts.[101] Government was more successful at eliminating restraints on trade which harmed the individual than in providing for safety in the workplace. The exception here was safety for female workers, the thin end of the regulatory wedge.[102] This fact caused some agonising amongst feminists: was it better to work for the amelioration of the lot of the working woman, or would that underline her inferiority and undermine the drive for equality?

What feminists did agree on was the need to fight for women's rights. One might have assumed that there would be a close connection between the women's rights movements in the two countries, as there was in the anti-slavery movements, but that was not the case. The two movements frequently differed over goals, strategies and tactics. Indeed, their political and social contexts were so different that their links were more episodic than continuous. In Great Britain, only one legislature had to be convinced in order to turn proposals into law, and the country was small enough for an interest group to be reasonably united. In the US, women's groups could either work for a national solution and try to get a Bill through Congress or, in the case of Prohibition and the right to vote, a constitutional amendment, or they could work state by state and try to get Bills through the various state legislatures. Indeed, the 'move-ment' in the US was hardly united under a single leadership; rather, there were local and state organisations as well as national ones, and even where the national organisation was of great importance, such as the Women's Christian Temperance Union, its success varied from state to state.[103] What was common in both countries was that, even among women, those supporting access and equality never constituted a majority.[104]

The campaigns for women's rights had various strands. One was the determination to gain equality before the law, an element of which was for women to control their own property. Another was to protect social purity, such as changing the age of sexual consent, and stopping the subjection of women to unfair, intrusive investiga-tion of their sexual health, when men with venereal disease were allowed to wander around and infect whomsoever they wished. A third was health and safety issues for women at work. A fourth was the need, shared by male social reformers, to find ways of making political institutions deal with the huge problems arising from mas-sive industrialisation and crowded, unhealthy cities.[105] And, most famously, there was the campaign for the right to vote. In all of these campaigns, a contention was that women could improve the lot of both women and men because they could apply feminine strengths, variously defined and described; by the early twentieth century, however, arguments for the absolute equality of women with men moved more to the fore.

It was frequently the case that women involved in campaigning for women's rights were also prominent in social reform movements. One example might be the widening perspective of those involved in the anti-slavery movement. In the US, feminism began to develop from the 1830s, with arguments equating racial and sexual slavery: once married, women lacked a legal identity, and surrendered con-trol of their persons, as well as of their homes and their children. In Great Britain, conversely, abolitionist activities did not ordinarily lead to feminism as such: rather, many involved wished to take part in public duties in order to apply feminine virtues and approaches, without necessarily wishing to vote. Indeed, the right to vote was not nearly as much of an issue in the middle part of the nineteenth century as it would later become; having said that, the 1840 London Conference was the occasion, as noted above, of the coming together of Elizabeth Cady Stanton and Lucretia Mott, two leaders of the American movement for female suffrage. It is also worth pointing out that support for one feminist goal did not imply support for others: because the movements in both countries at various times concentrated on single issues, it was possible to be a feminist over one issue and not over another.[106]

Christine Bolt has pointed out that 'in fighting for the vote, women in the two countries achieved their most pronounced degree of friendly rivalry and their most extensive personal links'.[107] Both countries saw fierce debates about what determined whether or not someone was a citizen and the relationship of the franchise to citizenship: were you truly a citizen if you could not vote? During the final third of the nineteenth century, the suffrage journals kept track of each other's activities, setbacks and achievements, whilst their leaders kept track of each other's pronouncements and worked in each other's campaigns. The Englishwomen saw themselves as better researchers and organisers; the Americans felt that their educational and political systems ensured that they were better speakers and agitators. The British penchant after the turn of the century for destroying property dismayed the Americans, since respect for property in the US was so strong that it seemed self-defeating to attack it. Furthermore, most American activists believed that you caught more flies with honey than with vinegar, and thought it counter-productive to harass politicians. Even so, some British activists became involved in the American organisations, whilst Americans were welcomed by the British as speakers, planners and protesters. In their turn, the Americans picked up new tactics from the British.[108]

British women were very pragmatic in working for the vote. They did unpaid work for the Liberal and Conservative parties, especially for the local associations, in order to demonstrate their capabilities. Neither political party supported female suffrage until after the First World War, and therefore women took advantage of openings in local government. In 1869, single women with property received the right to vote in towns and boroughs; from 1870 they were allowed to vote for and serve on school boards and from 1894, whether single or married, on parish councils and rural district councils. However, they did not receive the right to vote for Members of Parliament until 1918, and then only if they were over thirty and ratepayers (local property taxpayers) or the wives of ratepayers; the remainder had to wait until 1928.

In the US, it was a number of states which first gave women the right to vote. As in Britain, they began with the right to vote for and to serve as members of school boards; by 1887, fourteen states were allowing women to vote on school matters, and in these (plus another nine) they could themselves fill the school offices. According to James Bryce, the US differed from Great Britain in that no distinction was made between married and unmarried women, and 'the Americans always assume that wherever women receive the right of voting at the election to any office, they become as a matter of course eligible for the office itself'. But it must be said that most of these states were in the West and Midwest, and Bryce reported that in Massachusetts 'quite recently a Ladies' Anti-Suffrage League has been formed'.[109] The eastern US could be as conservative as Great Britain, and it took until 1920, with the Nineteenth Amendment to the Constitution, for all American women over twenty-one to receive the vote.

The drive for social reform in both countries came to a temporary halt when each joined the Great War. Over the long nineteenth century, there had been a number of social reform movements in both countries, a great majority of which emerged from evangelical Protestantism of one shade or another. After the Civil War, others, such as supporters of the Social Gospel and Christian Socialists, united with, or supplanted, the evangelicals. These reformers were joined increasingly by those driven by secular arguments rather than by those based on religion and morality – Great Britain in particular was alarmed by the stunningly poor physical quality of the recruits for the Boer War from 1899 to 1902. During this whole period, Anglo-American links between reformers and reform movements varied in their intensity and importance, but they were always there. The constant exchange of ideas and information and the frequent visits were vital in maintaining them. The British tended to look to the US for comparisons with home rather than for solutions to problems, although there were exceptions: the US was vastly ahead of Great Britain when it came to primary education, for example. The Americans, on the other hand, tended to look to the British for solutions to many of the same problems of public squalor, although the differences in the political systems ensured that it was never easy, and often impossible, to implement these reforms. This implementation would require the public acceptance of a more powerful Federal government, which came only with the New Deal in the 1930s.

V

There are several ways in which one can approach the literary relationship between Britain and the US. There is the publication and supply of the books themselves; there is the supply of authors who wrote the books; and there is the question of influence, both of the ideas of movements and of an author's style or ideas on another. As a general theme, until the beginning of the twentieth century, the influence was almost entirely in one direction, from Great Britain to America: the former was the English-language cultural hegemon. With the turn of the century, however, this began to change.

Whilst the US was part of the British Empire, American culture, unsurprisingly, was 'a steady, resolute, instinctive reproduction of contemporary English culture'.[110] As noted in Chapter 2, the first novel published in North America was Samuel Richardson's *Pamela, or Virtue Rewarded* in 1742. (Indeed, one early nineteenth-century author argued that 'in America the printer came into existence before the author'[111] – just about arguable as long as books of theology and sermons are excepted.) William Reitzel claims that 'in its essentials, European culture of the eighteenth century was so uniform, so marked by an easy exchange of ideas, that it is often a waste of time to try to distinguish between the French and the English as carriers of any particular sets of ideas'.[112] Looking at, for example, Voltaire, Montesquieu and Locke, they were all available in English, and thus tended to come by the English route. That this influence continued into the period of the Early Republic is attested to by

James Fenimore Cooper, author of *The Last of the Mohicans* (1826), a book which had a wide-ranging influence in Europe for the remainder of the century. In his *Notions of the Americans*, published anonymously in 1833, he confirms that 'Speaking the same language as the English, and long in the habit of importing their books from the mother country, the revolution effected no immediate change in the nature of their studies, or mental amusements.' Indeed, he goes further, claiming that 'so far as taste and forms alone are concerned, the literature of England and that of America must be fashioned after the same models. The authors, previously to the revolution, are common property, and it is quite idle to say that the American has not just as good a right to claim Milton, and Shakespeare, and all the old masters of the language, for his countrymen, as an Englishman.' He does, however, note one 'peculiarity' of American literature, which is 'connected with the promulgation of their distinctive political opinions'.[113] His book provides a background for the ferocious 'warfare of the mind'[114] then in full battle.

The American conviction that they had won the War of 1812 unleashed a tide of frenzied nationalism. The US was now entirely independent of Great Britain, and an independent country required an independent literature. As the new journal *The Portico* stated in January 1816, 'Dependence, whether literary or political, is a state of degradation, fraught with disgrace; and to be dependent on a foreign mind, for what we can ourselves produce, is to add to the crime of indolence, the weakness of stupidity.'[115] Newspapers and journals on both sides of the Atlantic, especially the *Quarterly Review* and, to a lesser extent, the *Edinburgh Review* and *Blackwood's Magazine* in Great Britain, eagerly leapt into the fray – the so-called Paper War[116] – American writers with ferocity, British writers with condescension. It was notable, however, that readers refused to follow the flag: once Sir Walter Scott had published *Waverly* in 1814, he became almost as widely read in the US as in Great Britain,[117] a position later held by Dickens and other British writers. It was an unusual occasion when Washington Irving published *The Sketch Book of Geoffrey Crayon, Gent.* in 1820 and an American author had a rapid and huge success in both countries.

Sydney Smith, in a review of Adam Seybert's *Statistical Annals of the United States of America* in the *Edinburgh Review* of January 1820, brought this particular war to a peak, writing words that reverberated in the US for decades. Smith treats the book very seriously, summarising many of the main points and quoting statistics in a manner frowned upon by today's editors. On the whole, the review is complimentary if patronising. But then he seems to lose control: 'Thus far we are the friends and admirers of Jonathan [the early equivalent of Uncle Sam]: But he must not grow vain and ambitious; or allow himself to be dazzled by that galaxy of epithets by which his orators and newspaper scribblers endeavour to persuade their supporters that they are the greatest, the most refined, the most enlightened, and the most moral people upon earth.' Next comes the passage which outraged the Americans, not least because what Smith wrote was then largely true:

> In so far as we know, there is no such parallel to be produced from the whole annals of this self-adulating race. In the four quarters of the globe, who reads an American book? or goes to an American play? or looks at an American picture or statue? What does the world yet owe to American physicians or surgeons? What new substances have their chemists discovered? or what old ones have they analyzed? What new constellations have been discovered by the telescopes of Americans? – what have they done in the mathematics? Who drinks out of American glasses? or eats from American plates? or wears American coats or gowns? or sleeps in American blankets? – Finally, under which of the old tyrannical governments of Europe is every sixth man a Slave, whom his fellow-creatures may buy and sell and torture?

With Americans presumably reeling from this onslaught, Smith gives them his final advice: 'When these questions are fairly and favourably answered, their laudatory epithets may be allowed: But, till that can be done, we would seriously advise them to keep clear of superlatives.'[118]

It was the sentence 'In the four quarters of the globe, who reads an American book?' which was the most piercing and the resentment about which was the longest lasting. Americans furiously pointed out that they had published many books, as well as plays, and poems both lyrical and epic. But whether anyone other than Americans themselves read them was open to question. Again, it was James Fenimore Cooper who tried to explain why so few American books were published. The reason, basically, was that there were too many English books published. He set out a number of 'powerful obstacles' which American literature had to conquer, before it 'can ever enter the markets of its own country on terms of perfect equality with that of England'.[119] A major, indeed almost overwhelming, problem was the lack of copyright protection. This had two effects. For the British writer, such as Dickens, it meant that he gained nothing other than fame from selling thousands of his books in the US.[120] For the American writer, it meant that it was difficult to be published at all. As Cooper put it, the fact that 'an American publisher can get an English work without money, must . . . have a tendency to repress a national literature. No man will pay a writer for an epic, a tragedy, a sonnet, a history, or a romance, when he can get a work of equal merit for nothing.'[121]

A 'capital American publisher' had told Cooper that 'there are not a dozen writers in this country, whose works he should feel confidence in publishing at all, while he reprints hundreds of English books without the least hesitation'. A subsidiary reason for publishing British rather than American books, then, was that 'the uniform hazard which accompanies all literary speculations' could be lessened by the fact that the American publisher had the advantage of 'seeing the reviews of every book he wishes to print, and, what is of far more importance, he knows . . . the decision of the English critics before he makes his choice. Nine times in ten, popularity, which is all he looks for, is a sufficient test of general merit.'[122] De Tocqueville, publishing only a year after Cooper, wrote that 'Citizens of the United States themselves seem so convinced that books are not published for them, that before settling on the merit of one of their writers, they ordinarily wait for him to have been sampled in England.'[123] In defence of the publishers, they faced an uncertain economic climate in which to produce books:

perhaps nothing in the nineteenth century so influenced the American book trade as the depression of 1837–43. Established firms faltered but somehow carried on. New publishers sprang up only to disappear a few years later amidst the ranks of debtors and insolvents . . . Prices for books and periodicals fell lower and lower, till proprietors began to wonder if it would not be cheaper to suspend business altogether. A mania for cheapness had descended upon the trade, and nothing would ever be the same again.[124]

Over the century, some American authors discovered that they were better off publishing in Great Britain, if they could find a publisher, because if they remained resident there they could hold on to British rights and contracts. Washington Irving did this with *The Sketch Book of Geoffrey Crayon, Gent.* in 1820, a book which had such a wild and sustained success in both Great Britain and the US that 'he became the best-known, best-rewarded, exemplary American writer'.[125] Later in the century, Mark Twain's *The Adventures of Huckleberry Finn* was first published in London (in December 1884), prompted by copyright concerns. By this time, residence in Britain was no longer necessary: as of 1835, a writer received British copyright protection if the work was published in Britain before any other country. However, that did not save authors from the depredations of the Americans, and this extended to plays and music. W.S. Gilbert and Sir Arthur Sullivan were repeated victims – as Gilbert said, after their *HMS Pinafore* was produced by innumerable pirate companies in the US, with their receiving not a penny: 'I will not have another libretto of mine produced if the Americans are going to steal it. It's not that I need the money so much, but it upsets my digestion.' International copyright law was still in a chaotic state, and in order to try to protect their rights to their next production, *The Pirates of Penzance*, on both sides of the Atlantic, they decided on almost simultaneous productions. Therefore, a few hours *before* the premiere of the New York production, which was scheduled for 31 December 1879, there was a quiet debut in Paignton, Devonshire, at 2 p.m. on 30 December. This 'copyrighting performance' secured the British rights. In the US they sent out their own companies to perform the operetta, thereby securing at least a portion of the proceeds.[126] In 1891 the urgent need for all of these stratagems was lessened by the passage of the Chace Act in the US, which gave protection to new works published there or in a foreign country, provided a copy was deposited in Washington by the day of publication. This was modified twenty years later, when up to thirty days was allowed for the deposit of an English-language work published abroad.

Cooper's second 'obstacle against which American literature has to contend . . . is in the poverty of materials', because anything which America could contribute to the imagination of the author could be found more richly in Europe. (He surely could not be referring to his own five *Leatherstocking Tales*, set on the moving frontier.) He also states that he had never seen 'a nation so much alike in my life, as the people of the United States' – no 'costume for the peasant, . . . no wig for the judge, no baton for the general, no diadem for the chief magistrate'. In short, there was nothing out of the ordinary, and thus little for an author to write about. Henry James famously felt that American culture could not itself inspire and support a serious writer, and that to remain in the US would condemn him to being a provincial writer.[127] Another commentator wrote in 1901 that 'the absence of any capital city, any acknowledged literary centre, in a country of vast area with scattered towns, the want of a large society exclusively occupied with culture and forming a world of its own, the uniformity of American life, and the little scope it gives to the refined ease and the graceful *dolce far niente* of European *beaux mondes*, all these have something to do with a low average of original literature'. Even the fact that a much higher proportion of Americans than Britons could read was a drawback, since 'the wider the reading public becomes, the lower is the average of literary culture'.[128] Ultimately, however, Cooper was hopeful, since 'notwithstanding the overwhelming influence of British publications, and all the difficulties I have named, original books are getting to be numerous in the United States. The impulses of talent and intelligence are bearing down a thousand obstacles.'[129] This seems a curious conclusion, given his earlier comments, but the idea that the US would be in permanent intellectual thrall to Great Britain was something which no American could countenance.

One problem which Cooper did not consider, and which was of particular importance to a number of serious American writers, was the unpalatable fact that they were often more highly regarded in Great Britain than in the US. Irving was an early and notable example. Another was Nathaniel Hawthorne. Few American critics praised his *The Blithedale Romance*, whilst British critics expressed 'enthusiasm and insight', and it is probable that this situation was not unimportant in his decision to accept the offer of a consulship at Liverpool.[130] Herman Melville, author of *Moby-Dick; or The Whale*, found that upon publication in 1851, much of the most searching praise came from British critics (later, D.H. Lawrence's consideration of Melville in the 1920s was instrumental in bringing his work back to notice[131]). For Walt Whitman, William Rossetti's edition of *Leaves of Grass*, published in 1868 as *Poems by Walt Whitman* in England, was a turning point in his struggle for recognition. He wrote to his representative in London that 'In my own country, so far, from the organs, the press, & from authoritative sources, I have received but one long tirade of shallow impudence, mockery, & scurrilous jeers. Only since the English recognition have the skies here lighted up a little.'[132] And for a final example, there is Twain's *Huckleberry Finn*, which, as noted above, was published first in London. It was the English critics who first recognised Twain as 'an authentic man of genius' and *Huckleberry Finn* as a masterpiece belonging 'among the greatest books of the world'. As Benjamin Lease has noted, 'American critics were much slower to recognize the greatness of this new fable of the West.'[133]

The question of authorial influence, whether unidirectional or reciprocal, is by its very nature difficult to ascertain. It can be ways of thinking or styles of writing. Sometimes explicit letters are written; sometimes it has to be teased out by comparing styles and their changes. This is not the place for an extended discussion, but there are interesting examples. One is the long-lasting and close relationship between Ralph Waldo Emerson and Thomas Carlyle. Emerson had long admired Carlyle's work, and when he travelled to England on Christmas Day 1832, he hoped to meet and talk with him. They met for a day and a night in August 1833, twenty-four hours of great importance to them both, with warmth on both sides (although

Emerson decided that Carlyle was deficient 'in insight into religious truth'). Emerson's response to *Sartor Resartus*, a German-influenced type of spiritual biography written in savage prose (published in serial form 1833–4), was to approve of Carlyle's approach and ideas, but to deprecate his method of writing – a 'grotesque teutonic apocalyptic strain'. Carlyle's answer was that men had to find new ways of saying things. Their correspondence over the following years demonstrated warmth of feeling but also the diverging viewpoints of the two men, yet it flourished. Their friendship was 'soon transformed into something resembling an Anglo-American alliance when Emerson supervised an American edition of *Sartor*' (1836) followed by American editions of other works. Carlyle, in turn, 'helped (in a less active way) in the British publication of *Nature* and the two volumes of *Essays*. These ventures in transatlantic "bibliopoly" (as Carlyle called it) came to a halt when literary piracy made them increasingly unprofitable.' Each aided the spread of the other's fame. In due course they were to grow apart, but they apparently never lost their fundamental friendship and respect for each other.[134] Another who was drawn under Carlyle's spell was Whitman, although he, too, wished that Carlyle's ideas had been written in a plainer style. Specialists have noted a number of examples of the influence of Carlyle's style on the younger man, and Lease states plainly that 'Carlyle, early and late, was a pervasive presence for Whitman and *Leaves of Grass*.'[135]

In the final third of the century, there developed a growing conviction that America required an American-focused literature produced by Americans, that she should break away from the British intellectual empire. The outcome of the Civil War had ensured that the US would remain one country. This was now unified by a transcontinental railway which defied mountains and rivers of awe-inspiring grandeur. The population was increasing rapidly. The growing power of the US was palpable, and this helped to stimulate attempts by writers to exemplify and express America. Whitman is a major example. In the poem 'I Hear America Singing', and in the final two lines of 'For You O Democracy', he does this very thing: 'For you these from me, O Democracy, to serve you ma femme!/For you, for you I am trilling these songs.'[136] Indeed, in his 'Song of

Myself', he identifies himself with and as America.[137] With the increasing self-confidence of American writers, it would not be long before there developed something of a missionary endeavour to try to bring to the Old World something of the new approaches and new ideas of the New. Nevertheless, it would not be an easy battle to win, even at home: in 1901, when the College Entrance Board selected sixteen books as essential reading for students when preparing for their literature exams, thirteen of the authors were British.[138]

VI

The nineteenth century is a curious and confusing period in Anglo-American relations. The two countries had finally separated, and, externally, the US now focused on the western part of the continent and on the lands to the south; by the same token, Britain concentrated, in fits and starts, on extending and developing her empire. Yet, neither could ignore the other. Indeed, later in the century, the activities of each country in various parts of the globe were sometimes of great importance to the other. What the British government had decided soon after the War of 1812 the American government only came to recognise in the last decades of the century: their interests, whilst often divergent, were frequently more closely aligned than with those of other countries.

At the same time, the populations of the two countries were in the habit of disliking each other. Indeed, much of this *was* habit, and habits tend not to change unless there is a reason for them to do so. Nevertheless, many worked together in business, where it would have been foolish to disdain a good customer, or on social reforms. With religion, it is arguable that deeply held beliefs tied people together more strongly than nationalism tore them apart, not surprising in those who saw the afterlife as infinitely more important than the here-and-now. There was also a certain perceived equality in these areas, since both sides contributed to the relationship.

In literature things were different. Arguments over it brought out American insecurities in a very public manner, and the resulting bluster could only cause contempt in Great Britain. Americans insisted that they had poets and novelists as good as those of Great Britain, and more of them, but this was not supported by American readers themselves, who preferred the novels of Scott and Dickens to those of Hawthorne and Melville. Indeed, it could be argued that Irving, Cooper, Hawthorne, Emerson, Melville and Twain could match in quality Scott, Dickens, Trollope, Eliot, Collins, Hardy and Conan Doyle. But for many Americans during the first half of the century, this was not enough: it was vital that the British *admit* that this was the case, and, even more, that American writers were better. The sky would fall in first, of course. During the later decades this competition was no longer so important; what became crucial now for many Americans was the importance of having an *American* literature, one that by definition was not British.

But the US as better by definition than Great Britain was an American theme that did not fade. Nor did the British perception of the US as a growing adolescent that needed to be schooled and guided by older and wiser heads. Those with economic or religious links, those dedicated to bettering their societies, those who wrote and read books and poetry, could carry on because these private relationships did not depend upon their perceptions of the state-to-state relationship. But in any case, after 1870, this relationship began to change.

What also began to change was the perception of the US as a rough, backward country with little to teach Great Britain, or, indeed, Europe. The portents were there from 1851, with the American exhibition at the fabled Great Exhibition of the Crystal Palace in London. According to Robert W. Rydell and Rob Kroes, at this fair, 'American exhibitors knocked British government officials, industrialists, and the broader public back on their collective heels with displays of Colt revolvers and McCormick reapers [a farm machine].'[139] This industrial and commercial power continued to make an impact at a number of world's fairs, reaching its apotheosis at the 1900 Universal Paris Exhibition. The US government had decided to increase its exhibition space to match those of Great Britain and Germany; the Exhibition was spread out to a number of venues around Paris, and the US seemed to be everywhere. There were exhibits of machinery, of everyday life and of culture. The manufacturing exhibits provided a port of entry to European markets, to the great benefit of American business expansion, but they also gave the European public a less desirable impression of American civilisation, which seemed to be driven by technology.[140]

American mechanical genius therefore made an impact, but there had been another great influence during the late nineteenth century, one which gave the British a different view of American civilisation: Buffalo Bill Cody and his Wild West show. Already a great success in the US, the show travelled to London in 1887. As the ship carrying the 220 performers, including 97 Indians, 180 horses, 10 elk, 5 steers, 4 donkeys and 2 deer steamed across the Atlantic, Cody's publicity team was plastering London with posters and using the press to create anticipation and even excitement. For several weeks prior to the show's opening, the upper classes visited the encampment and wandered amongst the Indians and animals. Then the Prince of Wales accepted Cody's invitation to bring his wife and daughters for a special preview performance on 5 May; delighted with it, he urged his mother, Queen Victoria, to attend a performance. On 11 May 1887 the Queen appeared at a public performance for the first time since her husband's death a quarter of a century earlier. Naturally, her attendance made news everywhere in the English-speaking world, in particular because it was her Golden Jubilee year. The occasion was spectacular: when the show began and a rider entered the arena carrying an American flag, the Queen stood and bowed. The rest of the audience then stood as well, and British soldiers and officers saluted. For Cody and his comrades, it was unforgettable.[141]

By the turn of the century, then, the British public could now see the US as having both a past of her own – the Wild West – and a future of technological inventiveness and power. Given the economic context of the huge growth in the American economy after 1870, the US embarked on a drive for economic expansion in Europe that was to make it both a threat to that continent and a provider of unknown delights. Victoria de Grazia has termed this the growth of a Market Empire, which she memorably describes as 'the rise of a great imperium with the outlook of a great emporium'.[142] A symbolic starting point was the speech of President Wilson on 10 July 1916 to the World Salesmanship Congress in Detroit, Michigan. Here,

Wilson combined the imperatives of spreading American business practices and American democratic principles around the world. In the midst of a bloody war he told the salesmen that America's 'democracy of business' had to take the lead in the 'struggle for the peaceful conquest of the world'. And he urged them that 'with the inspiration of the thought that you are Americans and are meant to carry liberty and justice and the principles of humanity wherever you go, go out and sell goods that will make the world more comfortable and more happy, and convert them to the principles of America'.[143] As a way of making the world safe for democracy, selling was infinitely preferable to shooting. It is difficult to imagine any other leader during that period, or any other, equating selling with citizenship.

Over the twentieth century, Britain was overwhelmed with the American way of life as represented by affordable cars, labour-saving appliances for the kitchen, gramophone records by American singers, Walt Disney cartoons, Coca-Cola, films, and myriad other products that widened experience or even transformed lives. This was American 'mass culture', a term which came into use in the 1930s. Yet, it was only after the Second World War, when it came on the back of American power, that it became chronic and pervasive. Indeed, by the 1990s, 'mass culture had become America's second most lucrative export, exceeded only by the output of the aerospace industry'. Richard Pells, however, argues that culture not only travelled in both directions but left both populations essentially unchanged.[144] Watching Disney did not turn most Britons into Americans.

The distinction is often made between high and popular culture. High culture includes literature, classical music and classical dance; popular culture includes film, television and popular music. During the twentieth century, American films and television programmes dominated not only Great Britain but the rest of the world. American popular music of whatever genre was very important in Britain, but there were periods when British music made huge inroads into the American market. In other words, because of the language, there were few obstacles in the way of the cultural flow in either direction, which varied according to time, circumstance and category.

VII

Literature, and especially poetry, is a supreme example of high culture. The change in the direction of influence between Britain and America can be tracked by looking at poetry. At the beginning of the twentieth century it was vital for an American poet to know what was happening in Great Britain; by the end, this need had, perhaps, nearly disappeared. A brief look at the career of Ezra Pound illustrates something of this journey. Born in Idaho in 1885, Pound decided at the age of fifteen that he would be a poet, and 'that at thirty he would know more about poetry than any man living'.[145] In 1907, ready for anything, he left for Europe, first for Paris and then in August 1908 for London. According to Pound, at that time the US was 'still a colony of London so far as culture was concerned [and] Henry James, Whitman and myself all had to come to the metropolis, to the capital of the US, so far as arts and letters were concerned'.[146] He came because of England's literary past; he found, in his eyes, a languid, etiolated present. These were the Georgian poets,[147] who distrusted any intellectualisation of poetry, who believed in an instinctive, creative poetic process on the part of the author and an instinctive recognition of the poem as poetry on the part of the reader. The Georgians, who included Rupert Brooke, Edmund Blunden and Edward Thomas,[148] amongst others, believed in the use of traditional forms, some practised since the fourteenth century, and they worked to master the forms before adapting them to their own original voices and feelings. They found their inspiration primarily in nature and the rustic life; they were happy to remain with their version of the past and reject the modern.[149]

Pound was disappointed with what he found. To him, poetry was an art which should be happy to confront the modern world, should strive for an exact description and evocation of mood, and should use everyday words. Whilst in Great Britain, he acted as a scout for the Chicago journal *Poetry*, and in 1912 he wrote to the founder and editor, Harriet Monroe, about his feelings for England: the Irish poet W.B. Yeats was a classic, but 'as for his English contemporaries, they are food, sometimes very good food, for anthologies'. In their turn, the English poets were not much interested in Pound, dismissing him as a 'poseur and a charlatan – or simply as an American'.[150]

Pound went to Britain and thence to Italy, where he spent most of his life, although he remained an American; T.S. Eliot travelled to Britain in 1914 but remained, taking British citizenship in 1927. He shared with Pound large ambitions for poetry, for what it could do and how it should be approached and written, and he also wanted to break its tradition and continuity, to force it to confront modernity. By contrast, the English poets of that generation felt the traditions in their bones, and saw no need to rip themselves away. But times were changing, and Eliot would help British poets to change. In 1925 he was invited to join the new firm of Faber and Gwyer, and 'with his own strong convictions, he was able to form the literary taste of a generation', publishing, amongst others, Pound, James Joyce, Wyndham Lewis and himself. The firm became Faber and Faber, and, until the mid-1960s, was the pre-eminent publisher of twentieth-century poetry.[151] He never forgot his roots: 'In a line deleted from a lecture that he gave in 1948, Eliot [called] himself an "English poet of American origin".'[152]

The most famous of the British poets who moved in the opposite direction was W.H. Auden. According to the novelist Christopher Isherwood, Auden told him in July 1938 that he wanted to emigrate, become an American citizen, and settle permanently in the US (probably, in New York City). Partly it was because of a growing dissatisfaction with England. Having spent the late 1920s and 1930s in left-wing politics, Auden had discovered that he was, in reality, a 'pink old Liberal'; he had never been happy with the English literary world, finding it stultifying because of its 'family atmosphere', which was too cosy to be challenging; and more significantly, according to his biographer, he believed that 'European society was finished. So he turned to America, not because he had any dream of it as the perfect society, but because he regarded it as a place where the options were still open, and where no set pattern of civilisation had yet been developed.' As Auden himself put it in July 1939, 'What England can give me, I feel it already has, and that I can never lose it. America is so vast.' He also, some years later, gave a practical reason: 'I came to America because it's easier to make money here, to live by your wits.'[153]

Steve Clark and Mark Ford argue that of all twentieth-century British poets, only Auden, who in any case did become an American citizen in 1946, had a really significant impact on American poetry. This took several paths. First and most important was the poetry itself, which had a crucial influence on John Ashbery, John Holloway and Elizabeth Bishop, amongst others.[154] Second, Auden was a judge for the extremely prestigious Yale Younger Poets Award, by which he helped to decide who was 'good' and who was not; according to one's taste, he could therefore open up the promised land or he could be a blight. Finally, he was a 'campus-hopping poetic superstar',[155] bringing stimulus and revelation to regions and localities. He also earned a lot of money in this way, as he noted in 'On the Circuit':

> I see,
> Dwindling below me on the plane,
> The roofs of one more audience
> I shall not see again.
> God bless the lot of them, although
> I don't remember which was which:
> God bless the USA, so large,
> So friendly, and so rich.[156]

Auden was not the only British writer to take advantage of the offers of American universities, particularly in the decade after the end of the Second World War. American universities had the resources, and British writers were attracted not only to the posts but by the energy, self-confidence, drive, power and strangeness of the US, the new 'cultural capital of the world'.[157] For some, it seemed as if they were travelling to the other half of England, since in language, liberal culture and institutions the two countries appeared strongly to resemble one another. And there was no alternative at home, since it was not until the 1990s that British universities and other institutions made tentative moves in the same direction. Amongst the poets who stepped westward with Auden were Thom

Gunn, Geoffrey Hill, Donald Davie and Paul Muldoon.[158] This gradual drawing-in of British poets is a theme of the post-1945 period.
For many of these writers, it was inconceivable that they would not
read deeply and widely in American poetry, with, for the lucky, a
post in an American university as a rite of passage.[159] But the
Americans did not return the compliment. The American critic
Keith Tuma argues that British poetry has come to signify in the US
a 'flip frivolity and Audenesque chattiness, a strangely sentimental
cynicism in regular measures, one or another post-Georgian pas-
toralism'. Therefore, in the years since 1945, 'British poetry has
been crossed off our map, or relegated to the zones of the quaint and
antiquarian; American poets and critics no longer feel the need to
read widely in contemporary British poetry.'[160]

The British author and critic Malcolm Bradbury, however, argued
for the interconnectedness of the British and American novel and
other writings. On the one hand, the economic and military power
and the cultural pervasiveness of the US led Continental and British
readers and critics to plunge into American literature past and present, with new titles selling in impressive numbers in several
languages. 'Fascination with American fiction, American literature,
American anything, became a dominant phenomenon of the post-
war European world', although it is useful to remember Gore Vidal's
observation that writers in powerful countries get more recognition
than they deserve, because their writing is supported by the simple
facts and systems of cultural power. Yet Bradbury underplayed this,
arguing that the overpowering influence of American literature arose
from its critical energy, the vigour of its imagination, the fact that it
explored the anxieties of the changing condition of western life and
thought – the horrors of the Second World War had changed the
world for ever – the alienation felt by many, and the concomitant
desire for a cultural renewal. 'Something like a common transatlantic culture was beginning to emerge, most easily in Britain, where
there was a shared linguistic and cultural link.'[161]

This was not a situation desired by all, as a widespread fear of
'Americanisation' made clear. In any case, Bradbury presented much
less evidence for American appreciation of British literature. Things
had changed over the century. An American innovation in the 1890s

was the fiction bestseller list, and on the first such list, seven of the top ten titles were pirated British works.[162] Perhaps the extent of the mutual attraction of each other's literature in 2003 can be indicated by comparing similar figures. In the US eighteen of the Top 200 Fiction titles sold were British; in the UK seventy-three of the Top 200 Fiction titles were American.[163] And although the Americans won this particular competition, what is more interesting is that the two literary streams were now divergent and distinct.

VIII

For those who see the US as an imperial power in the cultural sphere, as a spider at the 'centre of webs of control and communication that span the world' and whose 'cultural products reach the far corners', American films and television are overwhelmingly important cultural products.[164] This has been the case since the beginning of the twentieth century. Reynolds has written that 'Neither [the American nor the British] people knew much, in a systematic way, about each other. Ideas were derived from national stereotypes, mediated, above all, by the cinema.'[165] Whether the populations of either country really believed that films told the truth about the other is a difficult question. For most film producers, that was not the point: making money was.

At the beginning of the century, the clear leader in the industry was France, then the world's most prolific maker of motion pictures. The combination of the early invention by the Lumière brothers of the portable motion picture camera and the energy of French firms such as Pathé Frères, supported by large urban audiences and wealthy investors, meant that by 1907, 40 per cent of total film receipts from the US went to French firms.[166]

The US industry then fought back. It first secured protective tariff legislation to cripple the production and distribution of foreign films (Pathé had maintained their own studios in the US).[167] Then, in 1909, leading American film-makers banded together as the Motion Picture Patents Company and set out to capture foreign markets. A major weapon was a new type of film, the long 'feature film'. Although the first feature-length film had appeared in Europe on the eve of the First World War, Hollywood producers popularised the concept in the second decade of the twentieth century. A feature-length film should tell a story and typically last for about two hours, a model which was ultimately accepted by film-makers in the rest of the world.[168] An early example was the three-hour *Birth of a Nation* (1915) by D.W. Griffith, innovative in its film-making techniques but despicable in its content (it features an heroic Ku Klux Klan). Between 1909 and 1912, the Americans captured 60 per cent of the British film market. They benefitted even more from the First World War, which disrupted European film distribution networks, and by 1917, American films made up 73 per cent of the British market. Not content with that, they saturated the imperial market as well.[169]

By the early 1920s, Britain was Hollywood's best foreign customer; in 1925–6, for example, Hollywood reaped 35 per cent of its foreign revenues from Britain alone. American films never relinquished the dominant position which they had gained during the Great War, and during the 1920s Hollywood films outnumbered British films shown in the UK by seventeen to one.[170] Indeed, it has been claimed that 'the Hollywood assault virtually wiped out the British film industry'.[171] Soon came the realisation, as the film columnist for the *Daily Express* wrote on 18 March 1927, that the picturegoers 'go to see American stars. They have been brought up on American publicity. They talk America, think America, and dream America. We have several million people, mostly women, who, to all intent and purpose, are temporary American citizens.'[172] Then came the reaction, as the Films Act of 1927 imposed a quota system, but this does not seem to have worked terribly well. In the 1930s, US producers focused attention on the British and British Empire markets, as the increasing closure of other markets by the Japanese, Italian and German governments seriously cut their earnings. As Mark Glancy points out, during the 1930s and the war years, British earnings could mean the difference between profit and loss for American films.[173] The Americans were not about to let this market go.

After the war, the British government attempted to impose

another quota system. The Treasury did not feel that it could afford to 'waste' what few dollars it had on importing American movies, given that the British themselves could make perfectly good films. The government also wanted to protect the domestic film industry, so it imposed a 75 per cent customs tax on all new films, called the 'Dalton Duty' after the Chancellor, Hugh Dalton, which lasted from August 1947 until March 1948.[174] In response, the Americans not only stopped exporting to the UK, they also cut back production at their British facilities. The British public wanted to know where the American films had gone, since they preferred them to most British ones.[175] Because American film producers had to appeal to a wide variety of ethnic groups and social classes, they had had to develop techniques which did not depend overmuch on words: spell-binding plots, visual expressiveness – body language, use of the eyes – lots of action and spectacle, with the whole film driven by narrative, not discussions (rather like silent films, in fact, at which the Americans had also been very good). The idea was to entertain, and the British were duly entertained. Furthermore, American films were profitable for British distributors and theatre owners, and they, too, were hostile to quotas and anything else that might reduce imports. Within a few months, the government rescinded the tax and abolished the quotas. Pressure had come from the American government as well, in that one requirement for receiving Marshall Aid (see Chapter 8) was that part of it had to be used to import American films.

The government then tried to control the screen time devoted to American films, limiting it to 45 per cent of the total. The problem here was that British studios were unable to supply enough films to theatres, which meant that soon the restrictions were simply ignored. The government then blocked the export of much of Hollywood's earnings in Britain, so the studios used the funds instead to buy up British film studios and invest in British films. There was then an outcry that the independence of the British film industry was in grave danger, not to mention the British identity of domestic films (a recurring fear since the mid-1920s). In the end, none of these restrictions achieved what the government had desired: by 1951, American films occupied 70 per cent of British screen time.[176]

Little changed during the remainder of the century. In the 1960s

American production companies financed two-thirds of all films shot in Britain, and the argument can be made that without American money, many of those films would simply not have been made. As long as the technicians and casts were predominantly British, films sponsored by American companies qualified as British 'quota films' and were entitled to subsidies from the so-called Eady Levy,[177] a production fund set up by the government in 1950. The fund gained its resources from a levy on cinema tickets, which was then redistributed to producers of British-registered films, with the amount based on their earnings at the box office. So, for example, the American company United Artists registered its James Bond film *Thunderball* (1965) as British, and scooped 15 per cent of the fund, $2.1 million, because of its success.[178] Yet the overwhelming number of American films shown in Britain originated in the US, and in the 1990s, 93 per cent of all films shown in Britain were American-made.[179] It seems likely that this situation will continue indefinitely.

There was some reverse traffic, but it was never going to be comparable. As noted above, the Americans had nipped the possibility in the bud in the very early years of cinema with protective legislation. But even had there been an open market, the British simply did not produce enough films even to fill their own cinemas, let alone those of the US. The few British films which were distributed in America attracted a mixed reception. Those that dealt with topics which the Americans recognised as 'English' tended to do very well: *Nell Gwyn* (1926) – which had an American star, Dorothy Gish – *The Private Life of Henry VIII* (1933) and *Henry V* (1946) were three examples.[180] With the advent of the 'talkies', the fact that British films were in English, and thus required no dubbing, was an overwhelming advantage; furthermore, they were sufficiently 'foreign' to be interestingly not American.

After the Second World War British cinematic specialities were political satire and sophisticated (often black) comedies, 'the kind of movies that had flourished in Hollywood in the 1930s but were now conspicuously absent from the studios' repertoire'.[181] By the 1960s, the popularity of British comedies gave way to a series of 'caustic' films about class divisions in Britain.[182] According to Pells, 'these movies were peculiarly exhilarating in spite of their grim portraits of working-class life, particularly for American audiences unaccustomed to such harsh realism from Hollywood'.[183]

British films, as well as other foreign films, benefitted in the 1950s and 1960s from the development in the US of the 'art cinema', theatres primarily in cities and in university and college towns which showed foreign films to a largely elite audience. British films also, if more unexpectedly, benefitted from the rise in the 'drive-in theatre'. The importance of these two types of theatre was increased by the fact that they were independent, and thus were not tied to screening the films that the big distributors insisted be shown.[184] Another help was the fact that the 1960s saw a recession in American film-making, which gave more room for foreign films.

This was the prime period of James Bond films, which were wildly successful throughout the US,[185] but the popularity of British films usually varied according to the place where they were shown. Undoubtedly, they were more popular in the towns and cities, and in college towns, than in small towns and rural areas; the British accent was foreign, and many people did not like it. But the American film audience grew more tolerant, and a generation later some British films were extremely popular – one such was *Four Weddings and a Funeral* (1994), which included both American and British accents. It was also financed largely by American money. Individual hits aside, however, 'British' films have never made up much of the American market: in 2003–4 they comprised only 5.7 per cent of American ticket sales.[186] Yet audiences ordinarily do not look at the provenance of a film when deciding whether to watch it. They simply want to be entertained. And British and American film-making are entangled: after all, British films do not qualify as 'foreign' at the Academy Awards.

IX

Since about 1960, television has been more important than film in transmitting knowledge, ideas and influences from one country to another. It was a Scottish engineer, John Logie Baird, who in 1926 first demonstrated a working television set, and it was the British

Broadcasting Corporation which, on 2 November 1936, opened the world's first regular television service, broadcasting from Alexandra Palace in North London. It showed the coronation procession of King George VI on 12 May 1937 and the FA Cup Final on 30 April 1938. However, with the coming of the Second World War, the television service was closed for the duration of the conflict and all resources were devoted to radio. Television was then resuscitated, but the focus was still on radio, which was seen as much more important. The situation began to change on 2 June 1953, when television broadcast the coronation of Queen Elizabeth II: there were an estimated twenty-two million viewers, many of them crowded into the living rooms of friends and relatives who owned sets. Many of these visitors were then inspired to buy their own sets.

However, the BBC saw itself as a public service broadcaster, and it took this responsibility very seriously: it was conservative, uplifting, and controlling.[187] A movement grew for a commercial alternative, not least to give the BBC some competition. The (Independent) Television Act was passed in July 1954, and on 22 September 1955, ITV began broadcasting. Whilst the BBC was funded by a licence fee from all owners of radio and television sets (the radio licence fee was abolished in 1971), independent television lived by advertising. Just because it was not the BBC and was 'independent' did not mean that it was independent: it had to devote part of its output to public service broadcasting. The law required it to have a national news broadcast every night, local news shows in each region, and a certain proportion of its air time devoted to British-made programmes. It also had to endeavour not to be vulgar. Notwithstanding these requirements, it carried programmes which were more entertaining and different from those on the BBC.[188]

At first, television developed more slowly in the United States. The number of lines constituting the picture was standardised in 1941, but, as in Britain, development was halted with entry into the Second World War. Once the war was over, though, development was rapid. During the 1940s and 1950s, however, US television was largely a domestic phenomenon: most programmes were shown live, and therefore could not be syndicated or distributed outside of the US. But this had changed by the early 1960s, when most American programmes were recorded and thus could be exported. This coincided with a significant increase in the costs of making programmes, which the networks refused to cover, and thus foreign sales became very important. Because American television producers had to appeal to a wide variety of ethnic groups and social classes, their products could easily cross national boundaries. They did this by utilising the same techniques as had been developed for American films. The idea was to entertain, and, again, the British were entertained.

Costs were rising in Britain as well, especially with increasingly high rates of inflation in the 1960s, and it was cheaper to buy American programmes than to make one's own. Furthermore, British audiences, judging by ratings, clearly preferred American sitcoms, Westerns, police dramas and cartoons to the 'homegrown, high-toned, heavily informational programming offered by the BBC'.[189] However, there was a growing fear of too much American influence – on one Saturday in 1961, after three hours of sport, the period from 5.45 p.m. until 11.50 p.m. was taken up with *Disneyland*, *Oklahoma Kid*, *The Buccaneers* and *Rosemary Clooney*, which were all American imports.[190] This was one of the reasons for a reorganisation of public broadcasting several years later in Britain, with the result that there were now two BBC channels, with BBC2 more high-brow than BBC1, the continuance of the severely regulated ITV, and a reduction in the proportion of programmes and concepts imported from the US.[191]

The years 1989 and 1990 saw the advent in Britain of satellite channels, which from the beginning relied heavily on imports, not only of individual American series but of entire American channels, such as the Movie Channel, stocked with Hollywood films. In 1995 the Disney Channel arrived in Britain via Sky. By then, with BBC, commercial, cable and satellite television, Britain had thirty channels to fill. They all wanted American expertise and they all needed American money and programmes. At the end of the century, Britain was spending over one billion dollars annually on television imports.[192]

However, the impact on British terrestrial television was mixed. Taking the week of Sunday 22 April–Saturday 28 April 2007 as an example, of the 840 hours of viewing time only 20 per cent of the shows were American in origin. During prime time (6 p.m.–12 a.m.) this increased to 25 per cent. However, these broad numbers cover a great deal of variation. BBC1 and BBC2 produced almost all of their own prime-time programmes, and ITV was close to this, with just under 10 per cent of programmes from the US. With commercial Channel 4 and Five, however, things were very different. On Channel 4, the channel of choice for the under-25s, just over 40 per cent of prime time was devoted to American programmes, whilst for Five, it was just under 68 per cent.[193]

As with films, the traffic was not entirely one way, and British programmes were imported into the US. They were not ordinarily bound for the main commercial channels such as NBC, but for the Public Broadcasting System. Often they were showcased in the *Masterpiece Theatre*, introduced by the Anglo-American broadcaster Alistair Cooke. But the PBS had neither enough money nor sufficient viewers, and in the 1990s the BBC began to sell its programmes increasingly to cable networks, especially to the Arts and Entertainment and Discovery channels. In 1998, however, the situation changed again. British television became an independent presence in the US, when BBC Worldwide established BBC America as an American cable and satellite television network, broadcasting only British programmes.

X

From the 1920s to the 1950s, the giants of modern popular music were overwhelmingly American: songwriters included Cole Porter, Irving Berlin, and Richard Rodgers and Oscar Hammerstein, whilst performers included Bing Crosby, Frank Sinatra, Miles Davis and Elvis Presley. In the 1950s, 68 per cent of the recorded music broadcast by the BBC came from the US, a percentage which was even higher in commercial radio stations, such as Radio Luxembourg, which broadcast 'top forty' shows. British and other European composers and singers emulated (when they did not actively copy) US styles; of particular importance were jazz and ragtime, and blues singers.[194] But then British groups developed their own sound, and for a while they swept everything before them.

The years 1964 to 1966 saw what was termed the Second British Invasion of the US. By far the most important group were the Beatles, who arrived triumphantly in New York City on 7 February 1964. Two days later they appeared on *The Ed Sullivan Show*, a television variety show which had monumental influence; this appearance has been termed 'the breakthrough moment of the burgeoning British Invasion'.[195] That same month they had four hits in the US Top 40 simultaneously, the first time this had happened,[196] and later in the year they appeared on the cover of *Life* magazine. But the Beatles were only one of many British groups who enjoyed success. Fifteen per cent of all the hit records in the US that year were British.[197] American record producers saw Britain as a 'hotbed of musical innovation', and American companies rushed to sign up any British group they could find. These groups produced more than music: they demonstrated different accents, slang and fashion, and their personalities were deliciously non-American. 'The Beatles' first film, "A Hard Day's Night" (1964), further painted England as the center of the (rock) universe. American media took the bait and made Carnaby Street, London's trendy fashion center in the 1960s, a household name.' The apotheosis came in April 1966, when *Time* published a cover story on 'London: the Swinging City'.[198]

The following years saw other British movements or groups making a significant impact on the American music scene. In the late 1970s came the stars of the largely English-based, raw and iconoclastic punk movement. However, although punk had a significant and lasting influence on US popular music, it never had the profound impact it had in Britain.[199] British music had another push in 1981, with the formation of Music-TV (MTV). The new station needed videos to broadcast, and it 'used a disproportionately large number by British acts, whose videos were generally more image conscious and entertaining than their American counterparts'. As a result, British music again dominated the US charts, this time to an even greater extent than in 1964–6. In July 1983 over 50 per cent of the Billboard Hot 100 comprised foreign artists.[200] After this high-water mark, though, the popularity of British acts dwindled, and at one point in May 2002, there were no British artists in the US singles chart, the first time this had happened since 1963. Reasons suggested include the ending of MTV's urgent need for videos; the fact that tastes in the US and Britain diverged; and a fragmentation of musical styles, making the recurrence of a unified 'invasion' unlikely.[201]

The pervasiveness of American music in Britain has continued. Notwithstanding the popularity of specific groups, the early years of the twenty-first century saw the relative decline of British artists at home reflected in the British charts, as in the US: in 2003, for the first time, US acts outperformed British rivals in the British album charts, with the former selling 45 per cent of all albums compared with the latter's 42 per cent.[202] Listeners knew whether the artists to whom they were listening were American or British, but thought it immaterial: on the whole, the focus was on the style of music.

XI

Cultural influence can have a more focused impact. Governments are not blind to the effect that culture can have in, for example, furthering foreign policy objectives. The assumption is that if people like a country's culture, they will like the country. This is, of course, frequently wrong: for example, a liking for American popular music can easily coexist with a dislike of US government policies. Nevertheless, the influence of a country's culture – sometimes termed 'soft power' – can help.

Hard power comprises the military, financial and economic power through which one country can impose its will on another. By contrast, as Joseph S. Nye, Jr. has conceptualised it, soft power is the 'ability to get what you want through attraction rather than coercion or payment. It arises from the attractiveness of a country's culture, political ideals, and policies.'[203] During the nineteenth century, Great Britain possessed a combination of both types of power with regard to the US. The hard power was obvious: as described above, Americans felt that wherever they turned, they were confronted by a much more powerful country, militarily and economically. The soft power arose from the recognition of Great Britain as a reasonably tolerant and increasingly democratic country which had a literary and cultural life against which the US could not compete and which many Americans envied. Near the end of the century, the joint historical legacy, the assumption of shared democratic values and the sense amongst some of an 'Anglo-Saxon' identity, became increasingly invoked by public men. The general conclusion was that whilst the two countries might be different from each other, each was more like the other than like any other country.

American soft power in the nineteenth century was largely based on two factors. One was her growing economic power, particularly after 1870, when the end of the Civil War released energy and resources that could now be devoted to development. The second was the sheer attractiveness of the American Dream. It gave hope to multitudes that if only they could get to America, they, too, could better themselves. This was the attraction – unique in the world – of the concept that all men are created equal. It was the freedom of religion, which gave hope that pogroms could be left behind. It was the energy of the country, the feeling that obstacles could be overcome, that goals would be reached, that at the end of your life you would be better off than your father had been. By the twentieth century, these components of American soft power were joined by pervasive American cultural influence.

By 1945, American hard power had substantially outstripped that of Britain. With regard to soft power, however, the situation was much less unequal. Both countries were attractive as repositories of democracy, although Britain was viewed as rather more tolerant. The American McCarthy era in the early 1950s, which saw the subordination of civil liberties to a search-and-destroy exercise against domestic communists, was hugely damaging to the image of the US in Britain, not least because, for several years after the war, there was a Member of Parliament from the Communist Party, and the state had not shuddered. But the US was still a beacon for those who wanted to get ahead, to remake themselves, to live in a less socially conservative society, to break out.

One of the strongest components of British soft power was the BBC World Service, by most accounts more trusted the world over as a provider of truth about world affairs than any other organisation. It maintained a continual vigilance against government interference, which was sorely tested during the 1956 Suez Crisis, when the Prime Minister, Anthony Eden, expressed his belief that the duty of the BBC in a time of crisis was to support the policy of the government, rather than to indulge in 'objectivity'.[204] This reputation for probity has, on the whole, stood the test of time. Other perceptions of Britain also strengthened this power: she gained from her reputation for tolerance and for being open to the world and, not unconnected, for the quality of her university system, which attracted students from around the globe, including future national leaders. And the language was English, then the global language of aspirations.

American soft power also depended on the attractiveness of her policies, and here the decisive factor, naturally, was the extent to which one agreed with them. The Marshall Plan is seen as one of the most successful foreign policies which the US has ever conceived and implemented: not just the US herself but all of the countries involved benefitted, and this was the key to its continuing historic success. America emerged with a reputation for a caring generosity which contributed substantially to its attractiveness for decades. However, the intense dislike amongst many in Great Britain of the Vietnam and Iraq wars (Chapter 8) substantially undermined this perception. The importance was twofold: the American assumption was that the world likes, admires and wants to emulate the US, and it was distressing for Americans to discover that this was not always the case; and in foreign policy terms it was feared that the US government might find it more difficult to convince other countries that its leadership could be trusted. In short, although American hard power remained phenomenal, after 2003 its soft power lagged behind. If world reaction to the Vietnam War has any predictive value, it could take the reputation of the US a generation to recover.

CHAPTER 6

The Turning of the Tide: 1871–1945

The American, it seems to me, feels a greater distinction between himself and the Englishman of Britain than the Englishman of Britain feels between himself and the American.

Edward A. Freeman, *Some Impressions of the United States* (1883)[1]

Not many years ago the self-respecting 'man in the street' considered himself bound to declaim against Britain and everything British . . . He saw her hand in nearly every disaster, domestic or foreign; he suspected her interference in every election that ran counter to his wishes; he wished her harm, intensest harm, with a whole heart; he rejoiced over her misfortunes, crowed over her mistakes, and thanked God that he was not an Englishman.

Frederick C. de Sumichrast, *Americans and the Britons* (1914)[2]

Just before his death in 1898, Otto von Bismarck, when asked what was the decisive factor in modern history, had replied, 'The fact that the North Americans speak English.'

Winston Churchill, *News of the World* (22 May 1938)

Nervos belli, pecuniam infinitam.[3]

Cicero, *Philippic* V.ii.5

We are in the remarkable position of not wanting to quarrel with anybody because we have got most of the world already, or the best parts of it, and we only want to keep what we have got and prevent others from taking it away from us.

Admiral Sir Ernle Chatfield, 4 June 1934[4]

Allies are the most aggravating of people.

General Sir William Slim[5]

In 1871, Great Britain was the only truly global power. She had the largest empire in history, which by the turn of the century would include 20 per cent of the surface of the globe and a quarter of the world's population. The Royal Navy ruled the waves. With just 2 per cent of the world's population, she produced 20 per cent of its total manufactured output. Indeed, her 'dominance of the world economy in the mid-nineteenth century was greater than that of the USA at its peak a century later'.[6] The symbol and support of this was the pound sterling, the world's most important trading currency, and the weapon of the City of London, the financial capital of the world. And the United States in 1871? Her manufacturing output was one-quarter that of Britain's, her coal production one-eleventh, and her steel production almost non-existent.[7] Compared to Britain's, her army and navy were minuscule. Yet, over the final third of the century, the strength of the American economy increased phenomenally. She experienced her own industrial revolution, which, by the end of the century, left her with steel production twice that of Britain and a manufacturing output that had increased to 70 per cent of Britain's. But the American navy, whilst growing, was still vastly smaller than the Royal Navy; and her army, whilst admirably able, was, again, vastly smaller.[8] The United States was a great economic power, but not yet a Great Power: she did not possess the necessary military might, nor, apparently, the will to increase it.

From 1871 until 1895, the political and diplomatic relationship between the two countries was less rocky than had earlier been the case. In the years following the Civil War, her unity settled with the victory of the North, the US turned her attention to completing the conquest and settlement of the North American continent, striving to fulfil her 'manifest destiny'. Americans increasingly looked inwards to their own ideas and resources, and if they thought of Britain at all – and most people never think about foreign countries or foreign policy unless there is a crisis – they thought of her as an enemy. Conversely, towards the end of the century, the British felt increasingly threatened by hostile European powers, and looked more appreciatively at the US. Yet the curious combination of attraction and repulsion lost little of its grip on both populations. Nevertheless, the last decades of the century saw a growing chorus of writers, politicians and academics emphasising a commonality of interests. This was an idea held more by the British than by the Americans, but as the international arena darkened, Americans, or at least the presidents, secretaries of state and other members of the political elite, also looked at alternatives to a traditional and almost automatic resentment. The two countries were very different, but they were less different, many claimed, than any two others in the world.

A boundary dispute between Great Britain and Venezuela in 1895–6 was the occasion for the assertion by the US, in defiance of Britain and Germany, of hegemony over the Western Hemisphere. This was also the beginning of a period which saw the two English-speaking countries sorting out problems which threatened their relationship. Much of the stimulus for this came from the British, encouraged by their realisation that they were effectively sur-rounded by enemies on land and sea. Britain needed US support – or, at least, not her enmity – and over the following decade, she appeased her by conceding nearly every point of conflict between them. As a result, once the First World War began, whilst the US did not join in 1914, her neutrality was benevolent. Yet, when she did become a belligerent in April 1917, she refused to be an ally – she was officially an 'Associated Power'. For the Americans, distrust of Great Britain was never far below the surface.

During the inter-war period, the relationship was complicated and confusing. Britain, with her empire, was undeniably still one of the greatest powers in the world, given her territorial range, interna-tional trade and military, especially naval, power. As for the US, she revelled in her own wealth and power. Yet, while demanding that other Great Powers accede to her wishes, she refused to take on the responsibilities of being one herself. In short, she had the resources but not the sustained will. This maddened the British government, which could not ignore events on the Continent or in the Far East. But if the US would not exercise what military power she had – and it was still much less than that of Great Britain – her economic power threatened to damage British interests extensively. As the 1930s darkened, the American evasion of responsibility became intensely worrying to the British. The US herself was going through a crisis of identity: was she only an economic power or also a military power? Was she only an American power or a world power? If the latter, was she willing to exercise that power? Would doing so erode what made her 'American'? She was bombed and torpedoed into the Second World War, as she had been torpedoed into the First. The later war would determine the answers to these questions.

This chapter shows the arcs of power of the two countries. The question of the 'decline' of Great Britain is misconceived, as is that of the 'rise' of the United States. Decline and rise in relation to what? In absolute terms or relative to other countries? Whilst from 1871 to 1945 it was clear that the US was a growing power, until the middle of the Second World War, it was not entirely clear to many contemporaries that Britain was a terminally declining one. Furthermore, power, or the ability to force another country to do something which it may not wish to do, is never absolute. It is more likely to be specific to a locality, time or the nature of the opposition. Thus, Britain was not, and the US is not, the strongest power in every contingency, although perhaps by more general measurements. However, during the Second World War, when economic and military forces were the determining factors, there increasingly seemed to be no question. And there were consequences. Whilst it is true that the military alliance was unprecedented in its closeness and apparent trust, it is similarly true that the US treated Britain as a rival which had to be cut down. For Britain, survival came at great cost: at the end of the war, it was the US which was the predominant international power. Britain now had to co-opt that power in support of her own policies. She had been attempting to do this, one way or another, since the turn of the century; now it was seen as vital to her safety. And the US continued to do what she had done since 1914: try to balance her wish to remain the cat who walks by herself with the need for a dependable ally in the jungle of international relations.

I

If most Americans and Britons had been asked in 1871 whether they believed it possible that the two countries would ever be allies, the tenor of the answers would have been the same: no. However, the nature of their answers would probably have differed. Most

Americans, when they thought of the British, disliked, distrusted and sometimes feared them. Those who lived in the Great Plains, the South or the West, and especially those in rural areas, were strongly Anglophobic; as described in Chapter 5, many saw the British taking over their land, livestock and railroads, and threatening their livelihoods. Furthermore, the British insisted that gold, not silver, was the measure of a currency – they had been on the gold standard since 1821 – and for the silver miners in the West or the farmers who had to pay for mortgages on their land, a hard, gold-based currency, rather than a more inflationary, partly silver-based one, could undermine their economic independence. And because, for example, the prices of most commodities were set in London, British policy mattered. The nature of the currency was such an issue that from about 1884 to 1900, an agrarian reform movement called the Populists, centred in the Great Plains states, the Rocky Mountains and the cotton-belt southern states, grew to and exercised significant political power. In 1896 they joined with the Democratic Party to nominate the Nebraska Congressman William Jennings Bryan as President. The peroration of his speech at the convention, against a currency based solely on gold, electrified the delegates and horrified both conservative Americans and the British: 'You shall not press down upon the brow of labor this crown of thorns. You shall not crucify mankind upon a cross of gold!'[9] But he was defeated (by William McKinley), and with his defeat the campaign for a currency based on both silver and gold also faded away. However, his appointment as Secretary of State in 1912 was to cause some apprehension in the Foreign Office.

It was not just gold, and it was not just farmers and miners who hated and feared the British. Many Americans felt that whatever they wished to do, wherever they wished to expand their markets, whether in Latin America or the Far East or the British Empire itself, Great Britain was already there and ready to thwart them. Dislike of and even hatred for Britain was, furthermore, a tradition, a habit. Dislike of the country could, however, cohabit quite comfortably with a liking for the people or the landscape. It could even cohabit with the reluctant belief that Britain was probably a more admirable country than others, such as Russia. It is also fair to say that there was a strong strain of anglophilia amongst the social and cultural elites, particularly on the East Coast.

Most Britons, when they thought of the US, had less fervent feelings. They were, increasingly, commercial rivals, but they were not truly imperial rivals, as were the French, the Russians and, soon, the Germans. Many retained their amused contempt for the US and its citizens, but increasingly the idea of war between the two became unthinkable, even fratricidal. More and more, the term 'American cousins' came into use. Even Sherlock Holmes got in on the act: 'It is always a joy to me to meet an American, Mr. Moulton, for I am one of those who believe that the folly of a monarch and the blundering of a Minister in fargone years will not prevent our children from being some day citizens of the same world-wide country under a flag which shall be a quartering of the Union Jack with the Stars and Stripes.'[10] This gradual change had more than one source. It had been nearly a century since the Revolution. For the British, the war had been largely forgotten – after all, the loss of that part of the empire had been replaced by an even larger chunk of the globe – but for many, the concept of the mother country and her daughter was important. Indeed, as dislike waned, there grew a curious pride in the strength and accomplishments of the erstwhile colony: 'the English-speaking peoples', not just the British Empire, were the power on the globe. Then there were the economic, religious, reform and literary links (as set out in Chapter 5).

There was also the racial factor. According to Stuart Anderson, 'the twin forces of burgeoning nationalism and the new imperialism gave an enormous impetus to race-thinking in the late nineteenth century', and by the 1890s the three strands were interwoven. Thinkers along those lines were not noted for the precision of their arguments, and 'race' and 'nation' tended to be used interchangeably. Thus, the 'Anglo-Saxon nations', in this context Great Britain (sometimes with her white settler colonies) and the US, also constituted the 'Anglo-Saxon race', and were thereby linked.[11] In the 1890s and into the early twentieth century many Britons saw the US as an Anglo-Saxon country – notwithstanding the non-British immigrants; equally, some Americans saw the British as the other Anglo-Saxon power. This was a period when a debased Darwinism, with its soundbite of 'the survival of the fittest', permeated public discourse. Looking at the British and American empires, it seemed quite clear that they were the fittest. Thus, the two were racial as well as cultural cousins, and, as a race, the Anglo-Saxons were inherently superior to all other peoples.[12] This 'cult of Anglo-Saxonism' had, for a short period, some diplomatic ramifications. Anderson argues for its impact during the 1895–6 Venezuela crisis,[13] and it certainly influenced the US government during the 1899–1902 Boer War (see below). This type of fellow-feeling will seldom convince one statesman to sacrifice a national interest for a foreign counterpart, but it can encourage a favourable position in less important situations. And very importantly for Britain, as she felt increasingly threatened, the US became the country to which she might be able to turn for diplomatic if not military support.

For Americans, the idea that anyone could question the principles of the Founding Fathers – that the US was anything but the beacon of the world, and that Americans were exceptional, were God's chosen people – was unthinkable. But it was not enough that Americans themselves should believe this: woe betide any visitors who were less than fulsome in their praise. This constant need for praise was a mark of the US's youth and insecurity, because the country which is self-confident tends not to require the repeated reassurances of others. As the US grew in wealth and power, it also increasingly gained this self-confidence. The need to bellow defiance at Great Britain lessened, and it became easier for the two countries to co-operate, as they began to do in the Far East and elsewhere, against the other Powers, as the century drew to a close.

A dominant theme of the period from 1871 was the American drive for markets abroad. Inevitably, she came up against the British, and frequently the Germans, in her attempts to force entry into these markets. In South America Great Britain continued to reign supreme,[14] whilst she was joined by Germany in Central America. In the Far East Britain was joined by Germany, France and Russia, all of whom controlled various regions which the latter three largely closed off from the trade of others. Part of the US's anger derived from this competition for markets, since Americans were convinced that if only their producers had a fair and open market place, they could match and even drive out the competition. In addition, it seemed clear to many that Americans had the God-given right to extend their economic reach, particularly in Central and South America; it was not unknown for politicians, for example, to argue that this was one implication of the Monroe Doctrine. Until near the end of the century, this did not imply political control of territory, but it did imply American dominance of trade. This mutated from cant phrases about the glorious future of America to a blatant economic nationalism. America is exceptional because of the virtues of its system, God intends that the US will extend these virtues, and thus it is right that the US dominates, for example, Latin America. And who is there to stop her? As James S. Hogg, the Governor of Texas, asked rhetorically in 1884, 'Why is it that the seat of commerce and finance now in control of and dominating the United States and the whole world is located on the little island of England? Why does not the United States control both the finance and commerce and pro-claim herself mistress of the seas?'[15]

As this quotation implies, the need for dominance had more than a psychological origin. From the 1870s to the turn of the century, the US experienced many years of depression as well as growth. The depression of the early 1870s was crucial: the imposition of a high protective tariff was intended to keep foreign goods out, especially those of Britain, to allow American products to dominate the home market. This indeed happened, with British exports to the US plunging by nearly 25 per cent of total American imports over the following ten years,[16] but the home market was not enough, because there were ever-larger surpluses from American farms, mines and factories which required overseas markets.

In due course, in some places, it seemed increasingly evident to many American businessmen, farmers and politicians that in order to maintain economic opportunities for Americans against the probably unfair manoeuvres, or even the fair competition, of other countries, the extension of American political control was desirable. This never became a serious threat to the territorial interests of Britain, Russia, France or Germany (although the Germans perhaps had a different view of this), because Americans never lost their ambivalence about becoming a straightforwardly imperial power. But the nearly total economic dominance combined with extremely influential links with local elites, dignified by the term 'informal empire', became increasingly acceptable, and even desirable, to Americans as long as it was clothed with the rhetoric of the 'open door', of free competition for all. The primary arena for the US's informal empire in this period was Central America. Formal empire would come elsewhere, at the end of the century.

The position of Great Britain from 1871 to 1895 varied from that of the US in a number of ways. Of course, she already had an empire: as large as it was in 1871, by the end of the century it had increased by another third, with Britain having acquired, amongst other territories, Burma, the Malay States, North Borneo and Sarawak in South-East Asia; Egypt and the Sudan in North Africa; and Nigeria, the Gold Coast (Ghana), Zimbabwe, Malawi, Zambia, Kenya and Uganda south of the Sahara Desert. During this same period, the US acquired no more territory, being fully occupied in settling and consolidating what she already possessed (which included Alaska, purchased from Russia in 1867 for $7,200,000). There was also the difference in population, particularly important as a labour force and as the pool for military forces. The British population in 1871 was 31 million and in 1901 41 million, an increase of 24 per cent; by comparison, the US population was 40 million in 1870 and 76 million in 1901, an increase of 48 per cent, and close to double the population of Britain.[17] However, this massive disparity in population made surprisingly little difference in the forces which the two countries could mobilise, because Britain could utilise the Indian army, which had a ratio of two Indian soldiers to one British, although it was officered exclusively by the British. Her land forces stabilised at about 120,000, and were used primarily in the Empire, whether for conquest or for police actions. With the exception of the Crimean War (1854–6) which was fought around the Black Sea, British troops were not occupied anywhere in Europe between 1815 and 1914. She thus had no need for a mass army, which was just as well. According to Lord Salisbury, a future Foreign Secretary and Prime Minister, in 1871 the Austrians and Germans could each put a million men into the field, and the

Russians nearly a million and a half, whilst the most that the British could manage was a mere hundred thousand.[18] As Otto von Bismarck, the Chancellor of the German Empire, commented, if the British army landed on the German coast, he would send the local police force to arrest it.[19]

But if the British army was small, the American army was tiny. From a high of over two million men in 1865 (the Union Army only) at the end of the Civil War, within five years the numbers had plummeted to just fifty thousand. The Americans were no more keen on a standing army than were the British. By 1880, the numbers had fallen further still, to thirty-eight thousand, and there they remained until the Spanish–American War of 1898, when army manpower shot up to over a quarter million. Thereafter, the numbers never fell below a hundred thousand, but nor, until US entry into the First World War, did they rise appreciably.[20] As a quick comparison, in 1890 the British (plus Indian) army was roughly seven times the size of the American.[21]

The disparity between the two navies was even greater. In the 1880s, according to LaFeber, the Royal Navy had 367 modern warships, whilst the US navy was a 'pathetic fleet' of fewer than ninety ships, only forty-eight of which were capable of firing a gun and thirty-eight of which were made of wood. In 1882, Congress appropriated the funds to build four modern warships, but it was a near war with Germany over Samoa in 1889 that focused American attention on the embarrassing fact that the navy ranked twelfth in the world, below those of the Austro-Hungarian Empire, the Ottoman Empire and China, none of which was a celebrated naval power. The Secretary of the Navy, Benjamin Tracy, a fervent imperialist, stressed in his annual reports for 1889 and 1890 that the US as a matter of urgency must devote greatly increased resources to the navy, and he was successful in convincing Congress to agree to the funding of the first three US modern armoured battleships.[22]

A more important and longer-lasting influence on US naval policy, however, was a book: *The Influence of Sea Power upon History, 1660–1783* by Captain Alfred Thayer Mahan, published in 1890, when the Samoan crisis and Tracy's reports were live in the public mind. Mahan was a seminal thinker, and his impact was probably as profound in London (and Berlin and Tokyo) as in the US. He believed that he had discovered the key to the development of the Roman Empire: it was the control of the sea, not of land, that had 'determined crucial turns in Rome's imperial development'. From this, and his reading of more modern history, he developed certain principles which, he argued, should inform any plans centred on the development or maintenance of 'sea power'.[23] His primary theme was that the Great Power rivalries between 1660 and 1815 had been decided chiefly by campaigns at sea, rather than on the land. He deduced that large battle fleets and the concentration of force decided the control of the oceans; that the blockade was a very effective weapon which would, sooner or later, bring an enemy to its knees; that it was more useful to position bases on islands or on the edges of continents than to control huge land masses; that overseas colonies were vital for a country's prosperity and colonial trade was the best of all, presumably because it could be more easily controlled; and that the rise of a country to world power without sea power was virtually unthinkable.

In his other writings he extrapolated from this to argue for policies which would help to solve the central US problem of the late nineteenth century: what to do with the results of the huge increases in productivity of farms and factories. For Mahan, the answer was foreign trade. This in turn would require a great fleet of battleships that could protect this commerce, destroy an enemy's commerce in time of war, and annihilate that enemy's own fleet. To support this, the US required coaling stations and rest stops, and Mahan thus demanded the annexation of such bases in Hawaii and the Caribbean.[24]

His impact was great. In 1904, for example, a British visitor to the US saw fourteen battleships and thirteen armoured cruisers being built simultaneously in American shipyards.[25] Those Britons who supported the strengthening of the Royal Navy adopted his arguments, but they also appreciated that whilst Mahan naturally urged that the US needed her own strong navy, as a fervent Anglo-Saxonist he expected and hoped that the naval predominance of Great Britain would remain unassailable. A few Britons took note of the darker implications. As the Earl of Selborne, the First Lord of the

Admiralty, wrote to the Viceroy of India in April 1901, 'I would not quarrel with the United States if I could possibly avoid it. It has not dawned on our countrymen yet, but doubtless it has on you as it has on me, that, if the Americans choose to pay for what they can easily afford, they can gradually build up a Navy, firstly as large and then larger than ours and I am not sure that they will not do it.'[26]

However, any concern about a putative American threat in the later years of the nineteenth century was minor compared to that aroused by a resurgent threat: France. Ever since the British had occupied Egypt in 1882, the French had been implacably hostile around the globe, and especially in Africa. For several years France had been engaged on a shipbuilding programme which the British, convinced as they were of the unchallengeable supremacy of the Royal Navy, had hardly noticed. But in 1884 W.T. Stead, then editor of the *Pall Mall Gazette*, drawing on leaks from within the government,[27] revealed that the two fleets had almost equal numbers of first-class battleships. Public opinion was duly aroused and alarmed. The Liberal government under Prime Minister Gladstone was devoted to economy and had kept the army and naval estimates as low as possible, but now it had to commit several extra millions of pounds to ships and coaling stations.

In 1885 the Liberals gave way to the Conservative Party under the Marquis of Salisbury,[28] and although they, too, tried to limit military spending, events would not allow this. The French remained hostile, and they continued with a substantial fleet-building programme. But they were not the only enemy: now there was Russia, too. Britain and Russia had for decades been imperial rivals in Central Asia. The most important concern for Britain was India, and the government was alarmed at the clear intention of Russia to challenge the British position. After the Crimean War of 1854–6, when Russia had been defeated primarily by Britain and France in her attempt to gain overwhelming power over the Ottoman Empire and the Black Sea, she had turned to Central Asia and further east to expand her empire. Branches of the Trans-Siberian Railway snaked southwards towards Persia, which shared a border with India;[29] the British knew the railway was intended to transport troops and supplies.[30] Another route of attack was through Afghanistan and the

Khyber Pass into the North-West Frontier; since 1838, Russia and Britain had been in repeated conflict over which would exercise control of the Afghan tribesmen and their mountains. Russia was also building up her fleet, and appeared to be musing about coming to an agreement with France over their differences. This would be a grave threat: the French and Russian navies could catch the under-strength British Mediterranean Fleet in a pincer movement and cut off all lines of communication if there should be a war, as well as taking control of the Suez Canal.

This threat could not be ignored, and thus on 7 March 1889 the First Lord of the Admiralty, Lord George Hamilton, introduced the Naval Defence Act, a five-year programme of construction, which had two main thrusts: the Commons should agree that 'the establishment [of battleships] should be on such a scale that it should be at least equal to the naval strength of any two other countries', in this case the combined navies of France and Russia; and it should vote funds for the construction of ten battleships, forty-two cruisers and eighteen torpedo boats, as well as for other facilities. They agreed to both.[31] This was a huge expansion programme, but the press and public continued to urge that even more resources be put into the Royal Navy, so in 1894 the government announced that a further seven battleships and many smaller vessels would be built.[32] Policy-makers, if not the public, knew about the 'secret' Franco-Russian entente in 1892 and the military alliance in 1894, with the implied threat that Britain's two great imperial rivals would join together and attack the Empire. This fear would drive British naval policy for the remainder of the decade, when a further threat began to emerge: a German fleet intended to challenge the Royal Navy.

The latter, however, had more than ships: by the end of the century, Great Britain held the 'five strategic keys' that 'lock up the world': the great naval bases at Dover, Gibraltar, Alexandria, the Cape of Good Hope and Singapore.[33] (Significantly, there was no mention of Halifax, Canada.) But these bases alone would not have sufficed for global reach. In 1881 and 1882 the Carnarvon Commission had produced three major reports, stressing the need for secure bases to provide worldwide mobility for the Royal Navy. Steam power for ships had been utilised since the early 1860s, and from 1870 had rapidly supplanted the sail. As a result of the commission's findings, a network of coaling and repair stations had been developed, and by 1889 the Royal Navy controlled, or had access to, 157 principal coaling stations around the world, including Malta, Ascension Island, Buenos Aires, San Francisco and Hawaii.[34]

A peacetime navy costs much more to build and run than an army of equivalent size, and no matter what the wealth of Britain, from the 1880s the country would feel the strain of paying for the successive building programmes, and then manning and running the fleet. It is true that Britain had the huge advantage of having been the first industrial nation, with a lead of about a century over all other European countries, and was thus rich and able to maintain her military forces. This early industrialisation had been based on plentiful coal supplies; a continuing supply of labour from the countryside; a banking system unmatched in the world, including the existence of the Bank of England from 1694; manufacturing industries, pre-eminently textiles, whose products were in demand around the world; the strongest navy in the world to keep international trade routes open and safe; a wealthy upper class which did not shy away from investing in the new industries; and a transport infrastructure, first canals and then railways, which facilitated country-wide and overseas distribution.[35] But there were disadvantages to being first. One was a resistance to new technology, in great contrast to the US, where machines were built cheaply and then discarded for newer models. Another was resistance to new processes, again in contrast to the US, which pioneered mechanisation,[36] the standardisation and thus the interchangeability of parts, and mass production, clearly a much faster and cheaper process than when each worker produced an object from beginning to end. There was the catch-up syndrome, whereby those from behind can build on the ideas and processes pioneered by the leaders and leapfrog them in the process. Furthermore, with her financing of railways and other infrastructures in developing countries and her loans to governments and corporations, Britain herself was an important factor in the development of many future rivals: her financial power helped to undermine her own manufacturing lead. Furthermore the growth in the proportion of the population available for industry mattered. Britain had long since ceased to be primarily an agricultural country, with a majority already having left the land and moved to manufacturing centres. Thus there was no longer a large pool of labour to be tapped. By contrast, both Germany and the US had plentiful supplies of labour to staff their industries. Furthermore, it could be argued that Britain was not an industrialised country of a type which could easily increase her output. A significant proportion of firms were family based, financed from family resources, and thus limited in their size; even those which were not were often reluctant to invest, since acceptable profits were being made. Organisations with professional managers were the exception, not the norm; also, they had to contend with labour unions which were often as conservative in their resistance to change as were their employers.[37]

What Great Britain was, and would for decades continue to be, was a financial and commercial power. The major reason why she could afford to fight two centuries of wars, create an empire, develop the resources of the home islands and maintain a relatively liberal political system was the combination of the financial probity of the government and the financial and economic power of the private sector.[38] The Bank of England had been established by private gentlemen in 1694, during a war with France, to lend money to the government; in exchange, successive governments paid the interest on time and repaid fixed-term loans. This gave the government credibility, and it could raise the money it required to equip the country with an army and a navy; it also meant that a national debt was created which provided a safe investment for Britons over the centuries. They could then easily liquidate their investments in order to invest in, say, American or Argentinian railways, or a tea plantation, or the opium trade with China, or thousands of other possibilities abroad. This benefitted the country in at least two ways. First of all, the interest payments, shipping fees and insurance premiums from abroad greatly enriched sections of the population, particularly those who tended to reinvest. And secondly, these overseas investments provided the British with financial and economic, and sometimes political, power. This financial power was centred on the City of London, the financial capital of the world, which by means of the banking system – stretching from country banks, which funnelled surplus funds from Yorkshire or Sussex to London for investment, to the merchant banks, which loaned the money – effectively set the terms for the international financial system. The fact that the pound sterling had been 'as good as gold' since 1821 and was the currency of choice the world over gave the City a tool which could not be matched during the nineteenth century by any other country. Because much of the trade in the world was denominated in pounds, British merchants had an advantage. They also had the protection of the Royal Navy, which aided the extension of communication and trading links, especially with those initially unwilling to trade, such as China. The commodities and manufactured goods produced in the British Empire, made by companies that were frequently financed by London bankers, were carried in ships of a merchant marine which, at the turn of the century, was larger than the combined merchant fleets of the rest of the world.[39] These ships sailed along trade routes patrolled by the Royal Navy, and their cargoes were frequently either landed in Britain, where the goods might be sold, or they might have duty paid on them and then be re-exported. It was a system of unrivalled extent and power. Increasingly, Britain became more important as an entrepôt than as a manufacturing centre.

This was very fortunate, because over the same period she lost some of her former advantages to the new industrial powers. An example was her predominance in the mining of plentiful supplies of coal, the primary fuel for manufacturing textiles. Whilst in 1850, 57 million tons were mined in Britain, compared to 6 million tons in Germany and negligible quantities in the US, by 1900, although Britain's output had quadrupled to 228 million tons, Germany was producing 149 million tons and the US 212 million tons. Fourteen years later, Britain's production stood at 292 million tons, Germany's at 277 million tons, and the United States' at 455 million tons.[40] The trend was the same in steel production, fundamental to manufacturing prowess and military strength alike. According to Eric Hobsbawm, 'every major innovation in the manufacture of steel came from Britain or was developed in Britain',[41] but the owners simply refused to invest in new plant. In 1880, Great Britain produced 1.3 million tons of steel compared to Germany's 700,000 tons;[42] in 1900 the comparative amounts were 5 million tons for Britain, 6.7 million tons for Germany and 10 million tons for the US. In the US 'Andrew Carnegie was producing more steel than the whole of England put together when he sold out in 1901 to J.P. Morgan's colossal organization, the United States Steel Corporation.'[43] The next decade and a half saw Britain falling even more spectacularly behind: in 1914 her production had increased to only 6.5 million tons, compared to Germany's 14 million tons; and that year the USA produced 50 million tons, more than the combined steel production of all of Europe.[44] In short, in both coal and steel production, while Britain's output increased substantially over the forty-five years from 1870, in relative terms she fell far behind her two main industrial rivals.

Much ink has been consumed in debate over the causes of Britain's relative economic decline: was it the narrow base of her industrial revolution, her later resistance to technological change, her failure to develop new industries – such as chemicals – and desperate lack of investment in the old, the lack of status accorded to science and engineering, the manifold drawbacks of being first, her lack of many important natural resources, the fact that the funds flowing in from interest payments, fees and shipping (the so-called 'invisibles') masked a decline in the balance of trade, so that the danger was not obvious? Hateful as it is to consider anything in history inevitable, a position of such mastery held by a country with just 2 per cent of the world's population was unlikely to last: indeed, that underlines the importance to Great Britain of her empire, which supplied manpower, markets and raw materials. Coming back to a comparison of the US and Britain, Peter Mathias sums it up very nicely: 'when half a continent starts to develop then it can produce more than a small island.'[45]

II

During the mid-1890s Latin America witnessed a series of conflicts between Britain and Brazil, Nicaragua and Venezuela, in all of which the US intervened.[46] Of these, the one that redefined the Anglo-American relationship centred on Venezuela. The question at issue was the boundary between Venezuela and a British colony, British Guiana (now Guyana). In 1814 Britain had acquired the territory from the Netherlands, but the boundary between the two countries lay in dense jungle and was ill-defined. In 1835 Britain commissioned Robert Schomburgk, a surveyor and member of the Royal Geographical Society in London, to survey the western boundary of British Guiana; the result in 1840 was the Schomburgk Line, a boundary which effectively incorporated a further thirty thousand square miles within Guiana. The following year, Venezuela put forth her own claim, basing it on the territorial boundaries established when she gained her independence from Spain after the Napoleonic Wars; this included a boundary which extended east to the Essequibo River, thereby making a claim on two-thirds of the territory of British Guiana. When gold was discovered in the disputed territory in 1876, Britain claimed a further thirty-three thousand square miles west of the Schomburgk Line; Venezuela countered by increasing her claim. The whole matter was deeply complicated, involving not only gold but, for example, control of the mouth of the Orinoco River.

In 1887 Venezuelans seized a British ship and imprisoned the captain; in response, Prime Minister Salisbury sent part of the Royal Navy's West Indies Squadron to demand – and receive – satisfaction.[47] Venezuela broke off diplomatic relations with Britain and appealed to the US for assistance in convincing Britain to moderate her boundary claims, largely on the grounds that the Monroe Doctrine was being threatened. The US offered her services as arbiter between the two claims, but Britain refused.[48] Venezuela then asked the US either to intervene with force or to sponsor arbitration. The US expressed concern, and again unsuccessfully suggested arbitration to Britain, but did nothing further. In light of this circumspection by the US, one question must be asked: what had changed so dramatically by 1895 that she not only took up the Venezuelan cause seriously, but President Grover Cleveland, in a message to Congress, threatened war if Britain did not do what the US demanded? The answer is a combination of public opinion aroused by a lobbyist of impressive ability, Cleveland's political difficulties, and the determination of a new Secretary of State to assert

American power. But why did Great Britain, still massively more powerful than the US, not defend her position more strongly? The answer here is the relatively small importance of the issue in comparison with more urgent threats to her empire.

In 1895 Cleveland, a Democrat, was the target of increasingly ferocious Republican attacks, including over what they saw as his supine response to British activities in Latin America. Democratic jingoes were also in full cry, and with an election due in 1896, the President needed to be seen to be decisive in support of American interests. This was especially important in view of the fact that he was not particularly imperialistic, having, for example, refused to annex Hawaii in 1893. Public opinion was also being whipped up, partly by a pamphlet published in 1894 entitled *British Aggression in Venezuela, or The Monroe Doctrine on Trial*, written by William Scruggs. He had been the American Minister in Venezuela, but had been dismissed for bribing local politicians, including the Prime Minister; he was now employed by Venezuela to lobby on her behalf. His main theme was that Britain was using the boundary dispute to mask encroachments against Venezuela: once she had gained the land at the mouth of the Orinoco, Britain would control the commerce and ultimately the political life of the northern quarter of South America, not just of Venezuela. The appeal to commerce was wise, since the US was acutely aware of Britain's commercial dominance in most of South America. Furthermore, the idea of encroachments was a red rag, given that Britain seemed to be encroaching all over the globe, in China, the Middle East and South and East Africa. It was likely that this was the case in the Western Hemisphere as well, since the crisis in Nicaragua in March 1895 included a threat by the British to occupy a port unless the country came to terms. Therefore, Venezuela could be part of a pattern.

The pamphlet was sent to all Senators and Congressmen, and proved highly influential. As a result, on 5 April 1895, the Secretary of State, Walter Q. Gresham, sent to Thomas F. Bayard, the American Ambassador to London,[49] a copy of a joint resolution of Congress recommending that Britain and Venezuela submit their differences over the boundary to arbitration, a suggestion supported by Cleveland. Gresham noted that this was not the first time that the US had suggested this – she had proposed arbitration in 1884, 1887, 1890 and 1891[50] – and had repeatedly thereafter urged Great Britain as the stronger party to negotiate or arbitrate. Britain refused to initiate a restoration of diplomatic relations. Furthermore, she stated that only if Venezuela surrendered a substantial portion of the territory in question, including land at the mouth of the Orinoco River, would she agree to submit the balance to arbitration. The point of this was that British settlers had already moved into the gold fields, as well as other parts of the land claimed, and Britain held that lands already settled and administered by British subjects could not be submitted to arbitration. The situation was seen by Cleveland and Gresham as dangerous: if not resolved, Venezuela might go to war with Britain, and the Monroe Doctrine would force the US to take up arms to prevent the loss of territory in the hemisphere to a European power. In other words, Britain and the US could soon be at war. But Gresham was not a strong personality, and he wavered back and forth between asserting that the British position was 'palpably unjust' and accusing the Venezuelan government of trying 'to dump the controversy on us', suggesting that the Venezuelans settle with Great Britain as best they could.[51]

However, Gresham suddenly died, and his successor was Richard Olney, a brusque, opinionated lawyer from Boston with a temper who was unfamiliar with diplomatic language and practices. As soon as he was appointed, he set out to examine the whys and wherefores of the Venezuelan controversy. The more he looked into the matter – using as sources the Scruggs pamphlet, a compilation of correspondence between Britain, Venezuela and the US which had been put together for Congress in 1888, recent files of the State Department and messages of Presidents, but no submissions from Britain – the more Britain seemed to be the guilty party and Venezuela the innocent. Looking over a decade's correspondence between the US and Britain on the matter, Olney decided that soft words had been worthless. A speedy solution was needed, but the disparity in strength between Britain and Venezuela was too great to allow a clash. Therefore, 'instead of another note beseeching the British to deal justly with Venezuela, Olney proposed calling the

London government up short and demanding that it deal directly with the United States'. Venezuela was not consulted. President Cleveland agreed with Olney, specifying only that the American stand must 'squarely vindicate the Monroe Doctrine'. The President himself was not entirely sure what that involved, but he seems to have believed that invoking the sacred text would leave the British with no choice but to withdraw.[52]

On 20 July 1895, a despatch of some twelve thousand words was sent to Ambassador Bayard, which he was instructed to read to the British Foreign Secretary (and Prime Minister) Lord Salisbury, and then give him a copy. Olney began with a history of the boundary dispute, and an explanation as to why the US was involved. At issue was title to 'territory of indefinite but confessedly very large extent'; the disparity in strength between the two meant that Venezuela could only hope for a peaceful settlement; during the half-century of conflict over the boundary, Venezuela had tried repeatedly to reach a negotiated settlement, but had failed; because conventional means had failed, Venezuela had for twenty-five years pressed for arbitration; Britain had consistently refused to go to arbitration 'except upon the condition of a renunciation of a large part of the Venezuelan claim and of a concession to herself of a large share of the territory'; and the US, 'by the frequent interposition of its good offices' and by 'expressing its grave concern whenever new alleged instances of British aggression' had been brought to its notice, had 'made it clear to Great Britain and to the world that the controversy is one in which both its honor and its interests are involved and the continuance of which it cannot regard with indifference'. On behalf of the US, then, and as proof of American impartiality, Olney offered arbitration, which he considered would be a relatively straightforward task, turning, as it did, on 'simple and readily ascertainable historical facts'. The accuracy of the foregoing analysis, Olney stated with confidence, 'cannot, it is believed, be challenged'.[53]

The fundamental basis of the American position was the Monroe Doctrine. That America was no longer open to colonisation had long been universally conceded. However, there was another application, which was that 'no European power or combination of European powers shall forcibly deprive an American state of the right and power of self-government and of shaping for itself its own political fortunes and destinies'. Indeed, its application was apparently being extended to the condemnation of current European settlements: 'That distance and three thousand miles of intervening ocean make any permanent political union between an European and an American state unnatural and inexpedient will hardly be denied.' (Canada?) By contrast, the states of North and South America, by geographical proximity, similarity of governmental institutions and natural sympathy, were friends and allies. Furthermore, the US had a vital interest in the cause of popular self-government, and would not tolerate European political control of any of these states. Olney then issued a stark warning:

> To-day the United States is practically sovereign on this continent, and its fiat is law upon the subjects to which it confines its interposition. Why? It is not because of the pure friendship or good will felt for it. It is not simply by reason of its high character as a civilized state, nor because wisdom and justice and equity are the invariable characteristics of the dealings of the United States. It is because, in addition to all other grounds, its infinite resources combined with its isolated position render it master of the situation and practically invulnerable as against any or all other powers.[54]

Known as the Olney Doctrine, this came very close to claiming that might made right. When made public it also, not surprisingly, infuriated the Canadians and Latin Americans.[55] Finally, the President hoped, and expected,[56] that Britain would decide to go to arbitration, since not to do so would 'gravely embarrass the future relations' of the two countries. He wanted the British government to tell him so in time for him to lay the whole subject before Congress in his Annual Message in December.[57]

The history was bad and the language intemperate, but Olney was trying to make his case. He later explained that the note was designed 'effectually even if rudely' to dispel British complacency. Its phrases were of a 'bumptious order', but the 'excuse was that in English eyes the United States was . . . so completely a negligible quantity that it was believed only words the equivalent of blows would be really effective'.[58] Neither party's claim rested on a clear title. Venezuela's was based on Spain's original discovery of the region, whilst Britain's relied heavily on so-called 'prescriptive rights': long occupation, settlement and use of the land in question. Venezuela's charges should be met by Britain with proofs, Olney thought, not just denials and assertions; arbitration would require that these proofs be provided and they would resolve the dispute.

On 7 August, Ambassador Bayard tried to read the despatch to Salisbury, but after some time the Prime Minister intimated that it 'was evidently much too large and much too complicated an argument to deal with in course of conversation',[59] and expressed his 'regret and surprise' that the US had thought it 'necessary to present so far-reaching and important a principle and such wide and profound policies of international action in relation to a subject so comparatively small'.[60] It would be necessary to investigate the whole question very carefully, and it was unlikely that an early response could be provided. Salisbury could have expedited the reply, but there were events taking place elsewhere which made the American démarche seem of relatively minor importance. The two despatches dated 26 November from Salisbury to the British Ambassador in the US, Sir Julian Pauncefote, were only sent by steamer fully four months after Olney's note had been received, and American irritation at the delay is understandable. One dealt with the points of principle raised by Olney; the other concentrated on the history of the boundary dispute itself. Pauncefote laid both before Olney on 7 December, four days after Cleveland's Annual Message to Congress.

The despatches were written in the best Foreign Office manner, heavy with gravitas and ripe with the very sort of *de haut en bas* tone which might have been calculated to raise the hackles of the Americans:

> The contentions set forth by Mr Olney . . . are represented by him as being an application of the political maxims which are well known in American discussion under the name of the Monroe Doctrine . . . But international law is founded on the general consent of nations; and no statesman, however eminent, and no

nation, however powerful, are competent to insert into the code of international law a novel principle which was never recognized before, and which has not since been accepted by the Government of any other country.

As for Olney's assertion that it could not be denied that the three thousand miles of intervening ocean made any permanent political union between a European and an American state unnatural and inexpedient, 'Her Majesty's Government are prepared emphatically to deny it on behalf of both the British and American people who are subject to her Crown', which included Canada, Jamaica and Trinidad, British Honduras and British Guiana (in total a larger territory than that of the US itself). As for the present issue, the 'British Empire and the Republic of Venezuela are neighbours, and they have differed for some time past, and continue to differ, as to the line by which their dominions are separated. It is a controversy with which the United States have no apparent practical concern . . . It is simply the determination of the frontier of a British possession which belonged to the Throne of England long before the Republic of Venezuela came into existence.'[61] The second despatch, based on the British, Spanish and Dutch archives and setting out the history of the controversy, insisted that Britain 'cannot consent to entertain . . . claims based on the extravagant pretensions of Spanish officials in the last century, and involving the transfer of large numbers of British subjects'.[62] In short, the answer was no to the demands of both Venezuela and the US.

To what extent had the British government misinterpreted Olney's despatch? For one thing, he had not claimed that the Monroe Doctrine was part of international law; as he later explained, the doctrine was 'a matter of policy and not of right' and was 'without recognition in international law'. He had also made no claim that either Great Britain or Venezuela was at fault: rather, he had insisted that all lands in dispute should be subject to arbitration. From his previous experience as an arbitrator, he realised that one of the principal objections was the tendency of tribunals to split the difference. This was clearly the case with the British government, which feared that the settled part of the territory would also be split, and British subjects would be turned over to Venezuela. In fact, because 'prescriptive rights' of settlement carried greater weight than mere claims to territory, Olney expected a tribunal to award most of this land to Britain, and then to award Venezuela most of the unsettled land. Swept away by the rhetoric, the Foreign Office had missed much of Olney's message.[63]

President Cleveland had gone on a ten-day duck-shooting holiday and did not return to the White House until Sunday afternoon, 15 December. He and Olney then had a conference, after which he sat at his desk until dawn, in the white heat of composition. (Cleveland was described by a friend as 'mad clear through'.[64]) On the Tuesday he read the result to the Cabinet, and on the same day it was sent to Congress. He had clearly taken the British answer as a challenge to the integrity of the Monroe Doctrine: 'the doctrine on which we stand is strong and sound because its enforcement is important to our peace and safety as a nation, and is essential to the integrity of our free institutions and the tranquil maintenance of our distinctive form of government'. He found the British declination of arbitration 'far from satisfactory', and the dispute had now reached such a stage that it was incumbent upon the US to determine what the true boundary was. Therefore, he was suggesting that Congress should make the funds available for the Executive to set up a Commission to investigate and report.

> When such report is made and accepted it will, in my opinion, be the duty of the United States to resist by every means in its power as a willful aggression upon its rights and interests the appropriation by Great Britain of any lands or the exercise of governmental jurisdiction over any territory which after investigation we have determined of right belongs to Venezuela. In making these recommendations I am fully alive to the responsibility incurred and keenly realise all the consequences that may follow . . . [but] there is no calamity which a great nation can invite which equals that which follows a supine submission to wrong and injustice and the consequent loss of national self-respect and honor beneath which are shielded and defended a people's safety and greatness.[65]

The Senate chamber rang with applause. In traditional diplomatic exchanges between countries, the message was a call for war, and war between the US and Britain might indeed have been the consequence.

There was a range of reactions throughout the country to Cleveland's message, not the least of which was surprise: it was the first most Americans had heard about an Anglo-American crisis over Venezuela. The House of Representatives and the Senate gave the President the appropriations he had requested. Ex-President Benjamin Harrison called for war. A number of Civil War veterans offered their services, as did the future President Theodore Roosevelt – 'If there is a muss I shall try to have a hand in it myself! They'll have to employ a lot of men just as green as I am even for the conquest of Canada' – and newspapers predictably shouted for action. Irish-American organisations stated that they could put a hundred thousand men in the field, Democrats thought it would help them in the elections, and businessmen saw this as a weapon against British commercial supremacy. However, there were chastening developments. 'The pulpit thundered against the President', stock prices plummeted on the New York Stock Exchange on the 20th, with four hundred million dollars lost in two days, and people began to consider how defenceless coastal cities were against British naval power.[66] Canada began military preparations and looked to her defences.

In Britain Cleveland's threat also came as a surprise, shattering the indifference of most politicians as well as the public towards the US. It gave a fresh impetus to planning for the defence of Canada. (Indeed, the War Office decided that offence was the best defence, and a war plan was drawn up. In retrospect, it looks a bit batty: three British army corps were to invade the US from three directions, one to march from Montreal, and the other two to land at Boston and New York; the invading British forces, it was hoped, would be supported by a massive Indian uprising. More seriously, the Royal Navy would have swept American trade from the oceans.[67]) The reaction of the Prime Minister, however, appeared calm rather than concerned: he remarked to a fellow-member of the Cabinet that 'the American conflagration will fizzle away', and conveyed the same assessment to the Queen. He also refused to disturb members of the Cabinet during the Christmas recess, which would have raised the political temperature.

Salisbury's views of the US were not complimentary. Indeed, from an early age he had seen the country as a threat. He disliked America and most Americans, writing in an article in the 1850s ridiculing 'Manifest Destiny' that 'The Yankee, whose life is one long calculation, appears to have bombast for his mother tongue.' According to his biographer, he did not fear her military might, but rather democracy, which, presumably, he feared would be contagious. He also believed that Americans were instinctively anti-British, a belief that any reasonable Englishman might have held in the 1850s. He must have seen Olney's Note as bombastic, and the American reaction to the British response and Cleveland's speech as demonstrating undying anti-British sentiment. 'Privately calling it "Cleveland's electioneering dodge", Salisbury decided simply to sit the crisis out.' However, this did not mean that he dismissed the American threat entirely: on 2 January 1896 he wrote to the Chancellor of the Exchequer, Sir Michael Hicks-Beach, that 'A war with America – not this year but in the not distant future – has become something more than a possibility.'[68]

Salisbury's policy of haughty defiance of the US was not supported by his Cabinet. He was in any case losing the unquestioned control he had exercised over foreign policy in previous Conservative governments. He was becoming old and tired (he was sixty-five), and there was a new generation of politicians with different ideas about British foreign policy. Furthermore, his habit of spending much of his time in the country at Hatfield House, where he dealt with the contents of the Foreign Office's red boxes, was increasingly irritating to his colleagues. It should also be added, however, that the Cabinet was a relatively weak coalition of Conservatives and Liberal Unionists, not a united Conservative Party government, and this was significant.[69] A series of threats bombarding Britain ultimately lost Salisbury the support of his Cabinet.

There was the problem of the Ottoman Empire. The Turks in Constantinople and especially in Asia Minor were slaughtering thousands of Armenians: what, if anything, should the other Powers do?

The British wished to stop the murders, which had aroused a horri-fied and vocal response from the public, but there was little the government could do beyond Constantinople, since they had neither the military forces nor the will to engage in a police action in Anatolia. Moreover, the government needed to prevent Russia from taking advantage of the chaos in order to seize Constantinople and the Dardanelles Strait, which would allow her to move warships into the Mediterranean instead of remaining bottled up in the Black Sea. However, the Admiralty insisted that, in the new circumstances of the Dual (Franco-Russian) Alliance, Britain could not take the chance of forcing the Dardanelles Strait alone, the only means of stopping the Russians if they made a grab for the Strait.[70] According to T.G. Otte, it was Salisbury's failure to carry the Cabinet in the face of the Admiralty's objections that was the beginning of the end of his command of British foreign policy.[71]

There was also a crisis in South Africa. Conflict was threatening between the British Cape Colony and the two Boer republics, the Transvaal and the Orange Free State. Cecil Rhodes, the Prime Minister of the Cape, was keen to conquer the republics and, with the connivance of Joseph Chamberlain, the Secretary of State for the Colonies, planned an invasion of the Transvaal. This began prema-turely with what was called the Jameson Raid on 29 December 1895, a 'private' initiative and a fiasco of the first order. This was bad enough, but what turned it into a crisis was the reaction of Kaiser Wilhelm II of Germany. He decided to make an issue of it, not least to aid his domestic campaign for an increasingly large navy, and on 3 January 1896 he sent a public telegram to Paul Kruger, the President of the Transvaal. In a deliberately offensive manner, he congratu-lated Kruger on the way that 'you and your own people, without appealing to the help of friendly powers [such as Germany], have succeeded, by your own energetic action against the armed bands which have broken into your country as disturbers of the peace, and maintaining the independence of the country against attacks from without'.[72] The British were already acutely sensitive about German activities in South Africa, given that in January 1895 Kruger had toasted the Kaiser and spoken of the need for a closer relationship between the Boer republics and Germany. The response of the

British public to this further evidence of the German–Boer relation-ship was fierce: according to the head of the political section of the German Foreign Ministry, 'probably no single act in the years before 1914 did more to inflame British and German public opinions against each other than the sending of the Kruger telegram'.[73] Salisbury's answer was to send a squadron of ships to Delagoa Bay in Portuguese East Africa in case Germany planned to land marines, and for some days, the outcome was uncertain.

Finally, there was general tension and concern over relations with France and Russia. They were both ferocious imperial enemies, Russia in Central Asia, the Far East and the Ottoman Empire, France in the Far East, the Middle East and Africa. As noted above, they had concluded a secret (albeit defensive) military alliance in 1894, which meant that Great Britain might be in danger in the Mediterranean and elsewhere. In 1887 Britain had signed separate agreements with the Austro-Hungarian Empire and Italy to maintain the status quo in the Mediterranean against Russia, but in January 1896 Austria refused to renew her Agreement. This not only increased the danger to the Royal Navy, it also weakened a link to Germany. Austria-Hungary, Italy and Germany were united in the so-called Triple Alliance against France and Russia, and Salisbury had leaned towards this alliance as closely as possible without actu-ally joining it (Germany had repeatedly tried with menaces to convince Great Britain that she had no option but to join). Now the link to Germany through Austria had gone, and at the very moment when the Kruger telegram dominated public and political minds.[74]

In short, when the Cabinet met on 11 January 1896, the crisis with America over Venezuela was only one amongst several. Over the previous two days *The Times* had run a series of reports from European newspapers about British isolation, and in a wide-ranging discussion the Cabinet tried to settle as many of the outstanding problems as it could. It was agreed to try to sort out various issues with France, as well as deal with the fallout from the Jameson Raid. As for Venezuela, Salisbury did not want to retreat from his position that the Monroe Doctrine did not apply to the boundary dispute and that Britain would not negotiate with the US over the matter, but the Cabinet decided that this was not the time to follow a policy which might threaten war. Salisbury eventually agreed, although he reportedly exclaimed that 'if we were to agree unconditionally to American threats another Prime Minister would have to be found'. (According to C.J. Lowe and M.L. Dockrill, Salisbury was 'the last British statesman to feel sufficiently confident in British power to stand up to the USA'.[75]) Thereafter, the Cabinet did not deny that the US had the right to intervene; rather, the Foreign Office concentrated on limiting the territory which was to be submitted to arbitration. Salisbury's plan now was to play a waiting game, since the Americans might make a move which would damage their case before the commission.

The following months saw a two-pronged response by the British government to American plans. In January and February 1896 Cleveland appointed the commission to investigate and determine the boundary, and the State Department asked that Britain provide 'documentary proof, historical narrative, unpublished archives, or other evidence' for their claims. The immediate response of the British was to provide everything they could, confident that their claims would be upheld.[76] However, negotiations over an arbitration tribunal were repeatedly stymied – to Olney's irritation, since he wanted a quick decision – by the British refusal to agree that all of the territory claimed by either country should be thrown into the pot. Chamberlain wanted to keep the disputed settled territories out because they might contain gold; Salisbury was more concerned with the settlers, not wanting British subjects abandoned to the Venezuelans.[77] Furthermore, whilst he would like to settle the question, he told an American diplomat in June, he considered compulsory arbitration a dangerous precedent for the British Empire, because claims for territory might be constantly made against it by countries having nothing to lose and everything to gain. Moreover, he disliked leaving such far-reaching questions to the ultimate decision of one man, and that man a foreigner. There was the added alarm felt by Canada, after Olney's anathema against any permanent union between a European and an American state, that if arbitration were agreed over the matter of Venezuela and territory was subsequently lost, it might be dangerous.[78] In short, Salisbury's suspicions of arbitration were difficult to assuage.

At the end of June 1896 Olney left Washington for his summer cottage for a couple of months. At the same time, Ambassador Pauncefote returned to London until nearly the end of October. For three months, therefore, negotiations were suspended. The crisis was not yet over, and in London discussions continued, but it was hardly keeping statesmen up at night. A formula was required to break the deadlock over whether some or all of the territory in question should be submitted for arbitration. It was the Leader of the Opposition, Sir William Harcourt, who finally suggested to Salisbury that the 'settled districts . . . should be left to the decision of the arbiters'. The question now became the length of time of occupation necessary to create an 'excepted settlement', and by the end of the discussions amongst members of the Cabinet, the leading men of the Opposition, Ambassador Pauncefote and the American diplomat Henry White,[79] it was decided to propose that a period of forty years' continuous occupation should except a territory from arbitration. Upon Pauncefote's return to Washington, he met Olney, who refused both forty and forty-five years, saying that Venezuela would insist on a minimum of sixty years. Olney ultimately suggested fifty years, which, after some months, was accepted by all of the parties.

On 30 December 1896 Cleveland announced to Congress that the crisis in Anglo-American relations caused by Venezuela had been settled, a sentiment echoed in the Queen's Speech to Parliament on 15 January 1897. On 2 February a treaty was concluded between Great Britain and Venezuela, stipulating that the boundary should be decided by an arbitral tribunal, whilst a month later the commission set up by Cleveland published its report on the 'true divisional line'. The tribunal, consisting of two British subjects, two US citizens (representing Venezuela) and a Russian international lawyer, handed down its award on 3 October 1899. The frontier in the main followed the Schomburgk Line, as established in 1841, but with two substantial alterations in favour of Venezuela.[80] And so it ended.

In retrospect, the boundary question may seem like a rather small issue to take up so much time and energy between the two countries. But it was truly a turning point. For the United States – as a future Secretary of State would say about another enemy – they had come eyeball to eyeball with Great Britain and the other fellow blinked.[81] As a result, Britain was never again to be perceived as such a threat by the Americans. The US had established that the Western Hemisphere was her sphere of influence, and in December 1904 President Theodore Roosevelt would openly proclaim the right of the US to enforce American hegemony.[82] Meanwhile, as noted briefly below, the US pushed Britain back, or Britain voluntarily withdrew, from strategic positions in the Caribbean, although not from her commercial dominance in South America. For Britain, with the crisis coming as one of a group, Venezuela forced her politicians and officials to decide whether the US was to remain hostile, or whether she could be conciliated. Surrounded as Great Britain was by hostile Great Powers – France, Russia and increasingly Germany, with Austria-Hungary and Italy trotting along behind Germany – her so-called 'splendid isolation'[83] was no longer so splendid: rather, it was becoming increasingly dangerous. If the US would not be an ally, she might at least not be an enemy, and, as points of conflict came up over the following several years, conciliating her became a primary policy.

III

There is a certain unity about the period from 1896 to 1917. The term used by some historians to characterise it is 'rapprochement',[84] and this is probably fair, as long as it is not seen as a smooth upward line. However, the argument will be made that there was no decided change in the relationship until 1917, and that the usual date of 1914, in the context of Anglo-American relations, is not a significant signpost. Two wars of importance bore some responsibility for the turn: the Spanish–American War of 1898 and the Boer War of 1899–1902. What was common to both was isolation from the other Great Powers and some mutual support. Public opinion also began to change. The Americans were grateful for the practical support given by Great Britain against the Spanish. It was rather different for the Boer War, since American public opinion, unlike much of the elite, tended to support the Boers. But the acquiescence to American demands over the next several years was made easier for the British by the growing conviction that if and when there was trouble in the international jungle, the US might support them. However, this did not happen in 1914. Only when the US's own safety was attacked in 1917 did she join the war, and even then it was in a disjointed manner.

The Spanish–American War stemmed from a rebellion in Cuba, long a colony of Spain. There had been rebellions before, particularly from 1868 to 1878, but this one, which had broken out in 1895 after an economic depression caused by the 1894 American Tariff Act (which imposed a 40 per cent tariff on Cuban sugar in order to help Hawaiian sugar), seemed particularly nasty. In 1896 Spain sent out 150,000 troops led by General Valeriano ('the Butcher') Weyler, who ordered cruel reprisals, a policy as ineffective in Cuba as it was offensive to the Americans. A huge 'Cuba Libre' wave of sentiment washed over much of the US, and in January 1898 a move towards war with Spain began. On 12 January Spanish army officers destroyed a newspaper that had attacked Weyler, and street riots erupted in Havana. Madrid disavowed the attack and promised calm, but by this time President William McKinley had decided that Spain could no longer maintain order. He sent the battleship USS *Maine* to Havana Harbour to protect American citizens and property. On 15 February a tremendous explosion sent it to the bottom, killing 266 of its 354 personnel. When the news reached London, crowds gathered in front of the American Embassy to pay their respects.[85] On 21 March the navy reported, probably wrongly, that an underwater mine had caused the explosion; whatever the cause, it had been immediately assumed that the culprit was Spain. According to LaFeber, McKinley was not, as has long been assumed, driven into war by the shrieks of the 'yellow press', particularly those of William Randolph Hearst's *New York Journal* and Joseph Pulitzer's *New York World*, who were locked in a circulation war. McKinley never read those newspapers. What he wanted was an end to violence in Cuba, which offended him, partly for humanitarian reasons, but also because letting it continue would show the inability of the US to do anything about chaos on an island only ninety miles away. He was also concerned that Cuba was diverting attention from threatening events in China, where the US had substantial and growing economic interests, and which was in danger of being torn apart by the Great Powers: in November 1897 Germany had seized Kiao-Chow on the Shantung Peninsula for a naval base, and Russia had then sent a fleet to Port Arthur on the tip of the Liaotung Peninsula. McKinley made careful preparations for war, including having Congress provide funds for the army and navy, reassuring the business community, ensuring the support of religious leaders, and then, on 11 April 1898, sending a war message to Congress, which debated it over the following week. On 29 April war was declared on Spain, and by 22 July, Cuba and Puerto Rico, another Spanish colony, had been conquered.[86]

Meanwhile, in the Far East, Commodore George Dewey and the Asiatic Squadron had their moment of glory. The fleet had been concentrated in the British-controlled Hong Kong Harbour since the receipt of a cable dated 25 February, which instructed Dewey to prepare for an attack on Manila in the Philippines. This was not for commercial reasons or to build an empire: rather, the Navy Department intended to weaken Spain by depriving it of revenues from the islands. The squadron was first to destroy Spanish ships, then capture Manila, and thereafter blockade all of the principal ports in the islands.[87] Once war was declared, the fleet moved to Mirs Bay outside Hong Kong, which it used for refuelling and other services for the remainder of the war. The British authorities also allowed Dewey to maintain communications with Washington through the Hong Kong cable, the only transpacific link. The order to attack Manila was finally approved by the President on 24 April, and the squadron left Hong Kong for Manila Bay at the end of the month.

The Spanish fleet did not receive the same consideration from the British as had the American. Late in June a Spanish squadron left for the Philippines by way of Suez. In Alexandria, Rear Admiral Manuel de la Cámara sought permission to take on coal, water and other supplies, but Egypt was a British protectorate and the Egyptians were induced to refuse permission; a week later the fleet returned to Spain.[88] This was unfortunate for Spain, because the Spanish force in Manila Bay was so weak that its commander, 'anticipating destruction, anchored his ships in shallow water to minimise the loss of life. In a seven-hour bombardment of the sitting ducks, Dewey destroyed Spanish naval power in the Pacific. Washington learned of his success from [British Secretary for the Colonies Joseph] Chamberlain, who received the word from Singapore before Dewey could cable through Hong Kong.'[89] Neutral vessels, with Germany's the largest group – larger than the American squadron, in fact – arrived in Manila Bay to watch. The German fleet was there to claim the Philippines if the Americans did not want them, and Dewey and Vice-Admiral Otto von Diederichs came into conflict. To the anger of the Americans, the Germans were provocative, cutting in front of US ships, taking soundings of the harbour, landing supplies for the besieged Spanish, and refusing to salute the US flag, required by naval courtesy. Dewey called von Diederichs' bluff, threatening a fight if his aggressive activities continued, and the Germans backed down.[90]

When Dewey began to bombard Manila to soften it up before an American landing, the British commander, Captain Edward Chichester, moved two ships near by to observe the effects of the American fire. In doing so, he appeared to place the British deliberately between the American and German ships, thereby saving the Americans from a stab in the back, although it is highly unlikely that the Germans would have fired on the Americans in any case. Nothing that the Germans could say checked the growth of the legend, though, which received sustenance from an erroneous account published the following year in Henry Cabot Lodge's *Our War with Spain*. Further encouragement was given to this interpretation by the fact that only Chichester fired a twenty-one-gun salute when the American flag rose over the city. In any case, 'more than any real episode, this imaginary one contributed to the belief that England was the only friend America had during the war with Spain'.[91]

In one sense this was true. Whilst all of those European countries who valued American friendship remained neutral during the war, the European press did not, with almost all of the newspapers critical of the US and sympathetic towards Spain. The Germans were particularly bitter, probably because they had anticipated falling heir to that part of the Spanish Empire themselves. The reaction in Great Britain to the abuse was to stimulate public manifestations of support for the US, not only in the press but with speeches, resolutions, processions and the establishment of Anglo-American associations. 'It was not that Englishmen especially liked Americans, but continental ill-will had so often been directed against English imperialism that when this ill-will was turned against the United States, Englishmen felt that they and the Americans were on "the same side".'[92]

Once the war was over, it had to be decided how much, if any, of the Spanish Empire the US ought to annex. There was regret in various quarters of the US that Cuba could not be included – as noted in Chapter 3, both Thomas Jefferson and John Quincy Adams had hoped, and expected, that at some point Cuba would be absorbed, whilst for decades before the Civil War this had been pushed by the slave-owning states. But McKinley agreed to accept Congress's Teller Resolution, by which the US disclaimed 'any disposition or intention to exercise sovereignty, jurisdiction, or control' over Cuba, 'except for the pacification thereof'.[93] However, there was compensation, as the US acquired the area of Guantánamo for a naval base, and in any case the whole island became an economic colony, part of the American informal empire.

But the Philippines were different. First of all, they would provide a base for the American navy and merchant vessels sailing to the Far East, and were thus seen as strategically vital. Moreover, the Germans would certainly try to move in if they were left unclaimed, and would subsequently close them to American business and commercial interests. In addition, there was pressure from some religious leaders to civilise and Christianise the natives – never mind that under the Spaniards many of them had been Christians for centuries. But this was a Protestant pressure group, to which McKinley responded, as he explained to a group of clergymen on 21 November 1899:

When . . . I realized that the Philippines had dropped into our laps I confess that I did not know what to do with them . . . And one night late it came to me this way . . .: (1) That we could not give them back to Spain – that would be cowardly and dishonorable; (2) that we could not turn them over to France or Germany – our commercial rivals in the Orient – that would be bad business and discreditable; (3) that we could not leave them to themselves – they were unfit for self-government – and they would soon have anarchy and misrule over there worse than Spain's was; and (4) that there was nothing left for us to do but to take them all, and to educate the Filipinos, and uplift and civilize and Christianize them.[94]

And finally, there was the imperialistic urge. McKinley was a Republican – the Venezuelan crisis had not resulted in Cleveland's re-election – and the Republicans were pushing for an empire. Under McKinley, independent Hawaii was annexed in 1898, as was a chunk of Samoa; Guam would also be acquired from Spain. And the Philippines were taken over. This was not an easy task. Filipinos under Emilio Aguinaldo, who had led the fight for independence from Spain since 1896, at first supported the American attack against the imperial power. But once they realised that the US was not going to leave, they turned against the Americans. It took McKinley until the end of October to decide to keep all of the Philippines: Manila was vital as a strategic port; its defence against possible attacks by other powers required control of all of Luzon; and the defence of Luzon required control of the rest of the 7,100 islands. However, he was having great difficulty getting the peace treaty with Spain through the Senate until news was received on 4 February 1899 that Aguinaldo's troops and the American forces had exchanged gunfire. Two days later the Senate ratified the treaty, but the fighting continued for some years. The 1898 war had cost some five hundred American lives; the war to pacify the Philippines cost two thousand more, as well as the lives of two hundred thousand Filipinos.[95] There is an irony here: the US went to war partly because of the brutal counter-insurgency methods used by the Spanish in Cuba and then did much the same themselves in the Philippines. So, at the cost of several thousand American casualties and some treasure, the US acquired an empire in the Pacific. John Hay, the Ambassador to Great Britain, exclaimed that it had been a 'splendid little war'.[96]

The British on the whole supported the annexation. In February

1899, coinciding with the Senate debate on the ratification of the treaty with Spain, Rudyard Kipling wrote a poem to encourage the Americans. The first stanza of 'The White Man's Burden: The United States and the Philippine Islands' made his point:

> Take up the White Man's burden –
> Send forth the best ye breed –
> Go bind your sons to exile
> To serve your captives' need;
> To wait in heavy harness,
> On fluttered folk and wild –
> Your new-caught, sullen peoples,
> Half-devil and half-child.[97]

Some Britons, however, thought that the Americans had a lot to learn about running a colony. According to Mrs Campbell Dauncey, an Englishwoman who spent nine months in the Philippines, 'though you may have heard of the corruption of American political life, it does not strike one with such force when you read in papers as when it comes home to you in daily life . . . It does seem such a pity that a great and noble nation should not be better represented in the eyes of another – and, when all is said and done – an inferior race.'[98] Nevertheless, the government assumed that some country would take over the islands, and no more than the Americans did the British welcome the possibility of a French or German acquisition. The British government did not believe that its and American interests would come into conflict in the Far East – rather the reverse.[99] Therefore, they approved of the annexation. Besides, if the US became an imperial power, she could not continue to denigrate the British Empire without the British being able to respond *tu quoque*. Yet, the US never really saw herself as an imperial power: after all, she had come to civilise and protect. Given their own history, most Americans found it impossible to accept that they were following in the footsteps of Great Britain. Consequently, the US felt perfectly capable of continuing to attack the British Empire as a blot upon democratic civilisation.

A satisfying aspect of the annexation for both countries was that an 'open door' for trade could be instituted. However, although both called for this, their emphases were different. Britain remained a believer in free trade, including for herself. The US, conversely, was a protectionist country, with very high tariffs at home; what she called for was equal entry elsewhere, without the resident political power giving advantages to one country over others – what John Hay, by now Secretary of State, called a 'fair field and no favor'. In March 1898 Great Britain suggested to the US that they issue a joint call for an 'open door' in China.[100] However, in a reprise of John Quincy Adams' refusal to allow his country to be a 'cockboat in the wake of the British man-of-war', Hay issued his own Open Door Note in September 1899, calling for the Great Powers not to discriminate in setting port and railway rates, and not to eliminate existing commercial arrangements. Britain agreed after a delay, as did Japan, but it was only with great reluctance that Russia, Germany and France agreed to sign up.

Then the 'Boxers United in Righteousness', who wished to drive all foreigners out of China, stormed towards Peking, leaving behind them dead Christians and Western-owned property laid waste; after the German minister was killed in June 1900, the Empress of China felt obliged to join the Boxers by declaring war on 21 June against all of the Great Powers. This rebellion is understandable, given the German grab of Shantung, the Russian drive into Manchuria, the new French claims to the southern territory bordering on Indochina, and the British taking of Wei-hai-Wei Harbour on the Shantung Peninsula to offset the German acquisition there. (The Chinese had offered Great Britain a lease on Wei-hai-Wei in February 1898, but Salisbury had delayed his answer, partly because he wanted Russia to incur the odium by making a move first.[101]) US troops joined those of Japan, Great Britain, Russia, France, Germany, Italy and Austria to lift the siege of Peking, with McKinley sending five thousand of the total of twenty thousand from the new base at Manila.[102] On 3 July 1900 Hay issued another Open Door Note, this time asking the Great Powers to support China's 'administrative and territorial integrity', stating that the US would deplore the creation of new spheres of influence. Hay would have liked some kind of alliance with Britain, which 'would make our ideas prevail', but he recognised that this was politically impossible. Neither Note had any practical effect in China, since Washington threatened no sanctions against those who continued to carve out spheres of influence. In 1901 the Great Powers withdrew from Peking, pledging allegiance to open door principles, but they also demanded a huge indemnity from China to compensate for the massacres and destruction of property.[103]

Both Notes, however, brought Hay public acclaim. In the US, his friend Henry Adams wrote that the Secretary of State 'put Europe aside and set the Washington Government at the head of civilization . . . History broke in halves.' In Britain he also received praise, with *The Times* writing on 11 July 1900 that the Note deserved 'general approbation and welcome in this country . . . The reason is simple. In China the main interests of the United States and Great Britain are identical.' Privately, though, the British government was disappointed. Not only did the Note recognise rather than challenge existing spheres of influence, it also made it clear that the US would not co-operate with any other Power to enforce the American request.[104] This would not be the last time that Britain would be frustrated by an American penchant for words without supporting deeds. The best that can be said is that the Notes emphasised that the US intended to play a role in the world.

Great Britain's attention was not wholly focused on China, because at the same time she was engaged in the Boer War. In 1795 the British had taken over the Cape Colony from the Dutch, and from the beginning the Dutch settlers and their descendants were unhappy with British rule. They objected to the abolition of the slave trade in 1807 and to the abolition of slavery itself in 1833. Two years later Parliament passed the Cape of Good Hope Punishment Act, to stop white aggression against the natives and the seizure of their lands. This resulted in ten thousand Boers setting out on the 'Great Trek', which lasted from 1836 to 1840, moving from Cape Colony to lands beyond the Orange and Vaal rivers. Many settled in Natal, but in 1843 the British made it a colony, and the Boers upped stakes again to join those north of the Vaal. In 1854 they established the Orange Free State, whilst in 1856 those in the Transvaal set up the South African Republic, with its capital at Pretoria. Unfortunately for the Boers, in 1867 diamonds were discovered in the Orange River, and in 1871 the British annexed the diamond area. Just to tidy things up, in 1877 they annexed the South African Republic as well. In 1880 the Boers rose up, and, after only a few minor reverses, the British government under Gladstone recognised the independence of the South African Republic, to the dismay of British imperialists in South Africa.

The leading imperialist was Cecil John Rhodes, who wanted to open up South Africa to British imperial and commercial enterprise, and in particular to build a railway from the Cape to Cairo. The Boer republics were in the way, with Portuguese and German colonies on either side, and Rhodes feared that Boers, Portuguese and/or Germans would move into unclaimed land. His solution was to bring the Boer republics into Cape Colony. This might have been possible, given that the Boers already in the colony supported him, except for the opposition of Paul Kruger, a leader in the 1880 war who had become the President of the South African Republic in 1883. Kruger feared the growing numbers of foreigners (*'uitlanders'* in Afrikaans), who were moving into the Republic, seeing them as threats to traditional Boer values, religion and political independence. He might have been able to preserve the Republic's traditional isolation had not huge deposits of gold been discovered in the Transvaal. In a short time the population of the capital, Johannesburg, had exploded to a hundred thousand, half of them black workers and the remainder largely foreigners, a large proportion of whom were British. Kruger feared that they would be utilised to extend British control over the Republic, so he severely restricted their political and civil rights. The situation deteriorated badly, and Rhodes decided to exploit the disaffection of the *uitlanders* and overthrow the Kruger government, hoping for the support of the British government, since Joseph Chamberlain, Secretary for the Colonies, was also a strong imperialist. The fiasco of the Jameson Raid of 29 December 1895 and the subsequent Kruger telegram have been described above. Events deteriorated over the following several years, and on 11 October 1899 the Orange Free State and the South African Republic went to war against Britain.

Because of their initial numerical superiority and excellent equipment, and possibly because Britain was already occupied in China, the Boers won a number of early victories. The British were not used to warfare on the plains and their troops were of a poor standard.[105] Perhaps if the Boers had made a dash for the seaports, they might have prevented the landing of British reinforcements, but they hardly had the manpower for so vast an enterprise, not only to conquer the ports but to hold them against the might of the Royal Navy. Reinforcements therefore arrived unhindered, and by the spring of 1900 the British had defeated the Boer armies on the field of battle. The Boers then resorted to guerrilla warfare, and the British responded with a scorched-earth policy – a ruthless destruction of Boer farms and crops – and the herding of the Boer civilian population into concentration camps.[106] Of the 120,000 women and children assembled in these camps, approximately one-fifth died of disease and exposure in the first year. The war came to an end in 1902, facilitated by generous British peace terms, which were motivated by the desire to reconcile what were called the 'two white races' of South Africa. Both former Boer republics were given constitutions providing for representative government, although only adult white males of European descent could vote. In 1910 the Federal Union of South Africa was established.[107]

The US was the only power not to condemn Britain officially over her actions in South Africa. This policy of restraint was not motivated by public opinion: on the contrary, Irish-American political organisations vilified the British, as did a substantial proportion of both political parties, and it took a great effort by John Hay and others to prevent the Republican convention in 1899 from supporting the Boers. Convinced Anglo-Saxonists, however, made their views known. In essence, Republican condemnation was prevented by the fact that Hay was deeply anglophiliac. The American consul at Pretoria, initially Hay's son Adelbert, represented British interests,[108] and although the US remained officially neutral, the elder Hay's attitudes and comments revealed his pro-British convictions. He was complacent about the concentration camps, and almost contemptuous of the Boer request that the US intervene or mediate.[109] He did, however, wish that the British army would perform better against what was essentially a group of farmers. He was not alone in this. 'Believing as they did that civilization and the interests of the entire Anglo-Saxon race were wrapped up in the British war effort, American supporters of Britain were horrified at the terrible defeats inflicted on the British forces in December 1899. During the period known as "Black Week" (10–15 December 1899) – the most disastrous week for British arms in the nineteenth century' – the army suffered three defeats, enduring 'a frightful slaughter'.[110] Theodore Roosevelt's opinion in April 1900 was that 'the British have won only by a crushing superiority in numbers where they have won at all. Generally they have been completely outfought, while some of their blunders have been simply stupendous.'[111] Henry Cabot Lodge attributed the British defeats to 'the fact that they have been whipping hill tribes and Dervishes so long that they have forgotten how white men fight'.[112] But whilst Hay believed that a British victory and the continued existence of the Empire were vital to the US, because only then would 'civilization and progress' be ensured, Roosevelt's conclusion was that 'England is on the downgrade' and, consequently, the US was becoming the stronger member of the Anglo-American partnership.[113]

At the same time as the Boer War a new conflict arose between the US and Great Britain, this one – how familiar – over a Canadian–US boundary. Some Americans had never ceased to hope for a takeover of Canada, or at least a merger between the two countries; indeed, the Republican Party platform in 1896 had called for annexation via negotiation. Britain, of course, did not want to lose Canada, nor, fundamentally, did Canada want to be lost, irrespective of how often she complained about being sacrificed on the altar of amicable Anglo-American relations. However, neither did Britain want to quarrel over Canada, not least because, as the Committee of Imperial Defence concluded in July 1905, it would be virtually impossible to defend her should it come to blows.[114]

The dispute arose over the boundary between Canada and Alaska. The problem was the ambiguous language of the Anglo-Russian Treaty of 1825, which had fixed the boundary which the US inherited when she bought Alaska from the Russians in 1867. In 1825 the territory was almost unknown, and a survey carried out by the two countries left many ambiguities. On the whole, Canadian maps followed the boundary as set by the Americans, but in 1896 gold was discovered in Yukon. Canada demanded a much-increased area and asked for arbitration of the whole. She hoped that Great Britain would defend her claims, but even the Canadian Minister of the Interior admitted the strength of the American position.

In March 1898 President McKinley and Ambassador Pauncefote agreed to embark on negotiations on all outstanding Canadian–American issues; at the end of May a protocol was signed setting up the Joint High Commission. It was headed by Lord Herschell, the Lord Chancellor, appointed by London partly to keep control of the Canadians. Even Joseph Chamberlain was tepid in his support, writing to Henry White of the American Embassy that 'personally, I care very little for the points in dispute, but I care immensely for the consequential advantages of a thorough understanding between the two countries and the removal of these trumpery causes of irritation'.[115] Herschell hoped to settle the disputes by mutual concessions, but he wanted at least the appearance of not betraying Canada. At the same time, the US and Britain were also negotiating over an isthmian canal (see below), and the Canadians wanted British concessions on the canal to be matched by American concessions on the boundary. The British argued for this,[116] but deadlock ensued, and the commission was adjourned in February 1899 for tempers to cool. Herschell then died.

The Alaskan boundary had dominated the discussions within the Commission. The imperial representatives argued for arbitration, but the Americans rejected this on the grounds that arbitrators usually split the difference, even between just and unjust claims – precisely the argument made by Salisbury over the Venezuelan claims and rejected by the Americans. In the end, Canada's exaggerated claims, and Britain's desire to strengthen relations with the US, led the British to tell the Canadians that the American case was 'unassailable', and that if they delayed any further their position would only worsen. The Canadians were driven to accept arbitration, with settled areas, which were held by the Americans, exempt. Everything was going well, but then the Canadian Premier, Sir Wilfrid Laurier, decided that for domestic political reasons, he, too, would demand some exemptions. The result (as noted above) was the end of negotiations for two years.

In 1901, Hay reopened negotiations. He suggested a binational commission in April, and the British urged the Canadians to accept it. But the Canadians delayed, and then insisted on neutral arbitrators. This caused Theodore Roosevelt, who had become President after the assassination of President McKinley on 19 September 1901, to lose his temper, and after more negotiations and delay, he began to wonder if the British were really as friendly as they seemed. He anticipated, if gold was discovered in the disputed territory, that a clash would come; therefore, Britain, and especially Canada, must give way. He sent eight hundred cavalrymen to Alaska and, though at least partly intended for police duties, they made the intended impression, which was to convince Britain that the US meant business. This was followed up by a raft of letters from the President and other American friends of Great Britain warning the Cabinet that this was the case.

There were now negotiations, a convention signed on 24 January 1903 setting up a boundary commission, Anglo-American-Canadian diplomatic manoeuvres, a crisis caused by the Senate's objections to the wording, political 'skullduggery' by Henry Cabot Lodge as the chairman of the Senate Foreign Relations Committee, a political brouhaha over the choice of the American commissioners, more international suspicion and manoeuvres, more digging in of Canadian feet, and – finally – a decision on 20 October 1903 awarding victory to the Americans. The US did, in fact, have a strong legal claim to the territory, 'precisely what Ottawa sought to revise, in the aftermath of the discovery of gold in Yukon'. Nevertheless, the two Canadian representatives refused to sign the award, and the Canadians later refused to allow a mountain to be named after one of the British representatives. 'There were screams of protest in England, and for years this episode provided the chief talking point for those who maintained that the Americans consistently bullied England.' But after a few years, although the Canadians apparently never forgot this so-called British 'betrayal', they gradually became reconciled to the decision.[117] By 1908, Canada's frontier was defined by treaty, thereby removing a century-long source of Anglo-American conflict.

Coincident with the negotiations over the Alaskan boundary was a much more important conflict, that over the building and control of an isthmian canal. In 1850 the two countries had signed the Clayton–Bulwer Treaty, by which they had agreed that neither was to fortify or exercise control over any future railway or canal linking the two oceans via Central America. However, it did not take long for the Americans to regret it, with Congress in 1857 calling for its annulment. There was a crisis in 1879 when Ferdinand de Lesseps, who had built the Suez Canal a decade earlier, obtained from the Colombian government a concession to construct a canal across the Isthmus of Panama, one of Colombia's provinces, and then announced that his firm would build one. The response of President Rutherford B. Hayes was to warn in a message to Congress on 8 March 1880 that 'the policy of this country is a canal under American control', and to emphasise the point by sending two warships along the coasts of Panama and Nicaragua. In 1881 Secretary of State James G. Blaine told the British that the 1850 treaty had to be altered, arguing that the US now had paramount interests in the area, not least because of the growth of the Pacific states, which were 'imperial in extent' and required easy transit from the Atlantic because of their export trade. He also informed the British government that 'England as against the United States is always wrong'. Blaine's successor as Secretary of State, Frederick T. Frelinghuysen, decided that this particular international obligation was inconvenient, and he therefore ignored the treaty; in 1884 he signed the Frelinghuysen–Zavala Treaty with Nicaragua that gave the US exclusive right to a canal, but, to his chagrin, the Senate refused to ratify it.[118]

What made the question of a canal crucial to the US was the Spanish–American War, and particularly the long cruise the battleship USS *Oregon* was forced to make around Cape Horn in order to join in battle. In December 1898 Hay proposed to Ambassador Pauncefote that the two countries should discuss modification of the 1850 treaty. In London the Cabinet agreed, and by mid-January 1899 the two men, both devoted to a close Anglo-American relationship, had drawn up a draft convention. It was essentially an amended version of the old treaty, not a new one, and its principal change was to concede to the US the right to regulate and manage a canal. Hay feared that the Senate might baulk, and he asked Henry White at the American Embassy in London to urge the Foreign Office to consider the treaty as soon as possible: 'In the usual reckless manner of our Senate,' he wrote, 'they are discussing the matter with open doors every day, and are getting themselves so balled up with their own eloquences that it is greatly to be feared they will so commit themselves as to consider themselves bound to reject any arrangement that may be made.'[119]

In London, however, the Director of Military Intelligence was not happy: the construction would damage British naval supremacy, since the ability of the US Pacific and Atlantic Fleets to join up rapidly would essentially double the strength of the US navy. As for the Cabinet, they wanted the Alaskan boundary question to be settled, if possible, in the same treaty.[120] Although Pauncefote cabled to Salisbury that the US government would not agree to any link of the two issues, Salisbury decided that Britain would not sign the convention because she would be 'making a concession which would be wholly to the benefit of the United States at a time when they appeared to be so little inclined to come to a satisfactory settlement in regard to the Alaska frontier'.[121] There the matter rested for some months. By the end of the year, however, Britain's catastrophic reverses in the Boer War had made her vulnerable to American pressure, given that public opinion in Europe was urging intervention on behalf of the Boers, and that the Russian Foreign Minister, Mikhail Muraviev, was attempting to organise Continental intervention and trying to convince the US to associate herself with it. In the circumstances, Salisbury and the Cabinet were anxious to avoid causing offence to the US. Hay revived the negotiations in January 1900, and on 5 February Pauncefote signed the Convention.[122]

It was then submitted to the Senate for ratification, but to Hay's anger it was mauled, with the 'Davis amendment' stating that nothing in the treaty would apply to measures which the US might 'find it necessary to take for securing by its own forces the defense of the United States and the maintenance of public order'. In other words, they reserved the right to fortify the canal. Hay offered to resign, stopped trying to get the convention ratified, and obtained British agreement to extend for some months the period for ratification. (In any case the Cabinet would not have accepted the treaty as amended in spring 1900.) When Congress convened again on 3 December, the Senators not only insisted on the Davis amendment, but added two more. Essentially, rather than amending the Clayton–Bulwer Treaty, the Senate produced an entirely different animal from the one the British Cabinet had accepted the year before.[123]

Salisbury had now given up the Foreign Secretaryship, although he remained Prime Minister, and Lord Lansdowne succeeded him in the former role. Lansdowne had been Governor-General of Canada and thus, unlike Salisbury, he had a clear sense of the potential power of the US. He decided to come to an agreement, stating in a Memorandum for the Cabinet in mid-December that 'I am afraid that public opinion in the United States runs so high in favour of an American canal, defended by whatever measures of precaution may seem good to the United States, that we shall be unable to stem the tide.' Nevertheless, they should not just accept it without raising objections because, if they did so, it would follow that 'while the United States would have a Treaty right to interfere with the Canal in time of war, or apprehended war, . . . [Great Britain] would be absolutely precluded from resorting to any such action, or from taking measures to secure her interests in and near the Canal'.[124] He had already cabled Pauncefote the Cabinet's decision to reject the treaty if it included the Davis amendment,[125] and similarly warned the American Ambassador, Joseph Choate. However, this was in the expectation of securing an alternative proposal from the US, rather than closing off further discussion. On 11 March Pauncefote informed Hay of the Cabinet's decision. Lansdowne was correct, and Hay conceded the main British points, including that the conditions and charges would apply to all – that is, the US was not to allow American ships to pay lower charges. (Equitability of charges was important, because the British estimated that 60 per cent of the traffic through a canal would be theirs.) On 18 November 1901 the treaty was signed in Washington, with the Senate ratifying it by a majority of seventy-two to six a month later.[126]

This Treaty was of great importance for Anglo-American relations, because with it Great Britain effectively relinquished the custodianship of the Western Hemisphere to the US. The decision taken by the British Cabinet in January 1896 to agree to arbitration with Venezuela had been viewed as tactical rather than strategic: no member, surely, would have taken this decision had it been recognised as agreeing to the irrevocable passing of predominance. But it was, because once the Cabinet decided to meet the American demand for arbitration, even if they believed it was outrageous, a step had been taken down a new path. Britain had agreed to American hegemony, and it would be counter-productive to try to prevent the US from providing the means to defend it. It was better to accede gracefully than to object fruitlessly. Little did this Cabinet know that it was setting the pattern which its successors were often forced to follow.

IV

Although the focus has been on a series of Anglo-American diplomatic conflicts, their results at that point were of more importance to the US than to Britain. American concerns were primarily hemispheric, but those of the British were global. Great Britain needed to protect her empire and safeguard the sea lanes, the highways for her trade and for vital imports of raw materials and food, and the pressures were becoming very great. In the phrase made famous by Paul Kennedy, Britain was experiencing 'imperial overstretch'.[127] To meet the threats, she needed to consolidate her resources. Thus, the period from about 1898 to 1907 saw Great Britain carrying out both a diplomatic revolution and a strategic redeployment.

By 1900, the Great Powers of Europe were linked in two military alliances: the Triple Alliance of Germany, Austria-Hungary and Italy versus the Dual Alliance of France and Russia. Great Britain was part of neither, nor did she wish to be. Her traditional policy had been to maintain a balance of power on the Continent, which meant that she temporarily allied with other Great Powers against whichever Power was trying to dominate. For roughly eight hundred years France had been the traditional enemy on the Continent, and from the seventeenth century Britain's greatest imperial rival in

North America, India, Africa and the Far East. In the nineteenth century Russia had also become a threatening imperial rival in the Near East, Central Asia and the Far East; by the end of the century, because of her threat to India, she was probably the most dangerous.

Traditionally, Germany in its various guises was more likely to be an ally than an enemy. Germany had lacked a powerful navy and Britain a powerful army, and thus they were not direct threats to each other. Salisbury's inclination had been to work more or less closely with her, but from the early 1890s, German power and policies had been changing. The German Empire argued that part of the definition of a Great Power was to have colonies, and the Royal Navy was blocking her way. Her destiny was to exercise Weltmacht, or world power, and her hostility towards Britain increased. The combination of German activities during the Boer War, the German Navy Bill of 1900 (the preface of which stated that 'there is only one way of protecting Germany's commerce and colonial possessions: Germany must possess a fleet of such a strength that a war with her would shake the position of the mightiest naval Power'[128]) and a series of crises involving the three hostile powers in Africa, the Middle East and the Far East emphasised Britain's increasing exposure to danger and lack of any ally. Germany would not be seen as a serious threat, given her lack of a powerful navy, until the middle of the 1900s, and even then some members of the British government saw a larger German navy as a useful counterbalance to the French and Russian navies. But the public rhetoric was disturbing, and after 1904, Germany's aggressive attempts to force concessions from the other Great Powers would drive France and Great Britain closer together.

British public opinion towards Germany was also darkening. What Christopher Andrew calls the 'literary war' began in 1903 with the publication of Erskine Childers' bestselling novel, *The Riddle of the Sands*, in which Carruthers of the Foreign Office and his friend Davies, yachting off the Frisian Coast, uncover a German invasion plan. However, it was the books of a laughably appalling writer, William Le Queux, which bore greater responsibility for scaring the British public. Le Queux's *The Invasion of 1910*, published in 1906, sold over a million copies in twenty-seven languages ('though, to the fury of its author, the German translation ended with a German victory'). He also 'discovered' a vast network of German agents, which included hundreds of waiters and hairdressers, about whom he warned the public in 1910's *German Spies in England*.[129] He was supported by a number of soldiers, such as the ageing Field Marshal Lord Roberts of Kandahar, various politicians, and Alfred Harmsworth (the future Lord Northcliffe), founder of the *Daily Mail* newspaper, which cranked up the paranoia for all it was worth. The young P.G. Wodehouse made his own contribution, publishing in 1909 *The Swoop! Or How Clarence Saved England*, in which Clarence Chugwater, an alert boy scout, notices the first warning of an invasion, buried in the small print of the stop press news: 'Fry not out, 104. Surrey 147 for 8. A German army landed at Essex this afternoon. Loamshire Handicap: Spring Chicken, 1; Salome, 2; Yip-i-addy, 3. Seven ran.' No one believes him, but he mobilises the scouts, after which, as Clarence points out, 'our beloved England no longer writhes beneath the ruthless heel of the alien oppressor'. For the British public, apparently, the situation was too serious for mockery, and the book sank without trace. As ridiculous as most of the books – excepting Wodehouse's – seem in retrospect, the mood of the nation had to be right to receive them.

By 1902, Great Britain was feeling beleaguered because the world was becoming unbalanced. She counted for less than her power implied in Europe, because the other Great Powers did not always believe that she would fight. Thomas Otte argues that the Cabinet preferred drifting and partial intervention, and lacked the political will to play the role of a Great Power on the Continent. As a result, both Otto von Bismarck, the Chancellor of Germany, and Alexander Gorchakov, the Foreign Minister of Russia, thought that she had ceased to be a European Power, and thus was no longer a Great Power.[130] For Great Britain, the rise of the two extra-European Powers, Japan and the US, meant that a balanced Europe no longer protected her Empire in the same way as before. The outcome was a reconfiguration by two successive Foreign Secretaries, Lord Lansdowne and Sir Edward Grey, of British relations with other Powers, including the US. At the same time, Lord Selborne, the First Lord of the Admiralty, after some years of consideration of the situation by the Royal Navy and the Cabinet Defence Committee,

Thomas Jefferson, chief writer of the Declaration of Independence and third President, whose Embargo nearly destroyed the young Republic.

A British officer looks over the crew of an American merchantman, searching for deserters from the Royal Navy.

American depiction of the British burning Washington in 1814. This was partly in retaliation for the Americans' burning of the Canadian capital, York.

Francis Scott Key on a British ship, seeing at dawn the American flag still flying over Fort McHenry. The ultimate result was the American national anthem, 'The Star-Spangled Banner'.

Richard Rush, American Minister to the Court of St James's 1817–25, who hid his dislike of England.

Lord Castlereagh, one of Britain's greatest Foreign Secretaries, who cut his own throat with a razor.

John Quincy Adams, arguably America's greatest Secretary of State, and sixth President.

George Canning, Foreign Secretary, whose suggestion of a joint initiative with the US stimulated the Monroe Doctrine.

Mrs Frances Trollope, whose *Domestic Manners of the Americans* outraged even those Americans who had not read it.

Captain Basil Hall, British traveller in North America 1827–8, whose book angered Americans.

Captain Basil Hall's sketch of a steamboat on the Mississippi.

Charles Dickens, painted during his visit to
the US in 1842. The Americans detested
what he wrote about them.

American philosopher and essayist Ralph
Waldo Emerson had deep admiration for
England, but he knew that the US would
supplant her.

The writer Harriet Martineau, who hated
American slavery but still wrote favourably
of the American Republic.

William Lloyd Garrison,
the fierce American abolitionist.

HERE   AND   THERE;

Or, Emigration a Remedy.

1848 *Punch* cartoon showing the benefits of emigrating from Britain to the US.

Fight between the Union Ironclad steamer *Kearsarge* and the Confederate steamer *Alabama* off Cherbourg, 19 June 1864. The crisis over the depredations of the *Alabama* brought the US and Britain close to war.

The Americanisation
of England.

Punch in 1859 sums up the
Anglo-American relationship:
a self-satisfied John Bull
facing an American with a
chip on his shoulder.

"WHAT? YOU YOUNG YANKEE-NOODLE, STRIKE
YOUR OWN FATHER!"

Lord Randolph Churchill, son of the seventh Duke of Marlborough.

Jennie Jerome, around the time of her marriage to Lord Randolph Churchill.

The ninth Duke of Marlborough and the Duchess, the former Consuelo Vanderbilt, with their sons, the Marquess of Blandford and Lord Ivor Spencer-Churchill, at Blenheim Palace.

Washington Irving, the first American to
have a bestseller in both Britain and the US.

The American writer Henry James, who
became a British subject in 1916.

The American writer Mark Twain in his
Oxford University doctoral robes,
23 June 1907.

The British poet W.H. Auden, who became
an American citizen in 1945.

accepted that Great Britain no longer possessed the naval superiority she had enjoyed for nearly three-quarters of a century, and changed the shape of the Royal Navy to meet the new situation.

The essential thrust of both strategies was to make changes on the peripheries in order to concentrate resources near the home islands. Until the latter part of the nineteenth century, any competing naval powers were European. This meant that the main tasks of the Royal Navy in wartime were threefold: to sweep the oceans of enemy vessels, whether warships or merchant ships; to blockade the enemy fleets in their home ports; and to attack them if they tried to escape. British command of the four 'narrow seas' – the Channel, the North Sea, the Suez Canal and the mouth of the Mediterranean – enabled her warships to control access to and thus to control the world's oceans. After 1880, however, European naval powers strengthened their fleets and new non-European naval powers arose, specifically Japan and the US. With the safety of the shipping lanes and the British Empire increasingly at risk, and given that by 1895 she imported four-fifths of her wheat,[131] did Britain dare to cease trying to maintain global maritime dominance? Or should the Cabinet decide that the crucial thing was to retain superiority in the home waters in order to protect the British Isles themselves, and thus give up global pretensions?

The first change, both diplomatic and strategic, was fundamental: Britain signed a peacetime alliance for the first time in centuries. The Anglo-Japanese Alliance was agreed in 1902 and renewed in 1905 and 1911. The crux was to commit the Imperial Japanese Navy to combine with the Royal Navy to contain the other Great Powers, particularly the combined French and Russian fleets, in the Far East.[132] This allowed the Royal Navy to withdraw five battleships from the China Station. The second diplomatic change was with France, and the two countries set out to eliminate as many imperial points of conflict as possible (France was increasingly worried about Germany). In Africa, Britain was driving from south to north, from the Cape to Cairo, as well as south from Egypt to reconquer the Sudan, whilst France was claiming territories from West Africa to the east. Both wanted to control the Upper Nile, but a crisis at Fashoda in 1898 had left Britain the victor. In North Africa the British claimed dominance in Egypt against French opposition, whilst France claimed dominance in Morocco and Tunisia. By the 1904 Anglo-French Agreement, each recognised the other's dominance in those three North African countries and sorted out their claims in West Africa. They also settled the question of French access to the rich fishing grounds off Newfoundland. The result was the Anglo-French Entente Cordiale – a feeling, not an alliance – and, from December 1905, secret military staff talks.

The negotiations with Russia were rather more difficult. Britain's imperial rivalry with Russia in Central Asia – the so-called 'Great Game' – was of a more ferocious nature than that with France in Africa: what was at supreme stake was India and, to a lesser extent, Persia (now Iran). The importance of Persia was twofold. Crucially, it shared a border with North-west India (now Pakistan); and there was British-controlled oil there – increasingly important, because the Royal Navy would in 1913 take the decision to power its ships entirely with oil rather than coal. The outcome of the negotiations was the 1907 Anglo-Russian Agreement: Persia was divided into spheres of influence, with a buffer zone between; Afghanistan was to be neutral, with British overlordship; and Tibet was to remain neutral. Russia saw this as providing breathing-space whilst she built up her power, and thus the British were unable to relax their vigilance; indeed, the two countries were inching towards war in the summer of 1914.[133] However, the public assumption was that there was now an easing of Anglo-Russian relations.

It is easy to see the United States' place in this 'revolution'. The value of British commercial interests in the Western Hemisphere was high, and the extent of her colonial possessions was larger than the US. She had a position, and did not like resigning this to the US, but she did not fear that the US would attack her colonies (not even Canada). Furthermore, if the US insisted that she was the hegemon in the hemisphere, that meant that she took on the responsibility of keeping those countries in order, and that could only benefit those, including Britain, who had business and commercial interests there. So, in the face of greater dangers elsewhere, Britain accepted that the US now dominated the hemisphere. The angry American reaction in 1902–3 when Germany, with the initial co-operation of

Britain, attempted to enforce Venezuelan payment of debts under-lined this; even Germany, who was steadily increasing her already-strong commercial position in Central America, tacitly accepted the reality of American hegemony.

By 1907, then, the view of the world from the window of the British Foreign Office had changed considerably. Some dangerous conflicts had been settled with France and Russia, and, although relations with Russia continued to be tense, those with France grad-ually eased. Relations with the US had gone through the most complete transformation, in that by means of a series of agreements, almost without exception giving the US what she wanted, there were virtually no points of conflict left (although Mexico would cause difficulties a few years later). Furthermore, the changes in public opinion in both countries meant that their governments accepted that war between them was now virtually unthinkable. (The opinion of the British War Office was that 'the contingency of war with the United States should be avoided at all hazards'.[134]) In this situation, each could hope for at least neutrality from the other; indeed, from Britain, the US could count on firm support in almost any contingency. The odd man out in this new world order was Germany, with whom relations varied – note the Kruger telegram in 1896 but the Anglo-German Agreement over China just four years later – but were generally on a gradual downward trajectory. The worsening of the official relationship was underlined by a Franco-German crisis over Morocco in 1905–6, when Britain, to the frustration of the Germans, steadily supported France.

A major reason for these diplomatic changes was that the elimin-ation of imperial points of crisis would considerably lessen the need for the Royal Navy to maintain fleets around the world. As noted above, the Admiralty had concluded by September 1901 that past policies and ways of thinking would have to change. A major reason was financial, or, rather, the fears of the Chancellor of the Exchequer, Sir Michael Hicks Beach. In despair because of his conviction that Britain was coming to the end of her resources, he had quarrelled with his service colleagues and nearly broken up the Cabinet. Britain had been engaged in a naval arms race with France and Russia since the 1880s and especially since 1889. Between that year and 1897, expenditure on the navy had increased by 65 per cent,[135] and Hicks Beach now believed that the relentless growth in naval expenditure would lead 'straight to financial ruin'. He pointed out that expenditure between 1895–6 and 1901–2 had risen by 40 per cent, over half of which was accounted for solely by increased spending on the army and navy (in this he did not include the special costs of the Boer War). Public expenditure on military forces in 1901 was 58 per cent of total government expenditure, of which 15 per cent was spent on the navy (the army cost was much higher because of the Boer War). By 1903, with the growing German naval threat, the navy alone would account for 25 per cent of public expenditure.[136] A major reason for this was the growth in the cost of the ships themselves. Between 1895 and 1905 the cost of a first-class cruiser (a vessel with a long range and high speed that could scout ahead of the main battle fleet) nearly quadrupled.[137] Not only was this a significant amount in itself, but there would soon be intense competition for resources for social reforms.

Hicks Beach, 'a true Gladstonian Chancellor of the Exchequer',[138] personified rigid orthodoxy, and his reaction to the growth in taxation was to slam down the lid and sit on it. Yet, there would be a worse fate for Britain than raising the already-high tax rate, if a weakened Royal Navy meant that part of the Empire was lost. Lord Selborne, the First Lord of the Admiralty, did not believe that Britain was anywhere near the limits of her taxable capacity.[139] She was certainly not at the limit of her capacity to borrow. The National War Loan of March 1900 had been eleven times oversubscribed, whilst in February 1901 a Treasury issue of Exchequer bonds had been subscribed twice over.[140] In a memorandum for the Cabinet on 16 November 1901, written in response to Hicks Beach's, he reminded his colleagues that 'the growth of the Naval Estimates has been caused solely by the efforts of France and Russia to establish a naval superiority over this country'. Yet, he was increasingly concerned about a German threat, which the Germans themselves had spelled out in the previous year's Navy Bill. In the memorandum he wrote that the naval policy of Germany was 'definite and persistent', and that the Kaiser seemed determined that 'the power of Germany shall be used all over the world'.[141] In April 1902 Selborne admitted that 'I had not realised the intensity of the hatred of the German nation to this country,'[142] and by February 1904 he had concluded that, as he told the Cabinet, 'the great new German navy is being carefully built up from the point of view of a war with us'.[143]

On 6 December 1904, Selborne presented to the Cabinet a memorandum entitled 'Distribution and Mobilization of the Fleet'. One decision already taken in December 1903 was to withdraw from the Halifax and Esquimalt naval bases, thereby handing over the defence of Canada to the Canadians themselves.[144] There was really nothing to be done about any American threat, because in the Western Hemisphere, 'the United States are forming a navy the power and size of which will be limited only by the amount of money which the American people choose to spend on it'. Fortunately, there was not believed to be a threat from that quarter, only from France, Russia and Germany. This was being met by a consolidation and redistribution of the fleets. The Pacific and South Atlantic Squadrons entirely disappeared, whilst all but a flagship and an armoured cruiser (with their supporting smaller craft) were withdrawn from the North American and West Indian Station. Three of the four battle fleets were concentrated in European waters, the Channel Fleet plus an Armoured Cruiser Squadron based in England, the Atlantic Fleet plus an Armoured Cruiser Squadron based on Gibraltar, and the Mediterranean Fleet based on Malta; the China, East Indies and Australia Stations were combined into an Eastern Fleet based on Singapore.[145] To the dismay of the Foreign Office, masses of smaller, obsolete ships were also withdrawn from positions around the world, and so were no longer available for minor diplomatic incidents or to show the flag. And so, as a by-product of the threats from Europe, Great Britain had, after centuries, finally withdrawn the Royal Navy from the Western Hemisphere, leaving the Caribbean an American lake. This, at least, was how the Americans saw it, but the British viewed it differently: they had turned over to the Americans the task of defending the hemisphere, thereby incorporating the US navy into the British defence strategy.

Anglo-American relations now entered a relatively quiet phase. As Sir Edward Grey, the British Foreign Secretary, put it in his memoirs, 'In the years from 1905 to 1912 there was not much in the handling of public affairs between the Government of the United States and ourselves that retains sufficient interest to be described here.' Indeed, for some, this period was one of increasingly friendly relations. In a speech which Grey gave on 20 October 1905 to a Liberal audience in the City of London, he set out what he called three cardinal features of current British foreign policy, the first of which was 'the growing friendship and good feeling between ourselves and the United States'.[146] Interestingly, the 1912 edition of *Whitaker's Almanack*, a British reference book which is still published, changed the order in which its data about foreign countries was listed: the US was moved from its lowly alphabetical position to a place just after the British Empire and ahead of all other foreign countries.[147] On the other hand, in 1913, with the encouragement of President William Howard Taft, Congress passed a Bill exempting American ships carrying cargoes between the two coasts through the future Panama Canal from paying tolls,[148] a direct breach of the Hay–Pauncefote Treaty of 1901. After sustained British pressure, Taft's successor Woodrow Wilson requested that Congress repeal the Act, which in 1914, after much discussion, they did.[149] But there was a substantial and ill-tempered difference of opinion between the British government and Wilson over their opposite responses to the Mexican Revolution. The British recognised the new government led by General Victoriano Huerta, even though he had had the ex-President murdered, in order to restore stability; Wilson refused to follow suit, arguing that governments should be founded on a moral basis. They went their separate ways, but Grey's diplomacy ensured that the two did not stumble into a full-blown crisis.[150] Nevertheless, it was clear that this relationship was still a bit fragile.

V

Then came the war. By the end of 1915, Germany, Austria-Hungary, Turkey, Italy, Great Britain, France, Russia, Greece, Japan, Romania and Belgium had all entered the war: why had not the US? The more reasonable question is, why should she? She had purposely, throughout her independent history, kept out of European affairs;

their war aims were not hers; she owed nothing to Britain, France or Russia. She was girded by the Atlantic and Pacific oceans, with Canada to the north and Mexico to the south: how could she be harmed? There was nothing in 1914 to draw her into the war as a belligerent. The major role which the US was destined to play in the Great War was that of economic powerhouse and supplier of munitions, food, shipping and money to Britain and her allies. Her military role, once she finally entered the war, was limited. She held a quiet part of the line on the Western Front, but her major contribution there – which, fortunately, was not needed – would have been endless numbers of American boys to fight.

Great Britain, in common with the other belligerents, was unprepared for the scale or the duration of the war. The assumptions on which British pre-war strategic planning had been based were that she would utilise her superior naval power to blockade the Central Powers – the German, Austro-Hungarian and Ottoman empires and, later, Bulgaria – and slowly starve them of resources, sweep their ships from the oceans, and supply her own allies with subsidies and *matériel*. She would not provide a mass army of her own; rather, her allies were expected to provide the bulk of the land forces with Britain contributing only an Expeditionary Force of six divisions (150,000 men).[151] These assumptions were very quickly shown to be false. The Germans made it to the Channel Coast of Belgium and nearly made it to Paris, until they were stopped at the Battle of the Marne. France clearly could not defeat the Germans on her own, particularly once the latter had defeated the Russians in the Battle of Tannenberg in August 1914. Very soon into the war, Lord Kitchener, the Secretary of State for War, succeeded in persuading the Cabinet that it was vital that Britain should after all raise a mass army. Kitchener was almost alone in the highest reaches of government in envisaging a long war – the general public assumption was that it would all be over by Christmas 1914 – but such was his prestige that the Cabinet agreed to begin the necessary preparations.[152]

A mass army requires clothing, weapons and provisions, but only some of these supplies were immediately available in Britain. The natural place to turn for them was the US, by now the most powerful industrial economy in the world. President Wilson had proclaimed American neutrality, but that did not prohibit the selling of goods to the belligerents. The first order (for rifles) was placed in October 1914. Within two years the British had a war mission of ten thousand men working in the US. The latter had always been a quantity rather than a quality producer. Shells, rifles and various other munitions required precision from their makers so that they would not blow up in the faces of British, French and Russian soldiers, so British engineers travelled out to give advice to the manufacturers. Moreover, since the factories necessary to produce supplies often did not yet exist, the British government provided the capital to build them. (It did the same in Canada.) And, of course, the US was full of Germans – a million had emigrated there in the 1890s alone and they were the country's largest non-English-speaking minority. Some retained their loyalty to their homeland, and might well be tempted to sabotage the production and shipping of these supplies; a spy ring was certainly being run by the German Embassy. There were also millions of Irish immigrants and Irish-Americans of longer standing who had no reason to love Britain. Therefore, members of British missions inspected the *matériel* as it was produced in the factories, they guarded it on the trains to the docks, and they supervised its loading onto the ships. By October 1916, 40 per cent of all British spending on the war was spent in North America. But Britain was not only purchasing supplies for her own army, navy and civilian population: she was also financing in the US[153] the purchases of France, Russia, Belgium, Romania, Italy and Greece. The result was financial catastrophe.[154] There was another worry: as the Chancellor of the Exchequer, Reginald McKenna, reported to the Cabinet on 24 October 1916, 'If things go on as present, I venture to say with certainty that by next June or earlier, the President of the American Republic will be in a position, if he so wishes, to dictate his own terms to us.'[155] In due course, President Wilson would decide to do just that.

If a government needs domestic resources, it can raise taxes, or borrow, or simply print money or even commandeer the goods. If it is necessary to buy them abroad, the government needs to pay with foreign currency, in this case US dollars. Great Britain acquired these dollars by shipping gold, a total of £305 million worth (roughly

$1,500 million at the time, in those days a huge sum) between the outbreak of the war and July 1917.[156] Furthermore, she required her citizens, under the threat of penal taxation, to lend or sell to the Treasury their American, Latin American, Japanese and other foreign securities, which the Treasury then sold in New York. She also raised money in the New York money market, using, when necessary, some of these securities as collateral. But by 1916, it was becoming increasingly difficult to raise loans, because higher interest rates were required. A real problem was that much of the American investing public did not, in their hearts, believe that the Allies were going to win the war – and, of course, if they lost, no one would repay the investors.

Furthermore, by the autumn of 1916, relations between Britain and America were fraught with tension. There was growing American disgust and anger with the blockade of neutral ships, which the British suspected might be carrying goods to the Central Powers. Ships were required to call in at British ports, where they were inspected, and sometimes their goods seized, although the British always paid for them. This was all perfectly legal under international law – but shades of the War of 1812. The British had increased the pressure substantially by an Order-in Council of 11 March 1915; in response to the German declaration in February of unrestricted submarine warfare around the British Isles, the British embargoed all trade with Germany. American anger was heightened by British cable and mail censorship. Even before the war had begun, the British had cut all German ocean cables, and Great Britain now controlled the transit of information across the oceans. German traffic went through the Swedish cable, but this had to touch England, where it was tapped. The British response to the 1916 Easter Rising in Dublin, and particularly the decision to execute the leaders, was viewed with dismay by pro-Ally Americans and with real hatred by the politically important Irish-Americans. Finally, in an incredibly maladroit move, Britain published on 18 July 1916 a blacklist of some eighty-seven American and 350 Latin American firms accused or suspected of trading with the Central Powers. Wilson wrote to his friend and close adviser Colonel Edward M. House on 23 July that 'I am, I must admit, about at the end of my patience with Great Britain and the Allies. This blacklist business is the last straw . . . [and] I am seriously considering asking Congress to authorize me to prohibit loans and restrict exportations to the Allies.'[157]

That never happened, but the President did change the habit of a lifetime and call for 'incomparably the best navy in the world' (although he later admitted that he had been somewhat overenthusiastic and indiscreet). In September 1916 Wilson discussed with Colonel House the increasing strains in relations with Britain, declaring, 'Let us build a navy bigger than hers and do what we please.' Within three weeks, the General Board of the US navy had drawn up the plans for it to 'be equal to the most powerful maintained by any other nation' by 1925. This plan would have great repercussions on Anglo-American relations in the 1920s.[158]

A significant reason for Wilson's anger was the British (and French and German) response to his attempts to mediate peace. He had made this desire clear in a speech a fortnight after the beginning of the war: 'The people of the United States are drawn from many nations, and chiefly from the nations now at war . . . Such divisions among us . . . might seriously stand in the way of the proper performance of our duty as the one great nation at peace, the one people holding itself ready to play a part in impartial mediation and speak the counsels of peace and accommodation, not as a partisan, but as a friend.' The US should be neutral in fact as well as in name, and Americans impartial in thought as well as in action.[159] This, of course, was an impossible goal, but Wilson repeatedly attempted to raise his fellow Americans to his own moral heights.

In late 1914 there were discussions in Washington, particularly between Colonel House and the German Ambassador to the US, Count Bernstorff, about the possibilities of American mediation. House believed that Bernstorff supported his plans; Foreign Secretary Grey, therefore, could not refuse to consider them, for fear of damaging the Allied cause. Grey replied that whilst he himself would be prepared to consider the proposals, he was not so sanguine about Russia and France. Wilson and House were determined to explore the possibilities seriously, and Grey was forced to try to dampen the enthusiasm, sending a message to the President in

January 1915 that the time had not yet come for peace overtures. But Wilson would still not be put off, and House arrived in London on 6 February for talks. It seems quite clear that neither House nor Wilson truly understood the British. House thought that he could induce the British to agree to 'freedom of the seas' in exchange for Germany's disgorging Belgium. This meant that the British would cease stopping neutral traffic and blockading enemies. But these powers constituted two of the most significant weapons of the Royal Navy, and thus were of great importance in the defence of the United Kingdom. And this was to be surrendered for Belgium? Fortunately for Britain, though, after visiting Berlin, House decided that Germany was the obstacle to peace. He returned to London, where he remained throughout May, taking the social and political pulse and trying to dampen friction between the two countries. When he finally left for home at the beginning of June 1915, he was convinced that the US would 'inevitably drift into war with Germany and before long',[160] not least because a German submarine had sunk the British liner *Lusitania* on 7 May, with the loss of 128 American lives.

House and Wilson tried again in early 1916, with the former landing in London on 5 January, where he outlined to Grey and Arthur Balfour (the former Conservative Prime Minister and now First Lord of the Admiralty) his scheme for a settlement based on freedom of the seas and the elimination of militarism. Balfour wanted to know how Germany could be controlled, and House replied that a 'League of Nations' under the control of Great Britain and the US would keep her on the straight and narrow. House then departed for the Continent to talk to the German and French governments, and decided that the French were open to his plans for mediation. He then returned to London, where, unbeknownst to him, he was referred to by many as the 'Empty House'. Grey did not want to discourage him, for fear of alienating both him and Wilson, so after further talks the House–Grey Memorandum was drawn up, putting on paper House's conviction that 'Wilson was ready, on hearing from France and England that the moment was opportune, to propose that a Conference should be summoned to put an end to the war. Should the Allies accept this proposal, and should Germany refuse it, the United States would probably enter the war against Germany.'[161]

The sting, of course, was the weasel word 'probably', rendering the whole suggestion entirely useless to the Allies. Yet, even had Wilson and House wished to promise American aid, they could not, in all conscience, have done so, since it would be up to Congress to declare war. Nothing resulted.

Always the optimists, House and Wilson tried again. British Ambassador Sir Cecil Spring Rice reported to London late in September 1916 that Wilson was again considering mediation between the belligerents. This would be most disadvantageous to the Allies, however, since the Battle of the Somme, which had begun on 1 July, had failed to dislodge the Germans from northern France. David Lloyd George, the Secretary of State for War (following the drowning of Lord Kitchener earlier in the year), decided to take matters into his own hands. Through the interception of German cable traffic between Washington and Berlin, the British government knew that Wilson had told the German ambassador that it was 'in the interest of America that neither of the combatants should gain a decisive victory'.[162] Just as Wilson thought that world peace depended on him, many British leaders thought that not only their empire but western civilisation itself depended on the defeat of German militarism. Therefore, they would fight on until it was destroyed. Lloyd George was pro-American – or, at least, not anti-American – and 'genuinely believed that world peace depended on the creation of a Pax Anglo-Americana'.[163] But Wilson was in the midst of his campaign for re-election, and Lloyd George feared that he would 'take pre-emptive action to force negotiations upon the British' when they were in a militarily weak position.[164] In order to forestall this, and without consulting either the Prime Minister or the Foreign Secretary, he summoned Roy Howard of the United Press on 28 September and gave an interview which outlined the substance of the 'Knock-Out Blow' – that Great Britain would fight to the finish, and that there 'can be no interference at this stage'.[165]

The President got his revenge three months later. In November 1916, he was returned to office in a landslide, primarily because 'he kept us out of war'. Now enjoying security of tenure, he exercised his power. Ever since the beginning of the war, his constant desire had been to bring it to an end by mediation, with himself acting as mediator. His motives were humanitarian, but his treatment of the British was ruthless. By this time, he believed that relations with Britain were more strained than those with Germany.[166] There is no doubt that he was intensely angered by Lloyd George's pre-emptive strike to forestall an earlier peace move. In November 1916 the Allies had few points more vulnerable than their credit in the US, their only way of purchasing vital supplies. The President, along with others in his administration, was certain that the military stalemate meant that peace was imminent;[167] the Allies should be forced to accede to mediation; only supplies and credit from the US were keeping them going; undermine this credit and there would be no choice left.

The opportunity for doing this came when the Federal Reserve Board was told by a partner in J.P. Morgan & Co., the British government's financial agent in the US, that they planned to issue a huge amount of short-term debt as fast as the market could absorb it. The Federal Reserve was alarmed for all sorts of financial reasons, but also because they were worried that the US economy was too dependent on the war trade.[168] They decided to issue a warning that banks should not invest too heavily in short-term foreign securities; they then went to Wilson for approval. Wilson not only approved but strengthened the warning, adding that this type of security was not liquid, and could therefore prove very embarrassing if there was a change in American foreign policy. Furthermore, the warning should extend beyond the banks to the private investor. It was then handed to the press on 28 November 1916.

That day, the price of Allied war bonds and American war stocks plunged, as did the exchange rate of the pound; within a week, values in the securities market had fallen by one billion dollars. British credit was devastated, and the pound was in dire straits. The British coalition government under Prime Minister Herbert Asquith fell in the midst of all of this and Lloyd George took over as Prime Minister. At the first meeting of the new War Cabinet, one of the permanent secretaries of the Treasury was called in to report. John Maynard Keynes, then an official in the Treasury, later recalled the exchange: '"Well, Chalmers, what is the news?" said the goat [Lloyd George]. "Splendid," [Sir Robert] Chalmers replied in his high quavering voice, "two days ago we had to pay out $20 million; the next day was $10 million; and yesterday only $5 million." He did not add that a continuance at this rate for a week would clean us out completely.'[169]

Britain was now in a desperate financial crisis. German submarines were sinking merchant ships faster than they could be built, and she now had only three weeks' supply of wheat in the country. She was dependent on the US for food, munitions and other supplies, but she had now virtually lost the means to pay for these goods – and no payment, no goods. The Treasury immediately stopped the placement of all orders in the US, both to save dollars and to make it clear to the Americans the cost to their own employment and trade of the destruction of British credit. This soon had some effect.[170] But Great Britain could now do little but scrabble for funds and hope that the US would soon become a belligerent.

Fortunately for Britain, Germany came to the rescue. Earlier in the war, on 4 February 1915, Germany had announced that in two weeks, the waters around Great Britain and Ireland would become a war zone in which German submarines would seek to destroy all enemy merchant ships. 'Neutrals are therefore warned against further entrusting crews, passengers and wares to such ships.' Furthermore, since British vessels sometimes flew neutral flags, neutral vessels were warned to avoid entering the war zone. In response to Germany's use of submarines to attack without first stopping and searching merchant ships, Great Britain began to arm the vessels. Germany then began to sink ships indiscriminately, including passenger liners. As noted above, the *Lusitania* was one such victim. Her destruction of the liner had horrified Americans, and, in an attempt to head off calls for action, Wilson had declared three days later that 'There is such a thing as a man being too proud to fight. There is such a thing as a nation being so right that it does not need to convince others by force that it is right.'[171] After the sinking of the *Arabic* (with the loss of two American lives) on 19 August 1915, Germany pledged that submarines would not attack unarmed passenger ships unless they resisted or tried to escape. And in May 1916, under American pressure, she promised not to sink merchant ships without warning and without rescuing passengers and crew.

By October 1916, however, the German government was in deep internal discussion about a change of policy. The army was desperate to break the stalemate on land, and needed Britain knocked out of the war. The navy, with over one hundred U-boats, was confident that it could crush Britain within six months, largely by starving her into submission. There was also a conviction that, sooner or later, the US would enter the war on the side of the Allies, and it was thus vital that Britain not provide a staging post for an invasion of the Continent. Chancellor Theobald von Bethmann Hollweg warned his colleagues about the likely American response, but he was overborne. The statement made the previous day by Field Marshal Paul von Hindenburg, the Chief of the General Staff, had already convinced the Kaiser: 'We are counting on the possibility of war with the United States, and have made all preparations to meet it. Things cannot be worse than they are now.'[172] The decision was taken on 9 January 1917, and on the 31st the German Ambassador to the US informed the US government that unrestricted submarine warfare would resume the following day. Wilson suspended diplomatic relations with Germany on 3 February, but he continued to hope for peace, and emphasised that the US would not go to war over the sinking of Allied ships alone: only 'actual overt acts', he declared to Congress, could persuade him that Germany refused to respect American rights. He refused to arm American merchant ships, and, as U-boat attacks increased, they stayed in port, clogging docks all along the East Coast.

On 24 February the British revealed to the President the existence of the Zimmermann telegram, sent over the Swedish cable the previous month and decoded by the British (see Section VI for details of why this was so explosive). Two days later, Wilson asked Congress for authority to arm merchant ships, and when strong opposition developed, he released the Zimmermann telegram to the press, which published it on 1 March. A wave of anger rolled over the US: this publication began the mobilisation of public opinion behind the imminent war. On 18 March, word reached Washington of the sinking of three merchantmen with the loss of fifteen American lives, and Wilson then recognised that he had little choice. Fortunately, word had also reached Washington the previous week of revolution in Russia, with its leaders proclaiming democratic principles. The war could now, in all conscience, be deemed one of democracy against autocracy. Wilson, in his war speech to Congress on 2 April, did just that, proclaiming that 'the world must be made safe for democracy'.[173] Congress agreed, and four days later the US was at war.

The British government breathed a sigh of relief. It was desperate: shipping, money and men, and supplies of all sorts were required for both Britain and her allies. Merchant ships to carry supplies and destroyers to attack U-boats were vital. Britain was largely unsuccessful with regard to merchant shipping, primarily because the chairman of the United States Shipping Board in April and May 1917, William Denman, was ferociously anti-British, but considerably more successful in convincing the Navy Department to send destroyers, forty-eight of which had arrived at Queenstown in Ireland by 1 June. Britain also had to fight for supplies, since the Americans naturally wanted to use them to equip their own soldiers, and it took some time for them to be released.[174] As emphasised by the Commander-in-Chief of the British Expeditionary Force, General Sir Douglas Haig, Great Britain desperately needed soldiers. The Battle of the Somme and soon the third Battle of Ypres (Passchendaele) would claim tens of thousands more. Haig wanted rank upon rank of midwestern farm boys to gain some training in the US, in the manner prescribed by British military doctrine, and then shipped to France to receive further training, after which they would be fed into the ranks of the British army. The US army was led by generals with absolutely no experience in trench warfare, and beginning from scratch would significantly delay the time until their troops could join the fighting. However, the American Secretary of War, Newton D. Baker, agreed with General Tasker Bliss, soon to be Chief of the General Staff, that 'France and England should stand fast and wait until our reinforcements can come and give a shattering blow'.[175] Pushing at an open door, the American Commander-in-Chief, General John J. Pershing, convinced Wilson that the Americans should maintain their own army, trained according to their own doctrines. Only in this way would the US have the independent power to enforce her own policies at the eventual peace conference, something with which Wilson was in wholehearted accord. (This was one of the fears of the British, who were keen to win the war before the Americans had built up the predominant military force in France, not least because of imperial concerns in Africa and the Middle East.) The arguments between Pershing and the Allies in the Supreme War Council once he had arrived became intensely harsh.[176] Delays also arose because Wilson remained determined to impose a mediated peace on the belligerents, and worked hard to convince German liberals to agree to negotiation.

The result of all this was that it was not until March 1918, nearly a year after the US had entered the war, that the first substantial shipment of American soldiers, 120,000 fighting troops, sailed to France.[177] By then, Germany had begun her final dash westwards, hoping to drive France out of the war before the Americans could arrive, and Wilson finally recognised her predatory nature.[178] He also belatedly appreciated that, unless soldiers were sent immediately, the war might be lost before the Americans even reached the battlefield. Increasingly large numbers continued to arrive each month, the soldiers sleeping three to a bunk in shifts on board ship. Arguments continued over where to put them, by themselves or brigaded with the French or the British. In the end they took over a quiet part of the Western Front, where they were engaged in only one real fight, at Cantigny, and two smaller manoeuvres west of Château-Thierry and into Belleau Wood. However, their holding of their section of the line released experienced French and British soldiers to halt the German advance. David Woodward has pointed out that, whilst the 'military impact of these limited American engagements should not be exaggerated', the 'psychological consequences . . . were profound'.[179] Americans now knew that they were fighting a war, and so did the Germans.

Probably the most important battles between the British and the Americans were fought over the extent of US financial support for Britain. By the time the US joined the war, the British, financially speaking, were hanging on by their fingernails. Their great hope was that the US would take over the financing of British purchases and those of the other Allies in the US, and relieve her of the burden. But the US government still viewed Great Britain as the world's supreme financial power: why should the US pay her bills?

The Americans feared being taken advantage of by the crafty Europeans – and, indeed, in some sense they had cause, because the British certainly wanted the US to assume as large a share of the financial burden as possible. Great Britain presumed that a major war interest of *both* countries was to maintain *Britain's* financial power, a primary reason being that if the pound plummeted in value, it would cost a great deal more to purchase the same amount of supplies around the world.[180] As Balfour, now Foreign Secretary, wrote to House on 28 June 1917, 'we seem on the edge of a financial disaster which would be worse than a defeat in the field . . . You know that I am not an alarmist: but this is really serious.'[181]

The US, whilst not wishing Britain to crash in flames, saw no reason why American interests should be sacrificed to any British interests which were, as it saw matters, unconnected with the war. But the British were desperate; indeed, Lord Northcliffe, newspaper magnate and now the head of the British War Mission in the US, wrote to a London colleague in July 1917 that 'We are down on our knees to the Americans.'[182] Without American financial and other aid, Britain and the Allies would simply be unable to continue fighting on anything like the same scale as heretofore and might be forced to negotiate a disadvantageous peace with Germany still in occupation of northern France. The two, however, eventually agreed, after a heartfelt show of British brinkmanship, that the US should indeed shoulder much of the immediate burden of Allied purchases in the US by loaning – not granting – billions of dollars. This was the genesis of the war debts, which would bedevil Anglo-American relations for the next twenty years.[183]

Some elements in the American government now determined to exploit what all assumed to be temporary British financial dependence on the US in order to further American interests. According to House, the US Treasury wished the dollar to replace the pound as the supreme international currency, and for New York to supplant London as the world's financial centre.[184] J.M. Keynes summed up the bitterness felt in the British Treasury over the need to beg when he wrote that 'it almost looks as if they took a satisfaction in reducing us to a position of complete financial helplessness and dependence'.[185] Wilson, too, planned to use American financial strength against the

British, in his case to enforce his peace plans at the conclusion of the war. As he wrote in July 1917, at the height of the desperate British fight for sufficient American financial aid, 'England and France have not the same views with regard to peace that we have by any means. When the war is over we can force them to our way of thinking, because by that time they will, among other things, be financially in our hands.'[186] Wilson would soon discover that financial power does not automatically translate into political or diplomatic power. Nevertheless, the summer of 1917 was a profound turning point for both countries. The desperate British fight for financial aid was met by a US government determined not to be forced to be the Atlas of the Allies. The Secretary of the Treasury, William Gibbs McAdoo, wrote on 12 July to Foreign Secretary Balfour, 'American financial policy will be dictated by a desire to cooperate to the fullest extent possible with the several powers making war in common with Germany, but America's cooperation cannot mean that America can assume the entire burden of financing the war.'[187] This revealed a fundamental misunderstanding of the situation, since Britain was providing twice as much money to the Allies as she was receiving from the US.[188] But day by day, financial power passed from Great Britain to the US, and by the end of the First World War, the United Kingdom and the United States had changed places: the latter was now the supreme international financial power, and she would remain so for the rest of the century.

VI

Given the tension between the various government departments, missions and personalities, it was fortunate for wartime co-operation that there was a close link between the British and American governments through a representative of Great Britain in the US – but it was not such a straightforward link as Wilson and House believed. Sir William Wiseman, a baronet and officer in the Duke of Cornwall's Light Infantry, had been gassed at the first Battle of Ypres early in 1915 and invalided out. Before the war, after unsuccessful careers as a journalist and playwright, he had travelled to North

America to try his hand in various business ventures, and was therefore familiar with the US. Early in 1916, he was sent to New York as the head of station of MI1c, Britain's wartime foreign intelligence agency, which was camouflaged as part of the American and Transport Department of the Ministry of Munitions; publicly, he was head of the British Military Mission. MI1c's instructions were to counter German espionage and covert operations in North America and to keep an eye on leading Irish and Indian nationalists, who were using the US as a safe haven from which to foment rebellion back home. However, as Christopher Andrew points out, 'Wiseman's most remarkable achievement . . . was to win the confidence first of Colonel House, then of President Wilson.'

Wiseman's introduction to House came about by accident. The man whom British Ambassador Sir Cecil Spring Rice entrusted with delivering messages to House was away, and he asked Wiseman to convey them instead. At their first meeting, on 17 December 1916, Wiseman impressed House as 'the most important caller I have had for some time'. House needed a link to the new British government, a coalition made up predominantly of the Conservative and Unionist Party and a few Labour Party leaders, and headed by a Liberal, Lloyd George. Those with whom he had had close relations, in particular Grey, had left. Both House and the President disliked Spring Rice, who had close links with the Republicans – he had been best man at J.P. Morgan, Jr.'s wedding – and an acerbic wit which he used without due care. Keynes, who had travelled out to the US on a mission for the Treasury, wrote that 'Sir C. Spring-Rice could not be regarded as entirely mentally responsible. It is certain that his excitability, his nervousness, his frequent indiscretion, and also his absent-mindedness render the proper conduct of his business almost impossible.'[189]

It is, therefore, not difficult to see why the two Americans turned with relief to an alternative link with the British government. Any doubts they may have had – although none, apparently, were ever expressed – were probably assuaged by Wiseman's assurance to House on 26 January 1917: '[Wiseman] told me in the *gravest confidence* . . . that he is in direct communication with the Foreign Office, and that the Ambassador and other members of the Embassy are not aware of it. I am happy beyond measure over this last conference with him, for I judge that he reflects the views of his government.' But, as Andrew points out, not even Lloyd George was aware of Wiseman's existence; instead, he reported to the head of MI1c, 'who passed on to the Foreign Office and other Whitehall ministries what intelligence he judged appropriate'.[190] With a mole at the centre of the American government, the British government knew what Wilson and House were thinking, including in due course their plans for the peace conference. The two Americans never realised Wiseman's true position. He was a loyal British subject and worked to further British interests. But he rapidly became very close to the two men, especially to House, and he tried to bring the two countries closer together during his two and a half years as an agent.

Andrew argues that the foundations of an Anglo-American intelligence alliance were laid in London. In the summer of 1918 there was a meeting between Franklin D. Roosevelt, who as Assistant Secretary of the US Navy had responsibility for the Office of Naval Intelligence, and Captain Reginald 'Blinker' Hall, the British Director of Naval Intelligence. This 'made a profound impression on [Roosevelt] that still coloured his attitude toward British intelligence at the beginning of the Second World War.' Roosevelt himself wrote that 'Their intelligence unit is much more developed than ours, and this is because it is a much more integral part of their Office of Operations.'[191] The crucial figure was Hall, who was given his nickname because of his habit of blinking furiously when interested or excited, and who has been called 'the most successful intelligence agent of the First World War'.[192] He used the discovery of German and German-American activities in the US, including the funding and organisation of the bombing and sabotage of steel mills and munitions factories, to shock and awe the Americans. Intelligence-gathering by the Americans themselves was hampered by bitter rivalry between the separate organisations, the Bureau of Investigation, the Secret Service, the Office of Naval Intelligence, the Military Intelligence Department, and the State Department's intelligence operations, who often refused to co-operate with each other, a situation for which Wilson evaded any responsibility and took no action to resolve. (This lack of co-operation would be repeated during the Second World War, and was not unknown after 1945.)

The glaring deficiencies of American intelligence-gathering and counter-espionage served to highlight the quality of the British equivalents, and Wilson himself was particularly impressed by their ability to intercept and decrypt German diplomatic and naval radio (or wireless) traffic. But Hall did not want the Americans to realise just how skilled they were, so he disguised this command of signals intelligence as work by his agents on the ground. He especially did not want Wilson to realise that the British were doing the same thing with American intercepts: in fact, they found American codes and cyphers amusingly simple to decode. And it was not only the British who were listening. According to one code clerk in 1918–19, James Thurber, there was a story current at the time that 'six of our code books were missing and a seventh, neatly wrapped, firmly tied, and accompanied by a courteous note, had been returned to one or another of our embassies by the Japanese, either because they had finished with it or because they already had one'.[193] Especially simple were those codes concocted and used by the President himself to communicate with House during the latter's 'confidential' peace missions to Europe.[194]

Hall's group of cryptologists early in the war were housed in Room 40 of the Admiralty Old Building, and this name was soon used as shorthand for the entire operation. Arguably their most important coup was the interception and decryption of the Zimmermann telegram. This was sent on 17 January 1917 by Arthur Zimmermann, the German Foreign Minister, to the German Embassy in Washington for onward transmission to their Ambassador in Mexico City. (For a period in the winter of 1916–1917 the US allowed Germany to use its transatlantic cable for cable traffic sent from Germany via the Swedish cable, and since Room 40 tapped into it, they received both German and American traffic.) On the assumption that the US and Germany would soon be at war, the latter was offering Mexico an alliance, promising 'generous financial support and an understanding on our part that Mexico is to reconquer the lost territory in Texas, New Mexico and Arizona', which the US had seized in 1848 (there was no mention of California). This, of course, was dynamite. But how should it be used?

Hall had not told the Americans that Room 40 had broken the

German codes, for fear that they would draw the obvious conclusion about their own, and now he held back the telegram for a fortnight. But with Wilson breaking off diplomatic relations with Germany on 3 February while at the same time emphasising his desire to avoid war between the two countries, Hall felt he had to turn the decrypt over to the Foreign Office. However, he only did so with a warning that they must disguise the source. The British Ambassador in Mexico illicitly obtained from a Mexican agent a copy of a version of the telegram forwarded by the British Embassy in Washington, and Hall could thus pretend that it came from a British agent in the field. The Foreign Secretary handed over a copy to the American Ambassador, who in great excitement passed it on to Washington, where it arrived on the 24th. Wilson was 'as shocked and angry as Hall had hoped he would be' and it was released to the public on 1 March. According to Andrew, 'the publication of the Zimmermann telegram created an even greater sensation in the United States than the German invasion of Belgium or the sinking of the *Lusitania*', an assessment supported by Wilson's biographer, Arthur Link: 'No other event of the war to this point . . . so stunned the American people.' Just in case anyone doubted its authenticity, Zimmermann himself said on 3 March, 'I cannot deny it. It is true.'[195] The Zimmermann telegram did not bring the US into the war – the U-boats did that – but it did more than anything else to mobilise public opinion behind entry.

In June 1917 Wilson authorised the funds for the US and Russia to unite in a propaganda operation designed to keep the latter in the war, but this manifestly failed.[196] Meanwhile, Hall furnished the Americans with information on the Central Powers which he thought might be of interest or use to them, and there was very close co-operation between British military intelligence and their American counterparts during 1917–18 on the Western Front.[197]

During this period there was a huge expansion in the American intelligence effort, both in size and capability. This took place especially in the War Department's Military Intelligence Department, but the Navy Department's Office of Naval Intelligence also mushroomed. The State Department, too, expanded its intelligence operations, with an important post-war operation with the War

Department, the Black Chamber, created in 1919 as the first American peacetime unit devoted to encrypting and decrypting. However, during the inter-war period intelligence-gathering declined. The most famous incident was Secretary of State Henry Stimson's closing down of the Black Chamber in 1931 with the immortal words, 'Gentlemen do not read each other's mail.' He has been excoriated for this but, according to Robert Angevine, the Black Chamber was of little use in any case, suffering from a lack of leadership and with little to do. The military and naval efforts, however, continued, with their focus soon primarily on Japan,[198] and in September 1940 the US army's Signals Intelligence Service broke the Japanese PURPLE machine cypher, the decrypts of which were called MAGIC. These were of immeasurable use once the US joined the war.

In Britain considerable success was enjoyed in the inter-war years by the Government Code and Cypher School (GC&CS). This had been established early in 1919 by the decision of the War Cabinet to establish a peacetime cryptographic unit. During the 1920s it broke the diplomatic codes of a number of countries, including the US, although it did not get very far with German codes even before Germany introduced the Enigma machine cypher later in the decade. During the 1930s its main successes were with Japanese, Italian and Comintern (the USSR's organisation established to foment worldwide revolution) traffic. By 1930, Japanese signals were being intercepted and decrypted in ships of the Royal Navy on the China Station by GC&CS-trained cryptanalysts.[199] Nevertheless, knowing what the Japanese were doing did not mean that the British could usefully respond, given their lack of resources.

VII

Once the US entered the war, it was assumed by the Allies that victory would ineluctably follow, although it was also assumed that the war would continue into 1919. The US gradually increased its co-operation with various Allied committees, and had the war indeed continued for another year, there would have been a rather well-organised war effort. Except, of course, that Wilson refused to agree that the US was an ally: rather, she was an 'associated power', a relationship which did not tie the US to the Allies' arrangements for dividing up the three dying empires, the Russian, the Austro-Hungarian and the Ottoman, nor to France's plans to re-establish herself as the predominant power in Continental Europe. Instead, Wilson wished to remain free to impose his plans for a peace without a division of the spoils and to establish a new world order. In any case, his lack of desire to share the territorial aims of the Allies is hardly surprising. (Conversely, Theodore Roosevelt, an admirer of the British Empire, would not have passed up the chance to pick up another colony.)

When, in December 1917, the Inter-Allied Conference meeting in Paris became deadlocked over the issue of war aims, Wilson decided to make an independent statement, setting out the principles on which a peace treaty should be based. However, once again Lloyd George got in first with his own statement – although it is Wilson's menu which is remembered, not Lloyd George's. In October 1917, the Bolsheviks had overthrown the Russian government, and on 15 December they signed an armistice with the Germans at Brest-Litovsk, a Polish fortress town, which called for peace talks on the basis of no annexations or indemnities; they would also publish the secret treaties made between the Allies.[200] At the same time, the British were in secret negotiations with the Austrians, encouraging them, in essence, to make a separate peace, and Lloyd George thought that a statement of moderate British war aims might encourage this. Importantly, setting out the British peace terms would, it was hoped, prevent the other Allies, and Wilson, from dominating the peace conference agenda at the expense of the strategic needs of the Empire and Britain's other international interests. For a concatenation of reasons, then, in a speech to the Trades Union Congress in Caxton Hall in London on 5 January 1918, Lloyd George set out his wares. He spoke of reason and justice, the sanctity of treaties,[201] a territorial settlement based on the 'right of self-determination' and the establishment of an 'international organisation [as] an alternative to war as a means of settling international disputes . . . [to] limit the burden of armaments and diminish the probability of war'. He called for the establishment of an independent Poland and the restoration of Belgium, Serbia, Montenegro, Romania and occupied Italy and France, so France would recover Alsace–Lorraine. Mesopotamia, Armenia, Arabia, Palestine and Syria, all provinces of the Ottoman Empire, were to have separate national 'conditions', whilst Germany's colonies would also be subject to self-determination.[202] This all bore a startling resemblance to the future Fourteen Points of President Wilson (see below).

When Wilson received news of Lloyd George's speech, his reaction was mixed. On the one hand, he was pleased that his and London's views on war aims appeared to agree on so many points (although he was sceptical that they were truly at one with him); but on the other, he was depressed by the notion that the Prime Minister had stolen his thunder as the proposer of war aims with which all good men and true could agree. House cheered him up by insisting that Wilson's views, when announced, 'would so smother the Lloyd George speech that it would be forgotten and that he, the President, would once more become the spokesman for the Entente, and, indeed, the spokesman for the liberals of the world'. In the privacy of his diary, however, House revealed his contempt for Wilson's reaction: 'it is not so much general accomplishment that those in authority seem to desire so much as accomplishment which may redound to their own personal advantage'.[203]

Early on 8 January, 'members of the House of Representatives' Committee on Foreign Affairs were startled when a courier arrived announcing that the president proposed to address a joint session of Congress that very afternoon'.[204] It was there that Wilson made his Fourteen Points speech. The first five points set out principles on which international relations in the widest term ought to be conducted: 'open covenants openly arrived at' (i.e., no secret treaties); freedom of the seas in peace and war; removal of all economic barriers to free trade; disarmament; and a settlement of colonial claims which took into account the wishes of both the peoples and their imperial masters. These were followed by more specific territorial questions, among which were the return of Alsace-Lorraine to France, the return of Belgium to full sovereignty, full autonomy for the various ethnic peoples of Austria-Hungary, and an independent

Poland with access to the sea. Finally, there should be 'a general association of nations' to provide 'mutual guarantees of political independence and territorial integrity to great and small nations alike'.[205] The impact of Wilson's speech certainly owed something to the fact that it was made by the leader of a powerful nation, but it also undoubtedly touched a chord, raising the hope that the slaughter of the war would prove not to have been entirely in vain. It was also the basis on which Germany sued for an armistice on 6 October 1918, thereby appearing to give Wilson control of the agenda for peacemaking.

This possible control by the Americans, which Wilson expected to exercise, was a considerable worry for the British Cabinet. Its decision to sign an armistice in November 1918 owed a great deal to its recognition that otherwise the war would continue a good way into 1919. There was, of course, concern about more casualties, as well as the lack of manpower to replace them, but there was also the fear that the steady increase in American military power would ensure that the US was the dominant power at the peace conference. As Lloyd George had intimated to the War Policy Cabinet Committee back in June 1917, he 'did not want to have to face a Peace Conference some day with our country weakened while America was still overwhelmingly strong'.[206]

The Paris peace conference, which lasted from January to June 1919, was only one of six.[207] However, it was the most important because it dealt with Germany, and although the US and Britain disagreed during the negotiations over the subsequent treaties, the important and memorable arguments occurred in Paris. The two primary points of conflict were the traditional American insistence on freedom of the seas, the rights of neutral countries during wartime (number two of Wilson's Fourteen points), and the nature of an association of nations (the fourteenth). Disagreement over freedom of the seas erupted even before the conference began. In late October 1918, prior to the armistice with Germany, House travelled to London for discussions with the Allies. His assumption, he wrote to Wilson, was that 'England cannot dispense with us in the future', and he was therefore confident that 'the English I think will accept your fourteen points with some modification such as . . . making of the freedom of the seas conditional upon the foundation of the League of Nations'.[208] He was wrong. Britain would not accept the freedom of the seas without important changes and qualifications, and if it became part of the League of Nations, they would refuse to accept the League. The crux was the right to impose a blockade. House threatened a separate peace between the US and Germany; Wilson added that he might go before Congress and ask whether the US should fight for the Allies' war aims; and House told the British privately that the President believed that their position could trigger, in Godfrey Hodgson's words, the 'greatest naval building program the world had even seen'.[209] Lloyd George wrote reassuringly to House that the Allies would make peace on the basis of the Fourteen Points and those made in Wilson's later speeches, but he reiterated that they could not accept the freedom of the seas without changes and qualifications. Wilson then agreed that although the blockade power would have to be redefined, it need not be abolished. On 3 November Lloyd George told House that he was quite willing to discuss the matter, which House took as a great diplomatic victory.[210] The British believed that they had given away nothing whilst placating the Americans, with the result that they could now work together on other issues. Discussions on the subject died away.

The existence and nature of the League of Nations was a topic that came to dominate the peace conference. Wilson wanted it so badly that he eventually sacrificed other issues. As he told House on 14 December, he intended 'making the League of Nations the center of the whole program and letting everything revolve around that. Once that is a *fait accompli*, nearly all the very serious difficulties will disappear.'[211] The Allies knew this, and early on the British government determined to exploit this desire, with Lloyd George emphasising to his colleagues that the League 'was the only thing which [Wilson] really cared about', and that they should let him have his way and deal with it first, on the assumption that it would ease other matters, such as the German colonies, economic questions, and the Freedom of the Seas. (The Australian Prime Minister, Billy Hughes, put it more brutally: 'Give him a League of Nations and he will give us all the rest.')[212] Yet the British position was more complicated than this. The British had begun work on such an organisation before the Americans – there was even a pressure group, the League of Nations Union, with widespread support amongst the British public. The idea had come to the Americans from the British, with Foreign Secretary Grey writing to House on 22 September 1915 to ask, 'Would the President propose that there should be a League of Nations binding themselves to side against any Power which broke a treaty'? House had passed the request on to Wilson.[213] And, of course, Lloyd George had called for it in his Caxton Hall speech three days before Wilson had done so in his Fourteen Points speech. Beneath the surface accord, however, the two countries had very different approaches to such an organisation.

The President's approach has been well characterised by George Egerton:

> For Wilson, . . . the league cause had deep religious and national-ist wellsprings. His devout Presbyterian faith ramified his political ideals with a sense of responding to the call and directives of Providence, whereby he and his country were chosen to usher in a new age of justice and peace. The desired new international order, therefore, represented not just an international constitu-tional contract, but also a *covenant* for righteousness and justice sanctioned by God. The league project was viewed eschatologic-ally by Wilson as the 'final enterprise of humanity'.[214]

This moral and ideological approach was in sharp contrast to that of the British. It was not that the latter did not have a moral and ideo-logical strain: the principal British advocate of the League inside the government was Lord Robert Cecil, a younger son of Lord Salisbury, the Victorian Prime Minister, a man of such firm religious faith that he was to resign over the position of the Church of England in Wales. It was just that they did not believe that Wilson's insistence on including a guarantee of territorial integrity and polit-ical independence was either right or workable.[215] Indeed, the Lloyd George government, both civilian and military leaders, saw the League as alien, fundamentally flawed and unworkable; the only advantage, to which Lloyd George clung, was that it might facilitate future Anglo-American co-operation.

Wilson simply refused to consider the practicalities of the League, preferring not to design a structure but rather to cultivate firm support for it amongst all peoples, and then to let it develop with case law; it was difficult to see how this would work. The British on the other hand, steeped in the diplomatic tradition, were very concerned with how an international organisation would work – where was the power to lie, which countries would be members, and so on. Furthermore, they had a problem with Wilson's strong belief in the efficacy of collective security: where were the means of enforcement? Wilson believed fervently in the moral force of international public opinion, that such opinion would force governments to do the right thing. The British believed in a balance of power, skilful diplomacy and a strong Royal Navy. Britain continued to try to come up with a workable model for a League of Nations. Increasingly, they attempted to do what Wilson refused to do – incorporate answers to some of the objections of Republican Senators. Wilson wanted an automatic response of war if any member of the League were attacked; the Senators insisted that this would contravene the US Constitution, which gave to Congress the power to declare war. The Senators wanted a position given to the Monroe Doctrine; Wilson refused. But the President was weakened by the fact that he had called for the election of Democrats as a vote of confidence in his plans during midterm elections in November 1918, and the electorate had responded by giving the Republicans control of both the House and the Senate.[216] Wilson had also refused to have any Republicans in the Versailles delegation; this was short-sighted, because they therefore had no political stake in its success. After the Treaty of Versailles was signed in June 1919, the Senate refused to ratify it. Wilson had insisted that the League of Nations constitute part of the Treaty, and the Senate, rejecting the League, thereby rejected the Treaty. The President's awe-inspiring self-righteousness, when combined with a total inability to compromise, drove him to be a martyr and the destroyer of his own creation.[217] A League of Nations without the Americans, whilst useful in legal and financial matters, was doomed as an agent of peace and security.

VIII

During the inter-war period, relations between Britain and the US were often fraught, particularly during the 1920s. They were fighting for their positions. Great Britain, still the only global power although no longer financially pre-eminent, wished to remain the strongest, and it is worth remembering that the world regarded her as a damaged but not necessarily declining power. Her Empire was larger than ever, with the addition of League of Nations mandates for Mesopotamia (now Iraq), Palestine and Jordan, all from the Ottoman Empire, and German East Africa (now, combined with Zanzibar, Tanzania). Importantly, the Royal Navy remained the largest in the world, although the quality of its ships was variable. The US navy, conscious as never before of its actual and potential strength, and supported by many in the US government and the public, wanted to supplant the Royal Navy. However, that would require money to be spent on the armed forces and involvement in international politics, and that was a path which few Americans wished to follow. Domestic politics and a fear of communist subversion (there was a 'Red Scare' between 1917 and 1920 which attracted a particularly ferocious governmental reaction) demanded more attention in Washington than did foreign policy. According to Lord Curzon, the British Foreign Secretary, at the end of the Wilson administration 'Official relations with the American Government almost ceased to exist, and for ten months we practically did no business with America at all.'[218] This was merely a prelude to a decade of conflict. A statement made by Lord Selborne in November 1901 neatly summed up the problem for the government both then and years later: Great Britain's 'Credit and its Navy [are] the two main pillars on which the strength of this country rests, and each is essential to the other. Unless our financial position is strong, the Navy cannot be maintained. Unless the Navy is fully adequate for any call which may be made upon it, our national Credit must stand in jeopardy.'[219] And unless the Royal Navy was maintained, the British Empire and even the safety of the realm would be at risk. During the inter-war period, both seemed under attack by the US, and Britain, having lost her position of financial predominance to the US, was also forced to surrender naval supremacy and settle for formal parity.

Great Britain's financial power was not an arcane, obscure subject, of interest only to the banker or the economist. It had been the foundation of British world power for centuries, and the passing of her dominant position to the US was of central concern to the whole financial and political elite. Financial conflict had two strands: that between the two governments, and that centred in the private sector, which also included trade rivalry. The governmental conflict stemmed from the loans made to the British by the US Treasury after America entered the war. Briefly, the US wanted them repaid and Britain wanted them cancelled. The British had suffered roughly 947,000 deaths, the US roughly 115,000; Britain had lost 15 per cent of her pre-war investments, primarily American and other foreign securities, and had borrowed massively – by 1928, fully 40 per cent of government expenditure would be spent on servicing war debts[220] – whilst the US had become a huge economic power. France and Belgium had been occupied and damaged: was it right that they should use part of what little money they had to repay the US, which had barely suffered? Britain had loaned vastly more money to its allies than the US had loaned to her – $7.8 billion compared to almost $4.3 billion[221] – and offered to cancel those debts if the US would do the same. The US refused. If not always expressed with the crudity of President Calvin Coolidge – 'they hired the money, didn't they?' – there were few in the US who did not believe that Great Britain could and should pay. This was the great international financial power: how could the US believe other than that Britain was trying to take advantage? The upshot was that not only was the war debt funded (converted to a fixed-interest, repayable debt) in 1922, but the US also insisted that the British pay a higher rate of interest than any of the other debtor countries.[222] Britain struggled to meet the repayments; yet, because of the interest, the debt continued to increase. She had received $4,277,000,000 and repaid a total of $2,025,000,000; yet in 1933 the amount stood at over $4 billion. With the Depression having hit, she made her final repayment in December 1933, and then suspended payment.[223]

The private sector was a mixed story. On the one hand, US investment banks and British merchant banks, the organisations which
dominated the foreign and 'sovereign' (governmental) debt markets,
had traditionally worked together. This continued in the inter-war
period, because although New York had more money to lend, the
City of London had the experience and expertise, having been
active in the foreign bond markets since the late seventeenth century.[224] Furthermore, the US had a significant disadvantage, in that
it lacked a sizeable investing public with an appetite for foreign
loans. (New York bankers sometimes tried to get around this by
issuing the loan in New York and garnering the fees, and then selling on the bonds to investors in London.)[225] It should be noted that
the dominant international bank, the House of Morgan, had banks in
New York, London and Paris, and it certainly supported the continuance of British financial power. Yet, continuance did not mean
continued dominance, and the weight of capital told. During the
war, as mentioned above, a stream of gold had flowed from east to
west: in 1913 Europe had held 63 per cent of the world's total stock
and North America 24 per cent; by 1925, Europe held 35 per cent,
whilst North America held 45 per cent.[226] In the 1920s, when the
American economy was booming, the country's long-term investment rose by nearly nine billion dollars and 'accounted for about
two-thirds of world new investment'. Great Britain's total overseas
investments were less than half of those of the US. She never recovered her former leadership.[227]

On the other hand, there was ferocious competition in foreign
trade and investment. In the US, even during the war, Secretary of
the Treasury William McAdoo was a major figure in a growing consensus amongst business and political leaders on ways of expanding
American foreign trade and investment. As his biographer describes
it, 'by 1916 this consensus envisioned a number of preconditions for
growth, among them creation of an international economic system
that would enable the United States to supplant Britain as the linch-
pin of world commerce'. McAdoo's chief target was Latin America,
where in 1914 'the European colossus stood astride these markets'.
Once Britain was in deep financial difficulties, and had increasingly
to liquidate her foreign positions, American money moved into the

region.[228] This was a perfectly natural development, given the position the US already held in Central America, and the tradition she had of exporting her surpluses. But McAdoo and other politicians could not direct banks to do the same by, for example, establishing branches. Domestic American banks were wary about challenging British banking power when there was still plenty of money to be made at home.

The growing naval rivalry between the two countries, which caused 'the worst level of Anglo-American hostility in the twentieth century',[229] was of supreme importance to Britain and only slightly less to the US, which had fewer global interests than Britain but a widespread desire for its naval forces to reflect its new-found international status. It also needed to be able to defend itself against an enemy in war, and for much of the 1920s the US navy, in which anglophobia was rife, thought that enemy might be Britain. As noted above, in 1916 the US Naval Bill had reflected calls for 'a navy second to none', and by the end of the war it had sixteen dreadnoughts and a multitude of smaller warships in commission (equal to the combined navies of France, Italy and Japan). In addition, the Navy Department was now asking Congress for an eventual force of thirty-nine dreadnoughts and twelve battle cruisers, a navy to dwarf that of Britain.[230] It did not get them, but it did receive general support for at least naval parity with Britain. President Wilson wanted a great navy as a diplomatic weapon with which to intimidate the British, whilst others, such as the US navy itself, just wanted to be the biggest and the best.[231]

The Royal Navy, which had ended the war as still the greatest navy in the world, obviously wanted to retain that position, notwithstanding the American construction programme. But there was an almost insurmountable problem: money. Prime Minister Lloyd George and Chancellor of the Exchequer Stanley Baldwin both opposed naval construction through fear that it would set off an unaffordable arms race. Even the First Lord of the Admiralty, Walter Long, admitted that if the US 'chose to put all their resources into the provision of a larger Navy the competition between us would be impossible, and we should in the end be beaten from the point of view merely of finance'.[232] But even if Britain was being 'beaten', on realpolitik grounds this was acceptable, because the assumption continued to be that the US was not a threat. The result was that the Cabinet, to the dismay of many within the Royal Navy and without, decided on a one-power standard in battleships and battle cruisers with the US – that is, parity between the navies – thereby overturning a policy of decades.[233]

But unbeknownst – or at least barely considered – was the fact that, with the war over, the US public was losing interest in military affairs. What this meant to many congressmen was that they could stop 'wasting' money on the navy. On 14 December 1920 Senator William Borah of Idaho, a leading isolationist (he had fought against the League of Nations), introduced a resolution in the Senate calling for an Anglo-American-Japanese agreement to limit naval armaments. The new and powerful Secretary of State, Charles Evans Hughes (whom Wilson had defeated in the 1916 presidential election and who would in 1930 become Chief Justice of the Supreme Court), saw the fleet as the means to an end, which was the ending of the Anglo-Japanese Alliance. He feared that the Japanese were becoming increasingly hostile towards the US, and that the continued existence of the alliance would encourage them to mount a challenge. His strategy was to use a conference to lessen British apprehension of American plans and thereby talk them into refusing to renew the alliance (a refusal which the Japanese would take as an insult). Thus, on 11 July 1921 the new Republican President, Warren G. Harding, invited Great Britain, Japan, France and Italy to a conference in Washington to discuss naval arms control and security issues in the Pacific. The British Cabinet agreed to attend, but at the same time authorised another four battle cruisers, which would either be built or used as bargaining chips at the conference.[234]

The Conference on Limitation of Armaments, or simply the Washington Conference, opened on 12 November 1921 in the Continental Hall of the Daughters of the American Revolution. The British had assumed that the Americans would not be prepared: stunned, they discovered that they were. As Theodore Roosevelt, Jr., the Assistant Secretary of the Navy, noted in his diary, 'The plan is to spring everything, including our definite naval program on the opening day',[235] and they did. Secretary of State Hughes, in his opening speech, 'in a skilful and dramatic way . . . led up to his main proposals', which were that the US would scrap every capital ship laid down as part of the 1916 programme; that the British and Japanese would have to stop all capital ship construction and scrap a large number of older vessels; and that they would stabilise their capital ship strengths in a ratio of 5:5:3, with Japan being the 3. He suggested that the way to keep this balance was to institute a capital shipbuilding holiday for ten years and then to regulate subsequent building. The British response was to accept the plan with regard to capital ships and the ratio (the so-called 'Rolls-Royce:Rolls-Royce:Ford' ratio). But Lord Balfour, the head of the British delegation, stressed in his speech the following day Great Britain's need for cruisers and destroyers. For their part, the Japanese naturally wanted a higher ratio.[236]

Negotiations over the subsequent month modified the proposals, although the result adhered to the ratio, which was now 5:5:3:1.75:1.75 (with France and Italy filling the final two slots). Great Britain, however, with memories of the war still fresh, absolutely refused to accept a severe limitation on her cruisers, a significant number of which were needed for the defence of trade and sea communications and if need be to maintain a blockade. The American administration, unwilling to wreck the conference and happy to have achieved at least some measure of success in a naval agreement with Great Britain, agreed. The bottom line for the US was the abrogation of the Anglo-Japanese Treaty. This was a real concession, because the Lloyd George government on balance wanted to keep it, as it provided a check on Japan, and relieved Britain of some responsibility for patrolling the Far East. A Four-Power Treaty linking the US, Great Britain, Japan and France was substituted, which provided for mutual consultation with regard to regional security issues. In total the conference gave birth to nine treaties and twelve resolutions. It also, of course, stimulated the building of non-ratio ships, particularly cruisers, destroyers and submarines, but also aircraft carriers. For the US and Britain, it imposed a (temporary) check on their naval rivalry, although it must be said that the US navy continued to see Britain and her empire as a potential foe and by far the most formidable. Nevertheless, according to the Foreign Office, the outcome of the conference contributed to the 'curve of good feeling between the countries'.[237] Unfortunately, just over five years later it was crushed.

Calvin Coolidge, Harding's Vice-President, became President himself on 2 August 1923 after Harding suffered a fatal heart attack. One of his first announcements was his support of arms control, although it is not clear whether it was for moral reasons or because he was arguably the most parsimonious President the US has ever had. On 10 February 1927 he invited the British, French, Italians and Japanese to a disarmament conference at Geneva, with the intention of applying the capital ships ratio to cruisers and other auxiliary vessels.

The British reaction was cautious. The Admiralty based its position on the British reliance on trade. By 1927, Great Britain had recovered her former position as the world leader in shipping: her merchant shipping tonnage was almost twice that of the US, and made up more than one-third of the world's total.[238] Furthermore, Britain was the world's largest importer; conversely, the US exported food and was self-sufficient in oil, for both of which Britain was dependent on imports. The British Isles were therefore vulnerable to a blockade, as had been the case in the Great War, when German submarines had been slowly strangling her. For the Admiralty, these were compelling arguments for a greater number of cruisers than the Americans might desire or feel they needed. To be more precise, the Admiralty distinguished between two classes of cruiser: the so-called 'Washington-class', built up to the Washington Treaty's 10,000-ton limit and armed with 8-inch guns, which were ideal for fleet work, and which the Admiralty were willing to see fall within the 5:5:3 ratio; and those of less than 7,500 tons, with guns of 6 inches or less, which were ideal for commerce protection, being small and fast. The Admiralty wanted as little restriction as possible on numbers of the smaller class.

The Admiralty, however, did not control the Cabinet, which was hardly united in its approach to the conference. The leaders of the delegation were Lord Robert Cecil, committed to the arms-control process, and William Bridgeman, the First Lord of the Admiralty, a man of frequent indecision. Austen Chamberlain, the Foreign Secretary, was more interested in European questions, and admitted that he was not well informed on the conference issues, whilst

Winston Churchill, the Chancellor of the Exchequer, was determined to reassert the supremacy of the Royal Navy. Stanley Baldwin, the Prime Minister, hardly knew what he wanted.[239]

The Coolidge administration assumed that Britain would recognise America's right to parity in all sizes of ships. Although its position was not very strong – since 1921 the Americans had laid down only two cruisers whilst the British had laid down nine – the administration believed that 'it could get around this imbalance by using America's enormous latent power to compel the British to recognize America's right to equality'. It was believed that Great Britain would concede the *principle* of cruiser parity, as long as the US did not actually institute a building programme to match the strength of the Royal Navy. The US General Board of the Navy also saw the conference as an opportunity to reinvigorate the public's interest in naval construction.[240] The British, unintentionally, helped them to do just that.

The conference officially opened on 20 July 1927. It was supposed to discuss a number of issues, including further restrictions on capital ships and tonnage allowances for all other classes of ship. Essentially, the Americans wanted fewer but bigger cruisers, whilst the British wanted more but smaller. The US did not have to protect trade routes. Furthermore, lacking the British network of naval bases around the world, they wanted craft which could sail longer distances in case of, say, war with Japan. Britain had thousands of miles of sea routes to protect and a network of bases at which they could refuel and take on supplies. What was really at issue was the traditional conflict between the British intention to maintain their ability to enforce belligerent rights in opposition to the American desire to maintain neutral trading rights in time of war. Thus, they could not agree on cruiser limitation.[241]

Early in the negotiations, the British Cabinet had supported its two delegates in their statement to the Americans that Britain did not question their right to naval parity. Churchill, however, had never agreed, writing in June that 'There can be no parity between a Power whose Navy is its life and a Power whose Navy is only for prestige . . . It always seems to be assumed that it is our duty to humour the United States and minister to their vanity. They do nothing for us in return, but exact their last pound of flesh'[242] (clearly, Churchill was not always as pro-American as the myth implies). He saw the conference as the UK's last chance to assert 'strategic independence' from the US, and even proposed rejuvenating the Anglo-Japanese Alliance. He convinced the rest of the Cabinet that they could not agree to parity, and when Bridgeman and Cecil returned to Geneva on 28 July, they informed the Americans of this. The Americans immediately rejected the British proposals, and on 4 August the conference broke up.

As Phillips Payson O'Brien emphasises, 'the fallout from the collapse of the Geneva Conference was dramatic. For a while all trust between the British and American governments disappeared.' Insults flew: the British Foreign Secretary called the head of the American delegation a 'dirty dog', whilst the US Secretary of State accused the British of going back on their word and told Coolidge that there was no point negotiating with them. Cecil accused his own government, especially Churchill, of causing the break, saying that war was the only thing in politics that interested the Chancellor. Certainly Churchill welcomed the collapse of the conference.[243] Bridgeman seems not to have fully understood what had happened, later writing that when they returned to Geneva on 28 July, 'it was obvious that the American attitude had greatly stiffened against us, and I attribute it to the pronouncement on parity which may well have been thought a recession from our former attitude'.[244] But he blamed the Americans for the breakdown, saying that they had not prepared, and in any case had very little knowledge of cruiser limitation. Indeed,

> The real object with which they came was to try to get 'parity' on the cheap by forcing us to give up the numbers we require for security, and also to prevent us from intercepting contraband in wartime. They hoped to get a good election cry for Coolidge by saying they had not only made a further peace move, but also twisted the British Lion's tail by making him reduce his cruiser strength. If they could have got their own proposals agreed to as they stood, they would have settled, but I much doubt if they ever meant to agree to any other terms.[245]

His analysis was not far off the mark.

The US navy and the 'big navy party' were delighted by the break-down, because they now had presidential support for a huge new building programme, with Coolidge asking Congress for seventy-one new cruisers, including twenty-five of the Washington class. In March 1928 Congress authorised the construction of fifteen of the Washington-class, the largest American authorisation since the end of the Great War. Churchill had assumed that the administration would not be able to convince Congress, but he had miscalculated the depth of American anger which the British manoeuvres had inspired. Moderates in the British Cabinet now came forward and the result was an attempted Anglo-French compromise, in which gun calibre, not tonnage, would be the determinant, so that a country could have as many ten-thousand-ton cruisers as she wanted, but would be restricted in the number of ships that could carry guns larger than six inches. It was hoped that this would 'soothe the American navies'.

It did not. The Americans were by now so suspicious of, and antagonistic towards, the British that the unanimous view of the White House and the State and Navy departments was that the pro-posed compromise was 'sneaky and self-serving'. As far as the navy was concerned, this would 'neuter' a large number of their ships, since they would not be allowed to equip them with eight-inch guns, whilst prolonging the life of Great Britain's older, smaller cruisers. Coolidge himself was enraged, and on Armistice Day, 11 November 1928, he publicly condemned the British and called for American naval superiority.[246]

The British government reeled. Robert Craigie, former First Secretary at the British Embassy in Washington and now the head of the American Department of the Foreign Office,[247] had been draft-ing a magisterial memorandum on Anglo-American relations, which was now approved the following day, rapidly printed, and circulated to the Cabinet the following week. His opening sentence estab-lished the problem: 'It is probably safe to say that at no time since 1920 have Anglo-American relations been in so unsatisfactory a state as at the present moment.' He then reminded the Cabinet of some home truths, and the need to maintain good relations with the US, given their relative strengths:

Great Britain is faced in the United States of America with a phenomenon for which there is no parallel in our modern history – a
State twenty-five times as large, five times as wealthy, three times
as populous, twice as ambitious, almost invulnerable, and at least
our equal in prosperity, vital energy, technical equipment and
industrial science. This State has risen to its present state of development at a time when Great Britain is still staggering from the
effects of the superhuman effort made during the war, is loaded
with a great burden of debt and is crippled by the evil of unemployment. The interests of the two countries touch at almost every
point, for our contacts with the United States – political and economic, by land and sea, commercial and financial – are closer and
more numerous than those existing with any other foreign State.

Furthermore, 'the existence of satisfactory relations between Great
Britain and the United States must necessarily increase our influence
and prestige in the councils of Europe'. He agreed that dealing with
the US was frustrating, but 'in almost every field, the advantages
derived from mutual co-operation are greater for us than for them'.
At the same time, 'it is fully recognised that, as a general proposition,
firmness is essential in our relations with the United States. An
unnecessarily yielding attitude would not win American friendship
or respect.' In summary, Britain needed to spend a good deal of time
and effort sorting out the causes of Anglo-American antagonism
because, he pointed out starkly, 'war is *not* unthinkable between the
two countries. On the contrary, there are present all the factors which
in the past have made for wars between States.'[248]

The Cabinet took the point, and although Churchill spat and
thrashed about – Coolidge was a 'New England backwoodsman'
who would 'soon sink back into the obscurity from which only accident extracted him' – his dangerous lack of judgement had been
fully exposed. The main hope now was that the US would again fail
to build all of her allotted number of ships. Prime Minister Baldwin
decided that he should pay a visit to the US, and began dropping
hints in private and public that he would like to do so.[249] Alas for
him, the Conservatives lost the May 1929 general election to the
Labour Party, and thus on 5 June Ramsay MacDonald became Prime

Minister. For the sake of Anglo-American relations, this was fortunate, because the primary goal of his foreign policy was to remove the differences between the two countries.[250]

Herbert Hoover, elected President in November 1928, was a Quaker and a pacifist who, like Coolidge, wanted to spend as little money as possible on the armed forces. He appointed as Secretary of State Henry Stimson, who was determined to improve Anglo-American relations. (According to Sir Robert Vansittart, the Permanent Under-Secretary at the Foreign Office from 1929 to 1937, 'I never met anyone, American or British, who throughout Stimson's long life gave him less than full marks.'[251]) They wanted to settle the naval question, and Hoover came up with the 'yardstick' proposal: 'instead of using gross tonnage to establish cruiser parity, Hoover was willing to let the newer, more powerful American ships count for more than an equal tonnage of older and smaller ships'. As a result, the Royal Navy would have a higher cruiser tonnage allowance, but older vessels.

By the time the MacDonald government took over in Britain, both sides were eager to come to an agreement. MacDonald quickly made it clear to the US that Britain would accept the yardstick as the means of providing cruiser parity; to make it easier to come to an agreement, he also offered to reduce the number of cruisers to be built from seventy to fifty (admittedly by taking account of the fact that thirty-nine of Britain's battle cruisers would become obsolete in the following ten years). The warming of relations convinced MacDonald that he should visit Washington, and he did so from 4 to 10 October 1929. His purpose was to settle some outstanding problems between the two countries, especially that over cruisers. Yet, it had an importance beyond that: this was the first visit by either head of government to the other's country. It was significant that the Atlantic voyage was from east to west. Since the departure of Churchill and Coolidge from the scene, elite anti-Americanism and anglophobia had significantly lessened, at least publicly; Hoover and Stimson certainly agreed that war between the US and Great Britain was 'unthinkable'. The US navy did not share this view, though, and worked hard against any lowering of the number of cruisers to be built, but its influence was lessening, given the lack of 'crucial anti-British oxygen'.[252]

The London Naval Conference opened on 21 June 1930. It was a very different proposition from the Geneva Conference in that the preparation had been exemplary; British and American negotiators had been in contact for most of the previous nine months, and the framework of an agreement was in place even before the opening session. The result was the end of twelve years of intense naval rivalry. The key was the cruiser yardstick: the US was allowed 323,000 tons and up to eighteen Washington-class cruisers, whilst Britain got 339,000 tons but had to stop at fifteen of the big cruisers. The two sides also agreed on parity for submarines and destroyers. The agreement was rapidly approved by the Senate. The Japanese, however, were extremely unhappy, because they were again forced to limit their navy to a size smaller than those of the US and Great Britain, and to agree not to build any more Washington-class cruisers. As a result, Japanese nationalists were incensed, with unhappy consequences.[253]

IX

In spite of the cordiality at the 1930 conference, relations between the US and Great Britain during the 1930s were often fraught and even rancorous. A fundamental reason was that the US wanted to be a Great Power, with the attendant respect and deference, but it did not want the international responsibilities of such a position. A Great Power requires two things: the necessary resources and a sustained will to power. The US certainly had the resources, but she most emphatically did not have the will, as would be demonstrated in the Far East. She also wrapped herself in isolationism as though it were a duvet, ignoring the problems of the outside world and hoping that they would simply go away. But American isolationism was more complex than is usually recognised. The public wished to isolate themselves from European problems – they were told by Senator Gerald P. Nye, a Republican from North Dakota, that they had been lured into the First World War by bankers to safeguard loans to the Allies, and by arms manufacturers, the so-called 'merchants of death'.[254] Not only had nothing good come of it, more than fifty thousand American soldiers had died. Americans did not want to repeat the experience. But the US was very involved with trade in the Far East – why else the Philippines? – and she was an aggressive interventionist in Latin America. But, except for the latter, she did not wish to become militarily involved anywhere.

The US was, of course, experiencing a Depression so bad that it was capitalised, but her lack of involvement abroad had little to do with the economic and social welfare of the people. Rather, it was motivated by a geographical isolation and an abundance of natural resources which Americans frequently confused with a special dispensation from God: they were chosen, their form of government and politics was superior to all others, and if care were not taken, the contamination of the Old World could do irreparable harm to what made America great. In sum, most people saw no reason to become involved. All that should be done was to heighten the tariff walls to keep foreign goods out,[255] raise the fence against immigration to keep foreigners out,[256] and refuse to become involved abroad, whether the cause was just or unjust. Altogether, it was safer and cheaper that way. As a result, the active isolationists were able to mobilise this widespread sentiment to ensure that those who wished to become involved had little leeway to do so until very late in the day.

For Britain, relations with the US were difficult because of the combination of contempt and despair felt at the latter's inaction. Britain had myriad responsibilities but declining resources to carry them out, and the US evaded what Britain saw as the obligations of power. Britain's economic situation was such that she could no longer, after September 1931, keep the pound on the gold standard – the former symbol of her economic and international power. The floating of the pound actually stimulated economic growth, but the tax base was still not large enough to support the military forces necessary to fulfil her responsibilities. Britain was too close to Europe to ignore the Franco-German conflict, the menace of the Soviet Union and the rise of Hitler; the Suez Canal was too important to the British Empire to ignore the rise of Mussolini; and in the Far East Great Britain had extensive interests, including substantial economic interests in China, a number of colonies (such as Burma, Singapore, Malaya, North Borneo and Papua New Guinea) and the antipodean Dominions (Australia and New Zealand), all of which relied on the Royal Navy for protection. As the 1930s rolled past, Britain was increasingly faced with the possible catastrophe of a three-front war – Germany in Europe, Italy in the Mediterranean, and Japan in the Far East. She could not seem to convince the Americans that US interests were also involved, that such a conflagration could engulf them too, and that they should therefore help to prevent it. But Great Britain also tended to conflate her imperial interests with those of the rest of the right-thinking world, as the US would often do after 1945, and thus could not understand that, as far as the US was concerned, Britain was merely requiring her help to save the Empire, something she was not prepared to do.

During the 1930s, the Far East would prove to be a more important region for the relations of the two countries than Europe. Fundamentally, the US had little interest in Europe beyond business or commerce, and the unfolding of the European tragedy was a matter of indifference to many Americans – or, if not precisely indifference, it was a matter in which they believed that they should not become involved. The Far East was different. The US was hardly in the same imperial league as Britain, but she possessed the Hawaiian Islands, the Philippines and Guam, as well as long-standing commercial interests in China and elsewhere. Nevertheless, it was an episode in the Far East which convinced many British policy-makers that the US was worse than useless in a foreign crisis.

On 18 September 1931, violence erupted in Manchuria between the Japanese Kwantung Army, a private force which guarded the Japanese-owned railways, and troops loyal to the local Chinese warlord, who in turn owed fealty to China's leader, Chiang Kai-shek. Regular Japanese troops were then sent from their colony of Korea, and by mid-October they controlled most of the Manchurian railway system and were fanning out to conquer the remainder of the province. The Japanese had therefore violated the Nine-Power Treaty (one of the Washington treaties), which guaranteed the integrity of China, as well as the Covenant of the League of Nations, on which all the signatories had agreed, so on 21 September 1931 China had appealed to the League. Britain was in the midst of an acute financial crisis – the very day that China made its appeal was when she was forced off the gold standard – and an associated political crisis. But even had she not been, she could do little. As Vansittart wrote, '*We* are incapable of checking Japan in any way if she really means business and has sized us up, as she certainly has done. Therefore we must eventually be done for in the Far East unless the United States are eventually prepared to use force.'[257] Besides this, as Secretary of State Stimson pointed out in a press conference on 5 November, public opinion in Great Britain was pro-Japanese, as, it was suspected, was Sir John Simon, the Foreign Secretary.[258] In addition, some British officials felt that the Chinese had behaved so badly that it was not surprising that the Japanese had reacted as they had done. In mid-November, when the Cabinet met to discuss its options, it decided that it could not provide military forces. The only alternative was to conciliate the Japanese.

Stimson's first inclination was to act, but he was stymied by President Hoover, who was acutely aware of the support for isolationism. Although he thought that the US had to do something 'to uphold the moral foundations of international life', he would not even agree to economic sanctions through fear that they would lead to war. Nevertheless, when the Council of the League met in November and December, Stimson sent Charles G. Dawes, but Hoover would not allow him to join in the discussions, for fear of outraging the isolationists in Congress. Instead, he 'simply paced the lobby to show American solidarity with the League'.[259] This did not get things very far. American policy appeared so unfocused and lame that Stanley Baldwin, in his new role as Lord President of the Council, burst out to a friend: 'You will get nothing out of Washington but words, big words, but only words.'[260]

As it happened, Stimson was about to provide some words. He rose at 6 a.m. on 2 January 1932 and drafted what became known as the Doctrine of Nonrecognition, or the Stimson Doctrine. The key phrase was that the US 'did not intend to recognize any situation, treaty or agreement which may be brought about by means contrary to the Pact of Paris', that is, by armed aggression. He asked the British and French to join him, expecting the British at least to agree. They did not. Simon thought that they should work through the League, and joining the Americans in this announcement would complicate matters.[261] (Richard N. Gardner has argued that 'In no country of the world, perhaps, had there been greater devotion to the League of Nations, or greater interest generally in international institutions' than in Britain.[262]) On 7 January the Stimson Doctrine was delivered to the Japanese. It contained tough words, but there was no action to follow it up. Vansittart's assessment on 1 February was that 'It is universally assumed that the US will never use force.'[263] It was this episode as much as anything which convinced many British foreign policy-makers that it was prudent to work on the assumption that the US would shy away from standing up to the Japanese. They were correct. Very soon Japanese troops were landing in Shanghai, where both the US and Great Britain had extensive interests. Six per cent of British foreign investment was in China, with three-fifths of this in Shanghai, then Asia's greatest seaport.[264] On 5 February US and Royal Navy warships arrived to help defend the International Settlement, which included twenty-five to thirty thousand women and children. But the Japanese took the city in a bloody attack in which thousands of Chinese were killed (the latter put up a stiffer resistance than anyone had predicted), and the British and Americans restricted themselves to rescuing the foreign nationals. By March the conquest was complete, and a puppet government declared the independence of Manchukuo (Manchu-land).

Over Manchuria, the US had largely refrained from involvement with another country in a diplomatic crisis. In 1933 the new President, Franklin Delano Roosevelt, positively wrenched the US out of international economic discussions as well and then closed the door, thereby making it clear to the rest of the world that his primary focus was on domestic policy, and that he had little interest in events 'abroad'. Perhaps not surprisingly, he saw his main challenge as the breakdown of the American economy, with one-third of the workforce unemployed, a banking system which had collapsed, and a New York Stock Exchange which had suspended trading on 4 March 1933, the day of his inauguration. He had given a warning in his inaugural address when he had said that 'Our international trade relations, though vastly important, are in point of time and necessity secondary to the establishment of a sound national economy.'[265] Yet, he was so prone to hiding what he really thought – if, indeed, he himself always knew what he really thought – that it is no wonder that foreigners often found him unfathomable. According to David M. Kennedy, he believed that inflation was vital to bring the US out of the Depression. An inflated currency would also make the national debt produced by the sharp rise in public spending easier to repay.[266] This policy was partly motivated by pressure from Democratic majorities in Congress who were acutely concerned about the devastation of the rural economy.[267] However, Roosevelt was constrained by the gold standard, which could require deflating the economy by cutting back on public spending and balancing the budget, as Hoover had done, in order to retain confidence in the currency. Therefore, the US went off gold on 18 April. Nevertheless, when at a press conference the following day he was asked, 'Mr President, is it still the desire of the United States to go back on the international gold standard?', he answered, 'Absolutely; one of the things we hope to do is to get the world as a whole back on some form of gold standard.' A month later, in a round-robin letter to the sovereigns and presidents of the world, he insisted that they 'must establish order in place of the present chaos by a stabilization of currencies'.[268]

A World Economic Conference, one of the primary goals of which was to resuscitate the gold standard, met in London in July. This had been planned for some months, and the delegates naturally expected the US to take an important part. Roosevelt's radio message to the conference on 3 July, therefore, was a 'bombshell': the US would not return to the gold standard in the foreseeable future, because 'The sound internal economic system of a Nation is a greater factor in its well-being than the price of its currency in changing terms of the currencies of other Nations.' Furthermore, the US would not co-operate in re-establishing stable exchange rates, because 'old fetishes of so-called international bankers are being replaced by efforts to plan national currencies'.[269] And with that, the conference fell into acrimonious uproar. Prime Minister MacDonald expressed 'the most bitter resentment' against the man who just weeks earlier in Washington had personally assured him that he favoured stabilisation, whilst Neville Chamberlain, the Chancellor of the Exchequer, privately called the message 'most offensive'.[270] According to

Roosevelt himself, 'The immediate result was a somewhat petulant outcry that I had wrecked the Conference.'[271] Alonzo L. Hamby is much harsher: Roosevelt's performance revealed him at his worst, 'impetuous and uncomprehending, taking a monumentally important decision in isolation, disregarding his most competent advisers, composing the most important diplomatic document of his short presidency in a fit of petulance'.[272] Roosevelt's withdrawal signalled the last international attempt to end the Depression, since without the US, which had the largest economy in the world, it would have been very difficult to achieve.

For most of the remainder of the decade, relations between the US and Britain, at any level beyond the mundane, were episodic and usually fruitless. Consider a series of crises. First, the Abyssinian crisis. On 3 October 1935, in order to further Mussolini's desire for a New Roman Empire, Italian forces attacked Abyssinia (Ethiopia) from their East African colony of Eritrea. The League of Nations imposed economic sanctions on Italy, particularly an embargo on oil, and several times the Foreign Office asked the Americans whether they would abide by these sanctions. Even before the League acted, Roosevelt had embargoed arms, ammunitions and guns against both Italy and Abyssinia, but he did nothing about sanctions, other than to ask the oil companies to please not sell to Italy. In 1937 came the *Panay* crisis. On 12 December, a Japanese plane flying along the Yangtze River in China attacked an American gunboat, the *Panay*; at the same time, Japanese shore batteries shelled two Royal Navy riverboats, the *Bee* and the *Ladybird* (unusually non-assertive names for the Royal Navy). The *Panay* was escorting American-owned tankers and evacuating American Embassy staff; when those who could dived into the water to swim to safety, they were machine-gunned, resulting in three deaths and almost fifty wounded. Roosevelt immediately demanded an apology and reparations, and the Japanese government complied. The British hoped that Washington would now use its strength to draw a line in the sand, and suggested a joint response. Neville Chamberlain, by now the Prime Minister, wrote to his sister that 'It is always best & safest to count on *nothing* from the Americans except words' – thus far, rather like Baldwin's exclamation – but Chamberlain continued, 'but at this moment they are nearer "doing something" than I have ever known them and I cant [*sic*] altogether repress hopes.' These hopes were crushed, as the US refused.[273] Did anyone remember the sinking of the *Lusitania* by the Germans in May 1915, which the British had vainly hoped would bring the US into the war?

Of course, in neither case did the US want to become involved in a foreign war. Partly because of the conviction of a majority of Americans that they had been tricked into the Great War, great efforts were made by their legislators to ensure that it would not happen again. They passed a series of Neutrality Acts, forbidding Americans in a number of ways from becoming involved with belligerent foreigners. The first was in reaction to the cession of war debt repayments, with Britain making her last payment in December 1933 (only Finland completely repaid her debt). In April 1934 Roosevelt signed the Johnson Debt Default Act, which prohibited loans to any nation which had ceased repayment of First World War loans from the US government. The following August Senator Gerald P. Nye sponsored a Neutrality Act which was to last for six months: there was a mandatory embargo on 'arms, ammunition, or implements of war', a prohibition on ships carrying munitions to belligerent states, a denial of passports to Americans wishing to enter war zones, and discretion to the President to withdraw protection for Americans travelling on belligerent ships.[274]

On 3 October 1935, as noted above, Italian forces attacked Ethiopia, and Roosevelt rapidly invoked the Nye legislation; he also sought to levy a 'moral embargo' on general trade with the belligerents.[275] The following February Congress passed a second Neutrality Act which extended the 1935 Act and in addition forbade loans to belligerents and arms sales to states which entered an existing war. On 18 July 1936 the Spanish army in Spanish Morocco, led by General Francisco Franco, rose in revolt against the democratically elected government. The following January Congress passed a third Neutrality Act, in this case extending the arms embargo to civil wars, as well as giving the President discretion to withhold raw materials from belligerents.

The Spanish Civil War provides an example of Britain and the US working together during the 1930s. What they agreed on in this case was to do nothing. Britain and France proclaimed a non-importation agreement, with the intention of containing the war by refusing to supply the belligerents with *matériel*, and in August 1936 Roosevelt signed up America, again announcing a 'moral embargo' on shipments to either side. The result, of course, was that the Soviet Union supplied the government – which gave the democracies another excuse for refusing to do the same, the Germans and the Italians supplied Franco's rebels, and the conflagration horrified Europe. As one historian put it, the 'prevailing attitude in the State Department was that the United States did not have the available materials, the will, or the experience to disconnect its European policy from that of the British Foreign Office'.[276] It was ironic that Great Britain, which so wanted the US to acknowledge her responsibilities as a Great Power, had herself failed to act.

X

The time was fast approaching when the Americans would no longer be able to ignore what was going on across the Atlantic Ocean. The US's situation and its reaction to events were very different in 1939–41 from what they had been in 1914–17. In the years before the First World War, the US government and public largely ignored Europe; once the war began, there was still the conviction on the part of both that the country could remain neutral. The scene and the play were rather different for the Second World War. For one thing, it was clear to many Americans that there was an increasingly serious crisis in Europe – the war did not apparently blow up out of a clear sky as had been the case in 1914. But a more significant difference was that the US President decided at some point (probably in 1938) that, sooner or later, the US would have to fight. Because of this conviction, the American reaction to the desperate needs of Great Britain was lifesaving.

In retrospect, the march to war looks inexorable, and perhaps it was. But during the second half of the 1930s, and certainly under Chamberlain, the British government tried, with one expedient after another, to satisfy what many saw as legitimate German grievances.

They accepted the German army's taking up residence again in the Rhineland in March 1936 and the Anschluss with Austria in March 1938, even though both were in contravention of the Versailles Treaty. At Munich in September 1938 they agreed to the ripping of the Sudetenland out of Czechoslovakia. The balance against Germany was France, and the British link with France was ambiguous. On the one hand, they did not like France once again assuming an almost hegemonic position on the Continent; on the other, if there was a war, they wanted France as a shield against the onslaught whilst they prepared themselves. Again, the idea of encouraging a two-front war against Germany was difficult, because the Chamberlain government disliked the Bolsheviks as much as, if not more than, the Nazis. Furthermore, by 1938 Stalin had purged most of his generals and a substantial proportion of his army officer corps – was the Red Army even a viable fighting force any more?

The theory that Germany was a greater danger than Japan had been adopted as far back as 1934. Since Britain did not have the resources to fight two major wars in two theatres at the same time, it followed that Japan would have to be accommodated. The implication was that relations with Washington (and China) would be adversely affected, given the US's opinion of Japan, and the fact that Britain had abrogated the Anglo-Japanese Alliance at her insistence. Vansittart was not too unhappy about this, writing in early February 1934 that 'I will only repeat my strengthened conviction that we have been too tender, not to say too subservient, with the US for a long time past. It is we who have made all the advances, and received nothing in return.'[277] Yet, it increasingly seemed that war with Japan was not unlikely, and there were only two possible reactions: the US would join Britain against Japan in order to defend her own interests in the Far East, and they would defeat Japan; or the US would remain uninvolved, and the Japanese would destroy the British Empire in the Far East. The best that Britain could do over the decade was to try to keep their relations with the US in the Pacific on an even keel.

According to David Reynolds, over the winter of 1937–8 Roosevelt 'inclined increasingly towards carefully defined co-operation with the British'. In January 1938 he adopted the suggestion of Sumner

Welles, the Under-Secretary of State and a man profoundly suspicious of Britain, that he must bring American moral authority to bear and try to organise an international settlement in order to determine the 'essential and fundamental principles to be observed in international relations'. He proposed a two-step plan: first, he would call a meeting in Washington of ten small, neutral nations to draft such principles; then the results of their discussions would be circulated to other countries. Ideally, the culmination would be an international conference, at which all would agree on the draft principles. Once they were agreed, political adjustments would be easier. Welles and a colleague wanted to spring it on the world, thereby precluding any obstruction by London, but Secretary of State Cordell Hull insisted, and Roosevelt agreed, that London must approve the plan first.[278]

On 12 January at about 5:15, according to Sir Alexander Cadogan, who had succeeded Vansittart as Permanent Under Secretary at the Foreign Office, 'telegrams began to roll in from Washington – personal messages from Roosevelt to P.M. [Prime Minister Chamberlain]. Roosevelt has wild ideas about formulating a world settlement! But must know by *Monday* [17 January] whether we agree he should. Sent telegram down to P.M. with a hurried minute. This is not the way to transact such business!'[279] Welles had carried the message to Sir Ronald Lindsey, the British Ambassador, who had sent it on to the Foreign Office with his endorsement; delay or destructive criticism would accomplish little and create a very bad impression, he argued, and he urged a quick and cordial acceptance of 'this invaluable initiative'.[280] This, of course, is precisely what Chamberlain was not prepared to do. He had great hopes for discussions with Germany and Italy, and he feared that Roosevelt's initiative might cut across his own. Without consulting anyone else, therefore, he replied to the President the following day and asked whether he would 'consider holding his hand' whilst the British tackled 'some of the problems piecemeal'. When the Foreign Secretary, Anthony Eden, discovered what he had done, he was horrified, believing that the President had been snubbed, and urged that he be given greater encouragement.[281] (The incident contributed to Eden's decision to resign the following month.)

Roosevelt agreed to delay his initiative, but historians differ as to whether he was disappointed at Chamberlain's reaction. Reynolds believes that Roosevelt was never very enthusiastic about Welles's plan in the first place, and only suggested it because nothing else seemed to be happening to forestall a slip into war; he knew very little of Chamberlain's manoeuvres. He points out that on 14 January Roosevelt, once he had learned of Chamberlain's plans, 'readily agree[d]' to postpone action for a brief time. As a result of Eden's urging on 15 January, the Foreign Office on 21 January invited Roosevelt to proceed with his plan. However, nothing happened for nearly a fortnight, when Hitler's purge of the Berlin bureaucracy on 4 February killed it off. A positive result of the whole episode, however, was an informal agreement, suggested by Welles and Hull, that there be a greater sharing of political and diplomatic intelligence, particularly about Europe.[282]

The Munich crisis in September 1938 shocked Roosevelt. He had in general terms approved of what Chamberlain was trying to achieve in appeasing Hitler and Mussolini – and it is worth remembering that it was not then the derogatory term it has since become – although he had his doubts as to both its practicality and its morality. He now decided that war would come, that Hitler wanted to rule the world, and that if France and Great Britain were defeated, Germany would next turn on the US. The Germans could refuse to buy American and Latin American exports, which would seriously injure some of the Latin American states; he and his advisers were also concerned about Nazi propaganda, and about German military and commercial penetration of South America. 'Above all, F.D.R. feared that Germany might combine its subversion in Latin America with a direct invasion of the Western Hemisphere, perhaps after neutralizing the British and French fleets and securing European possessions in West Africa or the Caribbean.' What was particularly worrying was the lack of a US Atlantic fleet: since 1919 the US navy had concentrated on the Pacific Ocean, probably because Britain secured the Atlantic for both countries. This defect was remedied with the creation of an Atlantic fleet, which engaged in manoeuvres off the East Coast in February 1939.[283]

Roosevelt concluded that he had to aid Britain, although he was still severely constrained by an isolationist Congress bowing to iso-lationist public opinion. But during the period before Pearl Harbor, he succeeded in providing aid and comfort in a number of ways, both secret and open. The secret discussions and arrangements were mil-itary in nature and began in January 1938 (see Section XI); the open arrangements, which took time and required Roosevelt to squirm like an eel, were primarily financial, and began in 1940.

The chronology of events was as follows. In March 1939 all hope of avoiding war disappeared when the Germans marched into Prague and annexed the remainder of Czechoslovakia. Both France and Britain then gave a guarantee to Poland, and to Romania the fol-lowing month. On 23 August the USSR and Germany signed the Non-Aggression Pact, and nine days later the Germans invaded Poland. Two days after that, on 3 September, Great Britain declared war on Germany. Then came the 'Phoney War', which for Great Britain ended on 9 April 1940 with the German invasion of Denmark and its conquest in four hours, followed by Norway's surrender six weeks later. On 10 May the Blitzkrieg (lightning war) against the Low Countries and France began; it took four days to take care of the Netherlands, whilst Belgium surrendered on 28 May. The British Expeditionary Force was driven back to the Channel, and from 26 May to 3 June, 338,226 British, French and other Allied troops were evacuated from Dunkirk. Some British civilian vessels helped in this operation. The resulting 'Dunkirk spirit' significantly boosted civilian morale, and helped to involve the whole population in 'their' war. Then, on 27 June, the unthinkable happened: France surrendered. At war with both Germany and Italy, Great Britain now stood alone, the only enemy of Germany which remained unconquered.

XI

The Anglo-American relationship during the war, whilst by general agreement the closest and most successful in history, was neverthe-less bedevilled by widespread and apparently irradicable American suspicions of British motives. Their intensity varied. The relation-ship was closest in the European theatre; in the Far East, though, relations were often dire. The Commander-in-Chief of the US Fleet, Admiral Ernest J. King, was 'the most even-tempered man in the Navy. He is always in a rage.' He also 'had the greatest contempt for civilians and said that they should be told nothing until the war was over, and then only who had won'. King was convinced that the British were manipulating the Americans to recover their empire, and subordinates tend to take their cues from their commander. Reportedly, there was one Combined Chiefs of Staff meeting over Burma when 'Brooke got nasty and King got good and sore. King almost climbed over the table at Brooke. God, he was mad.'[284]

The development of the Anglo-American wartime relationship began whilst the US was still neutral. During 1937 the British Admiralty became increasingly convinced that they would have to fight a three-front war against the fleets of Germany, Italy and Japan, and their prime interest was to secure US help. Although the US had concentrated on country-by-country war plans, with the most likely enemy being Japan, in late 1937 the US navy began to anticipate a two-front war against Germany and Japan, and it too wanted to explore whether co-operation with Great Britain would be sensible and useful. It pressed Roosevelt, who, alarmed by the *Panay* incident on 12 December, agreed to the British suggestion of naval staff talks. The following month Captain Royal Ingersoll, the Director of Naval Plans, travelled to London to meet with his opposite number, Captain Thomas Phillips. The US insisted that the talks were non-committal, and thus the immediate outcome was limited, but the two sides exchanged information on, for example, fleet sizes, ship construction, and strategy and tactics against Germany and Japan. Arrangements were also made for the periodic updating of this type of technical information.

With 1939 and the annexation of Czechoslovakia by Germany, the tempo of co-operation gradually quickened. On 19 March the Foreign Office invited the US to resume naval talks. Two days later Roosevelt agreed, if they were kept secret – he feared congressional uproar if word got out – and held in Washington. As it happened, the British Admiralty at that point did not see the need for talks, since discussions had been held only two months before, but some weeks later it reconsidered because of uncertainty about what resources

Britain could devote to the Far East, given the likely threat in the Mediterranean. In mid-June, therefore, Commander T.C. Hampton travelled to Washington. To maintain secrecy, the discussions were held in the home of Admiral William Leahy, the Chief of Naval Operations, who was very pro-British. Hampton was undoubtedly relieved to discover that the two navies were thinking along the same lines. If there was a European war, the US was to concentrate its main fleet in Hawaii to deter Japan, whilst offering some cruiser assistance and the patrolling of the western Atlantic; there might, he thought, also be some help with the defence of Singapore. Another visitor that summer was King George VI. Whilst he was hardly in a position to speak for his government, he could return home with Roosevelt's outline of the help he planned to give to Britain, which included an Atlantic patrol. Roosevelt also indicated an interest in establishing some US bases in Newfoundland and the Caribbean.[285]

With the outbreak of war, the British Cabinet decided that it had to prepare for a three-year war, although the Treasury thought that they had resources for only two years. The assumption – hope – was that if worse came to worst, they could call upon the US, but, of course the latter's Neutrality Act barred the sale of arms to belligerents. On 21 September the President therefore began manoeuvres to change some of its provisions, although repeal would have been too long and bloody a process, given the strength of isolationist sentiment. He rapidly decided to leave the matter in the hands of the Senate Foreign Relations Committee, which at least ensured less of a senatorial knee-jerk reaction against the supposed enhancement of presidential powers. By 2 November the revision had been approved by Congress, and on the 4th the Act was signed by Roosevelt: the embargo against arms sales was repealed, but purchasers would have to pay cash for them – credit from either the US Treasury or private bankers was absolutely forbidden – and carry the goods away on their own ships (the 'cash-and-carry' provision).[286] The British Purchasing Commission was immediately set up, since Great Britain could now place orders in the US. Only time would tell for how long she would be able to pay for them.

On 15 May 1940, five days after the Germans had launched the Blitzkrieg and five days after he had become Prime Minister,

Churchill wrote to Roosevelt asking for 'the loan of forty or fifty of your older destroyers to bridge the gap between what we have now and the large new construction we put in hand at the beginning of the war'. They were required for anti-submarine escorts in the Atlantic, as well as generally for patrols against invasion. The former was important in keeping open the supply lanes to the Western Hemisphere, crucial now that the German drive to the sea had blocked off European sources of supply, and the Mediterranean and Suez Canal were effectively closed to merchant shipping.[287] Germany might destroy Britain either with guns or by starvation. It was difficult for Roosevelt to act. Popular sympathy and support were undoubtedly on the side of Great Britain, but Americans did not want to get involved in the war, and provision of the destroyers might well be seen as the first step. The fall of France at the end of June had shocked and shaken the US population. It also encouraged strong doubts that Britain could survive, with 95 per cent of Americans believing that she would be defeated[288] – and if she could not survive, it would be better if the US stayed out of it. Furthermore, with the passage of the National Defense Act in July, the US herself began to rearm, and it seemed foolish beyond per-mission to give existing American arms to a country which seemed to be on the verge of defeat.

However, the Battle of Britain demonstrated that Britain could survive. Since mid-June 1940 German aircraft had been attacking Channel shipping, but on 10 July wave after wave of German bombers, escorted by fighter aircraft, began bombing British coastal radar stations and airfields: they were preparing for a cross-Channel invasion, code-named Sealion. '"The Führer has ordered me to crush Britain with my Luftwaffe," German Air Minister Hermann Goering told his generals. "By means of hard blows I plan to have this enemy . . . down on his knees in the nearest future."'[289] But Britain was saved by the Hurricane and especially the Spitfire fighter aircraft, which had only entered service in any numbers in 1939, and by the pilots who flew them, celebrated by Churchill in a speech to the House of Commons: 'Never in the field of human conflict was so much owed by so many to so few.'[290] What gave the pilots a fight-ing chance was radar (radio detection and ranging). By 31 May 1935, a basic radar transmitter and receiver were operating at Orford Ness on the East Coast, and by 3 September 1939, eighteen stations throughout England were connected to Fighter Command at Stanmore, with two more operating in Scotland. Radar revealed the massing of German bombers in the Low Countries, enabling the pilots of Fighter Command to be directed to intercept them. In August 1940 the Luftwaffe began to target Royal Air Force airfields, but when this proved difficult to achieve they turned to bombing civilians in London, in the 'Blitz'.[291] On 7 September 1940 300 bombers, escorted by 600 fighters, attacked the capital; huge fires were left burning in the East End, providing beacons for the follow-up night attack by 180 aircraft. Until mid-November, an average of 200 aircraft bombed London each night but one, resulting in the deaths of over 43,000 civilians and a further 139,000 injured. 'Americans followed the drama keenly, tuning their radios to Edward R. Murrow's nicotine-lubricated voice reporting from BBC House. "London is burning," Murrow began nightly in his trademark funereal tone, and Americans anxiously awaited the apparently inevitable announcement of Britain's final subjugation.'[292] Secretary of State Hull wrote in his memoirs that 'Never have I admired a people more than I admired the British in the summer and autumn of 1940. Each man and woman and even the children seemed to realize that upon their indomitable spirit depended not only their own fate but also that of the whole democratic world.'[293] On 31 July Churchill pleaded again for the destroyers, which were said to be intended for use in the Channel against a German amphibious invasion.[294] Roosevelt was caught between isolationist attacks at home and the catastrophe of seeing Great Britain going down to defeat, but his conviction that if the latter happened the US herself would be in great peril decided him. (Hull referred to 'the spectre of Britain standing alone between the conqueror and ourselves'.[295]) He was aided in this decision by the British triumph against the Luftwaffe. On 17 September Sealion was indefinitely postponed because of the inability of the Luftwaffe to guarantee control of the air.[296] Great Britain would live to fight another day.

On 2 September the two countries signed the destroyers-for-bases agreement: Britain would receive the destroyers in exchange for ninety-nine-year leases on eight bases stretching from Newfoundland to the Caribbean. In campaigning for the presidential election due on 5 November Roosevelt said the deal enhanced American national security because the Caribbean was her inner defensive line. His concern, and that of others in the government, had been height-ened by the fear that the French and Dutch colonies in the West Indies would fall into German hands, since the Germans were already making threatening comments and encouraging pro-Axis activities in a number of Central and South American countries.[297] Indeed, when Churchill explained the agreement to the House of Commons on 20 August he emphasised the US need for the bases: 'we learned that anxiety was . . . felt in the United States about the air and naval defence of their Atlantic seaboard'. But, he continued, 'There is, of course, no question of any transference of sover-eignty – that has never been suggested.' Rather, Britain was granting 'defence facilities to the United States on a 99 years' lease-hold basis . . . Undoubtedly this process means that . . . the British Empire and the United States . . . will have to be somewhat mixed up together in some of their affairs for mutual and general advan-tage.'[298] Even though a number of people saw it as a hard bargain for Britain, the Cabinet viewed the arrangement not merely from the point of view of exchanging destroyers for naval bases. Much more significant was the hope (or even assumption) that it 'might well prove to be the first step in constituting an Anglo-Saxon *bloc*, or indeed a decisive point in history'.[299] It was just as well that the British government saw the destroyers more as a symbol of American support than as a valuable contribution to the Royal Navy: some of the ships were in such bad shape that they barely made it across the Atlantic, and only nine were in use by the end of the year.[300] Britain had received desperately needed symbolic sup-port, but the US, in practical terms, came out rather better in this particular deal.

The military relationship continued to develop. In September the two air forces agreed that both would train their air crews in the US; arrangements were also made to repair British warships in American shipyards. Then, in January 1941, an event of much greater importance took place: high-level American and British officers met secretly in Washington to develop a combined strategic plan, to be followed if the US joined the war. The suggestion had come from Admiral Harold R. Stark, the US Chief of Naval Operations, who wrote in a memorandum in November that American war plans, which were designed for war against a specific country and colour-coded (RED for Great Britain and ORANGE for Japan, for example), were badly out of date. He believed that they needed to be replaced by plans which would take into account the possibility of war against the entire Axis coalition of Germany, Italy and Japan. They also had to consider the British request for the revival of the Anglo-American naval staff talks which had taken place in January 1938 and June 1939, and, as requested in those talks but not provided, US naval assistance at Singapore. The Americans were suspicious of this final point – they were not prepared to help to defend the Empire. American military officials warned the negotiators that the proposals would probably 'have been drawn up with chief regard for the support of the British Commonwealth. Never absent from British minds are their post-war interests, commercial and military.'[301] The double standard is notable.

Stark believed that American security had always – and still did – 'depend upon a strong British navy and empire to maintain the balance of power and preclude the emergence of a hegemonic European power'. Support for Britain against Germany was therefore a vital American defence need. Without Britain, the US would be 'alone, and at war with the world'. Furthermore, Britain could not defeat Germany by herself, but would need American land, as well as naval, forces for a land offensive. What Stark proposed was Plan Dog: the US should assume the lead role in a strategic defensive policy against Japan in the Pacific, but her main focus, in conjunction with Britain, should be combined offensive action in the Atlantic/European theatre against Germany, the more dangerous foe for both countries. He called for high-level staff talks to gain agreement for the plan before the US entered the war. For the British, the Far East and the Pacific were important because of the interests of the Dominions and the wide geographical range of the British Empire. Malaya was crucial because of her raw materials, and the base at Singapore was absolutely vital to the defence of the entire region. However, the Americans refused to accept this as a commanding principle. Churchill, much as he was committed to the safety of Singapore, was even more concerned to lure the US into active participation; the Cabinet had already decided to instruct the British officers at the staff talks to abandon their call for American help at Singapore and to agree to American strategic plans.[302] They did so, but they also indirectly received help for Singapore, in that the US navy would for the present keep its main fleet in the Pacific to deter Japan, but some ships would steam to the Atlantic, which in turn would allow Britain to shift her ships to Singapore. (This was to no avail, however: Singapore fell to the Japanese on 15 February 1942.) The resulting agreement, known as ABC-1, was signed in March 1941. It became the strategic basis for the formal alliance, and for the conduct of the war.[303]

March 1941 was also notable for the equally important passage of the Lend–Lease Act. At its most basic, this provided a set of procedures intended to facilitate the transfer of American goods and services to Great Britain and the Commonwealth (and others, including the USSR) to enable them to fight the Axis powers. Separate from the procedures was the financial underpinning; separate again was the 'Consideration', which Britain was to render in recompense. Lend–Lease inherited a weight of history which determined its shape, the use made of it, and the results flowing from that use. There are immense resonances between Anglo-American financial relations in the First and Second World Wars, both in problems which arose and solutions imposed. Furthermore, Wilsonian aspirations unfulfilled in the First, such as free trade and freedom of the seas, were achieved in the Second, primarily by the use of American financial leverage against Britain.

As noted above, the modifications made to the Neutrality Act in November 1939 allowed Britain to buy munitions and supplies in the US, as long as she could pay for them and carry them away in her own ships. The question was how to pay for them? Because she was forbidden to borrow money in the US, Britain had to depend on shipping gold and mobilising securities to sell in New York, both of which she had done during the First World War. At the outbreak of the Second, Britain had gold and dollar reserves totalling £503 million ($2,028 million), which were gradually run down until, by March 1941, they stood at £70 million ($282 million); at their lowest point that spring, they stood at just £3 million ($12 million). These could be replaced only by acquiring more gold from South African mines – if the ships got through – or by earning dollars from exports, which became increasingly difficult as industry and labour were mobilised almost exclusively for war-related production. As for the securities, until the market collapsed with the invasion of Denmark and Norway, the British carried out a steady stream of sales. American officials made it clear that they expected the British to sell not only US but also South American securities, as well as direct investments in the US, such as insurance companies and manufacturing plant.[304]

In Great Britain during the Phoney War the Treasury emphasised economy, but once the Germans began their Blitzkrieg, the danger to Britain became so great and the need for munitions and supplies so urgent that on 24 May 1940, the Cabinet threw financial prudence to the winds: the government would buy all of the munitions and supplies which the US could provide until the dollars and gold ran out. R.S. Sayers points out, 'it seems likely that Treasury officials reconciled themselves to such prodigality only by private expectations that sooner or later America would loosen the purse-strings'.[305]

Nevertheless, massive orders now had to be paid for, especially as, after Dunkirk, most Americans thought that Britain was about to lose the war. Businessmen and manufacturers were no exception, and they demanded cash in advance and refused to sign contracts that called for payment only upon delivery of the goods. Thus, Great Britain's proportional costs accelerated, and the Treasury was forced to make hard decisions as to which orders were vital and which merely desirable. Naturally, the British government wanted to turn to the US for financial help; naturally, the American government wished to discourage this. Roosevelt, for one, did not believe that the British were in quite such dire straits as they claimed; he is quoted as commenting, after a quick glance at a US Treasury estimate of British dollar resources, 'Well, they aren't bust – there's lots of money there.'[306]

The British ambassador to the US, now Lord Lothian, urged

Churchill to make a personal appeal to Roosevelt once the 5 November 1940 election was over. Churchill would have to present a synoptic, wide-ranging view: it would call for help with shipping, which concerned the Prime Minister and others, and for financial help, which concerned the Treasury and others; and it would show the interdependence of British needs. The hope was that, having won the election and an unprecedented third term as President, Roosevelt would be more open to the British arguments. Therefore, the letter 'stressed very frankly our need for American support in obtaining the Irish naval bases, in guarding Singapore, in getting more ships and above all in buying munitions and aircraft on credit. It is intended to make R. feel that if we go down, the responsibility will be America's.'[307] It arrived in the Caribbean on 9 December. According to Harry Hopkins, Roosevelt's aide and confidant, the President 'read and re-read the letter and for about two days seemed unsure of what to do . . . Then the following day he came up with the Lend–Lease idea.' His Treasury Secretary, Henry Morgenthau, Jr., wrote in his diary that the President had told him that 'I have been thinking very hard on this trip about what we should do for England, and it seems to me that the thing to do is to get away from a dollar sign.'[308] Morgenthau was enthusiastic about the idea, and the President announced his own views to a press conference on 17 December (although 'announced' is probably too straightforward a word for the hints and suggestions which he employed). He used to good effect the so-called 'fire-hose analogy', first suggested to him the previous summer by Harold Ickes, the Secretary of the Interior, another close aide. The US would take over from Britain her orders for munitions and

> enter into some kind of arrangement for their use by the British on the grounds that it was the best thing for American defence, with the understanding that when the show was over, we would get repaid sometime in kind, thereby leaving out the dollar mark . . . If his neighbour's house was on fire, and the neighbour wanted to borrow his garden hose, he would not say that the hose had cost $15 and that he wanted $15 for it; rather, he would loan the hose and reclaim it after the fire.[309]

Nevertheless, there had to be some recompense – Congress would not agree to the scheme otherwise. Each country which received aid had to sign a Master Lend–Lease Agreement. It was almost a year before the agreement, then called the Mutual Aid (Lend–Lease) Agreement, with Great Britain was signed, with the stumbling block being the question of the 'Consideration'. Countries had to agree not to use Lend–Lease goods 'to enable their exporters to enter new markets or to extend their export trade at the expense of the United States exporters', nor could scarce materials of any kind be used to manufacture goods for export. In other words, the Americans were deeply suspicious that Great Britain would take advantage of American generosity to safeguard or expand commercial interests at the expense of American business. Therefore, the British had to mortgage their future.[310] Where London baulked, however, was at the American request that Britain agree (in Article VII) to the prohibition of discrimination in either country against any product originating in the other. In other words, Great Britain would be required to abandon 'imperial preference', by which members of the British Empire and Commonwealth set agreed preferential tariffs, and the closed Sterling Area, within which other currencies were tied to the pound. Instead, she had to embrace multilateralism, but would still face very high American tariffs. For the Americans, this would make it a level field for all; for the British, weakened by war, it would unfairly open up their markets to the dominant power of American business and commerce. The result could well be devastating for British industry and commerce. After extremely tough negotiations, the threat of the fragmentation of the Churchill coalition government and his resulting brinksmanship, a compromise was reached and the agreement was signed on 23 February 1942. However, the Americans would return to the subject at the end of the war, this time with more success.

Meanwhile, during the year of Lend–Lease negotiations, the links between the two countries tightened. In early July 1941 the US took her first step towards active intervention in the war when she sent troops to Iceland to join the British soldiers already there. Then, on 9 August, at the suggestion of Roosevelt, he and Churchill met at

Placentia Bay off the coast of Newfoundland. A number of Roosevelt's advisers feared that Britain and the USSR would come to an agreement that would trade Soviet help against Germany, both during and after the war, for British acquiescence in Soviet territorial gains in Eastern Europe. This recalled the Allied secret treaties of the First World War, 'which had assumed a sacred place in American diplomatic demonology',[311] and they wished to prevent it. There was also the desire to tie Great Britain down to other Wilsonian principles, such as self-determination. And there was the simple wish to meet and see how they worked together.

With HMS *Prince of Wales* nestled cosily next to the USS *Augusta*, the two leaders spent three days in discussion.[312] Churchill wanted a declaration of war; Roosevelt demurred. However, he agreed that the US navy would provide armed escorts as far as Iceland. The most public outcome was the so-called Atlantic Charter. Initiated by Roosevelt, and drafted in the first instance by Sir Alexander Cadogan, it pledged the two countries to seek a post-war world suffused with and dominated by the principles of self-determination, non-aggression, free trade, and the freedom of the seas. It was no accident that the final two were principles which the US had been trying to force on Great Britain for a century and a half, and which were currently causing difficulties in the negotiations over the Lend–Lease Consideration. The Atlantic Charter was a joint Anglo-American declaration of war aims; if not as welcome to the British as a declaration of war would have been, nevertheless it tied the neutral US more closely to Britain. This was Churchill's defence in Parliament when the Charter ran into substantial political difficulties, with charges that the Prime Minister had repeatedly surrendered British interests.[313]

But Great Britain did not have long to wait. On 7 December the airplanes of the Japanese First Fleet bombed Pearl Harbor, temporarily crippling the US Pacific Fleet, except for three aircraft carriers which were away at sea. On the following day, the US declared war on Japan, as did Britain. Obligingly, on 11 December Germany and Italy both declared war on the US. The US and Great Britain could now, finally, organise a proper alliance.

XII

The Second World War saw the destruction of Great Britain's global predominance and the United States' assumption of that role. Until mid-1943, when American military power reached full force, the relationship was not unequal: not only had Great Britain stood alone and fought off the might of Germany, but during 1942 and into 1943 she simply had more forces in the field. Furthermore, she was contributing her fair share in the Battle of the Atlantic, in Africa, Italy and elsewhere, and in her mastery of the breaking and interpreting of Germany's signals intelligence. But as the war went on, and the US became increasingly conscious of her immense power, she increasingly took decisions which benefitted her own interests and damaged those of Great Britain. This, of course, is what strong states have always done, and it was precisely what Great Britain herself had done in her own time of great power. Yet, the belief persisted on the British side that close allies ought not to behave in such a manner. The Americans, on the other hand, could be obsessed with the fear that the British were, yet again, going to 'outsmart' them. Particularly from 1943, conflicts over strategy were frequent, with discussions tense and sometimes unbridled. Nevertheless, while the alliance was frequently strained – particularly in the Far East – it was still fit for purpose.

One of Churchill's immediate worries was that, because of Pearl Harbor, the US would discard the agreement putting the defeat of Germany first and go after Japan. He therefore decided on 8 December to travel to the US. The resulting conference with Roosevelt was code-named Arcadia; it ran from 22 December to 14 January and in general terms it organised the war effort. It created the formal alliance, proclaimed to the world on New Year's Day 1942, and it confirmed the Germany-first decision; it then established many of the combined Anglo-American bodies which organised and administered the war.

At the Christmas Day meeting, the US Army Chief of Staff, General George C. Marshall, made a suggestion which transformed the nature of this and subsequent military alliances. Convinced that both inter-service and inter-Allied military co-operation were vital, he suggested that they adopt the principle of 'unity of command'; in South-east Asia and the South-west Pacific, they and the other Allies should place all of their army, navy and air forces under a single commander. Churchill offered some resistance, asking bluntly what an army officer could know about handling a ship. But Marshall insisted that they had to have unified control at the highest levels of Allied forces facing the Japanese. If they failed to do so, he warned, 'we were finished in the war'.[314] His logic was underlined by his willingness to make a British field marshal, Sir Archibald Wavell, the Allied commander in the area (although for Wavell, this was a 'poisoned chalice', since the following two months were an 'unmitigated disaster' for the British Empire and Commonwealth, culminating with the fall of Singapore on 15 February 1942). Henceforth, all British, American and other Allied ground, naval and air forces in a single theatre would serve under a single commander – 'a coordination unprecedented for major powers in military history'.[315]

At that same Christmas Day meeting, Marshall pointed out the importance of having a central Anglo-American body which would draw up strategy and direct the theatre commanders around the world. Roosevelt pushed for an inter-Allied council in Washington, whilst Churchill held out for an Anglo-American one with branches in both Washington and London. Both gave ground, and the result was an Anglo-American body situated in Washington, the Combined Anglo-American Chiefs of Staff (CCS), made up of the US and British army, navy and air force chiefs, which met in continuous session.[316] To this must be added economic co-ordination, based on various combined boards, such as the Combined Production and Resources Board, and Lend–Lease. To service all of these committees, missions and boards, large numbers of British officials crossed the Atlantic and took up residence; as one official historian wrote, 'the overseas administration . . . assumed such proportions as almost to suggest that the British government was functioning in duplicate on both sides of the Atlantic'.[317] There was also the united intelligence effort, but for this the American contingents frequently crossed to Britain. The officials of the two countries, both military and civilian, worked closely together, knew each other's families, shared telephone switchboards bringing good news and bad, and in general forged such close links that the feeling of unity carried through into the post-war world. As one diplomat put it, there was 'an integration of effort of truly astonishing proportions between two completely independent countries'.[318]

Yet, there was often conflict, personal and professional – how could it be otherwise? With the best will in the world, members of the boards and committees were, not surprisingly, concerned to defend their own national interests, which they sometimes saw as alliance interests (Churchill and Roosevelt were both very good at this). The two countries frequently put emphases on different theatres of war and timetables – the Americans on the Far East, the British on the Mediterranean; the Americans on an early invasion of France, the British desperate to hold back until they were more ready. And sometimes personalities clashed, or simply did not understand each other, or were insensitive to signs or atmospheres in negotiations. The British sometimes found the Americans unwilling to learn, overoptimistic about what could be achieved, and suspicious of British motives and abilities. The Americans sometimes found the British condescending, reeking with ineffable superiority. A classic formulation of this was by Harold Macmillan, the future Prime Minister. In 1943, when Minister Resident in the Mediterranean, Macmillan told a fellow-Briton that 'You will find the Americans much as the Greeks found the Romans, great, big, vulgar, bustling people, more vigorous than we are and also more idle, with more unspoiled virtues but also more corrupt. We must run A.F.H.Q. [Allied Forces Headquarters] as the Greek slaves ran the operations of the Emperor Claudius.' An alternative was an ambassador's apophthegm, that the Americans 'confused plumbing with civilization'.[319]

There was a hero who often saved the situation by brokering agreements, facilitating good relations, and explaining each side to the other. This was Field Marshal Sir John Dill. He had been Chief of the Imperial General Staff from mid-1940 to 1941, when Churchill, who disliked him intensely, 'retired' him. It has been said that one reason for this dislike was that Dill stood up to him: Roosevelt's aide, Harry Hopkins, who witnessed a confrontation in 1943, described it as Dill telling Churchill that he, Dill, 'was free, white, and twenty-one and was going to tell him what he thought whether he liked it or not'. Dill was sent to Washington in January

1942 as head of the British Joint Staff Mission and senior British representative on the Combined Chiefs of Staff Committee.

Dill saw his role as working for harmonious and productive Anglo-American relations. Fortunately, he found a soulmate in Marshall. According to Stimson, now Secretary of War, it was their close friendship which made it possible for the CCS to act 'not as a mere collecting point for individual rivalries between services and nations but as an executive committee for the prosecution of global war'.[320] The two men shone with integrity, both were calm and soft-spoken, both worked for the greater good of both countries: as Dill said, he worked for Britain, which meant working for the US. He also insisted, however, that he wanted to avoid 'frantic dancing to the American tune'. What was crucial was the building of trust. Each man trusted the other, and, further, each inspired the same trust in the other's colleagues. Such building of trust on the personal level was the most important element in cementing the alliance, and it was what made it unique. It also kept the alliance going after the war. But it did not come quickly or easily. The CCS was meant to be the mechanism by which decisions were taken on strategy, but the desires of the military establishments on both sides – not to mention those of Churchill and Roosevelt – meant that coming to decisions was usually a tortuous process. Anger and stalemate were not unknown. Even Dill could become exasperated, trying to explain the reasons for some of the conflict between them: '[The Americans] are quite the kindest and most fraternal people one could meet. But with the British they, or most of them, suffer from a serious inferiority complex. They feel that we are a homogeneous people with great traditions, great institutions and a lovely land. They long to persuade themselves that we are effete but they can't quite do it. And paradoxically this inferiority complex leads to much bally hoo about any American achievement which produces a spurious superiority complex.' Both sides turned to Dill because he was perceived to be impartial, and therefore trusted. He was also irreplaceable, a discovery made upon his death in late 1944. His stature in Washington was underlined by his burial in the US National Cemetery in Arlington, Virginia, the only non-American so honoured, with the US Joint Chiefs of Staff acting as honorary pallbearers.[321]

Military decisions on strategy tended to emerge from days, weeks, even months of sometimes full and frank discussions. The Allies had different views as to what the military priorities should be. The Americans, as exemplified by Marshall, believed that the Allies should roll up all of their strength into a ball and throw it directly at the Germans: only with their defeat would the war be won, and it was pointless to waste time and resources elsewhere. The British, as exemplified by Churchill, believed that the Americans underestimated what this would entail. They had not lost a generation of young men on the Western Front nor thousands on the sands of Dunkirk, as had the British, and the latter had no intention of condemning themselves to another such hell if it could be avoided. Rather, they wanted to pick off Germany's weaker ally, Italy, and then move north from there. The Americans were deeply suspicious of this argument, since it seemed to be directed at protecting British possessions in the Middle East and Africa, rather than at defeating Germany. Churchill did not believe that the one precluded the other.

The crux here became the question of opening a second front. For most of two years the USSR bore the brunt of the war with Germany, and Stalin from early on demanded that the Allies attack Germany from the west. The Americans, and especially Marshall, wished to oblige, but Churchill opposed SLEDGEHAMMER, the planned 1942 Channel crossing, even though he had agreed to it 'in principle' and Roosevelt had subsequently promised it to Stalin. Churchill told the Soviet Foreign Minister that he simply would not and could not do it. Britain would have to provide the bulk of the forces, since by September 1942 the US could have contributed only two and a half divisions; therefore the Prime Minister could, in essence, veto it. The U-boat menace was still very great, so how would the troops be transported safely to France; and, as they lacked landing craft, how would they disembark if they got there? For Churchill, the priority was to knock Italy out of the war and reopen the Mediterranean to shipping.

But by the end of 1943, the Battle of the Atlantic had been won and American soldiers and landing craft could now cross the ocean in relative safety. Churchill was now forced to agree that a second front was now the priority. The venue for his defeat was the Teheran Conference in November, and the whole experience was traumatic for him. By this time, it was apparent that the Soviet success against Germany, when combined with the certainty of Allied victory, meant that in the post-war world Soviet power would be enormous. At the same time, the decline in British power was palpable. Roosevelt looked at the situation and decided that it was crucial that the US and the USSR, rather than the US and Britain, should work together in both war and peace. He knew that Churchill was very suspicious of an overweening Soviet Union which would unbalance the Continent; he also recognised that the Soviets would assume that the US and Britain were likely to move together against them. So, Roosevelt decided, he had to prove to Stalin that he was now the important partner and that there was no Anglo-American front, and he did this by ostentatiously slighting Churchill. In Teheran he stayed at the Soviet rather than the British Embassy; furthermore, he met privately with Stalin but not with Churchill. Most crassly, he decided to humiliate Churchill publicly. 'When Stalin suggested shooting 50,000 German officers at war's end and Churchill vehemently objected, FDR humorously responded with a "compromise" proposal of 49,000 and his son Elliott with a toast in favour of the executions that led Churchill to stalk out of the room in anger.' On another occasion Roosevelt needled Churchill mercilessly 'about his Britishness, about John Bull, about his cigars, about his habits', until Churchill got red in the face and Stalin 'broke into a deep, hearty guffaw . . . I kept it up', Roosevelt later told a member of his Cabinet, 'until Stalin was laughing with me' – at Churchill's expense.[322] Stalin did not require Roosevelt's help in this arena: 'I can't understand you at all; in 1919 [the intervention in Russia] you were so keen to fight and now you don't seem to be at all? What happened? Is it advancing age? How many divisions do you have in contact with the enemy? What is happening to all those two million men you have in India?'[323]

Churchill really had no choice, because by this time the US and the USSR were determined, for strategic reasons, to push him into agreement. On 30 November 1943, the third day of the conference, he surrendered: OVERLORD would be launched in May 1944. That evening Churchill hosted his own birthday dinner (he was sixty-nine); in contrast to the previous evening, when he had been under attack by the other two, there were now a series of 'effusive' toasts, all sharing the recognition of an historic moment. But, for Churchill, the conference was a time of profound melancholy. It was at Teheran, Churchill used to remark, that he realised for the first time what a small nation Britain was. 'There I sat with the great Russian bear on one side of me, with paws outstretched, and on the other side the great American buffalo, and between the two sat the poor little English donkey who was the only one . . . who knew the right way home.'[324]

The other arguments arose over the Pacific War, and these could be ferocious. The US wanted to do the fighting and to control policy. There was conflict over the importance of China: Britain thought it not very, whilst the US saw it as the future centre of power in the Far East and an important ally, and they had great faith in Chiang Kai-shek. More immediately, the US wanted to be able to bomb Japan from Chinese soil; to get there, they wanted a land route opened through Burma. The task of rolling back the Japanese on land was taken on by the British, whilst the Americans concentrated on the ocean and the islands, such as Iwo Jima. Burma was a terrible struggle; the tropical climate, disease and the need to hack through jungle destroyed morale, and the campaign failed in 1943. According to Peter Lowe, this collapse 'encouraged American cynicism over the British role in the war which was seen increasingly as an American responsibility'. However, the reanimation of the British campaign by the Fourteenth Army under General Sir William Slim resulted in 1944 in the greatest land defeat suffered by the Japanese army during the war.[325] Ironically, by 1944, the vicious and incompetent leadership of Chiang had disillusioned the Americans, and China became a sideshow. Nevertheless, as far as the Americans, and especially the US navy, were concerned, the Pacific War was *their* war, and the British should stay out of it. The outcome was that the British concentrated on the land war, particularly the recovery of Burma, and, figuratively, stayed out of ships. As Christopher Thorne has memorably put it, 'Anglo-American relations in the context of the war against Japan were in many respects extremely poor, and . . . this in turn placed a considerable strain upon their war-time alliance

as a whole, as well as foreshadowing serious differences to come . . .
Here, if nowhere else, they were only allies of a kind.'[326]

A fundamental conflict between the two countries was over the
future of the British Empire. Churchill wanted to keep it in India
and the Middle East and to grab it back in the Far East. The
Americans wanted it dismantled, an ambition encouraged by the
British defeats in the Far East: in their opinion the Empire was both
wrong and incompetently run. Famously, in the 12 October 1942
issue of the American magazine *Life*, the editors addressed an 'Open
Letter' to the 'People of England'. Americans, they wrote, still
lacked a consensus on war aims, but 'one thing we are sure we are
not fighting for is to hold the British Empire together. We don't like
to put the matter so bluntly, but we don't want you to have any illu-
sions. If your strategists are planning a war to hold the British
Empire together they will sooner or later find themselves strategis-
ing all alone.' They then 'entreated the British to forsake "Your side
of the war", which included imperialism, and join "Our Side", which
meant the side fighting for freedom throughout the world'. Just as
famously, Churchill made his response on 10 November 1942 in a
speech at the Mansion House in London. After acclaiming the landing of American and British troops in North Africa, he denied that
the British had acquisitive ambitions there or anywhere else. 'Let
me, however, make this clear, in case there should be any mistake
about it in any quarter. We mean to hold our own. I have not become
the King's First Minister in order to preside over the liquidation of
the British Empire.' Churchill had let his rhetoric run away with
him, and his words shocked many British as well as most Americans.
He sounded reactionary, which bothered imperialists, since it failed
to convey the responsibility for their subjects in the colonies which
many felt; and he alarmed those who believed that Britain *should*
recognise that the time of empires had perhaps passed.[327]

Roosevelt had attempted to intervene over India earlier in the
year, telling Churchill that he had given 'much thought' to the country, since it was 'an untenable burden' to Britain; he suggested a
transition government, setting out its structures and duties. 'The
infuriated Prime Minister did not reply.' He had also, in May,
suggested to the Soviet Foreign Minister that perhaps British-owned

islands should be placed under international trusteeship, a suggestion to which he returned at Yalta in February 1945.[328] Roosevelt felt at liberty to make jibes. Hong Kong was repeatedly one focus of his attention. He favoured returning the colony to the Chinese, provided that they designated it a free port. In January 1945 Roosevelt nudged the British Colonial Secretary Oliver Stanley, 'I do not want to be unkind or rude to the British, but in 1841 [sic], when you acquired Hong Kong, you did not acquire it by purchase.' Stanley snapped back, 'Let me see, Mr. President, that was about the time of the Mexican War, wasn't it?'[329]

There was a real problem here, one of which most Britons seemed unaware. Many Americans split their perceptions of Great Britain roughly into two. On the one hand, the admiration for her as a bastion of representative democracy was undeniable. The First Amendment freedoms of speech, religion and assembly, thrived, and it was a tolerant society; furthermore, she had stood alone against the Nazis. But at the same time, Americans disliked, with greater or lesser intensity, the British Empire.[330] Why should they give Great Britain their support? The British seldom recognised this dichotomy.

An area which stimulated repeated arguments was Lend–Lease. It had been proposed by an administration which saw it as a means by which the US could defend herself by proxy – perfectly in the British tradition – and agreed to by a Congress which did not intend to give Great Britain and the other recipients something for nothing. Powerful components of the American government wanted to use the leverage it provided against British policies or activities. These included the Secretary of State, the Secretary of the Treasury and sundry military officers. Cordell Hull had been appointed Secretary of State by Roosevelt not because of his ability or his stamina (he was often ill), but because he touched parts of the Democratic Party that Roosevelt could not. But according to Randall Bennett Woods, he 'appeared to believe that the articulation of a lofty principle was tantamount to its realization'.[331] He was also convinced that political conflict was largely caused by economic rivalry, which he assumed would be obviated by multilateral free trade and convertible currencies. A main theme of his tenure at the State Department, therefore, was the attempt to force other powers, particularly Great

Britain, to change their economic policies. Hull had an exaggerated idea of British power. He believed that the Empire was a tightly integrated economic system controlled by London from which Britain reaped great benefits but which greatly harmed the prospects of American exporters. He therefore determined to end the system which was, in his eyes, no better than Germany's drive towards autarchy. His State Department team fully supported him in this, believing that the leverage provided by the Lend–Lease Consideration, at a time when British power was greatly diminished, was 'their only chance to do it'.[332] Their answer was Article VII of the Mutual Aid (Lend–Lease) Agreement, which required that both countries move towards ending discrimination. For Britain this meant that 'imperial preference' must be abandoned (see Section XI) whilst for the US it meant reducing tariffs and other trade barriers; neither provision was destined to be fully implemented. This was combined with the expansion of production, employment, and the exchange and consumption of goods, which meant that the US should combat any post-war depression so that Americans could afford to import as well as export goods.[333]

Secretary of the Treasury Morgenthau supported aiding Great Britain, but admitted in 1946 that his primary objective had been to 'move the financial center of the world from London and Wall Street to the United States Treasury and to create a new concept between the nations of international finance'. He also intended that the dollar would replace sterling as the dominant trading currency. In short, the Treasury intended to dominate the international financial system after the war, and thus needed to eliminate Britain as a viable rival. The way to achieve this was to keep Great Britain short of reserves, and therefore dependent on the US – or at least not financially strong enough to act against US wishes. Morgenthau and the Treasury, later joined by Leo Crowley and the Foreign Economic Administration (established by Roosevelt in 1943 to replace the Lend–Lease Administration), plotted to restrict Lend–Lease. The intention was to force the British to pay cash for whatever they required that was not a war-need narrowly defined, and thereby limit the size of the British reserves to between six hundred million and one billion dollars (the British insisted that they needed at least one and a half billion dollars).

By early 1944, Morgenthau and Crowley were purposely running down British balances by increasing the so-called 'take-outs', that is, specifying goods such as sugar, fish and paper for which Lend–Lease aid would not be available and for which they would thus have to pay cash. Hull and the State Department, however, were by now worried that Great Britain was going to end the war too weak to share in the work of what would become the UN nor would she be able to accept a multilateral economic order if she was not allowed to rebuild her reserves. By devious manoeuvres, therefore, the State Department provoked a crisis which gave Churchill a chance to protest to Roosevelt, and the Treasury had to agree that there would be no more take-outs. But, as with the State Department, the Treasury would achieve what it wanted at the end of the war.[334]

The third US government predator was the armed services, which saw opportunities not to be missed. In September 1944, for example, General Brehon Somerville, Chief of the Supply Services, suggested that Lend–Lease be used to force the British to turn over their bases in the Pacific to the US, because the latter would need these islands after the war, given their expectation of exercising wide control over the area. This was not imperialism, according to the General Board of the Navy, 'because the islands had no economic value'. Somerville also called for the conversion of the ninety-nine-year leases on bases in the Caribbean and the Atlantic into permanent transfers; he wanted to secure unconditional landing rights for US military and commercial aircraft at British bases around the world; and he wanted to prevent Britain from blocking American access to strategic materials in the Middle and Far East. The pressure would dramatically increase as Germany moved towards defeat.[335]

In March 1945, when Congress renewed Lend–Lease, it inserted a special proviso that no Lend–Lease funds should be used for post-war relief, rehabilitation or reconstruction. The death of Roosevelt in April removed a sympathetic higher authority, and 'From April onwards British officials in Washington, watching events closely at these lower levels, could see the brakes coming on slowly at many different points.' But what no one expected was the brutal suddenness with which Lend–Lease was ended. On 15 August the Japanese surrendered, four days later the British Food Mission in

Washington notified London that all loadings of Lend–Lease foodstuffs had been stopped, and the next day the White House announced the immediate termination of Lend–Lease – anything in the pipeline would have to be paid for. The British were profoundly shocked. 'That the United States Government, after years of closer co-operation with the United Kingdom than had ever before been known between Great Powers, should have taken such drastic measures unilaterally, without any prior negotiation, left British Ministers and officials gasping for breath.' The only path open to Great Britain was to apply for a loan. It was during the negotiations for this that the State Department and the Treasury achieved the collapse of British external economic policy which they had so long desired.[336]

The tale of Lend–Lease is not altogether a pretty one, and, indeed, the official British historian warns against the natural reactions of his readers at the outset: 'It is a story, above all else, of unexampled generosity on the part of the American nation. Unless this all-important fact is remembered throughout, these chapters are bound to convey a false impression, an impression insulting alike to the Americans who gave and to the British who strove to justify acceptance of the colossal stream of munitions, of food, of aircraft and of materials to sustain both direct war production and civilian life in these islands.'[337] What perhaps is not emphasised enough is that the traffic was not all one way: the US gave $27 billion in Lend–Lease to Britain and the Commonwealth, but Britain, in what was termed 'reverse-Lend–Lease', gave $6 billion to the US. Certainly those historians who lived and worked during the war and had close relations with the Americans present a view considerably more generous towards the US government and its manipulation of Lend–Lease than those of a later generation, who have to depend on the documents without the ameliorating gloss which human explanation can sometimes provide.

XIII

The post-war Anglo-American relationship is primarily a military alliance, although one of unusual closeness, and the bones of the alliance are the intelligence and nuclear links. The former did not begin until the Second World War, but the intelligence relationship had started as soon as the US had joined the First World War. The roots put down in 1917–18, however, were shallow and hardly survived the inter-war period. It was the Second World War which established the co-ordinated and combined effort which to some extent continued after 1945.

In 1939 the Government Code and Cypher School took up residence at Bletchley Park (known as Station X). The initial staff of 150 had expanded to about 3,500 by late 1942, when it was renamed Government Communications Headquarters (GCHQ). Besides the British, there were in due course French, Polish and American decryptors. In May 1940 Bletchley made the first major break in the Enigma machine cypher, the decrypts of which were known as ULTRA, when it cracked the Luftwaffe variant; this was followed in June 1941 by the naval variant. In July 1940 William 'Wild Bill' Donovan, the future head of the Office of Strategic Services (OSS) and later of the Central Intelligence Agency (CIA), travelled to Great Britain as Roosevelt's special envoy. Churchill briefed him, George VI met him, and most of the heads of intelligence included him in secret meetings. As a result, upon his return Donovan urged Roosevelt to sanction a 'full intelligence collaboration'.[338] It is worth noting that many of the important decisions in this context were taken whilst the US was still officially neutral.

At this point, however, Whitehall found it difficult to take the fragmented American intelligence effort entirely seriously. Not only did the three services refuse to work together, but there was neither a specialised foreign intelligence agency nor a centralised system of assessment. In 1940 the new head of station in New York, Sir William Stephenson (also known as 'Intrepid'), decided that he should guide the Americans into forming a united intelligence community (without, of course, their realising that they were being so guided). He cultivated Donovan, and when in June 1941 the latter was appointed Co-ordinator of Information (Intelligence), Stephenson took the credit. In the following summer, strongly influenced by Stephenson's advice, Donovan set up the OSS. But, ego aside, from Stephenson's contacts with Donovan and earlier ones with J. Edgar Hoover and the FBI 'sprang a full-blown Anglo-American human intelligence (humint) alliance'. However, Stephenson seems not to have succeeded in unifying the intelligence effort. The US army and navy argued over which service was to decrypt MAGIC – the army had broken it, but some of the decrypts dealt with naval matters. Roosevelt decided that the army would decrypt on odd dates whilst the navy would decrypt on even dates; nothing was done on weekday evenings or on Sundays. Churchill would not have stood for such a ramshackle effort.[339]

Meanwhile, there was an analagous construction of a signals intelligence (sigint) alliance, much more important than humint. At a meeting in London on 31 August 1940 between the British Chiefs of Staff and the American Military Observer Mission, it was decided that 'the time had come for a free exchange of intelligence' between the British and American governments. The following month, as noted above, the Americans broke the Japanese PURPLE code, and a few months later delivered a copy of a PURPLE machine to Bletchley Park and showed the code-breakers how it worked.[340] The British were more circumspect about what they revealed to the Americans. The British decryption of the Luftwaffe Ultra remained a deep, dark secret, for fear that it would leak in the US. Churchill also wanted it kept secret that the British were still decrypting American traffic (although this appears to have ceased once the US entered the war). British willingness to share sigint grew with the developing Anglo-American naval co-operation in the North Atlantic in the summer of 1941. After Bletchley Park broke the German Enigma naval variant, Churchill insisted that Washington should be given the contents of any decrypts that referred to American naval units. After Pearl Harbor, and then with the breaking of U-boat Enigma in December 1942, co-operation in naval sigint accelerated. On 27 December Washington opened the 'Secret Room', a submarine-tracking room on the British model, and from early 1943 the British and American cryptanalysis of naval Enigma was carried out according to a single programme co-ordinated by Bletchley. Communication via direct signal links between the U-boat tracking rooms in London, Washington and (from May 1943) Ottawa became so close that, for the remainder of the war, 'they operated virtually as a single organization'. During the Battle of the Atlantic, called the longest and most complex battle in the history of naval warfare, ULTRA made a major and possibly decisive contribution to the British and American victory.[341]

In the spring of 1943, Anglo-American co-operation was formalised by the signing of the BRUSA (British/USA) agreement on the treatment of sigint and by an exchange of missions between the US Special Branch and Bletchley Park. Both sides agreed to exchange completely all relevant information on signals, codes and cyphers used by the Axis powers; the US was to take care of Japan, whilst Britain would deal with Italy and Germany. The only problem of liaison which BRUSA failed to solve was not between the US and Britain, but between the American army and naval sigint agencies, which reflected a lack of central direction from the White House – Roosevelt neither knew nor cared about intelligence in the way that Churchill did. Nevertheless, the President's willingness to endorse such close collaboration laid the foundation for the enduring post-war sigint alliance, which was extended to include Australia, Canada and New Zealand. Negotiations took place episodically from February 1946 until the final text of the UKUSA Agreement (which is still classified) was signed in June 1948.[342]

If the intelligence alliance was well balanced during the war, the same could not be said for the nuclear equivalent. In essence, a combination of British and European scientists made the fundamental scientific discoveries, British-domiciled physicists outlined how the atomic bomb could be made, and the Americans built and used it. By the end of the war, the Americans were determined to maintain complete control of research, development and use of nuclear energy, a decision which surprised and appalled the British, and which was a direct reason for Britain's establishing and maintaining her own nuclear project after the war.

In the spring of 1940 two refugee scientists in Birmingham, Otto Frisch, one of the 'discoverers' of nuclear fission early in 1939,[343] and Rudolf Peierls, a distinguished theoretical physicist, wrote a memorandum of crucial importance, which set out the principles behind an atomic bomb and proposed an industrial method to produce the Uranium 235 necessary to build one.[344] This memorandum was sent to the Committees on the Scientific Survey of Air Defence and of Air Warfare, and they set up the Maud Committee, under whose wing research proceeded rapidly.[345] With the fall of France in June 1940, the work of the Maud Committee was reinforced by the dramatic arrival from Paris of Hans von Halban and Lev Kowarski, who had lugged along with them twenty-six five-litre cans containing the total world stock of heavy water, needed to 'moderate' the speed of neutrons during a chain reaction.[346]

Two Maud Committee reports of July 1941 showed that an atomic bomb was possible. The politicians gave the go-ahead, but the question then arose: was it possible to build the enormous plant in Great Britain, where most scientific resources were devoted to radar, and where it might be bombed? Meanwhile, in the US, two more refugee scientists, Leo Szilard and Albert Einstein, drafted a letter in 1939 for Roosevelt (with Edward Teller, the 'father of the hydrogen bomb', acting as amanuensis), which was signed by Einstein. In this letter, they presented the possibility of an atomic bomb and warned of the danger that the Nazis were already building one.[347] Research began, but it was desultory. In the summer of 1941, however, the British gave the Maud reports to the Americans. Shortly thereafter the latter reorganised their uranium project, putting it under the control of the army, partly because of the huge scale of construction and partly to ensure the utmost secrecy. Under the leadership – and command – of General Leslie R. Groves, the Manhattan Project was established.

The British were undecided as to what extent they should co-operate with the Americans: should the pilot plant be built in Britain or in North America? There was pressure to build it in Great Britain, not least because it was assumed that whoever had the plant would be able to dictate terms (this proved to be correct). At this stage, in autumn 1941, the Americans were conscious that the British were far ahead, and proposed a jointly controlled Anglo-American project. But the British treated this proposal very coolly, with Lord Cherwell, Churchill's scientific assistant, expressing the view of many in a memorandum to the Prime Minister: 'However much I may trust my neighbour, and depend on him, I am very much averse to putting myself completely at his mercy and would therefore not press the Americans to undertake this work: I would just continue exchanging information and get into production over here without raising the question of whether they should do it or not.'[348] In the US in November 1941, a Report of the Committee of the National Academy of Scientists confirmed the findings of the Maud reports, and an all-out effort on the development of the uranium bomb began. Within six months, the Americans had far outstripped the British effort. By mid-1942, the British realised that the Americans were forging ahead very quickly, whilst they themselves were having great difficulty in constructing even a few pilot plants for separating Uranium 235. The technological gap became painfully obvious. The British now wanted to become involved in the Manhattan Project as an equal partner, but the Americans no longer wanted them, not least because the project was now under military control.

Nearly a year of total breakdown in collaboration followed, during which the British, and especially Churchill, struggled to be allowed to rejoin the project. It was only in August 1943 that Roosevelt, on the advice of Harry Hopkins, decided to renew collaboration. The consequent Quebec Agreement enabled the British to rejoin and led to the joint purchase of uranium. The Agreement had three main provisions: neither the British nor the Americans would use the bomb without the other's consent; neither would give information to a third party without the other's consent; and the US had exclusive rights to commercial exploitation. This final provision was explicitly justified in the Agreement by the disproportionate effort put in by the two countries.[349] Once the Agreement was signed, co-operation rapidly improved. The physicists working on the Uranium 235 and fast neutron bomb calculations in Great Britain, roughly fifty in number, joined the Manhattan Project.

The British scientists worked on several parts of the project, with the largest contingent migrating to Los Alamos, where the bomb was fabricated. However, no Britons were allowed to cross the threshold of the reactors where plutonium, the alternative to Uranium 235 that would be used in the Nagasaki bomb, was produced. Concern in Great Britain about the need to continue co-operation after the war led to talks between Roosevelt and Churchill at Hyde Park in September 1944. As a result, an aide-mémoire was initialled which identified Japan as a possible target. Even more significant, the

British thought, Clause 2 stated that 'Full collaboration between the United States and the British Government in developing tube alloys [the code name for atomic research] for military and commercial purposes should continue after the defeat of Japan unless and until terminated by joint agreement.'[350] Unfortunately for Great Britain, Roosevelt died less than eight months later, and the single American copy had been filed away in the papers of his naval aide. The only others to know about it were Lord Cherwell and Dr Vannevar Bush, Director of the US Office of Scientific Research and Development, who argued against close bilateral nuclear relations with Great Britain in favour of better relations with the USSR and the development of international controls over nuclear development elsewhere. And – contrary to the Quebec Agreement – the decision to drop the bomb on Hiroshima was taken by the President: Britain was simply asked to agree to what was arguably the single most significant act of the war.

XIV

Once the US joined the war, it was assumed that the Allies would win, although few cared to predict when that would be. From the earliest days, however, consideration was given to the reconstruction of the post-war world, in both its political and economic aspects. There seems little evidence that policy-makers believed that the whole League of Nations experiment in collective security should be jettisoned, at least on the side of the western Allies. But what should be put in its place? From the meeting at Placentia Bay (August 1941) to the San Francisco Conference (April–June 1945), a series of high-level conferences were held during which decisions were taken on a replacement for the League of Nations. This would help to provide a structure for peaceful international relations. Even more fragmented was the international economic and financial system, which in truth no longer existed. A conference in July 1944 in Bretton Woods, New Hampshire (see below), established the principles and organisation of the International Monetary Fund and the International Bank for Reconstruction and Development (or World

Bank), which were to provide the support required to allow international economic relations to resume. In both sets of negotiations, conflict between Britain and the US was sometimes sharp, exacerbated by the concurrent strategic conflicts.

The establishment of the League of Nations after the First World War had been attended by many hopes that it would provide the means to limit war. It had undeniably failed but there were contrasting views as to why. Some said that the whole idea of collective security was absurd. Others blamed the way in which the League was structured and its lack of power. It still existed (and would continue to do so until the United Nations Organisation was established), but no one argued that it should be brought out of its suspended animation. Instead, an attempt was made to put together another organisation for collective security. One of the major supporters in the American administration was Cordell Hull; only gradually did Roosevelt himself come to accept that it might be a good idea. As for the British, Churchill was a balance-of-power man born and bred; but, as noted above, the British had been strong supporters of the League, and would expect to take a leading part in establishing its successor.

At Placentia Bay, Churchill's draft for the Atlantic Charter called for an 'effective world organization' to ensure the security of all states, although Roosevelt deleted it for fear that it would serve as a red flag to the isolationists in Congress. That year the Soviets also began developing ideas about ways and means of ensuring peace and security after the war. However, they did not envisage an organisation, but co-operation amongst the Great Powers based on specific and binding treaties and guarantees. In May 1942, when Soviet Foreign Minister Vyacheslav Molotov visited Washington, Roosevelt told him that instead of 'another League of Nations with 100 different signatories', he wanted the US, the USSR, Great Britain and possibly China (later referred to as the 'Four Policemen') to be responsible for international security. When Molotov enquired, not surprisingly, whether other countries might object, Roosevelt admitted that they just might possibly do so, but he did not retract his suggestion. As mentioned earlier, Roosevelt also suggested that islands held by weak nations, and perhaps those held by Great Britain, might be placed under international trusteeship, a possibility which he had yet to propose to Churchill. Molotov told Roosevelt that Stalin appreciated the President's proposals, and for the following two years the USSR's leader deferred to American policy on a post-war security organisation.[351]

Over the following year other ideas, many of them less than fully thought through, developed in the US and Britain. When Foreign Secretary Anthony Eden visited Washington in March 1943, Roosevelt proposed a general assembly, an advisory council of the Great Powers, and an executive council of the Big Three plus China. He also suggested that armaments be concentrated in the hands of the Big Three. (Eden thought this idea was ridiculous. How would the rest of the world be disarmed?) On the other hand, when the British proposed regional security councils, one each for Europe, the Americas and Asia, Hull vetoed it. He believed that the US should follow 'a diplomacy of principle – of moral disinterestedness instead of power politics'. Eden remarked in his memoirs that 'United States policy is exaggeratedly moral, at least when non-American interests are concerned'.[352] According to Diane Shaver Clemens, 'the "diplomacy of principle" for Hull meant Russia's and Britain's submission to American "principle" as interpreted in Washington'.[353] Negotiations over the following two years on a post-war security organisation, as in other areas, were clearly going to be difficult.

In the spring and summer of 1943, Roosevelt became increasingly worried about the Republican threat in the run-up to the next election, due to be held in November 1944. He feared that they might take control of post-war foreign policy away from the Democrats. In April 1943 Wendell Willkie, Roosevelt's opponent in the 1940 election, published *One World*, a bestselling book in which he pleaded for American co-operation to preserve peace in the world once the war had ended. At the Quebec meeting in mid-August, Roosevelt told Churchill, Eden and W.L. Mackenzie King, the Canadian Prime Minister, that he needed to make a pronouncement on post-war peacekeeping before the other candidates in the presidential election did. The vehicle was the Four-Power Declaration at the Moscow Foreign Ministers' Conference in October: the Allies promised to hold discussions about a world organisation, and recognised 'the necessity of establishing at the earliest practicable date a general international organisation, based on the principle of the sovereign equality of all peace-loving states, and open to membership by all such states, large and small, for the maintenance of international peace and security'.[354]

At the Teheran Conference a month later Roosevelt had a private meeting with Stalin during which he explained his evolving plans for the post-war organisation: there should be three main bodies, an assembly for discussions and recommendations, an executive committee to deal with all non-military questions, and the Four Policemen as the enforcing agency against acts of aggression. The addition of China to the Big Three was pushed by Roosevelt for a number of reasons, including the assumption that she would be a Great Power sooner or later; that she should be encouraged to provide a check on Japan; and that she could be expected to follow America's lead – or, as Churchill put it, would be the US's 'faggot vote' (based on a sham qualification). Stalin wanted to know whether American troops would be sent abroad as part of this Four Policeman concept, but Roosevelt replied that in the future, land armies would have to be provided by Britain and the USSR. Stalin, like Churchill, disliked the idea of a worldwide organisation, but at least the concept was now being discussed by the three leaders.[355]

Throughout the spring of 1944, the Allies circulated amongst themselves various ideas. Churchill was disturbed by Roosevelt's support for a world organisation, since he worried about the anti-colonial implications, telling Eden in May that 'we have no idea of three or four Great Powers ruling the world' – and especially not ruling the British Empire. The Cabinet distributed a paper drafted by the Foreign Office, 'Future World Organisation', recommending a three-part structure for the 'United Nations' (Eden's proposed name) comprising a council, an assembly and a secretariat. It was also proposed that member states provide military forces which, at the council's discretion, could be used to garrison or occupy specified areas.[356] Hull's ideas were essentially the same, and on 30 May he invited the Allies to a conference at Dumbarton Oaks in Washington to discuss the issues. Britain accepted quickly, but the USSR was unimpressed by the quality of the ideas outlined by Britain and the US, and delayed accepting until 9 July. By this time, Roosevelt had rejected the Soviet approach of a political/military organisation; he also now believed that the UN Organisation (UNO) should be fully representative rather than a 'coercive superstate', to which he had agreed in earlier conversations with Molotov and Stalin and to which Churchill had objected.[357]

All three countries prepared draft proposals, and on 19 August, two days before the conference was to begin, the State Department produced a 'check list' of the differences between them. The fundamental difference was that the USSR saw the UNO as primarily a security organisation, whilst the US and Britain thought that it should include arrangements for both security and economic and social co-operation. For example, the USSR thought that there should be an international air corps for taking urgent military measures, but neither of the other two supported this. Nevertheless, agreement was reached over its final structure, which would comprise General Assembly, Security Council, International Court of Justice, and Economic and Social Council. As Hull noted, it therefore incorporated 'all the essential points' of the American proposals.[358]

Two major issues, however, remained: its membership and the voting formula in the Security Council. Stalin disliked the positions of both the other Powers, especially that of the US, on these issues, and he strongly distrusted their intentions. On membership, for example, they all agreed that China should be a permanent member of the Security Council, and then they agreed to Churchill's proposal to include France as well (he wanted a stronger European presence, and hoped that a 'dependent' France would follow British leadership). But then Roosevelt overplayed his hand, and proposed adding Brazil, to give the US another dependent vote (or perhaps to have it as a card which he could withdraw). This backfired, with the Soviets interpreting it as an attempt to isolate them. From then on, Stalin insisted on an 'absolute veto' on the Security Council to prevent the others uniting against the USSR and forcing on her decisions which she did not want to take. Each side also tried to pack the General Assembly. Roosevelt had earlier suggested that the twenty-six countries which constituted the United Nations against the Axis powers should be the original members, and now proposed adding six Latin American republics plus Egypt and Iceland, all of whom he saw as leaning towards the Allies. Great Britain also wanted six members of the British Commonwealth as individual members. In defence, Stalin now proposed that all sixteen of the Soviet Socialist Republics be individual members, causing 'shock' to the US and Britain. These two issues remained unresolved until the Yalta Conference in February 1945.[359]

When the Big Three gathered at Yalta in the Crimea on 4 February 1945, the Americans considered the UNO to be the crucial issue, and they were prepared to push their views. On the other hand, both the Soviets and the British were increasingly worried about the gap between American principles and practices. The British were especially worried about American attempts to dismantle their empire; the Americans were hinting that British possessions which had fallen to the Japanese should be 'internationalised'. Indeed, in March 1943 during Eden's visit to Washington, Roosevelt had urged the British to 'give up Hong Kong as a gesture of good will'. Eden replied that he had not heard the President suggest any reciprocal gesture by the US. Churchill had to yell and scream before it was agreed that the question of 'trusteeships', which in concept were akin to League of Nation mandates, would be applied only to ex-enemy territories, not to Allied empires: 'I will not have one scrap of British Territory flung into that area. After we have done our best to fight in this war and have done no crime to anyone. I will have no suggestion that the British Empire is to be put into the dock and examined by everybody to see whether it is up to their standard.' Stalin backed Churchill on this, probably because he, too, had an empire – as Eden later wrote, 'the Prime Minister's vehemence . . . appeared to give the most pleasure to Stalin. He got up from his chair, walked up and down, beamed, and at intervals broke into applause.'[360] The US then confirmed that the only target was former enemy territory.

The US delegation did, however, achieve success for its proposal for voting on the Security Council. Any permanent member could veto any resolution, but none could block consideration of an issue, even if they were a party to it. In return, Roosevelt and Stalin both compromised on the latter's earlier request for more seats, agreeing to seats for the Ukraine and Byelorussia. Stalin and Churchill in return agreed that the US could have three votes, the latter in case this equality with the USSR was required for passage through Congress, but ultimately decided not to take up this offer. They then all agreed to hold a conference at San Francisco to establish the design and structure of the UNO.[361]

This was duly held from 15 April to 26 June. There were delegates from fifty countries, because another compromise was that all of those who had declared war on the Axis powers before 1 March 1945 could attend. (Chastened by Wilson's disastrous decision to have only Democrats at Versailles, Roosevelt included Republicans in the San Francisco delegation.[362]) During this conference, the structure of the organisation was agreed, but not before a final crisis caused by Stalin's arguing for a permanent member of the Security Council being able to veto *discussion* of any issue as well as the outcome (Harry Hopkins finally convinced him to withdraw the demand). The structure also included a Trusteeship Council to administer the colonies and mandates of the Axis powers. Finally, the UN Charter, based on the Dumbarton Oaks draft, was signed on 26 June. It was ratified on 24 October 1945 at the first session of the General Asssembly, held in London as a gesture to Great Britain. As had Wilson with the League, Roosevelt had anticipated that the new UNO would cushion any draconian peace settlements, but, as with Wilson, the reach exceeded the grasp.[363] Nevertheless, at the outset the hopes of the world were high.

The reconstruction of an international financial system, needed to facilitate a new international trading regime, produced far more conflict between Britain and the US than had the UNO. Essentially, plans were drawn up in both countries, one by J.M. Keynes in Great Britain and one by Harry Dexter White in the US. These were based on different assumptions and were intended to produce different outcomes. Each saw the other's plan in July 1942, and negotiations culminated in April 1944 with the 'Joint Statement by Experts on the Establishment of an International Monetary Fund'.

From the beginning, the US Treasury assumed the dominant role in determining American post-war international financial policy, beating off the pretensions of the State Department. Within the Treasury, the dominant personality was White, the Director of Monetary Research. 'He was widely considered to be a difficult personality –

aggressive, irascible, and with a remorseless drive for power. His general unpopularity might have provided an obstacle to the realization of his personal ambitions. But he was an indefatigable worker and his quick and active mind soon made a profound impression on . . . Morgenthau.' He was also a Soviet spy.[364] Morgenthau wanted the establishment of an inter-Allied stabilisation fund which would provide the basis for monetary stabilisation arrangements in the post-war period. He needed a plan for this, and thus a week after Pearl Harbor he asked White to draw one up. A fortnight later White suggested two new institutions, an international stabilisation fund and an international bank. Morgenthau intended that both of these, and especially the fund, would be controlled by the US Treasury and would in effect act as its surrogate in dealing with the financial policies of other countries.

There was no real opposition in Washington to the intentions of the Treasury, which were the long-standing desiderata of fixed exchange rates with convertible currencies, the end of discrimination, and trade expansion. These were viewed as requirements for American and world prosperity (the two were seen as one), and, as long argued by Hull, as a measure to prevent war. The British had objections to some of these principles, but even when they agreed in theory about their desirability they differed sharply with the Americans over how they should be implemented. For example, the Americans wanted the international financial system to be based on gold – of which the US held more than one-half of the world's stock. By contrast, the British, through Keynes, argued for the creation of an almost virtual international currency, which could be based on, for example, the amount of a country's trade. The US wanted an end to discriminatory tariffs, and especially to 'imperial preference', a system which she had found intolerable since its inception in 1932. Americans did not, however, view their own very high tariffs as discriminatory because they inflicted equal pain on everybody. This highlights an important difference between Britain and the US in their conceptions of free trade. In Britain this meant free trade into Britain as well as in the rest of the world; as for the US, a profoundly protectionist country, it was always difficult to lower her tariff and trade barriers. Thus, although the two countries agreed on the need for post-war trade expansion, only Britain believed that one way of achieving this was through the lowering of American tariff barriers. Of even greater importance to the British was maintaining high levels of employment (as set out in a 1944 White Paper on the subject). Conversely, for the Americans, influenced by their experiences in the nineteenth century, trade liberalisation was vital to maintaining employment, because American productivity had for decades produced more goods than could be absorbed by the US alone.

The negotiations leading to the Joint Statement were long, complicated and sometimes full and frank. Both sides gave ground. White and his colleagues, although convinced that they were acting to create the best of all possible monetary worlds, nevertheless knew that if they pressed the British too hard and forced them to make too many concessions, Parliament would throw out the agreement.[365] In the end, the International Monetary Fund embodied American requirements, not British. It was essentially based on gold, it had relatively little flexibility, and countries would not automatically be able to withdraw funds equal to the amount which they had put in as their quota without the agreement of the Fund's Executive Board, which the US expected to keep on the straight and narrow.[366] And, of course, it was situated in Washington.

Morgenthau had hoped that an inter-governmental conference could be held in Washington at the end of May 1944 to ratify the Joint Statement. He wanted to present a treaty setting up the IMF to Roosevelt at the Democratic National Convention in July.[367] However, the British government had not yet committed itself to the Joint Statement; it merely agreed to send a delegation to an international monetary conference. So, on 25 May, Hull sent out invitations to the forty-four countries of the United Nations to meet at Bretton Woods from 1 to 23 July. In total, seven hundred delegates attended.

However, before the conference, the British delegation, led by an increasingly unwell Keynes, met the American delegation, led by Morgenthau and White, at Atlantic City, New Jersey. For a week they attempted to reach agreement. According to Keynes, White 'was anxious to avoid the appearance of a stitch-up' between the

British and American Treasuries. So 'Keynes and White would try to agree a text behind the scenes, but present alternatives to the monkey-house [Bretton Woods], having agreed which alternatives they would drop or press'.[368] However, the two could not come to a complete agreement. Keynes insisted that the Articles of Agreement must explicitly recognise national sovereignty in monetary matters; White retorted that the point of the Fund was to secure stable exchange rates. As Keynes wrote to the Permanent Secretary to the Treasury, 'The essence of our plan is that there is no absolute obligation to obey the Fund in the matter of exchanges and that a member in the last resort has the power to take the matter into his own hands without having to go through the prior act of formally withdrawing from the Fund.' He believed that White agreed with him, but 'they are having the usual trouble which always occurs in this country and is one of the causes of preventing anything sensible being done; that is, they have to consult their lawyers, who are proving difficult. In this lawyer-ridden country . . . lawyers seem to be paid to discover ways of making it impossible to do what may prove sensible in future circumstances.' In this case White accepted Keynes' point.[369] By the time of the departure from Atlantic City to travel to Bretton Woods, most of the main issues had been agreed between the two countries.

However, there was one major issue still to be considered: the size of quota assigned to each country. The US would have the largest; voting power was determined by the size of the quota, and the US ensured that her own exceeded the total voting power of Great Britain and the British Commonwealth. But there was then the impossible task of satisfying all the other countries. The US had decided that the resources of the Fund should be announced as $8 billion, with the flexibility, kept secret, to go up to $8.4 billion. White had left quotas to be decided at Bretton Woods because he felt arguing over quotas would divert countries' attention from more important points. (As one of the American delegates, Dr Emanuel Goldenweiser from the Federal Reserve Board, put it to White, 'Just make one general rule, that anybody can talk as long as he pleases provided he doesn't say anything. Separate the business of the Committee from the talk.') To ensure this, White set up masses of commissions, committees and sub-committees, which met all day and into the night. He confidently predicted that this would allow him to maintain control because everybody else would be too busy and too tired to notice. Just in case this did not work, though, he had plenty of lawyers working for him. For example, the British and other delegations had insisted that their access to the Fund's resources was a matter of right, but the Americans had equally persistently argued that the Directors of the Fund had the power to refuse the facilities, even if the country's quota was available. The lawyers drafted the relevant clause so that 'it reads in a way that is not too easy to see if you read it quickly'. As White said, 'our lawyers have done a job'.[370] There would be virtually unanimous complaints that the final ninety-six-page agreement was almost impossible to understand.

In the end, however, agreement was reached. As Keynes said at a press conference on 6 July, if he wished to criticise the International Monetary Fund, he could make 'quite a good job of it', but all of the alternatives he had seen were much worse.[371] In truth, both the US and Great Britain backed a free-trading world (it had, after all, been a British policy for a century). Where they differed was how, and how soon, to achieve it. Basically, there was an agreement because both the US and Great Britain made certain that there was one. Every effort had been made to come to a prior accommodation at Atlantic City, and White and the US Treasury had then stage-managed the conference. The two principals were driven by desire: Morgenthau wanted to present the agreement to Roosevelt as an electoral gift, whilst Keynes wanted to 'lock the United States into a rule-based post-war financial order'[372] to prevent her from acting unilaterally.

> The conference ended with a grand banquet on the evening of Saturday 22 July. Keynes came in a little late 'and as he moved slowly towards the high table, stooping a little more than usual, white with tiredness, but not unpleased at what had been done, the whole meeting spontaneously stood up and waited, silent, until he had taken his place' . . . As Keynes left the dinner some of the delegates – presumably those from the Anglo-Saxon world – started singing 'For He's a Jolly Good Fellow'. The Soviet reaction to these strange rites is not recorded.[373]

The following day, the delegates left to return to their own countries. Whatever the point at issue at the conference, the Americans, driven by ideology and good intentions, had won, because they had the power.

On 12 February 1945, following an intense lobbying effort, Roosevelt sent a message to Congress urging the adoption of the Bretton Woods agreement. Three days later legislation was introduced in the House and the Senate suspending the Johnson Act (see Section IX) for countries joining the IMF and the World Bank. On 19 July the Bill passed its final hurdle. It had been driven through the Congress by what was described in the *New York Herald-Tribune* as 'the most high-powered propaganda campaign in the history of the country'.[374] Much more than that – naked force, as it happened – would be required to ensure the agreement of the British Parliament in early 1946.

XV

The seventy-five years after 1871 saw an utter transformation in the relationship between Great Britain and the United States. In 1871 the former was arguably the supreme international power, whilst the latter was a provincial country, a potential but not yet an actual Great Power. In 1945, after fighting two world wars from beginning to end, Great Britain was virtually on her knees, whilst the US was the supreme international power. In the long run, this was bound to happen, given the great disparities in the sizes of both territory and population, and the US's abundance of natural resources. But wars accelerated the process. As the Joint Permanent Secretary to the Treasury wrote in 1901 during the Boer War, 'Our commercial supremacy has to go sooner or later; of that I have no doubt; but we don't want to accelerate its departure accross the Atlantic.'[375] Great Britain fought relentlessly to maintain her position, but she also encouraged the US, often fruitlessly, to act as a Great Power by taking some responsibility for dealing with international conflicts. At the same time, she became increasingly conscious that her own power was no longer sufficient to defend her widespread interests. Her solution was to try to co-opt American power, a policy which would continue after 1945. It is undoubtedly a rare event in history for one predominant Great Power to hand this position straight to another without a war being fought between them. It was Great Britain's conviction that the interests of the two countries were sufficiently aligned and the historical and cultural links between them sufficiently strong that her own interests would not suffer unbearably. It was this conviction that enabled the transition to take place without dangerous recriminations and uproar.

One characteristic which Great Britain passed on to the US was self-righteousness. The presumption of many Britons, especially in the nineteenth century, that they were bringing civilisation to benighted natives, was soon shared by many Americans after their seizure of the Philippines. In addition, Americans' conviction that they were the guardians of democracy entrenched the self-perception of righteousness. A wonderful example of the clash of the two took place in the US in 1933. During a lecture tour, Harold Nicolson, diplomat and man of letters, was asked by a woman with a voice 'palpitating with up-lift' about the fate of the 'poor' Indians. 'Which Indians?' he replied, 'yours or ours? . . . Whereas we educated and multiplied our Indians you practically exterminated yours.'[376]

One theme which runs through the period is Great Britain's ignorance about how the American political system worked. Britons knew about the power of public opinion, and they knew that Bills had to be agreed to by both Congress and the President before they became law, but they seem to have misunderstood fundamental points, assuming that the President was stronger, had more independent power, than he in fact enjoyed. When the President and the majority of both Houses came from the same political party, they would compare it to Parliament in the same position, and could not always understand why things did not get done. The President proposes, but Congress disposes. Therefore, the inability of Roosevelt to depend upon his fellow-Democrats to carry out his wishes was seen as a lack of will rather than a lack of ability, which encouraged the British to see him frequently as untrustworthy if not mendacious.

The British also found it very difficult to see how the executive branch of the American government worked. Keynes once tried to explain it to London, as far as he understood it himself:

To the outsider it looks almost incredibly inefficient. One wonders how decisions are ever reached at all. There is no clear hierarchy of authority. The different departments of the Government criticise one another in public and produce rival programmes. There is perpetual internecine warfare between prominent personalities. Individuals rise and fall in general esteem with bewildering rapidity. New groupings of administrative power and influence spring up every day. Members of the so-called Cabinet make public speeches containing urgent proposals which are not agreed as part of the Government policy. In the higher ranges of government no work ever seems to be done on paper; no decisions are recorded on paper; no-one seems to read a document and no-one ever answers a communication in writing. Nothing is ever settled in principle. There is just endless debate and sitting around . . . Suddenly some drastic, clear-cut decision is reached, by what process one cannot understand, and all the talk seems to have gone for nothing, . . . the ultimate decision appearing to be largely independent of the immense parlez-vous, responsible and irresponsible, which has preceded it. Nothing is secret, nothing is confidential.[377]

The comparison with the comparatively well-oiled machine which was the British government could not have been more striking, and British officials, used to the hierarchy and the settled tasks of every member, sometimes felt, during the Second World War in particular, that they had entered a maelstrom.

Another important theme which runs through the period is the link between American self-perception and the exercise of power. Americans believed themselves a chosen people, with the God-given task of promoting liberty and democracy. The fundamental tenet of democracy was the expression and implementation of the will of the people. Because the United States exemplified both the democratic will and liberty, its interests were clearly identical with the interests of mankind in general. This tendency to arrogance and self-righteousness could make negotiations with the US somewhat difficult: if the position of the US was correct, and if the American people supported this position, the policy should be accepted by all; anyone opposed to it must be devious or wrong or even malevolent.

When the US possessed the power, it could be difficult for her to compromise, because that would be going against the right. The US had also become a Great Power without practice against equals. The European Great Powers, including Great Britain, had endured centuries of defeats as well as victories, had shared borders with both strong and weak states, and had some sense of the mutability of allies and enemies. The belief of most Americans was that the US had enjoyed only victories, and, for some, the possession of power allowed or even mandated the exercise of such power. Therefore, once it had great and then predominant power, she often used it without mercy, especially if it was seen as in the interests of both the US and the other party, whether that party liked it or not. Of course, these reactions were not universal, nor were relationships always so one-sided. But the tendency which became increasingly obvious after 1945 was already developing in this period: the US called for co-operation, but she meant to control.

However, this worked both ways. When predominant themselves, the British had often acted in the same manner. After all, it was self-evident, many Britons thought, that the Empire benefitted its subjects as well as the British themselves – it was the 'white man's burden'. Britain, too, could look solely to her own interests – she had not acquired the sobriquet 'perfidious Albion' in the eighteenth century for nothing. The self-perception of many of the members of her governing classes by the twentieth century in the face of growing American power was their role as the wise guide of a somewhat clumsy and ignorant adolescent. This could be maddening to Americans, who often sensed this assumption under the self-possession, wit and manners of their British counterparts. Furthermore, the Americans were frequently suspicious, and rightly so, of the British tendency to be less than candid about the resources which they could still command as they fought to maintain their international economic and political position. Good fellowship and suspicion walked together.

CHAPTER 7

Anglo-American Marital Relations: 1870–1945

[The British] come over here every day and trade us a second-class duke or a third-class earl for a first-class American girl, and get several million dollars to boot. And the very next day the entire outfit goes back to Liverpool on a British vessel. We didn't even get the freight back to Liverpool on the earl, the girl, or the money.

J. Potter to Richard Olney, 30 September 1895[1]

On 6 November 1895, the streets between 72nd Street and Fifth Avenue, New York City, were lined with spectators. They had come to see the journey to St. Thomas's Church of the principals in the newest of the international marriages, that between the American railway heiress Consuelo Vanderbilt and the 9th Duke of Marlborough. The choir was sixty strong, a symphony orchestra played the 'Wedding March', and a bishop conducted the proceedings. It was unfortunate that the bride's face was puffy from crying at her fate.

Beginning about 1870, the union of American money and the British aristocracy was a continuing theme in the Anglo-American relationship. This was a development which had its basis in economics – in American economic growth and British agricultural decline. However, it was probably the social aspects which mesmerised American public opinion over five decades. Indeed, such marriages continued thereafter, although usually attracting much less publicity – with the overwhelming exception of that between the former King Edward VIII and Mrs Wallis Warfield Simpson of Baltimore, Maryland (who admittedly was not an heiress) in 1938. Yet, there was something special about the earlier period. Perhaps it was the number of such unions or the amount of cash involved. Perhaps it was the sheer hardheadedness of many of the transactions. For whatever reasons, these fairy tales – or horror stories – provided the plot for many a newspaper article, novel and play.

But there was another tale, one less sprinkled with stardust and less immortalised in song and story. This was the saga of the war brides, the GI brides of the Second World War. The commanders of the American armed services, strongly supported by the British government, tried to prevent such marriages; American public opinion resented them. Frequently treated with contempt, prone to anxiety and despair, the experiences of the war brides is not the most admirable tale in Anglo-American relations.

I

From the end of the Civil War in 1865, the American economy surged. The completion of the transcontinental railways, and of the attendant North–South lines, meant that the entire country was now open to economic growth. The wheat grown on the Great Plains, for example, was available both to other parts of America and for easy export, whilst the development of refrigerated railway cars, and then of ships, meant that fresh and preserved meats could be sent from Chicago around the world. Silver mines expanded, the discovery and exploitation of oil went on apace, and hundreds of new industries were established and developed. Alongside all of these developments, the New York Stock Exchange, that jungle of wild beasts, saw massive fortunes made and lost.

One result of the spectacular growth in the economy over the next decades was the emergence of thousands of very wealthy men. They came from all over the country – the phenomenon was not limited to urban areas such as Chicago and San Francisco. Yet what very many of these men had in common were wives and daughters who burned to establish themselves socially in accordance with their newly acquired wealth. They had become dissatisfied with local society, and therefore many of these families moved to nearby cities and made furious efforts to break into the best circles. A number of the more adventurous, or richer, determined to brave the strongest social fortress of all: New York City. The Tower of London in the time of William the Conqueror would have been easier to storm. This was because two individuals, one with masses of money and determination and the other with a mind both strategic and tactical, had determined that certain rules would dictate who was and who was not worth knowing, in order to ensure that the riff-raff were kept out of the best New York society.

Traditionally, the 'best people' were the Knickerbockers, most of them descended from the early Dutch settlers, and named after their ancestors' knee-length breeches. Their ideal life was quiet, modest and conservative, and with no ostentation. The *nouveaux riches* horrified them: they were vulgar, flaunted their money, had no manners, no taste, no sense of the rightness of things. But there were lots of them with lots of money, and they might eventually overwhelm the social citadel. Something therefore had to be done to defend it, to control access. Cometh the hour, cometh the woman – but the woman in this case curiously combined the two worlds. Born Caroline Schermerhorn, daughter of an old Knickerbocker shipping family, she had married William Backhouse Astor, Jr., deemed acceptable because his 'new' money was fifty years old.[2]

But who was to determine, from all of the possible suppliants, the true best people? Mrs Astor would need help, and she found it in the form of Ward McAllister, 'The Autocrat of Drawing-Rooms', a southerner proud of his lineage. Having made a small fortune as a lawyer, he married a 'self-effacing heiress' and in 1853 they set off on a tour of Europe which was 'less honeymoon than social apprenticeship. He visited Windsor Castle, "dining at the village inn with Her Majesty's *chef*",' off partridges which he hoped had been shot by Prince Albert, and was given a peek at the dining-table actually laid for Queen Victoria, though his mystic communion was cut short by a flurry presaging her imminent arrival.' Upon McAllister's return in 1858, 'flushed with connoisseurship',[3] he set about transforming society in the resort of Newport, Rhode Island, and then in New York City. He fully agreed with Mrs Astor that it was necessary to keep out the parvenus, and he it was who came up with the method. First of all, he divided potential socialites into two categories, nobs and swells. The former were already members of the elect; the latter aspired to be so, but their only chance was to be wealthy, to be engaged in an acceptable occupation (such as banking, the law or commerce), and to have manners indistinguishable from members of old society. He then formed a committee of three men who, he believed, could best choose twenty-five such paragons, referred to by McAllister as 'Patriarchs', and defined by him as 'the leading representative men of the city, who had the right to create and lead society'.[4] His three judges met daily at McAllister's house to draw up their list.

To McAllister, the strength of his proposed new social elite would be the union of old families and acceptable new money – hence the need for the vetting of the swells. Eric Homberger agrees with this, commenting that 'the Patriarchs became a device by which changing relations within the upper strata of New York society were managed and accommodated'.[5] Each Patriarch would hold three balls a year, to which he could invite four ladies and five men, including himself; guests could also include distinguished strangers visiting New York, but no more than fifty. As McAllister later explained:

> The object was to make these balls thoroughly representative; to embrace the old Colonial New Yorkers . . . and men whose ability and integrity had won the esteem of the community, and who formed an important element in society. We wanted the money power, but not in any way to be controlled by it. Patriarchs were chosen solely for their fitness; on each of them promising to invite to each ball only such people as would do credit to the ball . . . We knew . . . that the whole secret of the success of these Patriarch Balls lay in . . . making it extremely difficult to obtain an invitation to them, and to make such invitations of great value; to make them the stepping-stone to the best New York society.[6]

By legend, Mrs Astor's ballroom held only four hundred people – and consequently the best society was dubbed the 'Four Hundred'. To provide for the daughters of desirable people who could not be fitted into the room, McAllister invented the Junior Patriarchs, known as the Family Circle Dancing Classes, or FCDCs.[7] It was all very effective, and terribly successful: unsuitable people were kept out, those kept out were desperate to be in, and those who were let in plumed themselves, making those kept out even more desperate and despairing.

But not everyone who was kept out was willing to leave it at that. If they were shunned by New York, why not go elsewhere – to Paris, for instance? Several did, and the story of one of the earliest to do so, Jennie Jerome, had a profound effect on British history.

Leonard Jerome, a speculator on the New York Stock Exchange, was successful enough to build a huge mansion, with small private theatre attached, in Madison Square. Referred to as the first of New York's private palaces, a 'great strawberry shortcake amid blocks of dull brown townhouses', it was to be the setting for the storming of the citadel of the Four Hundred by Mrs Clara Jerome and her three daughters Jennie, Clara and Leonie. She was unsuccessful, but she did not sit at home and mope: rather, in 1867 she informed her husband that she was unwell and wished to go to Paris.[8] He arranged for an apartment on the Boulevard Malesherbes and then returned home with a permanent invitation to visit them and a permanent requirement to pay their bills. The court of the Second Empire welcomed lively, attractive, well-dressed young girls, and the daughters were soon a success. But just as serious marital possibilities presented themselves, the Prussians invaded, heralding two years of war. Indeed, the Jerome sisters seem to have received advance notice. In June 1869 Clara 'had a disquieting experience. Count Hatzfeldt, a secretary at the German Embassy, drew her into an alcove to whisper, "I never saw their Majesties in better spirits than last night but God knows where they will be next year at this time."'[9] Leonard Jerome hastened over to Paris, collected his family, and reinstalled them, this time in Brown's Hotel in London. He then returned to New York – money had to be made and mistresses entertained.[10]

In London the girls were again a success, largely because their timing was good. The leader of society was Albert Edward, the Prince of Wales, who was always keen on lively and beautiful girls, particularly American ones (he had visited the United States in 1860, when he was a slender and handsome nineteen-year-old, and had had a wonderful time). The nineteen-year-old Jennie made her debut in 1872, and spent the summer with her mother and sisters at Cowes, on the Isle of Wight. In August she attended a ball in honour of the Prince and Princess of Wales and his uncle and aunt, the Tsar and Tsarina of Russia. At the ball she met Lord Randolph Churchill, the fascinating but somewhat ill-disciplined second son of the seventh Duke of Marlborough. For both it was a *coup de foudre*, and on their third meeting they became engaged. They had, however, neglected to involve their parents in this momentous decision, and immediately faced furious opposition from both sides.

For the Jeromes, it was unthinkable that they had not been consulted before such a decision had been taken; besides, Lord Randolph was only a second son and would therefore inherit very little and almost certainly not a title. For the Duke and Duchess of Marlborough, the news was even more shocking: an unknown American from a vulgar, parvenu family. Even the reputed Jerome wealth did not make up for these drawbacks; in fact, Lord Randolph's biographer does not believe that he married for money, as some contemporaries claimed, because the formerly very wealthy Jerome had just lost most of his fortune in the 1873 financial crash.[11] Certainly, once the Duke had had enquiries made in America, he was distinctly unimpressed. But the young lovers had a powerful ally in the Prince of Wales, who told the Marlboroughs that he knew about America and about the family, and not only was there nothing objectionable in the match, he positively endorsed it (Jennie was a favourite of his).[12] The Duke fought back, telling his son that he was forbidden even to see Jennie again until he had won a seat in the House of Commons; he was notoriously erratic, and his parents apparently assumed that he would wander off towards someone else. As it happened, Parliament was promptly dissolved and Lord Randolph became the Member of Parliament for Woodstock, the then little village in North Oxfordshire which nestles around Blenheim Palace, the premier seat of the Marlboroughs.[13]

The engagement now had to be accepted, but then came the financial negotiations. What dowry would Jennie bring with her in exchange for marriage into a family of such lustre? The groom had very little: as did most younger sons of the peerage and the gentry, he lived on an allowance from his father, which he was continually exceeding. Many younger sons went into the law, the Church, diplomacy or the armed forces, with the first three, at least, providing an independent income of sorts. But MPs were not paid. Therefore, most of the financial support of the young couple would have to come from her side of the match.

There were some tense negotiations, particularly when her father insisted on making Jennie a substantial allowance for her own use and under her control. Lord Randolph's lawyers were outraged, one writing to him that

> The Duke says that such a settlement cannot as far as you are personally concerned be considered any settlement at all, for . . . Miss Jerome would be made quite independent of you in a pecuniary point of view, which in my experience is most unusual . . . Although in America, a married woman's property may be absolutely and entirely her own, I would remark that upon marrying an Englishman, she loses her American nationality and becomes an Englishwoman so that I think that the settlement should be according to the law and custom here.[14]

Jerome refused to be cowed: 'I can but think that your English custom of making the wife so entirely dependent upon the husband, is most unwise.'[15] At one point Lord Randolph, backed by his father, told Jerome that unless all of the dowry capital came to him in the event of his future wife dying childless, 'all business between us was perfectly impossible and he could do what he liked with his beastly money'. He won his point and, in the end, agreement was reached. The eventual settlement involved £50,000 of capital, in various government and railway stocks, and a mortgage on a large landed estate, worth £60,000, yielding £2,000 a year to the couple. The Duke added £1,100 a year, which came out of £20,000 settled on Lord Randolph minus the amount needed to pay his debts.[16]

On 15 April 1874 the couple were married at the British Embassy in Paris, although without the groom's parents in attendance. After their honeymoon in France, they returned to England, where the new Lady Randolph Churchill assumed a prominent place in society. She also carried out, with commendable expedition, the duty of all wives of men of property: to produce an heir. Her eldest son Winston was born prematurely on 30 November 1874.[17] Indeed, she entirely lived up to expectations in this area and produced, in the phrase of a future American Duchess of Marlborough, both 'an heir and a spare' – should the elder die, there was a younger to take his place.

Although an early example, she was merely one of what would, just fifteen years later, be termed an 'invasion'. Here is Oscar Wilde's description of it, written in 1887 for the *Court and Society Review*:

> on the whole, the American invasion has done English society a great deal of good. American women are bright, clever, and wonderfully cosmopolitan . . . They insist on being paid compliments and have almost succeeded in making Englishmen eloquent. For our aristocracy they have an ardent admiration; they adore titles and are a permanent blow to Republican principles . . . Her sense of humour keeps her from the tragedy of a *grande passion*, and, as there is neither romance nor humility in her love, she makes an excellent wife.[18]

By 1914, sixty peers, and forty younger sons of peers, had married wealthy American women.[19] It is fairly clear why there was such a supply: the quest for social acceptability and even superiority; the attraction of a more sophisticated social milieu; the search for an alternative to Denver, Cleveland or Chicago, sometimes dismissed as rough, coarse and provincial; even, for the more daring, the simple attraction of the unknown. The British politician Joseph Chamberlain visited the US in late 1887, and his impressions were 'that if you want to be rich and then richer, this country is the best to live in . . . if you want real life and not the means of living, England is the place'.[20] But why was there such a demand for these girls? Naturally, some of the marriages were love matches, as was apparently the case with Lord and Lady Randolph Churchill. But many would-be grooms were more driven by economic need.

II

In 1873 four hundred peers and peeresses owned 5,729,000 acres of England and Wales, over 15 per cent of the total area.[21] Very little of it was farmed by the landlords themselves; rather, it was let to tenants, with the work being done largely by landless agricultural labourers. These estates were predominantly devoted to cereals. Over the previous century many improvements had been made, such as an increase in drainage and the adoption of reaping machines. Yet, in general there was a vast under-utilisation of poorly paid labour and a general conservatism about making changes. The major change of the previous thirty years had been the repeal of the Corn Laws, the elimination of tariffs against imported grain. This initially had relatively little effect, but the situation changed drastically from the 1870s.

There was a run of bad harvests during that decade. In the past, farmers had simply raised their prices to compensate, but now the trend for prices was downwards. It was clear to contemporaries that the cause was foreign competition, but the belief was that this was a temporary phenomenon caused by the coincidence of poor harvests in Great Britain and good harvests in North America. But conditions had changed, and now foreign suppliers could permanently undercut British farmers regardless of the weather. The increased production of grain in the US during the late 1870s meant that supplies could be provided to Britain at nearly normal prices, not the higher ones which British farmers had hoped to charge. As railway construction surged in the US and Eastern Europe in the 1880s, even greater supplies became available at much lower cost. Although British harvests improved during the 1890s, imports again surged and prices tumbled further. Steam ships with new methods of preservation and refrigeration also enabled imports of meat nearly to double between the late 1870s and the mid-1890s, with the obvious result of a drastic reduction in prices. It is ironic that the very economic developments which were enriching the American heiresses were helping to impoverish their future bridegrooms.

This continuing pressure on prices meant a growing call for reductions in rents. In the first years they were maintained, but in the 1880s, and particularly in the 1890s, landlords frequently had to choose between reducing rents or having a vacant farm. If, for example, rent of 28 shillings per acre equals 100, they fell from 101 between 1870 and 1874, to 94 between 1880 and 1884, to 79 between 1890 and 1894, and to 72 between 1900 and 1904 before rising to 75 in 1910–14. This average naturally concealed local variations: in some pastoral areas there was not much change, whilst in some arable areas rents fell to almost negligible sums. Two farms in Steeple in Essex, in total 638 acres, paid £760 in rent in 1873, £460 from 1883 to 1886, and just £1 a year from 1886 to 1891.[22] The consequences for the landlord are obvious.

This period saw the ending of the pre-eminence of agriculture amongst British industries. With this decline in economic status went a change in the conditions and activities of all classes connected to the land. The period saw large-scale rural decline and the crumbling of long-standing traditions of village society. The landowning class as a whole suffered a permanent loss of capital and income: immediately prior to the First World War it was estimated that the best they could hope to receive was a net income of 3 per cent on the reduced capital value of their estates.[23]

From this it might seem clear that all great estates suffered and all peers must needs marry for money. But this was not the case. Large landowners were not a conspicuous element in the transatlantic marriage stakes. They might well have had diversified sources of income – urban rents, mineral rights to coal on their lands, investments abroad, equities or government bonds – and therefore less need for inward investment from American heiresses. Only four peers with landed incomes in excess of fifty thousand pounds married Americans during this period. The middling ranks of landowning peers were more obvious in the lists; perhaps they were more at risk from changes in the economy and had less diversified income. A strong argument for the proposition that peers were attracted by American bankbooks rather than by American blue eyes can be based upon the personal amounts (personalty), as opposed to the estates themselves, left at death. For example, of the seven peers who made transatlantic marriages and left very small personal fortunes, four had been married to, and divorced by, wealthy American women. However, although in general evidence for mass numbers of loveless but lucrative transatlantic marriages is hard to find,[24] they did exist, and the huge amount of publicity they attracted helped to form the popular view.

The depression was uneven in its impact. It was worst in southern England, which for centuries had been the traditional wheat-growing area. The counties where the value of agricultural land fell most heavily in the 1880s and 1890s – by more than 30 per cent in fifteen years – formed a continuous block in the south-east quarter of the country (the counties closely surrounding London benefitted from supplying the capital).[25] In the middle of this block, sprawling in the country north of Oxford, was the estate of the Dukes of Marlborough, and it was the need of the 9th Duke to marry a fortune which resulted in what was possibly the most notorious marriage merger of them all.

In 1893, on a cruise to India in the family yacht, Consuelo Vanderbilt fell in love with Winthrop Rutherfurd, a New York lawyer who was rich, 'the handsomest bachelor in New York society', and impeccably bred.[26] Her passion was reciprocated, and this was to prove a worrying barrier to the plans of her mother, Alva Vanderbilt, for Consuelo to make a stunning aristocratic match. The following year the two ladies – or, rather, the lady and the girl, since Consuelo was only seventeen – arrived in London. Mrs Minnie Paget, an American who had in 1878 married an Englishman, Colonel Arthur Paget, a close companion of the Prince of Wales, would sponsor Consuelo and present her.[27] She arranged a little dinner party, with the twenty-four-year-old Duke of Marlborough as the principal guest. Lady Paget placed the Duke on her right and Consuelo on his – an entirely obvious manoeuvre. The young Duke needed to marry an heiress. Blenheim Palace, his ancestral home, needed repairs, maintenence, and glorification, and the family fortune did not extend to this. Nevertheless, he could not marry just anyone with money. The Duke was fastidious and had a high sense of what was due both to the estate and to the Marlborough name. He was stiff with family pride.

Back in New York City for the winter season, Consuelo was very carefully chaperoned, because her mother was determined to keep her and Winthrop Rutherfurd apart. However, during a bicycling party in March 1895, the two managed to escape from the others. Winthrop proposed marriage and Consuelo accepted. Then her mother, pedalling furiously, caught up with them. The next day

Consuelo and her mother departed for Europe. Winthrop followed them, but Mrs Vanderbilt was ruthless. In Paris he was forbidden to see Consuelo, his letters were confiscated, and she was relentlessly chaperoned. The two ladies returned to London in June, where they met the Duke again at a ball. He danced with Consuelo several times, a very promising sign, and invited her and her mother to Blenheim, probably to see if she could match up to her surroundings.

Consuelo had been raised to fill a great position. She was tall and slender with a swanlike neck and a cloud of black hair. She had beautiful posture – her mother had ensured this by making her wear a back brace for much of her childhood – and impeccable manners. She knew all about butlers and formal dinners, and something about art, literature and history. She had also been taught to speak French and German. The Duke drove her around the estate and guided her around the house. Mrs Vanderbilt then invited the Duke to visit them at their house in Newport, Rhode Island, the resort town of New York society, and he accepted.

When Consuelo and her mother returned to the United States in the summer, preparations for the Duke's visit were put in hand. Meanwhile, the regular round of balls and other social events continued. Consuelo and Winthrop managed to snatch a dance at a ball. Immediately afterwards, there was a showdown between Consuelo and her mother. Some years later her mother testified that 'when I issued an order nobody discussed it. I, therefore, did not beg, but ordered her to marry the Duke.'[28] Consuelo later dramatically described her response in her autobiography: 'Thinking it best no longer to dissemble, I told her that I meant to marry X., adding that I considered that I had a right to choose my own husband. These words, the bravest that I had ever uttered, brought down a frightful storm of protest.'[29] The following morning the house was unnaturally quiet. 'The family doctor was called in to tell Consuelo that her mother had a very bad heart, and that any grievous disappointment might prove fatal. "There was a terrible scene in which she told me that if I succeeded in escaping she would shoot my sweetheart and she would, therefore, be imprisoned and hanged and I would be responsible."'[30] This broke Consuelo, and she gave in.

But would the Duke ask her to marry him? Finally, Consuelo

later wrote, 'it was in the comparative quiet of an evening at home [in September 1895] that Marlborough proposed to me in the Gothic Room whose atmosphere was so propitious to sacrifice. There was no need for sentiment. I was content with his pious hope that he would make me a good husband and ran up to my mother with word of our engagement.' The following day, when she broke the news to her brothers, her younger brother Harold observed, 'He is only marrying you for your money', and 'with this last slap to my pride I burst into tears'.[31]

Then came the financial negotiations. The Marlborough solicitor, Sir George Lewis, 'crossed the seas with the declared intention of "profiting the illustrious family" he had been engaged to serve, [and] devoted a natural talent to that end'.[32] The Duke had $2.5 million (£500,000) in the form of 50,000 shares in the Beech Creek Railroad Company settled on him by Vanderbilt, and from this an annual dividend of 4 per cent – $100,000 (£20,000) -- was payable to the couple during their joint lives (this allowance continued even after he and Consuelo later separated). In addition Consuelo had settled on her enough of the same stock to pay her an annual sum of $100,000 'for her separate use'.[33] As a contemporary commentator was to write, 'The Marlborough title was an expensive one . . . All told, the Marlborough dukedom had cost William K. Vanderbilt, it was said, fully $10,000,000.'[34]

The marriage seemed to embody much of what many Americans were beginning to dislike about these transatlantic marriages. In earlier years some newspapers had expressed pleasure and even pride that sweet and pretty American girls had carried off all those aristocratic matrimonial prizes from under the noses of the English girls. At the same time, however, others pointed out that they were obviously being married only for their money. By the mid-1890s, the focus of opinion was the loss of capital. Newspapers printed lists of dowries being paid to English grooms: in December 1895 the *New York Morning Journal* ran the headline, 'We Pay the Freight: Seven Titles Purchased at a Cost of 75 Millions'; in September 1907 the *New York World* 'provided a list of eligible bachelors in the British aristocracy' for the information of American heiresses; and in May 1909 the *Omaha World Herald* published a table of foreign marriages entitled 'Heiresses Who Have Taken Themselves and Their Millions Out of America', with a column for the amount of dollars 'We Lost'. Gustavus Myers calculated that, up to 1909, as much as $220 million was drained from the US to Europe as a result of international marriages. The charge remained the same as in earlier years: once they were there with their money, they were exploited, being required to pay for the estates and entertainments of lazy or effete peers and their families. Indeed, along with the amount of the dowry, the most publicised feature of these marriages was the amount spent on entertainment.[35]

Linked with the idea that endless amounts of money were going to England to prop up and entertain impecunious peers – or to buy titles – was the growing argument that to marry a peer was to betray democratic principles. Why were these girls leaving a republic to live in a monarchy? Even worse, it was the best stock, as demonstrated by the ability to make such fortunes, which was going. Instead of supporting equality of opportunity, they were propping up a system of hereditary privilege. 'Certainly, by the turn of the century, marrying a foreign nobleman was denounced as unpatriotic.'[36] In short, by the time of the Vanderbilt/Marlborough marriage, transatlantic unions were attracting considerable criticism in America.

What about the reaction in Great Britain? It seems clear why the men of society courted and wed American girls. Granted that most of these wives were wealthy (although many were not heiresses – the British tended to conflate the two terms), they were also attractive to men, partly for the reasons listed by Oscar Wilde, but also because they tended to be more natural than English girls. The American girl was used to male friends, whilst the English maiden was kept separate and chaperoned, was relatively uneducated, and was taught to be shy and demure. As George W. Smalley, the *New York Tribune* correspondent in London, explained matters, 'The relations between the sexes in youth are ten times more natural, genuine, and right in America than in England. Life does not begin with the English girl on her coming out. She is still in the nursery or the school-room, is still the bread-and-butter miss, still the nonentity, still the shy, silent, unformed creature she was.'[37] It was also not the case that the traffic was entirely American girls travelling to England to trawl for aristocratic husbands. Even more Englishmen went to America, some to try their luck, but many just to see the place. (They were particularly keen to experience the Wild West.)[38] Both types sometimes met their fate there.[39]

Captain Cedric Errol, the youngest son of the Earl of Dorincourt, went to New York, accidentally met a lovely, sweet young woman, and married her. His father, who hated America and Americans, was appalled, and cut him off, forcing the young man to go out to work, for which he had not been educated. But he worked hard, the two of them loved each other, they lived in a small but pleasant house and they soon had a pretty young son. Then Captain Errol died. But the story carried on. The Earl's other two sons both died without heirs, and the young son of Capt. Errol, aged seven, was suddenly the heir to the earldom. The Earl wanted him raised as an Englishman, not as a savage, and thus he summoned him and his mother to England. The Earl soon discovered that his grandson was a model boy in all ways, and he rapidly became extremely fond of the little Lord Fauntleroy.

The author of the novel *Little Lord Fauntleroy* (1886),[40] Frances Hodgson Burnett, was an Englishwoman who emigrated to America with her family at the age of sixteen, lived for a portion of her life in each country, and died in America. She was only one of a number of authors who wrote about Anglo-American marriages. Indeed, another of her novels, *The Shuttle* (1906), tells of two such marriages, one of which goes horribly wrong, whilst the other is wonderfully right. Her conceit was the weaving of the two countries together. The story focuses on two extremely wealthy American sisters, one of whom marries a baronet, a cad of the first order, who bullies and nearly destroys her in order to gain control of her money, and the other of whom marries a noble but impecunious earl. The Baronet dies horribly of a stroke, whilst the Earl and his American wife undoubtedly found a new race of superior persons.[41]

If Burnett was positive about such relationships, other authors, such as Henry James, were more ambivalent. Or consider Edith Wharton, herself a somewhat renegade member of the best New York society. Her last, but unfinished, book, *The Buccaneers* (1938), tells the story of four American girls who, baulked of entry into New

York society, travel to England. There they pick up between them a duke, an earl, a younger son of a marquess, a baronet and a rising MP, but only two of them experience real happiness. Added interest is provided by the fact that at least two of the characters are apparently based on real people. Nan St George, who marries the Duke and then in despair leaves him for another man (the Baronet), is not unlike Consuelo Vanderbilt, who, having provided her husband with the requisite heir and spare, left him eleven years after their marriage.[42] Consuelo then spent some years engaged in social work and local politics, becoming a London County Councillor in 1917. In 1921 their divorce became final, and six years later she gained an annulment of the marriage (on the basis that she had been coerced into it) so that she could marry a French airman, Jacques Balsan, in the Catholic Church.[43] She then lived happily ever after. Another character in *The Buccaneers*, Lizzie Elmsworth, who married the rising MP Hector Robinson, was based on Jennie Jerome, Lady Randolph Churchill, whose husband would rise to be Chancellor of the Exchequer before throwing away his career. It is Robinson, appalled at the planning which is being devoted to catching the same duke for a newly arrived sister, who breathes to his wife, 'What a gang of buccaneers you are!' 'Buccaneers,' Lizzie reminded him gently, 'were not notorious for paying fortunes for what they took.'[44]

Robinson, however, was expressing a view which was common amongst a wide range of people, although it was by no means a blanket reaction. The very existence of so many American wives in society upset a great number of people, and especially other women, because they exemplified changes in society itself whilst seeming to threaten the composition and even the continuing existence of the aristocracy.

The British peerage was different from those of the Continent in various ways. First of all, because there was only one peer per family, with the eldest son having a 'courtesy' title, it meant more. As well, the system was very much more established and stable: a younger son of an eminent British aristocratic family was often a more attractive proposition than a down-at-heel French count. As the American Price Collier was to write in *England and the English*, 'England is still a commercial country and her aristocracy is still held, or holds itself, at the highest price. The foolish American mother, and the ambitious American girl, find that titles on the Continent may be bought by the dozen, while in England they still command a fair, though declining price, for each one.'[45]

Importantly, the British aristocracy was more fluid, and therefore it was considerably easier to move up and down the scale than it was in, say, France. New forms of money could eventually join. Merchant bankers were among the first – Barings, Rothschilds – but increasingly over the nineteenth century industrialists were ennobled. As the agricultural depression ate away at the economic basis of the traditional peerage, this newer form of wealth – and wealth was needed to support the way of life of a peer[46] – gained its reward. Between 1874 and 1885, 12 per cent of new peers were industrialists; between 1885 and 1895 it was 28 per cent; between 1895 and 1905 it was 30 per cent; and between 1905 and 1911, 40 per cent. A consequence was the loosening up of Society, with the lowering of social barriers, and this made it easier for American girls, wives and widows to be accepted.[47] These wealthy American wives, however, upped the ante. They could afford endless new dresses from Worth and hats from Virot, elaborate balls and other entertainments, jewels, huge estates and houses in London. The reaction of members of society who disapproved was that the Americans were commercialising society. However, the Americans were supported by the Prince of Wales, who liked expensive entertainments and loved to go to house parties where he received the best of everything. This required money on the part of the host, and this sometimes came courtesy of the wealth of the wife. At the same time this seemingly lowered the social barriers even more, with mere wealth becoming as, if not more, important than birth and breeding. For many of the old aristocracy, this was distasteful and even hateful. This mirrored the reaction of the Four Hundred in New York City to the threat of being socially overwhelmed by vulgar newcomers.

Of more importance to individual families was the fact that the Americans and their money were depriving English girls of husbands. As the economic position of many peers worsened, they simply had to marry wealth. It also meant that the allowances given to younger sons were often less than that required to support a wife in reasonable comfort; it also meant that daughters' portions were smaller. But why should the girl not marry a businessman? After all, peers had, not infrequently, married the daughters of bankers, nabobs and industrialists. But for a woman, it was different: her social status followed that of her husband. Should she marry a businessman, she would slide down the social ladder, and money seldom compensated for her decline in status in the world which was important to her. With a decent allowance, the daughter of a peer might well find the single life preferable to being married to someone so far beneath her, and indeed, by the turn of the century, fully one-third of the daughters of peers were spinsters.[48]

Not only did Americans take husbands away from English girls, they were a positive threat to the existence of the peerage itself, because they were failing to reproduce themselves. There were already difficulties amongst the British, as an article in the periodical *The Nineteenth Century and After* tried to make clear: 'our stable upper classes during the past fifty years have reduced their birth-rate by more than one-half, and have passed well below the point at which the number of births compensates for the number of deaths. Their extinction on these lines is clearly only a matter of a few generations.'[49] The dark suspicion was that the cause was birth control, the use of which went beyond the peerage to embrace the gentry and middle classes as well. As the eminent gynaecologist John W. Taylor wrote in the same periodical in 1906, 'I have no hesitation in . . . tracing the decline of the birth rate to the use of artificial checks or preventatives', which he called 'vicious and unnatural'.[50] Taylor blamed this use of 'prevention' on the wish for a better life, assailing 'many whose courage and manliness have been temporarily fouled by . . . sins of cowardly but comfortable living'.[51] Although expressed in more prosaic language, Taylor's arguments were supported by Sidney Webb. In a 1907 Fabian Society pamphlet, he ascribes the decline in the birth rate to 'deliberate volition in the regulation of the married state', and laments that it is concentrated especially in 'those sections of the population which give proofs of thrift and foresight', which include the industrious artisan class as well as the middle class. 'This can hardly result in anything but national deterioration; or, as an alternative, in this country gradually falling to the

Irish and the Jews [who do not limit their family size]. The ultimate future of these islands may be to the Chinese!'[52]

Anglo-American marriages occupied an ambiguous place in this argument. On the one hand, they brought in new blood. As the popular novelist Marie Corelli wrote, 'one should look upon the frequent marriages of American heiresses with effete British nobles as the carrying out of a wise and timely dispensation of Providence. New blood – fresh sap, is sorely needed to invigorate the grand old tree of the British aristocracy, which has of late been looking sadly as though dry rot were setting in.'[53] On the other hand, many accused them specifically of driving down the rate of reproduction of the upper classes, thereby depriving Great Britain of the best of the population and leaving the lower orders to breed irresponsibly. The basis of this charge was the observation that many of these Anglo-American marriages were childless, and certainly, from 1870 to the turn of the century, approximately one in every two transatlantic marriages was either childless or produced only one child.[54] As it happened, the American birth rate in, for example, 1880 was lower than that of any European country except France, and evidence of this sort gave rise to the conviction held by members of the British medical profession, as well as by many intellectuals, that the Americans must be practising birth control, known by many of the more moralistic among them as the 'American sin'.[55] If they did it in America, they would surely also do it in England.

But there was another possibility, even worse than the first, and this was that American women were genetically inferior and becoming increasingly sterile, which would account for the high number of childless marriages – the possibility of any sterility arising from the male side was seldom considered. This was the direct charge of an anonymous author writing in the *Contemporary Review* in 1905, who claimed that colonial marriages, such as those to Australians or Canadians, did not suffer the same problem. A major contribution to this supposed infertility was the tendency of American wives to be frivolous, restless and with no higher goal than 'having a good time'. A subordinate charge was that if they did manage to produce offspring, they neglected them, with the result that 'there was not a single distinguished peer's son with an American mother'.[56]

For some years concerns about the baleful effect of American brides on the nature and continued existence of the peerage continued to be expressed. The fears of their likely effect on the British gene pool also exercised the many believers in the pseudo-science of eugenics, although this died down as the fashion for eugenics declined. Perhaps closer to home, members of society continued to bewail the deleterious effects of the Americans both on the tone of society and on the marriage prospects of their daughters. Even the former Prince of Wales, now King Edward VII, complained that he had met too many Americans and he did not want to meet any more. Upon Edward's death in 1910, George V and Queen Mary made it clear that his father's way of life was not one which they were disposed to follow, with the consequence that American women no longer had such access to the court. In America itself such marriages had for some years been viewed rather sceptically, particularly since a number of them had ended in separation and even divorce. With the coming of the First World War, the phenomenon appeared to die away, not least because a substantial number of those eligible for such marriages died on the battlefields of France and Flanders.

III

After the war, however, and once transatlantic steamers resumed their regular and frequent crossings, the rate of Anglo-American upper-class marriages reached and even surpassed that of 1870 to 1914. In the earlier forty-four-year period sixty peers had married Americans, whilst in only twenty-four years between 1915 and 1939 there were another forty-four.[57] During the later period, however, they were not much of an issue, either in the US or in Great Britain. In the former, perhaps, the Roaring Twenties provided enough excitement and social possibilities at home. Now the focus for many Americans abroad was not London but Paris, where exciting artistic things were happening and the dollar went far. The newspapers in any case had lost interest in Anglo-American marriages. In Britain, meanwhile, the general public and the newspapers were obsessed with the Bright Young Things, not with American girls.

Yet, there was an American set, and in an unnerving repeat of history it circled around the Prince of Wales. Just as the future Edward VII had rebelled against the strict upbringing of his parents, the future Edward VIII did the same against the cold and frequently harsh rule of his father, George V. Born in 1894, the Prince of Wales was almost beautiful, with his blond hair, blue eyes and melancholy smile. He was also possessed of an extraordinary charm, united, in his days of youth and young manhood, with a strong desire to please and a short attention span. His father kept him on a very short rein, and therefore his post-war official visit to North America in 1919 was something of a turning point, as it had been for the future Edward VII in 1860. He felt an immediate affinity with the United States, possibly encouraged by his knowledge that the King was distinctly anti-American.[58] He discovered that he could turn crowds into adoring mobs, and learned the immense pleasure of living his life more as he liked to do, which involved pretty girls, dancing, drinking, late hours, golf and general hedonism. He was particularly attracted to bright, lively and fun-loving American girls. For a young man of twenty-five who was never really to grow up, this was all perfectly natural.

It is fair to say that for the next several years, he endeavoured to carry out the tasks required of him by his father, including touring the Empire. Yet, over the following decade and a half, he increasingly adopted a particularly irresponsible lifestyle. In one sense the cause of this was the same as for his grandfather: both Queen Victoria and King George V refused to allow their respective heirs any responsibility for affairs of state, or even to know what was going on. Not surprisingly, upon ascending the throne, neither greeted the work required of a monarch with alacrity, although Edward VII carried out his duties with rather more assiduity and good humour than did Edward VIII. The later Prince of Wales increasingly devoted his time to the inter-war equivalent of clubbing, as well as to the pursuit of women with 'hectic abandon'.[59] In this, of course, he was following the same road as all of the other aristocratic Bright Young Things. As one author has commented, 'large sections of society spent their time in pursuit of pleasure with a single-mindedness which marks this generation off from almost any other in history. In spite of his position . . . the Prince was a genuine product of his period', not least in his love of dancing.[60] Even in the general freneticism, it was noticeable that his set was particularly heedless, fun-loving and superficial. No one was more so than Thelma, Lady Furness, his American mistress for several years. She was married, as had been his first love, Mrs Dudley Ward, and as would be his last, Wallis Warfield Simpson.[61]

Lady Furness's place in history rests on the fact that she effectively turned the Prince over to her closest friend, the American Mrs Simpson. Wallis Simpson and the Prince first met in January 1931, and the friendship gradually ripened over the following three years. In January 1934, Lady Furness left for an extended visit to the United States. In her memoirs she describes how she asked Mrs Simpson to 'look after him while I'm away. See that he doesn't get into any mischief.'[62] Being such a good friend, Mrs Simpson did just that. Within a few months she had established her ascendancy: the Prince was wholly, abjectly, besotted with her, and remained so for the rest of his life. As Philip Ziegler has explained, 'he was frightened by Wallis Simpson, enjoyed being frightened by her, and accepted her lightest word as law'.[63] She needed to master and he needed to be mastered – the perfect couple.

The relationship was known amongst the elite but the affair was still far from a public scandal. She was unknown to all but a handful of people in the British Isles before the Prince came to the throne upon the death of King George V in January 1936. Some politicians, however, were becoming worried. Stanley Baldwin, the Prime Minister, told Duff Cooper, the Secretary of State for War, that 'if she were what I call a respectable whore', he would not mind. This was a description which Cooper took to mean 'somebody whom the Prince occasionally saw in secret but didn't spend his whole time with'.[64] But increasingly they appeared together in public, and the Prince openly took her on holiday with him. In due course it even affected his accent: 'the State Opening of Parliament in November [1936] was of interest as being the first occasion several people referred to the American accent which was increasingly replacing the Cockney that had in the past tinged his speech'.[65]

The Prince always claimed that Mrs Simpson had not been his

mistress, but she certainly was not his wife. He later told a friend that from 1934, he had been determined to marry her, but there was an inconvenient husband in the way. On 20 January 1936 George V died and the Prince became King Edward VIII. In early February Wallis's husband, Ernest Simpson, 'directly challenged the King and asked him what his intentions were. The King rose from his chair and answered: "Do you really think that I would be crowned without Wallis at my side?"' The King's biographer points out that 'the words were momentous as being the first definite indication that the King believed he would be able to marry Wallis and make her his Queen'. In July Simpson moved out of the house and left the field clear for the King.[66]

The question now was divorce. Would Simpson agree to it? He would have to provide evidence of his own adultery – not a problem – but there was also the very great danger of a public scandal engulfing the King. Edward VII had become involved with a number of married women, but then the need for discretion on both sides had been observed – and in any case he was happily married. His grandson either had no real sense that discretion was necessary or he just did not care. Even at this time, however, few people believed that the King would actually wed Wallis Simpson. They believed that he would tire of her, as he had tired of others, and that the crisis would blow over. The divorce was heard in late October, and a decree nisi, or provisional divorce, was granted. Another six months were required before it became absolute, at which point the principals could remarry. However, if there was any reason for the law to suspect collusion between the Simpsons, or any misconduct by Mrs Simpson, judicially the innocent party, the divorce would not be granted. Mrs Simpson therefore went to France for the six-month period, leaving the King alone and distraught.

One of the most surprising elements of the whole situation was the self-denying ordinance observed by the British press. The King asked Lord Beaverbrook, owner of Express Newpapers, to allow only minimal details about the Simpson divorce to appear in the press. The King implied that he did not intend to marry Mrs Simpson – the divorce was just to allow her to escape from an unsatisfactory marriage – and on these grounds Beaverbrook persuaded the other newspaper proprietors to forbid any mention of the affair. The Canadian press followed suit. But one national press did not: the American newspapers covered the divorce in lurid detail, and the *New York American* announced on 26 October that the King and Mrs Simpson would marry eight months later. Most of the newspapers were friendly towards the King – he was being democratic and choosing his own friends.[67]

The King for some time continued to believe that Mrs Simpson could be Queen, but finally accepted that this was impossible. The possibility of a morganatic marriage then arose. (A morganatic marriage is one between two people of unequal rank. In this case, any children would be legitimate but not royal, and Mrs Simpson herself would remain a commoner.) Prime Minister Baldwin, a Conservative, sounded out the leaders of the Labour Party. On the one hand, many socialists were attached to the King, because whilst he was Prince of Wales he had expressed strong support for helping the poor and unemployed. The Labour leadership, however, would have none of it. Clement Attlee, the Leader of the Opposition, told the Prime Minister that 'Labour voters would have no objection to an American marriage as such, but would not accept Mrs Simpson or a morganatic marriage', whilst Ernest Bevin, a trade union leader and future Foreign Secretary, was blunter: 'Our people won't 'ave it.' Baldwin then raised the issue in Cabinet, but a morganatic marriage had no support at all. Nor was there any support from the Dominions.[68] If there could not be a morganatic marriage, and if the King refused to lay aside the idea of marrying Mrs Simpson, there was only one outcome: he would have to follow the advice of his ministers and abdicate the throne. The choice was the King's.

As far as he was concerned, there was no choice to be made. He had not particularly enjoyed carrying out the duties of a King, and, after beginning reasonably well, had increasingly evaded them. Conversely, his need for Mrs Simpson grew so overwhelming that giving her up was unthinkable. Without her at his side, he would not be crowned. And so he was not. On 14 December 1936 he broadcast to the nation, and indeed to the world, the reason why he was giving up the throne: 'you must believe me when I tell you that I have found it impossible to carry the heavy burden of responsibility and to discharge my duties as King as I would wish to do without the help and support of the woman I love'.[69]

For Beaverbrook and the Archbishop of Canterbury, Cosmo Gordon Lang, the speech was better than they could have hoped. Many others of the elite found it vulgar, but those in pubs and working-class homes were more supportive. A report from San Francisco made it clear that the crisis had touched more than resident British hearts: 'A restaurant had been cleared and fitted with chairs to accommodate those who wanted to hear the speech. The place was crowded out, everyone weeping, and they all stood up and sang "God Save the King" at the end!'[70] This last comment arouses the suspicion that the listeners were members of the British expatriate community rather than Americans, none of whom would have known the words of the British national anthem (particularly since the same tune accompanies the words of a second American anthem, 'My Country, 'Tis of Thee').

The travails of the King, and the accompanying political crisis, were soon overshadowed by a far greater threat – the rise of Nazi Germany, Fascist Italy and militarist Japan. For Great Britain, war came on 3 September 1939 and for the United States on 7 December 1941. And with the latter's entry into the conflict came another phenomenon of Anglo-American relations, the war brides. Beginning in January 1942 with the arrival of 4,068 men, the number of American servicemen occupying Great Britain peaked in June 1944 at 1,650,000, before declining to just 62,000 at the end of November 1945.[71] The possibilities for sex, and even marriage, were endless. But so were the possibilities for misunderstandings, arising from the very different dating mores that existed in the two countries. As explained by one American serviceman, 'American adolescents were expected to make a pass on a date; the test for the girl was her adroitness in saying no. In Britain . . . girls expected the man to show restraint. A man's kiss was therefore regarded as a much more serious token of affection than the American might have intended.'[72] The problem was that incidents of this kind gave rise to one obvious element of the gibe that the Americans were 'overpaid, overfed, oversexed and over here'. Conversely, because they allowed themselves to be kissed, many local girls seemed cheap and forward to the GIs. One US soldier, in a letter home, referred to Britain as 'a nation of prostitutes'.[73]

The problem was so interesting that the American anthropologist Margaret Mead, after a visit to Britain in 1943, produced a theory of 'dating patterns', which was then set out in discussion pamphlets for the American and British armies.

> The initial reserve of the English, the preponderance of single-sex schools, and the surplus of women to men were all grist for Mead's mill. She argued that the Americanism 'to date' indicated that the main point was a social event rather than a personal relationship. Dates were 'a barometer of popularity' – the boy boosted himself by big talk, sounding as if the girl was bound to fall into his arms, whereas the girl 'proves her popularity by refusing him most or all of the favours which he asks for . . . If she kisses him back, he'll take as much as she will give and despise the girl, just as she will despise him if he doesn't ask for the kiss. A really successful date is one in which the boy asks for everything and gets nothing, except a lot of words, skilful, gay, witty words.' Mead went on to suggest that 'this game is confusing to the British'. Girls might be put off by the GI's wisecracking, speed, and assurance. Or they might confuse 'dating' with 'wooing' and kiss back 'with real warmth' or even 'think the Americans were proposing when they weren't and take them home to father'.[74]

If the initial misunderstandings were sorted out, and a couple became engaged, they then ran up against a huge and sometimes insuperable barrier: the attempts by both countries, and especially the US, to prevent such marriages. Whilst access to sex was widely considered highly desirable and even a necessity for armed forces – comfort girls for the Japanese army, brothels for the French – marriage interfered with the ability and even the willingness of the soldier to fight. For one thing, wives living near bases could distract soldiers' attention. Furthermore, it was unfair: soldiers were not allowed to bring their families with them from the United States, so why should others enjoy the comforts provided by 'local' marriages? And American soldiers were better off than most Britons; they had higher rates of pay, access to plentiful food of which the British could only dream, and much higher allowances for dependants. In short, 'gullible men are readily seduced by British girls, whose ulterior motive may be that of extra remuneration on the part of our Government as well as that of the soldier'.[75]

Meanwhile, the British government was worried that American soldiers might be taking advantage of innocent girls by engaging in bigamous unions, which could then be disclaimed at the end of the war. But even more important, apparently, was to prevent girls latching on to Americans as their passport to the American Dream.[76] In this the British leaders were at one with the American government, although for foreign policy reasons rather than out of deep concern for the girls involved: Anglo-American relations must be kept as smooth as possible.

American military officials could be quite brutal in their attempts to discourage these marriages. On 8 June 1942 the War Department issued Circular 179, which stated that 'No military personnel on duty in any foreign country may marry without the approval of the commanding officer of the United States Army forces stationed in such foreign country or possession.' The following month the even harsher European Theater of Operations (ETO) Circular 20 stipulated that officers and men could marry only with their commanding officer's permission and after written notice of three months; violation of this order would be a court-martial offence under the 96th Article of War – 'conduct of a nature to bring discredit upon the military service'. Furthermore, no privileges would follow upon such permission to marry. There would be no special treatment in living arrangements, for rental, food or travel allowances, or for medical expenses. The spouse would have to pay for all her travel, whether within Britain or to the US. And she would not become an American citizen by virtue of the marriage.[77]

Not surprisingly, Circular 20 provoked anger within the ETO, and three months later yet another circular was issued, Circular 66 of 22 October 1942. The provisions were less harsh, cutting the notice period to two months, and stating that the spouse would be 'entitled to all the allotments, insurance and other benefits' authorised to military wives and that, although marriage conferred no automatic citizenship, spouses would 'be exempted from immigration quotas and are entitled to speedier naturalization'.[78] Yet, officers in command could impose stringent requirements if they wished to do so. For example, the head of the Services of Supply, J.C.H. Lee, arbitrarily denied all requests except in the case of pregnancy. By the spring of 1943, senior ETO officers were concerned, fearing that this policy threatened to encourage immorality, given that it was clear that some couples deliberately put themselves in this situation in order to force the commanding officer to give permission to marry. The full imposition of such rules naturally varied with time and place, however: General Ralph Pulsifer, a senior ETO staff officer, 'took offence if he was not invited to the marriage of any members of his "official family"'. And in 1942–3, with hundreds of thousands of soldiers in Britain and little fighting to do, romance, sex and marriages could hardly be suppressed. Regulations were easier to enforce during certain periods in 1944, when real combat began. But during the final months of the war the whole policy fell apart.[79]

Until 1944, the number of war brides was small – by mid-February 1944, there had been only 4,093. But with the drive to real combat, the figures rose rapidly, with surges in the spring of both 1944 and 1945. The former was linked to D-Day. Everyone knew that an invasion of Europe was about to happen, and everyone also knew that many men would not be coming back. As a Canadian soldier later remembered, 'My God, but it was easy to fall in love in those two months before D-Day . . . There was a feeling that these were the last nights men and women would make love, and there was never any of the by-play or persuading that usually went on . . . I won't describe the scenes or sounds of Hyde Park or Green Park at dusk and after dark. They just can't be described. You can just imagine, a vast battlefield of sex.' The second, and larger, surge of marriages came with the defeat of Germany, when obstacles put in place by the US army weakened.[80]

But with the end of the war, what was to be done with all of these GI brides, by now numbering between 40,000 and 45,000? By law, they were entitled to passage to the US, but the priority for the American servicemen and the American public, and therefore for the

American government, was to bring the boys home as rapidly as possible. In response to pressure from soldiers in Britain, as well as from the American Embassy, it was announced by US Army Headquarters on 14 June 1945 that 'British girls who have married American soldiers are unlikely to get free shipping passages to the United States for 10 months to a year.'[81] The GI brides were becoming increasingly anxious, and as a result of the announcement the US Embassy was 'mobbed by desperate wives'.[82]

On 19 June, Mrs Kathleen Heywood of Salford wrote to the Prime Minister: 'This town has been a holiday place for resting American troops . . . Some of the Yanks married our girls, all in good faith & some of those marriages will be successful. We are asking What is the country going to do for 24,000 girls who are supposed to wait ten to twelve months before they can see their husbands again . . . Can something be done?' Nearly a month later the Foreign Office wrote to the US Embassy, and informed them that they were going to write to Mrs Heywood that it was an American, not a British, responsibility.[83] Indeed, the Foreign Office became increasingly concerned about the diplomatic implications of the problem, urged on by the British Embassy in Washington, which warned London in late July that 'these women will prove an increasingly important factor in Anglo-American relations', the fear being that the war brides might become 'a bad advertisement for Great Britain'.[84]

Of course, the marriages would not have a chance to work if the couple could not be together. It all became too much for many of the women, and on 11 October 1945 about a thousand brides held a protest meeting at Caxton Hall in Westminster, before marching on the US Embassy with cries of 'We want our husbands! We want ships!' The London papers gave it extensive coverage. Unbeknownst to the women, however, that very day conferences began in Paris and London which hammered out plans for sending the wives and their children to the US from January 1946. Further help came with the passage by Congress on 29 December of the War Brides Act, which enabled them to skip many of the normal immigration procedures.[85]

Getting registered, acquiring tickets, exchanging currency and surrendering ration cards, as well as enduring a medical examination, often while caring for a baby or toddler, made the whole process a nightmare for many of the women. There were two staging areas, the Carleton Hotel in Bournemouth and Tidworth Barracks.

> Many of the brides recalled Tidworth station in bleak mid-winter, struggling with bags and screaming children. At the barracks some GIs could not conceal their resentment at this unwelcome duty, which was delaying their return home. [One woman] never forgot the opening of a 'welcome' speech from one officer: 'You may not like conditions here, but remember no one asked you to come.' At first there were no cribs for the babies, until one inventive officer obtained file drawers and footlockers that he lined with pillows and rubber mattresses. Washing facilities were rudimentary, food often abysmal, and the obligatory physical exam proved a public humiliation. Women stood naked on the stage of the camp theatre while a doctor shone a flashlight between their legs to check for VD, watched from the back by a crowd of American officers.[86]

After strong protests from both the wives and their husbands already in America, conditions improved, and thirty ships were commandeered to take the women over. On 26 January 1946 the first 'war bride ship', the SS *Argentina*, left Southampton for New York, carrying 452 women and their children. They arrived in New York to the sounds of 'Here Comes the Bride' as they docked.[87] On 5 February the second ship followed. One member of her staff stumbled across the somewhat surreal sight of the huge indoor swimming pool drained and full of drying nappies (diapers). It is not surprising that the American press dubbed it 'Operation Diaper Run'.[88]

As the Embassy had feared, for many of the war brides, arrival in the US and the long-awaited reunions with their husbands was the beginning of months or years of unhappiness. Many men had exaggerated their economic and social positions; many now resented the responsibilities which a wife and family entailed. One unfortunate woman's story was sadly typical:

> It was getting dark when I got off the train [in a grimy town in Pennsylvania]. He was wearing one of those long overcoats like I'd seen people wearing in the old movies. He looked like Himmler.

I stared at him and thought, 'Lord! What have you married?' And his mother! I was shocked to find that she was German to the hilt. I looked at him and said, 'Am I really in America?' I woke up next morning and I told him, 'I'm going home. I don't like it here.' He said to me, 'You're not getting away. You're mine, you belong to me!' – and he meant it.

It was twenty-five years before she was able to get a divorce.[89]

But of course, there were also stories with happier endings. One English wife of an American sergeant had married against her parents' wishes, since, according to her husband, he was only a fisherman. She was even prepared to go out to work herself, still a rarity in those days. When she arrived in Redondo Beach, California, she found that her husband was indeed a fisherman; he had just neglected to tell her that he owned a fleet of five boats.[90] Presumably he had wanted to assure himself that she had wanted to marry him, not the good life. And she had.

By and large, the stories of these wartime Anglo-American marriages, emphatically not unions of heiresses and the peerage, were probably much the same emotionally as those of their elders and – in late nineteenth- and early twentieth-century terms – betters. Many survived, many did not. A major difference was that obtaining a divorce now made a woman less of an outcast than had earlier been the case in Britain. On the other hand, there was less money all round, and this could make rocky marriages even rockier. Furthermore, lack of money meant that the homesick, the unhappy or the deserted war bride often found it very difficult if not impossible to return to Britain. Much happiness was matched by much despair. In this sense, all Anglo-American marriages, for richer or poorer, were the same. As for the Foreign Office, their fear that these marriages would adversely affect Anglo-American relations was never borne out.

CHAPTER 8

The Alliance since 1945

In Washington Lord Halifax
Once whispered to Lord Keynes:
'It's true *they* have the moneybags
But *we* have all the brains.'[1]

There is some connexion
(I like the way the English spell it
They're so clever about some things
Probably smarter generally than we are
Although there is supposed to be something
We have that they don't – don't ask me what it is . . .)

John Ashbery, 'Tenth Symphony'[2]

Of course a unique relation existed between Britain and America – our common language and history insured that. But unique did not mean affectionate. We had fought England as our enemy as often as we had fought by her side as an ally.

Dean Acheson, *Present at the Creation* (1969)[3]

Rightly or wrongly the Americans tend to convince themselves that their policies have a moral validity of their own and thus deserve our support: this limits their sense of gratitude when such support is given.

Foreign Office (August 1964)[4]

More than one British Ambassador in the United States has quoted the story of the successful Foreign Office candidate who gave to the question: What three things matter most in the world? the reply 'God, Love and Anglo-American relations'.

H. Duncan Hall, *North American Supply* (1955)[5]

With the dawn of the post-war world, the relative positions of the UK and the US were starkly outlined. During the war the UK had been fighting to defend her freedom and independence, enduring continuous bombing by both manned and unmanned aircraft. Her economy was very badly damaged, having lost 25 per cent of its pre-war value.[6] Her people were exhausted. She was only too well aware of her need for US support, particularly economic but also diplomatic and, should it prove necessary, military. In contrast, the mainland US had suffered virtually no damage at all, her economy was unimaginably strong and prosperous, and the population was well fed and energetic. She was almost triumphalist and, whilst sometimes consulting others, and particularly the UK, she intended to lead, not to follow. Following the end of the war, the US continued for a short time to see the USSR as her partner in sorting out the problems of Europe, but with the final realisation of ineradicable Soviet hostility, the UK became for the US an irreplaceable ally.

The development of the relationship from 1945 was not uniform. Generally, it can be summarised as follows: the decade after the end of hostilities continued the wartime partnership, even if as senior and junior partners; the 1960s and 1970s saw a distinct cooling; the 1980s and 1990s saw a wavy upward trend; and the period from 2001 to 2007 saw a close relationship between the leaders but the growth of anti-Americanism in the UK, although the US was generally pro-British. From 1970, the UK was torn between links with the US and membership of the European Economic Community (later Union). As for the US, she wavered between a close relationship with the UK (as well as with other countries) and a desire to be the sole lawman in the Wild West town. But, as Gary Cooper knew in the film *High Noon*, even the bravest and best sometimes need help.

When considering the diplomatic relationship between the two countries, it is important to appreciate that they have different drivers of foreign policies and different methods of implementing these policies. For the US, the overwhelming driver is domestic pressure of myriad varieties. Decision-making can appear chaotic to the outsider, and decisions are often taken by a group at the top, primarily the President and his chosen advisers, ignoring the expertise available in the State, Defense and Treasury departments. The tendency of the US government has always been to act unilaterally, with varying levels of concern as to the impact of a decision on other countries. In the UK, conversely, domestic pressures can be important, but if an election is not imminent, and the party of government has a sufficient majority in the House of Commons, they can often be finessed. Normally, decision-making on foreign policy links the Foreign Office often with the Ministry of Defence, sometimes with the Treasury, and always with the Prime Minister, with greater or lesser involvement of other members of the Cabinet. All are aware of the need to work together with both the US and, since 1973, Europe.

The diplomatic and military links between the two countries were never broken, although at certain periods, in particular during the premiership of Edward Heath from 1970 to 1974, they became somewhat etiolated. But, for the general public in both countries, other elements of a linguistic, historical and cultural nature were even more important in weaving the two countries into a 'special relationship'. These were the everyday links, whether literary, musical, legal, educational or theatrical, or as a safe and interesting place to travel and shop. However, the newspaper and broadcasting media in the UK paid considerably more attention to news from the US than vice versa. This did not in itself, however, mean that the UK was unimportant to Americans, because normally, Americans paid very little attention to *any* foreign countries. Nevertheless, what attention the UK did attract was generally favourable: as a Senator said during a crisis in the 1980s, 'we support you because you are British'. It is, however, wise to recognise that although the two countries seemed rather alike, certainly in comparison with Continenal European countries, the common language masked great differences in culture, assumptions and expectations. In general, there was an arresting change: in the nineteenth century, when Great Britain was the dominant power, the American public was rather more aware of Great Britain than the British public was of the US; after 1945 those positions were reversed.

I

During the war, the US and the UK took very different approaches to planning for the post-war world. For Roosevelt, what was important was the broad brush, the establishing of international systems, and the reconfiguring of Allied relationships, so that all would recognise the intention of the US to work with the USSR, rather than with the UK, to sort out European problems. As described in Chapter 6, he took great pains to make his intentions clear to both Stalin and Churchill. But in general, the Americans wished to concentrate on the military task at hand, perhaps bolstered by the certainty that the US government would not find it difficult to achieve any policies believed important to American interests. The UK, conversely, had no such strength and no such certainty. It was a natural step for the Foreign Office to set up committees to work out future interests and policies with regard to the US, the Continent, the Empire and the rest of the world. In March 1944 it produced a memorandum which dealt with relations with the US. There was a clear assumption that the relationship was so close that it was almost domestic rather than external, but that this also made it a source of endless friction. Notable was the conviction that

> if we go about our business in the right way we can help to steer this great unwieldy barge, the United States of America, into the right harbour. If we don't, it is likely to continue to wallow in the ocean, an isolated menace to navigation. A strong American policy must therefore be based not on a determination to resist American suggestions or demands, but on an understanding of the way in which their political machinery works, and a knowledge of how to make it work to the world's advantage – and our own. Instead of trying to use the Commonwealth as an instrument which will give us the power to outface the United States, we must use the power of the United States to preserve the Commonwealth and the Empire.[7]

The UK persisted at least to the end of the premiership of Harold Macmillan (1957–63) in believing that, based on centuries of experience and greater expertise, she could guide the US in developing and implementing her foreign policies, precisely as Macmillan himself had set it out in his notorious 'Greeks and Romans' analogy (see Chapter 6). They were to find almost immediately at the end of the war that the US had her own ideas about the future, and this included treating the UK in a manner that wounded her self-respect and would almost wreck her economy a year later. This is not to deny that the US saw the UK as an important element in her plans after 1945, which were sometimes modified significantly to take British interests into account. For example, the US wished the UK to lead Europe, but reduced pressure when the UK made clear her disinclination to do so. And the US accepted the predominant place of the UK in the Middle East and the Indian Ocean. But with the Suez Crisis in 1956, all of that would change: in foreign policy, any sentimental links surviving from the comradeship of the war snapped.

Financial weakness effectively limited British foreign and military policy after 1945. The attempts by the two countries in 1945 to hammer out agreements to deal with this took place during a period when the American public wanted nothing more than to demobilise the troops, return to normality, enjoy a good standard of living, and forget 'abroad'. That the UK faced an altogether more ominous economic situation was not fully understood in Washington. The willingness to give yet more aid to Great Britain was virtually non-existent. There was anxiety caused by the election of a Labour Party government, with a warning to Congress by 'elder statesman' Bernard Baruch not to help foreign countries 'to nationalize their industries against us'; Congressman Emmanuel Celler insisted darkly that a loan to the UK would 'promote too damned much Socialism at home and too damned much Imperialism abroad'.[8] Besides, the UK had already received a significant amount of financial aid from the US. In the mood of the informed public in Great Britain as well as of Parliament, there was increasingly a sense of incredulity and then of rage that the US seemed once again prepared to ignore the price paid by Britain in a war which had been a joint effort – 'It is, of course, aggravating to find that our reward for losing a quarter of our total national wealth in the common cause is to pay tribute for half a century to those who have been enriched by the war' – and impose increasing financial burdens.[9] Regardless of the correctness of these perceptions, the negotiations, and especially the reactions in Congress and Parliament during the attempts to gain their consent to the agreements, were frequently bad tempered and sometimes ferocious. Anglo-American relations suffered a severe battering.

Great Britain had three finance-related problems, settlements for which had to be negotiated with the Americans: Lend–Lease claims, the sterling balances and a badly needed loan, all of which were dealt with in negotiations in Washington from September to December 1945. The British delegation was led by Lord Halifax, the British Ambassador to Washington, with Keynes as the dominant negotiator, whilst the Americans were led by Fred Vinson, the Secretary of the Treasury, a former Congressman from Kentucky, who was both conscientious and conservative. He was also acutely aware of the limitations imposed by the need for the approval of any agreement by Congress, a consideration of which Keynes took little account. The two men did not get along. Gardner decided that Vinson's chief criterion for judging Keynes's economic arguments was what would be accepted by his constituents at home: 'Mebbe so, Lawd Keynes, mebbe so,' Vinson would say after hearing some particularly brilliant contribution, 'but down where I come from folks don't look at things that way.' Keynes found Vinson as impossible as the American found him, and reacted by hurling shafts of wit at him. His colleagues warned him of the danger he was inviting, but that seemed only to drive him into further performances,[10] which did not incline Vinson to be flexible.

Lend–Lease was cut off abruptly at the end of the war, leaving Great Britain in a parlous state. At the end of 1945 the terms of the Lend–Lease settlement were agreed. Depending on the point of view, they were either of 'unprecedented generosity' or of unforgivable selfishness (the UK had to pay $650 million as against the cancellation of roughly $20 billion).[11] This writing-off was linked to British agreement to implement multilateral free trade, the Consideration required by Article VII of the Lend–Lease legislation.

Britain also needed help to deal with the sterling balances. During the war she had incurred huge debts denominated in sterling. She owed large amounts to countries in the British Empire and Commonwealth as well as to non-dollar countries for imports. She repaid the debts in sterling, and by and large these funds were banked in London. These were essentially current account liabilities, which could be withdrawn virtually without notice. By the end of June 1945 these sterling balances totalled $14 billion (roughly

£3,473 million), compared with British foreign currency and gold reserves of only $2.515 billion (£624 million),[12] and the reserves urgently had to be built up – a rapid withdrawal of the balances would dangerously threaten the financial system. The US felt strongly that the countries which had built up the balances should do something to reduce the amount, for fear that American aid would be diverted to deal with the balances instead of aiding British recovery,[13] and she urged the cancellation by Great Britain of a large proportion of the balances. There were objections to this. One was the question of honour, that a gentleman's word was his bond and one did not renege on an agreement, articulated particularly by the Bank of England; the Bank also believed, more prosaically, that such an agreement would greatly damage the pound as a reserve and trading currency and thus the position of London as a financial centre.[14] Both the Bank and the Treasury feared that a precipitate conversion of the balances into gold or dollars would strike at the reserves and weaken the exchange rate. Separately, the Board of Trade believed that the sterling balances encouraged countries who owned them to purchase goods in Great Britain, rather than elsewhere; the difficulty here was that Great Britain did not at that point produce much that these countries wanted to buy. Furthermore, she would receive only sterling in payment, whilst she needed dollars in order to buy goods in North America. Drafts of the Financial Agreement sent to London were returned with the clauses dealing with the balances taken out, and this eventually drove Keynes to cable that 'We are negotiating in Washington repeat Washington. Fig leaves that pass muster with old ladies in Threadneedle Street [Bank of England] wither in a harsher climate.'[15] Keynes had always believed that the balances should be blocked (i.e., that their owners could not require their conversion into gold or other currencies). Eventually there was agreement that, in rough proportions, 8 per cent could be immediately released, 31 per cent would be cancelled, and 62 per cent converted into long-term debt, with a transition period of five years.[16] However, the sterling balances would continue to be a problem, sometimes a dangerous one, for thirty-five years.[17]

Finally, Great Britain needed funds in order to carry out reconstruction, and to import food and raw materials.[18] She therefore needed financial aid of an immediate and concrete sort – an addition to resources, not a subtraction from liabilities. Therefore, the UK asked for a dollar loan, negotiations for which extended from June to December 1945.[19] Keynes was in an unenviable position. He had convinced the Cabinet that a generous American government would, because of Great Britain's sufferings in the common cause, grant a huge sum in aid. Yet, not only did he and his colleagues become subject to intense pressure in the US, which they had not expected, but they had to try to convince the Cabinet that Keynes had been too sanguine about American intentions. The Cabinet's response was to blame him for his failure to carry out its instructions, and thus the delegation had to cope with a government in London which did not see why it had to give up traditional positions merely for a few dollars.[20] The British Treasury itself was little better. The Chancellor of the Exchequer, Hugh Dalton, was thought even by his friends not to understand overseas finance, nor to be aware of the links between it and domestic finance.[21] Sir Wilfrid Eady, the Permanent Secretary in charge of the Overseas Finance Section of the Treasury, actually wrote to Keynes thanking him for the two years' instruction he had received from him during the war years. Keynes himself wrote to Halifax after it was all over that 'The ignorance was all embracing . . . And as for the insiders, so dense a fog screen had been created that such as the Chancellor and the Governor of the Bank had only the dimmest idea of what we had given away and what we had not . . . Political trouble there will be, for the Cabinet is a poor, weak thing.'[22]

In the end, Great Britain received not a grant, not an interest-free loan, but a loan carrying 2 per cent interest, although there was a 'waiver' clause attached, so that if the UK was in dire straits, the repayment of capital and interest could be postponed. (The interest rate, it should be noted, was lower than that imposed on returning American servicemen for housing loans.[23]) The loan itself was for $3,750 million (the British request shrank from $6,000 million to $4,000 million, whilst Vinson stuck at $3,500 million; the President split the difference), which Keynes thought would be barely sufficient if nothing went wrong. In exchange for this loan, the British agreed to try to deal with the sterling balances as described above, and, more ominously, also conceded that sterling would be fully convertible into dollars and other currencies within one year of the ratification of the Financial Agreement. (During the war, in order to control Britain's financial resources, the Treasury had refused to allow sterling to be converted into any other currency without its permission.) Either Britain yielded this point, or there would be no loan.[24] The Americans had determined to pin her down to convertibility, and, further, to the elimination of restrictions of imperial preferences within the Sterling Area.[25] They also insisted that the transition period should be only one year, rather than the five requested by the British. Negotiations nearly broke down over this, and it was only the stark realities of the situation that convinced the Cabinet to accept the Financial Agreement. As Halifax wrote to London on 5 December, 'I cannot think the practical disadvantage of accepting American Draft [of the Loan Agreement] comes anywhere near the grave mischief over many fields of Anglo-American relations that must be the inevitable and enduring consequences of rupture.'[26] As far as the Treasury was concerned, there was 'real consternation . . . , acute disappointment, and some resentment'.[27] For the Americans, however, who had been working towards this new world of convertible currencies, the elimination of preferences, and multilateral trading since the First World War, victory was sweet. The fiftieth and final repayment, of $100 million, was made in December 2006, sixty years after the loan was arranged.[28]

There was a real crisis, however, with the attempts to convince Parliament and the US Congress to ratify it. Both sides in the negotiations, and particularly the Americans, had been closely constrained by fears of going beyond what would be acceptable to their legislatures. Without the loan, the UK would not join Bretton Woods,[29] and the IMF and the World Bank would most likely be prevented from operating; conversely, if the UK declined to ratify Bretton Woods, the Americans would refuse the loan. A few days after the signing of the Financial Agreement, the Labour government presented Parliament with an omnibus resolution expressing approval of it, the Lend–Lease settlement and Bretton Woods. The deadline for British ratification was 31 December 1945, which allowed only three weeks for public discussion and Parliamentary debate. The government was never going to have a problem in the parliamentary vote, given Labour's large majority, but feelings ran high and the debate opened with a cascade of hostile comments. For the Conservative MP Robert Boothby, the Agreement was 'an economic Munich' and the government did not have a mandate from the people to 'sell the British Empire for a packet of cigarettes'.[30] As *The Economist* put it, 'In the complex of agreements that have been bound together – the Loan Agreement, Bretton Woods, and the commercial proposals – there is something to displease everybody.'[31] The worst point, not least because it could be understood by everybody, was that, once again, the US had chosen to charge interest on a loan to its wartime ally. Churchill declared himself 'astonished', whilst Keynes stated, 'I shall never so long as I live cease to regret that this is not an interest-free loan . . . The amount of money at stake cannot be important to the United States, and what a difference it would have made to our feelings and to our response!'[32] The defence of the Agreements by the government was weak: Great Britain needed the loan, and the effects of rejection would be alarming – less food and fewer raw materials than the country needed, and living standards would plummet. Furthermore (although this argument needed careful deploying), rejection of the Agreement would badly harm Anglo-American relations. As Dalton said during the debate in the Commons, 'We and the Americans, if peace is to be assured, must learn to live and work together. The rejection of these Agreements would not only be an economic and financial disaster for this country of ours, but it would be not less a disaster for the whole future of international co-operation.'[33]

In the end, the motion of approval was passed by the Commons 343 to 100, with 169 abstentions. According to Gardner, this vote gave 'an entirely inadequate picture of the divided character of Parliamentary sentiment. Churchill and the majority of the Conservative party abstained from voting', and seventy of them, mostly imperialists, defied their leaders and voted against the agreements. The government also faced a revolt in its own ranks,[34] with twenty-nine Labour MPs voting against. Even the supporters were mostly lukewarm, with *The Economist* summing up the general reaction: 'We are not compelled to say we like it . . . Our present needs are the dire consequence of the fact that we fought earlier, that we fought longest and that we fought hardest.'[35]

In the House of Lords, where Conservatives held the majority, the danger that they might delay the motion past the final hour was very real. Lord Woolton, the leader of the Conservative Party in the Lords, spoke of 'dollar dictation'.[36] Keynes, though, saved the day. Arriving from the US on 17 December, he went virtually straight to the Lords and sat through five hours of debate. He then opened the debate the following day. 'His aim was to dispel the ignorance and mistrust which had enveloped the speeches in both Houses. Even supporters of the loan treated it as a humiliating imposition and directed their wrath at the source – the United States.'[37] But Keynes argued that the Loan Agreement was a compromise between the US and the UK to enable the restoration of a liberal world economy, from which Britain stood to gain. He 'finessed the issue of unequal bargaining power and clashing national interests'.[38] They were two different countries with different national interests and different methods of achieving them. Keynes emphasised the 'complex politics of Congress', the 'remoteness' of public opinion, the contractual and commercial basis of American life in trying to explain the characteristic American approach to negotiating with the British. The Americans wanted everything cut and dried, the British preferred things left 'vaguer'; the package of deals represented a 'workable compromise between the certainty they wanted and the measure of elasticity we wanted'. The British, he admitted, should not have placed so much reliance on extracting help by parading their 'war medals'. 'Our American friends were interested not in our wounds, though incurred in a common cause, but in our convalescence. They wanted . . . to be told that we intended to walk without bandages as soon as possible.' Then he came to his final, profoundly important, statement: 'Some of us, in the tasks of war and more lately in those of peace, have learnt by experience that our two countries can work together. Yet it would be only too easy for us to walk apart. I beg those who look askance at these plans to ponder deeply and responsibly where it is they think they want to go.'[39] Finally, he sat back, exhausted. After a further five hours of debate, the House divided, and approved the Financial Agreement by a vote of ninety to eight,[40] with about one hundred peers abstaining; the Bretton Woods Agreement was approved without a vote. With the end of the political debate, the 'fever of controversy' in Britain subsided.[41]

But the Agreements now had to face an even more volatile institution. On 20 January 1946 President Harry S Truman sent the Financial Agreement to Congress with an appeal for speedy approval. But from the beginning, it was clear that passage was going to be very difficult. The public were largely indifferent, with domestic problems – high taxes, the rising cost of living, and a wave of strikes – in the forefront. Opposition to the Agreements came from a number of directions and were of a number of types, but the more substantial arguments fell, broadly, into two categories. First, there was the fear that such a loan would tie the US to an alliance with Britain. The US administration had already spent some time and effort in selling the UN as obviating the need for power blocs, which were accused of leading to war. Yet, here was the possibility of the United States' being sucked into just such a bloc, a threat which was underlined by the speech Churchill made in Fulton, Missouri, on 5 March 1946, referring to an 'Iron Curtain' falling across Europe and calling for 'a special relationship between the British Commonwealth and Empire and the United States'.[42] Such talk only agitated those Congressmen and Senators who feared that, in effect, they would be underwriting the British Empire.

The other concern was, did Britain actually need the money? As Gardner points out, 'the Bretton Woods debate had distracted attention from the grave character of Britain's transitional difficulties and the unique importance of British and Commonwealth policy in the organization of multilateral trade. Ignorance of Britain's economic difficulties had grown to appalling proportions.'[43] The question many were asking was, why did Britain deserve special privileges? Could she not borrow the money from her own citizens, or extract it from the resources of the Commonwealth? Furthermore, Congress was not encouraged to approve the Loan by the reaction in the UK to its terms. As Michigan Senator Arthur Vandenberg, chairman of the Senate Foreign Relations Committee, wrote to John Foster Dulles on 19 December 1945, the day after the the passage of the Agreement by the House of Lords, 'Our prospective debtors are already begining to "shylock us" before the papers are signed. We are notified in advance that we are going to get no good will out of this largesse. If we are not going to get good will what are we going to get?'[44]

For the administration, the goal was the construction of a system of multilateral trade, and Britain was a key country. But Congress had to be assured that the Loan was sufficient for the purpose: enough was enough. None the less, the legislators dragged their feet. The turning point in the Senate came with Vandenberg's speech on 22 April 1946, when he announced that he had decided to support the loan: 'If we do not lead some other great and powerful nation will capitalize our failure and we shall pay the price of our default.' On 10 May the Senate approved the Agreement by forty-six to thirty-four. The Agreement also faced great difficulties in getting through the House of Representatives. An unrepentant isolationist had just been elected Senator from Nebraska, which aroused fright amongst some Congressmen about the grass roots. There was also the current conflict between the UK and the US over the future disposition of Palestine, whose Mandate from the League of Nations was held by Britain. Truman, under strong pressure from American Zionists, was urging Britain to allow 100,000 Holocaust survivors into Palestine, despite British restrictions on Jewish immigration (the British had long tried to hold the ring between Arabs and Jews in Palestine). And, of course, there were all of the same anti-British pressures which had been focused on the Senate. Nevertheless, the Agreement passed by 219 to 155, and on 15 July Truman signed the legislation authorising the British loan.[45]

What had changed was the American perception of the Soviet Union, relations with which were steadily deteriorating. In early spring 1946 there had been a crisis over Iran. The Soviet Union had maintained troops in the north of the country in spite of the January 1942 Tripartite Treaty of Alliance between the UK, the USSR and Iran, in which they had all agreed to the evacuation of Allied troops within six months after the end of the war. In the autumn of 1945 the Kremlin had supported separatist movements in the Iranian provinces of Azerbaijan and Kurdistan, with Soviet troops preventing Iranian soldiers from putting down the uprisings (the Soviets were also demanding oil concessions). Iran insisted on the evacuation of Azerbaijan in north-western Iran by 2 March 1946, and the US strongly supported her, but Iran also engaged in quieter direct negotiations with the Soviets; Soviet troops finally left in May. Turkey was another flash point. The Soviets since March 1945 had been putting pressure on Turkey to grant a base on the Dardanelles Strait, which would control the waterway linking the Black Sea and the Mediterranean; they were also calling for the cession of Kars and Ardahan.[46] In March 1946 there was a difficult Foreign Ministers' meeting in Paris. At this point, the US administration held back from mobilising votes on an anti-Soviet platform, but some Congressmen were growing restless about the Soviet threat.

On 1 July, Stewart Alsop, one of the most influential American journalists, wrote in the *New York Herald-Tribune* that 'in view of the appalling world situation, the choice between a strong and friendly Britain and a weak and resentful Britain condemned to a future of endless austerity by a vote of Congress does not seem a difficult choice to make'.[47] It may have been that the Iranian crisis was crucial, in that the Soviet threat could no longer be ignored. In the final stages of the debate in the House the Speaker, Sam Rayburn of Texas, was compelling. In his speech on 12 July he 'intoned gravely': 'I do not want Western Europe, England, and all the rest pushed toward an ideology that I despise. I fear if we do not co-operate with our great natural ally that is what will happen . . . If we are not allied with the great British democracy, I fear that somebody will be and God pity us when we have no ally across the Atlantic Ocean and God pity them too.'[48]

Little was done by Britain about the sterling balances, which continued to loom threateningly over London. The Treasury, at least, was aware that in order to carry through safely, Britain would have to limit her imports, but here it ran into the economic policy of the rest of the Labour government. The Chancellor repeatedly warned his colleagues of the dangers inherent in the 'reckless pace'[49] of their expenditure, but the dollars provided by the American loan still drained away much more quickly than had been expected, a result hastened by a rapid rise in American prices.[50] And then came 15 July 1947, the date when, according to the Loan Agreement, the pound had to become fully convertible with all currencies, in particular the dollar. There was a huge run on the pound, as holders around the world rushed to sell sterling and buy dollars or gold. Britain did not have the foreign currency to meet the run for more than six weeks, and convertibility was suspended on 20 August 1947;[51] the country would not return even to partial convertibility until 1 January 1959.

In terms of multilateral trading and the convertibility of currencies, this was a turning point for both Britain and the US. The British immediately began to strengthen the barriers against the dollar and against imports from America, which they had agreed to lower in the Loan Agreement. The Commonwealth Foreign Ministers in September 1947 began the process which led to their countries combining to exclude dollar imports by rationing dollars, to restrict capital transfers outside of their group, and to foster dollar-saving trade amongst themselves[52] – back to imperial preference, so to speak, presumably to the horror of Cordell Hull. Meanwhile, the convertibility crisis brought home to the Americans both how necessary Britain was in their anti-Soviet scheme of things and how fundamentally weak she was. Therefore, they had a choice: they could have a multilaterally trading, non-discriminatory, but weak Britain, of little use as an ally; or they could have as an ally a Britain which, as leader of the Sterling Area and the British Commonwealth, appeared to be independently strong. The US chose the latter for the moment, but during the period of the Marshall Plan (1947 to 1952) she would still try to bend Britain more to her way of thinking.

II

The world view of the US government darkened inexorably between 1945 and 1947. From 1943 until his death in April 1945, Roosevelt had seen the future of the world as one to be guided by the united efforts of the US and the USSR – to his mind the two liberal and reformist powers.[53] The UK, the conqueror and possessor by force of a great empire, was relegated to the sidelines. Truman, however, encouraged by his advisers, did not see the world through Roosevelt's spectacles. From 1946 onwards, apprehension as to the intentions of the USSR grew. Melvyn Leffler argues that 'it is hard to overstate how portentous the international situation appeared to US officials in early 1946.' When Undersecretary of State Dean Acheson testified on behalf of the British loan on 6 March, he painted a bleak picture: 'The commercial and financial situation of the world is worse than any of us thought a year ago it would be. Destruction is more complete, hunger more acute, exhaustion more widespread than anyone then realized.'[54] There was pressure in Europe, with ominous hints of intended communist control not only of the Soviet Zone but of a united Germany, and of the rest of Eastern Europe. There were concerns about the Far East, with real fears over what was happening in China, which were to be confirmed in 1949 with the establishment of the People's Republic. There was pressure in many Third World countries, as nationalist movements seemed increasingly to be falling under the influence and even control of communists. How should the US fight back?

George Kennan, chargé d'affaires at the American Embassy in Moscow, had sent telegrams warning the State Department of Soviet intentions, but there had been little reaction. When, however, the Department wrote on 3 February 1946 that 'we should welcome receiving from you an interpretive analysis of what we may expect in the way of future implementation of these announced policies' (i.e., those contained in the pre-election speeches of Stalin and his associates), he grabbed the opportunity and on 22 February sent to Washington – in sections so as not to put off his readership by its length – what became known as the 'Long Telegram'. This was the intellectual origin of the policy of 'containment', the lodestar of American foreign policy during the Cold War. In the following three years Europe would see economic containment with the Marshall Plan and military containment with NATO.

The USSR, Kennan wrote, was aggressive and expansionist, and she would test and probe, taking advantage of opportunities and seeking to exploit any weaknesses in the west. She would continue to use governments or governing groups willing to work with the USSR to gain control over countries. Significantly, he argued that it would not be possible to negotiate with or placate the Soviets. So the US always had to respond, to make it abundantly clear to the Soviets that they would not be allowed to absorb more territory, and to threaten force if necessary – since the USSR was fundamentally weak, it would retreat if the west acted with determination. 'Impervious to logic of reason, . . . it is highly sensitive to logic of force.'[55] Leffler emphasises the sheer fragmentation of policy-making in Washington, with the President basically uninterested in foreign policy and the separate armed forces fighting amongst themselves, but united in contempt of the State Department's inability to take an overall view of the international situation.[56] Not the least of the reasons for the influence of the Long Telegram was the fact that it provided a unifying theme.

Less than two weeks later Churchill made his contribution to mobilising American public opinion. Truman feared the growth of Soviet power, but he was stymied by a public opinion which appeared not to support a firm policy towards the USSR and a press which was divided. Churchill's visit to the US in February and March 1946 provided the President with the opportunity to try to change public perception. On 5 March 1946 at Westminster College in Fulton, Missouri, with Truman sitting beside him, Churchill set out the issues and warned of the looming Soviet threat: 'We understand the Russians' need to be secure on her western frontiers from all renewal of German aggression . . . [Nevertheless,] From Stettin in the Baltic to Trieste in the Adriatic, an iron curtain has descended across the Continent . . . [Furthermore,] in a great number of countries, far from the Russian frontiers and throughout the world, Communist fifth columns are established and work in complete unity and absolute obedience to the directions they receive from the Communist centre.' The only sure defence, Churchill stated, was 'the fraternal association of the English-speaking peoples. This means a special relationship between the British Commonwealth and Empire and the United States.'[57] Churchill's speech had a profound impact both in the US and abroad. He was able to speak in easily understood language, emphasising an all-encompassing threat: Soviet expansion externally and communist subversion internally. Americans rejected Churchill's call for a military alliance but shivered at the menace he portrayed.

The British government, too, felt profound apprehension about the USSR. As noted above, Churchill feared the power of a USSR unconstrained by a defeated Germany, the country which had traditionally formed the barrier between Russia and Western Europe. His successor as Prime Minister, the Labour Party's Clement Attlee, had a short period with his Foreign Secretary, Ernest Bevin, of believing that left could speak to left. But Bevin, who essentially controlled British foreign policy,[58] soon shared Churchill's concerns about the USSR and the safety of the empire, given the lack of resources for safeguarding it. The government had to concentrate its forces, and to do this, it had to decide what was most vital to defend. Great Britain could not be separate from Europe, given the advent of missiles, but after the defence of the UK herself and her maritime communications, priority was given to the defence of the British Empire and Commonwealth. Britain would not again land soldiers on the Continent in time of war, and the Royal Air Force would normally fly only from bases in the UK.[59] By December 1947, the Chiefs of Staff had decided on the three pillars which had to be defended at all costs: the home islands, the sea communications to the US and the Dominions, and the Middle East.[60] The only way these could be safeguarded was by close co-operation with and the co-optation of the power of the US. As a group of British high officials, gathered together for an informal discussion on European co-operation in January 1949 during the negotiations over NATO, reaffirmed, 'Since post-war planning began, our policy has been to secure close political, military and economic co-operation with USA. This has been necessary to get economic aid. It will always be decisive for our security . . . We hope to secure a special relationship with USA and Canada . . . for in the last resort we cannot rely upon the European countries.'[61]

But the UK was also of use to the US. According to a State Department policy statement of 11 June 1948, 'The policies and actions of no other country in the world, with the possible exception of the USSR, are of greater importance to us.' A new appreciation of the value of the British Empire was one of the most spectacular changes in American perceptions of the world and of the UK's place in it to have occurred since the Revolution. Written during a period of very tense negotiations between the two countries over the

Marshall Plan (see below), the statement continues: 'British friendship and cooperation ... is necessary for American defense. The United Kingdom, the Dominions, Colonies and Dependencies, form a world-wide network of strategically located territories of great military value, which have served as defensive outposts and as bridgeheads for operations. Subject to our general policy of favoring eventual self-determination of peoples, it is our objective that the integrity of this area be maintained.'[62] Or, as it was later put by Frank Wisner, head of covert operations for the CIA, in a conversation with Foreign Office official and Soviet spy Kim Philby, 'whenever there is somewhere we want to destabilize, the British have an island nearby'.[63]

Two years later, just before the outbreak of the Korean War, the importance of the UK and the Commonwealth to the US was reaffirmed and widened:

> No other country has the same qualifications for being our principal ally and partner as the UK. It has internal political strength and important capabilities in the political, economic and military fields throughout the world. Most important, the British share our fundamental objectives and standards of conduct ... To achieve our foreign policy objectives we must have the cooperation of our allies and friends. The British and with them the rest of the Commonwealth, particularly the older dominions, are our most reliable and useful allies, with whom a special relationship should exist. This relationship is not an end in itself but must be used as an instrument of achieving common objectives. We cannot afford to permit a deterioration in our relationship with the British.[64]

Therefore, in the period from 1947 to 1956, the UK was the US's primary ally. For this reason, the US made efforts both to support the UK and very occasionally to give some precedence to British interests over what the Americans believed were the best interests of both the western world and themselves.

III

The supreme weakness for the UK in her attempt to maintain her status as a Great Power was the fragility of her economy. The US had overestimated Britain's economic strength, but the true situation was brought home by the British decision in February 1947 to withdraw the bulk of her troops from Greece.[65] When the German army had withdrawn, they had left a country devastated by war and divided between left and right. The British had immediately sought to restore order, contain the Greek left and revive the economy. But in late 1944, civil war had erupted, and British troops had to put down a communist-led uprising. This then allowed the right to consolidate power and wreak their revenge. Since late 1945 the British had asked for American aid, because their financial and military resources were stretched. During 1946 the US government continued to discourage the withdrawal of British troops, hoping that Britain would continue military aid whilst the US concentrated on economic aid.[66] But in 1945–1946, this military aid had cost Great Britain £132 million, and on 21 February 1947 the British told the Americans that their financial position was such that they could no longer provide assistance to Greece and Turkey: they planned to pull their troops out of Greece and to end their military aid to both countries.[67] The US government had decided eighteen months earlier that the Dardanelles, the eastern Mediterranean and the Middle East had to be kept free of Soviet influence, so something had to be done. In this case, the US would have to prevent the Greek communists from taking over and then aligning Greece with the USSR. As set out by William Clayton, Undersecretary of State for Economic Affairs, the problem was that the 'reins of world leadership are fast slipping from Britain's competent but now very weak hands. These reins will be picked up either by the United States or by Russia. If by Russia, there will almost certainly be war in the next decade or so, with the odds against us. If by the United States, war can almost certainly be prevented.'[68]

An even greater problem was to convince Congress and the American people that the US should pick up the reins in the eastern

Mediterranean. On 27 February 1947, President Truman, Secretary of State Marshall and Undersecretary of State Acheson met with Congressional leaders. Marshall began to explain the problem to the Congressmen and Senators, but he was clearly making little impression. Then Acheson broke in and described the situation in apocalyptic terms: 'I knew we were met at Armageddon . . . In the past eighteen months, I said, Soviet pressure on the Straits, on Iran, and on Northern Greece had brought the Balkans to the point where a highly possible Soviet breakthrough might open three continents to Soviet penetration . . . We and we alone were in a position to break up the play.' When he finished, there was a long silence. Finally Senator Vandenberg solemnly declared, '"Mr. President, if you will say that to the Congress and the country, I will support you and I believe that most of its members will do the same."'[69] Therefore, after a rapid public relations effort, Truman appeared before a joint session of Congress on 12 March 1947 to request $400 million for aid to Greece and Turkey, and to announce that 'I believe it must be the policy of the United States to support free peoples who are resisting attempted subjugation by armed minorities or by outside pressures. I believe that we must assist free peoples to work out their own destinies in their own way. I believe that our help should be primarily through economic and financial aid which is essential to economic stability and orderly political processes.'[70] Known as the Truman Doctrine, this became an important principle of American foreign policy.

There was nothing to indicate a geographic limit, although Acheson repeatedly explained to Congressmen that it was not meant to include China or to undermine Soviet control of Eastern Europe. None the less, Greece and Turkey were not the only problems. France and Italy, which had large domestic Communist parties and even Communist ministers in coalition governments, were also of great concern. Indeed, the dire economic situation in most of the Continental countries frightened many in the US government and the army: hungry and cold people were distressing in themselves, but even worse was the fear that they would succumb to Communist blandishments. It is unclear whether Truman's speech itself put an end to the meeting of the Council of Foreign Ministers then taking place in Moscow, but Marshall returned from the meeting convinced of the USSR's unremitting hostility towards the West in general and the US in particular. However, it certainly laid the foundation for one of the most famous, and successful, American foreign policy initiatives, the Marshall Plan.

The Marshall Plan, or European Recovery Program (to give it its formal title), saw the US granting or loaning some thirteen billion dollars over four years to sixteen European countries to enable them to reignite their economies. The US required a strong and integrated European economy to which American goods, both industrial and agricultural, could be exported; American strategic policy required a strong and united Western Europe to provide a barrier against further Soviet expansion westward; the US needed other liberal, capitalist democracies to exist lest the US cease to be one herself; and the altruistic strain in American political culture encouraged the desire to help the European countries get back on their feet. The Marshall Plan, therefore, was a defining episode in the Cold War, during which the Continent was split along the geopolitical line which remained in place until 1989; it was a defining episode in the early history of European integration; it was an important example of the overt use of economic power in foreign policy; and it was the first concerted attempt by the US government to transplant American culture abroad.[71]

Upon his return from Moscow, Marshall instituted a number of studies looking into the problems faced by a number of regions, particularly Western Europe. The new Policy Planning Staff, headed by George Kennan of the Long Telegram, wrote a memorandum setting out what the US might do to solve these problems; based on this, Marshall and his advisers developed a plan which could be presented to the Europeans.[72] In some haste they had to discuss the matter with important Congressmen and Senators, especially Arthur Vandenberg. They also had to ensure that the Europeans responded. On 4 June, Acheson invited to lunch Leonard Miall of the BBC, Malcolm Muggeridge of the *Daily Express* and Stewart McCall of the *News Chronicle*. He 'disclosed that the Secretary's Harvard speech [to be given the following day] was of the greatest importance and urged the correspondents to telephone the full text of the speech to

London as soon as it was released and to make arrangements with their editors in London to deliver the full text at once to Ernest Bevin, no matter where he was or what time it was.'[73]

And then, on 5 June 1947, Marshall spoke at the graduation ceremony at Harvard University. He described the collapse of the European economies, called for a programme of reconstruction rather than relief, asked the Europeans to take the initiative, and invited all European countries to participate, including, by implication, the Soviet Union and those of Eastern Europe.[74] This was a remarkable change. It is not even necessary to go back to the years after the end of the First World War, when the US could not withdraw from Europe fast enough. From the spring of 1945 to a year later, US military forces had demobilised to the extent that their numbers plummeted from 12.3 million to 1.5 million;[75] the expectation, and the intention, of most Americans was that they would leave European affairs behind and return home. Yet, within two years of the end of the war in Europe, Marshall was making his clarion call to arms.

After the delivery of the speech, 'Miall went on the air to Great Britain at 3 p.m. on June 5, saying what a tremendous proposal Marshall had made, and Muggeridge and McCall telephoned the text to their editors, who rushed it to Bevin at his home.'[76] Bevin contacted Georges Bidault, the French Foreign Minister, and the two invited Vyacheslav Molotov, the Soviet Foreign Minister, to meet in Paris to discuss the matter. The question as to whether the Americans wanted Soviet participation is only barely problematic: it would have been inconvenient, to say the least, but they did not themselves want to take the decision which might split Europe. The Soviets, who profoundly distrusted the whole idea, discussed it in Moscow, but decided that they could not countenance the Americans crawling all over their economy. Thus they refused, and forced those countries under their influence to do likewise (Poland, Finland and Czechoslovakia had wanted to participate).[77] Bevin certainly did not want Soviet participation, since he believed that their only desire would be to sabotage the scheme. Bidault agreed, but he was firm that it had to be a Soviet decision: the French Communist Party, which was worryingly large, would certainly try to rock France if it thought that the Soviets had been kept out.[78]

Bevin's primary strategic concern was to involve the US so closely in European affairs that she would not again be able to withdraw, a policy conceptualised by Geir Lundestad as an American 'empire by invitation'.[79] Coincidental with the Marshall Plan negotiations, Bevin was trying to lay the groundwork for an American military commitment (see below). But this was a beginning, and in answer to the joint invitation from Bevin and Bidault, the Conference on European Economic Co-operation, with representatives from sixteen countries, met in Paris from 17 July to 22 September 1947. With very great difficulty, they prepared a plan for American aid based on increased production in each country; this was then submitted to the Americans. It was essentially a shopping list of the separate country plans and the total requested, $29.2 billion, was far too high. The Americans were frustrated, and insisted that the countries integrate their independent submissions and come up with a smaller sum; indeed, there was the implicit threat that they would call the whole thing off if the Europeans did not comply. There had been a trade-off between the British and the French, in that the conference was held in Paris, but the British provided the chairman, Oliver Franks. His supreme chairing and negotiating skills enabled the Europeans to come up with a total that the State Department believed it could present to the Congress.[80] But after the Foreign Assistance Bill was presented to Congress on 19 December, it languished and nearly died. Ironically, the Soviets came to the rescue: between 20 February and 1 March 1948 Czechoslovakia changed from a democratic state into a Communist dictatorship. The reaction in Congress was to pass the Bill, and on 1 March it was signed by Truman; the appropriations were approved in June.

Meanwhile, during the spring, the European countries set up the Organisation for European Economic Co-operation, whose purpose was to co-ordinate the requests for funds from the individual countries, a condition of aid; the US would then decide which to accept. Sir Edmund Hall-Patch, Deputy Under-Secretary at the Foreign Office, became the chairman of the Executive Committee. As Bevin pointed out, 'by our occupation of the chair of the Executive Committee . . . we shall be able to exercise a guiding influence on the day to day work of the Organisation',[81] a position in exchange for

which the UK was entirely happy for the Organisation to be situated
in Paris. The US, for legal reasons, required each country to sign a
bilateral agreement, so during the same period, negotiations
between the US and the UK took place. During June 1948, they
became fraught and nerve-racking, to the extent that a memorandum was drafted setting out the extent to which the UK required
Marshall Aid, in order that Cabinet ministers would know the consequences if, as seemed entirely possible, they rejected it.[82]

The reaction of the Cabinet to the US draft, in fact, was that it was
unacceptable. Not only was the whole tone of the draft felt to be
insulting, but the US was insisting on three conditions which the
Cabinet found outrageous. First of all, the US was claiming the right
to force Britain to give most-favoured-nation (MFN) treatment to
US goods – that is, that they would be entitled to equal treatment
with the best conditions allowed to any other country, such as members of the British Commonwealth – whilst leaving the US free to
impose high tariffs. She was also requiring MFN treatment to be
accorded to Japan and Korea, the former of which had been Britain's
ferocious enemy only three years previously. And – worst of all – she
demanded the right to insist that Britain change the exchange rate of
the pound if she believed that the current rate was increasing
Britain's need for American help. There were other points as well,
several of which had significant implications.[83] In other words, elements in the American government were continuing the fight against
the position of the pound and against Britain's commercial policies.
Anglophobia on the whole dominated the US Treasury. The State
Department was more sympathetic, since it shared with the Foreign
Office the overriding perception of the USSR as the primary enemy,
and saw the UK as the main European power in the fight to contain
the Soviets.

The negotiations over the agreement nearly broke down on 17
June, after six gruelling hours in Washington. They were moved to
London and the British appealed to the American Ambassador,
Lewis Douglas, who was sympathetic to their position. Additional
help was provided by France, whose leaders refused to sign their
Bilateral Agreement until the British signed theirs; partly this was in
support, but it also indicated a refusal to accept less than the British

obtained. The deadlock was finally broken on 24 June. Both sides compromised, but Article X, which had given the US the right to dictate the exchange rate of the pound, was dropped entirely, and the others modified to such a degree that the British could live with them.[84] In the negotiations for the Loan in 1945, Britain had had to give way; by 1948, with the previous year's sterling crisis having brought home to the US the weakness of the British economy, the UK was allowed to prevail on those points which she believed were vital to her well-being.

Each country which received Marshall Aid had a resident ECA (Economic Co-operation Administration) mission. Their purpose was to work closely with the government of the recipient country, perhaps influence it, and to learn as much about the economic situation and policy of the country as the host government itself knew. The amount of interference in the affairs of the host country varied enormously; in Greece, for example, the country mission was practically a second government, whilst in the UK its influence was minimal.[85] Indeed, the ECA headquarters in Washington felt that there were special problems with the London mission. To be specific, Washington often felt that the mission had been captured by the British, and was more likely to argue the British case against Washington than vice versa.[86] The members of the mission certainly had great respect for British Treasury officials.

There were two main problems, one focusing on internal British financial policy and the other on British foreign policy. The first was the use of the 'counterpart' funds. Marshall Aid did not come as money but as goods. Each country had to provide the local currency equivalent of the cost; 5 per cent of this total (the counterpart fund) was to be set aside for the use of the country mission. (The American military establishment, against the wishes of the ECA, hijacked the bulk of the British 5 per cent to purchase strategic materials, such as tin, rubber, manganese and chrome, from the Empire.) The other 95 per cent was intended by the Americans to be used by each recipient government for monetary and financial stabilisation, for the stimulation of productive activity, and for the exploration and development of new sources of wealth. In general, the ECA hoped that countries would use it for investment. London, however, wished to use it instead to repay short-term debt, and the UK Treasury refused to budge on the issue. The ECA had to accept this.[87]

The other major Anglo-American conflict centred on the attempt by the US to convince the OEEC countries to use this organisation as a vehicle for closer integration, both economic and political. It is not too strong to say that the US was the midwife of an integrated Europe. Belgium was probably the keenest. Great Britain was undoubtedly the most reluctant, alongside Norway. The US was intensely frustrated, because she saw the UK as the leader of Europe – and there is no doubt that, had the UK acted as the US hoped that she would, she would indeed have been the leader. Other European countries, although not France, looked to the UK. She alone of the Western European countries involved in the war had been neither defeated nor occupied, and her economy, weakened as it was, was still stronger than most of the others, with the possible exception of Belgium's. She had the British Empire and Commonwealth, as well as an army, navy and air force. But for all of those reasons, and because she feared being considered by the US as just another Continental European country, the UK refused to throw in her lot with Europe. Indeed, she fought this tooth and nail, and only gradually came to compromise over certain proposals as a result of American assurances or after weighing her chances of fending off American threats.

Over the years of the Marshall Plan, Britain was repeatedly to fight American attempts to convince her to integrate with Europe. One reason was economic, the fear that various American plans for a European Payments Union would force Britain to a premature restoration of convertibility – ministers had been seared by the 1947 convertibility crisis.[88] Furthermore, she was actually engaged in more trade with the Sterling Area than with Europe. Another reason was the fear that European economic weakness might drag Britain down. But beyond this was the fear of future diminution of her world role. The British government believed that it was imperative that the US consider her a partner, even if only a junior one, to be consulted and have her opinion respected. It was the UK's basic need of the US for both economic and military support that motivated the British in the negotiations for Marshall Aid, and it was her basic distrust of Europe that, in the final analysis, made her unable to go as far as the US desired, and nearly required, towards European integration.

The US government in general understood this, even if ECA officials sometimes lost their sense of proportion (but even one high ECA official, Richard M. Bissell, wrote that it was not to the US's benefit for Britain to abandon her overseas orientation in favour of a European one).[89] This recognition was a major reason why the US never pushed the UK too far, and the former's sense of her need for the UK checked her use of Marshall Aid. As final proof, in order to ensure that Britain could continue her involvement in foreign affairs, she received the largest amount of Marshall Aid.[90]

IV

The American assumption had been that the US would provide economic and financial aid to shore up Western Europe, not military aid. But Bevin was convinced that grave danger threatened without an American military commitment as well. Thus from 1946 he worked for this, initially without much success, because entering into a peacetime alliance would overturn the traditional American approach to world affairs. But, as with the Marshall Plan, it was the February 1948 Soviet coup in Czechoslovakia which, allied with other Soviet threats, encouraged the Americans to change their minds and enter seriously into negotiations for a West European military alliance. It was Bevin who first proposed what became the North Atlantic Treaty Organization (NATO), the institution which committed the US, to the dismay of Kennan and others in the State Department, to the military containment of the USSR on the European continent.

On 15 December 1947, the London Conference of Foreign Ministers' meeting on the future of Germany, which had begun in November and involved Bevin, Marshall, Molotov and Bidault, broke down irretrievably. Two days later Bevin spoke separately to Bidault, Marshall and Norman Robinson, the Canadian High Commissioner in London. To Bidault in the morning, he spoke of the necessity of creating some sort of federation in Western Europe and of bringing in the Americans. To Robinson in the afternoon he said how unfortunate that the Americans had no contingency plan in place if the Conference broke down. Therefore, the UK had to produce such a plan. Then, in the evening, he saw Marshall. He told him of his conversation with Bidault, and said that there had to be a defence system comprising the Americans, France, Italy, the UK and the Dominions; this would not be a formal alliance, but an 'understanding backed by power, money and resolute action', a sort of 'spiritual federation of the West'. The purpose was to convince the USSR that her advance into Western Europe had now stopped. Marshall was willing for early discussions to begin, and Bevin said that he would discuss matters with the Cabinet, and return with more definite views. This was the somewhat unlikely origin of the North Atlantic Treaty Organisation, or NATO.[91]

Over the following weeks Bevin became even more convinced that it was urgently necessary to provide some security for Western Europe. Earlier, on 4 March 1947, Britain and France had signed the Treaty of Dunkirk, which bound them together in an alliance for fifty years against the revival of German aggression. On 13 January 1948 Bevin instructed the British Ambassador in Paris, Sir Oliver Harvey, to suggest to Bidault that they simultaneously approach Belgium, the Netherlands and Luxembourg (Benelux), offering them treaties on the Dunkirk line. His idea was that once there was a solid defence core in Western Europe, they might develop the system and invite other states, such as the Mediterranean and Scandinavian countries, to join. Bidault agreed immediately, and on 20 January an approach was made to the three Benelux countries. Meanwhile, Bevin had sent a letter to Marshall to tell him about the treaty proposals; Marshall answered that he would do what he could to assist the Europeans.

Bevin wanted an American commitment to Western European security, since he believed that without this, any Western European system would have little value. But he knew that there had to be some effective collaboration amongst the European countries themselves before the Americans would even consider solid support. As Nicholas Henderson, a British diplomat who took part in the NATO negotiations, points out, 'if he appealed prematurely for US support before anything had been built in Western Europe, he might frighten American opinion forever'.[92] In a debate on foreign affairs in the House of Commons on 22 January, Bevin warned MPs about deteriorating relations with the Soviets, and announced the talks with the Benelux countries. He wanted to jolt people into realising the dangers. This included the Americans, and the warm response to his speech, with the State Department taking 'the remarkable step' of issuing a statement on 23 January welcoming the proposed new treaties, encouraged an approach to the US government.[93]

But then came several discouraging weeks. Robert Lovett, Undersecretary and sometimes Acting Secretary of State, was monumentally cautious, and with reason, because he was receiving conflicting advice; in addition, there were other important issues to take into account. On 2 February he wrote to the British Ambassador, Lord Inverchapel, making it clear that before the US became in any way involved, the Europeans had to show through a formal arrangement that they were willing to act together to defend themselves. A primary cause of this unexpected reluctance to act was a growing division of opinion within the State Department between those who believed that the US should become involved and those who did not. Unfortunately for Bevin, those against the proposal were two of the most influential men in the Department, Kennan and Charles Bohlen, the latter Departmental Counsellor and one of the Department's chief Russian experts. They feared provoking the Russians, but even more, they feared that this would irrevocably split the Continent.[94] Bohlen in particular was closely listened to by Marshall and Lovett, and he recommended general encouragement but no commitment. In addition Marshall and Lovett had, at that point, other priorities: getting the Marshall Plan legislation through Congress, and ensuring that Germany's resources were controlled by the West. They were particularly disturbed about directing any Western European defence arrangement against Germany. According to Henderson, 'Bevin feared the drift of events into a vicious circle: the Western union failing to materialise for lack of any knowledge of American intentions, and America unwilling to make any move towards Western Europe until Western Europe had consolidated itself.'[95]

But then came the Czech coup. As the diplomat Lord Gladwyn later wrote, 'the great producer of union is . . . fear'.[96] And it was not the only warning: on 8 March the Norwegian Foreign Minister, Halvard Lange, informed the US and British Ambassadors in Oslo that he had received advance notice that the USSR planned to demand that Norway sign a defence pact on the lines of the one that the Finns were being forced to sign. Norway wanted to refuse, but the government needed to know what, if any, help the US and UK would provide if the Soviet Union attacked.[97] Negotiations over a new Western European treaty had stalled in February because the French wanted bilateral treaties with the Benelux countries, not a larger grouping, and they wanted them directed against Germany. They feared that any other arrangement would be unduly and dangerously provocative to the Soviets, given that they had no guarantee of American support. The Belgians thought that this was foolish – communism was more of a threat than Germany; and, in any case, they hoped that, one day, Germany would join a western union. But the French were shocked by the Czech coup and the Norwegian rumours, negotiations accelerated, and on 17 March the Five-Power Treaty, or Brussels Pact, was signed.[98] That very same day Truman publicly endorsed it, in the same speech to Congress in which he called for the first peacetime conscription and stated that American troops would remain 'until the peace is secured in Europe'.[99]

But this was not enough of an American commitment for Bevin. Given the news from Norway (the British and Americans had immediately promised the Norwegians full support if they resisted Soviet pressure – vital, given the near panic in Oslo[100]), he had already proposed on 12 March tripartite talks between the UK, the US and Canada to discuss Western European security. A few hours after receiving Bevin's message, Marshall had replied that 'we are prepared to proceed at once in the joint discussions on the establishment of an Atlantic security system. I suggest the prompt arrival of the British representative early next week.'[101] This was the signal for the beginning of negotiations. Tension was increased substantially by the Soviet blockade of Berlin, begun on 24 June 1948, and the subsequent nine-month airlift of supplies to the beleaguered city by US and British aircraft (in the first substantial Anglo-American military mission since the war). Proposals were produced and studied by the various countries. There was a pause, and then what Henderson calls a 'sprint', with a draft text of a treaty produced on 24 December 1948.

Reaching that point had been fraught with difficulties. Which countries should be involved? Just the Brussels Treaty powers plus the US and Canada? What about Scandinavia? Sweden was determined to produce a neutral Scandinavian defence bloc, one requirement of which was that the members must not join any military alliance; amongst other reasons, she feared provoking the USSR. But Norway decided that a Scandinavian bloc, whether neutral or armed, would not provide the security she believed vital, and opted for the North Atlantic Pact, as did Denmark. What about Italy? By no stretch of the imagination could she be considered a North Atlantic power, but she was eventually included not because of her strength – the UK rightly considered her a military liability – but because of her weakness: left out, she might drift towards the Eastern Bloc, thereby endangering the eastern Mediterranean. Given the strength of the Italian Communist Party, which came worryingly close to winning the general election on 18 April 1948, this was not so unlikely. What about Algeria? France insisted that she be included as part of metropolitan France, to which the others finally agreed. And Portugal? She was reluctant, fearing that her alliance with Spain, which was not asked to join, would be damaged. But the US saw her inclusion as vital, given her possession of the Azores, and she eventually agreed to sign up. Ireland was different. Her initial response to the invitation had been that she would join the talks as a united Ireland; the American response was that they would not allow the talks to be hijacked by an internal matter and that Ireland's attempt to do so showed that she was not seriously interested in membership. She was therefore not asked to sign the treaty.[102]

With the publication of the text came one of the most difficult parts of the task: winning the consent of the Senate. Acheson succeeded Marshall as Secretary of State on 20 January 1949, and took some days to acquaint himself, as far as possible in the time, with all of the problems cluttering up his desk. On 3 February he had a meeting with Vandenberg and Senator Tom Connally of Texas, now chairman of the Senate Committee on Foreign Relations, to find his way: he needed to secure a text that these two Senators and their colleagues on the committee would support. The strength of isolationist sentiment made the task of getting the treaty through Congress a tough one. There were a number of questions – Should it deal with more than military security? Which nations should sign? What commitments should there be? – but the most difficult problem was Article 5. Fundamentally, this determined what the treaty powers should do if there was an attack against a member. Should there be automatic involvement? This, of course, went against the US Constitution, which gave Congress the power to declare war. Yet, without such automatic response, how would the treaty deter any attacker?[103] In the end, the treaty echoed the three musketeers: all for one and one for all.[104] Military force was threatened: all of the signatories would come to the assistance of any of them attacked by taking 'forthwith' – a word much argued over as being too aggressive – 'individually and in concert with other Parties, such action as it deems necessary' – thereby taking out the automaticity and placating the Constitution – 'including the use of armed force, to restore and maintain international peace and security'.[105] The treaty was signed in Washington on 4 April 1949.

But it still had to get through the Senate. The hearings of the Committee on Foreign Relations took sixteen days, but the earlier consultations with the State Department and the modification of the original text had been so thorough that, after hearing ninety-six witnesses and spending much time on Article 5, it went through thirteen to zero. But the full Senate was a different matter. The subject attracted long and impassioned speeches, and a modicum of silliness. As described by the cynical Acheson:

John Foster Dulles, appointed to the Senate on July 7 by Governor Dewey of New York to fill a vacancy, in a maiden speech a few days later supported the treaty and lashed out at 'preposterous and dangerous interpretation[s]'. This brought shouted and angry interruptions from Senator Taft [a strong isolationist].

William Jenner of Indiana found the treaty shrouded in secrecy
and wanted to know the whole truth, though about what remained
vague. After ten days of such statesmanlike deliberation the vote
was taken and the treaty approved by 82 to 13.[106]

Bevin was now a happier man. The US was treaty-bound to
defend the other signatories: the UK, France (including Algeria),
Belgium, the Netherlands, Luxembourg, Italy, Portugal, Norway,
Denmark, Canada and Iceland.[107] They, of course, were also committed to defending the US, but this promise somehow weighed
less heavily on them. The organisation of the Combined Chiefs of
Staff, still working together, was eventually folded into the NATO
structure, so that bilateral military discussions no longer took place in
the same manner. But there is an interesting question here: why
did Great Britain fight for integration within NATO while fighting
against it in the OEEC? The answer is clear: NATO was, theoret-
ically, an organisation of equals – all for one, one for all – and of
sovereign states; conversely, the OEEC, if American wishes were
followed, was to become a supranational organisation, first economic
and then political, to which individual sovereignties were to be at
least partly surrendered. It would take a quarter-century for Britain
finally to fulfil American hopes and join Europe, but by this time it
was not quite the Europe the US had desired. Nor was it the end of
the matter for the many Britons who did not feel particularly
'European'.

V

The 1950s were a very difficult period for Anglo-American relations.
There were continuing conflicts between the two countries' policies
in the Far East: particular problems arose from the UK's recognition
of the People's Republic of China in January 1950, to the fury of the
Americans; in Korea until 1953; and in Taiwan in 1955. These placed
a massive strain on the relationship. The UK as an imperial and military power was in obvious and rapid decline; by 1948, India,
Pakistan, Nepal, Burma and Ceylon had all received their

independence.[108] Great efforts were made by the British to regain or at least retain as much as possible of their international power, but their attempts to influence the use of American power for this purpose met with varying success. At the same time, the US revelled in her own power. The massive expansion in her military forces was one element, but of almost equal importance was that in her intelligence capabilities. A mixed blessing was the growth in the size and power of the CIA, which early on began to devote itself to covert activities rather than intelligence-gathering. Not the least of the strains in the alliance was that caused by growing British apprehension that the US would push the USSR beyond endurance by her series of covert activities around the Soviet perimeter.

For decades the UK had sought to convince the US to take up the responsibilities of a Great Power. With the Marshall Plan and NATO, she fulfilled these hopes. But for the British, events threatened to spiral out of control. The crucial event was the Korean War, which began in June 1950 with the invasion of South Korea by North Korea. From this period, the US, buttressed by a huge and growing military force, supported by several intelligence agencies and driven increasingly by the desire to go beyond containment and 'win' the Cold War, caused increasing alarm in London.[109] In December 1950 Field Marshal Sir William Slim, the Chief of the Imperial General Staff, returned from a visit to Washington and warned his fellow service chiefs that 'The United States were convinced that war was inevitable, and that it was almost certain to take place within the next eighteen months; . . . This . . . was dangerous because . . . they might think that . . . the sooner we got it over with the better, and we might as a result be dragged unnecessarily into World War III.'[110] This visit had taken place because of the fear of Prime Minister Attlee that the US was contemplating the use of nuclear weapons in Korea. Had he known that two days after the war began, General Curtis LeMay, the commander of the Strategic Air Command, had advised the Joint Chiefs of Staff 'to declare atomic operations the top priority for Korea and eschew a conventional response' because he feared that 'conventional preparations might preclude effective atomic preparations',[111] Attlee would have been even more alarmed. Both governments believed that North Korea had been encouraged, if not directed, by the USSR, the ultimate enemy. The nub of the matter was that American contingency plans for a 'hot' war required that over half of her air strike on the USSR be launched from Great Britain, the US's 'unsinkable aircraft carrier'.[112]

By the Spaatz–Tedder Agreement in 1946, the British had undertaken to prepare five RAF bases in East Anglia – Lakenheath, Mildenhall, Scampton, Marham and Bassingbourn – for use by American B-29 'Superfortress' bombers in time of crisis. Atomic bomb-handling facilities in Britain were ready by 1947 (atomic weapons would first arrive in July 1950, a month after the outbreak of the Korean War). On 24 June 1948, the USSR closed off to the other three occupying powers of Germany all access routes to Berlin (the Berlin blockade). Four days later, a Cabinet committee agreed to the request of the US Ambassador that another three groups of heavy bombers be allowed to come to the UK as a temporary show of strength. But it seems clear that the US had more than a temporary sojourn in mind. As the US Defense Secretary, James Forrestal, wrote in his diary on 15 July, 'We have the opportunity *now* of sending these planes, and once sent they would become somewhat of an accepted fixture, whereas a deterioration of the situation in Europe might lead to a condition of mind under which the British would be compelled to reverse their present attitude.'[113] Bevin, of course, was so keen to have the US committed to European defence that he welcomed the suggestion. Indeed, somewhat to the bewilderment of the Americans, the UK did not even require an agreement as to their use. As the US Air Force commander in Britain had pointed out in 1949, 'Never before in history has one first-class power gone into another first-class power's country without any agreement.'[114] However, when the US asked to take over two airfields in Oxfordshire, the British government decided that an agreement was needed, stating the right of the UK to terminate it, and setting out her rights if the US wished to use the airfields before Britain herself was at war.[115] Britain, not the US, would be in the front line. For Britain, it was a complex situation. On the one hand, she needed to tie the US to her safety, and to do this, she had to give the US what that country needed. But there was another deep concern. Britain moved from a desire to contain the Soviet Union to a desire to contain the threat of war, and this implied the need to contain the US. The reaction of US civilian and military leaders to this was sometimes closer to contempt than to respect.[116]

Respect was similarly damaged by the obvious decline in Britain's relations with her colonies. The old British form of rule, based on a close relationship with monarchs and the local elites (what Richard Aldrich calls 'suggestible princes and pashas'[117]), was becoming increasingly untenable, given the rise of new nationalist movements. More force was having to be used, and British notions of superiority were being shown up for the faded and even tattered pieces of cloth that they were. To the American gut feeling that the British Empire was wrong was added a growing conviction that the British were no longer even competent to run it. The British out in the field could sense this. As Sir Henry Pelham, British Ambassador to Saudi Arabia, wrote on 17 December 1952, 'The Americans seem anxious to build their empire on their own, and in so far as they seek our co-operation at all . . . seem to find us embarrassing partners. Their attitude reminds me of those advertisements warning against bad breath.'[118] When the Americans looked at the British leaders, they could see why things were in such bad shape. Churchill, by the end of his premiership in 1955, had neither health nor full capability of mind. Anthony Eden, who succeeded him, also suffered badly from ill health and great pain, which was only controlled by the use of various medicines, and he was consequently subject to severe mood swings; he also repeatedly showed stunning and even dangerous errors of judgement.[119] One of these was when he decided to act as his own Foreign Secretary by replacing Harold Macmillan with the colourless and easily-controlled Selwyn Lloyd. Macmillan had enjoyed a very good relationship with the American Secretary of State, John Foster Dulles, whilst Eden and Dulles detested each other.

This swirl of resentment, contempt and apprehension all came together in the Middle East and specifically in the Suez Crisis of October–November 1956. The crisis has a resonance in many spheres beyond that of Anglo-American relations. For instance, severe damage was done to Britain's reputation amongst many long-standing allies and friends. A good example is Norway, for years one of Britain's closest and most loyal allies: Suez badly shook that loyalty. Another interesting point regarding the crisis was the dangerous role of MI6, nearly out of the control of its institutional head, the Foreign Office, and indulging, along with the CIA, in anti-Nasser plots which included assassination plans. There was also the amazing duplicity of Harold Macmillan, the Chancellor of the Exchequer, who was at least as responsible as Eden, if not more so, for propelling Britain into the crisis. And Suez provides a standard of comparison for Iraq in the first years of the twenty-first century as a crisis which split the British nation.

As noted above, the Middle East was deemed by the British to be one of their three pillars of security; the US saw the area as the responsibility of the British. But increasingly the latter feared that the UK by its actions was opening the Middle East to Soviet penetration and communist subversion. The British feared nationalists, who threatened the Empire; the US feared communists, who threatened the free world. The problem for Britain was that control of the Suez Canal, she believed, was fundamental to the maintenance of her sea communications to her South-east Asian colonies, and to Australia and New Zealand; of equal if not more importance, it was also the route for oil from the Persian Gulf. Furthermore, her base near Cairo was the centre of defence for her positions in the Mediterranean and Africa. Her claim to control of the canal rested on her position as the major shareholder in the Suez Canal Company, 44 per cent of whose shares had been purchased by the British government in 1876. In 1882 Britain had declared Egypt a protectorate, but she gave the country her independence in 1922, although binding her with strong treaty obligations. Nevertheless, British soldiers did not entirely vacate Egypt; in 1936 the Anglo-Egyptian Treaty ended British occupation of cities such as Cairo and Alexandria, but confirmed the British operation of the Suez Canal Base. During the Second World War this base, the largest in the world, was the centre of British military operations outside of the UK.

After the end of the war, events moved against the British. There was increasingly violent activity by nationalist groups, both against the British themselves and against their wayward puppet ruler, King Farouk. In July 1952 the Egyptian Revolution, or the Free Officer coup, led by General Mohammed Neguib and a group of middle-ranking, middle-class young officers (six of whom had studied in the US), successfully overthrew Farouk and took power. From this group emerged Colonel Gamel Abdel Nasser, who became President in March 1954. Nasser had been in touch with American officials since October 1951, and he maintained close relations with the CIA, his main channel for communications with Washington.[120] A new Anglo-Egyptian Treaty was signed on 19 October 1954, by which British troops were to leave the Suez Canal Zone (which contained the base) by June 1956, although – significantly for future events – they could re-enter in the event of war or the threat of war against any Arab state or Turkey. What the British did not then know was that the treaty had been drafted in the State Department:[121] the Americans did not trust either country, but particularly the British, not to exacerbate the situation. Nevertheless, American influence may well have been the reason for the existence of the clause allowing conditional British re-entry.

The Suez Crisis had manifold implications. The US and the UK had different defence strategies. Mention has been made of their links to different groups of Egyptians, with the British retaining their links with the old elites and the Americans fostering closer links with the nationalists, especially the growing and increasingly important middle classes. They also worked with different groups of countries in establishing a barrier to Soviet penetration. In January 1955 the Turks and Iraqis began to hold talks, encouraged at first by the Americans, and signed a pact. By the Treaty of Versailles in 1919, the UK had received Iraq as a Mandate, and even though that had ended, she still retained treaty rights to bases there. On 5 March 1955, Egypt, Syria and Saudi Arabia signed an agreement. Ten days later, Britain joined the Turkish–Iraqi Pact, now called the Baghdad Pact. It was later joined by Iran and Pakistan. At first, the intention was that the US would also adhere to the Pact, but this was during a period of attempts to mediate an Arab–Israeli agreement. If they succeeded, the Americans thought the Israelis could then also join the Pact and they would all face down the USSR together. However, once the mediation attempts failed, the Americans began to see the Pact as destabilising and, to the bewilderment and annoyance of the Foreign Office, suggested that the British hold back on the Pact. As it was now their primary defence arrangement in the Middle East, the British were not about to do so.[122] In any case, the US's closest relations in the Middle East were with Israel and Saudi Arabia, and Britain had somewhat frosty relations with the latter.[123]

Nasser reacted with fury to the Baghdad Pact, which promised to interfere with his project for pan-Arab unity, to be led by Egypt and himself. In September 1955 he announced the Egyptian purchase of arms from the Soviet bloc (on 26 September two high-ranking CIA officers had spent over three hours with Nasser, 'trying to find a placatory way of publicly announcing this shocking agreement').[124] Nasser pointed out that he had attempted more than once to purchase arms from the US, and it was only when he had been refused that he had turned to Czechoslovakia. (After the 1948 Arab–Israeli War, the US and the UK had imposed an arms embargo on both the Arabs and the Israelis.) Allen Dulles, the head of the CIA, strongly supported Nasser, seeing him as riding the crest of the wave of the future in the Middle East. In December the US and UK agreed to help fund the construction of the High Aswan Dam. By the following year, however, Allen Dulles's brother John Foster Dulles, the Secretary of State, had lost patience with Nasser and Egypt as insufficiently pro-western, and on 19 July 1956 Foster Dulles withdrew the offer of finance, followed by the British. The US's and UK's views on Nasser and the danger he posed to their interests had largely converged; unfortunately for Britain, however, the two countries' views as to how they should respond had diverged.

Nasser's response to the cancellation of the US and British offers of funding was to nationalise the Suez Canal, partly to use the tolls to finance the dam, but overwhelmingly to assert that it was Egypt's and prove that the country was entirely independent of British rule. The differing American and British responses to this opened a huge breach between the two powers. The US wanted a peaceful solution, and Foster Dulles embarked on a number of manoeuvres and arrangements, but little came of them. He spoke more fiercely in Washington than in London, but President Eisenhower, who controlled foreign policy, time and again emphasised that the US would not support the use of force. Neither Macmillan nor Eden believed him, assuming that the US merely wished to remain in the background, not that she would undermine the whole endeavour. Indeed, there is reason to believe that, had the British succeeded, the US would have accepted the situation: Foster Dulles later asked Foreign Secretary Lloyd, 'Selwyn, why did you stop? Why didn't you go through with it and get Nasser down?'[125]

Meanwhile, by 10 August 1956 the UK government had approved Operation Musketeer, presented to the Egypt Committee of the Cabinet by the Chiefs of Staff. Its mission was to occupy Egyptian cities and overthrow Nasser. (The plan would later be revised and some objectives added, but that of getting rid of Nasser would remain.) The French also wanted to oust Nasser, who was support-ing rebels in the French colony of Algeria, and on 1 September they hinted to the Israelis that they would like to co-ordinate joint action. By the 24th, there was a tripartite agreement. The plan was that Israel would attack Egypt, and the British and French, on the pre-text that they were separating the two sides, would then move in and take control of the Suez Canal Zone. Macmillan, then a hawk, told the Cabinet on 11 September that only force would work; con-versely, Foster Dulles announced in Washington that 'we do not intend to shoot our way through'.[126]

On 29 October the Israelis attacked Egypt. Thus began a rich, full week. The following day, Britain and France sent ultimata to the two sides, instructing them to withdraw ten miles to either side of the canal to allow Anglo-French occupation. The Anglo-French task force set sail from Malta, after which it was shadowed and even harassed by the US Sixth Fleet.[127] There was uproar in the House of Commons, and at the UN Britain and France vetoed a resolution calling for a ceasefire which had been proposed to the Security Council by the US. On the 31st the British and French attacked Egyptian airfields. On 2 November the UN called for a ceasefire. On 3 November Russian tanks rolled into Budapest to put down the Hungarian Uprising. On the 4th November, the Egyptians blocked the canal, and Britain was warned of oil sanctions against her. On the 5th British and French paratroopers were dropped to take Port Said and Port Fuad near the northern end of the canal; on the same day the Soviets threatened rocket attacks on Paris and London. The Soviet intervention deeply concerned Eisenhower, who worried 'that the Soviets, seeing their position and their policy failing so badly in the satellites, are ready to take any wild adventure'. Foster Dulles commented that the British and French had perhaps committed a worse crime in Egypt than the Russians had in Hungary, but they would soon bow to American wishes because 'there would be a strain on the British and French and it will be economic and quickly [*sic*].'[128]

The decisive date was 6 November, the day of the American presidential election. At dawn, Anglo-French troops landed in the Canal Zone, but back in London, the condition of the pound was critical. Britain had two major points of weakness, her oil supplies and her currency. When the invasion began, Nasser ordered the closing of the canal to halt the flow of oil, an action strengthened by the cutting by Arab nationalists of the oil pipelines from the Persian Gulf to the Mediterranean through Syria; Syria herself destroyed three of the Iraq Petroleum Company's pumping stations.[129] The US refused to make up the shortfall in oil, which was to prove decisive in forcing British capitulation.[130] By 5 November, the pound and the reserves were in dangerous shape. Both British and American authorities as well as the financial markets had long regarded two billion dollars as the danger point for sterling reserves; on 6 November the British prepared to ask the US for massive assistance and, in the expectation of receiving it, they decided to ignore the crucial two-billion-dollar point and to make propping up the exchange rate of the pound their first priority. But the expected aid did not materialise. 'Secretary of the Treasury, George Humphrey, strong in government and close to Eisenhower, gave the British Treasury a virtual ultimatum: as Londoners recall it, he posed the simple choice of an immediate cease-fire or war on the pound, with not a dollar to be had for oil supplies.'[131] When Macmillan telephoned Washington, he was told that only a ceasefire by midnight would secure American support for a loan. Macmillan reported this to the Cabinet, urging that the country faced financial disaster; the Cabinet decided at 9.45 a.m. that a ceasefire would take place at midnight, and British troops stopped twenty-three miles down the canal from Port Said. But financial pressure did not cease, and as long as British and French troops were left in Egypt, they would receive no help from the

Americans.[132] On 30 November the Cabinet accepted that with-drawal from Egypt was inevitable, and on 3 December the Foreign Secretary announced that British troops would be withdrawn from the Canal Zone. On 22 December the evacuation was complete.[133]

The Suez Crisis was a watershed in British history. It was the end of Britain as an independent great power. It was now clear that Britain could no longer implement any foreign policy which required the use of force without at least the acquiescence of the US.[134] Within five years Britain made her first application to join the European Economic Community. It accelerated Britain's withdrawal from her empire, both because she did not have the resources to maintain it and because public opinion was increasingly unsupport-ive. And it was the end of an era in the Anglo-American relationship. As Sir Harold Caccia, the British Ambassador to Washington, wrote, 'something has ended, and, in my view, three things: first, the senti-mental attachment, in the Administration, created by our wartime experience as crusaders in arms; second, the innate trust in our longer experience of international affairs and our reputation for dependability; third, our largely unquestioned right to a special posi-tion . . . Now the position is different.'[135] The US intended it to be different, and now preferred to deal with Britain and France through the machinery of NATO. But there were attempts by both Eisenhower and the new Prime Minister, Harold Macmillan – who had replaced Eden through collusion with the Americans – to rebuild the alliance. Indeed, Eisenhower, some time in the 1960s, was to tell his former Vice-President, Richard Nixon, that his worst foreign policy mistake was his failure to support Britain and France during Suez.[136] And one of his first moves, to the pleasure and relief of the British, was to reopen discussion of the nuclear relationship.

VI

While Anglo-American relations in the decade after the war may have been 'special' in a number of ways, in one case they most emphatically were not: the nuclear relationship. As described above, Britain had contributed vital knowledge and research prowess without which the atomic bomb would probably not have been ready to use before the end of the war; and the war itself would possibly have lasted much longer without it. Yet, for a number of reasons, the Americans, in spite of their agreement with the British, decided to restrict the exchange of all further information. Truman had early on decided that the US would control all knowledge about how to manufacture a bomb, which he later justified on the grounds that it was a trade secret. But there were other considerations. During this period there were significant attempts to establish international control of atomic energy, backed in particular by scientists,[137] and some officials feared that Anglo-American control would undermine these efforts. Others were concerned that a nuclear facility in the UK might be too tempting a target for the USSR. Would sensitive information be safe from Soviet spies? According to Robert Hathaway, Truman was preoccupied with securing civilian control over atomic energy, and this 'undoubtedly led him to disregard British protests, which in his mind only complicated an already complex political problem . . . [But] there was a specific anti-British element in this as well. A full interchange of information on atomic energy, the American military advised, would be tantamount to an outright alliance. Very few in the American government in 1946 were prepared for such a step.'[138] Furthermore, public opinion objected to sharing the secret of the bomb with other countries.[139] The legal vehicle was the Atomic Energy Act of August 1946, known as the McMahon Act, which effectively cut off all exchanges of information with any country, including the UK.

To the British this came as a shock. After the shock came anger, and after the anger came a determination to build their own bomb. As Bevin stated to the House of Commons on 16 May 1947, 'His Majesty's Government do not accept the view . . . that we have ceased to be a Great Power',[140] and the mark now of this status was to be a nuclear power. But there were other reasons, too. Prime Minister Clement Attlee later recalled that this was before NATO, and 'there was always the possibility of their [the US's] withdrawing and becoming isolationist once again. The manufacture of a British bomb was therefore at that stage essential for our defence.'[141] Furthermore, as a medium-sized country, she had to depend on her scientific and technological superiority for her defence against the USSR – the Cabinet believed that only British possession of the bomb would deter a nuclear-armed enemy.[142] But it must be said that the British wanted the bomb not only as a defence against an enemy but also as a defence against a friend – the US. Partly this was because they felt cheated by the US, a sentiment which was, in fact, shared by Acheson and Eisenhower.[143] But of overwhelming importance was the conviction of the Cabinet that if Britain did not possess the bomb, the US would pay no attention to British wishes in foreign policy. As Bevin emphasised, 'We could not afford to acquiesce in an American monopoly of this new development . . . we must develop it ourselves.' And therefore, at a meeting of the War Cabinet on 8 January 1947, the decision was taken to build the bomb.[144]

Nevertheless, this was to take five years, and in the interim the UK was wholly dependent on the American nuclear deterrent. Thus, as noted above, the rapid response to the 1946 American request for bases; the UK even surrendered her right – perhaps useless in the circumstances – to veto the American use of the bomb, in the vain hope that the US would soften her stance against the sharing of information. Meanwhile, research and development went on apace, and on 3 October 1952 the UK tested her first atomic bomb on the Australian island of Monte Bello. By then, however, research had moved on; in 1952 and 1953 the Americans and the Soviets tested their thermonuclear bombs, the hydrogen (or H-)bomb. In July 1954 the Cabinet decided that the UK had to have a comparable weapon, with Churchill arguing that 'we could not expect to maintain our influence as a world power unless we possessed the most up-to-date nuclear weapons'. The Chiefs of Staff had emphasised that a British H-bomb was vital because 'it would be dangerous if the United States were to retain their present monopoly since we would be denied any right to influence her policy in the use of this weapon'. Lord Salisbury, the Lord President of the Council, hoped that it would increase their influence over the Americans by ensuring 'more respect for our views': the 'adventurous action' demonstrated by the Americans in threatening to use the bomb during the Korean War, and perhaps against the Soviets, had seriously alarmed the British government.[145] And, above all, there were two compelling strategic arguments. Firstly, US bombs were directed against Soviet cities, but the UK wanted to attack Soviet air and submarine bases from which the Soviets could attack the UK; and secondly, with no certainty that the US would help to defend her, the UK had to possess her own serious deterrent.[146]

President Eisenhower, who succeeded Truman in 1953, was more sympathetic to British arguments, believing that closer co-operation would be beneficial to the US.[147] In December 1953, armed with a promise made by American officials in October 1952 to exchange data on the effects of nuclear weapons and with a copy of the original Hyde Park aide-mémoire (see Chapter 6), Churchill, again Prime Minister, met the President in Bermuda. The Eisenhower administration was hobbled by the McMahon Act, but agreements at a lower level were made through talks between the military establishments of the two countries; of particular importance were the senior officers of the two air forces. According to Simon Ball, they constituted a 'functional elite' dealing with nuclear delivery systems and the planning for their use.[148] On 12 March 1954, the two sides signed the Wilson–Alexander Agreement, the first joint targeting agreement.[149] Eisenhower promised to ask Congress to amend the McMahon Act, and in August it passed the Atomic Energy Act, which allowed nuclear co-operation with countries which had made significant advances in the field of nuclear energy, a requirement which could apply only to the UK.[150]

Two years later the Suez Crisis rent the alliance, but both sides moved rapidly to repair it, not least because of a deterioration in relations with the Soviet Union. Eisenhower knew that he had to take the first step, and in January 1957 the US proposed the deployment of a number of intermediate-range ballistic missiles (IRBMs) in the UK. The weapons and specialised equipment were to cost the UK nothing; furthermore, the British would take over the sites as soon as their personnel were trained. The British government welcomed the offer as proof of the restoration of good Anglo-American relations. Importantly, as Macmillan later wrote, the IRBMs 'would give us a rocket deterrent long before we could hope to produce one ourselves; moreover it would provide full training for our own men in these new and sophisticated armaments'.[151] The details were worked out at a meeting between Macmillan and Eisenhower on Bermuda in March 1957, which the President later described as 'the most successful international conference that I had attended since the close of World War II'.[152] The outcome of the meeting was that the UK was given sixty Thor missiles, which were deployed under a 'two-key system' in East Anglia; the US provided the missiles and warheads, the UK the support facilities.[153]

The next stage was stimulated by the shock of the launch by the Soviet Union in October 1957 of Sputnik, the world's first satellite. The USSR had thereby beaten the US in the development of an intercontinental-range missile delivery system, and the latter was now anxious for a closer alliance with the one other country which had developed nuclear weapons. In addition, the UK now had independent expertise to contribute. Because she had been cut off entirely from American help, she had developed her own H-bomb, successfully tested on Christmas Island in the Pacific in May 1957. In the other area of research, the peaceful use of nuclear energy, she was considerably ahead of the US. In 1955 the first Calder Hall reactor had come on stream. This was the first of the so-called 'Magnox reactors', which produced both electricity for commercial use and plutonium for bombs.[154] (The UK also had the first near-catastrophic nuclear reactor fire, at Windscale in Cumberland on 8 October 1957, an occasion kept secret from the world, including, it was hoped, the Americans.[155]) Eisenhower promised Macmillan that he would press Congress to repeal the McMahon Act, and it duly passed the 1958 Atomic Energy Act. This enabled the two countries to sign on 3 July 1958 the US–UK Mutual Defence Agreement. By this the UK received information from the US on the design and production of nuclear warheads as well as fissile material; it also authorised the transfer of materials, with the British, for example, supplying plutonium. However, the agreement did 'increase British dependence upon the United States without markedly increasing British influence in Washington'.[156]

The UK had been developing its own missile, Blue Streak, but the cost was huge and promised to become more so; furthermore, it was a liquid-fuel missile which took fifteen minutes to prepare for firing (both the US and the USSR were developing solid-fuel missiles, which did not require such lengthy preparation). In February 1960 the unanimous advice of the Chiefs of Staff was that the project be cancelled, and the Cabinet Defence Committee agreed. Yet, if it were cancelled, what would take its place? As it happened, the decision was made easier because the UK would be able to purchase Skybolt, an air-to-ground missile, from the US. This was still under development, but its use would extend the life of the British V-bomber force, since the missiles could be launched at a considerable distance from their targets. Macmillan visited Washington from 27 to 31 March 1960, and after talks with Eisenhower at Camp David he 'was able to secure a very valuable exchange of notes about Skybolt and Polaris'. The US would let the UK have Skybolt vehicles, and the UK would provide her own warheads. With regard to Polaris, a submarine-based nuclear ballistic missile, Macmillan later wrote that 'although Eisenhower was very helpful, he was unwilling to enter into a definite arrangement . . . It was certain, however, that we could obtain Polaris, although at a heavy cost, in one form or another when we might need it.'[157] At the same time, the President 'had mentioned his desire to station some Polaris submarines in Scotland so that fewer ships could do more work. The first British suggestion had been Gair Loch, but in the end they had agreed to the American preference for Holy Loch.'[158] Given Eisenhower's offer, upon his return to Great Britain Macmillan proposed to the Cabinet that they formally cancel Blue Streak and depend upon the 'firm agreement' for Skybolt to prolong the life of the V-bombers.[159]

The Minister for Defence, Harold Watkinson, went to Washington in May 1960 to finalise the formal agreement over Skybolt. There he found himself under strong pressure from the Americans to agree formally to their establishing a base for Polaris nuclear submarines at Holy Loch on the Clyde in Scotland; this was in line with earlier agreements allowing the forward deployment of US deterrent forces.[160] The British agreed with some reluctance. There was uproar, with anti-nuclear protesters coming out in force, but even those who did not object to nuclear weapons in principle found it disquieting to have the base situated so near a densely populated area with Glasgow at its heart.[161]

Over the following two years American doubts about the desirability of Skybolt increased. The missile failed five tests, making it the worst-performing of any US strategic missile system; to add insult to injury, it was also the most expensive. Hints of this dissatisfaction were given, but apparently were resolutely ignored by the British. Indeed, Macmillan and Peter Thorneycroft, his new Minister of Defence, made it clear that Skybolt was to be the foundation of the independent British nuclear deterrent.

October and November 1962 were difficult months for the Americans. Of supreme importance was the Cuban Missile Crisis, when, between 16 and 29 October, the world came very close to nuclear war. Although this was pre-eminently a US–USSR affair, President John F. Kennedy had a number of telephone discussions with Macmillan, and the British Ambassador to the US, David Ormsby-Gore (later Lord Harlech), who was an old friend, was frequently consulted by the President. 'Macmillan and Ormsby-Gore became de facto members of Kennedy's Executive Committee.'[162] There was also the concurrent Chinese invasion of India. Therefore, when Secretary of Defense Robert McNamara decided to cancel Skybolt, advice which Kennedy accepted on 7 November, he had little time to worry about the British response. Besides, 'neither side fully grasped the priorities, the political problems and the policy-making processes of the other'.[163]

This was manifestly the case with McNamara. In early December news of the imminent cancellation was published in the UK, which led to a surge of anti-American feeling. Then came the speech of Dean Acheson, ex-Secretary of State and now an elder statesman, at West Point on 5 December 1962, the British reaction to which may well be imagined: 'Great Britain has lost an Empire and has not yet found a role. The attempt to play a separate power role – that is, a role apart from Europe, a role based on a "special relationship" with the United States, a role based on being the head of a "Commonwealth" which has no political structure, or unity, or strength and enjoys a fragile and precarious economic relationship by means of the sterling area and preferences in the British market – this role is about to be played out.'[164] The British reaction may well be imagined. Although Kennedy personally telephoned Macmillan, 'urging him to grin and bear the outburst of a disillusioned man rather than be drawn into public debate', the force of British indignation compelled the Prime Minister 'to rebuke Acheson publicly for falling "into an error which has been made by quite a lot of people in the course of the last four hundred years, including Philip of Spain, Louis XIV, Napoleon, the Kaiser and Hitler"'.[165] By 18 December, and the beginning of a conference at Nassau between Kennedy, Macmillan and the Prime Minister of Canada, John Diefenbaker, 'the atmosphere between London and Washington had become electric, even explosive',[166] and Anglo-American relations were at breaking point.

The Nassau conference was the sixth in a series of routine meetings set up to discuss a number of foreign policy problems,[167] but Macmillan went to this one determined to return to Britain with an agreement for Polaris in his pocket. By all accounts, the beginning of the conference was the angriest of any Anglo-American post-war summit, with David Nunnerley describing it as 'one of the great confrontations in the history of Anglo-American relations'. When Macmillan arrived at the airport, he learned for the first time of Kennedy's scathing remarks about Skybolt on American television the previous evening. The President had said that he 'saw no point in spending two and a half billion dollars on Skybolt's development when "we don't think we are going to get two and a half billion dollars' worth of national security".' Here was another case, he said, where 'the British were simply going to reap the rewards of American labours',[168] a somewhat disingenuous statement, given that the Americans had developed Skybolt for their own use. The Americans had not thought it worthwhile to inform the British delegation of Kennedy's remarks.[169] According to Henry Brandon, veteran Washington correspondent of the *Sunday Times*, he found an atmosphere of 'resentment and suspicion of American intentions such as I have never experienced' in twenty years of Anglo-American conferences. George Ball, Undersecretary of State for Economic Affairs, later recalled that the mood of the British 'was not merely subdued but grim . . . and Thorneycroft, in particular, [was] suspicious and resentful almost to the point of hostility'. However, Sir Solly Zuckerman, Chief Scientific Adviser to the Ministry of Defence, responded that 'if anyone was grim, I would say that it was

Bob McNamara';[170] presumably the Secretary of Defense did not entirely trust the President to hold out against Macmillan. His suspicion proved correct.

There were strong forces in the American government urging Kennedy to deny Britain Polaris; it would extend Britain's status as a nuclear power, and powerful men wanted this to end. In the Pentagon McNamara based this on strategic grounds. He could hardly help but be uneasy when the British (and later the French) hinted (and sometimes stated explicitly) that their own nuclear force might be used to trigger American use of nuclear weapons in an East–West confrontation. More than once, and publicly at Ann Arbor, Michigan in June 1962, McNamara described independent, limited nuclear capabilities as 'dangerous, expensive, prone to obsolescence and lacking in credibility as a deterrent', although shortly afterwards he insisted that he had been referring to the French, not the British.[171] Nevertheless, he wanted the end of any pretence to nuclear independence on the part of the British.

This was connected to a growing interest in the US government in the concept of a European multilateral nuclear force (MLF). The idea here was to incorporate all of the nuclear capabilities of the NATO states into one unit. Important German politicians and others were insisting that Germany, too, should have her own nuclear forces, and the US wanted urgently to discourage this, but it was difficult, given the positions of Britain and France. Macmillan derided the whole concept, pointing out that 'if one imagined a tough Germany determined to have a nuclear deterrent it was doubtful if they would be satisfied to have one of 16 in a submarine crew'. Ball recalled that when he had stressed that any offer of Polaris needed to be linked to a nuclear fleet manned by crews of mixed nationalities, 'Macmillan said to me disdainfully, "You don't expect our chaps to share their grog with Turks, do you?" ... I replied, "Wasn't that exactly what they did on Nelson's flagship?"'[172] This failed to have any effect on Macmillan, who recognised that an MLF would be subject to American control. Indeed, for many American officials, the overriding object was simply to restore safe control to the United States of all nuclear arms in the western world.

The State Department had a different slant on the issue. For some years the US had tried to convince Great Britain to integrate with Europe, whether through the OEEC during the Marshall Plan period, the Coal and Steel Community in 1950 or the European Economic Community (EEC) in 1957. In 1961 Britain had finally applied to join the EEC, but the fear was that if the US provided Britain with Polaris, the French would decide that the UK was irrevocably committed to clinging to America and President Charles de Gaulle of France would veto her application. There had developed in the US government the concept of the Grand Design, called by some the 'dumb-bell theory' – two massive spheres connected by a thin rod – whereby a united Europe and a United States would be linked through a common forum such as the Organisation for Economic Co-operation and Development (OECD). Ball in particular was nearly evangelical in pushing the idea, but de Gaulle, resentful of Britain's close ties with the US and fearful that Britain would frustrate France's hopes of dominating Europe, would crush the idea for the time being by vetoing the British application in January 1963.[173]

The conference at Nassau opened on the morning of 19 December 1962 with Macmillan giving a brief account of Anglo-American co-operation over nuclear matters and especially Skybolt, ending with the warning that 'the difficulties which had been mentioned over the allies would be as nothing to the difficulties which would follow if the United States seemed to be using the SKYBOLT decision as a means of forcing Britain out of an independent nuclear capacity'. Both those in the UK who favoured an independent deterrent and those opposed to it would resent the fact that abandonment had not been decided by Britain but forced upon her. Kennedy agreed, but he emphasised in return the main American concern: Germany.[174] With the two leaders having set out their main positions, negotiations began.

Macmillan had serious political problems at home. First of all, he did not have full public support for the application to join Europe, with the nationalistic right wing of the Conservative Party and the trade unions, in particular, opposed. A Gallup Poll published on 1 August 1961 found that only 38 per cent of the population supported joining the EEC, with 23 per cent disapproving and a staggering

39 per cent 'don't knows'. The government was tired. Less than six months before, in the so-called 'night of the long knives', Macmillan had sacked a third of his Cabinet, but rather than being perceived as a measure of strength, it was seen as an admission of weakness. The Conservatives had just lost two by-elections, and, most humiliatingly, both the Prime Minister himself and the government were being mocked for their apparent total lack of influence in Washington during the Cuban Missile Crisis. As noted above, the UK did, in fact, have some influence,[175] but this was not known to the public in December 1962, and the British delegation came to Nassau trailing clouds of ridicule. Macmillan desperately needed a victory.

The Foreign Office record of the talks gives the gist of the discussions but omits much of the atmosphere. The official record reduces to one long paragraph what was, by all accounts, a masterly performance by Macmillan. He began by invoking all of the past glories of the Anglo-American alliance, reminded his audience of the vital British role in the development of the atomic bomb, alluded to the McMahon Act, pointed out how he and Eisenhower had restored the relationship, and stressed the political embarrassment his government had suffered because of the Holy Loch agreement, yet he had still welcomed the American presence in the UK. The British, he implied, stood by their agreements. 'He was at his most eloquent and emotional and his skilful presentation of his case greatly impressed the American delegation . . . Kennedy was moved by [his] articulation, phraseology, and historical perspective.'[176] The President tried to bring the discussions back to earth, and over the afternoon and the following day the US made offers and suggestions – for instance, the UK could have Skybolt practically for free – and the UK rejected them. As Macmillan said, with reference to Kennedy's public denial of Skybolt's efficacy, 'while the proposed marriage with Skybolt was not exactly a shot-gun wedding, the virginity of the lady must now be regarded as doubtful. There had been too many remarks made about the unreliability of Skybolt for anyone to believe in its effectiveness in the future.'[177]

According to Macmillan, 'the discussions were protracted and fiercely contested. They turned almost entirely on "independence" in national need. I had to pull out all the stops – adjourn, re-consider; refuse one draft and demand another, etc., etc.' Throughout the conference the British delegation sent drafts back to the Cabinet for their comments.[178] This was a more complex procedure than it might seem because Macmillan had left in London a group of ministers and civil servants who did not all share his belief in the desirability of a nuclear capability. These included the Chancellor of the Exchequer, Reginald Maudling, concerned about the cost; the Leader of the House of Commons, Iain Macleod, and the Home Secretary, Rab Butler, both sceptical about the political benefits; the Lord Privy Seal and chief European negotiator, Edward Heath, more concerned about Europe; and the Cabinet Secretary, Sir Norman Brook, who simply thought that there was no need for a nuclear capability at all.[179] Macmillan had not allowed protracted discussion, for fear of a resurgence of opposition; for this reason, too, he had initially fought to defend Skybolt, and this was his public position until he reached Nassau, when Kennedy's comments on television made it impossible. According to Lawrence Freedman and John Gearson, 'it was in Macmillan's interest to avoid any detailed discussion of the Skybolt problem in advance of his meeting with Kennedy. Once face to face with the President, he would thrash out a deal and face the cabinet with a fait accompli, and bounce them . . . into a Polaris deal.'[180]

And there was a deal. Macmillan had insisted that the UK would remain a nuclear power. 'Britain', he said, 'has had a great history and is not going to give up now.' If the US refused to help Britain, she would go it alone, 'whatever the cost'. And the climax: 'We have gone a long way in this nuclear business, . . . but if we cannot agree, let us not patch up a compromise. Let us agree to part as friends.'[181] In other words, this would be the end of the Anglo-American alliance. This might seem a hollow threat, had not the US at that point a sad lack of friends: the relationship with Germany was tense, whilst that with France was unspeakably bad. It would have been more than careless to have tossed Britain aside – as the Secretary of State, Dean Rusk, said, 'We have to have somebody to talk to in the world'. But Britain was never going to be abandoned because, unbeknownst to Macmillan, Kennedy had already decided on

16 December that, if absolutely necessary, the US would let the UK have Polaris.[182] In doing so, Kennedy went against the wishes of much of his administration, but the alliance with the UK was deemed of great importance. Much has been made of the personal relationship between the two men, and this was doubtless very helpful, not least when Macmillan made it clear that if he did not get Polaris, his government would probably fall. High-level politicians tend to sympathise with this dilemma. But beyond sympathy, the US would then be faced with a government, possibly anti-American, much less to their liking. At the end of the day, countries take decisions on the basis of national interest, and the interest of the US was to retain strong links with the UK. This story would be played out again two decades later with the Falklands War.

The Statement on Nuclear Defence Systems was 'a monument of contrived ambiguity',[183] since it had to reconcile interdependence and independence. On the one hand, it referred to the joint commitment by the US and the UK to establish a NATO multinational force – the pooling of national nuclear forces under a single command – and of a mixed-manned nuclear force. On the other hand, by Paragraph Eight, Britain's Polaris fleet would be 'used for the purposes of international defence of the Western Alliance in all circumstances', except 'when Her Majesty's Government may decide that supreme national interests are at stake'. Was it indeed independent? Nigel Ashton has concluded that, from the British side, 'interdependence was viewed as a form of partnership . . . From the US side, although the language of interdependence was also used, the concept meant more effective central, and hence American, control of Western defence efforts.'[184] Certainly the UK remained dependent on the US for the delivery system and targeting intelligence, but it is probable that a decision to threaten or to use the weapon in a supreme national emergency could be taken 'independently', that is, in the face of American reservations. From the mid-1980s on, the US government apparently accepted that this 'second centre of decision' actually strengthened NATO's deterrent posture.[185]

There was another phrase important for the future of the British nuclear capability, and for which Sir Solly Zuckerman takes the credit. In the statement 'the US will make available on a continuing basis Polaris missiles (less warheads) for British submarines', it was he who added 'on a continuing basis'. These four words made it 'legally straightforward' twenty-five years later for the US to sell the UK the Trident missile, since it could be regarded as part of the 'continuing basis'.[186] According to a former US ambassador, in 1979 'at the Guadeloupe summit Callaghan dropped by Carter's bungalow just as the President was about to take a nap, and with Carter seated in his underwear, Callaghan extracted an American commitment to supply the new Trident submarine to the British'.[187] Discussions begun in 2007 over the next generation of Trident made it likely that the nuclear relationship would continue to provide one of the major planks of the alliance.

VII

When the Labour government of Harold Wilson came to power on 15 October 1964 it inherited from the Conservatives a financial crisis of some magnitude: whilst the balance of payments deficit in 1963 had been £35 million, in 1964 it was estimated at £750–800 million. Devaluing the pound was one obvious remedy; this would make exports cheaper and imports dearer, thereby in due course improving the balance. However, virtually the first decision of the new government – or, rather, of three men, the Prime Minister, the Chancellor of the Exchequer James Callaghan and Secretary of State for Economic Affairs George Brown – was not to devalue. Wilson had been scarred by the 1949 devaluation, when the exchange rate of the pound had dropped from $4.03 to $2.80, and he was fearful that because the last two Labour governments had had to devalue, a third Labour devaluation would encourage the markets to expect that the election of his party was the signal for a sterling crisis. For Callaghan, it was a moral issue: if Britain devalued, she would betray the interests of the members of the Sterling Area. As for Brown, he believed strongly in the traditional position that devaluation hurt the working classes – food would be more expensive – and that the duty of a Labour government was to protect them and improve their conditions. The amount of the deficit was published on 26 October 1964, at the same time as the government imposed a Temporary Import Surcharge of 15 per cent on all imports save food and raw materials. But this was contrary to the rules of the General Agreement on Trade and Tariffs and of the European Free Trade Area, and there was an inevitable international outcry. Holders of sterling noted this, as well as the size of the deficit, and from this point onwards the pound came under recurring attack.[188]

Because of electoral considerations – they had won with a majority of just three – Labour needed to spend money. There had not been a Labour government since 1951, and the trade unions and the working classes, politicians believed, had a lot of ground to make up; it was also necessary to keep their support. This meant that uncomfortable decisions were repeatedly postponed and the economy lurched on, increasingly supported by borrowed money, especially during the repeated sterling crises. The American Embassy in London wrote to the Secretary of State on 26 May 1966 that the UK had a limited future as any sort of international power: perhaps the US should cease to help and allow her to find her natural level as a 'comparatively lesser middle state'.[189] By mid-July 1966 the US Secretary of the Treasury had decided that Britain's problems were now so acute that they threatened not only American interests but the free world's financial system. There were sterling crises in November 1964, July–August 1965 – the US played a critical role in supporting the pound in those two[190] – and July 1966, before the final crisis in November 1967.

The value of the pound was a prime US concern, and officials worked hard to support it. Both the pound and the dollar were reserve currencies; that is, they were major components of the reserves of central banks around the world. But speculators speculate, and if they succeeded in destroying the exchange rate of the pound by driving down its value relative to the dollar, American officials believed, they would next turn their attention to the dollar. The American economy was also in difficulties, in that attempts to pay for both the Vietnam War and the social reforms of President Lyndon B. Johnson's Great Society programme, without raising taxes, were causing alarming budget deficits, huge public borrowing requirements and inflationary pressures. And if the dollar went, many Americans feared, so too would the Bretton Woods system, with a return to trade and payments restrictions. Hence the importance to the Americans of the pledge by Callaghan to Henry Fowler, the Secretary of the Treasury, and Al Hayes, the chairman of the Federal Reserve Bank of New York, that he would never voluntarily devalue the pound; and hence the repeated efforts by the Americans to put together packages for its support.[191]

There was a second reason for American concern about the pound: the US's determination that the UK should not remove her forces from East of Suez (usually capitalised at the time because it became almost a concept as well as a geographical area). 'East of Suez' referred to the retention of British bases, aircraft and ships, and in some cases the deployment of troops, in Singapore and Malaysia, the Persian Gulf, Aden and the Indian Ocean. By the mid-1960s, these deployments were costing £320 million a year, or 25 per cent of the UK defence budget, with an additional £90 million annually spent in purchasing foreign currencies. There were 100,000 men deployed, with 55,000 fighting in Malaysia alone in the so-called 'confrontation' with insurgents backed by Indonesia. The US administration was genuinely alarmed at the prospect of the British departure. It valued the British bases at Singapore and Aden, thought it useful to have the Union Jack rather than the Stars and Stripes flying in the Indian Ocean and the Persian Gulf, did not want to be the only western power in East Asia, and feared that if the British withdrew their forces, congressional pressure to withdraw Americans would increase.[192]

But there was another American demand, and this related, as far as the Americans were concerned, less to British finances and more to British will. The Americans were becoming increasingly embroiled in Vietnam, as they fought alongside the dismayingly corrupt South Vietnamese government against local insurgents who were supported by communist North Vietnam. Both domestically and internationally, opposition to US involvement grew. The Americans wanted a major power to stand alongside them, and thus they became increasingly desperate for Great Britain to send even a token force. But there was strong opposition to the Vietnamese War in the House of Commons, and in June 1966, when the US began bombing the outskirts of Hanoi and Haiphong, over one hundred Labour MPs urged Wilson to make clear the government's disapproval. In the streets of Britain there were increasing numbers of anti-war demonstrators. On 27 October 1968 a crowd in Grosvenor Square tried to storm the American Embassy in what the police called 'the worst riot in memory'.[193]

Public support by the government for the Americans in Vietnam was therefore impossible. Wilson pointed out to Johnson that South Vietnamese soldiers were being trained in jungle schools in Malaysia, a medical relief team was being sent out, and the British were providing policemen in Saigon. But the Americans still called for some British soldiers by their side. Johnson asked, bitterly, could not the British send even a token force? 'A platoon of bagpipes would be sufficient; it was the British flag that was wanted.'[194] The Americans became increasingly blunt about their disappointment. Secretary of State Rusk told the journalist Louis Heren that 'All we needed was one regiment. The Black Watch would have done. Just one regiment, but you wouldn't. Well, don't expect us to save you again. They can invade Sussex, and we wouldn't do a damned thing about it.'[195]

Various defence reviews by the British government inched towards paring back its commitments East of Suez. In talks in December 1964 between McNamara and Denis Healey, the British Minister of Defence, McNamara had emphasised strongly the importance to the US of Britain's continuing presence. As Healey told the Cabinet on 11 December, the Americans did not want Britain to 'maintain huge bases but keep a foothold in Hong Kong, Malaya, the Persian Gulf, to enable us to do things for the alliance which they can't do. They think that our forces are much more useful to the alliance outside Europe than in Germany.'[196] But eventually, according to Healey, 'hard experience compelled me to recognise that the growth of nationalism would have made it politically unwise for Britain to maintain a military presence in the Middle East and South East Asia, even if our economic situation had permitted it'.[197] And as the UK moved more towards Europe, making a second application in 1967 to join the EEC, choices had to be made.

But the government was left with no choice as it was driven on to the rocks by a ferocious sterling crisis.

The pressure, building from early summer 1967, became inexorable. On 6 June the Arab–Israeli War began and on the following day the Suez Canal was closed, which immediately caused a flight from the pound and other currencies into the dollar, seen as a strong, safe financial haven. Closure also held up the flow of oil, which was exacerbated by the civil war in Nigeria. The UK was forced to buy oil from the Western Hemisphere at considerably higher prices, which worsened the balance of payments and deficit. In September dockers in Hull, Manchester, Liverpool and London announced an indefinite strike, causing a pile-up of goods on the docks and devastating exports. There followed a series of announcements and news which weakened the pound even more, and the result was the beginning of yet another sterling crisis. On 4 November, Wilson and Callaghan decided on devaluation, and Washington was notified. The Americans were horrified, and offered a loan of three billion dollars. But it was too short term and it came with strings attached: Britain would have to retain her external commitments. On 14 November the October trade figures showed the worst monthly deficit in British history, and sterling was again sold heavily. On the 16th the Cabinet agreed to devalue, on the 17th one billion dollars was lost from the reserves, and on the 18th the pound was devalued by 14.3 per cent, thereby dropping its dollar value from $2.80 to $2.40. By the time it was announced, Callaghan had placed his resignation in Wilson's hand.[198]

The devaluation accelerated withdrawal from East of Suez. The new Chancellor was Roy Jenkins, the former Home Secretary and a confirmed Europhile, who was highly critical of the 'outdated imperial pretensions' embodied in the East of Suez role. The coalition which had supported Britain's world role, pre-eminently Wilson and Callaghan (now Home Secretary), was weakened. Other changes also facilitated Jenkins' plans. In 1964, the three separate service departments had been merged into a Ministry of Defence. The Colonial Office had been abolished in 1966, and the Commonwealth Relations Office would go in 1968.[199] These reorganisations eliminated many political positions traditionally held by supporters of Britain's foreign role.[200] But it was the dire financial situation which ensured that Jenkins got his way.

On 16 January 1968, 'Black Tuesday' in the Ministry of Defence, the Cabinet's decision was announced: nearly all British forces were to be withdrawn from the Middle East and East Asia by the end of 1971, although the UK would retain her position in Hong Kong, amongst other things a valuable listening post for signals intelligence. The US administration was outraged. It was the ultimate betrayal by their closest ally and only partner in global policing, and it came at a time when the US herself was mired in Vietnam. Johnson fired off a letter to Wilson the same day, saying that if the UK abandoned her East of Suez commitments and rescinded an order for fifty F-111 fighter aircraft, the US would no longer consider the UK a valuable ally in any strategic theatre, including Europe. Wilson did not back down, in spite of the fact that he was also devastated by the decision. The British, he cabled Johnson, were 'sick and tired of being thought willing to eke out a comfortable existence on borrowed money'. The UK was not becoming neutralist; rather, she needed to find a military role which matched her resources.[201]

It was the end of an era. Great Britain, which had been a global power for three centuries, had now to settle for being a regional power. For many, it was difficult – one Cabinet minister at the time, Richard Crossman, refers in his diary to 'bursting through the status barrier . . . and it's terribly painful when it happens'.[202] Wilson regretted it not only because of the absolute loss of prestige, but also because it signalled the end, for many years, of a close Anglo-American relationship. Johnson remained contemptuous of Wilson until he left office in January 1969, having decided not to stand for re-election; the new Republican president, Richard Nixon, saw no reason to resume close ties, particularly since he 'distrusted' Wilson.[203] Countries ally because each has something to contribute to the relationship, but now the UK had relatively little to offer the US. Germany was stronger, and, the UK feared, was becoming the US's primary European ally.

VIII

It initially seemed as though relations between the leaders of the two countries would change for the better with the election on 19 June 1970 of the Conservative Edward Heath. According to Henry Kissinger, 'there was no foreign leader for whom Nixon had a higher regard, especially in combination with Sir Alec Douglas-Home, Heath's Foreign Secretary, whom Nixon positively revered'. But, alas, 'the relationship never flourished'. One reason was that Nixon and Heath never established any kind of personal rapport, both being cool and reserved. But a more important, and probably conclusive, reason was that 'of all the British leaders, Heath was probably . . . the least committed emotionally to the United States. It was not that he was anti-American. Rather, he was immune to the sentimental elements of that attachment forged in two world wars . . . [and] was persuaded that Britain's future was in Europe.'[204] Heath's biographer broadly agrees that 'his purpose was to realign the country's sense of identity irrevocably towards Europe'. But rather than being anti-American as such, he showed himself to be a proponent of the dumb-bell theory: an enlarged Europe 'should shoulder a larger role within NATO, becoming a true partner of the United States instead of a resentful dependent'; just as America had long wished.[205] The difficulty was that Kissinger, Nixon's National Security Adviser and from 1973 Secretary of State, frequently made it clear that the US did not want a partner but a militarily strong acolyte and Heath was determined that Britain would not occupy such a role. Indeed, time and again he sacrificed opportunities for Britain to influence the US, going so far as to instruct his officials to avoid private consultations with their US counterparts.[206] This led Kissinger to comment that 'for the sake of an abstract doctrine of European unity . . . something which had been nurtured for a generation was being given up'.[207] (A few years later, however, a closeness was re-established by Prime Minister Margaret Thatcher and President Ronald Reagan.) Nevertheless, as far as Heath and Nixon were concerned, 'the personal relationship ended in mutual contempt, and, once they left office, the old lions were barely civil to each other'.[208]

This was a significant decline in relations, especially as things had started so well. Shortly after Heath's election, the British Embassy in Washington had told the Foreign Secretary that Anglo-American relations were 'extremely good', with Nixon himself telling the Ambassador that he regarded Britain as his closest and most trusted ally, 'even more because Britain still counted for something in the world, was still looked up to by other nations; and because Britain "knew her way around" perhaps better than any other nation'.[209] He thereby confirmed the British self-perception of being an old and wise power which could help the US. And she did so in 1972–3. On 28 July 1972 Sir Burke Trend, the Cabinet Secretary, learned during a visit to Washington that, following a visit by Nixon to Moscow in May 1972, the USSR had proposed to the US that the two countries should come to an agreement on the prevention of nuclear war. This was alarming to the British: it would remove the main nuclear threat to Moscow and free the USSR to attack China with conventional forces, as well as severely weakening NATO. It might also make it difficult for Britain to continue to develop her own nuclear forces. On 10 August Sir Thomas Brimelow, a senior civil servant in the Foreign and Commonwealth Office, went to Washington to convey these doubts personally to Kissinger. But Brimelow became caught up in the latter's desire not to rebuff the USSR whilst presenting a counter-proposal more consonant with the western alliance's security requirements: not trusting his own State Department, Kissinger asked Brimelow to help to draft a revised text. Over several months Brimelow did just that, leading the British Ambassador in Washington, Lord Cromer, to note how he was 'struck by the astonishing anomaly of the most powerful nation in the world invoking the aid of a foreign government to do its drafting for it, while totally excluding its own Ministry for Foreign Affairs'.[210] This is a good example of the fact that, even though the two countries appeared to be moving apart in their approaches to world problems, the habit of working together was very difficult to break. As a later US ambassador wrote, 'in the unglamorous trenches of the bureaucracy, personal relations are usually undisturbed as the politicians at the top come and go'.[211]

But these relationships were about to be tested in the most

The Marquis of Salisbury, Prime Minister and Foreign Secretary, was forced by his cabinet to back down over the Venezuelan crisis in 1896.

Richard Olney, Secretary of State, forced the British government to back down over the Venezuelan crisis in 1896. He invoked the Monroe Doctrine.

Sir William Wiseman, Head of MI6 in the US 1915–18, and the mole in the White House.

Col. Edward M. House and Woodrow Wilson, twenty-eighth President 1912–20. House was his closest adviser during most of Wilson's two terms.

First World War recruiting poster picturing Lord Kitchener, Secretary of State for War from 1914 until his death from drowning in 1916, a hero of imperial wars.

First World War American recruiting poster showing Uncle Sam, clearly based on the British recruiting poster showing Lord Kitchener.

Your Song—My Song—Our Boys' Song
OVER THERE

WORDS AND MUSIC BY
GEORGE M. COHAN

LEO. FEIST INC. NEW YORK

Sheet music cover for American First World War song by George M. Cohan, 'Over There':
'Over there, over there,
Send the word, send the word over there –
That the Yanks are coming,
The Yanks are coming,
The drums rum-tumming
Ev'rywhere.
So prepare, say a pray'r,
Send the word, send the word to beware.
We'll be over, we're coming over,
And we won't come back till it's over
Over there.'

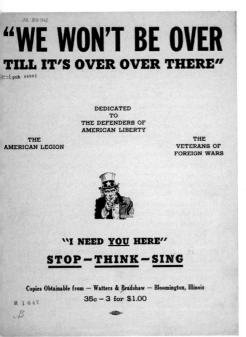

"WE WON'T BE OVER
TILL IT'S OVER OVER THERE"

DEDICATED
TO
THE DEFENDERS OF
AMERICAN LIBERTY

THE
AMERICAN LEGION

THE
VETERANS OF
FOREIGN WARS

"I NEED YOU HERE"

STOP – THINK – SING

Copies Obtainable from — Watters & Bradshaw — Bloomington, Illinois

35c – 3 for $1.00

LET'S NOT GO OVER THERE
Words and Music by THE DUNCAN SISTERS

D. L. WINTER

1940 sheet music reflecting the desire of many Americans to stay out of the war. The words are a parody of the First World War song, 'Over There'.

1941 American sheet music showing support for Britain.

Official US photo entitled 'Lend–Lease in Action: Vegetables for British Children', December 1941.

Helping to keep relations close.

Josef Stalin, Franklin D. Roosevelt and Winston Churchill, Teheran Conference, 1943. The body language demonstrates Roosevelt's rejection of Churchill in favour of Stalin.

Operation GI Bride gets underway: the first shipment sails to the US on SS *Argentina*, 26 January 1946. The exercise began after Congressional legislation allowing the brides exemption from the immigration quota.

Prime Minister Anthony Eden addresses
the nation on the Suez crisis, 1956.

"And now I want some for sending to the States,
with plenty of holly and not too much about
good will!" 1.xii.56.

Cartoon by Osbert Lancaster on 1 December
1956, shortly after the US government forced
the British, French and Israeli governments to
end their attacks on Egypt.

The first UK atomic bomb test, Hurricane,
at Montebello Island, 3 October 1952.

USS *George Washington* fires
the first Polaris missile ever
launched from an underwater
submarine on 20 July 1960.

1964 US *Life* magazine celebrating the Beatles, the heroes of the 'Second British Invasion'.

Royal Marines and paratroopers march and fight their way from San Carlos to Port Stanley during the 1982 Falklands War.

President Ronald Reagan and Prime Minister Margaret Thatcher; their rapport is obvious.

Prime Minister Tony Blair and President George W. Bush striding confidently together.

"You can spot the Americans a mile off."

serious crisis since the Cuban Missile Crisis in 1962: the 1973–4 Yom Kippur War and consequent Arab oil embargo. Both the US and the UK were at that point racked by domestic crises. Heath was at the centre of a conflict between the trade unions and the government, with its roots in the worsening economic situation. Nixon was embroiled in the Watergate Crisis, which involved his attempts to cover up the fact that the White House had been complicit in a break-in at the Democratic Party's national headquarters. Indeed, both leaders were to fall in 1974, Heath on 28 February when he lost the election and Nixon on 9 August when he resigned to avoid being impeached by Congress.

On 6 October 1973, the Egyptians launched a surprise attack against Israel across the Suez Canal, whilst the Syrians simultaneously drove into the Golan Heights. To the surprise of most western observers, the Israelis were driven back, and for some days the outcome was unclear. The American reaction to these events rapidly brought out the US's and UK's long-standing differences over Middle Eastern policy. Kissinger rang Ambassador Cromer on the 6th to tell him that the US planned to introduce in the UN Security Council a resolution calling for a ceasefire and an Arab withdrawal to the previous line, and he hoped that the UK would support it. Cromer had to tell him that whilst the UK would support a resolution calling for a ceasefire and urge the Secretary-General to promote negotiations, she would not support a call for the Arabs to withdraw from their own territory. As Cromer reported, 'Dr Kissinger reacted badly'.[212] The crisis then developed on three levels: the war itself; conflict between the US and her NATO allies, particularly with regard to oil; and a near confrontation between the US and the USSR.

On 10 October the Soviets began resupplying both Egypt and Syria. Pressure built in Congress for the US to do the same for Israel, and on the 13th a massive military supply operation duly began – according to Kissinger, the Israelis were almost out of ammunition. But to the rage of the Americans, only Portugal and the Netherlands allowed their bases to be used for the purpose.[213] The UK made it clear that the US should not ask to use British air bases to resupply Israel or even to make reconnaissance flights in the Middle East.[214]

Meanwhile, the members of the Organisation of Petroleum Exporting Countries (OPEC) had for some time been angry about the low prices which they were receiving for their oil, and in 1973 they enforced a sudden, substantial rise in the price. The Yom Kippur War, however, encouraged a number of Arab oil producers in addition to limit their production and impose an oil embargo upon those states deemed to be friendly to Israel. In the consequent turmoil the price rose from $2.59 a barrel in January 1973 to $5.12 on 6 October, the day the war began, to $11.65 by the end of the year – a quadrupling of the price. This directly threatened the European countries: Britain, for example, depended upon the Middle East for 65 per cent of her oil. 'Panic swept the industrialized nations', and as a result the Nine (members of the EEC, since the start of the year including Britain) were acutely concerned that they should not do anything which would encourage OPEC to tighten the screw further. As far as Kissinger was concerned, however, it was literally unbelievable that the Europeans were reluctant to support the US in its attempts to save Israel, its primary ally and the only democracy in the region, and to prevent the USSR from achieving a central position in the Middle East. The British concluded that Kissinger did not understand the vital importance of Arab oil to Europe, given America's near self-sufficiency. Furthermore, the perceptions of the US and her NATO allies were diametrically opposed: the Europeans regarded the war as round four in a regional dispute, whilst Kissinger saw it in terms of superpower relations.[215] For him, the crucial factor in the crisis was the USSR.

Real danger threatened when the Israelis began to drive back the initially successful Egyptian army, and then broke through to the west bank of the Suez Canal. On 22 October the UN adopted a Security Council resolution calling for a ceasefire, but this rapidly collapsed. President Anwar Sadat of Egypt requested Soviet and American troops to separate the two sides. (Disengagement of the forces along the Suez Canal would begin on 18 January 1974, whilst UN peacekeepers created a buffer zone between Syria and Israel on the Golan Heights in May.) According to Cromer, 'I was telephoned in the early hours of 25 October to be informed by Dr Kissinger of the receipt of a letter from Mr Brezhnev [the Soviet leader] inviting joint United States–Soviet military intervention to shore up the ceasefire, and threatening, in the event that the Americans declined, the despatch unilaterally of Soviet troops . . . Dr Kissinger said the President had decided to order forthwith a world-wide military alert as a strong counter-measure and signal.' The UK received an hour's notice at 1.15 a.m., but none of the other NATO members were informed; the American Permanent Representative to the NATO Council, Donald Rumsfeld, finally made a statement at the end of the NATO Council meeting on the 25th, well after reports of the alert had been broadcast on radio.[216] Not surprisingly, the allies protested at the lack of consultation and information, but Kissinger himself was angry with the allies. Whilst admitting at the NATO ministerial meeting at Brussels on 10–11 December that the Americans had 'occasionally' been guilty of oversights and mistakes, he insisted that the US 'remained committed to the view that the basic interests of America and Europe were indivisible and asked all the allies to be willing to rededicate themselves to the "great goal of Atlantic cooperation".'[217] In short, the US knew best and should not be challenged.

The UK had some sympathy for Kissinger since, with the President at bay because of Watergate, he was singlehandedly carrying the responsibility for American foreign policy. Nevertheless, the shaky relations during the Heath–Nixon period certainly owed something to Kissinger's ego. He seems to have decided that the combination of his intellectual prowess and American power could enable him – and Nixon, of course – to settle many outstanding problems in international relations. Pre-eminently, US relations with the USSR and with the People's Republic of China, and settling the Vietnam War, were so overwhelmingly important that all other problems paled. The British appreciated his desire to accomplish great things for the US and the free world, but they sometimes feared that his 'astonishing intellectual arrogance' encouraged him to act unilaterally and, since he seemed in March 1973 'to be taking an ever-widening interest in all issues of US policy', there was 'an increased danger that with so many balls in the air, one or other of them may come down with a nasty crash'.[218]

There were then two approaches which the British could take:

they could either redouble their efforts to follow the traditional path of acting as the US's closest ally and most dependable friend, or they could link themselves more closely with Europe and attempt to balance the overweening power of the US. In June 1970, presumably in response to Heath's election, Denis Greenhill, the top civil servant at the Foreign and Commonwealth Office (FCO), had written to Foreign Secretary Sir Alec Douglas-Home that 'We shall wish to keep our special links with the United States, e.g. in the intelligence and nuclear fields, so far as we can, but must recognise that unless we can find a new power base in Europe our influence in Washington is bound to decline and it will be necessary on occasion to demonstrate that for us Europe has priority.'[219] The UK would not, it was hoped, cease to be the US's closest ally, but this had to be based on her usefulness, including her increased influence in Europe, not on an independent power base which had effectively ceased to exist.

IX

By the start of the 1970s, the British economic situation had not improved, and nor had the American. On 15 August 1971 Nixon had decoupled the dollar from gold by which the Americans themselves formally killed Bretton Woods. As a result, world financial markets were thrown into turmoil. The fourfold increase in the oil price then dealt a massive blow to the world economy as a new phenomenon emerged: 'stagflation', the combination of high inflation and high unemployment. Unlike Germany and Japan, Britain increased public spending, partly to ward off deflation and partly to keep the support of the trade unions. This was also the period of huge wage increases, particularly in the public sector, as unions tried to leapfrog each other. By 1975, inflation was 24 per cent and rising, and Britain was being spoken of as a banana republic.[220]

The crisis came in 1976. The US was increasingly worried about Britain. Since the war, there had been alarming sterling crises, when holders of sterling had sold in massive amounts, in July–August 1947 (when convertibility was stopped), 1949 (ending in devaluation),

1951, 1955, 1956 (during the Suez Crisis), 1957, 1964, 1965, 1966, 1967 (another devaluation), 1972 (when she was forced out of the European monetary 'snake' after only two months) and 1975.[221] In short, sterling crises were a repeated and tedious fact of life. The British economy was in a deplorable state, Edwin Yeo, the Undersecretary for Monetary Affairs at the US Treasury, recalled that 'To our great dismay, . . . we realised we were going to have a major UK experience ahead . . . We feared that if a country like Britain blew up, defaulted on its loans, introduced foreign exchange controls and froze convertibility, we could have a real world depression. Our role was to persuade the British that the game was over. They had run out of string.' (All of the moves feared by Yeo, in fact, would subsequently be urged by various members of the Cabinet, led by Anthony Wedgwood Benn, the Secretary of State for Energy, and the leader of Labour's left wing.)[222] Furthermore, her armed services continued to decrease in size. Worst of all, the left wing of the Labour Party was threatening to take over the Party and hence power. This was frightening to the Americans for a number of reasons. It was feared that a left-wing government would almost certainly be anti-American, and might possibly require them to withdraw from their bases in Britain; Britain herself might withdraw from NATO and from Europe; and she might become anti-nuclear.[223] Indeed, Brent Scowcroft, President Gerald Ford's National Security Adviser, later commented that in 1976 the condition of Britain, and what might result from it, 'was considered by us to be the greatest single threat to the Western world'.[224]

Therefore, when the British on 4 June made what was by then a routine request to the US Federal Reserve and other central banks for a six-month line of credit in order to support the pound, the Governor of the Federal Reserve Board, Arthur Burns, and the US Treasury decided to use this request as a hook. They would extend the credit, but only on condition that Britain agree to turn to the IMF for a loan if she could not repay the credit within six months.[225] She could not, and this set in train a crisis during which the US exerted strong and public pressure on Britain to change her free-spending ways.

The flamboyantly public manner in which Britain had to

announce her turning to the IMF added to the pressure. At the beginning of September 1976 there was a wave of wildcat strikes[226] in the motor industry; on 8 September the National Executive Committee of the Labour Party announced proposals to nationalise major banks and insurance companies; and on the same day the National Union of Seamen called a strike. Sterling immediately came under pressure, but it was on 28 September 1976, as the Labour Party conference opened, that a sterling crisis exploded. The Chancellor of the Exchequer, now Denis Healey, was due to leave for Hong Kong and then Manila for an IMF meeting, but when he reached Heathrow Airport the news of the morning's trading was so appalling – sterling fell 4.5 cents that day to $1.63 – that he returned to London and telephoned the Prime Minister, now James Callaghan, at the conference in Blackpool. Healey told Callaghan that the Bank of England was forecasting that sterling would fall a cent a day until it reached $1.50, and it might not even stop there: in other words, the pound was in free fall. Later that day it was decided to apply to the IMF for a loan,[227] the third application in less than a year.

Meanwhile, Callaghan made his own contribution to steadying the markets with a speech at Blackpool which flashed around the world: 'For too long, perhaps ever since the war, . . . we have been living on borrowed time . . . We used to think that you could spend your way out of a recession and increase employment by cutting taxes and boosting government spending. I tell you in all candour that that option no longer exists, and that insofar as it ever did exist, it only worked on each occasion since the war by injecting a bigger dose of inflation into the economy, followed by a higher level of unemployment as the next step.' The Labour Party conference booed, but the Americans liked it.[228]

The mission from the IMF arrived in Britain on 1 November. When an IMF mission descended upon a country, its method was to respond to that country's plans and requests, not to produce its own. This method went awry in Britain. Fundamentally, most of the Treasury were outraged at the situation, and said that the IMF could come up with its own plans. Furthermore, the Cabinet under Callaghan was badly divided as to what should be done – should

IMF requirements be accepted or should they be defied and the country batten down the hatches? It received no clear signals from the Labour Party itself, which was similarly divided.[229]

Although this was nominally an IMF visitation, in reality it was an American one. Since the establishment of the IMF in 1944, the US, as the largest shareholder, has wielded predominant influence over its activities.[230] Indeed, it is not too much to say that, from the beginning, the IMF has acted as a foreign policy surrogate for the US. The only chance Britain had of fighting off its demands was to outflank it by convincing the German Chancellor or the American President that it was politically important that pressure on the UK be lifted. Therefore, Callaghan tried to convince Helmut Schmidt and Gerald Ford that the IMF should be reined back. The German manoeuvre failed, but Kissinger, who had retained his position of Secretary of State after Nixon's fall, was apprehensive enough about what the Treasury was trying to do to convince the President to lighten the pressure. In the end, although Britain had publicly to agree to the IMF demands, these demands were more tolerable than those which had first been proposed.[231] But Britain had still been humiliated, not only because this was the first case of a modern industrial country turning to the IMF for this type of loan, but also because she was treated the same as any other indigent country.

X

The 1960s and 1970s in general saw a steady decline in British military capabilities, as expenditure on the armed forces was repeatedly cut back. The US increasingly turned to a dynamic and affluent Germany as her primary European ally. It was not that the UK did not have a role to play in NATO and elsewhere: there was still a British army presence on the Rhine, and the Royal Navy carried out 70 per cent of the patrols of the Atlantic seaways. It was just that with repeated economic crises, armed forces which were declining in number and were increasingly under-equipped and almost no useful pieces of land left, Britain's attractions as the primary ally were less obvious to the Americans than they had once been. It would take the advent of Margaret Thatcher as Prime Minister in 1979, and the Falklands War in 1982, to modify this perception.

The relationship between Thatcher and President Ronald Reagan excited interest at the time and continues to do so. Margaret Thatcher became leader of the Conservative Party as the successor to Edward Heath in 1975; Reagan became the presidential candidate of the Republican Party only in the summer of 1979, and therefore he tended to look up to her as the senior conservative. As a member of the State Department once commented, they were ideological soulmates. They also had a great personal affection for each other. But was that personal relationship reason enough for the US to support the British during the Falklands War, a conflict over what Reagan memorably called 'that little bunch of ice cold land down there'?[232] For some weeks the issue seemed to be in the balance because it was not a cost-free decision for the US.

In 1833, encouraged by the Americans, the Falkland Islands were claimed for the British Crown. Argentina, however, had never relinquished her claim of sovereignty over what she calls Las Islas Malvinas. In March 1982 the Argentinian military junta which at that time controlled the country needed to provide a distraction: there was rioting on the streets of the capital, Buenos Aires; the economy was in a desperate state; and the long-held suspicions of the junta's waging of a 'dirty war', during which thousands had clandestinely disappeared (*los desaparecidos*, the 'disappeared ones'), were now seen as confirmed, and 'the mob was howling at the gate'. The junta therefore decided to create a situation which would unite the nation. Since the one point on which all Argentinians could agree was that Las Malvinas belonged to Argentina, their recovery would reunite the country.[233] Furthermore, the junta felt safe in invading the islands, because they believed that Britain would not fight to get them back: the previous year, the British government had announced the withdrawal of the patrol ship HMS *Endurance* from the South Atlantic, a result of the 1981 Defence Review which provided for significant reductions in Britain's surface fleet, and the junta drew the obvious conclusion.

The junta had apparently planned to land in the Falklands in

September 1982, but when the British government announced the despatch of a nuclear-powered submarine from Gibraltar on 26 March, they assumed it was coming south (although actually it was going north), and the timetable was brought forward.[234] On 19 March 1982, Constantino Davidoff, an Argentinian scrap merchant, and forty-one other men sailed in an Argentinian naval ship to South Georgia (a Falklands Islands dependency providing a base for the British Antarctic Survey) to dismantle an old whaling station. They raised the Argentinian flag and began displacing the men of the survey; they were soon joined by soldiers and other ships.[235] On 24 March, the British intelligence service in Buenos Aires discovered that Argentina was about to invade the Falklands; they also correctly predicted the date of landing.[236] By the 31st, the Argentinian fleet was on its way. Sir Nicholas Henderson, the British Ambassador to the US, took the intelligence reports to the American Secretary of State, Alexander Haig, and in a few hours American intelligence sources confirmed the accuracy of the British reports.[237] Thatcher asked Reagan to intervene with General Leopoldo Galtieri, the junta's leader. He attempted to do so, but was unsuccessful. On 2 April the Argentinians landed and the Governor of the Falklands, Sir Rex Hunt, and a small garrison of Royal Marines surrendered. The following day the same thing happened on South Georgia.

The British response was four-pronged. First of all, there was an immediate appeal to the Security Council of the UN, which convened on 3 April and adopted Resolution 502, calling for the Argentinians to leave the islands. This early success was invaluable for the UK's international legal and moral position, and was in great part due to the consummate diplomacy of the British Ambassador to the UN, Sir Anthony Parsons. He was opposed on this issue by Dr Jeane Kirkpatrick, the American Ambassador. Kirkpatrick was a Latin American specialist, who believed that the US should maintain friendly ties with right-wing authoritarian regimes, such as the Argentinian junta, on the grounds that they could provide support against totalitarian communist regimes.[238] The Argentinian military was then helping the US in Nicaragua and El Salvador, and this particular argument was influential in the State Department (according to a young Department official, it was 'obsessed' with El Salvador).[239]

The second prong was to mobilise support in Britain for war. An emergency session of the House of Commons met on 3 April, the day after the invasion, and, except for thirty Labour Party rebels, all sides strongly supported the government. One unexpected but vitally important supporter was the left-wing leader of the Labour Party, Michael Foot, who vehemently opposed Argentina as a 'fascist' dictatorship. The third prong was to launch a military response. On 5 April the task force steamed out of Portsmouth Harbour on its eight-thousand-mile journey south to the Falklands; at roughly the same time, members of the Special Air Service (SAS) slipped into the Falklands to carry out reconnaissance and identify possible points for large-scale landings. On 25 April South Georgia was recaptured and on 21 May British amphibious forces landed on East Falkland. And the fourth prong, of course, was to secure strong American support, which was far from inevitable: it 'had to be argued and fought for all the time'.[240] The task may be measured by the amused reaction of the State Department in the early hours of the crisis to what was 'perceived as a Gilbert and Sullivan battle over a sheep pasture between a choleric old John Bull and a comic dictator in a gaudy uniform'.[241]

There were conflicting American national interests involved. Since 1946 Argentina had enjoyed increasingly good relations with the Soviet Union, which had not ceased even with the coming to power of the military junta in 1976; for example, the Soviet Union and Cuba blocked all discussion in the UN's Commission on Human Rights of Argentina's deplorable human rights record.[242] There was real concern that the Soviets might take advantage of Argentinian anger at the US to convince them to withdraw their military support of American covert operations in Central America.[243] The US also needed the support of other Latin American countries in the continuing fight against communist influence in all of its forms, and this might be jeopardised by a failure to support Argentina. It was possible that the USSR would make inroads in terms of arms sales and other commercial arrangements; there was also the usual concern about communist influence on trade unions and other collective operations. Yet, arguably, the American national interest in helping secure a British victory was even stronger. Fundamentally, it was

overwhelmingly important that an attempt to use violence to settle
a territorial dispute should not be successful.[244] Some concerns were
institutional. There was NATO: what lessons might the USSR draw
if the US did not support her ally? This was of particular importance
in view of the suggestion that the US government 'saw the NATO
alliance as pivotally involving the US–British relationship'.[245] There
was the fear that lack of support might cause the fall of the
Conservative government and the accession of Foot's strongly left-
wing Labour Party. This again threatened withdrawal from NATO
and Europe and the closing of American bases in the UK, but it also
threatened unilateral nuclear disarmament and the consequent
refusal even to store American nuclear missiles.

But there were reasons specific to that period as well. There were
huge difficulties in Europe, involving the deployment of the neutron
bomb and widespread demonstrations against it. As described by a
State Department official,

> the one pillar . . . those of us back in Washington felt we could
> hang onto, was the UK. Not only because of the special relation-
> ship, but because of the special Prime Minister in that special
> relationship . . . We in the State Department said, 'Unless we can
> assure the Europeans that we will resume a process of nuclear
> arms control negotiations with the Soviets, it could break the
> alliance.' But we were losing, we were definitely losing that argu-
> ment [with Reagan]. And Thatcher made, I think it was just a
> simple, single phone call to Reagan telling him that '[y]ou will
> cause great damage if you do not resume the nuclear arms control
> process.' And from that point forward we did.[246]

In short, it was not just Reagan who saw Thatcher as virtually irreplaceable.

The Americans wanted to remain friends with both the
Argentinians and the British, and at the outset effectively declared
themselves neutral. Thus the desired outcome was no war. Secretary
of State Haig embarked on a mission to mediate between the two
sides. He was driven, and limited, by the fact that he only had the
time it would take for the task force to reach the South Atlantic to

effect an agreement. His mission was not a success. The Argentinians refused to believe that the British would fight, no matter how often, and how forcefully, Haig told them that they would.[247] As for the British, Thatcher's reaction when she was told that the Americans wanted to be 'evenhanded' can easily be imagined. But fundamentally, they were not: they would support Britain over Argentina. However, if mediation had succeeded, they would not have had to make the awkward choice.

As Sir Nicholas Henderson later pointed out, 'the nature of the American Government makes it very difficult to have one clear-cut and comprehensive fount of policy'.[248] The differences between the factions were significant. The State Department was split between the Latin Americanists and the Europeanists. From the outset, the Pentagon, under Secretary of Defense Caspar Weinberger, supplied Britain with virtually everything she needed in the way of *matériel*. As he later wrote, 'I therefore passed the word to the Department that all existing requests from the United Kingdom for military equipment were to be honored at once; and if the British made any new requests for any other equipment or other types of support, short of our actual participation in their military actions, those requests should also be granted, and honored immediately. I knew how vital speed would be',[249] not least because of the disaster which would ensue if they allowed a NATO ally to lose the war. The US navy, for one, feared that the UK might do so, since she was so ill-equipped to fight a war in the South Atlantic, lacking air surveillance, adequate satellite communications, an effective air-to-air missile for the Harrier jump-jets, and a base in the South Atlantic.[250] Weinberger did what he could to fill the gaps, with one of the most important provisions being the Sidewinder AIM-L air-to-air missile (which could be fired head-on at an enemy aircraft, rather than its being necessary to manoeuvre behind the target).[251] The range and amount of aid were impressive. Ascension Island, halfway to the Falklands, was British, but the Wideawake Air Base was American. However, after a short period of confusion, the British used it not only for resupplying but also as a base for their Vulcan bombers. In early June the Americans also moved a satellite over the South Atlantic.[252]

The White House was not particularly interested in the dispute as such, and tried not to take too public a position. Its primary concern, perhaps not surprisingly, was to minimise the damage done by the war both to the domestic standing of the President and to American foreign policy interests in Europe and Latin America.[253] Reagan had said to a group of journalists on 5 April that the US was friends equally with the UK and Argentina. This was perhaps why, according to Sir Anthony Parsons, 'We never thought in terms of Reagan and where he stood. We thought of Haig, Kirkpatrick, Weinberger, but not Reagan. We felt he was under the influence of the last person he spoke to and didn't think about it [the war] much one way or the other.'[254] By early June, Thatcher and Reagan had had three increasingly acrimonious telephone conversations, as the President pressed for negotiations – the Americans feared that the defeat and humiliation of Argentina would cause the fall of the government and the return of the left-wing Peronistas – and the Prime Minister refused until the UK had retaken the islands.[255] Nevertheless, it seemed inconceivable at the time that Reagan's government would have acted otherwise than to support the UK, not only because of his relationship with Thatcher but also 'because of his strategic view of the world and his strong personal commitment to the Anglo-American relationship . . . He brought it to the White House and he left with it.'[256] Furthermore, everyone on both sides remembered Suez, and they were determined that this time things would be different.

Reagan was joined in this commitment by Weinberger (who, like Reagan, was later awarded an honorary knighthood). Weinberger himself later emphasised the importance of personal relationships: 'basically, there was a trust and a friendship, personal friendship as well as professional friendships, all the way along the line'.[257] Louise Richardson also emphasises the importance of this, pointing out that the institutions and practices set up by the Second World War generation continued and reinforced the relationship; NATO was important here, because it provided opportunities for the military at all levels to work together. Thus when the Falklands War broke out, the middle and upper ranks of both the American and British military forces had served together in NATO and were often close personal friends. A prime example of this was the close friendship between Admiral Lord Lewin, the chief of the Defence Staff, and General David Jones, the chairman of the Joint Chiefs of Staff.[258]

The war was fought, but it was sometimes touch and go. The idea of Britain's losing was unacceptable to the higher reaches, both military and civilian, of the US government, but it was also assumed that, without American aid, Britain *would* lose. So she received generous support, not least because of overwhelmingly pro-British American public opinion (in mid-April a US opinion poll indicated that 83 per cent of the public supported Britain).[259] This was partly due to the hard work of the British Embassy, fronted by Ambassador Henderson, who became something of a fixture on news shows (he gave seventy-three televised interviews in seventy-four days).[260] An order of battle was drawn up, and the five hundred Embassy staff were divided into groups responsible for 'wooing' the executive, the Congress and the media. Every morning a 'prayer meeting' was held and priorities were established 'in the war to win public opinion'.[261] Henderson himself met with each of the hundred Senators and many of the Congressmen. This helped to ensure the support of Congress, which was in any case inclined to be pro-British: as Senator Joseph Biden said, 'we're with you because you're British'.[262] A hundred years earlier the feeling would have been precisely the reverse.

Prominent during the war was the range and depth of British interaction with the US government; the bewilderment manifested by British representation in Washington during the Second World War had been replaced by a clear-eyed worldliness. A State Department official once tried to describe the situation:

It's been said that there are on most major US national security decisions a number of important inter-agency viewpoints. There's what does the State Department think, what does the Defense Department think. What do the Joint Chiefs think . . . What does the intelligence community think about the facts, the analysis. And what does the British embassy think, or the British government, vicariously through the British embassy? I think that during this period . . . the British embassy was as effective as ever in Washington.[263]

It is worth noting that this closeness had to be carefully calibrated. It was (and is) vital for the UK that the British ambassador or the appropriate subordinate be in at the beginning of discussions on any topic, to be able to put forward the British point of view before decisions were made. The usual British approach was to come prepared with a solution to the problem – or at least to provide a list of options. As described by Kissinger, the British 'way of retaining great-power status was to be so integral a part of American decision-making that the idea of not consulting them seemed a violation of the natural order of things'.[264] But it was also vital that this be done – and be seen to be done – in an impartial and balanced manner. It would be disastrous for the Embassy to be seen to be taking sides, to be caught up in inter-agency quarrels. It was useful for the Americans to be able to call on the British for ideas, to use them as a sounding board when trying out ideas, and – as did Kissinger – to utilise their unrivalled expertise with the drafting pen.

On 15 June 1982 the Argentinian troops surrendered to British forces. The successful outcome of the war was important for the UK, and for Anglo-American relations. For the British, it boosted self-confidence, giving the reassurance that they were capable of carrying out a military expedition of unusual complexity and difficulty, that they could dare and win. George Shultz, who succeeded Haig as Secretary of State in June 1982, later wrote that 'the British decision to go to war . . . was the first marker laid down by a democratic power in the post-Vietnam era to state unambiguously that a free world nation was willing to fight for a principle. The world paid attention to this – and not just the Third World either; it was noted by the Soviets.'[265] The British performance was certainly appreciated by the USSR: 'Soviet analysts studied the battle [of Darwin–Goose Green] intensively, and decided on this basis that they had considerably underestimated the fighting power of the British Army of the Rhine. Beginning in the autumn of 1982 Warsaw Pact forces facing the British in northern Germany began to receive substantial reinforcements.'[266] The victory also meant that the cuts in the naval capability, announced in the 1981 Defence Review by the Secretary of State for Defence, John Nott, were quietly shelved. Indeed, the resources were increased, at least for the time being.[267]

As for the Americans, the assistant to the chairman of the Joint Chiefs of Staff testified that the war 'was an overall plus for the British–American relationship . . . [which] increased the stature of the British military at a time when a lot of us were losing confidence in their ability to do it. It was a military feat of some significance, a triumph of ingenuity in adversity.'[268] Ambassador Kirkpatrick agreed, writing that 'I believe Britain emerged from the Falklands war stronger, her reputation enhanced.'[269] And George Shultz was convinced that 'the war had made its mark on the Anglo-American alliance, now closer than at any time since World War II'.[270]

XI

How long would this new closeness last? In one sense it ended with the departure of Reagan from the presidency in January 1989 and his succession by George Bush, Reagan's Vice-President. Bush and Thatcher lacked the same rapport, as the latter rapidly found out. More seriously, perhaps, the Bush administration after 1990 saw a reunified Germany as its most important European ally, one whose increasing economic and political strength would make it the major influence on the Continent, particularly with regard to East–West relations and relations with the re-emerging Eastern and East Central European countries. Indeed, Bush publicly called Germany the US's 'partner in leadership'.[271] What was required to reanimate a close Anglo-American relationship in the upper reaches of government was another war, and one soon exploded: the Gulf War.

The cause was the desire of Saddam Hussein and many other Iraqis to conquer and absorb Kuwait. From 1932, when Iraq became an independent state, it had repeatedly challenged the territorial integrity of Kuwait. Once Kuwait itself became fully independent in June 1961, the pressure was sometimes intense. To the Iraqi leadership, then, Kuwait was an integral part of Iraq. But the conflict was about more than pride. Kuwait possessed a large natural harbour along with 120 miles of coastline, which would substantially increase Iraq's window on the Persian Gulf; it also had huge oil-based wealth. Once captured, Kuwait might also have provided a launch pad for even richer prizes: the movement of Iraqi troops to the Kuwaiti–Saudi Arabian border after the invasion seemed to show that Iraq intended to grab the latter's oil fields as well. Control of both would have given Iraq control of 40 per cent of the world's known oil reserves.[272]

On 2 August 1990, two Iraqi Republican Guard armoured divisions invaded Kuwait, rapidly crushing any resistance. It was not immediately clear to the US government how it should respond, although military force was not then seen by the National Security Council as a desirable option. Later the same day, President Bush flew to Aspen, Colorado, for a pre-arranged meeting with Thatcher, who had arrived the previous evening for a conference on international affairs. The UK had closer ties to the Gulf than any other western power except for the US, not least with Kuwait, where, until June 1961, she had had a base. Other factors brought in the UK, too: the recent British victory and the successful Anglo-American cooperation during the Falklands War; and, of course, Thatcher happened to be in the US as the crisis broke. She insisted that Iraqi aggression was comparable to that of Argentina against the Falklands; she highlighted the threat to the Saudi oilfields; she insisted on the need for a UN resolution imposing a full trade embargo on Iraq; and she emphasised the urgency of getting Turkey and Saudi Arabia to block the oil pipelines through which Iraq exported most of its oil. After a telephone call to President François Mitterrand of France, she was able to reassure Bush of France's military support.[273] At the press conference afterwards, Bush said that he and Thatcher were 'looking at it on exactly the same wavelength'.[274]

On the day of the invasion, at the request of the US government, the UN Security Council passed Resolution 660, the first of twelve dealing with the crisis. It condemned the Iraqi attack and demanded a complete and unconditional withdrawal. Thatcher and James Baker, the US Secretary of State, had differed over the approach to the UN: Thatcher had wanted to base the western response on Kuwait's right to seek aid for self-defence under Article 51 of the UN Charter; Baker had insisted on a separate resolution. King Fahd Ibn-Abd-al-Aziz of Saudi Arabia asked for help, and the US 82nd Airborne Division and fighter aircraft were sent. On 19 August two

Iraqi oil tankers on their way to Aden ignored shots fired across their bows by the US navy. In response, a week later the Security Council passed a resolution permitting enforcement of the embargo, which the UN had sanctioned. Bush telephoned Thatcher, and she urged that these powers had to be used to stop Iraqi shipping: 'this was no time to go wobbly'. The President's National Security Adviser, Brent Scowcroft, recalled Bush's amusement: 'We used the phrase almost daily after that.'[275]

Baker met NATO Foreign Ministers in Brussels on 10 September and emphasised the need for more tanks. Four days later, Thatcher told Bush that the UK would be sending 7th Armoured Brigade (the 'Desert Rats'), an offer particularly welcomed by Bush since none of the other NATO members were responding in the same way. When Thatcher admonished the other NATO members for their weak response to the Iraqi invasion, the Spanish Prime Minister, Felipe González, criticised her 'warmaking ardour'.[276] (The French later sent a brigade.[277]) The British forces' commander in the Middle East was Lieutenant General Sir Peter de la Billière, a former director of the SAS and commander of the SAS Group,[278] and vastly experienced in the Middle East. When he arrived at the coalition headquarters in Riyadh, the capital of Saudi Arabia, de la Billière's priority was to win the trust of the American commander, General Norman Schwarzkopf. 'He and I were going to have to trust each other completely and tell each other what was going on, even if it meant, on occasion, sharing information which our own governments might have preferred to keep to themselves.' Schwarzkopf agreed, even though they were both aware that 'America was running the show, that Schwarzkopf himself would always be the main source of information, and that I stood to gain most from our deal'.[279]

Some time was spent waiting to see if sanctions would work, but by late September the CIA had decided that they would not. Both Bush and Thatcher consulted their Chiefs of Staff. Both believed that incrementalism would not work, and on 30 October Bush decided to double the US forces in the Gulf, to ensure that the Iraqis would be pushed out of Kuwait. Thatcher believed that Iraqi aggression could be defeated only by force, but American public opinion was ambivalent, with only 40 per cent believing that Kuwait was worth a war. Democratic congressional leaders believed that sanctions should be given more time to work. Scowcroft's response to that was that if the Allies waited much longer, there would be little left of Kuwait, and they would soon be dealing with a nuclear-armed Iraq. (There was some evidence for this, as in March 1990 an Anglo-American customs team at Heathrow Airport had confiscated possible nuclear triggering material bound for Iraq.[280]) British public support was stronger than American, and most pro-war opinion thought that, in addition to freeing Kuwait, Saddam Hussein ought to be overthrown. In November there was a two-thirds majority in favour of the use of force. Once the war began, support in the UK rose to almost 90 per cent.[281]

But defeating Iraq would not be an easy task. The Iraqi forces appeared formidable: nearly a million men, 140,000 of whom had poured into Kuwait during the invasion, armed with French Mirage fighters and Exocet missiles, and Russian tanks, fighters and bombers.[282] On 10 November, in order to take a greater part in the campaign and thus give himself more influence on American strategy, de la Billière requested a second brigade. On 22 November the Cabinet approved the sending of 4th Armoured Brigade and extra artillery, which brought British strength up to a division.[283] However, this was also the day that Thatcher resigned as Prime Minister, for reasons unconnected with Iraq. According to de la Billière, it was 'a thunderbolt which sent shock waves through the entire Coalition. Her fall was a shattering blow for Arabs and Americans alike: they all had the highest regard for her and simply could not understand how it was possible for a leader of international stature, who had done so much for her country, to be evicted from office . . . just as Britain was preparing to fight a major war.'[284] As a leader, although perhaps not as a companion, she had also come to be fully appreciated by Bush.

The President decided that he needed another UN resolution in order to maintain support at home and hold the coalition together. On 29 November the Security Council passed a resolution authorising 'all necessary means' if Iraqi withdrawal had not been completed by 15 January 1991. Just after Thanksgiving, as he later wrote, Schwarzkopf presented his battle plan to de la Billière. 'It was no coincidence that I'd gone to him first: Great Britain had been our closest western ally in the crisis, and he and I had become good friends. I trusted his brains and judgement so much that I asked his advice on even the most sensitive military issues.'[285] The political leadership also had to find out if they could work together. Shortly before Christmas, the new Prime Minister, John Major, visited Bush at Camp David. Bush told Major that if the Iraqis were still in Kuwait on 15 January, he intended to order an all-out coalition air attack to reduce Iraqi resistance, to be followed by a ground offensive. The Americans were relieved to find that Major entirely agreed. They were also relieved that he did not try to hector the President: according to Raymond Seitz, 'Bush had come to think of meetings with Mrs Thatcher the same way he thought of visits to the dentist'. Soon the two leaders were in almost daily telephone contact.[286]

On 12 January 1991, as the deadline drew near, Bush decided that in order to maintain public support, he needed a congressional vote in favour of military action. The Democratic leadership still opposed it, but Bush won in both the House of Representatives (250–183) and the Senate (52–47). The debate in the House of Commons on 15 January over whether force should be used saw a majority of 534 to 57.[287] The deadline expired at midnight on 15 January, and Bush ordered the launch of the Allied air attack, which included RAF aircraft. Over the following month the coalition forces overwhelmed Iraqi defences. Meanwhile, the British 22nd SAS Regiment was engaged in deep reconnaissance operations inside Iraq, begun before the start of the air campaign, hunting out Scud missile launchers and exploring routes to be used later by the Allied invasion forces.[288] The ground war began on 24 February, when US marines broke through Iraqi minefields into Kuwait and began to fight their way northwards, directly towards Kuwait City. The American XVIII Corps, with a French brigade on their left flank, began an enveloping operation towards the Euphrates River valley deep in Iraq, designed to trap the Republican Guard divisions. The next day the British 1st Armoured Division joined the attack. The American 101st Airborne Division had already landed nearly fifty miles inside Iraq, and the US navy was shelling the coast as if preparing for an amphibious landing.

On 28 February, after only four days of ground combat, Bush decided to end the war. Kuwait had already been reconquered, and American public opinion disliked the air attacks on the retreating columns of Iraqi soldiers – it appeared to be turning into a massacre, with pilots referring to it as a 'turkey shoot'. Furthermore, he feared that the coalition might fall apart if it went beyond the stated war aim of liberating Kuwait. The UN mandate, flowing from Resolution 678, authorised the coalition to use all necessary means to eject the Iraqis from Kuwait; it did not have a mandate to invade Iraq, and if the Americans had done so, or tried to take the country over, the Arab members of the coalition would not have supported them. No Arab troops entered Iraqi territory during the campaign.[289] Although Douglas Hurd, the British Foreign Secretary, was in Washington and observed the meeting at which the decision to stop was taken, he was simply not consulted: he was informed that the coalition would not press on to oust Saddam Hussein. The British contribution to the Gulf coalition had been forty-five thousand troops, second only to that of the Americans, but the latter had fielded ten times as many.[290]

With the Gulf War, the US had returned from a post-Vietnam War withdrawal to play a more active role in international affairs. It was wreathed with the aura of unimaginable power, and able to wage an 'electronics war', producing missiles which could apparently fly down a street and turn left at the lights. So was the UK needed now as an ally? On the one hand, the two countries had, on the whole, worked very well together. As a former British Ambassador to the US has written, 'a lesson of the operations in the Gulf was the ability of the American and British armed forces to operate together in a more cohesive manner than any other allies could have done, due to long habits of cooperation, integrated command structures and access to the same real time intelligence. Politically, Britain had displayed from the outset a willingness to share the military risks involved in defeating Iraqi aggression, in contrast to all the other allies except France.'[291] Yet his opposite number, Raymond Seitz, who took up his position as American Ambassador to the UK just after the end of the war, saw matters differently: 'When I arrived in London, the partnership was already undergoing some stress. The success of the Gulf

War disguised this, but the Gulf War was the last hurrah of the old regime. My first private meeting with John Major was to inform him that the United States had decided to cancel a missile programme to which the British military had already committed itself. This was a small harbinger which the Prime Minister didn't fail to appreciate.'[292] (Did he also appreciate the fact that the US had done this before, with Skybolt?) Indeed, the very idea of a particularly close Anglo-American relationship appears to have occasioned some hilarity in the White House. A few weeks after President Bill Clinton's inauguration in 1993, Major went to Washington. According to one account, 'Just before the Prime Minister arrived at the White House, Clinton was sitting with a few aides in the Oval Office. "Don't forget to say 'special relationship' when the press comes in," one of them joked – a little like "don't forget to put out the cat". "Oh, yes," Clinton said. "How could I forget? The 'special relationship'!" And he threw his head back and laughed.'[293]

The disparity in strength was huge. Throughout her history, the US had usually preferred to act unilaterally if at all possible, only calling upon allies in time of real need: this was bred in the bones from the very start of the republic, characterised by Jefferson's warning against entangling alliances.[294] Indeed, any country prefers to work to its own agenda without having to consult another, since that might result in having to modify plans or expectations. The US had a special – some Americans might call it providential – position in that she was surrounded by two moats and two militarily weak countries. She therefore developed into a Great Power whilst assuming that it was normal not to consult other countries. Great Britain, conversely, has always been conscious of the threats posed by other Great Powers lying but a few miles to the south and east. For both aggression and defence, alliances with Powers on the Continent have been vital. Once one of the Great Powers became a superpower, only an alliance with the other superpower rendered life tolerably safe. Therefore, Great Britain's search for allies was necessary and automatic; the price was a lack of total freedom in making and implementing foreign policy.

The US and Great Britain had always been competitors, being driven together as allies only when there was a threat greater than either could handle alone. The twentieth century had seen two common enemies, Germany and the USSR. Both had been defeated. Military allies need such an enemy, and although the two countries were tied together by NATO, this did not necessarily imply close co-ordination at the top. The US did not believe that, as a matter of course, special attention had to be paid to the UK. But the UK could not take such a detached view. Both Major and his successor Tony Blair saw the Atlantic alliance as the absolute foundation of British security. It was therefore deemed to be dangerous to criticise the US publicly: neither that country's government nor her public took kindly to such admonishments.

Even so, this did not mean that the UK always followed in the wake of the US. There was, for example, a great deal of acrimony during the 1990s over Bosnia and Kosovo. In 1991 Yugoslavia as a state began to fragment. The primary cause was the drive by Slobodan Milošević to make Serbia, the largest component of Yugoslavia, the dominant power in the Balkans. In June 1991 Croatia and Slovenia both declared their independence, as did Bosnia-Herzegovina in April 1992. Bosnia was 44 per cent Muslim, 33 per cent Orthodox Serb and 17 per cent Catholic Croat, mirroring faithfully the complexity of ethnic and religious intermingling in the region. Once the Muslim-dominated government had declared independence, Bosnia was plunged into a three-cornered war. In the UK, Major and Hurd attributed the fighting to the re-emergence of 'ancient hatreds', and wanted to stay out of it. The most they would agree to do was to send two thousand lightly armed British soldiers to ensure that humanitarian relief was delivered to the victims of the fighting. Nor did Bush want to get involved; his ultimately unsuccessful campaign for re-election in November 1992 was taking up most of his time.[295]

The newly elected President Clinton, however, called for a 'lift and strike' strategy. The plan was to lift the arms embargo (which benefited the Serbs as the inheritors of the Yugoslav army whilst preventing the Bosnians from obtaining arms and building up a rival army), then, if the Serbs tried to prevent this, to send air strikes against them. Clinton did, however, insist there would be no American ground troops. Major was consequently horrified, anticipating that the British troops would come under attack. Even Clinton's ambassador in London referred to it as a 'cockamamie idea'.[296] Clinton therefore happily dropped it, declaring to Congress that he had proposed a bold plan to Great Britain and the other NATO allies, but that they would not agree to it. He then returned with relief to domestic politics. Seitz's conclusion was that the Anglo-American relationship was never going to be the same again: 'at a time of almost manic killing on European territory the British and Americans seemed unable to find common ground'.[297]

When, in March 1999, the Balkans conflict flared up again, this time over Kosovo, Tony Blair was now Prime Minister. His approach was the opposite of Major's: he was appalled at the Serbian massacres of Albanians in Kosovo, and he supported military intervention. But this would be intervention in the internal affairs of a sovereign country which had not attacked or even threatened any of those countries which might intervene, and for which there was no Security Council mandate. To resolve this problem, Blair came up with the idea of a 'doctrine of international community', which essentially meant that it was justified to intervene in the affairs of another country if genocide was being – or was about to be – carried out.[298] Most Americans, and especially Clinton, were not eager to use force; only Madeleine Albright, the Secretary of State, supported it.[299] The crisis had blown up when Milošević rejected a new autonomy agreement with Kosovo. Clinton finally agreed to a bombing campaign, which would have much less impact than the public was led to believe at the time, but still no ground troops would be sent. Blair's advocacy of ground troops irritated Clinton, but he was eventually worn down and agreed that sending troops was an option. Reynolds sees Blair as indulging in largely empty posturing, since if the US did not act, nor would the UK. Only the US really had the power to do so.[300] The bombing campaign, 80 per cent of which was carried out by the Americans, was not decisive; what brought Milošević to the negotiating table were public Anglo-American discussions about ground troops. By the agreement of June 1999, the Serbs withdrew their troops from Kosovo and NATO peacekeepers took their place.

For the US, there had been no vital interests at stake. Besides, it was in Europe, and European countries had spent the years since the early 1970s insisting that they could act together in their own interest. In this case, they had not. As for Britain, Major and Hurd had broadly agreed that she should not get involved in any Balkans conflicts, but then Blair had decided that Britain must get involved for the sake of humanity. This approach, – characterised by his first Foreign Secretary, Robin Cook, as an 'ethical foreign policy'[301] – was to dominate the remainder of Blair's period as Prime Minister.

XII

For the United States, darkness fell on 11 September 2001, when three aeroplanes were crashed into the World Trade Center in New York City and the Pentagon in Virginia. The US government focused on tracking down the perpetrators and eliminating them individually, collectively and territorially. The first target was Afghanistan, whose connection with the attacks had soon become clear. Afghanistan was ruled by the Taliban, an extremist, fundamentalist, Sunni Muslim sect, dedicated to the cleansing of modern Islam and returning it to the purity it had enjoyed a millennium before. They were drawn from the majority Pashtun ethnic group which had formerly ruled Afghanistan for three hundred years, and in 2001 they controlled roughly 90 per cent of the country. Al-Qa'ida, led by the Saudi Osama Bin Laden, was the extreme Islamist terrorist group which carried out the attacks. Its goal was to cleanse the Islamic world, in particular the Middle and Near East, of all non-Islamic influences and to re-establish the Muslim caliphate which had ruled the area for centuries. It was based in Afghanistan, but its fighters were drawn from about thirteen Arab states, and it had a global network spread over thirty-four countries. In September 2001 few others than specialists had heard of Al-Qa'ida.[302]

Public support in both the US and the UK for the attack on Afghanistan was very strong, and continued for some years. The invasion of Iraq in 2003 was a different matter. There was scepticism especially in the UK as to the veracity of the claim that Saddam Hussein was connected with Al-Qa'ida, and therefore with the

September 2001 attack. The decision to invade was intensely controversial, and it put an immense strain on the Anglo-American relationship at many levels.

The sympathy felt by most of the British public over what was soon termed '9/11' was deep and publicly expressed. The Queen was seen to weep. According to Christopher Meyer, the British Ambassador to the US,

> something happened that seized the American imagination like nothing else. On Thursday, 13 September, at the ceremony of the Changing of the Guard at Buckingham Palace, the band of the Coldstream Guards played the 'Star-Spangled Banner'. This was something without precedent. At the embassy we were inundated with phone calls, faxes, letters, and emails of gratitude and appreciation. Condi [Condoleezza] Rice [George W. Bush's National Security Adviser] later recounted how she had returned to her apartment that evening after another exhausting day, turned on the television, saw the Coldstreams playing, and, for the first time since 9/11, wept.[303]

The immediate and nearly universal worldwide reaction was one of sympathy and horror. On 12 September there were two significant statements: the North Atlantic Council invoked Article 5 of the NATO Treaty, which said, broadly, that an attack against one was an attack against all; and the UN Security Council and General Assembly passed resolutions condemning the terrorist attacks and calling on all members to bring the perpetrators to justice. On 14 September Congress authorised the use of force against the terrorists and appropriated forty billion dollars to finance it. A military build-up began with the despatch of fighter aircraft to bases in the Persian Gulf and the Indian Ocean, a naval task force, including an aircraft carrier group, to join the two that were already in the area, and a task force of marines. Within a few days, the US had reached agreements with Kazakhstan, Uzbekistan and Tajikistan to allow her to use bases in their territory for operations against the Taliban.[304]

Prime Minister Blair signalled very early on that he intended Britain to play a central role in the fight. (Many Britons had died in the attacks on the World Trade Center.) On 20 September he flew to Washington and had supper at the White House. He and President George W. Bush (who had been elected the previous year) discussed the preparations for the American response, with Bush outlining American military plans and Blair offering British troops and other military assistance. They agreed that international support was necessary, so Blair offered to fly to various capitals to help mobilise it. They then travelled together to the House of Representatives, where Blair was Bush's guest as the President addressed a Joint Session of Congress. The occasion was one of 'intoxicating, intense patriotism', and for the British Ambassador, two themes in Bush's speech stood out. The first was his Manichaean world view: 'Every nation, in every region, now has a decision to make. Either you are with us or you are with the terrorists.' There was no middle ground, echoing John Foster Dulles's pronouncement during the Cold War that 'neutrality is immoral'. The second theme was the challenge not simply to the terrorists but to the regions that harboured them: 'From this day forward, any nation that continues to harbor or support terrorism will be regarded by the United States as a hostile regime.' Bush turned to Blair and called him 'our truest friend', and the response was thunderous applause. The Prime Minister himself pledged that the UK would stand 'shoulder to shoulder' with the US. Ambassador Meyer's assessment was that Blair's relationship with Bush 'had been transported to a new and higher level of trust and friendship. It was a sea change. Blair had become an American hero. More than any other European politician he seemed to have understood the shocking impact on the United States of 9/11: on the President, on the administration, on the intelligence services and on the American people themselves.'[305]

Blair's speech to the Labour Party conference on 1 October 2001, which was transmitted live in the US, could only enhance his hero status: 'We were with you at the first. We will stay with you to the last.' Meyer was soon quoting it repeatedly, and has since said that it never failed to touch Americans 'at their core'. Indeed, sections of the speech were almost otherworldly, or perhaps Wilsonian: In a 'paean of praise to America's historic values', Blair said, 'I believe this is a fight for freedom, and I want to make it a fight for justice too, justice not only to punish the guilty but justice to bring those same values of democracy and freedom to people around the world.' This was an ethical foreign policy with a vengeance, and fully justified the *Newsweek* comment in its issue of 3 December 2001 (in a cover story on Blair) that 'George W. Bush may be commander in chief of the military campaign in Afghanistan. But Blair is its evangelist in chief.'[306] The Prime Minister always seemed happiest when he was part of a moral crusade.

The fighting did not last long. On 7 October British and American bombers made the first attacks against the Taliban in Afghanistan, and on the 19th ground operations began, when US Rangers and Special Forces, alongside local opponents of the Taliban, attacked the headquarters in Kandahar of the regime's leader, Amir Mullah Mohammed Omar. Over a period of two months, the Taliban were driven out of city after city, with victory over Kandahar coming on 7 December. Two days previously, agreement had been reached to establish an interim government in which all non-Taliban elements in Afghan national politics could participate. It would sit for six months whilst more permanent arrangements were devised.

However, the apparent rapidity and smoothness of the war against the Taliban could not hide conflicts amongst the allies, even between the US and the UK. One was the question of 'collateral damage', the modern euphemism for the killing of non-combatants. This was, for the Americans, a regrettable outcome of the bombing campaign which was at the centre of their strategy. The concept of 'force protection' was central to all American tactics. It meant that, next to victory, the most important imperative was to safeguard the lives of American soldiers. Thus, if the choice was either the death of foreign civilians or that of American servicemen, the former lost. War from the air, not on the ground, saved American lives. Many non-Americans found the results not only difficult to accept, but profoundly immoral, and a growing opposition to the US had its origins in this particular conundrum.

The US and the UK differed on other issues, such as what was the main intention in Afghanistan? The Americans wanted to track down the leaders of the Taliban and Al-Qa'ida (in which, however, they were unsuccessful); the British were more concerned with establishing a stable regime, on the grounds that the alternative would allow the Taliban and their allies back into the country. There were also the legal and moral issues centring on the status of the combatants and their treatment. The US insisted that non-military prisoners should be tried by secret military tribunals. The treatment of prisoners at Guantánamo Bay in Cuba, where the US maintained a prison in which it kept those men who it believed had fought for the Taliban and Al-Qa'ida, stimulated strong but unavailing criticism from Britain and other countries. (Strong criticism also came from within the US itself.) The concentration of the US government on the destruction of the forces which had given aid and succour to the terrorists apparently made foreigners' protests seem relatively unimportant: the US was strong enough to ignore them.

This attitude would surface during the preparations for the invasion of Iraq in 2003, which had been pushed by American right-wingers since the mid-1990s. There had certainly been contingency planning in the Pentagon before 9/11. The prospect was discussed in meetings of the National Security Council in Washington immediately after the terrorist attack, but the UK refused to agree to the invasion of any country which could not be proven to have been involved in it. This stance was clearly immaterial to the US. On 29 January 2002 Bush, in his State of the Union speech, announced that 'I will not wait on events while dangers gather'.[307]

Blair and the British Cabinet were not yet so certain about what to do. Over the next few months, Blair's justification for war with Iraq modulated from one of Iraqi involvement in 9/11 to one of Iraqi possession, or not, of weapons of mass destruction (WMDs). However, there was no clear consensus behind going to war. In 1998 Saddam Hussein had thrown out of Iraq UN weapons inspectors whose duty it had been to find out whether Iraq possessed or was developing WMDs. In early 2002 a report by the UK Joint Intelligence Committee showed little if any evidence of such development, although certainty was impossible because of the lack of co-operation from Saddam's regime. By the summer of 2002 Blair was beginning to emphasise the need to take the issue to the UN. If Iraq continued to refuse to co-operate, this increased the case for war, given that Saddam's previous use of chemical weapons had already violated international norms; furthermore, the departure of the inspectors had removed the only constraint on his development of such weapons. The question as to whether WMDs existed became increasingly serious, but unfortunately, sensible debate 'was lost in a frenzy of emotional grandstanding and governmental manipulation, in every country concerned'.[308] In September 2002 the British government published the dossier on WMDs: its conclusion was that Saddam did possess them and that they amounted to a 'current and serious' threat to UK security because they could, it was claimed, be ready to use in forty-five minutes. There was dissent in the Cabinet over whether the dossier justified war, but, according to Foreign Secretary Cook, Blair's response was that 'to carry on being engaged with the US is vital. The voices on both left and right who want to pull Europe and the US apart would have disastrous consequences if they succeeded.'[309] (Once the war was over the dossier was at the centre of a ferocious political controversy because no WMDs had been found.)

The development of British policy ran alongside the related attempts by Blair to influence American policy in a manner which would ensure greater international support for an invasion of Iraq. In April 2002 Blair had met with the President at the latter's ranch in Crawford, Texas. According to Peter Riddell, this was the point at which the British recognised the strength of Bush's determination to oust Saddam, most likely by military means. Blair had three objectives: he wanted to emphasise WMDs rather than regime change; to keep options open; and to convince Bush that there were great advantages to working with allies rather than going it alone. At a press conference on 6 April Bush stated, with admirable bluntness, 'I explained to the Prime Minister that the policy of my government is the removal of Saddam and that all options are on the table.' Since it was not yet British policy, Blair finessed it by emphasising WMDs as the criterion. However, Bush then trumped Blair's card by reiterating that Saddam had to go. The following day, in a speech at the Bush Presidential Library, Blair emphasised the desirability of seeking international support. This was partly for its own sake, but it was also an attempt to meet the criticisms of the Labour Party, many of whose members were increasingly worried about the development of unilateral American policies, and in particular of American plans for war against Iraq.[310]

Over the summer Blair tried to convince the Bush administration of the desirability of working through the UN. It would refocus international attention on Saddam and his unspeakable activities, provide the means of putting together an anti-Saddam coalition, ensure that an attack on Iraq was legal, provide cover for Blair in the UK from those, primarily with Labour, who were both anti-war and anti-American, facilitate the reintroduction of weapons inspectors into Iraq, ensure a role for the UN in post-war Iraq, and possibly even provide a means of avoiding war altogether.[311] However, he came up against the adamantine hatred for the UN of Vice-President Dick Cheney and others in the administration. They had decided on war, and going through the UN might dilute or divert the plan, or at the very least delay it. Blair's other argument was the threat from Iraq's WMDs, which he said must be addressed. In the US over the summer there were arguments between current and former powers: Cheney and Donald Rumsfeld, the Secretary of Defense, were all for war and ignoring the UN; Secretary of State Colin Powell told Bush on 5 August that the US should consider war only as part of an international coalition, rather than going it alone; Brent Scowcroft, James Baker and Henry Kissinger warned variously about the dangers of ignoring the UN, of going it alone, and of a doctrine of pre-emptive action.

When Blair returned to the UK from holiday in late August he found growing opposition to military engagement with Iraq, stimulated by the conflicting messages emanating from Washington. British public opinion supported trying to make international institutions, in particular the UN, work before resorting to force. It seems that Blair's political need, as well as desire, for a UN resolution helped to tip the President in that direction. Powell was also arguing for this, and Bush's decision was a notable victory for the Prime Minister and Secretary of State (and for Baker). On 7 September Blair flew to Camp David for the day, and he and the President talked for three hours. In the subsequent press conference, Bush emphasised the danger Saddam posed not only to the region, but to the US and Britain. Blair emphasised that the two countries had a shared strategy, and would approach the issue 'on the basis of the broadest possible international support'. It was decided that Bush would go to the Security Council to seek a resolution giving Saddam one more chance to comply with the UN weapons inspectors. If Iraq's leader then failed to do so, Blair would stand 'shoulder-to-shoulder' with Bush and commit military forces. There were still problems, however: many Labour MPs would oppose war whatever the case – the American journalist Bob Woodward called them 'a pacifist party at heart' – and the Washington hawks would call for war whatever Saddam did. At Camp David Blair had publicly committed Britain to supporting the US. For the Bush administration, this meant that he was committed to war if it should come, although Blair himself did not interpret it as an irrevocable decision to go to war.[312]

On 12 September, Bush addressed the UN General Assembly and called for a resolution demanding that Iraq readmit the weapons inspectors. Thereafter, for two months, Powell led the American delegation in the negotiations at the UN, and on 8 November 2002 there emerged UN Security Council Resolution 1441. Powell had had to watch his back in Washington, where attempts were made by the hawks to modify the proposed content of the resolution. He was helped by the British Ambassador to the UN, Jeremy Greenstock, and by the strong support of the pro-American Prime Ministers John Howard of Australia and José María Aznar of Spain. After a few days Saddam accepted the terms of the resolution, and later in November the inspectors, led by Dr Hans Blix, returned to Iraq after a four-year absence.

On 7 December Iraq declared her WMD holdings, but Washington judged it a lying rehash of earlier declarations. The Bush administration feared a long-drawn-out inspections process that would allow Saddam to slip through their fingers, but there was the danger that too great pressure on Blix would alienate the UN, destroy the consensus painfully built up around Resolution 1441, and seriously undermine any possibility of an international coalition. The US Administration rapidly lost patience and, according to Woodward, by early January 2003 Bush had decided on war. On the

29th, in his State of the Union address, he made this clear, devoting the final third of his speech to a condemnation of Saddam, including a list of weapons which the Iraqi leader had included in earlier declarations but which had not yet been discovered. There was also a call to rally around the flag. 'The destruction of Saddam was a crusade against evil to be undertaken by God's chosen nation: "The call of history has come to the right people."'[313]

Thereafter came a stumble to war. Many countries had been seriously alarmed by Bush's bellicose speech and its call for a unilateral response to Saddam's evil regime. Blair again tried to push the US towards seeking another Security Council resolution which would explicitly endorse an invasion, and Washington agreed to try; whatever the extent of Blair's influence, it was supported by the desire of the American public for as much sharing of the risk as was possible. But international support was fragmenting, with France, Germany and Russia, in particular, extremely reluctant to agree to a second resolution. Blair was therefore increasingly isolated in his support for the Americans. And even domestic support for Bush's call to arms was tepid. On the evening of 10 March Jacques Chirac, the President of France, made the startling announcement that his country would veto a second resolution, 'whatever the circumstances'. The following day Ambassador Greenstock reported to London that support for the resolution was dwindling. Geoff Hoon, the British Defence Secretary, telephoned Rumsfeld to warn him that, without the second resolution, Blair might be unable to muster the necessary support to send troops to Iraq. In a monumental misjudgement which humiliated Blair, Rumsfeld announced publicly that the US did not need British troops and could go it alone. (Blair's director of communications and strategy, Alastair Campbell, referred to it as a 'communications friendly fire'.) On 17 March the second resolution was formally withdrawn; on the same day Robin Cook resigned as Foreign Secretary.[314]

On the 18th there was a House of Commons debate to decide whether to go to war. Blair emphasised Britain's duty to back the US, but the government also played the 'French card' by citing Chirac's intransigence, and Jack Straw, newly installed as Foreign Secretary, urged Labour MPs to vote 'to keep this government in business'.

According to Woodward, 'Bush had never paid such close attention to a debate or vote in a foreign legislature as the one going on that day in the British Parliament. "What's the vote count?" he had asked a number of times during the day. Finally at 5:15 p.m. – 10:15 p.m. London time – the Parliament voted.' Blair won by 396 to 217. In the end, although 139 Labour MPs voted against, the House voted for war.[315] Great Britain was now part of the American 'coalition of the willing'.

XIII

When the history of the Blair premiership can be written properly – when archives are open and emotions are cooler – it is likely to be the period of the Iraq War which dominates the pages. And within that context, the nature and appropriateness of Blair's relationship with Bush will bulk large. What is clear from earlier chapters is that the Anglo-American relationship as expressed through and by the respective leaders has been of some importance since 1940. Although the Roosevelt–Churchill double-act could never have lived up to the consciously created Churchillian myth, nevertheless it was characterised by mutual respect in the earlier days, until Roosevelt decided that the relationship needed to be at least partially sacrificed in favour of a more useful one with Stalin. The Kennedy–Macmillan relationship developed a closeness that surprised them both, and it certainly facilitated the acquisition by Britain of Polaris. Kennedy himself found it useful and enjoyable to discuss matters great and small with Macmillan.[316] And there was genuine affection between them.

In the Reagan–Thatcher relationship an ideological identification, missing from the earlier examples, was reciprocal and complete. And whilst no British Prime Minister could be unaware of the disparity in resources and power, it is still difficult to imagine that Thatcher always saw herself as the junior partner. She and Reagan reinforced each other. Furthermore, on at least one important occasion – the Reykjavik summit of 1986 – she reined him back from a provisional agreement with the Soviet leader Mikhail Gorbachev which had come close to bargaining away nuclear weapons alto-gether. Without nuclear deterrence, Europe was at the mercy of the USSR, so she had to keep Reagan committed to Europe. She strongly defended Reagan in most things, but she did not have the aura of a subordinate in the way her successors did. She recognised the asymmetry – who could not? – but she did not bow to it. Her successors had little choice.

Blair was unusual because he made himself a close friend and comrade of two successive American Presidents who could hardly have been more different. According to Anthony Seldon, no foreign leader more impressed Blair or was so personally close to him as Clinton: 'both men challenged the prevailing orthodoxies within their parties, were non-ideologues captivated by the promise of finding a "third way" in politics, and they were both natural extroverts who wanted to reach out across conventional frontiers to win new converts to their cause'. However, there was a trajectory: first Blair was a junior partner, then a soulmate, and then, after Kosovo, a disillusioned lover.[317] Essentially, the relationship was clouded by their differing approaches to foreign policy, in particular since Blair sometimes treated it as a moral issue.

Clinton himself told Blair to 'get as close to George Bush as you have been to me', although, according to Riddell, the Prime Minister had already adopted the 'hug them close' approach.[318] This was hardly carving out a new path, given that Churchill had followed an identical strategy. For Blair, it appeared to have worked very well, but such a strategy always depends on a reciprocal embrace. With Bush, it worked probably for two reasons: the two men immediately took to each other; and Bush needed Britain, because the US required an ally able and willing to fight. In March 2003, according to Woodward, 'From Bush's perspective, Blair was the guy who had stuck his neck out, who had the "cojones" to be strong and steady. If his government went down, Bush would not only lose his chief ally but it would strengthen Saddam.' Bush rang Blair and offered him several escape routes, such as the British being the peacekeepers rather than the warriors in Iraq, but Blair's response was that 'I'm there to the very end.'[319] For a President who valued loyalty above most other qualities, Blair must have seemed a pearl beyond price.

But there can be a drawback to being best international friend, and this is a strong risk of being taken for granted. Leverage may be lost, and certainly the British Ambassador in Washington feared that the UK was reaping diminishing returns: 'There comes a point where, if you hug too close, it becomes an end in itself.' But his later conclusion was that 'the Americans really needed us by their side if it came to war', a conviction strengthened by the avowal of a powerful member of the Bush team that the UK was 'the only ally that mattered'.[320] It is undoubtedly the case that a President can give the lead on these matters and subordinates will usually follow. But the US government is made up of several layers of decision-makers perched on top of a huge bureaucracy, and the possibilities of delay or circumvention are legion. A relationship which is going to be productive for Britain or the US, that is made up of more than ritual obeisances to the 'special relationship', effectively needs more than a close relationship between the leaders, useful though that might be.

The period after 1945 saw the consequences of Great Britain's increasing economic weakness and her withdrawal from the Empire. Her decline from global to regional power had a tremendous impact on the formal relationship with the US, which had emerged from the Second World War as a global superpower of unparalleled wealth and strength. The relationship was bound to be asymmetrical. Britain tried to retain as much power and influence over the US as she could by exploiting her Empire, her military power, her nuclear and intelligence links, and her diplomatic expertise. As described above, the results were mixed. She needed the US more than the US needed her. It was a total reversal of the nineteenth-century relationship between the two countries.

For her part, the US saw herself as the leader and protector of the 'free world', with global responsibilities. In this order of things the UK sometimes hardly figured. She could help, but she could also hinder, and to a US which normally saw her own national interests as nearly identical with the interests of the whole western world, the insistence of Britain that she had interests which should be respected could appear parochial and even small-minded. The treatment of the UK by the US tended to vary relative to the region and the problem, and to the extent that America needed British aid. Both countries accepted that, in general, they had common ideals, common interests and common approaches to problems in foreign affairs, and this manifested itself in the very close links between the armed services, between the Foreign Office and the Department of State, and between the diplomatic corps in the field. On nearly a daily basis they consulted each other, and when necessary they worked together. But in dealing with conflicts of interest, the US could be ruthless in safeguarding and advancing her own. Her approach to foreign affairs was not helped by the lack of an institutional memory in the US government. The relationship was sometimes made particularly difficult by the need of the executive, which has responsibility for foreign policy, to accommodate the wishes of the legislature, which pays for it. Great Britain could be caught in the middle.

In these circumstances, it is a matter of some interest that the two countries managed to maintain such close relations. Fundamentally, when the occasion demanded it, there re-emerged the early twentieth-century assumption that, different from each other as they were in their cultures, interests and ability to project power, they were, nevertheless, more alike than any other two powers on the globe. And the instinctive feeling persists: there is a true love–hate Anglo-American special relationship.

Notes

Prologue – Looking Westwards

1 'An extract taken out of the map of Sebastian Cabot, cut by Clement Adams, concerning his discovery of the West Indies, which is to be seene in her Majesties privie gallerie at Westminster, a59 nd in many other ancient merchants houses', Irwin R. Blacker, ed., Richard Hakluyt, *Hakluyt's Voyages: The Principal Navigations, Voyages, Traffiques & Discoveries of the English Nation* (New York: Viking Press, 1965, 1st pub. 1600), pp. 19–20, quotation on p. 19.

2 Lines 25–30. Helen Gardner, ed., *The Elegies and the Songs and Sonnets of John Donne* (Oxford: Oxford University Press, 1965), pp. 14–16, quotation on p. 15.

3 The map, with its rectangular array of lines of longitude and latitude, is in Mercator's 'projection', published in its original form in 1569 and from 1700 or so the standard projection for mariners' maps. The map allows a mariner directly to read off the bearing – e.g., west, south-east or north-north-west, or whatever he needs to follow in order to travel between two points. This convenience is achieved at the expense, however, of a distortion of scale. The scale increases with increasing latitude (N or S), as the '1,000 mile' markings on the map show. (There are many other methods of projection, each of which must sacrifice something in the process of 'projecting' the earth's curved surface onto a flat piece of paper.) Grateful thanks to Michael Jewess.

4 'Dead reckoning' is an (inevitably approximate) method of determining the position of a point relative to a starting point on the basis of the direction of travel between the two points and an estimate of the speed. Thanks to Michael Jewess.

5 And Tolkien's Bilbo and Frodo departed with the elves for the west.

6 Throughout the fifteenth century sailors were discovering islands, and there seemed to be no reason why this should not go on indefinitely – a cloud bank at dusk can resemble an island. Imaginary islands dotted sea charts: St Brendan's Isle off Ireland; Brazil Rock (on Admiralty charts until 1873); and most famously, Atlantis or Antilla. Parry has related that this was 'the isle of seven cities, where seven Portuguese bishops were supposed to have migrated with their flocks, during the barbarian invasions, and where their descendants had lived in piety and great prosperity ever since. It was one of the dreams of fifteenth-century sailors to rediscover this mythical country, its Christian people and its gold.' J.H. Parry, *The Age of Reconnaissance: Discovery, Exploration and Settlement 1450–1650* (London: Phoenix Press, 2000), p. 5.

7 Plato, *Timaeus*, 24–5, in *Timaeus and Critias*, trans. Desmond Lee (London: Penguin, 1977), pp. 37–8.

8 On a map of the known world at the end of the seventeenth century, published in Edward Well's *New Sett of Maps* (Oxford, 1701), there is printed on the continent of North America the following: 'This Continent with the adjoining Islands is generally supposed to have been Anciently unknown, although there are not wanting some, who will have even the Continent its self to be no other, than the Insula ATLANTIS of the Ancients.' British Museum, illus. 57 in Parry, *Age of Reconnaissance*.

9 Seneca, *Medea*, trans. Frederick Ahl (Ithaca: Cornell University Press, 1986), p. 64.

10 From Seneca's comment that 'I am not born for one corner; the whole world is my native land', one gains the impression that he read about discoveries and other lands. Strabo (c. 58 BC– c. AD 24) was a Greek geographer who travelled widely throughout the Roman world and wrote

a description of it in his seventeen-volume *Geographia*. Polybius wrote *c.* 150 BC of the voyage made by Pytheas.

11 For Bjarni's sighting of North America, see the *Graenlendinga Saga*, pp. 51–4; for Leif Ericsson's planned exploration, see *ibid.*, pp. 54–6; for the date of sighting of North America, see *ibid.*, p. 7; for the first attempted colonisation by Thorfinn Karlsefni, see *ibid.*, pp. 6–7; the attribution to Leif Ericsson of the discovery of North America by the Norsemen can be found in the later *Eirik's Saga*, pp. 84–6; all in *The Vinland Sagas: The Norse Discovery of America*, trans. and Introduction by Magnus Magnusson and Hermann Palsson (London: Penguin, 1965). Thanks to Tristan Stansbury for Pytheas and the suggestions about the sagas. Chemical analysis of the Vinland Map has shown that the black ink of the parchment does not contain gallotannate, which was found in medieval inks, and therefore 'the Vinland Map, purportedly drawn in the mid-15th century showing the New World as discovered by Nordic explorers, is a fake from the early 20th century'. *Independent*, 31 July 2002.

12 Parry, *Age of Reconnaissance*, p. 5.

13 Sir John Mandeville, *The Travels of Sir John Mandeville*, trans. and Introduction by C.W.R.D. Moseley (London: Penguin, 1983), p. 137. And customs: 'There is another fair and good isle, full of people, where the custom is that when a woman is newly married, she shall not sleep the first night with her husband, but with another young man, who shall have ado with her that night and take her maidenhead, taking in the morning a certain sum of money for his trouble. In each town there are certain young men set apart to do that service, which are called *gadlibiriens*, which is to say "fools of despair". They say, and affirm as a truth, that it is a very dangerous thing to take the maidenhead of a virgin; for, so they say, whoever does puts himself in peril of death. And if the husband of the woman find her still virgin on the next night following (perchance because the man who should have had her maidenhead was drunk, or for any other reason did not perform properly to her), then shall he have an action at law against the young man before the justices of the land – as serious as if the young man had intended to kill him. But after the first night, when those women are so defiled, they are kept so strictly that they shall not speak to or even come into the company of those men. I asked him what the cause and reason was for such a custom there. They told me that in ancient times some men had died in that land in deflowering maidens, for the latter had snakes within them, which stung the husbands on their penises inside the women's bodies; and thus many men were slain, and so they follow that custom there to make other men test the route before they themselves set out on that adventure.' *Ibid.*, p. 175.

14 *Ibid.*, pp. 127–8.

15 Giles Milton, *The Riddle and the Knight: In Search of Sir John Mandevile* (London: Hodder & Stoughton, 2000, 1st pub. 1996), pp. 3–4, 55, 271–8.

16 It is worth noting that during the medieval period, Arab scholars were improving on Ptolemy's work, making significant advances in map presentation and accuracy.

17 For the Europeans, that is. Parry, *Age of Reconnaissance*, pp. 149–50; W.P.D. Wightman, *Science in a Renaissance Society* (London: Hutchinson, 1972), pp. 65–71; and Timothy Ferris, *Coming of Age in the Milky Way* (New York: Doubleday, 1988), pp. 54–7. Columbus also made the significant, but relatively minor, error of underestimating the distance to be travelled on the sea per degree of longitude. Grateful thanks to Michael Jewess.

18 Vespucci took part in four early expeditions to the New World, the accounts of which were published in 1507 by Waldseemüller. He was later pilot major, or head, of the Seville school of navigation, set up in the early sixteenth century to train and license navigators for the West Indian trades. Parry, *Age of Reconnaissance*, p. 96.

19 Parry refers to his globe as 'of beautiful workmanship and remarkable accuracy'. *Ibid.*, p. 110. Mercator was also the first to include magnetic bearings on globes. His true name was Gerhard Kremer, but he is known by the Latinised form.

20 As is shown by the map at the beginning of this Prologue, itself in Mercator's projection, the easy determination of bearing was achieved at the expense of varying the scale, which increases from the equator towards the poles. To estimate the distance to be travelled between starting-point and destination, one uses the scale at the mid-point of the line joining them. The '1,000 mile markings' on the map show the variation of scale. On this map Mercator incorporated some information from Mandeville – 'an author who, though he relates some fables, is not to be disregarded as concerns the positions of places'. Nicholas Crane, *Mercator: The Man Who Mapped the Planet* (London: Weidenfeld & Nicolson, 2002), p. 227. Mercator's book of maps published in 1595 was called *Atlas*, the first use of the term.

21 Wightman, *Science in a Renaissance Society*, p. 136; Parry, *Age of Reconnaissance*, pp. 112–13; and Crane, *Mercator*, pp. 289–90. The technical advantages of Mercator's projection are still appreciated by modern-day explorers (e.g., for recording the features of the planets as observed from space missions). However, world maps for the uninstructed reader are generally less likely nowadays to be in Mercator's projection than formerly. Such a reader, regarding the map at the beginning of the Prologue but disregarding the scale markings, would be surprised to learn that the area of India is in reality ten times that of Norway.

22 Kenneth R. Andrews, *Trade, Plunder and Settlement: Maritime Enterprise and the Genesis of the British Empire 1480–1630* (Cambridge: Cambridge University Press, 1991, 1st pub. 1984), pp. 43–4. A fifty-ton ship meant that it could, notionally, carry fifty barrels – i.e., tunnes – of cargo, particularly of wine.

23 *Ibid.*, pp. 43–7; Alan Smith, ed., *Virginia 1584–1607: The First English Settlement in North America* (London: Theodore Brun, 1957), p. xvii; Rodney Broome, *Amerike: The Briton Who Gave America its Name* (Stroud: Sutton, 2002), p. 125. At the end of the fifteenth century, a skilled artisan's wage was about seven pounds a year, so Cabot's pension was considerable.

24 James McDermott, *Martin Frobisher: Elizabethan Privateer* (London and New Haven, Conn.: Yale University Press, 2001), p. 447, ref. 4.

25 Sir Thomas More, *Utopia: Containing an Impartial History of the Manners, Customs, Polity, Government &c of That Island*, trans. Gilbert Burnet (Oxford: J. Newbery at the Bible and Sun in St Paul's Churchyard, London, 1751, 1st pub. 1515), p. 4.

26 Andrews, *Trade, Plunder and Settlement*, pp. 54–5.

27 *Ibid.*, pp. 9, 32–3.

28 Ben Jonson, John Marston and George Chapman, *Eastward Ho!* (London: Nick Hearn for the Royal Shakespeare Company, 2002), pp. 39–40.

29 J.H. Elliott, *The Old World and the New 1492–1650* (Cambridge: Cambridge University Press, 1992, 1st pub. 1970), *passim;* Susan Brigden, *New Worlds, Lost Worlds: The Rule of the Tudors 1485–1603* (London: Allen Lane, 2000), pp. 274–82; Andrews, *Trade, Plunder and Settlement*, pp. 54–7; Howard Mumford Jones, *O Strange New World. American Culture: The Formative Years* (New York: Viking Press, 1964), pp. 33–5. Anthony Grafton has pointed out that Tacitus' descriptions of the ancient Germans helped to shape European perceptions of barbarians. Tacitus describes, *inter alia*, how the Germans chose their commanders for their valour, and how these commanders relied on their example rather than on their authority (ch. 7); how the natives take less pleasure than most in possessing and handling gold and silver (ch. 5); and how on minor matters only the chiefs debate, but on major matters the whole community does so (ch. 11). Tacitus, *The Agricola and the Germania* (London: Penguin, 1970), pp. 107, 105, 110. He is, at least implicitly, comparing the virtues of the allegedly savage Germans with the corrupt Romans, and 'Tacitus can thus be said to be the intellectual great-grandfather of the concept of the Noble Savage.' Anthony Grafton, *New Worlds, Ancient Texts: The Power of Tradition and the Shock of Discovery* (Cambridge, Mass.: Belknap Press, 1995, 1st pub. 1992), p. 43.

30 Smith, *Virginia 1584–1607*, p. xx; McDermott, *Frobisher*, pp. 93–256; Hakluyt, *Hakluyt's Voyages*, pp. 175–8, 182–98, 199–209.

31 Nicholas Canny, ed., *The Origins of Empire: British Overseas Enterprise to the Close of the Seventeenth Century* (Oxford: Oxford University Press, 1998), p. 4.

32 Hakluyt, *Hakluyt's Voyages*, pp. 210–15.

33 Description by Edward Hayes, a gentleman of Liverpool, who had contributed to Gilbert's 1578 expedition, and contributed the *Golden Hind*, which he captained. Quoted in Andrews, *Trade, Plunder and Settlement*, pp. 194–7.

34 Quoted in Phil Jones, *Ralegh's Pirate Colony in America: The Lost Settlement of Roanoke 1584–1590* (Stroud: Tempus, 2001), p. 26, where the spelling has been modernised. The original source is not given.

35 Jack P. Greene, *The Intellectual Construction of America: Exceptionalism and Identity from 1492 to 1800* (Chapel Hill: University of North Carolina Press, 1993), pp. 36–8.

36 *Ibid.*, pp. 38–43; William H. Sherman, *John Dee: The Politics of Reading and Writing in the English Renaissance* (Amherst: University of Massachusetts Press, 1995), ch. 7.

37 Andrews, *Trade, Plunder and Settlement*, pp. 31–2.

38 Elliott, *The Old World and the New*, p. 42.

39 Andrews, *Trade, Plunder and Settlement*, pp. 37–8.

40 Hakluyt, *Hakluyt's Voyages*, pp. 279–85.

41 Andrews, *Trade, Plunder and Settlement*, p. 201.

42 Hakluyt, *Hakluyt's Voyages*, pp. 286–97, quotations on pp. 287 and 297.

43 Andrews, *Trade, Plunder and Settlement*, pp. 200–12. P. Hulton and D.B. Quinn, eds, *The American Drawings of John White*, 2 vols (London and Chapel Hill: University of North Carolina Press, 1964).

44 Hakluyt, *Hakluyt's Voyages*, pp. 298–300.

45 Jones, *Ralegh's Pirate Colony*, pp. 47–8 for the quotations from an earlier source. Colonists the following year put together the story from Indian reports. *Ibid.*, p. 48.

46 John C. Appleby, 'War, Politics, and Colonization, 1558–1625', in Canny, ed., *Origins of Empire*, p. 65.

47 Andrews, *Trade, Plunder and Settlement*, pp. 215–17.

48 *Ibid.*, pp. 217–30, quotation on p. 229.

49 *Ibid.*, pp. 218–20, quotation on p. 219. Jones, *Ralegh's Pirate Colony*, pp. 75–84.

Chapter 1 – Conquest and Colonisation: 1607–1763

1 'Newes from Virginia on the happy arrival of that Famous and Worthy knight, Sir Thomas Gates, and well reputed and Valiant Captain Newport, into England', *c.* 1610, in C.H. Firth, ed., *An American Garland: Being a Collection of Balads Relating to America 1563–1759* (Oxford: B.H. Blackwell, 1915), p. 13.

2 John C. Appleby, 'War, Politics, and Colonization, 1558–1625', in Nicholas Canny, ed., *The Oxford History of the British Empire, Volume I: The Origins of Empire: British Overseas Enterprise to the Close of the Seventeenth Century* (Oxford: Oxford University Press, 1998), p. 68.

3 *Ibid.*, p. 67. It is not really possible to say with any accuracy what the equivalent of this £200,000 would be today. In 1688, Gregory King estimated that for England and Wales, 'the country's annual income was £43,500,000, the annual expence [*sic*] was £41,700,000, yearly rents of the land equalled about £10m, the yearly produce of trade, arts and labour was about £30,500,000, and the whole value of the Kingdom was £650,000,000'. Gregory King, *Natural and Political Observations and Conclusions upon the State and Condition of England* (London, 1696), ch. 6. B.R. Mitchell and Phyllis Deane, *Abstracts of British Historical Statistics* (Cambridge: Cambridge University Press, 1962), p. 279, suggests that in 1700, imports were worth £5.8 million, domestic exports £3.7 million and exports plus re-exports £5.8 million.

4 Andrews, *Trade, Plunder and Settlement*, p. 310.

5 Alison Games, *Migration and the Origins of the English Atlantic World* (Cambridge, Mass.: Harvard University Press, 1999), p. 17.

6 Andrews, *Trade, Plunder and Settlement*, p. 311.

7 Among them were the Russia Company, set up in 1553 to trade with Muscovy; the Levant Company, set up in 1592 to trade in the eastern Mediterranean; and the most famous of all, the East India Company, set up in 1600 to trade with the Far East.

8 Quoted in Richard Middleton, *Colonial America: A History, 1585–1776* (Oxford: Blackwell, 1996 2nd edn), p. 15.

9 Quoted in Andrews, *Trade, Plunder and Settlement*, p. 327.

10 Middleton, *Colonial America*, p. 54; Appleby, 'War, Politics, and Colonization', p. 72.

11 From John Smith, *The General Historie of Virginia, New England and the Summer Isles* (London, 1624), in Smith, ed., *Virginia 1584–1607*, p. 80. It is worth bearing in mind that John Smith was not averse to editing and even fabricating material about his own activities.

12 The *Susan Constant*, captained by Newport, was a 120-ton ship; the *Godspeed* was 40 tons; and the pinnace *Discovery* was 20 tons. The other two captains were Bartholomew Gosnoll (the *Godspeed*), 'one of the first movers of this plantation, having many yeares solicited many of his friends', and John Ratcliffe (the *Discovery*), who 'is now called Sicklemore, a poore counterfeited imposture. I have sent you him home, least the company should cut his throat.' Quotations from John Smith, *Generall Historie*, in Smith, ed., *Virginia 1584–1607*, pp. 79, 94.

13 Warren M. Billings, *Jamestown and the Founding of the Nation* (Gettysburg, Penn.: Thomas Publications, n.d.), p. 31.

14 John Smith (1580–1631) was born in the village of Willoughby in Lincolnshire. Always an adventurer, he was successively a soldier in the Low Countries, a mercenary in Hungary, where he killed hordes of pagans, and then a captive and slave of the Turks.

15 Andrews, *Trade, Plunder and Settlement*, p. 315.

16 'The Proceedings . . . by William Simons', in Smith, ed., *Virginia 1584–1607*, p. 86.

17 Quoted in Andrews, *Trade, Plunder and Settlement*, p. 316.

18 'Although the countrie people be very barbarous, yet they have amongst them such government, as that their magistrats for good commanding, and their people for du subjection, and obeying, excell many places that would be counted very civill . . . Yet when he listeth his will is a law and must bee obeyed: not only as a king but as halfe a God they esteeme him. His inferiour kings whom they cal werowances are tyed to rule by customes, and have power of life & death.' Quoted in *ibid.*, p. 317. A weroan, according to the English, was 'a great Lorde of Virginia'. Billings, *Jamestown*, p. 23. The Tidewater encompasses all of Virginia between the Atlantic Ocean and the fall line, the point approximately 100 miles inland at which the eastern rivers are no longer tidal.

19 Quoted in Andrews, *Trade, Plunder and Settlement*, p. 318.

20 'The Proceedings . . . by William Simons', in Smith, ed., *Virginia 1584–1607*, p. 86.

21 *Ibid.*, pp. 87–90. Pocahontas's Indian name was Matoaka. The only source of the story was Smith's *General Historie*, published in 1624. When Smith and Pocahontas met in London in 1616, she barely remembered him.

22 Smith, ed., *Virginia 1584–1607*, pp. 97–8.

23 According to the Revels Accounts for 1611, 'Hallowmas nyght was presented at Whitehall before the kinges Maiestie a play Called the Tempest', in Stephen Orgel, ed., William Shakespeare, *The Tempest* (Oxford: Oxford University Press, 1987), p. 1. The description is from 'A true repetory of the wreck and redemption of Sir Thomas Gates, Knight, upon and from the islands of the Bermudas, his coming to Virginia, and the estate of the colony then and after the government of the Lord La Warre. July 15, 1610, written by William Strachey, Esquire', from *Purchas his Pilgrimes* (London, 1625), Part 4, Book 9, ch. 6 (pp. 1734 *et seq.*), printed (with spelling modernised) as Appendix B of the OUP *Tempest*.

24 Smith, ed., *Virginia 1584–1607*, pp. 98–9.

25 Billings, *Jamestown*, p. 44.

26 *Ibid.*, pp. 45–7. Both quotations from Raphe Hamor, *A True Discourse of the Present Estate of Virginia, and the successe of the affaires there til the 18 of June, 1614. Together, With a Relation of the several English townes and forts, the assured hopes of that countrie and the peace concluded with the Indians. The Christening of Powhatans daughter and her mariage with an English-man* (London, 1615), pp. 63, 24.

27 Quoted with modernised spelling in Middleton, *Colonial America*, p. 59. There exists near-contemporary reference to it in Hamor, *A True Discourse*, pp. 55–6.

28 Ann Uhry Abrams, *The Pilgrims and Pocahontas: Rival Myths of American Origin* (Boulder, Col.: Westview Press, 1999), pp. 20–1; quotation in parentheses from Andrews, *Trade, Plunder and Settlement*, p. 322.

29 *Ibid.*, p. 323.

30 Edward Waterhouse, 'A Declaration of the state of the Colonie and Affaires in Virginia', in Susan Myra Kingsbury, ed., *Records of the Virginia Company of London*, 4 vols (Washington, D.C., 1906–35), III, p. 551, quoted in Billings, *Jamestown*, pp. 51–3.

31 Middleton, *Colonial America*, pp. 67–8.

32 Billings, *Jamestown*, pp. 53–4; Andrews, *Trade, Plunder and Settlement*, pp. 325–6.

33 Quoted in Middleton, *Colonial America*, p. 67.

34 David Hackett Fischer, *Albion's Seed: Four British Folkways in America* (Oxford: Oxford University Press, 1991, 1st pub. 1989), p. 229.

35 *Ibid.*, p. 277.

36 Bernard Bailyn, *The Peopling of British North America: An Introduction* (New York: Alfred A. Knopf, 1986), pp. 99–102. Charles II had chartered the Royal Africa Company in 1663 to monopolise the supply of slaves to the English West Indies.

37 Fischer, *Albion's Seed*, pp. 212–14, quotation on p. 214.

38 *Ibid.*, pp. 212–25, quotation on p. 224.

39 Firth, ed., *An American Garland*, pp. 25–6.

40 The Puritans did not refer to themselves as such – they considered themselves as members of 'the godly'.

41 This was not an eccentric move. The Netherlands, of course, was a Protestant country, but beyond that, 'the sea linked East Anglia, Kent and Lincolnshire with each other, and also with the Netherlands, in a cultural nexus of great importance in the seventeenth century'. Fischer, *Albion's Seed*, p. 43.

42 William Bradford, *Bradford's History 'Of Plimoth Plantation'. From the Original Manuscript. With a Report of the Proceedings Incident to the Return of the Manuscript to Massachusetts* (Boston, Mass.: Wright & Potter, 1898), pp. 30, 31, 32–3. Bradford's work is the basis of all subsequent accounts, although others exist which are important.

43 Andrews, *Trade, Plunder and Settlement*, pp. 328–9, quotation on p. 329.

44 Printed (with modernised spelling) in Middleton, *Colonial America*, p. 77. *Ibid.*, pp. 75–8; Andrews, *Trade, Plunder and Settlement*, pp. 328–30. Because the *Mayflower* had previously been involved in carrying wine from Bordeaux to London, its hold was relatively 'sweet' and free from disease. As a consequence, the eight-week voyage to America was healthier than many others, and only five of those on board died. Andrew Barr, *Drink: A Social History of America* (New York: Carroll & Graf, 1999), p. 33, ref. 3.

45 But see Mary Beth Norton, *Founding Mothers and Fathers: Gendered Power and the Formation of American Society* (New York: Alfred A. Knopf, 1996). For an interesting assessment of the work, see Edmund S. Morgan, *The Genuine Article: A Historian Looks at Early America* (New York: W.W. Norton, 2004), pp. 43–9.

46 Bradford, *Of Plimmoth Plantation*, p. 111.

47 *Ibid.*, pp. 115–21, quotation on p. 116; Andrews, *Plunder and Settlement*, pp. 330–1.

48 This is now celebrated on the fourth Thursday in November. Virginia celebrated the first such Thanksgiving in 1614, by order of the Governor, but it was not a regular holiday. It remained primarily a local New England holiday until President Abraham Lincoln proclaimed it a national observance in 1862, during the Civil War.

49 Andrews, *Trade, Plunder and Settlement*, pp. 326–31; Middleton, *Colonial America*, pp. 75–80.

50 'And I will establish my covenant between me and thee and thy seed after thee in their generations for an everlasting covenant, to be a God unto thee, and to thy seed after thee. And I will give unto thee, and to thy seed after thee, the land wherein thou art a stranger, all the land of Canaan, for an everlasting possession; and I will be their God. And God said unto Abraham, Thou shalt keep my covenant therefore, thou, and thy seed after thee in their generations. This *is* my covenant, which ye shall keep, between me and you and thy seed after thee; Every man child among you shall be circumcised.' Genesis 17: 7–10, King James Version.

51 Fischer, *Albion's Seed*, pp. 23–4, quotations on p. 24.

52 Edmund S. Morgan, *The Puritan Dilemma: The Story of John Winthrop* (Boston, Mass.: Little, Brown, 1958 pb. edn), pp. 7–8. According to the American H.L. Mencken, the definition of Puritanism was 'the haunting fear that someone, somewhere, might be happy'.

53 Morgan, *The Puritan Dilemma*, pp. 26–9, quotation on p. 27. Arminianism was based on the teachings of the Dutch theologian Johann Arminius.

54 Games, *Migration*, pp. 18–19.

55 Bailyn, *The Peopling of North America*, pp. 25–6, quotations on p. 26. Bailyn's numbers are at variance with Fischer's. Bailyn writes that three times the 21,200 emigrants to Massachusetts emigrated to other colonies in America and the West Indies, and that 120,000 Englishmen and Scots migrated to Ireland. Fischer writes that during the period 1630–41, some 80,000 Englishmen and -women left England, about 20,000 each to Massachusetts, Continental Europe, other colonies in America and the West Indies, and Ireland. *Albion's Seed*, p. 16. In his statement that this relocation was not 'unique in the annals of migration', Bailyn is taking issue with Carl Bridenbaugh, who wrote that 'The exodus of the English Puritans to New England, 1629–42, was, and still is, unique in the annals of migration. This flight of groups whose members shared a religious ideal, a sense of destiny, and a firm conviction that God wanted them to depart from their corrupt homeland and settle in the New England Canaan, had no counterpart elsewhere, not even in the Puritan Providence Island experiment or the Bermuda Plantation.' *Vexed and Troubled Englishmen 1590–1642: The Beginnings of the American People* (Oxford: Clarendon Press, 1967), p. 434.

56 Morgan, *The Puritan Dilemma*, pp. 39–53; Middleton, *Colonial America*, pp. 82–4; Fischer, *Albion's Seed*, pp. 13–16, 33, 42–3. R.C. Winthrop, *Life and Letters of John Winthrop* (Boston, Mass.: Ticknor & Fick's, 1864), I, pp. 309–11, quoted in David Brion Davis and Steven Mintz, *The Boisterous Sea of Liberty: A Documentary History of America from Discovery through the Civil War* (New York: Oxford University Press, 1999, 1st pub. 1998), p. 64.

57 According to Fischer, this 20,000 (the number he uses) was about 25 per cent of those who left England during this period, perhaps fleeing what some historians have called the 'eleven years' tyranny'. Another quarter went to Ireland; a third quarter went to the Netherlands and the Rhineland; and the final quarter went to the West Indies. Fischer, *Albion's Seed*, pp. 16–17. Fischer also points out that large-scale immigration to Massachusetts did not resume until Irish Catholics began to arrive nearly two centuries later. See also Virginia DeJohn Anderson, *New England's Generation: The Great Migration and the Formation of Society and Culture in the Seventeenth Century* (Cambridge: Cambridge University Press, 1991).

58 Quoted in Davis and Mintz, *The Boisterous Sea of Liberty*, pp. 65–6; spelling modernised by the editors. 'Ye are the light of the world. A city that is set on an hill cannot be hid.' Matthew 5: 14. According to Fischer, this passage was often used by Puritans in East Anglia to describe the spiritual condition of the region: 'When John Winthrop described his intended

settlement in Massachusetts as "a city upon a hill", he employed a gospel phrase that had become a cliché in the communities of eastern England.' *Albion's Seed*, p. 47.

59 *Ibid.*, p. 55; spelling modernised, presumably by the author.

60 Middleton, *Colonial America*, pp. 84–5.

61 Morgan, *The Puritan Dilemma*, pp. 84–9, quotation on p. 88.

62 On three occupational lists, fewer than 5 per cent were identified as labourers and fewer than 25 per cent as servants (75 per cent for Virginia), and these servants were mostly members of households (rather than labour drafts as in Virginia). Eleven per cent of the so-called 'Winthrop Fleet' (i.e., the eleven ships of 1630) were classed as gentry. Fischer, *Albion's Seed*, pp. 27–8, quotation on p. 27.

63 Morgan points out that this was especially the case with a Puritan people educated by their ministers in the principle of government based on a covenant. *The Puritan Dilemma*, p. 95.

64 *Ibid.*, pp. 84–91.

65 Frank Lambert, *The Founding Fathers and the Place of Religion in America* (Princeton, NJ: Princeton University Press, 2003), p. 78. The Puritans developed a 'congregational' form of government, the opposite of rule by hierarchy, such as that of the Anglican Church or the Presbyterians. They developed a special process of public examination: 'First, the intending saint had to acknowledge humanity's innate depravity – God alone could save. Next the individual had to show true repentance and desire to be saved. Then followed the hardest part of the examination, justification, whereby the examinee had to convince the interrogators that the Holy Spirit had entered the soul and that the individual was open to God's covenant of grace. If the answers were satisfactory the fourth stage, sanctification, followed, indicating that the person was of the elect. Even then no relaxation was possible, for sin could quickly lead to a loss of grace.' Middleton, *Colonial America*, p. 86.

66 Lambert, *The Place of Religion in America*, pp. 84–5.

67 Morgan, *The Puritan Dilemma*, pp. 69–83, quotation on p. 71. For a graphic, if fictional, description of the righteous pressure of a New England community on one who had strayed, see Nathaniel Hawthorne's *The Scarlet Letter*, first published in 1850. The scarlet letter was the letter 'A' for adultery, which Hester Prynne was condemned to wear embroidered on the bodice of her dress. Hawthorne's ancestors had participated in the Salem witch trials and later in the Quaker persecutions, about which he always felt a sense of guilt.

68 Interestingly, 'when the General Court was preparing to ship him back to England in disgrace, it was Winthrop who forewarned him and suggested that he flee to Rhode Island'. Morgan, *The Genuine Article*, p. 13.

69 Middleton, *Colonial America*, pp. 99–101, quotations on pp. 100, 101.

70 Games, *Migration*, p. 203.

71 Middleton, *Colonial America*, pp. 88–96, quotation on p. 95.

72 In Britain, 5 November (Guy Fawkes' Night) is fireworks night, rather than 31 October (Hallowe'en), as in the USA.

73 Middleton, *Colonial America*, p. 105; Michael J. Braddick, 'The English Government, War, Trade, and Settlement, 1625–1688', in Canny, ed., *The Origins of Empire*, p. 297.

74 Middleton, *Colonial America*, pp. 105–8, quotation on pp. 107–8.

75 *Ibid.*, p. 111. The phrase 'in the free exercise thereof' reappears in the First Amendment to the Constitution.

76 John Miller, *The Stuarts* (London: Hambledon & London, 2004), pp. 203–11.

77 Producing beer was impossible, or at least impractical, because growing barley demanded a plough, and this required draft animals, prohibitively expensive to maintain.

78 Bailyn, *The Peopling of North America*, p. 98.

79 In Firth, ed., *An American Garland*, p. 41.

80 Fischer, *Albion's Seed*, p. 456.

81 Fox in 1672 canoed across Chowan River from Edenton to the head of Albemarle Sound in the future North Carolina. W.P. Cumming, S. Hillier, D.B. Quinn and G. Williams, *The Exploration of North America 1630–1776* (London: Paul Elek, 1974), p. 87.

82 After the Restoration of Charles II, the tradition of religious dissent was included as one of the defining tenets of the Whig Party; this included, *inter alia*, men such as the Earl of Salisbury and John Locke, who had supported Cromwell (and would be influential in the establishment of the Carolinas). It was the Whigs' distrust of monarchical power, combined with a hatred of Catholicism, which led to the Exclusion Crisis of 1681.

83 'In 1671, Penn was arrested . . . [and] . . . tried secretly in the Tower [of London] and sent to Newgate [Prison], where he refused the privileges of his rank and lived in a common cell . . . [He] was treated with deference by his persecutors, and affection by many of his jailors. He maintained warm personal relations with Charles II and the future James II. From his cell he courted and won the hand of Guilelma Springett . . . (Penn's rivals included London's leading Restoration rakes.)' Fischer, *Albion's Seed*, p. 459.

84 'Socage' meant that the possessor had to pay a small annual fee, known as quitrent, to the King, as opposed to 'fee simple', which was equivalent to owning the land outright. Modern English equivalents are the terms 'leasehold' for socage and 'freehold' for fee simple.

85 Middleton, *Colonial America*, pp. 161–3, quotation on p. 163; Fischer, *Albion's Seed*, pp. 451–9; Mary K. Geiter and W.A. Speck, *Colonial America: From Jamestown to Yorktown* (Houndsmills: Palgrave Macmillan, 2002), pp. 93–5.

86 Lambert, *The Place of Religion in America*, pp. 100–2.

87 Women came together with the men for meetings of worship, but had separate meetings for business. As Penn explained, 'Why should women meet apart? We think for a very good reason. The church increaseth, which increaseth the business of the church, and women whose bashfulness will not permit them to say or do much, as to church affairs before men, when by themselves, may exercise their gift of wisdom and understanding, in a direct care of their own sex.' William Penn, *Just Measures* (London, 1692), quoted in Fischer, *Albion's Seed*, p. 494. I consulted *Just Measures* myself in the British Library, but I was unable to find this quotation; presumably there was more than one printing and it was left out of the one I consulted.

88 *Ibid.*, pp. 426–9, quotations on pp. 426–7, 428.

89 Fox quoted in *ibid.*, p. 490; William Penn, *Some Fruits of Solitude: In Reflections and Maxims Relating to the Conduct of Human Life* (London: Thomas Northcott, 1693), p. 33. Fox argued that before Eve and Adam ate the apple, there was equality between the sexes, and that after their redemption through conversion, this equality returns: 'For man and woman were helpsmeet, in the image of God and in Righteousness and holiness, in the dominion before they fell; but, after the Fall, in the transgression, the man was to rule over his wife. But in the restoration by Christ into the image of God and His righteousness and holiness again, in that they are helpsmeet, man and woman, as they were before the Fall.' Quoted in Mary Maples Dunn, 'Women of Light', in Carol Ruth Berkin and Mary Beth Norton, eds, *Women of America: A History* (Boston, Mass.: Houghton Mifflin, 1979), p. 118.

90 Fischer, *Albion's Seed*, pp. 573–7, 492. Mary Dyer had a notable life as a dissenter. After emigrating to Massachusetts in 1634 or 1635, she became a follower of Anne Hutchinson, leaving the church and following her into exile in Rhode Island. She returned to England for a time in the 1650s, where she met Fox and became a Quaker, returning to the colonies in 1657. She began a public ministry in the New England Puritan communities which had previously banned her and was expelled from Boston and New Haven four times: even after Massachusetts had passed a law banishing Quakers under pain of death, she returned to Boston on four occasions. Once she was condemned to death but set free at the last moment as she stood under the gallows. On her fourth trip she was again sentenced to death, and this time the sentence was carried out. Maples Dunn, 'Women of Light', in Berkin and Norton, eds, *American Women*, p. 120.

91 James Boswell, *The Life of Samuel Johnson, LL.D, to which is added The Journal of a Tour to the Hebrides* (London: Bliss Sands & Co., 1897), p. 114 [3 July 1763].

92 Fischer, *Albion's Seed*, pp. 420–1. Others – although not many – went to Virginia and Maryland, New England and North Carolina.

93 Hugh S. Barbour, *The Quakers in Puritan England* (New Haven, Conn.: Yale University Press, 1964), p. 124.

94 Ephraim Pagitt, *Heresiography or A description of the Hereticks and sectaries of these Latter Times* (London, 1654 5th edn). This section, entitled 'The Shaker or Quaker', was a new addition, not appearing in the 4th edition of 1647. Barry Reay quotes from another enemy of the Quakers, H. Hallywell, who wrote in *An Account of Familism* (London, 1673), p. 124, that the Quakers were 'the Refuse of the World, Persons of the meanest Quality and lowest Parts and Education'. Reay, *Quakers and the English Revolution* (London: Temple Smith, 1985), p. 25. Penn himself took issue with Hallywell in *Wisdom Justified of Her Children, From the Ignorance & Calumny of H. Halywel, in his Book, Called, An Account of FAMILISM, as it is Revived and Propaged [?] by the QUAKERS* (London, 1673). The book is overwhelmingly an exercise in marshalling argument against argument, but Penn very occasionally reveals his anger at Hallywell's slanders, e.g. on p. 112: 'That a *Woman at* Weighton *in* York-shire *of that Goatish Herd* (as he is pleased to call them) *went Naked to another Woman's Husband's Bed, and bid him open his Bed to her, for the Father had sent her,* is a Slander hatcht in Darkness'.

95 Barbour, *The Quakers in Puritan England*, p. 74; Reay, *Quakers and the English Revolution*, p. 25 for the quotation; Fischer, *Albion's Seed*, pp. 445–6.

96 *Ibid.*, p. 442.

97 Ned C. Landsman, 'The Middle Colonies: New Opportunities for Settlement, 1660–1700', in Canny, ed., *The Origins of Empire*, p. 361.

98 Fischer, *Albion's Seed*, pp. 577–80.

99 *Ibid.*, pp. 590–2, quotation on p. 592. Gary B. Nash, *Quakers and Politics: Pennsylvania, 1681–1726* (Princeton, NJ: Princeton University Press, 1969), p. 24; Frederick Barnes Tolles, *Quakers and the Atlantic Culture* (London: Macmillan, 1960), p. 124; Wayne L. Bockelman, 'Local Government in Colonial Pennsylvania', in Bruce C. Daniels, ed., *Town and Country: Essays on the Structure of Local Government in the American Colonies* (Middletown, Conn.: Wesleyan University Press, 1978), pp. 216–37.

100 Lambert, *The Place of Religion in America*, pp. 115–20.

101 *Maryland Gazette*, 22 May 1755, taken from an unknown English magazine. Davis and Mintz, eds, *The Boisterous Sea of Liberty*, p. 128.

102 Cumming, *et al.*, *The Exploration of North America*, p. 87.

103 Robert M. Weir, '"Shaftesbury's Darling": British Settlement in the Carolinas at the Close of the Seventeenth Century', in Canny, ed., *The Origins of Empire*, p. 376. Some went involuntarily: as Alison Games has commented, 'so common was the practice of kidnapping servants for American destinations that a new verb was coined, to be Barbadosed, to describe this misfortune'. *Migrations*, p. 77.

104 Weir, 'British Settlement in the Carolinas', p. 379. Carteret and Lord Berkeley would soon share the gift of New Jersey from the Duke of York.

105 Geiter and Speck, *Colonial America*, pp. 102–3; Weir, 'British Settlement in the Carolinas', pp. 379–81.

106 An influence was probably a recently published book, James Harrington's *The Commonwealth of Oceana* (1655), which argued that power was based on landed property, that too much land made men too powerful, and that one cause of the Civil War had been an imbalance between the landed classes. Therefore, the Fundamental Constitutions set out a social hierarchy and the amount of land each type of colonist could hold. The scheme called for a three-tiered hereditary nobility, consisting of 'proprietors', 'land-graves' (a German title) and

'caciques' (a Spanish designation for an Indian chief, although it was not contemplated that Indians would be so endowed). This nobility would own 40 per cent of the colony's land and serve as a Council of Lords, whose duty would be to recommend all laws to an assembly elected by small landowners, who would own the other 60 per cent of the land. Middleton, *Colonial America*, pp. 138–9.

107 *Ibid.*, pp. 137–42, quotations on p. 139; Geiter and Speck, *Colonial America*, pp. 101–4; Weir, 'British Settlement in the Carolinas', p. 381.

108 One of the first governors at Charleston, Yeamans had apparently arranged the murder of a rival in Barbados and a few weeks later married his widow. Weir, 'British Settlement in the Carolinas', p. 385.

109 Geiter and Speck, *Colonial America*, pp. 104–6; Weir, 'British Settlement in the Carolinas', pp. 381–9, quotations on p. 384; John Locke, *The Second Treatise of Government*, ed. Thomas P. Peardon (Upper Saddle River, NJ: Prentice Hall, 1997), ch. 5, quotations on pp. 29, 20, 23.

110 Geiter and Speck, *Colonial America*, pp. 104–6; Middleton, *Colonial America*, pp. 204–5.

111 Weir, 'British Settlement of the Carolinas', p. 386.

112 *Ibid.*, pp. 388–91, quotation on p. 391.

113 Fischer, *Albion's Seed*, pp. 606–31, 642–50, quotations on p. 615. Bernard Bailyn, *Voyagers to the West: A Passage in the Peopling of America on the Eve of the Revolution* (New York: Knopf, 1986), pp. 26, 129–40, 189–93; Ian C.C. Graham, *Colonists from Scotland: Emigration to North America, 1707–1783* (Ithaca, NY: Cornell University Press, 1956).

114 Fischer, *Albion's Seed*, p. 615.

115 *Ibid.*, pp. 615, 639–68.

116 Henry Hudson *(c.* 1565–1611) first sought a north-west passage for the English Muscovy Company, but was blocked by polar ice. His mission for the Dutch East India Company was his second attempt. His third, again for the English, began in April 1610, during which he discovered Hudson Bay (in August) and wintered on St James Bay. The following spring his crew mutinied and left him marooned.

117 'One day, not so long after the little Dutch settlement started, a group of white men and Indians gathered under a tree. On the ground was a pile of colored cloth, some strings of wampum, knives, bells and other trinkets. The Dutch were trading these things for the island of Manhattan, on which the city of New York now stands. The land that is now worth millions [trillions?] of dollars was bought from the Indians for goods that were worth about twenty-eight dollars.' Alice Dalgliesh, 'Dutch Homes in New Netherlands', in Nora Beust, Phyllis Fenner, Bernice E. Leary, Mary Katherine Reely and Dora V. Smith, eds, *Stories of Early America* (Eau Claire, Wisconsin: E.M. Hale, 1958), p. 73. This is just one example.

118 Alan Taylor, *American Colonies: The Settling of North America* (London: Penguin, 2002, 1st pub. 2001), p. 257. The Dutch East Indies, part of the Dutch Empire until 1949, is now Indonesia.

119 Geiter and Speck, *Colonial America*, pp. 86–90; Middleton, *Colonial America*, pp. 114–19; Landsman, 'The Middle Colonies', pp. 351–4.

120 Middleton, *Colonial America*, p. 119.

121 J.R. Jones, *The Anglo-Dutch Wars of the Seventeenth Century* (London: Longman, 1996), pp. 150, 178; Middleton, *Colonial America*, pp. 127–8, quotation on p. 128.

122 Geiter and Speck, *Colonial America*, pp. 89–90, Penn quotation on p. 89; Landsman, 'The Middle Colonies', p. 357.

123 Geiter and Speck, *Colonial America*, pp. 89–91, quotations from Nicholls and James on p. 90; Middleton, *Colonial America*, pp. 130–5, quotation from grand jury on p. 134.

124 Richard S. Dunn, 'The Glorious Revolution and America', in Canny, ed., *The Origins of Empire*, p. 450.

125 Middleton, *Colonial America*, pp. 130–5, quotation from frame of government on p. 134, quotation from Middleton on p. 135.

126 *Ibid.*, p. 135; Dunn, 'The Glorious Revolution and America', pp. 458–63.

127 John J. McCusker and Russell R. Menard, *The Economy of British America, 1607–1789* (Chapel Hill: University of North Carolina Press, 1985), pp. 48–9, 38. Percentage increases: as the source of imported goods to England/Britain, from 3 per cent in 1633 to 12 per cent in 1663–9 to 37 per cent in 1772–4; as the destination of exports from England/Britain, from 8 per cent in 1663 to 42 per cent in 1772–4; and as the destination for re-exported goods, from 16 per cent in 1699 to 17 per cent in 1772. *Ibid.*, p. 40, Table 2.1. Stephen Conway points out that Great Britain was dependent on Scandinavia for crucial naval stores, such as timber and pitch; not only would supplies from America increase the quantity available, but they would force down the prices of Scandinavian supplies. 'Empire, Europe, and British Naval Power, *c.* 1763–*c.* 1833', unpublished lecture given in London, 24 October 2006.

128 For the former, see Charles Wilson, *Profit and Power: A Study of England and the Dutch Wars* (London: Longmans, Green, 1957); for the latter, see Jones, 'Introduction', in *The Anglo-Dutch Wars*. Jones concedes that important interest groups in England had pressed for anti-Dutch policies in 1650–2 and 1664–5, but he still sees power of the harder sort as commanding; he believes that these interest groups played no role at all in initiating the 1672–4 war. See *ibid.*, p. 179.

129 Taylor, *American Colonies*, p. 258; Jones, *The Anglo-Dutch Wars*, ch. 6.

130 McCusker and Menard, *The Economy of British America*, p. 47; Jones, *The Anglo-Dutch Wars*, chs. 7 and 8.

131 Patrick K. O'Brien, 'Inseparable Connections: Trade, Economy, Fiscal State, and the Expansion of Empire, 1688–1815', in P.J. Marshall, ed., *The Oxford History of the British Empire, Volume II: The Eighteenth Century* (Oxford: Oxford University Press, 1998), p. 71; McCusker and Menard, *The Economy of British America*, pp. 47–9, quotation on p. 49.

132 Quoted in Jack P. Greene, *Peripheries and Center: Constitutional Development in the Extended Politics of the British Empire and the United States, 1607–1788* (Athens: University of Georgia Press, 1986), p. 13.

133 *Ibid.*, pp. 10–12. See Michael Zuckerman, 'Identity in British America: Unease in Eden', in Nicholas Canny and Anthony Pagden, eds, *Colonial Identity in the Atlantic World, 1500–1800* (Princeton, NJ: Princeton University Press, 1987), pp. 115–57.

134 Ned C. Landsman, *From Colonials to Provincials: American Thought and Culture 1680–1760* (Ithaca, NY: Cornell University Press, 1997), pp. 152–8.

135 Quoted in Greene, *Peripheries and Center*, p. 12.

136 Imperial authority over the royal colonies in mainland America and the West Indies was exercised directly in the name of the monarchs: 1) it included royal approval of the relevant parliamentary legislation, royal proclamations, appointment and instruction of royal governors, reviews of acts passed by colonial legislatures, and the hearing of colonial legal appeals by the King-in-Council; 2) the Privy Council issued royal proclamations, reviewed laws passed by colonial Assemblies, and heard colonial petitions and legal appeals. The King was the legal authority and the Privy Council, with its bureaucracy and considerable records office, did the work. Ian K. Steele, 'The Anointed, the Appointed, and the Elected: Governance of the British Empire, 1689–1784', in Marshall, ed., *The Eighteenth Century*, p. 107.

137 Julian Hoppit, *A Land of Liberty? England 1689–1727* (Oxford: Clarendon Press, 2000), pp. 283–7; Steele, 'Governance of the British Empire, 1689–1784', p. 115; Geoffrey Holmes, *British Politics in the Age of Anne* (London: Hambledon, 1987 rev. edn), *passim*.

138 Hoppit, *England 1689–1727*, p. 139.

139 For a wonderful example of how party politics during the period of Queen Anne impinged upon the American colonies, see Patricia U. Bonomi, *The Lord Cornbury Scandal: The*

Politics of Reputation in British America (Chapel Hill: University of North Carolina Press, 1998). Edward Hyde, Viscount Cornbury, was Governor of New York and New Jersey from 1702 to 1708. He was alleged both to have looted the colonial treasury and to have indulged in public cross-dressing in New York City. In the collection of the New York Historical Society there is a portrait of, supposedly, Cornbury dressed in women's clothes. Bonomi locates his story within a society where 'raw passion often drove the struggle for power and interest. Yet the notion that rival elites might compete for political authority within some embryonic kind of party system was unimaginable in a regime based on hierarchy and royal prerogative . . . Competition there was – bitter, irrepressible competition; and in that preparty age there was as yet no accepted vocabulary with which to explain or justify it. Hence such activity could only be seen by anyone, even those engaged in it, as conspiratorial and sinister in intent.' *Ibid.*, p. 6.

140 'The Anglo-Saxons remained alone in thinking that the only good Indian is a dead Indian, since the Spanish, the Portuguese, and the French, once the period of slaughter had waned, altered their philosophy and incorporated the Indians into their colonial cultures in greater or lesser degree.' Mumford Jones, *O Strange New World*, p. 49.

141 Howard H. Peckham, *The Colonial Wars 1689–1762* (Chicago: University of Chicago Press, 1964), p. 18.

142 *Ibid.*, pp. 25–56. The attempt to conquer Quebec cost Massachusetts Bay more than £50,000. To pay the soldiers and sailors, the legislature issued paper money, as well as levying heavy taxes to redeem it. This was the first issue of paper money in America, and in the British Empire as a whole; it was a practice that recurred during successive wars in America, notably during the Revolution. *Ibid.*, p. 38.

143 *Ibid.*, pp. 51–2.

144 *Ibid.*, pp. 57–76. Readers may have noticed a certain terminological variation in this paragraph with regard to England/Great Britain: in the middle of the war, in 1707, England and Scotland united into Great Britain.

145 By agreement in 1713, Britons could sell slaves in the Spanish West Indies and one boatload of trade goods per year, but attempts to smuggle goods were endemic. The two countries had agreed on the mutual right to search each other's ships for contraband goods. Captain Robert Jenkins had been caught by the Spaniards in 1731 and punished by having one ear cut off. Spain's somewhat cruel and unusual punishment inflamed public resentment in Great Britain. In the spring of 1738, Jenkins appeared before a parliamentary committee and displayed his severed ear, which he had been carrying around with him for seven years. When asked what he did at the moment of mutilation, Jenkins answered, 'I commended my soul to God, and my cause to my country!' The statement naturally aroused the British to a war fever. *Ibid.*, p. 88.

146 *Ibid.*, pp. 97–119, quotation on pp. 118–19.

147 John Ferling, *Setting the World Ablaze: Washington, Adams, and Jefferson and the American Revolution* (Oxford: Oxford University Press, 2000), pp. 67–8. France had won military victories in the Low Countries, an acute strategic threat to the home islands; and thus for the British government, the return of Louisbourg was an acceptable price to pay. It is worth noting that Parliament gave Massachusetts £180,000 as reward and recompense for its 'extraordinary wartime effort', which the provincial government used to retire paper currency, although with severe deflationary results. John Shy, 'The American Colonies in War and Revolution, 1748–1783', in Marshall, ed., *The Eighteenth Century*, p. 310.

148 Fred Anderson, *Crucible of War: The Seven Years' War and the Fate of the Empire in British North America, 1754–1766* (London: Faber and Faber, 2000), pp. 11–41; Peckham, *The Colonial Wars*, pp. 120–54. One of the most popular novels ever written by an American, *The Last of the Mohicans; A Narrative of 1757* (1826) by James Fenimore Cooper, is set in 1757 and deals with the war.

149 Peckham, *The Colonial Wars*, pp. 153–5, quotation on p. 155; Anderson, *Crucible of War*, pp. 125–9; Daniel Marston, *The Seven Years' War* (Oxford: Osprey, 2001), pp. 29–77.

150 Peckham, *The Colonial Wars*, p. 157. The Royal Americans in due course became the King's Royal Rifle Corps. By the late nineteenth century, it had become one of the most aristocratic regiments in the army, almost on a par with the Household Brigade. It also attracted more than its fair share of highly intelligent/educated officers, with the result that it produced a considerable number of generals. In 1964, together with the Rifle Brigade and the Oxford and Buckinghamshire Light Infantry, it was amalgamated to form the Royal Green Jackets. (The rest of the army sometimes refers to this regiment as the 'Black Mafia' on account of their black buttons, and the fact that they are reputed to get each other good jobs.) Many thanks for the hard information to David French.

151 *Ibid.*, pp. 153–95; Marston, *The Seven Years' War*, pp. 33–77; and Anderson, *Crucible of War, passim.* Rupert Furneaux, *The Seven Years' War* (London: Hart-Davis-MacGibbon, 1973) has lots of illustrations. Success in the world war resulted in worldwide acquisitions and influence for the British Empire.

152 Landsman, *From Colonials to Provincials*, pp. 3–47.

153 Paul Langford, *Englishness Identified: Manners and Character 1650–1850* (Oxford: Oxford University Press, 2000), p. 88.

154 See in particular Paul Langford's *A Polite and Commercial People: England 1727–1783* (Oxford: Oxford University Press, 1989).

155 Landsman, *From Colonials to Provincials*, p. 39.

156 Benjamin Franklin, *Autobiography and Other Writings* (Oxford: Oxford University Press, 1993), pp. 15–16.

157 '. . . only some work in which the most thorough knowledge of human nature, the happiest deliniation of its varieties, the liveliest effusions of wit and humour are conveyed to the world in the best chosen language'. *Northanger Abbey* (1818), end of ch. 5.

158 Landsman, *From Colonials to Provincials*, pp. 46–8. These teacups were probably the first showing a non-political image which were widespread in popular culture. Thanks to R.S. Taylor Stoermer.

159 Bernard Bailyn, *The Ideological Origins of the American Revolution* (Cambridge, Mass.: Harvard University Press, 1992 enlarged edn, 1st pub. 1967), p. 27.

160 Frank Lambert, *Inventing the 'Great Awakening'* (Princeton, NJ: Princeton University Press, 1999), *passim.*

161 Lambert, *The Place of Religion in America*, pp. 139–43.

162 Stephen Conway, 'From Fellow-Nationals to Foreigners: British Perceptions of the Americans, *circa* 1739–1783', *William and Mary Quarterly*, 3rd Series, Vol. 59, No. 1 (January 2002), pp. 65–6.

Chapter 2 – The War for American Independence: 1763–1783

1 R.C. Simmons and P.D.G. Thomas, eds, *Proceedings and Debates of the British Parliaments Respecting North America, 1754–1783*, 6 vols (Millwood, NY: Kraus International Publications, 1982–7), V, pp. 234–5.

2 Burke's speech is known as 'On Conciliation with America'. *Ibid.*, p. 630.

3 Sung at the completion of the Concord Monument, 19 April 1836, which commemorated the beginning of the Revolutionary War at Lexington and Concord, 19 April 1775. Ralph Waldo Emerson, *The Concord Hymn and Other Poems* (New York: Dover, 1996), pp. 41–2. Emerson's grandfather, William Emerson, had watched this battle from the window of his nearby house, the Old Manse.

4 Lester J. Cappon, ed., *The Adams–Jefferson Letters: The Complete Correspondence between Thomas Jefferson and Abigail and John Adams*, 2 vols (Chapel Hill: University of North Carolina Press, 1961), II, p. 455.

5 *The Patriot*, a film set in the time of the American Revolution and released in 2000, is a

particularly appalling example of the deliberate falsification of history: the Americans were neither so white, nor the British so black, as they were portrayed. No Americans were ever herded into a church and burned alive, as depicted in the film; in fact, this event took place at Oradour-sur-Glâne in France, where the Nazi SS burned alive 642 inhabitants on 10 June 1944.

6 This was one of General le Comte de Rochambeau's aides de camp. John Trevor to Charles James Fox, 16 April 1782, Shelburne Papers, Vol. 34, No. 2, William Clements Library, Ann Arbor, Michigan, quoted in Piers Mackesy, *The War for America 1775–1783* (Cambridge, Mass.: Harvard University Press, 1993, 1st pub. 1964), p. 510.

7 Robert M. Bliss, *Revolution and Empire: English Politics and the American Colonies in the Seventeenth Century* (Manchester: Manchester University Press, 1993, 1st pub. 1990), p. 61.

8 *Ibid.*, pp. 62–3, quotations on p. 63.

9 Ian K. Steele, 'The Anointed, the Appointed, and the Elected: Governance of the British Empire, 1689–1784', in Marshall, ed., *The Eighteenth Century*, p. 121.

10 Conway, 'From Fellow-Nationals to Foreigners', pp. 82–3; Greene, *Peripheries and Center*, pp. 57–8.

11 Steele, 'Governance of the British Empire, 1689–1784', p. 112.

12 Greene, *Peripheries and Center*, pp. 57–8. For descriptions and analysis of the early use of transatlantic lobbying, see David S. Lovejoy, *The Glorious Revolution in America* (Middletown, Conn.: Wesleyan University Press, 1987, 1st pub. 1972), e.g., the activities of the agent for New York under Leisler, pp. 274–5. The classic text is Michael G. Kammen, *A Rope of Sand: The Colonial Agents, British Politics, and the American Revolution* (Ithaca, NY: Cornell University Press, 1968 pb. edn), which analyses the methods, resources and effectiveness of Anglo-American colonial agents at Whitehall and Westminster. Edmund Burke was appointed colonial agent by the New York Provincial Assembly in 1770; his performance was underwhelming. See Ross J.S. Hoffman, *Edmund Burke, New York Agent, with His Letters to the New York Assembly and Intimate Correspondence with Charles O'Hara, 1761–1776*, Memoirs of the American Philosophical Society, Vol. 41 (Philadelphia, Penn.: American Philosophical Society, 1956). James Delancy, a friend who was also one of his employers, wrote to him that the members of the Assembly were not satisfied with the letters he had been sending. Hoffman adds: 'One glance at these is enough to see that there was indeed little of interest in them.' *Ibid.*, p. 110. Burke replied to Delancy on 20 August 1772: 'I am extremely sorry that my correspondence has not been so pleasing as I could wish to the gentlemen of the Committee [of Correspondence]. It is very natural that they should desire a correspondent who might contribute to their entertainment by the frequency and agreeableness of his letters.' Fundamentally, they wanted more political information. *Ibid.*, pp. 212–17 for the letter, quotation on p. 214. Burke's New York Letter-Book covers letters from 9 June 1771–3 October 1775.

13 One of the strongest, Pondicherry, remained in French hands until 1778, when it fell to the British after a siege lasting seventy-seven days.

14 Middleton, *Colonial America*, pp. 444–6.

15 'And whereas it is just and reasonable and essential to Our Interest and the Security of Our Colonies, that the several Nations or Tribes of Indians with whom We are connected, and who live under Our Protection should not be molested or disturbed . . . no Governor . . . in any of Our other Colonies or Plantations in America, do presume for the present . . . to grant Warrants of Survey, or pass Patents for any Lands beyond the Heads or Sources of any of the Rivers which fall into the Atlantic Ocean . . . And whereas great Frauds and abuses have been committed in the purchasing Lands of the Indians, to the great Prejudice of Our Interests, and to the great Dissatisfaction of the said Indians; in order to prevent such irregularities for the future, and to the End that the Indians may be convinced of Our Justice and determined Resolution to remove all reasonable cause of Discontent, We do . . . enjoy and

require that no private Person do presume to make any Purchase from the said Indians of any Lands reserved to the said Indians.' Davis and Mintz, eds, *The Boisterous Sea of Liberty*, p. 146.

16 Stephen Conway, 'Britain and the Revolutionary Crisis, 1763–1791', in Marshall, ed., *The Eighteenth Century*, p. 326.

17 P.J. Marshall, 'The Case for Coercing America before the Revolution', in Fred M. Leventhal and Roland Quinault, eds, *Anglo-American Attitudes: From Revolution to Partnership* (Aldershot: Ashgate, 2000), p. 11.

18 As the Duke of Wellington later wrote, 'in such a country as America . . . military operations by large bodies are impracticable, unless the party carrying them has the uninterrupted use of a navigable river, or very extensive means of land transport, which such a country can rarely supply'. Wellington to Earl Bathurst, 22 February 1814, in Lt.-Col. John Gurwood, *Selections from the Dispatches of Field Marshal the Duke of Wellington during His Various Campaigns in India, Denmark, Portugal, Spain, the Low Countries, and France*, 8 vols (London: Parker, Furnivall, and Parker, 1844–7), VII, pp. 327–8, quotation on p. 327.

19 Stephen Conway, *The War of American Independence 1775–1783* (London: Edward Arnold, 1995), p. 5; Middleton, *Colonial America*, p. 446.

20 George III's first ministry, headed by his former tutor Lord Bute, had announced this decision to Parliament on 4 March 1763, 'optimistically' presuming that the costs would be borne by the colonies, as had long been the practice with the British army in Ireland. Steele, 'Governance of the British Empire, 1689–1784', p. 123. The reason given by Bute was France's decision to maintain 20,000 soldiers in its West Indian colonies; furthermore, there was the need to control Canada, with 90,000 new, and probably disaffected, subjects. The army would be garrisoned primarily in Canada, the Floridas, and the Ohio and Mississippi valleys, not in the old colonies. It was 10,000 for 1764, then 7,500 until 1770, when it was further reduced. Peter D.G. Thomas, 'The Grenville Programme, 1763–1765', in Jack P. Greene and J.R. Pole, eds, *The Blackwell Encyclopedia of the American Revolution* (Oxford: Blackwell, 1994, 1st pub. 1990), p. 107.

21 Peter D.G. Thomas, *Revolution in America: Britain and the Colonies, 1763–1776* (Cardiff: University of Wales Press, 1992), pp. 11–12.

22 Conway, 'Britain and the Revolutionary Crisis', p. 327.

23 Peter D.G. Thomas, *George III: King and Politician 1760–1770* (Manchester: Manchester University Press, 2002), p. 3.

24 Mackesy, *The War for America*, pp. 7–12, quotation on p. 7. Thomas, *George III*, pp. 3–4.

25 Robert A. Gross, *The Minutemen and Their World* (New York: Hill and Wang, 2001, 1st pub. 1976), p. 36.

26 Gordon S. Wood, *The American Revolution: A History* (London: Modern Library, 2002), pp. 39–40. The idea that women might vote was, of course, preposterous.

27 Thomas, 'The Grenville Programme', p. 108. Simmons and Thomas, eds, *Proceedings and Debates*, I, pp. 488–92, quotation on p. 489, 9 March 1764. It is worth remembering that the same year saw the passage of the Currency Act. This banned the issuing of paper money, forcing many colonists to resort to barter.

28 Benjamin Franklin pointed out on 13 February 1766, in response to questioning by a parliamentary committee, that with regard to the revenue raised, 'I know that it is appropriated by the act to the American service; but it will be spent in the conquered colonies, where the soldiers are, not in the colonies that pay it.' *Ibid.*, II, p. 236.

29 Marshall, 'The Case for Coercing America', p. 19 for the quotation; Thomas, *Revolution in America*, p. 17.

30 Thomas, 'The Stamp Act Crisis and its Repercussions, Including the Quartering Act Controversy', in Greene and Pole, eds, *American Revolution*, p. 114; Middleton, *Colonial America*, p. 451 for the quotations.

31 New Hampshire declined to attend, but later approved the Congress's decision; Virginia, North Carolina and Georgia were prevented from attending by the refusal of their governors to summon assemblies to select delegates. Delaware and New Jersey evaded this prohibition by an unofficial choice of delegates. Thomas, 'The Stamp Act Crisis', p. 115.

32 These were Resolves II–V. 'The Declarations of the Stamp Act Congress (19 October 1765)', in Merrill Jensen, ed., *English Historical Documents, IX: American Colonial Documents to 1776* (London: Eyre and Spottiswoode, 1955), pp. 672–3, quotations on p. 672.

33 Unlike the West Indian colonies, which were represented by a 'small but vocal and influential' group of proprietors – i.e., absentee landlords – in the Commons. Paul Langford, 'Property and "Virtual Representation" in Eighteenth-Century England', *The Historical Journal*, Vol. 31, No. 1 (March 1988), p. 114, ref. 71.

34 See Chapter 1.

35 Thomas Whately, *The Regulations Lately Made Concerning the Colonies and the Taxes Imposed on Them Considered* (London, 1765), pp. 108–9, quoted in Conway, 'Britain and the Revolutionary Crisis', pp. 328–9. Whately was Secretary to the Treasury under Grenville and a 'key' figure in the drafting of the Stamp Act. Bernard Bailyn, *The Ordeal of Thomas Hutchinson: Loyalism and the Destruction of the First British Empire* (London: Allen Lane, 1975), p. 225.

36 Pauline Maier, *From Resistance to Revolution: Colonial Radicals and the Development of American Opposition to Britain, 1765–1776* (London: Routledge & Kegan Paul, 1973), p. 58. One Son of Liberty was the silversmith Paul Revere, who might have made the special insignia worn by each member, a silver medal with a Liberty Tree and the words 'Sons of Liberty' engraved on its face. David Hackett Fischer, *Paul Revere's Ride* (Oxford: Oxford University Press, 1994), p. 22.

37 Simmons and Thomas, eds, *Proceedings and Debates*, II, pp. 9–17, quotation on p. 16.

38 John K. Alexander, *Samuel Adams: America's Revolutionary Politician* (Lanham, Md.: Rowman & Littlefield, 2004, 1st pub. 2002), pp. 25–6, quotation on p. 25.

39 Gary B. Nash, *The Urban Crucible: Social Change, Political Consciousness, and the Origins of the American Revolution* (Cambridge, Mass.: Harvard University Press, 1979), p. 294. Maier has explained that 'Eighteenth-century Americans accepted the existence of popular uprisings with remarkable ease. Riots and tumults, it was said, happened "in all governments at all times". To seek a world completely free of them was vain; it was to pursue "a blessing denied to this life, and reserved to complete the felicity of the next" [John Adams quoting Algernon Sidney]. Not that extra-legal uprisings were encouraged. They were not. But in certain circumstances, it was understood, the people would rise up almost as a natural force, much as night follows day, and this phenomenon often contributed to the public welfare . . . The existence of such a tradition meant, moreover, that the people, or, as their opponents said, the mob, entered the struggle with Britain as an established social force, not as an agency newly invented to serve the ends of radical leadership.' Maier, *From Resistence to Revolution*, p. 3.

40 Alexander, *Samuel Adams*, p. 26. Hutchinson was something of an unfortunate victim. Although personally opposed to Parliament's taxing the colonies – he thought that the Stamp Act and the Townshend Duties should never have been passed – he supported parliamentary authority; by insisting that customs regulations be carried out to enforce the Tea Act in 1773, he would precipitate the Boston Tea Party. He left for England in June 1774, where he died in 1780. Bailyn, *The Ordeal of Thomas Hutchinson*, pp. 172, 185, 261, 378–9.

41 Ray Raphael thought that it was not exactly class warfare, 'but the poorer had definitely been getting poorer as the rich got richer. Since the late 1600s, the richest 5 percent of the population had increased their share of the taxable assets from 30 percent to 49 percent, while the wealth owned by the poorest half of the population had decreased from 9 percent to a mere 5 percent.' Raphael, *The American Revolution: A People's History. How Common People Shaped the Fight for Independence* (London: Profile, 2001), p. 14. Pauline Maier, however, suggests a different explanation for the attack on Hutchinson and other wealthy men: it had little

to do with the Stamp Act but was more likely 'inspired by a group of merchants who feared they had been named in a set of recent depositions about smuggling'. Maier, *From Resistance to Revolution*, p. 58.

42 Wood, *The American Revolution*, pp. 29–30.

43 *Ibid.*, p. 43.

44 This was suggested by Benjamin Franklin during his examination in the House of Commons on 13 February 1766: Q. 'Considering the resolution of parliament, as to the right, do you think, if the stamp-act is repealed, that the North-Americans will be satisfied?' A. 'I believe they will . . . I think the resolutions of right will give them very little concern, if they are never attempted to be carried into practice.' Simmons and Thomas, eds, *Proceedings and Debates*, II, p. 241.

45 *Ibid.*, pp. 84–91, quotations on pp. 82, 85–6, 88, 91.

46 *Ibid.*, pp. 109–10 for the text of the petition.

47 *Ibid.*, p. 125 for the resolution, p. 150 for Pitt's remarks.

48 The decisive debate in the Commons had taken place on 21 February 1766, when, at nearly 2 a.m., the exhausted MPs voted for repeal, 275 to 167. *Ibid.*, pp. 280–7.

49 *Ibid.*, p. 240.

50 *Ibid.*, pp. 428–9.

51 *Ibid.*, p. 470, 13 May 1767. The revenue from the Tea Act was used in that manner from 1772. Conway, 'Britain and the Revolutionary Crisis', p. 335.

52 Simmons and Thomas, eds, *Proceedings and Debates*, II, p. 411.

53 Q. 'If the act is not repealed, what do you think will be the consequences?' A [Franklin]. 'A total loss of the respect and affection the people of America bear to this country, and of all the commerce that depends upon that respect and affection.' Q. 'How can the commerce be affected?' A. 'You will find, that if the act is not repealed, they will take very little of your manufactures in a short time.' Q. 'Is it in their power to do without them?' A. 'I think they may very well do without them.' Q. 'Is it their interest not to take them?' A. 'The goods they take from Britain are either necessaries, mere conveniences, or superfluities. The first, as cloth, &c. with a little industry they can make at home; the second they can do without, till they are able to provide them among themselves; and the last, which are much the greatest part, they will strike off immediately. They are mere articles of fashion, purchased and consumed, because the fashion in a respected country; but will now be detested and rejected. The people have already struck off, by general agreement, the use of all goods fashionable in mournings, and many thousand pounds worth are sent back as unsaleable.' Q. 'Is it their interest to make cloth at home?' A. 'I think they may at present get it cheaper from Britain, I mean of the same fineness and neatness of workmanship; but when one considers other circumstances, the restraints on their trade, and the difficulty of making remittances, it is their interest to make every thing.' *Ibid.*, pp. 242–3.

54 *Ibid.*, p. 464, 13 May 1767.

55 Robert J. Chaffin, 'The Townshend Acts Crisis, 1767–1770', in Greene and Pole, eds, *American Revolution*, p. 127.

56 Simmons and Thomas, *Proceedings and Debates*, II, p. 467 for the quotation; Middleton, *Colonial America*, p. 466.

57 Probably only Tom Paine's *Common Sense* had a greater popularity and circulation during the revolutionary period. Chaffin, 'Townshend Acts Crisis', p. 132.

58 Wood, *American Revolution*, p. 33.

59 Alexander, *Samuel Adams*, chs. 2–3. The Caucus was formed by Adams' father, Samuel Adams Sr., and about twenty others in 1724 as a way of controlling the politics of Boston. At the time of the Boston Massacre, there were three parts: for example, the North Boston Caucus, to which Paul Revere belonged, was made up of artisans and ships' captains 'who

exchanged delegates with the other Caucuses and settled on slates of candidates before town meetings'. Fischer, *Paul Revere's Ride*, p. 20. For details of the elder Adams' place in the foundation and growth of the Caucus, see Alexander, *Samuel Adams*, p. 2.

60 His large and bold handwriting later became the name and symbol of an American insurance company. According to James Truslow Adams, 'Hancock was the richest man in New England, and because of his wealth was later chosen President of the Continental Congress.' Adams, *The March of Democracy: A History of the United States, Volume I: The Rise of the Union* (New York: Charles Scribner's Sons, 1932), p. 146.

61 *Ibid.*, p. 146.

62 Middleton, *Colonial America*, p. 467.

63 A recipe of the 1750s for punch: one part rum to three parts water, sugar and lemon juice to taste; pour into a large bowl, take a hot poker from the fire, and plunge it into the bowl to heat the punch. It was most emphatically not a fruit juice concoction for children's birthday parties.

64 Joseph Harrison was the Collector of Customs. Benjamin Hallowell, a member of the American Board of Commissioners for Boston, was referred to by contemporaries as 'mulish' and 'ignorant and illiterate'. Maier, *From Resistance to Revolution*, p. 184. He left Boston when the British troops withdrew and in due course went to Canada and thence to London.

65 George Bancroft, the 'father of American history' and author of *History of the United States from the Discovery of the American Continent*, 10 vols (1834–74), which culminated in the American Revolution.

66 Benson J. Lossing, *Our Country, a Household History for All Readers*, 3 vols (New York: Johnson and Miles, 1877), II, pp. 643–4.

67 Douglas Edward Leach, 'The British Army in America, before 1775', in Greene and Pole, eds, *American Revolution*, p. 151. Even before the *Liberty* riot, the government had instructed Gage to send a garrison force, since Boston was at the forefront of American resistance to British taxes and the customs service; the effective difference the riot made was that the force sent was considerably stronger than originally planned. *Ibid.*

68 Maier, *From Resistance to Revolution*, p. x.

69 Fischer, *Paul Revere's Ride*, p. 23.

70 Chaffin, 'The Townshend Acts Crisis', p. 142.

71 *Ibid.*, pp. 140–1.

72 The trial was put off for nearly eight months, at the instigation of the defence lawyer, John Adams (later the second President of the US), in the face of the opposition of the radical leadership. Then he gained separate trials for the officer in charge, Captain Preston, and the eight soldiers. This allowed Adams to argue that the officer had not ordered the shooting, and he was acquitted. Then, during the trial of the soldiers, he argued that they were only following orders. (This type of stratagem is no longer permitted, since such a conflict of interest violates professional ethics.) At least one of the eight soldiers had not fired a shot, since only six or seven were fired. Evidence showed the identities of two who had fired, and they were convicted of manslaughter, although not hanged; the other six were acquitted. Ferling, *Setting the World Ablaze*, pp. 77–8. The military historian David French has pointed out that it is difficult to account for eleven casualities, given that a musket could fire only one shot at a time, and it took about thirty seconds to reload.

73 Bailyn, *The Ordeal of Thomas Hutchinson*, pp. 158–62, quotations on pp. 158, 159, 160, 162.

74 Thomas, *Revolution in America*, pp. 29–32 for the deprecation of the boycott; for the fall in British sales to the colonies, Davis and Mintz, eds, *The Boisterous Sea of Liberty*, p. 161.

75 The 7th baron, he succeeded his father as 2nd Earl of Guilford in 1790.

76 Conway, 'Britain and the Revolutionary Crisis', p. 334.

77 Rebecca K. Starr, 'Political Mobilization, 1765–1776', in Greene and Pole, eds, *American Revolution*, pp. 235–6.

78 The tea still drunk in the colonies was primarily smuggled Dutch tea. Jerome R. Reich, *British Friends of the American Revolution* (Armonk, NY: M.E. Sharpe, 1998), p. 50.

79 The company was engaged in frequent conflict in India, and needed the income from the sales of tea to finance it.

80 Two of the factors appointed by the company were the sons of the Governor of Massachusetts Bay, Thomas Hutchinson.

81 David L. Ammerman, 'The Tea Crisis and its Consequences, through 1775', in Greene and Pole, eds, *American Revolution*, pp. 198–200, quotation on p. 200.

82 Raphael, *The American Revolution*, p. 18 for both quotations.

83 Ammerman, 'The Tea Crisis and its Consequences', p. 201.

84 Raphael, *The American Revolution*, pp. 18–19.

85 *Ibid.*, p. 22.

86 *Ibid.*, p. 19. In total, 342 chests of tea with a value of £10,000 were taken from the three ships and thrown into the harbour. Davis and Mintz, eds, *The Boisterous Sea of Liberty*, p. 161.

87 Quoted in Walter Isaacson, *Benjamin Franklin: An American Life* (New York: Simon & Schuster, 2003), p. 275.

88 Ammerman, 'The Tea Crisis and its Consequences', p. 201; Thomas, *Revolution in America*, pp. 37–8.

89 Middleton, *Colonial America*, p. 474 for the quotation.

90 *Ibid.*, p. 474.

91 Conway, 'Britain and the Revolutionary Crisis', Marshall, ed., *The Eighteenth Century*, pp. 335–6; Thomas, *Revolution in America*, p. 41.

92 Alexander, *Sam Adams*, pp. 130–1.

93 *Ibid.*, pp. 131–5, quotation on p. 133. Interestingly, the Massachusetts towns overwhelmingly rejected the Covenant, opting instead to call for uniform, concerted action by all the colonies. Starr, 'Political Mobilization', p. 236 for the response of the towns, except for Williamsburg, which is described in the Williamsburg town guide.

94 Alexander, *Sam Adams*, p. 135.

95 Virginia, Maryland, New Hampshire, New Jersey, Delaware and North Carolina.

96 Galloway was a Philadelphia lawyer who was Speaker of the Pennsylvania Assembly, 1766–76; he became a Tory in the Revolution, was British administrator of Philadelphia, 1777–8, and in 1779 left for England, where he died in 1803.

97 George Washington was also a member of the Virginia delegation.

98 Royal government was collapsing in Massachusetts in summer 1774; the structure was replaced by the towns, who created county conventions made up of two elected delegates from each town. The Resolves emerged from a joint meeting of four of these county conventions and were gradually adopted by all nine of the conventions. Starr, 'Political Mobilization', p. 236.

99 Thomas, *Revolution in America*, pp. 44–5; Wood, *American Revolution*, pp. 48–9; Starr, 'Political Mobilization', pp. 235–7; Alexander, *Samuel Adams*, pp. 139–40, quotation from the Resolves on p. 140.

100 Thomas, *Revolution in America*, Document XI, pp. 76–8.

101 Ammerman, 'The Tea Crisis and its Consequences', pp. 203–4, quotations on both pages.

102 Wood, *American Revolution*, p. 49.

103 Quoted in Raphael, *The American Revolution*, p. 35.

104 Anne Hulton, *Letters of a Loyalist Lady* (Cambridge, Mass.: Harvard University Press, 1927), p. 71, quoted in *ibid.*, p. 324.

105 Jonathan Bouchier, ed., *Reminiscences of an American Loyalist 1738–1789. Being the Autobiography of the Revd Jonathan Bouchier, Rector of Annapolis in Maryland and afterwards Vicar of Epsom,*

Surrey, England (Boston, Mass.: Houghton Mifflin, 1925), pp. 105, 113, 121–4. The manuscript was edited and published by a descendant.

106 Middleton, *Colonial America*, p. 478.

107 The patrols were organised by Dr Joseph Warren, chairman of the Boston Committee of Safety and President of the Massachusetts Provincial Congress, who was to die at the Battle of Bunker Hill, 17 June 1775.

108 *The Lexington–Concord Battle Road: Hour-by-Hour Account of Events Preceding and on the History-Making Day April 19, 1775* (Concord, Mass.: Concord Chamber of Commerce, n.d.), p. 5.

109 The Loyalist was named Daniel Bliss, who lived near the centre of Concord. He left town with the soldiers and never returned.

110 After attending the Congress, they were staying with a Rev. Jonas Clarke in Lexington; if captured they would probably have been sent to Great Britain and tried (and likely executed) for treason.

111 There were two ways by which the soldiers could reach the road to Concord: they could march across the Neck through Roxbury or travel by boat across the Charles River to East Cambridge. As it happened, the soldiers went by boat.

112 'Paul Revere's Ride' was published in *Tales of a Wayside Inn* (1863). This collection of narrative poems is structured on the model of Chaucer's *Canterbury Tales,* in that a group is seated around the fireside of a New England tavern and each tells a tale. Reprinted in *The Poetical Works of Henry Wadsworth Longfellow* (London: George Routledge and Sons, 1877), pp. 457–60.

113 Longfellow wrote it in 1861 (the year of the beginning of the Civil War) as a 'call to arms'. Fischer, in his *Paul Revere's Ride*, devotes three pages to 'Longfellow's Myth of the Lone Rider', pp. 331–3. 'As an historical description of Paul Revere's ride, the poem was grossly, systematically, and deliberately inaccurate'. *Ibid.,* p. 331.

114 'He had to pass a narrow gate, closely guarded by British sentries who stopped all suspicious travelers. Dawes was remembered to have been "mounted on a slow-jogging horse, with saddle-bags behind him, and a large flapped hat upon his head to resemble a countryman on a journey."' *Ibid.,* pp. 97–8.

115 The signal was sent as a precaution against Revere's not being able to deliver the warning himself. The Longfellow account incorrectly has Revere already on the other side of the water, awaiting the signal.

116 Their oars were muffled by a petticoat 'yet warm from the body of a fair daughter of Liberty'. Quoted in *The Lexington–Concord Battle Road*, p. 9. Prosaically, Fischer refers to it as a folktale. Fischer, *Paul Revere's Ride*, p. 104.

117 They were made up of twenty-one crack companies: the flank companies of the Royal Welch Fusiliers, the 4th (King's Own) Foot, the Royal Irish, the 5th Foot (later the Northumberland Fusiliers), and other regiments, the 52nd, the 38th, the 47th, the 59th (later the East Lancashire Regiment), the 10th (later the Lincolnshire Regiment) and the 64th (later the Prince of Wales' North Staffordshire Regiment). There were also British marines. Included were a few volunteers and Loyalist guides. *Ibid.,* p. 114.

118 Legend has it that the ploughman was still at work when the British arrived. *The Lexington–Concord Battle Road*, p. 14.

119 Quoted in Robert A. Gross, *The Minutemen and Their World* (New York: Hill and Wang, 2001, 1st pub. 1976), p. 116.

121 *Ibid.,* p. 59.

121 Quoted in *The Lexington–Concord Battle Road*, p. 15.

122 *Ibid.,* p. 16.

123 Anyone who visits the battlefield scene now may find the skirmishes difficult to imagine: then, the area was mostly cleared fields; today much of it is covered with trees.

124 David L. Ammerman, 'The Crisis of Independence', in Greene and Pole, eds, *American Revolution*, pp. 212–13.

125 *Ibid.*, pp. 212–13. The garrison of Fort Ticonderoga only numbered fifty men. This was 'a formidable post when in French hands in the Seven Years' War, but by this stage [it was] run down and barely defensible'. Conway, *The War of American Independence*, pp. 75–8, quotation on p. 75.

126 According to Ferling, Adams, Washington and Thomas Jefferson were all ready for hostilities with Great Britain by the beginning of 1774. Ferling, *Setting the World Ablaze*, p. 88. Washington was already disaffected by the late 1760s: the British had refused him a commission in the regular army after the end of the French and Indian War in 1763; they had stationed their troops in areas other than Virginia, leaving the colony to cope alone with its blazing frontier; they had prevented Virginia from issuing paper money in the early 1760s, leaving it without enough of a medium of exchange; and they had announced that all lands west of the mountains belonged to the Crown, jeopardising Washington's title to an extensive tract of such lands. He was a Virginian, and he decided that the colony would never be able to control its own affairs, and its destiny, whilst it was part of the British Empire. *Ibid.*, pp. 65–7.

127 *Ibid.*, p. 97.

128 *Ibid.*, pp. 97–9. After the Revolution, Washington was offered a crown, and he refused. According to John Adams, John Hancock had coveted the post of Commander-in-Chief. Apparently, he had already designed a handsome uniform.

129 *Ibid.*, p. 103.

130 George Washington described them as 'an exceedingly dirty and nasty people', while 'their officers generally speaking are the most indifferent kind of People I ever saw'. Washington to Lund Washington, 20 August 1775, in J.C. Fitzpatrick, ed., *The Writings of George Washington from the Original Manuscript Sources, 1745–1799*, 39 vols (Washington, D.C.: US Government Printing Office, 1931–44), III, pp. 432–5, quotation on p. 433.

131 Hugh Bicheno, *Rebels and Redcoats: The American Revolutionary War* (London: HarperCollins, 2003), p. 30.

132 *Ibid.*, p. 33.

133 Army surgeons blamed the deaths of so many wounded on the metallic debris fired by the Americans, which indicated that many were using shotguns or antique blunderbusses. *Ibid.*, p. 34. To give some idea of the cost to the British army of the loss of over a thousand trained men, it should be seen as a proportion of the total. According to Conway, whilst the army's paper strength was 48,647, it could probably muster no more than 36,000, who were themselves scattered widely around the empire – Africa, Gibraltar, the West Indies, Ireland and Great Britain itself. India was largely protected by the private army of the East India Company, in 1771 some 64,000 officers and men. There were only 8,000 troops in the North American colonies, and 1,000 had just been lost. Conway, *The War of American Independence*, p. 44.

134 Mackesy, *The War for America*, p. 4; Conway, *The War of American Independence*, pp. 73–5; Bicheno, *Rebels and Redcoats*, pp. 29–36. As King Pyrrhus of Epirus reputedly said after winning a battle with the Romans in 279 BC, but at the cost of all of his best officers and many irreplaceable men, 'Another such victory and we are done.'

135 Quoted in *ibid.*, p. 36.

136 Quoted in Thomas, *Revolution in America*, p. 54.

137 Walter Bodham Donne, ed., *Correspondence of George III with Lord North from 1768 to 1783*, 2 vols (London: John Murray, 1867), I, pp. 214–15, quotation on p. 215.

138 Thomas, *Revolution in America*, pp. 54–5 and Document XVII, p. 86.

139 Conway, *The War of American Independence*, p. 177.

140 Simmons and Thomas, eds, *Proceedings and Debates*, VI, pp. 277–84.

141 Thomas, *Revolution in America*, pp. 55–9.

142 'Under the "mildness and equity of the *English* constitution", members of the Maryland Convention recalled on January 12, 1776, they and their ancestors had experienced a remarkable state of happiness because "of all known systems" British government was "best calculated to secure the liberty of the subject". Their felicity had lapsed when the "grounds of the present controversy were laid by the Ministry and Parliaments of *Great Britain*", but Maryland wanted above all else to recover the remembered peace and freedom of times past. Even the news of early January failed to shake that desire: the Convention instructed its Congressional delegates to do all they could to secure reconciliation with the Mother Country, and also explicitly precluded their voting for Independence or for measures that might lead toward Independence without its previous consent.' Pauline Maier, *American Scripture*, p. 30.

143 *Ibid.*, p. 29.

144 *Ibid.*, p. 30.

145 Simmons and Thomas, eds, *Proceedings and Debates*, VI, p. 69.

146 Scott Liell, *46 Pages: Thomas Paine, Common Sense, and the Turning Point to Independence* (Philadelphia, Penn.: Running Press, 2003), p. 84.

147 The twenty-five editions is from Wood, *The American Revolution*, p. 55; Paine's estimate of 120,000 copies and the estimate of 500,000 copies are both from the Introduction by Isaac Kramnick to *Common Sense* (Harmondsworth: Penguin, 1976), pp. 8–9.

148 Thomas Paine, *Common Sense* (Mineola, NY: Dover, 1997), p. 31. The Penguin edition, the second edition, gives it as 'the Royal—of Britain', p. 98.

149 'That the crown is this overbearing part in the English constitution needs not be mentioned, and that it derives its whole consequence merely from being the giver of places and pensions is self-evident . . . To the evil of monarchy we have added that of hereditary succession; and as the first is a degredation and lessening of ourselves, so the second, claimed as a matter of right, is an insult and an imposition on posterity.' Paine, ed. Kramnick, *Common Sense*, pp. 70, 76.

150 *Ibid.*, p. 87.

151 *Ibid.*, pp. 95–7, quotation on p. 97.

152 Maier, *American Scripture*, p. 34.

153 Henry Steele Commager and Richard B. Morris, eds, *The Spirit of 'Seventy-Six: The Story of the American Revolution as Told by its Participants* (Edison, N.J.: Castle, 2002), p. 301.

154 Maier, *American Scripture*, pp. 38–9, quotation on p. 39. Great Britain signed treaties in early 1776 with the rulers of four small German principalities to provide about 18,000 troops; almost 13,000 were sent from Hessen-Kassel alone in 1776. By the end of the war, six German principalities had sent about 30,000 soldiers to North America, about a third of the British strength. Great Britain also attempted to hire 20,000 troops from Russia, but Catherine the Great refused the request. Jonathan R. Dull, *A Diplomatic History of the American Revolution* (London: Yale University Press, 1985), pp. 46–7.

155 Conway, *The War of American Independence*, pp. 75–7.

156 Quoted in Maier, *American Scripture*, pp. 40–1.

157 Commager and Morris, eds, *The Spirit of 'Seventy-Six*, p. 302.

158 Livingston was a delegate from New York and John Jay's law partner. He would be the first Secretary of Foreign Affairs for the new country, 1781–3. Sherman was a delegate from Connecticut for most of the period 1774–84. Importantly for the future of the US, he proposed the 'Connecticut Compromise' at the Constitutional Convention of 1787, which advocated a two-chamber legislature, one based upon population and the other upon equal representation of the states, the first benefiting the large states and the second the small.

159 Maier, *American Scripture*, pp. 143–50, quotation on p. 149. The Congress deleted 630 words, almost a quarter of the whole, and added 146.

160 Produced for posterity by the early historian Jared Sparks. Isaacson, *Benjamin Franklin*, p. 313.

161 Maier, *American Scripture*, p. 156.

162 Bicheno, *Rebels and Redcoats*, p. 84.

163 Mackesy, *The War for America*, p. 134.

164 Conway, *The War of American Independence*, pp. 94–9; Bicheno, *Rebels and Redcoats*, pp. 108–10; Mackesy, *The War for America*, pp. 130–44; Don Higginbotham, 'The War for Independence, to Saratoga', in Greene and Pole, eds, *The American Revolution*, p. 306.

165 'Providing a direct subsidy was too dangerous, so the French government devised a stratagem to funnel military supplies to America. It loaned 1,000,000 *livres tournois* (about £40,000) to a trading company, which would purchase arms at reduced prices from government arsenals. The company would then sell the arms to the Americans on credit and would eventually be repaid in American tobacco.' Jonathan R. Dull, 'Diplomacy of the Revolution, to 1783', in Greene and Pole, eds, *American Revolution*, p. 322.

166 Dull, *The Diplomacy of the American Revolution*, pp. 59–63; Dull, 'Diplomacy of the Revolution', pp. 321–5, quotation on p. 325; Mackesy, *The War for America*, p. xv. Franklin was now deemed the American minister to France.

167 *Ibid.*, pp. 7–21.

168 *Ibid.*, p. 1.

169 Conway, *The War of American Independence*, pp. 157–8, Tables 1 and 2.

170 London learned of the departure on 27 April from a British agent in Paris and bankers in Amsterdam; the fact that the fleet was carrying provisions for a nine-month journey made it clear that the destination was outside Europe. Mackesy, *The War for America*, p. 197.

171 For example, between 1779 and 1783, eight British regular regiments and two Hanoverian battalions were sent to India to support the troops of the East India Company in the latter's war against France and their 'country' allies. Conway, *War of American Independence*, p. 150.

172 Mackesy, *The War for America*, pp. 159, 187–9, 219–20, with quotations on pp. 159 and 219–20; Esmond Wright, 'The British Objectives, 1780–1783: "If Not Dominion Then Trade"', in Ronald Hoffman and Peter J. Albert, eds, *Peace and the Peacemakers: The Treaty of 1783* (Charlottesville: University Press of Virginia, 1986), p. 5.

173 Conway, 'Britain and the Revolutionary Crisis', pp. 340–1.

174 According to Bicheno, the 'inspiring legend of true-hearted patriots bravely bearing hardship at Valley Forge . . . was largely an invention of the mid nineteenth-century Romantic Era. Only a small number of those who had nowhere else to go remained with Washington, and his army actually suffered even more during the following, truly dreadful winter at Morristown, New Jersey. What was remarkable about Valley Forge was that nothing whatever was done for the soldiers, not even payment of the pittance they were entitled to in devalued Continental paper money.' Bicheno, *Rebels and Redcoats*, p. 116. According to Ferling, 'Over 3,000 men died at Valley Forge. Food was always scarce. Housing was inadequate, consisting of jerry-built huts that were crowded, drafty, and cold. Nearly one-third of the men lacked shoes, and almost all were without blankets and sufficient clothing. Inevitably, disease – smallpox, typhus, dysentery, and scurvy – swept through Valley Forge . . . The few who were healthy, and had not deserted, spent much of their time burying their less fortunate comrades.' Ferling, *Setting the World Ablaze*, pp. 186–7.

175 Baron Friedrich Wilhelm Ludolf Gerhard Augustin von Steuben (1730–94) had served in the Prussian army as an infantry officer, a staff officer, and an aide to Frederick the Great. In Paris in 1777 he had offered his services to Franklin, who sent him to America. The Continental Congress in January 1778 accepted his offer to serve as a volunteer without rank, and sent him to Valley Forge, and in May he became Inspector-General of the army with the rank of major-general. 'Steuben trained first a "model company" and then the entire army according to a unique system based on European practices but modified to American circumstances.' 'Biographies', in Greene and Pole, eds, *American Revolution*, p. 781.

176 By 1780 his rage had 'subsided to a dull resignation'. Bicheno, *Rebels and Redcoats*, p. 225.

177 Conway, *The War of American Independence*, pp. 104–5.

178 Don Higginbotham, 'The War for Independence, after Saratoga', in Greene and Pole, eds, *American Revolution*, p. 309; Ferling, *Setting the World Ablaze*, p. 224. In *ibid.*, p. 214, Ferling says 5,500 men. Conway, *The War of American Independence*, p. 120.

179 Bicheno, *Rebels and Redcoats*, pp. 132–46.

180 Conway, *The War of American Independence*, pp. 116–19, quotations on pp. 117 and 118.

181 Ferling, *Setting the World Ablaze*, p. 202. Adams 'saw clearly that Vergennes aspired to "Keep us poor. Depress Us. Keep Us weak. Make Us feel our obligations. Impress our Minds with a Sense of Gratitude."' *Ibid.*, p. 217.

182 *Ibid.*, p. 223.

183 Conway, *The War of American Independence*, pp. 121–2.

184 Ferling, *Setting the World Ablaze*, pp. 216–17, 237–9; Dull, *A Diplomatic History of the American Revolution*, pp. 130–1.

185 Dull, 'Diplomacy of the Revolution', p. 326. Dull, *A Diplomatic History of the American Revolution*, pp. 107–15. The attempted invasion of Great Britain failed to happen, although a huge Franco-Spanish fleet of sixty-six ships of the line caused great panic when it appeared off Plymouth. *Ibid.*, p. 11. The contribution of the Spanish navy would be crucial to the outcome at Yorktown, and the Spanish army during 1779–81 under the Governor of Louisiana, Bernardo de Gálvez (the city of Galveston is named after him), cleared the lower Mississippi Valley and the Gulf Coast of British troops; this diverted British resources, and restricted supplies to the Indian tribes fighting on the borders of the southern states. He also captured the Bahamas in 1782. *Ibid.*, pp. 110–11.

186 Dull, 'Diplomacy of the Revolution', p. 327 for the quotation; Dull, *A Diplomatic History of the American Revolution*, pp. 124–30.

187 *Ibid.*, pp. 124–7, quotation on p. 126; Dull, 'Diplomacy of the Revolution', p. 327.

188 Reich, *British Friends of the American Revolution*, p. 148.

189 Bicheno, *Rebels and Redcoats*, pp. 233–4; Mackesy, *The War for America*, pp. 360–2; Ferling, *Setting the World Ablaze*, p. 219 for the quotation.

190 *Ibid.*, pp. 236–8.

191 Higginbotham, 'The War for Independence, after Saratoga', p. 312; Bicheno, *Rebels and Redcoats*, p. 197. Bicheno adds that 'More exculpatory piffle has been written about Greene than any other general in this war, which is saying a lot. He was absent from his command when disaster struck at Brooklyn Heights, he did not remain with his men when Fort Washington came under attack, he was competent under Washington's eye at Trenton and the Brandywine but mishandled independent command at Germantown.' *Ibid.*, p. 197.

192 North Callahan, *Daniel Morgan: Ranger of the Revolution* (New York: Hold Rinehart Winston, 1961), pp. 195–6.

193 He was also a farmer and a man of substance in his community (near Winchester, Virginia). Thomas J. Fleming, *Cowpens* (Washington, D.C.: National Park Service, 1988), p. 15.

194 Bicheno, *Rebels and Redcoats*, pp. 202–6, quotations on pp. 202, 206; Conway, *The War of American Independence*, pp. 122–4; Callahan, *Daniel Morgan*, pp. 194–225.

195 Higginbotham, 'The War for Independence, after Saratoga', p. 312; Conway, *The War for American Independence*, p. 126.

196 *Ibid.*, pp. 126–8; Bicheno, *Rebels and Redcoats*, pp. 241–6, quotation on p. 246.

197 Conway, *The War of American Independence*, pp. 127–8; Bicheno, *Rebels and Redcoats*, pp. 241–8, quotations on pp. 246 and 247. Hamilton's assault on Redoubt 10 was the last military operation of significance by the Continental Army. *Ibid.*, p. 248. Ferling, *Setting the World Ablaze*, p. 251, for quotation on terms of surrender. Dull, *A Diplomatic History of the American Revolution*, p. 111.

198 Bicheno, *Rebels and Redcoats*, p. 248.

199 Quoted in Wright, 'The British Objectives', pp. 9–10.

200 *Ibid.*, p. 9; Conway, 'Britain and the Revolutionary Crisis', pp. 342–3; Conway, *The War of American Independence*, p. 229; Dull, *A Diplomatic History of the American Revolution*, pp. 137–43.

201 Wright, 'The British Objectives', pp. 11–12.

202 Dull, *A Diplomatic History of the American Revolution*, p. 141; Wright, 'The British Objectives', pp. 19–20, quotation on p. 20.

203 Dull, *A Diplomatic History of the American Revolution*, pp. 139–44, quotations on p. 139.

204 Ferling, *Setting the World Ablaze*, p. 260.

205 'Instructions to the Commissioners for the Peace', quoted in Gregg L. Lint, 'Preparing for Peace: The Objectives of the United States, France, and Spain in the War of the American Revolution', in Hoffman and Albert, eds, *Peace and the Peacemakers*, p. 48.

206 Ferling, *Setting the World Ablaze*, p. 257. Jay himself had written to the President of Congress on 20 September 1781 that 'as an American I feel an interest in the dignity of my country, which renders it difficult for me to reconcile myself to the idea of the sovereign independent States of America submitting, in the persons of their ministers, to be absolutely governed by the advice and opinions of the servants of another sovereign, especially in a case of such national importance'. Furthermore, the instructions eliminated 'the power of your ministers to improve those chances and opportunities which in the normal course of human affairs happens more or less frequently to all men'. Quoted in Lint, 'Preparing for Peace', p. 49. Upon being summoned by Franklin to Paris, Adams doubted that negotiations would proceed rapidly and decided to remain in the Netherlands to complete the negotiations for the Dutch–American Treaty of Amity and Commerce before joining the other commissioners; he arrived in Paris on 26 October 1782. Jay had arrived from Spain in late June 1782, but was soon bedridden with influenza. Therefore, for the first few months, Franklin was the sole negotiator. Dull, *A Diplomatic History of the American Revolution*, pp. 139–40.

207 Adams to James Lovell, 26 July 1778, quoted in Lint, 'Preparing for Peace', p. 36.

208 *Ibid.*

209 Dull, *A Diplomatic History of the American Revolution*, pp. 141–8, quotation on p. 145.

210 Ferling, *Setting the World Ablaze*, p. 258.

211 According to Ferling, the 'distinction between a "liberty" and a "right" would cause problems for American fishermen for the next century'. *Ibid.*, pp. 261–2.

212 *Ibid.*, pp. 258–62.

213 Dull, *A Diplomatic History of the American Revolution*, pp. 150–1; for Shelburne's devotion to commerce, see Bradford Perkins, 'The Peace of Paris: Patterns and Legacies', in Hoffman and Albert, eds, *Peace and the Peacemakers*, p. 198; for the Vergennes quotation see *ibid.*, p. 215.

214 Merrill Jensen, *The New Nation: A History of the United States during the Confederation, 1781–1789* (New York: Knopf, 1950), p. 14, quoted in Perkins, 'The Peace of Paris', p. 200.

Chapter 3 – War and Rumours of War: 1783–1872

1. Francis Scott Key was an American lawyer and the occasion was the British attack on Baltimore during the War of 1812. Key had gone on board a British ship to try to secure the release of a friend, and whilst there he witnessed the bombardment of Fort McHenry, at the end of which the American flag was still flying. His poem 'The Defense of Fort McHenry' was first published anonymously as a broadside in 1814, and then in the newspaper the *Baltimore Patriot*. It was then set to music; the melody was 'To Anacreon in Heaven', first published in England about 1780. (This was a popular melody in the US during the War of 1812, and Key's was not the only patriotic song which used it.) When the sheet music was published in 1815, the title was changed to 'The Star Spangled Banner'. The army and navy first

adopted it as their own anthem, and it was not until 1931 that, by Act of Congress, it was deemed the American national anthem. To hear the melody as in 1780, consult <http://www.contemplator.com/america/ssbanner.html>.

2. J.F. Watts and Fred L. Israel, eds, *Presidential Documents: The Speeches, Proclamations, and Policies that Have Shaped the Nation from Washington to Clinton* (London: Routledge, 2000), p. 30.

3. According to Eliga H. Gould, even well-disposed Englishmen usually found it difficult to conceive of the US as Great Britain's diplomatic equal. 'The Making of an Atlantic State System: Britain and the United States, 1795–1825', in Julie Flavelle and Stephen Conway, eds, *Britain and America Go to War: The Impact of War and Warfare in Anglo-America, 1754–1815* (Gainesville: University Press of Florida, 2004), p. 258.

4. Bradford Perkins, *Castlereagh and Adams: England and the United States 1812–1823* (Berkeley: University of California Press, 1964), p. 1. The question was: could the US remain united? The Whiskey Rebellion of 1795, the Burr Conspiracy of 1807, the north-eastern opposition to the embargo of 1808 and the Hartford Convention of 1814 were all regional challenges to the centre.

5 Bradford Perkins, *Prologue to War: England and the United States 1805–1812* (Berkeley: University of California Press, 1968), p. 377. The point is also made in Francis D. Cogliano, *Revolutionary America 1763–1815: A Political History* (London: Routledge, 2000), p. 180.

6 <www.sewanee.edu/faculty/Willis/Civil_War/documents/HammondCotton.html>.

7 In 1818, 1825–6, 1841–2, 1845–6 and 1903.

8 By Article XI, Canada would be allowed to join, with all rights and privileges.

9 A number of historians have argued that the Constitution was the result of the failure of the Confederation to determine and execute a coherent foreign policy. One such is Walter LaFeber: 'Nothing contributed more directly to the calling of the 1787 Constitutional Convention than did the spreading belief that under the Articles of Confederation Congress could not effectively and safely conduct foreign policy.' LaFeber, 'The Constitution and United States Foreign Policy', *Journal of American History*, Vol. 74, No. 3 (December 1987), p. 697.

10 Boswell, *The Life of Samuel Johnson*, p. 343. This was recorded in 1778, but there is no reason to assume that he had changed his mind by the time of his death on 13 December 1784.

11 Cappon, ed., *The Adams–Jefferson Letters*, I, p. 43. This sentence was written in code.

12 Before the war, American vessels had been responsible for 63 per cent of the shipping to and from the British West Indies. Charles R. Ritcheson, *Aftermath of Revolution: British Policy towards the United States, 1783–1795* (Dallas, Tex.: Southern Methodist University Press, 1969), p. 129 for the statistic. See also Bradford Perkins, *The Cambridge History of American Foreign Relations, Volume I: The Creation of a Republican Empire, 1776–1865* (Cambridge: Cambridge University Press, 1995, 1st pub. 1993), p. 57.

13 Ritcheson, *Aftermath of Revolution*, pp. 4–23.

14 *Ibid.*, pp. 56–87, quotation on p. 81.

15 Late in the war, the British invaded Virginia, torched Richmond and some plantations, and carried off hundreds of slaves to be set free. John Lamberton Harper, *American Machiaveli: Alexander Hamilton and the Origins of US Foreign Policy* (Cambridge: Cambridge University Press, 2004), p. 56.

16 There were two at the head of Lake Champlain, at Dutchman's Point and Pointe-au-Fer, which secured the outlet of the lake and the old military passage from Montreal to Albany; of additional importance was the fact that this military route was developing into a valuable trade route. The three forts of Oswegatchie (Ogdensburg, NY), Oswego and Niagara controlled the navigation of the St Lawrence River, Lake Ontario and the connection with Lake Erie, and Detroit the straits between Lakes Erie and Huron. The fortified island of Machilimackinac, off

the northern tip of the Michigan Peninsula, controlled the entrance to three lakes, Huron, Michigan and Superior. Samuel Flagg Bemis, *Jay's Treaty: A Study in Commerce and Diplomacy* (New Haven, Conn.: Yale University Press, 1962 rev. edn, 1st pub. 1923), pp. 3–4. A copy of the Treaty of Peace is printed in *ibid.*, Appendix VI.A.

17 *Ibid.*, pp. 3–4.

18 *Ibid.*, pp. 3–13, quotations on pp. 6 and 9; Ritcheson, *Aftermath of Revolution*, pp. 75–7.

19 Adams to John Jay, 13 May 1785, in C.F. Adams, ed., *The Works of John Adams, Second President of the United States, with a Life of the Author, Notes and Ilustrations*, 10 vols (Boston, Mass.: Little, Brown, 1850–6), VIII, pp. 248–50; Ritcheson, *Aftermath of Revolution*, p. 77 for quotation.

20 David McCullough, *John Adams* (New York: Simon & Schuster, 2001, 2002 pb), p. 348.

21 Adams to Jay, 25 Aug. 1785, in Adams, ed., *Works of John Adams*, VIII, pp. 302–10, quotation on p. 303.

22 Ritcheson, *Aftermath of Revolution*, p. 83.

23 *Ibid.*, p. 84.

24 Quoted in Harper, *American Machiaveli*, p. 66.

25 Ritcheson, *Aftermath of Revolution*, p. 70.

26 *Ibid.*, pp. 186–227.

27 Harper, *American Machiaveli*, p. 106.

28 'President George Washington's Proclamation of Neutrality', 22 April 1793, in Watts and Israel, eds, *Presidential Documents*, p. 12.

29 Ritcheson, *Aftermath of Revolution*, pp. 273–88.

30 *Ibid.*, pp. 289–313, quotation on p. 299; Harper, *American Machiaveli*, pp. 124–33.

31 Ritcheson, *Aftermath of Revolution*, p. 310.

32 *Ibid.*, pp. 305–21; Harper, *American Machiaveli*, pp. 131–2. The Battle of Fallen Timbers led to a preliminary peace between the Americans and the Indians; this was later followed by the Treaty of Greenville, which opened up most of Ohio to white settlement.

33 All quotations are from Harper, *American Machiavelli*, pp. 133–4; John Ehrman, *The Younger Pitt: The Reluctant Transition* (London: Constable, 1983), p. 509.

34 Hamilton to Washington, 14 April 1794, in Harold C. Syrett and Jacob E. Cooke, eds, *The Papers of Alexander Hamilton*, 27 vols (New York: Columbia University Press, 1961–87), XVI, pp. 266–79, quotations on pp. 271, 272, 276.

35 Robert Liston to Grenville, 29 January 1799, FO 5/25A, Foreign Office Papers, UK National Archives, Kew, London (hereafter FO 5/25A).

36 Jay to Sally Jay, 19 April 1794, in Henry P. Johnston, ed., *The Correspondence and Public Papers of John Jay*, 4 vols (New York: G.P. Putnam's Sons, 1893), IV, p. 5.

37 As it happened, Jay wrote to Randolph on 19 November 1794, after agreement on the treaty had been reached, that 'great reserve and Delicacy has been observed respecting our Concerns with France:— The Stipulations in favor of existing Treaties was agreed to without hesitation: not an Expectation nor even a wish has been expressed that our conduct towards France should be otherwise than fair and friendly'. Despatches from US Ministers to Great Britain, 1791–1906, Record Group 59 (State Department Papers), US National Archives, Washington, D.C., Microfilm Series 30, Roll 2 (hereafter M30/2, etc.).

38 Randolph to Jay, 6 May 1794, Diplomatic and Consular Instructions of the Department of State, 1791–1801, Record Group 59, US National Archives, M28/2.

39 Ehrman, *The Younger Pitt*, p. 511.

40 When at one of their first meetings, Jay described how British ships had seized and mistreated American ships and sailors, Grenville told him that 'not a single case under the instructions of November had been laid before him', and requested that some of the strongest of those cases be furnished him. Jay to Randolph, 6 July 1794, M30/3. Jay had a list of captures, but no statement of reasons for the condemnations. As it happened, H.C. Higginson,

who had been sent to the West Indies to collect data, died of yellow fever while in the islands. The result was that Jay did not receive full and authoritative information in time to use it in the negotiations. Ritcheson, *Aftermath of Revolution*, p. 324.

41 Walter Stahr, *John Jay: Founding Father* (London: Hambledon and London, 2005), p. 320 for the Parisian deaths.

42 Bradford Perkins, *The First Rapprochement: England and the United States 1795–1805* (Philadelphia: University of Pennsylvania Press, 1955), p. 19.

43 Jay to Randolph, 6 July 1794, M30/3. Grenville and Jay 'soon became, and remained, firm friends'. Ehrman, *The Younger Pitt*, p. 511.

44 Copy of the note from Jay to Grenville, enclosed in Jay to Randolph, 31 July 1794, M30/3; also found in Jay to Grenville, 30 July 1794, FO 95/512, pp. 104–5.

45 Jay to Randolph, 31 July 1794, M30/3.

46 Note from Grenville to Jay, 1 August 1794, M30/3.

47 Grenville to Hammond, 8 August 1794, FO 115/3; Harper, *American Machiaveli*, p. 143 for second quotation.

48 Jay to Randolph, 13 September 1794, M30/2, contains Jay's 6 August note and Grenville's 30 August response, his two projets.

49 Stahr, *John Jay*, p. 328.

50 Bemis, *Jay's Treaty*, pp. 343 and 317.

51 Stahr, *John Jay*, p. 329.

52 C.F. Adams, ed., *Memoirs of John Quincy Adams. Comprising Portions of His Diary from 1795 to 1848*, 12 vols (Philadelphia, Penn.: J.P. Lippincott, 1874–7), I, p. 48 (22 October 1794).

53 Jay to Randolph, 19 November 1794, M30/2.

54 Bemis, *Jay's Treaty*, pp. 453–84 for text of treaty.

55 A.T. Mahan, *Sea Power and Its Relations to the War of 1812*, 2 vols (London: Sampson Low, Marston, 1905), I, pp. 43, 44 for the quotations. According to Paul Kennedy, Mahan was using history to appeal to the American people to build a larger navy. Kennedy, *The Rise and Fall of British Naval Mastery* (London: Macmillan, 1983 edn), p. 183.

56 Stahr, *John Jay*, p. 337.

57 Perkins, *First Rapprochement*, p. 12.

58 From 1795 to 1800 the increase was from $6 million to $19 million. US Bureau of the Census, *Historical Statistics of the United States, Colonial Times to 1957* (Washington: US Government Printing Office, 1960), p. 551; Perkins, *The First Rapprochement*, p. 12. 'British possessions' included the British West Indies, British North America and India, with exports to India increasing greatly after 1814; exports to the United Kingdom alone increased by 26 per cent over the same period. *Ibid.*

59 Quoted in Perkins, *First Rapprochement*, p. 15.

60 *Ibid.*, pp. 90–9.

61 Paul Leicester Ford, ed., *The Writings of Thomas Jefferson*, 10 vols (New York: G.P. Putnam's Sons, 1892–9), VIII, p. 145. Jefferson assumed that the French would read this and take the point.

62 Perkins, *Creation of a Republican Empire*, p. 115.

63 Perkins, *First Rapprochement*, pp. 176–81, quotations on p. 180.

64 James Madison had written in his 'Political Observations' of 1795 that 'War is the parent of armies; from these proceed debts and taxes; and armies, and debts, and taxes are the known instruments for bringing the many under the domination of the few.' Thomas Mason, Robert A. Rutland and Jeanne K. Sisson, eds, *The Papers of James Madison*, 17 vols (Charlottesville: University of Virginia Press, 1962–91), XV, 511–33, quotation on p. 518.

65 Perkins, *Prologue to War*, pp. 68–71. Napoleon's goal was partly to wreck the British ability to fight the war, but equally he wanted to exclude British goods from Europe and trans-

form it into a captive market for France. As he told Eugène de Beauharnais on 23 August 1810, 'You must never lose sight of the fact that, if England triumphs on the seas, it is because the English are stronger there. It is reasonable, therefore, that, as France is the strongest on land, French trade should . . . triumph there.' Charles J. Esdaile, *The Wars of Napoleon* (London: Longman, 1995), pp. 103–4, quotation on p. 104.

66 Perkins, *Prologue to War*, p. 89.

67 *Ibid.*, pp. 74–90, quotation on p. 90.

68 *Ibid.*, p. 141. Lord Grenville was apprehensive about Berkeley's selection, but 'the admiral's brother commanded a number of votes that marched into the ministerial lobby at division time, as did Berkeley himself between tours of sea duty'. *Ibid.*, p. 140.

69 Burton Spivak has an alternative explanation: in the aftermath of the attack on the *Chesapeake* and through the congressional session of October, Jefferson favoured war; when he called for an embargo in December, 'his request grew from the grim realization that French additions to the initial English problems had created a general Atlantic crisis for the American nation'. He wanted time to 'make manageable the nation's foreign crisis'. The two explanations, of course, are not wholly uncomplementary. Spivak, *Jefferson's English Crisis: Commerce, Embargo, and the Republican Revolution* (Charlottesville: University Press of Virginia, 1979), pp. x–xi, quotations on p. xi.

70 Perkins, *Prologue to War*, pp. 141–8, 191. Robert V. Remini, *John Quincy Adams* (New York: Henry Holt, 2002), p. 38.

71 For the text of the 11 November Order, see Privy Council Register 1 September–30 November 1807, PC/174, pp. 479–82, UK National Archives, Kew, London (hereafter PC/174).

72 Perkins, *Prologue to War*, pp. 197–202; Denis Gray, *Spencer Perceval: The Evangelical Prime Minister 1762–1812* (Manchester: Manchester University Press, 1963), pp. 168–73; Mahan, *Sea Power in Its Relations to the War of 1812*, I, p. 178.

73 Quoted in Perkins, *Prologue to War*, p. 199. Lloyds of London stopped quoting insurance rates entirely for voyages between Great Britain and the Continent, while the rates for Anglo-American voyages increased by 50 per cent. Gray, *Spencer Perceval*, p. 171.

74 Garry Wills, *James Madison* (New York: Harry Holt, 2002), pp. 4–5. In 1793 Madison had written about the use of an embargo: 'It would probably do as much good as harm at home, and would force peace on the rest of the world, and perhaps liberty along with it.' *Ibid.*, p. 51.

75 Spivak, *Jefferson's English Crisis*, p. 158.

76 Perkins, *Prologue to War*, pp. 160–1.

77 *Ibid.*, pp. 156–65, quotations on pp. 160–1.

78 Perkins, *Creation of a Republican Empire*, p. 131.

79 *Ibid.*, p. 131.

80 Perkins, *Prologue to War*, pp. 248–9.

81 Tecumseh's brother, Tenskwatawa (known to whites as the Old Prophet), preached a message of cultural and political renaissance; Tecumseh sought to forge a military alliance among the remaining eastern tribes in order to resist American expansion.

82 Perkins, *The Creation of a Republican Empire*, pp. 134–5.

83 As, apparently, is the case with British historians. Many of the standard British political histories when discussing the period contain few or no references to the US.

84 Gray, *Spencer Perceval*, pp. 214–74.

85 Esdaile, *Wars of Napoleon*, p. 152.

86 Gray, *Spencer Perceval*, pp. 391–412.

87 Perkins, *Prologue to War*, p. 316 for the statistics.

88 *Cobett's Parliamentary Debates* (London: T.C. Hansard, 1812), Vol. 21, Col. 770 (13 February 1812).

89 Perkins, *Prologue to War*, p. 321.

90 His fame was preserved by having a one-horse carriage named after him.

91 For example, he introduced a petition from Liverpool. *Cobbett's Parliamentary Debates,* Vol. 22, Col. 1066.

92 J.E. Cookson, *Friends of Peace: Anti-War Liberalism in England, 1793–1815* (Cambridge: Cambridge University Press, 1982), pp. 215–34.

93 Perkins, *Prologue to War,* p. 331.

94 *Ibid.,* pp. 384–6; Carl Benn, *The War of 1812* (Oxford: Osprey, 2002), p. 28.

95 Cogliano, *Revolutionary America,* p. 175 for the number of ships.

96 Watts and Israel, eds, *Presidential Documents,* pp. 45–7.

97 Perkins, *Prologue to War,* pp. 408–20; Perkins, *Creation of a Republican Empire,* p. 140 for the quotation.

98 Text of decree repealing the Orders-in-Council of 1 January 1807 and 26 April 1809; 23 June 1812 was date of formal repeal at the court at Carlton House and publication in the *Gazette.* The US also had to repeal any regulations against British shipping, including opening all American ports, within two weeks of learning about the British repeal. PC 2/193.

99 For the astonishment, see Wills, *James Madison,* p. 121. Jonathan Russell to James Monroe, the Secretary of State, 17 September 1812, M30/14.

100 Wills, *James Madison,* pp. 110–11, quotation on p. 111.

101 General Peter B. Porter of the New York Militia wrote to Secretary of War John Armstrong on 27 July 1813 that Dearborn was better than all the others in the North put together, but that even he had nothing. John K. Mahon, *The War of 1812* (Gainesville: University Presses of Florida, 1972 pb. edn), p. 154.

102 Jefferson to William Duane, 4 August 1812, in Ford, *Writings of Thomas Jefferson,* IX, pp. 365–7, quotation on p. 366.

103 Mahon, *War of 1812,* pp. 43–7, 76–81, 93–5.

104 The battle came too late to have any legitimate influence on the New York election; however, Tompkins' supporters sent around victory proclamations regardless, and the American general kept the New York troops at home to vote for the Governor. Tompkins was re-elected by 3,606 votes. Benn, *War of 1812,* p. 37. According to Wills, it was John Armstrong, the Secretary of War, who decided that 'some victory, any victory, had to be scored by Dearborn's army before the April elections for congressional and state offices'. Wills, *Madison,* p. 123.

105 Benn, *War of 1812,* pp. 78–80; Mahon, *War of 1812,* pp. 141–3. York was to be attacked and burned again three months later. *Ibid.,* p. 155.

106 *Ibid.,* pp. 165–75, quotations on pp. 174, 175. The second quotation – minus the list of boats – used to be one that every American schoolchild knew.

107 Perkins argues that the conquest of Canada was never a serious American war aim, citing this disbandment of the militia as evidence of the feeble desire for the permanent incorporation of Canada within the US. Perkins, *Prologue to War,* p. 426. He argues elsewhere that in 1812 both Madison and Monroe looked upon Canada as no more than a vulnerable target. Perkins, *Castlereagh and Adams,* p. 55.

108 Mahan, *Sea Power in Its Relations to the War of 1812,* I, pp. 328–35, 416–22; II, pp. 3–7. The *Guerrière* and the *Java* were both so damaged that they were burned at sea. The *United States* was captained by Stephen Decatur. The *Constitution* was blockaded in port for most of 1813 and 1814.

109 Perkins, *Creation of a Republican Empire,* p. 141.

110 The so-called *guerre de course,* commerce-destroying or plundering.

111 Benn, *War of 1812,* p. 55; Henry Adams, *History of the United States of America during the Administrations of James Madison* (New York: Library of America, 1986, 1st pub. 1889–91), p. 1034.

112 Christopher D. Hall, *British Strategy in the Napoleonic War 1803–15* (Manchester: Manchester University Press, 1992), pp. 197–8; *Historical Statistics of the United States*, pp. 563, 712; Benn, *War of 1812*, pp. 55–61.

113 Bathhurst to Ross, 1814, War Office Despatches, British Archives, described as such and quoted in Adams, *History of the United States*, pp. 997–8, 1000. Because Sir George Prevost, the Governor-General of Canada, had written to Vice-Admiral Sir Alexander Cochrane on 2 June 1814 suggesting that he should 'assist in inflicting that measure of retaliation which shall deter the enemy from a repetition of similar outrages' as had taken place in Canada, Cochrane had on 18 July issued an order to the blockading squadrons 'to destroy and lay waste such towns and districts upon the coast as you may find assailable'. The army, however, paid no attention to the order. Cochrane to Prevost, 22 July 1814, C. 684, p. 221 and Orders of Vice-Admiral Cochrane, 18 July 1814, C. 684, p. 204, both MSS. Canadian Archives, quoted in *ibid.*, pp. 998–1000.

114 Perkins, *Creation of a Republican Empire*, p. 141; Wills, *Madison*, pp. 132–3, quotation on p. 133.

115 Quoted in Benn, *War of 1812*, p. 59.

116 Mahan, *Sea Power in Its Relations to the War of 1812*, II, pp. 349–50.

117 Adams, *History of the United States of America*, p. 1016.

118 An Officer Who Served in the Expedition [G.R. Gleig], *A Narrative of the Campaigns of the British Army at Washington and New Orleans under Generals Ross, Pakenham, and Lambert, in the Years 1814 and 1815; With Some Account of the Countries Visited* (London: John Murray, 1821), p. 131.

119 *Ibid.*, pp. 124–7.

120 Benn, *War of 1812*, p. 59.

121 *Ibid.*

122 Adams, *History of the United States*, pp. 1027–8, quotation on p. 1028; Gleig, *Campaigns of the British Army*, p. 164.

123 *Ibid.*, pp. 175–88, quotation on p. 188.

124 *Ibid.*, pp. 188–96; Benn, *War of 1812*, p. 61.

125 *Ibid.*, pp. 62–4, quotations on p. 64.

126 For gripping details of the battle by a British officer, see Gleig, *Campaigns of the British Army*, pp. 316–32.

127 Monroe to Gallatin, Adams and Bayard, 15 April 1813, Diplomatic Instructions of the State Department 1801–1906, M77/2, p. 239.

128 Perkins, *Castlereagh and Adams*, pp. 20–3.

129 In his diary for 1823, Adams referred to Gallatin's 'usual shrewdness and sagacity'. C.F. Adams, ed., *Memoirs*, VI, p. 193.

130 Remini, *John Quincy Adams*, p. 45.

131 Monroe to Gallatin, Adams and Bayard, 15 April 1813, pp. 239–68 and Monroe to Adams, Bayard, Clay and Russell, 28 January 1814, p. 313 for the quotation, both M77/2.

132 Monroe to Gallatin, Adams and Bayard, 23 June 1814, p. 98, M77/2.

133 Monroe to Adams, Bayard, Clay and Russell, 28 January 1814, pp. 311–21, quotation on p. 321, M77/2.

134 Perkins, *Castlereagh and Adams*, pp. 60–1.

135 Adams, *History of the United States*, p. 1193; Perkins, *Castlereagh and Adams*, p. 63 for the quotation.

136 Castlereagh to the Commissioners, 28 July 1814, and Gallatin to Madison, 13 June 1814, both quoted in Adams, *History of the United States*, II, p. 1190; *ibid.*, p. 1197.

137 *Ibid.*, pp. 1195–1201; Perkins, *Castlereagh and Adams*, p. 65; J.E. Cookson, *Lord Liverpool's Administration: The Crucial Years 1815–1821* (Edinburgh: Scottish Academic Press, 1975), p. 21 for government expenditure.

138 Perkins, *Castlereagh and Adams*, pp. 99–100; thanks to Thomas Otte for information on the subsidies.

139 Perkins, *Castlereagh and Adams*, p. 100.

140 Clay to Thomas Bodley, 18 December 1813, James F. Hopkins *et al.*, eds, *The Papers of Henry Clay*, 11 vols (Lexington: University of Kentucky Press, 1959–92), I, pp. 841–2, quotation on p. 842.

141 Wellington to Liverpool, 9 November 1814, in Arthur R. Wellesley, ed., *Supplementary Despatches, Correspondence, and Memoranda of Field Marshal Arthur Duke of Wellington, K.G.*, 12 vols (London: John Murray, 1858–65), IX, pp. 424–6, quotation on p. 426.

142 Adams, *History of the United States*, pp. 1210–12.

143 *Ibid.*, pp. 1213–17. Thomas Otte argues that the importance of the Treaty of Ghent has been seriously underestimated, in that it laid the foundations for nineteenth-century Anglo-American relations, especially the habit of arbitrating disputes through joint commissions. Otte to the author, 30 September 2006.

144 Richard Rush, American minister to Great Britain from 1817 to 1825, wrote in his memoirs for 1818 that 'On the drop curtain at Covent Garden, are seen the flags of nations with whom England has been at war. They are in a tattered state, and represented as in subjection to England. That of the United States is among them . . . England has fame enough, military and of all kinds, without straining in small ways after what does not belong to her.' Rush, *Memoranda of a Residence at the Court of London* (Philadelphia, Penn.: Carey, Lea & Blanchard, 1833), p. 201.

145 Castlereagh to Liverpool, 2 January 1815, quoted in Perkins, *Castlereagh and Adams*, p. 152.

146 FO 7/148, in H.W.V. Temperley and L.M. Penson, eds, *The Foundations of British Foreign Policy 1792–1902* (London: Frank Cass, 1966), Document 6, quotations on pp. 54 and 63.

147 Quoted in Wendy Hinde, *George Canning* (London: Collins, 1973), p. 345.

148 Quoted in *ibid.*

149 The Russo-American Convention of 1824 and the Anglo-Russian Convention of 1825 both limited the Russian boundary south to the 54°40' line, thereby cancelling the ukase. H.W.V. Temperley, *Foreign Policy of Canning 1822–1827: England, the Neo-Holy Alliance, and the New World* (London: Frank Cass, 1966, 1st pub. 1925), p. 493.

150 Adams, ed., *Memoirs*, IV, p. 438 (16 November 1819).

151 Rush to Quincy Adams, 19 August 1823, No. 323, M30/25, pp. 2–3. Perkins, *Creation of a Republican Empire*, p. 162 for Stratford Canning quotation. Richard Rush, *Memoranda of a Residence at the Court of London, Comprising Incidents Official and Personal from 1819 to 1825. Including Negotiations on the Oregon Question, and Other Unsettled Questions between the United States and Great Britain* (Philadelphia, Penn.: Lea & Blanchard, 1845), p. 400.

152 Rush, *Memoranda* (1845), pp. 400–1. The despatch to Adams, dated 19 August, was less felicitously phrased. No. 323, M30/25, pp. 3–4.

153 Canning to Rush, Private and Confidential, 20 August 1823, enclosed in Rush to Adams, 23 August 1823, No. 325, M30/25.

154 Temperley, *Canning*, p. 112, quoting from Canning, *Speeches* (1836), VI, pp. 413–14.

155 Rush, *Memoranda* (1845), pp. 421–6, quotation on p. 421; Rush to Adams, 28 August 1823, No. 326, M30/25; Canning to Rush, Private and Confidential, 31 August 1823, enclosed in Rush to Adams, 8 October 1823, No. 330, M30/25.

156 Rush, *Memoranda* (1845), pp. 429–43, quotation on p. 435. The actual despatch has much more detail: Rush to Adams, 19 September 1823, No. 331, M30/25.

157 Rush to Adams, 2 October 1823, No. 334, M30/25. In a discussion with the British minister on 19 November, the Secretary of State confirmed that 'we could move in concert with Great Britain upon South American affairs only upon the basis of their acknowledged independence'. Adams, ed., *Memoirs*, VI, p. 191.

158 This apparently surprised Rush, who wrote to Adams on 10 October, 'I saw him [Canning] again at the foreign office yesterday, and he said not one single word relative to South America . . . I therefore consider that all further discussion between us in relation to it is now at an end . . . The termination of the discussion between us may be thought somewhat sudden, not to say abrupt, considering how zealously as well as spontaneously it was started on his side.' No. 336, M30/25.

159 Hinde, *Canning*, p. 351 for the quotation; Temperley, *Canning*, pp. 114–24.

160 Stanislaus Murray Hamilton, ed., *The Writings of James Monroe*, 7 vols (New York: G.P. Putnam's Sons, 1898–1903), VI, p. 324.

161 Ford, ed., *The Writings of Thomas Jefferson*, X, pp. 277–8.

162 Madison to Monroe, 30 October 1823, in Gaillard Hunt, ed., *The Writings of James Madison, Comprising His Public Papers and His Private Correspondence, Including Numerous Letters and Documents Now for the First Time Printed*, 9 vols (New York: G.P. Putnam's Sons, 1900–10), IX, pp. 157–8.

163 Perkins, *Creation of a Republican Empire*, p. 163.

164 Adams, ed., *Memoirs*, VI, pp. 177–9. The Tsar had requested that the US would continue to observe the neutrality between Spain and their former colonies announced on their recognition of the South American governments; Adams wanted the Russian minister to convey to the Tsar the desire of the US that, in return, the Tsar should continue to observe the same neutrality. *Ibid.*, p. 181. Interestingly, the British minister in Washington, Henry Addington, commented that ever since Adams had received Rush's despatches on 9 October, 'he has been singularly cheerful and complaisant, and assumed a frankness and unreservedness in deportment and conversation altogether unusual to him'. Addington to Canning, 20 November 1823, No. 20, FO 5/177.

165 Adams, ed., *Memoirs*, VI, pp. 186–8, quotation on p. 188.

166 Adams to Rush, 29 November 1923, No. 76 and Adams to Rush, 30 November 1823, No. 77, both M30/25; Rush, *Memoranda* (1845), pp. 479–80.

167 Adams wrote in his diary for 22 November 1823 that the 'ground that I wish to take is that of earnest remonstrance against the interference of the European powers by force with South America, but to disclaim all interference on our part with Europe'. Adams, ed., *Memoirs*, VI, pp. 197–8.

168 Watts and Israel, eds, *Presidential Documents*, pp. 55–6.

169 Adams, ed., *Memoirs*, VI, p. 210.

170 Russ to Adams, 6 January 1824, No. 356, M30/26. Hinde, *Canning*, pp. 353–4; Temperley, *Canning*, pp. 126–30; Rush, *Memoranda*, pp. 470–2. Christian J. Maisch, 'The Falkland/Malvinas Islands Clash of 1831–32: US and British Diplomacy in the South Atlantic', *Diplomatic History*, Vol. 24, No. 2 (Spring 2000), pp. 206–9.

171 Adams, ed., *Memoirs*, VI, p. 220; Hinde, *Canning*, p. 355 for the quotations.

172 Kenneth Bourne, *Britain and the Balance of Power in North America 1815–1908* (Berkeley: University of California Press, 1967), p. 9; C.P. Stacey, 'The Myth of the Unguarded Frontier', *American Historical Review*, Vol. 56, No. 1 (October 1950), p. 9; Perkins, *Castlereagh and Adams*, p. 240 for quotation.

173 C.K. Webster, ed., *Britain and the Independence of Latin America, 1812–1830*, 2 vols (London: Ibero-American Institute of Great Britain, 1938), I, p. 42.

174 Perkins, *Creation of a Republican Empire*, p. 208.

175 Perkins, *Castlereagh and Adams*, pp. 241–4.

176 *Ibid.*, p. 243 for quotation; Stacey, 'The Myth of the Unguarded Frontier 1815–1871', pp. 1–12. According to Stacey, the period following the Treaty of Ghent was the most active era of fort-building in Canadian history. *Ibid.*, p. 4. Richard Rush was then Secretary of State *ad interim* and Sir Charles Bagot was the British minister in Washington.

177 'In October, 1818, the astronomers carrying out the boundary survey prescribed in the Treaty of Ghent found that the line heretofore accepted as the forty-fifth parallel was some three quarters of a mile too far north, and the American forts had been built in Canada!' Stacey, 'The Myth of the Unguarded Frontier', p. 8.

178 Mowat, *Diplomatic Relations*, p. 78; Rush, *Memoranda* (1833), p. 409 for quotation; Rush to Adams, 4 February 1818, No. 6 and Rush to Adams, 14 February 1818, No. 7, both M30/18; and Rush to Adams, 25 July, No. 30, M30/19; Rush, *Memoranda* (1833), p. 345. When musing later on the negotiations, and writing of the failed proposals, Rush wrote, 'had Lord Castlereagh been in London, there would not have been a failure . . . I believe that he set a high value upon a good understanding with the United States; and that he was sincerely anxious, not in words only, but by deeds, to promote it. I never saw any little jealousy in him of their rising power and greatness, although awake to both; for he saw in Britain enough of both, to place him above little jealousies'. *Ibid.*, pp. 409–10.

179 *Ibid.*, pp. 353 and 363–4. Gallatin and Rush to Adams, 20 October 1818, M30/19.

180 Gallatin and Rush to Adams, 20 October 1818, M30/19; Frederick Merk, *The Oregon Question: Essays in Anglo-American Diplomacy and Politics* (Cambridge, Mass.: Harvard University Press, 1967), pp. 33–43; Rush, *Memoranda* (1833), p. 380.

181 David Paul Crook, *American Democracy in British Politics, 1815–1850* (Oxford: Oxford University Press, 1965), p. 203; Charles Vaughan, 'Effect or Result of War between the United States and Great Britain, July 1827', quoted in Bourne, *Balance of Power*, p. 69.

182 Perkins, *Creation of a Republican Empire*, p. 179.

183 Bourne, *Balance of Power*, p. 77.

184 R.W. Mowat, *The Diplomatic Relations of Great Britain and the United States* (London: Edward Arnold, 1925), pp. 117–20, quotation on p. 119; Bourne, *Balance of Power*, p. 75.

185 Perkins, *Creation of a Republican Empire*, pp. 180–5; Mowat, *Diplomatic Relations*, pp. 120–3; Bourne, *Balance of Power*, pp. 75–8.

186 Howard Jones, 'The *Caroline* Affair', *Historian*, Vol. 38, No. 3 (May 1976), pp. 485–502.

187 Quoted in Bourne, *Balance of Power*, pp. 79–81, quotation on p. 81.

188 *Ibid.*, pp. 75–80, quotation on p. 76.

189 Perkins, *Creation of a Republican Empire*, p. 211 for first quotation; Jones, 'The *Caroline* Affair', pp. 498–9; Bourne, *Balance of Power*, pp. 86–97, p. 86 for Palmerston quotation.

190 Edward Everett to Daniel Webster, 21 February 1842, No. 5, enclosing Everett to Aberdeen, 21 February 1842, M30/45.

191 Mowat, *Diplomatic Relations*, pp. 110–13, Jackson quotation on p. 110; Francis M. Carroll, *A Good and Wise Measure: The Search for the Canadian–American Boundary, 1783–1842* (Toronto: University of Toronto Press, 2001), pp. 245–9; Bourne, *Balance of Power*, p. 70 for Ashburton quotation; Perkins, *Creation of a Republican Empire*, p. 212; John O. Geiger, 'A Scholar Meets John Bull: Edward Everett as United States Minister to England, 1841–1845', *New England Quarterly*, Vol. 49, No. 4 (December 1976), pp. 582–6.

192 A motion of thanks had been voted to Aberdeen in Parliament, but this had been objected to by the opposition, with Palmerston, for example, referring to the treaty as the 'Ashburton Capitulation'. Everett to Buchanan, 16 April 1845, No. 302, M30/51. Merk, *The Oregon Question*, p. 193 for the quotation; Mowat, *Diplomatic Relations*, pp. 112–16, p. 115 for the quotation below. For the obsession of the American minister to London about the map, see George J. Gill, 'Edward Everett and the North-eastern Boundary Controversy', *New England Quarterly*, Vol. 42, No. 2 (June 1969), pp. 201–13. Events conspired to produce a situation which encouraged this: Jared Sparks, a historian working in Paris on his history of the American Revolution, discovered a map and letter by Benjamin Franklin which supported the British claims, which Webster showed with effect to the Governor of Maine, although not to the British; the director of the British Museum discovered in London a map which supported

the American claims, which Palmerston hid in the Foreign Office secret files and, since Aberdeen did not know about it, nor did Ashburton ('his [Aberdeen's] conscience, which was of the kind that always made him take the most unprofitable course, would have compelled him to send the . . . map to Washington'). Mount, *Diplomatic Relations*, p. 114.

193 Wilbur Devereux Jones, *The American Problem in British Diplomacy, 1841–1861* (London: Macmillan, 1974), pp. 38–46.

194 This occasioned 'excitement' in London, but was soon replaced by Irish problems. Everett to Buchanan, 3 March 1845, M30/51.

195 The 54 degrees, 40 minutes parallel had been fixed in the Convention of 1824 as the line dividing the claims of the US from those of Russia, which owned Alaska.

196 McLane to Buchanan, 3 February 1846, No. 34, M30/52.

197 McLane to Buchanan, 3 March 1846, No. 35, M30/52.

198 M.M. Quaife, ed., *The Diary of James K. Polk during His Presidency, 1845–1849, Now First Printed from the Original Manuscript in the Collections of the Chicago Historical Society*, 4 vols (Chicago: A.C. McClurg, 1910), I, p. 241.

199 Bourne, *Balance of Power*, pp. 147–61; John Seigenthaler, *James K. Polk* (New York: Henry Holt, 2003), pp. 122–8.

200 McLane to Buchanan, 18 May 1846, No. 44, and McLane to Buchanan, 3 July 1846, No. 58, both M30/52.

201 Merk, *The Oregon Question*, pp. 408–13.

202 Kinley J. Brauer, 'The United States and British Imperial Expansion, 1815–60', *Diplomatic History*, Vol. 12, No. 1 (Winter 1988), pp. 31–2.

203 Quoted in Perkins, *Creation of a Republican Empire*, p. 218.

204 Quoted in *ibid.*, p. 219; R.J.M. Blackett, *Divided Hearts: Britain and the American Civil War* (Baton Rouge: Louisiana State University Press, 2001), p. 4. See also Blackett, 'British Views of the Confederacy', Joseph P. Ward, ed., *Britain and the American South: From Colonialism to Rock and Roll* (Jackson: University Press of Mississippi, 2003), pp. 141–61.

205 Henry Adams, *The Education of Henry Adams* (Oxford: Oxford University Press, 1999, 1st pub. 1918), p. 100. John Stuart Mill, *Autobiography* (London: Longmans, Green, Reader, and Dyer, 1873), pp. 268–9.

206 Adams, *The Education of Henry Adams*, p. 106.

207 Quoted in Perkins, *Creation of an American Empire*, p. 221.

208 Mill, *Autobiography*, p. 270.

209 Lord Stanley to Lady Stanley, 6 December 1861, in Nancy Mitford, ed., *The Stanleys of Alderley: Their Letters between the Years 1851–1865* (London: Hamish Hamilton, 1968), p. 272. Bourne, *Balance of Power*, pp. 219–28.

210 Adams to Seward, 12 December 1861, No. 88; 3 December 1861, No. 82; and 6 December 1861, No. 84, all M30/74. Bourne, *Balance of Power*, p. 245 for American insanity, and p. 251 for final quotation.

211 Palmerston wrote to the Queen on 5 December 1861, 'If the Federal Government comply with the demands it will be honourable for England and humiliating for the United States. If the Federal Government refuse compliance, Great Britain is in a better state to inflict a severe blow and to read a lesson to the United States which will not soon be forgotten.' Quoted in James Chambers, *Palmerston: 'The People's Darling'* (London: John Murray, 2005 pb. edn), p. 487.

212 Perkins, *Creation of a Republican Empire*, pp. 225–6; Mowat, *Diplomatic Relations*, pp. 179–81 for Lyons and Seward working together; Bourne, *Balance of Power*, p. 219 for torrent quotation; Adams to Seward, 10 January 1862, No. 99, M30/74.

213 Quoted in Mowat, *Diplomatic Relations*, p. 184.

214 Perkins, *Creation of a Republican Empire*, pp. 226–7; Adams to Seward, 10 October 1862, No. 237 and Adams to Seward, 17 October 1862, No. 243, both M30/76.

215 Martin B. Duberman, *Charles Francis Adams 1807–1886* (Boston, Mass.: Houghton Mifflin, 1961), pp. 293–4. James D. Bulloch, *The Secret Service of the Confederate States in Europe or, How the Confederate Cruisers Were Equipped*(New York: Random House, 2001, 1st pub. 1884), pp. 162–89, quotation on p. 168.

216 Mowat, *Diplomatic Relations*, pp. 186–9; Chambers, *Palmerston*, pp. 490–2, quotation on p. 491.

217 Mowat, *Diplomatic Relations*, p. 206.

218 *Ibid.*, p. 209.

219 Lord Tenterden, 'Relations with the United States', 21 November 1870, FO 5/1331, p. 2. According to Tenterden, such a plan had already been contemplated, but nothing had yet come of it.

220 John Morley, *The Life of William Ewart Gladstone*, 3 vols (London: Macmillan, 1903), I, p. 401. Gladstone took an increasingly active part in the negotiations. Fish, as well as his mentors, John Quincy Adams and Seward, assumed that in due course Canada, Mexico, Cuba and perhaps others would voluntarily fall into America's lap. Walter LaFeber, *The Cambridge History of American Foreign Relations, Volume II: The American Search for Opportunity, 1865–1913* (Cambridge: Cambridge University Press, 1993), p. 61.

221 Mowat, *Diplomatic Relations*, pp. 216–20, quotation on p. 220.

222 Clarendon to Victoria, 1 May 1869, in G.E. Buckle, ed., *The Letters of Queen Victoria*, 2nd Series, 3 vols (London: John Murray, 1926), I, pp. 594–5. Thanks to Thomas Otte for the reference.

Chapter 4– Nineteenth-Century Travellers' Tales

1. *Society in America*, 2 vols (New York: Saunders and Otley, 1837 4th edn), I, p. 156.

2. Alexander Mackay, *The Western World; or, Travels in the United States in 1846–47: Exhibiting Them in Their Latest Development, Social, Political, and Industrial; Including a Chapter on California*, 3 vols (London: Richard Bentley, 1849), I, p. 18.

3. The name given on the title page is not Thomas Hamilton, but By the author of Cyril Thornton (Philadelphia, Penn.: Carey, Lea & Blanchard, 1833), p. 123. 'Brother Jonathan' was the generic term for Americans; it was eventually supplanted by 'Uncle Sam'.

4. (Boston: Houghton Mifflin, 1907, 1st pub. 1863), pp. xi–xii.

5. According to C. Vann Woodward, more than two hundred books by British visitors to America were published between 1835 and 1860. Woodward, *The Old World's New World* (New York: Oxford University Press, 1991), p. xvi.

6 J. Hector St John Crèvecoeur, *Letters from an American Farmer*, ed. Susan Manning (Oxford: Oxford University Press, 1997 pb.), pp. 43–4.

7 For a particularly acute, and funny, assessment of the whole phenomenon, see the novel by Laurence Sterne, *A Sentimental Journey* (Harmondsworth: Penguin, 2001, 1st pub. 1768).

8 Paul Langford, 'Manners and Character in Anglo-American Perceptions, 1750–1850', in Fred M. Leventhal and Roland Quinault, eds, *Anglo-American Attitudes: From Revolution to Partnership* (Aldershot: Ashgate, 2000), pp. 76–90.

9 Alexis de Tocqueville, *Democracy in America*, ed. and trans. Harvey C. Mansfield and Delba Winthrop (Chicago: University of Chicago Press, 2000, 1st pub. as *De la Démocratie en Amérique*, Vol. I 1835, Vol. II 1840), 'Introduction', p. 3.

10 *Ibid.*, p. 12.

11 *Ibid.*, I, part 1, ch. 3, p. 46.

12 From his diary, 'First Impressions', quoted in George Wilson Pierson, *Tocqueville in America* (Baltimore, Md.: Johns Hopkins University Press, 1996, 1st pub. 1938), pp. 69–70.

13 De Tocqueville, *Democracy in America*, II, part 2, ch. 4, p. 488.

14 Quoted in Patrice Higonnet, 'Alexis de Tocqueville 1805–1859', in Marc Pachter and

Frances Wein, eds, *Abroad in America: Visitors to the New Nation 1776–1914* (Reading, Mass.: Addison-Wesley for the National Portrait Gallery, 1976), p. 59.

15 Letter from de Tocqueville to his brother, quoted in Pierson, *Tocqueville in America*, p. 125.

16 De Tocqueville, *Democracy in America*, I, part 2, ch. 9, p. 282.

17 *Ibid.*, II, part 2, ch. 5, p. 489.

18 *Ibid.*, I, part 2, ch. 7, p. 236.

19 *Ibid.*, pp. 244 and 243.

20 *Ibid.*, II, part 3, ch. 16, p. 585.

21 Basil Hall, 'Tocqueville on the State of America', *Quarterly Review*, Vol. 57 (1836), pp. 132–62, quoted in Christopher Mulvey, *Anglo-American Landscapes: A Study of Nineteenth-Century Anglo-American Travel Literature* (Cambridge: Cambridge University Press, 1983), p. 234.

22 One example is Anthony Trollope, in his *North America*, 2 vols (London: Chapman & Hall, 1862), p. 3.

23 Hamilton, *Men and Manners*, p. iv. A century and a quarter later, the American humourist James Thurber found Hamilton's book deeply irritating. 'A Holiday Ramble', in James Thurber, *Alarms and Diversions* (New York: Harper and Brothers, 1957), pp. 45–7.

24 See David Paul Crook, *American Democracy in English Politics, 1815–1850* (Oxford: Oxford University Press, 1965), *passim*.

25 John Graham Brooks, *As Others See Us: A Study of Progress in the United States* (New York: Macmillan, 1908), p. 104.

26 (Edinburgh: Robert Cadell, 1830 3rd edn).

27 Mulvey, *Anglo-American Landscapes*, p. 149.

28 This was a contrast commented upon by many travellers. One example was Mackay in *The Western World*, I, p. 18.

29 Hall, *Travels in North America*, II, pp. 178, 282–3, 301.

30 *Ibid.*, pp. 306–7.

31 *Ibid.*, p. 203. Actually, it was only thirty-five years.

32 Chauncey A. Goodrich, 'Memoir of the Author', in Noah Webster, *An American Dictionary of the English Language* (Springfield, Mass.: George and Charles Merriam, 1851 rev. edn, 1st pub. 1828), p. xvii.

33 Hall, *Travels in North America*, II, pp. 203–4.

34 Hall, *Travels in North America*, III, p. 40.

35 *Ibid.*, p. 146.

36 *Ibid.*, pp. 204–7.

37 *Ibid.*, p. 209.

38 *Ibid.*, pp. 209–10.

39 *Ibid.*, pp. 210–11.

40 Frances Trollope, *Domestic Manners of the Americans* (London: Richard Bentley, 1839 5th edn, first pub. 1832), p. 295.

41 Auguste Hervieu, a French exile who taught drawing to her children and would later illustrate her books.

42 Pamela Neville-Sington, *Fanny Trolope: The Life and Adventures of a Clever Woman* (New York: Viking Penguin, 1997), p. 113.

43 '[I]t is impossible to imagine anything more striking than her appearance. Her tall and majestic figure, the deep and almost solemn expression of her eyes, the simple contour of her finely formed head, unadorned, excepting by its own natural ringlets; her garment of plain white muslin, which hung around her in folds that recalled the drapery of a Grecian statue, all contributed to produce an effect unlike anything I had ever seen before, or ever expect to see again.' Trollope, *Domestic Manners of the Americans*, p. 54.

44 *Ibid.*, pp. 107–15.

45 Neville-Sington, *Fanny Trolope*, pp. 121–2.

46 Trollope, *Domestic Manners of the Americans*, Preface to the 4th edn, n.p.

47 *Ibid.*, pp. 157, 117, 166, 194, 12, 14.

48 *Ibid.*, pp. 77–9.

49 *Ibid.*, p. 94.

50 *Ibid.*, p. 61.

51 *Ibid.*, p. 84.

52 *Ibid.*, p. 336.

53 Fanny Trollope, *Domestic Manners of the Americans*, ed. Pamela Neville-Sington (Harmondsworth: Penguin, 1997), p. vii.

54 Martineau, *Society in America*, I, p. 4.

55 Her return fare was paid by an anonymous American supporter.

56 Martineau, *Society in America*, II, p. 271.

57 Marghanita Laski, 'Harriet Martineau 1802–1877', in Pachter and Wein, eds, *Abroad in America*, p. 65.

58 Martineau, *Society in America*, II, p. 168.

59 *Ibid.*, I, p. 394.

60 Hamilton, *Men and Manners in America*, p. 317.

61 Charles Dickens, *The Life and Adventures of Martin Chuzzlewit and American Notes*, 2 vols (Boston, Mass.: Houghton Mifflin, 1894), II [*American Notes*], p. 579.

62 Christopher Mulvey, *Transatlantic Manners: Social Patterns in Nineteenth-Century Anglo-American Travel Literature* (Cambridge: Cambridge University Press, 1990), p. 78.

63 Neville-Sington, *Fanny Trolope*, p. 243.

64 Trollope, *Domestic Manners of the Americans*, pp. 195, 200.

65 Neville-Sington, *Fanny Trolope*, p. 240.

66 'Demerara', in *Ilustrations of Political Economy*, I; Deborah A. Logan, 'The Redemption of a Heretic: Harriet Martineau and Anglo-American Abolitionism in Pre-Civil War America', paper given in October 2001 at the Third Annual Gilder Center International Conference, Yale University, p. 2.

67 Maria Weston Chapman, ed., *Harriet Martineau's Autobiography*, 2 vols (Boston, Mass.: James R. Osgood, 1877), I, p. 352.

68 Martineau, *Society in America*, I, pp. 20–1.

69 *Ibid.*, II, pp. 226–7.

70 *Ibid.*, I, pp. ii–iii.

71 See, for example, the review in the *North American Review*, Vol. 45, issue 97 (October 1837), pp. 418–60.

72 Quoted in Laski, 'Harriet Martineau', p. 71.

73 All three quotations taken from Philip Collins, 'Charles Dickens 1812–1870', in Pachter and Wein, eds, *Abroad in America*, p. 84.

74 Dickens to John Forster, 13 September 1841, in Benjamin Lease, *Anglo-American Encounters: England and the Rise of American Literature* (Cambridge: Cambridge University Press, 1981), p. 88.

75 James J. Barnes, *Authors, Publishers and Politicians: The Quest for an Anglo-American Copyright Agreement 1815–1854* (London: Routledge & Kegan Paul, 1974), pp. 75–7.

76 Quoted in Malcolm Bradbury, *Dangerous Pilgrimages: Trans-Atlantic Mythologies and the Novel* (London: Penguin, 1996, 1st pub. 1995), p. 99.

77 Edwin Percy Whipple, 'Introduction', in Dickens, *Martin Chuzzlewit and American Notes*, I [*Martin Chuzzlewit*], p. xlvi.

78 2 vols (Boston: Houghton Mifflin, 1894).

79 Bradbury, *Dangerous Pilgrimages*, p. 102.

80 Dickens, *Martin Chuzzlewit and American Notes*, I [*Martin Chuzzlewit*], pp. 463–4.

81 *Ibid.*, II [*American Notes*], p. 598.

82 W.E. Adams, *Our American Cousins: Being Personal Impressions of the People and Institutions of the United States* (London: Walter Scott, 1883), p. 1.

83 Collins, 'Charles Dickens', p. 91.

84 2 vols (London: Macmillan, 1888), I, p. 3. According to Greg Kennedy, for the following half-century, all British diplomats sent to the US read *The American Commonwealth*.

85 Edmund Ions, 'James Bryce 1838–1922', in Pachter and Wein, eds, *Abroad in America*, p. 209.

86 *Ibid.*, p. 211. For the rise, methods and downfall of the notorious Tweed Ring of New York, see Bryce, *The American Commonwealth*, II, ch. 88.

87 *Ibid.*, p. 671.

88 *Ibid.*, I, p. 2.

89 *Ibid.*, II, pp. 322–3.

90 *Ibid.*, p. 677.

91 *Ibid.*, I, p. 608.

92 *Ibid.*, p. 2.

93 William Austin, *Letters from London: Written during the Years 1802 & 1803* (Boston, Mass.: W. Pelham, 1804), p. 39.

94 Matthew Arnold, *Civilization in the United States: First and Last Impressions of America* (Boston, Mass.: Cupples and Hurd, 1888), p. 190.

95 *Ibid.*, pp. 177–8. Great Britain had to wait another generation for a truly popular press.

96 See Chapter 7.

97 Brooks, *As Others See Us*, p. 132.

98 Anthony Trollope, *North America*, II, p. 462; Adams, *Our American Cousins*, p. iv; Arnold, *Civilization in the United States*, p. 71.

99 W.T. Stead, *The Americanisation of the World, On the Trend of the Twentieth Century: The Review of Reviews Annual*, 1902, p. 14.

100 Bradford Perkins, *The Great Rapprochement: England and the United States 1895–1914* (London: Gollancz, 1969).

101 The gardener was Frederick Lewis Olmstead, who was later to design Central Park in New York City. Olmstead, *Walks and Talks of an American Farmer in England* (New York: Putnam, 1852). Another genre was books of letters by ladies; one such lady was Elizabeth Davis Bancroft, wife of George Bancroft, the historian and US minister to Great Britain 1846–9, who published *Letters from England 1846–1849* (London: Smith, Elder, 1904), a book of notable tedium.

102 Washington Irving, *The Sketch Book of Geoffrey Crayon, Gent.*, 2 vols (London: John Murray, 1821 new edn).

103 *Ibid.*, II, p. 122.

104 *Ibid.*, p. 121.

105 Mulvey, *Anglo-American Landscapes*, pp. 75, 78–9.

106 Ralph Waldo Emerson, *English Traits* (Boston, Mass.: Phillips, Sampson, 1856), pp. 256 and 42.

107 Emerson, 'The American Scholar', in *Selected Essays*, ed. Lazar Ziff (Harmondsworth: Penguin, 1985), p. 104.

108 De Tocqueville, *Democracy in America*, I, part 2, ch. 5, p. 244.

109 Stead, *The Americanisation of the World*, p. 106. Stead wrote that Emerson's essays 'are probably read to-day [1902] in England more than those of any other English writer'. Emerson, *English Traits*, pp. 41–2.

110 *Ibid.*, pp. 179, 111, 119, 121, 143, 160, 165.

111 *Ibid.*, pp. 274–5.

112 Hawthorne, *Our Old Home*, p. 22.

113 *Ibid.*, p. 59.

114 *Ibid.*, pp. 440–59.

115 Lease, *Anglo-American Encounters*, pp. 115–16.

116 Mark Twain, *A Yankee at the Court of King Arthur* (London: Chatto & Windus, 1890), pp. 76–7.

117 Lease, *Anglo-American Encounters*, pp. 255–7, quotations on pp. 256 and 257.

118 His philosopher brother, William James, was the author of *Pragmatism.*

119 Henry James, *Hawthorne* (London: Macmillan, 1879), p. 43.

120 See, for example, *The Ambassadors* (1903), *The American* (1877), *Portrait of a Lady* (1881), and, in summation, *The Wings of the Dove* (1902), which exemplify these themes.

121 (New York: Weidenfeld & Nicolson, 1989).

122 Quoted in Mulvey, *Anglo-American Landscapes*, pp. 109–10.

123 Harriet Beecher Stowe, *Sunny Memories of Foreign Lands*, 2 vols (Boston, Mass.: Phillips, Sampson, 1854), I, pp. 14, 18. Phillips, Sampson also published Emerson's *English Traits* two years later.

124 Emerson, *English Traits*, p. 42.

Chapter 5– Some Elements of Everyday Life in the Nineteenth and Twentieth Centuries

1. 'The State of the Money Market', p. 605.

2. Sidney Smith, Review of Adam Seybert, *Statistical Annals of the United States of America, Edinburgh Review*, Vol. 33 (January 1820), p. 79.

3. Michael Bywater, *Lost Worlds: What Have We Lost, & Where Did It Go?* (London: Granta, 2004), p. 31.

4. Such conflict was a subject of the Rodgers and Hammerstein musical *Oklahoma!*

5. Stead, *The Americanisation of the World*, p. 107.

6. Probably his longest-lasting poem, however, was the Civil War-based 'Barbara Frietchie', written in 1864 about her bravely hanging the American flag out of her window in Frederick, Maryland, while southern soldiers marched by, which Winston Churchill frequently recited to any Americans he met. Thanks to Adam Smith. Every American schoolchild formerly could recite: '"Shoot if you must this old gray head, but spare your country's flag," she said.' Then the rebel military leader, Stonewall Jackson, his 'nobler nature' stirred, responds, '"Who touches a hair of yon gray head dies like a dog! March on!" he said.'

7. 27 per cent went to the rest of Europe and 27 per cent to the Americas, including Canada. *Historical Statistics of the United States*, pp. 551–2.

8. Over the period from 1854 (when the index begins) to 1900 raw cotton, wheat and tobacco made up a substantial proportion of American exports to Britain, rising from 65 per cent in 1854 to 80 per cent in 1860, and although this group of exports fell to 39 per cent in 1880, in 1900 it still made up a third. American exports to Great Britain 1860s–1890s averaged 53 per cent of the country's total exports. Raw cotton exports made up 58 per cent of American exports to Great Britain in 1854, 67 per cent in 1860, 63 per cent in 1870, plummeting to 19 per cent in 1880, then rising to 32 per cent in 1890, down to 22 per cent in 1900 and back to 42 per cent in 1910. *Ibid.*, pp. 555–6.

9 *Ibid.*, pp. 551–2, 555–6, 552–3.

10 Hansard, *Parliamentary Debates*, 1st Series, Vol. 33, 9 April 1816, p. 1099.

11 B.R. Mitchell and Phyllis Deane, *Abstract of British Historical Statistics* (Cambridge: Cambridge University Press, 1962), Table XII, pp. 313–27. From 1854, re-exports were distinguished from exports; for the purposes of this paragraph, they have been added together.

12 The absolute numbers for Great Britain were 2,410 in 1820 and 1,153 in 1830, while for Ireland they were from 3,614 to 2,721. German immigrants doubled in number, from 968 to 1,976. 'Other North-western countries', comprising Benelux, France and Switzerland, went from 452 to 1,305. The total numbers of immigrants were 8,385 in 1820 and 23,322 in 1830. *Historical Statistics of the United States*, p. 57.

13 In the tables 'Ireland' includes both the North and the South. In 1900 the largest percentages were Italy at 22 per cent and Poland at 26 per cent. All of the figures come from *ibid.*, pp. 56–7.

14 Charles R. Ritcheson, 'The British Role in American Life, 1800–1850', *History Teacher*, Vol. 7, No. 4 (August 1974), p. 587; Charlotte Erickson, *Invisible Immigrants: The Adaptation of English and Scottish Immigrants in Nineteenth-Century America* (Leicester: Leicester University Press, 1972), *passim*.

15 Frank Thistlethwaite, *The Anglo-American Connection in the Early Nineteenth Century* (Philadelphia: University of Pennsylvania Press, 1959), pp. 29–3 1, quotations on pp. 30, 31; Erickson, *Invisible Immigrants*, pp. 229–388.

16 Presidents James Monroe and Andrew Jackson both vetoed Bills providing for Federal support for such schemes.

17 W.H.B. Court, *A Concise Economic History of Britain: From 1750 to Recent Times* (Cambridge: Cambridge University Press, 1962), pp. 7 1–2; <www.cottontimes.co.uk/bridgewatero.htm>.

18 There had been earlier attempts, particularly by the James River Company in the late eighteenth century, which had been a partnership between public and private capital.

19 Leland H. Jenks, *The Migration of British Capital to 1875* (London: Thomas Nelson and Sons, 1963, 1st pub. 1927), pp. 78–85; quotation on p. 80, figures on p. 85.

20 This outflow normally occurred when people holding pounds wanted to trade them for gold at the bank; this usually took place during periods of economic downturn.

21 These were the so-called 'three Ws' – Wiggins & Co., Wilkes and Co., and Wilson & Co.

22 Jenks, *Migration of British Capital*, pp. 86–8.

23 *Ibid.*, pp. 95–9, quotation on p. 99.

24 Sydney Smith, *Humble Petition to the House of Congress in Washington*, pp. 98–9, quoted in H.C. Allen, *The Anglo-American Relationship since 1783* (London: Adam and Charles Black, 1959), p. 93.

25 R.G. McGrane, *Foreign Bondholders and American State Debts* (London: Macmillan, 1935), p. 59. Smith's reaction differs little from that of Dr Johnson, as described in Chapter 2.

26 Jenks, *Migration of British Capital*, p. 106.

27 Kathleen Burk, *Morgan Grenfel 1838–1988: The Biography of a Merchant Bank* (Oxford: Oxford University Press, 1989), pp. 11–12. Peabody had suffered personally from the reaction to the states' repudiations of their debts. In spite of his high standing – he was referred to by the London *Times* as 'an American gentleman of the most unblemished character' – he was refused admission to the Reform Club because he was a citizen of a country that did not pay its debts. Ralph W. Hidy, *The House of Baring in American Trade and Finance: English Merchant Bankers at Work 1763–1861* (New York: Russell & Russell, 1970), p. 309 for the quotation; Muriel Emmie Hidy, *George Peabody Merchant and Financier 1829–1854* (New York: Arno Press, 1978), p. 301 for the Reform Club.

28 Burk, *Morgan Grenfel*, p. 12. 'The revolutions in 1848 . . . led to a boom in US Treasury bonds in Europe in the late 1840s and early 1850s – bonds that were used to pay for the Mexican War.' Jay Sexton, *Debtor Diplomacy: Finance and American Foreign Relations in the Civil War Era 1837–1873* (Oxford: Oxford University Press, 2005), p. 245.

29 Stuart Bruchey, *Enterprise: The Dynamic Economy of a Free People* (Cambridge, Mass.: Harvard University Press, 1990), p. 201.

30 Douglass C. North, 'International Capital Flows and the Development of the American West', *Journal of Economic History*, Vol. 16, No. 4 (December 1956), p. 504.

31 Sexton, *Debtor Diplomacy*, p. 60; for investment numbers, see Dorothy R. Adler, *British Investment in American Railways: 1834–1898* (Charlottesville: University Press of Virginia, 1970), p. 22.

32 Mira Wilkins, 'Foreign Investment in the US Economy before 1914', *Annals of the American Academy of Political and Social Science*, Vol. 516 (July 1991), p. 14.

33 Sexton, *Debtor Diplomacy*, p. 234. Adams, Jr. was the son of the former American minister to Great Britain and thereby well known in London.

34 Adler, *British Investment in American Railways*, p. 119, although she throws some doubt on the claim; *Bankers' Magazine*, Vol. 29 (November 1869), p. 1120, quoted in Sexton, *Debtor Diplomacy*, p. 235.

35 *Ibid.*, p. 239 for the Panic of 1873; Wilkins, 'Foreign Investment in the US', p. 14 for quotation of securities. There is a distinction, in that British investors bought fixed-interest bonds, while American investors held the controlling stock.

36 Edward P. Crapol, *America for Americans: Economic Nationalism and Anglophobia in the Late Nineteenth Century* (Westport, Conn.: Greenwood Press, 1973), p. 107.

37 Walter LaFeber, *The American Search for Opportunity, 1865–1913* (Cambridge: Cambridge University Press, 1993), p. 28.

38 Crapol, *America for Americans*, pp. 101–2. The 1883 *Annual Report* of the Secretary of the Interior stated that there were 570,000 tenant farmers, the largest number in the world. Roger V. Clements, 'British Investment and American Legislative Restrictions in the Trans-Mississippi West, 1880–1900', *The Mississippi Valley History Review*, vol. 42, no. 2 (September 1955), p. 213. Presumably the discrepancy arises from the respective use of farms and farmers.

39 *Ibid.*, pp. 99–100. James D. Richardson, *Messages and Papers of the Presidents, 1789–1897* (Washington, D.C.: Government Printing Office, 1898), VIII, p. 309.

40 *House Reports*, No. 2308, 48th Congress, 2nd Session, 1–4, in Clements, 'Legislative Restrictions', pp. 216–17.

41 *Ibid.*, pp. 207–11.

42 *Ibid.*, p. 213; newspaper quotation from *Western Herald*, 26 March 1892.

43 'Report on Land Titles to Aliens in the United States', *House Reports*, No. 2308, 48th Congress, 2nd Session, 1–4, in Clements, 'Legislative Restrictions', pp. 216–17.

44 *Ibid.*, pp. 219–27.

45 'The Most Important Circumstances Which Affect the Present Value of the Funds', 27 October 1860, p. 1174. The missing phrase, however, is 'though not perhaps in reality', *The Economist* arguing that supply of and demand for the stock for the day is probably more important. However, it also admits the overwhelming importance of public perception.

46 Ritcheson, 'The British Role in American Life', p. 588.

47 Gordon S. Wood, 'American Religion: The Great Retreat', *New York Review of Books*, Vol. 53, No. 10 (8 June 2006), pp. 61–3, quotation on p. 63.

48 Probably the most famous sermon from this period, which sets out the core of the argument, is Jonathan Edwards' 'Sinners in the Hand of an Angry God', given on 8 July 1741 at Enfield, Connecticut, during 'the most intense phase of the Great Awakening'. David A. Hollinger and Charles Capper, eds, *The American Intellectual Tradition, Volume I: 1630–1865* (Oxford: Oxford University Press, 2006 5th edn), p. 65 for the quotation, pp. 67–76 for the sermon.

49 See, for example, Charles Grandison Finney, *Lectures on Revivals of Religion* (1835), 'The agency is the sinner himself. The conversion of a sinner consists in his obeying the truth. It is therefore impossible it should take place without his agency, for it consists in *his* acting right.' Hollinger and Capper, *The American Intellectual Tradition*, I, pp. 236–46, quotation on pp. 240–1.

50 *Ibid.*, quotations on pp. 235, 236.

51 See Chapter 4 for Mrs Trollope's horrified reaction to a camp meeting.

52 *Notions of the Americans: Picked up by a Travelling Bachelor*, 2 vols (Philadelphia, Penn.: Carey, Lea & Carey, 1833), II, p. 239. According to Edward Gibbon Wakefield, an Englishman writ-

ing on both the US and Great Britain, 'To overrate the crazy doings of a camp-meeting in the back woods would be impossible. Bodies writhing, arms swinging, legs dancing, eyes rolling; groans, shouts, howls, and shrieks; men knocking their own heads against trees, and women tearing the clothes off each other's backs; the congregation frantic with fear of the devil, and the preacher drunk with his own gibberish; it is all true, and of common occurrence.' Wakefield, *England and America: A Comparison of the Social and Political State of Both Nations* (New York: Augustus M. Kelley, 1967, 1st pub. 1834), p. 190.

53 Richard Carwardine, *Transatlantic Revivalism: Popular Evangelicalism in Britain and America, 1790–1865* (Westport, Conn.: Greenwood Press, 1978), pp. 28–171; Wood, 'American Religion: The Great Retreat', p. 63.

54 Daniel Walker Howe, 'Victorian Culture in America', in Daniel Walker Howe, ed., *Victorian America* (Philadelphia: University of Pennsylvania Press, 1976), pp. 4–5.

55 Emerson, *English Traits*, p. 227.

56 Ritcheson, 'The British Role in American Life', p. 590.

57 Herbert Schlossber, 'The Tractarian Movement', at <www.victorianweb.org/ religion/ herb7.html>.

58 Owen Chadwick, *The Victorian Church, Part One: 1829–1859* (London: SCM Press, 1971 pb. 3rd edn), pp. 64–9, quotation on p. 65.

59 Glenn Everett and George P. Landow, 'High Church: Tractarianism', at <www.victorian web/org/religion/tractarian.html>.

60 Chadwick, *The Victorian Church*, pp. 210–11.

61 *Tom Brown's School Days*, By an Old Boy (London: Macmillan, 1979, 1st pub. 1889), pp. 114–15, from Part I, ch. 7.

62 Larry Crockett, 'The Oxford Movement and the 19th-Century Episcopal Church: Anglo-Catholic Ecclesiology and the American Experience', *Quodlibet Online Journal of Christian Theology and Philosophy*, Vol. 1, No. 5 (August 1999), pp. 23, 8.

63 Ritcheson, 'The British Role in American Life', pp. 590–3; Charles Roll, 'The Quaker in Anglo-American Cultural Relations', *Indiana Magazine of History*, Vol. 45 (1949), pp. 137–8.

64 Chapman, ed., *Harriet Martineau's Autobiography*, I, p. 352. Chapman, a Boston abolitionist, was referred to as 'Garrison's lieutenant', William Lloyd Garrison being a charismatic, fanatical abolitionist leader.

65 Kenneth O. Morgan, 'The Future at Work: Anglo-American Progressivism 1890–1917', in H.C. Allen and Roger Thomson, eds, *Contrast and Connection: Bicentennial Essays in Anglo-American History* (London: G. Bell & Sons, 1976), p. 247.

66 Thistlethwaite, *The Anglo-American Connection*, pp. 103–6, quotation on p. 106.

67 *Ibid.*, pp. 106–7, quotations on p. 107.

68 Raymond English, 'George Thompson and the Climax of Philanthropic Radicalism, 1830–1842', unpublished dissertation, Kenyon College, Ohio, n.d., p. 409, quoted in *ibid.*, p. 107.

69 Christine Bolt, *The Anti-Slavery Movement and Reconstruction: A Study in Anglo-American Co-operation 1833–77* (London: Oxford University Press, 1969), p. 25.

70 William Lloyd Garrison, 'The American Colonization Society is the Enemy of Immediate Abolition', Section V of *Thoughts on African Colonization*, in Hollinger and Capper, eds, *The American Intellectual Tradition*, I, pp. 257–60. Many members believed that freed slaves would always be impoverished and unequal if they remained in the US. Thanks to Adam Smith.

71 <http://www.pbs.org/wgbh/aia/part4/4p1561.html>. Garrison's anti-slavery convictions did not extend as far as total equality for blacks: he shut down the *Liberator* upon the passage of the Thirteenth Amendment in 1865 rather than fight for their full civil rights.

72 Many of the black members celebrated 1 August, the date of British emancipation, rather than 4 July. Thanks to Adam Smith. See Frederick Douglass, 'What to the Slave is the Fourth of July?' (1852), for his comparison of the attitudes towards the anti-slavery

movement of the churches in England and the US, to the detriment of the latter. Hollinger and Capper, eds, *The American Intellectual Tradition*, I, p. 503.

73 Bolt, *The Anti-Slavery Movement*, p. 23.

74 Thistlethwaite, *The Anglo-American Connection*, p. 109.

75 Bolt, *The Anti-Slavery Movement*, pp. 23–4; Thistlethwaite, *The Anglo-American Connection*, p. 110 for the quotations.

76 <http://www.spartacus.schoolnet.co.uk/USAantislavery.htm>.

77 Annie Heloise Abel and Frank J. Klingberg, eds, *A Sidelight on Anglo-American Relations 1839–1858: Furnished by the Correspondence of Lewis Tappan and Others with the British and Foreign Anti-Slavery Society* (New York: Augustus M. Kelley, 1970, 1st pub. 1927).

78 Thistlethwaite, *The Anglo-American Connection*, pp. 126–7, quotation on p. 127.

79 *Ibid.*, pp. 113–16, 126–7, quotations on pp. 115 and 116.

80 Bolt, *The Anti-Slavery Movement*, p. 21.

81 Howard Jones and Donald A. Rakestraw, *Prologue to Manifest Destiny: Anglo-American Relations in the 1840s* (Wilmington, Del.: Scholarly Resources, 1997), pp. 71–3. Rush, *Memoranda* (1845), pp. 475–501.

82 Adams, ed., *Memoirs*, VI, p. 328, 12 May 1824.

83 Jones and Rakestraw, *Prologue to Manifest Destiny*, p. 74.

84 Adams, ed., *Memoirs*, VI, p. 37, 29 June 1822.

85 Allen, *The Anglo-American Relationship since 1783*, p. 123. In the USA the first year's sale was 150,000. *Ibid.*

86 Stead, *The Americanisation of the World*, p. 107.

87 Daniel T. Rodgers, *Atlantic Crossings: Social Politics in a Progressive Age* (Cambridge, Mass.: Harvard University Press, 1998), pp. 52, 127–8, quotation on p. 52.

88 *Ibid.*, p. 63.

89 The founding group were Christians who supported Chartism. This was a working-class movement demanding political equality; its demands, embodied in a Bill or 'charter' for parliamentary approval, were for manhood suffrage, equal electoral districts, voting by ballot, annual Parliaments, abolition of property qualifications for MPs and payment for MPs. The group met on 10 April 1848 as a result of the decision of the House of Commons to reject the third, 5,706,000-signature, Chartist Petition.

90 In *Tom Brown at Oxford* (New York: John W. Lovell Company, n.d., but pub. in England in 1861), pp. 129–30, Hughes wrote that, in comparison with men who were merely muscular, 'the least of the muscular Christians has hold of the old chivalrous and Christian belief, that a man's body is given him to be trained and brought into subjection, and then used for the protection of the weak, the advancement of all righteous causes, and the subduing of the earth which God has given to the children of men'. George P. Landow states that 'the muscular Christian is merely the latest Victorian embodiment of the ideal knight or the true gentleman. And this simultaneous delight in the physical and the need to spiritualize it is also particularly Victorian.' '*Tom Brown at Oxford* on Muscular Christianity', <www.victorianweb.org/authors/hughes/muscular.html>.

91 Melvyn Stokes, 'American Progressives and the European Left', *Journal of American Studies*, Vol. 17, No. 1 (1983), p. 14.

92 Paul A. Kramer, 'Empires, Exceptions, and Anglo-Saxons: Race and Rule between the British and United States Empires, 1880–1910', *Journal of American History*, Vol. 88, No. 4 (March 2002), p. 1326.

93 Rodgers, *Atlantic Crossings*, pp. 62–3, quotations on p. 63.

94 <http://www.spartacus.schoolnet.co.uk/Jstead.htm>.

95 Detailed description at <http://www.attackingthedevil.co.uk/worksabout/babylon.php>. George Bernard Shaw wrote, 'Nobody ever trusted him after the discovery that the case of

Eliza Armstrong in the *Maiden Tribute* was a put-up job, and that he himself had put it up.'
<http://www.attackingthedevil.co.uk/peers/shaw1.php>.

96 Stokes, 'American Progressives and the European Left', p. 8.

97 David A. Shannon, ed., *Beatrice Webb's American Diary 1898* (Madison: University of Wisconsin Press, 1963), p. 108.

98 Rodgers, *Atlantic Crossings*, p. 64.

99 Shannon, ed., *Webb's American Diary*, p. 109.

100 Rodgers, *Atlantic Crossings*, pp. 152–8.

101 *Ibid.*, pp. 198–207.

102 *Ibid.*, pp. 235–41.

103 Christine Bolt highlights the WCTU as attracting feminists and non-feminists alike, as the biggest recruiter in the 1870s and 1880s, and as 'confirming the enduring importance of religious motivations among female reformers in the United States, notwithstanding the steady secularization of reform endeavours as a whole'. Bolt, *Feminist Ferment: 'The Woman Question' in the USA and England 1870–1940* (London: UCL Press, 1995), p. 49.

104 *Ibid.*, pp. 101–2.

105 *Ibid.*, pp. 50–1.

106 *Ibid.*, pp. 13–20.

107 *Ibid.*, p. 85.

108 *Ibid.*, pp. 55–86.

109 Bryce, *American Commonwealth*, II, pp. 424–35, quotes on pp. 431 and 432.

110 William Reitzel, 'The Purchasing of English Books in Philadelphia, 1790–1800', *Modern Philology*, Vol. 35, No. 2 (November 1937), p. 159.

111 Cooper, *Notions of the Americans*, II, p. 94.

112 Reitzel, 'The Purchasing of English Books', p. 160.

113 Cooper, *Notions of the Americans*, II, quotations on pp. 99–100, 100, 101.

114 A comment attributed to John Quincy Adams in Perkins, *Castlereagh and Adams*, p. 174.

115 Quoted in Lease, *Anglo-American Encounters*, p. 3. For a later example, see the discussion of Emerson in Chapter 4.

116 Frank Luther Mott, *A History of American Magazines, 1741–1850* (Cambridge, Mass.: Harvard University Press, 1939), p. 188, quoted in *ibid.*, p. 3.

117 Perkins, *Castlereagh and Adams*, p. 174.

118 *Edinburgh Review*, Vol. 33 (January 1820), pp. 78–80.

119 Cooper, *Notions of the Americans*, II, p. 106.

120 The first American 'pirate' was probably Benjamin Franklin. He had published *Pamela*, and 're-published the works of British authors . . . without seeking their permission or offering remuneration'. Philip V. Allingham, 'Dickens' 1842 Reading Tour: Launching the Copyright Question in Tempestuous Seas', at <http://www.victorianweb.org/authors/dickens/pva/pva75.html>.

121 Cooper, *Notions of the Americans*, II, pp. 106–7.

122 *Ibid.*, p. 107.

123 *Democracy in America*, II, Part 1, ch. 13, p. 446.

124 Barnes, *Authors, Publishers and Politicians*, p. 1.

125 Bradbury, *Dangerous Pilgrimages*, p. 64.

126 Leslie Baily, *The Gilbert and Sulivan Book* (London: Spring Books, 1966, 1st pub. 1956), pp. 169–200, quotations on pp. 169 and 184. Thanks to Jane Card for the reference.

127 Stephen Spender, *Love–Hate Relations: A Study of Anglo-American Sensibilities* (London: Hamish Hamilton, 1974 pb. edn), p. 53.

128 Frederick Harrison, 'Impressions of America', *The Nineteenth Century and After*, vol. 49 (June 1901), p. 914.

129 Cooper, *Notions of the Americans*, II, pp. 114–15.

130 Lease, *Anglo-American Encounters*, p. 108.

131 *Ibid.*, p. 144. D.H. Lawrence, *Studies in Classic American Literature* (London: Penguin, 1977, 1st pub. in USA 1923, in Britain 1924), chs. 10–11.

132 Letter to Moncure D. Conway, n.d., quoted in Lease, *Anglo-American Encounters*, p. 237. He did, however, have the praise and support of Ralph Waldo Emerson, who called *Leaves of Grass* 'the most extraordinary piece of wit and wisdom that America has yet contributed'. Quoted in *ibid.*, p. 199.

133 *Ibid.*, p. 255. Susan Manning argues that Twain acquired early on a dislike of Walter Scott and his overwhelming influence on American literature (and politics), pointing out that the wrecked steamboat on the Mississippi was named *Walter Scott*. Manning, 'Did Mark Twain Bring Down the Temple?', in Janet Beer and Bridget Bennett, eds, *Special Relationships: Anglo-American Affinities and Antagonisms 1854–1936* (Manchester: Manchester University Press, 2002), *passim.*, reference on p. 11.

134 Lease, *Anglo-American Encounters*, pp. 178–207, quotations on pp. 182–3, 184.

135 See, e.g., Fred Manning Smith, 'Whitman's Debt to Carlyle's *Sartor Resartus*', *Modern Language Quarterly*, Vol. 3 (1942), pp. 51–5, cited in *ibid.*, pp. 230–4, quotation on p. 234.

136 Ernest Rhys, ed., *Leaves of Grass: The Poems of Walt Whitman* (London: Walter Scott, 1886), pp. 7 and 28.

137 Robert Weisbuch makes this a general point when he states that 'British insults encouraged anew the Puritan-derived idea of each individual as a microcosm of America'. Weisbuch, *Atlantic Double-Cross: American Literature and British Influence in the Age of Emerson* (Chicago: University of Chicago Press, 1986), p. xvii.

138 Perkins, *The Great Rapprochement*, p. 137.

139 Robert W. Rydell and Rob Kroes, *Buffalo Bill in Bologna: The Americanization of the World, 1869–1922* (Chicago: University of Chicago Press, 2005), p. 98.

140 *Ibid.*, pp. 98–104.

141 *Ibid.*, pp. 105–8.

142 Victoria de Grazia, *Irresistible Empire: America's Advance through Twentieth-Century Europe* (Cambridge, Mass.: Harvard University Press, 2005), p. 3.

143 *Ibid.*, pp. 1–2.

144 Richard Pells, *Not Like Us: How Europeans Have Loved, Hated, and Transformed American Culture since World War II* (New York: Basic Books, 1997), p. 211 for the quotation and p. 291.

145 Spender, *Love–Hate Relations*, p. 104.

146 Quoted in *ibid.*, p. 146.

147 He found the poets but not the name, which dates from the first publication in 1912 of Edward Marsh's biennial anthology, *Georgian Poetry* (George V came to the throne in 1910).

148 It was the American poet Robert Frost, who arrived in England in 1912, who encouraged Thomas to write poetry. Spender, *Love–Hate Relations*, p. 134. Thomas himself referred to Frost as the 'onlie begetter' of his verse. R. George Thomas, ed., *The Collected Poems of Edward Thomas* (Oxford: Oxford University Press, 1978), p. xv.

149 Spender, *Love–Hate Relations*, pp. 103–13, quotation on p. 111.

150 *Ibid.*, pp. 112–13, quotations on p. 113.

151 Peter Ackroyd, *T.S. Eliot* (London: Hamish Hamilton, 1984), p. 152.

152 Nicholas Jenkins, '"Writing without Roots": Auden, Eliot, and Post-national Poetry', in Steve Clark and Mark Ford, eds, *Something We Have That They Don't: British and American Poetic Relations since 1925* (Iowa City: University of Iowa Press, 2004), p. 76.

153 Humphrey Carpenter, *W.H. Auden* (London: George Allen & Unwin, 1981), pp. 242–6, quotations on pp. 245, 244, 246. According to Peter Conrad, Auden and Isherwood were,

by moving to the USA, formalising 'a change of faith' and 'repudiating a demoralized Europe'. Conrad, *Imagining America* (Oxford: Oxford University Press, 1980), p. 194.

154 For his influence on Bishop, see Bonnie Costello, '"A Whole Climate of Opinion": Auden's Influence on Bishop', in Clark and Ford, eds, *Something We Have That They Don't*, pp. 98–117.

155 Clark and Ford, eds, *Something We Have That They Don't*, p. 10.

156 <http://famouspoetsandpoems.com/poets/w_h_auden/poems/10129>. By this time, 1963, his fee for a lecture was often $2,000 ($21,600 or £10,800 in 2007 prices). Thanks to Michael Jewess. Carpenter, *Auden*, pp. 422–3.

157 Bradbury, *Dangerous Pilgrimages*, p. 413. For a fictional rendering of the phenomenon, see Bradbury's *Stepping Westward* (London: Arena, 1984, 1st pub. 1965). Michael Bywater points out that there is another phenomenon: in Britain a writer supports himself by journalism, whilst in America he could support himself in academia – a major difference in how writing is done in the two countries. Bywater to author, 25 April 2007.

158 Gunn's story is especially revealing. After leaving Cambridge, he went to Stanford University on a fellowship, encouraged by his love for an American man, a fellow-student at Cambridge. The two of them lived in San Francisco for the remainder of his life, Gunn crossing the Oakland Bay Bridge to teach at the University of California at Berkeley. He lived through the Aids epidemic of the late 1980s, which was the inspiration for one of his great books of poetry, *The Man with Night Sweats* (1992). His friend Clive Wilmer later characterised Gunn as a man who lacked a national identity: 'Though British, he lived in the United States and learned from modern American poetry. But he never became an American poet himself: to Americans he was indelibly British, while to some British readers his language lacked distinctiveness. He described himself as an Anglo-American poet, and to those who admired him this seemed a striking virtue – something new and necessary in the annals of literature.' Obituary of Thom Gunn in the *Independent*, 29 April 2004, p. 34.

159 Conrad suggests that the Atlantic crossing has become a rite of passage for British authors. Conrad, *Imagining America*, p. 194.

160 Keith Tuma, *Fishing by Obstinate Isles: Modern and Postmodern British Poetry and American Readers* (Evanston, Ill.: Northwestern University Press, 1998), p. 3, quoted in Clark and Ford, eds, *Something We Have That They Don't*, p. 14.

161 Bradbury, *Dangerous Pilgrimages*, pp. 427–30, quotations on pp. 429, 430.

162 John Sutherland, 'A Brave New World', *FT Magazine*, 9 October 2004, p. 26.

163 Four of the British Top Ten were Americans: Dan Brown at 4 and 5, Lauren Weisberger's *The Devil Wears Prada* at 8 and Elizabeth Kostova's *The Historian* at 10. There are also differences in the type of non-fiction each public buys: in the US the chart in 2006 was full of misery memoirs, self-help and business manuals; in the British chart about one-quarter were written by or about celebrities, and that did not include cookbooks, another staple. Thanks to Helen Graham of Little, Brown.

164 Rydell and Kroes, *Buffalo Bill in Bologna*, pp. 172–3, quotations on p. 173.

165 David Reynolds, *Rich Relations: The American Occupation of Britain 1942–1945* (London: HarperCollins, 1995), p. 30.

166 De Grazia, *Irresistible Empire*, p. 294.

167 Rydell and Kroes, *Buffalo Bill in Bologna*, p. 120.

168 Pells, *Not Like Us*, p. 207.

169 Rydell and Kroes, *Buffalo Bill in Bologna*, pp. 120–3.

170 Mark Glancy, 'Temporary American Citizens? British Audiences, Hollywood Films and the Threat of Americanization in the 1920s', *Historical Journal of Film, Radio and Television*, Vol. 26, No. 4 (October 2006), pp. 464–5.

171 Jeremy Turnstall and David Machin, *The Anglo-American Media Connection* (Oxford: Oxford University Press, 1999), p. 129.

172 Glancy, 'Temporary American Citizens?', p. 461.

173 Mark Glancy, 'The "Special Relationship" and the Cinema: Anglo-American Audiences and Film Preferences', paper given at the Conference on Anglo-American Relations from the Pilgrim Fathers to the Present Day, University College London, February 2005.

174 This was settled by the 1948 Anglo-American Film Agreement, by which American companies were permitted to take no more than $17 million from the earnings of their films out of Britain, plus dollars equivalent to the earnings of British films in the US. Sarah Street, *Transatlantic Crossings: British Feature Films in the United States* (London: Continuum, 2002), pp. 92–3.

175 Giora Goodman, '"Who is Anti-American?": The British Left and the United States, 1945–1956', Ph.D. thesis, University College London, 1996, pp. 67–8.

176 Pells, *Not Like Us*, pp. 217–19; Street, *Transatlantic Crossings*, p. 29.

177 Sir Wilfrid Eady was a Permanent Secretary to the Treasury.

178 Pells, *Not Like Us*, p. 226; Street, *Transatlantic Crossings*, p. 169. In later years, a number of notable, and lucrative, American films were made at Pinewood Studios in London, including the *Alien* franchise (from 1979), *Batman* (1989), *Mission: Impossible* (1996) and *Charlie and the Chocolate Factory* (2005). All of the *Harry Potter* films were also made in Britain.

179 Pells, *Not Like Us*, p. 229.

180 Street, *Transatlantic Crossings*, pp. 22–103 for details of their making, marketing and reception.

181 The British had studios, the Americans had the star system. What many of these films had in common, along with wit and irony, was the actor Alec Guinness (twenty years later, he was Ben Obi-Wan Kenobi in *Star Wars* (1977)). According to Pells, 'if any single actor could take credit for the postwar popularity of British films in the United States [it was] Guinness . . . [who] made robbery and murder seem like thoroughly civilized forms of behavior'. Pells, *Not Like Us*, pp. 222–3.

182 These included *Room at the Top* (1959), about a 'serpentine' social climber, *A Taste of Honey* (1961) and *The Loneliness of the Long Distance Runner* (1962). This was a cinema response to the 'Angry Young Men' of 'kitchen-sink drama', which began with John Osborne's play *Look Back in Anger* (1956).

183 Pells, *Not Like Us*, pp. 222–3.

184 The studios had been forced to sell off the theatre chains which they had owned in the 1948 anti-trust Paramount 'Divorcement Decrees' case. Street, *Transatlantic Crossings*, p. 114.

185 *Dr No* (1962), *From Russia with Love* (1963), *Goldfinger* (1964), *Thunderball* (1965), *You Only Live Twice* (1967) and *On Her Majesty's Secret Service* (1969).

186 *Whitaker's Almanack 2005*, p. 1134. Thanks to Miranda Jewess for her help with this section.

187 It was also a very good example of culture as a power-artefact.

188 'The other side' (as ITV was known) was regarded by middle- and upper-middle-class British families as 'common', possibly because of the adverts.

189 Pells, *Not Like Us*, p. 231.

190 Alfred P. Holman, 'Two for the Money: The Current British Television Scene', *English Journal*, Vol. 50, No. 9 (December 1961), p. 635.

191 Tunstall and Machin, *Anglo-American Media Connection*, p. 129.

192 *Ibid.*, pp. 129–30; Pells, *Not Like Us*, pp. 231–3.

193 Thanks to Miranda Jewess.

194 Pells, *Not Like Us*, pp. 318–19.

195 <http://en.wikipedia.org/wiki/British_Invasion>. When Elvis Presley appeared on *Ed Sullivan*, the bottom half of the screen was blanked out (to avoid public outrage about 'Elvis the Pelvis'). Personal recollection.

196 They were 'I Want to Hold Your Hand', 'She Loves You', 'Please Please Me' and 'I Saw Her Standing There'. 'Love Me Do' and others followed. Michael Bryan Kelly ('Doc Rock'), *The Beatle Myth: The British Invasion of American Popular Music, 1956–1969* (Jefferson, N.C.: McFarland, 1991), pp. 21–3.

197 *Ibid.*, p. 175.

198 Pells, *Not Like Us*, p. 319; <http://en.wikipedia.org/wiki/British_Invasion>.

199 See Jon Savage, *England's Dreaming: Sex Pistols and Punk Rock* (London: Faber and Faber, 2005 pb. edn, 1st pub. 1991), *passim.*

200 *Ibid.*

201 *Ibid.*

202 *Whitaker's Almanack 2005*, p. 1143.

203 Joseph S. Nye, Jr., *Soft Power: The Means to Success in World Politics* (New York: Public Affairs, 2004), p. x.

204 Tony Shaw, 'Eden and the BBC during the 1956 Suez Crisis: A Myth Re-examined', *Twentieth Century British History*, Vol. 6, No. 3 (1995), pp. 320–43.

Chapter 6 – The Turning of the Tide: 1871–1945

1 (London: Longmans, Green, 1883), p. 20. Freeman was a historian who in 1884 became the Regius Professor of Modern History at Oxford University.

2 (New York: Appleton, 1914), p. 277. De Sumichrast was an Englishman who had lived in the US for some years.

3 Strict translation: 'The sinews of war, endless money'.

4 Admiral Sir Ernle Chatfield, First Sea Lord, to Sir Warren Fisher, 4 June 1934, CHT/3/1, p. 62, Chatfield Papers, National Maritime Museum, Greenwich.

5 Diary of General Sir William Slim, Slim Papers, 5/2/2, Churchill College, Cambridge. This is found in a draft chapter for his unpublished memoirs, with no specific date given. Thanks to Sandra Marsh of the Churchill College Archives Centre.

6 David Reynolds, *Britannia Overruled: British Policy and World Power in the Twentieth Century* (London: Longman, 2000, 2nd edn), p. 8.

7 US steel production in 1871 was 73,214 long tons. *Historical Statistics of the United States*, p. 417.

8 In the late 1880s Lord Wolseley, the Adjutant-General of the British army (and from 1895 the Commander-in-Chief), called the 25,000 soldiers and 2,000 officers of the American army, man for man, the best in the world. Technology was important, with the use of railways and modern rifles. LaFeber, *The American Search for Opportunity*, pp. 35 and 55–6.

9 <http://historicalvoices.org/earliest_voices/bryan.html> for a sound recording of the speech as well as a transcript.

10 From 'The Adventure of the Noble Bachelor', first published in *Strand* magazine in 1892. Sir Arthur Conan Doyle, *Sherlock Holmes: His Adventures, Memoirs, Return, His Last Bow and The Case-Book: The Complete Short Stories* (London: John Murray, 1928), p. 246.

11 Stuart Anderson, *Race and Rapprochement: Anglo-Saxonism and Anglo-American Relations, 1895–1904* (London: Associated University Presses, 1981), pp. 17–18, quotation on p. 17.

12 This is a brief summary of a small part of a complicated situation and argument. See Paul A. Kramer, 'Empires, Exceptions, and Anglo-Saxons: Race and Rule between the British and United States Empires, 1880–1910', *Journal of American History*, Vol. 88, No. 4 (March 2002), *passim.*

13 Anderson, *Race and Rapprochement*, ch. 5.

14 D.C.M. Platt, *Finance, Trade and Politics in British Foreign Policy, 1815–1914* (Oxford: Oxford University Press, 1968), pp. 308–16. See also the discussion in Chapter 3 of this book.

15 From a speech by Hogg advocating an isthmian canal, given in Philadelphia on 2 July 1894. Robert C. Cotner, ed., *Addresses and State Papers of James Stephen Hogg* (Austin: University of Texas Press, 1951), p. 374, cited by Crapol, *America for Americans*, p. 219.

16 The British proportion of American imports fell from 42.5 per cent in 1871 to 27 per cent in 1881. *Historical Statistics of the United States*, p. 553.

17 For the British statistics, Mitchell and Deane, *British Historical Statistics*, pp. 6–7; for the American statistics, *Historical Statistics of the United States*, p. 7.

18 Reynolds, *Britannia Overruled*, p. 18.

19 Kennedy, *British Naval Mastery*, p. 201.

20 *Historical Statistics of the United States*, pp. 736–7.

21 The British regular army in 1880 was 131,859, in 1890 153,483, and in 1895 155,403. Chris Cook and Brendan Keith, *British Historical Facts 1830–1900* (London: Macmillan, 1975) p. 185.

22 LaFeber, *The American Search for Opportunity*, pp. 114–16.

23 *Ibid.*, pp. 115–16, quotation on p. 116; Kennedy, *British Naval Mastery*, pp. 182–3.

24 *Ibid.*, p. 182; LaFeber, *The American Search for Opportunity*, p. 116.

25 Kennedy, *British Naval Mastery*, p. 183.

26 Selborne to Lord Curzon, 19 April 1901, in D. George Boyce, ed., *The Crisis of British Power: The Imperial and Naval Papers of the Second Earl of Selborne, 1895–1910* (London: Historians' Press, 1990), p. 115.

27 Aaron L. Friedberg, *The Weary Titan: Britain and the Experience of Relative Decline, 1895–1905* (Princeton, N.J.: Princeton University Press, 1988), p. 146. According to Thomas Otte, the scare was generated by the Admiralty, which had been pressing for more ships since 1881. Otte to the author, 2 December 2006.

28 He preferred the French spelling to Marquess.

29 This part of India is now Pakistan.

30 Paul Kennedy points out that, for centuries, India was only accessible to a Great Power by sea, 'but by 1900 it appeared to be in deadly danger from the approaching Orenburg–Tashkent railway, to which the British simply had no answer'. Kennedy, *British Naval Mastery*, p. 197.

31 336 H.C. Deb., 3rd Series, p. 1171. The Act was passed on 21 May 1889, *ibid.*, p. 1609; the list of ships to be built was announced on 27 May by Lord Elphinstone, *ibid.*, p. 1080. Friedberg, *Weary Titan*, pp. 146–50. Although in 1889 the third-largest navy was Italian, not Russian, no one thought that Great Britain and Italy would go to war. Parliament authorised expenditure of £21,500,000, plus another £4,750,000 for dockyard work. Jon Tetsuro Sumida, *In Defence of Naval Supremacy: Finance, Technology, and British Naval Power, 1889–1904* (London: Routledge, 1993 pb. edn), p. 13.

32 Kennedy, *British Naval Mastery*, pp. 177–81.

33 That is, controlling or patrolling the Channel, the western entrance to the Mediterranean, the eastern Mediterranean and the Suez Canal, the route to the Indian Ocean and the South Pacific, and the Far East. Admiral Sir John Fisher, quoted in A.J. Marder, *From the Dreadnought to Scapa Flow: The Royal Navy in the Fisher Era 1904–1919, Volume I: The Road to War, 1904–1914* (London: Oxford University Press, 1961), p. 41.

34 A.N. Porter (ed.), *Atlas of British Overseas Expansion* (London: Routledge, 1991, 1994 pb.), p. 145, for a list of the coaling stations.

35 See Peter Mathias, *The First Industrial Nation: An Economic History of Britain 1700–1914* (London: Methuen, 1969 pb. edn) and N.F.R. Crafts, *British Economic Growth during the Industrial Revolution* (Oxford: Oxford University Press, 1985).

36 According to Charlotte Ericson, 'To the American employer, the scarcity of skilled labour, his unwillingness to train it, the difficulties of recruiting it abroad, and the unsatisfactory result in trade unions when he did, combined to recommend a policy of increasing mechanisation to free him from the demands of the skilled European workmen.' Or Brinley Thomas, who argues that heavy immigration encouraged the development of machines which could be used by semi-skilled or unskilled labour, thereby replacing more costly, and sometimes difficult, skilled labour. Both references in H.J. Habakkuk, *American and British Technology in the Nineteenth Century: The Search for Labour-Saving Inventions* (Cambridge: Cambridge University Press, 1962), p. 128.

37 *Ibid.,* chs. 2 and 6.

38 David French points out a third vital factor: the ability of British diplomats to persuade other powers to become allies.

39 Kennedy, *British Naval Mastery,* p. 181.

40 A.J.P. Taylor, *The Struggle for Mastery in Europe 1848–1918* (Oxford: Oxford University Press, 1954), p. xxix, Table VII; *Historical Statistics of the United States,* pp. 356–7. On the ground this did not matter, given her self-sufficiency in coal.

41 E.J. Hobsbawm, *Industry and Empire: An Economic History of Britain since 1750* (London: Weidenfeld & Nicolson, 1968), p. 152.

42 The US Index has no entry for that year.

43 Geoffrey Barraclough, *An Introduction to Contemporary History* (Harmondsworth: Penguin, 1967), p. 51, quoted in Kennedy, *British Naval Mastery,* p. 189. 'England' presumably includes Scottish steel production.

44 Taylor, *The Struggle for Mastery in Europe,* p. xxx, Table IX; *Historical Statistics of the United States,* p. 418.

45 Quoted in Kennedy, *British Naval Mastery,* p. 190. This is very reminiscent of Tom Paine's comment in *Common Sense:* 'there is something very absurd, in supposing a continent to be perpetually governed by an island'. Dover edn, p. 25.

46 LaFeber, *The American Search for Opportunity,* pp. 121–3; David Healy, 'A Hinterland in Search of a Metropolis: The Mosquito Coast, 1894–1910', *International History Review,* Vol. 3, No. 1 (January 1981), pp. 20–43.

47 Andrew Roberts, *Salisbury: Victorian Titan* (London: Weidenfeld & Nicolson, 1999), p. 615.

48 Phelps to Salisbury, 8 February 1887 and Salisbury to Phelps, 22 February 1887, *Parliamentary Papers* [Blue Book], February 1896, Cmmd Paper United States, No. 1, 'Correspondence Respecting the Question of the Boundary of British Guiana'.

49 In 1893 Great Britain upgraded her mission in Washington from a legation to an embassy and her representative from a minister to an ambassador. This was a shrewd public relations move on London's part: the upgrade came in the knowledge, and in advance, of an impending congressional decision to raise US legations to embassies. Thanks to Thomas Otte.

50 E.J. Phelps to Lord Salisbury, 8 February 1887, Robert L. Lincoln to Salisbury, 5 May 1890, and Salisbury to Sir Julian Pauncefote, 11 November 1891, Cmmd Paper United States, No. 1. Apparently Phelps, the American minister to London in February 1888, never delivered an 'earnest protest' against Britain for not agreeing to arbitration, sent by the then Secretary of State, Thomas Bayard, to the Foreign Secretary, on the grounds that unless the US was prepared to use force, the protest was useless. Not delivered, it lay in the files, and was printed in the 1888 volume of documents, *Foreign Relations of the United States.* Olney would have read it, and might have concluded that Great Britain had received but disregarded the protest; this possibly contributed to his idea that the UK needed a 'jolt'. R.W. Mowat, *The Life of Lord Pauncefote: First Ambassador to the United States* (London: Constable, 1929), p. 175.

51 Gresham to Bayard, 9 April 1895, M77/90; Gerald G. Eggert, *Richard Olney: Evolution of a Statesman* (University Park: Pennsylvania State University Press, 1974), pp. 197–201, quotations on p. 199.

52 *Ibid.*, pp. 201–2, quotations on p. 202.

53 Olney to Bayard, No. 222, 20 July 1895, fols. 291–9, with the six points on fol. 299, M77/90.

54 *Ibid.*, fols. 305–6 for the quotations.

55 'If Washington won its point with Salisbury, the Chilean minister to Washington observed, "the United States will have succeeded in establishing a protectorate over all of Latin America".' LaFeber, *The American Search for Opportunity*, p. 126.

56 Eggert, *Olney*, p. 208.

57 Olney to Bayard, No. 222, 20 July 1895, fol. 310, M77/90. 'According to usage Lord Salisbury would, in the light of this last request, have been at liberty to take the note as an ultimatum'. Mowat, *Pauncefote*, p. 179.

58 Quoted in Eggert, *Olney*, p. 212.

59 Salisbury to Gough, 7 August 1895, No. 12, Cmmd Paper United States, No. 1.

60 Quoted in J.A.S. Grenville, *Lord Salisbury and Foreign Policy: The Close of the Nineteenth Century* (London: Athlone Press, 1970 pb. edn), p. 61.

61 Salisbury to Pauncefote, 26 November 1895, No. 15, Cmmd Paper United States, No. 1.

62 Salisbury to Pauncefote, 26 November 1895, No. 16, *ibid.*

63 Eggert, *Olney*, pp. 210–13, quotations on p. 210.

64 Henry F. Graff, *Grover Cleveland* (New York: Henry Holt, 2002), p. 125.

65 Watts and Israel, eds, *Presidential Documents*, pp. 181–4.

66 Eggert, *Olney*, p. 223 for Roosevelt quotation; Graff, *Cleveland*, p. 125; Mowat, *Pauncefote*, pp. 186–7, pulpit quotation on p. 186.

67 WO 106/48, cited in Grenville, *Lord Salisbury*, pp. 422 and 370.

68 Roberts, *Salisbury*, pp. 46 and 617.

69 Zara S. Steiner, *The Foreign Office and Foreign Policy, 1898–1914* (Cambridge: Cambridge University Press, 1969), p. 24.

70 Grenville, *Lord Salisbury*, ch. 2.

71 T.G. Otte, 'A Question of Leadership: Lord Salisbury, the Unionist Cabinet and Foreign Policy Making, 1895–1900', *Contemporary British History*, Vol. 14, No. 4 (Winter 2000), pp. 4–9.

72 Translation in Grenville, *Lord Salisbury*, p. 102.

73 Quoted in John Charmley, *Splendid Isolation? Britain, the Balance of Power and the Origins of the First World War* (London: Hodder & Stoughton, 1999), p. 239.

74 Roberts, *Salisbury*, pp. 617–26; Grenville, *Lord Salisbury*, pp. 98–107.

75 Entry for 11 January 1896, Diary of Joseph Chamberlain, printed in J.L. Garvin, *The Life of Joseph Chamberlain 1836–1900, Volume III: 1895–1900: Empire and World Policy* (London: Macmillan, 1934), p. 161 for Salisbury quotation; C.J. Lowe and M.L. Dockrill, *The Mirage of Power, Volume I: British Foreign Policy 1902–14* (London: Routledge & Kegan Paul, 1972), p. 98.

76 Bayard to Salisbury, No. 18, 3 February, Salisbury to Bayard, No. 19, 7 February and Bayard to Salisbury, No. 20, 10 February, all 1896, Cmmd Paper United States, No. 1, pp. 32–3.

77 Eggert, *Olney*, p. 238.

78 Allan Nevins, *Henry White: Thirty Years of American Diplomacy* (New York: Harper & Brothers, 1930), pp. 114–15.

79 Mowat, *Pauncefote*, pp. 195–8, quotation from Harcourt on p. 198. A future ambassador to Italy and France and member of the US delegation to the 1919 Paris Peace Conference.

80 Mowat, *Pauncefote*, pp. 199–201. It is worth noting that there was a growing trend towards arbitration in Anglo-American relations. Under President William Howard Taft, an arbitration treaty with Great Britain was signed in 1911, but the Senate refused to ratify it. Thanks to Thomas Otte.

81 Dean Rusk about the USSR and the 1962 Cuban Missile Crisis.

82 This was the Roosevelt Corollary to the Monroe Doctrine, part of his Annual Message to Congress: 'Our interests and those of our southern neighbors are in reality identical . . . While they . . . obey the primary laws of civilized society they may rest asssured that they will be treated by us in a spirit of cordial sympathy. We would interfere with them only in the last resort, and then only if it became evident that their inability or unwillingness to do justice at home and abroad had violated the rights of the United States or had invited foreign aggression to the detriment of the entire body of American nations.' Watts and Israel, eds, *Presidential Documents*, p. 205.

83 On 26 February 1896, in a speech at Lewes in Sussex, Lord Goschen said, 'We have stood alone in that which is called isolation – our splendid isolation, as one of our colonial friends was good enough to call it.' The 'colonial friend' was Sir George Foster, who on 16 January 1896 in the Canadian House of Commons referred to 'In their somewhat troublesome days when the great Mother Empire stands splendidly isolated in Europe.' *The Oxford Dictionary of Quotations* (Oxford: Oxford University Press, 1979, 3rd edn), pp. 233, 217.

84 One example is Perkins, *The Great Rapprochement*.

85 David H. Burton, *British–American Diplomacy 1895–1917: Early Years of the Special Relationship* (Malabar, Fl.: Krieger, 1999), p. 20.

86 LaFeber, *The American Search for Opportunity*, pp. 129–44; Robert L. Beisner, *From the Old Diplomacy to the New, 1865–1900* (Arlington Heights, Ill.: Harlan Davidson, 1986 pb. edn), pp. 120–30; Perkins, *The Great Rapprochement*, pp. 36–44.

87 The plan was the work of officers from the Naval War College, including Mahan, and the Office of Naval Intelligence, and had been drawn up before Roosevelt was in office. John A.S. Grenville and George Berkeley Young, *Politics, Strategy, and American Diplomacy: Studies in Foreign Policy, 1873–1917* (New Haven, Conn.: Yale University Press, 1966), pp. 270–2. The real concern of many American naval officers was the growing hostility of Japan towards the US.

88 When American agents rifled the correspondence of a Spaniard in Montreal, removing a letter which spoke of organising an espionage ring, the US asked for his expulsion. This might have been refused, because the evidence was tainted by the method of its discovery, but the British induced the Canadian authorities to deport him and other Spaniards. Perkins, *The Great Rapprochement*, pp. 44–5.

89 *Ibid.*, p. 46.

90 <www.rms-gs.de/phileng/history/kap02.html>.

91 Perkins, *The Great Rapprochement*, p. 47.

92 *Ibid.*, pp. 42–3, quotation on p. 43.

93 Quoted in LaFeber, *The American Search for Opportunity*, pp. 143–4. He argues that McKinley had no interest in annexing the multiracial Cuba.

94 Watts and Israel, eds, *Presidential Documents*, pp. 194–5.

95 LaFeber, *The American Search for Opportunity*, pp. 156–68.

96 *Ibid.*, p. 145.

97 As it happened, publication of the poem in the February 1899 issue of *McClure's* magazine also coincided with the beginning of the war between the Americans and the Filipinos under Aguinaldo. Roosevelt sent a copy of the poem to Lodge.

98 Mrs Campbell Dauncey, *An Englishwoman in the Philippines* (London: John Murray, 1906), pp. 167–8.

99 On 11 April 1905 Prime Minister Arthur Balfour wrote to Lodge, 'I agree with you in thinking that the interests of the United States and of ourselves are absolutely identical in the Far East, and that the more closely we can work together, the better it will be for us and the world at large.' Add. MS 49742, fols. 175–6, Balfour Papers, British Library, London.

100 This approach to Washington was the third and least preferred option. Salisbury had worked for a rapprochement with Russia, which was unsuccessful; the other option was the seizure of a naval base in northern China. Thanks to Thomas Otte.

101 Grenville, *Lord Salisbury*, pp. 143–4. Salisbury delayed because he was pursuing an Anglo-Russian agreement on China, and Britain's taking of Wei-hai-Wei would have made such a deal impossible. Only when it was beyond reach did Salisbury accept the Chinese offer.

102 This was done without consulting Congress or declaring war, thereby creating a new presidential power. China had declared war on the US, but few in Washington seemed to pay it much notice.

103 LaFeber, *The American Search for Opportunity*, pp. 169–77, quotations on pp. 174, 175.

104 Perkins, *The Great Rapprochement*, pp. 209–15, quotations on p. 215.

105 One outcome of the troops' poor showing was a set of reforms of the army, the Haldane reforms, implemented in time to make a difference in 1914.

106 This was the origin of the term, but the intentions were rather different – to concentrate the population in easily guarded places – from those of the Nazis.

107 The Boers were the eventual victors over Great Britain: they dominated the Union, and in 1961, declaring South Africa a republic, they severed all connection with Britain and the Commonwealth.

108 Reginald Tower to Salisbury, 18 October 1899, No. 292, FO5/2352, fols. 21–4. The Germans had refused.

109 Kenton J. Clymer, *John Hay: The Gentleman as Diplomat* (Ann Arbor: University of Michigan Press, 1975), pp. 158–66.

110 Anderson, *Race and Rapprochement*, pp. 135–6 for the quotations; Thomas Otte, '"It's What Made Britain Great": Reflections on British Foreign Policy, from Malplaquet to Maastricht', in T.G. Otte, ed., *The Makers of British Foreign Policy from Pitt to Thatcher* (Basingstoke: Palgrave, 2002), p. 15.

111 Roosevelt to William Sewall, 24 April 1900, in Elting E. Morison, ed., *The Letters of Theodore Roosevelt*, 8 vols (Cambridge, Mass.: Harvard University Press, 1951–4), II, pp. 1269–70, quotation on p. 1270.

112 Anderson, *Race and Rapprochement*, p. 136.

113 Clymer, *Hay*, p. 159 for Hay quotation; LaFeber, *The American Search for Opportunity*, p. 190 for Roosevelt's.

114 Friedberg, *The Weary Titan*, pp. 196–9.

115 Nevins, *Henry White*, p. 146.

116 Clymer, *Hay*, p. 176.

117 David G. Haglund and Tudor Onea, 'Victory Without Triumph? Theodore Roosevelt, Honour, and The Alaska Panhandle Boundary Dispute', colloquium on Canada in the North Pacific, Association for Canadian Studies in the US, Anchorage, Alaska, September 2006. Perkins, *The Great Rapprochement*, pp. 161–72, for the remaining quotations, on pp. 165, 168, 172.

118 Mowat, *Pauncefote*, pp. 260–9; LaFeber, *The American Search for Opportunity*, pp. 72–4, quotations on p. 72 for the first and p. 73 for the next two.

119 Quoted in Clymer, *Hay*, p. 175.

120 Grenville, *Lord Salisbury*, pp. 376–7; Salisbury to Pauncefote, 2 February 1899, FO 55/392; Mowat, *Pauncefote*, pp. 277–9.

121 Salisbury to Pauncefote, 15 February 1899, FO55/392.

122 'Memorandum respecting the Negotiations leading to Conclusion of the Hay–Pauncefote Treaty of November 18, 1901, superseding the Clayton–Bulwer Treaty of 1850', 31 March 1905, FO 881/8448; Grenville, *Lord Salisbury*, pp. 379–81.

123 Pauncefote to Salisbury, 10 March 1900, FO 55/398 for the Davis amendment; Grenville, *Lord Salisbury*, pp. 381–5; 'Memorandum', FO 881/8448; Mowat, *Pauncefote*, pp. 282–4.

124 Lansdowne to Pauncefote, 22 February 1901, No. 36, FO 55/405; 'Memorandum', FO 881/8448.

125 'Memorandum', Lansdowne, 13 December 1900; Lansdowne to Pauncefote, 14 December 1900, both FO 55/399.

126 'Memorandum', FO 881/8448; Grenville, *Lord Salisbury*, pp. 387–8; Mowat, *Pauncefote*, pp. 283–91.

127 Paul Kennedy, *The Rise and Fall of the Great Powers: Economic Change and Military Conflict from 1500 to 2000* (London: Unwin Hyman, 1988), p. 515.

128 Quoted in Lord Selborne, 'Memorandum', 26 February 1904, CAB 23/22, printed in Boyce, ed., *The Crisis of British Power*, p. 171.

129 Christopher Andrew, *Secret Service: The Making of the British Intelligence Community* (London: Heinemann, 1985), pp. 36–42, quotation on p. 42.

130 Otte comments to the author.

131 Sumida, *In Defence of Naval Supremacy*, p. 10.

132 It was also to prevent an imminent Russo-Japanese rapprochement. George Monger, *The End of Isolation: British Foreign Policy 1900–1907* (Westport, Conn.: Greenwood Press, 1963), p. 47. Japan was to destroy the Russian Pacific and Baltic fleets in the 1904–5 Russo-Japanese War.

133 Jennifer Siegel, *Endgame: Britain, Russia and the Final Struggle for Central Asia* (London: I.B. Tauris, 2002), pp. 188–201.

134 Bourne, *Balance of Power*, p. 362.

135 Sumida, *In Defence of Naval Supremacy*, p. 18.

136 Chancellor of the Exchequer, 'Financial Difficulties: Appeal for Economy in Estimates', October 1901, CAB 37/58, Vol. 109, p. 8; Table 3-1, 'Gross Expenditures 1887–1907', in Friedberg, *Weary Titan*, p. 131.

137 Sumida, *In Defence of Naval Supremacy*, pp. 20–1 plus Figure 1, 'Expenditure on battleships and first-class cruisers, 1889–1904'. The newer ones were so much larger that the manning requirements of the Royal Navy grew much faster after 1897 than during the previous five years: 1889–90, 65,400; 1896–7, 93,750; 1904–5, 131,100. Expenditure on new works, such as barracks, docks and other port facilities, increased five times from 1897 to 1904–5. *Ibid.* Thanks to David French for the definition.

138 Steiner, *The Foreign* Office, p. 24. Gladstone, then Prime Minister, had resigned from the government on 1 March 1894 when his Cabinet colleagues had accepted the necessity of large increases in naval expenditure, believing that it would lead to financial disaster. 'Gladstone stood practically alone against all his colleagues. During the Cabinet meeting of 9 Jan. 1894, Gladstone spoke for nearly an hour in Cabinet, but his only supporter was J.G. Shaw-Lefevre, the First Commissioner of Public Works.' Philip Magnus, *Gladstone: A Biography* (London: John Murray, 1954), p. 417.

139 Selborne to Joseph Chamberlain, 21 September 1901, in Boyce, ed., *The Crisis of British Power*, p. 126.

140 Hamilton Diary, 16 May 1900, Add. MS 48676; Stephen Gladstone, Bank of England, to the Chancellor, 12 March 1900, T. 168/87; Burk, *Morgan Grenfel*, pp. 118–20.

141 'The Navy Estimates and the Chancellor of the Exchequer's Memorandum on the Growth of Expenditure', 16 November 1901, in Boyce, ed., *The Crisis of British Power*, pp. 129–36, quotations on pp. 131, 136.

142 Selborne to Balfour, 4 April 1902, Add. MSS 49707, fol. 105, Balfour Papers.

143 Selborne, Memorandum for the Cabinet, 26 February 1904, in Boyce, ed., *The Crisis of British Power*, p. 171.

144 Bourne, *Balance of Power*, pp. 364–5.

145 Boyce, ed., *The Crisis of British Power*, pp. 184–90. After the destruction of the Russian fleet by the Japanese at Tshushima in May 1905, as well as the Anglo-French 'defeat' of the Germans in the 1905 Moroccan Crisis, there was a further redistribution of the fleet, with the object of countering the German threat. Previously, there were sixteen battleships deployed as part of the Channel and Home fleets and seventeen in the Mediterranean and on the China Station. Afterwards, there were nine in the Mediterranean, none on the China Station, and twenty-four deployed with the Channel and Atlantic fleets. David French, *The British Way in Warfare 1 688–2000* (London: Unwin Hyman, 1990), p. 159.

146 Paul Knaplund, ed., *Speeches on Foreign Affairs, 1904–1914 by Sir Edward Grey* (London: George Allen & Unwin, 1931), p. 27. The other two features were the Anglo-Japanese Alliance and the Anglo-French Agreement. *Ibid.*, pp. 27–9.

147 Viscount Grey of Fallodon, *Twenty-Five Years*, 2 vols (London: Hodder & Stoughton, 1925), II, p. 85; Perkins, *The Great Rapprochement*, p. 296. In the 2005 edition, the US is back in alphabetical order, between the United Arab Emirates and Uruguay.

148 Mowat, *Pauncefote*, p. 290. It also authorised a president to fix preferential rates to other American ships, wherever they were bound.

149 Walter Hines Page, the American ambassador to Great Britain, received the news of the repeal at a ball at Buckingham Palace, and as the word spread many other guests sought him out to offer congratulations. Perkins, *The Great Rapprochement*, pp. 304–5.

150 Grey, *Twenty-Five Years*, II, pp. 83–97; Keith Robbins, *Sir Edward Grey: A Biography of Lord Grey of Falodon* (London: Cassell, 1971), pp. 275–7.

151 Two divisions were intended to remain in the country for home defence, but by early September all six divisions plus a cavalry division were in France.

152 Kitchener told Lord Esher that 'the war might last two or three years at least'. Entry for 13 August 1914, Diary of Lord Esher (original manuscript), Vol. 2, Folder 13, Esher Papers, Churchill College, Cambridge.

153 And for most of these countries, but not necessarily for France, elsewhere in the world. France tried to maintain her position as an equal and pay her own way. J.M. Keynes, then in the Treasury, commented in March 1916 that Britain had only one ally, France, and that the rest were mercenaries. *The Collected Writings of John Maynard Keynes, Volume XVI: Activities 1914– 1919*, ed. Elizabeth Johnson (London: Macmillan, 1971), p. 187.

154 For details as well as hundreds of references, see Kathleen Burk, *Britain, America and the Sinews of War 1914–1918* (London: Unwin Hyman, 1985). By October 1916, the Allies were largely or wholly dependent on the US for guns, shells, metals, explosives, machine tools, oils and petroleum, cotton, foodstuffs, raw materials and grains. Memorandum, 6 November 1916, Cab. 42/23/7, Cabinet Papers, National Archive, London. This was the outcome of an interdepartmental committee called by the Foreign Office on 30 September precisely to determine how far Britain was dependent on the US.

155 Cab. 37/157/40.

156 Diary of Sir Hardman Lever, head of the Treasury mission in the USA, 20 July 1917, T.17 2/430, fol. 4, Treasury Papers, National Archive, London; Treasury to Cabinet Secretariat, 7 July 1917, Cab. 21/123.

157 E.M. House Papers, Box 121, Yale University Library; Burk, *Sinews of War*, p. 80.

158 Phillips Payson O'Brien, *British and American Naval Power: Politics and Policy, 1900–1936* (Westport, Conn.: Praeger, 1998), pp. 116–17, quotations on p. 117.

159 Message to Congress, 63rd Congress, 2nd Session, Doc. 566, in Burton, *British–American Diplomacy 1895–1917*, Doc. 23, pp. 128–9.

160 Robbins, *Sir Edward Grey*, p. 319.

161 Grey, *Twenty-Five Years*, II, p. 123; Robbins, *Grey*, pp. 336–9; David French, *British Strategy and War Aims 1914–1916* (London: Allen & Unwin, 1986), pp. 190–5.

162 David Lloyd George, *War Memoirs of David Lloyd George*, 2 vols (London: Odhams, 1938), I, p. 413.

163 David R. Woodward, *Trial by Friendship: Anglo-American Relations 1917–1918* (Lexington: University Press of Kentucky, 1993), pp. 22–3.

164 *Ibid.*, p. 23.

165 Burk, *Sinews of War*, p. 80.

166 Charles Hamlin, Diary, Vol. 4, entry for 30 November 1916, Hamlin Papers, Library of Congress, Washington, D.C. Hamlin had been a member of the Federal Reserve Board from its beginning in 1914.

167 Lever Diary, 23 March 1917, fol. 76, T. 172/429.

168 Between 1914 and 1916 American trade in munitions alone jumped from $40 million to $1.3 billion; the sales for 1916 represented almost 24 per cent of all US exports. Samuel Wells, Jr. *The Challenges of Power: American Diplomacy, 1900–1921* (Lenham, Md: University Press of America, 1990 pb. edn), p. 78.

169 Keynes, XVI, p. 211. Kathleen Burk, 'The Diplomacy of Finance: British Financial Missions to the United States 1914–1918', *Historical Journal*, Vol. 22, No. 2 (1979), pp. 356–8. Lloyd George was referred to as 'the goat' because of his compulsive womanising. His principal mistress, Frances Stevenson, who was also his private secretary, sometimes had difficulties in keeping the typing pool in order. Comment to author from A.J.P. Taylor.

170 FO minutes on French government to British government, 4 December 1916, No. 245051, FO 371/2800 for intention; Hamlin Diary, Vol. 4, 4 January 1917 for effect.

171 Wells, *Challenges of Power*, pp. 83–6, quotations on pp. 83, 86.

172 *Ibid.*, p. 94.

173 Watts and Israel, eds, *Presidential Documents*, p. 234. Wells, *Challenges of Power*, pp. 94–7.

174 Burk, *Sinews of War*, pp. 110–26.

175 Bliss to Baker, 25 May 1917, Box 2, File 88, Woodrow Wilson Papers, Library of Congress.

176 See David F. Trask, *The United States in the Supreme War Council* (Middletown, Conn.: Wesleyan University Press, 1961), *passim*.

177 It had been decided in June 1917 that the US would send a division of the regular army as a token for the future, and that it would co-operate with the French. Burk, *Sinews of War*, p. 123. Some specialist auxiliaries were sent to co-operate with the British, including forestry men, some railway battalions to man the supply line in France, medical units, including six base hospitals, and trained and untrained pilots. G.T.M. Bridges to the Chief of the Imperial General Staff, 29 April and 3 May 1917, Cab. 26/53; Wilson to Baker, 3 May 1917, Box 4, Newton D. Baker Papers, Library of Congress. By late 1918, roughly 300,000 American soldiers a month were arriving in France.

178 Woodward, *Trial by Friendship*, pp. 149–66.

179 *Ibid.*, pp. 149–70, quotation on p. 170.

180 Chancellor of the Exchequer to William Gibbs McAdoo, Secretary of the Treasury, 30 July 1917, FO 371/3115.

181 Balfour to Sir William Wiseman, head of the British Military Mission and of MI6 in the US, to be passed on to House, FO 800/209.

182 Northcliffe to Geoffrey Robinson, 1 July 1917, File 1917, Northcliffe Papers, British Library.

183 Kathleen Burk, 'J.M. Keynes and the Exchange Rate Crisis of July 1917', *Economic History Review*, 2nd Series, Vol. 32, No. 3 (August 1979), pp. 406–7. US Treasury loans to Great Britain totalled $4.3 billion. Secretary of the Treasury, *Annual Report* (Washington, D.C.: US Government Printing Office, 1920).

184 House to Wiseman, 25 August 1917, 90/26, William Wiseman Papers, Yale University Library.

185 Keynes' first draft of Chancellor of the Exchequer to Reading, the British ambassador, 8 May 1918, T.172/445, fols. 11–14.

186 Wilson to House, 21 July 1917, Box 121, House Papers.

187 Department of State, *Papers Relating to the Foreign Relations of the United States, 1917, Supplement 2, The World War* (Washington, D.C.: United States Government Printing Office, 1932), pp. 543–5.

188 Chancellor of the Exchequer, Andrew Bonar Law, to William Hines Page, American ambassador to Great Britain, 23 July 1917, FO 371/3120, for passing on to McAdoo. McAdoo was Wilson's son-in-law.

189 Andrew, *Secret Service*, pp. 208–9; Christopher Andrew, *For the President's Eyes Only: Secret Intelligence and the American Presidency from Washington to Bush* (London: HarperCollins, 1995), p. 39 for the first quotation; W.B. Fowler, *British–American Relations, 1917–1918: The Role of Sir William Wiseman* (Princeton, N.J.: Princeton University Press, 1969), pp. 12–15, p. 13 for second quotation; Burk, *Sinews of War*, pp. 181–2; J.M. Keynes, 22 October 1917, fols. 127–8, T. 172/446.

190 Quoted in Andrew, *For the President's Eyes Only*, p. 39.

191 *Ibid.*, p. 78.

192 *Ibid.*, p. 34.

193 Thurber, 'Exhibit X', in *Alarms and Diversions*, p. 119. Thanks to Jane Card.

194 Andrew, *For the President's Eyes Only*, pp. 34–41.

195 *Ibid.*, pp. 41–5, first quotation on p. 41, second on p. 43, third on p. 44 and fourth on p. 45; Arthur S. Link, *Wilson: Campaigns for Progressivism and Peace, 1916–1917* (Princeton, N.J.: Princeton University Press, 1965), pp. 354–7, quotation on p. 354.

196 Andrew, *For the President's Eyes Only*, pp. 46–7.

197a Jim Beach, 'Origins of the Special Intelligence Relationship? Anglo-American Intelligence Co-operation on the Western Front, 1917–18', *Intelligence and National Security*, Vol. 22, No. 2 (April 2007), pp. 229–49.

198. Robert G. Angevine, 'Gentlemen Do Read Each Other's Mail: American Intelligence in the Interwar Era', *Intelligence and National Security*, Vol. 7,

No. 2 (April 1992), pp. 1–29, quotation on p. 17.

199. Andrew, *For the President's Eyes Only*, p. 70; Andrew, *Secret Service*, pp. 260, 353.

200. The Americans already knew about them. Balfour had told House about the secret treaties on 28 April 1917. House's response was 'that it was all bad and I told Balfour so. They are making it a breeding ground for future wars.' Future peace terms also dominated an after-dinner conversation at the White House between Wilson, House and Balfour on 30 April. House Diary, Vol. 10, entries for 28 and 30 April 1917, House Papers.

201 British entry into the war had been triggered by the German violation of Belgian neutrality, guaranteed by a treaty of 1839 which Germany (then Prussia) had signed.

202 Woodward, *Trial by Friendship*, pp. 128–9; George W. Egerton, 'Ideology, Diplomacy and International Organisation: Wilsonism and the League of Nations in Anglo-American Relations, 1918–1920', in B.J.C. McKercher, ed., *Anglo-American Relations in the 1920s* (London: Macmillan, 1991), p. 24.

203 Woodward, *Trial by Friendship*, p. 129 for the first quotation; Godfrey Hodgson, *Woodrow Wilson's Right Hand: The Life of Colonel Edward M. House* (New Haven, Conn.: Yale University Press, 2006), p. 165 for the second.

204 *Ibid.*, p. 166.

205 Between February and September 1918, Wilson made another three speeches in which he proposed another thirteen points, four of which were repeats. The Twenty-Three Points are listed in Wells, *Challenges of Power*, p. 109.

206 'Minutes of the 7th Meeting of the War Policy Cabinet Committee', 19 June 1917, CAB 27/6, p. 14.

207 The other five were those which resulted in the Treaty of Saint-Germain with Austria in September 1919; the Treaty of Neuilly with Bulgaria in November 1919; the Treaty of Trianon with Hungary in June 1920; the Treaty of Sèvres with the Ottoman Empire in August 1920; and the Treaty of Lausanne, which superseded the Treaty of Sèvres, with Turkey in July 1924.

208 Quoted in Hodgson, *House*, p. 31.

209 *Ibid.*, p. 189.

210 *Ibid.*, pp. 187–91.

211 Charles Seymour, *The Intimate Papers of Colonel House, Volume IV: The Ending of the War June 1918–November 1919* (London: Ernest Benn, 1928), p. 263.

212 Egerton, 'Ideology, Diplomacy, and International Organisation', p. 32 for first quotation, capitals in original; Reynolds, *Britannia Overruled*, p. 110 for second quotation.

213 Charles Seymour, *The Intimate Papers of Colonel House, Volume II: From Neutrality to War 1915–1917* (London: Ernest Benn, 1926), p. 88.

214 Egerton, 'Ideology, Diplomacy, and International Organisation', p. 22.

215 This was Article Ten, which set out the obligation 'to respect and preserve against internal aggression the territorial integrity and existing political independence' of all League members.

216 Lloyd George had emerged from the so-called 'coupon election' with a tremendous vote of confidence.

217 Lloyd R. Ambrosius, *Woodrow Wilson and the American Diplomatic Tradition: The Treaty Fight in Perspective* (Cambridge: Cambridge University Press, 1987), *passim.*

218 Comment on 22 June 1921, quoted in Erik Goldstein, 'The Evolution of British Diplomatic Strategy for the Washington Conference', in Erik Goldstein and John Maurer, eds, *The Washington Conference, 1921–22: Naval Rivalry, East Asian Stability and the Road to Pearl Harbor* (London: Frank Cass, 1994), p. 12.

219 Memorandum for the Cabinet, 'The Navy Estimates and the Chancellor of the Exchequer's Memorandum on the Growth of Expenditure', 16 November 1901, in Boyce, ed., *Crisis of British Power*, p. 130.

220 'Since the war [the British people] have been carrying a burden of indebtedness amounting to approximately £8,000,000 (40,000,000 dollars) or £178 (850 dollars) per head of their population, about one fifth of which represents war loans made to allied governments.' R.C. Lindsay, British ambassador to the US, to Cordell Hull, 4 June 1934, and passed on to Roosevelt, File War Debts, Box 190, p. 4, President's Secretary's Files [hereafter PSF], Franklin Roosevelt Papers, Franklin D. Roosevelt Presidential Library, Hyde Park, New York.

221 Burk, *Sinews of War*, Appendix IV, p. 266.

222 Britain paid 3.3 per cent, France 1.6 per cent and Italy 0.4 per cent.

223 Lindsay to Hull, 4 June 1934, File War Debts, 1934, Box 190, pp. 2, 10, PSF, Roosevelt Papers. The interest was fully met plus the repayments from 1922 to 1932. The funding agreement allowed her to miss payments, and she took advantage of this. Then she suspended. Thanks to Jeremy Wormell.

224 According to J.P. Morgan & Co., 'Our experience . . . showed that evidence of co-operation with Great Britain particularly was of great influence with the investors throughout this Country'. J.P. Morgan & Co. to Morgan Grenfell & Co., 23 January 1924, No. 2050, File 31, Box History 5, Morgan Grenfell Papers, London. Sir Otto Niemeyer of the Treasury believed that long-term loans would always be cheaper in London because of 'our greater skill in the foreign loan business'. Commentary by OEN on the Chancellor's Exercise, February 1925, T.172/1500A, fol. 45.

225 Paul Einzig, *The Fight for Financial Supremacy* (London: Macmillan, 1931), p. 52; Kathleen Burk, 'Money and Power: The Shift From Great Britain to the United States', in

Youssef Cassis, ed., *Finance and Financiers in European History, 1880–1960* (Cambridge: Cambridge University Press, 1992), pp. 363–4.

226 Committee on Finance and Industry, *Report*, Session 1930–1, Vol. 13, Cmd. 3897, June 1931, para. 141.

227 Kathleen Burk, 'The House of Morgan in Financial Diplomacy, 1920–1930', in McKercher, ed., *Anglo-American Relations in the 1920s*, p. 130. In 1920 assets of all reporting US banks totalled $53 billion, whilst by 1929 they had climbed to $72 billion, an increase of nearly 36 per cent. *Historical Statistics of the United States*, p. 624; Burk, 'Money and Power', p. 363.

228 John J. Broesamle, *William Gibbs McAdoo: A Passion for Change 1863–1917* (Port Washington, N.Y.: Kennikat Press, 1973), pp. 201–3, quotations on pp. 201, 202.

229 O'Brien, *British and American Naval Power*, p. 5.

230 Kennedy, *British Naval Mastery*, p. 263.

231 John R. Ferris, 'The Symbol and Substance of Seapower: Great Britain, the United States, and the One-Power Standard, 1919–1921', in McKercher, *Anglo-American Relations in the 1920s*, p. 59.

232 Long to Lloyd George, 16 February 1919, F/33/2, David Lloyd George Papers, House of Lords Record Office, London. In 1917 the Admiralty estimated that the US spent £240 million (about $11,420,000) on new construction alone, an amount greater than the total Royal Navy budget. O'Brien, *British and American Naval Power*, p. 152.

233 Ferris, 'Symbol and Substance of Seapower', pp. 57–61; O'Brien, *British and American Naval Power*, p. 162.

234 *Ibid.*, pp. 156–60. In addition China, the Netherlands, Portugal and Belgium were invited to take part in the discussions on Pacific and Far Eastern questions because they had territorial or economic interests there. Stephen Roskill, *Naval Policy between the Wars, Volume I: The Period of Anglo-American Antagonism 1919–1929* (New York: Walker, 1968), p. 302; Ferris, 'The Symbol and Substance of Seapower', p. 72.

235 Goldstein, 'The Evolution of British Diplomatic Strategy', pp. 26–8 for the British reaction to Hughes's speech and p. 27 for the Roosevelt quotation.

236 Roskill, *Naval Policy between the Wars*, pp. 310–24, quotation on p. 310; O'Brien, *British and American Naval Power*, p. 166.

237 Akira Iriye, *The Globalizing of America, 1913–1945* (Cambridge: Cambridge University Press, 1993), p. 82; Roskill, *Naval Policy between the Wars*, pp. 300–30; B.J.C. McKercher, '"The Deep and Latent Distrust": The British Official Mind and the United States, 1919–1929', in McKercher, ed., *Anglo-American Relations in the 1920s*, p. 223; O'Brien, *British and American Naval Power*, p. 181; R. Craigie, 'Outstanding Problems Affecting Anglo-American Relations', 12 November 1928, FO 371/12812, fol. 178. The treaties were signed by Great Britain on behalf of the British Empire; the 1926 Imperial Conference made a repetition impossible, and for the London Treaty of 1930 special wording had to be devised to protect the rights of the dominions. Roskill, *Naval Policy between the Wars*, p. 328, n. 6.

238 Great Britain also had considerably more cruisers and other smaller ships under construction, with 633,622 tons being built compared to the USA's 106,855 tons. O'Brien, *British and American Naval Power*, p. 187.

239 *Ibid.*, pp. 181–9.

240 *Ibid.*, quotation on p. 189.

241 Roskill, *Naval Policy between the Wars*, pp. 225–6, 498–502; B.J.C. McKercher, *The Second Baldwin Government and the United States, 1924–1929: Attitudes and Diplomacy* (Cambridge: Cambridge University Press, 1984), pp. 65–71.

242 Winston Churchill, 'Reduction and Limitation of Armaments: The Naval Conference', 29 June 1927, Cab 24/187, fols. 189, 190.

243 O'Brien, *British and American Naval Policy*, pp. 192–5, quotation on p. 194.

244 As though there could be any doubt. Diary, June–August 1927, in Philip Williamson, ed., *The Modernisation of Conservative Politics: The Diaries and Letters of William Bridgeman, 1904–1935* (London: Historians' Press, 1988), p. 209.

245 *Ibid.*, p. 207.

246 O'Brien, *British and American Naval Policy*, pp. 198–9, quotation on p. 199.

247 Both he and his predecessor, Robert Vansittart, had American wives.

248 'Outstanding Problems Affecting Anglo-American Relations', 12 November 1928, FO 371/12812.

249 O'Brien, *British and American Naval Power*, pp. 201–2, quotation on p. 201.

250 B.J.C. McKercher, *Transition of Power: Britain's Loss of Global Pre-eminence to the United States, 1930–1945* (Cambridge: Cambridge University Press, 1999), p. 33.

251 Lord Vansittart, *The Mist Procession: The Autobiography of Lord Vansittart* (London: Hutchinson, 1958), p. 386.

252 O'Brien, *British and American Naval Power*, pp. 210–12, quotations on each page.

253 *Ibid.*, pp. 210–15.

254 There was little hard evidence for this, but plenty of 'where there's smoke there's fire' assertions. The Nye Committee sat from 1934 to 1936, and then issued its report. United States Senate, 74th Congress, 2nd Session, Special Committee on Investigation of the Munitions Industry, *Munitions Industry*, Report No. 944, 7 vols (Washington, D.C.: United States Government Printing Office, 1936).

255 The Fordney–McCumber Tariff Act 1922 set an average tariff of 26 per cent, thereby excluding large quantities of European farm produce and chemical and manufactured goods. The Hawley–Smoot Tariff Act 1930 raised it to 40 per cent, and was driven by a beggar-thy-neighbour approach. It excluded an even larger volume of European exports, led to retaliatory tariffs against US exports, and was a major factor in stifling world trade. In 1934, however, Congress passed the Reciprocal Trade Act, which gave power to the administration to lower tariff rates by up to 50 per cent for any nation which reciprocated. There was high feeling in the UK Treasury in the 1920s that Britain was meant to pay its war debt, but the US tariffs did not allow the UK to export to the US to earn dollars. The US reply (including Hoover's) was that Britain could export to other countries (e.g., Malaya), which could export to the US (e.g., rubber), and gain dollars that way. It was also pointed out that US tourists could spend money in Europe, and Europe acquire dollars that way. For the US, 'open door' meant 'equally open door' everywhere except the US market. Thanks to Jeremy Wormell.

256 The Emergency Quota Act 1921 provided for highly restrictive quotas, with the annual number of immigrants capped. It was delimited by ethnic origins, with those from northern and western Europe preferred. The National Origins Act 1924 provided for stricter quotas on Mediterranean and Slavic immigrants. Admissions to the US fell from 4,107,200 in the 1920s to 528,400 in the 1930s.

257 Minute on Sir J. Pratt, 'The Shanghai Situation', 1 February 1932, in Rohan Butler, Douglas Dakin and M.E. Lambert, eds, *Documents on British Foreign Policy 1919–1939*, 2nd Series, Vol. 9, No. 238, pp. 281–3, quotation on p. 282; Norman Rose, *Vansittart: Study of a Diplomat* (London: Heinemann, 1978), pp. 105–8.

258 Lord Robert Cecil wrote to Baldwin on 12 December 1932 that Simon 'seems to have given everybody the idea that he was a thick and thin sup-porter of Japan, or else that we are so afraid of her that we dare not say anything she dislikes'. Keith Neilson, *Britain, Soviet Russia and the Collapse of the Versailles Order, 1919–1939* (Cambridge: Cambridge University Press, 2006), p. 65.

259 McKercher, *Transition of Power*, pp. 118–20, quotations on pp. 118, 120.

260 Thomas Jones, *A Diary with Letters 1931–1950* (London: Oxford University Press, 1954), p. 30.

261 Baldwin agreed, saying, 'We can't be going along one road, outside the League, with America, and also at the same time profess loyalty to the League and its procedure.' *Ibid.*, 27 February 1932, p. 30.

262 Richard N. Gardner, *Sterling–Dollar Diplomacy in Current Perspective: The Origins and the Prospects of Our International Order* (New York: Columbia University Press, 1980 expanded edn), p. 25.

263 Minute on Sir J. Pratt, 'The Shanghai Situation', quotation on p. 282. However, Vansittart went on to write that 'I do not agree that this is necessarily so. The same was said of the US in the Great War. Eventually she was kicked in by the Germans. The Japanese may end by kicking in the US too, if they go on long enough kicking as they are now.' *Ibid.*

264 Reynolds, *Britannia Overruled*, p. 120.

265 Watts and Israel, eds, *Presidential Documents*, p. 262.

266 David M. Kennedy, *Freedom from Fear: The American People in Depression and War, 1929–1945* (New York: Oxford University Press, 2001 pb. edn), p. 157.

267 See, for example, John Steinbeck's novel, *The Grapes of Wrath* (1939).

268 'The Thirteenth Press Conference (Excerpts), April 19, 1933', in Samuel I. Rosenman, compiler, *The Public Papers and Addresses of Franklin D. Roosevelt*, 13 vols (New York: Random House and Harper, 1938–50) (hereafter *PPA)*, II, pp. 137–41, quotation on p. 140; 'An Appeal to the Nations of the World for Peace by Disarmament and for the End of Economic Chaos. May 16, 1933', in *ibid.*, pp. 185–90, quotation on p. 186.

269 'A Wireless to the London Conference Insisting upon Larger Objectives than Mere Currency Stabilization. July 3, 1933', in *ibid.*, pp. 264–6, quotations on pp. 264–5; Patricia Clavin, '"The Fetishes of So-Called International Bankers": Central Bank Co-operation for the World Economic Conference', *Contemporary European History*, Vol. 1, No. 3 (November 1992), pp. 281–311.

270 Kennedy, *Freedom from Fear*, p. 156 for the first quotation; Alonzo L. Hamby, *For the Survival of Democracy: Franklin Roosevelt and the World Crisis of the 1930s* (New York: Free Press, 2004), p. 135 for the second.

271 'A Wireless to the London Conference', p. 266.

272 Hamby, *For the Survival of Democracy*, pp. 134–5.

273 Justus D. Doenecke and Mark A. Stoler, *Debating Franklin D. Roosevelt's Foreign Policies, 1933–1945* (Lanham, Md: Rowman and Littlefield, 2005), pp. 3 1–2; McKercher, *Transition of Power*, pp. 248–9, quotation on p. 248.

274 Kathleen Burk, 'The Lineaments of Foreign Policy: The United States and a "New World Order", 1919–39', *Journal of American Studies*, Vol. 26, No. 3 (1992), p. 380.

275 Doenecke and Stoler, *Franklin D. Roosevelt's Foreign Policies*, p. 21 for the quotation.

276 Richard P. Traina, *American Diplomacy and the Spanish Civil War* (Bloomington: Indiana University Press, 1968), p. 237.

277 Minute, 5 February 1934, FO 371/17593/A785, fol. 379.

278 David Reynolds, *The Creation of the Anglo-American Alliance 1937–41: A Study in Competitive Co-operation* (London: Europa, 1981), pp. 31–2, p. 31 for first quotation; William R. Rock, *Chamberlain and Roosevelt: British Foreign Policy and the United States, 193 7–1940* (Columbus: Ohio State University Press, 1988), p. 56 for second quotation.

279 David Dilks, ed., *The Diaries of Sir Alexander Cadogan O.M. 1938–1945* (New York: G.P. Putnam's Sons, 1972), p. 36.

280 Lindsey to Foreign Office, 12 January 1938, FO 371/21526, fols. 125–6, quoted in Rock, *Chamberlain and Roosevelt*, p. 57.

281 Foreign Office to Lindsey, 13 January 1938, FO 371/21526, fols. 128–31, quoted in *ibid.*, p. 58.

282 Reynolds, *Creation of the Anglo-American Alliance*, p. 32.

283 *Ibid.*, pp. 40–1, quotation on p. 41. The February 1939 exercise was intended to stop the German fleet from assisting a fascist-led revolt in Brazil. *Ibid.*

284 I.C.B Dear, ed., *The Oxford Companion to the Second World War* (Oxford: Oxford University Press, 1995), p. 651. The first comment was his daughter's. For the near-fight, see Mark A. Stoler, *Allies in War: Britain and America Against The Axis Powers 1940–1945* (London: Hodder Arnold, 2005), p. 139.

285 Reynolds, *Creation of the Anglo-American Alliance*, pp. 60–3; McKercher, *Transition of Power*, p. 270; John Baylis, *Anglo-American Defence Relations 1939–1984: The Special Relationship* (London: Macmillan, 1984 2nd edn), pp. 1–3; Stoler, *Allies in War*, pp. 3–17.

286 Rock, *Chamberlain and Roosevelt*, pp. 225–8; Kennedy, *Freedom from Fear*, pp. 432–4.

287 Warren F. Kimball, ed., *Churchill & Roosevelt: The Complete Correspondence, Volume I: Alliance Emerging: October 1933–November 1942* (Princeton, N.J.: Princeton University Press, 1984), p. 37 for the quotation. The threat of Italian submarines threatened the shipment of ore from North Africa and Spain, for example. *Ibid.* French Premier Paul Reynaud had written to Roosevelt with the same request the previous day, four days after the German invasion of France. Cordell Hull, *The Memoirs of Cordell Hull*, 2 vols (London: Hodder & Stoughton, 1948), I, p. 831; Kathleen Burk, 'American Foreign Economic Policy and Lend–Lease', in Ann Lane and Howard Temperley, eds, *The Rise and Fall of the Grand Alliance* (London: Macmillan, 1995), p. 49.

288 John Maynard Keynes, *Collected Writings, Volume III: Fighting for Britain 1937–1946*, ed. Robert Skidelsky (London: Macmillan, 2000), p. 95 for the statistic.

289 Quoted in Kennedy, *Freedom from Fear*, p. 452. For the Germans, 13 August was *Adlertag* or Eagle Day, the date on which the Battle of Britain began.

290 *A Speech by the Prime Minister the Right Honourable Winston Churchill in the House of Commons, August 20th, 1940* (London: Bayard Press, 1940), p. 10. This is the only copy of this speech in the British Library.

291 Hitler issued a directive on 5 September which ordered disruptive attacks on the population and air defences of major British cities by day and night.

292 Alfred Price, 'Blitz', in Dear, ed., *Second World War*, pp 138–40; Kennedy, *Freedom from Fear*, p. 453, for Murrow.

293 Hull, *Memoirs*, I, p. 870.

294 Strictly Secret and Personal for the President from Formal Naval Person (Churchill to Roosevelt), 31 July 1940, in Kimball, ed., *Churchill & Roosevelt*, I, p. 56.

295 Hull, *Memoirs*, I, p. 855.

296 A primary reason for the ending of the German attacks was the sheer loss of trained pilots. From 10 July–31 October the RAF lost roughly 788 planes, while the Luftwaffe lost roughly 1,294 (although these figures remain controversial). Malcolm Smith, 'Battle of Britain', in Dear, ed., *Second World War*, p. 163.

297 Hull, *Memoirs*, I, pp. 813–17.

298 *A Speech by Churchill, August 20th, 1940*, pp. 15–16.

299 J.R.M. Butler, *History of the Second World War: Grand Strategy, Volume II: September 1939–June 1941* (London: HMSO and Longmans, Green, 1957), p. 245.

300 Butler, *Grand Strategy*, p. 245. According to Hull, however, they were reconditioned, and stocked with munitions and food. *Memoirs*, I, p. 842.

301 Stoler, *Allies in War*, pp. 20–1, quotation on p. 21.

302 Peter Lowe, 'The War against Japan and Allied Relations', in Lane and Temperley, eds, *The Grand Alliance*, pp. 191–2. 'Our Delegation should open the discussion by saying that they recognised that the United States navy would be in charge of the Pacific and that the American views on strategy in that theatre must prevail. They would not be asking the Americans to come and protect Singapore, Australia and India against the Japanese but would offer

the use of Singapore to the Americans if they required it.' Note by the Secretary, 19 December 1940, Chief of Staffs Committee, 'British–United States Technical Conversations', COS (40) 1052, CAB 80/24, fol. 295.

303 Stoler, *Allies in War*, pp. 20–1. According to Stoler, the fall of Singapore was 'one of the most shattering and humiliating defeats in British history, and it dealt a severe blow to British Imperial prestige in Asia'. *Ibid.*, p. 57.

304 R.S. Sayers, *History of the Second World War: Financial Policy 1939–45* (London: HMSO and Longmans, Green, 1956), p. 496, Table 7: 'Gold and Dollar Reserves', pp. 364–70. According to *Parliamentary Papers, 1945. Statistical Material Presented during the Washington Negotiations*, Cmd. 6706 (1945), p. 5, the reserves in the spring of 1941 were down to twelve million dollars.

305 Burk, 'Lend–Lease', p. 51; Sayers, *Financial Policy*, p. 366.

306 Burk, 'Lend–Lease', p. 51; Warren F. Kimball, *The Most Unsordid Act: Lend–Lease, 1939–1941* (Baltimore, Md.: Johns Hopkins University Press, 1969), p. 103 for the quotation.

307 John Colville, *The Fringes of Power: Downing Street Diaries 1939–1955* (London: Hodder & Stoughton, 1985), entry for 12 November 1940, pp. 291–2. Colville was one of Churchill's private secretaries.

308 Henry Morgenthau Presidential Diary, Vol. 3, fol. 740, Franklin D. Roosevelt Presidential Library, Hyde Park, New York.

309 Roosevelt's reaction as described by Kimball on the basis of Hopkins' comments to various contemporaries, in *The Most Unsordid Act*, p. 119; report of the press conference in *The Times*, 18 December 1940.

310 Burk, 'Lend–Lease', pp. 55–6; quotation from 'Correspondence respecting the Policy of His Majesty's Government in connexion with the Use of Materials received under the Lend–Lease Act', Cmd. 6311, *Parliamentary Papers, 1940–41, VIII: United States No. 2 (10 September 1941)*, p. 424.

311 Reynolds, *Creation of the Anglo-American Alliance*, p. 257.

312 For a human-interest description and a true period piece, see the journalist H.V. Morton's *Atlantic Meeting: An Account of Mr Churchill's Voyage in HMS Prince of Wales, in August, 1941, and the Conference with President Roosevelt which Resulted in the Atlantic Charter* (London: Methuen, 1943).

313 Reynolds, *Creation of the Anglo-American Alliance*, pp. 258–61.

314 Stoler, *Allies in War*, p. 42.

315 Over 100,000 Britons in Singapore surrendered to a Japanese army of 30,000 after a brief siege. Ironically, the Japanese had almost run out of ammunition and the final siege of the campaign was based on bluff. Their speed and flexibility led General A.E. Perceval to believe that he was badly outnumbered. Peter Lowe, *Great Britain and the Origins of the Pacific War: A Study of British Policy in East Asia, 1937–1941* (Oxford: Oxford University Press, 1977), p. 280; Peter Lowe, 'The War against Japan and Allied Relations', in Lane and Temperley, eds, *The Grand Alliance*, p. 194 for the unmitigated disaster; Lowe, *Great Britain and the Origins of the Pacific War*, pp. 277–84; Stoler, *Allies in War*, p. 43 for 'coordination' quotation.

316 Stoler, *Allies in War*, p. 43.

317 H. Duncan Hall, *History of the Second World War: North American Supply* (London: HMSO and Longmans, Green, 1955), p. 60.

318 Paul Gore-Booth, *With Great Truth and Respect* (London: Constable, 1974), p. 121.

319 For the first quotation, it was said to Richard Crossman, Director of Psychological Warfare in Algiers, printed in the *Sunday Telegraph*, 9 February 1964, and quoted in Alistair Horne, *Macmillan 1894–1956: Volume I of the Official Biography* (London: Macmillan, 1988), p. 160; Alex Danchev, *Very Special Relationship: Field Marshal Sir John Dill and the Anglo-American Alliance 1941–44* (London: Brassey's, 1986), p. 41 for the second quotation.

320 Quoted in Baylis, *Anglo-American Defence Relations*, p. 10. In July 1944 Stalin suggested that a combined military staff be set up, but the idea, which was not received with much eagerness by the Americans or the British, expired at Yalta in February 1945. John Ericson, 'Stalin, Soviet Strategy and the Grand Alliance', in Lane and Temperley, eds, *The Grand Alliance*, p. 160.

321 Danchev, *Sir John Dill, passim.*, quotations on pp. 5 and 79; p. 1 for the apotheosis. In 1950 an equestrian statue of Dill was unveiled.

322 Stoler, *Allies in War*, pp. 140–2, quotations on pp. 141, 142.

323 Cadogan, *Diaries*, p. 582.

324 Stoler, *Allies in War*, p. 142 for the first quotation; Cadogan, *Diaries*, p. 582 for the second.

325 Anne Orde, *The Eclipse of Great Britain: The United States and British Imperial Decline, 1895–1956* (London: Macmillan, 1996), p. 141; Lowe, 'The War against Japan and Allied Relations', pp. 195–7, quotation on p. 195. The Fourteenth Army is sometimes referred to as the 'Forgotten Army', with historians and the public alike failing to give it the recognition it perhaps deserves. It was also 'British' only in shorthand, since it was a mixed imperial fighting force with many Indian, West and East African, and Dominion forces as well as British. Thanks to Giora Goodman.

326 Christopher Thorne, *Allies of a Kind: The United States, Britain, and the War against Japan, 1941–1945* (London: Hamish Hamilton, 1978), p. 725.

327 Wm. Roger Louis, *Imperialism at Bay: The United States and the Decolonization of the British Empire, 1941–1945* (Oxford: Oxford University Press, 1978), pp. 198–205, quotations on pp. 198, 200.

328 Doenecke and Stoler, *Franklin D. Roosevelt's Foreign Policies*, p. 53 for quotations; Diane Shaver Clemens, *Yalta* (London: Oxford University Press, 1970), pp. 46, 240–3. Orde, *The Eclipse of Great Britain*, p. 142. She points out that some Americans noted that 'America could not write the Empire out of existence and at the same time fight all over the world side by side with its armies and fleets.' *Ibid.*

329 Doenecke and Stoler, *Franklin D. Roosevelt's Foreign Policies*, pp. 54–5.

330 John E. Moser, *Twisting the Lion's Tail: Anglophobia in the United States, 1921–48* (London: Macmillan, 1999), p. 127.

331 Cadogan, *Diaries*, entry for 20 August 1943, p. 553; Randall Bennett Woods, *A Changing of the Guard: Anglo-American Relations, 1941–1946* (Chapel Hill: University of North Carolina Press, 1990), p. 13 for the quotation.

332 Burk, 'Lend–Lease', pp. 45–6. The comment was by Dean Acheson.

333 Gardner, *Sterling–Dollar Diplomacy*, p. 59.

334 Burk, 'Lend–Lease', pp. 45–7, 58–9, quotation on p. 45. Robert Skidelsky's assessment is that Morgenthau 'would do all he could to help Britain, but as a satellite, not as an ally'. In Keynes, III, p. 99.

335 Burk, 'Lend–Lease', p. 58; Orde, *Eclipse of Great Britain*, p. 143 for the quotation.

336 Burk, 'Lend–Lease', pp. 61–2; Hall, *North American Supply*, pp. 450 for first quotation; Sayers, *Financial Policy*, p. 480 for the second.

337 *Ibid.*, p. 375.

338 Christopher Andrew, 'Anglo-American–Soviet Intelligence Relations', in Lane and Temperley, eds, *The Grand Alliance*, pp. 108–9, quotation on p. 109. To keep things in perspective, 'Close German sigint collaboration with Italy, Hungary, Finland and the Baltic states in the 1930s proved more effective in penetrating Anglo-French systems in 1939–40, and in assisting German operational successes during the Norwegian campaign and the fall of France in June 1940, than the individual progress made separately by Poland, France, and the UK up to the outbreak of war.' John Chapman, 'Signals Intelligence Warfare', in Dear, ed., *Second World War*, p. 1005.

339 Andrew, 'Anglo-American–Soviet Intelligence Relations', pp. 110–15, quotation on p. 112.

340 Nevertheless, there was great ignorance about Japanese preparations for war, which was compounded by the inability to penetrate Soviet signals security enough to recognise the Soviet–Japanese commitment to mutual neutrality, without which Japan almost certainly would not have gone to war. Chapman, 'Signals Intelligence Warfare', p. 1005.

341 Andrew, 'Anglo-American–Soviet Intelligence Relations', pp. 110–12, quotation on p. 112. The official historian was F.H. Hinsley, author of *British Intelligence in the Second World War*.

342 *Ibid.*, pp. 118–21, 139, 162–3; Jeffrey T. Richelson and Desmond Ball, *The Ties That Bind* (Boston, Mass.: Unwin Hyman, 1990 2nd edn), pp. 4–7. 'The UKUSA Agreement is a tiered treaty in which the US is designated as the First Party, with the other nations designated as Second Parties, and thus the United States (and specifically the NSA [National Security Agency]) is recognized as the dominant party. This represents a reversal of the US–British SIGINT relationship that existed during the Second World War.' *Ibid.*, p. 7. Lack of confidence on both sides of the other's ability to maintain secrecy periodically emerged.

343 If neutrons collide with uranium nuclei, the uranium atom splits in two and releases very large amounts of energy, the process known as fission.

344 Rudolf Peierls, *Bird of Passage: Recollections of a Physicist* (Princeton, N.J.: Princeton University Press, 1985), pp. 152–5; Otto Frisch, *What Little I Remember* (Cambridge: Cambridge University Press, 1980 pb. edn, 1st pub. 1979), pp. 123–32.

345 For the amusing manner in which this committee got its name, see *ibid.*, p. 131.

346 It was the arrival of the French scientists, who were settled at the Cavendish Laboratory of Cambridge University, which gave the British a head start at the end of the war in designing and constructing slow neutron reactors which produced plutonium for both bombs and nuclear power.

347 Richard Rhodes, *The Making of the Atomic Bomb* (New York: Simon & Schuster, 1988 pb. edn, 1st pub. 1986), pp. 305–17.

348 Margaret Gowing, *Britain and Atomic Energy 1939–1945* (London: Macmillan, 1964), p. 97.

349 *Ibid.*, pp. 439–40 for the text of the agreement. Apparently one of the constraints on collaboration with Great Britain was congressional suspicion of her post-war plans, especially in the commercial energy field. Churchill and Sir John Anderson, the Lord President of the Council, drafted the agreement to give the Americans assurances as to Britain's commercial disinterestedness. Baylis, *Anglo-American Defence Relations*, pp. 19, 235.

350 Printed in *ibid.*, Appendix 3, p. 136.

351 Robert Dallek, *Franklin D. Roosevelt and American Foreign Policy, 1932–1945* (New York: Oxford University Press, 1979), p. 283 for the first quotation; Clemens, *Yalta*, p. 46 for the second.

352 *Ibid.*, p. 47 for Hull quotation; Anthony Eden, *The Reckoning* (London: Cassell, 1965), p. 328 or 343 or 370, quoted in Clemens, *Yalta*, p. 45.

353 *Ibid.*, p. 47.

354 Dallek, *Roosevelt and American Foreign Policy*, pp. 419–2 1; Cadogan, *Diaries*, p. 572 for the quotation.

355 Dallek, *Roosevelt and American Foreign Policy*, p. 434; Clemens, *Yalta*, p. 49.

356 Eden, *The Reckoning*, p. 514.

357 Clemens, *Yalta*, pp. 50–1; Eden, *The Reckoning*, p. 514; Dallek, *Roosevelt and American Foreign Policy*, p. 467.

358 'Check List of Essential Differences between the United States, the British, and the Soviet Proposals', 19 August 1944, File Dumbarton Oaks Conference I, Box 145, PSF, Roosevelt Papers; Hull, *Memoirs*, II, p. 1677.

359 Clemens, *Yalta*, p. 53.

360 *Ibid.*, pp. 218, 240–2; Robert E. Sherwood, *Roosevelt and Hopkins: An Intimate History* (New York: Harper & Brothers, 1950), p. 719 for Hong Kong; Eden, *The Reckoning*, p. 595.

361 Doenecke and Stoler, *Franklin D. Roosevelt's Foreign Policies*, p. 83; Stoler, *Allies in War*, p. 192.

362 Senator Tom Connolly, John Foster Dulles and Harold Stassen. Thorne, *Allies of a Kind*, p. 501.

363 Thomas M. Campbell and George C. Herring, eds, *The Diaries of Edward R. Stettinius, Jr., 1943–1946* (New York: Franklin Watts, 1975), chs. 9–12; Cadogan, *Diaries*, pp. 728–50; Gore-Booth, *With Great Truth and Respect*, pp. 138–43.

364 Gardner, *Sterling–Dollar Diplomacy*, p. 73 for the quotation; for a discussion of White and the evidence for his guilt, see Keynes, III, Appendix to ch. 7, 'Harry Dexter White: Guilty and Naive', pp. 256–63, in which he concludes that 'There is no question of treachery, in the accepted sense of betraying one's country's secrets to an enemy. But there can be no doubt that, in passing classified information to the Soviets, White knew that he was betraying his trust, even if he did not thereby think he was betraying his country.'

365 Armand Van Dormael, *Bretton Woods: Birth of a Monetary System* (London: Macmillan, 1978), p. 170.

366 *Ibid.*, p. 171.

367 Keynes, III, p. 339.

368 *Ibid.*, pp. 344–5.

369 Keynes to Sir Richard Hopkins, 30 June 1944, in John Maynard Keynes, *The Collected Writings, Volume XXVI: Activities 1941–1946: Shaping the Post-War World, Bretton Woods and Reparations*, ed. Donald Moggridge (London: Macmillan and Cambridge University Press, 1980), pp. 66–71, quotations on p. 68.

370 Van Dormael, *Bretton Woods*, pp. 168–83, quotations on pp. 176, 171, 172.

371 *Ibid.*, p. 185.

372 Keynes, III, p. 356.

373 *Ibid.*, pp. 355–6.

374 Van Dormael, *Bretton Woods*, p. 286.

375 Hamilton Diary, 14 April 1901, Add. MS 48678. By 1913, the US had overtaken Britain in virtually all production and consumption figures.

376 *Spectator*, 16 February 1940, p. 212. Thanks to Giora Goodman.

377 Keynes to Sir Kingsley Wood, the Chancellor of the Exchequer, 2 June 1941, in John Maynard Keynes, *The Collected Writings, Volume XXIII: Activities 1940–1943: External War Finance*, ed. Donald Moggridge (London: Macmillan, 1979), p. 106.

Chapter 7 – Anglo-American Marital Relations: 1870–1945

1 Potter was one of the founders of the National Association of Manufacturers. Olney Papers, cited in LaFeber, *The American Search for Opportunity*, p. 112.

2 Eric Homberger, *Mrs Astor's New York: Money and Social Power in a Gilded Age* (London: Yale University Press, 2002), pp. 237–54.

3 Dixon Wecter, *The Saga of American Society: A Record of Social Aspiration 1607–1937* (New York: Charles Scribner's Sons, 1937), pp. 210–11, sobriquet on p. 210, quotations on p. 211.

4 Ward McAllister, *Society as I Have Found It* (New York: Cassell, 1890), p. 212.

5 Homberger, *Mrs Astor's New York*, p. 185.

6 McAllister, *Society as I Have Found It*, pp. 214–15.

7 *Ibid.*, pp. 224–32; Ruth Brandon, *The Dollar Princesses: The American Invasion of the European Aristocracy 1870–1914* (London: Weidenfeld & Nicolson, 1980), p. 16.

8 Anita Leslie, *Lady Randolph Churchill: The Story of Jennie Jerome* (New York: Charles Scribner's Sons, 1969), pp. 14 (for the quotation), 23.

9 *Ibid.*, p. 24.

10 Elisabeth Kehoe, *Fortune's Daughters: The Extravagant Lives of the Jerome Sisters: Jennie Churchill, Clara Frewen and Leonie Leslie* (London: Atlantic Books, 2004), pp. 5–38.

11 R.F. Foster, *Lord Randolph Churchill: A Political Life* (Oxford: Oxford University Press, 1981), p. 17.

12 Gail MacColl and Carol McD. Wallace, *To Marry an English Lord* (New York: Workman, 1989), p. 39.

13 Kehoe, *Fortune's Daughters*, pp. 40–57.

14 MacColl and Wallace, *To Marry an English Lord*, pp. 40–2.

15 Kehoe, *Fortune's Daughters*, p. 59.

16 Quoted in Foster, *Lord Randolph Churchill*, p. 19.

17 Kehoe, *Fortune's Daughters*, pp. 62–73.

18 Oscar Wilde, *Complete Writings, Volume VI: Miscellanies* (New York: Nottingham Society, 1909), pp. 78–82.

19 Maureen E. Montgomery, *Gilded Prostitution: Status, Money, and Transatlantic Marriages 1870–1914* (London: Routledge, 1989), Appendices A and B, pp. 249–57.

20 Stephen Gwynn, ed., *The Letters and Friendships of Sir Cecil Spring Rice*, 2 vols (Boston, Mass.: Houghton Mifflin, 1929), I, p. 84. Spring Rice, during the First World War the British ambassador to the US, was then a young diplomat in his first term of duty in Washington. In a letter of 26 May 1887 he had written that the US 'is the dullest country in the world to be rich in, and the bitterest perhaps to be poor in'. *Ibid.*, p. 65.

21 John Bateman, ed. David Spring, *The Great Landowners of Great Britain and Ireland* (Leicester: University of Leicester Press, 1971, reprint of *The Acre-Ocracy of England – a List of al Owners of Three Thousand Acres and Upwards with Their Possessions and Incomes Arranged Under Their Various Counties. Also Their Collapses and Clubs. Culled from 'The Modern Domesday Book'*, 4th edn., 1883) p. 515.

22 From 1886 to 1891 the tenant rather than the landlord paid the tithe of £140 to the Church. *Victoria Country History: Essex* (London: Archibald Constable, 1907), II, p. 327. Another example was a farm in Braintree, also in Essex, which until 1884 paid rent of 72s. an acre, from 1885 to 1892 paid 8s. 3d and from 1893 to 1907 paid 5s. 9d. *Ibid.*, p. 328.

23 William Ashworth, *An Economic History of England 1870–1939* (London: Methuen, 1972 pb. edn, 1st pub. 1960), pp. 49–70.

24 Montgomery, *Gilded Prostitution*, pp. 119–24.

25 Ashworth, *Economic History*, pp. 67–8.

26 His father was Lewis Morris Rutherfurd, a distinguished astronomer and one of McAllister's Patriarchs. The family was 'old New York' as well as colonial New England, and were infinitely more socially established than were the Vanderbilts. They were rich old money. Jerry E. Patterson, *The Vanderbilts* (New York: Harry N. Abrams, 1989), p. 150.

27 Consuelo Balsan, *The Glitter and the Gold* (London: Heinemann, 1953), p. 38.

28 Wecter, *The Saga of American Society*, p. 408.

29 Balsan, *The Glitter and the Gold*, p. 46. Seven years later Winthrop married another heiress, Alice Morton, whose father, Levi P. Morton, was Vice-President of the US, Governor of New York, and a guest of honour at Consuelo's wedding. After her death, he married yet another wealthy and socially prominent woman, Lucy Mercer. He does not appear to have done much beyond riding to hounds. Amanda Mackenzie Stuart, *Consuelo & Alva: Love and Power in the Gilded Age* (London: HarperCollins, 2005), p. 154.

30 Evidence given to the Rota in 1926 when successfully applying for the annulment of her marriage. The above quotation of her mother (n. 28) is from the same source. Wecter, *The Saga of American Society*, p. 408.

31 Balsan, *The Glitter and the Gold*, pp. 50–1.

32 *Ibid.*, p. 52.

33 Indenture between Charles, Duke of Marlborough, and William Kissam Vanderbilt, 1895, quoted in Wecter, *The Saga of American Society*, p. 408.

34 Gustavus Myers, *History of the Great American Fortunes*, 2 vols (Chicago: Charles H. Kerr, 1909–11), II, p. 274, quoted in Montgomery, *Gilded Prostitution*, p. 168.

35 *Ibid.*, pp. 166, 111; Myers, *History of the Great American Fortunes*, II, p. 274, cited by Mackenzie Stuart, *Consuelo & Alva*, p. 522, ref. 87.

36 Montgomery, *Gilded Prostitution*, p. 31.

37 George W. Smalley, 'The American Girl in England and How It Happens That She Is Known in England', *New York Tribune*, 17 November 1888, reprinted in *London Letters and Some Others*, 2 vols (New York: Harper & Brothers, 1891), II, p. 104.

38 See, for example, Gertrude Atherton's *American Wives and English Husbands: A Novel* (New York: Dodd, Mead and Company, 1898), which a publisher of romantic novels might consider reprinting.

39 Smalley, 'The American Girl in England', p. 103.

40 Frances Hodgson Burnett, *Little Lord Fauntleroy* (London: Frederick Warne, 1886). She also wrote the more widely known *The Secret Garden*.

41 Frances Hodgson Burnett, *The Shuttle* (New York: Frederick A. Stokes, 1907), pp. 1, 2, 512. On the final page of text of my copy one former reader has written 'a great book', whilst on the back page another has written 'a fine story'.

42 Patterson, *Vanderbilts*, p. 239.

43 Mackenzie Stuart, *Consuelo & Alva*, pp. 383–92, 411–25.

44 Edith Wharton, *The Buccaneers*, completed by Marion Mainwaring (London: Fourth Estate, 1993), p. 404.

45 Price Collier, *England and the English* (London: Duckworth, 1913), p. 158. The legal definition of a peer was a man who had a right to a seat in the House of Lords.

46 The Marquess of Lansdowne and the Marquis of Salisbury had both turned down duke-doms because they felt that they 'lacked the resources to support the dignity'. David Cannadine, *The Decline and Fall of the British Aristocracy* (London: Papermac pb. edn, 1996), p. 17.

47 Leonore Davidoff, *The Best Circles: Society, Etiquette and the Season* (London: Cresset Library pb. edn, 1986, 1st pub. 1973), pp. 59–62; statistics from table 'Industrialists in the British Peerage', p. 60.

48 Patricia Otto, 'Daughters of the British Aristocracy: Their Marriages in the Eighteenth and Nineteenth Centuries with Particular Reference to the Scottish Peerage', Ph.D. dissertation, Stanford University, 1974, pp. 285, 199.

49 W.C.D. Whetham and C.D. Whetham, 'The Extinction of the Upper Classes', *Nineteenth Century and After*, Vol. 66 (1909), p. 100.

50 John W. Taylor, 'The Bishop of London on the Declining Birth Rate', *Nineteenth Century and After*, Vol. 59 (1906), quotations on pp. 223, 226.

51 *Ibid.*, p. 224.

52 Sidney Webb, *The Decline in the Birth-Rate*, Fabian Tract No. 131, March 1907, pp. 8, 6, 17.

53 Marie Corelli, *Free Opinions Freely Expressed on Certain Phases of Modern Social Life and Conduct* (London: Constable, 1905), p. 119.

54 Montgomery, *Gilded Prostitution*, Appendix J, pp. 294–5.

55 J. Reed, *From Private Vice to Public Virtue: The Birth Control Movement and American Society since 1830* (New York: Basic Books, 1978), p. 17. Carroll Smith-Rosenberg and Charles Rosenberg, 'The Female Animal: Medical and Biological Views of Woman and Her Role in Nineteenth-Century America', *Journal of American History*, Vol. 60 (1973), p. 334 for 'American sin'.

56 'Colonial', 'Titled Colonials versus Titled Americans', *Contemporary Review*, Vol. 87 (1905), pp. 861–9.

57 Montgomery, *Gilded Prostitution*, Appendix F, pp. 285–8.

58 Philip Ziegler, *King Edward VIII: The Official Biography* (London: Collins, 1990), p. 120.

59 *Ibid.*, p. 236.

60 Frances Donaldson, *Edward VIII* (London: Omega pb. edn, 1976, 1st pub. Weidenfeld & Nicolson, 1974), pp. 103–4.

61 Ziegler, *Edward VIII*, pp. 222–3.

62 Gloria Vanderbilt and Thelma Lady Furness, *Double Exposure* (London: Frederick Muller, 1959), p. 291, quoted in Ziegler, *Edward VIII*, p. 227.

63 *Ibid.*, p. 238.

64 Entry for 20 January 1936 in *The Duff Cooper Diaries 1915–1951*, ed. John Julius Norwich (London: Orion, 2006 pb. edn), p. 226.

65 Ziegler, *Edward VIII*, pp. 264–5.

66 *Ibid.*, p. 278, including the King's statement; p. 291 for Simpson's departure.

67 *Ibid.*, pp. 294–6.

68 *Ibid.*, pp. 304 (for quotation), 305.

69 Printed in Donaldson, *Edward VIII*, p. 295.

70 Ziegler, *Edward VIII*, p. 332.

71 Reynolds, *Rich Relations*, Tables 7.1, 22.1, 22.3. There were, of course, thousands of domestic war brides in the US, many of whom lived in less than desirable circumstances. See John Costello, *Love, Sex and War 1939–1945* (London: Pan, 1986), pp. 268–9.

72 Reynolds, *Rich Relations*, p. 265. Based on my memories of high school in California, this rings true. In particular, good girls *never* kissed on a first date.

73 *Ibid.*, p. 207.

74 *Ibid.*, p. 265.

75 Quotation cited in *ibid.*, p. 213.

76 *Ibid.*, pp. 2 13–14.

77 Quoted in *ibid.*, p. 210; FO Minute on Lord Inverchapel to FO, 27 July 1946, FO 371/95343/AN2306. Conversely, the foreign bride of a British serviceman gained British nationality by virtue of her marriage. *Ibid.*

78 Quoted in Reynolds, *Rich Relations*, p. 211.

79 *Ibid.*, pp. 211–15, quotation on p. 15.

80 Quoted in *ibid.*, pp. 413–16, quotation on pp. 413–14.

81 Announcement by US Army Headquarters in the UK, *Sunday Express*, 14 June 1945, FO 371/44657/95343/AN1989. The announcement had been recommended by a meeting in London on 7 June of the American Red Cross, which was attended by representatives of the American Embassy, the Ministry of Information, the US Office of War Information and members of the British American Liaison Board: 'Recommendation to be Presented to the Commanding General, US Army', 12 June 1945. *Ibid.* According to a Gallup poll published the following year, there was also some resentment of the brides themselves, who had captured American boys who ought to have married American girls, and who were now taking up space on passenger ships.

82 Reynolds, *Rich Relations*, p. 417.

83 Heywood to Prime Minister [Clement Attlee], 19 June 1945 and P.M. Broadmead, Foreign Office, to Waldemar J. Gallman, US Embassy, 16 July 1945, FO 371/95343/AN1988.

84 P.H. Gore-Booth to the FO, 30 July 1945, FO 371/44657/95343/AN2405.

85 Reynolds, *Rich Relations*, p. 418.

86 *Ibid.*, pp. 418–19.

87 Good Housekeeping Magazine, *A War Bride's Guide to the USA* (London: Collins & Brown, 2006), p. 6. This was originally published in June 1945 at the request of the US Office of War Information as a small pamphlet called *A Bride's Guide to the USA*.

88 Elfrieda Berthiaume Shukert and Barbara Smith Scibetta, *War Brides of World War II* (Novato, Calif.: Presidio Press, 1988), pp. 50–64.

89 Costello, *Love, Sex and War*, p. 350.

90 *Ibid.*

Chapter 8 – The Alliance since 1945

1 Found on a yellowing piece of paper salvaged from the first Anglo-American discussions in 1945 about post-war economic arrangements. Gardner, *Sterling–Dollar Diplomacy*, p. xiii.

2 John Ashbery, *Self-Portrait in a Convex Mirror* (Manchester: Carcanet Press, 1981, 1st pub. 1975), p. 46.

3 *Present at the Creation: My Years in the State Department* (New York: W.W. Norton, 1969), p. 387.

4 'An Anglo-American Balance Sheet', 1 August 1964, SC(64) 30 Revise, FO 371/177830/PLA24/7, p. 119.

5 p. 60.

6 This was stated as £7,300 million, made up primarily of physical destruction (£1,500 million), shipping losses (£700 million), internal disinvestment (£900 million), and external disinvestment (£4,200 million). The seriously worsening external position resulted mainly from the liquidation of external investments (£1,118 million), the increase in external liabilities (£2,879 million), and the loss of gold and dollar reserves (£152 million). Furthermore, exports at the end of 1944 were only one-third of their pre-war volume. UK Treasury, *Statistical Material Presented during the Washington Negotiations*, Cmd. 6706 (1945); Gardner, *Sterling–Dollar Diplomacy*, p. 178.

7 'The Essentials of American Policy', 21 March 1944, FO 371/38523/AN1538/16/45.

8 Gardner, *Sterling–Dollar Diplomacy*, p. 193 for the comment by Baruch and p. 237 for Celler (quoted in the *Daily Mail*, 7 December 1945).

9 'Second Thoughts', *The Economist*, Vol. 149, 15 December 1945, p. 850.

10 Gardner, *Sterling–Dollar Diplomacy*, pp. 199–201, quotation on p. 201.

11 *Ibid.*, pp. 208–9, quotation on p. 208. The US had supplied without charge some $27 billion worth of materials, receiving some $6 billion of 'reverse Lend–Lease' articles in return. *Ibid.*, p. 170. These included raw materials from the Empire, supplies for American forces stationed in Britain and the Empire, and oil for US forces in the Mediterranean. Stoler, *Allies in War*, p. 48.

12 $14 billion in frozen sterling credits in William Clayton to S.M. McAshan, Jr., 18 September 1945, quoted in *ibid.*, p. 205; £624 million from Sayers, *Financial Policy*, p. 496, Appendix 1, Table 7. Sayers gives 'liquid external liabilities' as £2,132 million for the Sterling Area and £3,354 million for 'all countries' (£1 = $4.03).

13 'Safeguards against use of our credit to repay blocked sterling balances', 13 November 1945, Box 148, File UK Loan – November 1945, Frederick Vinson Papers, University of Kentucky Library, Lexington, Kentucky.

14 Sir Hugh Ellis-Rees, 'The Convertibility Crisis of 1947', Treasury Historical Memorandum No. 4 (December 1962), pp. 51–3, T. 267/3.

15 Gardner, *Sterling–Dollar Diplomacy*, pp. 325–6, quotation on p. 205.

16 Kathleen Burk, 'Britain and the Marshall Plan', in Chris Wrigley, ed., *Warfare, Diplomacy and Politics: Essays in Honour of A.J.P. Taylor* (London: Hamish Hamilton, 1986), p. 215.

17 For the final settlement of the problem, see Kathleen Burk and Alec Cairncross, *'Goodbye, Great Britain': The 1976 IMF Crisis* (London: Yale University Press, 1992), ch. 4.

18 1) Money spent on reconstruction at home would increase demand, and this would spill over into increased imports and reduced exports; this would further increase the difficulty of the balance of payments on current account. 2) The destruction of physical capital, whether by enemy action or unreplaced depreciation, meant a lack of capacity to produce goods for export, to replace imports, and to replace physical capital (reconstruction). Thanks to Jeremy Wormell.

19 Burk, 'Britain and the Marshall Plan', pp. 214–15.

20 John Maynard Keynes, *The Collected Writings, Volume XXIV: Activities 1944–6: The Transition to Peace*, ed. Donald Moggridge (London: Macmillan, 1980), pp. 420–628; L.S. Pressnell, *External Economic Policy since the War, Volume I: The Post-War Financial Settlement* (London: HMSO, 1986), pp. 315–20; Box 148 in its entirety, Vinson Papers; Douglas Jay, *Change and Fortune: A Political Record* (London: Hutchinson, 1980), pp. 136–9; Alan Bullock, *Ernest Bevin: Foreign Secretary 1945–51* (London: Heinemann, 1983), pp. 121–5.

21 Ben Pimlott, *Hugh Dalton* (London: Jonathan Cape, 1985), p. 489 for example.

22 1 January 1946, in Keynes, XXIV, p. 626.

23 Gardner, *Sterling–Dollar Diplomacy*, p. 237.

24 Pressnell, *The Post-War Financial Settlement*, p. 324.

25 The Sterling Area comprised a group of countries which decided in 1931, when Great Britain went off the gold standard, to tie their currencies to sterling rather than to gold and to hold their currency reserves in the form of balances with the Bank of England. They included, besides the UK and the British Empire, all of the Commonwealth except Canada, plus Burma, Iceland, Ireland, Jordan, Libya and the Trucial States. During and after the war, the acute shortage of gold and dollars compelled the members to impose exchange controls, although there was freedom of exchange within the area.

26 Halifax to Attlee and Bevin, 5 December 1945, No. 155, in Roger Bullen and M.E. Pelly, eds, *Documents on British Policy Overseas, Series I, Volume III: Britain and America: Negotiations of the United States Loan 3 August–7 December 1945* (London: HMSO, 1986), p. 431.

27 Sir Richard Clarke, *Anglo-American Economic Collaboration in War and Peace 1942–1949*, ed. Sir Alec Cairncross (Oxford: Oxford University Press, 1982), pp. 61–3 for the quotation; Hugh Dalton, Diary, 7 December 1945, Vol. 33, Hugh Dalton Papers, British Library of Political and Economic Science, London School of Economics; Ellis-Rees, 'Convertibility Crisis', p. 4, T. 267/3.

28 There were to be fifty annual instalments beginning 31 December 1951 at 2 per cent interest. Pressnell, *The Post-War Financial Settlement*, Appendix 24.

29 It was made clear on several occasions by the Chancellor and other Cabinet ministers that the American Loan, as it was usually called, was a prerequisite to Bretton Woods. See Dalton's statement on this point during the Commons debate on the loan: 'the Loan Agreement is, for us, a condition of Bretton Woods'. 417 H.C. Deb. 431 (12 December 1945).

30 417 H.C. Deb. 468–9 (12 December 1945).

31 'Second Thoughts', *The Economist*, Vol. 159, 15 December 1945, p. 850.

32 For Churchill, 417 H.C. Deb. 713 (13 December 1945); for Keynes, 138 H.L. Deb. 784 (18 December 1945).

33 417 H.C. Deb. 443 (12 December 1945).

34 Gardner, *Sterling–Dollar Diplomacy*, p. 235.

35 Quoted in Keynes, III, p. 444.

36 138 H.L. Deb. 715 (17 December 1945).

37 Keynes, III, pp. 444–45.

38 *Ibid.*, p. 445.

39 138 H.L. Deb. 777–94 (18 December 1945), quotations on pp. 780, 783, 782 and 794.

40 138 H.L. Deb. 896 (18 December 1945).

41 Gardner, *Sterling–Dollar Diplomacy*, p. 235.

42 Baylis, *Anglo-American Defence Relations*, p. 9.

43 Gardner, *Sterling–Dollar Diplomacy*, p. 240.

44 *The Private Papers of Senator Vandenberg*, ed. Arthur H. Vandenberg, Jr. (Boston, Mass.: Houghton Mifflin, 1952), p. 231.

45 Gardner, *Sterling–Dollar Diplomacy*, pp. 238–52, quotation on p. 250.

46 Melvyn P. Leffler, *A Preponderance of Power: National Security, the Truman Administration,*

and the Cold War (Stanford, Calif.: Stanford University Press, 1992), pp. 79, 103–4; J.P.D. Dunbabin, *The Cold War: The Great Powers and Their Allies* (London: Longman, 1994), pp. 64–6.

47 Quoted in Gardner, *Sterling–Dollar Diplomacy*, p. 249. Henry Dexter White, then Assistant Secretary of the Treasury, in a speech on 9 April 1946, assured the audience that 'Consumption in England will still have to be kept down to something like war-time austerity.' Harry Dexter White Papers, Box 11, Folder 266, Princeton University Library.

48 Gardner, *Sterling–Dollar Diplomacy*, p. 251.

49 Chancellor of the Exchequer, 'Import Programme 1947/48', 28 May 1947, p. 11, CAB 129/19 for the quotation; Dalton Diary, 29 July 1947, Vol. 35.

50 Between December 1945 and March 1947, the US index of wholesale prices had risen by about 40 per cent. Ellis-Rees, 'Convertibility Crisis', p. 21, T. 267/3.

51 *Ibid.*, pp. 18–22, 28–32, T. 267/3; Dalton Diary, 17 August 1947, Vol. 35.

52 Susan Strange, *Sterling and British Policy* (Oxford: Oxford University Press, 1971), p. 62.

53 According to John Lewis Gaddis, Roosevelt 'saw some possibility that the Soviet and American systems of government might, through evolution, become similar', a 'trend toward convergence'. Gaddis, *The United States and the Origins of the Cold War, 1941–1947* (New York: Columbia University Press, 1972 pb. edn), p. 41.

54 Leffler, *A Preponderance of Power*, p. 101.

55 Kenneth M. Jensen, ed., *Origins of the Cold War: The Novikov, Kennan and Roberts 'Long Telegrams' of 1946* (Washington, D.C.: United States Institute of Peace, 1991), pp. 17–31, ref. 11, p. 69 for State Department request, p. 29 for Kennan quotation. A version was published in July 1947 as 'The Sources of Soviet Conduct' by X (Kennan) in the journal *Foreign Affairs*.

56 Leffler, *A Preponderance of Power*, pp. 104–7.

57 *Ibid.*, pp. 107–9; Churchill's speech is document 2.2 in Baylis, *Anglo-American Defence Relations*, pp. 41–5, quotations on pp. 42–3.

58 Significantly, there was no Cabinet Committee on Foreign Affairs. K.O. Morgan, *Labour in Power: 1945–1951* (Oxford: Oxford University Press, 1985), p. 236.

59 Martin H. Folly, 'Breaking the Vicious Circle: Britain, the United States, and the Genesis of the North Atlantic Treaty', *Diplomatic History*, Vol. 12, No. 1 (Winter 1988), pp. 64–5. There were, however, also plans for an air offensive against southern Russia from the Suez base. Thanks to David French.

60 COS Paper (47)227(0) Annex A, 19 December 1947, Chiefs of Staff Memorandum, DEFE 5/6, Ministry of Defence Records, the National Archive, Kew.

61 'Policy Towards Europe', 5 January 1949, in Clarke, *Anglo-American Economic Collaboration*. Those attending were Sir Edward Bridges, permanent secretary to the Treasury; Sir Henry Wilson-Smith, head of the Overseas Finance Division; F.G. Lee (later Sir Frank Lee, permanent secretary of the Treasury); D.H.F. Rickett (later Sir Denis Rickett, second permanent secretary to the Treasury); R.W.B. Clarke (later Sir Richard (Otto) Clarke, second permanent secretary to the Treasury); Roger Makins, Deputy Under-Secretary of State at the Foreign Office (later British ambassador to the USA and Lord Sherfield); Sir Percivale Liesching, Under-Secretary of State at the Dominions Office; Sir John Henry Woods, permanent secretary to the Board of Trade; and Sir Edwin (later Lord) Plowden, Chief Planning Officer of HMG.

62 'Department of State Policy Statement: Great Britain', 11 June 1948, *Foreign Relations of the United States* (hereafter *FRUS), 1948*, III, pp. 1091–108, quotations on pp. 1092 and 1091.

63 Richard J. Aldrich, *The Hidden Hand: Britain, America and Cold War Secret Intelligence* (London: John Murray, 2001), p. 305, quoting from Kim Philby's memoirs, *Silent War*, p. 117.

64 Paper prepared for the Department of State, 19 April 1950, *FRUS, 1950*, III, pp. 870–9.

65 The British maintained a military mission in Greece until 1952 to help to train the Greek National Army. They also played a covert role in some anti-bandit operations. Thanks to David French.

66 'The Americans knew for months in advance of the withdrawal from Greece and Turkey what our intentions were . . . As regards Greece, we can also make it plain to the Americans that we have now been there three years. When we first went in no one intended that we should stay there more than a few months. Moreover, when we went in there, we received no support from the US and certainly no kind words from them. We were tilted at and pulled to pieces in the US on all sides.' Memorandum by J.C.P. Henniker, 19 August 1947, FO 371/61003, fol. 28. According to Acheson, the Americans had known for forty-five days before receiving notification of withdrawal from the British that the Treasury and the Foreign Office were in disagreement as to whether Britain should leave or stay in Greece. Committee on Foreign Relations, *Hearings Held in Executive Session before the Committee on Foreign Relations, United States Senate, 80th Congress, 1st Session, on S. 938, A Bill to Provide for Assistance to Greece and Turkey*, 13 March–3 April 1947, p. 88.

67 For the cost of Greece to the British, see Dunbabin, *The Cold War*, p. 82; 'Aide-Mémoire', British Embassy to State Department, delivered 21 February 1947, pp. 32–5 for Greece; 'Aide-Mémoire', British Embassy to State Department, 21 February 1947, pp. 35–7 for Turkey; Loy W. Henderson, 'Memorandum of Conversation by the Director of the Office of Near Eastern and African Affairs', 24 February 1947, with the Secretary of State, Lord Inverchapel (British ambassador) and Herbert M. Sichel (first secretary, British Embassy), pp. 43–4; Memorandum by Under-Secretary of State Acheson to the Secretary of State [Marshall], 24 February 1947: re the British Notes, they 'point out that without aid, the independence of Greece and Turkey will not survive. . . I believe that the British are wholly sincere in this matter, and that the situation is as critical as they state', pp. 44–5, all *FRUS, 1947*, V.

68 Memo by Clayton, 3 March 1947, printed in Leffler, *A Preponderance of Power*, p. 143.

69 Dean Acheson, *Present at the Creation: My Years in the State Department* (New York: W.W. Norton, 1969), p. 219.

70 *Hearings. . . on S. 938*, pp. vii–xi, quotation on p. x.

71 For an outline of the historiography of the Marshall Plan, see Kathleen Burk, 'The Marshall Plan: Filling in Some of the Blanks', *Contemporary European History*, Vol. 10, No. 2 (July 2001), pp. 267–94; see also Burk, 'Britain and the Marshall Plan', pp. 210–30. According to John Foster Dulles, 'If most of the rest of the world becomes communistic and under Soviet domination, can we count on keeping it out of our own country?' 1 December 1948, Box 36, Folder European Recovery Program, John Foster Dulles Papers, Princeton University Library.

72 Acheson to Secretary of War Patterson, 5 March 1947, pp. 197–8; Memorandum by the State Department Members, State–War–Navy Coordinating Committee (Hildring), 17 March 1947, pp. 198–9; 'Report of the Special "Ad Hoc" Committee of the State–War–Navy Coordinating Committee, 21 April 1947, pp. 204–19; Memorandum by the Director of the Policy Planning Committee (Kennan), 16 May 1947; Kennan to Acheson, 23 May 1947, pp. 223–30; Memorandum by the Under-Secretary of State for Economic Affairs (William Clayton), 27 May 1947, pp. 230–2, all *FRUS, 1947*, III.

73 Joseph Marion Jones, *The Fifteen Weeks: An Inside Account of the Genesis of the Marshall Plan* (New York: Harcourt, Brace, 1955), pp. 255–6.

74 *Press Release Issued by the Department of State, June 4, 1947*, giving the text of Marshall's speech, *FRUS, 1947*, III, pp. 237–9.

75 Melvin Small, *Democracy and Diplomacy: The Impact of Domestic Politics on US Foreign Policy, 1789–1994* (Baltimore, Md.: Johns Hopkins University Press, 1996), p. 83.

76 Jones, *Fifteen Weeks*, p. 256.

77 *Ibid.*, pp. 252–3; Scott D. Parrish, *New Evidence on the Soviet Rejection of the Marshall Plan, 1947*, International History of the Cold War Working Paper No. 9 (Washington, D.C.: Smithsonian Institution, 1994); Kennan to Acheson, 12 May 1947, 6.i, p. 228 and 'Memorandum of Conversation, by the Counselor of the Department of State (Cohen)', ?18 June 1947, with the Polish

ambassador, pp. 260–1, both *FRUS, 1947*, III; Mikko Majander, 'The Limits of Sovereignty: Finland and the Marshall Plan in 1947', *Scandinavian Journal of History*, Vol. 19, No. 4 (1994), pp. 309–26; and Rudolf Jičín, Karel Kaplan, Karel Krátký and Jaroslav Šilar, eds, *Československo a Marshallův plán: Sborník dokumentů* (Praha: Sešity: Ústav pro soudobé dějiny ve spolupráci se Státním ústředním archivam, 1992) [summaries of Czech documents in English], pp. 117–27.

78 Bullock, *Bevin*, p. 405.

79 Geir Lundestad, *The American 'Empire' and Other Studies of US Foreign Policy in a Comparative Perspective* (Oslo: Norwegian University Press/Oxford University Press, 1992), pp. 54–62.

80 Alex Danchev, *Oliver Franks: Founding Father* (Oxford: Oxford University Press, 1993), ch. 4.

81 Bevin, 'Memorandum on European Economic Co-operation', 21 April 1948, C.P. (48) 109, PREM 8/980, Prime Minister's Papers, UK National Archive.

82 Sir Stafford Cripps, 'Economic Consequences of Receiving No E.R.P. Aid', 23 June 1948, C.P. 48 (161), PREM 8/495. This is a shortened version of a memorandum of the same title written in March 1948, PREM 8/768.

83 Douglas to Marshall, 23 June 1948, *FRUS, 1948*, III, pp. 1109–13.

84 'The Foreign Secretary pointed out that . . . the US draft in its present form was unacceptable'. Minute 4, Cab. E.P.C. (48) 20th meeting, 3 June 1948; Cab. E.P.C. (48) 48, 2 June 1948; Cab. E.P.C. (48), 21st Meeting, 8 June 1948 (the Chancellor called Article X 'exceedingly dangerous'); O. Franks, UK ambassador to the US, to the Foreign Office, 17 June 1948, No. 2898; and Franks to the FO, 19 June 1948, No. 2940; Cab. GEN 240/1st meeting, 24 June 1948, all PREM 8/768. The text of the Economic Co-operation Agreement is printed as Appendix B in Henry Pelling, *Britain and the Marshall Plan* (New York: St Martin's Press, 1988), pp. 153–65.

85 Transcript of interview with Thomas K. Finletter, chief of London Country Mission 1948–9, 25 February 1953, Box 1, File January–June 1953, H.B. Price Papers, Truman Presidential Library, Independence, Missouri; Apostolos Vetsoupoulos, 'The Economic Dimension of the Marshall Plan, 1947–52: The Origins of the Greek Economic Miracle', University College London PhD thesis, 2002.

86 Bissell to Foster and Hoffman, 13 July 1949, Box 24, Subject Files, File Countries-UK January–July 1949, Files of the Assistant Administrator, Programs, Economic Co-operation Administration Papers (Record Group 286), US National Archives.

87 H.B. Price interview with John Kenney, 18 September 1952, Box 1, File August–October 1952, Price Papers; 'Local Currency Counterpart Funds', 31 January 1949, Box 1, File Counterpart Funds and Harriman to Hoffman, and Finletter, REPTO 2048, 27 December 1949, Box 1, File Counterpart Funds, Use for Strategic Materials, both Policy Subject Files, Central Secretariat, ECA Papers; Hoffman to London, No. ECATO 188, 1 September 1948, Box 62, Country Files 1948–9, File UK Funds, ECA Papers. Norway was the other country which devoted her counterpart funds to debt reduction; German occupation forces had wreaked havoc on her finances and financial system.

88 Lincoln Gordon to Milton Katz on talk with Eric Roll, 5 April 1950, Box 87, Country Files 1949, File Material to be Filed, Comm. and Rec. Section, Office of the Special Representative Files, ECA Papers; Burk, 'Britain and the Marshall Plan', p. 223.

89 For the lack of proportion, see, e.g., Memorandum, probably by Theodore Geiger and Harlan Cleveland, 1 September 1949, for a proposal to bounce France, Italy and the Benelux countries into an economic union before their governments had 'time to think through in detail all of the consequences, dangers and repercussions', Box 1, Copies of Outgoing Letters, Reading File 7 October–30 September 1949, Assistant Administrator Programs, and Bissell Memorandum for Hoffman and Bruce, 22 September 1948, Interoffice Memoranda (April 1948–May 1950), Office of the Administrator Files, both ECA Papers.

90 She received $3,443 million 1948–52; France received $2,806 million, Italy $1,548 million, Germany $1,413 million, the Netherlands $1,079 million, with Iceland receiving the least, $30 million. Gerd Hardach, *Der Marshall-Plan: Auslandshilfe und Wiederaufbrau in Westdeutschland 1948–1952* (München: Deutscher Taschenbuch, 1994), Table 6, p. 244.

91 Bevin's conversations with Bidault and Marshall (but not Robinson), 17 December 1947, FO 371/67674/Z11009 for Marshall and *ibid.* /Z11010 for Bidault; Sir Nicholas Henderson, *The Birth of NATO* (London: Weidenfeld & Nicolson, 1982), pp. 1–2, quotations on p. 1. Henderson was Second Secretary at the British Embassy in Washington and a member of the Working Party; in the weeks following the signing of the treaty on 4 April 1949 he wrote this as a report for the Foreign Office. Leffler refers to Bevin's 'inchoate, grandiose' ideas in *Preponderance of Power*, p. 199.

92 Henderson, *Birth of NATO*, p. 6; Folly, 'Breaking the Vicious Circle', pp. 60–2.

93 446 H.C. Deb. 383–90; Henderson, *Birth of NATO*, p. 7 for the quotation.

94 Folly, 'Breaking the Vicious Circle', p. 71.

95 Henderson, *Birth of NATO*, pp. 8–10, quotation on p. 10; Folly, 'Breaking the Vicious Circle', pp. 62–4; Leffler, *Preponderance of Power*, pp. 202–3.

96 Gladwyn, *The Memoirs of Lord Gladwyn* (London: Weidenfeld, 1972), p. 220.

97 British Embassy to Department of State, 11 March 1948, *FRUS, 1948*, III, p. 46, ref. 2.

98 Folly, 'Breaking the Vicious Circle', p. 66.

99 Quoted in Henderson, *Birth of NATO*, p. 14.

100 'If such demands are made on Norway, . . . it is imperative that Norway adamantly resist such demands and pressures . . . [W]e are in communication with Brit Govt about Norwegian situation.' Marshall to Bay, 12 March 1948, *FRUS, 1948*, III, p. 51; Folly, 'Breaking the Vicious Circle', pp. 67–9.

101 Marshall to Inverchapel, 12 March 1948, *FRUS, 1948*, III, p. 48.

102 This is just a hint of the nature and complexity of the problems which had to be dealt with during the negotiations. Henderson, *Birth of NATO*, pp. 11–110; Acheson, *Present at the Creation*, pp. 277–9.

103 This recalls the League of Nations, the Treaty of Versailles and the Senate.

104 As implicitly characterised by Alex Danchev, *On Specialness: Essays in Anglo-American Relations* (Basingstoke: Macmillan, 1998), p. 152.

105 Text of the North Atlantic Treaty in Henderson, *Birth of NATO*, Appendix B, pp. 119–22.

106 Acheson, *Present at the Creation*, p. 286; Vandenberg, *Private Papers*, pp. 474–83.

107 Greece and Turkey joined in 1952, the Federal Republic of Germany in 1955, Spain in 1982, the reunited Germany in 1990, the Czech Republic, Hungary and Poland in 1999, and Bulgaria, Estonia, Lithuania, Latvia, Romania, Slovakia and Slovenia in 2004.

108 See the various chapters in Judith M. Brown and Wm. Roger Louis, eds, *The Oxford History of the British Empire: The Twentieth Century* (Oxford: Oxford University Press, 2001).

109 A fictional account of a Briton's apprehension that a CIA agent had hugely overstepped the boundary is Graham Greene, *The Quiet American* (Harmondsworth: Penguin, 1965, 1st pub. 1955).

110 Quoted in Aldrich, *Hidden Hand*, pp. 10–11.

111 Peter J. Roman, 'Curtis LeMay and the Origins of NATO Atomic Targeting', *Journal of Strategic Studies*, Vol. 16, No. 1 (March 1993), p. 53. SAC, however, did not have control of the bombs. *Ibid.*

112 Aldrich, *Hidden Hand*, p. 207. Duncan Campbell, *The Unsinkable Aircraft Carrier* (London: Michael Joseph, 1984), p. 28. American long-range bombers such as the B-36 (with a range of 4,000 nautical miles) began to appear only in 1951; before then, the US was desperate for air bases close to the USSR. Aldrich, *Hidden Hand*, pp. 207, 216.

113 Campbell, *The Unsinkable Aircraft Carrier*, p. 32; 'Summary of Considerations Affecting

the Decision to Send B-29 Bombers to England', in Walter Millis, ed., *The Forrestal Diaries: The Inner History of the Cold War* (London: Cassell, 1952), pp. 429–30.

114 Quoted in Christopher Hitchens, *Blood, Class and Empire: The Enduring Anglo-American Relationship* (New York: Nation Books, 2004), p. 350.

115 Baylis, *Anglo-American Defence Relations*, pp. 39–41; Margaret Gowing, *Independence and Deterrence: Britain and Atomic Energy 1945–1952, Volume I: Policy Making* (London: UK Atomic Energy Authority and Macmillan, 1974), pp. 310–13. An informal agreement was reached in 1950, but it did not include consultation on the use of US bombers. An agreement of sorts was reached between Truman and Attlee only in October 1951.

116 Aldrich, *Hidden Hand*, pp. 29 1–2. 'The long-term aims of United States policy are not clear . . . there are some indications that they rate the possibility of detaching the satellites by subversion and revolt a good deal higher than we do . . . There are very evident risks that subversive activities involving anti-Soviet elements in the satellite countries may at a certain stage get out of control . . . For it is clearly on the European nations rather than on the United States that the first repercussions would fall.' PUSC (51) 16 (Final), 'Future Policy towards Soviet Russia', Secret, 17 January 1952, ZP10/4, FO 371/125002, Doc. 14.5, in Richard J. Aldrich, *Espionage, Security and Intelligence in Britain 1945–1970* (Manchester: Manchester University Press, 1998), pp. 194–6, quotation on p. 195.

117 Aldrich, *Hidden Hand*, p. 12.

118 Quoted in James R. Vaughan, *The Failure of American and British Propaganda in the Arab Middle East, 1945–57: Unconquerable Minds* (London: Palgrave, 2005), p. 160.

119 Evelyn Shuckborough, *Descent to Suez: Diaries 1951–56* (London: Weidenfeld & Nicolson, 1986), examples on pp. 178, 327, 340, 365.

120 Aldrich, *Hidden Hand*, p. 478.

121 W. Scott Lucas, *Divided We Stand: Britain, the US and the Suez Crisis* (London: Hodder & Stoughton, 1996 pb. edn), p. 27.

122 *Ibid.*, pp. 45–50; Wm. Roger Louis, *Ends of British Imperialism: The Scramble for Empire, Suez and Decolonization* (London: I.B. Tauris, 2006), pp. 641–7.

123 Tore Tingvold Petersen, 'Anglo-American Rivalry in the Middle East: The Struggle for the Buraimi Oasis, 1952–1957', *International History Review*, Vol. 14, No. 1 (February 1992), pp. 7 1–91.

124 Aldrich, *Hidden Hand*, p. 478.

125 Selwyn Lloyd, *Suez 1956: A Personal Account* (London: Jonathan Cape, 1978), p. 219.

126 *New York Times*, 14 September 1956, quoted in Louise Richardson, *When Allies D iffer: Anglo-American Relations during the Suez and Falklands Crises* (New York: St Martin's Press, 1996), p. 51; 'Statement by the Secretary of State', 17 September 1956, Box 10, file Suez Canal Second Conference, John Foster Dulles Papers, Princeton University Library, Princeton, New Jersey.

127 Richardson, *When Allies Differ*, pp. 96–9.

128 Diane B. Kunz, 'The Importance of Having Money: The Economic Diplomacy of the Suez Crisis', in Wm. Roger Louis and Roger Owen, eds, *Suez 1956: The Crisis and Its Consequences* (Oxford: Oxford University Press, 1989), quotations on pp. 226–7.

129 Amin Hewedy, 'Nasser and the Crisis of 1956', in Louis and Owen, eds, *Suez 1956*, p. 167; Richardson, *When Allies Differ*, p. 95.

130 *Ibid.*, pp. 107–8.

131 Richard E. Neustadt, *Alliance Politics* (New York: Columbia University Press, 1970 pb. edn), p. 26.

132 Kunz, 'Economic Diplomacy', p. 227; Diane B. Kunz, *The Economic Diplomacy of the Suez Crisis* (Chapel Hill: University of North Carolina Press, 1991), *passim*.

133 'During the Suez rift . . . the two intelligence communities were closer than their political masters and it is interesting that . . . the CIA representative on the JIC [the UK

Joint Intelligence Committee] . . . was left as the sole US–UK channel when all other communications between the two governments had been broken off.' Percy Craddock, *Know Your Enemy: How the Joint Intelligence Committee Saw the World* (London: John Murray, 2002), p. 279.

134 'Against her opposition we can do very little (e.g. Suez) and our need for American support is a fact which we cannot ignore.' 'Planning paper on interdependence: the effects of Anglo-American interdependence on the long-term interests of the United Kingdom', 27 January 1958, Steering Committee SC (58) 8, p. 3, FO 371/132330. The diplomat Sir Pierson Dixon later wrote that the main result of the Suez debacle had been that at one stroke Great Britain had been reduced 'from a 1st class to a 3rd class power'. Piers Dixon, *Double Diploma: The Life of Sir Pierson Dixon* (London: Hutchinson, 1968), p. 278.

135 Caccia to Lloyd, 'The Present State of Anglo-United States Relations', 28 December 1956, pp. 4–5, PREM 11/2189.

136 Peter Golden, *Quiet Diplomat: A Biography of Max M. Fisher* (New York: Cornwall Books, 1992), p. xviii, for Eisenhower's regret. Henry Kissinger later wrote that the USSR noted the US's disavowal of its closest allies, whilst the Europeans drew the conclusion that the interests of the US and Europe did not always run together. The French decided that Europe had to be united in order to play a decisive role in world affairs, and both France and Britain decided that, because they could not always count on US support, they needed to gain and maintain their own nuclear deter-rents. Kissinger, *Diplomacy* (New York: Simon & Schuster, 1994), pp. 546–8.

137 Septimus H. Paul, *Nuclear Rivals: Anglo-American Atomic Relations 1941–1952* (Columbus: Ohio State University Press, 2000), p. 95.

138 Robert M. Hathaway, *Great Britain and the United States: Special Relations since World War II* (Boston, Mass.: Twayne, 1990), p. 19.

139 Paul, *Nuclear Rivals*, p. 94. Seventy per cent of citizens and 90 per cent of Congressmen were against sharing information; interestingly, over 80 per cent of the respondents did not think that the secret could remain an American monopoly for more than five years. *Ibid.*, pp. 94–5.

140 437 H.C. Deb. 1965.

141 Francis Williams, *Twilight of Empire: Memoirs of Prime Minister Clement Attlee, as Set down by Francis Williams* (Westport, Conn.: Greenwood Press, 1978), p. 119.

142 Gowing, *Independence and Deterrence*, I, p. 174.

143 Acheson, a man with realpolitik in his bones, later wrote: 'During the winter of 1945–46 I learned about a matter that was to disturb me for some years to come, for with knowledge came the belief that our Government, having made an agreement from which it had gained immeasureably, was not keeping its word and performing its obligations. Like all great issues it was not simple. Grave consequences might follow upon keeping our word, but the idea of not keeping it was repulsive to me. The analogy of a nation to a person is not sound in all matters of moral conduct; in this case, however, it seemed to me pretty close. Even in *realpolitik* a reputation for probity carries its own pragmatic rewards.' As for Eisenhower, he told Macmillan in 1957 that the Act was 'one of the most deplorable incidents in American history, of which he personally felt ashamed'. Acheson, *Present at the Creation*, p. 164; Harold Macmillan, *Riding the Storm 1956–1959* (New York: Harper & Row, 1971), p. 324.

144 Confidential Annex, Minute 1, Research in Atomic Weapons, GEN. 163/1st meeting, CAB.130/16. Bevin's comment is on p. 1.

145 Ian Clark and Nicholas J. Wheeler, *The British Origins of Nuclear Strategy, 1945–1955* (Oxford: Oxford University Press, 1989), Chiefs of Staff quotation on p. 214, Salisbury quotation and their own 'adventurous action' quotation on p. 215.

146 Thanks to David French for the bases point. Reynolds, *Britannia Overruled*, p. 171.

147 S.J. Ball, 'Military Nuclear Relations between the United States and Great Britain under the Terms of the McMahon Act, 1946–1958', *Historical Journal*, Vol. 38, No. 2 (1995), pp. 170–1.

148 He reveals that the USAF moved to circumvent the Atomic Energy Commission's ban on giving information about nuclear weapons to the UK. In December 1955 'Project E was set up to convert British planes to carry American atomic bombs. At about the same time an even more sensitive programme, known as Project X, was established to prepare the RAF to receive American hydrogen bombs. The USAF delivered twenty dummy bombs and details of their advanced low-altitude bombing system to the Royal Aircraft Establishment, Farnborough so that RAF Canberra bombers could be modified to carry American nuclear weapons. The British were thus in full possession of the data about the dimensions, weights and attachment systems that the AEC had attempted to deny them.' The UK Treasury, however, worried that because these were informal agreements between military leaders, there was nothing to prevent the USA from cancelling the arrangement; furthermore, even if the arrangement continued, there was a substantial risk that the UK would become dependent on American technology, thereby compromising the independence of the British nuclear force. Consequently, the Treasury denied funding to convert the V-bombers to carry the American atomic weapons. *Ibid.*, pp. 450–1, quotation on p. 450.

149 *Ibid.*, pp. 448–9.

150 *Ibid.*, p. 450. And the USSR, of course.

151 Macmillan, *Riding the Storm*, p. 245. In 1964 the UK became part of the American Ballistic Missile Early Warning System, a chain of radars that gave limited warning of early attack, with the construction of a station on Fylingdales Moor. Aldrich, *Espionage, Security and Intelligence*, p. 60.

152 Dwight D. Eisenhower, *The White House Years: Waging Peace 1956–1961* (London: Heinemann, 1966), p. 124. '[T]here was a noticeable atmosphere of frankness and confidence throughout the meeting. Our determination to rebuild our close understanding was aided, in part, by the fact that Harold and I were old comrades.' *Ibid.*

153 Baylis, *Anglo-American Defence Relations*, pp. 88–90.

154 I.G.C. Dryden, ed., *The Efficient Use of Energy* (Guildford: IPC Science and Technology Press, 1975), p. 319. Magnox was the name of the magnesium alloy used for the cans which contained the uranium fuel rods. Thanks to Michael Jewess.

155 Hitchens, *Blood, Class and Empire*, pp. 341–2.

156 Baylis, *Anglo-American Defence Relations*, pp. 90–1, quotation on p. 90. It was the 'Agreement for Co-operation on Uses of Atomic Energy for Mutual Defence Purposes'. Reynolds, *Britannia Overruled*, p. 200.

157 Harold Macmillan, *Pointing the Way 1959–1961* (New York: Harper & Row, 1972), p. 252 for the quotations. The RAF wanted Skybolt rather than Polaris because prolonging the life of the V-bomber force ensured the continuance of their premier role in the deterrent. The Royal Navy was apprehensive that if it asked for Polaris, it would have to pay for it; if the government to decided, it would then have to provide new money for it.

158 'Record of a Meeting Held at Bali-Hai, the Bahamas, at 9.50 a.m. on Wednesday, December 19, 1962', Prime Minister's Talks with President Kennedy and Mr Diefenbaker, December 18–22, 1962, PREM 11/4229, p. 8.

159 Harold Watkinson, *Turning Points: A Record of Our Times* (Salisbury: Michael Russell, 1986), pp. 122–4.

160 Baylis, *Anglo-American Defence Relations*, p. 247, ref. 47.

161 C.J. Bartlett, *'The Special Relationship': A Political History of Anglo-American Relations since 1945* (London: Longman, 1992), p. 98; Meredith Veldman, *Fantasy, the Bomb, and the Greening of Britain: Romantic Protest, 1945–1980* (Cambridge: Cambridge University Press, 1994), pp. 171–

2, 176, ref. 92; for the 1961 Holy Loch protests, Richard Taylor, *Against the Bomb: The British Peace Movement 1958–1965* (Oxford: Oxford University Press, 1988), pp. 170–7.

162 Ernest R. May and Philip D. Zelicow, eds, *The Kennedy Tapes: Inside the White House during the Cuban Missile Crisis* (Cambridge, Mass.: Harvard University Press, 1997), p. 692.

163 Bartlett, 'The Special Relationship', p. 99.

164 *New York Times*, 6 December 1962, in Ian S. McDonald, ed., *Anglo-American Relations since the Second World War* (Newton Abbot: David & Charles, 1974), Document 43, pp. 181–2; Douglas Brinkley, 'Dean Acheson and the "Special Relationship": The West Point Speech of December 1962', *Historical Journal*, Vol. 33, No. 3 (September 1990), pp. 599–608. The speech was actually on prospects for European unity.

165 David Nunnerley, *President Kennedy and Britain* (New York: St Martin's Press, 1972), pp. 1–2.

166 Henry Brandon, *Special Relationships: A Foreign Correspondent's Memoirs from Roosevelt to Reagan* (London: Macmillan, 1988), p. 163.

167 They also discussed Cuba, the Sino-Indian conflict and Berlin.

168 Nunnerley, *President Kennedy and Britain*, pp. 149–53, quotations on pp. 149, 152–3.

169 *Ibid.*, p. 153.

170 Henry Brandon, *Sunday Times*, 8 December 1963, quoted in Reynolds, *Britannia Overruled*, p. 202; George Ball, *The Past Has Another Pattern: Memoirs* (New York: W.W. Norton, 1982), p. 266; Solly Zuckerman, *Monkeys, Men and Missiles: An Autobiography 1946–88* (London: Collins, 1988), pp. 256–7.

171 Bartlett, 'The Special Relationship', p. 99; McNamara quoted in Baylis, *Anglo-American Defence Relations*, p. 102.

172 'Record of a Meeting . . . at 9.50 a.m. . . . on December 19, 1962', p. 11, PREM 11/4229 for quotation by Macmillan on Germany; Ball, *The Past Has Another Pattern*, p. 267.

173 *Ibid.*, pp. 208–22.

174 'Record of a Meeting . . . at 9.50 a.m. . . . December 19, 1962', pp. 9–10, PREM 11/4229.

175 L.V. Scott, *Macmillan, Kennedy and the Cuban Missile Crisis: Political, Military and Intelligence Aspects* (London: Macmillan, 1999), *passim.*; May and Zelikow, eds, *The Kennedy Tapes*, p. 692.

176 Nunnerley, *President Kennedy and Britain*, pp. 155–6, quotation on p. 155.

177 'Record of a Meeting held . . . at 9.50 a.m. . . . on December 19, 1962', p. 10, PREM 11/4229. Two days after Nassau, Skybolt successfully passed its sixth test.

178 Harold Macmillan, *At the End of the Day 1961–1963* (New York: Harper & Row, 1973), p. 360. The record of the meetings makes his use of these tactics manifestly clear. PREM 11/4229.

179 On 18 January 1961 Brook had concluded that 'on purely military grounds, and assuming continued cohesion between the United States and United Kingdom, there is no great need for an independent British contribution to the strategic nuclear deterrent of the West. And over the years ahead its military value to the West will decline.' Sir Norman Brooke, 'Some Aspects of Our Relations with the United States', CAB 133/244.

180 Lawrence Freedman and John Gearson, 'Interdependence and Independence: Nassau and the British Nuclear Deterrent', in Kathleen Burk and Melvyn Stokes, eds, *The United States and the European Alliance since 1945* (Oxford: Berg, 1999), pp. 195–6.

181 Nunnerley, *President Kennedy and Britain*, pp. 15 7–8.

182 Brandon, *Special Relationships*, pp. 163–4, quotation on p. 164.

183 Ball, *The Past Has Another Pattern*, p. 267.

184 Nigel Ashton, *Kennedy, Macmillan and the Cold War: The Irony of Interdependence* (London: Palgrave, 2002), p. 152. Kennedy proclaimed a Declaration of Interdependence between the US and a united Europe in a speech at Independence Hall, Philadelphia, on 4 July 1962.

185 Sir Roger Jackling, Second Permanent Under-Secretary at the Ministry of Defence 1996–2002, to the author, 22 April 2007.

186 President Kennedy and Prime Minister Macmillan, 'Statement on Nuclear Defense Systems', Joint Statement, Nassau, 21 December 1962, PREM 11/4229, pp. 59–61; Zuckerman, *Monkeys, Men and Missiles*, p. 259.

187 Raymond Seitz, *Over Here* (London: Weidenfeld & Nicolson, 1998), pp. 317–18. Seitz was the American Ambassador to the UK 1991–4.

188 Kathleen Burk, 'Outline of Events, 1967 Devaluation Symposium', *Contemporary Record* (Winter 1988), pp. 44–5.

189 Quoted in Bartlett, *'The Special Relationship'*, p. 116.

190 Jonathan Colman, *A 'Special Relationship'? Harold Wilson, Lyndon B. Johnson and Anglo-American Relations 'at the Summit', 1964–68* (Manchester: Manchester University Press, 2004), p. 114.

191 Burk, '1967 Devaluation Symposium', pp. 45–51. In order to protect the US balance of payments in the summer of 1965, the Americans threatened 'retaliatory action' against the UK if she devalued. Glen O'Hara, 'The Limits of US Power: Transatlantic Financial Diplomacy under the Johnson and Wilson Administrations, October 1964–November 1968', *Contemporary European History*, Vol. 12, No. 3 (August 2003), p. 261.

192 Hathaway, *Great Britain and the United States*, pp. 81–2.

193 *Ibid.*, p. 90.

194 Harold Wilson, *The Labour Government 1964–70* (Harmondsworth: Penguin, 1974, 1st pub. 1971), p. 635 and quotation on p. 341.

195 Louis Heren, *No Hail, No Farewell* (London: Harper & Row, 1970), p. 230.

196 Richard Crossman, *The Diaries of a Cabinet Minister, Volume I: Minister of Housing 1964–66* (London: Hamish Hamilton and Jonathan Cape, 1976), p. 95.

197 Denis Healey, *The Time of My Life* (London: Michael Joseph, 1989), p. 299.

198 Burk, '1967 Devolution Symposium', pp. 46, 51.

199 Their functions were taken over by the Foreign Office, which then became the Foreign and Commonwealth Office, or FCO.

200 Jeffrey Pickering, *Britain's Withdrawal from East of Suez: The Politics of Retrenchment* (London: Macmillan, 1998), pp. 168–86, quotation on p. 168.

201 *Ibid.*, p. 173.

202 Richard Crossman, *The Diaries of a Cabinet Minister, Volume II: Lord President of the Council and Leader of the House of Commons 1966–68* (London: Hamish Hamilton and Jonathan Cape, 1976), p. 639.

203 Henry Kissinger, *White House Years* (Boston, Mass.: Little, Brown, 1979), p. 933.

204 *Ibid.*, pp. 932–3.

205 John Campbell, *Edward Heath: A Biography* (London: Jonathan Cape, 1993), p. 336.

206 John Dumbrell, *A Special Relationship: Anglo-American Relations from the Cold War to Iraq* (London: Palgrave pb., 2006 2nd edn), p. 90.

207 Henry Kissinger, *Years of Upheaval* (Boston, Mass.: Little, Brown, 1982), p. 191.

208 Seitz, *Over Here*, p. 317.

209 John Freeman, 'United States Review for 1970. Mr Freeman's Farewell Despatch', 8 January 1971, FCO 42/82.

210 Brimelow was the Deputy Under-Secretary of State. The story is told in a series of documents extracted from *Documents on British Policy Overseas, Series III, Volume IV: The Year of Europe: America, Europe and the Energy Crisis 1972–1974* (London: HMSO, 2006) (hereafter *DBPO)* and published concurrently as *Operation Hullabaloo: Britain's Role in Kissinger's Nuclear Diplomacy.* The quotation is from Cromer to Brimelow, 7 March 1973, No. 44 in *DBPO*. As is made clear in the Preface, British involvement in the drafting of the agreement bordered 'on the bizarre. Brimelow was in effect to become Kissinger's desk officer for the Soviet Union, amending and putting into treaty form a bilateral US/Soviet arrangement for which neither he, nor his colleagues, had any genuine sympathy.' *Ibid.*, p. 2.

211 Seitz, *Over Here,* p. 323.

212 Cromer to Douglas Home, 'The Middle East War and US/UK Relations', 9 January 1974, FCO 82/304.

213 At first, supplies from American depots in Germany were sent to Israel through German and Dutch ports. When the Germans asked the US to stop using the bases as part of the supply route, 'the Nixon administration challenged the extent of West German sovereignty over the bases'. This, in turn, raised a more dangerous issue: were American troops in Europe there to defend NATO against Soviet aggression, or as a base for American activities elsewhere? Fiona Venn, 'International Co-operation versus National Self-Interest: The United States and Europe during the 1973–1974 Oil Crisis', in Burk and Stokes, eds, *The United States and the European Alliance,* p. 80.

214 Cromer to Douglas Home, 'The Middle East War and US/UK Relations'; 'Chronology of Anglo/American Contacts during the Middle East War', n.d., FCO 82/34. The US Embassy in London had told the State Department not to ask.

215 Venn, 'The 1973–1974 Oil Crisis', p. 72 for the 'panic' quotation; Cromer to Douglas Home, 'The Middle East War and US/UK Relations'. The need to gain or retain the political support of the very influential Jewish lobby was a consideration, but in this case strategic concerns predominated.

216 *Ibid.*

217 *Ibid.*

218 Cromer to Brimelow, 7 March 1973, No. 44, *DBPO,* III, Vol. 4.

219 Greenhill was the Permanent Under-Secretary. 'Summary of Current Problems in HMG's Foreign Policy', June 1970, PREM 15/064.

220 Burk and Cairncross, *'Goodbye, Great Britain',* pp. 12–17, 179–93; for inflation, Table 3, *ibid.,* p. 148.

221 Scott Pardee was the vice-president of the Federal Reserve Bank of New York, for international finance effectively the US central bank, and the man with responsibility for foreign exchange operations in 1976. Reflecting both his own feelings and those of his contacts on Wall Street, his reaction was that 'by this time a lot of people were fed up with sterling crises'. Interview with Scott Pardee, 26 July 1989.

222 Yeo quoted in Stephen Fay and Hugo Young, 'The Day the £ Nearly Died', *Sunday Times* (14, 21 and 28 May 1978), 14 May 1978, pp. 43–4. Benn called for 'import controls fed in by a period of import deposits, and exchange controls which would certainly be necessary in the short run. This would permit us to have a differential interest rate for official holders of sterling. We'd need a capital issues committee, control of bank borrowing and to keep an eye on the direction of investment – and planning agreements under reserve powers – more money for the NEB [the government's National Enterprise Board]. But the most important thing is that we should consult the TUC [Trades Union Congress].' Tony Benn, *Against the Tide: Diaries 1973–76* (London: Hutchinson, 1989), p. 665.

223 Kathleen Burk, 'The Americans, the Germans, and the British: The 1976 IMF Crisis', *Twentieth Century British History,* Vol. 5, No. 3 (1994), p. 352.

224 Fay and Young, 'The Day the £ Nearly Died', 21 May 1978, p. 34.

225 Interview with Sir Kit McMahon, 3 September 1991; scribbled notes by Burns of telephone conversations between Arthur Burns, Governor of the US Federal Reserve Board, Gordon Richardson, Governor of the Bank of England, and others, and reflections, 7 June 1976, and Burns to the Federal Reserve Open Market Committee, 3 June 1976, both Arthur Burns Papers, Box 113, File UK Loan from Group of 10, June 1976, Ford Presidential Library, Ann Arbor, Michigan. This had been discussed briefly on the previous day by Denis Healey, the Chancellor of the Exchequer, and Johannes Witteveen, the managing director of the IMF, but at that time Healey thought that Britain could repay the credit. Telephone conversation

between the Chancellor of the Exchequer and Witteveen, 'Note for the Record', 3 June 1976, PREM 16/796; Fay and Young, 'The Day the £ Nearly Died', 14 May 1978, p. 33; and Burk and Cairncross, *'Goodbye, Great Britain'*, pp. 40–4.

226 Led by local shop stewards in individual factories rather than organised by the national union.

227 Burk, 'The 1976 IMF Crisis', p. 359; entry for 23 September 1976, Manuscript Diary of Anthony Wedgwood (Tony) Benn, Benn Archives, London; Edmund Dell, *A Hard Pounding: Politics and Economic Crisis 1974–76* (Oxford: Oxford University Press, 1991), p. 236; Fay and Young, 'The Day the £ Nearly Died', 14 May 1978, p. 35; Margaret Garritsen de Vries, *The International Monetary Fund 1972–78: Cooperation on Trial, Volume I: Narrative and Analysis* (Washington, D.C.: IMF, 1985), p. 468. On 6 October Healey told Callaghan that 'there was a real fear in the markets that money supply was out of control'. 'Notes of a Meeting Held in 10 Downing Street at 10.30 a.m. on Wednesday 6 October 1976, to Discuss the Future of Sterling', PREM 16/798.

228 James Callaghan, *Time and Chance* (London: Collins, 1987), pp. 425–6; William Keegan and Rupert Pennant-Rea, *Who Runs the Economy?* (London: Maurice Temple Smith, 1979), p. 166; Burk and Cairncross, *'Goodbye, Great Britain'*, pp. 55–7; 'Transcript of a Telephone Conversation between the Prime Minister and President Ford on Wednesday 29 September [1976]', Prime Minister's Personal Message, T85C/76, PREM 16/798.

229 Burk, 'The 1976 IMF Crisis', p. 363; interviews with Sir Derek Mitchell, 12 February and 3 September 1991; interview with Sir William Ryrie, 28 July 1989; interview with Alan Whittome, 25 July 1989; 'Conversation between the Prime Minister and President Ford', 1 December 1976, Prime Minister's Personal Message, PREM 16/804; Fay and Young, 'The Day the £ Nearly Died', 21 May 1978, p. 34; Dell, *A Hard Pounding*, p. 252; and Burk and Cairncross, *'Goodbye, Great Britain'*, pp. 69–73, 82–110.

230 Joseph Gold, *The Stand-by Arrangements of the International Monetary Fund* (Washington, D.C.: IMF, 1970), pp. 7–15; Robert O. Keohane and Joseph S. Nye, *Power and Interdependence* (Glenview, Ill.: Scott, Foresman, 1989 2nd edn), pp. 125–6; Sidney Dell, 'On Being Grandmotherly: The Evolution of IMF Conditionality', *Princeton Essays in International Finance*, No. 144 (October 1981), pp. 1–10.

231 Burk, 'The 1976 IMF Crisis', pp. 362–6; interview with Dr Karl-Otto Pöhl, 15 December 1989; interview with Lord Lever, 4 May 1989; interview with Sir William Ryrie, 28 July 1989; briefing paper for Lord Lever's meeting with President Gerald Ford, 12 November 1976, and Callaghan to Ford, three-page letter, 12 November 1976, both File CO 160, White House Files, Gerald Ford Papers, Ford Presidential Library. The Callaghan letter is cited here as listed in the catalogue, but the author was unable to convince the National Archives to declassify it. The arguments, however, are clear from the Lever interview and other sources; Callaghan, *Time and Chance*, p. 438. At the outset, the IMF had asked for public spending cuts of £3 billion in 1977/8 and a further £4 billion in 1978/9; they settled for cuts of £1 billion in 1977/8 plus the sale of £500 million worth of government-owned British Petroleum shares, and a further £1 billion cuts in 1978/9. See Burk and Cairncross, *'Goodbye, Great Britain'*, pp. 102–8.

232 Press conference, 30 April 1982, quoted in Richardson, *When Allies Differ*, p. 121.

233 Sir Henry Leach, in 1982 the First Sea Lord and Chief of Naval Staff, 'The Falklands War', paper delivered at Centre for Contemporary British History seminar, 5 June 2002. Available at: <http://www.icbh.ac.uk/witness/falklands/>.

234 Sir Nicholas Henderson, in 1982 the British ambassador to the USA, in *ibid.;* Admiral Harry D. Train, the US Commander in Chief, Atlantic Command, 'Falklands Roundtable', Presidential Oral History Program, Miller Center of Public Affairs, University of Virginia, 15–16 May 2003. Available at: <http://millercenter.virginia.edu/index.php/academic/oralhistory/projects/special/falklands>.

235 Sir Lawrence Freedman, *The Official History of the Falklands Campaign, Volume I: The Origins of the Falklands War* (London: Routledge, 2005), pp. 172–90.

236 Richardson, *When Allies Differ*, pp. 113–16.

237 *Ibid.*, p. 117.

238 Dr Jeane Kirkpatrick in 'Falklands Roundtable'.

239 Nicholas Henderson, *Mandarin: The Diaries of an Ambassador 1969–1982* (London: Weidenfeld & Nicolson, 1994), p. 448.

240 'Actions of the SAS', http://www.stuff.themutual.net/talk.htm; Nicholas Henderson, quoted in Michael Charlton, *The Little Platoon: Diplomacy and the Falklands Dispute* (Oxford: Basil Blackwell, 1989), p. 176 for the quotation.

241 Alexander Haig, *Caveat: Realism, Reagan and Foreign Policy* (London: Weidenfeld & Nicolson, 1984), p. 266.

242 D. George Boyce, *The Falklands War* (London: Palgrave, 2005), p. 57.

243 Charlton, *The Little Platoon*, p. 168.

244 Interestingly, the comment against violence is by Thomas Enders, with Kirkpatrick the strongest Latinista in the State Department. *Ibid.*, p. 176.

245 General Paul Gorman, in 1982 assistant to the chairman, US Joint Chiefs of Staff, in 'Falklands Roundtable'.

246 David Gompert, deputy to the Under-Secretary for Political Affairs and part of Secretary of State Haig's mediation team, in 'Falklands Roundtable'.

247 Haig, *Caveat*, pp. 279, 291.

248 Nicholas Henderson, *Channels and Tunnels: Reflections on Britain and Abroad* (London: Weidenfeld & Nicolson, 1987), p. 107.

249 Caspar Weinberger, *Fighting for Peace: Seven Critical Years in the Pentagon* (New York: Warner Books, 1990), p. 205.

250 Henderson, *Mandarin*, p. 443.

251 Duncan Anderson, *The Falklands War 1982* (Oxford: Osprey, 2002), p. 43.

252 Sir Lawrence Freedman, *The Official History of the Falklands Campaign, Volume II: War and Diplomacy* (London: Routledge, 2005), p. 517.

253 Richardson, *When Allies Differ*, pp. 116–35.

254 Quoted in *ibid.*, p. 120.

255 Freedman, *Official History*, II, pp. 516–17.

256 Kirkpatrick, 'Falklands Roundtable'.

257 Weinberger in Leach, 'Falklands War'.

258 Richardson, *When Allies Differ*, pp. 127–8.

259 *Ibid.*, p. 138.

260 Henderson, *Mandarin*, pp. 451–3; Brandon, *Special Relationships*, p. 392.

261 Richardson, *When Allies Differ*, p. 139.

262 Quoted in *ibid.*, p. 202.

263 Gompert, 'Falklands Roundtable'.

264 Kissinger, *Years of Upheaval*, p. 140.

265 George P. Shultz, *Turmoil and Triumph: My Years as Secretary of State* (New York: Charles Scribner's Sons, 1993), p. 152.

266 Anderson, *The Falklands War*, p. 92. This may be based on *post hoc, propter hoc*, given that a member of the Ministry of Defence looked for such evidence and failed to find any. Sir Roger Jackling to the author, 22 April 2007.

267 John Nott, *Here Today, Gone Tomorrow: Recollections of an Errant Politician* (London: Politico's, 2002), pp. 242–3.

268 General Paul Gorman, 'Falklands Roundtable'. He added that 'it's difficult for me to imagine our proceeding much further with the current US military strategy without a British

ally, period'. However, Gorman had retired in 1985, and was possibly no longer *au courant* with current plans.

269 Kirkpatrick, 'Falklands Roundtable'.

270 Shultz, *Turmoil and Triumph*, p. 152.

271 Robin Renwick, *Fighting with Allies: America and Britain in Peace and War* (Houndmills: Macmillan, 1996), p. 258.

272 Lawrence Freedman and Efraim Karsh, *The Gulf Conflict 1990–1991: Diplomacy and War in the New World Order* (London: Faber and Faber, 1994 pb. edn), pp. 42–7; Renwick, *Fighting with Allies*, p. 260.

273 Margaret Thatcher, *The Downing Street Years* (London: HarperCollins, 1993 pb. edn), pp. 817–19.

274 Dumbrell, *A Special Relationship*, p. 207; Freedman and Karsh, *The Gulf Conflict*, p. 75 for the quotation.

275 Dumbrell, *A Special Relationship*, p. 207; Renwick, *Fighting with Allies*, p. 262 for the quotation; James Baker, *The Politics of Diplomacy: Revolution, War and Peace 1989–1992* (New York: G.P. Putnam's Sons, 1995), pp. 278–9; Thatcher, *Downing Street Years*, pp. 821, 824.

276 Renwick, *Fighting with Allies*, p. 263.

277 In his memoirs Baker bracketed the UK and France as having the same primary reason for their responses: both countries 'had a long and checkered history in the Middle East', and both 'saw in this crisis an opportunity to emphasize their heritage as global powers'. Baker, *The Politics of Diplomacy*, p. 281. However, he also wrote that 'Much has been written about the special relationship between the United States and Great Britain, and the bilateral ties forged between us over two centuries are every bit as durable as advertised. We have no better friends than the British.' *Ibid.*, p. 279.

278 The oldest of the Special Operations services, the SAS is principally employed in sabotage, raids, intelligence-gathering and other like tasks in 'denied' areas; it also trains friendly foreign resistance forces and the forces of friendly nations. <www.specialoperations.com/Foreign/United_ Kingdom/SAS/History.htm>.

279 Peter de la Billière, *Storm Command* (London: HarperCollins, 1992), quotations on pp. 39–40.

280 Dumbrell, *A Special Relationship*, p. 206.

281 Freedman and Karsh, *The Gulf Conflict*, pp. 346–7.

282 Renwick, *Fighting with Allies*, pp. 263–4.

283 De la Billière found that, for the British army, 'the effort of producing one fully operational armoured brigade had turned the whole system inside-out ... To bring 7th Armoured Brigade up to the strength which was needed to fight a desert campaign, we decided to take people and equipment away from other units in Germany; when 4th Armoured Brigade also moved out, those units remaining were left with barely enough men to guard their own installations ... In effect, the whole of BAOR became seriously degraded in operational terms, for as long as the campaign in the Gulf lasted.' De la Billière, *Storm Command*, p. 26.

284 *Ibid.*, pp. 123–4.

285 Norman Schwarzkopf, *It Doesn't Take a Hero* (London: Bantam Press, 1993 pb. edn), p. 478. Schwarzkopf described de la Billière as 'a legendary soldier and adventurer ... the most decorated officer in the British armed services'. *Ibid.*

286 Renwick, *Fighting with Allies*, pp. 266–7; Seitz, *Over Here*, p. 320.

287 Renwick, *Fighting with Allies*, p. 267, for Congressional votes; 183 H.C. Deb. 734–825, for the vote in the Commons.

288 <www.specialoperations.com/Foreign/United_Kingdom/SAS/History.htm>. The Delta Force, the elite commando unit of the US Joint Special Operations Command, remained in South Carolina.

289 De la Billière, *Storm Command*, pp. 304–5.

290 This is de la Billière's number; according to Freedman and Karsh, *The Gulf Conflict*, Table 16, p. 409, the Americans provided at the peak 541,000 personnel of all types and the coalition (undifferentiated) 254,000.

291 Renwick, *Fighting with Allies*, p. 270. De la Billière's diplomacy was also a factor in the close co-operation of the armed services.

292 Seitz, *Over Here*, p. 326.

293 *Ibid.*, p. 322.

294 Christopher Meyer, British ambassador to the USA 1998–2003, disagrees, writing that 'for all of their brave talk, the Americans would always prefer to act in the world with allies than without'. Meyer, *DC Confidential: The Controversial Memoirs of Britain's Ambassador to the US at the Time of 9/11 and the Iraq War* (London: Weidenfeld & Nicolson, 2005), p. 235. But as his own book shows, in the planning for the invasion of Iraq in 2003, the context for Meyer's comment, the final decision was the Americans'. *Ibid.*, ch. 22 *passim.*, especially p. 248.

295 Reynolds, *Britannia Overruled*, pp. 277, 280.

296 Seitz, *Over Here*, p. 328.

297 *Ibid.*, p. 330.

298 John Kampfner, *Blair's Wars* (London: Free Press, 2004 pb. edn), pp. 40, 50–3; Meyer, *DC Confidential*, pp. 103–4.

299 Madeleine Albright, *Madam Secretary* (New York: Miramax, 2003), pp. 394–5.

300 Reynolds, *Britannia Overruled*, pp. 292–4. The US provided one-third of the cost of the bombing campaign, whilst the UK provided one-seventh. *Ibid.*, p. 293.

301 Kampfner, *Blair's Wars*, pp. 14–15.

302 Ahmed Rashid, *Taliban: The Story of the Afghan Warlords* (London: Pan, 2001 new edn), pp. vii–xii. The country also provided sanctuary for extremist groups from more than two dozen countries.

303 Meyer, *DC Confidential*, p. 197. Support was not universal, and there was a minor spate of 'the US had it coming' comments, exemplified by the furore over exchanges in the *London Review of Books*. See Richard Crockatt, *America Embattled: September 11, Anti-Americanism and the Global Order* (London: Routledge, 2003), pp. 39–43.

304 *Ibid.*, pp. 146–7.

305 Meyer, *DC Confidential*, pp. 204–5, quotations on p. 205; Crockatt, *America Embattled*, p. 146 for 'shoulder to shoulder' and quotations from Bush's speech.

306 Woodrow, not Harold. Full text of Blair's speech in the *Guardian*, 2 October 2001; *Newsweek*, 3 December 2001, quotation on p. 43; both quoted in Crockatt, *America Embattled*, p. 149.

307 Dumbrell, *A Special Relationship*, p. 210; Bob Woodward, *Plan of Attack* (London: Pocket Books, 2004), pp. 89–93, quotation on p. 92.

308 Julie Flint, 'What Kelly Really Thought', *Observer*, 31 August 2003, p. 8.

309 Dumbrell, *A Special Relationship*, pp. 210–11.

310 Peter Riddell, *Hug Them Close: Blair, Clinton, Bush and the 'Special Relationship'* (London: Politico's, 2003), pp. 198–202, quotation on p. 199.

311 Meyer, *DC Confidential*, p. 249.

312 *Ibid.*, pp. 207–13; Woodward, *Plan of Attack*, pp. 163–79, quotation on p. 177. The President afterwards told Alastair Campbell, Blair's director of communications, that 'your man has got *cojones*', colloquial Spanish for balls; he remarked later that he would call the Camp David meeting with Blair 'the *cojones* meeting'. *Ibid.*, p. 178.

313 Meyer, *DC Confidential*, pp. 253–9, quotation on p. 259; Woodward, *Plan of Attack*, pp. 294–5.

314 Anthony Seldon, *Blair* (London: Free Press pb. edn, 2005), pp. 592–3, quotation on p. 592; Alastair Campbell, *The Blair Years: Extracts from The Alastair Campbell Diaries* (London: Hutchinson, 2007), p. 676.

315 Dumbrell, *A Special Relationship*, pp. 211–12; Woodward, *Plan of Attack*, p. 375.

316 One of the small ones is the famous discussion with Macmillan as to the strength of his sex drive, with Kennedy admitting that if he didn't have it at least three times a day, he got a headache.

317 Seldon, *Blair*, p. 365.

318 Riddell, *Hug Them Close*, p. 2.

319 Woodward, *Plan of Attack*, p. 338.

320 Meyer, *DC Confidential*, pp. 248, 250.

Bibliography

Primary sources

Manuscripts – Government Papers

UK National Archive (formerly Public Record Office), Kew, London
    Cabinet Records
    Foreign Office Records
    Ministry of Defence Records
    Prime Ministers' Records
    Treasury Records

US National Archives, Washington, D.C.
    Department of State Papers
    Department of the Treasury Papers
    Economic Co-operation Administration Papers

Bank of England Papers – Bank of England, London

Gerald D. Ford Presidential Library, Ann Arbor, Michigan
    Arthur Burns Papers
    Gerald Ford White House Papers

Franklin D. Roosevelt Presidential Library, Hyde Park, New York
    Henry Morgenthau Papers
    Map Room Files
    President's Secretary's Files

Harry S Truman Presidential Library, Independence, Missouri
    W.L. Clayton Papers
    H.B. Price Papers

Manuscripts – Private Papers

Newton D. Baker Papers – Library of Congress, Washington, D.C.
A.J. Balfour Papers – British Library, London
Anthony Wedgwood Benn Papers – Benn Archive, London
Ernle Chatfield Papers – National Maritime Museum, Greenwich
Hugh Dalton Papers – London School of Economics
John Foster Dulles Papers – Princeton University Library
Lord Esher Papers – Churchill College, Cambridge
Edward Hamilton Papers – British Library, London
Charles Hamlin Papers – Library of Congress

Edward M. House Papers – Yale University Library
Morgan Grenfell Papers – Guildhall Library, London
Arthur Lee Papers – Courtauld Institute
David Lloyd George Papers – House of Lords Record Office
Lord Northcliffe Papers – British Library
William Slim Papers – Churchill College, Cambridge
Frederick Vinson Papers – University of Kentucky Library
Harry Dexter White Papers – Princeton University Library
Woodrow Wilson Papers – Library of Congress
William Wiseman Papers – Yale University Library

Printed Sources – Government Papers

Bullen, Roger and M.E. Pelly, eds, *Documents on British Policy Overseas, Series I, Volume III: Britain and America: Negotiation of the United States loan 3 August–7 December 1945* (London: HMSO, 1986).

Cobbett's Parliamentary Debates (London: T.C. Hansard, 1812).

Department of State, *Foreign Relations of the United States, 1947, Volume III: The British Commonwealth; Europe* (Washington, D.C.: US Government Printing Office, 1972).

Department of State, *Foreign Relations of the United States, 1948, Volume III: Western Europe* (Washington, D.C.: US Government Printing Office, 1974).

Department of State, *Foreign Relations of the United States, 1950, Volume III: Western Europe* (Washington, D.C.: US Government Printing Office, 1977).

Department of State, *Papers Relating to the Foreign Relations of the United States, 1917, Supplement 2, The World War* (Washington, D.C.: United States Government Printing Office, 1932).

Documents on British Foreign Policy 1919–1939, 21 vols, Second Series (London: His/Her Majesty's Stationery Office, 1946–84).

Hamilton, Keith and Patrick Salmon, eds, *Documents on British Policy Overseas, Series III, Volume IV: The Year of Europe: America, Europe and the Energy Crisis 1972–1974* (London: Routledge, 2006).

Hansard, *Parliamentary Debates, House of Commons*, 4th and 5th Series.

Jensen, Kenneth M., ed., *Origins of the Cold War: The Novikov, Kennan and Roberts 'Long Telegrams' of 1946* (Washington, D.C.: United States Institute of Peace, 1991).

Parliamentary Papers, 1940–41, VIII: United States No. 2 (1941), Cmd 6311.

Parliamentary Papers, Committee on Finance and Industry, *Report*, Session 1930–1, Cmd. 3897, June 1931, in *Reports from Commissioners, Inspectors, and Others*, 8 vols, Session 28, 1930–7, pp. 2 19–547.

Secretary of the Treasury, *Annual Report* (Washington, D.C.: US Government Printing Office, 1920).

Sešity Ústavu pro soudobé dějiny, *Československo a Marshallův Plán: Sborník dokumentů* (Praha: Institute of Contemporary History, 1992). [Has English summaries]

Simmons, R.C. and P.D.G. Thomas, eds, *Proceedings and Debates of the British Parliament Respecting North America, 1754–1783*, 6 vols (Millwood, NY: Kraus International Publications, 1982–7).

A Speech by the Prime Minister the Right Honourable Winston Churchill in the House of Commons, August 20th, 1940.

UK Treasury, *Statistical Material Presented during the Washington Negotiations* (1945), Cmd. 6707 (London: His Majesty's Stationery Office, 1945).

US Bureau of the Budget, *Historical Abstracts of the United States: Colonial Times to 1957* (Washington, D.C.: US Government Printing Office, 1960).

United States Senate, 74th Congress, 2nd Session, Special Committee on Investigation of the Munitions Industry, *Munitions Industry*, Report No. 944, 7 cols (Washington, D.C.: United States Government Printing Office, 1936).

United States Senate, 80th Congress, 1st Session, Committee on Foreign Relations, *Hearings Held in Executive Session . . . on S. 938, A Bill to Provide for Assistance to Greece and Turkey* (Washington, D.C.: US Government Printing Office, 1973).

Printed Sources – Official Histories
Butler, J.R.M., *History of the Second World War: Grand Strategy, Volume II: September 1939–June 1941* (London: HMSO and Longmans, Green, 1957).

Freedman, Sir Lawrence, *The Official History of the Falklands Campaign*, 2 vols (London: Routledge, 2005).

Gowing, Margaret, *Britain and Atomic Energy 1939–1945* (London: Macmillan, 1964).

Gowing, Margaret, *Independence and Deterrence: Britain and Atomic Energy, Volume I: Policy Making* (London: UK Atomic Energy Authority and Macmillan, 1974).

Hall, H. Duncan, *History of the Second World War: North American Supply* (London: HMSO and Longmans, Green, 1955).

Pressnell, L.S., *External Economic Policy since the War, Volume I: The Post-War Financial Settlement* (London: HMSO, 1986).

Sayers, R.S., *History of the Second World War: Financial Policy 1939–45* (London: HMSO and Longmans, Green, 1956).

Printed Sources – Other
Abel, Annie Heloise and Frank J. Klingberg, eds, *A Side-Light on Anglo-American Relations 1839–1858. Furnished by the Correspondence of Lewis Tappan and Others with the British and Foreign Anti-Slavery Society* (New York: August M. Kelley, 1970, 1st pub. 1927).

Adams, Abigail *et al.*, *The Adams–Jefferson Letters: The Complete Correspondence between Thomas Jefferson and Abigail and John Adams*, ed. Lester J. Cappon, 2 vols (Chapel Hill: University of North Carolina Press, 1959).

Adams, Charles Francis, ed., *Memoirs of John Quincy Adams: Comprising Portions of His Diary from 1795 to 1848*, 12 vols (Philadelphia: J.B. Lippincott, 1874–7).

Adams, John, *The Works of John Adams, Second President of the United States, With a Life of the Author, Notes and Ilustrations*, ed. Charles Francis Adams, 10 vols (Boston: Little, Brown, 1850–6).

Aldrich, Richard J., *Documents in Contemporary History. Espionage, Security and Inteligence in Britain 1945–1970* (Manchester: Manchester University Press, 1998).

Baker, James A., III, *The Politics of Diplomacy: Revolution, War and Peace 1989–1992* (New York: G.P. Putnam's Sons, 1995).

Bateman, John and David Spring, eds., *The Great Landowners of Great Britain and Ireland* (Leicester: University of Leicester Press, 1971, reprint of *The Acre-Ocracy of England – a List of All Owners of Three Thousand Acres and Upward with their Possessions and Incomes Arranged Under Their Various Counties. Also Their Coleges and Clubs. Culled from 'The Modern Domesday Book'*, 4th edn., 1883).

Baylis, John, ed., *Documents in Contemporary History: Anglo-American Relations since 1939: The Enduring Alliance* (Manchester: Manchester University Press, 1997).

Benn, Tony, *Against the Tide: Diaries 1973–76* (London: Hutchinson, 1989).

Bradford, William, *Bradford's History 'Of Plimouth Plantation': From the Original Manuscript: With a Report of the Proceedings Incident to the Return of the Manuscript to Massachusetts* (Boston: Wright & Potter, 1898).

Bridgeman, William, *The Modernisation of Conservative Politics: The Diaries and Letters of Wiliam Bridgeman, 1904–1935*, ed. Philip Williamson (London: Historians' Press, 1988).

Burke, Edmund, *Edmund Burke, New York Agent, with His Letters to the New York Assembly and Intimate Correspondence with Charles O'Hara, 1761–1776*, ed. Ross J.S. Hoffman, Memoirs of the American Philosophical Society, Vol. 41 (Philadelphia: American Philosophical Society, 1956).

Burke, Edmund, *The Portable Edmund Burke*, ed. Isaac Kramnick (Harmondsworth: Penguin Books, 1999).

Cadogan, Sir Alexander, *The Diaries of Sir Alexander Cadogan O.M. 1938–1945*, ed. David Dilks (New York: G.P. Putnam's Sons, 1972).

Campbell, Alastair, *The Blair Years: Extracts From The Alastair Campbell Diaries* (London: Hutchinson, 2007).

Churchill, Winston *et al.*, *Churchill & Roosevelt: The Complete Correspondence*, ed. Warren F. Kimball, 3 vols (Princeton: Princeton University Press, 1984).

Clarke, Sir Richard, *Anglo-American Economic Collaboration in War and Peace 1942–1949*, ed. Sir Alec Cairncross (Oxford: Oxford University Press, 1982).

Colville, Sir John, *The Fringes of Power: Downing Street Diaries 1939–1955* (London: Hodder & Stoughton, 1985).

Commager, Henry Steele and Richard B. Morris, eds, *The Spirit of 'Seventy-Six: The Story of the American Revolution as Told by Its Participants* (Edison, N.J.: Castle Books, 2002).

Cook, Chris and Brendan Keith, *British Historical Facts 1830–1900* (London: Macmillan, 1975).

Forrestal, James, *The Forrestal Diaries: The Inner History of the Cold War*, ed. Walter Millis (London: Cassell, 1952).

George III, *Correspondence of George III with Lord North from 1768 to 1783*, ed. Walter Bodham Donne, 2 vols (London: John Murray, 1867).

Hakluyt, Richard, *The Portable Hakluyt's Voyages: 'The Principal Navigations, Voyages, Traffiques & Discoveries of the English Nation'*, ed. and intro. Irwin R. Blacker (New York: Viking Press, 1965).

Hamilton, Alexander, *The Papers of Alexander Hamilton*, ed. Harold C. Syrett and Jacob E. Cooke, 27 vols (New York: Columbia University Press, 1961–87).

Hamor, Raphe, *A True Discourse of the Present Estate of Virginia, and the successe of the affairs there till the 18th of June. 1614. Together, With a Relation of the severall English Townes and forts, the assured hopes of that countrie and the peace concluded with the Indians. The Christening of Powhatans daughter and her mariage with an English-man* (London: John Beale for William Weley, 1615).

Hollinger, David A. and Charles Capper, eds, *The American Intellectual Tradition*, 2 vols (Oxford: Oxford University Press, 2006 5th edn).

House, Edward M., *The Intimate Papers of Colonel House Arranged as a Narrative*, ed. Charles Seymour, 4 vols (London: Ernest Benn, 1926–8).

Jay, John, *The Correspondence and Public Papers of John Jay*, ed. Henry P. Johnston, 4 vols (New York: G.P. Putnam's Sons, 1893).

Jefferson, Thomas, *The Writings of Thomas Jefferson*, ed. Paul Leicester Ford, 10 vols (New York: G.P. Putnam's Sons, 1892–9).

Jensen, Merrill, ed., *English Historical Documents, IX: American Colonial Documents to 1776* (London: Eyre & Spottiswoode, 1955).

Keynes, John Maynard, *The Collected Writings of John Maynard Keynes, Volume XVI: Activities 1914–1919*, ed. Elizabeth Johnson (London: Macmillan, 1971).

Keynes, John Maynard, *The Collected Writings of John Maynard Keynes, Volume XXIII: Activities 1940–1943: External War Finance*, ed. Donald Moggridge (London: Macmillan, 1979).

Keynes, John Maynard, *The Collected Writings of John Maynard Keynes, Volume XXVI: Activities 1941–1946: Shaping the Post-War World: Bretton Woods and Reparations*, ed. Donald Moggridge (London: Macmillan and Cambridge University Press, 1980).

King, Gregory, Lancaster Herald, *Natural and Political Observations and Conclusions upon the State and Condition of England (London, 1696), 40 pp., To Which Is Prefixed, A Life of the Author, By George Chalmers, F.R.S.S.A., Author of 'Caledonia', 'An Estimate of the Comparative Strength of Great Britain,' &c. A New Edition* (London: J.J. Stockdale, 1810).

Locke, John, *The Second Treatise of Government*, ed. Thomas P. Peardon (Upper Saddle River, N.J.: Prentice-Hall, 1997, 1st pub. 1690).

Lucas, Scott, *Documents in Contemporary History: Britain and Suez: The Lion's Last Roar* (Manchester: Manchester University Press, 1996).

Madison, James, *The Papers of James Madison*, ed. Thomas Mason, Robert A. Rutland and Jeanne K. Sisson, 17 vols (Charlottesville: University of Virginia Press, 1962–91).

Madison, James, *The Writings of James Madison. Comprising His Public Papers and His Private Correspondence, Including Numerous Letters and Documents Now For the First Time Printed*, ed. Gaillard Hunt, 9 vols (New York: G.P. Putnam's Sons, 1900–10).

May, Ernest R. and Philip D. Zelikow, eds, *The Kennedy Tapes: Inside the White House during the Cuban Missile Crisis* (Cambridge, MA: Harvard University Press, 1998 pb. edn, 1st pub. 1997).

McDonald, Ian S., ed., *Anglo-American Relations since the Second World War* (Newton Abbot: David & Charles, 1974).

Menning, Ralph R., *The Art of the Possible: Documents on Great Power Diplomacy, 1814–1914* (New York: McGraw-Hill, 1996).

Mitchell, B.R. and Phyllis Deane, eds, *Abstract of British Historical Statistics* (Cambridge: Cambridge University Press, 1962).

Monroe, James, *The Writings of James Monroe*, ed. Stanislaus Murray Hamilton, 7 vols (New York: G.P. Putnam's Sons, 1898–1903).

The Oxford Dictionary of Quotations (Oxford: Oxford University Press, 1979, 3rd edn).

Paine, Thomas, *Common Sense* (Mineola, N.Y.: Dover, 1997, 1st pub. 1776).

Paine, Thomas, *Common Sense*, ed. Isaac Kramnick (Harmondsworth: Penguin, 1976).

Penn, William, *Just Measures* (London, 1692).

Penn, William, *Some Fruits of Solitude: In Reflections and Maxims Relating to the Conduct of Human Life* (London: Thomas Northcott, 1693).

Penn, William, *The Papers of William Penn*, ed. Mary Maples Dunn and Richard S. Dunn, 5 vols (Philadelphia: University of Pennsylvania Press, 1981–7).

Penn, William, *Wisdom Justified of Her Children, From the Ignorance & Calumny of H. Hallywell, in his Book, Called, An Account of FAMILISM, as it is Revived and Propagated by the QUAKERS* (London, 1673).

Plato, *Timaeus and Critias*, trans. and intro. Desmond Lee (London: Penguin, 1977).

Polk, James K., *The Diary of James K. Polk during His Presidency, 1845 to 1849, Now First Printed from the Original Manuscript in the Collections of the Chicago Historical Society*, ed. M.M. Quaife, 4 vols (Chicago: A.C. McClurg, 1910).

Porter, A.N., ed., *Atlas of British Overseas Expansion* (London: Routledge, 1994 pb. edn, 1st pub. 1991).

Richardson, James D., ed., *Messages and Papers of the Presidents, 1789–1897*, 10 vols (Washington, D.C.: Government Printing Office, 1898).

Roosevelt, Franklin D., *The Public Papers and Addresses of Franklin D. Roosevelt*, ed. Samuel I. Rosenman, 13 vols (New York: Random House and Harper, 1938–50).

Roosevelt, Theodore, *The Letters of Theodore Roosevelt*, ed. Elting E. Morison, 8 vols (Cambridge, MA: Harvard University Press, 1951–4).

Selborne, Second Earl, *The Crisis of British Power: The Imperial and Naval Papers of the Second Earl of Selborne, 1895–1910*, ed. D. George Boyce (London: Historians' Press, 1990).

Smith, Alan, ed., *Virginia 1584–1607: The First English Settlement in North America: A Brief History with a Selection of Contemporary Narratives* (London: Theodore Brun, 1957).

Spring Rice, Cecil, *The Letters and Friendships of Sir Cecil Spring Rice: A Record*, ed. Stephen Gwynn, 2 vols (London: Constable, 1929).

Stanley, Second Baron et al., *The Stanleys of Alderley: Their Letters between the Years 1815–1865*, ed. Nancy Mitford (London: Hamish Hamilton, 1968 rev. edn, 1st pub. 1939).

Stettinius, Edward R., *The Diaries of Edward R. Stettinius, Jr., 1943–1946*, ed. Thomas M. Campbell and George C. Herring (New York: Franklin Watts, 1975).

Tacitus, *The Agricola and the Germania*, trans. and intro. H. Mattingly, revised S.A. Handford (London: Penguin, 1970).

Vandenberg, Arthur, *The Private Papers of Senator Vandenberg*, ed. Arthur H. Vandenberg, Jr. (Boston: Houghton Mifflin, 1952).

Victoria, Queen, *The Letters of Queen Victoria*, ed. G.D. Buckle, Second Series, 3 vols (London: John Murray, 1926).

Washington, George, *The Writings of George Washington from the Original Manuscript Sources, 1745–1799*, ed. J.C. Fitzpatrick, 39 vols (Washington, D.C.: United States Government Printing Office, 1931–44).

Webb, Beatrice, *Beatrice Webb's American Diary 1898*, ed. David A. Shannon (Madison: University of Wisconsin Press, 1963).

Webb, Beatrice, *The Diary of Beatrice Webb, Volume II, 1892–1905: 'All the Good Things of Life'*, ed. Norman MacKenzie and Jeanne MacKenzie (Cambridge, MA: Harvard University Press, 1983).

Webster, Noah, *An American Dictionary of the English Language* (Springfield, MA: George and Charles, Merriam, 1851 rev. edn, 1st pub. 1828).

Wellington, Duke, *Selections from the Dispatches of Field Marshal the Duke of Wellington during His Campaigns in India, Denmark, Portugal, Spain, the Low Countries, and France*, ed. Lt. Col. John Gurwood, 8 vols (London: Parker, Furnivall, and Parker, 1844–7).

Wellington, Duke, *Supplementary Despatches, Correspondence, and Memoranda of Field Marshal Arthur Duke of Wellington, K.G.*, ed. Arthur R. Wellesley, 12 vols (London: John Murray, 1858–65).

Whitaker's Almanack 2005 (London: A & C Black, 2004).

Memoirs and Travels

Adams, Brooks, *America's Economic Supremacy* (New York: Macmillan, 1900).

Adams, Henry, *The Education of Henry Adams* (Oxford: Oxford University Press, 1999 pb. edn, 1st pub. 1918).

Albright, Madeleine, *Madam Secretary* (New York: Miramax, 2003).

Arnold, Matthew, *Civilization in the United States: First and Last Impressions of America* (Boston: Cupples and Hurd, 1888).

Austin, William, *Letters from London: Written during the Years 1802 & 1803* (Boston: W. Pelham, 1804).

Ball, George, *The Past Has Another Pattern: Memoirs* (New York: W. W. Norton, 1982).

Balsan, Consuelo, *The Glitter and the Gold* (London: Heinemann, 1953).

Bax, Emily, *Miss Bax of the Embassy* (Boston: Houghton Mifflin, 1939).

de la Billière, Peter, *Storm Command: A Personal Account of the Gulf War* (London: HarperCollins, 1992).

Bouchier, Jonathan, ed., *Reminiscences of an American Loyalist 1738–1789. Being the Autobiography of the Revd Jonathan Boucher, Rector of Annapolis in Maryland and afterward Vicar of Epsom, Surrey, England* (Boston: Houghton Mifflin, 1925).

Brandon, Henry, *Special Relationships: A Foreign Correspondent's Memoirs from Roosevelt to Reagan* (London: Macmillan, 1988).

Brooks, John Graham, *As Others See Us: A Study of Progress in the United States* (New York: Macmillan, 1908).

Bulloch, James D., *The Secret Service of the Confederate States in Europe or, How the Confederate Cruisers Were Equipped* (New York: Random House, 2001 pb. edn, 1st pub. 1884).

Cather, Thomas, *Thomas Cather's Journal of a Voyage to America in 1836* (London: Rodale Press, 1955).

Collier, Price, *England and the English from an American Point of View* (London: Duckworth & Co., 1913).

Cooper, James Fenimore, *England: With Sketches of Society in the Metropolis*, 3 vols (London: Richard Bentley, 1837).

Cooper, James Fenimore, *Notions of the Americans: Picked up by a Travelling Bachelor*, 2 vols (Philadelphia: Carey, Lea & Carey, 1833).

Corelli, Marie, *Free Opinions Freely Expressed on Certain Phases of Modern Social Life and Conduct* (London: Constable, 1905).

Crèvecoeur, J. Hector St John de, *Letters from an American Farmer* (Oxford: Oxford University Press, 1997, 1st pub. 1783).

Crossman, Richard, *The Diaries of a Cabinet Minister, Volume I: Minister of Housing 1964–66* and *Volume II: Lord President of the Council and Leader of the House of Commons 1966–68* (London: Hamish Hamilton and Jonathan Cape, 1976).

Dauncey, Mrs Campbell, *An Englishwoman in the Philippines* (London: John Murray, 1906).

Dixon, Piers, *Double Diploma: The Life of Sir Pierson Dixon* (London: Hutchinson, 1968).

Eden, Anthony, *Memoirs, Volume III: The Reckoning* (London: Cassell, 1965).

Eisenhower, Dwight D., *The White House Years: Waging Peace 1956–1961* (London: Heinemann, 1961).

Emerson, R.W., *English Traits* (Boston: Phillips, Sampson, and Company, 1856).

Franklin, Benjamin, *Autobiography and Other Writings* (Oxford: Oxford University Press, 1993).

Gleig, George Robert, *A Narrative of the Campaigns of the British Army at Washington and New Orleans under Generals Ross, Pakenham and Lambert, in the Years 1814 and 1815; With Some Account of the Countries Visited* (London: John Murray, 1821).

Gore-Booth, Paul, *With Great Truth and Respect* (London: Constable, 1974).

Grey, Edward, *Speeches on Foreign Affairs, 1904–1914*, ed. Paul Knaplund (London: George Allen & Unwin, 1931).

Grey of Fallodon, *Twenty-Five Years, 1892–1916*, 2 vols (London: Hodder & Stoughton, 1925).

Hall, Captain Basil, *Travels in North America in Years 1827 and 1828*, 3 vols (Edinburgh: Robert Cadell, 1830 3rd edn).

Hamilton, Thomas ['By the Author of Cyril Thornton, Etc.' on the title page, rather than his name], *Men and Manners in America* (Philadelphia: Carey, Lea & Blanchard, 1833).

Harrison, F., 'Impressions of America', *The Nineteenth Century and After*, Vol. 49 (June 1901).

Healey, Denis, *The Time of My Life* (London: Michael Joseph 1989).

Holmes, Oliver Wendell, Sr., *Our Hundred Days in Europe* (Boston: Houghton, Mifflin and Company, 1887).

Hull, Cordell, *The Memoirs of Cordell Hull*, 2 vols (London: Hodder & Stoughton, 1948).

Irving, Washington, *The Sketch Book of Geoffrey Crayon, Gent.*, 2 vols (London: John Murray, 1821 new edn).

James, Henry, *English Hours* (New York: Weidenfeld & Nicolson, 1989, 1st pub. 1905).

Jones, Joseph Marion, *The Fifteen Weeks (February 21–June 5, 1947): An Inside Account of the Genesis of the Marshall Plan* (New York: Harcourt, Brace, 1955).

Kipling, Rudyard, *American Notes* (Boston: Brown and Company, 1899).

Kissinger, Henry, *White House Years* (Boston: Little, Brown, 1979).

Kissinger, Henry, *Years of Upheaval* (Boston: Little, Brown, 1982).

Lloyd, Selwyn, *Suez 1956: A Personal Account* (London: Jonathan Cape, 1978).

Mackay, Alexander, *The Western World; Or, Travels in the United States in 1846–47: Exhibiting Them in Their Latest Development, Social, Political, and Industrial; Including a Chapter on California*, 3 vols (London: Richard Bentley, 1849).

Macmillan, Harold, *At the End of the Day 1961–1963* (New York: Harper & Row, 1973).

Macmillan, Harold, *Pointing the Way 1959–1961* (New York: Harper & Row, 1972).

Macmillan, Harold, *Riding the Storm 1956–1959* (New York: Harper & Row, 1971).

Bibliography 755

Martineau, Harriet, *Harriet Martineau's Autobiography*, ed. Maria Weston Chapman, 2 vols (Boston: James R. Osgood, 1877).

McAdoo, William Gibbs, *Crowded Years: The Reminiscences of William G. McAdoo* (London: Jonathan Cape, 1931).

McAllister, Ward, *Society as I Have Found It* (New York: Cassell, 1890).

Meyer, Christopher, *DC Confidential: The Controversial Memoirs of Britain's Ambassador to the US at the time of 9/11 and the Iraq War* (London: Weidenfeld & Nicolson, 2005).

Mill, John Stuart, *Autobiography* (London: Longmans, Green, Reader, and Dyer, 1873).

Morton, H.V., *Atlantic Meeting: An Account of Mr Churchill's Voyage in HMS Prince of Wales, in August, 1941, and the Conference with President Roosevelt which Resulted in the Atlantic Charter* (London: Methuen, 1943).

Nadal, Ehrman Syme, *Impressions of London Social Life, with Other Papers* (London: Macmillan, 1875).

Nevill, Ralph, ed., *Leaves from the Notebooks of Lady Dorothy Nevill* (London: Macmillan, 1907).

Nott, John, *Here Today, Gone Tomorrow: The Recollections of an Errant Politician* (London: Politico's, 2002).

Olmstead, Frederick Lewis, *Walks and Talks of an American Farmer in England* (New York: Putnam, 1852).

Paulding, James K., *The Bulls and the Jonathans; Comprising John Bull and Brother Jonathan and John Bull in America* (New York: Charles Scribner, 1867, from 1835 edn, probably 1st pub. 1812).

Peierls, Rudolf, *Bird of Passage: Recollections of a Physicist* (Princeton: Princeton University Press, 1985).

Rush, Richard, *Memoranda of a Residence at the Court of London* (Philadelphia: Carey, Lea & Blanchard, 1833).

Rush, Richard, *Memoranda of a Residence at the Court of London, Comprising Incidents Official and Personal from 1819 to 1825. Including Negotiations on the Oregon Question, and Other Unsettled Questions between the United States and Great Britain* (Philadelphia: Lea & Blanchard, 1845).

Schwarzkopf, H. Norman, *The Autobiography: It Doesn't Take a Hero* (London: Bantam pb. edn, 1992).

Seitz, Raymond, *Over Here* (London: Weidenfeld & Nicolson, 1998).

Shultz, George P., *Turmoil and Triumph: My Years as Secretary of State* (New York: Charles Scribner's Sons, 1993).

Smalley, George W., *London Letters and Some Others, Volume II: Notes on Social Life – Notes on Parliament – Pageants – Miscellanies* (New York: Harper & Brothers, 1891).

de Sumichrast, Frederick, *Americans and the Britons* (New York: D. Appleton, 1914).

Thatcher, Margaret, *The Downing Street Years* (London: HarperCollins, 1993 pb. edn).

Ticknor, George, *Life, Letters and Journals of George Ticknor*, ed. George S. Hillard, Mrs George Ticknor and Anna Eliot Ticknor, 2 vols (Boston: James R. Osgood, 1876).

Trollope, Anthony, *North America*, 2 vols (London: Chapman & Hall, 1862).

Trollope, Frances, *Domestic Manners of the Americans* (London: Richard Bentley, 1839 5th edn).

Vansittart, Robert, *The Mist Procession: The Autobiography of Lord Vansittart* (London: Hutchinson, 1958).

Wakefield, Edward Gibbon, *England and America: A Comparison of the Social and Political State of Both Nations* (New York: August M. Kelley, 1967, 1st pub. 1834).

Watkinson, Harold, *Turning Points: A Record of Our Times* (Salisbury: Michael Russell, 1986).

Weinberger, Caspar, *Fighting for Peace: Seven Critical Years in the Pentagon* (New York: Warner, 1990).

Wharton, Edith, *A Backward Glance* (New York: D. Appleton-Century, 1934).

Williams, Francis, *A Prime Minister Remembers: The War and Post-War Memoirs of the Rt. Hon. Earl Attlee Based on His Private Papers and on a Series of Recorded Conversations* (London: Heinemann, 1961).

Wilson, Harold, *The Labour Government 1964–70* (Harmondsworth: Penguin, 1974, 1st pub. 1971).

Secondary sources

Monographs

Ackroyd, Peter, *T.S. Eliot* (London: Hamish Hamilton, 1984).

Adams, Charles Francis, *Transatlantic Historical Solidarity* (Oxford: Oxford University Press, 1913).

Adams, Henry, *History of the United States of America During the Administrations of Thomas Jefferson and James Madison*, 2 vols (New York: Library of America, 1986, 1st pub. 1889–91).

Adams, James Truslow, *The March of Democracy: A History of the United States*, 6 vols (New York: Charles Scribner's Sons, 1932).

Adler, Dorothy R., *British Investment in American Railways 1834–1898* (Charlottesville: University Press of Virginia, 1970).

Aldrich, Richard J., *Espionage, Security and Intelligence in Britain 1945–1970* (Manchester: Manchester University Press, 1998).

Aldrich, Richard J., *The Hidden Hand: Britain, America and Cold War Secret Intelligence* (London: John Murray, 2001).

Alexander, John K., *Samuel Adams: America's Revolutionary Politician* (Lanham, MD: Rowman & Littlefield, 2004 pb. edn, 1st pub. 2002).

Anderson, Duncan, *The Falklands War 1982* (Oxford: Osprey, 2002).

Anderson, Stuart, *Race and Rapprochement: Anglo-Saxonism and Anglo-American Relations, 1895–1904* (London: Associated University Press, 1981)

Anderson, Virginia De John, *New England's Generation: The Great Migration and the Formation of Society and Culture in the Seventeenth Century* (Cambridge: Cambridge University Press, 1991).

Andrew, Christopher, *For the President's Eyes Only: Secret Intelligence and the American Presidency from Washington to Bush* (London: HarperCollins, 1995).

Andrew, Christopher, *Secret Service: The Making of the British Intelligence Community* (London: Heinemann, 1985).

Andrews, Kenneth R., *Trade, Plunder and Settlement: Maritime Enterprise and the Genesis of the British Empire 1480–1630* (Cambridge: Cambridge University Press, 1999 pb. edn, 1st pub. 1984).

Ashton, Nigel, *Kennedy, Macmillan and the Cold War: The Irony of Interdependence* (London: Palgrave, 2002).

Ashworth, William, *An Economic History of England 1870–1939* (London: Methuen & Co., 1972 pb. edn, 1st pub. 1960).

Bailyn, Bernard, *The Ideological Origins of the American Revolution* (Cambridge, MA: Harvard University Press, 1992 enlarged edn).

Bailyn, Bernard, *The Ordeal of Thomas Hutchinson: Loyalism and the Destruction of the First British Empire* (Cambridge, MA: Harvard University Press, 1974).

Bailyn, Bernard, *The Peopling of British North America: An Introduction* (New York: Alfred Knopf, 1986).

Bailyn, Bernard, *To Begin the World Anew: The Genius and Ambiguities of the American Founders* (New York: Alfred A. Knopf, 2003).

Bailyn, Bernard, *Voyagers to the West: A Passage in the Peopling of America on the Eve of Revolution* (New York: Knopf, 1986).

Barbour, Hugh S., *The Quakers in Puritan England* (New Haven: Yale University Press, 1964).

Barnes, James J., *Authors, Publishers and Politicians: The Quest for an Anglo-American Copyright Agreement 1815–1854* (London: Routledge & Kegan Paul, 1974).

Barr, Andrew, *Drink: A Social History of America* (New York: Carroll & Graf, 1999).

Bateman, J., *The Great Landowners of Great Britain and Ireland* (London: 1883 4th edn).

Baylis, John, *Anglo-American Defence Relations 1939–1984* (London: Macmillan, 1984 2nd edn).

Beer, Janet and Bridget Bennett, eds, *Special Relationships: Anglo-American Affinities and Antagonisms 1854–1936* (Manchester: Manchester University Press, 2002).

Beisner, Robert L., *From the Old Diplomacy to the New, 1865–1900* (Arlington Heights, IL: Harlan Davidson, 1986 2nd edn).

Bemis, Samuel Flagg, *Jay's Treaty: A Study in Commerce and Diplomacy* (New Haven: Yale University Press, 1962 rev. edn, 1st pub. 1923).

Benn, Carl, *The War of 1812* (Oxford: Osprey, 2002).

Berkin, Carol Ruth and Mary Beth Norton, eds, *Women of America: A History* (Boston: Houghton Mifflin, 1979).

Bicheno, Hugh, *Rebels and Redcoats: The American Revolutionary War* (London: HarperCollins, 2003).

Blackett, R.J.M., *Divided Hearts: Britain and the American Civil War* (Baton Rouge: Louisiana State University Press, 2001).

Bliss, Robert M., *Revolution and Empire: English Politics and the American Colonies in the Seventeenth Century* (Manchester: Manchester University Press, 1990).

Bolt, Christine, *The Anti-Slavery Movement and Reconstruction: A Study in Anglo-American Co-operation 1833–77* (Oxford: Oxford University Press, 1969).

Bolt, Christine, *Feminist Ferment: 'The Woman Question' in the USA and England, 1870–1940* (London: UCL Press, 1995).

Bonomi, Patricia U., *The Lord Cornbury Scandal: The Politics of Reputation in British America* (Chapel Hill: University of North Carolina Press, 1998).

Boswell, James, *The Life of Samuel Johnson, L.L.D., to which is added The Journal of a Tour to the Hebrides* (London: Bliss Sands & Co., 1897).

Bourne, Kenneth, *Britain and the Balance of Power in North America 1815–1908* (Berkeley: University of California Press, 1967).

Boyce, D. George, *The Falklands War* (London: Palgrave, 2005).

Bradbury, Malcolm, *Dangerous Pilgrimages: Trans-Atlantic Mythologies and the Novel* (London: Penguin, 1996, 1st pub. 1995).

Brandon, Ruth, *The Dollar Princesses: The American Invasion of the European Aristocracy 1870–1914* (London: Weidenfeld & Nicolson, 1980).

Brands, H.W., *The First American: The Life and Times of Benjamin Franklin* (New York: Random House, 2000).

Brewer, John, *The Sinews of Power: War, Money and the English State, 1688–1783* (New York: Alfred A. Knopf, 1989).

Bridenbaugh, Carl, *Vexed and Troubled Englishmen 1590–1642* (Oxford: Clarendon Press, 1968).

Brinkley, Douglas, ed., *Dean Acheson and the Making of US Foreign Policy* (Basingstoke: Macmillan, 1993).

Brogan, D.W., *The American Character* (New York: Alfred A. Knopf, 1944).

Brookings Institution, *Anglo-American Economic Relations: A Problem Paper* (Washington, D.C.: Brookings Institution, 1950).

Broome, Rodney, *Amerike: The Briton who Gave America Its Name* (Stroud: Sutton, 2002).

Brown, Judith M. and Wm. Roger Louis, eds, *The Oxford History of the British Empire: The Twentieth Century* (Oxford: Oxford University Press, 2001).

Bruchey, Stuart, *Enterprise: The Dynamic Economy of a Free People* (Cambridge, MA: Harvard University Press, 1990).

Bruchey, Stuart, *The Wealth of the Nation: An Economic History of the United States* (New York: Harper & Row pb. edn, 1988).

Bryce, James, *The American Commonwealth*, 2 vols (London: Macmillan and Co., 1888).

Burk, Kathleen, *Britain, America and the Sinews of War 1914–1918* (London: George Allen & Unwin, 1985).

Burk, Kathleen, *Morgan Grenfell 1838–1988: The Biography of a Merchant Bank* (Oxford: Oxford University Press, 1989).

Burk, Kathleen and Alec Cairncross, *'Goodbye, Great Britain': The 1976 IMF Crisis* (London: Yale University Press, 1992).

Burk, Kathleen and Melvyn Stokes, eds, *The United States and the European Alliance since 1945* (Oxford: Berg, 1999).

Butler, Jon, *Becoming America: The Revolution before 1776* (Cambridge, MA: Harvard University Press, 2000).

Callahan, North, *Daniel Morgan: Ranger of the Revolution* (New York: Holt, Rinehart and Winston, 1961).

Cameron Watt, D., *Succeeding John Bull: America in Britain's Place 1900–1975: A Study of the Anglo-American Relationship in the Context of British and American Foreign-Policy-Making in the Twentieth Century* (Cambridge: Cambridge University Press, 1984).

Campbell, John, *Edward Heath: A Biography* (London: Jonathan Cape, 1993).

Cannadine, David, *The Decline and Fall of the British Aristocracy* (London: Papermac, 1996).

Canny, Nicholas, ed., *The Oxford History of the British Empire, Volume I: The Origins of Empire: British Overseas Enterprise to the Close of the Seventeenth Century* (Oxford: Oxford University Press, 1998).

Canny, Nicholas and Anthony Pagden, eds, *Colonial Identity in the Atlantic World, 1500–1800* (Princeton: Princeton University Press, 1989, 1st pub. 1987).

Carpenter, Humphrey, *W.H. Auden* (London: George Allen & Unwin, 1981).

Carroll, Francis M., *A Good and Wise Measure: The Search for the Canadian–American Boundary, 1783–1842* (Toronto: University of Toronto Press, 2001).

Cassis, Youssef, ed., *Finance and Financiers in European History, 1880–1960* (Cambridge: Cambridge University Press, 1992).

Carwardine, Richard, *Transatlantic Revivalism: Popular Evangelicalism in Britain and America, 1790–1865* (Westport, CT: Greenwood Press, 1978).

Chadwick, Owen, *The Victorian Church, Part One: 1829–1859* (London: SCM Press, 1971 pb. 3rd edn).

Chambers, James, *Palmerston: 'The Peoples' Darling'* (London: John Murray, 2005 pb. edn).

Charmley, John, *Splendid Isolation? Britain, the Balance of Power and the Origins of the First World War* (London: Hodder & Stoughton, 1999).

Clark, Ian and Nicholas J. Wheeler, *The British Origins of Nuclear Strategy, 1945–1955* (Oxford: Oxford University Press, 1989).

Clark, Steve and Mark Ford, eds, *Something We Have That They Don't: British and American Poetic Relations since 1925* (Iowa City: University of Iowa Press, 2004).

Clark, William, *Less than Kin: A Study of Anglo-American Relations* (London: Hamish Hamilton, 1957).

Clymer, Kenton J., *John Hay: The Gentleman as Diplomat* (Ann Arbor: University of Michigan Press, 1975).

Cogliano, Francis D., *Revolutionary America 1763–1815: A Political History* (London: Routledge, 2000).

Colman, Jonathan, *A 'Special Relationship'? Harold Wilson, Lyndon B. Johnson and Anglo-American Relations 'at the Summit', 1964–68* (Manchester: Manchester University Press, 2004).

Conrad, Peter, *Imagining America* (New York: Oxford University Press, 1980).

Conway, Stephen, *The British Isles and the War of American Independence* (Oxford: Oxford University Press, 2000).

Conway, Stephen, *The War of American Independence 1775–1783* (London: Edward Arnold, 1995).

Cookson, J.E., *Lord Liverpool's Administration: The Crucial Years 1815–1822* (Edinburgh: Scottish Academic Press, 1975).

Cookson, J.E., *The Friends of Peace: Anti-War Liberalism in England, 1793–1815* (Cambridge: Cambridge University Press, 1982).

Costello, John, *Love Sex and War 1939–1945* (London: Pan, 1986).

Court, W.H.B., *A Concise Economic History of Britain: From 1750 to Recent Times* (Cambridge: Cambridge University Press, 1962).

Cradock, Percy, *Know Your Enemy: How the Joint Intelligence Committee Saw the World* (London: John Murray, 2002).

Crapol, Edward P., *America for Americans: Economic Nationalism and Anglophobia in the Late Nineteenth Century* (Westport, CT: Greenwood Press, 1973).

Cumming, W.P., S.E. Hillier, D.B. Quinn and G. Williams, *The Exploration of North America 1630–1776* (London: Paul Elek, 1974).

Dallek, Robert, *Franklin D. Roosevelt and American Foreign Policy, 1932–1945* (New York: Oxford University Press, 1979).

Danchev, Alex, *On Specialness: Essays in Anglo-American Relations* (Basingstoke: Macmillan, 1998).

Danchev, Alex, *Very Special Relationship: Field Marshal Sir John Dill and the Anglo-American Relationship 1941–44* (London: Brassey's Defence, 1986).

Daniels, Bruce C., ed., *Town and Country: Essays on the Structure of Local Government in the American Colonies* (Middletown, CT: Wesleyan University Press, 1978).

Davidoff, Leonore, *The Best Circles: Society Etiquette and the Season* (London: Century Hutchinson, 1986 pb. edn, 1st pub. 1973).

Dear, I.C.B., ed., *The Oxford Companion to the Second World War* (Oxford: Oxford University Press, 1995).

Dell, Edmund, *A Hard Pounding: Politics and Economic Crisis 1974–76* (Oxford: Oxford University Press, 1991).

Dilks, David, ed., *Studies in British Foreign Policy of the Twentieth Century, Volume II: After 1939* (London: Macmillan, 1981).

Doenecke, Justus D. and Mark A. Stoler, *Debating Franklin D. Roosevelt's Foreign Policies, 1933–1945* (Lanham, MD: Rowman & Littlefield, 2005).

Douglas, Edward Leach, *Roots of Conflict: British Armed Forces and Colonial Americans, 1677–1763* (Chapel Hill: University of North Carolina Press, 1986).

Dryden, I.G.C., ed., *The Efficient Use of Energy* (Guildford: IPC Science and Technology Press, 1975).

Duberman, Martin B., *Charles Francis Adams 1807–1886* (Boston: Houghton Mifflin, 1961).

Dull, Jonathan R., *A Diplomatic History of the American Revolution* (London: Yale University Press, 1985).

Dunbabin, J.P.D., *The Cold War: The Great Powers and Their Allies* (London: Longman, 1994).

Eggert, Gerald G., *Richard Olney: Evolution of a Statesman* (University Park: Pennsylvania State University Press, 1974).

Ehrman, John, *The Younger Pitt: The Reluctant Transition* (London: Constable, 1983).

Elliott, J.H., *The Old World and the New 1492–1650* (Cambridge: Cambridge University Press pb, 1970).

Ellis, Joseph J., *After the Revolution: Profiles of Early American Culture* (New York: W.W. Norton, 2002 pb. edn, 1st pub. 1979).

Erickson, Charlotte, *Invisible Immigrants: The Adaptation of English and Scottish Immigrants in Nineteenth-Century America* (Leicester: Leicester University Press, 1972).

Esdaile, Charles, *The Wars of Napoleon* (London: Longman, 1995).

Ferling, John, *Setting the World Ablaze: Washington, Adams, Jefferson, and the American Revolution* (Oxford: Oxford University Press, 2000).

Ferris, Timothy, *Coming of Age in the Milky Way* (New York: Doubleday pb. edn, 1988).

Fischer, David Hackett, *Albion's Seed: Four British Folkways in America* (New York: Oxford University Press, 1991 pb. edn, 1st pub. 1989).

Fischer, David Hackett, *Paul Revere's Ride* (New York: Oxford University Press, 1994).

Fisher, Todd, *The Napoleonic Wars: The Empires Fight Back 1808–1812* (Oxford: Osprey, 2001).

Flavell, Julie and Stephen Conway, eds, *Britain and America Go to War: The Impact of War and Warfare in Anglo-America, 1754–1815* (Gainesville: University Press of Florida, 2004).

Fleming, Thomas J., *Cowpens* (Washington, D.C.: National Park Service, 1988).

Foster, R.F., *Lord Randolph Churchill: A Political Life* (Oxford: Oxford University Press, 1981).

Fowler, W.B., *British–American Relations, 1917–1918: The Role of Sir William Wiseman* (Princeton: Princeton University Press, 1969).

Freedman, Lawrence and Efraim Karsh, *The Gulf War 1990–1991: Diplomacy and War in the New World Order* (London: Faber and Faber, 1994 pb. edn).

French, David, *British Strategy & War Aims 1914–1916* (London: Allen & Unwin, 1986).

French, David, *The British Way in Warfare 1688–2000* (London: Unwin Hyman, 1990).

French, David, *The Strategy of the Lloyd George Coalition, 1916–1918* (Oxford: Oxford University Press, 1995).

Frisch, Otto, *What Little I Remember* (Cambridge: Cambridge University Press, 1980 pb. edn, 1st pub. 1979).

Gaddis, John Lewis, *The United States and the Origins of the Cold War, 1941–1947* (New York: Columbia University Press, 1972 pb. edn).

Games, Alison, *Migration and the Origins of the English Atlantic World* (Cambridge, MA: Harvard University Press, 1999).

Gardner, Richard N., *Sterling–Dollar Diplomacy in Current Perspective: The Origins and the Prospects of Our International Order* (New York: Columbia University Press, 1980 expanded edn).

Garritsen de Vries, Margaret, *The International Monetary Fund 1972–78: Cooperation on Trial*, 3 vols (Washington, D.C.: IMF, 1985).

Garvin, J.L., *The Life of Joseph Chamberlain 1836–1900, Volume III: 1895–1900: Empire and World Policy* (London: Macmillan, 1934).

Geiter, Mary K. and W.A. Speck, *Colonial America: From Jamestown to Yorktown* (London: Palgrave, 2002).

Gerbi, Antonello, *The Dispute of the New World: The History of a Polemic, 1750–1900* (Pittsburgh: University of Pittsburgh Press, 1973 English edn, 1st pub. 1955).

Gerlach, Murney, *British Liberalism and the United States: Political and Social Thought in the Late Victorian Age* (Basingstoke: Palgrave, 2001).

Giles, Paul, *Virtual America: Transnational Fictions and the Transatlantic Imaginary* (Durham, N.C.: Duke University Press, 2002).

Gold, Joseph, *The Stand-by Arrangements of the International Monetary Fund* (Washington, D.C.: IMF, 1970).

Golden, Peter, *Quiet Diplomat: A Biography of Max M. Fisher* (New York: Cornwall Books, 1992).

Goldstein, Erik, *The First World War Peace Settlements 1919–1925* (London: Longman, 2002).

Goldstein, Erik and John Maurer, eds, *The Washington Conference, 1921–22: Naval Rivalry, East Asian Stability and the Road to Pearl Harbor* (London: Frank Cass, 1994).

Good Housekeeping, *A War Bride's Guide to the USA* (London: Collins & Brown, 2006, 1st pub. 1945 for the US Office of War Information).

Gordon, George Stuart, *Anglo-American Literary Relations* (London: Oxford University Press, 1942).

Graff, Henry F., *Grover Cleveland* (New York: Henry Holt, 2002).

Grafton, Anthony, *New Worlds, Ancient Texts: The Power of Tradition and the Shock of Discovery* (Cambridge, MA: Belknap Press, 1995 pb. edn, 1st pub. 1992).

Graham, Ian C.C., *Colonists from Scotland: Emigration to North America, 1707–1783* (Ithaca, NY: Cornell University Press, 1956).

Gray, Denis, *Spencer Perceval: The Evangelical Prime Minister 1762–1812* (Manchester: Manchester University Press, 1963).

Grazia, Victoria de, *Irresistible Empire: America's Advance through Twentieth-Century Europe* (Cambridge, MA: Harvard University Press, 2005).

Grenville, J.A.S., *Lord Salisbury and Foreign Policy: The Close of the Nineteenth Century* (London: Athlone Press, 1970 pb. edn).

Grenville, John A.S. and George Berkeley Young, *Politics, Strategy, and American Diplomacy: Studies in Foreign Policy, 1873–1917* (New Haven: Yale University Press, 1966).

Gross, Robert A., *The Minutemen and Their World* (New York: Hill and Wang pb. edn, 2001, 1st pub. 1976).

Habakkuk, H.J., *American and British Technology in the Nineteenth Century* (Cambridge: Cambridge University Press, 1962).

Hall, Christopher, *British Strategy in the Napoleonic War 1803–15* (Manchester: Manchester University Press, 1992).

Hardach, Gerd, *Der Marshall-Plan: Auslandshilfe und Wiederaufbau in Westdeutschland 1948–1952* (München: Deutscher Taschenbuch, 1994).

Harper, John Lamberton, *American Machiavelli: Alexander Hamilton and the Origins of US Foreign Policy* (Cambridge: Cambridge University Press, 2004).

Hemphill, C. Dallett, *Bowing to Necessities: A History of Manners in America, 1620–1860* (Oxford: Oxford University Press, 1999).

Henderson, Sir Nicholas, *Channels and Tunnels: Reflections on Britain and Abroad* (London: Weidenfeld & Nicolson, 1987).

Henderson, Sir Nicholas, *The Birth of NATO* (London: Weidenfeld & Nicolson, 1982).

Hidy, Muriel Emmie, *George Peabody Merchant and Financier 1829–1854* (New York: Arno Press, 1978).

Hidy, Ralph W., *The House of Baring in American Trade and Finance: English Merchant Bankers at Work, 1763–1861* (New York: Russell & Russell, 1970, 1st pub. 1949).

Hinde, Wendy, *George Canning* (London: Collins, 1973).

Hitchens, Christopher Blood, *Class and Empire: The Enduring Anglo-American Relationship* (New York: Nation Books, 2004).

Hobsbawm, E.J., *Industry and Empire: An Economic History of Britain since 1750* (London: Weidenfeld & Nicolson, 1968).

Hodgson, Godfrey, *The Colonel: The Life and Wars of Henry Stimson 1867–1950* (New York: Alfred A. Knopf, 1990).

Hodgson, Godfrey, *Woodrow Wilson's Right Hand: The Life of Colonel Edward M. House* (London: Yale University Press, 2006).

Hoffman, Ronald and Peter J. Albert, eds, *Peace and the Peacemakers: The Treaty of 1783* (Charlottesville: University Press of Virginia, 1986).

Holmes, Geoffrey, *British Politics in the Age of Anne* (London: Hambledon, 1987 rev. edn).

Homberger, Eric, *Mrs Astor's New York: Money and Social Power in a Gilded Age* (New Haven: Yale University Press, 2002).

Horne, Alistair, *Macmilan 1894–1956: Volume I of the Official Biography* (London: Macmillan, 1988).

Howe, Daniel Walker, ed., *Victorian America* (Philadelphia: University of Pennsylvania Press, 1976).

Ions, Edmund, *James Bryce and American Democracy* (London: Macmillan, 1968).

Iriye, Akira, *The Globalizing of America, 1913–1945* (Cambridge: Cambridge University Press, 1993).

Isaacson, Walter, *Benjamin Franklin: An American Life* (New York: Simon & Schuster, 2003).

James, Henry, *Hawthorne* (London: Macmillan, 1879).

Jenks, Leland H., *The Migration of British Capital to 1875* (London: Thomas Nelson and Sons, 1963, 1st pub. 1927).

Jennings, Francis, *Benjamin Franklin, Politician: The Man and the Mask* (New York: W.W. Norton, 1996).

Jones, Howard and Donald A. Rakestraw, *Prologue to Manifest Destiny: Anglo-American Relations in the 1840s* (Wilmington: Scholarly Resources, 1997).

Jones, J.R., *The Anglo-Dutch Wars of the Seventeenth Century* (London: Longman, 1996).

Jones, Wilbur Devereux, *The American Problem in British Diplomacy, 1841–1861* (London: Macmillan, 1974).

Jupp, Peter, *Lord Grenville 1751–1834* (Oxford: Oxford University Press, 1985).

Kampfner, John, *Blair's Wars* (London: Free Press, 2004 pb. edn).

Keegan, William and Rupert Pennant-Rea, *Who Runs the Economy?* (London: Maurice Temple Smith, 1979).

Kehoe, Elizabeth, *Fortune's Daughters: The Extravagant Lives of the Jerome Sisters: Jennie Churchill, Clara Frewen and Leonie Leslie* (London: Atlantic, 2004).

Kelly, Michael Bryan ('Doc Rock'), *The Beatle Myth: The British Invasion of American Popular Music, 1956–1969* (Jefferson, N.C.: McFarland, 1991).

Kennedy, David M., *Freedom from Fear: The American People in Depression and War, 1929–1945* (New York: Oxford University Press, 2001 pb. edn, 1st pub. 1999).

Kennedy, Paul, *The Rise and Fall of British Naval Mastery* (London: Macmillan, 1983 edn).

Kennedy, Paul, *Strategy and Diplomacy 1870–1945* (London: Fontana pb. edn 1984, 1st pub. George Allen & Unwin, 1983).

Kennedy, Paul, *The Rise and Fall of the Great Powers: Economic Change and Military Conflict from 1500–2000* (London: HarperCollins, 1988).

Keohane, Robert O. and Joseph S. Nye, *Power and Interdependence* (Glenview, IL: Scott, Foresman, 1989 2nd edn).

Kimball, Warren F., *The Most Unsordid Act: Lend–Lease, 1939–1941* (Baltimore: Johns Hopkins University Press, 1969).

Kissinger, Henry, *Diplomacy* (New York: Simon & Schuster, 1994).

Kunz, Diane B., *The Economic Diplomacy of the Suez Crisis* (Chapel Hill: University of North Carolina Press, 1991).

Lacey, Robert, *Sir Walter Ralegh* (London: Phoenix Press, 2000, 1st pub. 1973).

LaFeber, Walter, *The Cambridge History of American Foreign Relations, Volume II: The American Search for Opportunity, 1865–1913* (Cambridge: Cambridge University Press, 1993).

Lambert, Frank, *Inventing the 'Great Awakening'* (Princeton: Princeton University Press, 2000 pb. edn, 1st pub. 1999).

Lambert, Frank, *The Founding Fathers and the Place of Religion in America* (Princeton: Princeton University Press, 2003).

Landsman, Ned C., *From Colonials to Provincials: American Thought and Culture 1680–1760* (Ithaca, NY: Cornell University Press, 1997).

Lane, Ann and Howard Temperley, eds, *The Rise and Fall of the Grand Alliance, 1941–45* (London: Macmillan, 1995).

Langford, Paul, *A Polite and Commercial People: England 1727–1783* (Oxford: Oxford University Press, 1989).

Langford, Paul, *Englishness Identified: Manners and Character 1650–1850* (Oxford: Oxford University Press, 2000).

Lease, Benjamin, *Anglo-American Encounters: England and the Rise of American Literature* (Cambridge: Cambridge University Press, 1981).

Leffler, Melvyn P., *A Preponderance of Power: National Security, the Truman Administration, and the Cold War* (Stanford: Stanford University Press, 1992).

Lenman, Bruce P., *England's Colonial Wars 1550–1688: Conflicts, Empire and National Identity* (London: Longman, 2001).

Leslie, Anita, *Lady Randolph Churchill: The Story of Jennie Jerome* (New York: Charles Scribner's Sons, 1969).

Leventhal, Fred M. and Roland Quinault, eds, *Anglo-American Attitudes: From Revolution to Partnership* (Aldershot: Ashgate, 2000).

The Lexington–Concord Battle Road: Hour-by-hour account of events preceding and on the History-making day April 19, 1775 (Concord: Concord Chamber of Commerce, n.d.).

Louis, Wm. Roger, *Imperialism at Bay: The United States and the Decolonization of the British Empire, 1941–1945* (Oxford: Oxford University Press, 1978).

Louis, Wm. Roger, *Ends of British Imperialism: The Scramble for Empire, Suez and Decolonization. Colected Essays* (London: I.B. Tauris, 2006).

Louis, Wm. Roger and Roger Owen, eds, *Suez 1956: The Crisis and Its Consequences* (Oxford: Oxford University Press, 1989).

Lovejoy, David S., *The Glorious Revolution in America* (Middletown, CT: Wesleyan University Press, 1987 pb. edn, 1st pub. 1972).

Lowe, C.J. and M.L. Dockrill, *The Mirage of Power: British Foreign Policy 1902–14*, 2 vols (London: Routledge & Kegan Paul, 1972).

Lowe, Peter, *Great Britain and the Origins of the Pacific War: A Study of British Policy in East Asia, 1937–1941* (Oxford: Oxford University Press, 1977).

Lucas, W. Scott, *Divided We Stand: Britain, the US and the Suez Crisis* (London: Hodder & Stoughton, 1996 pb. edn).

Lundestad, Geir, *The American 'Empire' and Other Studies of US Foreign Policy in a Comparative Perspective* (Oslo: Norwegian University Press/Oxford University Press, 1992).

MacColl, Gail and Carol McD. Wallace, *To Marry an English Lord* (New York: Workman, 1989).

Mackenzie Stuart, Amanda, *Consuelo & Alva: Love and Power in the Gilded Age* (London: HarperCollins, 2005).

Magnus, Philip, *Gladstone: A Biography* (London: John Murray, 1954).

Mahan, A.T., *Sea Power in Its Relations to the War of 1812*, 2 vols (London: Sampson Low, Marston, 1905).

Mahon, John K., *The War of 1812* (Gainesville: University Press of Florida, pb. edn, n.d., 1st pub. 1972).

Maier, Pauline, *American Scripture: Making the Declaration of Independence* (New York: Vintage pb. edn, 1998, 1st pub. Random House, 1997).

Maier, Pauline, *From Resistance to Revolution: Colonial Radicals and the Development of American Opposition to Britain, 1765–1776* (London: Routledge & Kegan Paul, 1973).

Malcolm, Joyce Lee, *To Keep and Bear Arms: The Origins of an Anglo-American Right* (Cambridge, MA: Harvard University Press, 1994).

Marder, A.J., *From the Dreadnought to Scapa Flow: The Royal Navy in the Fisher Era 1904–1919, Volume I: The Road to War, 1904–1914* (London: Oxford University Press, 1961).

Marshall, P.J., *The Making and Unmaking of Empires* (Oxford: Oxford University Press, 2005).

Marshall, P.J., ed., *The Oxford History of the British Empire, Volume II: The Eighteenth Century* (Oxford: Oxford University Press, 1998).

Marston, Daniel, *The Seven Years' War* (Oxford: Osprey, 2001).

Martin, Judith, *Star-Spangled Manners: In Which Miss Manners Defends American Etiquette (For a Change)* (New York: W.W. Norton, 2003).

Mathias, Peter, *The First Industrial Nation: An Economic History of Britain 1700–1914* (London: Methuen pb. edn, 1969).

McCullough, David, *John Adams* (New York: Simon & Schuster, 2002 pb. edn, 1st pub. 2001).

McCusker, John J. and Russell R. Menard, *The Economy of British America, 1607–1789* (Chapel Hill: University of North Carolina Press, 1985).

McFarlane, Anthony, *The British in the Americas 1480–1815* (London: Longman, 1994).

McKercher, B.J.C., ed., *Anglo-American Relations in the 1920s* (London: Macmillan, 1991).

McKercher, B.J.C., *The Second Baldwin Government and the United States, 1924–1929: Attitudes and Diplomacy* (Cambridge: Cambridge University Press, 1984).

McKercher, B.J.C., *Transition of Power: Britain's Loss of Global Pre-eminence to the United States 1930–1945* (Cambridge: Cambridge University Press, 1999).

Merk, Frederick, *The Oregon Question: Essays in Anglo-American Diplomacy and Politics* (Cambridge, MA: Harvard University Press, 1967).

Middleton, Richard, *Colonial America: A History, 1585–1776* (Oxford: Blackwell, 1996 2nd edn).

Millgate, Helen D., *Got Any Gum Chum? GIs in Wartime Britain 1942–1945* (Thrupp: Sutton, 2001).

Milton, Giles, *The Riddle and the Knight: In Search of Sir John Mandeville* (London: Sceptre pb. edn, 2001).

Montgomery, Maureen E., *Gilded Prostitution: Status, Money, and Transatlantic Marriages 1870–1914* (London: Routledge, 1989).

Morgan, Edmund S., *Benjamin Franklin* (London: Yale University Press, 2002).

Morgan, Edmund S., *The Puritan Dilemma: The Story of John Winthrop* (Boston: Little, Brown, 1958 pb. edn).

Morley, John, *The Life of William Ewart Gladstone*, 3 vols (London: Macmillan, 1903).

Moser, John E., *Twisting the Lion's Tail: Anglophobia in the United States, 1921–48* (London: Macmillan, 1999).

Mowat, R.B., *The Diplomatic Relations of Great Britain and the United States* (London: Edward Arnold, 1925).

Mowat, R.B., *The Life of Lord Pauncefote: First Ambassador to the United States* (London: Constable, 1929).

Mulvey, Christopher, *Anglo-American Landscapes: A Study of Nineteenth-Century Anglo-American Travel Literature* (Cambridge: Cambridge University Press, 1983).

Mulvey, Christopher, *Transatlantic Manners: Social Patterns in Nineteenth-Century Anglo-American Travel Literature* (Cambridge: Cambridge University Press, 1990).

Nagel, Paul C., *John Quincy Adams: A Public Life, a Private Life* (Cambridge, MA: Harvard University Press, 1997).

Nash, Gary B., *Quakers and Politics: Pennsylvania, 1681–1726* (Princeton: Princeton University Press, 1969).

Neale, R.G., *Great Britain and United States Expansion: 1898–1900* (Ann Arbor: Michigan State University Press, 1966).

Neilson, Keith, *Britain, Soviet Russia and the Collapse of the Versailles Order, 1919–1939* (Cambridge: Cambridge University Press, 2006).

Neustadt, Richard E., *Alliance Politics* (New York: Columbia University Press, 1970 pb. edn).

Neville-Sington, Pamela, *Fanny Trollope: The Life and Adventures of a Clever Woman* (New York: Viking, 1998).

Nevins, Allan, *Henry White: Thirty Years of American Diplomacy* (New York: Harper and Brothers, 1930).

Nicolson, Harold, *Good Behaviour: Being a Study of Certain Types of Civility* (Garden City, NY: Doubleday, 1956).

Norton, Mary Beth, *Founding Mothers and Fathers: Gendered Power and the Formation of American Society* (New York: Alfred A. Knopf, 1996).

Nunnerley, David, *President Kennedy and Britain* (New York: St Martin's Press, 1972).

Nye, Joseph S., Jr., *Soft Power: The Means to Success in World Politics* (New York: Public Affairs, 2004).

Otte, T.G., ed., *The Makers of British Foreign Policy: From Pitt to Thatcher* (Basingstoke: Palgrave, 2002).

Pachter, Marc and Frances Wein, eds, *Abroad in America: Visitors to the New Nation 1776–1914* (Reading, MA: Addison-Wesley and National Portrait Gallery, Washington, 1976).

Parrish, Scott D., *New Evidence on the Soviet Rejection of the Marshall Plan, 1947*, International History of the Cold War Working Paper No. 9 (Washington, D.C.: Smithsonian Institution, 1994).

Parry, J.H., *The Age of Reconnaissance: Discovery, Exploration and Settlement 1450–1650* (London: Phoenix Press, 2000, 1st pub. 1963).

Patterson, Jerry E., *The Vanderbilts* (New York: Harry N. Abrams, 1989).

Paul, Septimus H., *Nuclear Rivals: Anglo-American Atomic Relations, 1941–1952* (Columbus: Ohio State University Press, 2000).

Pelling, Henry, *Britain and the Marshall Plan* (New York: St Martin's Press, 1988).

Pells, Richard, *Not Like Us: How Europeans Have Loved, Hated, and Transformed American Culture since World War II* (New York: Basic Books, 1997).

Perkins, Bradford, *Castlereagh and Adams: England and the United States 1812–1823* (Berkeley: University of California Press, 1964).

Perkins, Bradford, *Prologue to War: England and the United States 1805–1812* (Berkeley: University of California Press, 1968 pb. edn, 1st pub. 1961).

Perkins, Bradford, *The Cambridge History of American Foreign Relations, Volume I: The Creation of a Republican Empire, 1776–1865* (Cambridge: Cambridge University Press, 1995 pb. edn, 1st pub. 1993).

Perkins, Bradford, *The First Rapprochement: England and the United States 1795–1805* (Philadelphia: University of Pennsylvania Press, 1955).

Perkins, Bradford, ed., *The Causes of the War of 1812: National Honor or National Interest* (Malabar, FL: Robert E. Krieger, 1983).

Pettegree, Andrew, *Europe in the Sixteenth Century* (Oxford: Blackwell, 2002).

Ponting, Clive, *Breach of Promise: Labour in Power 1964–1970* (London: Hamish Hamilton, 1989).

Raphael, Ray, *The American Revolution: A People's History: How Common People Shaped the Fight for Independence* (London: Profile, 2001).

Raphael, Ray, *The First American Revolution: Before Lexington and Concord* (New York: The New Press, 2002).

Rashid, Ahmed, *Taliban: The Story of the Afghan Warlords* (London: Pan, 2001 new edn).

Reay, Barry, *Quakers and the English Revolution* (London: Temple Smith, 1985).

Reed, John, *From Private Life to Public Virtue: The Birth Control Movement and American Society since 1830* (New York: Basic Books, 1978).

Rees, David, *Harry Dexter White: A Study in Paradox* (London: Macmillan, 1973).

Reich, Jerome R., *British Friends of the American Revolution* (Armonk, NY: M.E. Sharpe, 1998).

Remini, Robert V., *John Quincy Adams* (New York: Henry Holt, 2002).

Renwick, Robin, *Fighting with Allies: America and Britain in Peace and War* (Basingstoke: Macmillan, 1996).

Reynolds, David, *Britannia Overruled: British Policy and World Power in the 20th Century* (London: Longman, 2000 2nd edn).

Reynolds, David, *The Creation of the Anglo-American Alliance 1937–41: A Study in Competitive Co-operation* (London: Europa, 1981).

Reynolds, David, *Rich Relations: The American Occupation of Britain 1942–1945* (London: HarperCollins, 1995).

Rhodes, Richard, *The Making of the Atomic Bomb* (New York: Simon & Schuster, 1988 pb. edn, 1st pub. 1986).

Richardson, Louise, *When Allies Differ: Anglo-American Relations during the Suez and Falklands Crises* (New York: St Martin's Press, 1996).

Richelson, Jeffrey T. and Desmond Ball, *The Ties That Bind: Intelligence Cooperation between the UKUSA Countries, the United Kingdom, the United States of America, Canada, Australia, and New Zealand* (Boston: Unwin Hyman, 1990 pb. 2nd edn).

Riddell, Peter, *Hug Them Close: Blair, Clinton, Bush and the 'Special Relationship'* (London: Politico's, 2003).

Ritcheson, Charles R., *Aftermath of Revolution: British Policy towards the United States, 1783–1795* (Dallas: Southern Methodist University Press, 1969).

Robbins, Keith, *Sir Edward Grey: A Biography of Lord Grey of Fallodon* (London: Cassell, 1971).

Roberts, Andrew, *Salisbury: Victorian Titan* (London: Weidenfeld & Nicolson, 1999).

Rock, William R., *Chamberlain and Roosevelt: British Foreign Policy and the United States, 1937–1940* (Columbus: Ohio State University Press, 1988).

Rodgers, Daniel T., *Atlantic Crossings: Social Politics in a Progressive Age* (Cambridge, MA: Harvard University Press, 1998).

Rose, Norman, *Vansittart: Study of a Diplomat* (London: Heinemann, 1978).

Rosenberg, Emily S., *Spreading the American Dream: American Economic and Cultural Expansion, 1890–1945* (New York: Hill and Wang, 1982).

Russett, Bruce M., *Community and Contention: Britain and America in the Twentieth Century* (Cambridge, MA: MIT Press, 1963).

Rydell, Robert W. and Rob Kroes, *Buffalo Bill in Bologna: The Americanization of the World, 1869–1922* (Chicago: University of Chicago Press, 2005).

Savage, Jon, *England's Dreaming: Sex Pistols and Punk Rock* (London: Faber and Faber, 2005 pb. edn, 1st pub. 1991).

Savell, Isabelle K., *Wine and Bitters: An account of the meetings in 1783 at Tappan, NY and aboard HMS Perseverance between George Washington and Sir Guy Carleton, commanding generals of American and British forces at the close of the American Revolution* (Rockland County, NY: The Historical Society of Rockland County, 1975).

Schröder, Hans-Jürgen, ed., *Confrontation and Cooperation: Germany and the United States in the Era of World War I* (Providence: Berg, 1993).

Schukert, Elfrieda Berthiaume and Barbara Smith Scibetta, *War Brides of World War II* (Novato, CA: Presidio Press, 1988).

Schulzinger, Robert D., ed., *A Companion to American Foreign Relations* (Oxford: Blackwell, 2006 pb. edn, 1st pub. 2003).

Scott, L.V., *Macmillan, Kennedy and the Cuban Missile Crisis: Political, Military and Intelligence Aspects* (London: Macmillan, 1999).

Seigenthaler, John, *James K. Polk* (New York: Henry Holt, 2003).

Sexton, Jay, *Debtor Diplomacy: Finance and American Foreign Relations in the Civil War Era 1837–1873* (Oxford: Oxford University Press, 2005).

Sherwood, Robert E., *Roosevelt and Hopkins: An Intimate History* (New York: Harper and Brothers, 1950).

Shy, John, *A People Numerous and Armed: Reflections on the Military Struggle for American Independence* (Ann Arbor: University of Michigan Press, 1990 pb. rev. edn).

Siegel, Jennifer, *Endgame: Britain, Russia and the Final Struggle For Central Asia* (London: I.B. Tauris, 2002).

Skidelsky, Robert, *John Maynard Keynes, Volume III: Fighting for Britain 1937–1946* (London: Macmillan, 2000).

Small, Melvin, *Democracy and Diplomacy: The Impact of Domestic Politics on US Foreign Policy, 1789–1994* (Baltimore: Johns Hopkins University Press, 1996).

Smith, Graham, *When Jim Crow Met John Bull: Black American Soldiers in World War II Britain* (New York: St Martin's Press, 1988).

Spender, Stephen, *T.S. Eliot* (New York: Viking Press, 1976).

Spivak, Burton, *Jefferson's English Crisis: Commerce, Embargo, and the Republican Revolution* (Charlottesville: University Press of Virginia, 1979).

Stahr, Walter, *John Jay: Founding Father* (New York: Hambledon and London, 2005).

Steiner, Zara S., *The Foreign Office and Foreign Policy, 1898–1914* (Cambridge: Cambridge University Press, 1969).

Stoler, Mark A., *Allies in War: Britain and America against the Axis Powers 1940–1945* (London: Hodder Arnold, 2005).

Strange, Susan, *Sterling and British Policy* (Oxford: Oxford University Press, 1971).

Street, Sarah, *Transatlantic Crossings: British Feature Films in the United States* (London: Continuum, 2002).

Sumida, Jon Tetsuro, *In Defence of Naval Supremacy: Finance, Technology, and British Naval Policy, 1889–1914* (London: Routledge, 1993 pb. edn).

Taylor, A.J.P., *Struggle for Mastery in Europe 1848–1918* (Oxford: Oxford University Press, 1954).

Taylor, Alan, *American Colonies: The Settling of North America* (Harmondsworth: Penguin, 2001).

Taylor, Richard, *Against the Bomb: The British Peace Movement 1958–1965* (Oxford: Oxford University Press, 1988).

Temperley, H.W.V., *The Foreign Policy of Canning 1822–1827: England, the Neo-Holy Alliance, and the New World* (London: Frank Cass, 1966, 1st pub. 1925).

Thistlethwaite, Frank, *The Anglo-American Connection in the Early Nineteenth Century* (Philadelphia: University of Pennsylvania Press, 1959).

Thomas, Peter D.G., *George III: King and Politicians 1760–1770* (Manchester: Manchester University Press, 2002).

Thomas, Peter D.G., *Revolution in America: Britain and the Colonies 1763–1776* (Cardiff: University of Wales Press, 1992).

Thorne, Christopher, *Allies of a Kind: The United States, Britain, and the War against Japan, 1941–1945* (London: Hamish Hamilton, 1978).

Tilchin, William N., *Theodore Roosevelt and the British Empire: A Study in Presidential Statecraft* (London: Macmillan, 1997).

Tolles, Frederick Barnes, *Quakers and the Atlantic Culture* (London: Macmillan, 1960).

Traina, Richard P., *American Diplomacy and the Spanish Civil War* (Bloomington: Indiana University Press, 1968).

Trask, David F., *The United States in the Supreme War Council* (Middletown, CT: Wesleyan University Press, 1961).

Tulloch, Hugh, *James Bryce's 'American Commonwealth': The Anglo-American Background* (Woodbridge: Boydell Press for the Royal Historical Society, 1988).

Tunstall, Jeremy and David Machin, *The Anglo-American Media Connection* (Oxford: Oxford University Press, 1999).

Van Dormael, Armand, *Bretton Woods: Birth of a Monetary System* (London: Macmillan, 1978).

Van Vugt, William E., *Britain to America: Mid-Nineteenth-Century Immigrants to the United States* (Urbana: University of Illinois Press, 1999).

Vaughan, James R., *The Failure of American and British Propaganda in the Arab Middle East, 1945–57: Unconquerable Minds* (London: Palgrave, 2005).

Veldman, Meredith, *Fantasy, the Bomb, and the Greening of Britain: Romantic Protest, 1945–1980* (Cambridge: Cambridge University Press, 1994).

The Victoria History of the Counties of England: A History of the County of Essex, Volume II (London: Archibald Constable, 1907).

Villiers, Brougham and W.H. Chesson, *Anglo-American Relations 1861–1865* (London: T. Fisher Unwin, 1919).

Walmsley, Andrew Stephen, *Thomas Hutchinson and the Origins of the American Revolution* (New York: New York University Press, 1999 pb. edn).

Ward, Joseph P., *Britain and the American South: From Colonialism to Rock and Roll* (Jackson: University Press of Mississippi, 2003).

Webb, Sidney, *The Decline in the Birth-Rate* (London: Fabian Society, 1907).

Wecter, Dixon, *The Saga of American Society: A Record of Social Aspirations 1606–1937* (London: Scribner's, 1937).

Weeks, William Earl, *John Quincy Adams and American Global Empire* (Lexington: University Press of Kentucky, 1992 pb. edn).

Weintraub, Stanley, *The London Yankees: Portraits of American Writers and Artists in England 1894–1914* (New York: Harcourt Brace Jovanovich, 1979).

Weisbuch, Robert, *Atlantic Double-Cross: American Literature and British Influence in the Age of Emerson* (Chicago: University of Chicago Press, 1986).

Wells, Samuel F., Jr., *The Challenges of Power: American Diplomacy, 1900–1921* (Lanham, MD: University Press of America, 1990).

Wightman, W.P.D., *Science in a Renaissance Society* (London: Hutchinson, 1972).

Wilson, Charles, *Profit and Power: A Study of England and the Dutch Wars* (London: Longmans, Green, 1957).

Winfield, Pamela, *Melancholy Baby: The Unplanned Consequences of the GIs' Arrival in Europe for World War II* (Westport, CT: Bergin & Garvey, 2000).

Wood, Gordon S., *The American Revolution: A History* (New York: The Modern Library, 2002).

Woods, Randall Bennett, *A Changing of the Guard: Anglo-American Relations, 1941–1946* (Chapel Hill: University of North Carolina Press, 1990).

Woodward, C. Van, *The Old World's New World* (New York: Oxford University Press, 1991).

Articles and Chapters

Adam, Thomas, 'Transatlantic Trading: The Transfer of Philanthropic Models between European and North American Cities during the Nineteenth and Early Twentieth Centuries', *Journal of Urban History*, Vol. 28, No. 3 (March 2002), 328–51.

Angevine, Robert G., 'Gentlemen Do Read Each Other's Mail: American Intelligence in the Interwar Era', *Intelligence and National Security*, Vol. 7, No. 2 (April 1992), 1–29.

Appleby, John C., 'War, Politics, and Colonization, 1558–1625', in Nicholas Canny, ed., *The Oxford History of the British Empire, Volume I: The Origins of Empire: British Overseas Enterprise to the Close of the Seventeenth Century* (Oxford: Oxford University Press, 1998), 55–78.

Ball, S.J., 'Military Nuclear Relations between the United States and Great Britain under the Terms of the McMahon Act, 1946–1958', *Historical Journal*, Vol. 38, No. 2 (1995), 439–54.

Bartlett, C.J. and Gene A. Smith, 'A "Species of Milito-Nautico-Guerilla-Plundering Warfare": Admiral Alexander Cochrane's Naval Campaign against the United States, 1814–1815', in Julia Flavelle and Stephen Conway, eds, *Britain and America Go to War: The Impact of War and Warfare in Anglo-America, 1754–1815* (Gainesville: University Press of Florida, 2004), 173–204.

Beach, Jim, 'Origins of the Special Intelligence Relationship? Anglo-American Intelligence Co-operation on the Western Front, 1917–18', *Intelligence and National Security*, Vol. 22, No. 2 (April 2007), 229–49.

Beloff, Max, 'Historical Revision No. CXVIII: Great Britain and the American Civil War', *History*, Vol. 37 (February 1952), 40–8.

Blackett, R.J.M., 'British Views of the Confederacy', in Joseph P. Ward, ed., *Britain and the American South: From Colonialism to Rock and Roll* (Jackson: University Press of Mississippi, 2003), 141–61.

Bockelman, Wayne L., 'Local Government in Colonial Pennsylvania', in Bruce C. Daniels, ed., *Town and Country: Essays on the Structure of Local Government in the American Colonies* (Middletown, CT: Wesleyan University Press, 1978), 216–37.

Bolt, Christine, 'Was There an Anglo-American Feminist Movement in the Earlier Twentieth Century?', in Fred Leventhal and Roland Quinault, eds, *Anglo-American Attitudes: From Revolution to Partnership* (Aldershot: Ashgate, 2000), 195–211.

Burk, Kathleen, 'American Foreign Economic Policy and Lend–Lease', in Ann Lane and Howard Temperley, eds, *The Rise and Fall of the Grand Aliance, 1941–5* (London: Macmillan, 1995), 43–68.

Burk, Kathleen, 'The Americans, the Germans, and the British: The 1976 IMF Crisis', *Twentieth Century British History*, Vol. 5, No. 3 (1994), 351–69.

Burk, Kathleen, 'Britain and the Marshall Plan', in Chris Wrigley, ed., *Warfare, Diplomacy and Politics: Essays in Honour of A.J.P. Taylor* (London: Hamish Hamilton, 1986), 210–30.

Burk, Kathleen, 'The Diplomacy of Finance: British Financial Missions to the United States 1914–1918', *Historical Journal*, Vol. 22, No. 2 (1979), 351–72.

Burk, Kathleen, 'Great Britain in the United States, 1917–1918: The Turning Point', *International History Review*, Vol. 1, No. 2 (April 1979), 228–45.

Burk, Kathleen, 'The House of Morgan in Financial Diplomacy 1920–1930', in B.J.C. McKercher, ed., *Anglo-American Relations in the 1920s: The Struggle for Supremacy* (London: Macmillan, 1991), 125–57.

Burk, Kathleen, 'J.M. Keynes and the July 1917 Exchange Rate Crisis', *Economic History Review*, 2nd Series, Vol. 32, No. 3 (August 1979), 405–16.

Burk, Kathleen, 'The Lineaments of Foreign Policy: The United States and a "New World Order", 1919–39', *Journal of American Studies*, Vol. 26, No. 3 (1992), 377–91.

Burk, Kathleen, 'The Marshall Plan: Filling in Some of the Blanks', *Contemporary European History*, Vol. 10, No. 2 (July 2001), 267–94.

Burk, Kathleen, 'Money and Power: The Shift from Great Britain to the United States', in Youssef Cassis, ed., *Finance and Financiers in European History, 1880–1960* (Cambridge: Cambridge University Press, 1992), 359–69.

Burton, David H., 'Theodore Roosevelt and His English Correspondents: The Intellectual Roots of the Anglo-American Alliance', *Mid-America*, Vol. 53, No. 1 (January 1971), 12–34.

Burton, D.H., 'Theodore Roosevelt and the "Special Relationship" with Britain', *History Today*, Vol. 23 (1973), 527–35.

Campbell, Charles S., Jr., 'The Dismissal of Lord Sackville', *Mississippi Valey Historical Review*, Vol. 44 (March 1968), 635–48.

Canny, Nicholas, 'England's New World and the Old, 1480s–1630s', in Nicholas Canny, ed., *The Oxford History of the British Empire, Volume I: The Origins of Empire: British Overseas Enterprise to the Close of the Seventeenth Century* (Oxford: Oxford University Press, 1998), 148–69.

Clavin, Patricia, '"The Fetishes of So-Called International Bankers": Central Bank Cooperation for the World Economic Conference, 1932–3', *Contemporary European History*, Vol. 1, No. 3 (November 1992), 281–311.

Clements, Roger V., 'British Investment and American Legislative Restrictions in the Trans-Mississippi West, 1880–1900', *The Mississippi Valley Historical Review*, Vol. 42, No. 2 (September 1955), 207–28.

'Colonial', 'Titled Colonials versus Titled Americans', *Contemporary Review*, Vol. 87 (1905), 861–9.

Conway, Stephen, 'Britain and the Revolutionary Crisis, 1763–1791', in P.J. Marshall, ed., *The Oxford History of the British Empire, Volume II: The Eighteenth Century* (Oxford: Oxford University Press, 1998), 325–46.

Conway, Stephen, 'Empire, Europe, and British Naval Power, c.1763–c.1833', unpublished lecture given in London at the Conference on the Empire and Sea Power, 24 October 2006.

Crapol, Edward P., 'From Anglophobia to Fragile Rapprochement: Anglo-American Relations in the Early Twentieth Century', in Hans-Jurgen Schröder, ed., *Confrontation and Cooperation: Germany and the United States in the Era of World War I, 1900–1924* (Providence: Berg, 1993), 13–31.

Crapol, Edward P., 'Coming to Terms with Empire: Historiography of Late Nineteenth-Century American Foreign Relations', *Diplomatic History*, Vol. 16, No. 4 (Fall 1992), 573–97.

Crawford, Martin, 'Anglo-American Perspectives: J.C. Bancroft Davis, New York Correspondent of *The Times*, 1854–1861', *New York Historical Society Quarterly*, Vol. 62, No. 3 (July 1978), 191–217.

Crockett, Larry, 'The Oxford Movement and the 19th-Century Episcopal Church: Anglo-Catholic Ecclesiology and the American Experience', *Quodlibet Online Journal of Christian Theology and Philosophy*, Vol. 1, No. 5 (August 1999).

Doenecke, Justus D., 'The Roosevelt Foreign Policy: An Ambiguous Legacy', in Justus D. Doenecke and Mark A. Stoler, eds, *Debating Franklin D. Roosevelt's Foreign Policies, 1933–1945* (Lanham, MD: Rowman & Littlefield, 2005), 5–89.

Dull, Jonathan R., 'Benjamin Franklin and the Nature of American Diplomacy', *International History Review*, Vol. 5, No. 3 (August 1983), 346–63.

Dunn, Mary Maples, 'Women of Light', in Carol Ruth Berkin and Mary Beth Norton, eds, *Women of America: A History* (Boston: Houghton Mifflin, 1979), 114–36.

Dunn, Richard S., 'The Glorious Revolution and America', in Nicholas Canny, ed., *The Oxford History of the British Empire, Volume I: The Origins of Empire: British Overseas Enterprise to the Close of the Seventeenth Century* (Oxford: Oxford University Press, 1998), 445–66.

Ericson, John, 'Stalin, Soviet Strategy and the Grand Alliance', in Ann Lane and Howard Temperley, eds, *The Rise and Fall of the Grand Alliance, 1941–45* (London: Macmillan, 1995), 136–73.

Fay, Stephen and Hugo Young, 'The Day the £ Nearly Died', *Sunday Times* (14, 21 and 28 May 1978).

Folly, Martin H., 'Breaking the Vicious Circle: Britain, the United States, and the Genesis of the North Atlantic Treaty', *Diplomatic History*, Vol. 12, No. 1 (Winter 1988), 59–77.

Freedman, Lawrence and John Gearson, 'Interdependence and Independence: Nassau and the British Nuclear Deterrent', in Kathleen Burk and Melvyn Stokes, eds, *The United States and the European Alliance since 1945* (Oxford: Berg, 1999), 179–203.

Geiger, John O., 'A Scholar Meets John Bull: Edward Everett as United States Minister to England, 1841–1845', *New England Quarterly*, Vol. 49 (December 1976), 577–95.

Gill, George J., 'Edward Everett and the Northeastern Boundary Controversy', *New England Quarterly*, Vol. 42, No. 2 (June 1969), 201–13.

Glancy, Mark, 'Temporary American Citizens? British Audiences, Hollywood Films and the Threat of Americanization in the 1920s', *Historical Journal of Film, Radio and Television*, Vol. 26, No. 4 (October 2006), 461–84.

Gormly, James L., 'The Washington Declaration and the "Poor Relation": Anglo-American Atomic Diplomacy, 1945–46', *Diplomatic History*, Vol. 8, No. 2 (Spring 1984), 125–43.

Gould, Eliga H., 'The Making of an Atlantic State System: Britain and the United States, 1795–1825', in Julie Flavell and Stephen Conway, eds, *Britain and America Go to War: The Impact of War and Warfare in Anglo-America, 1754–1815* (Gainesville: University Press of Florida, 2004), 241–65.

Haglund, David G. and Tudor Onca, 'Victory Without Triumph? Theodore Roosevelt, Honour, and the Alaska Panhandle Boundary Dispute', paper presented to the Association of Canadian Studies in the United States, Anchorage, Alaska, September 2006.

Hall, David D., 'The Victorian Connection', in Daniel Walker Howe, ed., *Victorian America* (Philadelphia: University of Pennsylvania Press, 1984), 81–94.

Harrison, Frederick, 'Impressions of America', *The Nineteenth Century and After*, Vol. 49 (June 1901).

Healy, David, 'A Hinterland in Search of a Metropolis: The Mosquito Coast, 1894–1910', *International History Review*, Vol. 3, No. 1 (January 1981), 20–43.

Hewedy, Amin, 'Nasser and the Crisis of 1956', Wm. Roger Louis and Roger Owen, eds, *Suez 1956: The Crisis and its Consequences* (Oxford: Oxford University Press, 1989), 161–72.

Holman, Alfred P., 'Two for the Money: The Current British Television Scene', *English Journal*, Vol. 50, No. 9 (December 1961), 635–7.

Hutson, James H., 'Intellectual Foundations of Early American Diplomacy', *Diplomatic History*, Vol. 1, No. 1 (Winter 1977), 1–19.

Johnson, Richard R., 'Growth and Mastery: British North America, 1690–1748', in P.J. Marshall, ed., *The Oxford History of the British Empire, Volume II: The Eighteenth Century* (Oxford: Oxford University Press, 1998), 276–99.

Jones, Howard, 'The *Caroline* Affair', *The Historian*, Vol. 38, No. 3 (May 1976), 485–502.

Kaplan, Lawrence S., 'Jefferson as Anglophile: Sagacity or Senility in the Era of Good Feelings?', *Diplomatic History*, Vol. 16, No. 3 (Summer 1992), 487–94.

Kramer, Paul A., 'Empires, Exceptions, and Anglo-Saxons: Race and Rule between the British and United States Empires, 1880–1910', *Journal of American History*, Vol. 88, No. 4 (March 2002), 1315–53.

Kunz, Diane B., 'The Importance of Having Money: The Economic Diplomacy of the Suez Crisis', in Wm. Roger Louis and Roger Owen, eds, *Suez 1956: The Crisis and Its Consequences* (Oxford: Oxford University Press, 1989), 215–32.

LaFeber, Walter, 'The Constitution and United States Foreign Policy', *Journal of American History*, Vol. 74 (1987–8), 695–717.

Landsman, Ned C., 'The Middle Colonies: New Opportunities for Settlement, 1660–1700', in Nicholas Canny, ed., *The Oxford History of the British Empire, Volume I: The Origins of Empire: British Overseas Enterprise to the Close of the Seventeenth Century* (Oxford: Oxford University Press, 1998), 351–74.

Langford, Paul, 'Manners and Character in Anglo-American Perceptions, 1750–1850', in Fred M. Leventhal and Roland Quinault, eds, *Anglo-American Atttitudes: From Revolution to Partnership* (Aldershot: Ashgate, 2000), 76–90.

Langford, Paul, 'Property and "Virtual Representation" in Eighteenth-Century England', *Historical Journal*, Vol. 31, No. 1 (March 1988), 83–115.

Larsen, Peter, 'Sir Mortimer Durand in Washington: A Study in Anglo-American Relations in the Era of Theodore Roosevelt', *Mid-America*, Vol. 66, No. 2 (April–July 1984), 65–78.

Maisch, Christian J., 'The Falkland/Malvinas Islands Clash of 1831–32: US and British Diplomacy in the South Atlantic', *Diplomatic History*, Vol. 24, No. 2 (Spring 2000), 185–209.

Majander, Mikko, 'The Limits of Sovereignty: Finland and the Marshall Plan in 1947', *Scandinavian Journal of History*, Vol. 19, No. 4 (1994), 309–26.

Manning, Susan, 'Did Mark Twain Bring down the Temple on Scott's Shoulders?', in Janet Beer and Bridget Bennett, eds, *Special Relationships: Anglo-American Affinities and Antagonisms 1854–1936* (Manchester: Manchester University Press, 2002), 8–27.

Marshall, P.J., 'The Case for Coercing America before the Revolution', in Fred M. Leventhal and Roland Quinault, eds, *Anglo-American Attitudes: From Revolution to Partnership* (Aldershot: Ashgate, 2000), 9–22.

Muller, Dorothea R., 'The Social Philosophy of Josiah Strong: Social Christianity and American Progressivism', *Church History*, Vol. 28, No. 2 (June 1859), 183–201.

Neilson, Keith, '"Greatly Exaggerated": The Myth of the Decline of Great Britain before 1914', *International History Review*, Vol. 13, No. 4 (November 1991), 695–725.

North, Douglass C., 'International Capital Flows and the Development of the American West', *Journal of Economic History*, Vol. 16, No. 4 (December 1956), 493–505.

O'Brien, Patrick K., 'Inseparable Connections: Trade, Economy, Fiscal State, and the Expansion of Empire, 1688–1815', in P.J. Marshall, ed., *The Oxford History of the British Empire, Volume II: The Eighteenth Century* (Oxford: Oxford University Press, 1998), 53–77.

O'Hara, Glen, 'The Limits of US Power: Transatlantic Financial Diplomacy under the Johnson and Wilson Administrations, October 1964–November 1968', *Contemporary European History*, Vol. 12, No. 3 (August 2003), 257–78.

Otte, T.G., 'A Question of Leadership: Lord Salisbury, the Unionist Cabinet and Foreign Policy Making, 1895–1900', *Contemporary British History*, Vol. 14, No. 4 (Winter 2000), 1–26.

Otte, T.G., '"It's What Made Britain Great": Reflections on British Foreign Policy, from Malplaquet to Maastricht', in T.G. Otte, ed., *The Makers of British Foreign Policy from Pitt to Thatcher* (Basingstoke: Palgrave, 2002), 1–34.

Pagden, Anthony, 'The Struggle for Legitimacy and the Image of Empire in the Atlantic to c. 1700', in Nicholas Canny, ed., *The Oxford History of the British Empire, Volume I: The Origins of Empire: British Overseas Enterprise to the Close of the Seventeenth Century* (Oxford: Oxford University Press, 1998), 34–54.

Petersen, Tore Tingvold, 'Anglo-American Rivalry in the Middle East: The Struggle for the Buraimi Oasis, 1952–1957', *International History Review*, Vol. 14, No. 1 (February 1992), 71–91.

Ritcheson, Charles R., 'The British Role in American Life', *History Teacher*, Vol. 7, No. 4 (August 1974), 574–96.

Ritcheson, C.R., 'The Earl of Shelburne and Peace with America, 1782–1783: Vision and Reality', *International History Review*, Vol. 5, No. 3 (August 1983), 322–45.

Roll, Charles, 'The Quaker in Anglo-American Cultural Relations', *Indiana Magazine of History*, Vol. 45 (1949), 135–46.

Roman, Peter J., 'Curtis LeMay and the Origins of NATO Atomic Targeting', *Journal of Strategic Studies*, Vol. 16, No. 1 (March 1993), 46–74.

Rothstein, Morton, 'America in the International Rivalry for the British Wheat Market, 1860–1914', *Mississippi Valley Historical Review*, Vol. 47, No. 3 (December 1960), 401–18.

Shy, John, 'The American Colonies in War and Revolution, 1748–1783', in P.J. Marshall, ed., *The Oxford History of the British Empire, Volume II: The Eighteenth Century* (Oxford: Oxford University Press, 1998), 300–24.

Small, Melvin, 'The United States and the German "Threat" to the Hemisphere, 1905–1914', *The Americas*, Vol. 28, No. 3 (January 1972), 252–70.

Smalley, George W., 'The American Girl in England and How It Happens That She is Known in England', *New York Herald Tribune*, 17 November 1888, reprinted in Smalley, *London Letters and Some Others*, II, 101–6.

Smith-Rosenberg, Carroll and Charles Rosenberg, 'The Female Animal: Medical and Biological Views of Woman and Her Role in Nineteenth-Century America', *Journal of American History*, Vol. 60, No. 2 (September 1973), 332–56.

Stead, W.T., 'The Americanisation of the World', *Review of Reviews Annual* (1902), 1–170.

Steele, Ian K., 'The Anointed, the Appointed, and the Elected: Governance of the British Empire, 1689–1784', in P.J. Marshall, ed., *The Oxford History of the British Empire, Volume II: The Eighteenth Century* (Oxford: Oxford University Press, 1998), 105–27.

Stewart, Gordon T., '"A Special Contiguous Country Economic Regime": An Overview of America's Canadian Policy', *Diplomatic History*, Vol. 6, No. 4 (Fall 1982), 339–57.

Stokes, Melvyn, 'American Progressives and the European Left', *Journal of American Studies*, Vol. 17, No. 1 (1983), 5–28.

Sutherland, John, 'A Brave New World', *FT Magazine*, 9 October 2004, 26

Taylor, J.W., 'The Bishop of London on the Declining Birth Rate', *Nineteenth Century and After*, Vol. 59 (1906), 219–29.

Tilchin, William N., 'Theodore Roosevelt, Anglo-American Relations, and the Jamaica Incident of 1907', *Diplomatic History*, Vol. 19, No. 3 (Summer 1965), 385–405.

Tulloch, H.A., 'Changing British Attitudes towards the United States in the 1880s', *Historical Journal*, Vol. 20, No. 4 (December 1977), 825–40.

Weeks, William Earl, 'New Directions in the Study of Early American Foreign Relations', *Diplomatic History*, Vol. 17, No. 1 (Winter 1993), 73–96.

Weir, Robert M., "'Shaftsbury's Darling": British Settlement in the Carolinas at the Close of the Seventeenth Century', in Nicholas Canny, ed., *The Oxford History of the British Empire, Volume I: The Origins of Empire: British Overseas Enterprise to the Close of the Seventeenth Century* (Oxford: Oxford University Press, 1998), 375–97.

Whetham, W.C.D. and C.D. Whetham, 'The Extinction of the Upper Classes', *Nineteenth Century and After*, Vol. 66 (1909), 97–108.

Wilkins, Mira, 'Foreign Investment in the US Economy before 1914', *Annals of the American Academy of Political and Social Science*, Vol. 516, 'Foreign Investment in the United States' (July 1991), 9–21.

Wood, Gordon S., 'American Religion: The Great Retreat', *New York Review of Books*, Vol. 53, No. 10 (8 June 2006), 60–3.

Zuckerman, Michael, 'Identities in British America: Unease in Eden', in Nicholas Canny and Anthony Pagden, eds, *Colonial Identity in the Atlantic World, 1500–1800* (Princeton: Princeton University Press, 1987), 115–57.

Beles-Lettres, Novels and Poems

Ashbery, John, *Self-Portrait in a Convex Mirror* (Manchester: Carcanet New Press, 1985, 1st pub. 1975).

Atherton, Gertrude, *American Wives and English Husbands: A Novel* (New York: Dodd, Meade and Company, 1898).

Beust, Nora, Phyllis Fenner, Bernice E. Leary, Mary Katherine Reely and Dora V. Smith, eds, *Stories of Early America* (Eau Claire, WI: E.M. Hale, 1958).

Burnett, Frances Hodgson, *Little Lord Fauntleroy* (London: Frederick Warne, 1888).

Burnett, Frances Hodgson, *The Making of a Marchioness* (London: Smith, Elder, & Co., 1901).

Burnett, Frances Hodgson, *The Shuttle* (New York: Frederick A. Stokes, 1907).

Bywater, Michael, *Lost Worlds: What Have We Lost, & Where Did It Go?* (London: Granta, 2004).

Cooper, James Fenimore, *The Last of the Mohicans; A Narrative of 1757* (Oxford: Oxford University Press, 1994 new edn).

Donne, John, *The Elegies and the Songs and Sonnets of John Donne*, ed. Helen Gardner (Oxford: Oxford University Press, 1965).

Drayton, Michael, *The Works of Michael Drayton, Esq.* (London: J. Hughs, 1748).

Emerson, Ralph Waldo, 'Concord Hymn', in *The Concord Hymn and Other Poems* (New York: Dover, 1996).

Firth, C.H., ed., *An American Garland: Being a Colection of Balads Relating to America 1563–1759* (Oxford: B. H. Blackwell, 1915).

Greene, Graham, *The Quiet American* (Harmondsworth: Penguin, 1965, 1st pub. 1955).

Hawthorne, Nathaniel, *The Scarlet Letter* (New York: Barnes & Noble, 1993 2nd edn, 1st pub. 1850).

Hughes, Thomas, *Tom Brown's School Days, by an Old Boy* (London: Macmillan, 1979 facsimile of 1889 1st edn).

James, Henry, *The Golden Bowl* (Harmondsworth: Penguin, 1966, 1st pub. 1904).

Longfellow, Henry Wadsworth, 'Paul Revere's Ride', in *The Poetical Works of Henry Wadsworth Longfellow* (London: George Routledge & Sons, 1877).

Seneca, *Medea*, trans. and intro. Frederick Ahl (Ithaca, N.Y.: Cornell University Press, 1986).

Thomas, Edward, *The Collected Poems of Edward Thomas*, ed. R. George Thomas (Oxford: Oxford University Press, 1978).

Twain, Mark, *A Yankee at the Court of King Arthur* (London: Chatto & Windus, 1890).

Wharton, Edith, completed by Marion Mainwaring, *The Buccaneers* (London: Fourth Estate, 1993).

Whitman, Walt, *Democratic Vistas* (New York: Liberal Arts Press, 1949).

Whitman, Walt, *Leaves of Grass: The Poems of Walt Whitman* (London: Walter Scott, 1886).

Oscar Wilde, *The Complete Writings of Oscar Wilde*, 10 vols (New York: Nottingham Society, 1909).

Periodicals

The Americans
Annals of the American Academy of Political and Social Science
Church History
Contemporary Review
Diplomatic History
The Economist
English Journal
FT Magazine
The Historian
Historical Journal
Historical Journal of Film, Radio and Television
History
History Teacher
History Today
Indiana Magazine of History
Intelligence and National Security
International History Review
Journal of American History
Journal of American Studies
Journal of Economic History
Journal of Strategic Studies
Journal of Urban History
Mid-America
Mississippi Valley Historical Review
Modern Philology
New England Quarterly
New York Historical Society Quarterly
New York Review of Books
Nineteenth Century and Nineteenth Century and After
North American Review
Quodlibet Online Journal of Christian Theology and Philosophy
Review of Reviews
Sunday Times
Twentieth Century British History

Ph.D. Dissertations

Goodman, Giora, '"Who is anti-American?": The British Left and the United States, 1945–1956', University College London, 1996.

Miller, James N., 'Wartime Origins of Multilateralism, 1939–1945: The Impact of Anglo-American Trade Policy Negotiations', Cambridge University, 2003.

Otto, Patricia, 'Daughters of the British Aristocracy: Their Marriages in the Eighteenth and Nineteenth Centuries with Particular Reference to the Scottish Peerage', Stanford University, 1974.

Vestopoulos, Apostolos, 'The Economic Dimensions of the Marshall Plan in Greece, 1945–52: The Origins of the Greek Economic Miracle', University College London, 2002.

Interviews

Sir Derek Mitchell, 12 February and 3 September 1991
Dr Karl Otto-Pöhl, 15 December 1989

Scott Pardee, 26 July 1989
Sir William Ryrie, 28 July 1989
Alan Whittome, 25 July 1989

Websites

Allingham, Philip V., 'Dickens' 1842 Reading Tour: Launching the Copyright Question in Tempestuous Seas', www.victorianweb.org/authors/dickens/pva/pva75.html
Everett, Glenn and George P. Landow, 'High Church: Tractarianism', www.victorian web.org/religion/tractarian.html
Landow, George P., *Tom Brown at Oxford* on Muscular Christianity', www.victorianweb.org/authors/hughes/muscular.html
Schlossber, Herbert, 'The Tractarian Movement', www.victorianweb.org/religion/herb7.html
Scott, Donald, 'Evangelicalism, Revivalism, and the Second Great Awakening', www.nhc.rtp.nc.us:8080/tserve/nineteen/nkeyinfo/nevanrev.htm
www.attackingthedevil.co.uk/peers/shaw1.php
www.attackingthedevil/worksabout/babylon.php
www.contemplator.com/america/ssbanner.html
www.cottontimes.co.uk/bridgewatero.htm
http://famouspoetsandpoems.com/poets/w_h_auden/poems/10129
http://historicalvoices.org/earliest_voices/bryan.html
www.icbh.ac.uk/witness/falklands
www.millercenter.virginia.edu/index.php/academic/oralhistory/projects/special/falklands
www.pbs.org/wgbh/aia/part4/4p1561.html
www.spartacus.schoolnet.co.uk/USAantislavery.htm
www.spartacus.schoolnet.co.uk/Jstead.htm
www.specialoperations.com/Foreign/United_Kingdom/SAS/History.htm
www.stuff.themutual.net/polk.htm
http://en.wikipedia.org/wiki/British_Invasion

Index

Tuma, Keith 367
Turkey 573, 579, 580
Tuscarora, USS 273
Twain, Mark 278, 304–5, 356, 358
Tweeddale, Marquis of 321

UKUSA agreement 1948: 511, 726n342
Ulster 68, 77–8
Ultima Thule 3
Unitarians 327–8
United Nations (UN) 507, 515–20, 571,
     600, 623–4, 631–2, 639–41, 643, 648,
     651, 653–4, 744n238
United States
  British cattle ranchers 321–2
  British cultural influence 310
  British ownership of land 309, 321–3
  capital imports 312
  class distinctions 283–4, 291
  commitment to Western European
     security 588–9
  conformism 282
  containment policy 575
  corrupt municipal government 346–7
  debt to Britain post-Independence 193–9
  democracy 280
  desire for praise 282
  economic depression – Panic of 1837:
     315–17, 356
  economic depression – Panic of 1857: 319
  economic depression – Panic of 1873: 320
  economic depression – the 'Long
     Depression' 320
  economic depression – the Depression 474
  egalitarianism 294, 298
  emphasis on liberty 281
  enclosures 321
  exports 311
  Fallen Timbers, Battle of 204
  federal and state securities 316
  Federal Reserve System 347
  foreign policy 561–2
  Germany as key European ally 629
  immigration 312
  imports 311–12
  individualism 281
  intelligence cooperation with Britain
     451–2, 509
  intelligence operations and activities
     451–4
  isolationism 382–3, 473–4
  'mass culture' 363, 368
  middle class 280
  mining 313, 323
  municipal corruption 298

naval rivalry with Britain 464–7, 473
need for constant praise 386
newspapers 294, 295, 299
nuclear relationship with Britain 511–14
perception of being better than Britain
     by definition 361
popular culture 363, 368
railroads 318–20
recognition by Britain 187–8
relationship with Britain from 1945
     summarised 561
religious enthusiasm 281, 289–90
self-perception and power 527–8
slavery 285–6, 291–3
Tippecanoe, Battle of 223
tobacco chewing 289, 296
trade with Britain post-Independence
     192–4
trade with France 213–14
Treasury anglophobia 584
tyranny of the majority 281–2
USSR relationships post World War II
     563, 574, 595–6
United States – legislation
  Atomic Energy Act 1954: 605
  Chace Act 1891: 357
  Embargo Act 1807: 219–22
  enclosures on public domain 321
  Johnson Debt Default Act 1934: 480
  Macon's No. 2 Act 1810: 222
  McMahon Act 1946: 603
  National Defense Act 1940: 488
  Neutrality Act 1935: 480
  Neutrality Act 1936: 481
  Neutrality Act 1937: 481
  Neutrality Act 1939: 487
  Non-Importation Act 1806: 219
  Non-Intercourse Act 1809: 222
  Owen-Glass Act 1913: 347
  Sherman Antitrust Act 1890: 347
United States army 497, 555, 557
United States navy 167, 213, 229–30,
     234–5, 237, 267, 272–3, 381, 389–91,
     412–13, 415, 426, 435, 440, 446, 451,
     454, 461, 464–5, 467–70, 473, 484–6,
     492, 496, 498, 503, 507, 510, 634,
     639, 642, 685n1, 688n55, 720n232,
     723n302
United States, USS 234
Universal Paris Exhibition 1900: 361–2
US-UK Mutual Defence Agreement 1958:
     606
uti possidetis 183
Utrecht, Treaty of 89, 98
Uzbekhistan 648